Business Sustainability Practices in Society 5.0

Kittisak Jermsittiparsert
Shinawatra University, Thailand

Ismail Suardi Wekke
Institut Agama Islam Negeri, Sorong, Indonesia

Pannee Suanpang
Suan Dusit University, Thailand

Published in the United States of America by
IGI Global
701 E. Chocolate Avenue
Hershey PA, USA 17033
Tel: 717-533-8845
Fax: 717-533-8661
E-mail: cust@igi-global.com
Web site: https://www.igi-global.com

Copyright © 2025 by IGI Global. All rights reserved. No part of this publication may be reproduced, stored or distributed in any form or by any means, electronic or mechanical, including photocopying, without written permission from the publisher. Product or company names used in this set are for identification purposes only. Inclusion of the names of the products or companies does not indicate a claim of ownership by IGI Global of the trademark or registered trademark.

Library of Congress Cataloging-in-Publication Data

CIP Data Pending
ISBN:979-8-3693-9230-0
eISBN:979-8-3693-9232-4

Vice President of Editorial: Melissa Wagner
Managing Editor of Acquisitions: Mikaela Felty
Managing Editor of Book Development: Jocelynn Hessler
Production Manager: Mike Brehm
Cover Design: Phillip Shickler

British Cataloguing in Publication Data
A Cataloguing in Publication record for this book is available from the British Library.

ll work contributed to this book is new, previously-unpublished material.
he views expressed in this book are those of the authors, but not necessarily of the publisher.

Table of Contents

Preface xix

Chapter 1
Sustainable Development: What? Why? and How? 1
    Samanan Rattanasirivilai, Suan Sunandha Rajabhat University, Thailand
    Sippaphat Rotjanawasuthorn, Association of Legal and Political Studies, Thailand
    Sirinapattha Sirinapatpokin, Association of Legal and Political Studies, Thailand
    Puthisat Namdech, Association of Legal and Political Studies, Thailand
    Kittisak Jermsittiparsert, Shinawatra University, Thailand

Chapter 2
Behavioral Insights and AI for Enhancing Productivity in Society 5.0: A Path to Sustainable
Development 37
    Noor Wazikhaz Madia Wazi, Universiti Sultan Zainal Abidin, Malaysia
    Fazida Karim, Universiti Sultan Zainal Abidin, Malaysia
    Noor Aina Amirah Mohd Noor, Universiti Sultan Zainal Abidin, Malaysia
    Ismahafezi Ismail, Universiti Sultan Zainal Abidin, Malaysia
    Wan Mohd Amir Fazamin Wan Hamzah, Universiti Sultan Zainal Abidin, Malaysia
    Mokhairi Makhtar, Universiti Sultan Zainal Abidin, Malaysia
    Mohd Hafiz Yusoff, Universiti Sultan Zainal Abidin, Malaysia

Chapter 3
Business Information Systems, Importance of Information, Business Intelligence, Corporate
Excellence, and ICTs Within the Development of Organizations 61
    Aytaç Gökmen, Çankaya University, Turkey
    Dilek Temiz, Çankaya University, Turkey

Chapter 4
Entrepreneurial Passion or Machiavellianism? Exploring the Factors Affecting Entrepreneurial
Intention 73
    Jean Paolo Gomez Lacap, City College of Angeles, Philippines
    Mavy De Joseph, Polytechnic University of the Philippines, Philippines
    Karen Claire Solano, Polytechnic University of the Philippines, Philippines
    Mary Jane Legaspi, Polytechnic University of the Philippines, Philippines
    Mark Anthony Visca, Polytechnic University of the Philippines, Philippines

Chapter 5
From Theory to Practice: Essential Competencies for Success in International HRM 99
    Seema Bhakuni, Doon Institute of Management and Research, India

Chapter 6
Human Resource Analytics and Organizational Performance: Mediating Role of Evidence-Based Management...123
    Shivani Thapliyal, Christ University, India

Chapter 7
Integrating Work-Based Education: Bridging Academic Knowledge and Practical Experience for Workforce Readiness 137
    Sakunthai Pommarang, Loei Rajabhat University, Thailand
    Sanya Kenaphoom, Rajabhat Maha Sarakham University, Thailand

Chapter 8
Role of Diversity and Inclusion in Employee Engagement Among Different Sectors of India 177
    Vinita Sinha, Symbiosis Centre for Management and Human Resource Development,
        Symbiosis International University (Deemed), India

Chapter 9
Staff Behavior and Physical Environment Quality as Antecedents of Brand Loyalty: The Mediating Roles of Brand Passion and Satisfaction 195
    Francis Ion Sangil, University of the Visayas, Philippines
    Jean Paolo Gomez Lacap, City College of Angeles, Philippines
    Maureen Rivera, Polytechnic University of the Philippines, Philippines
    Bernadith Radaza, University of the Visayas, Philippines
    Mary Ruth Quintero, University of the Visayas, Philippines

Chapter 10
Strengthening Sustainable Development Goal 5: Role of Gender Diversity and Creativity in Selected Women-Owned Informal Small Businesses in Africa 219
    Timilehin Olasoji Olubiyi, Babcock University, Nigeria

Chapter 11
Guidelines for Generating Income Through Local Identity Products for Widows in the Southern Border Provinces, Thailand 237
    Nutnapha Lekhavichit, Yala Rajabhat University, Thailand

Chapter 12
The Development of Products From Budi Brown-Rice Flour to Promote Gluten-Free Brownies in Budi Subdistrict, Yala Province, Thailand 255
    Sutida Lekhawichit, Yala Rajabhat University, Thailand
    Wiroj Phaiboonvessawat, Yala Rajabhat University, Thailand
    Ubol Tansom, Yala Rajabhat University, Thailand
    Sasithorn Pangsuban, Yala Rajabhat University, Thailand
    Kurosiyah Yamirudeng, Yala Rajabhat University, Thailand

Chapter 13
Harnessing Business Analytics for Influencer Marketing: Enhancing Decision-Making and Performance in Society 267
    Sreethi Rebeka R., Christ University, India
    Rejoice Thomas, Christ University, India

Chapter 14
Evaluating the Degree of Risk Perception Among Kumbakonam Town Users of E-Commerce Platforms Using Artificial Intelligence 279
    K. Nalini, SASTRA University (Deemed), India
    G. Revathy, SASTRA University (Deemed), India

Chapter 15
Please Don't Stop the Music! Exploring the Factors Affecting Continuous Usage Intention in a Music Streaming Platform 299
    Jean Paolo Gomez Lacap, City College of Angeles, Philippines
    Jessalyn Alqueza, University of the Visayas, Philippines
    Jebe Mag-usara, University of the Visayas, Philippines
    Jessell Tandugon, University of the Visayas, Philippines

Chapter 16
Intention to Use E-Wallet Services, User Satisfaction and Loyalty: The Mediating Role of Trust and the Moderating Effects of Technological Stress.. 321
    Avelino Gonzales, Holy Angel University, Philippines
    Jean Paolo Gomez Lacap, City College of Angeles, Philippines

Chapter 17
Sustainable Travel Behavior: The Influence of Digital Marketing and Social Media 343
    Suraj Jaywant Yadav, D.Y. Patil Education Society, India

Chapter 18
Impact of Social Media on the Development of Religious Tourism Industry 359
    Mohammad Badruddoza Talukder, International University of Business Agriculture and
        Technology, Bangladesh
    Iva Rani Das, University of Dhaka, Bangladesh
    Mohammad Nurul Afchar, Daffodil International University, Bangladesh

Chapter 19
Tourism Industry Amidst COVID-19 With Special Reference to National Capital Region of India 379
    Rama Verma, Amity University Online, India
    Kuldeep Singh, Amity University, Haryana, India
    Arnab Gantait, Independent Researcher, India
    Susanta Ranjan Chaini, Shiksha 'O' Anusandhan University, India

Chapter 20
The Allure of Tranquillity: How Less-Crowded Destinations in Bangladesh are Captivating
International Tourists 399
    Mohammad Badruddoza Talukder, International University of Business Agriculture and
        Technology, Bangladesh
    Dil Afrin Swarna, Independent Researcher, Bangladesh
    Musfiqur Rahoman Khan, Daffodil Institute of IT, Bangladesh

Chapter 21
Kuakata Reimagined: Forecasting Economic Growth and Future Potential of Coastal Hub in
Bangladesh 419
    Mohammad Badruddoza Talukder, International University of Business Agriculture and
        Technology, Bangladesh
    Dil Afrin Swarna, Independent Researcher, Bangladesh
    Musfiqur Rahoman Khan, Daffodil Institute of IT, Bangladesh

Chapter 22
Integrating Sustainability With Dark Tourism 435
    Tripti Arvind, Christ University, India

Chapter 23
Defining Street Food 461
    Ninnart Daorattanahong, University of Canterbury, New Zealand
    Michael Colin Hall, University of Canterbury, New Zealand
    Girish Prayag, University of Canterbury, New Zealand
    Yaling Liu, University of Canterbury, New Zealand

Compilation of References 497

About the Contributors 607

Index 611

Detailed Table of Contents

Preface xix

Chapter 1
Sustainable Development: What? Why? and How? 1
    Samanan Rattanasirivilai, Suan Sunandha Rajabhat University, Thailand
    Sippaphat Rotjanawasuthorn, Association of Legal and Political Studies, Thailand
    Sirinapattha Sirinapatpokin, Association of Legal and Political Studies, Thailand
    Puthisat Namdech, Association of Legal and Political Studies, Thailand
    Kittisak Jermsittiparsert, Shinawatra University, Thailand

Sustainable development is a global agenda set together a century ago that countries will follow and achieve in the first half of this century. The answer to the big question "What are the conditions that will make a country successful or unsuccessful in sustainable development?" has arisen and continues today. To answer these questions with empirical data, this paper synthesizes documents in the Scopus database published from 2013 to the present and highlights how current knowledge answers these questions: 1) What is sustainable development? 2) Why is it necessary for the country to develop sustainably? 3) What is the current situation of sustainable development in the world? 4) What are the conditions and methods that will enable the country to move away from unsustainable development? 5) What are the conditions and methods for achieving sustainable development in a country? And lastly, 6) What are the conditions and methods for maintaining a sustainable level of development? The answer to each question is explained and discussed accordingly.

Chapter 2
Behavioral Insights and AI for Enhancing Productivity in Society 5.0: A Path to Sustainable Development 37
    Noor Wazikhaz Madia Wazi, Universiti Sultan Zainal Abidin, Malaysia
    Fazida Karim, Universiti Sultan Zainal Abidin, Malaysia
    Noor Aina Amirah Mohd Noor, Universiti Sultan Zainal Abidin, Malaysia
    Ismahafezi Ismail, Universiti Sultan Zainal Abidin, Malaysia
    Wan Mohd Amir Fazamin Wan Hamzah, Universiti Sultan Zainal Abidin, Malaysia
    Mokhairi Makhtar, Universiti Sultan Zainal Abidin, Malaysia
    Mohd Hafiz Yusoff, Universiti Sultan Zainal Abidin, Malaysia

This chapter examines the mutually beneficial connection between behavioural insights and artificial intelligence (AI) in order to enhance productivity within the framework of Society 5.0. Society 5.0 is a conceptual framework that seeks to establish a balanced integration of economic progress and social well-being via the process of digital transformation. The chapter highlights the vital importance of AI technologies, such as machine learning, natural language processing (NLP), predictive analytics, human-AI collaboration, and generative AI, in attaining sustainable development. When combined with knowledge from psychology, economics, and neuroscience, these technologies have a crucial function. The approaches used include real-life case studies across many industries, illustrating the impact of these technologies on decision-making, policy formation, and intervention design, while aligning with authentic human behaviours. The ethical dimensions of integrating AI with behavioural insights, with a specific emphasis on privacy, data security, and biases in AI systems, are also explored. The actual implementations of these technologies in real-life situations demonstrate significant improvements in organisational productivity and efficiency. The chapter ends with practical suggestions for leaders and policymakers to synchronise AI-based plans with sustainable development objectives, with a particular focus on the welfare of humans.

Chapter 3
Business Information Systems, Importance of Information, Business Intelligence, Corporate Excellence, and ICTs Within the Development of Organizations 61
    Aytaç Gökmen, Çankaya University, Turkey
    Dilek Temiz, Çankaya University, Turkey

An important shift takes places in organizations which is the shift in priorities to strategic management and increasing human demand for reliable information to run the business competitively in the global context. Nevertheless, executives and managers are exposed to a considerable amount of information which is both invaluable, as well as difficult to acquire, process, store, disseminate and utilize. Therefore, the objective of this study is to focus on the subjects as business information systems, information systems, business intelligence, corporate excellence, business intelligence, ICTs and other topics related to these issues in order to emphasize the importance of information and knowledge in the 21st century.

Chapter 4
Entrepreneurial Passion or Machiavellianism? Exploring the Factors Affecting Entrepreneurial
Intention 73
    Jean Paolo Gomez Lacap, City College of Angeles, Philippines
    Mavy De Joseph, Polytechnic University of the Philippines, Philippines
    Karen Claire Solano, Polytechnic University of the Philippines, Philippines
    Mary Jane Legaspi, Polytechnic University of the Philippines, Philippines
    Mark Anthony Visca, Polytechnic University of the Philippines, Philippines

This chapter examines how entrepreneurial passion (EP) and Machiavellianism affect entrepreneurial intention (EI). Moreover, it investigates the moderating effects of entrepreneurial creativity (EC) on the link between EP and EI, and of entrepreneurial self-efficacy (ES) on the relationship between Machiavellianism and EI. The participants were MBA (n = 304) students from several universities in Metro Manila, Philippines and they were identified using purposive sampling. The hypothesized relationships were evaluated through a causal-predictive research design and via path modeling using partial least squares. The results show that EP has a significant and positive influence on EC and EI. On the other hand, Machiavellianism has a significant but small direct effect on ES. It was likewise found that both EC and ES contribute to the formation of EI. After moderation analysis, the finding reveals that EC indirectly affects the link between EP and EI.

Chapter 5
From Theory to Practice: Essential Competencies for Success in International HRM 99
    Seema Bhakuni, Doon Institute of Management and Research, India

International Human Resource Management is the coordination amongst three aspects of managing resources; the types of employees involved, HR related activities and the location of operations. The challenges arise because the workforce comes from and work in different countries. The essential abilities required for the success of IHRM are investigated in this research. HR professionals are required to manage difficult cultural, legal, and economic situations across international boundaries. The essential talents concisely related to IHRM identified are cultural intelligence, global talent management, strategic thinking, and ethical awareness. The actual implementation of these competencies in global organisations by drawing from recent research and case studies based on real-world situations is illustrated here. The results highlight the need of continual learning and flexibility for human resource practitioners. A complete framework for HRM professionals to improve their international HRM competencies is the goal of this research.

Chapter 6
Human Resource Analytics and Organizational Performance: Mediating Role of Evidence-Based Management.. 123
    Shivani Thapliyal, Christ University, India

HR Analytics (HRA) is very crucial aspect of human resource management and drawing more attention each year. It has emerged as a powerful tool contributing towards organizational performance. However the literature work on HR analytics would appear to be more focused on the influence of HR analytics on organizational performance but the questions like how and why are still need to be explored. This research paper aims at understanding how HR analytics improves the organizational performance and systematically unfolds the mechanism how it happens. Data is collected from three organizations of different sectors and structure equation modelling is used to examine the chain mediation model connecting human resource analytics, evidence-based management and organizational performance. This research work extends our understanding of how HR analytics and evidence based management improves organizational performance.

Chapter 7
Integrating Work-Based Education: Bridging Academic Knowledge and Practical Experience for Workforce Readiness 137
    Sakunthai Pommarang, Loei Rajabhat University, Thailand
    Sanya Kenaphoom, Rajabhat Maha Sarakham University, Thailand

Work-based education (WBE), which bridges the gap between academia and industry, increases graduates' employability by giving them practical experience and industry-specific knowledge, better preparing them for the demands of the workforce. This paper aims to investigate the integration of WBEs. WBE is essential to modern education because it prepares graduates for the workforce by fusing academic knowledge with real-world experience. WBE better aligns educational objectives with labor market demands by fusing cutting-edge methods like competency-based and project-based learning with digital tools and virtual simulations. Its ongoing development is anticipated to improve its efficacy and better prepare graduates for the fast-paced labor market. This development will be aided by global collaborations and emerging technologies. In conclusion, utilizing cutting-edge technology and international collaborations, WBE combines theory and practical skills to better align education with the changing demands of the labor market and increase its overall impact.

Chapter 8
Role of Diversity and Inclusion in Employee Engagement Among Different Sectors of India 177
   Vinita Sinha, Symbiosis Centre for Management and Human Resource Development,
      Symbiosis International University (Deemed), India

Diversity and inclusion have become one of the main challenges and top priority for recruitment and other HR departments. Different sectors have different workforce diversity and organizational inclusion practices. It helps an organization to attract talented employees and drive the engagement of employees. The concept of diversity management and inclusion policies have been a focus for many companies for years now, and they have become more and more of a trending research topic. Although the literature on diversity and inclusion has been increasing in quantity, there remained a gap in the explaining the importance of diversity management and inclusion policies in the engagement of employees in the different Indian sector. The main aim of carrying out this research study is to investigate the association of various diversity and inclusion practices with an important aspect of the workplace, i.e. employee engagement among different sectors in India.

Chapter 9
Staff Behavior and Physical Environment Quality as Antecedents of Brand Loyalty: The
Mediating Roles of Brand Passion and Satisfaction 195
   Francis Ion Sangil, University of the Visayas, Philippines
   Jean Paolo Gomez Lacap, City College of Angeles, Philippines
   Maureen Rivera, Polytechnic University of the Philippines, Philippines
   Bernadith Radaza, University of the Visayas, Philippines
   Mary Ruth Quintero, University of the Visayas, Philippines

This chapter uses the Stimulus-Organism-Response (SOR) theory to examine how staff behavior and physical environment quality impact brand loyalty in the fast-food industry, including the roles of brand passion and satisfaction as mediators. Data from 434 customers of a major fast-food chain in the Philippines were analyzed using Partial Least Squares Structural Equation Modeling (PLS-SEM). The study finds that staff behavior affects brand passion, satisfaction, and loyalty, while physical environment quality influences brand passion and satisfaction but not directly brand loyalty. Brand passion and satisfaction are key mediators in these relationships. The study highlights the importance of staff training and an appealing physical environment in building brand loyalty.

Chapter 10
Strengthening Sustainable Development Goal 5: Role of Gender Diversity and Creativity in
Selected Women-Owned Informal Small Businesses in Africa 219
    Timilehin Olasoji Olubiyi, Babcock University, Nigeria

The post-pandemic business landscape in Africa has recently been characterised by business non-effectiveness, lack of employee creativity, and ma. Therefore, this study investigates gender diversity and organisational creativity in selected women-owned informal small businesses in Lagos State, Nigeria. The study adopted a survey research design. The chapter focuses on women-owned businesses as the target population comprising 497 randomly selected companies operating international trades in Lagos State, Nigeria. selected women-owned informal small businesses in Lagos State, Nigeria. The study concluded that owner-managers of small businesses should focus on gender diversity and organisational creativity priorities as factors that will enhance workplace diversity and international trade. Therefore, the study recommends that owner-managers encourage peaceful coexistence and participation of employees irrespective of gender to improve organisational creativity and international trade.

Chapter 11
Guidelines for Generating Income Through Local Identity Products for Widows in the Southern
Border Provinces, Thailand 237
    Nutnapha Lekhavichit, Yala Rajabhat University, Thailand

The ongoing unrest in Thailand's southern border provinces has led to significant loss, leaving some women widowed and responsible for their families. This research focused on 1) generating income for widows through local identity products, 2) developing their online marketing skills, and 3) managing networks to enhance their business potential. The study involved 30 widows from Narathiwat, Pattani, and Yala, using in-depth interviews, observations, and content analysis. Findings revealed that widows prefer home-based work with sufficient income, with online sales identified as a key avenue for business success. Skills like making wedding trays were promoted, and a network with wedding event planners was established, boosting their income.

Chapter 12
The Development of Products From Budi Brown-Rice Flour to Promote Gluten-Free Brownies in
Budi Subdistrict, Yala Province, Thailand 255
    Sutida Lekhawichit, Yala Rajabhat University, Thailand
    Wiroj Phaiboonvessawat, Yala Rajabhat University, Thailand
    Ubol Tansom, Yala Rajabhat University, Thailand
    Sasithorn Pangsuban, Yala Rajabhat University, Thailand
    Kurosiyah Yamirudeng, Yala Rajabhat University, Thailand

This research to development of products from Budi brown rice flour to promote gluten-free brownies in Budi Subdistrict, Yala Province. The study combines a mixed-method approach combined with (PAR). The quantitative research utilized questionnaires, with the study population comprising consumers interested in or purchasing the product. The sample group included consumers interested in or purchasing the product. It was found that the development of the product's form to suit the target group, the quality of the product, and the characteristics of the product such as color, aroma, taste, texture, and packaging should be appropriately aligned with the product. The qualitative research involved in-depth interviews using a structured interview guide with key informants. The research findings suggest that participation in strengthening the enterprise allows community organizations to play a role and represent their network in expanding distribution channels. The development process:1) Innovation development, 2) Utilizing online media or processes, 3) Creating differentiation and recyclable

Chapter 13
Harnessing Business Analytics for Influencer Marketing: Enhancing Decision-Making and
Performance in Society 267
    Sreethi Rebeka R., Christ University, India
    Rejoice Thomas, Christ University, India

Business analytics has enhanced decision-making and performance across social sectors in the evolving digital technology and artificial intelligence (AI) landscape. This chapter explores the transformative role of business analytics, focusing on its application in influencer marketing. By leveraging data-driven insights, businesses can strategically navigate the complexities of consumer behaviour, optimize engagement strategies, and drive measurable outcomes. Key themes include the strategic integration of AI and machine learning, ethical considerations in data usage, and the impact of analytics on shaping future marketing strategies. As organizations embrace analytics tools to harness the power of influencer partnerships, they position themselves to innovate, adapt, and thrive in the competitive digital marketplace, ultimately driving the future of social sector initiatives through informed decision-making and impactful digital strategies.

Chapter 14
Evaluating the Degree of Risk Perception Among Kumbakonam Town Users of E-Commerce Platforms Using Artificial Intelligence 279
    K. Nalini, SASTRA University (Deemed), India
    G. Revathy, SASTRA University (Deemed), India

The rapid proliferation of e-commerce platforms has transformed traditional shopping behaviors, offering unparalleled convenience and accessibility. However, with these benefits come various perceived risks that can influence consumer adoption and usage patterns. This study aims to evaluate the degree of risk perception among users of e-commerce platforms in Kumbakonam town. Through a comprehensive survey and data analysis, we examine the factors contributing to risk perception, including concerns over financial security, privacy, product authenticity, and transaction reliability. By understanding the nuances of these risk perceptions, the study provides insights into how e-commerce businesses can address user concerns and enhance trust. The findings will help inform strategies to improve user experience and promote safer online shopping environments, ultimately contributing to the growth and sustainability of e-commerce in smaller towns like Kumbakonam.

Chapter 15
Please Don't Stop the Music! Exploring the Factors Affecting Continuous Usage Intention in a Music Streaming Platform 299
    Jean Paolo Gomez Lacap, City College of Angeles, Philippines
    Jessalyn Alqueza, University of the Visayas, Philippines
    Jebe Mag-usara, University of the Visayas, Philippines
    Jessell Tandugon, University of the Visayas, Philippines

This chapter aims to examine the motivators of users and subscribers regarding their continuing intention to use music streaming platforms, including brand involvement, technology affinity, brand trust, and compatibility. Cross-sectional quantitative data was collected from 301 qualified respondents via an online survey questionnaire. Data was analyzed and validated using a partial least squares (PLS) structural equation model (SEM) to examine the relationship between the endogenous and exogenous variables. The proposed model posits that the level of user-brand involvement and technology affinity substantially impacts the intention to continue using the platform. Moreover, brand trust and compatibility play a crucial role in mediating the intention to continue using the music streaming service, while users' affinity towards technology and their involvement with the brand significantly and positively affect the users' intention to continue using the platform.

Chapter 16
Intention to Use E-Wallet Services, User Satisfaction and Loyalty: The Mediating Role of Trust and the Moderating Effects of Technological Stress.. 321
Avelino Gonzales, Holy Angel University, Philippines
Jean Paolo Gomez Lacap, City College of Angeles, Philippines

Grounded in the Technology Acceptance Model (TAM) and the Stimulus-Organism-Response (SOR) model, this chapter investigates consumers' intentions to adopt e-wallet services, as well as their satisfaction and loyalty. Using purposive sampling and partial least squares (PLS) path modeling, the results demonstrate that perceived usefulness, perceived ease of use, perceived COVID-19 risk, and government support positively influence the intention to use e-wallet services. Furthermore, the intention to use e-wallet services leads to consumer satisfaction, which, in turn, enhances trust, ultimately resulting in loyalty. Trust is also found to mediate the relationship between consumer satisfaction and loyalty.

Chapter 17
Sustainable Travel Behavior: The Influence of Digital Marketing and Social Media 343
Suraj Jaywant Yadav, D.Y. Patil Education Society, India

Sustainable travel behavior has become crucial as tourism's environmental impact grows. Digital marketing and social media play vital roles in promoting sustainable tourism. This study explores how digital marketing campaigns influence consumers' sustainable travel choices and the role of social media in shaping these behaviors. It identifies key digital marketing strategies that encourage sustainable decisions and examines the impact of user-generated content (UGC) on social media. The results indicate that high social media usage and digital marketing exposure are strong predictors of sustainable travel behaviors, with females showing higher awareness. Digital marketing's effectiveness in promoting sustainable travel is highlighted by significant relationships and logistic regression findings ($\chi^2 = 15.34, p = 0.000$). Findings revealed high social media usage (mean = 4.1) and moderate awareness of sustainable travel (mean = 3.5), and digital marketing exposure, with odds ratios of 1.73 and 3.32, respectively, highlighting their potential to promote sustainable practices.

Chapter 18
Impact of Social Media on the Development of Religious Tourism Industry 359
Mohammad Badruddoza Talukder, International University of Business Agriculture and Technology, Bangladesh
Iva Rani Das, University of Dhaka, Bangladesh
Mohammad Nurul Afchar, Daffodil International University, Bangladesh

This chapter investigates the impact of social media on religious tourism, exploring its role in destination marketing, visitor experiences, and community engagement. A comprehensive literature review was conducted to examine the influence of social media on religious tourism development. Academic databases were searched using relevant keywords, and findings were structured around key themes. Social media enhances accessibility, information sharing, and community engagement in religious tourism but presents challenges regarding authenticity and privacy. Case studies illustrate successful social media strategies employed by stakeholders. Insights from this chapter inform stakeholders on leveraging social media to promote religious heritage and sustainable tourism practices, fostering visitor experiences and interfaith dialogue. This chapter offers a holistic understanding of social media's impact on religious tourism, combining theoretical insights with practical examples to guide industry stakeholders.

Chapter 19
Tourism Industry Amidst COVID-19 With Special Reference to National Capital Region of India 379
   Rama Verma, Amity University Online, India
   Kuldeep Singh, Amity University, Haryana, India
   Arnab Gantait, Independent Researcher, India
   Susanta Ranjan Chaini, Shiksha 'O' Anusandhan University, India

Travel and Tourism is one of the leisure and service-based industries that survive to facilitate people around the globe; at the same time, it is a loaf of bread for millions. The outbreak of the Novel Coronavirus devastated the industry for a period of time. In view of the severe impact, the study focuses on the strategy for the revival and survival of the industry and its industry professionals. The area is particularly in the Delhi NCR region of India. The major objective of the study is to showcase and measure the outcome of the impact in the selected area, the strategies implemented so far, and the plans to inculcate ways to overcome any such occurrence in the near future. Also, to analyze the impact of this region on the entire world, The study uses a quantitative method to analyze it with the help of the One-way ANNOVA technique. Probable suggestions provide a survival platform for the industry in times of crisis.

Chapter 20
The Allure of Tranquillity: How Less-Crowded Destinations in Bangladesh are Captivating International Tourists 399
   Mohammad Badruddoza Talukder, International University of Business Agriculture and
      Technology, Bangladesh
   Dil Afrin Swarna, Independent Researcher, Bangladesh
   Musfiqur Rahoman Khan, Daffodil Institute of IT, Bangladesh

This paper explores the effect of low-populated areas on international travelers to Bangladesh. It identifies the transition patterns in tourists' behavior from crowded, conventional places to untouched, unconventional structures, reshaping tourism architecture in Bangladesh. The chapter is thus informed on surveys gathered from past literature concerning international tourists visiting several off-the-beaten-path sites in Bangladesh. These tourists aim for less touristy, quiet, and genuine experiences and tend not to fall under overtourism. The analyzed work emphasized these areas' cultural and psychological features, resulting in better satisfaction due to a better image of Bangladesh as a tourist destination. We found that an optimal level of crowding contributes to long-term, grassroots roots and responsible tourism. Some recommendations have been given to policymakers and the tourism industries to improve and strengthen these areas for tourism significance in Bangladesh, which is essential for national image building and country positioning on the international travel map.

Chapter 21
Kuakata Reimagined: Forecasting Economic Growth and Future Potential of Coastal Hub in Bangladesh 419

    Mohammad Badruddoza Talukder, International University of Business Agriculture and Technology, Bangladesh
    Dil Afrin Swarna, Independent Researcher, Bangladesh
    Musfiqur Rahoman Khan, Daffodil Institute of IT, Bangladesh

Kuakata is a naturally gifted tourist spot in the Patuakhali district in the southern region of Bangladesh. It is particularly famous for its beautiful sunrise and sunset view over the Bay of Bengal. We aim to predict Kuakata's economic performance and prospects as the best tourist destination, as indicated in the literature review. The main aspects cover natural resources, archeological and historical points of interest, and current construction and improvements to tourist attractions and amenities. The outcome of our chapter on the elements of decision-making in the choice of strategies for theme park business reveals long-term planning, new attraction, partnership with the private sector, active community involvement, and technological innovation as fundamental strategies for economic growth. It is suggested that more focus must be given to sustainability, promotion, training, and extensive study. Thus, addressing these aspects, Kuakata can go for balanced development with economic upliftment and set its place as one of the most significant tourist spots in the face of Bangladesh.

Chapter 22
Integrating Sustainability With Dark Tourism 435

    Tripti Arvind, Christ University, India

The chapter examines the role of sustainability within dark tourism, including places that are associated with death, tragedy, and morbid. It is thus important to understand that although dark tourism offers educative and emotional values, it raises ethical and environmental issues. It also focuses on primary areas that include war zones, disaster sites, and memorials besides presenting an ethical concern and commercialization of suffering. So, it is crucial to find the middle ground by maintaining site dignity and focusing on storytelling. For sustainability, some of the most important focuses are environmental concerns, means reducing ecological footprint, and community engagement, also inclusion of communities in planning and project development. The chapter also covers how sustainable dark tourism can add value to learning process and raise consciousness of present consequences of historical occurrences, and helps with a clear framework of how sustainable strategies could be implemented in the future, which will become valuable for policymakers, tourism operators, academics.

Chapter 23
Defining Street Food 461
    Ninnart Daorattanahong, University of Canterbury, New Zealand
    Michael Colin Hall, University of Canterbury, New Zealand
    Girish Prayag, University of Canterbury, New Zealand
    Yaling Liu, University of Canterbury, New Zealand

Street food is a culinary attraction and cultural representation that includes a wide range of food and beverage options sold in public areas. However, despite growing interest in street food no clear and common definition exists. Based on a comprehensive literature review, this research examines the multifaceted dimensions of street food across six main themes to provide a comprehensive understanding of the street food context: type of street food, location of sale, street food vending structure, form of business, street food characteristics, and features of street food. A scoping literature review methodology was applied to investigate journal articles published between 1984 and 2024 in Thai and English to clarify the definition of street food. Overall, the study enhanced understanding of the comprehensive role of street food in society and provides substantial insights into the culinary diversity, social and economic importance, and cultural value of street food in urban areas.

Compilation of References 497

About the Contributors 607

Index 611

Preface

In today's rapidly evolving world, the concept of business success has shifted dramatically. Gone are the days when success was measured solely by financial performance over a short period. Instead, we are now tasked with the challenge of fostering continuous, long-term performance while ensuring that our actions are beneficial to society and the environment. As we enter the era of *Society 5.0*, where technology permeates every aspect of life, the goal is no longer just business efficiency, but creating a harmonious relationship between technological advancement, societal well-being, and sustainable practices.

This edited volume, *Business Sustainability Practices in Society 5.0*, brings together insights and research from experts across the globe who have dedicated their work to answering one critical question: how can businesses thrive in this new age while remaining sustainable? The competition in today's market is fierce, driven by unprecedented technological advancements. In this context, sustainability is not an option but a necessity.

In compiling this book, we have sought to provide readers with the most current research and emerging trends on sustainability practices that are tailored for a super-smart society. The chapters included range from foundational theories to practical applications across a variety of fields, making this a versatile resource for readers with diverse interests. Whether you are an academic, researcher, or practitioner in business administration—encompassing fields such as strategic management, entrepreneurship, information systems, human resources, operations management, marketing, tourism, or international business—this book offers valuable insights. Moreover, it is particularly relevant for professionals in the technology sector, especially those interested in the business dimensions of artificial intelligence and its role in shaping a sustainable future.

We believe that this book will not only serve as an essential academic resource but also inspire further interdisciplinary research and innovation. We are confident that the ideas presented here will spark discussions and actions that push the boundaries of business sustainability in the age of Society 5.0.

CHAPTER OVERVIEW

In Chapter 1, we delve into the historical context of sustainable development, tracing its evolution as a global agenda. The chapter rigorously analyzes empirical data from the Scopus database, addressing fundamental questions regarding the essence of sustainable development, its necessity, the current global landscape, and the conditions required for countries to transition from unsustainable practices. This synthesis sets the stage for understanding how nations can effectively achieve and maintain sustainable development throughout this century.

Chapter 2 shifts focus to the intersection of behavioral insights and artificial intelligence (AI) within the framework of Society 5.0. This chapter presents a forward-looking exploration of how AI technologies can enhance productivity and tackle social challenges through human-centric approaches. By integrating psychological, economic, and neuroscientific insights, it offers a compelling case for using behavioral data in decision-making, thereby demonstrating practical applications that drive sustainable growth.

In Chapter 3, we address the critical role of strategic management in organizations amid an information-saturated environment. This chapter emphasizes the significance of business information systems and corporate excellence in leveraging knowledge for competitive advantage in the global marketplace. It underscores the necessity for executives and managers to refine their information-handling capabilities to thrive in the 21st century.

Chapter 4 investigates the psychological dimensions of entrepreneurship, examining how entrepreneurial passion (EP) and Machiavellianism shape entrepreneurial intention (EI). The chapter employs a robust research design involving MBA students in Metro Manila, revealing the moderating effects of entrepreneurial creativity and self-efficacy. The findings illuminate the intricate interplay between personal traits and entrepreneurial aspirations, contributing to a deeper understanding of the entrepreneurial process.

Chapter 5 focuses on International Human Resource Management (IHRM) and the complex dynamics of managing a diverse workforce across borders. By identifying essential competencies such as cultural intelligence and strategic thinking, this chapter offers valuable insights for HR professionals navigating the challenges of global operations, emphasizing the importance of adaptability and ongoing learning in international settings.

In Chapter 6, we explore the transformative potential of HR Analytics (HRA) within organizations. This chapter systematically unpacks the mechanisms through which HRA enhances organizational performance, utilizing data from various sectors to build a comprehensive understanding of evidence-based management. The findings advance the discourse on how analytics can inform HR practices to drive strategic outcomes.

Chapter 7 discusses the pivotal role of work-based education (WBE) in bridging the gap between academia and industry. The chapter highlights the integration of practical experience with academic knowledge, advocating for innovative teaching methodologies that align educational objectives with market demands. It outlines how emerging technologies and global partnerships can enhance the efficacy of WBE, ultimately improving graduates' employability.

In Chapter 8, the focus shifts to diversity and inclusion as paramount concerns for HR departments. This chapter investigates the impact of diverse workforce practices on employee engagement across various sectors in India. By addressing gaps in existing literature, it presents a thorough analysis of how effective diversity management fosters a more engaged and productive workforce.

Chapter 9 utilizes the Stimulus-Organism-Response (SOR) theory to analyze brand loyalty in the fast-food industry, highlighting the influence of staff behavior and environmental quality. Through rigorous data analysis, the chapter reveals that both staff training and a positive physical environment are crucial for enhancing brand loyalty, emphasizing the importance of customer experience in competitive markets.

Chapter 10 examines the intersection of gender diversity and organizational creativity within women-owned informal businesses in Lagos, Nigeria. The study highlights how prioritizing gender diversity can enhance creativity and international trade opportunities, providing actionable recommendations for small business owners to cultivate inclusive workplaces.

In Chapter 11, we explore the entrepreneurial journeys of widows in Thailand's southern border provinces, focusing on income generation through local identity products and online marketing. This research highlights the importance of community networks and skill development in fostering economic independence for marginalized groups.

Chapter 12 presents a study on the development of gluten-free products using Budi brown rice flour, illustrating the integration of community engagement in product innovation. The chapter emphasizes the need for aligning product characteristics with consumer preferences to enhance market viability, showcasing a participatory approach to entrepreneurship.

Chapter 13 investigates the impact of business analytics on influencer marketing, emphasizing the strategic use of data-driven insights to optimize engagement. The chapter discusses ethical considerations and the future of marketing strategies as organizations leverage analytics to navigate consumer behavior effectively.

In Chapter 14, we evaluate consumer perceptions of risks associated with e-commerce platforms, particularly in Kumbakonam. This study identifies key factors influencing risk perception and offers strategic insights for e-commerce businesses to enhance user trust and safety, thereby promoting sustainable growth in digital markets.

Chapter 15 examines the motivations behind continued use of music streaming platforms, analyzing factors such as brand involvement and technology affinity. By employing structural equation modeling, this chapter elucidates the complex relationships that drive user loyalty in the competitive music streaming landscape.

Chapter 16 explores the adoption of e-wallet services through the lenses of the Technology Acceptance Model and the SOR model. The findings reveal significant predictors of consumer intention, satisfaction, and loyalty, offering insights for service providers on enhancing user experiences in the digital payment sphere.

Chapter 17 highlights the role of digital marketing in promoting sustainable travel behavior. By analyzing the influence of social media on consumer choices, this chapter identifies effective marketing strategies that encourage environmentally responsible travel, providing a blueprint for industry stakeholders to adopt sustainable practices.

In Chapter 18, we investigate the impact of social media on religious tourism, examining its role in destination marketing and visitor experiences. The chapter provides a nuanced understanding of how social media facilitates community engagement while addressing ethical concerns regarding authenticity and privacy in tourism promotion.

Chapter 19 addresses the challenges and strategies for reviving the travel and tourism industry in the Delhi NCR region post-COVID-19. Through quantitative analysis, this chapter assesses the impact of the pandemic and outlines actionable recommendations for industry stakeholders to enhance resilience and sustainability in future crises.

Chapter 20 examines the behavioral shifts of international travelers towards low-populated areas in Bangladesh, emphasizing the desire for authentic experiences away from overtourism. The chapter suggests that a balanced approach to tourism development can enhance cultural appreciation and satisfaction, offering recommendations for sustainable practices in the sector.

In Chapter 21, we turn our attention to Kuakata, a scenic tourist destination in Bangladesh. The chapter forecasts its economic potential by analyzing natural resources and ongoing developments, advocating for strategic planning and community involvement as essential components for sustainable tourism growth.

Finally, Chapter 22 explores sustainability in the context of dark tourism, addressing the ethical implications of visiting sites associated with tragedy. This chapter proposes strategies for maintaining site dignity while promoting educational value, underscoring the need for community engagement in the development of sustainable dark tourism practices.

In Chapter 23, we conclude with an examination of street food as a cultural and culinary phenomenon. By analyzing the multifaceted dimensions of street food, this chapter enriches our understanding of its social and economic significance, paving the way for future research and policy development in urban culinary tourism.

These chapters collectively provide a rich tapestry of insights and strategies for navigating the complexities of sustainable development in diverse contexts. Each contribution adds depth to our understanding of the multifaceted challenges and opportunities that lie ahead.

CONCLUSION

In concluding this preface, we reflect on the transformative nature of business sustainability in the context of Society 5.0. As we navigate the intersection of technology, societal needs, and environmental stewardship, the contributions within this volume illuminate diverse pathways to achieving sustainable success. The varied perspectives presented in these chapters not only underscore the urgency of integrating sustainability into core business practices but also highlight the innovative solutions emerging across industries.

As editors, we believe that the insights gathered here will serve as a catalyst for further exploration and discourse. By fostering a deeper understanding of the challenges and opportunities inherent in sustainable practices, we hope to inspire academics, practitioners, and policymakers alike to embrace collaborative efforts towards a more sustainable future.

We encourage our readers to engage critically with the ideas and research presented in this book. Each chapter offers valuable lessons that can be adapted and applied in different contexts, reinforcing the notion that sustainable business is not merely a trend but a fundamental necessity in our rapidly evolving world. Together, let us strive for a harmonious coexistence of technological advancement and societal well-being, paving the way for resilient and thriving communities in the years to come.

We thank all the contributors for their dedication and insights, which have enriched this volume. May this work inspire meaningful change and foster a commitment to sustainability that resonates far beyond the pages of this book.

Kittisak Jermsittiparsert
Shinawatra University, Thailand

Ismail Wekke
Institut Agama Islam Negeri (IAIN) Sorong, Indonesia

Pannee Suanpang
Suan Dusit University, Thailand

Chapter 1
Sustainable Development:
What? Why? and How?

Samanan Rattanasirivilai
Suan Sunandha Rajabhat University, Thailand

Sippaphat Rotjanawasuthorn
Association of Legal and Political Studies, Thailand

Sirinapattha Sirinapatpokin
Association of Legal and Political Studies, Thailand

Puthisat Namdech
Association of Legal and Political Studies, Thailand

Kittisak Jermsittiparsert
https://orcid.org/0000-0003-3245-8705
Shinawatra University, Thailand

ABSTRACT

Sustainable development is a global agenda set together a century ago that countries will follow and achieve in the first half of this century. The answer to the big question "What are the conditions that will make a country successful or unsuccessful in sustainable development?" has arisen and continues today. To answer these questions with empirical data, this paper synthesizes documents in the Scopus database published from 2013 to the present and highlights how current knowledge answers these questions: 1) What is sustainable development? 2) Why is it necessary for the country to develop sustainably? 3) What is the current situation of sustainable development in the world? 4) What are the conditions and methods that will enable the country to move away from unsustainable development? 5) What are the conditions and methods for achieving sustainable development in a country? And lastly, 6) What are the conditions and methods for maintaining a sustainable level of development? The answer to each question is explained and discussed accordingly.

DOI: 10.4018/979-8-3693-9230-0.ch001

Copyright ©2025, IGI Global. Copying or distributing in print or electronic forms without written permission of IGI Global is prohibited.

WHAT IS SUSTAINABLE DEVELOPMENT?

Sustainable development refers to a development approach that meets the needs of the present without compromising the ability of future generations to meet their own needs (Lind et al., 2016; Sato, 2015; Dernbach & Cheever, 2015; Conca & Dabelko, 2018; Voukkali et al., 2014). It encompasses two key concepts: prioritizing the essential needs of the world's poor and recognizing the limitations imposed by technology and social organization on the environment's ability to meet present and future needs (Lind et al., 2016).

Sustainable development encompasses economic, environmental, social, and policy perspectives, each of which is crucial for achieving a balanced and inclusive approach to development. Here are the key principles and perspectives of sustainable development, supported by insights from academic documents.

Key Principles of Sustainable Development

1) Integration of Environmental Protection, Social Justice, and Economic Development: Sustainable development requires the consideration and achievement of environmental protection, social justice, and economic development (Ryan, 2017; Villarreal, 2014). This integration ensures that decisions about social and economic development incorporate environmental protection, and decisions about environmental quality consider social justice and economic viability (Ryan, 2017).

2) Fairness and Equity: Fairness is a fundamental principle of sustainable development, encompassing the rights of future generations to adjust to the current generation's bequeathal and the rights of all present generations to enjoy democratic rights and sustained livelihoods (Rai & Fulekar, 2023; Batalhão et al., 2021). This principle emphasizes intergenerational and intragenerational equity (Batalhão et al., 2021).

Economic Perspectives on Sustainable Development

1) Resource Accounting and Sustainable Growth Modeling: Economic approaches to sustainable development utilize resource accounting based on potential externalities, sustainable growth modeling, and the conceptual definition of strong and weak sustainability (Hasslöf, 2014; Dernbach & Cheever, 2015).

2) Environmental Limits and Precautionary Principle: Economic perspectives emphasize the importance of not exceeding environmental limits and adopting the precautionary principle in cases of doubt (Batalhão et al., 2021; Hasslöf, 2014).

Environmental Perspectives on Sustainable Development

1) Lean Attitude towards Ecosystem and Green Technologies: The ecological component of sustainable development focuses on a lean attitude towards the ecosystem and the development of "green" technologies to support innovative growth and protect the environment for future generations (Villarreal, 2014; Jordan & O'Riordan, 2023).

2) Environmental Justice and Equity: The social dimension, particularly environmental justice and equity, is considered crucial to the concept of sustainable development, contributing to the paradigm of Just Sustainability (Mantaeva et al., 2021).

Social Perspectives on Sustainable Development

1) Intragenerational and Intergenerational Equity: The concept of sustainable development requires both intragenerational equity, focusing on the relief of poverty and decent living standards, and intergenerational equity, ensuring fairness to future generations (Batalhão et al., 2021; Conca & Dabelko, 2018).
2) Education for Sustainable Development: Education for Sustainable Development is essential for promoting pluralistic views of sustainability and addressing conflicting perspectives on the intertwined dimensions of sustainable development (Van Den Bergh, 2014).

Policy Perspectives on Sustainable Development

1) Shifts in Focus: Policies and programs for sustainable development have shifted focus from production and the firm to products and consumption, and then to structural issues shaping systems of production and consumption (López et al., 2018).
2) Multi-Stakeholder Process: The international diplomatic conference on sustainable development, Rio+20, portrays sustainable development as a multi-stakeholder process aimed at increasing the well-being of present and future generations in an inclusive, equitable, and environmentally balanced fashion (Capper et al., 2014).

Why Is It Necessary for the Country to Develop Sustainably?

Sustainable development is crucial for countries due to several key reasons, as supported by academic documents.

1) Long-term resilience: Sustainable development enables countries to face crises effectively, as seen in China's transformation from a third world country to a major country after achieving sustainable development (Al-Dabbagh, 2020).
2) Preservation of resources: With the increasing global population, sustainable development is necessary to ensure the well-being of people and preserve resources for future generations (Li et al., 2017; Nezamova et al., 2023).
3) Human capital and well-being: Sustainable development relies on human capital, including health and education, as these factors significantly influence individual and community behavior and the efficiency of labor (Rahayu, 2017).
4) Environmental impact: Ignoring environmental interests in development can lead to environmental degradation and resource depletion, emphasizing the need for balanced economic, environmental, and social interests (Attfield, 2015).

5) Interconnectedness of natural resources and society: The sustainable development of humanity is closely linked to managing impacts on natural resources and the environment, which is essential for maintaining quality of life and well-being (Ciobotaru, 2015; Podaşcă, 2016).

Advantages of Sustainable Development for the Country

Economic Benefits of Sustainable Development: Sustainable development aims to balance economic, environmental, and social interests to increase people's welfare (Kumaran et al., 2022). It promotes a green economy, which enables economic growth and investment while increasing environmental quality and social inclusiveness (Zorpas, 2014). The transition to a green economy is intended to enable sustained, inclusive, and equitable economic growth and job creation (Henriksen et al., 2021).

1) Economic Benefits of Sustainable Development for the Country: Attaining economic growth through sustainable measures benefits society in the long run (Schoenaker et al., 2015). Sustainable economic development enhances equitable local income and employment growth without endangering the environment or contributing to global climate change (Dutta & Saha, 2023). Sustainable development policies and incentives can enhance conservation, recycling, and the use of renewable resources, promoting a bioeconomy that produces renewable products (Pais et al., 2019). Investments in nature, such as environmental capital, have a positive impact on economic growth and can lead to effective strategies and policies for sustainable development (Batalhão et al., 2021).
2) Contribution to GDP and Economic Growth: Economic development indicators, such as GDP, may not measure all dimensions of society's progress, leading to the need for alternative measurement systems to evaluate sustainable development (Yaprakli & Özden, 2021). Economic complexity is significantly affected by sustainable development's economic indicators, such as GDP, foreign direct investment (FDI), and research and development (R&D) expenditure, suggesting that investments in the green economy foster economic complexity while ensuring stability (Batrancea et al., 2023). The relationship between financial development and sustainable development is essential, as financial development fosters eco-friendly investment, financial inclusion, and economic growth, contributing to sustainable development (Shepelev et al., 2024). Energy consumption and the consumption of renewable energy have a positive impact on sustainable economic growth, indicating a relationship between energy usage and economic growth (Wang et al., 2023).
3) Long-Term Economic Implications: The effect of the financial crisis is verified immediately in GDP, in contrast to the lagged effect observed in the Genuine Progress Indicator (GPI), emphasizing the importance of considering long-term implications of economic growth and sustainability (Kartsan et al., 2023). Sustainable growth modeling and the conceptual definition of strong and weak sustainability are important in achieving sustainable development, as they assess and anticipate conditions and trends to avoid future economic, environmental, and social problems (Zilberman et al., 2018). Effective climate policy entails analysis that incorporates present and future changes in both capital and Total Factor Productivity (TFP), revealing the role of key parameters in determining economic values (Chapple, 2014).
4) Key Economic Indicators: Genuine Progress Indicator (GPI) is an alternative measurement needed to evaluate sustainable development, as it provides valuable information for policymakers seeking to achieve both economic growth and sustainable development (Kartsan et al., 2023). Economic

indicators and impacts are essential for sustainable development practices, but a comprehensive approach to economic assessment in the sustainable development perspective must guide indicators in a systematic way (Zilberman et al., 2018). The economic mechanisms for environmental protection, such as environmental taxes, emissions trading, and subsidies, are crucial for achieving sustainable development by preserving natural systems and maintaining the environment's quality (Lampert, 2021).

Social Well-being Implications:

Sustainable development contributes to social well-being by striving to achieve sustainable happiness and life satisfaction (Prizzia, 2017). It emphasizes the importance of social sustainability in bringing satisfaction and happiness to society (Prizzia, 2017). The concept of sustainable development promotes equality, independence, collaboration, and empowerment, aiming to improve the quality of life for people worldwide (Alam & Razzaque, 2015).

1) Economic Benefits of Sustainable Development for Social Well-being: Sustainable development is linked to the innovative development of environmentally friendly technologies and the international diffusion of innovations in the field of "green economy" (Rossi et al., 2024). It involves the availability of new technologies of the "green economy," productivity of resource-saving industries, and government support for environmental entrepreneurship (Rossi et al., 2024). The sustainable development goals (SDGs) aim at reconciling economic and social with ecological goals, which can influence strategic choices of policymakers to develop potential improvements (Rodzoś, 2019).
2) Impact on Health and Healthcare System: Sustainable development is associated with the health-related Sustainable Development Goal (SDG-3) which aims to ensure 'good health and well-being' for all (Gallardo-Vázquez & Folgado-Fernández, 2020). There is a significant relation between SDG-3 and subjective well-being scores, suggesting a holistic approach to economic development for improving citizen well-being (Gallardo-Vázquez & Folgado-Fernández, 2020). The 17 SDGs aim at promoting equilibrium between socio-economic development and environmental conservation, which can influence the well-being of countries with poorly progressed SDGs (Dasgupta, 2024).
4) Environmental and Ecological Benefits: Sustainable development is essential for guaranteeing that a population's present needs can be met without compromising future generations' well-being (Nezamova et al., 2023). It involves stable development of economic, environmental, and social spheres to improve the standard of living and preserve resources for future inhabitants of the earth (Pokorný & Palacká, 2023). The goals of sustainable development are oriented around the "three E's"—environmental protection, economic growth, and social equity, which correlate with quality-of-life considerations (Cusack, 2019).
5) Social and Cultural Impacts: Social development strategies include ensuring a satisfactory level of education while fostering an adequate quality of life and long-term sustainability (Nezamova et al., 2023). The concept of social capital and resilient communities is gaining significance in sustainable development, emphasizing the need to develop communities that can face challenges and adapt to new conditions in an active way (Kovalevsky et al., 2020). Human well-being is a prerequisite for achieving sustainable development, and specific indicators of human well-being

have an impact on the reported level of sustainability achieved on a macroeconomic scale (Du et al., 2024).

Environmental Advantages:

Sustainable development requires maintaining the value of renewable resources and ecosystems, integrating environmental protection into decisions about social and economic development (Dernbach & Cheever, 2015; Addai et al., 2024). It emphasizes the need to reduce carbon emissions and ecological footprints, with a focus on renewable energy and institutional quality to promote environmental sustainability (Voronina et al., 2024). The concept of a green economy and green growth are considered as tools for linking economic and environmental goals, promoting sustainable growth and providing prospects for new economic opportunities (Rahayu, 2017).

1) Sustainable Development and Environmental Protection: Sustainable development aims to meet the needs of the present generation while ensuring the ability of future generations to meet their own needs, emphasizing the protection of the environment (Zorpas, 2014; Kumaran et al., 2022). It promotes ecological balance, which is essential for environmental sustainability (Zorpas, 2014). The case study of Andhra Pradesh demonstrates a model for balancing development and environmental protection through measures such as observing environmental laws, expediting environmental clearance processes, and systematizing solid waste management (Zorpas, 2014).
2) Energy Consumption and Environmental Impact: Unsustainable energy production systems have a significant impact on the environment, leading to global warming and air pollution (Venkateswarlu et al., 2020). Sustainable development seeks to improve the standard of living economically and environmentally over the long term by finding new, clean energy alternatives and increasing societal awareness of environmental issues (Venkateswarlu et al., 2020).
3) Climate Change and Vulnerability: Sustainable development is crucial for addressing climate change, which poses a severe challenge to achieving sustainable development goals (Ozturkm & Yuksel, 2016). Vulnerability to climate change varies across nations and is influenced by social, economic, cultural, and environmental factors (Ozturkm & Yuksel, 2016).
4) Promotion of Green Technologies: The development of "green" technologies, such as hydropower, wind energy, solar energy, and bioenergy, is emphasized as a key point of economic growth without harming the environment (Mantaeva et al., 2021).

In conclusion, sustainable development offers various benefits for a country, including economic growth, social well-being, and environmental protection. It aims to create a balance between economic, environmental, and social needs, promoting inclusive and equitable growth while ensuring the well-being of present and future generations. The evidence from the documents supports the multifaceted advantages of sustainable development, highlighting its potential to address global challenges and foster a more sustainable and equitable society.

Disadvantages of Unsustainable Development for the Country

Unsustainable development leads to large-scale financial crises caused by irresponsible banking and changes in the global climate due to dependence on fossil fuel-based energy sources (Wallace, 2014; Balaji et al., 2022). It results in environmental unsustainability due to specific patterns of production and consumption, as well as population growth, leading to severe consequences for the natural environment (Taylor et al., 2015). The concept of unsustainable consumption and production patterns endangers global development more than ever (Brand et al., 2021).

Economic Impact of Unsustainable Development:

Economic development, at least thus far, has been decidedly unsustainable, leading to environmental degradation and resource depletion (Narain, 2016). Inequality and unsustainability are linked, and the world needs environmental solutions that are affordable and inclusive to meet the needs of all (Singh, 2022). Unsustainable economic development can lead to vulnerabilities in society and failures in governance, making individuals and ecosystems vulnerable to external perturbations and social crises (Adger & Winkels, 2014; Gordon, 2015).

1) Economic Consequences of Unsustainable Development: Unsustainable development can have adverse effects on a country's GDP and overall economic growth (Salotti & Trecroci, 2016; Dutta & Saha, 2023). It may lead to persistent poverty, rising income inequalities, perpetual gender disparities, environmental degradation, and impacts of climate change, hindering economic progress (Salotti & Trecroci, 2016).
2) Impact on Trade Balance and International Competitiveness: Unsustainable development can affect a country's trade balance and international competitiveness by leading to a negative impact on productivity growth and private investment, thus affecting the overall economy (Dung, 2024). Trade liberalization may have a negative impact on productivity growth in developing countries, potentially diminishing innovation and affecting international trade openness (Jha & Srinivasan, 2023).
3) Long-Term Fiscal Implications: Unsustainable development can pose long-term fiscal challenges, especially in the face of population ageing and climate change, which are likely to contribute to rising fiscal pressures (Gök & Sodhi, 2023; Auerbach, 2016). High public debt can adversely affect both aggregate investment spending and productivity growth, leading to fiscal challenges (Dung, 2024).
4) Sector-Specific Impacts: Unsustainable development can have sector-specific impacts on industries such as agriculture, manufacturing, and services, potentially leading to environmental degradation and social inequality (Lopez-Claros, 2014). It can also influence the technological gap of a small developing nation, affecting its productivity growth and economic policies (Jha & Srinivasan, 2023).

Social Implications of Unsustainable Development:

Unsustainable development has led to widening income gaps, stagnant economic growth, and deepening economic polarization, affecting both developing and developed countries (Domaracká et al. 2018). Vulnerabilities created by unsustainable resource use and exploitation affect individuals, communities, and ecosystems, emphasizing the need to address underlying vulnerabilities in society (Gordon, 2015).

1) Social Inequality and Unsustainable Economic Growth: The capitalist system creates insecurity and inequality for social classes, leading to social pressure on the political class to execute change for a better future (Okonjo-Iweala, 2017). Unsustainable economic growth and development contribute to social inequality in countries, impacting the well-being of the population (Masilo, 2022).
2) Impact on Marginalized Groups: Social exclusion and marginalization in developing countries deny many people access to education and perpetuate poverty, breaching human rights and hindering economic potential (Latchem, 2018).
3) Gender Disparities: Women in Sub-Saharan Africa face constraints in accessing basic assets and resources, impacting economic development and growth potential (Tikhomirova & Sukiasyan, 2021).
4) Population Growth and Socio-Economic Stability: Uncontrolled population growth in South Africa has led to a decline in socio-economic stability, affecting access to basic services and exacerbating challenges such as poverty and unemployment (Bran et al., 2014).

Environmental Consequences of Unsustainable Development:

Unsustainable economic growth and population growth have led to environmental damage, affecting climate change, global warming, and environmental pollution (Kopnina, 2016). Unsustainable development trends have resulted in resource depletion, waste disposal, climate change, extinction of species, and challenges to the integrity of ecosystems (McGregor, 2014). The consequences of unsustainable economic development include altering the provisioning and regulating functions of the Earth's ecological systems, leading to resource shortages and a changing climate (Milićević et al., 2023).

1) Ecological Consequences of Unsustainable Development Practices on Biodiversity and Ecosystems: Unsustainable development practices, such as land use change, deforestation, and habitat fragmentation, have led to the loss of biodiversity and ecosystem services (Cordella et al., 2022). Environmental externalities, lack of property rights, and asymmetrical information are indirect causes of ecosystem degradation (Cordella et al., 2022). Overexploitation of natural resources, driven by flawed development paradigms and simplistic metrics such as GDP, has resulted in the decline and extinction of species, leading to an increase in zoonotic pandemics (Bhattacharya & Managi, 2015). The loss of biodiversity alters the integrity and functioning of ecosystems, affecting ecosystem services and resilience (Brownlie et al., 2013).
2) Economic Impacts of Unsustainable Development Practices on Biodiversity and Ecosystems: Economic growth and industrial development have caused significant biodiversity loss and damage to ecosystems (Roy & Mukhopadhyay, 2015). Businesses impact ecosystems and services through their activities, and their survival depends on biodiversity and ecosystem services as inputs to their

production (Roy & Mukhopadhyay, 2015). Unsustainable practices of production and consumption have put nature in crisis, negatively affecting human wellbeing (Srinivasan & Shanker, 2021).

3) Social Implications of Unsustainable Development Practices on Biodiversity and Ecosystems: Loss of biodiversity and ecosystems has adverse effects on ecosystems' resilience and the well-being of local communities (Cordella et al., 2022). Overexploitation of biological resources has disrupted ecosystems and declined ecosystem services, impacting the well-being of local people (Carlucci et al., 2017). Development projects applying the mitigation hierarchy should consider related social impacts, as restrictions on access to biodiversity and ecosystem services can affect local well-being (Kluvankova et al., 2019).

In conclusion, unsustainable development poses significant disadvantages for a country, including economic instability, environmental degradation, and social vulnerabilities. The evidence from the academic documents underscores the multifaceted nature of these disadvantages and the urgent need for sustainable development initiatives to address these challenges.

The Current Situation of Sustainable Development in the World

The current situation of sustainable development on a global scale is characterized by the evolution of the concept over the past few decades, with a focus on the integration of economic, social, and environmental aspects (Kwatraet al., 2020; Bobylev, 2017; Dernbach & Cheever, 2015; Zhang, 2022). Key indicators of sustainable development on a global scale include the United Nations' goals for sustainable development, such as the Adjusted Net Savings Index developed by the World Bank (Kwatraet al., 2020). The concept of sustainable development emphasizes the need to balance economic growth, social equity, and environmental integrity (Wang et al., 2019; Noble, 2015). Different regions of the world vary in their progress towards sustainable development, with Asia being highlighted as a crucial region due to its dominant role in the global economy (Medvedev et al., 2023). The study of 44 Asian nations revealed hidden development dimensions and a mega-index of sustainable development, showcasing the complexity of sustainable development indicators at a regional level (Medvedev et al., 2023). The challenges hindering sustainable development on a global scale are multifaceted, including high-energy utilization, fossil-fuel consumption, environmental pollution, weak governance, natural resource overexploitation, and loss of traditional culture (Shaqour & Farzaneh, 2021; Shaker & Mackay, 2021). The global context, including the global governance system, the North-South debate, and global trade liberalization, presents obstacles to the implementation of sustainable development (Bakari, 2015). International policies and agreements play a crucial role in promoting sustainable development worldwide, as evidenced by the United Nations' sustainability summit in 2015, which introduced the 17 SDGs and the Paris Agreement aimed at addressing climate change and GHG emission mitigation (Capper et al., 2014; Noble, 2015).

Key Indicators of Sustainable Development on a Global Scale:

The United Nations' goals for sustainable development, including the Adjusted Net Savings Index developed by the World Bank, are crucial indicators of sustainable development (Kwatraet al., 2020). Sustainable development emphasizes the need to balance economic growth, social equity, and environmental integrity (Wang et al., 2019; Noble, 2015).

Comparison of Different Regions in Terms of Progress Towards Sustainable Development:

Asia, as the most populous continent and a dominant player in the global economy, is a crucial region for understanding global change and sustainable development (Medvedev et al., 2023). A study of 44 Asian nations revealed hidden development dimensions and a mega-index of sustainable development, showcasing the complexity of sustainable development indicators at a regional level (Medvedev et al., 2023).

Major Challenges Hindering Sustainable Development on a Global Scale:

Challenges include high-energy utilization, fossil-fuel consumption, environmental pollution, weak governance, natural resource overexploitation, and loss of traditional culture (Shaqour & Farzaneh, 2021; Shaker & Mackay, 2021). The global context, including the global governance system, the North-South debate, and global trade liberalization, presents obstacles to the implementation of sustainable development (Bakari, 2015).

Role of International Policies and Agreements in Promoting Sustainable Development Worldwide:

The United Nations' sustainability summit in 2015 introduced the 17 SDGs, and the Paris Agreement aimed at addressing climate change and GHG emission mitigation, highlighting the role of international policies and agreements in promoting sustainable development worldwide (Capper et al., 2014; Noble, 2015).

The Progress of Sustainable Development in Developed Countries

Composite Sustainable Development Index (SDI) is used to assess the progress made by advanced economies towards achieving sustainable development goals. It reveals that advanced economies had a satisfactory level of sustainability, especially since the adoption of the Paris Agreement in 2015 (Lior et al., 2018). A study evaluating the level of sustainable development in European Union member states found that countries like Sweden, Luxembourg, and Denmark showed the highest level of sustainable development, while others like Portugal and Bulgaria had lower levels (Bujanowicz-Haraś et al., 2015). The United Nations has put forward a set of indicators to monitor and evaluate the progress of global sustainable development, but these indicators may not apply to tracking the progress of sustainable development at the national level. However, a system of evaluation indicators has been built to assess the progress of sustainable development at the national level in China (Zhu et al., 2019). The European Union has made significant progress in implementing sustainable development strategies, especially among new member states that joined after 2004 (Balcerzak & Pietrzak, 2017).

Key Indicators for Measuring Sustainable Development in Developed Countries:

The United Nations has put forward a set of indicators to monitor and evaluate the progress of global sustainable development, which are internationally comparable but may not apply to tracking the progress of sustainable development at the national level (Schoenaker et al., 2015). The Genuine Progress Indicator (GPI) is an alternative measurement used to evaluate sustainable development, considering the limitations of gross domestic product (GDP) in quantifying welfare and sustainability (Lior et al., 2018). The indicators used to measure sustainable development encompass economic, social, environmental, and institutional-political domains, and are aimed at providing a comprehensive assessment of progress (Pais et al., 2019). Composite Sustainable Development Index is a tool designed to assess the progress made by advanced and emerging economies towards achieving sustainable development goals, considering indicators related to economy, society, governance, and environment (Rocchi et al., 2022).

Comparison of Sustainable Development Progress between Developed and Developing Countries:

Results from a study of 28 Organisation for Economic Co-operation and Development (OECD) countries suggest that the richest countries are not always the most sustainable, and the effect of the financial crisis is immediately observed in GDP but with a lagged effect in the GPI (Lior et al., 2018). The level of sustainable development in highly developed countries is evaluated using different sets of indicators compared to medium-developed and poor countries, indicating the need for separate indicator sets based on the level of development (Salamon, 2019). The success or failure in the implementation of sustainable development largely depends on the national implementation effort, and the measure of progress allows the consistency among the different dimensions of sustainable development to be assessed (Kaniaru, 2016).

Challenges and Barriers to Achieving Sustainable Development in Developed Countries:

The trade-off between preserving the environment and economic growth has been a growing concern reflected in academic literature, highlighting the need for new measurements to evaluate sustainable development due to the limitations of GDP in quantifying welfare and sustainability (Lior et al., 2018). The analysis of 55 sustainable development indicator (SDI) sets shows a great degree of agreement on the most popular indicators and themes, emphasizing the need for harmonization of measurement systems and flexibility at country level (Zhu et al., 2019). The concept of sustainable development is recognized as a common agenda for both developed and developing countries, providing the only feasible basis for assured common development (Yoon, 2014).

Role of Government Policies in Driving Sustainable Development Progress in Developed Countries:

The success of the 2030 Agenda and Sustainable Development Goals largely depends on the national implementation effort, and the measure of progress allows the consistency among the different dimensions of sustainable development to be assessed (Kaniaru, 2016). The democratic aspect of political systems and government administration, as well as the vitality of trade, are critical conditions for successful sustainable development policies, highlighting the importance of government policies in driving sustainable development progress (Koilo, 2020).

THE PROGRESS OF SUSTAINABLE DEVELOPMENT IN DEVELOPING COUNTRIES

Measuring Progress of Sustainable Development in Developing Countries:

The United Nations has put forward a set of indicators to monitor and evaluate the progress of global sustainable development, aimed for global and regional progress, but with a disadvantage that it does not apply to tracking the progress of sustainable development at the national level (Zhu et al., 2019). A study developed a Composite SDG Index to represent the comprehensive performance of achieving SDGs, using 108 indicators to assess the performance of achieving SDGs for 15 countries along the "Belt and Road," providing various national development models and related policy recommendations (Ite, 2018).

Level of Progress of Sustainable Development in Developing Countries:

Sustainable development is a significant challenge for governments, companies, and households due to the need for additional investments, innovations, and changes in production and consumption habits (Ermilova et al., 2019). The United Nations has set 17 Goals of Sustainable Development, and countries measure their sustainable development in different ways based on their development levels and social, economic, and environmental problems (Ermilova et al., 2019). A study on European Union countries proposed the SDGs achievement index (SDG-AI), a multicriteria-based index, to evaluate the results accomplished by these countries in achieving SDGs, highlighting the differences across the EU countries and assessing the contribution of different dimensions to the result (Bulis & Onževs, 2023).

Challenges of Sustainable Development in Developing Countries:

Academic literature reflects increasing concerns about the trade-off between preserving the environment and economic growth, emphasizing the need for new measurements to evaluate sustainable development, given the limitations of gross domestic product (GDP) in quantifying welfare and sustainability (Rocchi et al., 2022). The absence of globally accepted indicators for measuring progress towards a Sustainable Economy (SE) presents a significant challenge in achieving the SDGs in a timely and comprehensive manner (Pais et al., 2019).

Impact of Sustainable Development on Economic Growth in Developing Countries:

The study of 50 countries over 50 years indicated that attaining economic growth through sustainable measures benefits the overall society in the long run, with nitrous oxide emissions significantly influencing the economic growth level of these countries (Al-Thani & Koç, 2024). The concept of sustainable development emerged from global public pressure in the 1980s and is now embraced as the global standard for measuring development objectives and performance in both developed and developing countries, with the oil and gas industry playing a central role in sustainable development in many national economies (Huan et al., 2021).

Role of Technology in Sustainable Development in Developing Countries:

Technology plays a crucial role in the developmental activities of every nation, impacting many dimensions of societal and economic aspects like education, health, and quality of life, and contributing to the improvement of the ecosystem as a whole (Batrancea et al., 2023). The development and application of global sustainable development goals in the economy of each country contribute to improving the quality of life of the population and conservation of nature, with innovative activities related to technology impacting the economic and social status of nations (Batrancea et al., 2023).

THE PROGRESS OF SUSTAINABLE DEVELOPMENT IN UNDERDEVELOPED COUNTRIES

Level of Progress of Sustainable Development in Underdeveloped Countries:

The measurement of sustainable development performance of countries is necessary to apply the right sustainable development strategies and track the process (Collodel & Kotzé, 2014). A new approach for measuring sustainable development levels of countries has been demonstrated using a cumulative belief degree approach, enabling the use of incomplete data, which is critical in measuring sustainability (Collodel & Kotzé, 2014).

Factors Influencing Sustainable Development Progress in Underdeveloped Countries:

Economic growth has been the exception rather than the rule in developing and least-developed nations, despite large influxes of foreign aid (Pais et al., 2019). Rural entrepreneurs have been identified as the main factors driving societal renewal and accelerating economic liberalization in some cases, rather than international aid or government intervention (Pais et al., 2019).

Challenges Hindering Sustainable Development in Underdeveloped Countries:

Academic literature reflects increasing concerns about the trade-off between preserving the environment and economic growth, highlighting the need for new measurements to evaluate sustainable development (Huang & Quibria, 2015). The limitations of gross domestic product (GDP) in quantifying welfare and sustainability have led to the assessment of sustainable development using alternative measurements such as the Genuine Progress Indicator (GPI) (Huang & Quibria, 2015).

Role of International Aid in Promoting Sustainable Development in Underdeveloped Countries:

Despite the vast amount of foreign aid spent annually, very little headway has been made in addressing the poverty of millions of people and the economic decline of underdeveloped countries (Zhu et al., 2019). Foreign aid has been found to have a significantly positive influence on sustainable development in aid recipient countries, likely going through channels related to growth, resources, and technology with respect to energy intensity (Feng et al., 2023).

Comparison of Sustainable Development Progress Between Underdeveloped and Developed Countries:

The analysis of specific issues in the application of the global sustainable development indicators framework has been focused on meeting the goals and targets of the UN and building a system of evaluation indicators to assess the progress of sustainable development at the national level in China (Ünlüçay et al., 2017). The disparities between resource-rich and resource-scarce countries have profound implications for sustainable development, emphasizing the critical importance of addressing the resource divide for sustainable development (Farny & Calderon, 2015).

WHAT ARE THE CONDITIONS AND METHODS THAT WILL ENABLE THE COUNTRY TO MOVE AWAY FROM UNSUSTAINABLE DEVELOPMENT?

Conditions That Will Enable the Country to Move Away from Unsustainable Development

Conditions for Moving Away from Unsustainable Development:

Sustainable development is essential for balancing economic, environmental, and social interests (Kopnina, 2016). Development should be pursued in harmony with the changing productive potential of the ecosystem to ensure enduring sustainability (Roy & Goll, 2014). The desired state of a society is a moving target, and development must not compromise the survival of future generations (Roy & Goll, 2014).

Economic Policies for Promoting Sustainable Development:

Economic policies play a significant role in sustainable development (Serem & Kara, 2015). Expansionary monetary policy, fiscal policy, and effective regulatory policy have a significant impact on the level of sustainable development (Serem & Kara, 2015). Sustainable development can be achieved through changes in monetary and regulatory policies (Serem & Kara, 2015).

Role of Technology in Enabling Sustainable Development:

Transitioning to sustainability requires technological innovations in the short term (Balaji et al., 2022). Technology plays a crucial role in enabling sustainable development in the long term, along with cultural change to embrace traditional and Indigenous ideas of respect, responsibility, sufficiency, and reciprocity to reduce consumption (Balaji et al., 2022).

Influence of Social and Cultural Factors on Sustainable Development:

National culture influences various facets of a country's sustainability indicators, including environmental performance, human development, and the avoidance of corruption (Ozili, 2024). Cultural dimensions such as performance-based culture and gender egalitarianism culture positively influence environmental performance and human development (Ozili, 2024).

Environmental Implications of Moving Away from Unsustainable Development:

Unsustainable consumption and production patterns are endangering global development (Rahayu, 2017). Environmental unsustainability is due to specific patterns of production and consumption, as well as population growth (Ramankutty, 2023). The achievement of sustainable development goals is unlikely to lead to greater social equality and economic prosperity, but to a greater spread of unsustainable production and consumption (Ramankutty, 2023).

In conclusion, the conditions for moving away from unsustainable development involve pursuing sustainable development in harmony with the changing productive potential of the ecosystem and ensuring that the desired state of society does not compromise the survival of future generations. Economic policies, including expansionary monetary and fiscal policies, play a significant role in promoting sustainable development. Technology is crucial for enabling sustainable development in both the short and long term, along with cultural change. Additionally, social and cultural factors, such as national culture, influence various facets of a country's sustainability indicators. Moving away from unsustainable development has significant environmental implications, and addressing unsustainable consumption and production patterns is crucial for achieving sustainable development.

METHODS THAT WILL ENABLE THE COUNTRY TO MOVE AWAY FROM UNSUSTAINABLE DEVELOPMENT

Economic Strategies for Transitioning to Sustainable Development:

Transitioning to sustainability will require technological innovations in the short term, but also cultural change to embrace traditional and Indigenous ideas of respect, responsibility, sufficiency, and reciprocity to reduce consumption in the long term (Bertschek et al., 2024). The study of alternatives to the conventional economic growth paradigm, such as negative, zero, and positive economic growth, provides insights into the feasibility and policy perspective in relation to the transition toward sustainable development (Abraham, 2017).

Environmental Policies for Facilitating the Shift Towards Sustainable Development:

The discourses of sustainability are linked to the influence of technology in shaping the future. Information and Communication Technology (ICT) plays a crucial role in understanding the environment and human impacts, as well as in finding solutions to mitigate climate change (Ryan, 2017). The efficacy of environmental policies and their implications for global environmental health and social wellbeing are examined, showing that some environmental policies, particularly protected areas and sustainable forest certification, are linked with environmental improvements, mainly in forest and water ecosystems (Syagga, 2023).

Social and Cultural Factors Influencing the Transition to Sustainable Development:

The transition to sustainable development involves a negotiation and learning process, with diverse societal groups attempting to reconcile their various economic, environmental, and social needs and interests, reach agreement on a common development vision, and undertake concerted action to realize that vision through both collective action and coordinated individual initiative (Fairbrass et al., 2024). Education is highlighted as the key to fostering changes in behavior patterns, with tailored approaches needed to promote shifts to alternative options, such as the reduction of harmful practices like burning grass, bushes, and trees in Sub-Saharan Africa (Makhosheva et al., 2018).

Technological Innovations Supporting the Move Towards Sustainable Development:

Sustainable development seeks to evaluate all costs, including economic gain, environmental impact, and human health, to develop new technologies that provide economic opportunity while enhancing the environment or the health of the human population (Kumar et al., 2024). The imperative for development to be sustainable is emphasized, with the application of innovative developments in all spheres of human activity seen as crucial for shifting to a new type of economic growth without causing damage to the natural environment (Luis Soberon, 2023).

If there is no direct answer in the documents, but a response can be inferred from the information provided, it is important to consider the multifaceted nature of sustainable development, which requires a balanced approach that integrates economic, environmental, and social considerations (Ramankutty, 2023). While the documents provide insights into economic strategies, environmental policies, social and cultural factors, and technological innovations, it is important to note that sustainable development is a complex and interconnected process that requires collaboration and cooperation among various stakeholders (Mammino, 2020; Adamo & Willis, 2022; Harangozo et al., 2018).

WHAT ARE THE CONDITIONS AND METHODS FOR ACHIEVING SUSTAINABLE DEVELOPMENT IN A COUNTRY?

Critical Conditions for Achieving Sustainable Development in a Country

Economic Factors Influencing Sustainable Development:

Sustainable development is influenced by economic factors at a national level, with a focus on cross-country comparisons and economic indicators (Baporikar, 2023). The study emphasizes the need to minimize harm to future resource use while considering economic development (Veselovská, 2017). Economic development is found to positively influence green growth, while trade openness may have a detrimental effect (Tawiah et al., 2021).

Environmental Considerations for Sustainable Development:

The interdependence and challenges of environmental, social, and economic systems are crucial for sustainable development, emphasizing the need for environmental protection integrated into social and economic decisions (Dernbach & Cheever, 2015). The Sustainable Development Strategy focuses on sustainable production and consumption, recognizing the importance of improving energy efficiency and investing in resource-efficient technologies (Nezamova et al., 2023). Renewable energy consumption significantly improves green growth, highlighting the importance of sustainable energy practices (Tawiah et al., 2021).

Social Aspects of Sustainable Development:

Social equity, diversity, and social quality of life are newly added themes to the social dimension of sustainability, creating complexity in social sustainability assessment (López et al., 2018). The social dimension of sustainability includes meeting basic needs, power relations, and ensuring safety and security from a social perspective (Güney, 2017). The social dimension, particularly environmental justice and equity, is considered crucial to the concept of sustainable development, contributing to the paradigm of Just Sustainability (Talan et al., 2020).

Policy and Governance for Sustainable Development:

Governance has a positive effect on sustainable development, with an emphasis on the rule of law, bureaucratic quality, and government effectiveness (Filipowicz, 2023). The study of governance is crucial for organizational success and sustainable development, improving organizational performance through increased efficiency, productivity, and innovation (Pažėraitė & Kunskaja, 2023). The UN governance system for sustainable development is described as a process-based approach, providing a model for decision-makers in multilevel governance for sustainable development (Popescu & Mandru, 2022).

METHODS FOR ACHIEVING SUSTAINABLE DEVELOPMENT IN A COUNTRY

Economic Strategies for Achieving Sustainable Development:

Sustainable corporate practices, clean energy breakthroughs, and natural resource conservation are essential economic strategies for achieving sustainable development (Fairbrass et al., 2024). The sufficiency and subsistence approaches offer paths to sustainability by questioning the growth paradigm and promoting a structural transition in society (Singh & Bhatt, 2023). The green economy, emphasizing investments, jobs, and skills, provides a macroeconomic strategy for sustainable economic growth (Mölders et al., 2014).

Environmental Policies Contributing to Sustainable Development:

Environmental policies play a crucial role in sustainable development by addressing environmental pressures, linking to environmental improvements, and delivering social benefits through healthy environments (Bull & Frate, 2018). Resource efficiency, sustainable consumption, and production, as well as the green economy, contribute to sustainable development by reducing resource consumption, waste generation, and emissions (Mölders et al., 2014).

Social Factors Impacting Sustainable Development:

Social, economic, and environmental aspects are interrelated areas of policy that contribute to sustainable development (Agarwal, 2024; Kumar et al., 2024). Social sustainability is essential for achieving long-term, sustainable social well-being, and social impact assessment is crucial for evaluating the social impacts of new projects (Salvador, 2017).

Technological Innovations Supporting Sustainable Development:

Sustainable development is fueled by technological advancement, and integrating technology can promote environmental sustainability and operational efficiencies (Khan, 2020). Systems modeling and optimization have been proposed as powerful means for achieving sustainable development by examining the interplay between technology, economy, environment, and society (Segger, 2017).

In addition to the specific strategies and policies mentioned in the documents, it is important to note that achieving sustainable development requires a holistic approach that integrates economic, environmental, and social considerations (Fairbrass et al., 2024). Cooperation, holistic thinking, and integration of these dimensions are crucial for creating a world that is prosperous, environmentally resilient, and socially just (Fairbrass et al., 2024).

While the documents provide valuable insights into economic, environmental, social, and technological aspects of sustainable development, they do not explicitly address the comprehensive integration of these dimensions. However, it can be inferred that a comprehensive approach to sustainable development should consider the synergistic relations between economic, social, and environmental factors (Azapagic, 2016).

In conclusion, the evidence from the documents suggests that achieving sustainable development requires a multifaceted approach that encompasses economic strategies, environmental policies, social factors, and technological innovations, while also emphasizing the interconnectedness of these dimensions. However, it is important to note that the documents do not provide a comprehensive overview of specific technological innovations or detailed social factors impacting sustainable development.

INITIATIVES THAT THE TOP-RANKED COUNTRY IN SUSTAINABLE DEVELOPMENT IMPLEMENTED TO ACHIEVE ITS STATUS

Initiatives for Sustainable Development:

The top-ranked countries for sustainable development, such as Sweden, Norway, and Switzerland, have been identified through a composite multi-dimensional index that assesses the strengths and weaknesses of socio-economic development and environmental criticalities worldwide (Aflaki et al., 2018). These countries have been recognized for their potential environmental performance relative to their wealth, indicating a high degree of sustainability that they should achieve given their level of affluence (Campagnolo et al., 2018).

Key Environmental Policies and Regulations:

The implementation of environmental SDGs has been analyzed in various countries, revealing promising engagement with environmental SDGs in these countries, albeit with limited progress and impressionistic practices in reportage of successes compared with challenges (Derendiaeva, 2022). The study specifically highlights the critical environmental goals and areas for practical actions to accomplish Agenda 2030 moving forward, emphasizing the need for immediate actions in climate action (SDG13) and affordable and clean energy (SDG7) (Derendiaeva, 2022).

Measurement and Tracking of Progress Towards Sustainability:

A sophisticated SDG performance measurement tool has been developed to support the analysis of progress towards achieving sustainable development goals for each country, automatically processing the entire UN Global SDG Indicators database with exploratory data analysis, frequent item mining, and network analysis supported (Fang et al., 2023). The tool allows for the comparison of changes over time, enabling countries to be grouped according to their current states and derive values of the indicators achievable by 2030 (Fang et al., 2023).

Economic Strategies and Investments for Promoting Sustainability:

The Belt and Road Initiative (BRI) has been found to have profound implications for the sustainable development of the involved countries, with more than 90% of the BRI nations being at least halfway towards reaching the best performance of SDGs as of 2019 (Moses et al., 2022). The BRI showed high, medium, and low scores in achieving the economic, social, and environmental SDGs, respectively, indicating the need for more attention to be paid to the environmental dimension, particularly to SDG 15 (life on land) (Moses et al., 2022).

Social and Cultural Initiatives for Supporting Sustainable Living:

The study of environmental trends in leading countries, such as the United States, China, and Great Britain, emphasizes the importance of studying the involvement of various representatives of society, including the government and the private sector, in the implementation of environmental policy (Sebestyén & Abonyi, 2021). The study also highlights the analysis of project financing as a key aspect of a comprehensive assessment of the environmental policy of states (Sebestyén & Abonyi, 2021).

In conclusion, the top-ranked countries for sustainable development, such as Sweden, Norway, and Switzerland, have implemented various initiatives, policies, and regulations to achieve their status. These include the development of sophisticated measurement tools, engagement with environmental SDGs, and the implementation of the Belt and Road Initiative. However, the need for immediate actions in critical environmental areas and the involvement of various representatives of society in environmental policy implementation have been highlighted as key aspects of promoting sustainability.

WHAT ARE THE CONDITIONS AND METHODS FOR MAINTAINING A SUSTAINABLE LEVEL OF DEVELOPMENT?

Economic Conditions and strategies for Maintaining Sustainable Development

Economic Conditions for Sustainable Development:

International Economic System Restructuring: The adoption of sustainable principles by industrial enterprises is essential for sustainable economic development (Sukanya, 2016). Economic Security and Sustainable Development: Economic security, including economic, geopolitical, and environmental conditions, is crucial for sustainable economic development and the improvement of the population's quality of life (Galkina & Sorokin, 2020). Environmental Impact of Economic Growth: Economic growth through increased productive activity affects the environment, leading to environmental and ecological degradation, which affects the sustainability of development and human life quality (Ivanov et al., 2022).

Strategies for Maintaining Sustainable Development:

Resource Conservation and Socio-Economic Development: Strategies for sustainable development should consider resource conservation and socio-economic development as mutually reinforcing goals (Reshetnikova et al., 2023). Financing the Green Economy: The financing of the green economy contributes to economic growth while reducing the negative impact on the environment and conserving natural resources for future generations (Tarasyev et al., 2021). Promoting Sustainable Production and Consumption: The focus is on promoting consumption and production with minimal environmental impact to meet the basic needs of humanity (Pažėraitė & Kunskaja, 2023).

ENVIRONMENTAL CONDITIONS AND STRATEGIES FOR MAINTAINING SUSTAINABLE DEVELOPMENT

Environmental Conditions for Sustainable Development:

Importance of Environmental Protection: The protection of the environment is crucial for sustainable development (Venkateswarlu et al., 2020; Vidishcheva et al., 2020; Prizzia, 2017). Renewable Resource Consumption: Sustainable development involves consuming renewable natural resources while continuously renewing life-sustaining resources (Vidishcheva et al., 2020). Impact of Environmental Degradation: Environmental degradation poses a significant threat to sustainable development and human well-being (Osipov, 2019; Zhang, 2014).

Strategies for Maintaining Sustainable Development:

Sustainable Production and Consumption: The focus is on promoting consumption and production with minimal environmental impact (Dernbach & Cheever, 2015; Smol, 2023). Integration of Environmental Protection: Environmental protection must be integrated into decisions about social and economic development for sustainable development (Opschoor, 2018). Policy Integration and Stakeholder Participation: Good practices for sustainable development include policy integration, stakeholder participation, and monitoring and evaluation (Pažėraitė & Kunskaja, 2023).

SOCIAL CONDITIONS AND STRATEGIES FOR MAINTAINING SUSTAINABLE DEVELOPMENT

Social Conditions for Sustainable Development:

Fair Distribution of Income and Access: Sustainable development requires fair distribution of income and access to resources (Gallardo-Vázquez & Folgado-Fernández, 2020). Role of Universities: Universities play a crucial role in promoting education and fostering a sense of belonging, contributing to the sustainability of a region (Opschoor, 2018). Influence of Social Development: Social development strategies, including education and quality of life, are essential for sustainable development (Opschoor, 2018). Challenges and Measurement: Challenges for the social dimension of sustainable development include inequality, labor conditions, and meeting basic needs, which can be measured using various indicators (Roy, 2020; Kumar et al., 2024).

Strategies for Maintaining Sustainable Development:

Integration of Social, Economic, and Environmental Objectives: Strategies for sustainable development integrate social, economic, and environmental objectives, considering their implications for different socioeconomic groups and future generations (Filipowicz, 2023). Balancing Economic Growth, Ecological Stewardship, and Social Justice: The need to achieve a balance between economic growth, ecological stewardship, and social justice is crucial for sustainable development (Podaşcă, 2016). Role of Institutions: Introducing institutions in social and economic interactions is essential to change globalization to become conducive to sustainable and more human development (Gallardo-Vázquez & Folgado-Fernández, 2020).

POLITICAL CONDITIONS AND STRATEGIES FOR MAINTAINING SUSTAINABLE DEVELOPMENT

Critical Conditions for Sustainable Development:

The literature review suggests that institutional capacity, democracy, and government administration are critical conditions for successful sustainable development policies (Biscotti & D'Amico, 2016). Cross-national time-series analyses for 118-119 countries during 2000-2010 indicate that the democratic aspect of political systems and the vitality of trade are crucial for successful sustainable development policies (Biscotti & D'Amico, 2016).

Role of Political Leaders:

Political leaders play a significant role in addressing environmental matters, with cognitive and motivational factors shaping their environmental intentions (Wydra & Pülzl, 2015). The pursuit of sustainable development is largely driven by political concerns at the country level, and strategies need to be developed to deal constructively with uncertainties involved (Wydra & Pülzl, 2015; Grunwald, 2017).

Linkage Between Democracy and Sustainable Development:

While sustainable development seemingly does not need democratic forms of governance, research on democracy, human rights, and sustainable norms needs to be better linked to each other to implement the political requirements simultaneously (Luis Soberon, 2023).

Challenges and Options for Sustainable Development:

Achieving sustainable development requires balancing social, economic, and environmental objectives, which involves negotiation and learning processes among diverse societal groups (Yoon, 2014).

CONCLUSION

In conclusion, sustainable development has been the main global development agenda for the past half century. Without a doubt, a review of the academic documents of the past decade confirms that it is imperative for countries to transition from unsustainable to sustainable development. Although there are many conditions, obstacles, and challenges, reforming the structure and related mechanisms, including the role of technology, can help the country move closer and closer to sustainability in development. However, this chapter is only a broad proposal based on a review of academic documents in a single database over the past decade. Therefore, it does not provide very deep details on each issue. The direction of future studies can be to either 1) expand on some of the interesting points to reveal deeper details or 2) test these propositions with interesting case studies to prove their validity.

REFERENCES

Abraham, M. (2017). *Encyclopedia of Sustainable Technologies*. Elsevier.

Adamo, G., & Willis, M. (2022). Technologically mediated practices in sustainability transitions: Environmental monitoring and the ocean data buoy. *Technological Forecasting and Social Change*, 182, 121841. DOI: 10.1016/j.techfore.2022.121841

Addai, G., Amegavi, G., & Robinson, G. (2024). Advancing environmental sustainability: The dynamic relationship between renewable energy, institutional quality, and ecological footprint in the N-11 countries. *Sustainable Development (Bradford)*, sd.3096. Advance online publication. DOI: 10.1002/sd.3096

Adger, W., & Winkels, A. (2014). Vulnerability, poverty and sustaining well-being. In Atkinson, G., Dietz, S., Neumayer, E., & Agarwala, M. (Eds.), *Handbook of Sustainable Development* (2nd ed., pp. 206–216). Edward Elgar Publishing Ltd. DOI: 10.4337/9781782544708.00023

Aflaki, S., Basher, S., & Masini, A. (2018). Is your valley as green as it should be? Incorporating economic development into environmental performance indicators. *Clean Technologies and Environmental Policy*, 20(8), 1903–1915. DOI: 10.1007/s10098-018-1588-1

Agarwal, A. (2024). Understanding green economy. In Castanho, R. (Ed.), *Green Economy and Renewable Energy Transitions for Sustainable Development* (pp. 1–22). IGI Global. DOI: 10.4018/979-8-3693-1297-1.ch001

Al-Dabbagh, Z. (2020). Sustainable development and its role in containing crises: Corona virus pandemic crisis (COVID-19) in China as a model. *Journal of Public Affairs*, 20(4), e2339. DOI: 10.1002/pa.2339 PMID: 32904918

Al-Thani, M., & Koç, M. (2024). In Search of Sustainable Economy Indicators: A Comparative Analysis between the Sustainable Development Goals Index and the Green Growth Index. *Sustainability (Switzerland)*, 16(4), 1372.

Alam, S., & Razzaque, J. (2015). Sustainable development versus green economy: The way forward? In Alam, S., Atapattu, S., Gonzalez, C., & Razzaque, J. (Eds.), *International Environmental Law and the Global South* (pp. 609–624). Cambridge University Press. DOI: 10.1017/CBO9781107295414.030

Attfield, R. (2015). Sustainability and Management. *Philosophy of Management*, 14(2), 85–93. DOI: 10.1007/s40926-015-0008-4

Auerbach, A. (2016). Long-term fiscal sustainability in advanced economies. *Asia & the Pacific Policy Studies*, 3(2), 142–154. DOI: 10.1002/app5.131

Azapagic, A. (2016). ESCAPE-ing into a sustainable future: Can we optimise our way to sustainable development? *Computer-Aided Chemical Engineering*, 38, 2403. DOI: 10.1016/B978-0-444-63428-3.50405-7

Bakari, M. (2015). Sustainable Development in a Global Context: A Success or a Nuisance? *New Global Studies*, 9(1), 27–56. DOI: 10.1515/ngs-2014-0003

Balaji, M., Jiang, Y., Bhattacharyya, J., Hewege, C., & Azer, J. (2022). An Introduction to Socially Responsible Sustainable Consumption: Issues and Challenges. In Bhattacharyya, J., Balaji, M., Jiang, Y., Azer, J., & Hewege, C. (Eds.), *Socially Responsible Consumption and Marketing in Practice: Collection of Case Studies* (pp. 3–14). Springer. DOI: 10.1007/978-981-16-6433-5_1

Balcerzak, A., & Pietrzak, M. (2017). Sustainable Development in the European Union in the Years 2004–2013. *Eurasian Studies in Business and Economics*, 7, 193–213. DOI: 10.1007/978-3-319-54112-9_12

Baporikar, N. (2023). *Leadership and Governance for Sustainability*. IGI Global. DOI: 10.4018/978-1-6684-9711-1

Batalhão, A., Eustachio, J., Caldana, A., & Choupina, A. (2021). Economic approaches to sustainable development: Exploring the conceptual perspective and the indicator initiatives. In Singh, P., Verma, P., Perrotti, D., & Srivastava, K. (Eds.), *Environmental Sustainability and Economy* (pp. 151–169). Elsevier. DOI: 10.1016/B978-0-12-822188-4.00007-5

Batrancea, L., Rathnaswamy, M., Rus, M., & Tulai, H. (2023). Determinants of Economic Growth for the Last Half of Century: A Panel Data Analysis on 50 Countries. *Journal of the Knowledge Economy*, 14(3), 2578–2602. DOI: 10.1007/s13132-022-00944-9

Bertschek, I., Bünstorf, G., Cantner, U., Häussler, C., Requate, T., Welter, F., Arndt, E., Dreier, L., Erdsiek, D., Rieger-Fels, M., Dauchert, H., Eilers, L., & Heiny, F. (2024). Transformative R&I Policy using the Example of New Technologies in Agriculture and Social Innovations. *Wirtschaftsdienst (Hamburg, Germany)*, 104(4), 225–229.

Bhattacharya, T., & Managi, S. (2015). An assessment of biodiversity offsets and mitigation actions: Case studies on mining, energy and paper and pulp sectors in India. In Managi, S. (Ed.), *The Routledge Handbook of Environmental Economics in Asia* (pp. 401–420). Routledge.

Biscotti, A., & D'Amico, E. (2016). What are political leaders' environmental intentions? The impact of social identification processes and macro-economic conditions. *Ecological Economics*, 129, 152–160. DOI: 10.1016/j.ecolecon.2016.06.004

Bobylev, S. (2017). Sustainable development: Paradigm for the future. *World Economy and International Relations*, 61(3), 107–113. DOI: 10.20542/0131-2227-2017-61-3-107-113

Bran, F., Bodislav, D., Radulescu, C., & Ioan, I. (2014). Corporate governance intervention for a sustainable socio-economic model. *Revista de Cercetare si Interventie Sociala*, 46, 216–226.

Brand, A., Furness, M., & Keijzer, N. (2021). Promoting policy coherence within the 2030 agenda framework: Externalities, trade-offs and politics. *Politics and Governance*, 9(1), 108–118. DOI: 10.17645/pag.v9i1.3608

Brownlie, S., King, N., & Treweek, J. (2013). Biodiversity tradeoffs and offsets in impact assessment and decision making: Can we stop the loss? *Impact Assessment and Project Appraisal*, 31(1), 24–33. DOI: 10.1080/14615517.2012.736763

Bujanowicz-Haraś, B., Janulewicz, P., Nowak, A., & Krukowski, A. (2015). Evaluation of sustainable development in the member states of the European Union. *Problemy Ekorozwoju*, 10(2), 71–78.

Bulis, A., & Onževs, O. (2023). Measurement of sustainable development in Latvia. *Vide. Tehnologija. Resursi - Environment, Technology. Resources*, 1, 29–32.

Bull, A., & Frate, M. (2018). Social capital in the development of the agro nocerino-sarnese. In Sforzi, F. (Ed.), *The Institutions of Local Development* (pp. 141–173). Routledge.

Campagnolo, L., Eboli, F., Farnia, L., & Carraro, C. (2018). Supporting the UN SDGs transition: Methodology for sustainability assessment and current worldwide ranking. *Economics*, 12(1), 2018–10. DOI: 10.5018/economics-ejournal.ja.2018-10

Capper, G., Holmes, J., Jowsey, E., Lilley, S., McGuinness, D., & Robson, S. (2014). Sustainability. In Jowsey, E. (Ed.), *Real Estate Concepts: A Handbook* (pp. 402–429). Routledge.

Carlucci, R., Maglietta, R., Buscaino, G., Cipriano, G., Milella, A., Pollazzon, V., Bondanese, P., De Leonardis, C., Mona, S., Nitti, M., Papale, E., Reno, V., Ricci, P., Stella, E., & Fanizza, C. (2017). Review on research studies and monitoring system applied to cetaceans in the gulf of taranto (northern ionian sea, central-eastern mediterranean sea). *2017 14th IEEE International Conference on Advanced Video and Signal Based Surveillance, AVSS 2017*, 8078473.

Chapple, K. (2014). Strategies for growing green business and industry in a city. In Mazmanian, D., & Blanco, H. (Eds.), *Elgar Companion to Sustainable Cities: Strategies, Methods and Outlook* (pp. 116–132). Edward Elgar Publishing Ltd. DOI: 10.4337/9780857939999.00011

Ciobotaru, A. (2015). Rural sustainable development requires healthy and educated population. *Quality - Access to Success*, 16, 743–745.

Collodel, A., & Kotzé, D. (2014). The Failure of Cross-country Regression Analysis in Measuring the Impact of Foreign Aid. *Journal of Developing Societies*, 30(2), 195–221. DOI: 10.1177/0169796X14525527

Conca, K., & Dabelko, G. (2018). *Green planet blues: Critical perspectives on global environmental politics*. Routledge. DOI: 10.4324/9780429493744

Cordella, M., Gonzalez-Redin, J., Lodeiro, R., & Garcia, D. (2022). Assessing impacts to biodiversity and ecosystems: Understanding and exploiting synergies between Life Cycle Assessment and Natural Capital Accounting. *Procedia CIRP*, 105, 134–139. DOI: 10.1016/j.procir.2022.02.023

Cusack, C. (2019). Sustainable Development and Quality of Life. In Sinha, B. (Ed.), *Multidimensional Approach to Quality of Life Issues: A Spatial Analysis* (pp. 43–58). Springer. DOI: 10.1007/978-981-13-6958-2_3

Dasgupta, S. (2024). *Economic crisis of 2008-09 and subjective well-being: An empirical analysis of some selected countries*. International Trade, Economic Crisis and the Sustainable Development Goals., DOI: 10.1108/978-1-83753-586-620241003

Derendiaeva, O. (2022). Analysis of environmental trends on the example of the leading states: The USA, Great Britain and China in the context of the implementation of sustainable development goals. *IOP Conference Series. Earth and Environmental Science*, 979(1), 012148. DOI: 10.1088/1755-1315/979/1/012148

Dernbach, J., & Cheever, F. (2015). Sustainable development and its discontents. *Transnational Environmental Law*, 4(2), 247–287. DOI: 10.1017/S2047102515000163

Domaracká, L., Torres, M., Fonseca, N., Sokolova, A., & Yazevich, M. (2018). Mining Region Environmental Management in Transition to Sustainable Development. *E3S Web of Conferences, 41*, 02018.

Du, J., Liu, Y., Xu, Z., Duan, H., Zhuang, M., Hu, Y., Wang, Q., Dong, J., Wang, Y., & Fu, B. (2024). Global effects of progress towards Sustainable Development Goals on subjective well-being. *Nature Sustainability*, 7(3), 360–367. DOI: 10.1038/s41893-024-01270-5

Dung, N. (2024). How Productivity and Trade Liberalization Can Affect the Economies of Developing Nations is Illustrated by the Vietnamese Manufacturing Sectors Case. *Organizations and Markets in Emerging Economies*, 15(1), 109–126. DOI: 10.15388/omee.2024.15.6

Dutta, K., & Saha, M. (2023). Does financial development cause sustainable development? A PVAR approach. *Economic Change and Restructuring*, 56(2), 879–917. DOI: 10.1007/s10644-022-09451-y

Ermilova, M., Maksimova, T., Zhdanova, O., & Zohrab, D. (2019). Improvement of innovation systems in sustainable economic development. *E3S Web of Conferences, 135*, 04027.

Fairbrass, A., O'Sullivan, A., Campbell, J., & Ekins, P. (2024). The SDGs Provide Limited Evidence That Environmental Policies Are Delivering Multiple Ecological and Social Benefits. *Earth's Future, 12*(5), e2024EF004451.

Fang, K., Xu, A., Wang, S., Jia, X., Liao, Z., Tan, R., Sun, H., & Su, F. (2023). Progress towards Sustainable Development Goals in the Belt and Road Initiative countries. *Journal of Cleaner Production*, 424, 138808. DOI: 10.1016/j.jclepro.2023.138808

Farny, S., & Calderon, S. (2015). Entrepreneurship: The missing link for democratization and development in fragile nations? In Kyrö, P. (Ed.), *Handbook of Entrepreneurship and Sustainable Development Research* (pp. 99–129). Edward Elgar Publishing Ltd. DOI: 10.4337/9781849808248.00013

Feng, Y., Hu, J., Afshan, S., Irfan, M., Hu, M., & Abbas, S. (2023). Bridging resource disparities for sustainable development: A comparative analysis of resource-rich and resource-scarce countries. *Resources Policy*, 85, 103981. DOI: 10.1016/j.resourpol.2023.103981

Filipowicz, K. (2023). The social dimension of sustainable development. In Kuźniarska, A., Mania, K., & Jedynak, M. (Eds.), *Organizing Sustainable Development* (pp. 46–62). Routledge. DOI: 10.4324/9781003379409-6

Galkina, E., & Sorokin, A. (2020). Quality Management and Sustainable Economic Development. *Russian Engineering Research*, 40(7), 577–578. DOI: 10.3103/S1068798X2007014X

Gallardo-Vázquez, D., & Folgado-Fernández, J. (2020). Regional economic sustainability: Universities' role in their territories. *Land (Basel)*, 9(4), 102. DOI: 10.3390/land9040102

Gök, A., & Sodhi, N.Sr. (2023). Do Emerging Market Economies Have Sustainable Development?: A Panel Vector Autoregression Analysis. In Das, R. (Ed.), *Social Sector Spending, Governance and Economic Development: Perspectives from across the World* (pp. 140–157). Routledge. DOI: 10.4324/9781003245797-10

Gordon, R. (2015). Unsustainable development. In Alam, S., Atapattu, S., Gonzalez, C., & Razzaque, J. (Eds.), *International Environmental Law and the Global South* (pp. 50–73). Cambridge University Press. DOI: 10.1017/CBO9781107295414.004

Grunwald, A. (2017). Technology assessment and policy advice in the field of sustainable development. In Zacher, L. (Ed.), *Technology, Society and Sustainability: Selected Concepts, Issues and Cases* (pp. 203–221). Springer. DOI: 10.1007/978-3-319-47164-8_14

Güney, T. (2017). Governance and sustainable development: How effective is governance? *The Journal of International Trade & Economic Development*, 26(3), 316–335. DOI: 10.1080/09638199.2016.1249391

Harangozo, G., Csutora, M., & Kocsis, T. (2018). How big is big enough? Toward a sustainable future by examining alternatives to the conventional economic growth paradigm. *Sustainable Development (Bradford)*, 26(2), 172–181. DOI: 10.1002/sd.1728

Hasslöf, H., Ekborg, M., & Malmberg, C. (2014). Discussing sustainable development among teachers: An analysis from a conflict perspective. *International Journal of Environmental and Science Education*, 9(1), 41–57.

Henriksen, H., Thapa, D., & Elbanna, A. (2021). Sustainable Development Goals in IS Research Opening the agenda beyond developing countries' research. *Scandinavian Journal of Information Systems*, 33(2), 97–102.

Huan, Y., Liang, T., Li, H., & Zhang, C. (2021). A systematic method for assessing progress of achieving sustainable development goals: A case study of 15 countries. *The Science of the Total Environment*, 752, 141875. DOI: 10.1016/j.scitotenv.2020.141875 PMID: 33207501

Huang, Y., & Quibria, M. (2015). The global partnership for sustainable development. *Natural Resources Forum*, 39(3-4), 157–174. DOI: 10.1111/1477-8947.12068

Ite, U. (2018). Embedding and operationalizing sustainable development goals in the Nigerian oil and gas industry. *Society of Petroleum Engineers - SPE Nigeria Annual International Conference and Exhibition 2018, NAIC 2018,* SPE-193396-MS.

Ivanov, R., Grynko, T., Porokhnya, V., Pavlov, R., & Golovkova, L. (2022). Model substantiation of strategies of economic behavior in the context of increasing negative impact of environmental factors in the context of sustainable development. *IOP Conference Series. Earth and Environmental Science*, 1049(1), 012041. DOI: 10.1088/1755-1315/1049/1/012041

Jha, S., & Srinivasan, P. (2023). What Drives the Quality of Growth? An Empirical Analysis. *Sustainable Development Goals Series*, F2767, 275–293. DOI: 10.1007/978-981-19-9756-3_13

Jordan, A., & O'Riordan, T. (2023). Sustainable Development: The Political and Institutional Challenge. In Kirkby, J., O'Keefe, P., & Timberldke, L. (Eds.), *The Earthscan Reader in Sustainable Development* (pp. 287–289). Routledge. DOI: 10.4324/9781003403432-42

Kaniaru, D. (2016). The development of the concept of sustainable development and the birth of UNEP. In Kuokkanen, T., Couzens, E., Honkonen, T., & Lewis, M. (Eds.), *International Environmental Law-making and Diplomacy: Insights and Overviews* (pp. 127–143). Routledge.

Kartsan, I., Kartsan, P., Matyunina, M., Zhukov, A., & Kolosov, A. (2023). Economic mechanisms of environmental protection. *E3S Web of Conferences, 420*, 08008.

Khan, I. (2020). Critiquing social impact assessments: Ornamentation or reality in the Bangladeshi electricity infrastructure sector? *Energy Research & Social Science*, 60, 101339. DOI: 10.1016/j.erss.2019.101339

Kluvankova, T., Brnkalakova, S., Gezik, V., & Maco, M. (2019). Ecosystem services as commons? In Hudson, B., Rosenbloom, J., & Cole, D. (Eds.), *Routledge Handbook of the Study of the Commons* (pp. 208–219). Routledge. DOI: 10.4324/9781315162782-17

Koilo, V. (2020). A methodology to analyze sustainable development index: Evidence from emerging markets and developed economies. *Environment and Ecology*, 11(1), 14–29. PMID: 32122337

Kopnina, H. (2016). The victims of unsustainability: A challenge to sustainable development goals. *International Journal of Sustainable Development and World Ecology*, 23(2), 113–121. DOI: 10.1080/13504509.2015.1111269

Kovalevsky, S., Khouri, S., Gasanov, E., Lozhnikova, A., & Konovalova, M. (2020). Sustainable Development and Humanization of Economic Growth: Environmental and Social Well-Being. *E3S Web of Conferences, 174*, 04049.

Kumar, P., Sharma, L., & Sharma, N. (2024). Sustainable development balancing economic viability, environmental protection, and social equity. In Paul, B., & Poddar, S. (Eds.), *Sustainable Partnership and Investment Strategies for Startups and SMEs* (pp. 212–235). IGI Global. DOI: 10.4018/979-8-3693-2197-3.ch012

Kumaran, V., Haron, N., Ridzuan, A., Shaari, M., Saudi, N., & Sapuan, N. (2022). Evaluating climate change towards sustainable development. In Asif, M. (Ed.), *Handbook of Energy and Environmental Security* (pp. 377–398). Elsevier. DOI: 10.1016/B978-0-12-824084-7.00014-X

Kwatra, S., Kumar, A., & Sharma, P. (2020). A critical review of studies related to construction and computation of Sustainable Development Indices. *Ecological Indicators*, 112, 106061. DOI: 10.1016/j.ecolind.2019.106061

Lampert, A. (2021). Discounting as a double-edged sword: The values of both future goods and present economic growth decrease with the discount rate. *Journal of Environmental Economics and Policy*, 10(1), 43–53. DOI: 10.1080/21606544.2020.1775709

Latchem, C. (2018). The disabled, refugees, displaced persons and prisoners. *SpringerBriefs in Open and Distance Education,* 107-119.

Li, Y., Grainger, A., Hesley, Z., Hofstad, O., Sankhayan, P., Diallo, O., & Ati, A. (2017). Using GIS techniques to evaluate community sustainability in open forestlands in sub-saharan Africa. In Deakin, M., Dixon-Gough, R., & Mansberger, R. (Eds.), *Methodologies, Models and Instruments for Rural and Urban Land Management* (pp. 146–163). Routledge.

Lind, T., Yanyan, H., & Jäppinen, H. (2016). Sustainability and energy efficiency in the pulp and paper industry. *Paper Asia*, 32(3), 21–23.

Lior, N., Radovanović, M., & Filipović, S. (2018). Comparing sustainable development measurement based on different priorities: Sustainable development goals, economics, and human well-being—Southeast Europe case. *Sustainability Science*, 13(4), 973–1000. DOI: 10.1007/s11625-018-0557-2

López, I., Arriaga, A., & Pardo, M. (2018). The social dimension of sustainable development: The everlasting forgotten? *Revista Espanola de Sociologia*, 27(1), 25–41.

Lopez-Claros, A. (2014). Fiscal Challenges after the Global Financial Crisis: A Survey of Key Issues. *Journal of International Commerce. Economic Policy*, 5(2), 1450004.

Luis Soberon, A. (2023). Concertación: Integrated Planning and Development in Peru. In Schnurr, J., & Holtz, S. (Eds.), *The Cornerstone of Development: Integrating Environmental, Social, and Economic Policies* (pp. 263–279). CRC Press.

Makhosheva, S., Rud, N., Kandrokova, M., Israilov, M., & Shinahova, F. (2018). The paradigm of sustainable development and innovation in the region. *Espacios*, 39(47), 28.

Mammino, L. (2020). *Biomass Burning in Sub-Saharan Africa: Chemical Issues and Action Outreach*. Springer. DOI: 10.1007/978-94-007-0808-2

Mantaeva, E., Slobodchikova, I., Goldenova, V., Avadaeva, I., & Nimgirov, A. (2021). Green technologies as a factor in the sustainable development of the national economy. *IOP Conference Series. Earth and Environmental Science*, 848(1), 012133. DOI: 10.1088/1755-1315/848/1/012133

Masilo, M. (2022). Panoramas of Regulating the Right to Reproductive Health: A Remedy to Socio-Economic Challenges in South Africa. *Journal of Educational and Social Research*, 12(3), 162–171. DOI: 10.36941/jesr-2022-0075

McGregor, J. (2014). Human wellbeing and sustainability: Interdependent and intertwined. In Atkinson, G., Dietz, S., Neumayer, E., & Agarwala, M. (Eds.), *Handbook of Sustainable Development* (2nd ed., pp. 217–234). Edward Elgar Publishing Ltd. DOI: 10.4337/9781782544708.00024

Medvedev, S., Sokolova, E., & Dudin, P. (2023). Analysis of the "sustainable development" concept. *E3S Web of Conferences, 420*, 06005.

Milićević, D., Šelmić, R., & Petrović, Z. (2023). The One Health concept: A comprehensive approach to the function of a sustainable food system. *Metals Technology*, 64(2), 242–247.

Mölders, T., Szumelda, A., & von Winterfeld, U. (2014). Sufficiency and subsistence - On two important concepts for sustainable development. *Problemy Ekorozwoju*, 9(1), 21–27.

Moses, O., Nnam, I., Olaniyan, J., & Tariquzzaman, A. (2022). Sustainable Development Goals (SDGs): Assessment of Implementation Progress in BRICS and MINT. *Advances in Environmental Accounting and Management*, 10, 11–44. DOI: 10.1108/S1479-359820220000010002

Narain, S. (2016). Consequences of inequality for sustainability. *IDS Bulletin*, 47(2A), 113–115. DOI: 10.19088/1968-2016.185

Nezamova, O., Polukarov, N., Zdrestova-Zakharenkova, S., & Yamshchikov, A. (2023). Preparing the transition to sustainable development of territories. *E3S Web of Conferences, 402*, 09013.

Noble, K. (2015). Education for sustainability in primary school humanities and social sciences education. In Taylor, N., Quinn, F., & Eames, C. (Eds.), *Educating for Sustainability in Primary Schools: Teaching for the Future* (pp. 135–175). Sense Publishers. DOI: 10.1007/978-94-6300-046-8_8

Okonjo-Iweala, N. (2017). The role of women in Africa's economic development. In Kalu, K. (Ed.), *Agenda Setting and Public Policy in Africa* (pp. 167–185). Routledge.

Opschoor, J. (2018). Sustainable human development and the north-south dialogue. In Darkoh, M., & Rwomire, A. (Eds.), *Human Impact on Environment and Sustainable Development in Africa* (pp. 495–518). Routledge. DOI: 10.4324/9781315192963-21

Osipov, V. (2019). Sustainable Development: Environmental Aspects. *Herald of the Russian Academy of Sciences*, 89(4), 396–404. DOI: 10.1134/S1019331619040087

Ozili, P. (2024). Economic Policy for Sustainable Development: Role of Monetary Policy, Fiscal Policy and Regulatory Policy. *Circular Economy and Sustainability*. Advance online publication. DOI: 10.1007/s43615-024-00406-1

Ozturkm, M., & Yuksel, Y. (2016). Energy structure of Turkey for sustainable development. *Renewable & Sustainable Energy Reviews*, 53, 1259–1272. DOI: 10.1016/j.rser.2015.09.087

Pais, D., Afonso, T., Marques, A., & Fuinhas, J. (2019). Are economic growth and sustainable development converging? Evidence from the comparable genuine progress indicator for organisation for economic co-operation and development countries. *International Journal of Energy Economics and Policy*, 9(4), 202–213. DOI: 10.32479/ijeep.7678

Pažėraitė, A., & Kunskaja, S. (2023). Consumption Behaviour in the Context of Sustainable Energy: Theoretical Approach. *Springer Proceedings in Earth and Environmental Sciences*, (Part F639), 77–85. DOI: 10.1007/978-3-031-25840-4_11

Podaşcă, R. (2016). Sustainable development in the new economy. *Quality - Access to Success*, 17, 289–293.

Pokorný, J., & Palacká, A. (2023). Well-being as a Prerequisite for Sustainability on a Macroeconomic Scale? Case of V4 Countries. *Quality Innovation Prosperity*, 27(3), 141–153. DOI: 10.12776/qip.v27i3.1945

Popescu, M., & Mandru, L. (2022). A Model for a Process Approach in the Governance System for Sustainable Development. *Sustainability (Basel)*, 14(12), 6996. DOI: 10.3390/su14126996

Prizzia, R. (2017). Sustainable Development in an International Perspective. In Thai, K., Rahm, D., & Coggburn, J. (Eds.), *Handbook of Globalization and the Environment* (pp. 19–42). Routledge. DOI: 10.4324/9781315093253-2

Rahayu, M. (2017). Sustainable development in the perspective of Sundanese cultural wisdom. *Journal of Engineering and Applied Sciences (Asian Research Publishing Network)*, 12(18), 4657–4660.

Rai, A., & Fulekar, M. (2023). Environment and Sustainable Development. In Fulekar, M., & Dubey, R. (Eds.), *Climate Change and Sustainable Development* (pp. 117–128). CRC Press. DOI: 10.1201/9781003205548-7

Ramankutty, N. (2023). Both technological innovations and cultural change are key to a sustainability transition. *PLoS Biology*, 21(9), e3002298. DOI: 10.1371/journal.pbio.3002298 PMID: 37733652

Reshetnikova, N., Gornostaeva, Z., Khodochenko, A., Bugaeva, M., & Tregulova, N. (2023). Financing the Green Economy in the Context of Global Sustainable Development. *Environmental Footprints and Eco-Design of Products and Processes*, 531-540.

Rocchi, L., Ricciolini, E., Massei, G., Paolotti, L., & Boggia, A. (2022). Towards the 2030 Agenda: Measuring the Progress of the European Union Countries through the SDGs Achievement Index. *Sustainability (Basel)*, 14(6), 3563. DOI: 10.3390/su14063563

Rodzoś, J. (2019). The concept of human needs in sustainable development of cities. *Problemy Ekorozwoju*, 14(2), 91–99.

Rossi, L., Pasca, M., Arcese, G., & Poponi, S. (2024). Innovation, researcher and creativity: A complex indicator for territorial evaluation capacity. *Technology in Society*, 77, 102545. DOI: 10.1016/j.techsoc.2024.102545

Roy, A., & Goll, I. (2014). Predictors of various facets of sustainability of nations: The role of cultural and economic factors. *International Business Review*, 23(5), 849–861. DOI: 10.1016/j.ibusrev.2014.01.003

Roy, M. (2020). *Sustainable Development Strategies: Engineering, Culture and Economics*. Elsevier.

Roy, S., & Mukhopadhyay, R. (2015). Participatory biodiversity management: Approaches to institution building to improve ecosystem services and well being. *International Journal of Economic Research*, 12(3), 851–860.

Ryan, C. (2017). Eco-innovative cities Australia: A pilot project for the ecodesign of services in eight local councils. In Tukker, A., Charter, M., Vezzoli, C., Stø, E., & Andersen, M. (Eds.), *System Innovation for Sustainability 1: Perspectives on Radical Changes to Sustainable Consumption and Production* (pp. 197–213). Routledge.

Salamon, J. (2019). The Measurement of Sustainable Development Level in the Aspect of Selection of Indicators and Measurement Methods. In Krakowiak-Bal, A., & Vaverkova, M. (Eds.), *Infrastructure and Environment* (pp. 328–336). Springer. DOI: 10.1007/978-3-030-16542-0_41

Salotti, S., & Trecroci, C. (2016). The Impact of Government Debt, Expenditure and Taxes on Aggregate Investment and Productivity Growth. *Economica*, 83(330), 356–384. DOI: 10.1111/ecca.12175

Salvador, S. (2017). Strengthening capacity to link environment and health in the context of the FTAA. In Segger, M., & Reynal, M. (Eds.), *Beyond the Barricades: The Americas Trade and Sustainable Development Agenda* (pp. 169–180). Routledge.

Sato, M. (2015). Measuring sustainable development in Asia. In Managi, S. (Ed.), *The Routledge Handbook of Environmental Economics in Asia* (pp. 285–298). Routledge.

Schoenaker, N., Hoekstra, R., & Smits, J. (2015). Comparison of Measurement Systems for Sustainable Development at the National Level. *Sustainable Development (Bradford)*, 23(5), 285–300. DOI: 10.1002/sd.1585

Sebestyén, V., & Abonyi, J. (2021). Data-driven comparative analysis of national adaptation pathways for Sustainable Development Goals. *Journal of Cleaner Production*, 319, 128657. DOI: 10.1016/j.jclepro.2021.128657

Segger, M. (2017). Enhancing social and environmental cooperation in the Americas. In Segger, M., & Reynal, M. (Eds.), *Beyond the Barricades: The Americas Trade and Sustainable Development Agenda* (pp. 181–223). Routledge. DOI: 10.4324/9781351162647

Serem, D., & Kara, A. (2015). The role of Maasai Mara University in promoting sustainable development. In Jacob, W., Sutin, S., Weidman, J., & Yeager, J. (Eds.), *Community Engagement in Higher Education: Policy Reforms and Practice* (pp. 269–285). Sense Publishers. DOI: 10.1007/978-94-6300-007-9_16

Shaker, R., & Mackay, B. (2021). Hidden patterns of sustainable development in Asia with underlying global change correlations. *Ecological Indicators*, 131, 108227. DOI: 10.1016/j.ecolind.2021.108227

Shaqour, A., & Farzaneh, H. (2021). The Urban Sustainable Development Index: A Comparative Analysis of Low Emission Strategies in Urban Areas. In Farzaneh, H., Zusman, E., & Chae, Y. (Eds.), *Aligning Climate Change and Sustainable Development Policies in Asia* (pp. 19–39). Springer Nature. DOI: 10.1007/978-981-16-0135-4_2

Shepelev, I., Goncharova, O., Ermolina, L., & Gorokhova, N. (2024). Investing in nature: analysis of the relationship between environmental capital and economic growth. *E3S Web of Conferences, 531*, 05024.

Singh, R., & Bhatt, V. (2023). Technological advancement in industrial revolution 4.0 for sustainable development of India: Understanding linkages in theory and practice. In Mehta, K., & Sharma, R. (Eds.), *Sustainability, Green Management, and Performance of SMEs* (pp. 57–72). De Gruyter. DOI: 10.1515/9783111170022-004

Singh, V. (2022). Sustainable Development and Climate Change. In *Research Anthology on Measuring and Achieving Sustainable Development Goals, 3* (pp. 944–964). IGI Global. DOI: 10.4018/978-1-6684-3885-5.ch050

Smol, M. (2023). Global directions for the green deal strategies—Americas, Europe, Australia, Asia, and Africa. In Prasad, M., & Smol, M. (Eds.), *Sustainable and Circular Management of Resources and Waste Towards a Green Deal* (pp. 39–46). Elsevier. DOI: 10.1016/B978-0-323-95278-1.00019-X

Srinivasan, U., & Shanker, K. (2021). Making nature count: Reflections on the dasgupta review. *Ecology, Economy and Society*, 4(2), 5–12.

Sukanya, N. (2016). Fostering sustained economic development in India- the economic angle. *International Journal of Economic Research*, 13(3), 989–998.

Syagga, P. (2023). Supplying Clean Water to the Citizens of Nairobi. In Schnurr, J., & Holtz, S. (Eds.), *The Cornerstone of Development: Integrating Environmental, Social, and Economic Policies* (pp. 205–220). CRC Press.

Talan, A., Tyagi, R., & Surampalli, R. (2020). Social Dimensions of Sustainability. In Surampalli, R., Zhang, T., Goyal, M., Brar, S., & Tyagi, R. (Eds.), *Sustainability: Fundamentals and Applications* (pp. 183–206). Wiley. DOI: 10.1002/9781119434016.ch9

Tarasyev, A., Agarkov, G., & Tarasyeva, T. (2021). Dynamic modeling of risks and threats to the development of economic system. *AIP Conference Proceedings*, 2343, 040004. DOI: 10.1063/5.0047833

Tawiah, V., Zakari, A., & Adedoyin, F. (2021). Determinants of green growth in developed and developing countries. *Environmental Science and Pollution Research International*, 28(29), 39227–39242. DOI: 10.1007/s11356-021-13429-0 PMID: 33751350

Taylor, N., Quinn, F., & Eames, C. (2015). *Educating for Sustainability in Primary Schools: Teaching for the Future*. Sense Publishers. DOI: 10.1007/978-94-6300-046-8

Tikhomirova, T., & Sukiasyan, A. (2021). Comparative estimates of human potential taking into consideration the risks of social inequality. *CEUR Workshop Proceedings*, 2830, 63–76.

Ünlüçay, H., Ervural, B., Ervural, B., & Kabak, Ö. (2017). Cumulative belief degrees approach for assessment of sustainable development. *Intelligent Systems Reference Library*, 113, 257–289. DOI: 10.1007/978-3-319-42993-9_12

Van Den Bergh, J. (2014). Sustainable development in ecological economics. In Atkinson, G., Dietz, S., Neumayer, E., & Agarwala, M. (Eds.), *Handbook of Sustainable Development* (2nd ed., pp. 41–54). Edward Elgar Publishing Ltd. DOI: 10.4337/9781782544708.00011

Venkateswarlu, A., Adilakshmi, A., & Alapati, R. (2020). Sustainable development vs environment protection- Achieving a fine balance: A case study of Andhra Pradesh. *International Journal of Advanced Research in Engineering and Technology*, 11(6), 106–112.

Veselovská, L. (2017). Factors influencing countries on their path to sustainable development: Implications for organizations. *Problems and Perspectives in Management, 15*(2Continue3), 474-485.

Vidishcheva, E., Dreizis, Y., & Kopyrin A. (2020). The impact of ecological aspects on sustainable development of resort territories (example of the Krasnodar region, Russia). *E3S Web of Conferences, 175*, 14010.

Villarreal, R. (2014). Enterprise architecture of sustainable development: An analytical framework. In *Human Rights and Ethics: Concepts, Methodologies, Tools, and Applications, 1* (pp. 440–483). IGI Global.

Voronina, Y., Lopushynskyi, I., Grechanyk, B., Vahonova, O., Kondur, A., & Akimov, O. (2024). Economic and environmental component in the field of sustainable development management. *Quality - Access to Success*, 25(201), 7–14.

Voukkali, I., Pantelitsa, L., & Zorpas, A. (2014). Definitions of sustainability. In Zorpas, A. (Ed.), *Sustainability behind Sustainability* (pp. 1–6). Nova Science.

Wallace, W. (2014). *Working to engineer infrastructure resiliency in a changing operating environment* (Vol. 235). Geotechnical Special Publication. DOI: 10.1061/9780784413289.008

Wang, W., Wei, K., Kubatko, O., Piven, V., Chortok, Y., & Derykolenko, O. (2023). Economic Growth and Sustainable Transition: Investigating Classical and Novel Factors in Developed Countries. *Sustainability (Basel)*, 15(16), 12346. DOI: 10.3390/su151612346

Wang, Y., Wu, N., Kunze, C., Long, R., & Perlik, M. (2019). Drivers of Change to Mountain Sustainability in the Hindu Kush Himalaya. In P. Wester, A. Mishra, A. Mukherji & A. Shrestha (eds.). *The Hindu Kush Himalaya Assessment: Mountains, Climate Change, Sustainability and People* (pp. 17-56). Cham: Springer.

Wydra, D., & Pülzl, H. (2015). Sustainability governance in democracies. In *Public Affairs and Administration: Concepts, Methodologies, Tools, and Applications, 1* (pp. 270–293). IGI Global. DOI: 10.4018/978-1-4666-8358-7.ch013

Yaprakli, S., & Özden, E. (2021). The effect of sustainable development on economics complexity in OECD countries. *International and Multidisciplinary Journal of Social Sciences*, 10(2), 51–80. DOI: 10.17583/rimcis.7949

Yoon, J. (2014). Conditions for successful public policies of sustainable development: Institutional capacity, democracy, and free trade. *International Review of Public Administration*, 19(3), 252–266. DOI: 10.1080/12294659.2014.936547

Zhang, C. (2014). The research on the strategies for sustainable development and environmental protection. *Advanced Materials Research*, 869-870, 786–790. DOI: 10.4028/www.scientific.net/AMR.869-870.786

Zhang, Z. (2022). Introduction. *SpringerBriefs in Applied Sciences and Technology,* 1-3.

Zhu, J., Sun, X., He, Z., & Zhao, M. (2019). Are SDGs suitable for China's sustainable development assessment? An application and amendment of the SDGs Indicators in China. *Zhongguo Renkou Ziyuan Yu Huanjing*, 17(1), 25–38. DOI: 10.1080/10042857.2018.1544753

Zilberman, D., Gordon, B., Hochman, G., & Wesseler, J. (2018). Economics of sustainable development and the bioeconomy. *Applied Economic Perspectives and Policy*, 40(1), 22–37. DOI: 10.1093/aepp/ppx051

Zorpas, A. (2014). *Sustainability behind Sustainability*. Nova Science.

Chapter 2
Behavioral Insights and AI for Enhancing Productivity in Society 5.0:
A Path to Sustainable Development

Noor Wazikhaz Madia Wazi
https://orcid.org/0009-0008-9067-8726
Universiti Sultan Zainal Abidin, Malaysia

Fazida Karim
Universiti Sultan Zainal Abidin, Malaysia

Noor Aina Amirah Mohd Noor
Universiti Sultan Zainal Abidin, Malaysia

Ismahafezi Ismail
Universiti Sultan Zainal Abidin, Malaysia

Wan Mohd Amir Fazamin Wan Hamzah
Universiti Sultan Zainal Abidin, Malaysia

Mokhairi Makhtar
Universiti Sultan Zainal Abidin, Malaysia

Mohd Hafiz Yusoff
Universiti Sultan Zainal Abidin, Malaysia

ABSTRACT

This chapter examines the mutually beneficial connection between behavioural insights and artificial intelligence (AI) in order to enhance productivity within the framework of Society 5.0. Society 5.0 is a conceptual framework that seeks to establish a balanced integration of economic progress and social well-being via the process of digital transformation. The chapter highlights the vital importance of AI technologies, such as machine learning, natural language processing (NLP), predictive analytics, human-AI collaboration, and generative AI, in attaining sustainable development. When combined with knowledge from psychology, economics, and neuroscience, these technologies have a crucial function. The approaches used include real-life case studies across many industries, illustrating the impact of these technologies on decision-making, policy formation, and intervention design, while aligning with authentic human behaviours. The ethical dimensions of integrating AI with behavioural insights, with a specific emphasis on privacy, data security, and biases in AI systems, are also explored. The actual implementations of these technologies in real-life situations demonstrate significant improvements in organisational productivity and efficiency. The chapter ends with practical suggestions for leaders and policymakers to synchronise AI-based plans with sustainable development objectives, with a particular

DOI: 10.4018/979-8-3693-9230-0.ch002

Copyright ©2025, IGI Global. Copying or distributing in print or electronic forms without written permission of IGI Global is prohibited.

focus on the welfare of humans.

INTRODUCTION

Society 5.0, a concept initiated by Japan, seeks to establish an advanced society that integrates the digital and physical domains to tackle societal challenges and emphasise human-centric development. Society 5.0 represents a significant shift from previous social systems by integrating economic progress with the resolution of social issues via advanced digital transformation (Cabinet Office of Japan, 2018). The examination of human behaviour and the use of new technological innovations, including artificial intelligence (AI), are crucial for developing sustainable and inclusive societies.

In the epoch of Society 5.0, which aims to cultivate a human-centric society that harmonises economic progression with the efficient resolution of social challenges, the examination of human behaviour and the implementation of technical innovations are paramount. Society 5.0 anticipates a future in which digital transformation and advanced technology are used to resolve social challenges, leading to a sustainable and inclusive community. By adopting sustainable development concepts, society may establish a harmonious balance between economic progress and environmental health (Vivien, 2023).

Recent years have seen a growing recognition of the need of understanding human behaviour to achieve beneficial outcomes in several domains. This method, known as "behavioural insights," employs findings from psychology, economics, and neuroscience to influence decision-making and improve organisational strategy. Behavioural insights pertain to the use of understanding human behaviour to achieve advantageous results in many contexts, particularly within organisational environments. The concepts derived from psychology, economics, and neuroscience emphasise understanding the genuine cognitive processes and behaviours of people, as opposed to their anticipated cognitive processes and behaviours (Korteling & Toet, 2022; Kahneman, 2011). By identifying and mitigating cognitive biases, emotions, and social influences on behaviour, organisations may formulate more effective policies, strategies, and interventions that correspond with their objectives, resulting in enhanced results.

The beginnings of behavioural insights may be traced to the pioneering study of psychologists Daniel Kahneman and Amos Tversky in the 1970s. Their groundbreaking research on cognitive biases, including loss aversion and the availability heuristic, laid the groundwork for understanding the frequent divergence of human judgements from rationality (Kahneman & Tversky, 1979). The understanding has evolved into the field of behavioural economics, significantly influencing other domains like as public policy, health, and organisational management (Thaler & Sunstein, 2008). The use of behavioural insights in management has become more important as businesses seek to influence employee behaviour, enhance decision-making processes, and improve overall productivity (Ariely, 2008). Simultaneously with the advancement of behavioural insights, the field of AI has undergone significant transformations. In his seminal essay "Computing Machinery and Intelligence" published in 1950, Alan Turing proposed the concept of artificial intelligence, positing that computers may potentially replicate human cognition (Turing, 1950). Notable progress in artificial intelligence transpired throughout the 1950s and 1960s with the inception of the first AI systems, such as the Logic Theorist and ELIZA. Subsequently, in the 1980s, expert systems were developed to replicate human expertise in certain domains. The advent of machine learning in the 2000s, driven by abundant data and enhanced computer power, initiated a new era in the progression of artificial intelligence. This facilitated the development of more sophisticated models capable of learning from data and generating predictions (Goodfellow, Bengio, & Courville, 2016).

Artificial intelligence (AI) technologies augment operational efficiency and decision-making via the utilisation of data and analytics. Artificial intelligence technologies, including machine learning, natural language processing (NLP), predictive analytics, human-AI collaboration, and generative AI, have significantly improved managerial methods. These technologies have facilitated work automation, improved decision-making, and offered personalised suggestions (Russell & Norvig, 2016; Agrawal, Gans, & Goldfarb, 2018). The amalgamation of AI with behavioural insights in modern management may substantially enhance productivity and creativity, resulting in a more efficient and adaptive organisational environment (Doshi-Velez & Kim, 2017).

AI technologies have transformed management practices by automating tasks, optimising processes, and enhancing decision-making, leading to substantial productivity improvements. Machine learning algorithms use data to improve performance progressively, facilitating activities such as forecasting staff attrition, optimising supply chains, and customising marketing efforts (Agrawal, Gans, & Goldfarb, 2018). Natural Language Processing (NLP) facilitates computers in comprehending and interpreting human language via chatbots and virtual assistants, hence improving communication and customer service (Jurafsky & Martin, 2018). Predictive analytics use statistical algorithms and machine learning to ascertain the probability of future occurrences based on historical data, facilitating strategic planning and risk management (Siegel, 2016).

Human-AI collaboration amalgamates human and AI competencies, augmenting productivity by enabling AI to manage data-intensive responsibilities while people concentrate on creativity and strategic planning. Generative AI facilitates the development of innovative solutions, promotional material, and product design. Organisations may create user-centric and efficient systems that correspond with human behaviour, hence improving productivity via the integration of AI and behavioural insights (Doshi-Velez & Kim, 2017).

The integration of behavioural insights and AI technologies in contemporary management practices represents a profound and revolutionary shift. Artificial intelligence technologies, such as machine learning, natural language processing (NLP), predictive analytics, human-AI interaction, and generative AI, have radically altered the operational processes of organisations. These technologies enhance efficiency in repetitive tasks, optimise operations, and provide data-driven insights that refine decision-making and strategic planning (Agrawal, Gans, & Goldfarb, 2018). Integrating behavioural insights allows AI systems to be tailored to align with human cognitive processes, hence improving effectiveness and user acceptance. AI-generated prompts may be designed to reduce cognitive biases in decision-making, leading to more rational and beneficial outcomes (Sunstein, 2014).

The integrated methodologies examined has broader applicability beyond just organisational management. They may also be used in sectors like as education and healthcare. AI-driven adaptive learning systems in education use behavioural data to customise the learning experience for individual students, hence enhancing engagement and improving outcomes (Baker & Yacef, 2009). Predictive analytics, informed by behavioural insights, are used in healthcare to develop early diagnosis models and customised treatment methods, therefore improving patient outcomes and operational efficiency (Topol, 2019). These examples illustrate the flexibility and capacity to effect substantial change via the integration of behavioural insights with AI across several sectors.

Moreover, the ethical implications of integrating AI with behavioural insights must not be overlooked. The increasing influence of AI systems on essential sectors such as healthcare, finance, and public policy has raised significant concerns around privacy, data security, and algorithmic bias. Researchers and practitioners must stress fairness and transparency in the design of these systems. They must ensure the prevention of propagating existing prejudices and safeguard against any adverse outcomes (O'Neil, 2016).

As we go into the era of Society 5.0, it is essential to integrate behavioural insights with AI technology to create more streamlined, efficient, and inclusive organisational environments. This holistic strategy guarantees that technological advancement aligns with strategies that emphasise human requirements while promoting sustainable development by addressing complex societal issues. By using the benefits of artificial intelligence and behavioural insights, companies may adeptly navigate the uncertainties of the modern world, achieving sustainable growth and enhancing the welfare of individuals and communities.

In conclusion, as we go into the Society 5.0 age, comprehending and using behavioural insights with AI technology is essential for fostering a more efficient, productive, and inclusive organisational environment. This cohesive strategy harmonises technical advancement with human-centric methodologies, fostering sustainable growth and tackling the intricate difficulties of contemporary society.

This chapter offers extensive background information and a literature analysis on the amalgamation of behavioural insights and AI in the framework of Society 5.0 and sustainable development. The writers use many academic disciplines, such as psychology, economics, and neuroscience, to substantiate their conclusions. Citations of prominent scholars like Kahneman, Thaler, and Sunstein enhance the credibility of the literature review. The chapter would benefit from a succinct historical overview of the evolution of behavioural insights and AI, providing readers with a clearer comprehension of the convergence of both domains. Furthermore, including summaries of pivotal research and significant experiments would enhance the literature review, offering tangible proof of the themes addressed. The chapter emphasises organisational contexts; however, including insights from other domains, such as education or healthcare, might enhance the study and demonstrate the wider relevance of these principles.

DEFINITION AND IMPORTANCE OF BEHAVIOURAL INSIGHTS AND THE OVERVIEW AND IMPACT OF AI IN MANAGEMENT: THE THEORETICAL FOUNDATIONS

Behavioural insights is the systematic use of knowledge on human behaviour, derived from psychology, economics, and neuroscience, to influence decision-making and improve outcomes in organisational settings. The beginnings of behavioural insights may be traced to Herbert Simon's studies in the 1950s. Simon introduced the concept of bounded rationality, challenging the traditional economic assumption that decision-makers consistently behave in a fully rational fashion (Simon, 1955). This concept laid the groundwork for further exploration into the discrepancies between actual decision-making and the notion of rationality, leading to the development of behavioural economics, as popularised by Daniel Kahneman and Amos Tversky in their studies on cognitive biases (Kahneman & Tversky, 1979). These insights assist organisations in formulating more successful policies, plans, and interventions based on real thoughts and actions rather than assumed behaviours. Comprehending behavioural insights is essential, since human behaviour often exhibits irrationality and is shaped by cognitive biases, emotions, and social influences (Kahneman, 2011; Thaler & Sunstein, 2008).

Psychology examines individual behaviour and cognitive processes, improving comprehension of human thought, perception, and action. Economics analyses decision-making and resource distribution, emphasising departures from the rational conduct posited by conventional economic theories. Recent studies in behavioural economics have shown that humans often diverge from the rational behaviour anticipated by traditional economic models. The Royal Swedish Academy of Sciences (2017) highlighted that behavioural economics, including psychological insights, has recorded consistent departures from the rational behaviour posited by traditional neoclassical economics. This domain has profoundly affected several subfields of economics by elucidating the role of cognitive biases and heuristics on decision-making processes (Royal Swedish Academy of Sciences, 2017). Neuroscience investigates the brain processes that govern behaviour, offering a scientific foundation for comprehending decision-making (Loewenstein, 2000). Incorporating these viewpoints allows organisations to develop holistic solutions that successfully impact decision-making.

The integration of Artificial Intelligence (AI) into management science practices has become an essential strategy for improving efficiency in the modern company environment (Wazi, Karim, & Noor, 2024). Artificial intelligence technologies, including machine learning, natural language processing, predictive analytics, human-AI collaboration, and generative AI, have revolutionised management practices via work automation, process optimisation, and improved decision-making, resulting in significant productivity improvements. Artificial intelligence may discern trends, predict occurrences, and provide tailored suggestions via the analysis of extensive information, facilitating more informed and efficient decision-making (Russell & Norvig, 2016; Agrawal, Gans, & Goldfarb, 2018).

Advancements in AI technology have evolved with the development of behavioural insights. The inception of AI started with the progress in symbolic AI in the 1950s. The 1980s saw the emergence of expert systems, designed to replicate human expertise in certain domains. In the 21st century, machine learning gained prominence owing to improvements in computational capacity and the availability of vast datasets. This resulted in significant progress in areas such natural language processing (NLP) and predictive analytics (Goodfellow, Bengio, & Courville, 2016). These technology advancements have profoundly impacted management practices by enabling organisations to automate tasks, optimise processes, and make data-driven decisions.

Machine learning algorithms use data to enhance performance progressively, facilitating tasks such as forecasting staff attrition, optimising supply chains, and customising marketing initiatives (Agrawal, Gans, & Goldfarb, 2018). Natural Language Processing (NLP) facilitates computers in comprehending and interpreting human language via chatbots and virtual assistants, hence improving communication and customer service (Jurafsky & Martin, 2018). Predictive analytics use statistical algorithms and machine learning to ascertain the possibilities of future events based on historical data, facilitating strategic planning and risk management (Siegel, 2016).

Traditional management strategies have relied on hierarchical structures, intuitive decision-making, and manual processes. While these methods may be advantageous in certain contexts, they are often limited by human cognitive biases, inefficiencies, and the inability to process large volumes of data (Mintzberg, 1973). Conversely, the use of AI and behavioural insights in management processes offers a more objective and data-driven methodology that mitigates biases and enhances decision-making. AI systems has the capacity to analyse extensive datasets to identify patterns and predict outcomes. Furthermore, behavioural insights may be used to develop treatments aligned with human cognitive processes, hence improving employee engagement and productivity (Ariely, 2008).

Conventional management strategies often faced challenges arising from human cognitive limitations, including the inability to consistently make optimal decisions due to cognitive biases such as overconfidence, anchoring, and confirmation bias (Bazerman & Moore, 2012). AI technology has effectively mitigated these limitations by providing objective, data-driven insights that improve human decision-making. In supply chain management, AI-driven predictive models can forecast demand with more precision than traditional methods. This results in enhanced inventory management and reduced operational expenses (Chopra & Meindl, 2016).

Human-AI collaboration amalgamates human and AI competencies, augmenting productivity by enabling AI to manage data-intensive responsibilities while people concentrate on creativity and strategic planning. Generative AI facilitates the development of innovative solutions, marketing materials, and product designs. Organisations may create user-centric and efficient systems that correspond with human behaviour, hence improving productivity via the integration of AI and behavioural insights (Doshi-Velez & Kim, 2017).

ENHANCING PRODUCTIVITY THROUGH BEHAVIORAL INSIGHTS: NUDGING AND DECISION-MAKING

This section offers a comprehensive overview of cognitive biases and their effects on workplace efficiency, heavily referencing psychological research. The use of established notions such as status quo bias, loss aversion, and the availability heuristic, bolstered by citations of foundational studies by experts like Kahneman and Tversky, augments the credibility of the literature review. Nevertheless, the pragmatic implementation of these notions inside organisational contexts, especially via nudging and behavioural interventions, has garnered increasing interest in recent years.

The notion of "nudging," as proposed by Thaler and Sunstein, discreetly influences choices while preserving autonomy of choice. Nudging entails little strategic modifications in the environment that affect behaviour in a foreseeable manner. Organisational nudges, like reminders for breaks, default settings that encourage ideal work practices, and ambient designs that decrease distractions, may markedly improve attention, alleviate stress, and increase overall productivity (Thaler & Sunstein, 2008).

Default configurations in workplace settings may be modified to encourage healthier and more efficient practices. Altering the default selections in the corporate cafeteria to healthier alternatives or configuring computer systems to energy-efficient settings may promote improved habits without necessitating deliberate effort from workers. Customised prompts, such as tailored reminders about meetings or deadlines, can augment productivity. Minor modifications informed by behavioural insights may result in significant enhancements in employee happiness and productivity (Sunstein, 2014).

Numerous case studies illustrate the efficacy of nudging in enhancing productivity. The Behavioural Insights Team (BIT) discovered that tailored reminders enhanced attendance in training sessions by 20%. Nudges promoting frequent breaks mitigate burnout and sustain elevated productivity throughout the workday (Behavioural Insights Team, 2019). These examples emphasise the practical use of nudging in organisational contexts, demonstrating its capacity to cultivate a more productive and engaged staff.

Behavioural insights are essential for improving employee engagement and motivation. Comprehending the factors that drive individuals—such as acknowledgement, independence, and purposeful work—empowers organisations to cultivate surroundings that fulfil these requirements. Enhancing employee motivation via professional development opportunities and consistent feedback significantly increases productivity (Deci & Ryan, 2000). Recognition programs that acknowledge and recognise employee accomplishments inspire others and create a culture of ongoing development.

Granting workers more control over their activities and schedules fosters autonomy, so augmenting ownership and accountability. Aligning work with workers' beliefs and objectives enhances job happiness and performance (Pink, 2009). Open office layouts and access to collaborative tools enhance productivity by fostering cooperation and creativity. Policies that promote work-life balance, such as flexible hours and remote work alternatives, improve general well-being and job satisfaction, hence decreasing turnover rates and enhancing productivity (Fredrickson, 2001).

Organisations may use gamification to augment motivation and engagement. Gamification integrates game components, like points, leaderboards, and prizes, into non-gaming environments to enhance engagement and enjoyment of activities. Research indicates that gamification may enhance motivation, engagement, and performance across many contexts, such as workplace training, health initiatives, and educational settings (Deterding et al., 2011). Organisations may enhance engagement and productivity in the workplace via the use of gamification.

Furthermore, behavioural insights may guide the development of workplace interventions that enhance physical and mental health. Implementing standing desks, promoting consistent physical exercise, and offering mindfulness training may enhance employee health and productivity. Studies indicate that workers who engage in physical activity and maintain mental well-being exhibit higher productivity, less absenteeism, and a decreased likelihood of experiencing burnout (Biddle et al., 2015).

Incorporating behavioural insights into workplace design helps mitigate prevalent cognitive biases that influence decision-making and performance. The availability heuristic, in which humans depend on easily accessible information instead of all pertinent facts, may be alleviated by providing thorough information and context for decision-making. Likewise, confirmation bias, in which people seek information that validates their pre-existing opinions, may be mitigated by promoting multiple viewpoints and critical analysis. Recent study underscores the need of delivering counter-attitudinal information and involving participants in activities that confront their preconceived notions to successfully reduce confirmation bias (McSweeney, 2021). By cultivating an atmosphere that encourages multiple perspectives and promotes critical thinking, organisations may assist people in transcending confirmation bias and making more balanced and informed choices.

In summary, using behavioural insights and nudging within organisational contexts may markedly improve productivity and well-being. By comprehending and mitigating the elements that affect behaviour, organisations may cultivate environments that foster optimum performance, engagement, and satisfaction. This comprehensive strategy enhances both individual and organisational results while aligning with overarching objectives of sustainable development and social welfare.

UNDERSTANDING HUMAN BEHAVIOR IN THE WORKPLACE: COGNITIVE BIASES AND THEIR IMPACT ON PRODUCTIVITY AND SOCIAL AND EMOTIONAL FACTORS

This section provides a thorough examination of cognitive biases and the use of behavioural ideas to address them successfully. The chapter cites foundational studies by Kahneman and Tversky, highlighting critical cognitive biases like status quo prejudice, loss aversion, and the availability heuristic. The literature study is comprehensively supported by references to seminal publications, demonstrating a profound understanding of the subject topic. It would be beneficial for the chapter to include a broader array of interdisciplinary perspectives, including insights from behavioural economics and organisational behaviour, to provide a more thorough and inclusive outlook. Furthermore, including a discourse on the evolution of strategies to mitigate cognitive biases across time will augment the foundational knowledge.

Cognitive biases are systematic deviations from rationality that significantly influence behaviour and decision-making in professional settings. Organisations must recognise these biases to implement strategies that mitigate their impact and enhance productivity. A difficulty in organisational change initiatives is the status quo bias, which denotes individuals' aversion to change and inclination towards existing conditions. This cognitive bias may hinder the adoption and implementation of innovative technologies or processes, even when they provide better outcomes (Samuelson & Zeckhauser, 1988). To alleviate this prejudice, organisations may emphasise the lasting benefits of the change, provide clear and detailed information on its implementation, and offer support and training to aid employees' adaptation.

Loss aversion is a cognitive bias characterised by a pronounced preference for avoiding losses over acquiring equal gains. This may render employees hesitant to embrace changes they see as dangerous, despite the possible advantages outweighing the associated dangers (Kahneman & Tversky, 1979). Organisations may effectuate changes by highlighting prospective benefits and downplaying perceived drawbacks to mitigate loss aversion. Recent study demonstrates that presenting incentives as possible losses instead of rewards may markedly affect decision-making and behaviour. A research by Mrkva, Johnson, Gächter, and Herrmann (2020) shown that loss framing might significantly enhance the probability of persons engaging in desirable activities by emphasising potential losses. This strategy leverages the psychological concept of loss aversion, wherein individuals are motivated to evade losses by participating in the desired behaviour.

The availability heuristic, a cognitive bias recognised by Tversky and Kahneman in 1973, denotes the inclination of individuals to make judgements based on readily available information instead of evaluating all relevant data. This prejudice may adversely affect decision-making in the workplace. For instance, if a company has just had a notable security breach, employees may overrate the likelihood of further breaches and advocate for unnecessarily stringent security measures. Providing unbiased, evidence-based information on actual threats and the effectiveness of proposed measures may mitigate this prejudice and foster more rational decision-making. Recent studies underscore the importance of accurate and thorough communication in mitigating biases and enhancing decision-making processes. Grossi (2023) examines strategies for reducing bias in clinical algorithms, highlighting the need of transparent information distribution and the use of optimum procedures to guarantee that judgements are founded on precise and unbiased data.

Methods for mitigating cognitive biases have evolved, using insights from behavioural economics, psychology, and organisational behaviour. Thaler and Sunstein introduced the notion of nudging, which provides innovative strategies for subtly shaping employee behaviour to conform to organisational goals (Thaler & Sunstein, 2008). Nudging is making subtle changes to the work environment or decision-making procedures to encourage more rational and efficient behaviour. Default configurations in decision-making frameworks, such as the automatic enrolment of employees in advantageous programs like retirement savings plans, may successfully mitigate inertia and promote enhanced long-term outcomes.

Emotions significantly influence workplace behaviour, including motivation, engagement, and productivity. Positive emotions, like pleasure, pride, and satisfaction, may enhance creativity, problem-solving, and collaboration. Conversely, adverse emotions, such as tension and anxiety, may hinder performance. Promoting a supportive and positive work environment improves employee well-being and productivity. Fredrickson (2001) asserts that policies fostering work-life balance reduce stress levels and improve job satisfaction.

Workplace conduct is significantly shaped by social factors, including peer influence and societal norms. Employees are more predisposed to adopt new behaviours when they see their peers actively engaging in them. In an organisation that promotes sustainability initiatives, employees are more likely to participate in similar behaviours, such as recycling or reducing energy use. Fostering a culture that prioritises continuous development and recognises group achievements may motivate employees to embrace best practices and strive for outstanding performance (Cialdini, 2001).

Understanding emotional and social factors enables organisations to create solutions that address individual behaviour and foster a positive, collaborative organisational culture. Establishing a work environment that aligns with employees' intrinsic motivations and social connections enhances productivity and job satisfaction. Furthermore, recognising and mitigating cognitive biases may lead to improved decision-making and better organisational outcomes.

The status quo bias may provide considerable challenges in organisational restructuring or the adoption of new technologies. Certain workers may have a predilection for established routines and show reluctance to changes, even when such modifications might improve efficiency and productivity. Organisations may prioritise emphasising the lasting benefits of the change, offering clear and detailed information on the implementation process, and providing support and training to aid employees' adaptation (Samuelson & Zeckhauser, 1988).

Similarly, loss aversion may hinder the adoption of beneficial practices or inventions. Employees may emphasise the potential negative consequences associated with change over the possible beneficial ones. To mitigate complaints and enhance acceptance of a new performance management system, it is prudent to emphasise its capacity to promote individual and career development, acknowledge achievements, and provide incentives. Research demonstrates that effectively communicating the advantages of change, especially about personal and professional objectives, significantly increases acceptance and diminishes resistance.

It is essential to understand and address cognitive biases, emotions, and social factors in the workplace to enhance productivity and organisational success. Organisations may foster a constructive and cooperative culture that enhances performance and job satisfaction by adopting interventions that include these elements. This holistic method improves both individual and organisational outcomes while aligning with broader goals of sustainable development and social welfare.

APPLYING BEHAVIORAL INSIGHTS TO ADDRESS COGNITIVE BIASES

This section provides a thorough examination of cognitive biases and the use of behavioural insights to address them. This book cites seminal works by Kahneman and Tversky, highlighting critical biases such status quo bias, loss aversion, and the availability heuristic. The literature study is comprehensively supported by references to significant publications, demonstrating a profound understanding of the topic. However, the chapter might be improved by including a broader spectrum of interdisciplinary perspectives, including concepts from behavioural economics and organisational behaviour, to provide a more holistic approach. Furthermore, including a discourse on the evolution of methods to mitigate cognitive biases across time will augment the foundational knowledge.

The status quo prejudice, a well-researched cognitive bias, favours the maintenance of the current order of affairs. This complicates the ability of organisations to initiate new initiatives or adopt new technologies, even when such actions might be advantageous (Samuelson & Zeckhauser, 1988). This prejudice may significantly hinder organisations' ability to innovate and adapt. To minimise this bias, organisations must effectively communicate the benefits of the new condition and reduce perceived risks associated with the change.

Organisations may use many strategies to address status quo bias. Employing communication strategies that clearly convey the advantages of change and provide a compelling vision for the future is essential. In the shift to new software systems, offering comprehensive training sessions, accessible instructions, and endorsements from early adopters may serve as additional incentives. These techniques illustrate the advantageous impact of the transition on others' work and depict the change as an opportunity for personal and professional growth, so increasing the appeal of the new circumstances. By explicitly addressing the inclination to prefer the status quo, organisations increase the likelihood of successfully and broadly executing changes that are positively accepted (Kahneman, 2011).

Loss aversion, the tendency to prioritise the avoidance of losses above the acquisition of equal gains, significantly influences resistance to change within organisations. Employees often demonstrate resistance to changes seen as dangerous, even when the potential benefits outweigh the associated risks (Kahneman & Tversky, 1979). Organisations may alleviate loss aversion by framing changes to emphasise potential advantages while minimising perceived disadvantages. Providing guarantees on job stability and clarifying the long-term advantages of the change may alleviate apprehensions and reduce resistance.

Recent study underscores the need of transparent communication and the active engagement of employees to mitigate resistance throughout the transition process. Agile Ideation (2023) posits that clearly articulating the objectives and benefits of a change, together with offering continuous assistance and training, may mitigate uncertainty and enhance trust among employees. Organisations may foster a more inclusive and dedicated workforce by emphasising how the change will promote personal development and improve professional progression.

Loss framing strategies may be helpful in alleviating loss aversion. These tactics highlight the potential negative consequences of not implementing the change, hence creating a feeling of urgency. Demonstrating the repercussions of failing to embrace breakthrough technology, such as the potential to fall behind rivals, may create a feeling of urgency and encourage its implementation. Providing incentives for early acceptance or phased implementation may simplify the transition and mitigate perceived risks, so cultivating a more favourable environment for change (Mrkva et al., 2020).

The availability heuristic is a cognitive bias wherein judgements are influenced by readily available instances instead of taking into account all relevant information. This often leads to an exaggerated perception of the likelihood of significant events based on recent or notable instances (Tversky & Kahneman, 1973). This cognitive bias may distort risk perception, causing individuals to base decisions only on anecdotal evidence instead of doing a thorough assessment of the associated risks and benefits.

Effective and clear communication, together with comprehensive education, are crucial in mitigating the effects of the availability heuristic. A recent research by Vandeberg et al. (2022) demonstrates that using good communication strategies, such as conveying factual information via narratives, might mitigate the impact of cognitive biases, including the availability heuristic. This strategy enhances memory retention and the effectiveness of extensive information, aiding employees in making better informed decisions.

Organisations may use statistical data to provide a precise assessment of the risks and benefits associated with new initiatives. Case studies and success stories may be used to alleviate the impact of adverse events, diminishing their effect on attitudes. Encouraging employees to interact with other information sources might diminish their dependence on readily accessible examples, so improving their capacity to provide more objective assessments.

Emotions significantly influence individuals' behaviour in the workplace. Positive emotions, like happiness and pleasure, enhance motivation and productivity, while negative emotions, such as fear and anxiety, hinder performance. Creating a supportive and positive work environment may improve workers' physical and emotional well-being and increase their productivity. Enacting rules that promote work-life balance has been shown to significantly reduce stress levels and improve job satisfaction (Fredrickson, 2001).

Behaviour may also be affected by social factors, including peer influence and societal norms. Employees are more likely to adopt new behaviours when they see their peers actively engaging in them. The social influence may enhance the effectiveness of behavioural therapy. Fostering a culture that encourages continuous development and recognises team achievements may incentivise employees to embrace best practices and strive for superior performance (Cialdini, 2001).

Understanding emotional and social factors enables organisations to create interventions that address individual behaviour and foster a positive, collaborative organisational culture. Establishing a work environment that aligns with employees' intrinsic motivations and social connections enhances productivity and job satisfaction.

In times of organisational upheaval, providing chances for peer support and facilitating open communication alleviates fears and cultivates a collective sense of purpose. Leaders has the capacity to model commendable behaviours and engage with personnel to demonstrate their commitment to the new direction. Furthermore, recognising and celebrating little accomplishments and progress sustains motivation and reinforces the positive emotions associated with the shift.

Integrating behavioural insights into change management strategies may significantly improve the effectiveness of organisational transformations. Organisations may improve the resilience and flexibility of their workforce in a rapidly changing environment by addressing cognitive biases, emotional responses, and social dynamics.

Furthermore, the advancement of strategies to mitigate cognitive biases has led to the emergence of sophisticated approaches, such decision architecture and nudging, to gently and successfully influence behaviour (Thaler & Sunstein, 2008). These strategies not only assist in mitigating biases but also in promoting more rational and effective conduct within organisational settings.

Employing behavioural insights to address cognitive biases is essential for enhancing efficiency and decision-making inside organisations. Organisations may foster a more adaptable and innovative work environment by understanding and mitigating biases, including status quo prejudice, loss aversion, and the availability heuristic. The management of cognitive biases may be improved by integrating many interdisciplinary perspectives and using strategies such as nudging and decision architecture, resulting in increased outcomes in sustainable development and organisational well-being.

INTEGRATING BEHAVIORAL INSIGHTS WITH AI TECHNOLOGIES

This section provides a comprehensive analysis of the integration of behavioural insights with AI technology, illustrating the potential to enhance information processing and decision-making inside organisations. This book integrates foundational ideas from behavioural sciences with artificial intelligence, referencing notable writers such as Kahneman, Tversky, and esteemed AI experts like Russell and Norvig. The literature study thoroughly examines the theoretical underpinnings of machine learning, natural language processing (NLP), predictive analytics, and the collaboration between humans and artificial intelligence (AI). This chapter also presents a historical overview of the history and convergence of these technologies, using ideas from interdisciplinary fields such as cognitive neuroscience and data science to provide a holistic perspective and enrich the context.

The amalgamation of behavioural insights with AI technology significantly enhances information processing capabilities. Machine learning models based on behavioural data, including user interaction patterns and engagement levels, improve the precision and pertinence of predictions. An example of this is the enhancement of recommendation systems on e-commerce platforms by the analysis of consumer behaviour patterns, resulting in more effective and personalised recommendations (Agrawal, Gans, & Goldfarb, 2018).

Machine learning algorithms use behavioural data to reveal hidden patterns and trends, developing complex models that accurately predict user needs and preferences. Machine learning may be used in business to analyse employee performance data and identify traits correlated with high productivity and work satisfaction. This study may subsequently inform treatments that promote good behaviours.

The amalgamation of behavioural data with machine learning enables the development of user-focused products and services. Healthcare professionals use behavioural insights to build personalised treatment programs that include patient behaviours and preferences. This method enhances patient outcomes and fosters compliance with treatment protocols. The integration of machine learning with behavioural data yields more effective and customised solutions (Doshi-Velez & Kim, 2017).

Behavioural insights are crucial for enhancing NLP technologies, including chatbots and virtual assistants, by augmenting their ability to understand and respond to client requirements. Natural Language Processing (NLP) systems analyse the emotional sentiment and contextual details of user queries, providing accurate and empathetic replies. An example of this is a customer service chatbot that can recognise consumer displeasure. This chatbot may prioritise the customer's request and provide empathic responses, hence improving the overall user experience (Jurafsky & Martin, 2018).

Behavioural insights improve the usability and intuitiveness of NLP applications by informing their design. NLP technology in educational settings assess student interactions and provide tailored learning experiences. These technologies promote engagement and improve learning results by tailoring feedback to individual needs (Jurafsky & Martin, 2018).

Predictive analytics involves using statistical algorithms and machine learning techniques to forecast future events by examining historical data. When combined with behavioural insights, these predictions become more accurate and applicable. By understanding employee behaviour and engagement levels, organisations may predict turnover probability and proactively implement retention initiatives to mitigate future issues (Siegel, 2016).

Analysing behavioural indicators, like training participation, collaboration frequency, and communication patterns, provides valuable insights into employee performance and well-being. By incorporating these indications into predictive models, organisations may identify early signs of possible issues and execute preventive measures. The use of predictive analytics to identify people at elevated risk of burnout may prompt organisations to implement wellness programs and workload management strategies (Siegel, 2016).

Predictive analytics in marketing may evaluate customer behaviour and preferences, enabling the development of more targeted and effective campaigns. Marketers may improve customer happiness and loyalty by understanding the factors that affect purchase choices and creating personalised offers that resonate with customers. The amalgamation of behavioural insights with predictive analytics enhances decision-making and strategy planning (Siegel, 2016).

Enhancing human-AI collaboration requires the development of interfaces and protocols that align with human behaviour. Understanding the cognitive processes and decision-making mechanisms of persons offers critical insights for the creation of AI systems, allowing them to augment human capabilities and reduce limits. AI systems that provide clear reasons for their recommendations in collaborative settings may improve user trust and acceptance (Doshi-Velez & Kim, 2017).

AI technologies in healthcare may provide physicians detailed explanations, enhancing informed decision-making during the diagnosis of conditions. This collaborative approach integrates AI's analytical skills with human expertise and judgement, leading to a more effective diagnostic process (Doshi-Velez & Kim, 2017).

Integrating behavioural insights into human-AI collaboration enhances the design of training programs and user interfaces. Instructing AI systems to recognise and adapt to human preferences improves usability and engagement. In industrial environments, AI-enabled robots that work alongside human employees may understand and swiftly respond to their needs, promoting efficient and harmonious working circumstances (Doshi-Velez & Kim, 2017).

The integration of behavioural insights with generative AI, which employs algorithms to produce novel content or solutions, augments its capacity to provide outputs that resonate with human creativity and preferences. Generative design methodologies in architecture use human preferences and behavioural patterns to create visually appealing and highly functional solutions. Understanding the origins and evaluation of human ideas offers critical insights for the development of AI systems that enhance and support the creative process (Agrawal, Gans, & Goldfarb, 2018).

Generative AI is used in creative industries to produce music, art, and literature that aligns with consumer preferences and trends. AI algorithms can provide engaging content that appeals to diverse audiences by identifying trending subjects and styles. This method enhances the creative process and provides innovative tools and inspiration for artists and designers (Agrawal, Gans, & Goldfarb, 2018).

Generative AI is crucial in product development, since it generates innovative ideas by evaluating customer feedback and market trends. AI enables the rapid evaluation and improvement of new goods by integrating customer preferences and usability data, resulting in the creation of effective and user-centric solutions. Generative AI fosters innovation and creativity across several industries via the application of behavioural insights (Agrawal, Gans, & Goldfarb, 2018).

The integration of behavioural insights with AI technology may significantly enhance organisational decision-making and efficiency. Organisations may improve the efficacy of AI systems by addressing the psychological factors that influence human behaviour, so ensuring these systems are more aligned with human needs and objectives. It is crucial to examine the ethical implications of this integration, especially with equality, secrecy, and transparency. This strategy enables organisations to use artificial intelligence to actively promote the primary goals of Society 5.0, cultivating a future that is ecologically sustainable and focused on human needs.

ETHICAL CONSIDERATIONS IN THE INTEGRATION OF AI AND BEHAVIORAL INSIGHTS

As organisations progressively integrate AI technology with behavioural insights, it is essential to scrutinise the ethical ramifications of this amalgamation. Although these advances provide prospects for improved decision-making and organisational efficiency, they also present several ethical dilemmas, especially with privacy, prejudice, and transparency. It is essential to address these challenges to guarantee that the combination of AI and behavioural insights is ethical and socially responsible.

The extensive use of behavioural data in AI systems raises considerable privacy issues. Behavioural data, including user interactions, preferences, and decision-making habits, is often gathered without the express awareness or agreement of people. This data is then used to train machine learning algorithms, customise user experiences, and guide decision-making processes. The potential for data abuse is a considerable worry, since it may result in privacy invasions, data breaches, and unauthorised person profiling (Zarsky, 2019).

Organisations must use transparent data gathering and utilisation policies to mitigate privacy issues. Informed permission must be acquired from people prior to the collection and use of their behavioural data. Furthermore, organisations must guarantee that data is anonymised and encrypted to avert unauthorised access or exploitation. The establishment of stringent data protection legislation, such as the General Data Protection Regulation (GDPR), may provide a foundation for safeguarding privacy in AI systems. These requirements require organisations to disclose the data they gather and use, provide people authority over their data, and establish safeguards against unauthorised access (GDPR, 2018).

A significant ethical concern is prejudice in artificial intelligence systems. AI algorithms, especially those developed using historical data, might unintentionally reinforce existing biases present in the data. Such biases might result in inequitable or discriminatory results, especially when AI systems are used in decision-making processes that impact people' lives, like employment, lending, or criminal justice. If an AI system is trained on data that embodies historical prejudices against certain demographic groups, it may provide biassed results that disproportionately impact those groups (O'Neil, 2016).

Organisations must take proactive measures to guarantee that the data used for training AI systems is representative and devoid of bias to prevent bias in these systems. Fairness audits may be performed to evaluate the potential for bias in AI systems, and bias-mitigation strategies may be implemented to diminish the effects of biassed data. Furthermore, organisations have to include numerous teams in the creation and supervision of AI systems to guarantee that various views are integrated into the design and execution of these technologies (Bolukbasi et al., 2016).

Transparency becomes a fundamental ethical concern in the integration of AI and behavioural insights. AI systems are often regarded as "black boxes," indicating that their decision-making processes are not consistently accessible or comprehensible to users. The absence of transparency may undermine confidence in AI systems, especially when users are impacted by judgements made by these systems without a clear comprehension of the decision-making process (Burrell, 2016).

To mitigate transparency issues, organisations must emphasise explainability in artificial intelligence systems. AI systems must be built to enable users to comprehend the decision-making process and the variables that drove those judgements. Articulating transparent rationales for AI-generated judgements may enhance confidence and accountability in AI systems. Moreover, algorithmic transparency must be included into the design of AI systems, guaranteeing that the methodologies and data used to derive conclusions are available and comprehensible to both users and stakeholders (Doshi-Velez & Kim, 2017).

Frameworks for ethical decision-making must be established to facilitate the integration of AI and behavioural insights. These frameworks must adhere to the ideals of equity, openness, accountability, and privacy. The principle of algorithmic responsibility mandates that organisations are liable for the results generated by AI systems. Organisations must be equipped to elucidate and rationalise choices made by AI, especially when these decisions have substantial consequences for persons or communities (Cath, 2018).

A further significant concern is the possibility for manipulation when integrating behavioural insights with AI. Behavioural insights aim to affect decision-making by understanding and using cognitive biases. Although these approaches may foster beneficial results, such as promoting healthy behaviours or enhancing productivity, they also represent the potential of being used for manipulative ends. Companies may use behavioural insights to develop AI systems that leverage customers' cognitive biases to enhance sales or promote addictive behaviours (Sunstein, 2014).

To reduce the possibility of manipulation, organisations must comply with ethical norms that prioritise the welfare of people and communities. Behavioural treatments must be crafted to respect individual autonomy and facilitate informed decision-making. Furthermore, organisations must maintain transparency on the use of behavioural insights in AI systems and guarantee that these methodologies adhere to ethical norms (Thaler & Sunstein, 2008).

Data security is a significant ethical concern in the integration of AI and behavioural insights. AI systems dependent on extensive personal data are susceptible to security breaches, potentially resulting in the disclosure of sensitive information. Organisations must enforce rigorous data security protocols to safeguard the data used in AI systems. This include routine security assessments, encryption of confidential information, and the use of secure data storage and transfer techniques (Zarsky, 2019).

Moreover, the ethical incorporation of AI and behavioural insights must take into account the possible social ramifications of these technologies. As AI systems proliferate, they may intensify current inequities or generate new types of societal stratification. AI-driven decision-making in employment or financing may disproportionately harm certain demographic groups, resulting in uneven access to opportunities or resources (O'Neil, 2016).

Organisations must implement measures to guarantee that the use of AI technology fosters social justice and does not exacerbate existing inequities. This entails doing impact assessments to analyse the possible societal ramifications of AI systems and instituting efforts to alleviate any adverse effects. Furthermore, organisations must include stakeholders, particularly marginalised populations, to guarantee that the development and use of AI systems embody various viewpoints and foster inclusive results (Crawford & Calo, 2016).

In conclusion, the amalgamation of AI with behavioural insights has considerable promise for improving decision-making and productivity, although it also introduces certain ethical dilemmas. Organisations must confront issues pertaining to privacy, prejudice, transparency, and manipulation to guarantee the responsible and ethical use of these technologies. Organisations may use the promise of AI and behavioural insights to foster beneficial social outcomes and mitigate risks by adopting ethical frameworks and instituting strong safeguards to safeguard individual rights.

CASE STUDIES: PRACTICAL APPLICATIONS OF BEHAVIORAL INSIGHTS AND AI IN VARIOUS INDUSTRIES

The integration of behavioural insights with AI technology has shown considerable success across several sectors, providing pragmatic solutions that improve productivity, decision-making, and consumer engagement. This section emphasises significant case examples from healthcare, education, finance, and retail, demonstrating the collaboration of behavioural insights with AI in tackling intricate difficulties and fostering favourable results.

The incorporation of predictive analytics and behavioural insights in the healthcare industry has led to substantial improvements in patient care and results. A notable instance is the use of AI-driven prediction models to assess patient behaviour and pinpoint those at elevated risk for chronic illnesses, such diabetes or cardiovascular disease. Predictive analytics systems may uncover trends indicating a patient's risk for certain health outcomes by combining behavioural data, such as lifestyle decisions, medication adherence, and involvement with healthcare professionals (Topol, 2019).

Healthcare providers use AI algorithms to analyse behavioural data and forecast patient adherence to treatment programs. By comprehending patterns of non-adherence, like missing visits or irregular prescription consumption, healthcare practitioners may engage proactively to enhance patient outcomes. Furthermore, behavioural insights inform the creation of individualised treatment plans that take into account patients' distinct preferences, behaviours, and risk factors, resulting in enhanced care delivery (Steinhubl, Muse, & Topol, 2015).

Additionally, behavioural nudging strategies, including reminders and rewards for healthy behaviours, have been included into AI-driven systems to promote patient compliance with treatment regimens. A healthcare practitioner may use an AI-driven application to provide personalised reminders, prompting patients to adhere to their drug regimen or attend follow-up visits. These approaches markedly enhance adherence rates and result in improved long-term health outcomes (Volpp et al., 2017).

The education industry has gained advantages from the use of AI and behavioural insights. Recently, adaptive learning systems have developed that use machine learning algorithms to assess student behaviour, learning patterns, and engagement levels. These platforms may provide customised learning trajectories aligned with each student's skills, limitations, and interests, facilitating a more efficient and personalised educational experience (Luckin et al., 2016).

AI-driven solutions like Knewton and DreamBox use behavioural insights to detect deficiencies in a student's understanding and modify the curriculum appropriately. If a learner has difficulty with a certain mathematical subject, the system will provide further tasks, resources, or elucidations to aid the student's comprehension. This tailored method has shown a substantial improvement in educational results, particularly for pupils who may have lagged in conventional classroom environments (Pane et al., 2017).

AI-driven solutions may personalise learning experiences, analyse student engagement, and detect early indicators of disengagement or dropout risk. By monitoring metrics like as attendance, engagement, and assignment fulfilment, these systems may identify at-risk students and suggest interventions to maintain their progress. A university may use an AI system to observe student behaviour and provide prompts to those who are often absent or failing to achieve academic standards, urging them to seek academic assistance or consult with their advisers (Zawacki-Richter et al., 2019).

In the banking sector, AI algorithms integrated with behavioural insights have markedly enhanced the precision and efficacy of fraud detection. Conventional fraud detection systems often depend on inflexible rule-based methodologies that are susceptible to false positives and may overlook more intricate forms of fraud. AI systems can identify tiny irregularities indicative of fraudulent behaviour by combining behavioural data, including transaction history, spending trends, and account activity (Ngai, Hu, Wong, Chen, & Sun, 2011).

Financial institutions use machine learning algorithms to examine consumer behaviour and detect trends that diverge from standard activity. Should a consumer, typically engaged in little local purchases, unexpectedly execute a substantial overseas transaction, the AI system may identify the transaction as possibly fraudulent and notify either the customer or the institution for additional scrutiny. Through the ongoing assimilation of fresh data, these AI systems enhance their capabilities over time, increasing their accuracy in fraud detection while reducing false positives (Buczak & Guven, 2016).

Furthermore, AI-driven analysis of consumer behaviour is used to enhance financial services and goods by comprehending client preferences, requirements, and behaviours. Financial organisations use AI technologies to assess consumer expenditure patterns and provide tailored financial solutions, such loans or investment options, that correspond with personal objectives. This customised strategy improves customer satisfaction and boosts retention rates (Jagtiani & Lemieux, 2019).

Artificial intelligence and behavioural insights are revolutionising consumer interaction and personalised marketing techniques in the retail industry. Retailers use AI algorithms to examine customer behaviour, including browsing history, purchasing trends, and preferences, to provide tailored product suggestions and promotions. This empirical methodology has resulted in significant enhancements in conversion rates and consumer satisfaction (Davenport, Guha, Grewal, & Bressgott, 2020).

E-commerce sites such as Amazon and Alibaba use AI-driven recommendation algorithms that anticipate the goods a client is most inclined to buy based on their prior experiences with the platform. These suggestions are tailored for each user, enhancing the probability of a transaction. Moreover, dynamic pricing algorithms modify prices instantaneously according to consumer behaviour, market trends, and demand, enabling merchants to refine pricing strategies and enhance revenue (Chen, Mislove, & Wilson, 2016).

Retailers are utilising behavioural nudging strategies to promote preferred actions, such as completing a purchase or enrolling in loyalty programs. AI systems may dispatch tailored reminders or provide time-sensitive discounts to motivate client action. An online store may use AI to dispatch a personalised message to a consumer who has forsaken their shopping basket, providing a discount to incentivise the completion of the transaction. Nudging strategies have shown efficacy in enhancing conversion rates and fostering client loyalty (Sunstein, 2014).

SUSTAINABLE DEVELOPMENT THROUGH BEHAVIORAL INSIGHTS AND ARTIFICIAL INTELLIGENCE

This section examines the integration of behavioural insights and artificial intelligence (AI) in the pursuit of sustainable development objectives. Behavioural insights, particularly via nudging tactics, are essential for promoting sustainable behaviours, while AI provides creative methods to optimise resource use, boost energy efficiency, and improve environmental monitoring. Collectively, these disciplines provide a robust approach to promoting eco-friendly behaviours and executing sustainable development plans.

Behavioural insights are crucial for enhancing resource efficiency and sustainable practices by motivating people and organisations to embrace environmentally beneficial behaviours. Resource efficiency emphasises optimising production while reducing resource use, a fundamental tenet of sustainable development. The notion of nudging, as articulated by Thaler and Sunstein (2008), involves modest interventions aimed at influencing behaviour without limiting choice, and has shown efficacy in decreasing energy use. Behavioural nudges, such as reminders to deactivate lights or modify energy settings, may substantially reduce energy use. Likewise, establishing default settings for energy conservation practices, such as duplex printing, minimises resource depletion.

Promoting sustainable practices among workers and customers is essential for attaining sustainability objectives. Behavioural insights provide the means to create interventions that encourage acts like recycling, energy saving, and the choice of sustainable goods. Studies indicate that social norms, especially those emphasising peer behaviours, significantly motivate individuals to emulate like patterns. Cialdini (2001) revealed that highlighting the sustainable actions of peers is a significant incentive for adopting environmentally beneficial behaviours. Positioning recycling bins in prominent areas and using prompts to promote less plastic use helps cultivate a workplace ethos of sustainability.

It is essential to address cognitive biases that impede the adoption of sustainable behaviours. Status quo prejudice and loss aversion are prevalent biases that hinder progress. Samuelson and Zeckhauser (1988) discovered that people often choose to preserve existing habits, despite the availability of more advantageous sustainable alternatives. Emphasising the benefits of sustainable practices and delineating explicit processes for adopting environmentally friendly methods might mitigate this opposition. Likewise, loss aversion, the tendency for people to prioritise the avoidance of losses above the acquisition of equal gains, may be mitigated by presenting sustainable initiatives in terms of prospective savings, such as decreased energy expenses. Beam et al. (2022) shown that framing sustainability incentives as possible costs, rather than advantages, successfully promotes beneficial behaviours.

An interdisciplinary approach that integrates environmental psychology and ecological economics provides a more comprehensive framework for applying behavioural insights to sustainability. Environmental psychology investigates individuals' perceptions and interactions with their surroundings, guiding efforts to enhance the appeal and accessibility of sustainable behaviours. Ecological economics examines the interplay between economic systems and ecological health, offering insights into how market processes might be harmonised with sustainability objectives.

The efficacy of behavioural insights in advancing sustainability is shown across several sectors. In the energy industry, utilities have used social comparison nudges to promote conservation by supplying consumers with reports that compare their energy usage to that of their neighbours. This method utilises social norms to induce behavioural change, resulting in substantial decreases in energy use (Allcott, 2011). In agriculture, behavioural interventions advocating crop rotation and organic farming in India have been bolstered by peer networks, emphasising the enduring advantages of sustainable methods (World Bank, 2018). Urban planning in places such as Copenhagen has used behavioural nudges and infrastructure design to encourage cycling, leading to decreased automobile usage and less carbon emissions (Gössling, 2013).

Artificial intelligence (AI) is essential for advancing sustainable development via the optimisation of resource use, enhancement of energy efficiency, and stimulation of creativity. Artificial intelligence technologies, including machine learning, examine patterns of resource utilisation, detect inefficiencies, and provide practical suggestions for improvement. Predictive maintenance use AI to anticipate equipment breakdowns, facilitating prompt repairs that decrease downtime and mitigate waste. In manufacturing, artificial intelligence enhances production schedules and supply chain logistics, leading to decreased resource utilisation and waste output (Russell & Norvig, 2016).

The capacity of AI to analyse extensive data sets in real time facilitates substantial advancements in environmental management. For instance, AI may evaluate data from sensors integrated into industrial machinery to forecast maintenance requirements, therefore averting expensive failures and resource exhaustion. Artificial intelligence enhances equipment performance, allowing organisations to diminish their environmental impact by optimising energy use and resource efficiency.

In smart cities, artificial intelligence fosters sustainable practices by scrutinising data from energy meters, transportation networks, and waste management systems to pinpoint chances for minimising environmental effect. AI can suggest energy-efficient routes for public transport and enhance traffic flow to reduce emissions. AI improves the sustainability and liveability of urban areas by delivering real-time information.

Artificial intelligence significantly contributes to promoting innovation for sustainability. Machine learning expedites the creation of novel materials and products that reduce environmental impact. AI can enhance solar panel performance by examining sunshine patterns and material characteristics, resulting in more efficient renewable energy solutions. Moreover, AI facilitates the design of goods with sustainability considerations, guaranteeing their eco-friendliness throughout the whole lifespan, from manufacture to disposal.

Although AI has promise for sustainable development, it presents problems and ethical dilemmas that need attention. A significant concern is the energy consumption linked to training extensive AI models, which may undermine the environmental advantages that AI aims to provide. As artificial intelligence increasingly integrates into sustainability initiatives, it is essential to create energy-efficient AI models and investigate methods to mitigate their environmental impact.

Another issue is the potential for AI to intensify existing disparities, especially if access to AI technology is not egalitarian. Ensuring the accessibility of AI and associated technologies across all societal sectors is crucial for fostering inclusive sustainable development. Furthermore, AI systems should be developed with an emphasis on openness and responsibility. An AI system intended to enhance resource efficiency may unintentionally favour short-term benefits at the expense of long-term sustainability, leading to adverse environmental effects.

An interdisciplinary approach is crucial for properly harnessing AI's promise in sustainable development. Integrating ideas from environmental science, sustainability studies, and artificial intelligence research enables the development of solutions that are both efficient and scalable. Ecological modelling may use AI's capacity to analyse extensive information, allowing more precise forecasts of environmental changes. AI may enhance environmental economics by reconciling economic viability with ecological sustainability.

The combination of behavioural insights with artificial intelligence offers significant prospects for promoting sustainable development objectives. These technologies can tackle the intricate environmental concerns of the 21st century by enhancing resource efficiency, promoting innovation, and advocating for sustainable practices. It is essential to evaluate the ethical ramifications of its use and guarantee that sustainability programs are inclusive, transparent, and congruent with overarching societal objectives.

To optimise the advantages of these technologies, continuous cooperation among developers, environmental scientists, politicians, and the public is vital. Utilising a multidisciplinary approach guarantees the ethical, successful use of AI and behavioural insights in alignment with sustainable development goals. This encompasses the creation of AI systems that are resource-efficient, ecologically sustainable, and universally accessible. The integration of AI and behavioural insights has the capacity to foster a more sustainable and fair future for everyone.

CONCLUSION: THE FUTURE OF AI AND BEHAVIORAL INSIGHTS IN ENHANCING PRODUCTIVITY

The integration of behavioural insights with AI technology provides organisations with a robust toolkit to improve productivity, decision-making, and overall performance. Organisations across many sectors may use insights into human behaviour in conjunction with modern AI systems to create more effective interventions, enhance processes, and cultivate a more engaged and motivated workforce. This chapter has delineated the theoretical underpinnings of behavioural insights and artificial intelligence, while illustrating practical applications in healthcare, education, banking, and retail. The integration of these disciplines signifies a crucial advancement towards realising the objectives of Society 5.0—a society in which technology and human-centered innovation coexist synergistically to promote sustainable development.

The potential for AI and behavioural insights to significantly boost productivity in the future is substantial. Progress in machine learning, natural language processing (NLP), and predictive analytics will further enhance the capabilities of AI systems, allowing them to analyse greater datasets, provide more precise predictions, and yield deeper insights into human behaviour. This progression will enhance user personalisation, improve decision-making, and refine corporate processes across several industries.

Furthermore, the advancement of generative AI presents novel opportunities for creativity and innovation. Through the incorporation of behavioural insights, generative AI may generate outputs that correspond with human preferences, values, and aspirations, facilitating the development of more intuitive and user-centric solutions. Generative AI has the capacity to transform creation and innovation across architecture, design, marketing, and product development.

As AI capabilities expand, the ethical issues about its use also increase. Concerns about privacy, prejudice, and openness will continue to be essential in the ethical use of AI systems. Organisations must persist in adopting ethical frameworks that emphasise justice, responsibility, and privacy in the design and use of AI technology. It is essential for AI systems to be transparent, explainable, and connected with overarching social equality objectives to ensure their effectiveness in improving productivity without increasing disparities or violating human rights.

The collaboration between humans and AI will assume an increasingly significant role in creating the future of work. AI systems are designed to augment human capabilities by automating monotonous jobs, analysing extensive data sets, and offering insights that facilitate improved decision-making. This partnership will enable people to concentrate on advanced, creative, and strategic endeavours, fostering innovation and enhancing overall productivity. As AI systems increasingly integrate into the workplace, it is essential to ensure that people possess the requisite skills to collaborate effectively with AI, hence optimising the advantages of this partnership.

The domain of behavioural insights will further develop as further study is undertaken into human behaviour, decision-making, and the determinants of productivity. Organisations that comprehend cognitive biases, emotions, and social influences on behaviour will be more adept at crafting interventions that correspond with workers' inherent inclinations, resulting in enhanced performance, job satisfaction, and overall well-being. The use of nudging tactics and other behaviourally informed strategies will continue to be essential in promoting desirable behaviours and results within organisational contexts.

The prospects for AI and behavioural insights in augmenting productivity are promising. As these technologies advance, organisations may use their potential to foster sustainable development, innovation, and employee engagement. By using a human-centered approach to AI, grounded on behavioural insights, organisations may guarantee that their technological applications enhance productivity while also conforming to wider social objectives of inclusiveness, equity, and well-being. The way ahead is using the potential offered by AI and behavioural insights while maintaining awareness of the ethical implications associated with their incorporation into society.

REFERENCES

Agrawal, A., Gans, J. S., & Goldfarb, A. (2018). *Prediction machines: The simple economics of artificial intelligence*. Harvard Business Review Press.

Wazi, N. W. M., Karim, F., & Noor, N. A. M. (2024). *Productivity modern management science practices in the age of AI: AI driven productivity. Modern Management Science Practices in the Age of AI.* IGI Global.

Allcott, H., & Rogers, T. (2014). The short-run and long-run effects of behavioral interventions: Experimental evidence from energy conservation. *The American Economic Review*, 104(10), 3003–3037.

Amabile, T. M. (1996). *Creativity in context: Update to the social psychology of creativity*. Routledge.

Ariely, D. (2008). *Predictably irrational: The hidden forces that shape our decisions*. HarperCollins.

Bandura, A. (1977). *Social learning theory*. Prentice Hall.

Batty, M., Axhausen, K. W., Giannotti, F., Pozdnoukhov, A., Bazzani, A., Wachowicz, M., & Portugali, Y. (2012). Smart cities of the future. *The European Physical Journal. Special Topics*, 214(1), 481–518.

Behavioural Insights Team. (2019). Annual report.

Biddle, S. J. H., Mutrie, N., & Gorely, T. (2015). *Psychology of physical activity: Determinants, well-being, and interventions*. Routledge.

Cialdini, R. B. (2001). *Influence: Science and practice* (4th ed.). Allyn & Bacon.

Deci, E. L., & Ryan, R. M. (2000). The "what" and "why" of goal pursuits: Human needs and the self-determination of behavior. *Psychological Inquiry*, 11(4), 227–268.

Deterding, S., Dixon, D., Khaled, R., & Nacke, L. (2011). From game design elements to gamefulness: Defining "gamification." In *Proceedings of the 15th International Academic MindTrek Conference: Envisioning Future Media Environments* (pp. 9-15).

Doshi-Velez, F., & Kim, B. (2017). Towards a rigorous science of interpretable machine learning.

Ericsson, K. A., Krampe, R. T., & Tesch-Römer, C. (1993). The role of deliberate practice in the acquisition of expert performance. *Psychological Review*, 100(3), 363–406.

Fredrickson, B. L. (2001). The role of positive emotions in positive psychology: The broaden-and-build theory of positive emotions. *The American Psychologist*, 56(3), 218–226.

Goodfellow, I., Bengio, Y., & Courville, A. (2016). *Deep learning*. MIT Press.

Jurafsky, D., & Martin, J. H. (2018). *Speech and language processing* (3rd ed.). Prentice Hall.

Kahneman, D. (2011). *Thinking fast and slow*. Farrar, Straus and Giroux.

Kahneman, D., & Tversky, A. (1979). Prospect theory: An analysis of decision under risk. *Econometrica*, 47(2), 263–291.

Kirkpatrick, D. L., & Kirkpatrick, J. D. (2006). *Evaluating training programs: The four levels* (3rd ed.). Berrett-Koehler Publishers.

Loewenstein, G. (2000). Emotions in economic theory and economic behavior. *The American Economic Review*, 90(2), 426–432.

Pink, D. H. (2009). *Drive: The surprising truth about what motivates us*. Riverhead Books.

Russell, S., & Norvig, P. (2016). *Artificial intelligence: A modern approach* (3rd ed.). Prentice Hall.

Samuelson, W., & Zeckhauser, R. (1988). Status quo bias in decision making. *Journal of Risk and Uncertainty*, 1(1), 7–59.

Siegel, E. (2016). *Predictive analytics: The power to predict who will click, buy, lie, or die* (2nd ed.). Wiley.

Sunstein, C. R. (2014). *Why nudge? The politics of libertarian paternalism*. Yale University Press.

Thaler, R. H., & Sunstein, C. R. (2008). *Nudge: Improving decisions about health, wealth, and happiness*. Yale University Press.

Tilman, D., Cassman, K. G., Matson, P. A., Naylor, R., & Polasky, S. (2002). Agricultural sustainability and intensive production practices. *Nature*, 418(6898), 671–677.

Tversky, A., & Kahneman, D. (1974). Judgment under uncertainty: Heuristics and biases. *Science*, 185(4157), 1124–1131.

Wilson, H. J., & Daugherty, P. R. (2018). *Human + machine: Reimagining work in the age of AI*. Harvard Business Review Press.

Zuboff, S. (2019). *The age of surveillance capitalism: The fight for a human future at the new frontier of power*. PublicAffairs.

Vivien, S. (2023). Sustainable development: Balancing economic prosperity and environmental concerns. *Journal of Economics and Economic Education Research*, 24(4), 1–3.

Korteling, J. E., & Toet, A. (2022). Cognitive biases and how to improve sustainable decision-making. *Frontiers in Psychology*, 13, 1242809.

UN DESA. (2023). *The sustainable development goals report 2023* (Special edition). Department of Economic and Social Affairs, United Nations.

Mrkva, K., Johnson, E. J., Gächter, S., & Herrmann, A. (2020). Loss aversion and the willingness to take risks: A large-scale field experiment. *Journal of Economic Behavior & Organization*, 179, 177–190.

McSweeney, B. (2021). Fooling ourselves and others: Confirmation bias and the trustworthiness of qualitative research – Part 1 (the threats). *Journal of Organizational Change Management*, 34(5), 1063–1075.

Grossi, G. (2023). Review details strategies for mitigating bias in clinical algorithms. *The American Journal of Managed Care*.

Vandeberg, L., Meppelink, C. S., Sanders, J., & Fransen, M. L. (2022). Facts tell, stories sell? Assessing the availability heuristic and resistance as cognitive mechanisms underlying the persuasive effects of vaccination narratives. *Frontiers in Psychology*.

Royal Swedish Academy of Sciences. (2017). Nobel Prize in Economics document: Richard Thaler's contributions to behavioral economics.

McKinsey & Company. (2024). Performance management that puts people first.

Agile Ideation. (2023). Overcoming resistance to change in the workplace: Managing the transition to a generative culture.

Beam, E. A., Masatlioglu, Y., Watson, T., & Yang, D. (2022). *Loss aversion or lack of trust: Why does loss framing work to encourage preventative health behaviors?* National Bureau of Economic Research.

Chapter 3
Business Information Systems, Importance of Information, Business Intelligence, Corporate Excellence, and ICTs Within the Development of Organizations

Aytaç Gökmen
https://orcid.org/0000-0002-8985-3776
Çankaya University, Turkey

Dilek Temiz
Çankaya University, Turkey

ABSTRACT

An important shift takes places in organizations which is the shift in priorities to strategic management and increasing human demand for reliable information to run the business competitively in the global context. Nevertheless, executives and managers are exposed to a considerable amount of information which is both invaluable, as well as difficult to acquire, process, store, disseminate and utilize. Therefore, the objective of this study is to focus on the subjects as business information systems, information systems, business intelligence, corporate excellence, business intelligence, ICTs and other topics related to these issues in order to emphasize the importance of information and knowledge in the 21st century.

1. INTRODUCTION

The competitive environment of organizations is in a position of continuous change resulting from some factors as; decline of market frontiers, intensifying competition, appreciation of knowledge and information, differentiation customer habits, quick change of organizations and widening goods and service portfolio. The need to respond to the changes rises the role of decision support and managers shall depend on the available information throughout their decision-making process. Market players might have complete information. On the other hand, corporate managers may not enjoy all the necessary

DOI: 10.4018/979-8-3693-9230-0.ch003

Copyright ©2025, IGI Global. Copying or distributing in print or electronic forms without written permission of IGI Global is prohibited.

information to make decisions in the extensive cases. Sources are indispensable for business operations. These indispensable sources could be classified as human resources, raw materials, energy, capital and information. Henceforth, information stimulates decision-making as a factor in declining uncertainty. Information could be considered as a source when corporate interests can be constituted. Information utilization is composed of three closely correlated factors as decision-making, communication and the operation of processes. From a corporate point of view, decisions are to constitute new information. The organizational information systems serve information purposes. The goal of organizations is to provide target-focused information systematization and processing. Its duty is to fulfill stakeholders' information necessities. The information needs of organizations can be categorized as external and internal classifications; internal information is generated inside of the organization; therefore, it can only be accessed by means of its own information system, on the other hand external information could be installed into the corporate information system. Improvement of plans shall be applied to the users having optimal freedom while utilizing the information which is in disposal. To achieve this an information system (IS) offers a variety of solutions contemplated to enhance the decision-making process. Information systems are essential frameworks, technologies and tools devised to convert data to information, transfer information into knowledge and translate knowledge into plans for conducting a profitable business. Additionally, to the development of information systems, the main goal behind developing information management is the affective administration of information of sources and the capability of the organization to supply everything necessary for the use of information systems having access to information and the proper assistance of end users. The need to take advantage of the opportunities supplied by the information environment and the necessity create the information acquisition is intended to develop the performance administrative targets (Görsci, Szeles, 2018; Tvrdikova, 2016; Kim, 2022; Shrestha, Saatchandra, 2023).

A system is a group of entities and networks brought together to constitute a whole greater than the sum of its parts. An information system is a set of components which correlated to collect, store and process data and supply information and knowledge that stimulate decision making and control of an organization. An information system could be incorporated by their parts namely – organizations/process, individuals & information technology – and is an important means for constituting value for an organization. ISs have been becoming complex elements and are designated to supply comprehensive information which is not provided by a single system. In this regard, individuals demand systems which can be integrated to meet their needs, functioning as a single system and providing more than the information itself. When composed managerially and operationally an independent information system that leads to several other information systems that function together to accomplish mutual business targets. The significance of the correlation between these interoperable information systems due to the fact that organizations could be able to sustain themselves and produce more value if those systems are better scrutinized and understood. Systems which operate in isolation avoid the automation of information transfer and synchronization, decrease the association and sharing between systems communication obstacle among different sectors, bringing about an organization to provide inconsistent information to its consumers. Additionally, the lack of information system rises functional and administrative/coordination costs. Therefore, affectively enhance organizations' business processes, existing information systems are supposed to be integrated. Organizations shall endeavor to constitute value in their goods and services by cooperating with each other complement their common limitations and rise their impact and business advantages (da Silva Oliveria, 2022; Tvrdikova, 2016; Harum, Ali, 2022).

2. INFORMATION SYSTEMS, CORPORATE EXCELLENCE & EMPLOYEE PERFORMANCE

The IS is a component which is interconnected with the process of formation and conveying information in organizations, that processes inputs in the form resource data, afterwards processed with component hardware, software as well as brainware and generate information as output. Data and information are two different concepts that are interconnected. Data is raw material from the information generated. IS is the process of gathering, processing, screening and distributing information for specific purposes. A system of an organization which composes the daily processing and transplantation that fortifies the functional operation organization which is managerial with the activities. ISs are interconnected constituents which collect, store, process and disseminate information to enhance decision-making and monitoring in an organization. ISs also assist supervisors and employees sort out problems, delineate sophisticated issues, also constitute new products as well as innovations. The IS involves significant information in the form of individuals, places/locations and other major matters related to organization and its environment outside the organization. A set of factors which are correlated and function together to accomplish multiple roles. Additionally, other understanding of the system is involved factors and inputs and also processing an output. Furthermore, the system could simply be explained as a collection or set of organized factors or variables, interacting and mutually-dependent with each other. Once devised, the system is introduced and implemented in an organization. If the system which is applied is utilized, then, the system application could be comprehended as accomplished (Mahendra, 2023; Görsci, Szeles, 2018; da Silva Oliveria, 2022; Tvrdikova, 2016).

An organization's information system significantly impacts on business operations in the contemporary management environment. The information systems considerably forge the way the organizations function and their performance is embodied and realized by means of those systems. The quick penetration of information technology has resulted in considerable attention on digital data and organizational intelligence as well as the enabled digital connection has altered how business and employees work, exploring the dissemination of business information systems to enhance efficiency, value and innovation facilities. Henceforth, modern organizations shall be innovative and their core means are supposed to secure competitive advantage. Moreover, organizations undergo unprecedented technological alternations with their informative systems. Business systems face new technological alternations such as infrastructure which enable them to work remotely, executing remote commerce, virtual meetings, privacy protection, data analytics, cybersecurity and data-driven decision-making processes. Nevertheless, it becomes significant for businesses to embody the new system in desired organizational applications and processes, while accomplished continued system utilization. Information systems is a process by means of organizations identifying information technology applications portfolio to accomplish its business goals and to assist to execute its organizational targets. Changing business environments compel businesses to entail important investments from their revenue and research and development budgets to improve strategic information systems. Forecasting the effectiveness of the investments has been the major target of strategic planning for information systems and information technology decision-makers (Kim, 2022; Harum, Ali, 2022).

Furthermore, targeted performance generated from the information systems in which the entire sources are shared and connected with users is important for businesses. Henceforth, today's businesses involve information systems which are essential processes to development, searching for best efficiency and effectiveness available. An organization's management can take into account numerous methodological approaches to detect and evaluate the priorities in developing an information system and one of the essential issues to choose the best suited for the stakeholders of an organization. In researching the organizational necessities for information systems, different analytical frameworks and methods could assist executives find into maximizing organizational effectiveness (Kim, 2022; Harum, Ali, 2022).

2.1. Corporate Excellence

The competitive excellence of an organization is that the competitive advantage is the ability that is acquired by means of the character and sources of an organization to enjoy a higher performance than other organization in the same industry or market. Competitive advantage is an organization composition strategy devised to accomplish opportunities that cannot be imitated by rivals to improve profits and benefits. On the other hand, corporate excellence (CE) is when a company can do something which the rivals want, then organizations enjoys competitive advantage and do it better than competitors. CE in businesses is a strategy which places the businesses strong against rivals henceforth that gives the business a very robust competitive advantage. CE is the ability of a business to respond to the consumer expectations effectively and efficiently that goods and services have more value or at a lower cost. Competing strategies are targeted to sustain profit levels and dispositions facing rivalry (Mahendra, 2023)

2.2. Employee Performance

Performance is the output of a work correlated to organizational targets as efficiency, quality and performance other from effectiveness. Performance is a definition of the level of accomplishment of the application of a program of operation of policies accomplishing the goals, objectives, mission and visions of an organization. Performance is also the work on a basis of quality and quantity which one accomplishes implementing out one's duties in compliance with the responsibilities given to him or her. Performance is an accomplished achievement of a predetermined target of an organization. The information of organizational performance is very significant to appraise whether the performance level implemented by the organization is in line with the aim targeted or not. Performance which is a result of a work accomplished by an individual who is fitted to his or her role or task which an individual in an organization is associated with precise vale (Mahendra, 2023).

2.3. Inventory Management

Inventories are products which are stored to sell in the organizations' normal operations which are either in the manufacturing process or been stored for one target. Organizations shall have minimal needs in one goods inventory information system. The inventory information system involves information necessitated by a carefully arranged information. The inventory information system assists employees when researching information for services directly correlated the database. The aim and benefit of an inventory information system is to improve productivity and effectiveness in an organization. Inventories are acknowledged assets possessed by an organization for sale in everyday operations of an organization or inputs to be utilized manufacturing the merchandise beforehand (Mahendra, 2023).

3. BUSINESS INFORMATION SYSTEMS, THEIR INTEGRATION TO BUSINESS INTELLIGENCE & ENTERPRISE RESOURCE PLANNING

With the development in technology, organizations shall take into consideration new technologies such as business intelligence (BI) as an inevitable necessity for survival. In today's fast changing world of business, organizations are supposed to be innovative and competitive in order to create value for their stakeholders. The business information systems (BIS), supply a tool to the information necessities of organizations adequately. One way the organizations could accomplish this is to utilize methods as interactive graphical data analysis, data mining and predictive analytics. These tools are parts of a discipline considered as business information systems. A business information system is an appropriate approach to respond to the current issues in organizations. Business information systems are contemporary information technologies which assists organizations to collect, manage and analyze structural or non-structural data. The major goal of business information systems is to assist organizations to enhance their functions and develop their competitive advantage in the markets which they operate. Business systems help organizations in decision-making by means of appraise the operations and functions which may result in the enhancement of business systems. The most efficient function of business information systems is to provide possible access to organizational structure and process a large volume of data and convey corelated subsets of data to the business' administrators continuously. Decision-making and analysis are rested on the realty of business systems which effect entire organizations. Availability and dependable information are one of the benefits for business systems. Despite the amount of improper data, unsuitable data and oftentimes contradictory data, new technologies and methods assist decision-makers to take precise decisions for the benefit of organizations. Some businesses help their managers by producing relevant and convenient information which is presented in easy and understandable formats. Such businesses utilize the benefits of business information systems well and the effect is witnessed in the business at operational levels with its advantages. Accomplished business information systems help companies to make the most correct decisions at the most effective time by means of integrating data with decision support systems (Zafary, 2020; Mahendra, 2023; bin Rodzoan et al.; Tvrdikova, 2016).

Receiving the correct information at the suitable time is the basis for accomplished decisions and survival of the business. Successful business information provides the suitable information to proper managers by means of the organization framework to empower strategic and tactical decisions. The tool of business information systems supplies a perspective of the past, present and future. Application of business information systems approaches elevate the gap between intermediate managers and senior managers from information communication point of view and supplies the supervisors the required information in each level with high quality (Zafary, 2020; da Silva Oliveria, 2022; Alagic et al.).

On the other hand, another important issue of enterprise resource planning (ERP) could be regarded as major method for business intelligence, especially to gather and incorporate knowledge into a central database. Accomplished enterprise resource planning is able to act as a pillar for business information systems at organizations, for, it is capable of giving supervisors an integrated approach of inside processes. These systems and frameworks trigger time reductions in process and information sharing within the business, therefore, organizations can adapt the everchanging consumer needs. Some of the knowledge is acquired from outside the operational systems, or even outside of the organization by means of market information. The most significant advantage stemming from business information systems is the possibility of direct access to knowledge by decision-makers at all phases of the firm, therefore, they can interact with the knowledge and analyze it. Nevertheless, they can manage the organization, enhance effectiveness, determine opportunities and perform their goals with better efficiency (Zafary, 2020; Görsci, Szeles, 2018).

3.1. The Integration of Information Systems

The integration of business systems to organizations gave a high capacity of information proliferation all over the organization. It assisted better decision-making rested on complete information. The basic benefits of information system integration in organizations are developments in efficiency, cost reduction, better decision-making, and integrated services. Integration of information systems is an integrator for the quantification of the information components. Integrated information systems involve integrated manual and computer parts which are designed for acquiring, storing and controlling of information as well as to make sure the accuracy of information flow in the organization. The goals of integrated information systems in the organization are: 1. performing major and repetitive operations in an intelligent manner with the ease of operational functionalities; 2. Performing internal controls of the major activities in an intelligent manner; 3. fast access to categorized information for decision-making; 4. constitution of the field of constant and punctual reporting in the organization and the establishment of cultural background of the economic and financial discipline; and 5. saving more time for information processing (da Silva Oliveria, 2022; Zafary, 2020; Görsci, Szeles, 2018).

3.2. Business Intelligence and Correlation to Business Systems

Business Intelligence is a precipitating process for structured determination and analysis of specific knowledge to determine the process or the patterns by means of acquiring a specified view or conclusions. Business intelligence is regarded the acquisition, incorporation, analysis and bring forward organizational information, technology, implementation and applications. Business intelligence systems are data-driven decision support systems. Business intelligence could be a solution to develop the method of acquiring and processing data in accordance with conceptual processes. Business intelligence is a collection of technologies, abilities, approaches and tools which accommodate executives to comprehend organizational conditions. Business intelligence includes process and tools which convert data into knowledge. Furthermore, mangers and experts could develop their operations by utilizing simple facilities and acquire better results. The major goal of business intelligence is to enhance effectiveness in decision making by transforming data to knowledge for the development of decision-making (Zafary, 2020; bin Rodzoan et al.).

In general, the goal of business intelligence is, a. detecting organization orientation of the firms which results in the focus of the company on major goals without wasting time and energy; b. making market foresight which lead to new market advantages and benefits for the organization before rivals to take over the market; c. the improvement of the effectiveness on the organization on transparency in key process trend; d. standardization and establishment of compatibility among the firm structure; e. improving decision-making as one of the major goals of business intelligence; f. and eventually early determination of risks and detection of organizational opportunities (Zafary, 2020).

3.3. Enterprise Resource Planning

Enterprise resource planning (ERP) is a system devised for the constitution of a suitable base for complete management of an organization. By utilizing enterprise resource planning, communication facilities among business units, an executive of a firm could be able to supervise the entre issues of the firm involving financial, human resources and manufacturing affairs. This system enables the entire components of a firm and its operations to get integrated in one computer system which can meet all the necessities of the business. The major benefits and advantages of the enterprise resource planning involve organizational integration of standardization of standard organizational processes, quick installation of knowledge as well as the possibility or ease of extension of the new structural systems and technologies. With the development of enterprise development system, different goals, processes and tasks such as quality control, repair, maintenance, finance and accounting become integrated to productive systems (Zafary, 2020).

4. SUSTAINING THE IMPORTANCE OF INFORMATION SYSTEMS WITH ICTS, CORPORATE PERFORMANCE & COMPETITIVE INTELLIGENCE

Information systems and information and communication technologies (ICTs) have become the pillar for conducting firms in various field. The quantity of tools presented in the field of ICTs is enlarging at an increasing rate and making it difficult to understand them. The term ICT is used to delineate all the methods included in the information processing, telecommunicating equipment and suitable software within the organizational framework. There is an increasing correlation between information systems and business capacities. Alternations in rules, business plans, strategies and business processes require to changes in hardware, software, telecommunications equipment and storage sites. Often times, if a firm tries to do something on the market, this business issues are closely correlated with the information technology and know-how of firms. Information and communication technologies could be used to increase competitiveness, increase the capacities of organizations to create employment opportunities and instigate sales volumes by means of having access to new markets (Tvrdikova, 2016; Alagic, et al.; Wrerder, Werder, 2022).

The stability of organizations and firms make them to be flexible so that they can react fast, quickly and effectively to external changes. If an organization is not capable of adapting to quickly changing business environment, the management cannot return to the behavior of the socio-economic system to the steady state and the existence of the firm or organizations in danger. The flexible information system of management is supposed to obtain the necessary information for survival. Organizations are supposed to find out contemporary type and extent of information properly collected, effectively processed and efficiently distributed. Henceforth, one can state that this can be ensured by only means of an effective information system (Tvrdikova, 2016; da Silva Oliveria, 2022).

Information system and system control could be considered intertwined and one complete the other one. One thing is common in both of the terms, they assure equilibrium in the functioning of organizations and businesses. Moreover, information systems involve components to operate which are denoted below (Tvrdikova, 2016):

- Hardware; component systems of different types and sizes which should be completed with the essential peripherals which are interconnected through a network of computers and connected to a memory system to run large volumes of data.
- Software; the system programs monitoring the computer and programs enabling effectively acting with data, programs allowing the computer system to operate with the real world and application systems which are related to specific tasks for certain users.
- Orgware; involves a set of standards and regulations which delineate the conditions of operation, the utilization of information systems and information and communication technologies.
- Peopleware meaning the quality of conditions for adopting effective functioning of employees in the digital environment.
- Real world indicates alternations in political and social environments, information resources, business standards as well as scientific and technological improvements within the frame of information systems.

4.1. Corporate Performance Management and Contemporary Issues in Information & Communication Technologies (ICTs)

Businesses and organizations have been endeavoring to obtain the necessary information capital for constant innovation and operations of information systems. These issues continue in every business whether big or small. Moreover, a frequent source of issues is the lack of information which the business management does not enjoy establishing high quality ICTs. Therefore, it is essential to improve managers' awareness of the probabilities of information and communication technologies in enhancing their decision-making and search for new means to enable the implementation of new ICTs in practice. Executives and entrepreneurs who work for private, public or non-profit organizations have access to a substantial amount of data resulting from wide variety of resources. While making decisions, they are in need of means which assist them process data to acquire the essential information (Tvrdikova, 2016; Mahendra, 2023).

4.1.1. Corporate Performance Management

Corporate performance management is a managerial approach which can be used to manage and monitor the performance of the whole firm by means of information technologies. The major purpose of corporate performance management is to oversee how a business performs, also, how to develop its performance. It ensures responses focused on future. Corporate performance management is an answer to the question whether the organization enjoys the correct task. Corporate performance management can also be delineated as a set of activities such as collection, definition, analyzing and disseminating information about customers, rivals and about the entire aspects of the external environment around the firm and organization. This could be termed as early signal analysis and enables early detection of opportunities and risks in the market before they become obvious. Corporate performance management has essentially been the field of medium and large businesses which function on a global scale. Their sources enable them to invest in personnel and information and communication technologies which carry out corporate performance management (Tvrdikova, 2016).

4.1.2. The importance of ICTs and Current Trends

Extending the virtualization of all phases of a structure as a proven technology and a dependable connection of users to communication networks greatly stimulate the improvement of information technologies. In the establishment of an organization, information systems and information communication technologies are considerable with the trends as (Tvrdikova, 2016):

- Consolidation of storage virtualization; enables decreasing the number of physical data servers while enhancing the resilience to failures. Virtualization of computer abilities ensure a greater flexibility in acquiring better computing performance.
- Standardization and transparency of business processes; greater flexibility and optimization of the essential functions in organizations which can be accomplished while decreasing the costs as well as improve maintenance and development.
- Digital virtualization: this can simplify management, develop security and empower compliance with standards.
- Increasing performance and mobility of individual operations and services; develop businesses and organizations whose administration and supervisory operations function among several centers. Virtualization means enable conveying virtual machines running services without interruption.

Contemporary trends in information and communication services related to the administration of organizations and businesses are (Tvrdikova, 2016):

- Reinforcing the relationship between organizations and ICT; managing the organization – information relationship within the framework of information and technology services.
- Process management of organizations and their information and communication necessities; endeavors of efficiently and uniquely related to information and communication technologies with the business culture, business model and business processes.
- Separation of duties for the benefits and costs of information and communication technologies between firm executives and information and communication managers.
- Multiplying the share of external information and communication service supplies such as outsourcing, application service providers and clod computing.
- Continuity of information systems which serve as linkages between information technology and process implementation.

By means of information technologies clients are provided with applications which are accessible anytime and anywhere. The contemporary utilization of communication technologies ensure multi-tenant framework in which implementation is devised to serve multiple organizations and beneficiaries. The service provider enjoys executive control over operations. Moreover, the information technologies are responsible from installation, updating, safety and maintenance. Information technologies are models supplying entire sources for creating and sustaining custom applications available by benefiting from information sources and the Internet. Information technology service providers procure the computing infrastructure in the desired configuration in a virtualized form. Clients are supplied with a virtual hardware which could operate as a complete information and communication structure. The information technology provider is in charge of delivering the ordered computing power and its connection to the information and communication network. The clients then install operating systems and install every component themselves in accordance with their requirements (Tvrdikova, 2016; Kim, 2022; Mijailovic et al.).

5. CONCLUSION

Today's business world is changing at an enormous rate and competition intensifies as well as the business are not immune of this issue. Moreover, in order to be competitive in the intensifying global business conditions, organizations must have contemporary business systems and applications. First, enjoying true information in organizations is vital. Information is an essential tool to have competitive framework in business. Then organizations are supposed to associate the information efficiently with their business information systems in order to act competitively against their rivals. Moreover, these developments are also supposed to be empowered tools as quality, timeliness, reliability and relevance. However, such issues are not enough to be strong in the competitive business in the globe. Moreover, managers and supervisor are exposed to substantial amount of information which is very valuable as well as difficult to acquire, process, store, disseminate and utilize. Therefore, it is indispensable to use business information systems, business intelligence, information and communication technologies, corporate excellence and enterprise resource planning in organizations in the ever-changing business environment.

REFERENCES

Alagic, A., Turulja, L., & Bajgoric, N. (2021). Identification of Information System Audit Quality Factors. *Journal of Forensic Accounting Profession*, 1(2), 1–28. DOI: 10.2478/jfap-2021-0006

Bin Rodzoan, A. (2022). Business Intelligence Capabilities and Critical Success Factors in Public Sector Company of Malaysia. *Journal of Science and Technology*, 27(1), 29–44. DOI: 10.20428/jst.v27i1.1985

Da Silva, O. L., Vieira, V. A. P., & dos Santos, R. P. (2022). A systems-of-Information Identification Method Based on Business Process Models Analysis. *Journal of Management & Technology*, 22(4), 90–115. DOI: 10.20397/2177-6652/2022.v22i4.2309

Görsci, G., & Szeles, S. (2018). Examining Business Toll that Characterize the Corporate Internal Information System and Their Impact on Corporate Performance. *Forum on Business & Economics*, 21(135), 50–65. DOI: 10.46300/91014.2021.15.11

Harum, K. M., & Ali, H. (2022). Factors Effecting Operation Information Systems: Strategy, Software and Huamn Resources. *Dinasti International Journal of Digital Business Management*, 4(1), 94–104. DOI: 10.31933/dijdbm.v4i1.1601

Kim, S. (2022). Critical Success Factors Evaluation by Multi-Criteria Decision-Making: A Strategic Information System Planning and Strategy-As-Practice Perspective. *Information (Basel)*, 13(6), 270–296. DOI: 10.3390/info13060270

Mahendra, R. (2023). Effect of Corporate Competitive Excellence, Employee Performance and Inventory Information on the Resource Information System. *Dinasti International Journal of Management Science*, 4(3), 509–520. DOI: 10.31933/dijms.v4i3.1549

Mijaliovic, D., Klochov, Y., Misic, M., Djordjevic, A., Stojcetovic, B., Pavlovic, A., & Djodrevic, M. Z. (2021). ICT Leadership ss Enabler of Business Performances: An Integrative Approach. *International Journal of Qualitative Research*, 16(1), 177–192. DOI: 10.24874/IJQR16.01-12

Shrestha, A., & Saratchandra, M. (2023). A Conceptual Framework toward Knowledge Ambidexterity Using Information Systems and Knowledge Management. *Journal of Information Systems*, 37(1), 143–167. DOI: 10.2308/ISYS-2021-013

Tvrdikova, M. (2016). Increasing the Business Potential of Companies by Ensuring Continuity of the Development of their Information Systems by Current Information Technologies. *Journal of Business Economics and Management*, 17(3), 475–489. DOI: 10.3846/16111699.2013.839475

Werder, K., & Richter, J. (2022). A Meta-Analysis on the Effects of IT Capability toward Agility and Performance: New Directions for Information Systems Research. *PLoS One*, 17(10), 1–23. DOI: 10.1371/journal.pone.0268761 PMID: 36301914

Zafary, F. (2020). Implementation of Business Intelligence Considering the Role of Information Systems Integration & Enterprise Resource Planning. *Journal of Intelligence Studies in Business*, 10(1), 59–74. DOI: 10.37380/jisib.v1i1.563

Chapter 4
Entrepreneurial Passion or Machiavellianism?
Exploring the Factors Affecting Entrepreneurial Intention

Jean Paolo Gomez Lacap
City College of Angeles, Philippines

Mavy De Joseph
Polytechnic University of the Philippines, Philippines

Karen Claire Solano
Polytechnic University of the Philippines, Philippines

Mary Jane Legaspi
https://orcid.org/0000-0001-8982-3860
Polytechnic University of the Philippines, Philippines

Mark Anthony Visca
Polytechnic University of the Philippines, Philippines

ABSTRACT

This chapter examines how entrepreneurial passion (EP) and Machiavellianism affect entrepreneurial intention (EI). Moreover, it investigates the moderating effects of entrepreneurial creativity (EC) on the link between EP and EI, and of entrepreneurial self-efficacy (ES) on the relationship between Machiavellianism and EI. The participants were MBA (n = 304) students from several universities in Metro Manila, Philippines and they were identified using purposive sampling. The hypothesized relationships were evaluated through a causal-predictive research design and via path modeling using partial least squares. The results show that EP has a significant and positive influence on EC and EI. On the other hand, Machiavellianism has a significant but small direct effect on ES. It was likewise found that both EC and ES contribute to the formation of EI. After moderation analysis, the finding reveals that EC indirectly affects the link between EP and EI.

DOI: 10.4018/979-8-3693-9230-0.ch004

Copyright ©2025, IGI Global. Copying or distributing in print or electronic forms without written permission of IGI Global is prohibited.

INTRODUCTION

Entrepreneurship has always been one of the most significant themes of interest in public policy as it promotes national economic development (Lounsbury & Glynn., 2019; Wu et al., 2019). Scholars have examined entrepreneurship because entrepreneurial activities appear to result in various positive outcomes, including creating employment opportunities, incubating technical innovation, and promoting business and economic growth (O'Connor et al., 2018; Sergi et al., 2019; Zhang & Stough, 2013). In addition, according to Montiel and Clark (2018), entrepreneurship has long been regarded as essential to a country's or region's economic, political, and social environment. As a result, many studies demonstrate that individuals develop an EI and subsequently become entrepreneurs (Do & Dadvari, 2017; Wu et al., 2019; Zhang Xiu'e & Zhang Kun, 2018). In other words, EI is a strong predictor of future entrepreneurial activity for people who want to start a new business (Newman et al., 2021).

Previous studies show that entrepreneurial action follows the formation of EI, which focuses on the mentality that directs an individual's attention and experience toward intended entrepreneurial behavior (Do & Dadvari, 2017; Judge & Douglas, 2013; Wu et al., 2019; Zhang Xiu'e & Zhang Kun, 2018). Recently, the predictive effect of individual personality traits on EI has become a focal point in entrepreneurial research when discussing why people aspire to establish a business (Do & Dadvari, 2017). According to Wu et al. (2019), positive and negative personality traits may contribute to entrepreneurial motivation (Klotz & Neubaum, 2016; Miller, 2015). As such, it is acceptable to hypothesize that all personality traits, whether positive or negative, can influence an individual's propensity to participate in entrepreneurial ventures (Kenny, 2016).

While emerging evidence suggests that certain personality traits may play a slightly more significant role in the origins of entrepreneurial success, the factors influencing an individual's willingness to become an entrepreneur remain unclear (Wang et al., 2016). Existing literature primarily focused on positive, well-known personality factors (Anton, 2014), such as self-efficacy (Wang et al., 2016), creativity (Bellò-Pintado et al., 2018), and EP (Cardon et al., 2013). Furthermore, passion is at the heart of entrepreneurship because it fuels entrepreneurs' persistence and plays a vital role in developing novel ideas and exploiting new business opportunities (Cardon et al., 2013; Cardon & Kirk, 2015).

On the other hand, the opposite of a proactive personality also has an essential effect on EI. According to Miller (2015), dark personality traits may also contribute to EI because people have multiple characters, and dark personality traits can have a positive side. Machiavellianism is one of the three sub-structures of the Dark Triad. It is a self-interested, deceptive, strategic, and manipulative personality trait (Al Ain et al., 2013; Zettler et al., 2011). Individuals with Machiavellian personality traits can have strong adaptability. They can hide their true intentions, which means that they are better at making decisions strategically and this is what entrepreneurship favors more, being uncertain and unpredictable (Sesen, 2013). Furthermore, researchers analyzed the impact of EP (Campos, 2017; Cardon and Kirk, 2015; Drnovsek et al., 2016; Li et al., 2020; Mueller et al., 2017; Thorgren & Wincent, 2015) and Machiavellianism (Collison et al., 2018; Jacobs & Keegan, 2016; Mueller et al., 2017; Rauthmann & Will, 2011) to EI. There is, however, noticeably limited research on how these traits both purportedly affect EI. Hence, this topic has little in-depth study in the Philippines. Consequently, the study mainly fills a gap in the writings, so understanding how these two variables affect EI in specific contexts is critical.

LITERATURE REVIEW

The current study is based on the theory of planned behavior (TPB) that Ajzen presented in 1985. TPB is a psychological theory claiming that all actions are controlled by intention (Mumba, 2016). This concept is commonly applied to research in a variety of fields like entrepreneurship since becoming an entrepreneur is seen as a conscious activity, and intention is thought to be a state of mind (Sabah, 2016). The theory advances that planned behaviors such as launching a business are intentional and best forecasted by the intentions toward the behavior (Ajzen, 1991). Entrepreneurs may face uncertainties and problems, but they can surpass these through ES (Hechavarria et al., 2012; Zhao et al., 2005). In business, ES is vital to perform tasks and attain goals efficiently. ES is also a key indicator of EI (Krueger et al., 2000) and promotes an entrepreneurial attitude by increasing the individual's intention (Chen et al., 1998; Schlaegel & Koenig, 2014). Individuals interested in entrepreneurship must have a strong EI and a firm commitment to starting a business. A person's entrepreneurial attitude and intentions are strongly correlated with their creative disposition (Anjum et al., 2021). EC is engaging in creative concepts and turning these into profitable business activities (Belyh, 2019). It can be seen as a determinant for entrepreneurial behavior or intent because it is linked to the process of finding opportunities (Hills et al., 1999). Fostering these variables from this theory is significant in starting a business. Thus, we used this theory to analyze what gives rise to EI.

We also utilized the social cognitive theory (SCT), which explains human actions through the reciprocal interaction between personal factors, behavior, and environmental determinants (Bandura, 1986). One of the critical concepts of SCT we employed in this study is self-efficacy, which refers to the individual's belief in his capabilities to perform a behavior (LaMorte, 2019). Results from previous studies demonstrated that socio-cognitive characteristics like self-efficacy are essential factors for entrepreneurial behavior (Baron, 2006; Rauch & Frese, 2007; Welpe et al., 2012). In entrepreneurship, self-efficacy refers to entrepreneurs' confidence in their abilities to start and manage a new business (McGee et al., 2009). According to Laplume and Yeganegi (2021), there is a higher possibility that someone will intend to start and complete their goal if they believe they can. Moreover, individuals with ES continue their tasks despite uncertainty and lack of resources (Trevelyan, 2009). With that, people with ES have high EI (Neneh, 2020).

Meanwhile, EP is under the personal factor of the SCT model (Wood and Bandura, 1989). EP is a motivating influence that enables people to overcome challenges and remain dedicated to established entrepreneurial goals (Cardon et al., 2009). In connection with this, EP can lead a person to pursue entrepreneurial endeavors and concentrate on venture formation (Biraglia & Kadile, 2017). Hence, we used the theory to examine the proposed correlations in this study to identify what influences EI.

Entrepreneurial Passion (EP)

Entrepreneurial passion (EP) is associated with entrepreneurship (Bignetti et al., 2021; Sriyakul & Jermsittiparsert, 2019). Precedent studies identify the significance of passion in defining the entrepreneurial process (Cardon et al., 2009; Collewaert et al., 2016; Laaksonen et al., 2011; Murnieks et al., 2014; Smilor, 1997). Additionally, EP is knowingly accessible to strong positive feelings felt by engaging in entrepreneurial events linked with tasks relevant to the entrepreneur's self-identity (Cardon et al., 2009). Moreover, according to Newman et al. (2021), academics have studied EP due to the importance of entrepreneurial behavior to social and economic development. In essence, passion is fundamental to entrepreneurship, for it brings creativity and the identification of new knowledge trends, which are essential for the discovery of profitable opportunities for businesses (Cardon et al., 2013).

Entrepreneurial Creativity (EC)

According to Amabile (1997), most individuals think that creativity has a connection with business. Being creative and innovative is an important entrepreneurship personality trait (Luca et al., 2013; Ward, 2004). Literature indicates that creative individuals will probably engage in entrepreneurial behavior (Ward, 2004). Baldacchino (2009) describes creativity as a catalyst of change that can result in developing new business and improving products, allowing enterprises to be more competitive. Furthermore, creativity can be viewed as a significant consideration for entrepreneurship due to its relationship to the process of identifying opportunities (Bignetti et al., 2021). Therefore, people should be allowed to prove that they can come up with new and valuable ideas to help them succeed as entrepreneurs (Darini et al., 2011).

Based on the writings of Syed et al. (2020), EP affects creativity. Passion is a strong need for action derived from personal preferences and important considerations (Azavedo & Gogatz, 2021). Moreover, creativity is the ability to generate innovative ideas, which drives individuals to seek unique solutions (Liu & Gu, 2017). A recent research study stated that EP boosts the person's level of chance for enhancing creative ideas (Li et al., 2020). In addition, findings of Davis et al. (2017) show that creativity depends on the entrepreneur's passion. Furthermore, Campos (2017) claimed a positive relationship between EP and EC. Therefore, we hypothesized that:

H1a. Entrepreneurial passion has a significant and direct effect on entrepreneurial creativity.

Entrepreneurial Self-efficacy (ES)

Entrepreneurial self-efficacy (ES) is the individual's confidence in their ability to perform a task successfully (Bandura, 1989). It is associated with passion (Bandura, 1989; Johri & Misra, 2014) and is a direct determinant of intention and behavior (Neneh, 2020). A strong sense of self-efficacy is a significant factor in achieving greater skills and success (Bandura, 1989). According to Trevelyan (2009), individuals with high self-efficacy still persevere in their activities despite uncertainty and scarcity of resources. It is attaining the desired goal with persistence and strong determination (Ardichvili et al., 2003). ES is an antecedent to the development of intention. If a person thinks that they can accomplish their goal, there is a chance that they will achieve it (Laplume & Yeganegi, 2021).

Entrepreneurial Intention (EI)

Entrepreneurial intention (EI) is a conscious state of mind that guides attention, experience, and activity toward a specific goal (Bird, 1988; Hamidi et al., 2008; Kajornatthapol et al., 2023). It is also the entrepreneur's basic knowledge, preference, and behavioral tendency to create a new business (De Noble et al., 1999). Moreover, it is a psychological state that guides an individual's attention in achieving specific business goals to attain entrepreneurial results (Jarinto et al., 2019; Thompson, 2009). Krueger and Carsrud (1993) further argued that individuals with intentions to start a new business have the potential to be ready and more successful compared to those who do not have an initial intention.

Previous research has confirmed that EP can create confidence and positively influence EI in individuals who are not yet actively engaged in entrepreneurship (De Mol et al., 2020; Karimi, 2019). It also encourages entrepreneurs to recognize opportunities in engaging to new businesses, and shows that it is an integral part of business motivation. Success leads to EI (Collewaert et al. 2016; Murnieks et al. 2014). Similarly, Hubner et al. (2019) stated that EP is essential in achieving motivation and success and predicting EI. For instance, Karimi (2019) used data from 310 Iranian public university students from various courses to investigate the direct role of EP in EI, and the findings showed that EP successfully assisted students in developing EI. Therefore, we hypothesized that:

H1b. Entrepreneurial passion has a significant and direct effect on entrepreneurial intention.

Machiavellianism

Machiavellianism can be an organization's positive or negative attribute depending on how it is performed (Hartzell, 2012). On the positive side, people with this personality have strong adaptability and a better decision-making strategy (Wu et al., 2019), which is an advantage in a competitive setting. They can easily persuade others, successfully attain their goals, and win more (Hartzell, 2012). In contrast, Machiavellians are self-centered, cynical, and devious characters that focus only on their interests and exploit others' desires to achieve their respective goals (Wu et al., 2019). Moreover, they are dishonest (Jones & Paulhus, 2017), manipulative (Braginsky, 1970), power-hungry (Kessler et al., 2010), opportunistic (Czibor et al., 2017), exploitative, and unethical (Bereczkei & Czibor, 2014; Jones & Kavanagh, 1996). It is a component of the Dark Triad, along with narcissism and psychopathy (Paulhus & Williams, 2002). Its behavioral outcomes captured the research community's attention (Geis & Moon, 1981; Jones & Paulhus, 2014). Machiavellianism is generally uncooperative, devoid of social values, and indifferent to the collective good, believing that the ends justify the means (Bereczkei & Czibor, 2014).

Dahling et al. (2009) believe that people who exhibit high levels of Machiavellianism typically show a strong desire for power and achievement, a high degree of result orientation, and a solid drive to achieve goals. Additionally, they can use dishonest tactics for their advancement (Do & Dadvari, 2017). For instance, they can manipulate others to achieve their expected results (Hechavarria et al., 2012; Zhao et al., 2005). This characteristic may increase the possibility that individuals with Machiavellian traits will succeed in their entrepreneurial endeavors. Whether the method to follow is good or bad, they will utilize it, believing that the end justifies the means (Bereczkei & Czibor, 2014). Therefore, we hypothesized that;

H2a. Machiavellianism has a significant and direct effect on entrepreneurial self-efficacy.

According to Wu et al. (2019) and Hartzell (2012), Machiavellians possess characteristics vital in starting a business, such as solid adaptability and better decision-making strategies. In addition, Zettler et al. (2011) emphasize that people with Machiavellian traits may be more likely to want to start their own businesses. Persons with high Machiavellianism are often eager to pursue personal goals and have confidence in their ability to overcome obstacles (Hechavarria et al., 2012; Zhao et al., 2005). Machiavellians use deception and any means necessary to get what they want (Al Ain et al., 2013). They make unethical choices and even succeed at the expense of others (Buckels et al., 2013). However, these habits benefit the business environment (Klotz & Neubaum, 2016). Therefore, we hypothesized that:

H2b. Machiavellianism has a significant and direct effect on entrepreneurial intention.

Creativity is a vital element of entrepreneurship since individuals need to be creative to identify and utilize opportunities (Anjum et al., 2021). It pertains to the individual ability to generate new and innovative solutions to current issues (Amabile, 1997). An earlier study found that entrepreneurship effectively fosters creativity, supporting EI (Shabab et al., 2019). The previous research shows the direct effect of creativity on entrepreneurial intent (Zampetakis & Moustakis, 2006). Moreover, according to Bellò-Pintado et al. (2018), EC positively influences EI. Thus, an entrepreneur's self-perception of creativity promotes creative thinking that can predict increased EI levels (Zampetakis & Moustakis, 2006). Therefore, we hypothesized that:

H3. Entrepreneurial creativity has a significant and direct effect on entrepreneurial intention.

The essential impact of self-efficacy on human behavior led scholars to employ the idea in entrepreneurship. Researchers emphasized the important influence of self-efficacy on different factors of new business processes (Pihie & Bagheri, 2013). Prior studies noted that ES strongly affects one's intention and capability to become an entrepreneur (Boyd & Vozikis,1994; Chen et al., 1998; Trevelyan, 2011). In entrepreneurship, ES is an important determinant of an individual starting a business (Neneh, 2020). Additionally, ES enables entrepreneurs to surpass challenges in the business process like identifying the opportunity, gathering resources, and developing the business' performance (Barbosa et al., 2007; Bryant, 2006; Markman & Baron, 2003; McGee et al., 2009; Tumasjan & Braun, 2012). According to Naktiyok et al. (2009), Pihie and Bagheri (2013), and Tsai et al. (2016), ES is a vital requirement of EI. If a person thinks that they can accomplish their goal, there is a likelihood that they will have the intention to accomplish the goal (Laplume & Yeganegi, 2021). ES affects the person's decision to choose an entrepreneurial career and controls how the company will perform in the future (Bandura, 2000; McGee et al., 2009). ES affects the person's decision to start a business and controls their future performance in managing the business (Bandura, 2000; McGee et al., 2009). Neneh (2020) assumed that people with the capacity to successfully start a business are considered to have high EI. Therefore, we hypothesized that:

H4. Entrepreneurial self-efficacy has a significant and direct effect on entrepreneurial intention.

Creativity is another core concept at the beginning of the entrepreneurial process since it involves identifying opportunities, designing market products, and utilizing resources (Gielnik et al., 2012; Zhou, 2008). Moreover, creativity is a crucial motivator of EI (Hamidi et al., 2008; Fatoki, 2010). Entrepreneurship is a way to create value that requires much creativity, and active, creative thinking is a crucial trait of entrepreneurs that requires a high EI level (Zhang et al., 2018). EI is a conscious state of mind that precedes action and focuses on entrepreneurial activities (Moriano et al., 2012). Specific attention has been given by Sriyakul and Jermsittiparsert (2019) as they examined the role of passion for work as a perception of one's ability to be a successful entrepreneur; the results of their survey revealed that passion enhances the influence on EI. Prior studies have supported this view, showing that creativity mediates EP and EI (Bhansing et al., 2018; Campos, 2017). Therefore, we hypothesized that:

H5. Entrepreneurial creativity has a mediating effect on the link between entrepreneurial passion and entrepreneurial intention.

Entrepreneurship is a complex procedure beginning with intention and ending in business establishment along with other factors (Gielnik et al., 2014). According to earlier studies, self-efficacy is a relevant variable (McGee et al., 2009) and mediator in the development of EI (Tsai et al., 2016). Self-efficacy mediates variables including risk propensity, previous entrepreneurial experience, and personality traits (Yu et al., 2017; Zhao et al., 2005). Personality impacts EI, which may also stem from less positive or ideological motives, such as Machiavellianism. A study supported the assumption that the dark triad

(Jonason et al., 2009) relates to EI and motives (Hmieleski & Lerner, 2016). Thus, self-efficacy is a mediator between EI and MA. Therefore, we hypothesized that:

H6. Entrepreneurial self-efficacy has a mediating effect on the link between Machiavellianism and entrepreneurial intention.

The research framework highlights the five constructs and their potential linkages in light of substantial literature review and hypotheses. Figure 1 illustrates the direct effect of EP, Machiavellianism, EC, and ES on EI. Furthermore, the present study examines the mediating effect of EC on the relationship of EP to EI and ES and the link between Machiavellianism and EI.

Figure 1. Conceptual framework

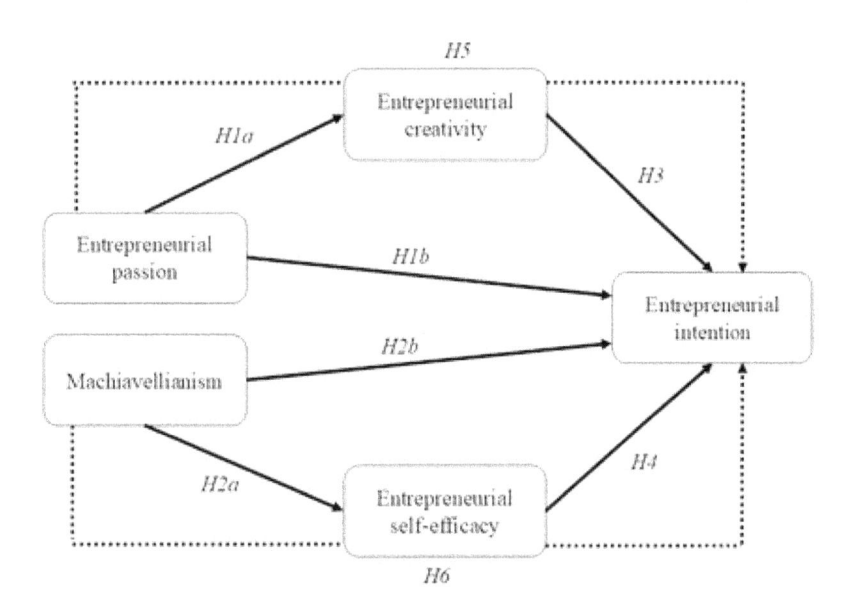

METHODS

Participants

The respondents of the study are MBA students in Metro Manila, Philippines. Metro Manila is the country's National Capital Region and has several universities and colleges that offer MBA programs. These universities and colleges provide entrepreneurial studies that equip students to pursue a career in higher-level management or manage their businesses. The Global Entrepreneurship Monitor 2021/2022 global report shows that higher educational attainment links to higher entrepreneurial activity. The report also presented that younger adults (<35 years old) have a higher chance of starting a new business than older adults (35 to 64 years old) (Hill et al., 2022). According to Murray (2014), more MBA students are becoming entrepreneurs instead of corporate employees. In addition, Byrne (2016) discovered that a growing number of MBA graduates are confident enough to launch their own businesses. The Global University Entrepreneurial Spirit Students Survey (GUESS), participated by 58 countries and more than 267,000 students, resulted in a stable 82.8 percent (direct, intentional entrepreneurs) of the respondents aiming to be entrepreneurs (Sieger et al., 2021). For this reason – the relevance of the research constructs to students, the MBA students in Metro Manila are the ideal participants of this study.

As for the inclusion and exclusion criteria, respondents must be of legal age (at least 18 years old) since the present study measures EI. Therefore, the capacity to establish a business is considered for the age requirement. Respondents must be currently enrolled in an MBA program within Metro Manila. Because of the Covid-19 pandemic, where mobility is restricted, we collected the data remotely using Google form and disseminated it via Meta messenger. The Google Form included informed consent, and respondents signified their voluntary participation in the questionnaire. The data distribution period was from May 27 to June 16, 2022.

The study collected 319 responses, of which 304 were valid (95% response rate). We used the inverse square root and gamma-exponential methods to determine the sufficiency of the study's sample size (Kock & Hadaya, 2016). The minimum recommended sample size of the inverse square root is 275, while the gamma-exponential method is 262 with a minimum absolute significant path coefficient of 0.15, a level of significance of 0.05, and a power level of 0.80. Thus, 304 respondents are robust enough to test the structural model.

The 304 respondents were currently enrolled MBA students (academic year 2021 – 2022) in different higher education institutions in Metro, Manila, Philippines.

Figure 2. Post-hoc sample size estimation

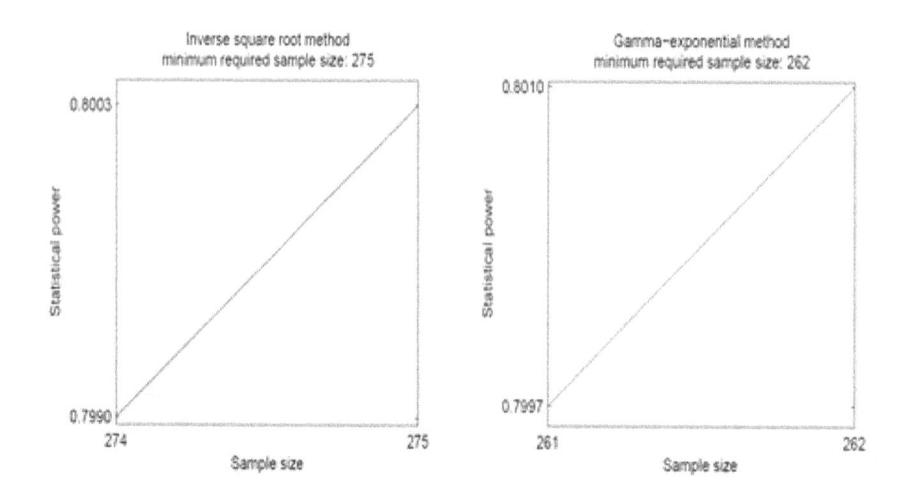

Research Instrument

The online self-administered survey is composed of two parts. The first part deals with the MBA student's profile in Metro Manila. The demographic characteristics collected are the following: school, type of school, legal age, gender, and civil status. The second part deals with the latent constructs of the study – EP, Machiavellianism, ES, EI, and EC.

The items of each construct were adopted from different studies (see Table 1) and were measured using a five-point Likert scale where 5 means strongly agree, and 1 means strongly disagree.

Table 1. Sources of latent reflective constructs

Latent reflective construct	Source
Entrepreneurial passion (4 items)	Cardon et al. (2013)
Machiavellianism (4 items)	Jonason and Webster (2010)
Entrepreneurial creativity (8 items)	Hills et al. (1997); Puhakka (2005)
Entrepreneurial self-efficacy (5 items)	De Noble et al. (1999); Liñan (2008)
Entrepreneurial intention (6 items)	Liñan et al. (2011); Tsai et al. (2016)

Data Analysis

The current undertaking employed a predictive-causal design to measure the hypothesized relationships. The study examined the direct and indirect effects of the model. The direct effects measured are H1a entrepreneurial passion and entrepreneurial creativity, H1b entrepreneurial passion and entrepreneurial intention, H2a Machiavellianism and entrepreneurial self-efficacy, H2b Machiavellianism, and entrepreneurial intention, and H3 entrepreneurial creativity and entrepreneurial intention, and H4 entrepreneurial self-efficacy and entrepreneurial intention. In contrast, we gauged the indirect effects based on the H5 mediating role of entrepreneurial creativity in the relationship between entrepreneurial passion and entrepreneurial intention and the H6 mediating part of entrepreneurial self-efficacy in the relationship between Machiavellianism and entrepreneurial intention.

The statistical test used in the study is partial least squares path modeling or partial least squares structural equation modeling (PLS-SEM) to measure the model's parameters. PLS-SEM is a variance-based approach (Hair et al., 2019) established through the composite model (Hair et al., 2017). It is a predictive-oriented method used for exploratory and confirmatory research (Sarstedt et al., 2014) focused on the interplay between prediction and theory testing (Gregor, 2006). This statistical approach simultaneously evaluates hypothesized relationships and enables researchers to measure complex models with many constructs (Hair et al., 2019). Therefore, PLS-SEM is a powerful tool appropriate for causal-predictive research design.

To run the PLS-SEM, we used the WarpPLS version 8.0 program (Kock, 2022); we evaluated the descriptive statistics using IBM SPSS Statistics Version 25.0. (IBM SPSS Statistics for Windows, 2017).

Results

Scrutiny of Measurement Model

The assessment of the measurement model comprises reliability and convergent validity (Hair et al., 2019). We used composite reliability (CR) to assess the constructs' reliability. The values of CR must be at least 0.70 to express good reliability (Fornell & Larcker, 1981; Kock, 2014; Kock & Lynn, 2012; Nunnally, 1978; Nunnally & Bernstein, 1994). Table 2 reveals that EP (CR = 0.871), Machiavellianism (CR = 0.917), ES (CR = 0.887), EI (CR = 0.942), and EC (CR = 0.930) are all above suggested level of 0.70 and achieved the criterion for reliability of research constructs.

We used average variance extracted (AVE) and factor loading to test the convergent validity. The values of AVE must be at least 0.50 (Amora, 2021), while factor loading must be at least 0.50, and the p-value must be equal to or less than 0.05 (Amora, 2021) to reflect convergent validity. Table 3 shows that all AVE and loadings are more significant than the required thresholds; thus, all constructs have convergent validity.

Table 2. Reliability and convergent validity

Latent construct	Item	Loading*
Entrepreneurial passion: AVE = 0.631; CR = 0.871		
	EP1	0.851
	EP2	0.867
	EP3	0.654
	EP4	0.790
Machiavellianism: AVE = 0.736; CR = 0.917		
	MA1	0.844
	MA2	0.882
	MA3	0.825
	MA4	0.878
Entrepreneurial self-efficacy: AVE = 0.616; CR = 0.887		
	ES1	0.583
	ES2	0.840
	ES3	0.811
	ES4	0.861
	ES5	0.797
Entrepreneurial intention: AVE = 0.764; CR = 0.942		
	EI1	0.863
	EI2	0.877
	EI3	0.866
	EI4	0.856
	EI5	0.907

continued on following page

Table 2. Continued

Latent construct	Item	Loading*
Entrepreneurial creativity: AVE = 0.626; CR = 0.930		
	EC1	0.779
	EC2	0.765
	EC3	0.797
	EC4	0.813
	EC5	0.829
	EC6	0.695
	EC7	0.810
	EC8	0.831

*all loadings are significant (p<0.001)

Furthermore, we evaluated the constructs' discriminant validity using heterotrait-monotrait (HTMT) ratios. The required HTMT ratio is less than 0.85 (Clark & Watson, 1995; Henseler et al., 2015; Kline, 2011; Voorhees et al., 2015). Teo et al. (2008) and Gold et al. (2001) claimed that HTMT ratios should not hit 0.90 and above. In Table 3, all values are equal to or less than 0.85. With that, all constructs have discriminant validity.

Table 3. Discriminant validity using HTMT ratios

	EP	MA	ES	EI	EC
EP					
MA	0.083				
ES	0.704	0.080			
EI	0.854	0.050	0.674		
EC	0.623	0.136	0.777	0.631	

EP-entrepreneurial passion; MA-Machiavellianism; ES-entrepreneurial self-efficacy; EI-entrepreneurial intention; EC-entrepreneurial creativity.

Scrutiny of the Structural Model

The second phase of PLS-SEM analyzes the structural model (Hair et al., 2019). Figure 3, Tables 4, and 5 present the direct and indirect effects of the PLS-SEM model. The results reveal that EP significantly and positively influences EC ($\beta = 0.543$, $\rho < 0.001$) and EI ($\beta = 0.545$, $\rho < 0.001$). Moreover, the data show a positive relationship between EP and EC with a medium effect ($f^2 = 0.295$) and EP and EI with a large effect ($f^2 = 0.401$). Thus, H1a and H1b are supported.

Figure 3. The structural model with parameter estimates

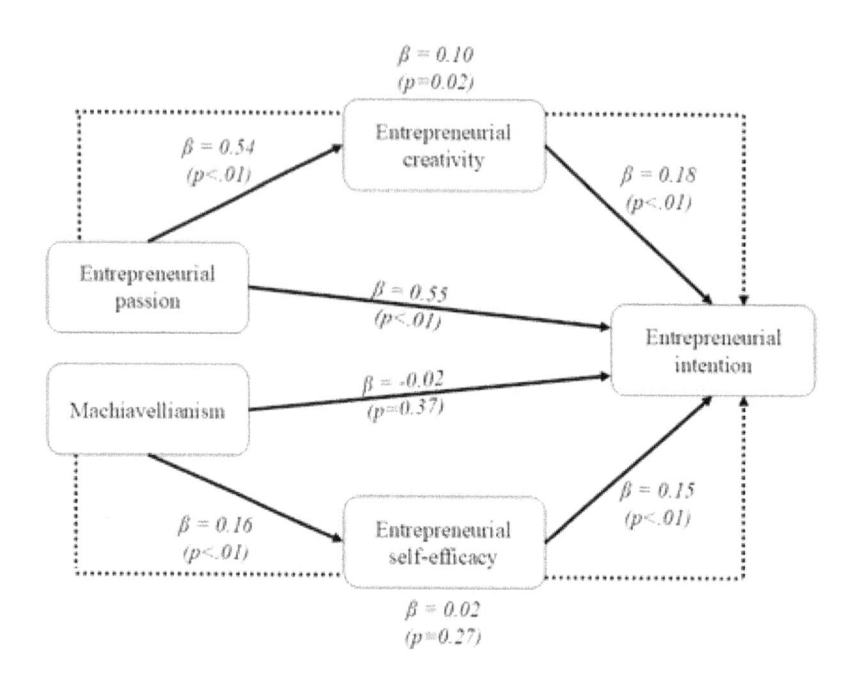

```
                              β = 0.10
                              (p=0.02)
                         ┌──────────────┐
         β = 0.54        │Entrepreneurial│      β = 0.18
         (p<.01)         │  creativity  │      (p<.01)
                         └──────────────┘
    ┌──────────────┐         β = 0.55          ┌──────────────┐
    │Entrepreneurial│─────────(p<.01)─────────▶│Entrepreneurial│
    │   passion    │                           │  intention   │
    └──────────────┘                           └──────────────┘
    ┌──────────────┐         β = -0.02
    │Machiavellianism│───────(p=0.37)
    └──────────────┘
         β = 0.16         ┌──────────────┐      β = 0.15
         (p<.01)          │Entrepreneurial│      (p<.01)
                          │ self-efficacy│
                          └──────────────┘
                              β = 0.02
                              (p=0.27)
```

The findings also exhibit that Machiavellianism significantly and directly influences ES ($β = 0.162$, $ρ = 0.002$) with a small effect ($f^2 = 0.026$). Therefore, H2a is supported. On the contrary, the results showed that Machiavellianism has no significant effect on EI ($β = -0.019$, $ρ = 0.371$). Thus, H2b is not supported.

Table 4. Hypothesis testing – direct effects

Hypothesis	Path coefficient	p	t-ratio	Effect size	Decision
H1a. EP → EC	0.543	<0.001	10.306	0.295	Supported
H1b. EP → EI	0.545	<0.001	10.348	0.401	Supported
H2a. MA → ES	0.162	0.002	2.896	0.026	Supported
H2b. MA → EI	-0.019	0.371	-0.329	0.003	Not supported
H3. EC → EI	0.181	<0.001	3.244	0.105	Supported
H4. ES → EI	0.150	0.004	2.686	0.090	Supported

In addition, the direct links between EC and EI ($β = 0.181$, $ρ < 0.001$), and ES and EI ($β = 0.150$, $ρ = 0.004$) showed to be significant. The data also showed a positive relationship between EC and EI with a small effect ($f^2 = 0.105$) and ES and EI with a small effect ($f^2 = 0.090$). Hence, H3 and H4 are supported.

Table 5. Hypothesis testing – indirect effects

Hypothesis	Path coefficient	p	SE	Effect size	Decision
H5. EP → EC → EI	0.098	0.007	0.040	0.072	Supported
H6. MA → ES → EI	0.024	0.273	0.040	0.004	Not supported

Furthermore, the results showed that EC mediates the relationship between EP and EI ($\beta = 0.098$, $\rho = 0.007$) with small effect size ($f^2 = 0.072$). On the other hand, ES was found to have no indirect effect on the relationship between MA and EI ($\beta = 0.024$, $\rho = 0.273$). Therefore, H5 is supported while H6 is not supported.

DISCUSSION

The current study shows that EP significantly and positively affects EC and EI. It implies that passion stimulates creativity and innovation. Individuals who are passionate about something will give more effort to develop their creative abilities. Additionally, it illustrates how individuals with a strong passion for entrepreneurship can apply creative thinking. These results support Ward (2004) study, which claimed that creative individuals are more likely to engage in entrepreneurial action. Moreover, this research also reveals that passion is a significant factor in developing an individual's EI. Passion supports an individual's intention to pursue entrepreneurship. It is evident in Thompson's (2009) study, which found that intention is a psychological state that focuses a person's attention on pursuing defined business goals in order to achieve entrepreneurial results. In addition, an individual's passion helps to boost their motivation, which drives them to pursue entrepreneurship. Prior research supports these findings (Baron, 2008; Bignetti et al., 2021; Campos, 2017; Cardon et al., 2009; Cardon et al., 2013; Collewaert et al., 2016; Davis et al., 2017; Laaksonen et al., 2011; Murnieks et al., 2014; Smilor, 1997; Saif, 2020; Syed et al., 2020).

Moreover, our findings suggest that Machiavellianism significantly and positively influences ES. This result indicates that when a person possesses more Machiavellian traits, they will demonstrate higher ES. It is natural for individuals with Machiavellian characteristics to have confidence in their capacity to carry out an undertaking successfully, like starting a business. Furthermore, they can be deceitful for their advancement and manipulate others to obtain their desired outcomes. The more a Machiavellian exhibits these characteristics, the higher their chances of achieving their goals. This was supported by previous research, which found that people with Machiavellian qualities have a higher demand for success (Wu et al., 2019). On the contrary, the results showed no link between Machiavellianism and EI. It suggests that Machiavellianism does not make people want to start their businesses. Machiavellianism is self-centered, lying, thinking ahead, and manipulating others. The same has been evident in earlier research that reveals how Machiavellians use dishonesty and other immoral methods to achieve their objectives and how they can potentially succeed at the expense of others (Al Ain et al., 2013; Hechavarria et al., 2012). In addition, individuals with Machiavellian traits show less emotion in social interactions, put themselves first, and rarely think about those around them. The more these Machiavellian characteristics are present, the less likely a person will start a business, as these traits are undesirable in an entrepreneurial setting. According to prior research, the correlation between Machiavellianism and EI was not yet established as Machiavellianism negatively affects EI. (Hmieleski & Lerner, 2016; Kramer et al., 2011).

This study also shows that EC significantly and positively impacts EI. The results revealed that an individual's perception of creativity encourages innovative thinking, which raises their EI. Innovative thinking is the capacity to generate fresh concepts and original solutions to issues that will open opportunities to launch a business. Thus, it will potentially contribute to individuals with a higher intention to pursue entrepreneurial activities. Additionally, research found that being creative is an important factor for business owners because it is part of the entrepreneurial process (Melati et al., 2018). Furthermore, earlier studies confirmed that high levels of creativity contribute to the formation of entrepreneurial intentions and are more likely to become an entrepreneur. (Hamidi et al., 2008; Zhang et al., 2018; Bellò-Pintado et al., 2018).

Another finding indicates that ES has a significant influence on EI. It implies that ES impacts people's decision-making if they want to be entrepreneurs. Additionally, ES serves as an indicator of what product or service these aspiring entrepreneurs can offer. Moreover, individuals who exhibit ES have confidence that they will succeed in their endeavor and strengthen their intention to launch a business. The greater the ES of an individual, the higher the probability they will engage in business. Previous studies supported the importance of ES and how it directly influenced individuals' EI (Neneh, 2020; Nowinski et al., 2019; Trevelyan, 2009; Zhao et al., 2005).

Furthermore, EC as a mediator between EP and EI indicated a significant effect in the current study. Data analysis shows that EC drives the entrepreneurship process, and that innovation mediates the link between EP and EI. As a result, when an individual has a high EC, EP and EI become relevant. Therefore, EC is an important part of EP that contributes to the formation of EI. This research supports previous findings (Bhansing et al., 2018; Gielnik et al., 2012; Hamidi et al., 2008; Khedhaouria et al., 2015; Zhang et al., 2018).

In addition, the mediation analysis showed that ES does not serve as a link between Machiavellianism and EI. Although ES significantly connects with Machiavellianism and entrepreneurial intent individually, it fails as a mediator between the stated variables. Through ES, Machiavellian individuals have the determination and perseverance to complete tasks in the same manner that drives an individual's intention to start a business. However, since self-centered and unethical individuals will not necessarily pursue entrepreneurial endeavors, individuals' confidence in their ability is irrelevant. In contrast to previous findings of Wu et al. (2019) stating that ES mediates the dark triad and EI, our study revealed unsupported results. It suggests that EI and Machiavellianism do not drive an individual's confidence in achieving entrepreneurial tasks.

Study's Implications, Limitations, and Future Research Directions

The current research provides a deeper understanding of how positive and negative traits influence EI. Mainly, this study aims to establish the effect of EP and Machiavellianism on EI. It also intends to provide practical evidence on the other factors, such as EC and ES, and how they influence EI. Moreover, the results showed that several factors in the proposed model, such as EC, EP, and ES, contribute to understanding individuals' future intentions in starting a new business. It suggests that universities and other higher education institutions should provide discussions, training, and programs promoting entrepreneurial education. Additionally, it is essential to encourage academe to create activities, particularly for EC, as they greatly contribute to the formation of entrepreneurial intentions of individuals. On the other hand, individuals with Machiavellian characteristics have weak significance on EI. Educators in business schools should pay special attention to these students and provide entrepreneurial encouragement and guidance whenever possible. In addition, these individuals have a higher EI because they are less fearful than other students and prefer to take risks. Hence, individuals with Machiavellianism traits are more inclined to start a business. Furthermore, government and big start-up companies may work together to promote entrepreneurship in the country, increase the enthusiasm of prospective entrepreneurs, and help them identify business opportunities. Lastly, MBA students should be encouraged to participate in business expos, conferences, and networking events for SMEs, start-ups, and entrepreneurs. These activities will help them demonstrate, develop, and strengthen their creativity, passion, and self-efficacy.

A key theoretical contribution of this study establishes the importance of behavior such as EC and ES as mediators between EP and Machiavellianism to EI. The research supports the theory of planned behavior (TPB) by illustrating the direct impact of ES on EI. It means that an individual with confidence in solving business challenges can be an entrepreneur. Moreover, EC was proven to influence EI. It signifies that individuals who can creatively make new ideas, develop favorable relationships with prospective customers, and are sensitive to identifying problems have greater intent to be involved in entrepreneurship. This study also supports the social cognitive theory (SCT), wherein ES positively influences EI. It indicates that if a person thinks they can succeed, there is a greater likelihood that they will intend to launch a business. Additionally, EP, which falls under the personal factor of SCT, was discovered to have an immediate effect on EI. It denotes that EP is a motivating force that encourages people to persevere through difficulties and stay committed to their established business goals. Thus, an individual who displays a high level of passion will more likely pursue starting a business.

This study contains limitations and suggests approaches for future researchers. First, this study only involves MBA students in Metro Manila. Future researchers can probe the EI of college students or graduates in other cities of the Philippines and potentially abroad. Second, it covers EC and ES as mediators in assessing the model. In future research, scholars could replace the existing mediators with other intervening variables to expound the EI model. Prior studies have emphasized the significance of entrepreneurship education and entrepreneurial experience, and these mediators can be possible substitutes for raising students' knowledge in founding a business. Third, most variables and mediators reflect positive characteristics, which might result in social desirability bias. Scholars could consider other elements of the dark triad to assess its effects on establishing business ventures. Therefore, this highlights the study's primary objective of measuring and understanding the factors influencing EI in fostering future entrepreneurs.

ACKNOWLEDGMENT

The authors would like to acknowledge Janica Anne G. Plaza, Xhyrlynn L. Gaño, Clain Darrenne B. Mendoza, and Rogie Ann I. Arcilla for their contributions in the data collection phase of this study, and for providing useful feedback to better improve the undertaking.

REFERENCES

Ajzen, I. (1985). From Intentions to Actions: A Theory of Planned Behavior. In Kuhl, J., & Beckmann, J. (Eds.), *Action Control. SSSP Springer Series in Social Psychology* (pp. 11–39). Springer., DOI: 10.1007/978-3-642-69746-3_2

Ajzen, I. (1991). The theory of planned behavior. *Organizational Behavior and Human Decision Processes*, 50(2), 179–211. DOI: 10.1016/0749-5978(91)90020-T

Al Aïn, S., Carré, A., Fantini-Hauwel, C., Baudouin, J. Y., & Besche-Richard, C. (2013). What is the emotional core of the multidimensional Machiavellian personality trait? *Frontiers in Psychology*, 4. Advance online publication. DOI: 10.3389/fpsyg.2013.00454 PMID: 23885245

Amabile, T. M. (1997). Entrepreneurial Creativity Through Motivational Synergy. *The Journal of Creative Behavior*, 31(1), 18–26. DOI: 10.1002/j.2162-6057.1997.tb00778.x

Amora, J. T. (2021). Convergent validity assessment in PLS-SEM: A loadings-driven approach. *Data Analysis Perspectives Journal*, 2(3), 1–6.

Anjum, T., Heidler, P., Amoozegar, A., & Anees, R. T. (2021). The Impact of Entrepreneurial Passion on the Entrepreneurial Intention; *Moderating Impact of Perception of University Support. Administrative Sciences*, 11(2), 45. DOI: 10.3390/admsci11020045

Anton, R. (2014). Sustainable Intrapreneurship-*The GSI Concept and Strategy-Unfolding Competitive Advantage via Fair Entrepreneurship*, 1-46.

Ardichvili, A., Cardozo, R., & Ray, S. (2003). A theory of entrepreneurial opportunity identification and development. *Journal of Business Venturing*, 18(1), 105–123. DOI: 10.1016/S0883-9026(01)00068-4

Azavedo, M., & Gogatz, A. (2021). The developing specialty coffee businesses of Bangkok, Thailand and Penang, Malaysia. A story of entrepreneurial passion and creativity? *Journal of Entrepreneurship, Management and Innovation,* 17(1), 203–230. ttps://DOI: 10.7341/20211717

Baldacchino, L. (2009). Entrepreneurial creativity and innovation. *First International Conference on Strategic Innovation and Future Creation*, 1–15, 22-23.

Bandura, A. (1986). Social foundations of thought and action. A social cognitive theory. Englewood Cliffs, NJ, 23-28.

Bandura, A. (1989). Regulation of cognitive processes through perceived self-efficacy. *Developmental Psychology*, 25(5), 729–735. DOI: 10.1037/0012-1649.25.5.729

Bandura, A. (2000). Exercise of human agency through collective efficacy. *Current Directions in Psychological Science*, 9(3), 75–78. DOI: 10.1111/1467-8721.00064

Barbosa, S. D., Gerhardt, M. W., & Kickul, J. R. (2007). The Role of Cognitive Style and Risk Preference on Entrepreneurial Self-Efficacy and Entrepreneurial Intentions. *Journal of Leadership & Organizational Studies*, 13(4), 86–104. DOI: 10.1177/10717919070130041001

Baron, R. A. (2006). Opportunity Recognition as Pattern Recognition: How Entrepreneurs "Connect the Dots" to Identify New Business Opportunities. *The Academy of Management Perspectives*, 20(1), 104–119. DOI: 10.5465/amp.2006.19873412

Baron, R. A. (2008). The Role of Affect in the Entrepreneurial Process. *Academy of Management Review*, 33(2), 328–340. DOI: 10.5465/amr.2008.31193166

Bello-Pintado, A., Kaufmann, R., & Merino Diaz De Cerio, J. (2018). Firms' entrepreneurial orientation and the adoption of quality management practices. *International Journal of Quality & Reliability Management*, 35(9), 1734–1754. DOI: 10.1108/IJQRM-05-2017-0089

Belyh, A. (2019, September 23). How Entrepreneurial Creativity Leads to Innovation. Cleverism. Retrieved June 30, 2022, from https://www.cleverism.com/entrepreneurial-creativity-leads-innovation/

Bereczkei, T., & Czibor, A. (2014). Personality and situational factors differently influence high Mach and low Mach persons' decisions in a social dilemma game. *Personality and Individual Differences*, 64, 168–173. DOI: 10.1016/j.paid.2014.02.035

Bhansing, P. V., Hitters, E., & Wijngaarden, Y. (2018). Passion Inspires: Motivations of Creative Entrepreneurs in Creative Business Centres in the Netherlands. *The Journal of Entrepreneurship*, 27(1), 1–24. DOI: 10.1177/0971355717738589

Bignetti, B., Santos, A. C. M. Z., Hansen, P. B., & Henriqson, E. (2021). The influence of entrepreneurial passion and creativity on entrepreneurial intentions. *Revista de Administracao Mackenzie*, 22(2). https://doi.org/DOI: 10.1590/1678-6971/ERAMR210082

Biraglia, A., & Kadile, V. (2017). The Role of Entrepreneurial Passion and Creativity in Developing Entrepreneurial Intentions: Insights from American Homebrewers. *Journal of Small Business Management*, 55(1), 170–188. DOI: 10.1111/jsbm.12242

Bird, B. (1988). Implementing Entrepreneurial Ideas: The Case for Intention. *Academy of Management Review*, 13(3), 442–453. DOI: 10.2307/258091

Boyd, N. G., & Vozikis, G. S. (1994). The Influence of Self-Efficacy on the Development of Entrepreneurial Intentions and Actions. *Entrepreneurship Theory and Practice*, 18(4), 63–77. DOI: 10.1177/104225879401800404

Braginsky, D. D. (1970). Machiavellianism *and manipulative interpersonal behavior in children. Journal of Experimental Social Psychology*, 6(1), 77–99. DOI: 10.1016/0022-1031(70)90077-6

Bryant, P. T. (2006). Improving entrepreneurial education through self-regulatory skills. In Venture Well. Proceedings of Open, the Annual Conference (p. 279). National Collegiate Inventors & Innovators Alliance.

Buckels, E. E., Jones, D. N., & Paulhus, D. L. (2013). Behavioral Confirmation of Everyday Sadism. *Psychological Science*, 24(11), 2201–2209. DOI: 10.1177/0956797613490749 PMID: 24022650

Byrne, J. A. (2016, June 26). MBAs Doing Startups at Nearly Four Times the Rate Previously Thought. Poets & Quants. Retrieved June 30, 2022, from https://poetsandquants.com/2016/06/26/mba-employment-reports-understate

Campos, H. M. (2017). Impact of entrepreneurial passion on entrepreneurial orientation with the mediating role of entrepreneurial alertness for technology-based firms in Mexico. *Journal of Small Business and Enterprise Development*, 24(2), 353–374. DOI: 10.1108/JSBED-10-2016-0166

Cardon, M. S., Gregoire, D. A., Stevens, C. E., & Patel, P. C. (2013). Measuring entrepreneurial passion: Conceptual foundations and scale validation. *Journal of Business Venturing*, 28(3), 373–396. DOI: 10.1016/j.jbusvent.2012.03.003

Cardon, M. S., & Kirk, C. P. (2015). Entrepreneurial Passion as Mediator of the Self–Efficacy to Persistence Relationship. *Entrepreneurship Theory and Practice*, 39(5), 1027–1050. DOI: 10.1111/etap.12089

Cardon, M. S., Wincent, J., Singh, J., & Drnovsek, M. (2009). The Nature and Experience of Entrepreneurial Passion. *Academy of Management Review*, 34(3), 511–532. https://Doi.Org/10.5465/Amr.2009.40633190. DOI: 10.5465/amr.2009.40633190

Chen, C. C., Greene, P. G., & Crick, A. (1998). Does entrepreneurial self-efficacy distinguish entrepreneurs from managers? *Journal of Business Venturing*, 13(4), 295–316. DOI: 10.1016/S0883-9026(97)00029-3

Clark, L. A., & Watson, D. (1995). Constructing validity: Basic issues in objective scale development. *Psychological Assessment*, 7(3), 309–319. DOI: 10.1037/1040-3590.7.3.309

Collewaert, V., Anseel, F., Crommelinck, M., de Beuckelaer, A., & Vermeire, J. (2016). When Passion Fades: Disentangling the Temporal Dynamics of Entrepreneurial Passion for Founding. *Journal of Management Studies*, 53(6), 966–995. DOI: 10.1111/joms.12193

Collison, K. L., Vize, C. E., Miller, J. D., & Lynam, D. R. (2018). Development and preliminary validation of a five-factor model measure of Machiavellianism. *Psychological Assessment*, 30(10), 1401–1407. DOI: 10.1037/pas0000637 PMID: 30047746

Corp, I. B. M. (2017). IBM SPSS Statistics for Windows (Version 25.0) [Computer software]. IBM Corp. https://www.ibm.com/analytics/spss-statistics-software

Czibor, A., Szabo, Z. P., Jones, D. N., Zsido, A. N., Paal, T., Szijjarto, L., Carre, J. R., & Bereczkei, T. (2017). Male and female face of Machiavellianism: Opportunism or anxiety? *Personality and Individual Differences*, 117, 221–229. DOI: 10.1016/j.paid.2017.06.002

Dahling, J. J., Whitaker, B. G., & Levy, P. E. (2009). The Development and Validation of a New Machiavellianism Scale. *Journal of Management*, 35(2), 219–257. DOI: 10.1177/0149206308318618

Darini, M., Pazhouhesh, H., & Moshiri, F. (2011). Relationship between Employee's Innovation (Creativity) and time management. *Procedia: Social and Behavioral Sciences*, 25, 201–213. DOI: 10.1016/j.sbspro.2011.10.541

Davis, B. C., Hmieleski, K. M., Webb, J. W., & Coombs, J. E. (2017). Funders' poise reactions to entrepreneurs' crowdfunding pitches: The influence of perceived product I've creativity and entrepreneurial passion. *Journal of Business Venturing*, 32(1), 90–106. DOI: 10.1016/j.jbusvent.2016.10.006

De Mol, E., Cardon, M. S., de Jong, B., Khapova, S. N., & Elfring, T. (2020). Entrepreneurial passion diversity in new venture teams: An empirical examination of short- and long-term performance implications. *Journal of Business Venturing*, 35(4), 105965. DOI: 10.1016/j.jbusvent.2019.105965

De Noble, A. F., Jung, D., & Ehrlich, S. B. (1999). Entrepreneurial Self-Efficacy: The Development of a Measure and Its Relationship to Entrepreneurial Action. In *Frontiers of Entrepreneurship Research* (pp. 73–87). Babson College.

Do, B. R., & Dadvari, A. (2017). The influence of the dark triad on the relationship between entrepreneurial attitude orientation and entrepreneurial intention: A study among students in Taiwan University. *Asia Pacific Management Review*, 22(4), 185–191. DOI: 10.1016/j.apmrv.2017.07.011

Drnovsek, M., Cardon, M. S., & Patel, P. C. (2016). Direct and Indirect Effects of Passion on Growing Technology Ventures. *Strategic Entrepreneurship Journal, 10*(2), 194 213. DOI: 10.1002/sej.1213

Fatoki, O. O. (2010). Graduate entrepreneurial intention in South Africa: Motivations and obstacles. *International Journal of Business and Management*, 5(9), 87.

Fornell, C., & Larcker, D. F. (1981). Evaluating structural equation models with unobservable variables and measurement error. *JMR, Journal of Marketing Research*, 18(1), 39–50. DOI: 10.1177/002224378101800104

Geis, F. L., & Moon, T. H. (1981). Machiavellianism and Deception. *Journal of Personality and Social Psychology*, 41(4), 766–775. https://Doi.Org/10.1037/0022-3514.41.4.766. DOI: 10.1037/0022-3514.41.4.766

Geisser, S. (1974). A predictive approach to the random effects model. *Biometrika*, 61(1), 101–107. DOI: 10.1093/biomet/61.1.101

Gielnik, M. M., Barabas, S., Frese, M., Namatovu-Dawa, R., Scholz, F. A., Metzger, J. R., & Walter, T. (2014). A temporal analysis of how entrepreneurial goal intentions, positive fantasies, and action planning affect starting a new venture and when the effects wear off. *Journal of Business Venturing*, 29(6), 755–772. DOI: 10.1016/j.jbusvent.2013.09.002

Gielnik, M. M., Frese, M., Graf, J. M., & Kampschulte, A. (2012). Creativity in the opportunity identification process and the moderating effect of diversity of information. *Journal of Business Venturing*, 27(5), 559–576. DOI: 10.1016/j.jbusvent.2011.10.003

Gold, A. H., Malhotra, A., & Segars, A. H. (2001). Knowledge management: Organizational Capabilities Perspective. *Journal of Management Information Systems*, 18(1), 185–214. DOI: 10.1080/07421222.2001.11045669

Gregor, S. (2006). The Nature of Theory in Information Systems. *Management Information Systems Quarterly*, 30(3), 611–642. DOI: 10.2307/25148742

Hair, J. F., Matthews, L. M., Matthews, R. L., & Sarstedt, M. (2017). PLS-SEM or CB-SEM: Updated guidelines on which method to use. *International Journal of Multivariate Data Analysis*, 1(2), 107–123. DOI: 10.1504/IJMDA.2017.087624

Hair, J. F., Risher, J. J., Sarstedt, M., & Ringle, C. M. (2019). When to use and how to report the results of PLS-SEM. *European Business Review*, 31(1), 2–24. DOI: 10.1108/EBR-11-2018-0203

Hamidi, D. Y., Wennberg, K., & Berglund, H. (2008). Creativity in entrepreneurship education. *Journal of Small Business and Enterprise Development*, 15(2), 304–320. DOI: 10.1108/14626000810871691

Hartzell, S. (2012) Machiavellianism in Organizations: Justifying the Means by the Ends. Retrieved September 19, 2012 from https://study.com/academy/lesson/machiavellism-in-organizations-justifying-the-means-by-the-ends.html

Hechavarria, D. M., Ingram, A., Justo, R., & Terjesen, S. (2012). Are Women More Likely to Pursue Social and Environmental Entrepreneurship? *In Global Women's Entrepreneurship Research*, 135–151. DOI: 10.4337/9781849804752.00016

Henseler, J., Ringle, C. M., & Sarstedt, M. (2015). A new criterion for assessing discriminant validity in variance-based structural equation modeling. *Journal of the Academy of Marketing Science*, 43(1), 115–135. DOI: 10.1007/s11747-014-0403-8

Hill, S., Ionescu-Somers, A., Coduras, A., Guerrero, M., Roomi, M. A., Bosma, N., & Shay, J. (2022, February). Global Entrepreneurship Monitor 2021/2022 Global Report: Opportunity Amid Disruption. In *Expo 2020 Dubai*.

Hills, G. E., Lumpkin, G. T., & Singh, R. P. (1997). Opportunity recognition: Perceptions and behaviors of entrepreneurs. *Frontiers of Entrepreneurship Research*, 17(4), 168–182.

Hills, G. E., Shrader, R. C., & Lumpkin, G. T. (1999). Opportunity recognition as a creative process. In Bygrave, W. D. (Eds.), *In Frontiers of entrepreneurship research, 19(19), 216–227*. Babson College Press.

Hmieleski, K. M., & Lerner, D. A. (2016). The dark triad and nascent entrepreneurship: An examination of unproductive versus productive entrepreneurial motives. *Journal of Small Business Management*, 54, 7–32. DOI: 10.1111/jsbm.12296

Hubner, S., Baum, M., & Frese, M. (2019). Contagion of Entrepreneurial Passion: Effects on Employee Outcomes. *Entrepreneurship Theory and Practice*, 44(6), 1112–1140. DOI: 10.1177/1042258719883995

Jacobs, G., & Keegan, A. (2016). Ethical Considerations and Change Recipients' Reactions: 'It's Not All About Me'. *Journal of Business Ethics*, 152(1), 73–90. DOI: 10.1007/s10551-016-3311-7

Jarinto, K., Jermsittiparsert, K., & Chienwattanasook, K. (2019). The Influence of Innovation and self-employment on entrepreneurial inclination: The moderating effect of the role of universities in Thailand. *International Journal of Innovation. Creativity and Change*, 10(1), 174–197.

Johri, R., & Misra, R. K. (2014). Self-efficacy, Work Passion and Wellbeing: A Theoretical Framework. *The IUP Journal of Soft Skills*, 8(4).

Jonason, P. K., Li, N. P., Webster, G. D., & Schmitt, D. P. (2009). The dark triad: Facilitating a short-term mating strategy in men. *European Journal of Personality*, 23(1), 5–18. DOI: 10.1002/per.698

Jonason, P. K., & Webster, G. D. (2010). The dirty dozen: A concise measure of the dark triad. *Psychological Assessment*, 22(2), 420–432. DOI: 10.1037/a0019265 PMID: 20528068

Jones, D. N., & Paulhus, D. L. (2014). Introducing the Short Dark Triad (SD3). A Brief Measure of Dark Personality Traits. *Assessment*, 21(1), 28–41. DOI: 10.1177/1073191113514105 PMID: 24322012

Jones, D. N., & Paulhus, D. L. (2017). Duplicity among the dark triad: Three faces of deceit. *Journal of Personality and Social Psychology*, 113(2), 329–342. DOI: 10.1037/pspp0000139 PMID: 28253006

Jones, G. E., & Kavanagh, M. J. (1996). An Experimental Examination of the Effects of Individual and Situational Factors on Unethical Behavioral Intentions in the Workplace. *Journal of Business Ethics*, 15(5), 511–523. Retrieved June 30, 2022, from https://www.jstor.org/stable/25072775. DOI: 10.1007/BF00381927

Judge, W. Q., & Douglas, T. J. (2013). Entrepreneurship as a leap of faith. *Journal of Management, Spirituality & Religion*, 10(1), 37–65. DOI: 10.1080/14766086.2012.758047

Kajornatthapol, P., Prayoon, A., & Kamolthip, K. (2023). Investigating the social entrepreneurial intention among Thai population. *Asian Administration & Management Review,* 6(2), 107-118. https://doi.org/DOI: 10.14456/aamr.2023.23

Karimi, S. (2019). The Role of Entrepreneurial Passion in the Formation of Students' Entrepreneurial Intentions. *Applied Economics*, 52(3), 331–344. DOI: 10.1080/00036846.2019.1645287

Kenny, G. (2016, June 21). Strategic plans are less important than strategic planning. Harvard Business Review. https://hbr.org/2016/06/strategic-plans-are-less-important-than-strategic-planning

Kessler, S. R., Bandelli, A. C., Spector, P. E., Borman, W. C., Nelson, C. E., & Penney, L. M. (2010). Re-Examining Machiavelli: A Three-Dimensional Model of Machiavellianism in the Workplace. *Journal of Applied Social Psychology*, 40(8), 1868–1896. DOI: 10.1111/j.1559-1816.2010.00643.x

Khedhaouria, A., Gurău, C., & Torrès, O. (2015). Creativity, self-efficacy, and small-firm performance: The mediating role of entrepreneurial orientation. *Small Business Economics*, 44(3), 485–504. https://www.jstor.org/stable/43553764. DOI: 10.1007/s11187-014-9608-y

Kline, R. B. (2011). *Principles and practice of structural equation modeling*. Guilford Press.

Klotz, A. C., & Neubaum, D. O. (2016). Article commentary: Research on the dark side of personality traits in entrepreneurship: Observations from an organizational behavior perspective. *Entrepreneurship Theory and Practice*, 40(1), 7–17. DOI: 10.1111/etap.12214

Kock, N. (2014). Advanced mediating effects tests, multi-group analyses, and measurement SEM: An illustration and recommendations. *Journal of the Association for Information Systems*, 13(7), 546–580. DOI: 10.17705/1jais.00302

Kock, N. (2015). Common method bias in PLS-SEM: A full collinearity assessment approach. *International Journal of e-Collaboration*, 11(4), 1–10. DOI: 10.4018/ijec.2015100101

Kock, N. (2022). *WarpPLS user manual: Version 8.0*. Script Warp Systems.

Kock, N., & Hadaya, P. (2016). Minimum sample size estimation in PLS-SEM: The inverse square root and gamma-exponential methods. *Information Systems Journal*, 28(1), 227–261. DOI: 10.1111/isj.12131

Kock, N., & Lynn, G. S. (2012). Lateral collinearity and misleading results in variance-based model assessments in PLS-based SEM. *International Journal of e-Collaboration*, 10(3), 1–13.

Kramer, M., Cesinger, B., Schwarzinger, D., & Golléri, P. (2011). "Investigating entrepreneurs' dark personality: how narcissism, Machiavellianism, and psychopathy relate to entrepreneurial intention," in *Proceedings of the 25th Conference on ANZAM*. Wellington: Australia and New Zealand Academy of Management.

Krueger, N. F., & Carsrud, A. L. (1993). Entrepreneurial intentions: Applying the theory of planned behavior. *Entrepreneurship and Regional Development*, 5(4), 315–330. DOI: 10.1080/08985629300000020

Krueger, N. F.Jr, Reilly, M. D., & Carsrud, A. L. (2000). Competing models of entrepreneurial intentions. *Journal of Business Venturing*, 15(5–6), 411–432. DOI: 10.1016/S0883-9026(98)00033-0

Laaksonen, L., Ainamo, A., & Karjalainen, T. (2011). Entrepreneurial passion: An explorative case study of four metal music ventures. *Journal of Research in Marketing and Entrepreneurship*, 13(1), 18–36. DOI: 10.1108/14715201111147923

LaMorte, W. W. (2019, September 9). The Social Cognitive Theory. Behavioral Change Models. https://sphweb.bumc.bu.edu/otlt/mph-modules/sb/behavioralchangetheories/BehavioralChangeTheories5.html#headingtaglink_1

Laplume, A., & Yeganegi, S. (2021). Entrepreneurship Theories. Independently published.

Li, C., Murad, M., Shahzad, F., Khan, M. A. S., Ashraf, S. F., & Dogbe, C. S. K. (2020). Entrepreneurial Passion to Entrepreneurial Behavior: Role of Entrepreneurial Alertness, Entrepreneurial Self-Efficacy and Proactive Personality. *Frontiers in Psychology*, 11, 1611. Advance online publication. DOI: 10.3389/fpsyg.2020.01611 PMID: 32973593

Liñán, F. (2008). Skill and value perceptions: How do they affect entrepreneurial intentions? *The International Entrepreneurship and Management Journal*, 4(3), 257–272. DOI: 10.1007/s11365-008-0093-0

Liñán, F., Urbano, D., & Guerrero, M. (2011). Regional variations in entrepreneurial cognitions: Start-up intentions of university students in Spain. *Entrepreneurship and Regional Development*, 23(3-4), 187–215. DOI: 10.1080/08985620903233929

Liu, J., & Gu, J. (2017). The Role of Entrepreneurial Passion and Creativity in Entrepreneurial Intention: A Hierarchical Analysis of the Moderating Effect of Entrepreneurial Support Programs. *JEP*, 8(36).

Lounsbury, M., & Glynn, M. A. (2019). Cultural Entrepreneurship: A New Agenda for the Study of Entrepreneurial Processes and Possibilities. *Administrative Science Quarterly*, 64(4), 33–35. DOI: 10.1177/0001839219862938

Luca, M. R., Cazan, A. M., & Tomulescu, D. (2013). Entrepreneurial Personality in Higher Education. *Procedia: Social and Behavioral Sciences*, 84, 1045–1049. DOI: 10.1016/j.sbspro.2013.06.696

Markman, G. D., & Baron, R. A. (2003). Person–entrepreneurship fit why some people are more successful as entrepreneurs than others. *Human Resource Management Review*, 13(2), 281–301. DOI: 10.1016/S1053-4822(03)00018-4

McGee, J. E., Peterson, M., Mueller, S. L., & Sequeira, J. M. (2009). Entrepreneurial self-efficacy: Refining the measure. *Entrepreneurship Theory and Practice*, 33(4), 965–988. DOI: 10.1111/j.1540-6520.2009.00304.x

Melati, I. S., Arief, S., & Baswara, S. Y. (2018). Does Financial Background Affect Entrepreneur Students' creativity: An Investigation of How Rich and Poor Students Start Their Businesses. *Journal of Entrepreneurship Education*, 21(1), 1–11.

Miller, D. (2015). A Downside to the Entrepreneurial Personality? *Entrepreneurship Theory and Practice*, 39(1), 1–8. DOI: 10.1111/etap.12130

Montiel, O., & Clark, M. (2018). The dark side of entrepreneurship: A reflection on their multidimensionality. In *Proceedings of the 60th Annual Southwest Academy of Management Conference*, 7-10. Albuquerque: USA.

Moriano, J. A., Gorgievski, M., Laguna, M., Stephan, U., & Zarafshani, K. (2012). A Cross-Cultural Approach to Understanding Entrepreneurial Intention. *Journal of Career Development*, 39(2), 162–185. DOI: 10.1177/0894845310384481

Mueller, B. A., Wolfe, M. T., & Syed, I. (2017). Passion and grit: An exploration of the pathways leading to venture suaccess. *Journal of Business Venturing*, 32(3), 260–279. DOI: 10.1016/j.jbusvent.2017.02.001

Mumba, M. N. (2016). Icek Ajzen's Theory of Planned Behavior: A theoretical framework. Sigma Repository. Retrieved June 30, 2022, from https://sigma.nursingrepository.org/handle/10755/602080

Murnieks, C. Y., Mosakowski, E., & Cardon, M. S. (2014). Pathways of Passion. *Journal of Management*, 40(6), 1583–1606. DOI: 10.1177/0149206311433855

Murray, S. (2014, November 10). 22% Of Full-Time Mba Graduates Become Start-Up Founders Business. BusinessBecause. Retrieved June 30, 2022, from https://www.businessbecause.com/news/entrepreneurs/2901/22pc-of-fulltime-mba-graduates-become-startup-fouders#:~:text=Some%2022%25%20of%20full%2Dtime,stable%2C%20high%2Dsalary%20jobs

Naktiyok, A., Nur Karabey, C., & Caglar Gulluce, A. (2009). Entrepreneurial self-efficacy and entrepreneurial intention: The Turkish case. *The International Entrepreneurship and Management Journal*, 6(4), 419–435. DOI: 10.1007/s11365-009-0123-6

Neneh, B. N. (2020). Entrepreneurial passion and entrepreneurial intention: The role of social support and entrepreneurial self-efficacy. *Studies in Higher Education*, 47(3), 587–603. DOI: 10.1080/03075079.2020.1770716

Newman, A., Obschonka, M., Moeller, J., & Chandan, G. G. (2021). Entrepreneurial passion: A review, synthesis, and agenda for future research. *Applied Psychology*, 70(2), 816–860. DOI: 10.1111/apps.12236

Nowiński, W., Haddoud, M. Y., Lančarič, D., Egerová, D., & Czeglédi, C. (2019). The impact of entrepreneurship education, entrepreneurial self-efficacy and gender on entrepreneurial intentions of university students in the Visegrad countries. *Studies in Higher Education*, 44(2), 361–379. DOI: 10.1080/03075079.2017.1365359

Nunnally, J. C. (1978). *Psychometric theory*. McGraw Hill.

Nunnally, J. C., & Bernstein, I. H. (1994). *Psychometric theory*. McGraw-Hill.

O'Connor, A., Stam, E., Sussan, F., & Audretsch, D. B. (2018). Entrepreneurial Ecosystems: The Foundations of Place-based Renewal. *International Studies in Entrepreneurship*, 1–21. DOI: 10.1007/978-3-319-63531-6_1

Paulhus, D. L., & Williams, K. M. (2002). The Dark Triad of personality: Narcissism, Machiavellianism, and psychopathy. *Journal of Research in Personality*, 36(6), 556–563. DOI: 10.1016/S0092-6566(02)00505-6

Pihie, Z. A. L., & Bagheri, A. (2013). Self-Efficacy and Entrepreneurial Intention: The Mediation Effect of Self-Regulation. *Vocations and Learning*, 6(3), 385–401. DOI: 10.1007/s12186-013-9101-9

Puhakka, V. (2005). The role of intellectual capital in opportunity recognition of entrepreneurs. In 50th World conference of ICSB, Washington, DC.

Rauch, A., & Frese, M. (2007). Let's put the person back into entrepreneurship research: A meta-analysis on the relationship between business owners' personality traits, business creation, and success. *European Journal of Work and Organizational Psychology*, 16(4), 353–385. DOI: 10.1080/13594320701595438

Rauthmann, J. F., & Will, T. (2011). Proposing a Multidimensional Machiavellianism Conceptualization. *Social Behavior and Personality*, 39(3), 391–403. DOI: 10.2224/sbp.2011.39.3.391

Sabah, S. (2016). Entrepreneurial Intention: Theory of planned behavior and the moderation effect of start-up experience. *In Entrepreneurship-Practice-Oriented Perspectives*. DOI: 10.5772/65640

Saif, H. A. A. (2020). Entrepreneurial passion for founding as a mediator of the career anchors to entrepreneurial behavior relationship. *Journal of Public Affairs*, 22(1), e2408. Advance online publication. DOI: 10.1002/pa.2408

Sarstedt, M., Ringle, C. M., Henseler, J., & Hair, J. F. (2014). On the Emancipation of PLS-SEM: A C commentary on Rigdon (2012).*Long Range Planning*, 47(3), 154–160. DOI: 10.1016/j.lrp.2014.02.007

Schlaegel, C., & Koenig, M. (2014). Determinants of Entrepreneurial Intent: A Meta–Analytic Test and Integration of Competing Models. *Entrepreneurship Theory and Practice*, 38(2), 291–332. DOI: 10.1111/etap.12087

Sergi, B. S., Popkova, E. G., Bogoviz, A. V., & Ragulina, J. V. (2019). Entrepreneurship and Economic Growth: The Experience of Developed and Developing Countries. *Entrepreneurship and Development in the 21st Century*, 3–32. DOI: 10.1108/978-1-78973-233-720191002

Sesen, H. (2013). Personality or environment? A comprehensive study on the entrepreneurial intentions of university students. *Education + Training*, 55(7), 624–640. DOI: 10.1108/ET-05-2012-0059

Shahab, Y., Chengang, Y., Arbizu, A. D., & Haider, M. J. (2019). Entrepreneurial self-efficacy and intention: Do entrepreneurial creativity and education matter? *International Journal of Entrepreneurial Behaviour & Research*, 25(2), 259–280. DOI: 10.1108/IJEBR-12-2017-0522

Sieger, P., Raemy, L., Zellweger, T., Fueglistaller, U. & Hatak, I. (2021). Global Student Entrepreneurship 2021: Insights From 58 Countries. (2021 GUESS Global Report).

Smilor, R. W. (1997). Entrepreneurship: Reflections on a subversive activity. *Journal of Business Venturing*, 12(5), 341–346. DOI: 10.1016/S0883-9026(97)00008-6

Sriyakul, T., & Jermsittiparsert, K. (2019). The mediating role of entrepreneurial passion in the relationship between entrepreneur education and entrepreneurial intention among university students in Thailand. *International Journal of Innovation. Creativity and Change*, 6(10), 193–212.

Stone, M. (1974). Cross-validatory choice and assessment of statistical predictions. *Journal of the Royal Statistical Society. Series B, Statistical Methodology*, 36(2), 111–133. DOI: 10.1111/j.2517-6161.1974.tb00994.x

Syed, I., Butler, J. C., Smith, R. M., & Cao, X. (2020). From entrepreneurial passion to entrepreneurial intentions: The role of entrepreneurial passion, innovativeness, and curiosity in driving entrepreneurial intentions. *Personality and Individual Differences*, 157, 3–4. DOI: 10.1016/j.paid.2019.109758

Teo, T. S. H., Srivastava, S. C., & Jiang, L. (2008). Trust and Electronic Government Success: An Empirical Study. *Journal of Management Information Systems*, 25(3), 99–132. DOI: 10.2753/MIS0742-1222250303

Thompson, E. R. (2009). Individual Entrepreneurial Intent: Construct Clarification and Development of an Internationally Reliable Metric. *Entrepreneurship Theory and Practice*, 33(3), 669–694. DOI: 10.1111/j.1540-6520.2009.00321.x

Thorgren, S., & Wincent, J. (2015). Passion and habitual entrepreneurship. *International Small Business Journal*, 33(2), 216–227. DOI: 10.1177/0266242613487085

Trevelyan, R. (2009). Entrepreneurial Attitudes and Action in New Venture Development. *International Journal of Entrepreneurship and Innovation*, 10(1), 21–32. DOI: 10.5367/000000009787414271

Trevelyan, R. (2011). Self-regulation and effort in entrepreneurial tasks. *International Journal of Entrepreneurial Behaviour & Research*, 17(1), 39–63. DOI: 10.1108/13552551111107507

Tsai, K. H., Chang, H. C., & Peng, C. Y. (2016). Extending the link between entrepreneurial self-efficacy and intention: A moderated mediation model. *The International Entrepreneurship and Management Journal*, 12(2), 445–463. DOI: 10.1007/s11365-014-0351-2

Tumasjan, A., & Braun, R. (2012). In the eye of the beholder: How regulatory focus and self-efficacy interact in influencing opportunity recognition. *Journal of Business Venturing*, 27(6), 622–636. DOI: 10.1016/j.jbusvent.2011.08.001

Voorhees, C. M., Brady, M. K., Calantone, R., & Ramirez, E. (2015). Discriminant validity testing in marketing: An analysis, causes for concern, and proposed remedies. *Journal of the Academy of Marketing Science*, 44(1), 119–134. DOI: 10.1007/s11747-015-0455-4

Wang, B., Abdalla, E., Atrio-Barandela, F., & Pavón, D. (2016). Dark matter and dark energy interactions: Theoretical challenges, cosmological implications, and observational signatures. *Reports on Progress in Physics*, 79(9), 096901. DOI: 10.1088/0034-4885/79/9/096901 PMID: 27517328

Ward, T. B. (2004). Cognition, creativity, and entrepreneurship. *Journal of Business Venturing*, 19(2), 173–188. DOI: 10.1016/S0883-9026(03)00005-3

Welpe, I. M., Spörrle, M., Grichnik, D., Michl, T., & Audretsch, D. B. (2012). Emotions and Opportunities: The Interplay of Opportunity Evaluation, Fear, Joy, and Anger as Antecedent of Entrepreneurial Exploitation. *Entrepreneurship Theory and Practice*, 36(1), 69–96. DOI: 10.1111/j.1540-6520.2011.00481.x

Wu, W., Wang, H., Zheng, C., & Wu, Y. J. (2019). Effect of Narcissism, Psychopathy, and Machiavellianism on Entrepreneurial Intention—The Mediating of Entrepreneurial Self-Efficacy. *Frontiers in Psychology*, 10, 360. DOI: 10.3389/fpsyg.2019.00360 PMID: 30846958

Xiu'e, Z., & Kun, Z. (2018). The Relationship between Creativity and Entrepreneurial Intention: A Moderated Mediating Effect Model. *Foreign Economics & Management*, 40(03), 67–78.

Yu, X., Roy, S. K., Quazi, A., Nguyen, B., & Han, Y. (2017). Internet entrepreneurship and "the sharing of information" in an Internet-of-Things context. *Internet Research*, 27(1), 74–96. DOI: 10.1108/IntR-02-2015-0060

Zampetakis, L. A., & Moustakis, V. (2006). Linking creativity with entrepreneurial intentions: A structural approach. *The International Entrepreneurship and Management Journal*, 2(3), 413–428. DOI: 10.1007/s11365-006-0006-z

Zettler, I., Friedrich, N., & Hilbig, B. E. (2011). Dissecting work commitment: The Role of Machiavellianism. *Career Development International*, 16(1), 20–35. DOI: 10.1108/13620431111107793

Zhang, T., & Stough, R. (Eds.). (2013). *Entrepreneurship and Economic Growth in China*. World Scientific., DOI: 10.1142/7296

Zhao, H., Seibert, S. E., & Hills, G. E. (2005). The Mediating Role of Self-Efficacy in the Development of Entrepreneurial Intentions. *The Journal of Applied Psychology*, 90(6), 1265–1272. DOI: 10.1037/0021-9010.90.6.1265 PMID: 16316279

Zhou, J. (2008). New look at creativity in the entrepreneurial process. *Strategic Entrepreneurship Journal*, 2(1), 1–5. DOI: 10.1002/sej.38

Chapter 5
From Theory to Practice:
Essential Competencies for Success in International HRM

Seema Bhakuni
https://orcid.org/0000-0002-3885-9860
Doon Institute of Management and Research, India

ABSTRACT

International Human Resource Management is the coordination amongst three aspects of managing resources; the types of employees involved, HR related activities and the location of operations. The challenges arise because the workforce comes from and work in different countries. The essential abilities required for the success of IHRM are investigated in this research. HR professionals are required to manage difficult cultural, legal, and economic situations across international boundaries. The essential talents concisely related to IHRM identified are cultural intelligence, global talent management, strategic thinking, and ethical awareness. The actual implementation of these competencies in global organisations by drawing from recent research and case studies based on real-world situations is illustrated here. The results highlight the need of continual learning and flexibility for human resource practitioners. A complete framework for HRM professionals to improve their international HRM competencies is the goal of this research.

INTRODUCTION

The world has now become a global village. Any business which deems to operate in such an environment, has to maintain its international mindset and operations. It consists of successfully handling employees who come from diverse backgrounds of different countries, getting the most appropriate employee and making them work abroad. In other words, it is the management of a countrywide diverse workforce. While managing them, the challenge lies in managing different cultural background, language or the legalities prevailing in their home country. It is in fact, the management of HRM which is highly

DOI: 10.4018/979-8-3693-9230-0.ch005

diverse in all aspects. In IHRM, employees are appointed, placed, onboarded, developed as per needs and helped to acclimatise as per their prospective roles.

The geographical location of a country is just a political phenomenon these days if talked about the economic expansion prevalent today. The world has been termed as a global village in the contemporary world which also reflects the state of business today. If business is talked about, it reaches beyond the set boundaries. This has resulted into the formation of many transnational and multinational firms, which poses the requirement on HR managers to change their perspective from Human Resource Management to International Human Resource management.

The firms dealing internationally, must ensure that the HR policies they have formulated must cater to the needs of all the employees coming from diverse backgrounds. The HR managers must understand that they are managing people who have faced different culture, government regulations and an entirely different environment in the workplace since different countries have different culture, values, taxation, work hours, rights and norms based on the country specific circumstances.

It is necessary for human resource managers to possess particular competencies, both personally and professionally, to be successful in the global arena. These competencies are necessary for them to contribute to the organisation. Careful implementation of International Human Resource Management is important in the context that the expenditure associated with dealing and training with an expatriate is so high that it becomes difficult for some companies to bear the cost of the same easily and its failure can lead to fatal lose to the company. Other than that, as per (Dowling and Welch, 2004) there are certain other factors which cannot be controlled by the internal experts of the company i.e. governmental regulations or pressure from highly influential groups which could have vested or social interest in this spectrum.

Although it is still in its infancy as a business discipline and as a field of study at academic institutions, "International Human Resource Management" (IHRM) is pretty genuine and has been firmly established (Adler & Ghadar, 1990). IHRM research examines how different companies are dealing with the present HRM; is it with the olden policies or they have changed themselves to formulate new policies. The previous research done on IHRM reflects that IHRM is a broader phenomenon, so they focused on how MNCs and MNEs work to get positive IHRM. Very soon it was understood that companies who have started working internationally, have to work differently to pace up with the changing scenario. The need of managing expatriates in a different way was felt during this phase, as research made it clear that the management of local nationals is completely different from international workers and that has to be tackled differently. The companies who are working internally must have the HRs who are aware of the rules and regulations followed in different countries and the possible problems the employees could face in a different country and draft the training accordingly for the employees who they plan to send to any other country for work. At the same time, all these plans and processes should be under the budgetary constraints of the company.

Lags in the previous studies

The previous studies have been done in the context of how IHRM works but this study will not only focus on the work but the challenges IHRM face while dealing with the expatriates, the policies or the other factors related to it. The various paths of progress factors within organizations, unique cultural aspects, preferences and connections of those involved, have displayed unwavering strength to adapt themselves to changing scenarios over time. This has led to a range of viewpoints on defining the realm of International Human Resource Management (IHRM) and its crucial factors within an expanding collection of writings despite it being considered new. (Welch,1994). Despite all the studies focusing on getting into the details related to IHRM, it is still in its infancy and most of it is left for exploration. The present challenges are completely different from the previous one because of the ever dynamic nature of the world. Since Laurent classified the field of human resource management as being in its infancy in the 1980s only, there is little doubt that the empirical and theoretical foundations of IHRM, together with their implementation in practice, have made significant advancements (Björkman and Stahl, 2006) since then. Furthermore, in a recent survey of the topic, (Thomas, D. C., & Lazarova, M. B., 2013) presents an optimistic argument, claiming that "as a field of research, IHRM is vibrant and diverse and has grown even more so in the past decade" (Schuler et al., 2002; Scullion, 2004; Björkman and Stahl, 2006; Lazarova, 2006). This is an upbeat and positive argument. It would have been beyond the scope of this study to provide a comprehensive assessment of the current condition of the field of human resource management (IHRM) at the beginning of the 21st century.

What's new in the present study?

The past studies have given an insight on the IHRM practices followed in MNCs in the past decade but since then many changes have come into force. They have posed the working conditions of the international HR managers. Rather, this chapter will present an overview of some significant challenges in IHRM and concentrate on the future possibilities for IHRM within the field. This is because it would be beyond the scope of this study to offer such an assessment (Scullion et al., 2007). The IHRM studies have mainly centered on staff, so it's crucial for upcoming research to consider the entire workforce of multinational enterprises (MNEs) and even extend further to encompass their CSR strategy. This will help in catering to the requirements of individuals who are experiencing heightened levels of insecurity, disempowerment and vulnerability due, to the pandemic. (Caligiuri, P., De Cieri, H., Minbaeva, D., Verbeke, A., & Zimmermann, A., 2020).

In the beginning, this study will discuss international human resource management (IHRM) in a broad sense. After that, the focus will be on significant differences that exist between IHRM and domestic HRM. In the second part of this chapter, we cover the topic of generating new issues in international human resource management (IHRM). These concerns include development and the challenges of implementing IHRM in the context of globalisation, as well as the advantages and disadvantages of effectively localising a firm. As a third point, we discuss talent management in particular, in addition to other topics that are related with integrated human resource management. In such settings HR tasks tend to increase due to the need to handle activities, that are not typically required in a local context. These activities include dealing with taxation, assisting with relocation and integration into cultures managing relationships, with host governments and providing language translation services. Moreover, managing HR on a bigger scale, demands an extensive viewpoint as international HR managers must take into account a diverse set of factors when making decisions. (Morley, Michael & Heraty, Noreen & Collings, David., 2006). An analysis of the future of integrated human resource management (IHRM) as both a subject of study and an important component of management practice is presented in the last section of his article. In today's changing economy it is becoming more common to see multinational corporations (MNCs) taking the lead. However, as these MNCs grow and operate in countries they encounter hurdles especially in managing their international human resources effectively. (Schipper, M. 2023).

International HRM: Important characteristics

1. International Human Resource Management (IHRM) focuses on hiring the candidates for specific roles regardless of where they are located geographically.
2. It involves creating a HR plan that aligns effectively with the goals of the organization, over an extended period.
3. Providing employees with a set of skills is essential, for those who are required to operate across international borders. It necessitates the determination of compensation to cater to individuals, from backgrounds including locals, residents and foreigners considering factors relevant to each country.
4. Establishing reporting structures worldwide to enhance the exchange of information promptly.
5. Implementing both informal techniques to merge different segments of the global business.
6. Setting up an evaluation system to evaluate employee performance across locations and countries efficiently.
7. Recognizing the aspects of host countries that impact HR operations is crucial.
8. Maintaining communication among all sectors and individuals within the organization at a scale, is vital.
9. The value related perception of HR activities, often varies across international company locations.

IHRM: The varied functions associated with it.

Globalization, which involves aligning a company's activities and plans across cultures, and the products and concepts, is influencing the responsibilities of human resource managers. Previously focused on how local matters affect staff members human resources now need to take into account the impacts of diversity, in the workforce legal constraints and the connection between training and career growth within the company. Therefore, understanding the various functions relevant to today's human resource management is crucial for effectively running a business.

Attracting, hiring and retaining employees are the different aspects associated with human resources management. This involves tasks such as elaborating on job related details, conducting interviews, extending job offers and discussing compensation packages. Organizations that understand the importance of their workforce, give importance to the recruitment process in the HR processes. This emphasis is justified, as having a competent team can enhance the company's reputation drive towards profitability and ensure smooth operations.

When a company hires workers, there is usually a need for some form of on-the-job training that the HR department is responsible for providing. This is because each organization carries out tasks in its own way. There could be possible differences on two company's tackling of the same jobs or the way of working. Regardless of the processes within the organization, HR must play an innovative role in delivering contemporary useful training to the employees. The importance of training becomes more pronounced, when an organization operates globally across locations. Having standardized processes across these locations makes communication and resource sharing much easier to manage.

Professional development which is closely linked to training, also falls under HRs purview. While training focuses on the organizations' operations and procedures, professional development focuses on offering employees the chances for their development and education. Many HR departments provide development opportunities by disseminating funds for employees to attend productive conferences, external skills training sessions or industry trade shows. This beneficial arrangement helps employees feel valued and supported within the team while enabling the organization to benefit from their enhanced skill set and motivation.

Giving benefits and compensation and managing them properly, has always been an aspect of Human Resource. However, with the increasing globalization of companies in the new era, HR now faces the challenge of adapting to methods of providing employee benefits which cannot be challenged and considered just and fair. Offering traditional perks like flexible work schedules, paternity leave, extended vacations and remote work options serve as effective ways to motivate current staff members and attract top talent. Striking a balance between compensation and benefits for employees is crucial in HR.

Another indispensable function of human resource management which holds importance, is compliance with labour laws and tax regulation. Ensuring compliance with labour laws and tax regulations is essential for the organizations' sustainability. Both federal and local governments impose regulations on companies regarding employees' working hours, tax deductions, mandated breaks, minimum wage requirements and anti-discrimination policies. Staying informed about these laws and guidelines while ensuring adherence is a critical responsibility that falls under human resource and holds more importance in IHRM.

To conclude on this particular aspect of HRM and the functions associated with it, we can say that the manager's job has become significantly different because the world is becoming a global village. No one can be contented with the limited knowledge he has attained as per the HRM of one country. With the opening of many MNCs and inter country wide corporations, it has become apparent that the HR manager must poses capabilities to deal with the employees having different cultural backgrounds, languages, attitudes and behavioural variations. HRM deals with recruitment, training, development, legal compliances and many more. So, HR manager cannot be limited to having the knowledge of one country's people and regulations when it is obvious that the world is coming together with the advent of many transnational ventures, which need someone who can deal efficiently with the culture and employees of a different country employed in any organisation of any other country.

International vs. Domestic HRM

During the early stages of the academic investigation that surrounded "International human resource management (IHRM)," a number of researchers proposed that IHRM is distinct from its domestic equivalent in terms of a number of differences. (Dowling, 1988). This viewpoint is brought up to date by the following. A study by (Scullion, H, Collings, D, Gunnigle I. P., 2007) stated that similarities in world-wide systems are brought out by external competitions which include approved best practices like benchmarking, information security tools and systems. Since the day IHRM has become a subject of deep insight, many researchers suggest that IHRM is completely different from HRM and how it is handled in the domestic arena. (Dowling, 1988). It is also discovered that IHRM is a not so simple phenomenon as compared to its domestic counterpart because the employees in an international setup come from diverse backgrounds but they act together in an organisational setup and follow the same rules and regulations as formulised by any organisation. (Smerek, Lukáš and Vetrakova, Milota and Šimočková, Ivana., March 2021). The expansion of business operations, into countries, known as globalization has an impact on various aspects such, as employment, human resource development (HRD) compensation and labour relations. The international Human Resource Management (HRM) model consists of three factors; HR practices, the country where operations are conducted and the characteristics of employees involved. There are four approaches used while making international recruitment – ethnocentric, polycentric, geocentric and regiocentric.

The practice of human resource management (HRM) in the international setting is distinct from its counterpart in the domestic context in a number of ways, and it deems mandatory to be aware of this fact. The IHRM department of a multinational corporation is included in this category. (1) having responsibility for a higher variety of activities, such as the administration of overseas assignees, which involves elements such as foreign taxes and work permits, as well as providing thorough support with family relocations to foreign places; (2) requiring the expansion of its areas of competence to include a somewhat larger viewpoint, which includes knowledge of employment regulations in other nations; (3)based on the factual information that the company is moving personnel from one nation to another, it is immensely significant to become much more engaged in the lives of employees and their families than is ever required in a scenario that is solely domestic in nature; (4) being associated with a far larger and more diverse pool of personnel, which adds a significant amount of complexity to the process of managing human resources; (5) being forced to deal with a greater number of external influences, such as dealing with problems that originate from a variety of nations and cultures; and as a consequence, (6)having to deal with a significantly increased number of challenges and obstacles, and thus, being exposed to a much higher number of possible liabilities for making errors in human resource choices (for instance, the cost of a failed overseas assignment may be as high as one million dollars in the United States) (Claus, 1998; Tarique et al., 2015).

When we become inclined towards learning about and managing the new foreign obligations, the average domestic human resource manager in the United States does not have the relationships or networks that are required. As a general rule, he or she does not have any prior experience with the business and social conventions that are necessary for interacting effectively with colleagues from other countries, nor does he or she have any prior knowledge of the organisational structures that are used to pursue international plans (such as joint ventures or cross-border acquisitions). (Tarique et al., 2015). The core principle of managing International Human Resource Management (IHRM) involves assigning employees and managers so that they could oversee operations at both subsidiary and parent company levels. These individuals should possess an understanding of the tasks at hand, demonstrate awareness and take accountability for the outcomes of their work. (Smerek, Lukáš and Vetrakova, Milota and Šimočková, Ivana., March 2021).

Furthermore, the still relatively small body of literature as well as the publicly accessible seminars and training programmes make it far more challenging to build the competences that are necessary for effectively managing the intra-organizational human resource management role.

Conclusion

Thus, it can be summed up with the discussion that HRM and IHRM are different in many aspects with the former being dealing with the people who posses most of the characteristics as his own and the latter has to deal with people who come from diverse countries, backgrounds and cultures. What might be considered good in a country, may have wrong implications in a different country. In the organisations set up in different countries, there is a mix of home country, host country or third country nationals. This poses serious responsibilities on the manager to deal with people, things and conflicts in an entirely analytical and dexterous way. HRM needs important traits and characteristics that the manager must posses but it becomes easier in the home country if compared to IHRM where the manager has to sometimes deal with the cultural shock also.

Emerging Issues in IHRM

In managing the International Human Resource Management (IHRM) processes, the key focus is on ensuring that both the subsidiaries and the main company are staffed with employees and managers, who grasp the nature of their roles, possess a perspective and bear responsibility of the work done and its outcomes. The globalisation of human resource management has given rise to a multitude of problems, including the following: (1) The Evolution of Integrated Human Resource Management, (2) Challenges Facing Human Resource Management Around the World, (3) Problems Associated with Globalisation and Localization, (4) The Effective Method of Localization in IHRM, (5) The Benefits of Effective Human Resource Localization in International Human Resource Management, and (6) There are certain drawbacks associated with successful HR localization in IHRM. Globalization significantly affects employment patterns by businesses to structure their operations around their strengths, in order to effectively address competitive challenges. (Krishna. Vaishali, 2021). In our examination of the evolving landscape of International Human Resource Management (IHRM), we delve into a theme regarding the ongoing relevance of the conventional expatriate assignments. This discussion arises in light of challenges such as rising demand for assignees and a diminishing pool of candidates. (Collings, D.G., Scullion, H. and Morley, M.J., 2007). Financial gains and opportunities for career advancement linked to varied assignments are often those factors that motivate employees to embrace international opportunities. (Holden, 1997;685) explores various bodies of literature that gives deeper insight on HRM in international settings and its appropriate implementation. He identifies deeper insight to the literature related to HRM including international management, which he notes can be observed both nationally and internationally and maintains that international HRM literature focus on comparative issues relevant to single nation; literature on comparing industrial and employment relations; discussions centered around multinational corporations; and studies on culture and acculturation. A key takeaway from these sources as per Holden is the idea that IHRM can be examined within organizational and national contexts by comparing them both.

Conclusion

According to Wong (2000) there are ten tasks that international HR managers need to handle; including planning for assignments and costs, selecting candidates, documenting assignment, terms and conditions managing relocation and vendors providing language orientation/training, administering compensation, processing payroll, managing taxes, planning career development, addressing spouse and dependent issues as well as handling immigration processes. With that, the discussion concludes with the fact that IHRM has its own set of problems. It is not as comfortable to deal with human resources in the home country with having all the like-minded people coming for work from more or less the same homogeneous background. The problems can pop-up even when the manager himself is trying to accommodate to the new surroundings. The challenges could be related to cultural shock, recruitment, work-hours, norms, legal compliances, rules of the country, informal groups in the organisation or such other factors.

The Development of IHRM

Managers of human resources in almost every kind of company are able to and do encounter issues that are associated with international human resources. The extent to which this participation is involved will vary to a great extent based on a wide range of various conditions, and it will always increase over the course of time. While this is going on, it is projected that human resource managers will be required to provide an increasing amount of expertise to the process of internationalisation of businesses. This is because the breadth and intensity of internationalisation of companies will continue to increase (Tarique et al., 2015).

The ability to identify (either through recruitment or training) human resource managers who are capable of effectively interacting with and managing individuals from contrasting cultural base, despite their own cultural upbringing and experience, is the unavoidable fundamental challenge that must be overcome in order to achieve successful human resource management. On top of that, these managers need to be able to devise and put into action efficient human resource policies and procedures across a variety of business contexts in which the company works. Furthermore, it is necessary for them to provide assistance to firm leaders in the process of planning and managing efficiently within these many contexts concurrently (Harris et al., 2003).

Interpersonal and Human Resource Management (IHRM) is still in its embryonic years, both as a discipline of study in the academic world and as a functional area of business. This may be ascribed, at least in part, to the generally limited role that human resource management plays inside a great number of significant firms, even enormous multinational corporations (some of which is due to HR managers themselves. (Kopp, 1993). Human resource professionals have been called upon to handle a variety of new operations all of a sudden during the course of the last twenty years or more, as a result of the fast internationalisation of business in general. These activities include the organisation of assignees who live abroad, the management of HR mangers belonging to other countries, and the adaptation of HR methods to multi-cultural and cross-cultural situations. Additional activities include the management of employees who have been assigned work internationally (Clause, 1998). To improve operations using International Human Resource Management (IHRM) policies and practices, it's essential to align HR strategies, with the organization's approach, local customs and legal framework. (Hofstede, 1998).

The delayed awakening of international commerce in US firms and its dominance on human resources has been linked to a range of various explanations, which have been put forth in order to explain the phenomena (Clause, 1998, 1999). Additionally, schools imparting business education and professional human resource organisations have been cautious to include courses in international human resources into their educational offerings. To a large extent, professionals working in human resources have not been successful in incorporating globalisation into their development strategies (Laurent, 1986). In fact, they have only just begun to comprehend the significance of carrying out such an endeavour. In addition, human resource managers are frequently the last members of their companies to lay stress on the manifesting globalised economy, the last members of the management team to accept international assignments, and consequently, the last members of the management team to be productive as fully-fledged strategic counterparts in the process of internationalising their businesses. This is because human resource managers are the ones who are responsible for managing human resources (Tarique et al., 2015).

The lack of professionalisation of international human resources (IHR) and the wide bifurcation of variety of functional areas within HR practice, leads to giving less importance based on evaluation to international activities by other HR practitioners, the lag and lack of deep insight about varied cultural issues by domestic or in-home HR practitioners are some of the many reasons that lead to the delayed awakening of HR managers towards the importance of international HRM. (Clause, 1998, 1999).

Conclusion

It is clear that there is a separate body with updated knowledge about the recent trends worldwide that acts as a very crucial starting point in the area of international human resource management (IHRM). To provide just one example, the International Journal of Human Resource Management is one of the few periodicals that focuses only on this subject matter. There are few more which devote not specifically yet broadly devoted to human resources, have either formed specific sections that are dedicated to IHR or have additional newsletters or articles that are more often devoted to IHR. Both of these approaches are examples of how IHR has been incorporated into other publications. There has been a consistent increase in readings and texts, as well as in the number of seminars and courses that are being provided by educational institutions, corporate consulting firms, and training groups. Furthermore, the quantity of readings and texts has steadily increased over the course of an extended period of time (Caliguiri, 1999).

In general, there are two very distinct points of view that might be held while investigating topics pertaining to IHRM (Tarique et al., 2015). These comprises the following:

1. Discussions of human resource policies and procedures, as well as the human resource function and department inside the multinational corporation, with a particular emphasis on managing the company's personnels as well as concerns about the organization's overall strategy and organisational structure.
2. Discussions about human resource practices and policies in different nations as well as features of those countries which are particularly centred on the phenomenon of "comparative" human resource management.

International Human Resource Management: The challenges

When it comes to increasing their foreign direct investment (FDI), the majority of businesses face a significant challenge in the form of effectively integrating managers from the host country national (HCN) into the management of their subsidiaries situated in any other foreign land as well as the management structure of the larger corporation (Keeley, 2001). This is a challenge that they face because it is a significant obstacle. Businesses confront a variety of issues that are related with the adoption of HCN managers when it falls in the preview of internationalisation of human resource management (HRM). Managers of human resources are expected to analyse and determine the degree to which HCN managers are really involved in the management processes as an outcome based on that. In order to do this, it becomes indispensable to address the challenges that are connected with international human resource management (IHRM), management that takes into consideration diverse cultures, and management that is multinational. The increasing worldwide unpredictability influences the assumptions about talent management, particularly while selecting and evaluating criteria for an enterprise's talent pool. Even though there have been advancements in acknowledging the significance of such context yet it remains a matter of debate. (Vaiman, Sparrow, Schuler & Collings, 2018). The overall management method of the parent company, the transferability of management practices from the parent company to overseas subsidiaries, and other issues that are linked to these themes that are now being discussed are among the most significant topics. Analysing and interpreting the role of HCN managers not only sheds light on the method in which multinational companies (MNCs) manage their overseas operations but also provides insights into international human resource management (IHRM) from the perspective of the HCN managers themselves. This is what makes the investigation of HCN managers so valuable (Keeley, 2001). The challenges which managers face while tackling the employees:

Cultural differences: Managing cultural diversity poses a hurdle, for International Human Resource Management (IHRM) in Multinational Corporations (MNCs). The varying cultural norms can result in communication challenges, misunderstandings and hindered cross cultural interactions. It is crucial for MNCs to acknowledge and value the cultures of their workforce, clients and partners, across nations. Failure to navigate these differences appropriately could result in missed business prospects, reduced employee morale and potential legal conflicts.

Language barriers: Navigating language differences can pose a hurdle, in managing resources within multinational corporations. With operations spanning across countries, it's crucial for MNCs to establish communication channels with their staff, clients and partners. Failing to communicate in the tongue can result in misinterpretations reduced employee involvement and challenges, in executing company initiatives. (Damodharan & Ravichandran, 2019).

Compensation and benefits: Multinational corporations often encounter difficulties when crafting and enforcing compensation and benefit packages that are equitable and suitable across countries. Disparities in labour regulations, tax laws and cultural practices, can result in differences in wages and perks among employees stationed in nations. Such variations may contribute to dissatisfaction among employees, higher turnover rates as diminished morale and drive. Moreover, maintaining employee retention poses a challenge for International Human Resource Management (IHRM) within corporations. The budgetary limitations linked with turnover, recruitment costs, training investments and the degradation of expertise, can be substantial for MNCs. To address this issue effectively MNCs need to offer avenues for growth learning opportunities and clearly defined pathways, for career progression to their employees. (Meijer, S., 2003).

Conclusion

Unlike HRM, IHRM is a wide aspect which needs substantial concentration from the end of all those who are involved in multi-national organizations. Other than language, culture, rewards based on diverse attitudes, there are manifold factors which poses challenge to IHRM. The manager who deals with IHRM has to learn about different cultures, the barriers, attitude of people in different countries, legal compliances and every minute detail of the expatriates so as to tackle the conflicting and crucial situations aptly. IHRM is a broad concept. Its spectrum can be judged on the basis of the tasks and processes it handles which are boundary-less in the sense that it has no limit of culture constraints, nothing to do with the regulations of one country and dealing with people having entirely different characteristics due to their diverse upbringing.

The Globalization and Localization Issues

Over the course of the last several years, it has become more usual for national and multinational businesses (MNCs) to concurrently work in such a manner that both global and local goals are achieved. Multiple multinational companies (MNCs) should work towards the goal of achieving global efficiency and competitive advantage by integrating their various processes all over the world to the greatest degree that is practically possible. It is essential for them to give some thought to the ways in which they may best utilise their resources, be it the materials or human, in the utmost productive and effective manner that is possible. If an organisation has such a mission, it indicates that it will overlook the factor of national origin when it comes to the acquisition and utilisation of available resources (human resource included), and it will have a universal agreement on the acquisition and utilisation of resources. (Meyer, 2006) deems that an MNC act as an interconnection between finances, thoughts, value system, ideals and knowledge base world-wide which brings underdeveloped, developed and developing economies together.

Multinational businesses (MNCs), on the contrary, need to make it a top priority to be attentive to and responsive to the reality of local communities. In the framework of a strategy for global integration, they need to take into consideration, to the maximum degree feasible, the requirements and preferences of the people who live in the area (Bartlett and Ghoshal, 1989; Scullion& Collings, 2006).

Because Japanese corporations have significantly expanded their worldwide operations during the course of the 1980s and 1990s, there is now a shortage of professional Japanese PCN managers who are able to take management positions at overseas subsidiaries. This need has resulted in a shortage of Japanese PCN managers. Additionally, the extravagant expenditure of maintaining such a large number of PCN managers at foreign subsidiaries alongwith the complaints from HCN workers and local authorities, underscore the need of integrating HCNs into the management process, which has important ramifications. The majority of Japanese and Asian multinational firms have a significant quantity of data that indicates the need to work a lot prior to reaching that level (Lazarova, 2006). This is because the majority of these corporations have not yet reached the degree of organisational development that they possess. Because they are taking part in significant amounts of foreign direct investment (FDI), firms are becoming more global. In accordance with Wingrove, her conclusions are derived from an examination of well-known Japanese firms that are now operating in the United Kingdom. Mitsubishi Electric, Hitachi Power Tools, Kobe Steel, and Mitsui & Company are some of the firms that fall under this category (Yoshihara, 1994; Kopp, 1993). She made the striking discovery that practically all of the uppermost executive positions are held by Japanese citizens who are now residing outside of Japan. Furthermore, Wingrove contends that even in situations when decision-making is rests with the managers in European markets, the Japanese culture of consensus still necessitates complete engagement with the head office in Japan (Wingrove, 1997, Keeley, 2001). It is her belief that Japanese parent firms have a high degree of control over the operations of their overseas subsidiaries, and that a considerable percentage of Japanese overseas manufacturing subsidiaries have not evolved beyond the level of a screwdriver plant. She also states that the Japanese parent corporations have strong control over the operations of their host country subsidiaries. In terms of internationalisation, Japanese corporations are ten to twenty years behind their international counterparts, according to Shoichiro Irimajiri, senior managing director of Honda, who was cited as stating this by (Keeley, 2001).

Conclusion

As a consequence of the alterations that have taken place in the global environment over the course of the past twenty years, the vast majority of firms are being compelled to give globalisation and localization problems a more serious thought. Companies of all sizes have created or extended their manufacturing operations in other nations as a consequence of a variety of circumstances, including the higher value of a country's currency and the friction that occurs in trade. These factors were contributary to the growth of these establishments (Keeley, 2001). (Walker, 1992;93) highlights that international HRM presents challenges compared to HRM, such, as managing a wider range of functional tasks due, to varying taxation and regulatory landscapes facilitating global employee relocation and onboarding and navigating language and cultural diversity.

Successful Localization in IHRM

IHRM in human resource management relates to managing employees who live in wide distances across the globe probably in very different locations from the one which they originally belong to. (Natter 2020). Hence, expanding recruitment efforts not only improves product quality and attracts top talent but also secures a critical role in enhancing brand visibility across different nations. This means that recruiting initiatives can serve as both a strategy to elevate brand recognition in markets and a method to establish connections within talent pools benefiting both recruitment and marketing endeavors. (Lander n.d.). As stated by the International Human Resource Management (IHRM), the process of localization has developed into a key challenge in the management of multinational businesses. Each and every human resource manager is obligated to take into account this matter as a significant and essential component in the approaching employment procedure (Evans et al., 2002). Nevertheless, the concept is often addressed in broad terms, without any specific dentition being specified at any point. Hideo Sugiura, a former vice-chairman of Honda, proposed a differentiation between four separate types of localization in this context (Scullion & Collings, 2006). These forms of localization are as follows: localization of products, localization of profit, localization of production, and localization of people. For the sake of the objectives that are there, this chapter devotes a significant amount of attention to the problem of the localization of persons. As far as this perspective is concerned, the word "localization" (which is often addressed as "labour nationalisation," "host country national development," or "indigenization") is defined as "the extent to which jobs that were initially filled by expatriates are filled by local employees who are competent to perform the job" (Selmer, 2004). If talked about the employment policies of many nation-states, localization is generally regarded to be one of the key variables that contributes to the decision-making process. The relationships that the state has with international organisations that are striving to function inside their national limitations are also impacted by localization (Evans et al., 2002). This is another way in which localization's influence may be seen.

Conclusion

The process of localization is described as the one in which systematic investments are made in the recruitment, development, and retention of local individuals. Out of the many important aspects, one important aspects of the globalisation plan that multinational firms use is this vital component (Scullion & Collings, 2006). Hence, the localisation of the IHR manager is a big challenge as it cannot be expected from a human being to attain expertise in all the international assignments and deal with the expatriates without fail in any aspect of his diversity.

Benefits of HR Localization That Works in IHRM

A capable human resources manager should discuss with other key management strategic decision makers within the organisation, a comparison of the benefits and disadvantages of various expatriate and local employment methods. This comparison helps to select the plan that is most suitable for the multinational corporation. A variety of benedictions that are beneficial to the company are brought about as a consequence of the use of local staff rather than foreigners to fill critical jobs within international operations. These benefits are often overstated, particularly for topmost positions, for reasons that are sometimes based on racial or national stereotypes. This is especially true for senior positions. Additionally, this in particular, is true for positions of seniority. (Banai, 1992).

There are at least four major advantages that come along with the successful implementation of localization policy. To begin, the localization of human resources has the ability to develop relationships between the governments of host nations and national investors from other countries. This is achieved via the utilisation of human resources (Selmer, 2004). Therefore, from the perspective of the multinational corporation (MNC), a localization plan may be of assistance in ensuring that overseas operations are carried out with minimal levels of friction with the authorities of the host country, while simultaneously gaining more buy-in and assistance from the government of the host country. The second advantage of localising human resources is that it has the ability to improve communication channel and, finally, the performance of enterprises in the country that is hosting the firm. The communication that takes place between natives is, in general, more effective than the communication that takes place between foreigners and natives (Black and Gregerson 1992). Temporary workers, even if they remain in the nation for a lengthy amount of time, have a conflicting loyalty and almost certainly perceive their ultimate objective as being in a different location. Third, labour from the host country is often a more stable resource if compared to temporary employees. Fourth, from the economic point of attention, the organisation is able to increase the capital gain of the local people by responding to the needs of the local community, notably by investing money and hiring local workers. This is important because it allows the organisation to grow the remuneration of the local people. The ability of the local populace to acquire products and services that are provided by local companies is therefore improved as a result of this. In spite of the fact that the market is relatively small and has not yet matured, there is still the chance of major growth and long-term profit (Prahalad, 2004; Scullion & Collings, 2006).

Conclusion

Localisation has a significant impact on IHRM where positive outcome can be attained through assistance from the government of the host country for which the company has to work before setting up the organisation overseas, the IHR manager must be aware of the local culture and attitude people carry and he must have skills to adapt to the different circumstances so that he is able to counsel his employees to align their culture with the organisational aim and respect the policies of the parent country also, the communication that takes place between natives and the expatriates must be transparent and they must be ready to understand and value the differences.

Benefits and drawbacks of HR localization for IHRM

When it is related to the process of developing a localization policy, there are four key negatives that are linked with it. In the beginning, it is necessary to invest a reasonable quantity of time, effort, and financial resources in order to get an understanding of the native market. Second, there are negatives connected with the challenges that generate the focus towards making modifications to work policy and practice in order to comply to the circumstances that are widespread in the local region (Yoshihara, 1994). These adjustments are necessary in order to cope up with the existing conditions. Third, when there is a need to managing without expatriates, there is less effective coordination from the headquarters' point of view, and there may be more difficulties in connecting with the headquarters from the subsidiary's point of view. In the fourth place, top headquarters managers are very concerned about the possibility of losing their intellectual property rights when it reaches to the preview of the localization plan. This is especially true in developing countries, where people have the impression that anything can be replicated. This is what (Selmer, 2004) refers to as a "agency problem," and he believes that the presence of expatriates may assist to prevent local managers from following their own personal self-interests when it comes to managing the subsidiary or from making choices that does not align with the organization's overall plan (Scullion & Collings, 2006). Localizing content is a task that hinges on planning and the formulation of a sound strategy. Executing this strategy effectively necessitates backing from management and the establishment of HR policies that align with both the strategy and the local environment. When these criteria are fulfilled, localization can become a component of a corporation's global expansion approach. (Scullion, H & Colling, G. D, 2006)

Conclusion

If we see from the negative aspects, like any other factor, HRM has its own negative side. This does not mean that we must give up on the basis of its negatives but it gives us a firm foundation to work on the possible negatives. There could be financial, time related and other constraints because setting up a corporation in any other country, would have an investment of extra capital. On top of that, spending on the training of manager would come as an extra expenditure. The company's own well established policies need to be accommodated according to the host country. But these issues can be taken care of by systematically working on them. A team specifically consisting of expatriates and local people, must be appointed for devising pre-plans for any such issues which are likely occur in future related to IHRM.

International Talent Management Issues in IHRM

Numerous significant global issues that companies confront today are closely linked to challenges with resources. This realization is increasingly acknowledged by human resource professionals and consultants who are working for companies on a global level. (Tarique, Ibraiz & Schuler, Randall., 2010). Due to the necessity to handle the increased mobility of labour in a more streamlined way, the majority of top multinational corporations are increasingly seeking to combine local recruiting methods with a universal strategy in this era of globalisation. This way of working is only set to intensify in the future decade. In order to achieve effective management in new volatile markets, human resource managers need to take into consideration not only the credentials of workers and their appropriate job experience, but also the abilities of other employees and their entire potential (Patel, 2002). The challenges surrounding the training of managers, the under-representation of women in international management roles and the limitations faced by companies in retaining international talent are all pressing concerns. These issues are gaining importance as companies grapple with a shortage of professionals who are competent in navigating global business strategies effectively. (Scullion, 1992).

Conclusion

With the advent of more and more international companies, it has become evident that more of multi dexterous managers are required for handling the international corporations. International organisations need employees who are efficient in their field and that has broken barriers of boundaries, gender or cultural gap. It has led to the participation and employment of anyone irrespective of culture, gender, geographical boundaries, language or other significant differences.

Employer branding and the talent pipeline: Challenges for effective IHRM

The observation that in order for international human resource managers to effectively manage talent in an international setting, it's a prerequisite that they must deeply understand that there is an alignment between the aim of business and the present competence of the most intellectual and talented employees of the organisation. It must also be understood that how many of these talented employees wish to mobilise for further development. (Sparrow et al.2004). (Wright and McMahan, 1992) have stated that he amalgamation of systems, processes and practices within the organization, effectively protects the efficiency of talent management. Regarding talent development, international assignments are used to upskill global talent as assignees, to immerse such talent in a host culture, and to teach them how to be effective global leaders within the MNE (Welch 2003). Through vast experience in International Human Resource Management (IHRM), we have gained insights into the various difficulties which the individuals encounter in diverse Multinational Enterprise's (MNEs) work setups. These challenges include varied roles, virtual global work environments, collaboration in project teams and regular international travel. (Shaffer, Kraimer, Chen & Bolino, 2012). Additionally, talent management on a global scale has some broader elements, which illustrates that, in fact, talent markets continue to work very much inside the national settings of the various countries. This is especially true in the case of the United States (Harris et al., 2003). Working in international companies, present hurdles for global teams as they must navigate across various boundaries including countries, regions, cultures, institutions and different units within the company. (Zimmermann, 2011).

Conclusion

From the ongoing discussion, it can be concluded that the value of talent management heavily relies on the comprehending skills of human resource management. This is because the business agenda is directly related to the present potential of the highly talented people in the organisation. This "calibration" attempt of talent on a worldwide level often requires multinational firms, especially HR personnel, to take care of talent on a wider basis, and also to think deeply into "who they are" and "what they stand for".

Benefits and Drawbacks of MNCs Using Host Country Managers

Four underlying assumptions, all of which lead to the same conclusion, provide support for the significance of the efficient integration of HCNs via their successful integration (Keeley, 2001). There is a tendency that is both helpful and widespread among multinational companies (MNCs) nationwide, and that trend is the globalization of human resource management policies and procedures. (Selmer, 2004) states that the involvement of expatriates play a critical part in helping the localization process to work smoothly. Expatriates not only bring in skills and knowledge but also serve as role models passing on their attitudes, behaviors and standards for locals to follow. If an expatriate is non-cooperative, sceptical or incapable it can delay the implementation of localization efforts. It lies with an expatriate that he creates a foundation of trust between them and the local employees (Home country nationals) so that localization stands a better chance of achieving its goals, particularly where there is a climate of trust between expatriate and HCNs. With regard to competitiveness, multinational corporations (MNCs) that do not globalize their activities in an appropriate manner may divulge into certain disadvantage in comparison to their peers. In the second place, "International human resource management (IHRM) offers competitive advantages, which can only be fully exploited by making use of the expertise of human capital directors (HCN). Multinational businesses (MNCs) need to have an understanding of how to create and maintain strong human capital managers to ensure their long-term success. HCN managers should be given a prominent role in the administration of foreign subsidiaries, regardless of whether such subsidiaries are situated in their home country, at the parent company, or in a third nation, based on the capabilities that they possess. (Patel, 2002).

On the other hand, the opinion that if the parent company is unable to effectively incorporate HCN managers into the management process of foreign subsidiaries, this might potentially result in major negative impacts for the parent company. Concerns that fall under this category include poor productivity, low morale, internal unrest, and high personnel turnover. Other considerations include low morale. Additionally, discrimination against HCNs and/or the failure to provide just and equal chance for qualified HCNs so that they could take up positions of managerial responsibility may result in issues with the government authorities of the host country (for example, Japanese businesses have become notorious for their violations in this regard and have been facing the outcome of their actions that have been brought about by their actions. (Keeley, 2001).

Conclusion

It can be validated by this discussion that the hiring of HCNs in management roles offers a number of advantages to the multinational business (MNC), forming on to the advantages that are enjoyed by the nation that is hosting the HCNs. HCN managers often possess a natural knowledge of the local language(s) and culture(s) in the locations in which they are located. When compared to a parent country national (PCN) who is on his or her first task in the host country, it is more likely that they are acquainted with the local business and regulatory environment. This is because they have established a relationship with the local community. On top of that, the costs that are associated with the employment of HCNs are often a great deal cheaper than the costs that are associated with the employment of PCNs. As an added benefit, the hiring of HCN managers leads to the establishment of more opportunities for white-collar professionals working in the HCN. The country that is hosting the multinational firm receives extra benefits, including the transfer of managerial knowledge and expertise, as well as the enhancement of public relations related to the multinational organization being viewed as a good corporate citizen.

Towards an IHRM Future

There is a high probability that the future will bring about new strategic obstacles that multinational corporations (MNCs) will need to address and that will push new directions in the field of human resource management (IHRM). This is in addition to the strategic human resource management (IHRM) issues and challenges that MNCs are currently facing. The reason for this is because dynamic difficulties, such as an increasing number of foreign workers moving to the United States in quest of better salaries and a higher quality of life that they can supply for themselves, are causing this situation. Certain policies and practices in International Human Resource Management (IHRM) have attracted high levels of research focus in the areas of recruitment and training. We have highlighted areas for research to make gradual progress in these specific domains as well as in areas that have received less attention historically. It is crucial to establish connections between HRM policies and the behavioral and financial results or performance of individual business units and the organization as a whole. (Becker et al. 2001). Additionally, the related geographical dispersion (as a result of people transferring) would lead to increasing cross-cultural issues, notably for expatriate workers and staff, which would affect the relative benefits for the majority of countries. (Keating, Mary & Thompson, Karen., 2004) say that they recognize the importance of starting a theory that combines the three aspects of International Human Resource Management (IHRM) within a framework that incorporates disciplinary perspectives, cross-cultural discussions and literature related to this field. By exchanging ideas and methods between these aspects of research in the present field can be an inclusive approach to theory development that encompasses all related disciplines. They proposed that by engaging in comparative and cross-cultural discussions, research can yield valuable benefits. The global corporations will be compelled to deal with a necessity for competence and sensitivity that is not present in the local firms as a consequence of these difficulties that are now existent and those that are currently growing (Claus, 1998).

(Scullion, Hugh & Collings, David & Gunnigle, Patrick., 2007) stated that the organisations which are focusing on making themselves globally acclaimed, stress more on developing their people for taking up jobs as expert expatriates and global leaders. In the future, the personal and professional attitudes and views of the international human resources manager will be substantially enlarged in order to deal with the different nations and cultures that are faced in the worldwide arena. This is necessary in order to cope with the confrontations that come from working in the international arena. As per (Noruzi, Mohammad Reza & Rahimi, Gholam, 2010) Human resource managers whether working on a local scale or internationally, will consistently face national, social, cultural, educational, managerial and governmental structures within multinational enterprises. Therefore, they must receive training to equip themselves with skills which are crucial and expertise to effectively tackle this evolving challenge. In order to effectively manage their obligations in the area of human resources (IHR) and to make a positive contribution to the international business plans of their respective firms, this will be done. These dispositions and points of view will go beyond those that the domestic human resources manager has to cultivate in order to become an international human resources manager (Tarique et al., 2015).

In addition, from the perspective of human resource management, internationalization is likely to take on a variety of forms. It is crucial to prioritize procedures, particularly while crafting an International Human Resource Management (IHRM) system with an emphasis on international talent management.

The talent pool segment considers variations amongst employees based on their diverse background they had been associated with. When we talk about talent management, the significance of employees' contribution cannot be ignored who must demonstrate responsibility and remain proactive in helping the HR manager as this can help decrease the company's expenses. (Smerek, Lukáš and Vetrakova, Milota and Šimočková, Ivana, 2021).

It's not surprising that human resource management is highly valued for enhancing relations globally in the international business or academic contexts. This helps the community in positive ways and help them to address a wide range of challenges. The impact of international relations on businesses especially concerning economical and human capital resources is significant, because human capital is dynamic and constantly evolving. (Krishna, V., 2021).

CONCLUSION

For all intents and purposes, human resource managers in the vast majority of various sorts of firms will be compelled to cope with at least certain chosen aspects of internationalization and the changes brought about by multinational corporations. Resting our belief that globalization and technological considerations will provide "no place to hide," these developments will contribute to the formation of small and medium companies (SMEs). As a consequence of this, human resource professionals have the potential to become involved in international human resource management (IHRM) issues, and as a consequence, they are required to have an understanding of these issues. These circumstances include human resource management jobs in all kinds of companies, not simply international HR positions inside the kinds of companies that are normally focused on, such as working at the headquarters of a multinational business (MNE) or in the operations of the parent country. In every case, the international aspects of the issue increase the human resource managers' exposure and liabilities, and they put ever-increasing demands on them to learn new skills that are focussed on growing their worldwide awareness (Yoshihara, 1994). In addition, the international aspects of the problem heighten the risk of the problem. With multinational businesses (MNEs), human resource managers will continue to be presented with a broad diversity of national, social, cultural, educational, managerial, and governmental systems. In the future workforce, there will be heightened emphasis on creativity, critical thinking, effective decision making and the skill to handle information comprehensively. (Smerek, Lukáš and Vetrakova, Milota and Šimočková, Ivana., March 2021). This is true for both domestic and foreign human resource managers. As a consequence of this, they need to be educated and well-prepared with the skills and abilities that are required to effectively tackle this expanding challenge.

All in all, the management of talent in the global arena is a challenging task. It cannot be avoided as it is the need of the hour also. While managing talent or even getting the expatriates ready to work in any other country than their own, it becomes important to be vigilant towards the attitude, aptitude and potential of an employee otherwise it can end up with having a stressed employee. The trainer must be trained for that and they must possess the traits which helps them tom accommodate themselves with the changing scenario and changing people in a different country.

Recommendation

For the vast majority of companies that are deeply focusing on their "talent-pipeline," the ideas of employer branding and talent management in IHRM are deeply felt. A number of elements are pointing towards the fact why organizations must strive to coordinate their talent streams towards IHRM on a more international scale. Among these factors to take into account are the following:

- Talent is now more mobile than ever before so it needs to be dealt with utmost care in a systematic manner.
- The degree of competitive enthusiasm with other employers has evolved from the national level to the regional and global levels, and it has gotten more general over this time period.
- In order to meet the requisite for gender related and nationality related diversity, it becomes mandatory to get away from the attitude of a headquarters.
- Both economies of scale and global networks have the potential to facilitate the transfer of best practices from one nation to another. IHRM has a variety of similar answers to issues that arise from tying the talent pipeline to global biases.
- Collaborating with present and future workers as well as agencies to do research on "local peoples' insights."
- In order to take a more proactive and strategic approach to recruiting, talent management on an international level is recommended.
- Raising awareness at educational institutions and other businesses in order to attract the individuals who are ready to take up international assignments without much training.
- Advancing internal talent pools and future IHR managers in different parts of the business.
- Creating competent evaluators all across the world.
- The management of recruiting providers on a worldwide scale.
- Communicating messages about the employer brand via the use of electronic technologies.

With these recommendations, the study sums up with the need of change or update in the present methodology of IHRM operations. Since it is a broad aspect, it cannot be dealt with just one approach. It needs to be worked upon, with foreign collaborations and interventions by the policy makers, in the international organisation and in the country, so the expatriates don't face problems of accommodating themselves in the new scenario and managers do not have to spend much time on making them work towards the organisational goal.

REFERENCES

Adler, N. J., & Ghadar, F. (1990) Strategic human resource management: A global perspective, in: R. Pieper.

Banai, M. (1992). The ethnocentric staffing policy in multinational corporations: A self-fulfilling prophecy. *International Journal of Human Resource Management*, 3(3), 451–472. DOI: 10.1080/09585199200000159

Becker, B., Huselid, M., & Ulrich, D. (2001). *The HR Scorecard*. Harvard Business School Press.

Björkman, I., & Stahl, G. (2006). International human resource management research: an introduction to the field. In Stahl, G., & Björkman, I. (Eds.), *Handbook of Research in International Human Resource Management*. Edward Elgar. DOI: 10.4337/9781845428235.00005

Black, J. S., & Gregerson, H. B. (1992). Serving two masters: Managing the dual allegiance of expatriate employees. *Sloan Management Review*, 33(4), 61–71.

Caligiuri, P., De Cieri, H., Minbaeva, D., Verbeke, A., & Zimmermann, A. (2020). International HRM insights for navigating the COVID-19 pandemic: Implications for future research and practice. *Journal of International Business Studies*, 51(5), 697–713. DOI: 10.1057/s41267-020-00335-9 PMID: 32836500

Caligiuri, P. M. (1999). The ranking of scholarly journals in the field of international human resource management. *International Journal of Human Resource Management*, 10(3), 515–518. DOI: 10.1080/095851999340468

Claus, L. (1998). The role of international human resource management in leading a company from a domestic to a global corporate culture. *Human Resource Development International*, 1(3), 309–326. DOI: 10.1080/13678869800000040

Claus, L. (1999) "People Management and Globalization," presentation to the fifty-first annual conference and exposition of the Society of Human Resource Management, Atlanta, GA, June.

Collings, D. G., Scullion, H., & Morley, M. J. (2007). Changing Patterns of Global Staffing in the Multinational Enterprise: Challenges to the Conventional Expatriate Assignment and Emerging Alternatives. *Journal of World Business*, 42(2), 198–213. DOI: 10.1016/j.jwb.2007.02.005

Damodharan, P., & Ravichandran, C. S. (2019). Applicability evaluation of web mining in healthcare E-commerce towards business success and a derived cournot model. *Journal of Medical Systems*, 43(8), 268. DOI: 10.1007/s10916-019-1395-1 PMID: 31273541

. Dowling, P. & Welch, D.E. (2004). International human resource management: Managing people in a multinational context.

Dowling, P. J. (1988) "International and domestic personnel/human resource management: Similarities and differences," in R.S. Schuler, S.A. Youngblood, and V.L. Huber (eds), *Readings in Personnel and Human Resource Management*, 3rd edition, St Paul, MN: West Publishing. Also discussed in Dowling *et al*. (1999).

Evans, P., Pucik, V., & Barsouxm, J. L. (2002). *The Global Challenge: Frameworks for International Human Resource Management*. McGraw-Hill.

Harris, H., Brewster, C., & Sparrow, P. R. (2003). *International Human Resource Management*. Chartered Institute of Personnel and Development.

Hofstede, G. (1998). Organizationl culture. In Poole, M., & Warner, M. (Eds.), *The ICBM Handbook of Human Resource Management* (pp. 237–255). ITP.

Keating, M., & Thompson, K. (2004). International human resource management: Overcoming disciplinary sectarianism. *Employee Relations*, 26(6), 595–612. DOI: 10.1108/01425450410562191

Keeley, T. D. (2001). *International Human Resource Management in Japanese Firms*. Palgrave Macmillan (UK). DOI: 10.1057/9780230597655

Kopp, R. (1993). *Koyo Masatsu. (Employment Friction)*. Sanno Institute of Management Press.

Krishna, V. (2021). Evaluating the Qualitative Significance of Human Resource Management in Promoting International Relations. *Journal of Research in Business and Management.*, 9(8), 56–63.

Lander, S. (n.d.), "The Importance of Global Recruitment Strategies", Small Business-Chron.com, https://smallbusiness.chron.com/effect-globalization-hr-60492.html

Laurent, A. (1986). The cross-cultural puzzle of international human resource management. *Human Resource Management*, 25(1), 91–103. DOI: 10.1002/hrm.3930250107

Lazarova, M. L. (2006). International human resource management in global perspective. In Morley, M. J., Heraty, N., & Collings, D. G. (Eds.), *International Human Resource Management and International Assignments*. Palgrave Macmillan. DOI: 10.1007/978-1-349-72883-1_2

Meijer, S. (2003). The challenges of international human resource management in multinational corporations. *Journal of Research in International Business and Management.*, 10(2), 1–2.

Meyer, K. E. (2006). Perspectives on multinational enterprises in emerging economies. *Journal of International Business Studies*, 35(4), 259–276. DOI: 10.1057/palgrave.jibs.8400084

Morley, M. & Heraty, N. & Collings, D. (2006). Introduction: International Human Resource Management and International Assignments. .DOI: 10.1007/978-1-349-72883-1_1

Natter, E. (2020), "Effects of Globalization on Human Resources Management", Small Business-Chron.com, July 8, https://smallbusiness.chron.com/effects-globalization-human-resources-management-61611.html

Noruzi, M. R., & Rahimi, G. (2010). Exploring successful International Human Resource Management: Past, present, and future directions, *IEEE Xplore Conference: Advanced Management Science (ICAMS)*, 2010 IEEE International Conference, 3. 757 - 758. DOI: 10.1109/ICAMS.2010.5553305

. Patel, D. (2002) "Managing talent", *HR Magazine*, March

Prahalad, C. K. (2004). *The Fortune at the Bottom of the Pyramid: Eradicating Poverty Through Profits*. Wharton School Publishing/Pearson.

Schuler, R. S., Budhwar, P. S., & Florkowski, G. W. (2002). International human resource Management: Review and critique. *International Journal of Management Reviews*, 4(1), 41–70. DOI: 10.1111/1468-2370.00076

Schuler (2003). United Nations Conference on Trade and Development (UNCTAD), *World Investment Report 1998*, New York: United Nations (1999).

Scullion, H. (1992). Strategic recruitment and development of the international manager: Some European considerations. *Human Resource Management Journal*, 3(1), 57–69. DOI: 10.1111/j.1748-8583.1992.tb00302.x

Scullion, H. (2004). Introduction. In Scullion, H., & Linehan, M. (Eds.), *InternationalHuman Resource Management: A Critical Text*. Palgrave.

Scullion, H., Collings, D., & Gunnigle, P. (2007). International Human Resource Management in the 21st Century: Emerging Themes and Contemporary Debates. *Human Resource Management Journal*, 17(4), 309–319. DOI: 10.1111/j.1748-8583.2007.00047.x

. Scullion, H. & Collings, D.G. (2006) Global Staffing, published in the Taylor & Francis e-Library, 2006.

Selmer, J. (2004). Expatriates' hesitation and the localization of Western business operations in China. *International Journal of Human Resource Management*, 15(6), 1094–1107. DOI: 10.1080/09585190410001677322

Shaffer, M. A., Kraimer, M. L., Chen, Y. P., & Bolino, M. C. (2012). Choices, challenges, and career consequences of global work experiences: A review and future agenda. *Journal of Management*, 38(4), 1282–1327. DOI: 10.1177/0149206312441834

. Smerek, Lukáš and Vetrakova, Milota and Šimočková, Ivana. (March 2021). International Human Resource Management System, pp.125. isbn: 978-83-7351-914-5

Sparrow, P. R., Brewster, C., & Harris, H. (2004). *Globalizing Human Resource Management*. Routledge. DOI: 10.4324/9780203614129

Tarique, I., Briscoe, D. R., & Schuler, R. S. (2015). *International human resource management: Policies and practices for multinational enterprises*. Routledge.

Tarique, I., & Schuler, R. (2010). Global talent management: Literature review, integrative framework, and suggestions for further research. *Journal of World Business*, 45(2), 122–133. DOI: 10.1016/j.jwb.2009.09.019

Thomas, D. C., & Lazarova, M. B. (2013). *Essentials of international human resource management: Managing people globally*. Sage Publications.

Vaiman, V., Sparrow, P., Schuler, R., & Collings, D. G. (Eds.). (2018). *Macro talent management: A global perspective on managing talent in developed markets*. Routledge. DOI: 10.4324/9781315200200

Walker, J. (1992), Human Resource Strategy, New York: McGraw Hill.

Welch, D. (1994). Determinants of international human resource management approaches and activities: A suggested framework. *Journal of Management Studies*, 31(2), 139–164. DOI: 10.1111/j.1467-6486.1994.tb00769.x

Welch, D. E. (2003). Globalisation of staff movements: Beyond cultural adjustment. *MIR. Management International Review*, ●●●, 149–169.

Wong, N. (2000). Mark your calendar! Important tasks for international HR. *The Personnel Journal*, 79, 72–74.

Wright, P. M., & McMahan, G. C. (1992). Theoretical perspectives for strategic human resource management. *Journal of Management*, 18(2), 295–320. DOI: 10.1177/014920639201800205

Yoshihara, H. (1994). *Gaishikei Kigyo. (Foreign Firms)*. Dobunkan Shuppan.

Zimmermann, A., & Ravishankar, M. N. (2011). Collaborative IT offshoring relationships and professional role identities: Reflections from a field study. *Journal of Vocational Behavior*, 78(3), 351–360. DOI: 10.1016/j.jvb.2011.03.016

Chapter 6
Human Resource Analytics and Organizational Performance:
Mediating Role of Evidence-Based Management

Shivani Thapliyal
https://orcid.org/0000-0002-7285-2830
Christ University, India

ABSTRACT

HR Analytics (HRA) is very crucial aspect of human resource management and drawing more attention each year. It has emerged as a powerful tool contributing towards organizational performance. However the literature work on HR analytics would appear to be more focused on the influence of HR analytics on organizational performance but the questions like how and why are still need to be explored. This research paper aims at understanding how HR analytics improves the organizational performance and systematically unfolds the mechanism how it happens. Data is collected from three organizations of different sectors and structure equation modelling is used to examine the chain mediation model connecting human resource analytics, evidence-based management and organizational performance. This research work extends our understanding of how HR analytics and evidence based management improves organizational performance.

1. INTRODUCTION

The area of human resource management has evolved dramatically from personnel management to HRM to strategic management. Now with the application of data analytics in the area of human resource management, we are moving towards human resource analytics. Today's organizations are using data analytics in the field of human resource management along with evidence based management to make informed decisions for the benefit of the organization. According to Kim et al (2021) employee data is

DOI: 10.4018/979-8-3693-9230-0.ch006

Copyright ©2025, IGI Global. Copying or distributing in print or electronic forms without written permission of IGI Global is prohibited.

generated in massive amount which leads to the increased use of technology in HR system like human resource information system (HRIS), and cloud platforms.

The implementation of analytics in HR management has increasingly capturing the attention of researchers with the aim to understand how the combination of people, data and technology can create wonders in the field of HR management. The HR managers are trying to improve the accuracy of their decisions by implementing HR analytics and are making more informed decisions which are very important for an organization's success.

Furthermore, the present organizations are using people data, analytics and evidence based management for making data driven decisions to enhance performance. HR analytics focuses on using analytics on employee data to address HR issues and evidence based management to make informed decisions. The significant development of Human resource analytics including cloud platforms and human resource information system (HRIS) has equipped the HR managers with the ability to collect, store and analyse the enormous amount of employee data compared to earlier IT systems resulting in the adoption of HR analytics in HR departments (Kim et al., 2021). Orientation towards analytics will give a competitive advantage to the organizations deploying it. HR analytics not only focuses on improving the human resource management but also couple the analytical techniques with HR data to make informed decisions and improve overall organizational performance. In addition to this, to improve the recruitment cycle, Google's HR team has developed an evidence based approach by identifying several KPIs that can predict the likelihood of a candidate's high performance ((Harris et al., 2011; Shrivastava et al., 2018).

To date, the literature on HR analytics has covered many areas including the challenges and benefits (Boudreau and Cascio, 2017; Jeske and Calvard, 2020) and the importance of analytical skills in many areas. Despite the advancement of literature in the area of HR analytics, proving the impact of HR analytics on organizational performance (Fernandez and Gallardo-Gallardo, 2020; Karekar, P and Jiby, B. 2022), research on investigating how and to what extent HR analytics influences organizational performance remains scarce (Minbaeva, 2018). On this basis, the present research paper seeks to investigate how and why HR analytics influences organizational performance. By theorizing the chain model between HR analytics, evidence based management, access to HR technology and organizational performance, the present research work extends the understanding of how and why HR analytics leads to improved organizational performance.

Various researchers and professionals are keen to understand how the usage of data leads to improved organizational performance that further raises the demand of understanding the concept of data and analytics in the field of management (Chierici et al. 2019; Santoro et al. 2019; Singh & Del Giudice, 2019). Furthermore the growth of HR technology that includes cloud platforms and human resource information system (HRIS) has made the functioning of HR department really smooth by collecting, storing and processing all the employee rated data in large volumes as compared to previously used IT systems (Bondarouk and Brewster, 2016; 2017; Kim et al., 2021). HR technology has acted as a driver of HR analytics that increased its usage and adoption in the human resource departments.

The present research work is divided into subsequent sections like the review of literature and hypotheses formulation. The next section describes the research methodology followed by research analysis and findings. The last section is about discussion and theoretical contribution of the research work followed by limitations and areas for future research.

2. LITERATURE REVIEW AND HYPOTHESES FORMULATION

2.1 Human Resource Analytics (HRA) and Evidence Bases Management (EBM)

The present research study adopts the HR analytics definition given by Marler and Boudreau (2017), where HR analytics is *"an HR practice enabled by information technology that uses descriptive, visual, and statistical analyses of data related to HR processes, human capital, organizational performance, and external economic benchmarks to establish business impact and enable data driven decision-making"* (p. 15). HR analytics also known as people analytics use employee data and statistical tools to resolve organizational challenges that effects the manpower (Marr, 2016). However researchers like Marler & Boudreau (2017) and Huselid (2018) highlighted that HR analytics is not a new concept and has its root in the area of social science research focused on workforce measurement. Jac Fitz-Enz (1984) "How to measure human resource management" book is one of the most significant and highly cited work by the pioneering research work in the domain quantitative analysis of human resource management.

However, a concept that is mostly associated with HR analytics, is evidence-based management. Evidence based management is one of the best approach for an organization to make evidence based decisions that combines both rational decision making and intuitive decision making. Although the evidence based management approach has emerged from the field of medical science and health care sector wherein it was used for the purpose of decision making regarding patients health, on the basis of evidence present (Biglan & Ogden, 2008; Wan, 2006; Walshe & Rundall, 2001).

According to Briner & Rousseau, 2011, practitioner uses four sources of information ""*practitioner expertise and judgment, evidence from the local context, a critical evaluation of the best available research evidence, and the perspectives of those people who might be affected by the decision."* Evidence based management uses the combination of HR data, research and analysis to establish the connection between practices of HR management and outcomes like quality, profitability and customer satisfaction (Reddy & Keerthi, 2017). It has transformed the whole idea of HR management which started with supervising to instinct based decisions to right evidence based decisions. Furthermore, there is a emergence of creating a culture of evidence based management to create HR analytics capabilities (Minbaeva, 2018). Also the literature available on evidence based management gives a number of reasons for explaining why it is difficult for managers to use evidence based management and the reasons found to be are lack on analytical or research skills, limited access to quality data and misfit of the evidence with managerial judgement (Briner & Rousseau, 2011).

The data that generates from HR analytics is not solely sufficient for having competitive edge, instead businesses should incorporate evidence effectively (Lin and Wu, 2014; Fu et al., 2017). There is enormous amount employee data present with HR department which generally remains unused and does not serve the purpose for which it is being collected. HR analytics helps in the appropriate usage of the collected HR data and helps the management in taking data driven decisions (Sheth, 2023). Kepes et al. (2014) found that HR analytics and evidence based HR practices were found to be positively correlated. HR data analytics also contributes in improving evidence based HR practices (Ma et al.; 2018). Another research is of Coron (2021) that suggests evidence based HRM relies on HR metrics and data to increase knowledge that leads to improved HR decision making. Accordingly, it is proposed that HR analytics generate organizational facts that contribute to evidence creation and anticipate a positive relationship between HR analytics (HRA) and evidence based management (EBM). Therefore, it is hypothesizing:

H1. HRA has a significant association with EBM

2.2 Evidence Based Management (EBM) and Organizational Performance (OP)

In 1990s, evidence based management is originally derived from the healthcare sector and and it is highly recommended by many researchers to use evidence based management in especially health care sector as well as in many others sectors (Arndt & Bigelow,2009). EBM allows the organizations to make smarter choices based on organizational data and reduce the risk of failure. According to CEBMA (Center for Evidence-Based Management) *"Evidence-based management is defined as making decisions about the management of employees, teams, or organizations through the conscientious, explicit, and judicious use of the best available scientific evidence, organizational data, professional experiential evidence, and stakeholders' values and concerns"*. So we can say that evidence based management is a way to govern the methods of data gathering, processing and coming up with more reliable information that supports in the process of managerial decision making. According to Luhmann (2000), the father of social system theory stated that "organizations are made of decision" this means that one right decision can either make or break the organization. One of the basic responsibilities of a manager involves decision making and in a day a manager is taking 'n' no. of decisions. Although, many decision maker support their decisions on the basis of intuition, gut feeling and experience or expertise (Baba and Hakem Zadeh, 2012). Many scholars have emphasised on the shift of organizations decision making process towards evidence based decisions (Morrell and Learmonth, 2015; Rousseau, 2006; Rynes and Bartunek, 2017).

Evidence based management (EBM) can help the managers or any stakeholder in improving their decision making quality leading to the higher organizational productivity ((Briner *et al.*, 2009; Kovner & Rundall, 2006). This is evidenced in many research studies that focuses on how HR analytics equips the management with the right evidence that further contributes in making right choices leading to high organizational performance (Buttner and Tullar, 2018; Gelbard et al., 2018; Minbaeva, 2018; Rasmussen and Ulrich, 2015). Evidence based management has contributed in uplifting the management practices by providing a frame for better and informed decisions perhaps less influenced by ill-founded advice and management's fads (Criado-Perez et al., 2023). Based on this review, it is hypothesising:

H2. EBM has a significant association with organizational performance

2.3 Human Resource Analytics (HRA) and Organizational Performance (OP)

HRA is considered as a very important tool for the organization as it helps in assessing the large amount of employee data which is used for analysis employee's contribution, manpower forecasting and workforce utilization to improve the organizational performance (Kailash & Prathyusha, 2020). According to a study conducted by Kale, et al (2022), human resource analytics helps in analysing the influence of HR functions on the overall organizational performance. It also helped many organizations in gaining competitive advantage and utilise it human capital in the best possible way (Masese & Uttam, 2020).

Human resource analytics can also be used to improve the performance of business processes and implementation of strategies which further contributes in improving business outcomes (Jain et al., 2022). Further Lochab et al. (2018) assessed the effectiveness of human resource analytics (HRA) on the functioning and performance of an organization by conducting literature analysis. It was found that the organizations must understand the importance of HR analytics as a tool that can be employed to make important HR related decisions. HR analytics is a tool that contributes in enhancing the effectiveness of the processes wherever it is applied. In support of the following statement, it was found in a study conducted by Sharma and Sharma (2017), when HR analytics is used in the process of performance appraisal, it helped in improving the employee's satisfaction level which in turn improved their productivity and contributed towards organization's productivity.

HR analytics is not only contributing in improving the performance and productivity of an organization but also adding towards gaining competitive advantage by transforming the human resource of the organization (Fred & Kinange, 2015). Their study reported that the utilization of HR analytics also makes the employees more engaged. According to a study conducted by Trkaman et al, (2010) it was concluded that analytical skills and performance are significantly influenced by each other. The relation between HR analytics and performance is found to be moderated by many variables like HR professional's analytical skills (Marler & Boudreau, 2017), data collection and effective use of data (Levenson, 2013 and Pape, 2016), human resource information technology (Aral, et al, 2012 and Lawler III, et al 2004).

Based on this review, it is hypothesising:

H3. HRA has a significant association with organizational performance

2.4 Evidence Based Management (EBM), Human Resource Analytics (HRA) and Organizational Performance (OP)

According to a research conducted by Kane 2015, to improve the organization's HR functions and outcomes, BOA (Bank of America in collaboration with an HR analytics software provider (Humanyze) used HR analytics. Based on the analysis and solutions given by Humanyze (HR analytics software provider), BOA has implemented the solutions in their business operations and improved the productivity by 23% as suggested by Kane, 2015.

Patil and Priya (2024) have conducted a research on HR analytics and evidence based practices in IT sector and suggested that future research may study the role of HR analytics in influencing HR decision making which further contributes to better organizational performance. When organizations use the insights derived from HR analytics in the decision making process, it is like to contribute towards effectiveness of organizational performance (Buttner and Tullar, 2018; McIver et al., 2018). Another study conducted by McCartney and Fu (2022), wherein data was gathered from 155 Irish organizations and it was reported that using HR technology supports HR analytics that facilitates evidence based management and all these factors contributes towards improving organizational performance. Mushtaq et al (2024) examined the relationship between HR analytics, evidence based management and firm performance in the manufacturing sector of a developing economy. The study suggested that evidence based management works as a mediator between HR analytics and firm performance and HRA has a positive relationship with firm performance.

Accordingly it is proposed that EBM plays a mediating role between HR analytics and Organizational Performance. There it is hypothesising:

H4. EBM mediates the association between HRA and organizational performance.

Figure 1. The proposed conceptual model

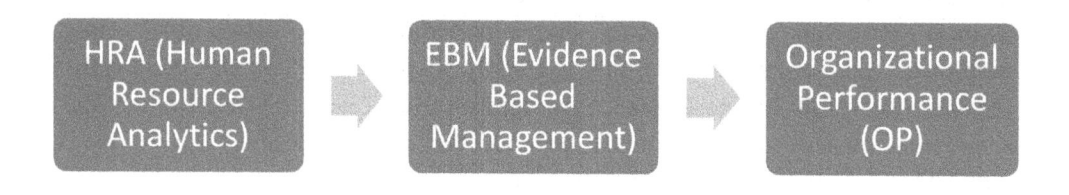

HRA (Human Resource Analytics) → EBM (Evidence Based Management) → Organizational Performance (OP)

3. RESEARCH METHODOLOGY

3.1 Data Collection and Sample Profile

The present research study has used online survey method for the purpose of data collection. The targeted population was consisting of three organizations from different industries in Delhi NCR. Out of three, there was one from IT industry, second from cement and construction and third one from financial services. Probability sampling technique is used to identify the sample. Employees working in the HR department like HR managers, HR executives, HR administers, etc. was among the targeted population. A total of 100 questionnaires were sent in the each organization so the sample size was of 300. Out of 300 we have received 268 acceptable responses. Among the accepted responses, 67% were male and 33% were female employees.

3.2 Measuring Instruments

HRA: To measure the human resource analytics, a structured questionnaire developed by Opatha and Dayarathna (2024) is adapted with a cronbach's alpha value of 0.947.

EBM: To measure the evidence based management, a structured questionnaire developed by McCartney and FR (2022) is adapted with a cronbach's alpha value of 0.93.

Organizational Performance: To measure organizational performance, a structured questionnaire developed by Delaney and Huselid (1996) is adapted with a cronbach's alpha value of 0.87.

Control Variables: In the present study, several contextual variables that can potentially influence the usage of HRA, EBM and organizational performance were controlled. Among them one is the size of the organization, having three categories where in organization having less than 50 employees (small organization), between 50 and 200 (medium organization) and above 200 (large organization) were there. Second is the organization type, dummy variables are used like 0 for domestics and 1 for multinational organization. Third is the industry where in 1 represents IT, 2 represents cement and construction and 3 represents the financial services.

4. RESULTS

4.1 Descriptive Statistics

Table 1. The descriptive statistic of the core variables results including mean, standard deviation and correlations

	Mean	SD	1	2	3	4	5	6
Organizational performance	3.26	.89	1					
HRA	3.23	.62	.54**	1				
EBM	3.10	.78	.52**	.497*	1			
Org. Size	1.38	.91	.03	-.01	-.03	1		
Org. Type	0.35	.92	-.12	-.05	-.01	-.04	1	
Industry	1.45	.88	-.20	.00	.04	.02	.11	1

Note(s): N= 268 (listwise) **p < 0.01 *p < 0.05

4.2 Structural Models and Hypotheses Testing

In the present study, analysis was conducted using SPSS 26 and SEM (structure equation modelling) is utilized for the hypothesis testing. Figure 2 represents the structural model where in the beta coefficient values are provided.

Figure 2. SEM values

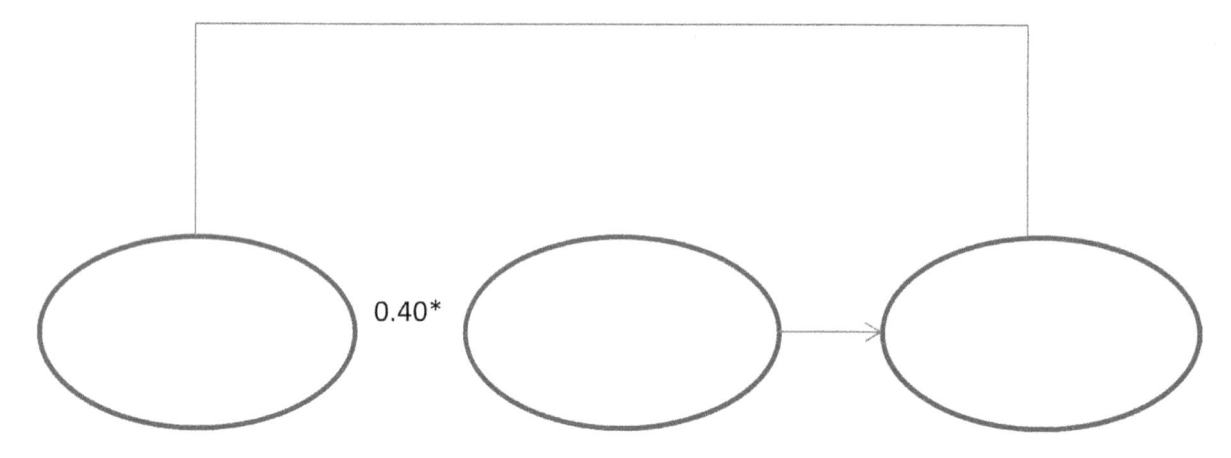

0.40*

Hypothesis 1 HRA has a significant association with EBM

The results from Figure 2 shows that HR analytics has a positive and significant association with evidence based management ($\beta = 0.40$, $p < 0.05$). Therefore H1 is accepted.

Hypothesis 2 EBM has a significant association with organizational performance

Figure 2 shows that evidence-based management has a positive and significant association with organizational performance ($\beta = 0.52$, $p < 0.05$). Hence H2 is accepted.

Hypothesis 3 HRA has a significant association with organizational performance

Figure 2 represents that HR analytics has a positive and significant association with organizational performance ($\beta = 0.37$, $p < 0.05$). Therefore, H3 is accepted

Hypothesis 4 EBM mediates the association between HRA and organizational performance.

For conducting a mediation analysis, three conditions need to be tested: First there should be a significant association between the independent variable and the mediating variable, Second, there should be a significant association between the mediating variable and the dependent variable. And the third condition is there should be a significant relationship between the independent and the dependent variable (Baron and Kenny, 1986; Hayes, 2013). The testing of H1 and H2 has fulfilled the first two conditions and H3 has met the third condition. The direct association between HRA and organizational performance comes out to be positive and significant ($\beta = 0.37$, $p < 0.05$) and in the presence of the mediating variable i.e., evidence based management, the association comes out to be significant ($\beta = 0.22$, $p < 0.05$). Hence, it can be concluded that EBM mediates the association between HRA and organizational performance. Therefore, H4 is accepted.

Hence from Figure 2, it can be concluded that H1 to H4 confirms the significant influence of human resource analytics on evidence based management which further influences organizational performance.

5. DISCUSSION AND CONCLUSION

Human resource management is considered as one of the important pillar for the survival of any organization. And a managerial profile involves a lot a decision making. Earlier decisions taken by the management were either intuitive, based on gut feeling or can be an experience based decision. But with the emergence of human resource analytics, we are moving towards taking such decisions which can be supported on the basis of evidence as well. According to Baesens et al., (2017), Marler and Boudreau (2017) and Greasley and Thomas (2020), the concept HRA has gained a lot of importance, despite the research on the role of human resource analytics for organizational performance is still need to be explored. In a research conducted by McIver et al. (2018), it has been proved that, organizations are still not aware of how to use HRA for improving organizational performance. The present research examines the association between HRA and organizational performance considering EDM as the mediator wherein it is proved that EDM mediates the association between HRA and organizational performance. So we can conclude that, understanding the impact of HR decision on organizational performance, it is time to realise the importance of evidence based management that is taking management decisions on the basis of right evidence. The present work sheds light on the association between HR analytics and organizational performance. The HR manager can only reap the benefits of human resource data analytics if they will be provided with right training and knowledge and if executed wisely by the HR manager for organizational benefit. The results of the present study has also supported by the studies conducted by Bassi *et al.* (2012), Boakye and Ayerki Lamptey (2020), Green, 2017 and Shabbir and Gardezi (2020) where they concluded that manager's with higher analytical skills always generate quality evidences and use them in organizational decision making that further leads to improved organizational performance. According to McAfee and Brynjolfsson (2012) and Rousseau and Barends (2011) the potential benefits of evidence based management on firm performance have been the topic of interest still the empirical evidences are limited. Hence the present research work has addressed this gap.

The present research work has contributed towards HR analytics research by analysing the mediation effect of evidence based management between the relationship of HR analytics and organizational performance. The findings of the present work offer several implications suggesting the implementation of HR analytics and focusing towards evidence based management can contribute towards organizational performance. Lastly the present research also suggests the managers that establishing a culture focused on decision making has a significant contribution in improving the organizational performance. Thus it can be concluded that the organizations and the management must employ organizational facts that are being generated with the help of HR analytics and must incorporate them in the process of decision making.

Recommendation

Organization's use several types of HR technologies like HRIS (human resource information system) and Excel for HR data analytics. Accordingly, future research can focus on the HR technologies as the enablers of HR analytics. Furthermore, research on HR analytics can also move forward to understand how analytics can enhance or develop human resource practices and their further effect on organizational efficiency.

Further, it is recommended to the organizations that in order to reap full benefits of analytics, HR managers should get proper training and skills so that HR analytics can be effectively executed in the organizations. If HR analytics is properly understood then only it can be wisely executed by the HR managers to achieve the highest level of organizational productivity. Future research work can also focus on the total value created by human resource analytics for all the stake holders like line managers, employees, suppliers, customers, etc. Thus future research recommendations could help to explore the black box of human resource analytics and its influence on other organizational factors.

REFERENCES

Aral, S., Brynjolfsson, E., & Van Alstyne, M. (2012). Information, technology and information worker productivity. *Information Systems Research*, 23(3), 849–867. DOI: 10.1287/isre.1110.0408

Arndt, M., & Bigelow, B. (2009). Evidence-based management in health care organizations: A cautionary note. *Health Care Management Review*, 34(3), 206–213. DOI: 10.1097/HMR.0b013e3181a94288 PMID: 19625822

Baba, V. V., & HakemZadeh, F. (2012). Toward a theory of evidence based decision making. *Management Decision*, 50(5), 832–867. Advance online publication. DOI: 10.1108/00251741211227546

Baesens, B., De Winne, S., & Sels, L. (2017). Is your company ready for HR analytics? *MIT Sloan Management Review*, 58(2), 20–21. DOI: 10.1016/j.jsmc.2005.11.006

Baron, R. M., & Kenny, D. A. (1986). The moderator–mediator variable distinction in social psychological research: Conceptual, strategic, and statistical considerations. *Journal of Personality and Social Psychology*, 51(6), 1173–1182. DOI: 10.1037/0022-3514.51.6.1173 PMID: 3806354

Biglan, A., & Ogden, T. (2008). The evolution of evidence-based practices. *European Journal of Behavior Analysis*, 9(1), 81–95. DOI: 10.1080/15021149.2008.11434297 PMID: 21461128

Boakye, A., & Ayerki Lamptey, Y. (2020). The rise of HR analytics: Exploring its implications from a developing country perspective. *Journal of Human Resource Management*, 8(3), 181–189. DOI: 10.11648/j.jhrm.20200803.19

Briner, R. B., Denyer, D., & Rousseau, D. M. (2009). Evidence-based management: Concept cleanup time? *The Academy of Management Perspectives*, 23(4), 19–32. DOI: 10.5465/AMP.2009.45590138

Briner, R. B., & Rousseau, D. M. (2011). Evidence-based I–O psychology: Not there yet. *Industrial and Organizational Psychology: Perspectives on Science and Practice*, 4(1), 3–22. DOI: 10.1111/j.1754-9434.2010.01287.x

Buttner, H., & Tullar, W. (2018). A representative organizational diversity metric: A dashboard measure for executive action. *Equality, Diversity and Inclusion*, 37(3), 219–232. DOI: 10.1108/EDI-04-2017-0076

Center for Evidence-Based Management. What is evidence-based management? 2015. Available at: http://www. cebma.org/#what-is evidence-based-management.

Chatterjee, S., Chaudhuri, R., & Vrontis, D. (2021). Does data-driven culture impact innovation and performance of a firm? An empirical examination. *Annals of Operations Research*, 17(2), 1–26. DOI: 10.1007/s10479-020-03887-z

Chierici, R., Mazzucchelli, A., Garcia-Perez, A., & Vrontis, D. (2019). Transforming big data into knowledge: The role of knowledge management practice. *Management Decision*, 57(8), 1902–1922. DOI: 10.1108/MD-07-2018-0834

Criado-Perez, C., Jackson, C., & Collins, G., C. (. (2023). Evidence collection and use when making management decisions. *Applied Psychology*, •••, 1–21. DOI: 10.1111/apps.12503

Fitz-Enz, J. (1984). *How to measure human resources management*. McGraw-Hill.

Fred, M., & Kinange, U. (2015). Overview of HR Analytics to maximize Human capital investment. *International Journal of Advance Research and Innovative Ideas in Education*, 1(4), 118–122.

Fu, N., Flood, P. C., Bosak, J., Rousseau, D., Morris, T., & O'Regan, P. (2017). High performance work systems in professional service firms: Examining the practice-resources-uses performance linkage. *Human Resource Management*, 56(2), 329–352. DOI: 10.1002/hrm.21767

Gelbard, R. et al. (2018) "Sentiment analysis in organizational work: towards an ontology of people analytics", (July 2017), pp. 1-15, .DOI: 10.1111/exsy.12289

Greasley, K. and Thomas, P. (2020) "HR analytics: the onto-epistemology and politics of metricised HRM", (December 2019), pp. 1-14, .DOI: 10.1111/1748-8583.12283

Green, D. (2017). The best practices to excel at people analytics. *Journal of Organizational Effectiveness*, 4(2), 137–144. DOI: 10.1108/JOEPP-03-2017-0027

Gupta, M., & George, J. F. (2016). Toward the development of a big data analytics capability. *Information & Management*, 53(8), 1049–1064. DOI: 10.1016/j.im.2016.07.004

Hayes, A. (2013). *Introduction to Mediation, Moderation, and Conditional Process Analysis*. The Guilford Press.

Jain, G. R., Jain, S. G., & Babu, R. (2022). HR analytics and business performance – a mediation model. *Academy of Marketing Studies Journal*, 26(S2), 1–7.

Kane, G. (2015). People analytics through super- charged ID. *MIT Sloan Management Review*, 56(4), •••. https://sloanreview.mit.edu/article/people-analytics-through-supercharged-id-badges/

Kepes, S., Bennett, A. A., & McDaniel, M. A. (2014). Evidence-based management and the trustworthiness of our cumulative scientific knowledge: Implications for teaching, research, and practice. *Academy of Management Learning & Education*, 13(3), 446–466. DOI: 10.5465/amle.2013.0193

Kim, S., Wang, Y., & Boon, C. (2021). Sixty years of research on technology and human resource management: Looking back and looking forward. *Human Resource Management*, 60(1), 229–247. DOI: 10.1002/hrm.22049

Kovner, A. R., & Rundall, T. G. (2006). Evidence-based management reconsidered. *Frontiers of Health Services Management*, 22(3), 1–3. DOI: 10.1097/01974520-200601000-00002 PMID: 16604900

Lawler, E. E.III, Levenson, A., & Boudreau, J. W. (2004). HR metrics and analytics–uses and impacts. *Human Resource Planning Journal*, 27(4), 27–35.

Levenson, A. (2013). The promise of big data for HR. *People & Strategy*, 36, 22–26.

Levenson, A. (2018). Using workforce analytics to improve strategy execution. *Human Resource Management*, 57(3), 685–700. DOI: 10.1002/hrm.21850

Lin, Y., & Wu, L. Y. (2014). Exploring the role of dynamic capabilities in firm performance under the resource-based view framework. *Journal of Business Research*, 67(3), 407–413. DOI: 10.1016/j.jbusres.2012.12.019

Lochab, A., Kumar, S., & Tomar, H. (2018). Impact of Human Resource Analytics on Organizational Performance: A Review of Literature Using R-Software. *International Journal of Management, Technology And Engineering*, 8, 1252–1261.

Ma, L., Huang, X., & Chen, S. (2018). Does human resource analytics lead to evidence-based human resource management? Evidence from China. *Journal of Business Research*, 91, 366–375.

Marler, J. H., & Boudreau, J. W. (2017). An evidence-based review of HR analytics. *International Journal of Human Resource Management*, 28(1), 3–26. DOI: 10.1080/09585192.2016.1244699

Marr, B. (2016), "A-brief-history-of-people-analytics", Forbes, available at: www.forbes.com/sites/bernardmarr/2016/12/08/a-brief-history-of-people-analytics/?sh=6b4f4fa6608f

McAfee, A., & Brynjolfsson, E. (2012). Big data: The management revolution. *Harvard Business Review*, 90(10), 60–68. PMID: 23074865

McCartney, S., & Fu, N. (2022). Bridging the gap: Why, how and when HR analytics can impact organizational performance. *Management Decision*, 60(13), 25–47. DOI: 10.1108/MD-12-2020-1581

McIver, D., Lengnick-Hall, M. L., & Lengnick-Hall, C. A. (2018). A strategic approach to workforce analytics: Integrating science and agility. *Business Horizons*, 61(3), 397–407. DOI: 10.1016/j.bushor.2018.01.005

Minbaeva, D. B. (2018). Building credible human capital analytics for organisational competitive advantage. *Human Resource Management*, 57(3), 701–713. DOI: 10.1002/hrm.21848

Morrell, K., & Learmonth, M. (2015). Against evidence-based management, for managementlearning. *Academy of Management Learning & Education*, 14(4), 520–533. DOI: 10.5465/amle.2014.0346

Mushtaq, N., Xing, M.-J., Bakhtawar, A., & Mufti, M. A. (2024). Elevating the influence of HR analytics on organizational performance: An empirical investigation in Hi-Tech manufacturing industry of a developing economy. *Journal of Chinese Human Resource Management*, 15(2), 3–40. DOI: 10.47297/wspchrmWSP2040-800501.20241502

Pape, T. (2016). Prioritising data items for business analytics: Framework and application to human resources. *European Journal of Operational Research*, 252(2), 687–698. DOI: 10.1016/j.ejor.2016.01.052

Patil, B. S., & Priya, M. R. (2024). "HR data analytics and evidence based practice as a strategic business partner", Vilakshan - XIMB. *Journal of Management*, 21(1), 114–125.

Rasmussen, T., & Ulrich, D. (2015). Learning from practice: How HR analytics avoids being a management fad. *Organizational Dynamics*, 44(3), 236–242. DOI: 10.1016/j.orgdyn.2015.05.008

Reddy, R. P., & Keerthi, L. P. (2017). 'Hr Analytics' - An Effective Evidence Based HRM Tool [IJBMI]. *International Journal of Business and Management Invention*, 6(7), 23–34.

Rousseau, D. M. (2006). Is there such a thing as 'evidence-based management'? *Academy of Management Review*, 31(2), 256–269. DOI: 10.5465/amr.2006.20208679

Rousseau, D. M., & Barends, E. G. R. (2011). Becoming an evidence-based HR practitioner. *Human Resource Management Journal*, 21(3), 221–235. DOI: 10.1111/j.1748-8583.2011.00173.x

Rynes, S. L., & Bartunek, J. M. (2017). Evidence-based management: Foundations, development, controversies and future. *Annual Review of Organizational Psychology and Organizational Behavior*, 4(1), 235–261. DOI: 10.1146/annurev-orgpsych-032516-113306

Santoro, G., Fiano, F., Bertoldi, B., & Ciampi, F. (2019). Big data for business management in the retail industry. *Management Decision*, 57(8), 1980–1992. DOI: 10.1108/MD-07-2018-0829

Shabbir, M. Q., & Gardezi, S. B. W. (2020). Application of big data analytics and organizational performance: The mediating role of knowledge management practices. *Journal of Big Data*, 7(1), 1–17. DOI: 10.1186/s40537-020-00317-6

Shamim, S., Zeng, J., Shariq, S. M., & Khan, Z. (2019). Role of big data management in enhancing big data decision-making capability and quality among Chinese firms: A dynamic capabilities view. *Information & Management*, 56(6), 1–16. DOI: 10.1016/j.im.2018.12.003

Sharma, A., & Sharma, T. (2017). HR analytics and performance appraisal system. *Management Research Review*, 40(6), 684–697. DOI: 10.1108/MRR-04-2016-0084

Sheth, H. (2023). HR analytics – An evidence based HR process. *International Journal of Creative Research Thoughts*, 11(10), 849–854.

Singh, S. K., & Del Giudice, M. (2019). Big data analytics, dynamic capabilities and firm performance. *Management Decision*, 57(8), 1729–1733. DOI: 10.1108/MD-08-2019-020

Trkman, P., McCormack, K., De Oliveira, M. P. V., & Ladeira, M. B. (2010). The impact of business analytics on supply chain performance. *Decision Support Systems*, 49(3), 318–327. DOI: 10.1016/j.dss.2010.03.007

Walshe, K., & Rundall, T. G. (2001). Evidence-based management: From theory to practice in health care. *The Milbank Quarterly*, 79(3), 429–457. DOI: 10.1111/1468-0009.00214 PMID: 11565163

Wan, T. T. H. (2006). Healthcare informatics research: From data to evidence-based management. *Journal of Medical Systems*, 30(1), 3–7. DOI: 10.1007/s10916-006-7397-9 PMID: 16548408

Chapter 7
Integrating Work-Based Education:
Bridging Academic Knowledge and Practical Experience for Workforce Readiness

Sakunthai Pommarang
Loei Rajabhat University, Thailand

Sanya Kenaphoom
https://orcid.org/0000-0002-9833-4759
Rajabhat Maha Sarakham University, Thailand

ABSTRACT

Work-based education (WBE), which bridges the gap between academia and industry, increases graduates' employability by giving them practical experience and industry-specific knowledge, better preparing them for the demands of the workforce. This paper aims to investigate the integration of WBEs. WBE is essential to modern education because it prepares graduates for the workforce by fusing academic knowledge with real-world experience. WBE better aligns educational objectives with labor market demands by fusing cutting-edge methods like competency-based and project-based learning with digital tools and virtual simulations. Its ongoing development is anticipated to improve its efficacy and better prepare graduates for the fast-paced labor market. This development will be aided by global collaborations and emerging technologies. In conclusion, utilizing cutting-edge technology and international collaborations, WBE combines theory and practical skills to better align education with the changing demands of the labor market and increase its overall impact.

INTRODUCTION

Work-Based Education (WBE) is an educational approach designed to help students meet the demands of the professional world by fusing academic knowledge with real-world work experience. WBE includes a range of educational opportunities that let students put theory into practice in real-world situations, in-

DOI: 10.4018/979-8-3693-9230-0.ch007

cluding industry projects, cooperative education, apprenticeships, and internships (Smith & Betts, 2000). This type of instruction aims to close the knowledge gap between classroom instruction and workforce skills, making graduates competent and knowledgeable in their fields of study (Billett, 2001). WBE is significant because it can improve students' employability and preparedness for the workforce. Work-Based Education (WBE) is an educational approach designed to help students meet the demands of the professional world by fusing academic knowledge with real-world work experience. WBE includes a range of educational opportunities that let students put theory into practice in real-world situations, including industry projects, cooperative education, apprenticeships, and internships (Smith & Betts, 2000). This type of instruction aims to close the knowledge gap between classroom instruction and workforce skills, making graduates competent and knowledgeable in their fields of study (Billett, 2001). WBE is significant because it can improve students' employability and preparedness for the workforce. WBE contributes to the development of a workforce that is more skilled and adaptable by matching academic programs with real-world workplace requirements. Employers, who can rely on a consistent supply of graduates who are adequately prepared to meet their staffing needs, as well as students and educators, gain from this alignment (Toner, 2011). Therefore, Work-Based Education (WBE) is an educational approach that integrates academic learning with practical work experience, aiming to enhance students' employability and career readiness."

To close the knowledge gap that exists between classroom theory and the practical skills required in the workplace, Work-Based Education (WBE) is essential. Students can apply academic concepts in real-world settings thanks to this educational approach, which gives them real-world experiences. Students can obtain practical experience that improves their comprehension of their field of study by participating in cooperative education, internship, and apprenticeship programs (Schaap, Baartman, & de Bruijn, 2012). In addition to enhancing academic knowledge, experiential learning fosters the development of critical thinking and problem-solving abilities, all of which are crucial in professional settings (Smith & Betts, 2000).

WBE's effect on employability is one of its main advantages. Because they have developed professional behaviors and pertinent skills that employers value, students who engage in work-based learning programs are frequently more prepared for the workforce (Jackson, 2015). These students have the chance to network professionally and learn about the industry, which may result in job offers after graduation. Employers also gain from work-based learning (WBE) since it gives them access to a pool of prospective workers who have already proven their abilities and fit in with the company during work-based learning experiences (Toner, 2011). The overall efficacy and efficiency of workforce development are improved by this mutual gain. WBE also promotes closer ties between academic institutions and the business community. Through these partnerships, educational curricula are kept up to date with industry demands and incorporate the newest methods and technologies (Coll et al., 2009). Maintaining the relevance of educational programs and making sure that students have up-to-date, employable skills depend on this kind of alignment. Additionally, collaborative research projects, innovative teaching strategies, and ongoing advancements in industry and academic practices can result from these partnerships. Thus, WBE's integration of academic and real-world experiences promotes an education system that is responsive and dynamic, able to change to meet the changing needs of the global workforce (Billett, 2001).

Even though work-based education (WBE) has been shown to improve student employability and close the knowledge gap between theory and practice, there is still a large body of research to help determine the best ways to incorporate WBE into academic curricula. A large portion of the literature currently in publication concentrates on the benefits of WBE, such as increased skill acquisition and job readiness (Jackson, 2015; Toner, 2011). Less focus has been placed on the institutional frameworks and pedagogical approaches that enable the smooth integration of WBE into various educational contexts. More specifically, extensive research is required to investigate how various WBE models can be modified and applied in a variety of fields and educational settings, ranging from higher education to vocational training (Schaap, Baartman, & de Bruijn, 2012). Furthermore, little research has been done on the long-term effects of WBE on employers and students. While the short-term advantages of WBE, like fast job placement and initial skill development, are well-established (Smith & Betts, 2000), more research is needed to determine the long-term effects of WBE on career advancement, professional development, and lifelong learning. Gaining an understanding of these long-term results can help one better understand how WBE supports ongoing professional development and adaptability in a labor market that is changing quickly. Additionally, not enough research has been done to examine employers' viewpoints on how well WBE programs fulfill industry demands and expectations. By addressing these gaps, mixed-methods research and longitudinal studies can help design more successful WBE programs and policies that better match learning goals with changing workforce demands (Coll et al., 2009). Therefore, this paper aims to investigate the integration of Work-Based Education.

LITERATURE REVIEW

Teaching

In the framework of Work-Based Education (WBE), teaching entails the intentional blending of in-class learning with practical application. To ensure that students can understand the relevance of their academic studies in real-world settings, this pedagogical approach attempts to close the gap between theoretical knowledge and practical application (Smith & Betts, 2000). For teachers to teach WBE effectively, their curricula must include opportunities for students to participate in tasks related to their line of work in addition to covering the necessary academic material. This could include industry placements, project-based learning, and simulations that let students use what they've learned in real-world situations. To prepare students for the complexities of the working world, it is intended to establish a learning environment in which they can enhance their practical and cognitive skills (Coll et al., 2009).

Academic Service

In WBE, academic service is the term used to describe how instructors and students interact with the community and business sector through partnerships and service-learning initiatives. This idea highlights how universities may improve student learning while simultaneously meeting societal demands (Bringle & Hatcher, 1996). Students have the chance to put their academic knowledge to use by taking part in projects that tackle real-world issues through academic service. For instance, business students could help nearby non-profits with strategic planning, while engineering students might work on infrastructure projects for the community. These encounters enhance students' education while also encouraging civic engagement and a sense of responsibility (Furco, 2010).

Research

Since research helps shape and improve educational practices and policies, it is an essential part of WBE. By conducting research, teachers can determine the most effective ways to incorporate work-based learning into the curriculum and assess the success of WBE programs (Billett, 2001). In this context, research can take many different forms. For example, educators can use action research to improve their teaching methods, and formal studies can be used to evaluate the effects of Work-Based Education (WBE) initiatives on student learning and employability. Researchers can improve the quality and efficacy of these programs and guarantee that they satisfy the needs of employers and students by methodically examining the effects of WBE and offering evidence-based recommendations (Coll et al., 2009).

Networking

WBE relies heavily on networking to create links between academic institutions, business partners, and the community at large. According to Schaap, Baartman, and de Bruijn (2012), efficient networking guarantees that WBE programs are in line with industry demands and that students have access to important resources and opportunities. Creating advisory boards with representatives from the industry, planning networking events and job fairs, and creating internship and apprenticeship programs are a few examples of networking activities. Through these initiatives, academic institutions can remain current with industry demands and trends, and students can develop professional networks that improve their chances of landing a job. Additionally, networking fosters cooperation on cooperative research projects and initiatives that benefit the business and academic communities (Toner, 2011).

Practical Experience

WBE's core component is practical experience, which gives students the chance to use their academic knowledge in real-world situations. The development of the skills and competencies needed in the workplace depends on experiential learning (Jackson, 2015). A person can gain practical experience through a variety of programs, such as industry projects, cooperative education, apprenticeships, and internships. Through these experiences, students can learn more about the vocations they want to pursue, hone professional demeanors, and compile a portfolio of their work that prospective employers can view. In addition, hands-on learning facilitates students' comprehension of their professional interests and objectives, thereby enhancing their knowledge and drive upon entering the workforce (Smith & Betts, 2000).

THE FRAMEWORK OF WORK-BASED EDUCATION

1. Historical Context and Evolution of Work-Based Education (WBE)

The origins of work-based education (WBE) can be found in the medieval apprenticeship programs, which taught young people trades by having them work alongside seasoned artisans. To transfer skills and knowledge across different trades and professions, this practical training was essential (Grollmann & Rauner, 2007). Vocational training changed over time as societies became more industrialized and as the need for a workforce with more formal education increased. To better match educational outcomes with the demands of industrial economies, many nations had established formal apprenticeship programs and vocational schools by the late 19th and early 20th centuries (Billett, 2011).

With the rise of higher education and the growing complexity of job roles requiring more advanced skill sets, the mid-20th century saw significant changes in WBE. Cooperative education initiatives became a major innovation during this time, especially in the US and Canada. These programs gave students the chance to obtain real-world experience while pursuing their degrees by combining academic study with paid work placements (Wilson, 2014). The emergence of internships and other experiential learning opportunities during this period led to their standardization as elements of numerous academic curricula. The realization that traditional classroom-based education was insufficient to prepare students for the realities of the workforce was what spurred the change.

The evolution of WBE has been impacted in recent decades by labor market demands, technological advancements, and globalization. More flexibility and variety in program formats, such as project-based learning, virtual internships, and broad industry partnerships, are characteristics of modern WBE programs (Coll et al., 2009). The emphasis now includes lifelong learning and adaptability in a world that is changing quickly, rather than just getting students ready for the workforce. In addition, contemporary WBE places a strong emphasis on the development of soft skills like problem-solving, cooperation, and communication—all of which are necessary for success in the collaborative and multidisciplinary work environments of today (Jackson, 2015). The constant development of WBE is a reflection of the ongoing endeavor to develop more adaptable and dynamic educational frameworks that can satisfy employers' demands in an intricately linked global economy as well as those of students.

2. Core Principles and Goals of Work-Based Education (WBE)

2.1 Integration of Experiential Learning with Formal Education

Integrating experiential learning with formal education is one of the core tenets of work-based education (WBE). This theory is predicated on the notion that learning occurs most efficiently when students can immediately apply their theoretical knowledge to real-world scenarios. Experiential learning theories highlight the value of practical experiences in enhancing comprehension and solidifying academic concepts (Kolb, 2014). Students can contextualize and solidify their academic learning through participation in real-world tasks and projects, increasing its relevance and applicability to their future careers. This integration guarantees that students are competent in applying their knowledge in real-world contexts in addition to being knowledgeable.

2.2. Collaboration Between Educational Institutions and Industry Partners

WBE also emphasizes cooperation between academic institutions and business partners. For educational programs to be in line with the expectations and standards of the modern industry, this partnership is essential. According to Smith and Betts (2000), these kinds of partnerships are crucial for making sure that the curriculum is current and that students are prepared with the skills that employers value. Industry partners can help develop curricula, offer opportunities for internships and apprenticeships, and offer insights into the newest trends and technologies. This partnership guarantees that employers have access to a workforce that is well-prepared while also improving the employability of graduates.

2.3. Development of Soft Skills

Apart from the technical and subject-specific skills, WBE emphasizes cultivating critical soft skills like problem-solving, teamwork, and communication. According to Jackson (2015), employers highly value these skills and they are necessary for success in any professional setting. Students have the chance to develop and practice these skills in real-world scenarios through work-based learning experiences. Working in teams, negotiating workplace dynamics, and resolving real-world issues all assist students in developing the cognitive and interpersonal abilities necessary to succeed in the workplace. The intention is to generate graduates who can work well in a variety of work settings, collaborate with others, and adjust in addition to being technically proficient.

2.4. Lifelong Learning and Adaptability

Preparing students for adaptability and lifelong learning is another important objective of WBE. According to Boud and Solomon (2001), the capacity for ongoing learning and adaptation is essential for long-term career success in a labor market that is changing quickly. WBE programs are made to help students develop these skills by putting them in front of real-world problems and pushing them to adopt a growth mindset and problem-solving techniques. Students who participate in lifelong learning and learn to adapt to new circumstances during their schooling are more equipped to manage the changing demands of the workplace and pursue continuous professional development throughout their careers.

2.5. Enhancing Employability

WBE's main objective is to increase graduates' employability. This entails giving students the professional demeanor and technical proficiency needed in their chosen fields. According to Billett (2011), the goal of WBE programs is to produce graduates who are prepared for the workforce and can make an instant impact on their employers. WBE improves students' readiness for the workforce by giving them exposure to industry practices, opportunities to build a professional network and hands-on experience. By emphasizing employability, graduates are guaranteed to be both academically qualified and equipped to handle the real-world demands of their careers.

Figure 1 Core principles and goals of Work-Based Education (WBE)

Core Principles and Goals of Work-Based Education (WBE)
• Integration of Experiential Learning with Formal Education
• Collaboration Between Educational Institutions and Industry Partners
• Development of Soft Skills
• Lifelong Learning and Adaptability
• Enhancing Employability

From Figure 1, a fundamental component of education in the changing "next normal," where equity, creativity, and adaptability are critical, is digital literacy. For both educators and students to successfully navigate and thrive in an increasingly technologically-driven educational environment, mastery of digital literacy is imperative. Education can fully utilize technology by fostering digital literacy, guaranteeing fair access, and equipping students with the skills they will need to thrive in a world where technological innovations rule the day.

3. The Role of Work-Based Education (WBE) in Modern Education Systems

Work-Based Education (WBE) is essential to contemporary educational systems because it responds to the changing demands of the global labor market and the changing needs of the global economy. By combining theoretical instruction with real-world application, WBE offers a pragmatic approach to preparing students for the intricacies of today's job markets, as traditional education models that only emphasize classroom-based learning become more and more inadequate. Students benefit from this integration by gaining academic knowledge as well as the skills and competencies needed to succeed in the workplace (Kolb, 2014).

WBE's main responsibility is to increase graduates' employability. There is tremendous pressure on today's educational systems to turn out graduates who are capable of stepping into professional roles with ease. WBE offers students hands-on experience in their fields through internships, apprenticeships, and cooperative education programs. This allows students to network with professionals in the field and gain industry-specific insights. Studies show that students who take part in work-based experience (WBE) programs have a higher chance of finding employment soon after graduation than their counterparts who do not have such experiences (Jackson, 2015). WBE helps close the knowledge gap between education and employment by interacting directly with workplace demands and expectations. This guarantees that students have the knowledge and transferable skills that employers look for.

WBE also encourages responsiveness and creativity in educational systems. Educational institutions can maintain their curricula current with the newest practices, technologies, and trends by forming partnerships with industry stakeholders. This dynamic interplay guarantees that the instruction given is pertinent and in line with the demands of the economy, both now and in the future. Additionally, it makes it possible to create customized courses that are matched to particular business needs, improving the general caliber and relevance of education (Smith & Betts, 2000). Furthermore, these collaborations frequently result in joint research opportunities that can spur creativity and aid in the creation of novel concepts and methods across a range of disciplines.

4. Case Study

To illustrate these principles in action, let's examine a case study of successful WBE implementation, A case study: Bachelor's degree program in Modern Business Management, Faculty of Management Science, Rajabhat Loei University, Thailand has signed an MOU with CP All Public Company Limited, Thailand found that the teaching and learning management in the form of work-based education that CP ALL Public Company Limited has developed and is a model for the Thai education management system according to the needs of entrepreneurs, the management of the curriculum according to the agreement between the company and the university is considered to be very successful. Currently, there are universities and educational institutions jointly producing graduates according to the cooperation agreement starting from 2009 to the present, there are 56 network universities and educational institutions participating, with a total of 7,513 students, and in the academic year 2024, there are 1,214 students (Kingkaew & Saengchompoo, 2024).

The Bachelor's Degree Program in Modern Business Management, Faculty of Management Science, Loei Rajabhat University is another program that has developed a curriculum to produce graduates jointly according to the Memorandum of Understanding (MOU) between Loei Rajabhat University and CP All Public Company Limited and its subsidiaries in the academic year 2019. The course name; Bachelor of Business Administration Program in Modern Trade Business Management; B.B.A (Modern Trade Business Management. which seeks to produce graduates who are exceptional in both academic and practical domains through joint theory and practice study. There are two systems used for teaching and learning, each semester, students will be divided into two equal groups, designated Group A and Group B, by the curriculum, in order to learn on the basis of work as a basis (Work-based Education). Every group will alternate between three months of theory study and three months of practice. The internship will take place in Bangkok's 7-Eleven convenience stores. The course offers several benefits, such as 70% scholarships from the company, pay for the internship, free transportation and lodging, a mentorship program that teaches the job step-by-step, and an immediate hiring opportunity from CP All Public Company Limited after the course ends. Previous to this, in the academic years 2022 and 2023, the program graduated 32 students in two batches, and every graduate immediately obtained employment. It is clear from the cooperation agreement with CP All Public Company Limited that the program has been successful in producing graduates who obtain education based on the workplace. This is because improving professional skills and fully preparing for the workforce to meet employer demands is in line with the student development plan. Additionally, those who complete the course and are given the chance to work are seen as capable, ready, and accepted by the company under the given circumstances. They are also people who are happy to learn and possess the essential life skills for the twenty-first century (Kingkaew & Saengchompoo, 2024).

TEACHING THROUGH WORK-BASED EDUCATION

1. Curriculum Design and Implementation in Work-Based Education (WBE)

1.1. Alignment with Industry Needs

Ensuring alignment with industry needs is a crucial component of curriculum design in Work-Based Education (WBE). This alignment ensures that the knowledge and abilities imparted in educational programs are up to date and satisfy the needs of the labor market. Coll et al. (2009) state that identifying the competencies employers demand and incorporating them into the curriculum require close cooperation with industry stakeholders. This process entails continuing market research, frequent industry representatives' consultations, and course content adaptations to take into account industry trends and technological advancements. In addition to improving graduates' employability, this alignment makes sure that academic institutions continue to adapt to the changing needs of the economy.

1.2. Integration of Experiential Learning

A cornerstone of WBE is the inclusion of experiential learning opportunities in the curriculum. With the help of project-based learning, internships, and apprenticeships, students can gain practical experience in addition to their academic studies. According to Kolb (2014), experiential learning helps students apply what they have learned in the classroom to real-world situations by bridging the theory-practice gap. Well-designed curricula provide students with opportunities to do real-world work, think back on their experiences, and get feedback. By making the learning process more dynamic and contextually relevant, this integration improves student preparation for challenges in the workplace.

1.3. Development of Soft Skills

One of the main objectives of WBE curriculum design is the development of soft skills, such as problem-solving, teamwork, and communication. Employers place a high value on these abilities, which are necessary for professional success. Jackson (2015) emphasizes how crucial it is to include tasks and activities in the curriculum that develop these competencies. This can include group projects, speeches, and activities involving solving problems in the real world. Education programs make sure that students are not only technically competent but also capable of navigating interpersonal and organizational dynamics by incorporating the development of soft skills into the curriculum.

1.4. Assessment and Evaluation

The successful implementation of WBE curricula depends on the use of assessment and evaluation strategies that are effective. To provide a thorough assessment of student's performance, these strategies ought to assess both academic knowledge and practical skills. According to Billett (2011), a mix of formative and summative evaluations should be used, such as traditional exams, project reports, reflective journals, and performance reviews from work placements. A comprehensive approach like this guarantees that in addition to academic performance, students are evaluated on their capacity to integrate and apply knowledge in real-world situations. Frequent feedback from these tests promotes ongoing learning by assisting students in identifying areas for development.

1.5. Continuous Improvement and Adaptation

For curriculum design in WBE to stay current and useful, it must be continuously improved upon and adjusted. This entails routinely evaluating and revising the curriculum, instructional strategies, and learning objectives in response to input from instructors, industry partners, and students. According to Smith and Betts (2000), it is critical to use a cyclical approach to curriculum development in which iterative improvements are made using feedback. By doing this, the curriculum is kept up to date with industry standards, new information and technologies are incorporated, and any gaps in the teaching process are filled. Practices for continuous improvement create a flexible learning environment that can adapt to shifts in educational research and the labor market.

2. Pedagogical Strategies for Integrating Work-Based Learning

2.1. Project-Based Learning

Project-based learning (PBL) is an effective teaching approach that complements work-based learning by involving students in practical projects that call for the application of their academic knowledge and abilities. Under this method, students often collaborate with industry partners to work on complex, open-ended projects that mirror professional tasks (Thomas, 2000). PBL promotes deep learning by involving students in worthwhile tasks that foster creativity, critical thinking, and problem-solving, claim Barron and Darling-Hammond (2008). This approach not only closes the knowledge gap between theoretical ideas and real-world applications but also aids in the development of soft skills that are vital in the workplace, like communication and teamwork.

2.2. Simulations and Role-Playing

Effective pedagogical techniques that give students a safe space to practice and hone their skills include role-playing and simulations. According to Beard and Wilson (2006), these techniques imitate real-world situations in which students can participate in decision-making, problem-solving, and role-specific activities. By engaging in role-playing games and simulations, students get practical experience and fast performance feedback. Simulations improve learning by creating immersive experiences that aid students in comprehending intricate systems and processes (Garris, Ahlers, & Driskell, 2002). These tactics are especially helpful in professions like business, healthcare, and engineering where application of practical knowledge and prompt decision-making are essential.

2.3. Industry-Based Mentoring

Students are paired with seasoned professionals who offer advice, encouragement, and feedback throughout their work-based learning experiences as part of industry-based mentoring. By providing students with individualized insights and guidance from business experts, this tactic improves learning (Cox, 2005). Mentors assist students in establishing professional networks, learning how to function in the workplace, and developing career skills. Effective mentoring relationships can have a significant impact on students' career development and job satisfaction by giving them access to professional role models and practical knowledge (Allen, Eby, Poteet, Lentz, & Lima, 2004). This method also facilitates the integration of academic knowledge with practical application by assigning students to mentors who can offer guidance and significance to their academic pursuits.

2.4. Reflective Practice

Students can gain new insights and enhance their performance by systematically reflecting on their work-based learning experiences through the use of the reflective practice technique. This approach fosters critical analysis of students' decisions, deeds, and outcomes, which enhances their learning and professional development (Schön, 1983). Reflective practice includes journaling, participating in group discussions, and receiving feedback from teachers and peers. According to Moon (2004), students benefit from reflective practice when it comes to developing their self-awareness, problem-solving skills, and understanding of their educational experiences. This methodology, which fosters the establishment of links between scholarly ideas and real-world experiences, excels in uniting theoretical understanding with pragmatic implementation.

2.5. Competency-Based Learning

The goal of competency-based learning is to make sure that students gain particular skills or learning objectives from their work-based experiences. The goal of this strategy is to guarantee that students gain the abilities and information required to succeed in their chosen fields (Spady, 1994). According to Stark and Lowther (1988), competency-based learning entails defining precise performance criteria, offering chances for real-world application, and rating students according to their capacity to exhibit competencies rather than just finishing coursework. Boud and Falchikov (2006) claim that by emphasizing practical skills and real-world applications, this approach encourages deeper learning and better equips students for the demands of the workplace.

3. Case Studies of Effective Teaching Methods in Work-Based Education (WBE)

3.1. Cooperative Education Programs

One well-known example of a successful teaching strategy in WBE is the cooperative education (co-op) initiatives run by universities such as Northeastern University. Students can switch between academic terms and paid work placements through these programs that combine classroom instruction with paid work experience. Wilson's (2014) study demonstrates how Northeastern University's co-op program has effectively improved students' employability by giving them real-world experience related to their academic fields. Students apply their academic knowledge in practical settings, build professional networks, and receive insightful industry insights. Co-op programs are structured to guarantee that students are not only working but also learning from their experiences. Regular assessments and reflection opportunities are part of this structure.

3.2. Industry Partnerships and Capstone Projects

The capstone project approach from the University of Waterloo is an additional useful strategy for incorporating work-based learning. Under this model, students complete their final year of study working on projects sponsored by the industry. According to a study by Eames and Cates (2018), these capstone projects give students the chance to apply their knowledge and skills in the real world by letting them take on problems that industry partners pose. Students receive mentorship from faculty and professionals in the industry, and the projects are made relevant and challenging through collaboration with industry partners. This approach improves students' capacity for problem-solving, collaboration, and preparedness for the workforce.

3.3. Simulations and Role-Playing in Healthcare Training

Role-playing and simulations are used successfully in the healthcare industry to get students ready for actual clinical situations. For example, medical students at the University of Miami's School of Medicine receive training in high-fidelity simulation labs. These simulations give students immersive, hands-on experiences in a controlled setting, enabling them to practice clinical skills, make decisions, and get feedback, as shown by a case study by Issenberg et al. (2005). By bridging the knowledge gap between theory and practice, simulations improve students' clinical competencies and self-assurance in real-world scenarios.

3.4. Mentoring and Industry-Based Learning in Business Education

The application of industry-based mentoring programs in business education has shown to be successful. A mentorship program has been established by the University of Melbourne's Business School, matching students with seasoned business professionals. Such mentoring programs offer students career guidance, networking opportunities, and insights into industry practices, according to a study by Kram (1985). Mentors support students in applying their academic knowledge to real-world business challenges, help them navigate their career paths, and provide guidance on professional development. This individualized approach improves the educational process and gets students ready for lucrative careers in business.

3.5. Problem-Based Learning (PBL) in Engineering Education

Work-based learning has been successfully integrated into engineering education through the use of Problem-Based Learning (PBL). PBL is used at McMaster University to get students involved in solving challenging engineering problems that mimic real-world issues. PBL encourages students to actively engage in learning by identifying problems, researching solutions, and presenting their findings, as demonstrated by a case study by Barrows (1996). This method not only helps students become more adept at solving problems and using critical thinking, but it also gets them ready for the multidisciplinary and collaborative nature of modern engineering practices.

Figure 2. Teaching through work-based education

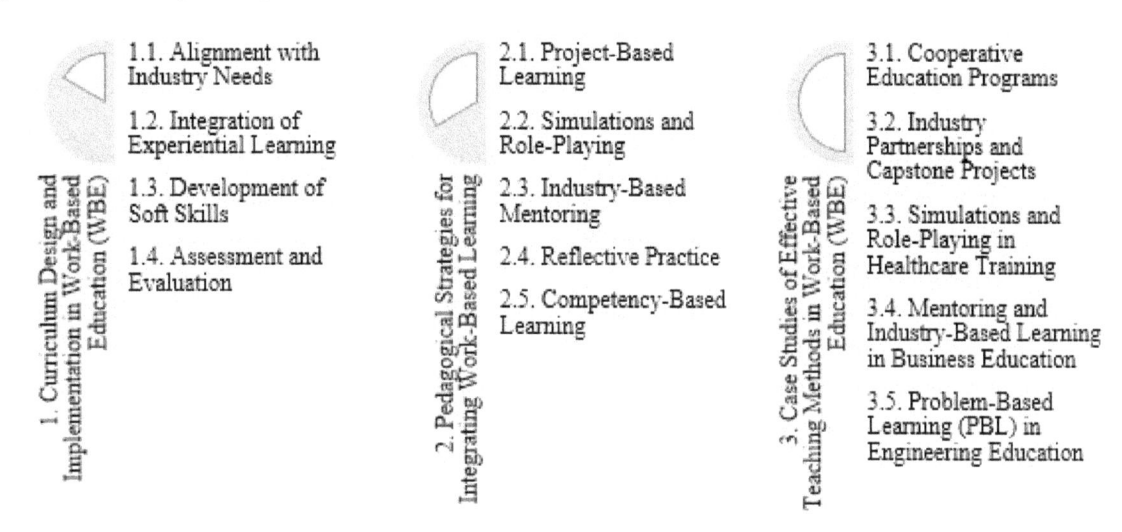

1. Curriculum Design and Implementation in Work-Based Education (WBE)
- 1.1. Alignment with Industry Needs
- 1.2. Integration of Experiential Learning
- 1.3. Development of Soft Skills
- 1.4. Assessment and Evaluation

2. Pedagogical Strategies for Integrating Work-Based Learning
- 2.1. Project-Based Learning
- 2.2. Simulations and Role-Playing
- 2.3. Industry-Based Mentoring
- 2.4. Reflective Practice
- 2.5. Competency-Based Learning

3. Case Studies of Effective Teaching Methods in Work-Based Education (WBE)
- 3.1. Cooperative Education Programs
- 3.2. Industry Partnerships and Capstone Projects
- 3.3. Simulations and Role-Playing in Healthcare Training
- 3.4. Mentoring and Industry-Based Learning in Business Education
- 3.5. Problem-Based Learning (PBL) in Engineering Education

From Figure 2, work-based education (WBE) emphasizes curriculum design, pedagogical strategies, and the application of experiential learning to effectively bridge the gap between academic learning and industry requirements. WBE makes sure that students are ready for the workforce by integrating experiential learning, coordinating educational programs with industry needs, and encouraging the development of soft skills. The use of various pedagogical techniques, such as project-based learning, role-playing, and mentorship, improves students' practical abilities and competencies. Case studies from a variety of fields show how effective these approaches are, emphasizing the value of industry collaborations and hands-on learning in preparing students for obstacles they may face in the real world. All things considered, work-based learning is an essential strategy for giving students the knowledge and experience they need to pursue successful careers.

ACADEMIC SERVICE IN WORK-BASED EDUCATION

1. Collaboration with Industry and Community Partners

1.1. Enhancing Curriculum Relevance through Industry Collaboration

In Work-Based Education (WBE), academic service necessitates close cooperation between academic institutions and industry partners to guarantee curricula that are current and relevant to industry demands. By incorporating real-world knowledge and cutting-edge trends into the curriculum, this kind of collaboration assists in matching academic programs with the demands of business. These collaborations make it easier to integrate real-world problems and technological advancements into academic courses, which improves the relevance and engagement of the learning process for students (Smith and Betts, 2000). Teachers can create and deliver a curriculum that not only satisfies academic requirements but also gets students ready for the particular demands and expectations of their future careers by collaborating closely with industry experts. Graduates with this alignment will find it easier to find employment because they will have knowledge and skills that are immediately useful in their chosen fields.

1.2. Facilitating Experiential Learning Opportunities

Establishing opportunities for experiential learning, like internships, apprenticeships, and service-learning initiatives, is made easier through cooperation with business and community partners. Through practical experiences in real-world settings, students can apply their theoretical knowledge in real-world situations. According to Billett (2011), these kinds of experiences are essential for gaining real-world knowledge and comprehending work settings. Community organizations may offer service-learning opportunities that address regional needs and issues, while industry partners can offer students worthwhile work placements and projects that mimic actual job functions. Through these interactions, students can expand their professional networks, acquire invaluable experience, and get a deeper understanding of their subject areas, all of which are beneficial to their overall academic and career development.

1.3. Building Stronger Community and Industry Connections

Collaborating with industry and community partners to provide academic service benefits students and fortifies the bonds between academic institutions and their larger communities. Educational institutions can address community needs, support regional economic development, and instill social responsibility in students by collaborating with local businesses and organizations. As per Wankel and Blessinger's (2013) findings, industry, and community partners can offer resources, expertise, and real-world learning contexts, while educational institutions can produce skilled graduates and creative solutions to local problems. These partnerships can result in mutually beneficial outcomes. This cooperative method fosters a feeling of common purpose and dedication to community development while enhancing the social impact of education.

2. Service Learning and Community Engagement in Work-Based Education

2.1. Integration of Service Learning into Academic Programs

A pedagogical strategy called "service learning" combines academic instruction with community service to give students the chance to apply what they've learned in practical ways while meeting needs in the community. By encouraging a deeper comprehension of academic concepts through real-world application, this method improves the educational experience (Eyler & Giles, 1999). Service learning initiatives frequently entail working with neighborhood associations and community groups, giving students the chance to get hands-on experience with real-world problems and contribute to important solutions. Service learning fosters social awareness and civic responsibility in addition to reinforcing classroom learning by tying academic goals to community service.

2.2. Benefits to Students and Communities

There are many advantages to service learning for communities and students alike. It provides students with practical experience that improves their comprehension of academic material and fosters the development of transferable skills like leadership, teamwork, and problem-solving (Billig, 2002). Serving the community enables students to make the connection between their academic understanding and practical applications, increasing the relevance and impact of their education. Students' services, which can address local needs and promote community development, are beneficial to communities (Zlotkowski, 2004). Through service learning, communities receive invaluable support and creative solutions to urgent problems, and students develop a greater understanding of social issues and a commitment to civic engagement.

2.3. Challenges and Strategies for Effective Implementation

Although there are many benefits to service learning, there are also drawbacks. These include the need to manage logistics, make sure projects are in line with academic goals, and sustain meaningful community partnerships (Kendall, 1990). Careful planning and cooperation between educational institutions, community organizations, and students are necessary for effective implementation. Establishing precise learning objectives, designing well-organized reflection exercises, and keeping lines of communication open with community partners are some strategies for overcoming these obstacles (Furco, 1996). Institutions can improve service-learning programs' efficacy and guarantee that communities and students get the results they want by tackling these issues.

3. Benefits of Academic Service for Students and Stakeholders

3.1. Enhanced Learning and Practical Skills for Students

Students gain substantial advantages from academic service, especially when it comes to work-based learning and service learning, as it improves their learning opportunities and transferable skills. Students' comprehension of academic concepts is enhanced when they apply theoretical knowledge in real-world settings through real-world projects and community service (Eyler & Giles, 1999). In addition to supporting classroom learning, this practical experience aids in the development of critical thinking, problem-solving, and professional communication skills in students. For example, Billig (2002) emphasizes that through hands-on application and reflection on their experiences, students engaged in service learning frequently develop greater self-confidence and a deeper understanding of their academic subjects. Through this hands-on experience, their education becomes more engaging and relevant, preparing them for their future careers.

3.2. Strengthened Community Partnerships and Impact

Academic service helps everyone involved—including community organizations—by fostering stronger bonds and effectively addressing needs in the community. Through work-based learning and service learning, educational institutions collaborate with community partners to provide valuable services and solutions. Zlotkowski (2004) claims that these collaborations help communities solve pressing problems by providing them with access to students' innovative ideas and problem-solving skills. Better local services and greater community involvement are among the many benefits that these partnerships typically bring to the area. Student contributions can also assist community organizations in achieving their goals and forging mutually beneficial alliances that further educational and community goals.

3.3. Increased Institutional Reputation and Community Support

Academic service helps educational institutions by improving their standing and bolstering community support. Participating in work-based learning and service learning shows that an institution is committed to community involvement and social responsibility. Increased support from nearby companies, organizations, and potential donors may result from this proactive involvement (Furco, 1996). Institutions that successfully incorporate academic service into their curricula frequently see increases in public perception and stronger ties with stakeholders in the community, according to Kendall (1990). This stellar reputation can draw in more students, boost the standing of the institution, and create enduring community relationships that advance social and academic goals.

Figure 3. Academic service in work-based education

1. Collaboration with Industry and Community Partners
- 1.1. Enhancing Curriculum Relevance through Industry Collaboration
- 1.2. Facilitating Experiential Learning Opportunities
- 1.3. Building Stronger Community and Industry Connections

2. Service Learning and Community Engagement in Work-Based Education
- 2.1. Integration of Service Learning into Academic Programs
- 2.2. Benefits to Students and Communities
- 2.3. Challenges and Strategies for Effective Implementation

3. Benefits of Academic Service for Students and Stakeholders
- 3.1. Enhanced Learning and Practical Skills for Students
- 3.2. Strengthened Community Partnerships and Impact
- 3.3. Increased Institutional Reputation and Community Support

From Figure 3, working together with partners in the community and industry is essential to enhancing the curriculum, promoting experiential learning, and fortifying ties between the educational system, business community, and the community. There are several advantages to incorporating service learning and community involvement into work-based learning, such as improved student learning, the development of employable skills, and beneficial community impact. Even with implementation challenges, strategic approaches guarantee successful results. All things considered, academic service strengthens ties with the community, improves the standing of the institution, and aids in students' overall development, making it an important part of contemporary educational initiatives.

RESEARCH WITHIN WORK-BASED EDUCATION

However, researchers must be mindful of ethical considerations, such as ensuring fair treatment of student participants and addressing potential conflicts of interest with industry partners.

1. Areas of Research Focus in Work-Based Education (WBE)

1.1. Efficacy of Work-Based Learning Models

An important field of study in Work-Based Education (WBE) is the effectiveness of different work-based learning models, such as apprenticeships, co-ops, and internships. Scholars investigate the effects of various models on student outcomes, including academic performance, skill acquisition, and employability. Research has examined the impact of structured internships on students' career development and professional preparedness, for instance (Jackson, 2015). Research frequently compares the efficacy of various models, identifies best practices, and comprehends how elements like length, kind of work experience, and mentorship affect these programs' overall success. To better serve the needs of industry and education, this research aids in the optimization and refinement of WBE models.

1.2. Impact on Student Learning Outcomes

Evaluating the effect of work-based learning on student learning outcomes is a crucial sector of WBE research. This involves assessing the effects that students' involvement in WBE activities has on their academic performance, skill growth, and preparedness for the workforce. To measure these outcomes, researchers employ a variety of methodologies, such as interviews, surveys, and longitudinal studies (Billett, 2011). Research has investigated how practical problem-solving exercises and hands-on projects improve students' critical thinking and problem-solving skills. Institutions can create more effective programs and enhance the alignment of academic and professional learning by having a better understanding of the relationship between work-based learning experiences and educational outcomes.

1.3. Integration of WBE with Academic Curriculum

Effective ways to incorporate WBE into the academic curriculum are also the subject of research. This field looks at ways to make sure that students' work experiences make sense about their coursework and that work-based learning is in line with academic objectives (Kolb, 2014). Research in this area examines methods for designing curricula that include experiential learning in academic programs, like project-based learning and simulations. Researchers look into the best ways to combine theoretical and practical elements to preserve academic rigor and optimize learning outcomes. This research is essential for creating curricula that support students' comprehensive and coherent learning journeys while also integrating work-based experiences.

1.4. Role of Industry and Community Partnerships

Industry and community partnerships' role in WBE is another crucial area of research. This includes looking into how partnerships between academic institutions and businesses or neighborhood associations improve the efficacy of work-based learning initiatives (Smith & Betts, 2000). The nature of these collaborations, the resources they offer, and their effects on partners and students are all examined by research in this field. Research frequently looks at how these alliances can be set up to benefit all parties involved, including the most efficient ways to form and keep them. Comprehending these dynamics enables educational institutions to cultivate more robust relationships with business and community associates, resulting in more fruitful and significant work-based learning opportunities.

1.5. Assessment and Evaluation of WBE Programs

A key component of WBE research is assessment and evaluation, which focuses on how to gauge and assess the efficacy of work-based learning initiatives. According to Garris, Ahlers, and Driskell (2002), this entails creating measures and instruments to evaluate program outcomes, student performance, and overall program quality. Scholars investigate diverse evaluation techniques, including performance assessments, reflective journals, and feedback mechanisms, to ascertain the degree to which Work-Based Education (WBE) programs fulfill their intended goals in terms of education and career advancement. Sustaining improvement and guaranteeing that WBE programs offer students worthwhile and pertinent learning experiences depend on efficient assessment procedures.

2. Methodologies and Approaches for Work-Based Education (WBE) Research

2.1. Qualitative Research Methods

In WBE research, qualitative research methods are frequently employed to obtain a comprehensive understanding of participants' experiences and perspectives. Researchers can investigate how students, educators, and industry partners experience and perceive work-based learning programs through various techniques like focus groups, interviews, and case studies. Interviews with employers and students, for example, can yield rich, contextual data regarding the effects of coops and internships on skill development and career readiness (Yin, 2018). Program improvements can be informed by the common themes and difficulties that participants in focus groups reveal. When examining intricate phenomena, deciphering the subtleties of work-based learning opportunities, and formulating research questions, qualitative approaches are especially helpful.

2.2. Quantitative Research Methods

Quantitative research methods are used to measure and analyze variables systematically related to WBE programs. Surveys, questionnaires, and statistical analyses are commonly used to assess the efficacy of work-based learning initiatives and their impact on student outcomes. For example, researchers may use pre- and post-program surveys to measure changes in students' employability, confidence, or skill sets (Creswell, 2014). Statistical techniques can be used to analyze data on program participation, career outcomes, and academic achievement. Using this approach, researchers can identify trends, linkages, and root causes, providing a solid basis for evaluating the impact of WBE initiatives on student achievement and program effectiveness.

2.3. Mixed Methods Approaches

Qualitative and quantitative methods are combined in mixed methods research to give a thorough understanding of WBE programs. Researchers can take advantage of each methodology's advantages and obtain a more comprehensive understanding of work-based learning experiences by combining the two forms of data (Tashakkori & Teddlie, 2010). For instance, a study may employ qualitative interviews to delve deeper into participant experiences and viewpoints and quantitative surveys to gauge program outcomes. Through triangulation, this approach enables researchers to validate findings and obtain insights into the contextual factors as well as the measurable impacts affecting WBE programs.

2.4. Longitudinal Studies

Studies with a long follow-up period monitor participants to evaluate the long-term effects of work-based learning on their professional and academic growth. To track changes and results over time, this methodology entails gathering data at several points in time (Menard, 2002). To assess how experiences affect professional trajectories, researchers could, for instance, track students from the time they first enroll in a work-based learning program until they graduate and launch their careers. Studies with a longitudinal design offer significant insights into the long-term impacts of work-based learning and facilitate the identification of variables associated with sustained success.

2.5. Comparative Studies

Comparative studies are used to assess the relative efficacy of various WBE models, programs, or practices. Scholars may examine differences in program design between various institutions or industries, or compare the results of internships versus co-ops (Garris, Ahlers, & Driskell, 2002). This method aids in identifying best practices and comprehending the various aspects that affect work-based learning program success. Researchers can offer suggestions for improving program design and implementation to improve student learning and career outcomes by comparing various models.

3. Impact of Research on Educational Practices and Policies in Work-Based Education (WBE)

3.1. Informing Program Design and Curriculum Development

Curricula and program design in Work-Based Education (WBE) are greatly influenced by research. Through the provision of empirically grounded insights into the efficacy of diverse work-based learning models, research facilitates the design of programs that better serve the needs of industry and educational objectives by educators and policymakers. For instance, studies comparing the effects of various work-based learning models, like internships versus apprenticeships, help determine which models are best suited to meet particular learning goals (Jackson, 2015). Furthermore, research on effective program elements and best practices directs educational institutions in the incorporation of work-based learning components into their curricula, guaranteeing that academic programs stay current and adaptable to the needs of the labor market.

3.2. Shaping Policy and Funding Decisions

Policymakers can make decisions about funding and educational policies because research in work-based learning (WBE) gives them information about the advantages and efficacy of WBE programs. The results of research on how WBE affects student outcomes, employability, and career readiness can be used to support and justify the funding of these initiatives (Billett, 2011). For example, research demonstrating the benefits of work-based learning on employment placement and graduation rates can result in more financing and policy support for these kinds of programs. Research helps policymakers make well-informed decisions about whether to expand and support work-based education programs, which improves their impact on workforce development and the educational system.

3.3. Enhancing Collaboration between Educational Institutions and Industry

The advantages and difficulties of working together between academic institutions and business partners are highlighted by research on WBE, which has an impact on how these alliances are set up and run. Research on productive industry-academia partnerships offers important insights into how organizations can create and sustain partnerships that improve work-based learning opportunities (Smith & Betts, 2000). This study encourages academic institutions to form strategic alliances that benefit industry partners as well as students, improving program outcomes and better coordinating with industry demands. Because of this, organizations are more likely to take part in fruitful partnerships that improve the outcomes of work-based learning initiatives and fortify ties between higher education and the workforce.

3.4. Guiding Assessment and Evaluation Practices

The effectiveness of work-based learning programs can be assessed and evaluated using frameworks and methodologies that are provided by research. Research on tools and strategies for assessment aids in the development and application of efficient evaluation techniques by educators to gauge program impact, overall quality, and student performance (Garris, Ahlers, & Driskell, 2002). This evidence-based strategy guarantees that evaluation procedures give accurate feedback on the efficacy of programs and are in line with educational goals. Institutions can improve work-based learning programs and their contributions to student learning and career preparation by integrating research findings into assessment and evaluation practices.

3.5. Driving Innovation and Continuous Improvement

Work-based learning (WBE) research identifies new technologies, work-based learning strategies, and emerging trends that spur innovation and continuous improvement in educational practices. For instance, studies on the application of virtual simulations and digital tools in work-based learning shed light on how technology can improve learning objectives and experiences (Kolb, 2014). Educators and policymakers can improve the efficacy of work-based education by embracing innovative practices and making data-driven decisions by staying up to date on the latest research findings. This continuous process of translating research into practice guarantees that work-based learning initiatives stay flexible, current, and able to adapt to changing demands from the business and education sectors.

Figure 4. Research within work-based education

1. Areas of Research Focus in Work-Based Education (WBE)

1.1. Efficacy of Work-Based Learning Models

1.2. Impact on Student Learning Outcomes

1.3. Integration of WBE with Academic Curriculum

1.4. Role of Industry and Community Partnerships

1.5. Assessment and Evaluation of WBE Programs

2. Methodologies and Approaches for Work-Based Education (WBE) Research

2.1. Qualitative Research Methods

2.2. Quantitative Research Methods

2.3. Mixed Methods Approaches

2.4. Longitudinal Studies

2.5. Comparative Studies

3. Impact of Research on Educational Practices and Policies in Work-Based Education (WBE)

3.1. Informing Program Design and Curriculum Development

3.2. Shaping Policy and Funding Decisions

3.3. Enhancing Collaboration between Educational Institutions and Industry

3.4. Guiding Assessment and Evaluation Practices

3.5. Driving Innovation and Continuous Improvement

From Figure 4, research in work-based education (WBE) is essential to enhance student outcomes, incorporate WBE into academic curricula, and boost the effectiveness of learning models. Research offers crucial viewpoints that impact educational policies and practices by looking at issues like industry partnerships, program evaluation, and the efficacy of work-based education models. The use of a variety of research methodologies, including mixed methods, quantitative, and qualitative approaches, makes it possible to fully understand the impact of WBE. Through program design, funding and policy decisions, and industry-academic collaboration, the results of WBE research stimulate innovation and continuous improvement in education.

NETWORKING WITH BUSINESS SECTOR AND PARTNERS

1. Building and Sustaining Industry Partnerships in Work-Based Education

1.1. Establishing Effective Initial Connections

The first step in creating a solid industry partnership is for businesses and educational institutions to effectively connect. Finding possible industry partners who share the institution's needs and goals for education is part of this process. Using alumni networks, going to business gatherings, and reaching out to possible partners directly are all effective tactics (Wankel & Blessinger, 2013). Creating a concise value proposition that highlights shared advantages is essential to luring and securing business partners. Institutions, for instance, can show how cooperation can give businesses a pool of graduates who are ready for the workforce while giving students important exposure to business and career opportunities.

The initial focus of meetings and conversations should be on defining shared goals, coordinating objectives, and summarizing each partner's possible contributions.

1.2. Developing Structured Partnership Agreements

After the first contacts are made, it is crucial to draft formal partnership agreements that specify each party's expectations as well as their roles and responsibilities. The scope of the collaboration should be outlined in these agreements, along with information on work-based learning opportunities like internships, cooperative placements, or joint projects (Smith & Betts, 2000). Good agreements also have channels for evaluation, feedback, and communication to make sure the collaboration stays fruitful and on course. Institutions and industry partners can ensure that there are no misunderstandings and that both parties benefit from the partnership by formalizing these agreements and establishing a framework for ongoing collaboration.

1.3. Maintaining Ongoing Communication and Engagement

It takes constant communication and proactive participation from educational institutions as well as industry partners to maintain industry partnerships. Maintaining a strong relationship and addressing any new issues or changes in goals is facilitated by holding regular meetings, updates, and feedback sessions (Billett, 2011). Organizations ought to set up channels of communication, like working groups, advisory boards, and digital platforms, that promote cooperation and information sharing. Maintaining the partnership's vitality and relevance requires ongoing participation in cooperative endeavors like industry-sponsored events, guest lectures, and networking opportunities. Acknowledging and applauding the partnership's accomplishments can also improve ties and highlight the importance of continued cooperation.

1.4. Evaluating and Adjusting the Partnership

Maintaining the partnership's efficacy and sustainability requires regular evaluation. Institutions and business partners should evaluate the partnership's results and effects regularly to see if it is accomplishing its objectives and benefiting both sides (Garris, Ahlers, & Driskell, 2002). Surveys, interviews, and performance metrics are examples of evaluation techniques that are used to determine how well work-based learning opportunities are going, how satisfied participants are, and how effective the partnership is as a whole. The partnership's operations, procedures, and structure can all be improved by making changes in response to the evaluation's findings. This iterative process aids in upholding a fruitful and flexible collaboration that keeps up with changing goals and needs.

1.5. Leveraging Technology for Partnership Management

Industry partnerships are managed and sustained in large part by technology. The efficiency and efficacy of the collaboration can be increased by leveraging digital tools and platforms for data sharing, project management, and communication (Kolb, 2014). For example, project management software can manage tasks and track progress, while online collaboration tools can help arrange regular meetings and conversations. Technology also makes it possible to gather and analyze data about the partnership's results, which aids in the decision-making and adjustment-making processes of institutions and industry partners. Institutions can ensure that the partnership stays responsive to the needs of both parties, improve coordination, and streamline processes by incorporating technology into partnership management.

2. Role of Networking in Enhancing Work-Based Education (WBE) Programs

2.1. Expanding Professional Opportunities for Students

Through the expansion of students' professional opportunities, networking is essential to the improvement of Work-Based Education (WBE) programs. Educational institutions can create connections that result in internships, job placements, and mentorship opportunities through strategic networking with industry professionals, alumni, and community leaders (Friedman, 2015). These relationships increase students' employability and career readiness by giving them access to a wider range of career opportunities and industry insights. Through networking events, industry conferences, and alumni gatherings, for instance, students can interact with industry experts and potential employers, receiving advice and job leads that may not be obtained through more conventional job search techniques.

2.2. Strengthening Industry and Academic Partnerships

Building stronger relationships between academic institutions and business requires networking. Institutions can establish and preserve strong relationships with industry partners by actively participating in industry associations, professional groups, and community organizations (Smith & Betts, 2000). These connections are essential to the development and maintenance of work-based learning opportunities like cooperative projects, internships, and co-ops. Through networking, educational institutions can stay up to date on market trends, match student needs to industry demands, and make sure that partnerships work both ways. Frequent engagement with industry stakeholders via advisory boards and networking events enables universities to obtain input and modify their WBE programs as needed.

2.3. Facilitating Knowledge Exchange and Best Practices

Networking facilitates the sharing of best practices and knowledge between academic institutions, business associates, and other WBE stakeholders. Teachers and business professionals can exchange experiences, ideas, and creative approaches to work-based learning through professional networks and forums (Wankel & Blessinger, 2013). Collaboration among institutions facilitates the adoption of effective strategies, enhances program design, and addresses shared challenges. Networking, for instance, can give access to case studies, research results, and effective program models that improve and inform WBE practices. Working with a larger group of professionals and specialists encourages innovation and ongoing development in work-based learning.

2.4. Enhancing Student and Alumni Engagement

To engage students and alumni with WBE programs, networking is also essential. Current students can benefit from networking opportunities, career guidance, and mentorship offered by alumni networks and professional associations, which can further their education and professional growth (Kolb, 2014).

Establishing strong ties with alumni and incorporating them in WBE programs via panel discussions, networking events, and guest lectures allows institutions to build a community that is beneficial to both current students and graduates. Alumni can help close the gap between academic learning and practical application by sharing their career experiences and providing insightful commentary from the industry.

2.5. Supporting Program Promotion and Recruitment

Successful networking increases awareness of and highlights the benefits of work-based learning initiatives, which aids in the recruitment and promotion of WBE programs. Institutions can showcase their successful programs, draw in prospective students, and establish a good reputation in the industry by utilizing professional networks and industry connections (Garris, Ahlers, & Driskell, 2002). Through networking events like industry presentations, educational fairs, and cooperative projects, universities can interact with potential partners and students and showcase the advantages of their WBE programs. Institutions can improve their overall program offerings, draw in top talent, and increase their visibility by using these networks for promotional purposes.

3. Examples of Successful Business-Education Collaborations

3.1. IBM and P-TECH Schools

A good example of a business-education partnership is IBM's work with the Pathways in Technology Early College High School (P-TECH) program. P-TECH is an educational model that integrates professional training, college, and high school into a single pathway. It was introduced in 2011. Through industry projects and internships with IBM and other partner companies, students in the program gain work experience while earning both an associate degree and a high school diploma in a STEM field (P-TECH, 2022). Through this partnership, employers can fill in skills gaps by giving students real-world experience and credentials that are highly sought after. Because of P-TECH's success, it has spread to other states and nations, proving how well industry partnerships can be incorporated into education.

3.2. Google and the Grow with Google Program

Grow with Google by Google is another excellent example of business and education working together. This program was started in 2017 to give organizations and individuals access to free resources and training to help them become more digitally literate. Grow with Google provides workshops, online courses, and certification programs in subjects like digital marketing, data analysis, and web development through collaborations with academic institutions, libraries, and community organizations (Google, 2022). Google supports workforce development and bridges the digital skills gap by working with a variety of educational and community partners. This shows how business-education partnerships can improve career readiness and economic opportunity.

3.3. Cisco Networking Academy

One well-known illustration of a business-education partnership that succeeds in promoting technology education is Cisco Networking Academy. This program, which was started in 1997, offers curriculum, materials, and assistance to educational institutions so they can teach networking and information technology. Cisco, through its curriculum and online resources, provides students with practical training in networking technologies, cybersecurity, and IoT (Internet of Things) in partnership with schools and colleges worldwide (Cisco, 2022). Millions of students worldwide have benefited from The Networking Academy's industry-relevant training and certification programs, which increase their employability in the technology sector.

3.4. Microsoft and the Microsoft Philanthropies Global Skills Initiative

Through education and training initiatives, Microsoft Philanthropies Global Skills Initiative seeks to close the skills gap in the world. This initiative, which was started in 2020, collaborates with government organizations, nonprofits, and educational institutions to offer free access to learning materials, certifications, and assistance with job placement. The program includes partnerships with companies like LinkedIn and Coursera to offer courses and certifications, and it focuses on in-demand digital skills like cloud computing, artificial intelligence, and data science (Microsoft, 2022). This partnership serves as an example of how companies can use their networks and resources to promote extensive workforce development and education initiatives.

3.5. Siemens and the Siemens Technical Academy

One effective business-education partnership that focuses on vocational training is Siemens' Technical Academy. Through its academy programs, Siemens collaborates with academic institutions and technical and vocational schools to offer training in technical and engineering fields. The academy provides specialized training in fields like energy management, robotics, and automation, as well as apprenticeships and internships (Siemens, 2022). By working together, we can make sure that students acquire real-world experience and industry-specific skills that meet Siemens' operational requirements. We also hope to contribute to the creation of a skilled labor force for the larger industrial sector.

Figure 5. Networking with business sector and partners

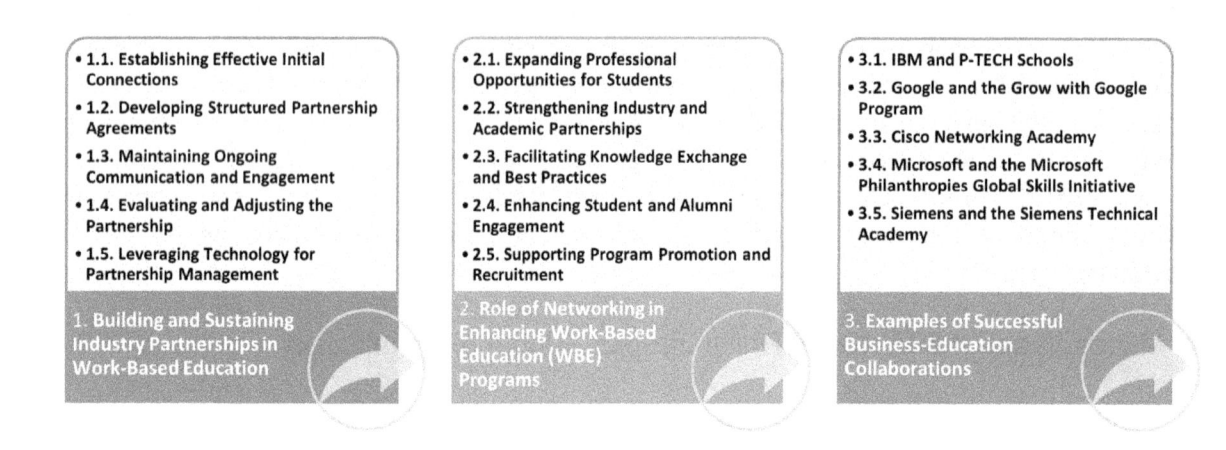

1. Building and Sustaining Industry Partnerships in Work-Based Education	2. Role of Networking in Enhancing Work-Based Education (WBE) Programs	3. Examples of Successful Business-Education Collaborations
• 1.1. Establishing Effective Initial Connections • 1.2. Developing Structured Partnership Agreements • 1.3. Maintaining Ongoing Communication and Engagement • 1.4. Evaluating and Adjusting the Partnership • 1.5. Leveraging Technology for Partnership Management	• 2.1. Expanding Professional Opportunities for Students • 2.2. Strengthening Industry and Academic Partnerships • 2.3. Facilitating Knowledge Exchange and Best Practices • 2.4. Enhancing Student and Alumni Engagement • 2.5. Supporting Program Promotion and Recruitment	• 3.1. IBM and P-TECH Schools • 3.2. Google and the Grow with Google Program • 3.3. Cisco Networking Academy • 3.4. Microsoft and the Microsoft Philanthropies Global Skills Initiative • 3.5. Siemens and the Siemens Technical Academy

From Figure 5, creating and maintaining industry partnerships is essential to the success of programs focused on work-based education (WBE). Long-term collaboration hinges on forging solid early bonds, creating well-organized agreements, and keeping lines of communication open. By creating more professional opportunities, fostering stronger partnerships, and promoting knowledge exchange, networking plays a crucial role in further enhancing WBE. Promising partnerships between business and education, like those between IBM, Google, Cisco, Microsoft, and Siemens and educational institutions, provide valuable learning experiences and equip students for their future careers. These partnerships serve as a reminder of how crucial strategic alliances are to fostering innovation and raising student achievement in WBE programs.

INTEGRATING ACADEMIC KNOWLEDGE AND PRACTICAL EXPERIENCE

1. Models and Approaches for Effective Integration

1.1. Theoretical Frameworks for Integration

To effectively integrate academic knowledge with practical experience, educational program design and implementation must be guided by a strong theoretical framework. Kolb's Experiential Learning Theory is a well-known model that highlights the cyclical nature of experience-based learning. Effective learning, according to Kolb (2014), entails a never-ending cycle of active experimentation, abstract conceptualization, reflective observation, and concrete experience. By encouraging students to apply theoretical concepts in real-world settings, reflect on their experiences, and modify their understanding based on practical feedback, this model supports the integration of academic knowledge and practical experience. Institutions can design programs that close the knowledge gap between classroom instruction and practical application by coordinating educational activities with Kolb's framework. This will increase the relevance and power of educational experiences.

1.2. Work-Integrated Learning (WIL) Models

Models of work-integrated learning, or WIL, are a useful way to combine academic knowledge with real-world experience. WIL includes a range of experiential learning opportunities, such as industry projects, co-ops, and internships. These models, according to Billett (2011), give students the chance to participate in worthwhile work experiences that enhance their academic coursework. For instance, co-op programs enable students to apply what they learn in the classroom to real-world professional settings by alternating between periods of academic study and paid work experience. Through real-world application, these models not only improve students' employability and practical skills but also help them grasp academic concepts more deeply. Strong collaborations between academic institutions and business, well-defined learning goals, and organized reflection procedures that assist students in making the connections between their professional experiences and course material are characteristics of successful WIL programs.

1.3. Project-Based Learning (PBL) Approaches

PBL, or project-based learning, is another powerful method for fusing academic understanding with real-world application. PBL entails students working on practical projects that call for applying abstract ideas to solve challenging issues. Thomas (2000) claims that PBL gives students the chance to participate in inquiry-based, cooperative learning that is similar to what professionals do. Through projects that tackle real-world industry issues or community needs, students learn practical skills and hone their critical thinking, problem-solving, and collaboration abilities. PBL methods frequently entail collaborations with outside organizations, which can offer insightful information, helpful resources, and insightful criticism. Students' learning is made more engaging and effective when academic content is combined with real-world tasks, which helps them understand the relevance of their studies and gets them ready for challenges in the real world.

2. Challenges and Solutions in Bridging Theory and Practice

2.1. Disconnect Between Academic Content and Industry Needs

The gap between academic content and business needs is a major obstacle to bridging theory and practice. Curricula from educational institutions are frequently created using theoretical frameworks that might not be entirely in line with the knowledge and skills that employers are looking for. Graduates who close this gap may be knowledgeable in theory but deficient in the real-world abilities required by employers (Beinecke et al., 2013). Institutions can address this problem by implementing curriculum modifications that take into account input from industry stakeholders, conducting routine reviews of the curriculum, and making sure that academic programs are adaptable to shifting trends in the industry. Enhancing industry relationships through advisory boards and joint projects can also help match course material to real-world needs, better-preparing students for the rigors of their future employment.

2.2. Limited Opportunities for Practical Experience

Providing enough opportunities for students to gain practical experience is another challenge. Due to funding shortages, a dearth of industry connections, or logistical challenges, many academic programs find it difficult to provide worthwhile work-integrated learning experiences (Billett, 2011). Institutions can overcome this obstacle by forming creative alliances with companies and neighborhood associations to expand the availability of internships, cooperative education, and project-based learning opportunities. Institutions can also use technology to offer remote work opportunities and virtual simulations that give students real-world experience without having to travel far. The inclusion of organized work-based learning activities in the curriculum guarantees that every student will have access to worthwhile real-world experiences that will enhance their academic learning.

2.3. Ensuring Effective Reflection and Integration

Making sure that students properly reflect on and integrate their practical experiences with academic learning is a crucial challenge in bridging theory and practice. Without formalized reflection procedures, students might find it difficult to make the connection between their practical experiences and theoretical ideas, which could result in a cursory comprehension of both (Kolb, 2014). Teachers can solve this problem by creating reflective exercises that help students reflect on and explain their learning, like journals, talks, and presentations. Encouraging and assisting students in engaging in reflective practices enables them to draw significant connections between their practical experiences and academic knowledge. Furthermore, incorporating assessment techniques that gauge students' theoretical comprehension and practical application guarantees that students can integrate what they have learned and show how it applies to real-world situations.

3. Student Outcomes and Success Stories in Work-Based Education

3.1. Enhanced Employability and Career Advancement

Work-Based Education (WBE) programs offer industry-relevant skills and practical experience, which greatly improve students' employability and career advancement. According to Jackson's (2015) study, for instance, students who take advantage of work-integrated learning opportunities—like internships and co-ops—frequently see higher employment and career progression rates than their peers. Through these programs, students can build professional networks within their chosen industries, apply theory knowledge in practical settings, and develop essential professional skills. Success stories, like graduates landing jobs at top companies right out of WBE programs, highlight how important these experiences are for improving long-term success and career readiness.

3.2. Improved Academic Performance and Learning Outcomes

Improvements in learning outcomes and academic performance are also a result of participation in WBE programs. According to research by Billett (2011), students who participate in work-based learning frequently exhibit improved problem-solving skills and a deeper comprehension of academic concepts. Students become more motivated and achieve better academically when they can see the relevance of their studies through the practical application of knowledge in work settings. Success stories from a variety of universities show that students who combine work experience with their coursework usually achieve better academically because they can make the connection between their theoretical knowledge and practical applications and develop a more thorough understanding of their subjects.

3.3. Development of Critical Soft Skills and Professional Competencies

Employers place a high value on professional competencies and critical soft skills, both of which are developed through WBE programs. Students who participate in work-based learning opportunities frequently show improvements in their communication, teamwork, and problem-solving abilities, per a study by Jackson (2017). Through the opportunity to work in professional settings, these programs give students the ability to hone their interpersonal skills and obtain real-world experience overcoming obstacles in the workplace. Alumni success stories that credit their WBE experiences for their professional development and smooth career transitions emphasize the significance of these programs in cultivating critical soft skills and competencies that support overall career success.

Figure 6. Integrating academic knowledge and practical experience

1. Models and Approaches for Effective Integration	2. Challenges and Solutions in Bridging Theory and Practice	3. Student Outcomes and Success Stories in Work-Based Education
• 1.1. Theoretical Frameworks for Integration • 1.2. Work-Integrated Learning (WIL) Models • 1.3. Project-Based Learning (PBL) Approaches	• 2.1. Disconnect Between Academic Content and Industry Needs • 2.2. Limited Opportunities for Practical Experience • 2.3. Ensuring Effective Reflection and Integration	• 3.1. Enhanced Employability and Career Advancement • 3.2. Improved Academic Performance and Learning Outcomes • 3.3. Development of Critical Soft Skills and Professional Competencies

From Figure 6, work-based education (WBE) must integrate theory and practice in order to give students the skills required for the modern workforce. Strong theoretical foundations, Work-Integrated Learning (WIL) models, and Project-Based Learning (PBL) techniques are necessary for effective integration. While there are obstacles to overcome, such as the mismatch between industry demands and academic content and the scarcity of real-world opportunities, improvements in integration and reflection can help close these gaps. Students' increased employability, academic achievement, and acquisition of critical soft skills are clear results of WBE, highlighting the importance of well-designed WBE programs in promoting success in both the classroom and the workplace.

PRODUCING WORK-READY GRADUATES

1. Competencies and Skills Developed through Work-Based Education (WBE)

1.1. Technical and Job-Specific Skills

Programs for work-based education (WBE) are essential for fostering the development of job-specific and technical skills that are immediately usable in the workplace. Through experiential learning opportunities like industry projects, internships, and apprenticeships, students acquire real-world knowledge and skills related to their chosen fields. For instance, WBE gives students the chance to work with industry-standard tools, technologies, and practices in fields like engineering, healthcare, or information technology (Smith & Betts, 2000). By directly applying academic knowledge to real-world situations, students are guaranteed to gain the specialized skills necessary for success in their future careers in addition to a thorough understanding of theoretical concepts. WBE participants' success stories frequently showcase their increased technical proficiency and preparedness to take on industry-specific challenges after graduation.

1.2. Soft Skills and Professional Competencies

WBE programs support the development of critical soft skills and professional competencies in addition to technical skills. These include problem-solving, teamwork, communication, and time management, all of which are essential for success in the workplace. According to Jackson's (2015) research, students who participate in WBE frequently show improvements in their capacity for problem-solving, teamwork, and interpersonal skills. Students are forced to navigate challenging situations, collaborate with diverse teams, and handle a variety of responsibilities in the workplace, which helps them hone their soft skills in real-world situations. Graduates often state that these WBE-developed competencies greatly improve their performance in professional roles and employability.

1.3. Professional Etiquette and Workplace Adaptability

WBE programs foster workplace flexibility and professional manners, both of which are essential for succeeding in a variety of professional settings and integrating into the workforce. Students who are exposed to real-world work environments, according to Billett (2011), learn how to navigate organizational cultures, follow industry standards, and adjust to various workplace dynamics. Students who receive this exposure are better able to manage professional relationships, comprehend workplace expectations, and cultivate a professional manner. WBE participants' success stories frequently showcase their seamless entry into the workforce, crediting their preparedness and flexibility to the hands-on training and professional experiences they received during their programs. Graduates from these programs are better equipped to manage the intricacies of today's workplaces and make valuable contributions to their companies.

2. Assessment and Evaluation of Graduate Readiness

2.1. Competency-Based Assessments

Work-Based Education (WBE) programs must use competency-based assessments to evaluate graduates' preparedness for the workforce. The main goal of these tests is to determine whether or not students have acquired the particular knowledge and abilities needed for their chosen fields. Competency-based assessments, according to Docherty et al. (2015), are intended to evaluate practical skills as well as theoretical knowledge, including problem-solving, industry-specific practices, and technical proficiency. To evaluate students' preparedness for professional roles, instruments like performance-based assignments, skill demonstrations, and real-world problem-solving scenarios are employed. With this strategy, graduates are guaranteed to be able to meet the expectations of their future employers and apply their knowledge in practical settings.

2.2. Employer Feedback and Industry Surveys

Surveys of the industry and employer input are useful resources for gauging graduate preparedness from the viewpoint of employers of WBE program graduates. Jackson (2016) claims that gathering employer feedback regarding graduates' performance and readiness offers valuable insights into how well WBE programs are fulfilling industry demands. Employer surveys and interviews can provide insight into whether graduates have the professional qualities, expertise, and knowledge that employers value. To ensure that graduates are capable of making valuable contributions to their organizations and are well-prepared for the workforce, educational institutions use this feedback to identify program strengths and areas for improvement.

2.3. Self-Assessment and Reflective Practices

In WBE programs, self-evaluation and reflective practices play a significant role in determining graduate readiness. Students who are encouraged to evaluate themselves critically are better able to analyze their abilities, experiences, and areas in need of improvement. The integration of academic and practical learning through reflection is endorsed by Kolb's (2014) experiential learning theory. Students who reflect on their work-related experiences are better able to pinpoint their areas of strength, pinpoint areas where they need to grow, and explain how their experiences have helped them in their careers. Instructors can assess their students' preparedness and offer extra help or direction as necessary based on their self-assessments and reflective reports.

2.4. Comprehensive Capstone Projects

Capstone projects combine academic knowledge with real-world application to provide a thorough way to evaluate graduate readiness. Students are frequently required to solve real-world issues or finish substantial research projects that are relevant to their field of study for these assignments (Wankel & Blessinger, 2013). A variety of competencies, such as project management, critical thinking, and the application of theoretical knowledge, are evaluated through capstone projects. Students exhibit their capacity to integrate and apply their knowledge in a real-world setting by presenting their projects to academic staff and professionals from the business world. This type of evaluation offers a comprehensive picture of students' preparedness for careers and their ability to make valuable contributions to the industries they have chosen.

2.5. Longitudinal Tracking and Alumni Outcomes

Alumni outcomes analysis and longitudinal tracking are useful tools for evaluating graduates' long-term success and preparedness. Monitoring graduates' professional accomplishments, employment rates, and career advancement over time offers important insights into how successful WBE programs are (Smith & Betts, 2000). Educational institutions can assess how well their programs prepare students for long-term career success and spot any gaps that need to be filled by looking at alumni outcomes. Through program improvement and better alignment with industry expectations, institutions can improve the readiness and success of future graduates by using this data-driven approach.

3. Long-Term Career Impact on Graduates

3.1. Enhanced Career Trajectories

Because Work-Based Education (WBE) programs equip graduates with highly sought-after experience and skills in the labor market, they frequently have a substantial long-term impact on their career trajectories. According to research by Jackson (2017), graduates who take advantage of work-based learning opportunities—like internships or co-ops—tend to advance in their careers more quickly than their contemporaries. Graduates can strengthen their resumes, expand their professional networks, and acquire industry-specific skills through these experiences, all of which can result in increased starting salaries, speedier promotions, and more career opportunities. A competitive edge in the labor market is facilitated by the practical knowledge and real-world experience acquired through WBE programs, which also promote long-term career success and stability.

3.2. Increased Job Satisfaction and Retention

WBE initiatives have a favorable effect on employees' retention and long-term job satisfaction. A study by Billett (2011) found that graduates who participated in work-based learning typically reported higher job satisfaction because their roles and career expectations were more aligned. Graduates can more closely match their skills and interests to positions thanks to the practical experience they've gained through WBE, which lowers the risk of job dissatisfaction and career changes. Additionally, the professional skills acquired during WBE improve job satisfaction and performance, which in turn improves long-term career stability and job retention. A more stable and satisfying career trajectory is promoted by this alignment of job roles with career aspirations.

3.3. Development of Professional Networks and Industry Connections

The industry ties and professional networks that graduates of WBE programs form have a major impact on their long-term career impact. WBE offers networking opportunities for graduates to connect with professionals, mentors, and future employers through internships and industry projects (Smith & Betts,

2000). These relationships may open doors to joint ventures, career progression, and employment in the future. Alumni who uphold and utilize these networks frequently see sustained professional advancement as well as access to important business opportunities and insights. Effectively navigating and utilizing professional networks is essential for long-term career success and career advancement.

3.4. Enhanced Skills and Continued Professional Development

WBE programs help graduates succeed in their careers over the long term by encouraging the acquisition of transferable skills and a dedication to lifelong learning. Kolb (2014) asserts that WBE graduates gain critical thinking, problem-solving, and adaptability skills that are useful in their careers as a result of the experiential learning process. With these abilities, graduates can pursue opportunities for lifelong learning, adjust to changing industry trends, and manage career transitions. WBE programs give graduates the foundation of real-world experience and skill development they need to pursue leadership positions, additional education, and advanced certifications, which improves their prospects for employment and long-term professional development.

3.5. Contribution to Industry and Professional Practice

The contributions graduates make to business and professional practice are another aspect of the long-term effects of WBE. Graduates from WBE programs frequently contribute insightful viewpoints, creative solutions, and useful knowledge to their fields. Professional advancement and industry practice improvements can result from their capacity to apply academic knowledge to real-world problems (Jackson, 2015). Graduates can drive innovation, influence professional standards, and contribute to the overall development of their industries by utilizing their practical experience and industry knowledge. This effect demonstrates the wider significance of WBE in influencing not just individual careers but also the professional environment.

Figure 7. Producing work-ready graduates

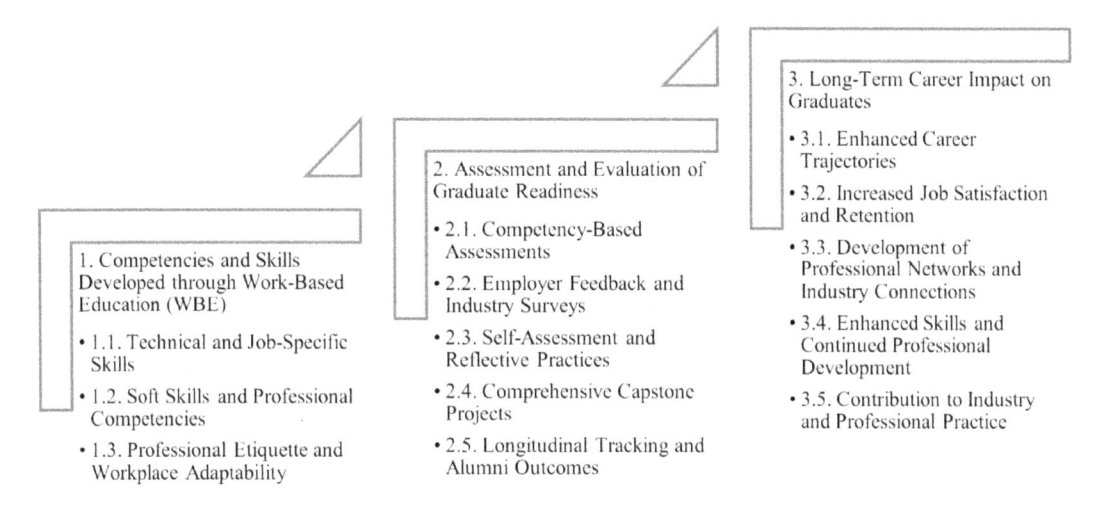

1. Competencies and Skills Developed through Work-Based Education (WBE)
- 1.1. Technical and Job-Specific Skills
- 1.2. Soft Skills and Professional Competencies
- 1.3. Professional Etiquette and Workplace Adaptability

2. Assessment and Evaluation of Graduate Readiness
- 2.1. Competency-Based Assessments
- 2.2. Employer Feedback and Industry Surveys
- 2.3. Self-Assessment and Reflective Practices
- 2.4. Comprehensive Capstone Projects
- 2.5. Longitudinal Tracking and Alumni Outcomes

3. Long-Term Career Impact on Graduates
- 3.1. Enhanced Career Trajectories
- 3.2. Increased Job Satisfaction and Retention
- 3.3. Development of Professional Networks and Industry Connections
- 3.4. Enhanced Skills and Continued Professional Development
- 3.5. Contribution to Industry and Professional Practice

From Figure 7, a wide range of competencies and skills, such as technical proficiency, soft skills, and workplace adaptability, are developed through work-based education (WBE). WBE makes sure that graduates are prepared for the workforce by using extensive assessment techniques like competency-based evaluations, employer feedback, and capstone projects. WBE has a major long-term impact on graduates, resulting in improved career paths, higher levels of job satisfaction, and robust professional networks. By promoting ongoing skill development and deep industry connections, this strategy not only helps the individual but also advances industry and professional practice.

EDUCATIONAL INNOVATION THROUGH WORK-BASED EDUCATION

Artificial Intelligence (AI) is poised to revolutionize WBE. AI could personalize learning experiences, automate assessment processes, and provide real-time feedback to students during their work placements.

1. Innovative Practices and Trends in WBE

Innovative approaches are helping Work-Based Education (WBE) advance in terms of efficacy and relevance. The incorporation of project-based learning (PBL), in which students work on real-world projects supplied by industry partners, into WBE programs is one noteworthy trend. With this method, students can apply their theoretical knowledge to real-world issues, hone their critical thinking abilities, and generate observable results (Thomas, 2000). Utilizing competency-based education (CBE) frameworks, which place more emphasis on evaluating students' mastery of particular skills and competencies than traditional credit hours, is another innovation (Streckfuss & Martinez, 2017). This change improves students' preparedness for the workforce by ensuring that their evaluations are based on their capacity to complete tasks relevant to their jobs. Personalized learning experiences are also becoming more and more important. By allowing students to customize their WBE activities to match their interests and career goals, this approach helps to create more engaged and motivated learners (Billett, 2011).

2. Role of Technology in Enhancing WBE

Technology is essential to improving work-based education because it offers new platforms and tools that make learning and industry integration easier. A flexible and scalable approach to skill development, virtual simulations, and digital labs enable students to participate in real-world experiences without being restricted by physical settings (Agarwal & Bowers, 2015). Students can work on industry projects remotely, communicate with professionals, and efficiently manage tasks with the help of online collaboration tools and project management software. Additionally, analytics-enabled learning management systems (LMS) can monitor student progress, offer tailored feedback, and modify learning paths in response to individual performance (Siemens, 2013). According to Chui et al. (2018), the integration of cutting-edge technologies like machine learning and artificial intelligence into WBE programs is also opening up new possibilities for specialized learning and advanced skill development. Digital literacy is emerging as a cornerstone of education in the evolving "next normal," where creativity, equity, and adaptability are paramount. Mastery of digital literacy is essential for both educators and students, enabling them to effectively navigate and thrive in an increasingly technology-driven educational environment. By promoting digital literacy, education can harness the full potential of technology, ensuring equitable access and preparing students to succeed in a future dominated by digital advancements (Janthapassa et al, 2024).

3. Future Directions and Potential for Educational Innovation

Work-based education is expected to undergo additional innovation in the future as universities and business partners investigate novel approaches and tools. Growing international partnerships is one promising path that will enable students to learn about various industry practices and obtain international experience (Cunningham et al., 2020). Enhancing practical skills and simulating real-world scenarios, the integration of augmented reality (AR) and virtual reality (VR) into Work-Based Education (WBE) programs provides immersive learning experiences (Chen et al., 2018). Furthermore, a safe and authentic record of students' accomplishments and competencies may be provided by using blockchain technology for credentialing and competency tracking (Tapscott & Tapscott, 2016). These developments point to a future in which WBE programs are more globally focused, technologically sophisticated, and networked, leading to notable gains in academic performance and workforce preparedness.

CONCLUSION

With the integration of academic knowledge and real-world experience, work-based education (WBE) has become an essential part of contemporary educational systems, producing graduates who are prepared for the workforce. The evaluation of WBE practices revealed several important conclusions, one of which being that it can improve students' employability by giving them relevant, practical experience and skills unique to the industry. The alignment between educational outcomes and the demands of the labor market is getting better thanks to innovative practices like competency-based education, project-based learning, and personalized learning. Furthermore, the utilization of virtual simulations, online collaboration tools, and advanced learning analytics by technology is crucial in augmenting Work-Based Education. These developments are improving student readiness for the workforce by revolutionizing the way that hands-on learning is imparted and evaluated. There are important ramifications for policymakers, institutions, and educators. To develop more captivating and successful WBE programs, educators should adopt cutting-edge techniques and incorporate technology. This entails creating industry partnerships, incorporating real-world projects into curricula, and enhancing learning outcomes through the use of digital tools. Prioritizing the alignment of academic programs with industry needs is imperative for institutions to ensure that students acquire the necessary skills and competencies. The role of policymakers in facilitating the integration of work-based learning into educational systems, creating frameworks for industry collaboration, and providing funding are critical in supporting work-based learning (WBE) initiatives. To fully realize the benefits of WBE and overcome obstacles like the gap between academic content and industry requirements, cooperation amongst all stakeholders is crucial. There is a ton of room for innovation and impact in work-based learning in the future. WBE programs should grow more complex and integrated as academic institutions and business partners keep investigating new approaches and technologies. Exciting developments that have the potential to completely transform WBE include the growth of international partnerships, the use of augmented and virtual reality, and the use of blockchain technology for credentialing. These developments should improve the efficacy and relevance of educational programs, increasing graduates' adaptability and readiness for a changing labor market. WBE can dramatically improve educational outcomes and workforce readiness by staying on the cutting edge of these trends and focusing on real-world, industry-aligned learning experiences. This could have a significant impact on how education and employment are shaped in the future.

REFERENCES

Agarwal, R., & Bowers, A. (2015). The impact of digital tools on education: Enhancing learning and collaboration. *Journal of Educational Technology & Society*, 18(3), 112–122.

Allen, T. D., Eby, L. T., Poteet, M. L., Lentz, E., & Lima, L. (2004). Career benefits associated with mentoring for protégés: A meta-analysis. *The Journal of Applied Psychology*, 89(1), 127–136. DOI: 10.1037/0021-9010.89.1.127 PMID: 14769125

Barron, B., & Darling-Hammond, L. (2008). Teaching for meaningful learning: A review of research on inquiry-based and cooperative learning. *The Rose Foundation*. Retrieved from https://www.edutopia.org

Barrows, H. S. (1996). Problem-based learning in medicine and beyond A brief overview. *New Directions for Teaching and Learning*, 1996(68), 3–12. DOI: 10.1002/tl.37219966804

Beard, C., & Wilson, J. P. (2006). *Experiential learning: A handbook for education, training, and coaching*. Kogan Page.

Beinecke, R., Cummings, T., & Williams, R. (2013). Bridging the gap between academic learning and practical application. *Journal of Higher Education Policy and Management*, 35(3), 244–259.

Billett, S. (2001). *Learning in the workplace: Strategies for effective practice*. Allen & Unwin.

Billett, S. (2011). *Vocational education: Purposes, traditions and prospects*. Springer. DOI: 10.1007/978-94-007-1954-5

Billig, S. H. (2002). Research on K-12 service learning. In Furco, A., & Billig, S. H. (Eds.), *Service learning: The essence of the pedagogy* (pp. 73–106). Information Age Publishing.

Boud, D., & Falchikov, N. (Eds.). (2006). *Aligning assessment with learning outcomes: The impact of a competency-based assessment system*. Routledge.

Boud, D., & Solomon, N. (Eds.). (2001). *Work-based learning: A new higher education?* Society for Research into Higher Education & Open University Press.

Bringle, R. G., & Hatcher, J. A. (1996). Implementing service learning in higher education. *The Journal of Higher Education*, 67(2), 221–239. DOI: 10.1080/00221546.1996.11780257

Chen, C. M., & Huang, T. C. (2018). The impact of augmented reality on learning effectiveness: A case study. *Journal of Educational Technology*, 15(4), 33–44.

Chui, M., Manyika, J., & Miremadi, M. (2018). What AI can and can't do (yet) for your business. *The McKinsey Quarterly*.

Cisco. (2022). *Cisco Networking Academy*. Retrieved from https://www.netacad.com/

Coll, R. K., Eames, C., Paku, L., Lay, M., Hodges, D., Bhat, R., & Ram, S. (2009). An exploration of the pedagogies employed to integrate knowledge in work-integrated learning. *The Journal of Cooperative Education and Internships*, 43(1), 14–35.

Cox, E. (2005). *Coaching and mentoring: Practical methods to improve performance*. Routledge.

Creswell, J. W. (2014). *Research design: Qualitative, quantitative, and mixed methods approaches* (4th ed.). Sage Publications.

Cunningham, J., & Harlow, M. (2020). Global partnerships in education: Enhancing learning opportunities through international collaborations. *International Journal of Educational Management*, 34(2), 45–60.

Docherty, P., Gibb, J., & Lee, M. (2015). Competency-based assessment: An evaluation of effectiveness. *Assessment & Evaluation in Higher Education*, 40(3), 330–344.

Eames, C., & Cates, J. (2018). Capstone projects in engineering education: A case study from the University of Waterloo. *International Journal of Engineering Education*, 34(2), 649–661.

Eyler, J., & Giles, D. E. (1999). *Where's the learning in service-learning?* Jossey-Bass.

Friedman, T. L. (2015). *Thank you for being late: An optimist's guide to thriving in the age of accelerations*. Farrar, Straus and Giroux.

Furco, A. (1996). Service-learning: A balanced approach to experiential education. In Tayler, B., & Rhoads, R. (Eds.), *Experiential education: Principles and practices* (pp. 2–10). National Society for Experiential Education.

Furco, A. (2010). The community as a resource for learning: An analysis of academic service-learning in primary and secondary education. In Taylor, B. B., & Gallardo, R. M. C. (Eds.), *Service-learning: Research and practice* (pp. 45–67). IAP.

Garris, R., Ahlers, R., & Driskell, J. E. (2002). Games, motivation, and learning: A research and practice model. *Simulation & Gaming*, 33(4), 441–467. DOI: 10.1177/1046878102238607

Google. (2022). *Grow with Google*. Retrieved from https://grow.google/

Grollmann, P., & Rauner, F. (2007). The European perspective on advanced vocational education and training. In Clarke, L., & Winch, C. (Eds.), *Vocational education: International approaches, developments, and systems* (pp. 121–139). Routledge.

Issenberg, S. B., McGaghie, W. C., Petrusa, E. R., Gordon, D. L., & Scalese, R. J. (2005). Features and uses of high-fidelity medical simulations that lead to effective learning: A BEME systematic review. *Medical Teacher*, 27(1), 10–28. DOI: 10.1080/01421590500046924 PMID: 16147767

Jackson, D. (2015). Employability skill development in work-integrated learning: Barriers and best practice. *Studies in Higher Education*, 40(2), 350–367. DOI: 10.1080/03075079.2013.842221

Jackson, D. (2016). Evaluating the effectiveness of graduate employability: A focus on employer feedback. *Journal of Education and Work*, 29(2), 155–175.

Jackson, D. (2017). Developing employability skills and competencies through work-based learning: The impact on graduates' careers. *Journal of Education and Work*, 30(3), 293–313.

Janthapassa, S., Chanthapassa, N., & Kenaphoom, S. (2024). The Role of Digital Literacy in Shaping Education in the Next-Normal. *Asian Education and Learning Review*, 2(1), 29–41.

Kendall, J. (1990). *The meaning of service: A resource guide for the development of service-learning.* The National Society for Experiential Education.

Kingkaew, A., & Saengchompoo, J. (2024). *Information of universities and network educational institutions that have signed the agreement to produce graduates with CP All Public Company Limited.* Interview 8 August 2024.

Kolb, D. A. (2014). *Experiential learning: Experience as the source of learning and development.* FT Press.

Kram, K. E. (1985). *Mentoring at work: Developmental relationships in organizational life.* University Press of America.

Menard, S. (2002). *Longitudinal research* (2nd ed.). Sage Publications. DOI: 10.4135/9781412984867

Microsoft. (2022). *Microsoft Philanthropies Global Skills Initiative.* Retrieved from https://www.microsoft.com/en-us/philanthropies/global-skills

Moon, J. A. (2004). *A handbook of reflective and experiential learning: Theory and practice.* Routledge.

P-TECH. (2022). *P-TECH model.* Retrieved from https://www.ptech.org/the-p-tech-model/

Schaap, H., Baartman, L., & de Bruijn, E. (2012). Students learning processes during school-based learning and workplace learning in vocational education: A review. *Vocations and Learning*, 5(2), 99–117. DOI: 10.1007/s12186-011-9069-2

Schön, D. A. (1983). *The reflective practitioner: How professionals think in action.* Basic Books.

Siemens, G. (2013). Learning analytics: The importance of a comprehensive approach. *Journal of Educational Technology & Society*, 16(1), 24–34.

Siemens. (2022). *Siemens Technical Academy.* Retrieved from https://www.siemens.com/global/en/home/company/career/technical-academy.html

Smith, C., & Betts, M. (2000). Learning as partners: Realising the potential of work-based learning. *Journal of Vocational Education and Training*, 52(4), 589–604. DOI: 10.1080/13636820000200147

Spady, W. G. (1994). The concept of outcome-based education. In Spady, W. G. (Ed.), *Outcome-based education: Critical issues and answers* (pp. 11–26). American Association of School Administrators.

Stark, P. B., & Lowther, M. A. (1988). *Competency-based education and training: Concepts and practices.* American Council on Education.

Streckfuss, T., & Martinez, A. (2017). Competency-based education: Assessing the effectiveness of new learning paradigms. *Journal of Higher Education Theory and Practice*, 17(4), 15–25.

Tapscott, D., & Tapscott, A. (2016). *Blockchain revolution: How the technology behind Bitcoin is changing money, business, and the world.* Penguin.

Tashakkori, A., & Teddlie, C. (2010). *Sage Handbook of mixed methods in social & behavioral research* (2nd ed.). Sage Publications. DOI: 10.4135/9781506335193

Thomas, J. W. (2000). *A review of research on project-based learning*. Autodesk Foundation.

Toner, P. (2011). Workforce skills and innovation: An overview of major themes in the literature. OECD Education Working Papers, No. 55, OECD Publishing.

Wankel, C., & Blessinger, P. (Eds.). (2013). *Increasing student engagement and retention using immersive interfaces: Virtual worlds, gaming, and simulation*. Routledge.

Wilson, J. W. (2014). A history of the integration of work experience and learning in higher education. In Coll, R. G., & Zegwaard, K. E. (Eds.), *International handbook for cooperative and work-integrated education: International perspectives of theory, research, and practice* (pp. 3–14). World Association for Cooperative Education.

Yin, R. K. (2018). *Case study research and applications: Design and methods* (6th ed.). Sage Publications.

Zlotkowski, E. (2004). Service-learning and the scholarship of engagement. In Zlotkowski, E. (Ed.), *Service-learning and the liberal arts* (pp. 23–36). Anker Publishing.

Chapter 8
Role of Diversity and Inclusion in Employee Engagement Among Different Sectors of India

Vinita Sinha
https://orcid.org/0000-0002-4195-2257
Symbiosis Centre for Management and Human Resource Development, Symbiosis International University (Deemed), India

ABSTRACT

Diversity and inclusion have become one of the main challenges and top priority for recruitment and other HR departments. Different sectors have different workforce diversity and organizational inclusion practices. It helps an organization to attract talented employees and drive the engagement of employees. The concept of diversity management and inclusion policies have been a focus for many companies for years now, and they have become more and more of a trending research topic. Although the literature on diversity and inclusion has been increasing in quantity, there remained a gap in the explaining the importance of diversity management and inclusion policies in the engagement of employees in the different Indian sector. The main aim of carrying out this research study is to investigate the association of various diversity and inclusion practices with an important aspect of the workplace, i.e. employee engagement among different sectors in India.

1. INTRODUCTION

Diversity and inclusion have been a focus for many companies for years now, and they have become more and more of a trending research topic. Maintaining diversity and inclusion have become one of the main challenges and top priority for recruitment and other HR departments in the organization. When diversity is included in the operations of the organization, it helps to encourage growth and provide better solutions for a particular problem in the organization (Ayega & Muathe; 2018). Different sectors have different workforce diversity and organizational inclusion practices. It helps an organization to attract talented employees and drive employee engagement. Present workforce perceives that they are not an

DOI: 10.4018/979-8-3693-9230-0.ch008

Copyright ©2025, IGI Global. Copying or distributing in print or electronic forms without written permission of IGI Global is prohibited.

important and valuable part of the company and develop the feeling of exclusion (MorBarak, 2000; Ibarra, 1993). Several research works supports the fact that effective management facilitates inclusion in the workplace (Shore el al., 2010; Greenberger et al., 1989; Jones et al., 2005).

A lot has been spoken about the topic of diversity and inclusion in the recent year. It can be observed that most companies see the diversity management and inclusion practices as an event that can be done on a monthly basis and contribute very less for the rest of the year. Various studies argued that if there is a high level of involvement in local and international companies, then it will help in the retention of talented workforce, customer loyalty, an increased value of stakeholders and effective organizational performance (Wilson, 2009; Markos and Sridevi, 2010). Remarkably, India's top employer studies consider diversity and inclusion only recently as a key factor to being the top employer. It is little wonder that there is less effort to concentrate efforts in this area. The reality of course, is that in this unpredictable marketplace, businesses that function carefully and in an organized way will have an advantage in the battle for talent and be able to foster a dramatically different culture that will be respected by workforces. Today, diversity in the workforce has become an inseparable part of the HRM (Davis, Frolova, and Callahan; 2015). Thus, the connection between workforce diversity, inclusion and employee engagement can't be overlooked.

The research work conducted in this topic emphasizes on fostering a working culture where diverse people feel included (Bilimoria, Joy, and Liand, 2008; Roberson, 2006). Although the literature on diversity and inclusion has been increasing in quantity, there remains a gap in the knowledge of the impact of diversity management and inclusion practices in employee engagement among different sectors in India. The main aim of carrying out this study is to investigate the association of diversity and inclusion with an important aspect of the workplace, i.e. employee engagement among different sectors in India.

The current study scrutinizes the factors of workforce diversity and inclusion and its effect on engaging employees. Pertinent literature on workforce diversity, inclusion and engagement is studied which laid down the base for the development of the model.

Research Gap:

The extensive reviews of the above literature suggests that the majority of research on employee engagement has focused on its various definitions and the factors that determine the employee engagement like diversity-inclusion management, climate of trust, etc., but very few studies have been carried out on the impact of diversity-inclusion practices in promoting employee engagement among various sectors. The above studies indicates that all those businesses which embraced and carried out various exceptional diversity interventions at each level are considered to be successful. In any case, strategy implementation cannot be considered to be a sole and isolated methodology; it changes in accordance with the vision, mission, and the objectives of the organization (Arrendondo, 1996). Still there is strong dearth in terms of exploring the pivotal role of diversity management and inclusion on employees' attitude and behavior. It involves cautious determination of advanced interventions and drives attached to necessities of organization. Obviously, scholars recognized that organizations must essentially evaluate and reevaluate its diversity and inclusion techniques and regard it as a continuous cycle (Carnevale and Stone, 1994; 1995). Hence the above reviews of literature suggests that there is a strong need to explore appropriate diversity management and inclusion practices specific to the various sectors. The present study is an attempt to explore and address the following research questions by reviewing the related literature and collecting and analyzing data from 80 employees 10 each from the 8 sectors- viz: IT, manufacturing, education, financial services, tourism, health and insurance.

Research questions

1) What are the practices of diversity management in different sectors?
2) What inclusion practices are adopted at different companies and in different sectors?
3) What are the various challenges faced by the companies in diversity and inclusion management?
4) What role does diversity management and inclusion play in the employee engagement?

2. LITERATURE REVIEW

The author Shore et al. (2011) explains that a substantial amount of study has been carried out on workforce diversity, yet researchers and scholars have only recently concentrated on inclusion practices. The paper thus uses Brewer's optimal distinctiveness theory to define the workers' inclusiveness in the work environment based on the fulfilment of the needs of a sense of belonging and uniqueness. A framework of inclusion is presented and the contextual factors linked with inclusion are recommended for future research.

Nishi, L .H. (2013) in her paper focused on both diversity and inclusion as it involves removing relational sources of bias by making sure that the status of the identity group is not related to utilities, and creating paths for diverse people to ensure personalized relationships and forming ideas with solving issues. Qualitative methodology is used to formulate conceptually distinct definitions.

The different kinds of diversity strategies usually followed by firms – Multiculturalism and color blindness which have clear advantages but also leads to the feeling of ostracization by various stakeholders of the organization (Stevens, F.G., Plaut, V.C. and Sanchez-Burks, J, 2008). The paper deals with the issues thrown by the two methods and provides an alternate model. The authors such as Bilimoria, D., Joy, S., & Liang, X. (2008) in their paper have discussed the importance of breaking down the cultural and gender barriers to create an inclusive workplace. It also recommended various program initiatives, facilitating factors along with a changing model that every organization could make use of, in order to build a diverse and productive work environment.

Author Paluck, E. L. (2006) dealt with various methods to tackle the diversity issues using diversity training and studies the impact of such programs on organizations. Cunningham, G. B. (2008) in his article highlighted the past diversity models emphasized on the required final state of diversity strategies, but have failed to establish proper methods to create such a change and the paper proposed a model that addresses this gap. Contemporary organizations continue to spend significant amounts of money on diversity training without considering the tendency of training to fail most of the time (Chavez et al. (2008). This paper introduced an alternative, strategic approach which emphasizes attitudinal and cultural transformation by breaking cultural barriers, moving away from diversity management and moving towards managing for diversity to create a more inclusive workforce.

Sabhrawal, M. (2014) asserts that the idea of organizational inclusion is more than just managing diversity and the study states that an organization cannot enhance its overall performance by just managing the diversity at the workplace. It emphasizes an approach that promotes self- esteem of all the employees and creates an inclusive productive environment for work with the aid of supportive leadership and other important resources. According to Cho, S., & MOR Barak, M. E. (2008), there is a significant amount of evidence which suggests that inclusion and diversity are important indicators of job performance and employee engagement. A survey was conducted in a sample of 381 employees to examine the link between inclusion and diversity and work performance. It is evident from the results that the diversity and inclusion had a important effect on job performance and employees commitment towards organization.

Diversity management and inclusion

With globalization, the concept of inclusion and diversity also gained much attention and realized its necessity in serving and satisfying the stakeholders globally. Managerial researchers indicated that in the future the composition of the workforce in the organization might rise to 90% of minorities and women; of which many migrants can result in the increased challenge in communication and also many companies would include racial groups as part of (Griggs, 1995, Johnston & Packer, 1987, Caudron, 1990). Companies that realize the necessity and importance of training and developing entire sections of their workforce to confirm competitive advantage are indulged in various methods to manage their diverse labor force. (Jamieson & O' Mara, 1991).

Different research works have contributed in providing the definition for the term diversity in many ways. ASTD, 1996a; 1996b states that diversity is more than just the traditional philosophy like gender, disabilities and race. It is in fact, defined as all the ways in which individuals vary from each other (Hayles, 1996).The broad definition of diversity explains that it comprises of all the features of people such as gender, age, physical attributes, nationality, race, language, lifestyle, ethnicity, educational background, geographical location, marital status, beliefs, economic status and tenure of job. (Wheeler, 1994; Triandis, 1994; Carr, 1993; Thomas, 1992; Caudron, 1992). Morrison (1992) describes the four levels of diversity. They are: sexual, ethnic and racial balance; different culture values; acceptance of other cultures; and the broad view of inclusion.

Griggs (1995) Described workplace diversity as the combined effort of primary and secondary dimensions. The primary dimension is concerned with shaping the self-image of a person on others and the word and is unchangeable while the secondary dimension is adjustable. This dimension is subject to adjustment with the change in tenure of job, geographical location, educational background and many more (Shown in Table 1). The definition of diversity is evolutionary, dynamic and broad and it has a long-term impact on individuals and businesses. (Tommervik, 1995).

Table 1. The dimensions of the diversity management

• Race, • Ethnicity, • Sex, • Age, • Disability	• Religion, • Culture, • Sexual orientation, • Political orientation, • Geographical origin, • Family status, • Lifestyle, • Education, • Experience, • Nationality, • Language, • Thinking ability	• Beliefs, • Assumptions, • Perceptions, • Attitudes, • Values, • Feelings, • Norms

Source: (Mazur, 2010)

Scholars have defined a term diversity so broadly that it is comprehensive and considers everybody as an important part of the organization (Griggs, 1995; Johnson, 1995). Broad definition of the concept moved the attention from some towards all in order to make an effort to maximize diversity to attain goals at both individual and organizational level.

According to scholars Mor-Barak & Cherin, inclusion is the extent to which the workforce perceives that they are a critical part of the organizational process. Researchers anticipated that if diversity and inclusion is well adopted at the workplace, then the organization would achieve an added advantage of employee commitment and increase in productivity (Davidson & Ferdman, 2002; Ferdman et al., 2006). It doesn't matter whether the idea of diversity management and inclusion is looked at as individual, organizational or societal concerns, it is not possible to disregard demographic changes and it is also subject to significant change in the future (Jackson & Associates, 1992). Such changes have guided many organizations in the investigation of the business consequences and also have provided a strong base on how to manage and value workplace diversity. Organizational scholars describe that management of diversity and inclusion is not just concerned with empowerment of employees rather it is more than that (Thomas, 1992).

In order to include all the dimensions, inclusion recommends philosophically broad approaches; stresses on managerial guidelines and abilities in the achievement of goals both at individual and organizational level (Henderson, 1994a); discovering suitable work culture for all the groups by bringing changes in the standard operational process (Triandis et al., 1994). It is important to value diversity and inclusion for various individual, profitability, social and legal reasons (Hayles, 1992).

Employee engagement

The term employee engagement is a new concept in academic research. The work carried out by many consultants and practitioners focused on explaining how to create and leverage employee engagement (Macey & Schneider, 2008). We can see from the literature that employee engagement is concerned with the measurement of emotional commitment of employees towards their job and organization (Waldman, 2016). A study conducted by Liu, F (2024) presented the mechanisms through which leadership influences engagement in digital contexts, offering insights for leaders to foster a more committed and psychologically invested workforce. Kahn (1990), also known as the father of employee engagement, did the remarkable work on the employee engagement. (Kahn, 1990, p.692) on the basis of theory of intrinsic motivation developed the concept of "personal engagement and personal disengagement". The personal engagement has been explained as the difference in the association level of an individual in terms of cognitive, physical and emotional attributes of work roles and personal disengagement is defined as the act of disassociating the presence of own self from work functions (p. 693).Khan (1990) in order to know more about the applicability of the engagement to work, implemented the qualitative research method with a sample of sixteen architectures. These samples were collected from different firms and sixteen summer camp counselors. Kahn conducted two qualitative studies in which the first study was carried out with the method of open-ended questionnaire and another survey was carried out with a method of an in-depth interview.

Sukphon, N. (2022) suggested the strategies for building employee engagement in the organization consisted of 4 strategies: strategy 1- organizational culture improvement, strategy 2- compensation and benefit management, strategy 3- upgrading proactive human resources department, and strategy 4- improvement of quality of life in safety, occupational health, and working environment.

A study conducted by Rattanasirivilai, et.al, (2020) examined the role of gender difference with regards to perceptions of CSR and employee engagement. Employees working in various sectors in Thailand. The role of gender as moderator in the relationship between corporate social responsibility and employee engagement was also examined. Findings indicated that the relationship between corporate social responsibility and male is stronger than female.

Research conducted by Oentoro (2018) examines the effects of high-performance work practices (HPWPs) on service performance, moderated by employee engagement. The findings suggests that employee engagement moderates the relationship between HPWPs and service recovery performance.

Kerdpitak & Jermsittiparsert (2020) found in the research that employee engagement positively mediates the relationship among the practices of HRM such as employees training, learning practices and employee selection and competitive advantage.

Employee engagement is differentiated as work and organization engagement by Saks (2006). The multi-dimensional method focused on both individual and organization and identified that engagement is the extent of an individual's passionate and intellectual commitment to their work and company (Richman, 2006; Saks, 2006; Baumruk, 2004; Shaw, 2005). Consequently, Saks (2006) described employee engagement as the association of intellectual, behavior and emotional components that are connected with role performances of an individual.

Further, Saks (2006) conducted empirical research with a sample of 102 employees. These employees were selected from different job positions and from numerous organizations. The study identified that organization engagement and job engagement are different from each other. It also specified that managerial support envisions both the job engagement and the organization engagement.

Also, the concerned study acknowledged that engagement at the job and the engagement in organization acts as a facilitator between antecedents (perceived organizational support, procedural justice, job characteristics, distributive justice) and repercussions (intent to quit, the dedication to organization, job satisfaction) (Saks, 2006 p. 604).(Macey & Schneider, 2008) explained that the concept of the engagement was divided into three categories. These categories are: a) The psychological state engagement – it is concerned with an individual's own involvement in the work and job; b) Behavioral engagement – it is concerned with the reinforcement towards organizational effectiveness and innovation; c) The trait engagement – it is related to the personality characteristics of an individual. The concept of the engagement further seemed to be more than the job characteristics of an individual and the study failed to deliver the supportive arguments (Newman & Harrison, 2008).

To summarize, studies on engagement suggested that the notion of the engagement doesn't include a final consensus. But researchers are trying to find out more clarification by associating the engagement with managerial characteristics. Dell et al., (2001) recommended that the academic work of each scholar appears to concentrate on several elements of the construct rather than all at once nonetheless contributing to the nomological space. Therefore, the employee engagement is regarded as a mental state and embraces numerous associated managerial traits. Thus, the engagement is concerned with the passion and commitment of employees as well as willingness to work with full zeal and enthusiasm to outperform the expectation from job and contribute to the overall growth and development of the organization.

The influence of inclusion practices and diversity management on employee engagement

Many organizational scholars have provided evidence of the noteworthy positive relationship between employees that are highly engaged and the performance of the organization (Avigdor et al., 2007; Fernando, Pedro, Deloitte 2015 & Gonzalo 2013). The study result depicts that about 96 percent of higher-level executives agree to the fact that inclusion and diversity in the workplace boosts the scores of engagement and also improves organizational performance. (Ferry, 2013). Conversely, businesses which don't give much importance to the idea of inclusion and diversity while developing strategy are found to have a high number of disengaged employees (Riffkin & Harter, 2016).

Jones & Harter (2005) conducted a study which described that the likelihood of employees' leaving the organization would be high if there is a difference between managers and employees in terms of race which ultimately results in employee disengagement. However, if the organization is capable of strategically handling these discrepancies and fostering favorable organizational climate then the employees may want to stay longer with the company which ultimately increases the engagement of employees in the organization.

Gallup's study states that there is a strong association between employee engagements and workplace inclusion. This is because a high employee engagement develops a sense of belongingness among employees and they develop a perception that their organization highly values different opinions, ideas and acts to the issues related to discrimination. But only 3 percent of actively disengaged or engaged employees are found to agree with these statements (Riffkin & Harter, 2016). Sodexo conducted an employee engagement survey which confirmed that inclusion and diversity practices boosts scores of engagements and ranked diversity and inclusion as the top two indicators of employee engagement (Anand, 2013).

Although consultants and researchers conducted several studies and identified many advantages of inclusion and diversity, there are numerous organizations and the top-level management who still don't realize the need and significance of diversity management and inclusion practices at the different levels of organization. They also lack a proper knowledge and assistance in implementing the diversity and inclusion practices in the workplace. (Skalsky & McCarthy, 2009)

Diversity-Inclusion Management Business cases

The strategy of inclusion and diversity management at Walmart is based on "think globally and serve locally". In order to foster a culture of valuing diversity and promoting inclusion in the workplace, Walmart focuses on seeking, attracting, and hiring talents from diverse backgrounds. The Diversity & Inclusion report (2015), of Walmart states that out of the total workforce 57 percent of the workforce represents women and 41 percent of them are in managerial positions, 40 percent of the total workforce represented different color people, of which 30% are in managerial positions and 22 percent are indulged in corporate activities.

Walmart is additionally engaged with different useful projects like Veterans' gladly received home commitment, mentoring programs for the career development, and the worldwide series of women developments are some popular projects that Walmart carries out in order to implant diversity and inclusion across the organization to achieve remarkable results of business operation. Constant effort to cultivate an inclusive climate based on trust for the employees so that they feel associated and upheld to one another.

Apple considers that 'the most creative organization should likewise be the most diversified organization'. The growth and success of any organization depends on the creation and execution of new and innovative thoughts to manage and overcome diversity.

Starbuck is notable and all around the world acknowledged brand in business sectors by individuals. As per Starbucks (2011), business morals and consistency, effectively fosters a climate that includes all cultures, all things considered, and their exclusive capacities, qualities, and dissimilarities and stimulates diversity as an important factor for corporate advantage (Morais et al., 2014, p. 41). Starbuck sees that competency in culture is fundamental, so it ought to be instituted mainly by high level executives which, thus impacts the managerial behavior and also its workforce all through the company (Tracey, Elder et al., 2014; Hinkin, 2010). The high-level administration at Starbucks has given the alternative to their representatives to work for extra hours during non-weekend days to manage their working days (Hinkin and Tracey, 2010). Additionally, flexible work timetables meet their companion's timetables and support people with disabilities in the working environment (Marques, 2008, p. 253). Additionally, workers of Starbucks should consider legal practices and qualities while dealing with clients and staff. High level management makes fundamental decisions in preparing their supervisors as well as workers in taking care of stakeholders who belong to diverse cultures and societies (Tracey, 2010 and Marques, 2008; Hinkin).

Diversity Management and Inclusion Practices

During the last two decades, numerous businesses have understood that the conventional presumptions made about diversity in workforce were crucial to growing in the present business setting (Loden and Rosener, 1991; Walker 1991; Beilinson, 1991 ;).

The Conference Board directed exploration on 166 leading organizations and recorded some significant drivers of diversity, for example, – 1) development activities and career planning, 2) change in culture, performance, and responsibility, 3) participation of employees, 4) communication, 5) learning and development activities (Winterle, 1992). Further, Gottfredson (1992) explained three diversity issues identified with gender and ethnicity, for example, – measures to decrease sex and nationality issues during changes in organizational environment, in accommodating migrants, and in building career results. Two issues of diversity identified with differences in individual, for example, – methodology to accept individual differences and local conditions among the workforce. Additional investigation led by The Conference Board on 69 diversity supervisors, scientists and specialists tracked down that creating diversity action plans, cultivation of diversity into mission statement, responsibility, employee contribution in all capacities, professional development, activities of local area outreach, and long-standing culture change creativities were seven advanced diversity inclusion drives (Wheeler, 1995).

Likewise, researchers recognized different methodologies as well as techniques for diversity management and inclusion at the working environment. As indicated by Louw (1995), handling diversity comprises of five stages: (1) recognizing the requirements and studying them in detail; (2) planning the methodology of diversity; (3) outlining exclusive initiatives of diversity and interventions; (4) carrying out the mentioned three phases; (5) consistent assessment and observation of diversity procedure measure. Some significant normal practices are – key objectives; regular checking of all HR frameworks; environmental situation; preparing and reskilling as a hierarchical need; compensates and upgrading benefits dependent on outcomes; reinforcing the recruiting and promotion frameworks according to the need and objective of the organization (pp. 166-167).

Conceptual Framework derived from the Literature:

Figure 1. Conceptual framework

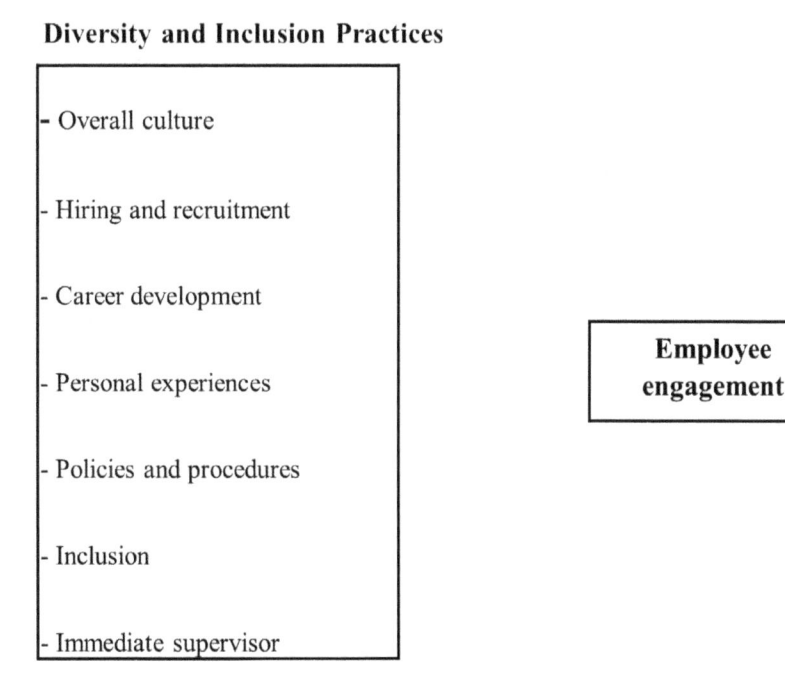

Diversity and Inclusion Practices

- Overall culture
- Hiring and recruitment
- Career development
- Personal experiences
- Policies and procedures
- Inclusion
- Immediate supervisor

Employee engagement

3. RESEARCH METHODS

Sample

Data for study is collected from around 80 employees working in different sectors. A structured questionnaire containing 20 questions on all the seven constructs was employed under study, whereby 80 questionnaires were completely filled. The questionnaire was circulated to the respondents through Google forms link and mail. The participants were assured confidentiality and anonymity of the information collected.

Data Collection

The objective of the study was to cover employees from different sectors in India. For this purpose, an online questionnaire was designed and the samples were informed to respond to the questionnaire. 110 employees were able to fill up the questionnaire. However, after screening the questionnaire for the completeness of the responses, it was found that 80 respondents responded to all the questions. Consequently, for final analysis, these 80 responses were taken into the consideration.

Table 2 shows the demographic profile of respondents. The sample represents 67.5- percent males (54) and 32.5percent females (26). It also represents the wide range of ages (31.25 percent were between the ages of 20-25; 43.75 percent between the ages of 25-30; 12.50 percent were between the ages of 30-35, 5.0 percent were between 35-40 and 7.5 percent were more than 40 years). The tenure of the job of the participants which is less than 5 years was 68.75 percent (55), between 5-10 years was 18.75 percent (15) and 12.5 percent (10) of the respondents had an experience of more than 10 years from the different sectors.

Table 2. The demographic profile of respondents

Classification	Category	Number of respondents	Sample Percentage
Age	20-25	25	31.25%
	25-30	35	43.75%
	30-35	10	12.50%
	35-40	4	5.00%
	40+	6	7.50%
Gender	Female	26	32.50%
	Male	54	67.50%
Tenure of Job	Less than 5 year	55	68.75%
	5-10 years	15	18.75%
	more than 10 years	10	12.50%

Instruments

The scale for assessing the employee engagement was developed according to important inclusion and diversity practices. The inclusion and diversity practices that are considered as prime factors that influence employee engagement are: overall culture, hiring and recruitment, career development, personal experiences, policies and procedures, inclusion practices and behavior of immediate supervisor.

A questionnaire to be used for collecting responses from the sample employees consisted of the above mentioned 8 diversity and inclusion practices. The questionnaire included 20 items i.e. 4 items for overall culture, 2 items for hiring and recruitment, 3 items for career development, 2 items for personal experiences, 3 items for policies and procedures, 4 items for inclusion practices and 2 items for behavior of immediate supervisor. A 7-point Likert scale was used to record the responses of the participants were 1, 2, 3,4,5,6 and 7 indicates strongly disagree, moderately disagree, slightly disagree, neutral, slightly agree, moderately agree and strongly agree. Here, the lowest score was 1 and the highest score was 7.

For testing the reliability of the questionnaire, Cronbach's alpha was used which generated a score of 0.97. The Cronbach's alpha (internal consistency) for "overall culture", " hiring and recruitment", "career development," " personal experiences", " policies and procedures", "inclusion practices" and "immediate supervisor" were 0.94, 0.78, 0.88, 0.83, 0.88, 0.88 and 0.87 respectively. The developed instrument was able to meet the standard level of reliability and therefore, was considered to be appropriate for being used in research.

4. RESULTS

The study recorded the views of the respondents on various aspects of diversity and inclusion practices that influence employee engagement in the workplace. The data was collected from 80 employees and Cronbach's Alpha was applied to test the reliability of the instrument which generated a score of 0.97. The Cronbach's alpha (internal consistency) for "overall culture", "hiring and recruitment", "career development," " personal experiences", " policies and procedures", "inclusion practices" and "immediate supervisor" were 0.94, 0.78, 0.88, 0.83, 0.88, 0.88 and 0.87 respectively and all these values fall in the acceptable range.

Table 3 represents values of mean, standard deviation and internal consistencies of the variables under study. From the data we can observe that the diversity and inclusion aspects were positively interrelated i.e. $r = 0.40$. The data collected from 20 item instrument from 80 employees across 8 sectors was analyzed to assess the employee engagement in different sectors of India. The responses of the participants were collected with the help of a 7-point Likert scale with anchors 1-Strongly disagree, 2- Moderately Disagree, 3-Slightly Disagree, 4- Neutral, 5- Slightly agree, 6- Moderately agree and 7- Strongly Agree. Here, the lowest score was 1 and the highest was 7. Thus, the possible lowest cumulative score from a participant was 20 if all 20 items in the instrument if a respondent gives the lowest score 1. Also, the highest cumulative score possible was 140 if all 20 items were given the highest score of 7 in the study.

Table 3. Means, standard deviations, and internal consistencies

Variable	M	SD	Alpha	1	2	3	4	5	6	7
1.Overall Culture	4.08	0.94	0.94	1.00						
2.Hiring and Recruitment	3.97	0.93	0.78	.81**	1.00					
3.Career Development	3.99	0.99	0.88	.84**	.76**	1.00				
4.Personal Experiences	4.06	0.96	0.83	.82**	.74**	.83**	1.00			
5.Policies and Procedures	4.01	0.97	0.88	.87**	.82**	.84**	.87**	1.00		
6.Inclusion Practices	4.09	0.89	0.88	.83**	.77**	.84**	.81**	.81**	1.00	
7.Immediate Supervisor	4.08	1.01	0.87	.84**	.81**	.83**	.80**	.84**	.83**	1.00

**. Correlation is significant at the 0.01 level (1-tailed).

On the basis of the scores obtained from the participants, that ranges 20 to 140, all the respondents were divided into three groups:

- **Disengaged employees**- This category comprises the employees who feel disconnected with the organization and have a score of less than or equal to 60.
- **Neutral employees**- neutral employees are those who sleepwalk the day and have a score ranging from 61 to 80.
- **Engaged employees**- They are the employees who feel connected to the organization and have a score above 80.

Table 3 illustrates the status of engagement (i.e., from being highly disengaged to highly engage) of the employees from the 8 sectors included in the study on the basis of recorded scores.

Gallup (2010) States that the number of employees that are engaged or disengaged determine the organizational rating as a world class organization, the average organization or sub-average organization.

- World Class Organization- an organization is said to be world class if it the percentage of engaged employees in this organization is more than 67% and the percentage of highly disengaged employees is less than 7%.
- Average Organization- An average organization has engaged employees ranging from 33% to 67% and highly disengaged employees ranging from 7% to 18%
- Below Average Organization- the percentage of engaged employees in these organizations is below 33% and the percentage of highly disengaged employees is above 18%

From Table 3, we can see that the sectors like Information Technology and Healthcare have 74.5% and 68.5% engaged employees and 3.5% & 6.8% highly disengaged employees respectively. This indicates that these two sectors belong to world class organizations. The sectors like tourism, education and retail have 59.3%, 44.4% and 59.8% engaged employees and 10.5%, 16.5% & 10% highly disengaged employees. Therefore, these sectors (i.e., tourism, education and retail) fall under the category of average organizations. Other sectors like manufacturing, financial services and insurance fall under the category of below average organizations as these sectors have 26.8%, 29.8% and 28.1% of employees who are engaged and 21.3%, 21.2% and 22% of employees who are highly disengaged respectively. Thus, we can conclude that the organizations that belong to Information Technology (IT) sector have a better employee engagement followed by the Healthcare sector.

Challenges faced by the organizations in implementing diversity-inclusion practices in organizations

An organization consists of people from different nationalities, backgrounds and religions, etc. For promoting diversity and inclusion practices, management needs to accept and respect this diverse workforce. Although there are numerous benefits of including diversity and inclusion in an organization, management faces certain challenges in its effective implementation. Some of the challenges that organizations face in the implementation of diversity and inclusion practices are listed below:

- Communication barrier is one of the biggest issues that companies face in diversity and inclusion management. This problem occurs because of different languages spoken by a diverse workforce. People from different cultures and locations may not be able to communicate effectively.
- Organizations face issues in the implementation of various workplace diversity and inclusion policies and procedures for the diversified workforce.
- Another challenge is the difference in age and generation. This difference creates problems for people in understanding the problems of each other.
- Native employees may not prefer the cultural diversity of diverse employees. This may lead to discrimination in the workplace.
- People may hesitate to accept and provide respect to people from diverse backgrounds. Sometimes they may also feel jealous of other employees. This reduces the performance and productivity of employees in the company.
- Most of the time, people may not be willing to change themselves according to the culture of their organization. This hinders the efforts of an organization towards introducing diversity and inclusion policies in the organization.
- Sometimes the managers may favor a particular group of people. This biasness again acts as a biggest challenge for the organization.

Recommendations to enhance diversity-inclusion practices in the organizations

- An organization should develop clear and effective policies and procedures for better diversity-inclusion management.
- Management should communicate the policies and procedures to all the employees in the organization.
- For the successful implementation of diversity and inclusion practices, managers should provide the employees with training and development programs.
- In order to develop the feeling of belongingness in the employees, employee engagement should be kept on top priority.
- Managers should collect regular feedback and suggestions from the diverse workforce to ensure the employees' level of satisfaction.
- All the employees should be encouraged and motivated to freely share and discuss their issues with managers or the concerned person in the company.
- Respect and dignity should be shown to the diverse workforce working for the betterment of their organization.

From the study, we can observe that the sectors like Information Technology and Healthcare falls under the category of world class organizations. The sectors like tourism, education and fall under the category of average organizations. Other sectors like manufacturing, financial services and insurance fall under the category of below average organizations.

Thus, when we do a comparative analysis among these sectors, it can be seen that the organizations that belong to Information Technology (IT) sector are highly involved in creating strategies and practices for employee engagement. After IT sector, the organizations in health sectors are indulged effectively in employee engagement practices.

5. DISCUSSION

The research paper studied the effect of workplace diversity-inclusion practices in the engagement of employees. The results showed that an organization's inclusion and diversity policies have a positive impact on engagement of employees.

The analysis clearly shows that the sectors like IT and Healthcare show appreciable diversity and inclusion practices to keep its employees engaged whereas sectors like tourism, education and retail have to make ample amounts of changes in their policies to increase the employees' level of engagement. Organizations in manufacturing, financial services and the insurance need to introspect their practices and make changes accordingly to come into the category of world class organizations.

Indeed, as a potential strategy for enhancing employee trust and engagement, this research highlights the importance of encouraging diversity and inclusivity in businesses. Diversity is no longer just about attracting and retaining people from different backgrounds. It is about including employees by modifying entire corporate processes to include minorities and incorporating all employees' opinions into its core goals (Nishii, Rich, & Thomas & Ely, 1996; Woods, 2006). It is critical to promote greater levels of participation. This research demonstrates that it goes beyond diversity and inclusion practices for practitioners, and in fact, could be a necessary prerequisite for businesses to reap the benefits of diversity\s practices. These findings support the importance of inclusion and diversity factors for practitioners to consider in their organizations. Organizations with competent leadership teams will place a greater emphasis on performance rather than individual distinctions such as gender, color, age or sexual orientation, enhancing the company's competitiveness. Management must design diversity-inclusion policies that encourage and support unbiased and equal dealing with all employees and aid as role models for a superior workplace in which everyone can participate.

6. CONCLUSION

Diversity and inclusion practices of a company have a significant positive association with employee engagement. The study found out the role and significance of diversity management and inclusion practices on employee engagement. Yeh, 2013; Huong et al., 2016 states that in the current economic scenario, the study of employee engagement is crucial. This is because satisfied and engaged employees tend to perform better in organizations. The study revealed that diversity and inclusion practices are a good indicator of engaged employees and employee engagement in turn is a good indicator of high performance and productivity.

REFERENCES

American Society for Training and Development (ASTD). (1996a). *ASTD buyer's guide &consultant directory*. Author.

Anand, R. (2013, February 26). How Diversity and Inclusion Drive Employee Engagement. Princeton, NJ: Academic Press.

Apple. (2017). Inclusion and Diversity. Retrieved 08 14, 2017, from https://www. apple.com/diversity/ : https://www.apple.com/diversity/

April, K., & Blass, E. (2010). Measuring Diversity Practice and Developing Inclusion. *Dimensions*, 1(1), 59–66.

ASTD. (1996b). *National report on human resources*. Author.

Ayega, E. N., & Muathe, S. (2018). Critical Review of Literature on Cultural Diversity in the Workplace and Organizational Performance: A Research Agenda. *Journal of Human Resource Management*, 6(1), 9–17. DOI: 10.11648/j.jhrm.20180601.12

Barber, A. E., & Daly, C. L. (1996). Compensation and diversity: new pay for a new workforce? In Kossek, E. E., & Lobel, S. A. (Eds.), *Managing Diversity: Human Resource Strategies for Transforming the Workplace*. Blackwell.

Bilimoria, D., Joy, S., & Liang, X. (2008). Breaking barriers and creating inclusiveness: Lessons of organizational transformation to advance women faculty in academic science and engineering. Human Resource Management: Published in Cooperation with the School of Business Administration, The University of Michigan and in alliance with the Society of Human Resources Management, 47(3), 423-441.

Bunny. (2007, September 13). Bunny's Story. Starbucks Barista Victimized by Age

Carnevale, A. P., & Stone, S. C. (1995). *The American mosaic*. McGraw-Hill.

Caudron, S. (1992). U.S. West finds strength in diversity. *The Personnel Journal*, 71(3), 40–44.

Chavez, C. I., & Weisinger, J. Y. (2008). Beyond diversity training: A social infusion for cultural inclusion. Human Resource Management: Published in Cooperation with the School of Business Administration, The University of Michigan and in alliance with the Society of Human Resources Management, 47(2), 331-350.

Cho, S., & Barak, M. O. R. (2008). Understanding of diversity and inclusion in a perceived homogeneous culture: A study of organizational commitment and job performance among Korean employees. *Administration in Social Work*, 32(4), 100–126. DOI: 10.1080/03643100802293865

Cunningham, G. B. (2008). Creating and sustaining gender diversity in sport organizations. *Sex Roles*, 58(1-2), 136–145. DOI: 10.1007/s11199-007-9312-3

Dell, D., & Ainspan, A. Nathan, Bodenberg, A., & Thomas. (2001). Engaging Employees through Your Brand. The Conference Board

Deloitte. (2015). *Global Human Capital Trends 2015 Leading in the new world of work*. Deloitte University Press.

Discrimination. Industrial Workers of the World. Retrieved 04 12, 2017, from http:// www.iww.org/node/3649

Ferdman, B. M., & Davidson, M. N. (2002). Inclusion: What can I and my organization do about it? *The Industrial-Organizational Psychologist*, 29(4), 80–85.

Fernando, M. A., Pedro, M. R., & Gonzalo, S. G. (2013). Workforce diversity in strategic human resource management models. *Cross Cultural Management*, 20(1), 39–49. DOI: 10.1108/13527601311296247

Findler, L., Wind, L. H., & Barak, M. O. R. (2007). The challenge of workforce management in a global society: Modeling the relationship between diversity, inclusion, organizational culture, and employee well-being, job satisfaction, and organizational commitment. *Administration in Social Work*, 31(3), 63–94. DOI: 10.1300/J147v31n03_05

Gallup. (2006). Gallup study: Engaged employees inspire company innovation: national survey finds that passionate workers are most likely to drive organisations forward. The Gallup Management Journal.

Hayles, V. R. (1996). Diversity training and development. In *The ASTD training and development handbook* (pp. 104–123). McGraw-Hill.

Ibarra, H. (1993). Personal networks of women and minorities in management: A conceptual framework. *Academy of Management Review*, 18(1), 56–87. DOI: 10.2307/258823

Kerdpitak, C., & Jermsittiparsert, K. (2020). The Impact of Human Resource Management Practices on Competitive Advantage: Mediating Role of Employee Engagement in Thailand. *Systematic Reviews in Pharmacy*, 11(1), 443–452.

Liu, F., Khong-Khai, S., Leelapattana, W., & Tsai, C. (2024). Analyzing the Influence of Leadership Style on Employee Engagement in Digital Economy. *Asian Administration and Management Review*, 7(2), 31–44.

Nishii, L. H. (2013). The benefits of climate for inclusion for gender-diverse groups. *Academy of Management Journal*, 56(6), 1754–1774. DOI: 10.5465/amj.2009.0823

Oentoro, W. (2018). High Performance Work Practices and Service Performance: The Influence of Employee Engagement in Call Center Context. *International Journal of Interdisciplinary Research*, 7(1), 1–14.

Paluck, E. L. (2006). Diversity training and intergroup contact: A call to action research. *The Journal of Social Issues*, 62(3), 577–595. DOI: 10.1111/j.1540-4560.2006.00474.x

Rattanasirivilai, S., Somjai, S., & Deeprasert, D. (2020). The Role of Gender as a Moderator Linking Corporate Social Responsibility Perception to Employees Engagement: A Study in the Services Sector of Thailand. *SSRN*, 7(2), 1–14. DOI: 10.2139/ssrn.3898422

Roberson, Q. M. (2006). Disentangling the meanings of diversity and inclusion in organizations. *Group & Organization Management*, 31(2), 212–236. DOI: 10.1177/1059601104273064

Sabharwal, M. (2014). Is diversity management sufficient? Organizational inclusion to further performance. *Public Personnel Management*, 43(2), 197–217. DOI: 10.1177/0091026014522202

Saks, A. (2008). The Meaning and Bleeding of Employee Engagement: How Muddy Is the Water? *Industrial and Organizational Psychology: Perspectives on Science and Practice*, 1(1), 40–43. DOI: 10.1111/j.1754-9434.2007.00005.x

Saks, A. M. (2006). Antecedents and consequences of employee engagement. *Journal of Managerial Psychology*, 21(7), 600–619. DOI: 10.1108/02683940610690169

Scott, K. A., Heathcote, J. M., & Gruman, J. A. (2011). The diverse organization: Finding gold at the end of the rainbow. *Human Resource Management*, 50(6), 735–755. DOI: 10.1002/hrm.20459

Starbucks. (2003). Living our values. Corporate Social Responsibility. Fiscal 2003. Annual Report. Author.

Starbucks. (2011). Business ethics and compliance. Author.

Starbucks. (2014). Diversity and inclusion. Author.

Stevens, F. G., Plaut, V. C., & Sanchez-Burks, J. (2008). Unlocking the benefits of diversity: All-inclusive multiculturalism and positive organizational change. *The Journal of Applied Behavioral Science*, 44(1), 116–133. DOI: 10.1177/0021886308314460

Sukphon, N.Strategic Management and Employee Engagement in Organization. (2022, July 1). Asian Administration &. *Management Review*, 5(2), 1–10.

Waldman. (2016). The Importance of Diversity and inclusion on Employee Engagement. The Employee Engagement Blog.

Walker, B. A. (1991). Valuing differences: The concept and a model. In Smith, M. A., & Johnson, S. J. (Eds.), *Valuing differences in the workplace* (pp. 23–44). ASTD Press.

Walmart. (2015). Diversity & Inclusion. Global Office of Diversity and Inclusion.

Wheeler, M. L. (1994). *Diversity training*. The Conference Board.

Wheeler, M. L. (1995). *Diversity: Business rationale and strategies*. The Conference Board.

Wilson, K. (2009). A survey of employee engagement. (Doctoral dissertation, University of Missouri)

Winter, M. (1992). *Workforce diversity: Corporate challenges*. The Conference Board.

Chapter 9
Staff Behavior and Physical Environment Quality as Antecedents of Brand Loyalty:
The Mediating Roles of Brand Passion and Satisfaction

Francis Ion Sangil
https://orcid.org/0009-0000-5927-9817
University of the Visayas, Philippines

Jean Paolo Gomez Lacap
City College of Angeles, Philippines

Maureen Rivera
https://orcid.org/0009-0000-5911-6698
Polytechnic University of the Philippines, Philippines

Bernadith Radaza
University of the Visayas, Philippines

Mary Ruth Quintero
University of the Visayas, Philippines

ABSTRACT

This chapter uses the Stimulus-Organism-Response (SOR) theory to examine how staff behavior and physical environment quality impact brand loyalty in the fast-food industry, including the roles of brand passion and satisfaction as mediators. Data from 434 customers of a major fast-food chain in the Philippines were analyzed using Partial Least Squares Structural Equation Modeling (PLS-SEM). The study finds that staff behavior affects brand passion, satisfaction, and loyalty, while physical environment quality influences brand passion and satisfaction but not directly brand loyalty. Brand passion and satisfaction are key mediators in these relationships. The study highlights the importance of staff training and an appealing physical environment in building brand loyalty.

DOI: 10.4018/979-8-3693-9230-0.ch009

INTRODUCTION

In recent years, the fast-food sector in the Philippines has rapidly expanded, becoming a key part of the nation's economy and business landscape (Prasetyo et al., 2023; Alvarez, 2020). In 2021, the food-service industry led in revenue, reaching PHP 203 billion with 4,411 establishments (Philippine Statistics Authority, 2018). This growth is driven by food's cultural significance and changes in income, lifestyles, and preferences (Gabriel, 2001; Mina & Campos, 2017; Rahkovsky et al., 2018). To foster customer loyalty and ensure profitability, fast-food restaurateurs must refine their marketing strategies, enhance product offerings, and improve customer experience (Mubarok et al., 2023). Understanding the factors behind customers' fast-food choices is crucial for achieving this goal (Shahzadi et al., 2018).

Brand loyalty has been extensively examined in marketing and consumer behavior research, being recognized as a critical asset for organizational success (Mills et al., 2022). Understanding the factors that drive customer loyalty is essential for marketers and entrepreneurs, as it significantly influences profitability, competitiveness, and long-term business success (Del Mar Garcia-De los Salmones et al., 2005; Ngobo, 2016; Kim et al., 2020). Brand loyalty not only fosters strong, long-term customer relationships but also reflects customers' repeated purchases and emotional attachment to a brand (Rather et al., 2018; Zhang et al., 2020; Sahagun & Vasquez-Parraga, 2014).

Research has highlighted that staff behavior and physical environment quality are significant determinants of brand loyalty. Attributes such as friendly, attentive, and respectful staff positively impact customer loyalty and dining experience (Yurt & Sağir, 2023). Similarly, factors like store design and cleanliness are crucial for maintaining customer loyalty (Sun & Moon, 2023). Additionally, customer satisfaction plays a significant mediating role in the relationship between physical environment quality and brand loyalty. Studies have shown that customer satisfaction significantly influences this relationship (Ali et al., 2021; Rajput & Gahfoor, 2020). These findings are further supported by a range of studies within the fast-food industry, which consistently highlight the importance of both staff behavior and physical environment quality in fostering brand loyalty (Achamadi et al., 2023; Javed et al., 2021; Villanueva et al., 2023).

While staff behavior and physical environment quality are well-established as key drivers of brand loyalty, with customer satisfaction serving as a mediator, contemporary literature has not extensively explored the impact of brand passion—customers' emotional attachment to the brand. Despite extensive research on the direct effects of staff behavior on brand loyalty, the role of brand passion as a mediator remains underexamined. As noted by Hyken (2022), emotional connections with a brand can significantly enhance customer preference. Incorporating brand passion into existing research is important due to its unclear relationship with other brand loyalty constructs (Albert et al., 2013). This study aims to address this gap by introducing a model that examines brand passion and customer satisfaction as mediators in the relationship between staff behavior, physical environment quality, and brand loyalty. The findings will provide valuable insights for entrepreneurs and marketers, helping them focus on strategies that enhance customer satisfaction, strengthen brand loyalty, and improve performance in the competitive fast-food industry.

LITERATURE REVIEW

Mehrabian and Russell's (1974) Stimulus-Organism-Response (S-O-R) theory explains how stimuli affect cognitive and emotional states, which in turn influence behavioral responses (Islam & Rahman, 2017). In this framework, "stimuli" refer to environmental factors impacting an individual's cognitive and emotional responses (Eroglu et al., 2001), while the "organism" represents the internal emotional and cognitive processes triggered by these stimuli (Bagozzi, 1986; Bagozzi & Yi, 1988). "Response" encompasses the consumer's final decisions or behaviors, which may include positive actions like continued engagement or negative behaviors such as avoidance (Ridgway et al., 1990).

In consumer behavior and service marketing, stimuli include various marketing and environmental factors that affect emotional responses (Bagozzi, 1986). Feedback represents the consumer's ultimate response, influencing behaviors such as purchasing or avoiding (Bagozzi, 1986).

This study applies the S-O-R theory to explore how brand passion and satisfaction mediate the relationships between staff behavior, physical environment quality, and brand loyalty. Specifically, brand passion acts as an emotional mediator, affecting customer attachment and loyalty, while satisfaction serves as a psychological mediator, reflecting overall service evaluation and its impact on loyalty. By examining these mediating roles, this study aims to deepen the understanding of brand loyalty determinants in the foodservice industry, highlighting the interplay between external stimuli, internal processes, and final consumer responses.

Brand Loyalty

Brand loyalty is crucial for marketing success, encompassing both repeat purchases and positive attitudes toward a brand (Lacap et al., 2021). It is not only about customer retention but also about fostering affection for the brand, which supports long-term growth (Sahagun & Vasquez-Parraga, 2014). Core factors driving brand loyalty include trust and commitment, which are reinforced through exceptional service and effective handling of service failures (Delgado-Ballester & Munuera-Alemán, 2005; Morgan & Hunt, 1994; Hess & Story, 2005).

In competitive sectors like the fast-food industry, brand loyalty is particularly valuable, leading to higher profitability and customer investment beyond mere price considerations (Flavián & Guinalíu, 2006; Khorasani & Almasifard, 2017). Effective marketing strategies focus on building and maintaining this loyalty to capture market share and enhance profits (Ergün & Kitapci, 2018). Modern research emphasizes that strong brand loyalty ensures long-term customer satisfaction and financial stability, encourages brand advocacy, and adapts to a rapidly changing competitive landscape (Cardoso et al., 2022; Tanveer et al., 2021). Understanding these factors is essential for marketers to develop strategies that nurture enduring customer relationships in the competitive fast-food market (Djayapranata & Setyawan, 2022).

Staff Behavior

In the fast-food sector, staff behavior is integral to shaping customer satisfaction and overall dining experience (Fitria & Yuliati, 2020). Positive interactions and effective service by employees significantly impact customer perceptions and contribute to business success (Park & Kim, 2020). Given the competitive nature of the industry, high employee performance and professionalism are essential for enhancing the customer experience (Yurt & Sağir, 2023).

Research highlights that staff attitudes and interactions play a crucial role in fostering brand passion. Employees who exhibit positive behavior and emotional engagement can trigger customers' emotional attachment to the brand (Mostafa & Kasamani, 2020). Customer satisfaction, driven by staff reliability, responsiveness, and empathy, strengthens this emotional bond, leading to increased brand passion (Lin & Mattila, 2010; D' Lima, 2018). Staff enthusiasm and dedication further enhance this connection, deepening customer engagement and attachment to the brand (Wentzel, 2009). Thus, effective staff behavior is pivotal in cultivating strong brand loyalty and passion (Hemsley-Brown & Alnawas, 2016). Based on this literature, it is hypothesized that:

H1a. Staff behavior has a significant influence on brand passion.

In the context of hospitality industry, employees exhibit many varieties of behavior or sequences of actions towards the customers. Considering the importance of human contact in fast-food industry, staff behavior can positively and negatively influence customer satisfaction (Ivkov et al., 2016) and repeat patronage (Weiss et al., 2004). As moted by Javed et al (2021), staff behavior, as one of the components of service quality, plays a crucial role on forming consumer behavior. Attributes such as friendliness, courtesy, efficiency in service delivery, and wait times, are determinants of the customers' intention to return in a restaurant. Customer satisfaction can be fostered when employees understand the customers' needs, anticipate and meet expectations, and respond appropriately to inquiries and requests (Jones & Shandiz, 2015). As proven by Abdullah & Rozario, 2009, customer satisfaction is a crucial contributing factor in determining customer satisfaction in the food services industry. With this, it is hypothesized that:

H1b. Staff behavior has a significant influence on brand satisfaction.

There is a vast amount of literature proving the significant impact of staff behavior on brand loyalty. Staff behavior and service quality has a substantial impact on customer happiness, which fosters the growth of customer loyalty (Setyadi et al., 2023; Zhang, 2023). In the hospitality industry, a lot of studies indicate that enhancing all several facets of staff behavior leads to increased customer satisfaction, loyalty, and repurchase intent (Phijaranakul, 2022; Villanueva et al., 2023). This was also proven by Rajput and Gahfoor (2020) that good staff behavior and quality service exhibited by employees are important triggers of customer loyalty and revisit intention in the context of fast-food restaurants. Following the logic presented above, it is reasonable to anticipate the following outcomes in the fast-food industry:

H1c. Staff behavior has a significant influence on brand loyalty.

Physical Environment Quality

Physical environment quality is a pivotal factor in establishing a competitive advantage (Shamah et al., 2018). This encompasses various elements such as exterior and interior design, lighting, cleanliness, ambiance, and overall aesthetic appeal (Shamah et al., 2018; Ha & Jang, 2012). A well-maintained and appealing physical environment significantly influences a restaurant's reputation and attractiveness, playing a crucial role in drawing customers (Ngah et al., 2022).

Brand passion, which involves an emotional attachment to the brand, can be significantly influenced by the physical environment of a restaurant. Research indicates that an attractive and thoughtfully designed interior and exterior, including seating arrangements and overall building design, are essential for cultivating brand passion (Nyamekye et al., 2021). Such elements enhance the customer's emotional experience and attachment to the brand. On the other hand, a poorly designed or unappealing environment can generate negative emotions, undermining customers' positive feelings and diminishing their emotional connection to the brand (Jani & Han, 2015; Jang & Namkung, 2009). This negative impact can lead to decreased brand passion and reduced customer loyalty. Recent studies, such as that by Hemsley-Brown (2022), further support the idea that high-quality physical environments are crucial in fostering strong brand passion among customers. Therefore, it is hypothesized that:

H2a. Physical environment quality has a significant influence on brand passion.

Physical environment quality plays a critical role in shaping customer satisfaction in the service industry (Zhong & Moon, 2020). In restaurant settings, atmospheric elements such as lighting, ambiance, décor style, cleanliness, seating comfort, and noise significantly influence customer experiences and behavioral intentions (Pei & Ayub, 2015). A well-designed and welcoming restaurant environment enhances overall impressions, fosters customer confidence, and builds loyalty among diners (Samlejsin & Kookkaew, 2022; Siswanto et al., 2019).

Conversely, an unattractive or poorly designed physical environment can elicit negative feelings, diminishing customer satisfaction and emotional well-being (Jani & Han, 2015). Factors like cleanliness, seating arrangement, space adequacy, lighting, and aroma directly impact brand loyalty through customer satisfaction (Rodhiah & Ervina, 2024). Rajput and Gahfoor (2020) confirm that high-quality physical environments significantly enhance customer loyalty in fast-food restaurants. Additionally, research by Daries Ramón et al. (2018) shows that perceptions of the physical surroundings are strong indicators of customer satisfaction and loyalty, while Çetinsöz (2019) finds a positive effect of physical environment quality on both satisfaction and loyalty in upscale restaurants. Thus, the related hypotheses are as follows:

H2b. Physical environment quality has a significant influence on brand satisfaction.

H2c. Physical environment quality has a significant influence on brand loyalty.

Brand passion refers to a strong emotional attachment and enthusiasm for a particular brand (Albert et al., 2013). It is characterized by a highly positive attitude and infatuation with the brand, leading to increased customer loyalty and preference. Research shows that brand passion drives positive outcomes such as higher revisit intentions, increased social media engagement, and favorable word-of-mouth (Hemsley-Brown & Alnawas, 2016; Matzler et al., 2007). Customers who are passionate about a brand often become brand advocates, enhancing loyalty and promoting the brand to others (Zhang et al., 2020). This relationship has been confirmed across various industries, including sports and luxury (Hossain et al., 2021; Pourazad et al., 2019). Therefore, the following hypothesis is proposed:

H3. Brand passion has a significant influence on brand loyalty.

Brand satisfaction is a pivotal construct in understanding consumer behavior, as it gauges how well a product or service meets or exceeds customer expectations. Rooted in Expectancy Confirmation Theory, this concept posits that customer satisfaction arises when actual performance surpasses expectations, leading to positive disconfirmation, whereas negative disconfirmation occurs when performance falls short (Javed et al., 2021). In the service industry, enhancing customer satisfaction is vital for driving profitability and fostering brand loyalty (Hiranrithikorna et al., 2019; Slack et al., 2020).

Satisfaction plays a key role in building trust, which is essential for developing customer loyalty (Sharma et al., 2020). High satisfaction levels not only increase the likelihood of repeat purchases but also encourage customers to share positive experiences and advocate for the brand (Hidayat et al., 2019). Research indicates that satisfied customers are more likely to be loyal, reinforcing the importance of customer satisfaction in maintaining strong brand relationships (Akmal et al., 2023). Therefore, it is hypothesized that:

H4. Brand satisfaction has a significant influence on brand loyalty.

Studies have shown that staff behavior and the physical environment significantly impact brand loyalty by shaping customer experiences, fostering emotional connections, and building trust (Bihamta et al., 2017). According to S-O-R theory, brand passion—characterized by emotional attachment and deep engagement—can mediate the effects of staff behavior and physical environment quality on brand loyalty. Research by De Nisco and Warnaby (2014) indicate that customer emotions mediate the relationship between store atmosphere and behavioral intentions. Jang and Namkung (2009) found that staff behavior influences customer emotions, which in turn affects behavioral intentions. Koo and Kim (2013) demonstrated that store environmental factors enhance emotional attachment, which predicts brand loyalty. Hemsley-Brown and Alnawas (2016) confirmed that brand passion fully mediates the impact of both staff behavior and physical environment quality on brand loyalty. Therefore, to enhance brand loyalty, businesses should focus on improving staff performance and the physical environment. Thus, the following hypotheses are proposed:

H5. Brand passion mediates the relationship between staff behavior and brand loyalty.

H6. Brand passion mediates the relationship between physical environment quality and brand loyalty.

Numerous studies highlight that both physical environment quality and staff behavior significantly impact brand loyalty by shaping customer experiences and fostering emotional connections (Gill et al., 2021). Recent research also underscores that customer satisfaction mediates these relationships. Rajput and Gahfoor (2020) found that customer satisfaction mediates the link between physical environment quality and brand loyalty, supporting the S-O-R theory by showing that external stimuli affect internal responses, which in turn influence loyalty and revisit intentions. Ali et al. (2021) demonstrated that customer satisfaction mediates the relationship between service quality, price, restaurant environment, and brand loyalty. Devi and Yasa (2021) further validated this by showing that customer satisfaction mediates the effect of service quality on brand loyalty, aligning with earlier findings by Joudeh & Dandis (2018) and Yacob et al. (2016). Additionally, and Ashraf et al. (2018) confirmed that customer satisfaction mediates the impact of service quality on brand loyalty. Studies by Javed et al. (2021) and Ikramuddin and Mariyudi (2021) also emphasize the critical role of customer satisfaction in linking service quality and perceived value to brand loyalty. Thus, it is proposed that:

H7. Brand satisfaction mediates the relationship between physical environment quality and brand loyalty.

H8. Brand satisfaction mediates the relationship between staff behavior and brand loyalty.

The conceptual framework in Figure 1 outlines the study's variable relationships, incorporating the SOR Theory. It posits that staff behavior (H1a, H1b, H1c) and physical environment quality (H2a, H2b, H2c) significantly affect brand passion, satisfaction, and loyalty. The framework further suggests that brand passion (H3) and brand satisfaction (H4) impact brand loyalty. Additionally, it proposes that brand passion (H5, H6) and brand satisfaction (H7, H8) mediate the relationships between staff behavior and brand loyalty, as well as between physical environment quality and brand loyalty.

Figure 1. Conceptual framework

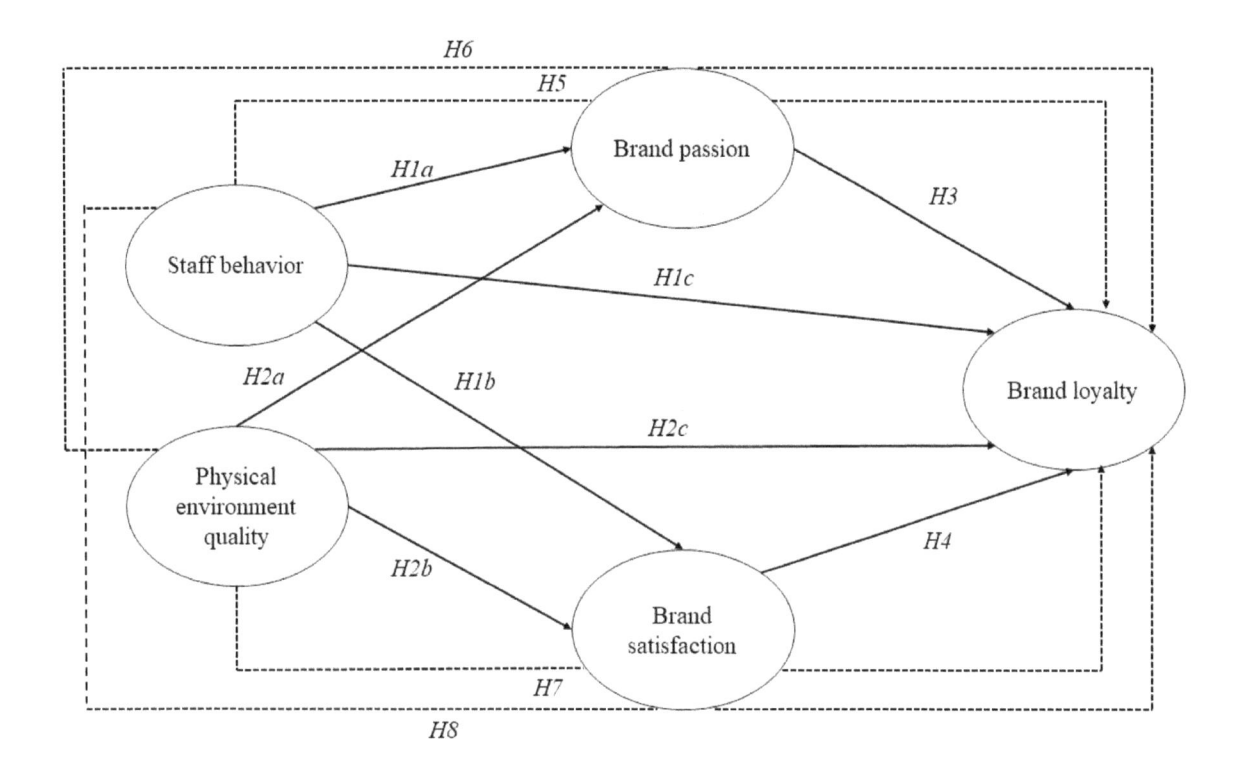

METHODS

Respondents

The study targeted Filipino customers from Cebu Province, Southern Leyte, and Zamboanga del Norte. To be included in the research, respondents needed to meet specific criteria: they had to be at least 18 years old, must be customers of one of the major fast-food brands in the Philippines, and should have made a purchase from the brand in question. A total of 434 respondents were surveyed. The study utilized purposive sampling, also known as judgment sampling, where participants are selected based on predetermined qualities or characteristics (Tongco, 2007). To capture genuine feedback about their experiences, the intercept method was used for data collection. This method involves approaching respondents in real-time at locations like restaurants or shopping malls to gather their opinions immediately after their interactions with the brand. This approach helps ensure that the feedback is accurate and reflects their experiences before any emotions might have faded (Phonthanukitithaworn & Sellitto, 2016).

Research Instrument

To measure these constructs, questions have been adopted from various established sources, and a 5-point Likert scale where 5 means strongly agree and 1 means strongly disagree was used.

Table 1. Research constructs, items, and sources

Constructs and Items	Sources
Staff Behavior	Ekinci & Dawes, (2009)
SB 1. Employees of this fast-food restaurant listen to me.	
SB 2. Employees of this brand are helpful.	
SB 3. Employees of this brand are friendly.	
SB 4. Employees of this fast-food brand always understand my needs.	
SB 5. Employees always have my best interests in mind.	
Physical Environment Quality	Nam et al. (2011)
PE 1. This brand has modern-looking equipment.	
PE 2. This brand's facilities are visually appealing.	
PE 3. This brand gives you a visually attractive room.	
PE 4. This fast-food is beautifully coordinated with great attention to detail.	
Brand Passion	Thomson et al. (2005)
BP 1. I am passionate about this fast-food brand.	
BP 2. I have real trust in this fast-food brand.	
BP 3. I feel really close this fast-food brand.	
BP 4. This fast-food brand is really appealing to me.	
BP 5. This fast-food brand makes me feel great delight.	
Brand Satisfaction	Erciş, A., et al. (2012)
BS 1. Overall, I am satisfied with my transactions on this fast-food.	
BS 2. This fast-food brand is the best choice for me	
BS 3. This fast-food brand has met my expectations	
Brand Loyalty	Harris and Goode (2004) and Chaudhuri and Holbrook (2001)
BL 1. I will continue to choose this fast-food brand before other brands.	

BL 2. I would continue to favor the offerings of this fast-food brand before others.
BL 3. I am willing "to go the extra mile" to choose this fast-food brand.
BL 4. I would rather stay with this fast-food than try a different fast-food I am unsure of.
BL 5. Next time I am looking for somewhere to eat, I will stay with fast-food brand.
BL 6. I will recommend this fast-food brand to someone who seeks my advice.
BL 7. I am very committed to this fast-food brand.

In order to measure the constructs of the study, research instruments were adopted from various sources. For instance, the Staff Behavior Scale, which comprises five questions, was adopted from Ekinci & Dawes, (2009). The four questions of the Physical Environment Quality Scale were adopted from Nam et al. (2011). The survey questionnaire on Brand Passion was adopted from the study of Thompson et al. (2005). The Brand Satisfaction Scale, comprising 3 questions, has been adopted from Erciş et al. (2012). Finally, the Brand Loyalty Scale, consisting of 7 questions, has been adopted from Harris and Goode (2004) and Chaudhuri and Holbrook (2001). See Table 1 for summary.

Research Design and Data Analysis

The present study is under quantitative research. Specifically, a predictive research design was utilized. A predictive research design aims to measure hypothesized interrelationships between exogenous, endogenous, and intervening variables by using contemporary statistical and data mining methodologies (Waljee et al., 2014). This research design predicts future outcomes based on a proposed path model of a theory (Chin et al., 2020)

Partial Least Squares – Structural Equation Modelling was used to prove the hypothesis based on the path model. With the complex nature of predictive studies, PLS-SEM is usually utilized in this type of research since it allows the researcher simultaneous analysis of relationships between observed and latent variables in complex cause–effect relationship models (Hair et al., 2019).

RESULTS

Measurement Model Assessment

The validity and reliability of the variables in this study were assessed using composite reliability (CR), discriminant validity, and convergent validity. Composite reliability values of 0.70 or higher are necessary to confirm the internal consistency of reflective constructs (Cheung et al., 2023). As indicated in Table 2, the CR values for staff behavior (CR = 0.894), physical environment quality (CR = 0.900), brand passion (CR = 0.916), brand satisfaction (CR = 0.915), and brand loyalty (CR = 0.943) exceeded the threshold of 0.70, confirming that all constructs are reliable and exhibit adequate internal consistency. Convergent validity was evaluated through item loadings and average variance extracted (AVE). According to Fornell and Larcker (1981) and Hair et al. (2009), item loadings and AVE should be at least 0.50 and statistically significant ($p < .05$). The results presented in Table 2 show that all constructs meet these criteria, indicating that they possess convergent validity.

Table 2. Reliability measure and convergent validity

Reflective latent construct	Item	Item loading
Staff behavior: AVE = 0.627; CR = 0.894		
	SB1	0.771
	SB2	0.804
	SB3	0.766
	SB4	0.844
	SB5	0.772

continued on following page

Table 2. Continued

Reflective latent construct	Item	Item loading
Physical Environment Quality: AVE = 0.693; CR = 0.900	PE1	0.799
	PE2	0.863
	PE3	0.848
	PE4	0.819
Brand Passion: AVE = 0.686; CR = 0.916	BP1	0.826
	BP2	0.819
	BP3	0.821
	BP4	0.862
	BP5	0.813
Brand Satisfaction: AVE = 0.783; CR = 0.915	BS1	0.882
	BS2	0.866
	BS3	0.905
Brand Loyalty: AVE = 0.702; CR = 0.943	BL1	0.845
	BL2	0.851
	BL3	0.841
	BL4	0.838
	BL5	0.868
	BL6	0.751
	BL7	0.865

All item loadings are significant ($p < 0.001$)

Table 3 presents the assessment of discriminant validity for the study's constructs, utilizing heterotrait-monotrait (HTMT) ratios. According to Henseler et al. (2014), an HTMT ratio of less than 0.85 is considered acceptable for structural equation modeling (SEM), although some sources suggest a threshold of 0.90 (Hamid et al., 2017). The data in Table 4 indicate that all HTMT ratios for the constructs in this study are below the recommended thresholds, thus confirming the discriminant validity of the constructs.

Table 3. Discriminant validity

	SB	PE	BP	BS	BL
SB					
PE	0.702				
BP	0.644	0.663			
BS	0.698	0.665	0.822		
BL	0.537	0.491	0.732	0.744	

SB-staff behavior; PE-physical environment quality; BP-brand passion; BS-brand satisfaction; BL-brand loyalty.

Structural Model Assessment

Table 4 provides an evaluation of the proposed model by analyzing coefficients (β), p-values, standard errors (SE), and effect sizes (f²), and determining the acceptance or rejection of each hypothesis. The results demonstrate that staff behavior significantly influences brand passion (H1a: β = 0.344, p < 0.001) with a medium effect size (f² = 0.197). Additionally, staff behavior significantly affects brand satisfaction (H1b: β = 0.400, p < 0.001) with a medium effect size (f² = 0.246) and also positively impacts brand loyalty (H1c: β = 0.103, p < 0.001), albeit with a small effect size (f² = 0.052).

Regarding physical environment quality, it significantly influences both brand passion (H2a: β = 0.362, p < 0.001) and brand satisfaction (H2b: β = 0.320, p < 0.001) with medium effect sizes of f² = 0.209 and f² = 0.189, respectively. However, it does not significantly affect brand loyalty (H2c: β = -0.029, p = 0.288). Brand loyalty is positively and significantly impacted by both brand passion (H3: β = 0.364, p < 0.001) and brand satisfaction (H4: β = 0.363, p < 0.001), with medium effect sizes of f² = 0.252 and f² = 0.251, respectively.

Figure 2. The study's structural model

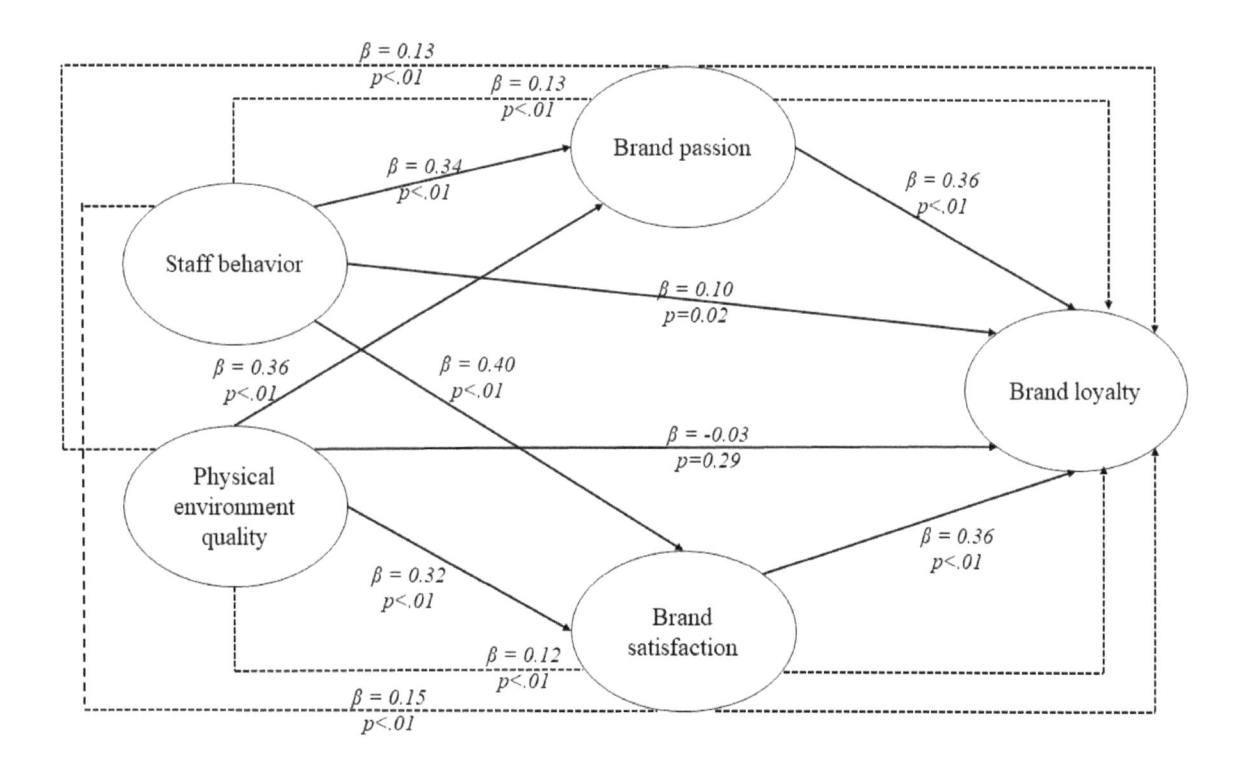

Mediation analyses reveal significant indirect effects of brand passion and brand satisfaction. Specifically, brand passion mediates the relationship between staff behavior and brand loyalty (H5: β = 0.125, p < 0.001) and between physical environment quality and brand loyalty (H6: β = 0.132, p < 0.001), with weak effect sizes of f² = 0.060 and f² = 0.060. Additionally, brand satisfaction mediates the relationship between physical environment quality and brand loyalty (H7: β = 0.116, p < 0.001) and between staff behavior and brand loyalty (H8: β = 0.145, p < 0.001), with small effect sizes of $f^2 = 0.053$ and $f^2 = 0.074$, respectively.

Table 4. Direct and mediating effects

Hypothesis	β	p	SE	f^2	Decision
Direct effects					
H1a. SB → BP	0.344	<0.001	0.049	0.197	S
H1b. SB → BS	0.400	<0.001	0.049	0.246	S
H1c. SB → BL	0.103	0.021	0.051	0.052	S
H2a. PE → BP	0.362	<0.001	0.049	0.209	S
H2b. PE → BS	0.320	<0.001	0.049	0.189	S
H2c. PE → BL	-0.029	0.288	0.051	0.013	NS
H3. BP → BL	0.364	<0.001	0.049	0.252	S
H4. BS → BL	0.363	<0.001	0.049	0.251	S
Mediating effects					
H5. SB → BP → BL	0.125	<0.001	0.036	0.064	S
H6. PE → BP → BL	0.132	<0.001	0.036	0.060	S
H7. PE → BS → BL	0.116	<0.001	0.036	0.053	S
H8. SB → BS → BL	0.145	<0.001	0.036	0.074	S

SB-staff behavior; PE-physical environment quality; BP-brand passion; BS-brand satisfaction; BL-brand loyalty.

β-path coefficient; p-p-value; SE-standard error; f^2=effect size; S-supported; NS-not supported. Effect sizes evaluation (Cohen, 1988): 0.02 – small; 0.15 – medium; 0.35 – large.

In summary, the hypotheses H1a, H1b, H1c, H2a, H2b, H3, and H4 are supported. Hypothesis H2c is not supported. Furthermore, brand passion and brand satisfaction are confirmed as mediators in the relationships between staff behavior, physical environment quality, and brand loyalty, supporting hypotheses H5, H6, H7, and H8.

DISCUSSION

The study investigates the impact of staff behavior and physical environment quality on brand passion, satisfaction, and loyalty. It hypothesizes that brand passion and satisfaction directly affect brand loyalty, and that brand passion and satisfaction mediate the relationships between staff behavior, physical environment quality, and brand loyalty.

The results from Partial Least Squares Structural Equation Modeling (PLS-SEM) indicate that staff behavior significantly influences brand passion (H1a: β = 0.344, p < 0.001) and brand satisfaction (H1b: β = 0.400, p < 0.001), with medium effect sizes ($f^2 = 0.197$ and $f^2 = 0.246$, respectively). Staff behavior also impacts brand loyalty (H1c: β = 0.103, p < 0.001), albeit with a smaller effect size ($f^2 = 0.052$). These findings align with previous research emphasizing the role of positive employee interactions in fostering brand passion and satisfaction (Mostafa & Kasamani, 2020; Wentzel, 2009) and improving customer loyalty (Rajput & Gahfoor, 2020).

Physical environment quality positively affects both brand passion (H2a: β = 0.362, p < 0.001) and brand satisfaction (H2b: β = 0.320, p < 0.001), with medium effect sizes (f^2 = 0.209 and f^2 = 0.189, respectively). These results highlight the importance of store design and maintenance in enhancing emotional connections and satisfaction (Nyamekye et al., 2021). However, physical environment quality does not significantly impact brand loyalty (H2c: β = -0.029, p = 0.288), a finding consistent with studies suggesting that factors beyond physical environment may influence customer loyalty (Atsnawiyah et al., 2021; Purwadi et al., 2020; Shin & Yu, 2018). Variability in customer preferences may affect the relationship between physical environment quality and loyalty (Ryu & Han, 2011).

The study also confirms significant positive relationships between brand passion and brand loyalty (H3: β = 0.364, p < 0.001) and between brand satisfaction and brand loyalty (H4: β = 0.363, p < 0.001), both with medium effect sizes (f^2 = 0.252 and f^2 = 0.251, respectively). These findings underscore the role of emotional attachment and satisfaction in enhancing customer loyalty (Pourazad et al., 2019; Sharma et al., 2020).

Mediation analyses reveal that brand passion mediates the relationships between staff behavior and brand loyalty (H5: β = 0.125, p < 0.001) and between physical environment quality and brand loyalty (H6: β = 0.132, p < 0.001), with weak effect sizes (f^2 = 0.060). Additionally, brand satisfaction mediates the relationships between staff behavior and brand loyalty (H8: β = 0.145, p < 0.001) and between physical environment quality and brand loyalty (H7: β = 0.116, p < 0.001), with small effect sizes (f^2 = 0.074 and f^2 = 0.053). These results support the notion that emotional factors and satisfaction play crucial roles in mediating customer-brand relationships (Hemsley-Brown & Alnawas, 2016; Ali et al., 2021; Devi & Yasa, 2021; Gill et al., 2021; Rajput & Gahfoor, 2020).

Overall, the study supports hypotheses H1a, H1b, H1c, H2a, H2b, H3, and H4, while hypothesis H2c is not supported. It also confirms the mediating roles of brand passion (H5, H6) and brand satisfaction (H7, H8) in the relationships between staff behavior, physical environment quality, and brand loyalty.

CONCLUSION AND IMPLICATIONS

In the Philippine context, the fast-food industry is experiencing notable growth driven by increasing demand for convenient dining options, influenced by evolving lifestyles and urbanization. A critical challenge for this sector, however, is the prevalent lack of customer loyalty, as consumers frequently rotate among various establishments rather than showing consistent preference for a single one (Raquel, 2014). Filipinos, known for their adventurous dining habits, exhibit discernment in their patronage, suggesting that factors beyond food quality play a crucial role in fostering customer loyalty.

This study offers valuable insights for fast-food industry stakeholders. The findings underscore that brand loyalty is influenced not only by food quality and taste but also by the quality of interactions with restaurant staff. Effective staff behavior significantly impacts the overall dining experience, emphasizing the importance of human connection in an increasingly technology-driven industry. Despite advancements such as online kiosks, robotic servers, and AI-assisted ordering systems, personal interaction remains a pivotal component of a successful dining experience (). Consequently, it is essential for fast-food establishments to prioritize hiring qualified staff and implementing comprehensive training programs to enhance customer service skills. Additionally, a well-structured performance appraisal system is critical for ensuring adherence to service standards.

Furthermore, maintaining a clean, attractive, and well-designed physical environment is vital. As the first and last points of contact with customers, the store's interior and exterior significantly impact customer satisfaction and can influence both retention and acquisition (Walter & Edvardsson, 2012). An appealing physical environment can create positive impressions and foster customer satisfaction.

In summary, effective management in the fast-food industry must balance both environmental and human resource considerations. Investing in high-quality staff and maintaining an appealing physical environment are crucial strategies for enhancing customer satisfaction, building brand loyalty, and establishing a positive reputation in the competitive fast-food market.

Theoretical Contribution

The theoretical contribution of this study centers on validating the applicability of the Stimulus-Organism-Response (SOR) model within the specific context of Filipino fast-food consumers. The research elucidates the dynamics of consumer-brand relationships by demonstrating how stimuli—such as staff behavior (human factor) and physical environment quality (physical factor)—directly impact brand loyalty (response) within the highly competitive fast-food sector in the Philippines. Furthermore, this study investigates the role of brand passion and customer satisfaction as mediating factors (organism), thereby providing insights into the psychological and emotional mechanisms underpinning these relationships. By offering empirical evidence on the mediating role of brand passion, which has been insufficiently explored in existing marketing literature, this research contributes to a deeper understanding of consumer-brand relationship constructs.

Limitations of the Study

Despite its contributions, this study has several limitations. Firstly, its focus on the fast-food industry may restrict the generalizability of the findings to other sectors. Secondly, the respondents were exclusively from three provinces in the Philippines, and the study concentrated on a single Filipino fast-food chain, omitting other significant players in the industry. Thirdly, the predominance (83.41%) of respondents aged 18 to 30 limits the demographic diversity of the sample. Lastly, the study solely considered staff behavior and physical environment as exogenous variables, despite their extensively documented roles in fostering loyalty within the marketing literature, both locally and internationally.

Future Research Directions

Based on the limitations identified in this study, several avenues for future research can be explored. Firstly, future researchers could adopt a comparative approach by investigating similar relationships in industries beyond the fast-food sector. Additionally, to mitigate the limitation of the geographic scope of the study, future research could broaden the scope of data collection to include respondents from a more extensive range of regions in the Philippines. Instead of focusing solely on one fast-food chain, future studies could adopt a broader industry-wide perspective by including respondents from other significant competitors in the fast-food industry. While this study primarily focused on staff behavior and physical environment quality, future research could explore the influence of additional understudied variables on brand loyalty.

REFERENCES

Abdullah, D. N. M. A., & Rozario, F. (2009). Influence of service and product quality towards customer satisfaction: A case study at the staff cafeteria in the hotel industry. *World Academy of Science, Engineering and Technology*, 53, 185–190.

Achamadi, R., Eviana, N., & Soerjanto, S. (2023). Increase Brand Loyalty Through Customer Satisfaction at Restaurants. *African Journal of Hospitality, Tourism and Leisure*, 12(1), 98–113. DOI: 10.46222/ajhtl.19770720.356

Akmal, E., Panjaitan, H. P., & Ginting, Y. M. (2023). Service quality, product quality, price, promotion, and location on customer satisfaction and loyalty in CV. Restu. *Journal of Applied Business and Technology*, 4(1), 39–54. DOI: 10.35145/jabt.v4i1.118

Albert, N., Merunka, D., & Valette-Florence, P. (2013). Brand passion: Antecedents and consequences. *Journal of Business Research*, 66(7), 904–909. DOI: 10.1016/j.jbusres.2011.12.009

Ali, B. J., Saleh, P. F., Akoi, S., Abdulrahman, A. A., Muhamed, A. S., Noori, H. N., & Anwar, G. (2021). Impact of Service Quality on the Customer Satisfaction: Case study at Online Meeting Platforms. *International Journal of Engineering Business Management*, 5(2), 65–77. DOI: 10.22161/ijebm.5.2.6

Ali, D., Alam, M. W., & Bilal, H. (2021). The influence of service quality, price, and environment on customer loyalty in the restaurant's industry: The mediating role of customer satisfaction. *Journal of Accounting and Finance in Emerging Economies*, 7(1), 143–154. DOI: 10.26710/jafee.v7i1.1587

Alvarez. (2020). Marketing Strategies of Food Service Industry in the Province of Isabela, Philippines. *The Mattingley Publishing Co., Inc.*, 83, 1736–1749.

Ashraf, S., Ilyas, R., Imtiaz, M., & Ahmad, S. (2018). Impact of Service Quality, Corporate Image and Perceived Value on Brand Loyalty with Presence and Absence of Customer Satisfaction: A Study of four Service Sectors of Pakistan. *International Journal of Academic Research in Business & Social Sciences*, 8(2). Advance online publication. DOI: 10.6007/IJARBSS/v8-i2/3885

Atsnawiyah, D., Rizan, M., & Rahmi, R. (2021). The influence of cafe atmosphere and food quality on customer satisfaction in building customer loyalty of Masalalu Café Rawa Domba Jakarta. *Pedagogi: Jurnal Penelitian Pendidikan/Pedagogi*, 5(1), 113–138. https://doi.org/DOI: 10.21009/JDMB.05.1.6

Bagozzi, R. P. (1986). Attitude formation under the theory of reasoned action and a purposeful behaviour reformulation. *British Journal of Social Psychology*, 25(2), 95–107. DOI: 10.1111/j.2044-8309.1986.tb00708.x

Bagozzi, R. P., & Yi, Y. (1988). On the evaluation of structural equation models. *Journal of the Academy of Marketing Science*, 16(1), 74–94. DOI: 10.1007/BF02723327

Bihamta, H., Jayashree, S., Rezaei, S., Okumus, F., & Rahimi, R. (2017). Dual pillars of hotel restaurant food quality satisfaction and brand loyalty. *British Food Journal*, 119(12), 2597–2609. DOI: 10.1108/BFJ-07-2016-0344

Cardoso, A., Gabriel, M., Figueiredo, J., Oliveira, I., Rêgo, R., Silva, R., Oliveira, M., & Meirinhos, G. (2022). Trust and Loyalty in Building the Brand Relationship with the Customer: Empirical Analysis in a Retail Chain in Northern Brazil. *Journal of Open Innovation*, 8(3), 109. DOI: 10.3390/joitmc8030109

Çetinsöz, B. C. (2019). Influence of physical environment on customer satisfaction and loyalty in upscale restaurants. *Journal of Tourism and Gastronomy Studies*, 7(2), 700–716. DOI: 10.21325/jotags.2019.387

Chaudhuri, A., & Holbrook, M. B. (2001). The Chain of Effects from Brand Trust and Brand Affect to Brand Performance: The Role of Brand Loyalty. *Journal of Marketing*, 65(2), 81–93. DOI: 10.1509/jmkg.65.2.81.18255

Cheung, G. W., Cooper–Thomas, H. D., Lau, R. S., & Wang, L. C. (2023). Reporting reliability, convergent and discriminant validity with structural equation modeling: A review and best-practice recommendations. *Asia Pacific Journal of Management*. Advance online publication. DOI: 10.1007/s10490-023-09871-y

Chin, W., Cheah, J., Liu, Y., Ting, H., Lim, X., & Cham, T. H. (2020). Demystifying the role of causal-predictive modeling using partial least squares structural equation modeling in information systems research. *Industrial Management + Data Systems. Industrial Management & Data Systems*, 120(12), 2161–2209. DOI: 10.1108/IMDS-10-2019-0529

Cohen, J. (1998) Statistical Power Analysis for the Behavioural Sciences. Lawrence Erlbaum Associates, Hillsdale. - References - Scientific Research Publishing. (n.d.). https://www.scirp.org/reference/referencespapers?referenceid=1341443

D'lima, C. (2018). Brand passion and its implication on consumer behaviour. *International Journal of Business Forecasting and Marketing Intelligence*, 4(1), 30–42. DOI: 10.1504/IJBFMI.2018.10009307

Daries Ramón, N., Cristobal-Fransi, E., Ferrer-Rossell, B., & Marine-Roig, E. (2018). Behaviour of culinary tourists: A segmentation study of diners at top-level restaurants. *Intangible Capital*, 14(2), 332–355. DOI: 10.3926/ic.1090

De Nisco, A., & Warnaby, G. (2014). Urban design and tenant variety influences on consumers' emotions and approach behavior. *Journal of Business Research*, 67(2), 211–217. DOI: 10.1016/j.jbusres.2012.10.002

Del Mar García De Los Salmones, M., Crespo, A. H., & Del Bosque, I. R. (2005). Influence of corporate social responsibility on loyalty and valuation of services. *Journal of Business Ethics*, 61(4), 369–385. DOI: 10.1007/s10551-005-5841-2

Delgado-Ballester, E., & Munuera-Alemán, J. L. (2005). Does brand trust matter to brand equity? *the Journal of Product & Brand Management. Journal of Product and Brand Management*, 14(3), 187–196. DOI: 10.1108/10610420510601058

Devi, A. D. T., & Yasa, N. N. K. (2021). role of customer satisfaction in mediating the influence of service quality and perceived value on brand loyalty. *International Journal of Management. IT and Social Sciences*, 8(3), 315–328. DOI: 10.21744/irjmis.v8n3.1786

Djayapranata, G. F., & Setyawan, A. (2022). The antecedents in forming loyalty in the Fast-Food industry. In *Advances in economics, business and management research* (pp. 769–777). https://doi.org/DOI: 10.2991/978-94-6463-008-4_97

Ekinci, Y., & Dawes, P. L. (2009). Consumer perceptions of frontline service employee personality traits, interaction quality, and consumer satisfaction. *Service Industries Journal/˜the œService Industries Journal*, 29(4), 503–521. DOI: 10.1080/02642060802283113

Erciş, A., Ünal, S., Candan, F. B., & Yıldırım, H. (2012). The effect of brand satisfaction, trust and brand commitment on loyalty and repurchase intentions. *Procedia: Social and Behavioral Sciences*, 58, 1395–1404. DOI: 10.1016/j.sbspro.2012.09.1124

Ergün, G. S., & Kitapci, O. (2018). The impact of cultural dimensions on customer complaint behaviours: An exploratory study in Antalya/Manavgat tourism region. *International Journal of Culture, Tourism and Hospitality Research*, 12(1), 59–79. DOI: 10.1108/IJCTHR-01-2017-0010

Eroglu, S. A., Machleit, K. A., & Davis, L. M. (2001). Atmospheric qualities of online retailing: A conceptual model and implications. *Journal of Business Research*, 54(2), 177–184. DOI: 10.1016/S0148-2963(99)00087-9

Fitria, N. A., & Yuliati, E. (2020). The impact of behavior of restaurant employees on word of mouth intention: The mediating role of customer satisfaction. *Iptek/Majalah IPTEK Institut Teknologi Sepuluh Nopember 1945 Surabaya*, 31(1), 91. DOI: 10.12962/j20882033.v31i1.6328

Flavián, C., & Guinalíu, M. (2006). Consumer trust, perceived security and privacy policy. *Industrial Management + Data Systems. Industrial Management & Data Systems*, 106(5), 601–620. DOI: 10.1108/02635570610666403

Fornell, C., & Larcker, D. F. (1981). Evaluating Structural Equation Models with Unobservable Variables and Measurement Error. *JMR, Journal of Marketing Research*, 18(1), 39–50. DOI: 10.1177/002224378101800104

Gabriel, Y. (2001). Fast food enterprises. In *Elsevier eBooks* (pp. 5415–5418). DOI: 10.1016/B0-08-043076-7/04326-6

Gill, A. A., Abdullah, M., & Ali, M. H. (2021). A Study to Analyze the Determinants of Fast-food Restaurant Customer Loyalty through Mediating Impact of Customer Satisfaction. *Global Economic Review*, VI(I), 214–226. DOI: 10.31703/ger.2021(VI-I).16

Ha, J., & Jang, S. (2012). The effects of dining atmospherics on behavioral intentions through quality perception. *Journal of Services Marketing/the Journal of Services Marketing*, 26(3), 204–215. DOI: 10.1108/08876041211224004

Hair, J. F., Black, W. C., Babin, B. J., & Anderson, R. E. (2009). *Multivariate data analysis*. Prentice Hall.

Hair, J. F., Sarstedt, M., & Ringle, C. M. (2019). Rethinking some of the rethinking of partial least squares. *European Journal of Marketing*, 53(4), 566–584. DOI: 10.1108/EJM-10-2018-0665

Hamid, M. R. A., Sami, W., & Sidek, M. H. M. (2017). Discriminant Validity Assessment: Use of Fornell & Larcker criterion versus HTMT Criterion. *Journal of Physics: Conference Series*, 890, 012163. DOI: 10.1088/1742-6596/890/1/012163

Harris, L. C., & Goode, M. M. (2004). The four levels of loyalty and the pivotal role of trust: A study of online service dynamics. *Journal of Retailing*, 80(2), 139–158. DOI: 10.1016/j.jretai.2004.04.002

Hemsley-Brown, J., & Alnawas, I. (2016). Service quality and brand loyalty. *International Journal of Contemporary Hospitality Management*, 28(12), 2771–2794. DOI: 10.1108/IJCHM-09-2015-0466

Hemsley-Brown, J., & Oplatka, I. (2022). Corporate brand communication in the higher education sector. In *The Emerald Handbook of Multi-Stakeholder Communication: Emerging Issues for Corporate Identity, Branding and Reputation* (pp. 11-29). Emerald Publishing Limited. DOI: 10.1108/978-1-80071-897-520221004

Henseler, J., Ringle, C. M., & Sarstedt, M. (2014). A new criterion for assessing discriminant validity in variance-based structural equation modeling. *Journal of the Academy of Marketing Science*, 43(1), 115–135. DOI: 10.1007/s11747-014-0403-8

Hess, J., & Story, J. (2005). Trust-based commitment: Multidimensional consumer-brand relationships. *the Journal of Consumer Marketing. Journal of Consumer Marketing*, 22(6), 313–322. DOI: 10.1108/07363760510623902

Hidayat, A., Adanti, A. P., Darmawan, A., & Setyaning, A. N. A. (2019). Factors influencing Indonesian customer satisfaction and customer loyalty in local Fast-Food restaurant. *International Journal of Marketing Studies*, 11(3), 131. DOI: 10.5539/ijms.v11n3p131

Hiranrithikorna, P., Jermsittiparsertb, K., & Joemsittiprasertd, W. (2019). The importance of conscious idleness & intellectual entrench in gauging brand loyalty toward smartphone brands. *International Journal of Innovation. Creativity and Change*, 8(8), 160–177.

Hossain, M., Alim, M., & Shanta, S. (Eds.). (2021). The Robustness of Brand Passion and Brand Loyalty in Social Media and Consumers' Luxury Brands Purchase Intention (1st ed.). *4th International Conference on Management & Entrepreneurship*.

Hyken, S. (2022, October 24). Customer loyalty comes from an emotional connection. *Forbes*. https://www.forbes.com/sites/shephyken/2022/10/23/customer-loyalty-comes-from-an-emotional-connection/

Ikramuddin, I., & Mariyudi, S. (2021). The mediating role of customer satisfaction and brand trust between the relationship of perceived value and brand loyalty. Asian Journal of Economics. *Business and Accounting*, 21(19), 21–33.

Islam, J. U., & Rahman, Z. (2017). The impact of online brand community characteristics on customer engagement: An application of Stimulus-Organism-Response paradigm. *Telematics and Informatics*, 34(4), 96–109. DOI: 10.1016/j.tele.2017.01.004

Ivkov, M., Blesic, I., Simat, K., Demirovic, D., Bozic, S., & Stefanovic, V. (2016). Innovations in the restaurant industry: An exploratory study. *Ekonomika Poljoprivrede*, 63(4), 1169–1186. DOI: 10.5937/ekoPolj1604169I

Jang, S., & Namkung, Y. (2009). Perceived quality, emotions, and behavioral intentions: Application of an extended Mehrabian–Russell model to restaurants. *Journal of Business Research*, 62(4), 451–460. DOI: 10.1016/j.jbusres.2008.01.038

Jani, D., & Han, H. (2015). Influence of environmental stimuli on hotel customer emotional loyalty response: Testing the moderating effect of the big five personality factors. *International Journal of Hospitality Management*, 44, 48–57. DOI: 10.1016/j.ijhm.2014.10.006

Javed, S., Rashidin, M. S., & Jian, W. (2021). Predictors and outcome of customer satisfaction: Moderating effect of social trust and corporate social responsibility. *Future Business Journal*, 7(1), 12. Advance online publication. DOI: 10.1186/s43093-021-00055-y

Jones, J. L., & Shandiz, M. (2015). Service Quality Expectations: Exploring the Importance of SERVQUAL Dimensions from Different Nonprofit Constituent Groups. *Journal of Nonprofit & Public Sector Marketing*, 27(1), 48–69. DOI: 10.1080/10495142.2014.925762

Joudeh, J. M. M., & Dandis, A. O. (2018). Service quality, customer satisfaction and loyalty in an internet service providers. *International Journal of Business and Management*, 13(8), 108. DOI: 10.5539/ijbm.v13n8p108

Khorasani, S. T., & Almasifard, M. (2017, July 12). *Evolution of Management Theory within 20 Century: A Systemic Overview of Paradigm Shifts in Management*. https://econjournals.com/index.php/irmm/article/view/4719

Kim, J., Lee, H., & Lee, J. (2020). Smartphone preferences and brand loyalty: A discrete choice model reflecting the reference point and peer effect. *Journal of Retailing and Consumer Services*, 52, 101907. DOI: 10.1016/j.jretconser.2019.101907

Koo, W., & Kim, Y. (2013). Impacts of store environmental cues on store love and loyalty: Single-Brand Apparel Retailers. *Journal of International Consumer Marketing*, 25(2), 94–106. DOI: 10.1080/08961530.2013.759044

Lacap, J. P. G., Cham, T. H., & Lim, X. J. (2021). The influence of corporate social responsibility on brand loyalty and the mediating effects of brand satisfaction and perceived quality. *International Journal of Economics and Management*, 15(1), 69–87.

Lin, I. Y., & Mattila, A. S. (2010). Restaurant servicescape, service encounter, and perceived congruency on customers' emotions and satisfaction. *Journal of Hospitality Marketing & Management*, 19(8), 819–841. DOI: 10.1080/19368623.2010.514547

Matzler, K., Pichler-Luedicke, E., & Hemetsberger, A. (Eds.). (2007). *Who is spreading the word? The influence of extraversion and openness on consumer passion and evangelism* (1st ed.). American Marketing Association's Winter Educators' Conference 2007. https://www.researchgate.net/publication/234023910_Who_is_spreading_the_word_The_influence_of_extraversion_and_openness_on_consumer_passion_and_evangelism

Mehrabian, A., & Russell, J. (1974). *An approach to environmental psychology*. MIT Press.

Mills, M., Oghazi, P., Hultman, M., & Theotokis, A. (2022). The impact of brand communities on public and private brand loyalty: A field study in professional sports. *Journal of Business Research*, 144, 1077–1086. DOI: 10.1016/j.jbusres.2022.02.056

Mina, J., & Campos, R.Jr. (2017). Promotional mix and industry practices of leading fast–food industry in the Philippines: A case of NE Pacific Mall, Cabanatuan City, Nueva Ecija. *American International Journal of Business Management*, 3(12). https://www.aijbm.com/wp-content/uploads/2020/12/B3120818.pdf

Morgan, R. M., & Hunt, S. D. (1994). The Commitment-Trust theory of relationship Marketing. *Journal of Marketing*, 58(3), 20–38. DOI: 10.1177/002224299405800302

Mostafa, R. B., & Kasamani, T. (2020). Brand experience and brand loyalty: Is it a matter of emotions? *Asia Pacific Journal of Marketing and Logistics*, 33(4), 1033–1051. DOI: 10.1108/APJML-11-2019-0669

Mubarok, E. S., Subarjo, B., Raihan, R., Wiwin, W., & Bandawaty, E. (2023). Determinants of customer satisfaction and loyalty Waroeng Steak Restaurant in DKI Jakarta. *Cogent Business & Management*, 10(3), 2282739. Advance online publication. DOI: 10.1080/23311975.2023.2282739

Nam, J., Ekinci, Y., & Whyatt, G. (2011). Brand equity, brand loyalty and consumer satisfaction. *Annals of Tourism Research*, 38(3), 1009–1030. DOI: 10.1016/j.annals.2011.01.015

Ngah, H. C., Rosli, N. F. M., Lotpi, M. H. M., Samsudin, A., & Anuar, J. (2022). A Review on the Elements of Restaurant Physical Environment towards Customer Satisfaction. *International Journal of Academic Research in Business & Social Sciences*, 12(11). Advance online publication. DOI: 10.6007/IJARBSS/v12-i11/15621

Ngobo, P. V. (2016). The trajectory of customer loyalty: An empirical test of Dick and Basu's loyalty framework. *Journal of the Academy of Marketing Science*, 45(2), 229–250. DOI: 10.1007/s11747-016-0493-6

Nyamekye, A. P., Tian, Z., & Cheng, F. (2021). Analysis on the contribution of agricultural sector on the economic development of Ghana. *Open Journal of Business and Management*, 09(03), 1297–1311. DOI: 10.4236/ojbm.2021.93070

Park, J., & Kim, H. J. (2020). Customer mistreatment and service performance: A self-consistency perspective. *International Journal of Hospitality Management*, 86, 102367. DOI: 10.1016/j.ijhm.2019.102367

Pei, K. J., & Ayub, A. B. (2015). Measuring Customer Satisfaction towards Cafeteria Services in Primary Health Care Setting: A Cross-Section Study among Patients and Health Care Providers in Bintulu, Sarawak. *OAlib*, 02(04), 1–11. DOI: 10.4236/oalib.1101361

Phijaranakul, P. (2022). Moderated Mediation Model: Factors That Effect Brand Loyalty in Medical Aesthetic Clinics in Thailand. *Asian Administration & Management Review*, 5(2), 141-154. https://doi.org/DOI: 10.14456/aamr.2022.22

Philippine Statistics Authority. (2018). 2016 Annual Survey of Philippine Business and Industry (ASPBI). https://psa.gov.ph/content/2016-annual-survey-philippine-business-and-industry-aspbi-accommodation-and-food-service-0

Phonthanukitithaworn, C., & Sellitto, C. (2016). A reflection on intercept survey use in Thailand: Some cultural considerations for Transnational studies. *Electronic Journal of Business Research Methods*, 14(1). https://academic-publishing.org/index.php/ejbrm/article/view/1341/1304

Pourazad, N., Stocchi, L., & Pare, V. (2019). The power of brand passion in sports apparel brands. *the Journal of Product & Brand Management. Journal of Product and Brand Management*, 29(5), 547–568. DOI: 10.1108/JPBM-12-2018-2164

Prasetyo, Y. T., Susanto, K. C., Asiddao, S. M. A., Benito, O. P., Liao, J., Young, M. N., Persada, S. F., & Nadlifatin, R. (2023). Determining Marketing Strategy for Coffee Shops with Conjoint Analysis. *2023 IEEE International Conference on Industrial Engineering and Engineering Management (IEEM)*. DOI: 10.1109/IEEM58616.2023.10406308

Purwadi, P., Devitasari, B., & Darma, D. C. (2020). Store atmosphere, SERVQUAL and consumer loyalty. *SEISENSE Journal of Management*, 3(4), 21–30. DOI: 10.33215/sjom.v3i4.385

Rahkovsky, I., Young, J., & Carlson, A. (2018). Consumers balance time and money in purchasing convenience foods. *Economic Research Report, 251*. DOI: 10.22004/ag.econ.276227

Rajput, A., & Gahfoor, R. Z. (2020). Satisfaction and revisit intentions at fast food restaurants. *Future Business Journal*, 6(1), 13. Advance online publication. DOI: 10.1186/s43093-020-00021-0

Raquel, M. (2017). Customer loyalty in the fast food industry in the Philippines. *World Journal of Management and Behavioral Studies*, 5(2), 47–53.

Rather, R. A., Tehseen, S., & Parrey, S. H. (2018). Promoting customer brand engagement and brand loyalty through customer brand identification and value congruity. *Spanish Journal of marketing-ESIC*, 22(3), 319–337. DOI: 10.1108/SJME-06-2018-0030

Ridgway, N. M., Dawson, S. A., & Bloch, P. H. (1990). Pleasure and arousal in the marketplace: Interpersonal differences in approach-avoidance responses. *Marketing Letters*, 1(2), 139–147. DOI: 10.1007/BF00435297

Rodhiah, R., & Ervina, E. (2024). Service recovery on loyalty through customer satisfaction at fast food restaurant "X" in North Jakarta. *International Journal of Social Science Research and Review*, 6(3). Advance online publication. DOI: 10.47814/ijssrr.v6i3.951

Ryu, K., & Han, H. (2011). New or repeat customers: How does physical environment influence their restaurant experience? *International Journal of Hospitality Management*, 30(3), 599–611. DOI: 10.1016/j.ijhm.2010.11.004

Sahagun, M. A., & Vasquez-Parraga, A. Z. (2014). Can fast-food consumers be loyal customers, if so how? Theory, method and findings. *Journal of Retailing and Consumer Services*, 21(2), 168–174. DOI: 10.1016/j.jretconser.2013.12.002

Samlejsin, C., & Kookkaew, P. (2022). Integrated Marketing Communication and Service Quality Influencing on Brand Loyalty of Customer a Company that Produces and Distributes Chemical Fertilizers Under the ABC Brand. *PSAKU International Journal of Interdisciplinary Research, Forthcoming, Asian Administration &. Management Review*, 5(1), 7–16. DOI: 10.14456/aamr.2022.2

Setyadi, B., Helmi, S., & Mohamad, N. S. I. B. S.Syed Ismail bin Syed Mohamad. (2023). Customer satisfaction mediates the influence of service quality on customer loyalty in Islamic banks. [IJIBEC]. *International Journal of Islamic Business and Economics*, 7(1), 25–36. DOI: 10.28918/ijibec.v7i1.6924

Shahzadi, M., Malik, S. A., Ahmad, M., & Shabbir, A. (2018). Perceptions of fine dining restaurants in Pakistan. *International Journal of Quality and Reliability Management. International Journal of Quality & Reliability Management*, 35(3), 635–655. DOI: 10.1108/IJQRM-07-2016-0113

Shamah, R. A., Mason, M. C., Moretti, A., & Raggiotto, F. (2018). Investigating the antecedents of African fast food customers' loyalty: A self-congruity perspective. *Journal of Business Research*, 86, 446–456. DOI: 10.1016/j.jbusres.2017.05.020

Sharma, A., Gupta, J., Gera, L., Sati, M., & Sharma, S. (2020). Relationship between customer satisfaction and loyalty. Social Science Research Network. DOI: 10.2139/ssrn.3913161

Shin, Y., & Yu, L. (2018). The influence of quality of physical environment, food and service on customer trust, customer satisfaction, and loyalty And Moderating Effect of Gender: An Empirical Study on Foreigners in South Korean restaurant. [IJACT]. *International Journal of Advanced Culture Technology*, 8(3), 172–185.

Siswanto, B., Rahmawati, & Kuleh, J. (2019). The influence of food quality and physical environment on behavior intention through customer satisfaction at visitors to McDonald's store in Samarinda. [IJBMI]. *International Journal of Business and Management Invention*, 11(12).

Slack, N., Singh, G., & Sharma, S. (2020). The effect of supermarket service quality dimensions and customer satisfaction on customer loyalty and disloyalty dimensions. *International Journal of Quality and Service Sciences*, 12(3), 297–318. DOI: 10.1108/IJQSS-10-2019-0114

Solnet, D., Subramony, M., Ford, R. C., Golubovskaya, M., Kang, H. J., & Hancer, M. (2019). Leveraging human touch in service interactions: Lessons from hospitality. *Journal of Service Management*, 30(3), 392–409. DOI: 10.1108/JOSM-12-2018-0380

Sun, K., & Moon, J. (2023). Assessing antecedents of restaurant's brand trust and brand loyalty, and moderating role of food healthiness. *Nutrients*, 15(24), 5057. DOI: 10.3390/nu15245057 PMID: 38140316

Tanveer, M., Kaur, H., Thomas, G., Mahmood, H., Paruthi, M., & Yu, Z. (2021). Mobile Phone Buying Decisions among Young Adults: An Empirical Study of Influencing Factors. *Sustainability (Basel)*, 13(19), 10705. DOI: 10.3390/su131910705

Thomson, M., MacInnis, D. J., & Park, C. W. (2005). The Ties that Bind: Measuring the strength of consumers' emotional attachments to brands. *Journal of Consumer Psychology*, 15(1), 77–91. DOI: 10.1207/s15327663jcp1501_10

Tongco, M. D. C. (2007, December 31). *Purposive sampling as a tool for informant selection*. https://ethnobotanyjournal.org/index.php/era/article/view/126

Villanueva, M. C. C., Alejandro, A. F., & Ga-An, M. L. L. P. (2023). Measuring the Service Quality, Customer Satisfaction, and Customer Loyalty of Selected Fast-Food Restaurants during the COVID-19 Pandemic. *Open Journal of Business and Management*, 11(03), 1181–1207. DOI: 10.4236/ojbm.2023.113066

Waljee, A. K., Higgins, P. D. R., & Singal, A. G. (2014). A primer on predictive models. *Clinical and Translational Gastroenterology*, 5(1), e44. DOI: 10.1038/ctg.2013.19 PMID: 24384866

Walter, U., & Edvardsson, B. (2012). The physical environment as a driver of customers' service experiences at restaurants. *International Journal of Quality and Service Sciences*, 4(2), 104–119. DOI: 10.1108/17566691211232864

Weiss, R., Feinstein, A. H., & Dalbor, M. (2004). Customer satisfaction of theme restaurant attributes and their influence on return intent. *Journal of Foodservice Business Research*, 7(1), 23–41. DOI: 10.1300/J369v07n01_03

Wentzel, D. (2009). The effect of employee behavior on brand personality impressions and brand attitudes. *Journal of the Academy of Marketing Science*, 37(3), 359–374. DOI: 10.1007/s11747-009-0140-6

Yacob, Y., Ali, J. K., Baptist, C. J., Nadzir, H. M., & Morshidi, M. H. (2016). How far members' satisfaction mediated members' loyalty? Investigating credit cooperative in Sarawak Borneo. *Procedia: Social and Behavioral Sciences*, 224, 376–383. DOI: 10.1016/j.sbspro.2016.05.391

Yurt, İ., & Sağir, Y. E. (2023). The effect of staff behaviors in food and beverage establishments on customer's eating and drinking experience. *Gastroia: Journal of Gastronomy and Travel Research*, 7(2), 448–460. DOI: 10.32958/gastoria.1360913

Zhang, J. (2023). Causal effects of service quality on China merchants bank brand equity loyalty through consumer customer satisfaction. *Procedia of Multidisciplinary Research*, 1(10), 66–66.

Zhang, J., Zheng, W., & Wang, S. (2020). The study of the effect of online review on purchase behavior. *International Journal of Crowd Science*, 4(1), 73–86. DOI: 10.1108/IJCS-10-2019-0027

Zhong, Y., & Moon, H. C. (2020). What drives customer satisfaction, loyalty, and happiness in Fast-Food restaurants in China? Perceived price, service quality, food quality, physical environment quality, and the moderating role of gender. *Foods*, 9(4), 460. DOI: 10.3390/foods9040460 PMID: 32276425

Chapter 10
Strengthening Sustainable Development Goal 5:
Role of Gender Diversity and Creativity in Selected Women–Owned Informal Small Businesses in Africa

Timilehin Olasoji Olubiyi
https://orcid.org/0000-0003-0690-7722
Babcock University, Nigeria

ABSTRACT

The post-pandemic business landscape in Africa has recently been characterised by business non-effectiveness, lack of employee creativity, and ma. Therefore, this study investigates gender diversity and organisational creativity in selected women-owned informal small businesses in Lagos State, Nigeria. The study adopted a survey research design. The chapter focuses on women-owned businesses as the target population comprising 497 randomly selected companies operating international trades in Lagos State, Nigeria. selected women-owned informal small businesses in Lagos State, Nigeria. The study concluded that owner-managers of small businesses should focus on gender diversity and organisational creativity priorities as factors that will enhance workplace diversity and international trade. Therefore, the study recommends that owner-managers encourage peaceful coexistence and participation of employees irrespective of gender to improve organisational creativity and international trade.

INTRODUCTION

Recent research on women's entrepreneurship has emphasised the need to focus on the factors that impact establishing and expanding women-owned businesses(Roca, Suárez, & Meléndez-Rodríguez, 2023). The COVID-19 pandemic has caused disruptions and has had negative impacts on hospitals the world over. Africa and, indeed, Nigeria have a weak standing concerning gender equality in entrepreneurial and small business activity. Workplace gender diversity can significantly contribute to acquiring essential resources for fostering innovation in women-owned enterprises, including technological and market expertise, financial resources, and legitimacy. (Olubiyi, 2023). The gender diversity within the

DOI: 10.4018/979-8-3693-9230-0.ch010

Copyright ©2025, IGI Global. Copying or distributing in print or electronic forms without written permission of IGI Global is prohibited.

small business ecosystem's creativity environment has not been extensively documented, particularly in developing nations and Africa. Very little is known concerning the relationship between gender diversity and creativity in small businesses, and there are many low-level female creatives. This research attempts to fill this gap. Olubiyi, Jubril, Sojinu, and Ngari (2022) assert that there is a growing recognition that the Sustainable Development Goals (SDGs) have the potential to safeguard the environment, mitigate inequality, and address poverty. Nevertheless, numerous small company owners and entrepreneurs in Africa continue to perceive it as a state of extreme unhappiness or suffering. The SDG objectives were designed to aid nations in overcoming the issues that weigh them down, such as poverty and inequality. The primary focus of this study is to examine Goal Five (5), which calls for gender equality, and how it relates to business creativity in Africa. Gender equality is an essential entitlement of every individual and a crucial basis for fostering a harmonious, thriving, and enduring global society (Olubiyi, Jubril, Sojinu, & Ngari, 2022). Gender discrimination may manifest in several forms, such as biased hiring practices, disparities in pay and compensation, unequal opportunities for advancement, and inequitable access to products and facilities based on gender (Gauci, Elmir, O'reilly, & Peters, 2021). Scholars at different times have conducted studies on gender discrimination and employee creativity in different contexts, countries and organisations (Babaita, & Aliyu, 2019; Coffman, Exley, & Niederle, 2021; Ge, Knittel, Heilman, & Caleo, 2018; Parker, & Funk, 2017; Ma, & Jiang, 2018; Pitafi, Khan, Khan, & Ren, 2020; Verniers, & Vala, 2018). However, the level at which gender diversity affects organisational creativity in the banking industry in Nigeria may not have been given adequate research attention. Consequently, organisations emphasise diversity and inclusion initiatives in the modern workplace to strengthen organisational effectiveness and adaptability, gain competitive advantage and reduce employee turnover. Despite this trend, many organisations still struggle with racial and ethnic discrimination and policymaking. There is, however, a dearth of research conducted on the subject matter in Nigeria's small business sector. However, corporate bodies have begun aligning priorities to focus on factors that will enhance workplace diversity and creativity. Still, these factors are less noticed in small businesses even though they are adjudged as the sector that is vital in the modern economic world. It has also been observed that the linkage between gender diversity and organizational creativity has not been fully established within the small business ecosystem in Nigeria, the trade hub and Africa's largest economy. This may be attributable to their inability to manage diversity in their business operations. Hence, it is essential to examine the effect of gender diversity on employee creativity in selected women-owned informal small businesses in Lagos State, Nigeria. Because less attention in the literature reviewed has been given to gender diversity on employee creativity within the small business landscape (Acar, Tarakci, & van Knippenberg, 2019; Channar, Abbassi, & Ujan, 2011; Bassett-Jones, 2005; Batey, 2012; Crewe, & Wang, 2018; Mensa, & Grow, 2022). On this basis, the present study hypothesized that:

H_{01}: Gender diversity does not have a significant effect on organisational creativity in selected women-owned informal small businesses in Lagos State, Nigeria.

Sustainable Development Goals and Goal Five (5)

In recent years, the concept of Sustainable Development Goals (SDGs) has attracted considerable interest from researchers, policymakers, and practitioners. The SDGs have emerged as a successor to the Millennium Development Goals (MDGs) and signify a worldwide commitment to tackling our time's most urgent economic, social, and environmental concerns. The genesis of the Sustainable Development Goals may be traced back to the United Nations Conference on Environment and Development in 1992, where the notion of sustainable development was initially codified. The formation of the Millennium Development Goals in 2000 paved the way for a more focused approach to global development. This ultimately resulted in the formulating and acceptance of the 17 Sustainable Development Goals in 2015. According to Olubiyi, Jubril, Sojinu, and Ngari, (2022), The United Nations (U.N.) adopted a comprehensive framework of 17 Sustainable Development Goals (SDG) in 2015, aiming to eradicate inequality and poverty, safeguard the environment, and promote prosperity. This undertaking was a component of a sustainable development agenda, aiming to be completed by 2030. Regrettably, the Sustainable Development Report for 2023 by the United Nations revealed sluggish advancement in achieving 50 per cent of the goals, while no development or even a decline was observed in 30 percent of the targets. Evidently, further action is required. Although reporting on their impact on the Sustainable Development Goals (SDGs) is prevalent among large organizations, small and medium-sized enterprises are generally less familiar with these goals. Although small and medium-sized firms (SMEs) may not be able to pursue objectives in the same manner as giant corporations or governments, they nonetheless have the potential to create a significant effect. Indeed, the global count of small enterprises exceeds 400 million, constituting a considerable portion of the world's workforce and accounting for over 50% of total employment, yet still increasing (Olubiyi, Jubril, Sojinu, & Ngari, 2022).

Gender Diversity

Disparities between men and women in terms of well-being, status, and access to resources are frequently institutionalized via law, justice, and social norms and tend to favor men (Oguzie, 2020). Diversity within an organizational context can manifest in various ways, including but not limited to physical conditions, gender, ethnicity, race, age, and religion (Smeds & Aulivola, 2020). Organizational diversity refers to variations and distinctions among staff members concerning factors such as sexual orientation, ethnicity, religion, age, culture, physical abilities and disabilities, and religion (Cunningham, 2019; Mensa, & Grow, 2022). Rezina and Mahmood (2016) assert that gender bias in the workplace has been a pervasive issue globally, particularly in developing and underdeveloped nations, for an extended period of time. At each stage of their professional lives, women must exert more significant effort to survive than to attain equal rights. They are not even acknowledged for their laboriousness and efficacy in comparison to their male counterparts.

Gender inequity, which pertains to professional opportunities that exhibit gender-based discrimination, and gender inequality, which concerns the absolute number of males and females in contrast, are fundamental components of gender diversity (Abdellatif, Ding, Jalal, Nguyen, Khorshed, Rybicki, & Khosa, 2020). In addition to fostering a more balanced representation of the workforce, equal gender representation among employees may promote safer work environments, increased employee innovation, and harmonious coexistence (Chung & Van der Lippe, 2020). Enforcing policies that improve gender diversity in the workplace or business is an economic and moral imperative that must be implemented globally. Segregation can impede the competitiveness and growth potential of businesses and nations by causing financial losses and a decline in innovation (Gonas, Wikman, Vaez, Alexanderson, & Gustafsson, 2019). For this reason, the United Nations (U.N.) and other international organizations acknowledge gender diversity and inequality as substantial and persistent global issues that impact the pursuit of sustainable development (George, Howard-Grenville, Joshi, & Tihanyi, 2016). Furthermore, corporate, and public policy leaders worldwide should address these issues worldwide (United Nations Population Fund, 2016).

Organisational Creativity

Organisational creativity refers to the collaborative generation of a valuable and practical novel product, service, concept, technique, or process within a complex social system (Blomberg, Kallio, & Pohjanpää, 2017). Organisational creativity focuses on the effect of persons and internal circumstances, which are more or less favorable to individual creativity (De Vasconcellos, Garrido, & Parente, 2019). Dechamp and Szostak (2016) identify three primary internal elements that are emphasised in organisational creativity. The first factor is the personal dedication to the innovative process of generating novel concepts. The factors that contribute to creativity include motivation and personality traits that are conducive to creativity, such as independence, curiosity, emotional sensitivity, strong conviction, the ability to bring together different ideas, self-confidence, a preference for complex and risky situations, the ability to think in unconventional ways, experience, and specialised knowledge (Mikalef & Gupta, 2021). Aside from the person, the organisational setting also exists, which is demonstrated by the organisational climate and is defined by the level of trust among individuals, the amount of time dedicated to generating ideas, the encouragement of taking risks, and the autonomy granted to employees. This entails considering the organization's dedication to the creative process, such as during the assessment of the concept (Deng & Grow, 2018). The third internal component pertains to the organization's capacity for self-renewal (Acar, Tarakci, & van Knippenberg, 2019). This is shown by effectively using and capitalising on novel concepts that have emerged during the process (Mensa & Grow, 2022), as well as the organization's capacity for acquiring knowledge (Bassett-Jones, 2005; Batey, 2012; Mensa & Grow, 2022). Creativity may be defined as the act of introducing novel methods or approaches by an individual or a collective inside an organisation with the aim of optimising human effort and effectively attaining goals (Mensa & Grow, 2019). Organizational creativity refers to the process of producing original and useful ideas that are crucial for the survival and efficiency of a company. The employee's creativity may be described as an individual who generates novel ideas for their job and work style and is adaptable to working collaboratively in a team rather than alone completing a project (Siddiqi & Qureshi, 2016). An innovative person possesses enhanced comprehension abilities and is very flexible, enabling them to quickly adapt and effectively use new technologies offered inside the organisation (Runco, 2004).

EMPIRICAL REVIEW

Gender Diversity and Organisational Creativity

Multiple studies have been undertaken by scholars and researchers on the relationship between gender diversity and employee innovation. The research conducted by Joshi and Ganji (2020) demonstrated that gender discrimination has a deleterious and crucial influence on work happiness, employee engagement, and organisational identity, while also exerting a beneficial and substantial impact on workplace stress. The research conducted by Abbas, Hameed, and Waheed (2011) examines the impact of gender discrimination on employee performance and productivity. Data is collected by 200 telecommunications supervisors from the Pakistani business in order to comprehend the impact of prejudice on employees' performance. The data is analysed using quantitative methods such as correlation and regression. The study found that there is a negative correlation between gender inequalities in hiring, gender bias in promotion, and gender diversity in the supply of products and facilities, and productivity. This conclusion aligns with the research conducted by Joshi and Ganji (2020), which also revealed that gender discrimination has had a negative and crucial influence on work happiness, employee engagement, and organisational identity, while simultaneously exerting a favourable and noteworthy impact on workplace stress. Memon (2015) conducted research where data was gathered from 192 workers working at public universities located in upper Sindh. The data was analysed using the quantitative approach of regression. The findings indicate that gender discrimination does not significantly impact employee performance, except for one specific aspect: gender discrimination in promotion. However, the correlation between gender discrimination in promotion and employee performance/productivity was found to be weak. In addition, the research conducted by Kim, Kim, Lee, Sim, Kim, Yun, and Yoon (2020) revealed that women who encountered gender discrimination in the workplace had an increased likelihood of experiencing depressive symptoms. This was seen independent of the specific form of discrimination, such as biased hiring practices, unfair advancement opportunities, inequitable job assignments, unequal pay, or unjust termination. The patterns of these relationships were stable among women under the age of 40 in relation to recruitment, advancement, compensation, and termination, but they were not consistent among women above the age of 40. The research conducted by Lucifora and Vigani (2021) demonstrates that having a female boss is linked to a decrease in gender discrimination. This effect is particularly beneficial for female subordinates, especially in occupations with a larger proportion of women and more intricate work structures. The existence of more adaptable work schedules and an improved equilibrium between work and personal life further strengthens the alleviating impact of female leadership on prejudice. The findings were found to align with the existing data on disparities in income and career progression across genders, and were also found to be resilient when subjected to various sensitivity analyses. The research conducted by Triana, Jayasinghe, Pieper, Delgado, and Li (2019) revealed a significant inverse correlation between perceived gender discrimination and employment attitudes, physical health outcomes, behaviours, psychological health, and work-related outcomes (both job-based and relationship-based). The associations between perceived workplace gender discrimination and physical health outcomes and behaviours were more pronounced in countries that had well-integrated labour regulations and strict enforcement of labour practices aimed at promoting gender equality. Correlations were more pronounced in nations that have a greater emphasis on gender equality in their cultural practices, in connection to various employee outcomes related to the perception of gender discrimination in the workplace. In Yang's (2016) study, it was shown that men with high power and women with low power had the strongest support for gender stereotypes and sexist views. The study revealed that the relatively inconsequential outcomes of discrimination also implied the occurrence of climate change in the workplace, where there is less tolerance for hostile working settings targeting women. Prior research on the relationship between gender diversity and organisational creativity utilised a survey research design, specifically employing either a descriptive or cross-sectional survey design (Acar, Tarakci, & van Knippenberg, 2019; Auh, & Menguc, 2005; Bassett-Jones, 2005; Batey, 2012; Mensa, & Grow, 2022).

THEORETICAL REVIEW

Equity Theory

The study utilised equity theory as its basis since it promotes the concept of establishing a productive workforce founded on fairness and justice. John Stacey Adams, a workplace and behavioural psychologist, introduced the concept of Equity theory in 1963 as part of his employment incentive theory. The reference is Anderson and Patterson (2008). Adams (1963) posits that individuals engage in social comparison by evaluating their efforts and rewards in relation to those of relevant persons. Perceptions of relative fairness in incentives have a significant impact on individuals' motivation (Kokkoniemi & Isomöttönen, 2020). The concept emerged after years of advocating for fair and just compensation for all bank employees. When individuals see that the ratio of their labour to the rewards, they receive is equal to that of the people they identify with, they engage in contemplation of equity. Perceiving a disparity in the ratio of work to reward compared to others can lead individuals to experience a sense of inequality, usually in a negative manner. This research is founded upon the premise of this concept, which is rooted in extensive advocacy for fair and impartial compensation and perks for all employees. According to the idea, which is divided into two parts, individuals assess the equity of their situations by comparing them to those of others. According to this theory, an individual (P) assesses their own ratio of perceived outcomes (O = salary, benefits, working conditions) to perceived inputs (I = commitment, skill, experience) in comparison to those of another person (O) - external inequality pays. The validity of the fundamental principles of equity theory has been called into doubt. Academics have raised doubts about the model's simplicity, arguing that various demographic and physiological factors impact individuals' fairness perceptions and social interactions. However, a significant portion of the research that supports the fundamental principles of equity theory has been carried out in controlled laboratory environments, casting doubt on its relevance to real-world situations (Brimhall & Palinkas, 2020). Within a corporate setting, an individual may see their salary to be equitable when compared to that of their colleagues. However, Farkas and Anderson (1979) argue that the whole compensation scheme may be deemed unfair. The issue of subjectivity in the comparative method, as stated by Ng 'ethe, Namasonge, & Mike (2012), is a significant challenge within this theory. According to Huseman, Hatfield, & Miles (1987), humans often misinterpret their inputs, particularly in terms of effort, which complicates the task of comparing their levels of dedication to their work. Another drawback of the equity theory is that after a person has experienced all three stages, they become highly dissatisfied with their employment and seem to be irreversibly unable to return to a normal, positive state where they can contribute productively to the organisation. Notwithstanding the criticism, some scholars have supported this concept as it exemplifies the significance of justice, namely the equality and fairness that employees desire in exchange for their contributions to the workplace (Adams & Freedman, 1976; Kokkoniemi & Isomöttönen, 2020). Advocates of this concept contended that it would result in enhanced performance, employee retention, retention of skilled individuals, enriched perspectives via diversity, and improved financial outcomes. Equity theory, as described by Ng'ethe, Namasonge, & Mike (2012), focuses on individuals' perceptions of how they are viewed relative to others. As per the author's findings, employees make an effort to achieve a balance between the contributions they make to their job (such as education, time, experience, engagement, and effort) and the rewards they receive from it (such as promotion, appreciation, and increased pay), in relation to what they perceive other employees to contribute and receive. Ng 'ethe, Namasonge, & Mike (2012) endorsed the theory, asserting that it acknowledges the importance of acknowledging individual contributions such as education, experience, and dedication in a manner that ensures fairness. They also argued that the absence of fairness leads to various behaviours, including employees leaving the Bank. The equity theory demonstrates another advantage in its ability to perceive and respond to sensitivity, as highlighted by Farkas and Anderson (1979). The personal evaluations of workers directly evaluated the fairness of work relationships, as well as their judgements of how they were treated in the workplace by colleagues and supervisors (Farkas, & Anderson, 1979). An additional benefit of the equity theory is that it requires a worker to go through the three phases of the theory - benevolent, sensitive, and entitled - before facing any adverse repercussions in the workplace. The authors Adams and Freedman published a work in 1976.. Consequently, this study sought to bridge the gap and hypothesised thus:

H_{o1}: There is no significant impact of gender diversity on organisational creativity in selected women-owned informal small businesses in Lagos State, Nigeria, post-pandemic.

Conceptual Model

Figure 1. Author's conceptual model (2024)

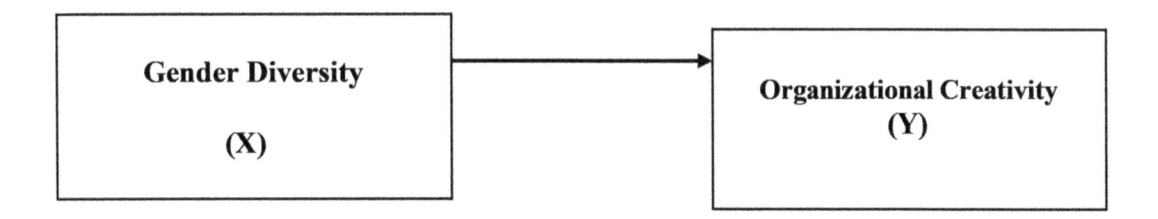

Gender Diversity (X) → **Organizational Creativity (Y)**

The model sheds light on the relationship between gender diversity and organizational creativity, which is the research framework. This research's independent and dependent variables are gender diversity (X) and organizational creativity(Y), respectively. This can be deduced mathematically since organizational creativity is a function of gender diversity; $y=f(x_1\text{-----------}x_n)$.

Hypothesis:

$$y_{1i}=\alpha_0 + \beta_{1x1} + \mu_i \quad \ldots\ldots\ldots\ldots\ldots\ldots\ldots\ldots\ldots\ldots\text{Regression equation (1)}$$

Materials and Methods

The research context of this study is the women-owned informal SME in Lagos State, Nigeria. The study employed a survey research methodology. The survey approach is employed to assess the opinions, attitudes, and feelings of various groups, allowing them to offer more dependable and honest input regarding the issue under inquiry. This study adopted the research methodology utilized by Adeyemi and Olubiyi, (2023), Arokodare, Falana, and Olubiyi, (2023), Olowoporoku, and Olubiyi,(2023), Olubiyi, (2023a), Olubiyi,(2023b), Olubiyi, (2022a), Olubiyi, Lawal, & Adeoye, (2022), Olubiyi, (2022b) and Olubiyi, (2022c) Olubiyi, Adeoye, Jubril, Adeyemi, and Eyanuku (2023) as well as Uwem, Oyedele, and

Olubiyi, (2021) with cross-sectional have adopted this method in their respective studies and found it helpful. The study aims to investigate gender diversity and its impact on creativity among women-owned small businesses, focusing on Lagos State, the economic hub of Nigeria and one of the fastest-growing economies in Africa, as the research sites. The study centers on female entrepreneurship, and the sample comprises specifically chosen female proprietors of small firms willing to participate in the questionnaire. Nevertheless, a crucial condition for being included is the strict adherence to the criteria set by U.N. Women (2017) for a women-owned enterprise, which entails being independent from businesses not owned by women, having at least 51 percent unequivocal ownership by one or more women, and having complete control over both long-term and day-to-day decision-making. The target population consisted of 497 respondents selected from businesses operating in Lagos State, Nigeria. The location was chosen based on its relevance, its influence on the surrounding area, and the high level of economic activities carried out by women in the geographical area. A statistical sample is a smaller, representative subset of a larger population that is used to gather information on the population's characteristics (Olubiyi, Egwakhe, & Akinlabi, 2019). The parameters for selecting the sample align with the research conducted by Akinbami and Aransiola in 2016. The primary data was collected from manufacturing, services, information technology, transport, trading, and communications organizations. The decision was made to use judgmental sampling in order to select the respondent from the population. Given the time constraints and challenges associated with assessing the comprehensive list of all small and medium-sized enterprises provided by the authorities, a subjective evaluation method was employed. Nevertheless, the sample was selected from several groupings within the population, with size, area, and industry being the three criteria used for classification. The rationale behind this approach is that it allows the researchers to gather unrestricted information, examine the thoughts, emotions, and convictions of the participants regarding the Sustainable Development Goals (SDGs), specifically goal five (5), and thoroughly investigate individual business concerns in relation to gender inequality in small businesses. The researchers and research assistants obtained more accurate data on women's viewpoints on creativity and attitudes toward sustainable development goals due to the selected research strategy.

Results

The response rate refers to the proportion of individuals who participated in the survey by providing their responses and submitting completed questionnaires. The researcher disseminated a total of 497 copies of the questionnaire to the participants: Out of the 497 copies distributed by the researcher and trained research assistants, 480 copies of the questionnaire were completed and returned for analysis. This represents a response rate of 97.76%. The remaining replies either were not returned or had incomplete information. The specific details of these responses are displayed in Table 1.

Table 1. Response rate

Response Rate	Frequency	Percentage
Filled and returned complete	480	97.80%
Incomplete or unreturned	17	2.20%
Total	497	100%

Source: Researcher's computation (2024)

Restatement of Research Objective and Research Question

Objective: To evaluate the impact of gender diversity on organisational creativity in selected women-owned informal small businesses in Lagos State, Nigeria.

Research Question: What is the effect of gender diversity on organisational creativity in selected women-owned informal small businesses in Lagos State, Nigeria.?

The study's objective is to examine the effect of gender diversity on organisational creativity in selected women-owned informal small businesses in Lagos State, Nigeria. The respondents were required to rate their responses about airline safety management and passenger satisfaction on a scale of (Very Low) to 6 (Very High). The results are presented in Table 3, followed by an analysis and interpretation.

Restatement of Research Hypothesis

H_{01}: Gender diversity does not have a significant effect on organisational creativity in selected women-owned informal small businesses in Lagos State, Nigeria.

A basic linear regression analysis was employed to evaluate the hypothesis. Gender diversity is considered the independent variable in the study, whilst organisational creativity is regarded as the dependent variable. The data for the variables were derived by aggregating the replies of the items within each variable, resulting in an index that measures both gender diversity and organisational innovation. Table 2 displays the findings of the analysis..

Table 2. Summary of regression of the effect of gender diversity and organisational creativity of the selected women-owned informal small businesses in Lagos State, Nigeria

Variables	B	T	Sig	R	R^2	Std. Error of the Estimate
(Constant)	27.240	49.971	0.000	0.141[a]	0.020	4.017
Gender Diversity	-0.092	-2.710	0.007			

a. Dependent Variable: Organisational creativity
Source: Researcher's Findings (2024)

Table 3 presents the result of the simple linear regression analysis that was carried out to test the effect of gender diversity on the organisational creativity of the selected women-owned informal small businesses in Lagos State, Nigeria. The result of the regression analysis indicated that gender diversity has a negative but significant effect on the organisational creativity of the selected women-owned informal small businesses in Lagos State, Nigeria (β = -0.092, t = -2.710, p < 0.05). The correlation coefficient (R) was 0.141, implying a positive relationship between gender diversity and organisational creativity. The coefficient of determination (R^2) was 0.020, which shows that gender diversity accounted for 2.0% of the changes in the organisational creativity of the selected women-owned informal small businesses in Lagos State, Nigeria. According to the test model, 98.0% of the changes in organisational creativity could not be explained by the model. Therefore, further studies should be done to establish the other factors that affect organisational creativity. This indicates that the model effectively predicted the relationship between gender diversity and organisational creativity. The regression equation from the result is given as follows:

$$OC = 27.240 - 0.092 + \mu_i \dots\dots\dots\dots\dots\dots\dots\dots\dots\dots\dots\dots\dots\dots\dots\dots\dots\dots\dots eq.i$$

Where O.C. = Organizational Creativity

G.D.   = Gender Diversity

The regression model presented above revealed that when gender diversity is constant at zero, organisational creativity of the selected women-owned informal small businesses would be 27.240, which means that without the influence of gender diversity, organisational creativity of the selected women-owned informal small businesses in Lagos State, Nigeria would still be 27.240 which is positive. The regression results show that gender diversity positively influences the organisational creativity of the selected women-owned informal small businesses in Lagos State, Nigeria. The result further indicates that a unit change in gender diversity will lead to -0.092 unit increase in organisational creativity of the selected women-owned informal small businesses in Lagos State, Nigeria and this is significant at a 95% confidence level. From the simple linear regression results, gender diversity is an essential determinant of organisational creativity of the selected women-owned informal small businesses. Therefore, the null hypothesis, which states that gender diversity has no significant effect on organisational creativity of the selected women-owned informal small businesses in Lagos State, Nigeria was rejected.

DISCUSSIONS

The study objective determined the effect of gender diversity on organisational creativity in selected women-owned informal small businesses in Lagos State, Nigeria. The hypothesis was tested using simple linear regression, and the results revealed that gender diversity significantly affected organisational creativity in selected women-owned informal small businesses in Lagos State, Nigeria. ($\beta = -0.092$, $t = -2.710$, $R^2 = 0.020$, $p < 0.05$). The results indicated that gender diversity had a substantial influence on the level of innovation within women-owned informal small companies in Lagos State, Nigeria. Triana, Jayasinghe, Pieper, Delgado, and Li (2019) argued that perceived workplace gender diversity refers to an individual's opinion of being treated unequally in the workplace based on their gender. Mehta and Wilson (2020) have linked gender diversity to factors such as behavioural compatibility, communication style, communal/agentive qualities, and gender reference group identification during childhood and adolescence. Women's occupational distribution shifts have exhibited more prominence compared to men's (Crewe & Wang, 2018; Gonäs, Wikman, Vaez, Alexanderson, & Gustafsson, 2019). Various scholars and researchers have empirically done several investigations on the relationship between gender diversity and employee innovation. The research conducted by Joshi and Ganji (2020) demonstrated that gender discrimination has a deleterious and crucial influence on job satisfaction, employee engagement, and organisational identity, while also exerting a beneficial and substantial impact on job-related stress. The research conducted by Abbas, Hameed, and Waheed (2011) examines the impact of gender discrimination on employee performance and productivity. The study found that there is a negative correlation between gender disparities in recruitment, gender prejudice in advancement, and gender inclusivity in the provision of resources and amenities, and productivity. This conclusion aligns with the research conducted by Joshi and Ganji (2020), which also revealed that gender discrimination has had a negative and crucial influence on work satisfaction, employee engagement, and organisational identity, while simultaneously exerting a beneficial and substantial impact on workplace stress. In the study of Memon (2015), Results show that gender discrimination factors are not much to employee performance, the only single variable that is gender discrimination in promotion, is positively related with employee performance, but the strength of the relationship between gender discrimination in promotion and employee performance/productivity was found to be weak. In addition, the research conducted by Kim, Kim, Lee, Sim, Kim, Yun, and Yoon (2020) revealed that women who faced gender discrimination in the workplace had a greater likelihood of experiencing depressive symptoms, irrespective of the specific form of discrimination such as hiring, promotion, job assignments, salaries, or termination. The patterns of these correlations were stable among women under the age of 40 in relation to recruitment, advancement, salary, and termination, but they varied among women above the age of 40. The research conducted by Lucifora and Vigani (2021) demonstrates that having a female boss is linked to a decrease in gender discrimination. This effect is particularly beneficial for female subordinates, especially in occupations with a larger proportion of women and more intricate work structures. The existence of more adaptable work schedules and an improved equilibrium between work and personal life strengthens the ability of female leadership to reduce prejudice. The findings were found to align with the existing data on gender disparities in wages and professional progression and were also found to be resilient when subjected to various sensitivity analyses. The research conducted by Triana, Jayasinghe, Pieper, Delgado, and Li (2019) revealed a significant inverse correlation between perceived gender discrimination and employment attitudes, physical health outcomes, behaviours, psychological health, and work-related outcomes (both job-based and relationship-based). The associations between perceived workplace gender discrimination and physical health outcomes and behaviours were more pronounced in countries that have well-integrated labour regulations and strictly implemented labour practices aimed at advancing gender equality. Correlations were more pronounced in nations that had a higher degree of gender equality in their cultural practices, in connection to various employee outcomes regarding reported gender discrimination in the workplace. In Yang's (2016) study, it was shown that men with high power and women with low power were the most likely to firmly support gender stereotypes and sexist beliefs. The study revealed that the little impact of discrimination also indicated the possibility of climate change occurring in the workplace, where there is less tolerance for hostile working settings targeting women. In principle, the findings of this study align with the assumptions of Equity theory. According to the hypothesis, workers experience less exploitation, increased motivation, and improved interpersonal interactions. This ensures that the staff stays sustainable and prepared to enhance performance in the future. Equity theory posits that workers should receive equal treatment and fair compensation in accordance with their contributions to the Bank's performance. Employees form perceptions regarding what is considered a just and impartial compensation for their efforts in their respective roles. Employees form perceptions of what is considered a just and impartial compensation for their efforts in their respective roles. Based on the equity hypothesis, employees are likely to take action if they perceive inequality in the workplace, leading to negative consequences like job dissatisfaction, lack of interest, and difficulty in displaying positive behaviours. Therefore, considering the existing support from previous literature in terms of concepts, empirical evidence, and theories, this study confirms that gender diversity has a significant impact on organisational creativity in women-owned informal small businesses in Lagos State, Nigeria.

CONCLUSION AND RECOMMENDATION

In conclusion the study and literature have been provided with evidence of the association between gender diversity and organisational creativity. Through the combination of these variables, a new conceptual viewpoint was established. This study improves the understanding of the extent at which these concepts affect organisations. Another contribution was the conceptual model which enlightened the strength of each of the variables with gender diversity and organisational creativity being the strongest. The test of hypothesis indicated that gender diversity explained 2.0% variation in organisational creativity as indicated by (R^2) of 0.020. The result indicated that the overall model was statistically significant. This was supported by (β = -0.092, t = -2.710, R^2 = 0.020, $p < 0.05$). Therefore, since the study established that gender diversity had significant effect on organisational creativity in selected women-owned informal small businesses in Lagos State, Nigeria, therefore the study recommends that female owned small businesses should encourage peaceful coexistence and participation of employees irrespective of gender to improve organisational creativity.

SUGGESTIONS FOR FURTHER RESEARCH

In light of the findings and limitations of this study, future research should explore the following areas. Firstly, studies can be conducted in other industries and sectors of the economy in Nigeria to give a more holistic view of the relationship between gender diversity and creativity in selected women-owned informal small businesses in Nigeria Secondly, a comparative study on the relationship between gender diversity and creativity in other form of business ventures in other states in Nigeria is required. Thirdly, a longitudinal study on the relationship between gender diversity and creativity in the Southwest, Nigeria could be conducted. Lastly, the study was limited to women-owned SMEs, future studies could be done using family-owned and even other business sectors such as Hospitality, Manufacturing. Education etc.

REFERENCES

Abbas, Q., Hameed, A., & Waheed, A. (2011). Gender discrimination & its affect on employee performance/productivity. *Managerial and Entrepreneurial Developments in the Mediterranean Area*, 15(1), 170–176.

Abdellatif, W., Ding, J., Jalal, S., Nguyen, T., Khorshed, D., Rybicki, F. J., & Khosa, F. (2020). Lack of gender disparity among administrative leaders of Canadian health authorities. *Journal of Women's Health*, 29(11), 1469–1474. DOI: 10.1089/jwh.2019.7852 PMID: 32091966

Acar, O. A., Tarakci, M., & van Knippenberg, D. (2019). Creativity and innovation under constraints: A cross-disciplinary integrative review. *Journal of Management*, 45(1), 96–121. DOI: 10.1177/0149206318805832

Adams, J. S. (1963). Wage Inequities. *Industrial Relations*, 3(1), 9–16. DOI: 10.1111/j.1468-232X.1963.tb00805.x

Adams, J. S., & Freedman, S. (1976). Equity Theory Revisited: Comments and Annotated Bibliography. *Advances in Experimental Social Psychology*, 9, 43–90. DOI: 10.1016/S0065-2601(08)60058-1

Adeyemi, O. S., & Olubiyi, T. O. (2023). The Impact of Brand Awareness on Customer Loyalty in Selected Food and Beverage Businesses in Lagos State Nigeria. *Jurnal Multidisiplin Madani*, 3(3), 541–551. DOI: 10.55927/mudima.v3i3.3095

Ali, M., Grabarski, M. K., & Konrad, A. M. (2021). Trickle-down and bottom-up effects of women's representation in the context of industry gender composition: A panel data investigation. *Human Resource Management*, 60(4), 559–580. DOI: 10.1002/hrm.22042

Arokodare, M. A., Falana, R. B., & Olubiyi, T. O. (2023). Strategic agility, knowledge management and organisational performance in a post-pandemic era: A mediation analysis. *Journal of Family Business and Management Studies*, 27, 83–108.

Auh, S. Y., & Menguc, B. (2005). Top management team diversity and innovativeness: The moderating role of interfunctional coordination. *Industrial Marketing Management*, 34(3), 249–261. https://doi.org/ . indmarman.2004.09.005DOI: 10.1016/j

Babaita, I. S., & Aliyu, M. O. (2019). Gender Discrimination and Employment Decision: A Study of Selected Banks in Kano State, Nigeria. *African Journal of Management Research*, 2(6), 91–106.

Bassett-Jones, N. (2005). The paradox of diversity management, creativity and innovation. *Creativity and Innovation Management*, 14(2), 169–175. DOI: 10.1111/j.1467-8691.00337.x

Batey, M. (2012). The measurement of creativity: From definitional consensus to the introduction of a new heuristic framework. Creativity Research Journal, 24(1), 55–65. https://doi.org/. 649181DOI: 10.1080/10400419.2012

Blomberg, A., Kallio, T., & Pohjanpää, H. (2017). Antecedents of organizational creativity: Drivers, barriers or both? *Journal of Innovation Management*, 5(1), 78–104. DOI: 10.24840/2183-0606_005.001_0007

Brimhall, K. C., & Palinkas, L. (2020). Using mixed methods to uncover inclusive leader behaviors: A promising approach for improving employee and organizational outcomes. *Journal of Leadership & Organizational Studies*, 27(4), 357–375. DOI: 10.1177/1548051820936286

Channar, Z. A., Abbassi, Z., & Ujan, I. A. (2011). Gender discrimination in workforce and its impact on the employees [PJCSS]. *Pakistan Journal of Commerce and Social Sciences*, 5(1), 177–191.

Chung, H., & Van der Lippe, T. (2020). Flexible working, work–life balance, and gender equality: Introduction. *Social Indicators Research*, 151(2), 365–381. DOI: 10.1007/s11205-018-2025-x PMID: 33029036

Coffman, K. B., Exley, C. L., & Niederle, M. (2021). The role of beliefs in driving gender discrimination. *Management Science*, 2(5), 225–244. DOI: 10.1287/mnsc.2020.3660

Crewe, L., & Wang, A. (2018). Gender inequalities in the city of London advertising industry", Environment and Planning A. *Environment & Planning A*, 50(3), 671–688. DOI: 10.1177/0308518X17749731

Cunningham, G. B. (2019). *Diversity and inclusion in sport organizations: A multilevel perspective*. Routledge. DOI: 10.4324/9780429504310

De Vasconcellos, S. L., Garrido, I. L., & Parente, R. C. (2019). Organizational creativity as a crucial resource for building international business competence. *International Business Review*, 28(3), 438–449. DOI: 10.1016/j.ibusrev.2018.11.003

Dechamp, G., & Szostak, B. L. (2016). Organisational creativity and the creative territory: The nature of influence and strategic challenges for organisations. *M@n@ gement, 19*(2), 61-88.

Deng, T., & Grow, J. M. (2018). Gender segregation revealed: Five years of red books data tell a global story. *Advertising and Society Quarterly*, 19(3). Advance online publication. DOI: 10.1353/asr.2018.0024

Farkas, A. J., & Anderson, N. H. (1979). Multidimensional input in equity theory. *Journal of Personality and Social Psychology*, 37(6), 879–896. DOI: 10.1037/0022-3514.37.6.879

Gauci, P., Elmir, R., O'reilly, K., & Peters, K. (2021). Women's experiences of workplace gender discrimination in nursing: An integrative review. *Collegian (Royal College of Nursing, Australia)*.

Gonäs, L., Wikman, A., Vaez, M., Alexanderson, K., & Gustafsson, K. (2019). Gender segregation of occupations and sustainable employment: A prospective population-based cohort study. *Scandinavian Journal of Public Health*, 47(3), 348–356. DOI: 10.1177/1403494818785255 PMID: 29974817

Heilman, M. E., & Caleo, S. (2018). Combatting gender discrimination: A lack of fit framework. *Group Processes & Intergroup Relations*, 21(5), 725–744. DOI: 10.1177/1368430218761587

Huseman, R. C., Hatfield, J. D., & Miles, E. W. (1987). A New Perspective on Equity Theory: The Equity Sensitivity Construct. *Academy of Management Review*, 12(2), 222–234. DOI: 10.2307/258531

Ivancevich, J. M. (1998). Human Resource Management 7th Ed. Boston: Irwin McGraw-Hill Ivancevich JM, Lorenzi P, Skinner SJ, Crosby PB (1994). Management Quality and Competitiveness. Boston, Massachusetts: Richard D. Irwin, Inc.

Joshi, B. P., & Ganji, F. A. (2020). Impact of gender discrimination on the employees (Ghalib Private University in herat, Afghanistan as a case study). *European Journal of Molecular and Clinical Medicine*, 7(6), 1967–1980.

Kim, G., Kim, J., Lee, S. K., Sim, J., Kim, Y., Yun, B. Y., & Yoon, J. H. (2020). Multidimensional gender discrimination in workplace and depressive symptoms. *PLoS One*, 15(7), e0234415. DOI: 10.1371/journal.pone.0234415 PMID: 32673322

Kokkoniemi, M., & Isomöttönen, V. (2020). Project education and Adams' theory of equity. 2020 IEEE Frontiers in Education Conference, 1–5. DOI: 10.1109/FIE44824.2020.9274126

Lucifora, C., & Vigani, D. (2021). What if your boss is a woman? Evidence on gender discrimination at the workplace. *Review of Economics of the Household*, 7(9), 1–29.

Mehta, C. M., & Wilson, J. (2020). Gender segregation and its correlates in established adulthood. *Sex Roles*, 83(3), 240–253. DOI: 10.1007/s11199-019-01099-9

Memon, M. (2015). (Forthcoming). Gender discrimination and its impact on employee productivity/performance (A study on government universities of upper sindh). *International Journal of Management Sciences and Business Research*, 4(6), 36–40.

Mensa, M. & Grow, J.M. (2019).Women creatives and machismo in Mexican advertising *European Review of Latin American and Caribbean Studies/Revista Europea de Estudios Latinoamericanos* yDel Caribe, 107, (27-53).

Mensa, M., & Grow, J. M. (2022). Now I can see': Creative women fight against machismo in Chilean advertising. *Gender in Management*, 37(3), 405–422. DOI: 10.1108/GM-04-2021-0098

Mikalef, P., & Gupta, M. (2021). Artificial intelligence capability: Conceptualization, measurement calibration, and empirical study on its impact on organizational creativity and firm performance. *Information & Management*, 58(3), 103434. DOI: 10.1016/j.im.2021.103434

Ng'ethe, J. M., Namusonge, G. S., & Iravo, M. A. (2012). Influence of leadership style on academic staff retention in public universities in Kenya. *International Journal of Business and Social Science*, 3(21).

Oguzie, A. E. (2020). Counselling: An Advocacy for Balancing Gender Disparity for Sustainable National Development. *Sapientia Global Journal of Arts. Humanities and Development Studies*, 3(2), 1–13.

Olowoporoku, A., Asikhia, O., & Makinde, O. (2021). The Role of Organisational Capabilities in the Competitiveness of Hotels in Southwest Nigeria. Journal of Research in Business, Economics and Management, 16(1), 52- 70. Retrieved from http://scitecresearch.com/journals/index.php/jrbem/article/view/2049

Olowoporoku, A. A., & Olubiyi, T. O. (2023). Evaluating Service Quality and Business Outcomes Post-Pandemic: Perspective from Hotels in Emerging Market, Sawala. *Jurnal Administrasi Negara*, 11(2), 182–201. DOI: 10.30656/sawala.v11i2.6975

Olubiyi, O. T., Lawal, A. T., & Adeoye, O. O. (2022). Succession Planning and Family Business Continuity: Perspectives from Lagos State, Nigeria. *Organization and Human Capital Development*, 1(1), 40–52. DOI: 10.31098/orcadev.v1i1.865

Olubiyi, T. O. (2020). Knowledge management practices and family business profitability: Evidence from Lagos state, Nigeria [Nigerian Chapter]. *Arabian Journal of Business and Management Review*, 6(1), 23–32.

Olubiyi, T. O. (2022a). An Investigation of Technology Capability in Small and Medium-Sized Enterprises (SMEs) [ABS ranking]. *Journal of Management Sciences*, 9(2), 21–31.

Olubiyi, T. O. (2022b). Measuring technological capability and business performance post-COVID Era: Evidence from Small and Medium-Sized Enterprises (SMEs) in Nigeria. *Management & Marketing Journal*, xx(2), 234–248. DOI: 10.52846/MNMK.20.2.09

Olubiyi, T. O. (2022c). An investigation of sustainable innovative strategy and customer satisfaction in small and medium-sized enterprises (SMEs) in Nigeria. *Covenant Journal of Business and Social Sciences*, 13(2), 1–24.

Olubiyi T. O. (2023a). Leveraging competitive strategies on business outcomes post-covid-19 pandemic: Empirical investigation from Africa. Journal of Management and Business: Research and Practice, DOI: 10.54933/jmbrp-2023-15-2-1

Olubiyi, T. O. (2023b). Unveiling the role of workplace environment in achieving the Sustainable Development Goal Eight (SDG8) and employee job satisfaction post-pandemic: Perspective from Africa. *Revista Management & Marketing Craiova*, XXI(2), 212–228. DOI: 10.52846/MNMK.21.2.02

Olubiyi, T. O., Adeoye, O. O., Jubril, B., Makinde, G. O., & Eyanuku, J. P. (2023). Measuring Inequality in Sub-Saharan Africa Post-Pandemic: Correlation Results for Workplace Inequalities and Implication for Sustainable Development Goal ten. *International Journal of Professional Business Review*, 8(4), e01405. DOI: 10.26668/businessreview/2023.v8i4.1405

Ostroff, C., & Bowen, D. E. (2016). Reflections on the 2014-decade award: Is there strength in the construct of H.R. system strength? *Academy of Management Review*, 41(2), 196–214. DOI: 10.5465/amr.2015.0323

Osundina, K., & Opeke, R. (2017). Patients' waiting time: Indices for measuring hospital effectiveness. *International Journal of Advanced Academic Research for Social & Management Sciences*, 3(10), 1–18.

Owoseni, J., Gbadamosi, G., Ijabadeniyi, O., & Adekunle, D. (2016). Population growth and challenges in access to healthcare facilities in Urban Ekiti, Nigeria. *Unique Research Journal of Medicine and Medical Sciences*, 4(5), 51–58.

Parker, K., & Funk, C. (2017). Gender discrimination comes in many forms for today's working women. *Economic Journal (London)*, 12(5), 109–134.

Pitafi, A. H., Khan, A. N., Khan, N. A., & Ren, M. (2020). Using enterprise social media to investigate the effect of workplace conflict on employee creativity. *Telematics and Informatics*, 55, 101451. DOI: 10.1016/j.tele.2020.101451

Rezina, S., & Mahmood, F. (2016). Gender disparity in Bangladesh and its impact on women in workplaces. *Scholar journal of Business and social science,* 2(2), 27-34.

Roca, D., Suárez, A., & Meléndez-Rodríguez, S. (2023).Female creative managers as drivers for gender diversity in advertising creative departments: a critical mass approach, Gender in Management, Vol. ahead-of-print No. ahead-of-print. DOI: 10.1108/GM-09-2022-0291

Runco, M. A. (2004). Creativity. Annual Review of Psychology, 55, 657 687. https://doi.org/DOI: 10.1146/annurev.psych.55.090902.141502

Siddiqi, H., & Qureshi, M. (2016). The impact of employee creativity on performance of the firm.

Smeds, M. R., & Aulivola, B. (2020). Gender disparity and sexual harassment in vascular surgery practices. *Journal of Vascular Surgery*, 72(2), 692–699. DOI: 10.1016/j.jvs.2019.10.071 PMID: 32067879

Triana, M. D. C., Jayasinghe, M., Pieper, J. R., Delgado, D. M., & Li, M. (2019). Perceived workplace gender discrimination and employee consequences: A meta-analysis and complementary studies considering country context. *Journal of Management*, 45(6), 2419–2447. DOI: 10.1177/0149206318776772

Ukabi, O. B., Uba, U. J., Ewum, C. O., & Olubiyi, T. O. (2023). Measuring Entrepreneurial Skills and Sustainability in Small Business Enterprises Post-Pandemic: Empirical Study From Cross River State, Nigeria. *International Journal of Business. Management and Economics*, 4(2), 132–149. DOI: 10.47747/ijbme.v4i2.1140

United Nations Population Fund. (2016). ICPD beyond 2014 high-level global commitments. UNFPA. Retrieved from https://www.unfpa.org/sites/default/files/pub-pdf/ICPD_UNGASS_REPORT_for_website.pdf

Uwem, E. I., Oyedele, O. O., & Olubiyi, O. T. (2021). Workplace green behavior for sustainable competitive advantage. In human resource management practices for promoting *Sustainability IGI Global*. (248–263).

Verniers, C., & Vala, J. (2018). Justifying gender discrimination in the workplace: The mediating role of motherhood myths. *PLoS One*, 13(1), 19–36. DOI: 10.1371/journal.pone.0190657 PMID: 29315326

Veronesi, G., Kirkpatrick, I., & Vallascas, F. (2014). Does clinical management improve efficiency? Evidence from the English National Health Service. *Public Money & Management*, 34(1), 35–41. DOI: 10.1080/09540962.2014.865932

Xie, Z., & Or, C. (2017). Associations between waiting times, service times and patient satisfaction in an endocrinology outpatient department: A time study and questionnaire survey. *Inquiry*, 54, 1–10. DOI: 10.1177/0046958017739527 PMID: 29161947

Yang, J. (2016). The impact of power status on gender stereotypes, sexism, and gender discrimination toward women in the workplace and the career identity development of women. (Unpublished Dissertation).

Chapter 11
Guidelines for Generating Income Through Local Identity Products for Widows in the Southern Border Provinces, Thailand

Nutnapha Lekhavichit
Yala Rajabhat University, Thailand

ABSTRACT

The ongoing unrest in Thailand's southern border provinces has led to significant loss, leaving some women widowed and responsible for their families. This research focused on 1) generating income for widows through local identity products, 2) developing their online marketing skills, and 3) managing networks to enhance their business potential. The study involved 30 widows from Narathiwat, Pattani, and Yala, using in-depth interviews, observations, and content analysis. Findings revealed that widows prefer home-based work with sufficient income, with online sales identified as a key avenue for business success. Skills like making wedding trays were promoted, and a network with wedding event planners was established, boosting their income.

1. INTRODUCTION

1.1 Background and Significance of the Research

The southern border provinces of Thailand have been plagued by unrest and violence since 2004, which continues to impact the lives and properties of the local population, resulting in significant losses. Numerous citizens have been injured or killed due to attacks targeting government officials, creating a pervasive atmosphere of fear and insecurity. This situation has severely disrupted the residents' livelihoods, reduced their income, and led to financial struggles as they find it difficult to make ends meet (Aphirat Bunsiri, 2016). The prolonged conflict in the region has particularly affected daily life, with men often

DOI: 10.4018/979-8-3693-9230-0.ch011

being the targets of violence, leaving many women widowed (McCargo, 2008). Consequently, the number of widows has risen sharply, with reports indicating over 7,000 deaths, many of which involved men who either died or disappeared, leaving behind families headed by women (McCargo & Pathmanand, 2005). The loss of a husband forces widows to face significant economic challenges and social pressures. In Muslim society, where women typically take on the roles of homemakers, caring for the home, children, and elderly parents, the death of a husband means they must shoulder the responsibility of supporting their families on their own (Othman, 2015). This situation has led to widows becoming more reliant on themselves and their communities for survival.

Technical Promotion and Support Office 11 Songkhla, Ministry of Social Development and Human Security (2020), noted that in addition to the ongoing unrest affecting the economy, the three southern border provinces are among the poorest in the country. The COVID-19 pandemic has further exacerbated economic decline, deepening the poverty in this region. The most significant issue arising from the pandemic has been a reduction in income, with 43.96% of the population experiencing a total loss of income. Women and families are among the hardest hit groups, facing severe financial hardship. Although various organizations have attempted to develop the skills of widows by promoting women's group occupations, these efforts have largely failed. This is partly because the skills training provided does not align with the needs or abilities of the widows in the area or with the labor market demands.

This research aimed to develop the potential of communities for widows in Thailand's three southern border provinces to promote household and community economies. This guideline is seen as a way to alleviate some of the challenges in the region, as widows are among those most severely affected by the loss of family heads due to the ongoing unrest. Many Muslim women in the area marry at a young age, have multiple children, and lack opportunities to develop vocational skills while their husbands are still alive. As a result, when they lose their husbands, families lose their primary source of income, and women are forced to take on the role of family head and sole provider (International Crisis Group, 2009). The loss of their husbands leaves these women facing significant economic hardships and social pressures. Widows often have to seek employment to support their families, facing challenges in balancing multiple jobs, such as handicrafts, farming, or small-scale trading (Ismail, 2021). However, insufficient income and limited economic opportunities continue to keep these widows in difficult circumstances (Kasim, 2018).

The ongoing unrest in Thailand's southern border provinces has caused widespread violence, particularly affecting men, leading to a significant increase in the number of widows. These women, who are typically homemakers in Muslim society, are now forced to become the sole providers for their families, facing severe economic and social challenges. The situation is worsened by the region's poverty, further exacerbated by the COVID-19 pandemic, which has led to a significant loss of income. Despite efforts to develop widows' vocational skills, many initiatives have failed due to a mismatch with the widows' needs and market demands. This research focuses on enhancing the potential of communities to support widows, aiming to promote household and community economies and alleviate some of the challenges they face.

The researcher is; therefore, interested in studying ways to generate income for widows in the three southern border provinces through the production of local identity products. The research aimed to find methods to increase household income for these widows, develop vocational skills that align with their interests and abilities, and enhance their online marketing skills to support the sale of the local identity products they produce. In addition, the study seeks to build cooperative networks to enhance the business potential of these widows, thereby strengthening their businesses, fostering mutual support within the community and networks, and generating income for both the widows and their communities. This approach is intended to promote sustainable livelihoods, improve the quality of life, and provide widows with the potential to engage in viable occupations, secure income for themselves and their families, and live stable lives while taking care of their families.

2. LITERATURE REVIEW

2.1 Local Identity Products

Local identity products refer to goods developed from local resources and knowledge, characterized by unique attributes that reflect the cultural identity of the community (Cultural Identity Product). Creating local identity products is a method of promoting local economies and cultural tourism (Muñoz, 2021).

Developing these products requires consideration of several factors, including the uniqueness of the product, the use of local materials, the creation of a narrative and brand communication, and community involvement (Brown & Davis, 2018). Additionally, collaboration with both governmental and private organizations is essential to strengthen the identity of products (White, 2022). The development of local identity products supports the growth of local economies and increases community income, particularly in the tourism and export sectors (Smith, 2019). These products can convey the story of local culture, fostering a sense of connection and pride among consumers (Johnson, 2020). Studies on local identity products are abundant worldwide. For example, in Thailand, research often focuses on the efficient use of natural resources and local culture (Thongkhao & Chaiyawat, 2021) to add value to communities. In Japan, the development of local identity products emphasizes aesthetically pleasing and functional designs (Nakamura, 2020).

Johnson's (2020) study discusses the connection between identity products and consumer behavior, revealing that consumers tend to choose products that reflect their identity and values. The research also indicates that identity products can enhance brand loyalty. Moreover, the study by Kim et al. (2021) highlights the importance of marketing that focuses on building identity, which fosters more sustainable relationships between brands and consumers. Social media is emphasized as a key tool in creating and promoting these identities. Local identity products are crucial for promoting local economies and cultural tourism. Developing such products requires community involvement and collaboration between the public and private sectors to ensure that the products are valuable and competitive in the market.

2.2 Muslim Wedding Dowries

In Muslim culture, the wedding dowry, known as "Mahr," is a gift that the groom presents to the bride as a sign of love and respect. In Islamic law, the dowry is an obligation that the groom must fulfill before marriage, and it is the bride's absolute right (Ahmad, 2015). The Muslim dowry, or "Khan Maak," in Thailand's three southern border provinces, is a tradition that reflects both local customs and Islamic principles. The Muslim wedding dowry set symbolizes the love, respect, and bond between the two families (Ahmad, 2020). The items included in the dowry have specific meanings and serve as symbols of prosperity, happiness, and abundance in married life (Rahman, 2019).

Components of the Muslim Wedding Dowry

The preparation of the wedding dowry and the associated ceremonies in Muslim culture are conducted under Islamic traditions and customs. The gathering of family and relatives, along with the ceremonial procession, often involves singing and dancing that reflects local cultural practices, creating a festive and familial atmosphere. The wedding dowry is a significant part of the wedding ceremony in Malay-Muslim culture, especially in Thailand's three southern border provinces: Yala, Pattani, and Narathiwat. The Muslim wedding dowry set in this region is distinctive, reflecting the local traditions and culture. The components of the Muslim wedding dowry in these provinces typically include:

1. **Mahr:** Mahr is the wealth or money that the groom must present to the bride either before or during the marriage ceremony, as it is the bride's absolute right according to Islamic law. Mahr signifies the groom's sincerity and respect for the bride (Ahmad, 2015). Mahr can be in the form of cash, gold, jewelry, land, or other valuable assets, with the amount determined by mutual agreement between the families of both parties.
2. **Clothing and Attire:** Clothing and attire symbolize honor and readiness for marriage. These typically include the garments that the bride will wear on the wedding day or in the future, such as a Hijab (headscarf), a bridal dress, and everyday clothing. Beads or beautiful lace often embellish these garments (Halim, 2018).
3. **Sweets and Food**: Sweets and food in the Muslim wedding dowry symbolize sweetness and abundance in married life. The food items often include local sweets with cultural significance, such as traditional desserts like "Buto Gamoh" (a local Muslim dessert) or other sweet treats, beautifully arranged on trays or platters (Rahman, 2019).
4. **Jewelry**: Jewelry represents wealth and the commitment to love. The groom typically gives jewelry, such as necklaces, rings, or earrings made of gold or silver, as a gift to the bride on the wedding day. These pieces are usually intricately designed and hold cultural significance (Aishah, 2020).
5. **Al-Quran**: The Al-Quran symbolizes the teachings and way of life according to Islamic principles. Giving the Al-Quran emphasizes the importance of religion in married life. It is often wrapped in a beautiful cloth or placed in an ornate box and is included as part of the wedding dowry that the groom presents to the bride (Yusuf, 2017).
6. **Flowers and Incense**: Flowers and incense in the Muslim wedding dowry symbolize purity, happiness, and peace in married life. These typically include fresh flowers such as roses, jasmine, or champak, arranged beautifully on trays, along with Arab or Muslim incense like frankincense (Halim, 2018).

The components of the Muslim wedding dowry reflect both religious and cultural significance. The inclusion of Mahr, clothing and attire, sweets and food, jewelry, the Al-Quran, and flowers and incense symbolizes love, respect, and readiness for married life. In the southern border provinces, the Muslim wedding dowry also features special elements that reflect the local Malay culture, such as the use of local pottery and desserts in decorating the dowry set (Ismail, 2021). Additionally, traditional trays made from bamboo, rattan, or other natural materials are often used to present gifts, a practice rooted in local customs (Abdullah, 2022).

2.3 Online Marketing

Online Marketing refers to the process of promoting and selling products or services through various online platforms, such as websites, social media, email, and search engines (Kotler & Armstrong, 2018). In the digital age, online marketing is crucial because it significantly enhances the ability to reach a broad audience, targeting specific demographics effectively (Chaffey & Ellis-Chadwick, 2019).

Online marketing has a substantial impact on small and medium-sized enterprises (SMEs), as it reduces marketing costs compared to traditional marketing methods. Additionally, it allows businesses to expand their market reach, particularly in international markets (Tiago & Veríssimo, 2014). By utilizing appropriate online marketing tools, SMEs can enhance their competitive advantage in a highly competitive market (Leeflang et al., 2014).

Popular tools in online marketing include Search Engine Optimization (SEO), Pay-Per-Click (PPC) advertising, Social Media Marketing, and Content Marketing (Ryan, 2020). Effective online marketing also relies on data analysis and the measurement of marketing outcomes, which are used to continuously refine marketing strategies (Kingsnorth, 2019). Social media is a critical tool for brand building and customer engagement, allowing businesses to communicate directly with customers, foster brand loyalty, and increase awareness of products and services (Tuten & Solomon, 2017). Moreover, using social media in marketing enables the creation of highly targeted marketing campaigns that can better respond to consumer behavior (Barker et al., 2020).

2.4 Networking

Networking refers to the process of building and maintaining relationships with individuals or groups that influence success in life and work. Networking is a crucial component for enhancing business opportunities, knowledge exchange, and the development of social relationships (Granovetter, 1973). Effective networking can increase success in both personal and professional life, especially in the digital age, where connections between individuals can be established quickly and easily (Burt, 2000).

Networks can be categorized into several types, such as business networks, social networks, and professional networks. Business networks play a vital role in enhancing business opportunities and accessing necessary resources, and information. Social networks are important for building strong relationships and support in various areas (Lin, 2001). Professional networks help individuals develop their careers and access diverse job opportunities (Powell & Smith-Doerr, 1994).

A strong business network is essential for business growth and success. It enables access to information, news, business opportunities, and necessary resources. Additionally, networking plays a role in building trust and good relationships with partners, customers, and colleagues, which are indispensable in business operations (Coleman, 1988). However, while networking has advantages in strengthening business operations, it also presents challenges, such as maintaining long-term relationships, managing time for building and sustaining networks, and selecting networks that align with needs and goals (Burt, 2000). Therefore, effectively managing networks is crucial for enhancing long-term opportunities and success.

The literature review highlights the significance of local identity products, Muslim wedding dowries, online marketing, and networking in the context of economic development and social resilience. Local identity products, developed from unique cultural resources, play a crucial role in promoting local economies and cultural tourism, requiring collaboration between communities and various sectors. Muslim wedding dowries, deeply rooted in Islamic and local traditions, symbolize love and respect, with components that reflect both religious and cultural values. Online marketing is essential for reaching broader audiences, especially for SMEs, offering cost-effective tools for expanding market reach and building brand loyalty. Networking is critical for enhancing business opportunities, accessing resources, and building strong relationships, though it requires effective management to maximize long-term success. These interconnected elements contribute to the socio-economic empowerment of communities, particularly in challenging regions.

Research Conceptual Framework

Figure 1. Research conceptual framework

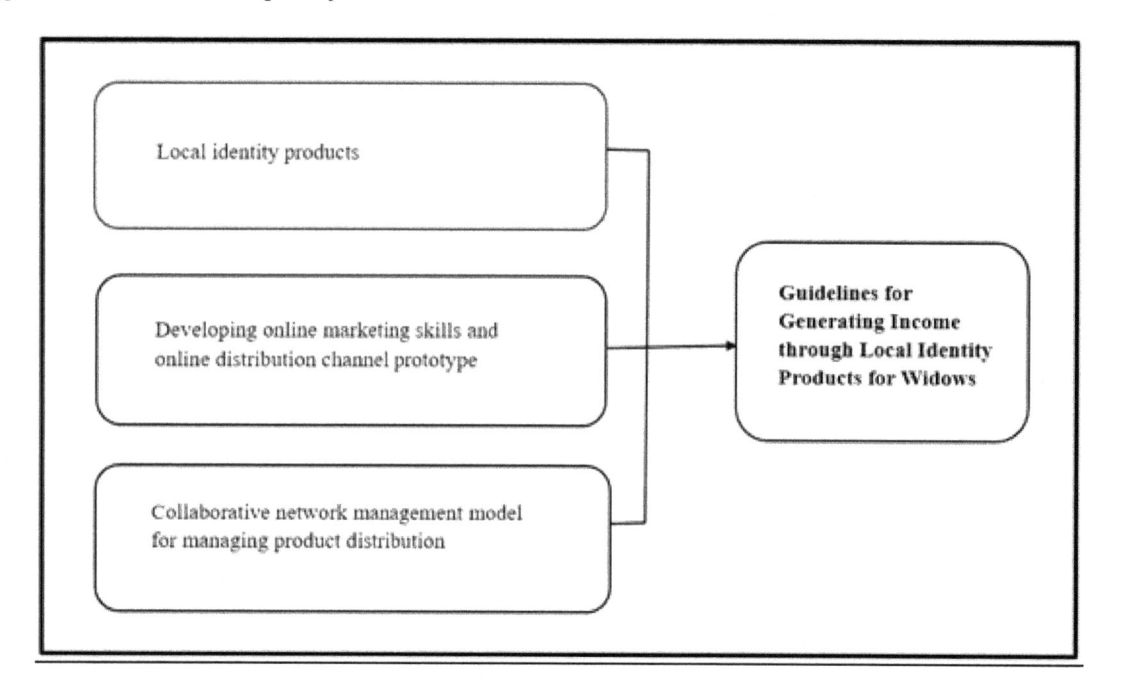

3. RESEARCH METHODOLOGY

A Study Area

In this research, the researcher chose a specific area for study using purposive sampling. The selected area is the Sustainable Economic Village Project and Demonstration Farm in Ban Rotan Batu, Moo 7, Ban Rotan Batu, Kaluwao Sub-district, Muang Narathiwat District, Narathiwat Province. This village was chosen because it hosts widows who represent all three southern border provinces. The Sustainable Economic Village Project and Demonstration Farm in Ban Rotan Batu is an initiative by Her Majesty the Queen to support the families of officials and citizens affected by unrest in the southern border provinces. The project aims to provide housing and land for cultivation, focusing on community development based on the principles of a sufficiency economy. It incorporates technology and agricultural innovations for farm development, crop cultivation, livestock, and fisheries (Chaiyaphum, 2019). This demonstration farm serves as a learning center and technology transfer hub for farmers and communities in the area. A survey in 2010 found that over 30% of families in the village were headed by widows, earning the village the nickname "Widow Village" (Srisompob & Panyasak, 2012). The widows living in the Demonstration Farm project in Ban Rotan Batu are those who lost their husbands due to the unrest in the southern border provinces. After losing their family heads, these widows have to find work to support their families, sometimes juggling multiple jobs, such as general labor, handicrafts, farming, or small-scale trading (Ismail, 2021). However, insufficient income and a lack of economic opportunities continue to keep the widows in difficult circumstances (Kasim, 2018).

Sample Group

The research was conducted as a participatory study under the academic service project for widows living in the Sustainable Economic Village Project and Demonstration Farm in Ban Rotan Batu, Narathiwat Province. The sample group consisted of 30 people, including one group leader from the widows in Ban Rotan Batu and twenty-nine other widows from the village.

Data Collection

This research involved qualitative data collection through informal interviews and focus group discussions, as follows:

Informal Interviews: The researcher engaged in casual conversations with the widows about general topics such as their current occupations, living conditions, preferred activities, and training received from various government projects. Discussions also covered general topics to create a relaxed atmosphere and reduce tension between the researcher and the interviewees.

Focus Group Discussions: Meetings were held to exchange opinions between the researcher and the sample group to select local products and plan skill development activities for the widows. These activities included product manufacturing skills and online marketing skills.

Data Analysis

The data analysis involved analyzing the basic data of the sample group through descriptive analysis or summary analysis, obtained from interviews and inquiries. This data was then analyzed using analytic induction by grouping the information according to key issues such as employment needs, professional skills, communication device skills, and community identity products.

4. RESEARCH RESULTS

4.1 Qualitative Data Analysis Results

The qualitative data analysis from the interviews with the leader of the widow group in the Sustainable Economic Village Project and Demonstration Farm in Ban Rotan Batu allowed the researcher to summarize the findings into the following points:

1. Current Income and Living Conditions: The current income is sufficient for a modest living. The villagers live within their means and do not spend excessively. The expenses in the village are minimal, allowing for a happy and content life.
2. Main Income Sources: The primary income comes from selling agricultural products from the land allocated by the project. Additionally, there is income from working at the project's ceramic factory, earning 150 baht per day.
3. Utilization of Allocated Land: The land allocated by the project is used by those skilled in agriculture to grow vegetables or raise ducks and chickens. However, some people are not skilled in agriculture and therefore do not fully utilize the land to generate sufficient income.
4. Skill Development Projects: Various skill development projects have been introduced by different agencies, but sometimes these do not align with individual needs and skills.
5. Desire for Craft Skills Training: There is a desire for training in craft skills that could provide additional income. The widows wish to use their spare time from farming or working at the ceramic factory to engage in craft work for extra earnings.

The qualitative data analysis from focus group discussions with the sample group of widows in the Sustainable Economic Village Project and Demonstration Farm in Ban Rotan Batu allowed the researcher to summarize the findings according to the following issues:

Employment Needs: The summary of the employment needs of the widows in the project and the potential of community identity products in Narathiwat Province.

Table 1. Key questions and findings

Key Questions	Summary of Findings
Employment Needs (Narathiwat Province)	1. **Desired Additional Learning**: Learn how to process local raw materials and make long-lasting baked goods, such as bakery items. Develop skills in sewing clothes and bags from scrap fabric. Gain knowledge in organic farming, and learn about online sales. 2. **Desired Professions for the Sample Group:** Craftwork, Food preparation, such as making crispy roti and fried bananas, Bakery items, Sewing (clothing and bags), and Online business

Employment Potential: The summary of the potential for employment, including both professional skills and the readiness for online business, of the widows in the Sustainable Economic Village Project and Demonstration Farm in Ban Rotan Batu.

Table 2. Key questions and findings

Key Questions	Summary of Findings
Employment Potential	1. **Basic Skills and Competencies Necessary for Employment**: Skills and knowledge in sales techniques or online sales are essential. Expertise in the specific area is required. 2. **Limitations in Employment for the Sample Group:** Funding for business development is a constraint. Physical Limitations: Incomplete physical health (not 100%); poor health conditions; distance issues. However, most individuals are generally ready to engage in employment if needed. 3. **Readiness of Basic Communication Systems in the Community:** The community has comprehensive communication systems, including internet and telephone services. 4. **Readiness of Goods Transport Systems in the Community**: Transportation systems are generally well-prepared with good and safe roads. However, some transportation services are located far from homes and require travel to the city. 5. **Local Raw Materials That Can Add Value or Be Developed into Products for Employment**: Notable local raw materials include coconut, duck eggs, durian, and Garcinia cambogia (tamarind). These can be used in business and confectionery. Some materials need to be purchased from stores, such as pottery. 6. **Employment Potential for Widows**: The sample group has existing skills from previous domestic work or occupations. Some still lack certain professional skills but live in a community with good communication, internet, and transportation systems. However, transportation access is not always ideal for everyone. 7. **Conditions or Factors Driving This Issue**: Development of basic knowledge and skills for employment by integrating existing skills of the widows and their willingness to learn for development. The readiness of communication and transportation systems in the community can enable widows to leverage these basic factors to create online selling careers.

The Potential of Community Identity Products: The Summary of Findings on the Potential of Community Identity Products in the Three Southern Border Provinces with the potential for developing community identity products in the Southern Border Provinces that can be used to create employment and generate income for the sample group of widows in the Sustainable Economic Village Project and Demonstration Farm in Ban Rotan Batu.

Table 3. Key questions and findings

Key Questions	Summary of Findings
Potential of Community Identity Products	1. **Products with Prominent Features and Income Potential:** Seasonal fruits such as durian and langsat. Processing of durian (e.g., durian Monthong). Processing of agricultural products. 2. **Sales and Profit Potential**: Current monthly income from existing occupations is approximately 2,000 - 3,000 baht. Income from selling products: Confectionery made from corn/coconut (processed) with coconut water being sold at 7-10 baht per coconut. Pottery is sold at 500 baht per set, with a production cost of 300 baht. 3. **Popular Tourist Attractions in the Community:** Ao Manao Beach, Yala Pae Waterfall, Ta Po Waterfall, Sai Buri River Bridge (a tourist spot for Malaysians), Rafting, Sipo Waterfall, Erawan Learning Center, Riverside Pavilion (open to tourists year-round) 4. **Interesting Products for Business Development:** Processing local raw materials such as coconut, duck eggs, corn, lime, banana, and durian.

Community Identity Products: The researcher analyzed data from interviews and group discussions to select community identity products for creating employment and generating income for widows. The criteria were 1) The product must be a local identity product. 2) The product should be something the widows have the skills to produce. 3) The product should meet the widows' needs for creating employment. 4) The product should be suitable for the current lifestyle of the widows, i.e., it should have low production costs, allow for the use of free time from daily tasks, and be producible at home without needing to travel. The consensus from the group discussions for a local identity product to create employment for widows was "organizing traditional wedding sets (Khan Maak)."

4.2 Guidelines for Generating Income for Widows with Local Identity Products

After concluding that "organizing traditional wedding sets (Khan Maak)" is the local identity product for creating income for widows, the researcher developed a curriculum for income generation. This involved collaboration with local event planning businesses, online business operators, and IT experts to develop a short-term curriculum for creating income through traditional wedding sets. The developed curriculum was then used to advance the development of local identity products and online marketing skills for widows.

Results of Developing Local Identity Products:

The research team organized a career development activity focused on making traditional wedding sets to enhance skills and create employment for widows by using leftover materials and local natural resources to add value and generate income.

From the development of traditional wedding sets made from leftover materials, it was found that:

1) Product Development: Various types of traditional wedding sets were developed from local natural materials, such as bamboo, banana leaves, local flowers, or fabric with local patterns. Each product type had unique features and benefits, was practical, and aligned with local traditions. Additionally, the products were affordable and could be customized to meet the target audience's needs and budget.
2) Economic Impact: Developing these products provided income for widows, reduced household expenses, and promoted community economic development. It added value to local natural materials by integrating them into traditional wedding sets, thereby enhancing the overall value of local products.
3) Social Impact: Making traditional wedding sets not only provided income but also promoted mental health by allowing widows to work together, reducing stress from primary occupations. It also helped preserve and promote valuable local traditions more widely.
4) Environmental Impact: The development of these products reduced waste and promoted the efficient use of local resources. It also contributed to reducing environmental pollution.

Figure 2. Traditional wedding sets (Khan Maak) products from waste materials

Development of Online Marketing Skills

The study on digital market development revealed that most widows have communication devices, such as phones, which they use for keeping in touch with close contacts and engaging with social media platforms like Facebook, Line, Instagram, and TikTok. Some use social media to promote their products, but they still lack skills in using these devices for online marketing. To address this, the research team organized activities to educate widows about using social media for marketing. The training included: creating online content as a sales channel; photography techniques and composition for marketing purposes; and running ads to reach a broader customer base. As a result, the widows set up a Facebook page for online marketing to sell and take orders for traditional wedding sets.

Figure 3. Online marketing skills development activities

1. Developing Careers for Widows: Develop careers for widows by utilizing their existing skills and abilities, while promoting new techniques and knowledge for product development. This approach will help widows learn and enhance their production capabilities quickly. Additionally, forming groups to produce wedding gifts allows them to come together during their free time from daily tasks. This not only generates additional income but also provides opportunities for social interaction and recreation, fostering love and unity within the group. It also enhances the recreational atmosphere, allows for playful conversation among members, and helps relieve stress and worries related to their profession and daily life.
2. Product Manufacturing Using Local and Recycled Materials: Manufacturing products by applying recycled and locally sourced materials helps reduce production costs and adds value to these materials.
3. Activities to Inspire Widows: Organizing activities to inspire widows will help enhance their creativity in both product manufacturing and online marketing processes.
4. Developing Diverse Product Lines: Develop a diverse range of products to cover both wedding gift sets and souvenirs for various occasions, with different price levels to meet the diverse needs of customers.
5. Building Networks with Wedding Planners: Establish partnerships with wedding planners to use as distribution channels for products made by widows.

4.3 Developing Online Marketing Skills for Widows:

The activities aimed at developing online marketing skills have shown that widows can create online sales channels through common social media platforms such as Facebook, Line, Instagram, and TikTok. However, they still lack skills and creativity in marketing communication. Therefore, widows should be given opportunities to study and participate in activities that enhance creative skills for creating content suited to various marketing objectives. Alternatively, a course on online marketing skills should be created to help widows develop their online marketing capabilities comprehensively, enabling them to conduct effective online marketing activities and achieve results in customer base building, sales, and income generation.

4.4 Guidelines for Managing Collaborative Networks to Enhance Business Capabilities for Widows

Although widows have good skills in product manufacturing, they lack marketing skills, are unaware of current market demands, and cannot access major markets or customer groups. Initially, the distribution of products needs to involve creating networks or partnerships for the widows' group. This can be achieved by inviting experts who are wedding planners to teach widows how to make wedding gifts and by creating networks with wedding planners for ordering products from the widows' group in Narathiwat. Since the products are not yet well-known to target customers, creating a supportive network between wedding planners and product manufacturers will help establish a market for the wedding gifts produced by the widows and reduce the cost of procuring wedding gifts and souvenirs for wedding planners.

5. CONCLUSION AND DISCUSSIONS

This research explored ways to generate income for widows in the southern border provinces of Thailand through the development of local identity products. The findings indicate that local identity products, rooted in the region's cultural and religious heritage, are valuable resources for income generation. This aligns with other research emphasizing the importance of cultural products in community economic development (Muñoz, 2021). By leveraging local materials and traditions, widows in these provinces can create unique products that are marketable both locally and internationally. The development of local identity products is crucial for promoting local economies and cultural tourism. Products reflecting community identity and culture not only help increase income but also preserve and promote local culture to the broader public (Muñoz, 2021). Furthermore, the study found that training widows in crafting wedding gifts enhances their ability to pursue occupations and generate supplemental income effectively. This approach utilizes local resources and cultural practices efficiently, which is consistent with Brown and Davis's (2018) research emphasizing the need for product uniqueness, local materials, and community involvement.

The research results also reveal that widows can independently generate income, even if it is not substantial enough for a comfortable living. The widows do not experience stress from the impact of violence in the region anymore, having lived through it for many years. Although they have not forgotten past violence, they are no longer distressed by their current life situation. Being part of the sample farm project in Ban Rotan Batu has made them feel safe and has developed their occupational skills, allowing them to generate income independently. Living in the sample farm village promotes a self-sufficient lifestyle, leading to contentment under their means. This is consistent with Lim's (2018) study, which shows that sufficient income can result in happiness and life satisfaction. The connection with the philosophy of sufficiency economy illustrates that the happiness of widows in Ban Rotan Batu arises not only from adequate income but also from satisfaction with the simplicity of life that matches their resources and capabilities. In addition, Supaporn et al. (2020) highlighted that sufficiency economy villages are effective learning centers for managing resources and income, enhancing household economic resilience and community happiness. Even though the income might not be high, it meets the basic needs of life, demonstrating how the sufficiency economy philosophy can be applied to improve the well-being of local communities.

One significant finding from this study is the potential of online marketing to expand the reach of these products. Online platforms, such as social media and e-commerce websites, can serve as crucial tools for connecting widows with a broader consumer base, increasing opportunities for income generation. This finding is consistent with Kim et al. (2021), who emphasized the importance of digital marketing in enhancing brand identity and expanding markets for local products. Moreover, Johnson (2020) noted that contemporary consumers value products reflecting cultural identity and authenticity, supporting the marketability of locally produced products by these widows.

Building business networks is thus crucial for the success and sustainability of the widows' wedding gift enterprises. Not only does it help enhance business operations, but it also plays a role in strengthening the local community in the long term. Since the widows' group faces limitations in resources and market access (Smith & Lohrke, 2008), creating networks facilitates the exchange of information, knowledge, and resources, leading to new business opportunities and market expansion. Lyons et al. (2012) also noted that business networks help small entrepreneurs maintain competitiveness by fostering trust and collaboration within the business community. Networking with other entrepreneurs, such as wedding product retailers or wedding equipment suppliers, can increase market expansion opportunities and stabilize the business (Granovetter, 1985).

Furthermore, developing essential skills in product creation, branding, and marketing is critical for the long-term sustainability of these businesses. Brown and Davis (2018) emphasized that the success of local identity products depends not only on the uniqueness of the products but also on the producer's ability to maintain quality and interact effectively with consumers. However, challenges remain, particularly concerning safety and resource access. Ongoing conflict in the southern border provinces may hinder business activities, aligning with Ismail's (2021) findings that political and social unrest is a significant barrier to economic development, especially for vulnerable groups like widows. The need for supportive policies and interventions from both government and non-profit organizations is crucial to address these issues, as White (2022) discussed the positive role of government-private sector collaboration in enhancing economic stability in conflict-affected areas.

Knowledge contribution

Here are some findings on the career development opportunities for widows in the three southern border provinces of Thailand, specifically focusing on local identity products

1. Cultural and Local Identity Products

Local Identity Products: Southern Thailand's cultural products include handwoven fabrics, batik textiles, and handicrafts reflecting the region's unique cultural heritage. These products are often inspired by traditional patterns, natural dyes, and motifs rooted in the region's Islamic and Malay cultures.

Cultural Significance: These products embody the rich traditions and cultural diversity of the area, serving as symbols of local identity and pride. They are not only functional items but also carry deep cultural narratives and are part of the community's intangible heritage.

2. Potential Careers for Widows

Handicraft Production: Widows in the region could be involved in creating handwoven textiles, batik, and other handicrafts. This work can be done from home, allowing flexibility and accommodating personal circumstances.

Entrepreneurship and Small Businesses: By establishing small businesses, widows can market and sell local identity products, either directly to consumers or through local markets and online platforms. This provides economic independence and strengthens local economies.

Tourism-Related Opportunities: Cultural tourism in southern Thailand is growing, and there are opportunities for widows to engage in guiding tours, selling cultural products, or even offering workshops on traditional crafts.

3. Support from Government and Non-Governmental Organizations

Various government initiatives and NGOs are working towards promoting local identity products. Providing widows with access to these programs can help them gain the necessary skills, resources, and market access. For instance, training in product design, quality control, and marketing strategies can enhance the competitiveness of their products.

4. Community Involvement and Networking

Creating networks among widows and with other community members can help in the sharing of resources, ideas, and markets. Cooperatives and community-based enterprises can be formed to strengthen their bargaining power and reduce costs.

5. Challenges and Considerations

Security and Social Issues: The ongoing conflict in the southern border provinces poses significant challenges, including safety concerns and limited access to markets. Widows, especially those with limited resources, may face difficulties in starting and sustaining businesses.

Support Systems: Effective programs that offer financial aid, training, and access to markets are crucial. NGOs and government initiatives play an essential role in empowering these women by providing the necessary support.

Recommendation

1. **Training and Education** Providing widows with training in business management, marketing, and production techniques can enhance their skills and enable them to produce high-quality products that can compete in broader markets.
2. **Market Access** Develop strategies to enhance market access, including participation in trade fairs, online marketplaces, and partnerships with larger businesses.
3. **Community-Based Initiatives** Encouraging community-based cooperatives can help in pooling resources, sharing knowledge, and creating a stronger collective market presence. This can mitigate some of the risks associated with individual entrepreneurship.
4. **Promotion of Local Products** Developing branding strategies that highlight the unique cultural aspects of the products can attract more buyers, especially in niche markets interested in authentic cultural goods.

These insights should help guide the development of sustainable careers for widows in the three southern border provinces, leveraging the region's rich cultural heritage and local identity products.

REFERENCES

Abdullah, F. (2022). Bamboo and Rattan in Malay Handicrafts. *Craft and Tradition*, 10(3), 67–85.

Ahmad, R. (2015). The Concept of Mahr in Islamic Law. *Journal of Islamic Studies*, 12(3), 45–60.

Ahmad, S. (2020). Islamic wedding traditions: The significance of wedding gifts. *Journal of Islamic Culture*, 15(2), 89–101.

Aishah, N. (2020). The Symbolism of Jewelry in Muslim Marriages. *Cultural Symbols*, 3(2), 88–99.

Barker, M., Barker, D., Bormann, N., & Neher, K. (2020). *Social media marketing: A strategic approach* (3rd ed.). Cengage Learning.

Boonshiri, A. (2016). The lifestyle of families and the impact of unrest in the Southern Border Provinces: A case study of the Southern Border Special Development Zone in Songkhla Province from 2004 to 2014. *Journal of Humanities and Social Sciences*. *Thaksin University*, 11(1), 237–254.

Brown, A., & Davis, L. (2018). Community-based branding: Strategies for cultural identity products. *Journal of Local Economy*, 33(2), 123–135.

Brown, C., & Davis, J. (2018). The importance of local identity in product development. *. *Cultural Identity and Economic Development*, 9(2), 134–145.

Burt, R. S. (2000). The network structure of social capital. *. *Research in Organizational Behavior*, 22, 345–423. DOI: 10.1016/S0191-3085(00)22009-1

Chaffey, D., & Ellis-Chadwick, F. (2019). *Digital marketing: Strategy, implementation, and practice* (7th ed.). Pearson.

Coleman, J. S. (1988). Social capital in the creation of human capital. *. *American Journal of Sociology*, 94, S95–S120. DOI: 10.1086/228943

Granovetter, M. (1985). Economic action and social structure: The problem of embeddedness. *. *American Journal of Sociology*, 91(3), 481–510. DOI: 10.1086/228311

Granovetter, M. S. (1973). The strength of weak ties. *. *American Journal of Sociology*, 78(6), 1360–1380. DOI: 10.1086/225469

International Crisis Group. (2009). Southern Thailand: Moving Towards Political Solutions? Asia Report No. 181.

Ismail, A. (2021). Local Traditions in Malay Weddings. *The Journal of Ethnic Studies*, 8(1), 112–130.

Ismail, H. (2021). Economic challenges faced by Muslim widows in Southern Thailand. *. *Journal of Southeast Asian Studies*, 52(1), 89–102.

Ismail, N. (2021). Livelihood strategies of widowed women in Southern Thailand. *Journal of Community and Family Studies*, 18(3), 98–110.

Johnson, L. (2020). Consumer behavior and cultural identity products. *. *The Journal of Consumer Research*, 46(5), 1021–1035.

Johnson, M. (2020). Cultural heritage and product branding: The consumer's perspective. *Marketing Insights*, 15(4), 45–59.

Johnson, R. (2020). Consumer behavior and identity products: A comprehensive study. *. *The Journal of Consumer Research*, 45(3), 233–245. DOI: 10.1086/709129

Kasim, H. (2018). Economic impacts of widowhood on women in rural Thailand. *Asian Economic Journal*, 22(4), 345–357.

Kim, S.. (2021). The impact of online marketing on brand identity. *. *International Journal of Marketing Studies*, 13(4), 67–78.

Kim, S., Park, J., & Lee, H. (2021). The role of identity in brand loyalty: A social media perspective. *. *Marketing Science*, 40(2), 189–205. DOI: 10.1287/mksc.2021.1297

Kingsnorth, S. (2019). *Digital marketing strategy: An integrated approach to online marketing* (2nd ed.). Kogan Page.

Kotler, P., & Armstrong, G. (2018). *Principles of marketing* (17th ed.). Pearson.

Leeflang, P. S. H., Verhoef, P. C., Dahlström, P., & Freundt, T. (2014). Challenges and solutions for marketing in a digital era. *. *European Management Journal*, 32(1), 1–12. DOI: 10.1016/j.emj.2013.12.001

Lim, S. (2018). The relationship between sufficient income and life satisfaction in rural communities. *. *International Journal of Rural Studies*, 14(2), 123–135.

Lin, N. (2001). *Social capital: A theory of social structure and action*. Cambridge University Press. DOI: 10.1017/CBO9780511815447

Lyons, T. S., Alter, T. R., Audretsch, D., & Augustine, D. (2012). Networking as a driver of firm growth: The impacts of social capital and social effectiveness. *. *Small Business Economics*, 39(4), 117–135.

McCargo, D. (2008). *Tearing Apart the Land: Islam and Legitimacy in Southern Thailand*. Cornell University Press.

McCargo, D., & Pathmanand, U. (2005). *The Thaksinization of Thailand*. NIAS Press.

Muñoz, A. (2021). Cultural identity products and local economic growth. *. *Economic Development Quarterly*, 35(1), 45–58.

Muñoz, R. (2021). Cultural identity products: Economic impact and cultural preservation. *Economic Development Review (Schiller Park, Ill.)*, 28(3), 67–82.

Nakamura, H. (2020). Design and functionality in cultural identity products: A Japanese perspective. *Design Studies*, 41(1), 89–103.

Nurul, I. (2018). Economic Empowerment Programs for Widows in Southern Thailand. *Development in Practice*, 28(6), 789–803.

Othman, N. (2015). Women and Conflict in Muslim Societies. *Journal of Islamic Studies*, 20(4), 55–70.

Rahman, F. (2019). Symbolism in Muslim wedding rituals: An analytical study. *Journal of Cultural Symbolism*, 11(3), 45–58.

Rahman, S. (2019). Culinary Traditions in Malay Weddings. *Southeast Asian Cultural Studies*, 6(4), 56–72.

Ryan, D. (2020). *Understanding digital marketing: Marketing strategies for engaging the digital generation* (5th ed.). Kogan Page.

Smith, A., & Lohrke, F. (2008). Entrepreneurial network development: Trusting in others' capabilities. *. *Journal of Business Venturing*, 23(2), 109–122.

Srisompob, J., & Panyasak, S. (2012). The Impact of Insurgency on Local Communities in Southern Thailand. *Journal of Asian Security and International Affairs*, 5(1), 89–108.

Sukree, P. (2019). Government Initiatives to Support Conflict-Affected Women in Thailand. *International Journal of Social Work*, 63(4), 402–417.

Supaporn, P.. (2020). Sufficiency economy villages: Enhancing local skills and resources for household economic stability. *. *Journal of Thai Local Development*, 7(1), 67–84.

Thongkhao, S., & Chaiyawat, P. (2021). Sustainable development of cultural identity products in Thailand. *Journal of Southeast Asian Studies*, 52(2), 210–229.

Tiago, M. T. P. M. B., & Veríssimo, J. M. C. (2014). Digital marketing and social media: Why bother? *. *Business Horizons*, 57(6), 703–708. DOI: 10.1016/j.bushor.2014.07.002

Tuten, T. L., & Solomon, M. R. (2017). *Social media marketing* (3rd ed.). SAGE Publications.

White, R. (2022). Partnerships in product development: Government and private sector collaboration. *Journal of Public Policy and Administration*, 19(1), 54–78.

White, R. (2022). Public-private partnerships in developing local identity products. *. *Journal of Economic Policy*, 29(3), 345–367.

Yusuf, H. (2017). Marriage Customs in Southern Thailand: A Study of Mahr. *Islamic Culture Journal*, 14(2), 90–105.

Chapter 12
The Development of Products From Budi Brown-Rice Flour to Promote Gluten-Free Brownies in Budi Subdistrict, Yala Province, Thailand

Sutida Lekhawichit
Yala Rajabhat University, Thailand

Wiroj Phaiboonvessawat
Yala Rajabhat University, Thailand

Ubol Tansom
Yala Rajabhat University, Thailand

Sasithorn Pangsuban
Yala Rajabhat University, Thailand

Kurosiyah Yamirudeng
Yala Rajabhat University, Thailand

ABSTRACT

This research to development of products from Budi brown rice flour to promote gluten-free brownies in Budi Subdistrict, Yala Province. The study combines a mixed-method approach combined with (PAR). The quantitative research utilized questionnaires, with the study population comprising consumers interested in or purchasing the product. The sample group included consumers interested in or purchasing the product. It was found that the development of the product's form to suit the target group, the quality of the product, and the characteristics of the product such as color, aroma, taste, texture, and packaging should be appropriately aligned with the product. The qualitative research involved in-depth interviews using a structured interview guide with key informants. The research findings suggest that participation in strengthening the enterprise allows community organizations to play a role and represent their network

DOI: 10.4018/979-8-3693-9230-0.ch012

in expanding distribution channels. The development process:1) Innovation development, 2) Utilizing online media or processes, 3) Creating differentiation and recyclable

INTRODUCTION

Currently, there is a growing demand for gluten-free (GF) products among specific consumer groups, driven by the increasing number of diagnosed celiac disease patients and their need to eliminate allergenic proteins from their diets. This trend has led to rapid growth in the gluten-free market (Gao et al., 2018). Additionally, research by Di Nardo et al. (2019) highlights the risk of nutritional deficiencies in children with celiac disease, who may face issues such as high fat intake and deficiencies in fiber, iron, vitamin D, and calcium.

Jnawali et al. (2016) reviewed the literature on food product development, emphasizing the importance of considerations during the development of gluten-free foods. These include finding alternative gluten sources, ensuring nutritional and sensory quality, and adhering to regulatory guidelines. Capriles et al. (2023) and Penjumras et al. (2021) studied consumer sensory evaluations, which play a crucial role in the research and development of gluten-free products, aiming to understand consumer preferences and satisfaction. The continuous growth of this market and the increasing research into gluten-free products have significant implications for future food industry developments.

Wimarnaya et al. (2021) analyzed the demand for brownie products among SMEs in Indonesia using the Kano model to assess consumer satisfaction levels and guide product development based on customer feedback. Stoin et al. (2021) studied the development of gluten-free confectionery and pasta products by exploring alternative ingredients to meet consumer demands for innovative products. The use of novel ingredients in the market helps improve taste and diversify multipurpose flour products. Pio Ávila et al. (2019) investigated the recipe adjustments, ingredients, and components of brownie products that cater to consumers with Celiac disease, whose preferences differ from the general population. The study found that the color and texture of the flour are crucial sensory attributes for consumers when adjusting brownie recipes. They experimented with mixing rice flour and lentil flour as a gluten- and lactose-free alternative.

In business operations and increasing market share for food and confectionery products containing rice flour, various processing techniques and development methods using food processing technology and innovation are employed. These methods aim to develop a comprehensive production process to meet modern consumer demands by using whole grains or rice by-products, such as flour, to create various food products. This research project aims to produce innovative products from local rice varieties with unique genetic traits found in Yala Province. These innovative products can be promoted as signature goods of Yala Province, with strategic marketing and distribution channels for local rice products. The research will benefit academically by incorporating projects that focus on the distinctiveness of the rice varieties, nutritional value, product development, packaging development, and the extension of marketing strategy research. In addition to the academic benefits, there are commercial advantages. Highlighting the unique qualities of Yala's local rice varieties will increase the value of rice-based products, thereby boosting the community's income and improving the overall well-being of the community. Moreover, there are policy benefits for local government agencies. Promoting local economic development and enhancing the community's capacity for self-reliance and management based on the philosophy of sufficiency economy will drive the local economy and increase the community's competitiveness.

Due to the recognition of the trends and situations of local rice varieties in Yala Province, there has been diverse and varied production management. Over time, the quality of these groups has been continuously developed, including ongoing knowledge transfer to farmers through farmer school processes, such as changing the age of seedlings, using wire traps for rice field rats, and processing rice into products like "Budi Rice," rice milk, and brown rice flour cookies. These efforts help the group preserve Thai culture, and create, and develop careers towards success. Therefore, it is essential to develop pesticide-free local rice flour products, improve packaging, and enhance the marketing communication for pesticide-free local rice flour products used in ready-made bakery products. This development will bring academic and commercial benefits by highlighting the distinctive qualities of local rice varieties, increasing the value of products derived from these varieties, boosting the community's income in Yala Province, and enhancing the local community's capacity for development, self-reliance, and self-management based on the philosophy of sufficiency economy. This forms the basis for this research.

RESEARCH OBJECTIVE

To Develop of Products from Budi Brown-Rice Flour to Promote Gluten-Free Brownies in Budee Subdistrict, Yala Province

Research Methodology

This study employed a mixed-methods approach combined with Participatory Action Research (PAR). For the quantitative research, the population includes consumers interested in or purchasing the products. The sample group consists of these consumers, and due to the inability to determine the exact number of the sample population, the researcher calculated the sample size using a formula for unknown population size (Kalaya Vanichbuncha, 2005: 26). With a 95% confidence level and a margin of error not exceeding 5% or .05, the sample size is 385, with an additional 15 samples collected as reserves, totaling 400 samples. For qualitative research, the key informants were selected based on specific criteria, including members of the community enterprise group of organic indigenous rice farmers in Budi who have at least five years of experience. The data was collected through in-depth interviews with 13 key informants, including 1) 10 members, including the president and vice president, of the community enterprise group for organic native rice farming (Budi rice), and 2) 3 experts in rice product promotion in Yala Province.

1. **Quantitative Research:** The researcher used a questionnaire to collect data from respondents. The questionnaire was divided into five parts: 1) General Information: This section includes checklist-type questions with a nominal scale, covering gender, age, education level, occupation, average monthly income, and experience. 2) Opinions on Product Development Capability: This section used a rating scale based on the Likert scale to measure opinions on awareness, environmental consciousness, public participation, and integration of diversity. 3) Product Development Information: This section also used a rating scale to measure opinions on product standards and group mobilization. 4) Marketing Promotion: This section used a rating scale to measure opinions on product quality improvement, suitable packaging, target market product design, value addition, and combining local wisdom with modern technology. 5) Product Development Guidelines: This section focused on guidelines for

developing rice products to promote marketing. Closed-ended questions using a 5-point Rating Scale on an Ordinal Scale were used (Napaporn Chansap et al., 2002). The evaluation criteria were based on the Class Interval principle, dividing the highest possible score into five levels. The highest score was 5, and the lowest was 1. The median range was calculated using the formula for the range of the interval.

2. **Qualitative Research:** The researcher used an interview guide for in-depth interviews, following these steps: 1) Studying Theory and Related Research: Gathering information to develop interview questions. 2) Setting Main and Sub-Topics: Ensuring the questions align with the research objectives. 3) Improving Questions: Incorporating feedback from advisors and experts before data collection.

3. **Participatory Action Research Process:** The researcher and the community enterprise group participated in all research stages, including planning, decision-making, implementation, monitoring, and benefiting from the process. The steps included: **Pre-research Phase:** The criteria for selecting the research area included: 1) The community enterprise must produce rice-based products and have diversified its product forms. 2) The area must have supportive community leaders, heads of community enterprises, marketing agencies, residents, and business operators willing to provide information for the research. 3) The researcher must be able to travel to and from the area conveniently and safely. After considering these criteria, the researcher selected the community enterprise group of pesticide-free local rice farmers - Budi Rice. This area was chosen because it is a community enterprise hub for rice products and has the potential for targeted market channels. The selection was made using purposive sampling due to the following reasons: 1) The researcher conducted a preliminary field survey to gather basic information about the community and the community enterprise group of pesticide-free local rice farmers - Budi Rice. This area was identified as having rice product production capabilities and the potential for diverse market channels. 2) The area lacked adequate group efforts to develop and enhance product appeal. 3) The community enterprise leaders were prepared to cooperate in the research and suggest ways to develop products and conduct the research effectively. **Research Phase:** During the research phase, the researcher worked on building a relationship between the research team and the community enterprise. This involved defining roles between the researchers and community leaders to ensure a clear understanding of the research objectives, goals, and expectations. The aim was to develop strategies for enhancing rice product marketing and assessing the feasibility of existing rice products within the community, particularly those based on local wisdom.

Research Phase

During the research phase, the researcher worked on building a relationship between the research team and the community enterprise. This involved defining roles between the researchers and community leaders to ensure a clear understanding of the research objectives, goals, and expectations. The aim was to develop strategies for enhancing rice product marketing and assessing the feasibility of existing rice products within the community, particularly those based on local wisdom. Collecting basic community data and identifying issues through cooperative efforts from all community members. This information was used to formulate plans for addressing challenges and enhancing rice products for market promotion. These steps ensured active community involvement, facilitating the identification of practical solutions for developing and marketing rice products effectively. **Planning Phase:** the researcher formulated plans based on the data gathered from the participatory problem analysis. The chosen solutions were analyzed in the context of the community enterprise's capabilities, considering its limitations and conditions. The plans included detailed projects and activities, emphasizing participation and responsibility distribution. Then, conduct training sessions for community leaders to educate them about their roles and responsibilities, and teach collaborative working methods with community enterprises. Next, creating a plan for tracking and evaluating the project's progress, the researcher participated in meetings with community leaders, enterprise groups, and business operators to monitor activities and prepare leaders for their tasks, using informal evaluation methods, such as casual conversations and informal interviews, to gather feedback and ensure leaders understood their responsibilities. By integrating these steps, the researcher ensured that the community enterprise could effectively develop and market rice products, leveraging local wisdom and collaborative effort to achieve sustainable development. **Implementation Phase:** In the implementation phase, the plans developed during the research phase are put into action. This phase emphasizes community participation in developing rice products by the Budi Organic Indigenous Rice Farmers Community Enterprise. **Monitoring and Evaluation Phase:** Monitoring and evaluating the progress of projects or activities in line with marketing promotion involves tracking operations by collecting data on actions already taken, activities that have not yet been implemented according to the plan, satisfactory performance results, encountered obstacles in the operations, and required assistance and support. Then, participate in planning future operations by using the collected information to improve operations. Additionally, evaluate the activities according to marketing promotion, assess the satisfaction of stakeholders, leaders, enterprises, and entrepreneurs, and conduct interviews regarding the operations, among other things.

The research concluded with the presentation of the gluten-free brownie product made from Budi brown rice flour, summarizing the success, obstacles, factors, and conditions for success from the participatory action research, validated by five experts through content analysis to guide future product development.

DATA ANALYSIS AND STATISTICAL METHODS

Quantitative Research: The researcher validated and checked the completeness of the data from the 400 questionnaires. The data was analyzed using a statistical software package with the following steps: 1) Coding: The questionnaires were coded according to predetermined codes. 2) Data Processing: The coded data was processed using various statistical methods. 3) The data collected from the questionnaires was analyzed descriptively using: Frequency, Percentage, Mean, and Standard Deviation. These statistics were used to describe the variables and were presented in tables along with descriptive explanations of the study results.

Qualitative Research: The researcher conducted a preliminary analysis of the interview data simultaneously with data collection. The information from notes and transcriptions was separated into different themes. The researcher ensured the completeness of the data and sought additional information as needed to achieve a comprehensive dataset. The data was then analyzed and synthesized using descriptive analysis, categorized, and organized by themes to draw clear conclusions that answer the research questions. These results were written and described for further presentation.

Research Results

For the development of gluten-free brownies from Budi brown rice flour in Budi subdistrict, Yala province, the community enterprise group of organic indigenous rice farmers aims to improve product quality to promote income from environmentally friendly products. The study emphasized enhancing management processes to achieve effective operations. It also examined the management context, processes, and development strategies to raise awareness within the enterprise group about the benefits and value-creating methods that inspire their professional practices.

Products Development

Figure 1. Development of gluten-free brownies from Budi brown rice flour in Budi subdistrict, Yala Province: community enterprise group of organic indigenous rice farmers - Budi rice

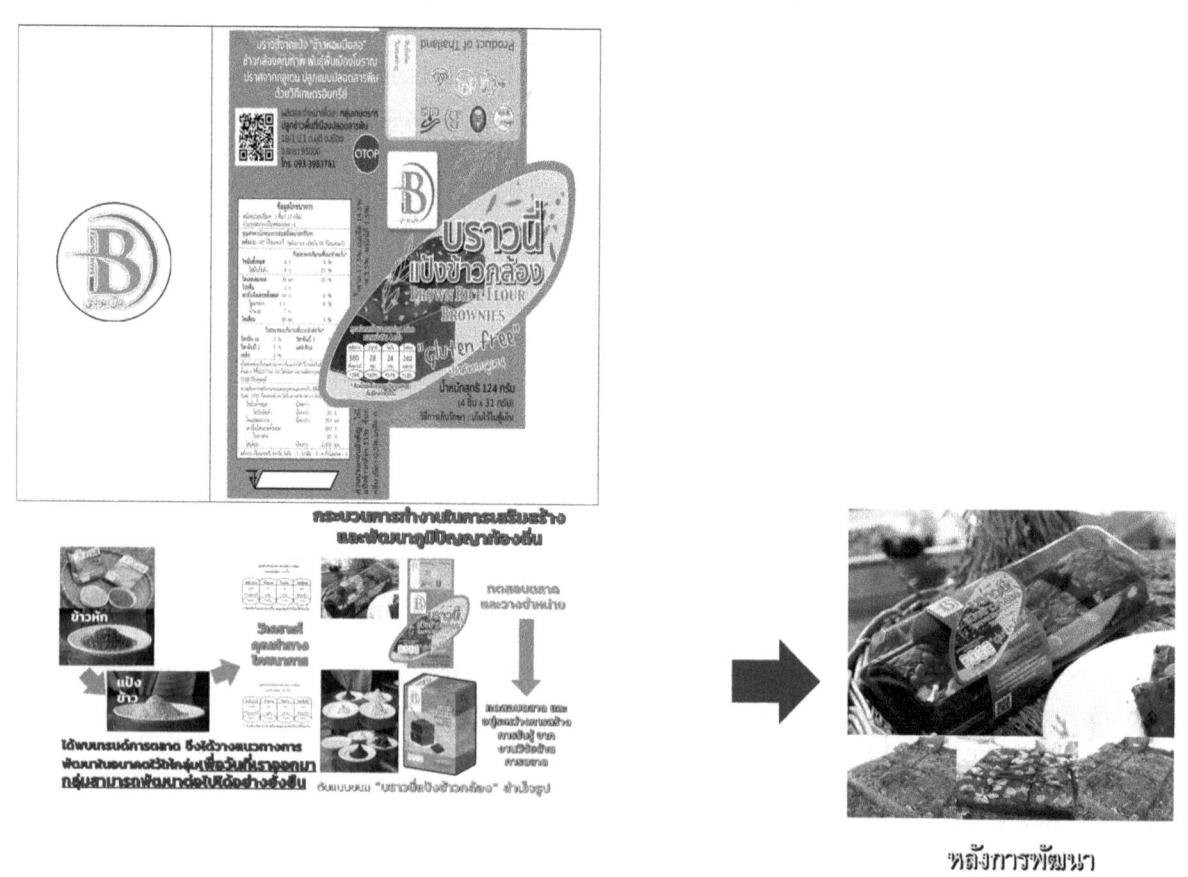

Qualitative Research Findings: The research team identified significant management issues within the community enterprise, as illustrated by the interview excerpts: "I have followed the procedures according to the enterprise policy, but at the same time, raising awareness within the group about product control is essential." Furthermore, "a key identity of the local products involves considering diverse rice varieties or other unique processing methods. There is also a need to emphasize financial planning for sustainable enterprise operations." Regarding product management strategies, it has been suggested that "through our participation in forming the group, we recognize the importance of the product's usage and foster enthusiasm in problem-solving, which includes: 1) Creating awareness of using rice efficiently to minimize waste, 2) Creating awareness in production from start to finish to ensure utilization and meet the needs of the homemaker group, and 3) Raising awareness about environmental conservation alongside operations to prevent environmental harm." Additionally, I believe that raising awareness and involving all sectors can help develop or integrate rice products and modify packaging to be environmentally friendly, which are all crucial factors throughout the operations of the community enterprise.

In summary, active participation in strengthening the enterprise allows community organizations to engage and represent network organizations, leading to expanded distribution channels. The development process can include: 1) Innovation and Technology: Integrating modern changes while maintaining environmental control. 2) Distribution Channels: Utilizing online media or processes for enhanced learning and communication, thus improving income generation. 3) Creating Value: Ensuring the products meet consumer demands with novelty, diverse flavors, and reusable packaging.

Data Analysis of Gluten-Free Brownies Development from Budi Brown Rice Flour in Budi Subdistrict, Yala Province: The analysis used mean ($\bar{x}$) and standard deviation (S. D.), presented in Table 1.

Table 1. Development of gluten-free brownies from Budi brown rice flour in Budi subdistrict, Yala Province

Development of Gluten-Free Brownies from Budi Brown Rice Flour in Budi Subdistrict, Yala Province (Overall)	Opinion Level			
	$\bar{x}$	S.D.	Opinion	Order
1. Product quality improvement	4.10	0.34	High	2
2. Packaging development appropriate for the product	3.62	0.45	High	4
3. Product design development suitable for the target group	4.31	0.11	High	1
4. Adding value to the product	3.33	0.65	Moderate	5
5. Creating new products by integrating local wisdom with modern technology in the production process	3.21	0.97	Moderate	6
6. Product characteristic development, such as color, smell, taste, and texture	3.97	0.52	High	3
Overall	4.03	0.64	High	

Product Development of Gluten-Free Brownies from Budi Brown Rice Flour in Budi Subdistrict, Yala Province (Overall): The overall development of gluten-free brownies from Budi brown rice flour in Budi Subdistrict, Yala Province, was rated at a high level ($\bar{x}$ = 4.03, S.D. = 0.64). When considering individual items, four aspects received high ratings: product design development suitable for the target group ($\bar{x}$ = 4.31, S.D. = 0.11), followed by quality improvement ($\bar{x}$ = 4.10, S.D. = 0.34), product characteristics development such as color, smell, taste, and texture ($\bar{x}$ = 3.97, S.D. = 0.52), and packaging development suitable for the product ($\bar{x}$ = 3.62, S.D. = 0.45). Adding value to the product received a moderate rating ($\bar{x}$ = 3.33, S.D. = 0.65), as did the integration of local wisdom with modern technology in the production process ($\bar{x}$ = 3.21, S.D. = 0.97).

Product Development Framework: The product development should initiate from a business group that integrates the ideas of its members to create uniqueness. Additionally, the business group should consider consumer demands by using hygienic production processes and employing knowledgeable personnel. Natural or locally sourced materials should be utilized to maximize benefits. Logos and text on packaging should be redesigned to be clear and attractive, highlighting product features. Expanding marketing channels through online media is recommended to increase the customer base. The business group should establish a knowledge-sharing platform for continuous learning and innovation. Training activities should focus on using raw materials and improving production technology quality.

DISCUSSIONS

Research on the development of gluten-free brownies from Budi brown rice flour in Budi Subdistrict, Yala Province, highlights the importance of community participation in strengthening business enterprises. Community organizations should have the opportunity to engage and represent networks to expand distribution channels. The development process includes: 1) Integrating innovation or technology to achieve modern changes while maintaining environmental control. 2) Using online media for product distribution to enhance learning and communication, leading to better income generation. 3) Creating value and importance aligned with consumer demands, offering unique flavors and reusable packaging. The findings were that high levels of feedback were received for product design suitable for the target group, followed by quality improvement, product characteristics (color, smell, taste, texture), and packaging development. These findings were consistent with Kotler & Armstrong (2016) and Natthaphat Sawangsap (2018), who emphasized that marketing mix is a strategic tool for achieving marketing objectives. For community enterprises processing Kluai Leb Mu Nang bananas in Chumphon Province, marketing factors influencing operational efficiency include 1) Product factors: High-quality, standardized, diverse products with attractive packaging. 2) Price factors: Reasonable pricing with clear price tags. 3) Distribution channels: Convenient locations with appropriate operating hours. 4) Marketing promotion: Special activities during festivals, discounts, giveaways, fast service, and advertising through various media.

Figure 2. Development of products from Budi brown-rice flour to promote gluten-free brownies in Budee subdistrict, Yala Province

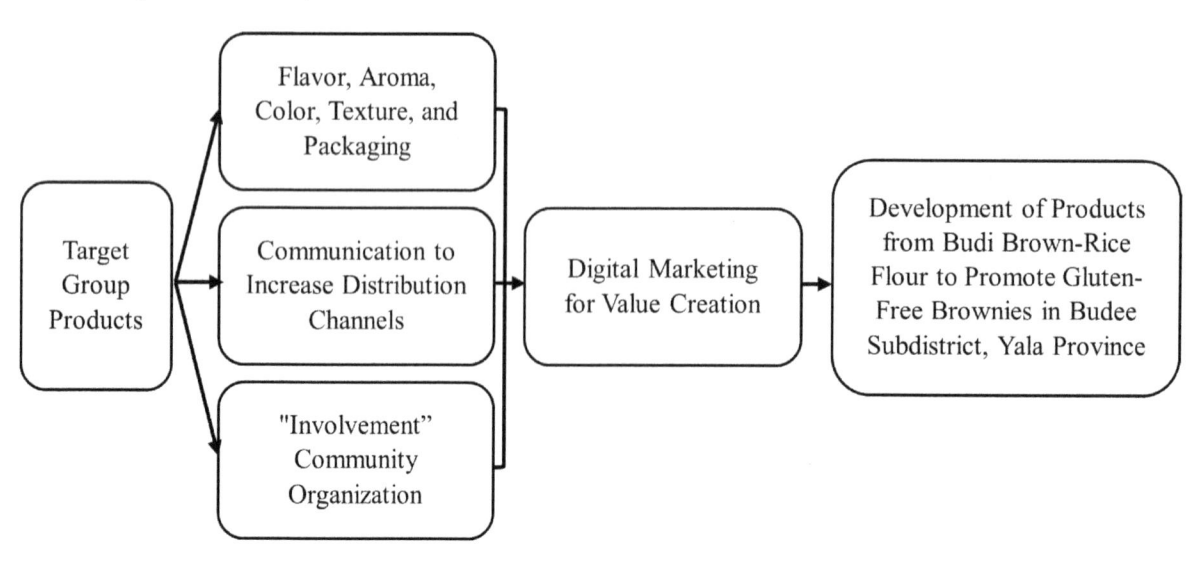

CONCLUSION

The study on the development of gluten-free brownies from Budi brown rice flour in Budi Subdistrict, Yala Province, suggests that agricultural housewives should focus on environmentally friendly products and community participation. Activities and idea exchanges with network organizations are crucial. Additionally, analyzing the internal and external problems of community enterprises can enhance business potential.

Recommendations

Participation Process and Entrepreneurship: Building networks to facilitate surveys and fieldwork can be a tool to enhance learning among local populations and promote awareness and consideration of environmentally friendly products. Key recommendations from agencies and entrepreneurs include **Participation in Innovation Transfer**: Engaging in the dissemination of innovations for developing or creating diverse, eco-friendly products. Currently, this has not been implemented as much as it should be. **Continuous Promotion of Entrepreneurship**: Elevating local and provincial individuals, promoting the export of products abroad, developing product mixes, and enhancing competitiveness to achieve better performance and the best products. **Skill and Career Development**: Supporting and enhancing skill and career development to integrate the creation of eco-friendly products within the community.

ACKNOWLEDGMENTS

This research was supported by the Faculty of Management Sciences, Yala Rajabhat University, through a research grant. We extend our sincere thanks to the university administrators, distinguished experts, and research advisors for their guidance, which made this research successful. The findings can be applied as a development guideline to effectively promote the business groups and farmers in Budi Subdistrict, Yala Province.

REFERENCES

Capriles, V. D., de Aguiar, E. V., Dos Santos, F. G., Fernández, M. E. A., de Melo, B. G., Tagliapietra, B. L., & Conti, A. C. (2023). Current status and prospects of sensory and consumer research approaches to gluten-free bakery and pasta products. *Food Research International*, 173, 113389. DOI: 10.1016/j.foodres.2023.113389 PMID: 37803727

Chanthasap, . (2002). *Basic Research Methods*. Dhurakij Pundit University Press.

Di Nardo, G., Villa, M. P., Conti, L., Ranucci, G., Pacchiarotti, C., Principessa, L., & Parisi, P. (2019). Nutritional deficiencies in children with celiac disease resulting from a gluten-free diet: A systematic review. *Nutrients*, 11(7), 1588.

Gao, Y., Janes, M. E., Chaiya, B., Brennan, M. A., Brennan, C. S., & Prinyawiwatkul, W. (2018). Gluten-free bakery and pasta products: Prevalence and quality improvement. *International Journal of Food Science & Technology*, 53(1), 19–32. DOI: 10.1111/ijfs.13505

Jnawali, P., Kumar, V., & Tanwar, B. (2016). Celiac disease: Overview and considerations for development of gluten-free foods. *Food Science and Human Wellness*, 5(4), 169–176. DOI: 10.1016/j.fshw.2016.09.003

Kotler, P., & Keller, K. L. (2016). *Marketing Management* (13th ed.). Pearson Prentice Hall.

Penjumras, P., Thongfathamrong, P., Umnat, S., Chokeprasert, P., Wattananapakasem, I., & Phaiphan, A. (2021, May). Gluten-free brownies made with composite rice flour. []. IOP Publishing.]. *IOP Conference Series. Earth and Environmental Science*, 756(1), 012075. DOI: 10.1088/1755-1315/756/1/012075

Pio Ávila, B., Cardozo, L. O., Alves, G. D., Gularte, M. A., Monks, J., & Elias, M. C. (2019). Consumers' sensory perception of food attributes: Identifying the ideal formulation of gluten-and lactose-free brownie using sensory methodologies. *Journal of Food Science*, 84(12), 3707–3716. DOI: 10.1111/1750-3841.14845 PMID: 31665555

Saengthap, N. (2018). *Marketing mix factors and post-purchase behavior of consumers in community markets in Thanyaburi District, Pathum Thani Province. Independent study*. Rajamangala University of Technology Thanyaburi.

Sawangsub, N. (2018). Marketing Mix Factors and Post-Purchase Behavior of Consumers at Community Markets in Thanyaburi District, Pathum Thani Province. [Master's thesis, Business Administration, Pathum Thani] Rajamangala University of Technology Thanyaburi.

Stoin, D., Jianu, C., Poiana, M. A., Alexa, E. C., & Velciov, A. B. (2021). Current trends in the use of unconventional raw materials for the development of gluten-free bakery and pastry products with high nutritional value: A review. *Journal of Agroalimentary Processes and Technologies*, 27(4), 378–391.

Wanichbancha, A. (2005). *Advanced Statistical Analysis with SPSS for Windows* (4th ed.). Thammasarn.

Wimarnaya, V. W., Fauza, G., Prasetyo, H., Muhammad, D. R. A., Affandi, D. R., & Ariviani, S. (2021, July). Analysis of Customer Needs for Food Products Using Kano Model, A Case Study of Steamed Brownies. []. IOP Publishing.]. *IOP Conference Series. Earth and Environmental Science*, 828(1), 012057. DOI: 10.1088/1755-1315/828/1/012057

Chapter 13
Harnessing Business Analytics for Influencer Marketing:
Enhancing Decision-Making and Performance in Society

Sreethi Rebeka R.
Christ University, India

Rejoice Thomas
https://orcid.org/0000-0002-8701-6720
Christ University, India

ABSTRACT

Business analytics has enhanced decision-making and performance across social sectors in the evolving digital technology and artificial intelligence (AI) landscape. This chapter explores the transformative role of business analytics, focusing on its application in influencer marketing. By leveraging data-driven insights, businesses can strategically navigate the complexities of consumer behaviour, optimize engagement strategies, and drive measurable outcomes. Key themes include the strategic integration of AI and machine learning, ethical considerations in data usage, and the impact of analytics on shaping future marketing strategies. As organizations embrace analytics tools to harness the power of influencer partnerships, they position themselves to innovate, adapt, and thrive in the competitive digital marketplace, ultimately driving the future of social sector initiatives through informed decision-making and impactful digital strategies.

INTRODUCTION

The advent of digital technology and artificial intelligence has revolutionized the landscape of marketing, particularly with the emergence of influencer marketing as a powerful tool for brands to connect with their target audience. Social media platforms have become the epicentre of influencer marketing, offering businesses a unique opportunity to engage with consumers more personally and authentically. This chapter explores influencer marketing within social sectors, examining its role in shaping consumer behaviour and driving purchase decisions(Davlembayeva et al., 2024). Influencer marketing, characterized

DOI: 10.4018/979-8-3693-9230-0.ch013

Copyright ©2025, IGI Global. Copying or distributing in print or electronic forms without written permission of IGI Global is prohibited.

by endorsements and product placements from individuals with a substantial social media following, has grown exponentially over the past decade. Influencers ranging from celebrities and industry experts to micro-influencers with niche audiences can sway public opinion and consumer choices (Abhishek & Srivastava, 2021). This dynamic form of marketing taps into the trust and credibility influencers have built with their followers, making it a potent tool for brands aiming to increase their reach and impact. The rise of influencer marketing can be attributed to several factors. Firstly, traditional advertising methods have become less effective as consumers grow weary of direct marketing tactics. Influencer marketing, by contrast, provides a subtler and engaging approach, seamlessly integrating products into the everyday lives of influencers. This method captures potential customers' attention and builds a sense of relatability and trust (Joshi et al., 2023).

Secondly, the proliferation of social media platforms such as Instagram, YouTube, TikTok, and Twitter has created fertile ground for influencers to thrive. These platforms offer influencers a stage to share content, interact with followers, and promote products in creative and diverse ways. Brands, in turn, benefit from the direct line of communication with consumers, allowing for immediate feedback and a more interactive marketing experience (Abhishek & Srivastava, 2021). Furthermore, the application of business analytics in influencer marketing has enabled brands to measure the effectiveness of their campaigns with unprecedented precision. Through analytics, companies can track engagement metrics, conversion rates, and return on investment, providing valuable insights into consumer behaviour and campaign performance. This data-driven approach helps refine marketing strategies, optimize influencer partnerships, and ultimately enhance decision-making and business performance (Abhishek & Srivastava, 2021; Joshi et al., 2023).In the social sectors, including health, education, and public services, influencer marketing has shown remarkable potential in driving positive change. Influencers can raise awareness about important issues, promote beneficial behaviours, and mobilize communities. For instance, health influencers can advocate for healthy lifestyles, educational influencers can support learning initiatives, and public service influencers can champion civic engagement (Vrontis et al., 2021).

This chapter aims to delve deeper into the mechanics of influencer marketing within these social sectors, supported by empirical research and case studies. By analyzing the impact of influencers on consumer behaviour and decision-making, we will uncover the nuances of this marketing approach and its broader implications for businesses and society. Through a comprehensive exploration, we aim to understand better how influencer marketing can be leveraged to enhance decision-making processes and drive performance in the digital era.

LITERATURE REVIEW

Influencer marketing has evolved from traditional celebrity endorsements to a more democratized form of promotion, where individuals with significant social media followings can impact consumer choices. Early studies highlighted the credibility and relatability of influencers as central to their effectiveness. Unlike traditional celebrities, influencers often cultivate a sense of authenticity and personal connection with their audience, making their endorsements appear more genuine (Joshi et al., 2023). Influencer marketing significantly impacts consumer behaviour, particularly in the context of purchase intentions. For instance, studies have found that the perceived popularity of an influencer can enhance brand perceptions and purchase intentions.

Similarly, influencer credibility, attractiveness, and content quality are critical factors that drive consumer engagement and conversion rates (Ao et al., 2023). Social media platforms play a pivotal role in the dissemination and success of influencer marketing campaigns. Platforms such as Instagram, YouTube, and TikTok offer various features that enable influencers to create engaging content, from stories and live videos to sponsored posts and product reviews. The interactive nature of social media allows consumers to engage with content in real-time, fostering a sense of community and enhancing the impact of influencer marketing (Joshi et al., 2023).

Integrating business analytics in influencer marketing has transformed how campaigns are designed, executed, and evaluated. Analytics tools enable businesses to track key performance indicators (KPIs) such as engagement rates, click-through rates, and return on investment (ROI). This data-driven approach allows for more strategic decision-making and optimization of marketing efforts (Vrontis et al., 2021). Influencer marketing has also shown promise in various social sectors, including health, education, and public services. For example, influencers have effectively promoted healthy behaviours and raised awareness about medical conditions. Influencers can support learning initiatives by sharing educational content and engaging with students.

Similarly, in public services, influencers can mobilize communities and advocate for civic engagement (Joshi et al., 2023). While influencer marketing presents numerous opportunities, it poses challenges and ethical considerations. The authenticity of influencer endorsements can sometimes be questioned, mainly when financial incentives are involved. Additionally, the potential for misleading or deceptive content requires brands and influencers to adhere to ethical guidelines and regulatory standards (Zniva et al., 2023).

The literature on influencer marketing underscores its significant impact on consumer behaviour and business performance. By leveraging business analytics, companies can enhance the effectiveness of their influencer marketing campaigns, leading to more informed decision-making and improved outcomes. As this marketing strategy continues to evolve, it will be essential for businesses to navigate its complexities and ethical challenges while harnessing its potential to drive engagement and influence in the digital age.

THE EFFECT OF INFLUENCER MARKETING ON PURCHASE INTENTION AND DECISION OF ONLINE CONSUMERS

Influencer marketing has emerged as a significant driver of consumer behaviour in the digital age, particularly in influencing purchase intentions and decisions among online consumers. This section examines the mechanisms through which influencer marketing impacts these aspects. One of the primary factors driving the effectiveness of influencer marketing is the credibility and trust that influencers build with their audience. Influencers often share their personal experiences and opinions, which resonate with their followers and create a sense of authenticity. According to experts, credibility combines expertise, trustworthiness, and attractiveness. When an influencer is perceived as credible, their endorsements are more likely to be persuasive, leading to higher purchase intentions among consumers (Wiedmann & Von Mettenheim, 2020). Social proof, a psychological phenomenon where people conform to the actions of others, plays a crucial role in influencer marketing. When consumers see influencers they admire using and endorsing products, they are more likely to perceive these products as desirable and worth purchasing.

Studies indicate that endorsements from influencers serve as a form of social proof, reducing perceived risk and uncertainty associated with online purchases. This effect is powerful when the influencer is seen as similar to the consumer, reinforcing the notion of peer influence (Jhawar et al., 2023).

Influencers often cultivate solid emotional connections with their followers through consistent interaction and engagement. This emotional bond enhances the persuasive power of their endorsements. Studies highlight that emotional engagement with an influencer can lead to positive attitudes towards the promoted products and increased purchase intentions. The interactive nature of social media platforms, where influencers can directly communicate with their followers, further amplifies this effect (Joshi et al., 2023). The quality and relevance of the content influencers share are critical determinants of their impact on consumer purchase decisions. High-quality, visually appealing, and informative content can capture consumer attention and generate interest in the promoted products. Content perceived as valuable and relevant to consumers' needs and interests is more likely to influence their purchase intentions (Ao et al., 2023). Business analytics plays a vital role in optimizing influencer marketing strategies. Businesses can identify which influencers are most effective in driving purchase intentions and decisions by analyzing consumer interactions, engagement rates, and conversion metrics. This data-driven approach allows for more targeted and efficient marketing efforts, maximizing the return on investment (Bansal et al., 2024).

Influencer marketing profoundly influences online consumers' purchase intentions and decisions. Businesses can effectively shape consumer behaviour and drive sales by leveraging the credibility, emotional connection, and social proof influencers provide. The integration of business analytics further enhances the precision and impact of these marketing efforts, enabling brands to optimize their strategies and achieve better outcomes. As influencer marketing evolves, understanding its mechanisms and effects will be crucial for businesses aiming to thrive in the digital marketplace.

CASE STUDIES

Case Study 1: Health Sector - Promoting Healthy Lifestyles

A health and wellness brand sought to increase awareness and sales of its organic nutritional supplements. The brand partnered with health and fitness influencers on Instagram, who had a solid following among health-conscious consumers. The influencers were selected based on their credibility, engagement rates, and relevance to the brand's target audience. They were provided with free products and compensated for their promotional efforts. The influencers shared personal stories and testimonials about how the supplements improved their health, accompanied by high-quality images and videos. Using advanced analytics tools, the brand tracked vital performance metrics such as engagement, click-through, and conversions. The data revealed which influencers generated the most engagement and sales, allowing the brand to refine its strategy and focus on the most effective partnerships.

The campaign resulted in a 35% increase in online sales and a significant boost in brand awareness. The analytics also revealed that content featuring personal stories and visual demonstrations of the product's benefits performed best. The brand's follower count on social media grew by 25%, indicating increased consumer interest and engagement.

Case Study 2: Education Sector - Supporting Online Learning

An online education platform aimed to increase enrollment in its new coding and programming courses. The platform partnered with educational influencers and tech enthusiasts on YouTube who were known for their expertise in technology and education. The influencers created detailed review videos and tutorials showcasing the platform's courses, highlighting their unique features and benefits. They also hosted live Q&A sessions where viewers could ask questions and receive real-time answers about the courses. The platform used analytics to monitor video views, subscriber growth, and enrollment rates. The platform identified which videos and influencers drove interest and enrollment most effectively by analyzing viewer demographics and engagement patterns.

The campaign led to a 50% increase in course enrollments and a 40% rise in website traffic. The most successful videos provided in-depth tutorials and practical demonstrations, resonating with potential students. The platform also experienced a 30% increase in YouTube subscribers, indicating heightened interest in its educational content.

Case Study 3: Public Services - Encouraging Civic Engagement

A local government agency wanted to promote a new recycling initiative to reduce waste and increase the community's recycling rates. The agency collaborated with environmental influencers on Twitter who were passionate about sustainability and eco-friendly practices. The influencers shared educational content about the importance of recycling and practical tips for reducing waste. They used hashtags and engaged with their followers through discussions and Twitter polls to create buzz around the initiative. The campaign included a challenge where followers could share their recycling efforts and win eco-friendly products. The agency employed analytics to track hashtag usage, tweet impressions, and engagement rates. Sentiment analysis was also used to gauge public opinion and feedback on the initiative. The data provided insights into the campaign's reach and effectiveness in fostering community participation.

The initiative saw a 20% increase in recycling rates within the first three months. The campaign's hashtag trended locally on Twitter, generating over 10,000 mentions and substantial community engagement. The sentiment analysis showed a positive reception, with many residents expressing support and commitment to the recycling efforts.

Case Study 4: Retail Sector - Boosting Fashion Sales

A fashion retailer aimed to increase sales of its new clothing line targeting young adults. The retailer partnered with fashion influencers on Instagram and TikTok, which had a large following among the desired demographic. Influencers were given exclusive previews of the new clothing line and encouraged to create styling videos and posts showcasing different outfits. They used discount codes and links to drive traffic to the retailer's online store. Influencers also engaged with their followers through comments and live sessions to build excitement around the new collection. The retailer used analytics to measure the impact of influencer posts on website traffic, conversion rates, and sales. Detailed reports on consumer demographics and purchasing behaviour helped the retailer understand the campaign's effectiveness and adjust strategies accordingly. The campaign resulted in a 45% increase in sales for the new clothing line and a 50% increase in website traffic. Posts that featured creative styling tips and interactive content, such as polls and Q&A sessions, were particularly influential in driving engagement. The retailer's social media following grew significantly, enhancing its brand presence and customer base.

These case studies illustrate the power of influencer marketing and business analytics in various sectors. By leveraging the credibility and reach of influencers, businesses can effectively shape consumer behaviour and drive performance. Integrating business analytics further enhances these efforts by providing valuable insights and enabling data-driven decision-making. These examples demonstrate that when executed strategically and supported by robust analytics, influencer marketing can lead to significant business success and positive social impact.

RECOMMENDATIONS AND SOLUTIONS

Implementing practical recommendations is crucial for optimizing influencer marketing campaigns in today's competitive landscape. Strategic influencer selection begins with prioritizing relevance and aligning influencers whose content and audience resonate with your brand values and target demographic. Credibility is equally vital; partnering with influencers perceived as trustworthy and knowledgeable enhances consumer trust and positively influences purchase decisions. Emphasizing engagement metrics over sheer follower counts ensures influencers can effectively connect with their audience and drive meaningful actions. Leveraging business analytics provides actionable insights into campaign performance, consumer interactions, and influencer effectiveness. Businesses can gauge campaign success and refine strategies by tracking engagement, click-through, and ROI KPIs. Understanding consumer demographics and behaviours through data analysis further enables tailored content and influencer partnerships. Creating high-quality, authentic content remains pivotal; encouraging influencers to showcase genuine experiences with products builds credibility and fosters audience trust. Visual appeal and interactive formats like live videos and Q&A sessions enhance engagement and community interaction. Continuous campaign optimization through A/B testing and feedback loops ensures strategies evolve based on real-time insights, maximizing effectiveness. Ethical practices, including transparent disclosures and authentic content presentation, uphold brand integrity and consumer trust, ensuring sustainable success in influencer marketing.

Developing a comprehensive influencer marketing strategy begins with defining clear goals and objectives tailored to specific outcomes, such as increasing brand awareness, driving sales, or delivering a particular message. Utilizing influencer marketing platforms and analytics tools becomes pivotal in identifying influencers who align closely with brand values and resonate with target audiences. Building solid partnerships with influencers involves providing the necessary support, resources, and creative autonomy to promote the brand authentically. Simultaneously, investing in advanced analytics tools enhances campaign effectiveness. Leveraging platforms like Hootsuite, Sprout Social, and Google Analytics offers deep insights into campaign performance metrics, enabling businesses to gauge impact and make informed adjustments. Custom dashboards consolidate data from multiple sources, providing a comprehensive overview, facilitating data-driven decision-making, and integrating predictive analytics, which aids in forecasting trends and consumer behaviours and empowering businesses to plan and optimize future influencer marketing initiatives strategically. By implementing these strategies, companies can strengthen their influencer marketing efforts, achieve measurable results, and drive sustained growth in the competitive digital landscape.

Enhancing cross-platform integration in influencer marketing involves strategic approaches to maximize brand visibility and audience reach across various social media channels. Businesses can start by developing a unified influencer marketing strategy that aligns messaging cohesively across platforms, ensuring consistency in brand communication and reinforcing brand identity. Tailoring content to suit each platform's specific features and audience preferences is crucial; for example, creating short, engaging videos for TikTok and detailed, informative posts for Instagram can optimize content relevance and engagement. Additionally, implementing cross-promotion strategies where influencers promote brands across different platforms amplifies visibility and expands audience reach effectively. By integrating these tactics, businesses can leverage the strengths of each platform, enhance cross-platform synergy, and achieve more significant impact and engagement in their influencer marketing campaigns.

Businesses can implement several key strategies to foster community engagement effectively in influencer marketing. Firstly, encouraging user-generated content from followers enhances authenticity and builds a sense of community around the brand. Businesses can create buzz and deepen connections with their followers by actively involving their audience through engagement campaigns such as contests, challenges, and interactive Q&A sessions. Additionally, focusing on community building involves consistent engagement, responding to comments, showing appreciation for customer support, and cultivating a loyal and engaged following. When combined with strategic influencer selection, leveraging business analytics, and consistently delivering high-quality content, these strategies can significantly enhance decision-making and performance in influencer marketing. Ethical practices and continual optimization based on data-driven insights are crucial for long-term success in the ever-evolving digital landscape. By adopting these approaches, businesses can effectively navigate the complexities of influencer marketing and leverage its potential to achieve meaningful outcomes in the digital era.

DISCUSSION

In today's rapidly evolving digital landscape, businesses across social sectors increasingly turn to business analytics to enhance their decision-making processes and improve overall performance. This chapter explores the transformative role of business analytics in leveraging data-driven insights to optimize strategies, mainly focusing on influencer marketing within digital technology and artificial intelligence.

Business analytics is pivotal in influencer marketing by providing essential insights into consumer behaviour, campaign effectiveness, and return on investment (ROI). Leveraging data analytics tools and techniques enable businesses to achieve several critical objectives. Firstly, they can effectively segment and target audiences using demographic and behavioural data, ensuring alignment between influencers and ideal customer profiles. This targeted approach enhances engagement and boosts conversion rates. Secondly, analytics facilitate precise performance measurement by tracking real-time KPIs such as engagement and conversion rates. Platforms like Google Analytics and social media analytics tools offer actionable metrics that empower businesses to evaluate campaign success and make informed adjustments. Thirdly, companies can optimize their content strategies by analyzing performance metrics to determine which content resonates most with their audience. Through A/B testing, they can refine messaging, formats, and creative elements to maximize impact. Finally, predictive analytics models enable businesses to forecast future trends and consumer behaviours by analyzing historical data patterns. This proactive approach allows enterprises to adopt influencer marketing strategies preemptively, ensuring they remain competitive and responsive in a rapidly evolving marketplace. Overall, business analytics empowers businesses in influencer marketing to make data-driven decisions, optimize performance, and achieve sustainable growth.

Integrating artificial intelligence (AI) and machine learning (ML) technologies significantly enhances business analytics within influencer marketing. AI-driven algorithms are crucial in analyzing extensive datasets to derive comprehensive audience insights, including preferences, interests, and purchase behaviours. This capability allows businesses to refine influencer partnerships and content strategies, tailoring them to effectively engage specific audience segments with targeted messaging. Furthermore, AI-powered sentiment analysis tools monitor real-time social media conversations, providing valuable insights into public sentiment towards brands and influencer campaigns. This real-time feedback enables businesses to gauge brand perception, identify potential issues, and pivot marketing strategies accordingly. ML algorithms enhance these capabilities by personalizing content recommendations based on individual consumer behaviours and interactions, optimizing engagement and driving higher conversion rates. By leveraging AI and ML technologies in influencer marketing, businesses can achieve deeper audience understanding, enhance brand relevance, and foster meaningful connections with consumers in the digital age.

While integrating business analytics and AI in influencer marketing brings substantial benefits, businesses must focus intensely on ethical considerations and transparency. Adhering to regulatory guidelines and industry standards is essential, particularly in disclosing influencer partnerships and sponsored content to foster consumer trust and comply with advertising regulations. Robust data protection measures are critical to safeguard consumer data privacy and confidentiality. Obtaining explicit consent for data collection and usage and strict adherence to data privacy laws ensures that businesses maintain consumer trust while navigating the complexities of digital marketing. By prioritizing ethical practices and transparency, companies can uphold integrity in influencer relationships, bolster brand reputation, and foster long-term consumer loyalty in an increasingly data-driven landscape.

Looking ahead, the future of business analytics in influencer marketing promises significant growth and innovation. Continued advancements in analytics technologies such as AI, machine learning, and predictive analytics will enable businesses to refine targeting, personalize content, and optimize influencer marketing strategies with greater precision. Emerging platforms like virtual reality (VR), augmented reality (AR), and live streaming present new opportunities for immersive and interactive influencer experiences, enhancing consumer engagement and brand affinity. Cross-channel integration across digital platforms will be crucial, allowing brands to create cohesive narratives and maximize their reach effectively. Fueled by data-driven insights and ethical standards, business analytics will continue to drive decision-making and performance enhancement in the digital and AI-driven social sectors. By embracing these advancements and anticipating future trends, businesses can achieve sustainable growth, innovation, and competitive advantage in an evolving digital marketplace, delivering meaningful value to brands and consumers.

FUTURE RESEARCH PROSPECTS

As businesses increasingly leverage business analytics to enhance decision-making and performance in influencer marketing within the digital landscape, future research avenues emerge that promise to advance understanding and capabilities in this domain. One key area of exploration involves the integration of artificial intelligence (AI) and machine learning (ML) technologies in influencer marketing. Research could delve into how AI-driven content personalization strategies can analyze consumer data to deliver tailored influencer campaigns, as well as investigate the predictive capabilities of AI and ML models in forecasting campaign outcomes and consumer behaviour trends. Ethical implications surrounding AI use, such as data privacy and algorithmic bias, warrant examination to ensure responsible implementation. Additionally, exploring cross-platform analytics and omnichannel strategies becomes crucial with the proliferation of digital platforms. Studying the effectiveness of cross-platform influencer campaigns and developing methodologies for measuring omnichannel performance will optimize engagement and ROI across diverse channels. Furthermore, investigating the impact of emerging technologies like virtual reality (VR), augmented reality (AR), and blockchain on influencer marketing strategies and analytics offers opportunities to innovate immersive experiences, enhance transparency, and build brand loyalty. These research directions hold promise for shaping the future landscape of influencer marketing, enabling businesses to adapt and thrive in a rapidly evolving digital ecosystem.

Exploring consumer behaviour and psychographics in influencer marketing offers valuable insights for businesses aiming to optimize engagement and effectiveness. Investigating psychological factors that shape consumer perceptions, attitudes, and purchase decisions in response to influencer content can provide a more profound understanding of what drives consumer actions. Conducting longitudinal studies is crucial to track how consumer behaviour and sentiment towards influencer marketing evolve, especially in changing digital trends and societal norms. These studies help businesses adapt their strategies to align with shifting consumer preferences, enhancing the relevance and impact of influencer campaigns. By delving into these aspects, companies can leverage data-driven insights to tailor their influencer partnerships and content strategies more effectively, fostering stronger connections with their target audiences.

Exploring ethics and regulation in influencer marketing analytics reveals crucial considerations for businesses and researchers. Analyzing their impact on influencer marketing practices becomes essential as regulatory frameworks evolve. Business analytics is pivotal in ensuring compliance with advertising standards and data privacy laws, highlighting its importance in maintaining ethical practices. Developing ethical guidelines for data analytics in influencer marketing promotes transparency, fairness, and consumer trust, which are crucial for sustaining long-term relationships. Looking forward, the future of research in business analytics within influencer marketing holds promise for growth and innovation. By addressing these areas, researchers can advance knowledge, establish best practices, and shape ethical standards in a rapidly evolving digital landscape. Interdisciplinary collaboration and technological advancements will drive influencer marketing analytics forward, shaping its strategic and ethical dimensions for years.

CONCLUSION

The integration of business analytics has emerged as a pivotal force in transforming decision-making and enhancing performance across social sectors, particularly within influencer marketing. This chapter has highlighted the impact of leveraging data-driven insights to optimize strategies, foster consumer engagement, and drive business outcomes in the dynamic digital landscape. Critical insights into the transformative role of business analytics in influencer marketing highlight its impact on strategic decision-making, consumer engagement, performance optimization, and ethical considerations. Business analytics empowers organizations to make informed decisions through comprehensive data analysis, enabling them to identify trends, understand consumer behaviour, and tailor strategies to meet market demands effectively. By leveraging influencer marketing and analytics, businesses can create personalized content that resonates with audiences, fostering more profound engagement, building brand loyalty, and driving conversions. Analytics tools, including AI and machine learning, facilitate real-time performance measurement, allowing businesses to track KPIs, assess campaign effectiveness, and refine strategies for maximum ROI and sustainable growth. Amidst these advancements, maintaining ethical standards and transparency in influencer partnerships is crucial, ensuring consumer trust, regulatory compliance, and safeguarding long-term brand reputation.

Looking ahead, the future of business analytics in influencer marketing holds promising avenues for exploration. Continued advancements in AI, machine learning, and predictive analytics will unlock new capabilities in content personalization, consumer targeting, and campaign optimization. Exploring cross-platform analytics and omnichannel strategies will be essential in delivering cohesive brand experiences and maximizing engagement across digital channels. Research into emerging technologies like VR, AR, and blockchain will shape innovative strategies, redefining consumer-brand interactions. Influencer marketing, supported by robust business analytics, represents a strategic imperative for businesses in the digital era. By harnessing data-driven insights, organizations can navigate competitive landscapes, anticipate market shifts, and forge meaningful connections with consumers. This transformative potential will drive interdisciplinary collaboration and continuous innovation, paving the way for sustainable growth and impactful social sector initiatives.

REFERENCES

Abhishek, N., & Srivastava, M. (2021). Mapping the influence of influencer marketing: A bibliometric analysis. *Marketing Intelligence & Planning*, 39(7), 979–1003. DOI: 10.1108/MIP-03-2021-0085

Ao, L., Bansal, R., Pruthi, N., & Khaskheli, M. B. (2023). Impact of social media influencers on customer engagement and purchase Intention: A Meta-Analysis. *Sustainability (Basel)*, 15(3), 2744. DOI: 10.3390/su15032744

Bansal, R., Saini, S., Ngah, A. H., & Prasad, T. D. (2024). Proselytizing the potential of influencer marketing via artificial intelligence: Mapping the research trends through bibliometric analysis. *Cogent Business & Management*, 11(1), 2372889. Advance online publication. DOI: 10.1080/23311975.2024.2372889

Davlembayeva, D., Chari, S., & Papagiannidis, S. (2024). Virtual Influencers in Consumer Behaviour: A Social Influence Theory Perspective. *British Journal of Management*, 1467-8551.12839. Advance online publication. DOI: 10.1111/1467-8551.12839

Jhawar, A., Varshney, S., & Kumar, P. (2023). *Sponsorship Disclosure on social media: literature review and future research agenda*. Management Review Quarterly., DOI: 10.1007/s11301-023-00342-8

Joshi, Y., Lim, W. M., Jagani, K., & Kumar, S. (2023b). Social media influencer marketing: Foundations, trends, and ways forward. *Electronic Commerce Research*. Advance online publication. DOI: 10.1007/s10660-023-09719-z

Vrontis, D., Makrides, A., Christofi, M., & Thrassou, A. (2021). Social media influencer marketing: A systematic review, integrative framework and future research agenda. *International Journal of Consumer Studies*, 45(4), 617–644. DOI: 10.1111/ijcs.12647

Wiedmann, K., & Von Mettenheim, W. (2020). Attractiveness, trustworthiness and expertise – social influencers' winning formula? ˜the œJournal of Product & Brand Management. *Journal of Product and Brand Management*, 30(5), 707–725. DOI: 10.1108/JPBM-06-2019-2442

Zniva, R., Weitzl, W. J., & Lindmoser, C. (2023b). Be constantly different! How to manage influencer authenticity. *Electronic Commerce Research*, 23(3), 1485–1514. DOI: 10.1007/s10660-022-09653-6

ADDITIONAL READING

Akkaya, B., Jermsittiparsert, K., & Gunsel, A. (Eds.). (2021). *Handbook of Research on Current Trends in Asian Economics, Business, and Administration* (pp. 1–497). IGI Global., DOI: 10.4018/978-1-7998-8486-6

Apaydin, A., Çelik, D., & Elçi, A. (2010). Semantic image retrieval model for sharing experiences in social networks. In *Proceedings of the 34th Annual IEEE International Computer Software and Applications Conference Workshops, COMPSACW 2010* (pp. 1-6). IEEE. DOI: 10.1109/COMPSACW.2010.11

Bitirim, Y., & Ertuğrul, D. (2020). An analysis of user behaviours on the search engine results in pages based on demographic characteristics. *KSII Transactions on Internet and Information Systems*, 14(7). Advance online publication. DOI: 10.3837/tiis.2020.07.006

Ertuğrul, D. Ç., & Ulusoy, D. Ç. (2021). Using personal data and observed symptoms, a knowledge-based self-pre-diagnosis system to predict COVID-19 in smartphone users. *Expert Systems: International Journal of Knowledge Engineering and Neural Networks*, 39(3). Advance online publication. DOI: 10.1111/exsy.12716

Hurbean, L., Militaru, F., Muntean, M., & Danaiata, D. (2023). The impact of business intelligence and analytics adoption on decision-making effectiveness and managerial work performance. *Scientific Annals of Economics and Business*, 70(SI, S1), 43–54. DOI: 10.47743/saeb-2023-0012

Narayanasamy, S., Muruganantham, D., & Elçi, A. (2019). Crisis and Disaster Situations on Social Media Streams: An Ontology-Based Knowledge Harvesting Approach. *Interdisciplinary Journal of Information, Knowledge, and Management*, 14, 343–366. DOI: 10.28945/4420

KEY TERMS AND DEFINITIONS

Analytics: The systematic computational analysis of data or statistics, often used to uncover meaningful patterns and insights for informed decision-making.

Behaviour: The actions and reactions exhibited by individuals or groups, influenced by various factors, including social, psychological, and environmental stimuli.

Business: An organization or enterprise engaged in commercial, industrial, or professional activities to generate profit or achieve specific objectives.

Consumer: An individual or entity that purchases goods or services for personal use or consumption, often influenced by preferences, needs, and perceptions.

Decision-Making: The process of selecting the best course of action from multiple alternatives based on analysis, intuition, or a combination of both.

Influencer: A person, typically on social media platforms, who can affect the purchasing decisions and opinions of their followers due to their perceived authority, knowledge, or popularity.

Marketing: The activities and processes of promoting and selling products or services, including market research, advertising, and customer engagement strategies.

Social Media: Online platforms and websites that enable users to create and share content, participate in social networking, and engage in digital communication and interaction.

Chapter 14
Evaluating the Degree of Risk Perception Among Kumbakonam Town Users of E-Commerce Platforms Using Artificial Intelligence

K. Nalini
https://orcid.org/0009-0000-1346-1146
SASTRA University (Deemed), India

G. Revathy
https://orcid.org/0000-0002-0691-1687
SASTRA University (Deemed), India

ABSTRACT

The rapid proliferation of e-commerce platforms has transformed traditional shopping behaviors, offering unparalleled convenience and accessibility. However, with these benefits come various perceived risks that can influence consumer adoption and usage patterns. This study aims to evaluate the degree of risk perception among users of e-commerce platforms in Kumbakonam town. Through a comprehensive survey and data analysis, we examine the factors contributing to risk perception, including concerns over financial security, privacy, product authenticity, and transaction reliability. By understanding the nuances of these risk perceptions, the study provides insights into how e-commerce businesses can address user concerns and enhance trust. The findings will help inform strategies to improve user experience and promote safer online shopping environments, ultimately contributing to the growth and sustainability of e-commerce in smaller towns like Kumbakonam.

DOI: 10.4018/979-8-3693-9230-0.ch014

Copyright ©2025, IGI Global. Copying or distributing in print or electronic forms without written permission of IGI Global is prohibited.

INTRODUCTION

The act of buying products or services online as opposed to going to stores in person is known as online shopping. Online shopping is becoming more and more popular, not just in India but all across the world, thanks to its conveniences. These days, customers may purchase anything online, including food, prescription drugs, clothing, furniture, electronics, books, equipment for the home, and gadgets. For many people, the neighborhood supermarket remains a convenient spot to pick up food. The increasing globalization of the global economy presents numerous opportunities for marketers. This has increased corporate competitiveness at the same time, prompting many businesses to think about non-traditional marketing approaches. Internet marketing is one such unconventional approach to marketing that many companies have used. The use of the carries a number of dangers.

DEVELOPMENT OF ONLINE SHOPPING

In India, the growth of online shopping has been sluggish and rather chaotic, and it hasn't recovered as much as it might have. The primary causes of this are the extremely low internet penetration rate and, more crucially, the lack of customer awareness. In addition, buyers are unwilling to assume the risk of buying a thing before personally inspecting it. India's population has traditionally had a traditional attitude to purchasing. Before acquiring anything, they want to handle, feel, and test items for their attributes. Early in 1995, when the Internet was first introduced in India, online shopping began.

Because of the auction website bazee.com, online purchasing gained popularity in 1999–2000. Jeff Bezos launched Amazon.com, an online bookshop that attracted attention right away for being the first to operate exclusively online. Several other physical libraries also created an online presence on the Internet following Amazon's success. The popularity of online shopping has grown quickly, leading to the launch of numerous new websites, including Amazon, Flipkart, Snapdeal, Gadgets Guru, Myntra, Craft Villa, and others. Indian consumers now have more options for online shopping thanks to several sites, including Rediff.com, Yahoo.com, and Indiatimes.com. Compared to traditional retail, online purchasing offers more convenience, speed, and affordability. Currently, internet booking is available for purchasing tickets for buses, trains, and airplanes. A website can be purchased more easily by logging in, as opposed to having to wait in line for your turn to purchase a ticket. Online shopping is preferred even though there may be a cost involved occasionally because it is much more comfortable. People prefer to purchase things online because it's convenient, even though it may cost more than the real ticket price. Take the example of booking movie tickets online.

BENEFITS OF ONLINE SHOPPING

Online shopping could be a fantastic choice for people looking to save money and increase their selection of purchases, according to Donna L. Montaldo (2020). When it comes to pricing, online businesses aggressively compete with physical storefronts.

By reading evaluations left by previous customers on price comparison websites, people can find the best online stores with the best brand image, which facilitates transactions. It offers the following benefits also:

Time and Money Saved, Services available around the clock, Comparing the product with other products, Numerous options, No annoyance Sales people, Clients may choose to shop in private, Discount coupons are available.

DIFFICULTIES CONSUMERS ENCOUNTER WHILE MAKING INTERNET PURCHASES

Order variant:

Even though internet purchasing has numerous advantages, there are drawbacks as well, and the surprise aspect is one of them. When making purchases online, consumers typically do so after viewing product photographs and specifications on the online store. However, frequently, the item they receive differs from what they initially saw on the website. If clients are placing orders from normally lesser-known online retailers whose legitimacy may be questioned, there may be some more shocks or surprises.

Delivery of product delay

Although it occurs very infrequently, there is still a potential that the item will be delivered later than expected and that their communication will be hindered. Order tracking is typically available to customers of online shops, though it's not always the case. The product may be delivered by the delivery person if the customers are not home. Delivery of the product will be rescheduled in this case. If this occurs more than three times, customers' orders will be returned to the vendor. From time to time, a product will become misplaced in order.

Issues in logistics

A sizable section of the Indian populace and rural cities, where most internet retailers do not transport goods, makes it impossible for them to make purchases online and store the goods in different places.

Problems in visibility

Due to screen size or resolution limitations, users can only see what fits on one webpage at a time; but, if they visit a nearby store, they will be able to view many more items at once.

Issues in the quality of goods

When customers purchase online, one of their most frequent grievances is that the product is of low quality. There is no assurance that buyers shopping online will receive high-quality products. Product reviews should not be the only source of information used by customers, as they are not reliable. A lot of websites only serve as the agent for the seller. Because of this, there is a significant chance that dishonest sellers would register on websites and offer to sell fake goods under the names of well-known companies. Because of the enormous amount of goods sold every day, internet retailers cannot inspect every single item that is provided. In certain situations, sellers may decline to replace a damaged item and give a refund. sites that offer fake products.

Poor network performance

Poor net quality can make it take longer for customers to browse and choose an item to buy. When they do decide to buy there are lots of struggles to place an order, and the speed is so slow that the payment gateways fail, making the entire experience awful.

Absence of product touch

Customers cannot truly engage in touch and feel shopping when they shop online. They are limited to believing what the vendor has posted on the internet in terms of photographs.

Dress fittings are not in size

While ordering online we cannot touch and feel the clothes. So there are problems with fittings. The size of the clothes doesn't suit the customers. Customers may get irritation due to this type of activity occurring in online shopping. This creates a problem with purchasing online. The product will be replaced or returned to its particular website. Sometimes the product can cancelled by the customers due to fit problems.

Problems in returns

When the customers don't like the goods they send them back to the shop and the return amount is also not added to the bank account or wallet. Sometimes, consumers won't purchase on websites. The shop member should bear the cost of the goods.

Fraudulent payments

Online payments are still not completely safe, even though they are becoming easier and more secure every day. When making online payments, there's a chance that your bank account or credit card information could be compromised. Debit and credit card fraud is also a possibility. Remember to keep certain things in mind when purchasing online, such as making sure the website's URL contains the words whenever you make a payment. To enter passwords, use simulated online consoles. Another extra security measure to prevent fake workouts is a one-time secret code. Finally, be certain that the computer you are using has an updated antivirus program that provides you with real-time online security. Frauds are rising on every platform.

Worries about security

The data of consumers are hacked by third parties like data theft, hacking, collecting data from searches, and following them in applications.
Lack of personal contact

During the time of network shopping, there is no direct contact between customers and sellers. If any issues occur, they cannot be resolved instantly, and is unable to identify the customer's inquiries.

Competition between sellers

It is challenging for businesses to classify themselves and cover the customers efficiently, it increases competition and dilutes the market.

PERCEIVED RISK

The word "perceived risk" refers to how people subjectively assess the potential downsides of a specific option or course of action, such as purchasing a product or service. It comprises risks associated with money, performance, safety, social contact, psychology, time, and convenience, among other factors. These perceived risks have an impact on customer behaviour, influencing decision-making and product selection. Customers weigh the obvious benefits of a product or service against any potential downsides or unknowns, considering factors such as product quality, dependability, safety, and cost-effectiveness.

OBJECTIVES OF THE STUDY

1. To aware of perceived risks associated in E-Commerce platforms.
2. To analyse the level of various risks associated and their influences.
3. To predict the ways to avoid the risks in E-Commerce platforms.
4. To offer suitable suggestions to improve the level of services by reducing risks.

SOURCES OF ANALYSIS

Primary Data

Primary data is collected through a questionnaire depending on the respondent's comfort.

Secondary Data

Secondary data are gathered from websites, journals, newspapers, reports, and other sources.

LITERATURE SURVEY

Even though the number of Internet users in Nigeria is increasing, a study revealed that buyers' perceptions of risks represent a significant obstacle to the expansion of online commerce. Nigeria's Lagos State was the location of this study. The goal of this study's research was to identify the different obstacles that customers mentioned facing when they shop online. The 262 respondents' responses to a questionnaire that they provided served as the basis for the study. Multiple regression analysis was used in this study to examine the hypothesis. The study's findings demonstrate how perceived product risk, perceived time risk, and perceived delivery risk harm online purchase intentions.

Tatiana Marceda Bach et.al (2020) have researched South Brazil's consumers. Examining the effects of different risks related to internet shopping on customer trust and intent to buy is the main objective of this research. The researcher used a survey for this investigation. The quantitative and qualitative approaches to the examination of primary data form the basis of this work. Finding the influence of factors is one of the study's goals. Akinbode Mosunmola (2019) Examines how perceived value proportions—such as hedonic and utilitarian value—affect attitudes, perceived risk, buy intention, and online buying trust. The research also elucidates the function of individual qualities such as masculinity/femininity, individualism/collectivism, and uncertainty avoidance, and their influence on perceived risk, intention to purchase online, and perceived value, or trust. In the end, the study finds that trust, perceived risk, and buy intention are significantly influenced by perceived value and individual qualities when it comes to online shopping.

Khalfan et. al (2019) examined the variables influencing Omani consumers' propensity to shop online, with a particular emphasis on business-to-consumer interactions. The four elements that were found as predictors of customers' intention to purchase online web trust, perceived risk, privacy protection, and user experience all contributed to the determination of these consumers' intentions.

Nawi (2019) This study employs a stimulus-organization-response (SOR) model to examine past trends and different risk factors that impact Malaysian consumers' online shopping decisions. In this study, 330 respondents from Malaysia had their data cross-sectionally evaluated. The research findings demonstrate that online buying behavior in Malaysia is influenced by after-sales, financial, psychological, and social risks.

Anam Bhatti et al (2019) studied online purchase intention while conducting research in Pakistan. The examination of this study demonstrates that Pakistanis' outlook.

Table 1. Occupation of the respondents

S.NO	OCCUPATION	NO OF RESPONDENTS	PERCENTAGE
1	Government employee	9	7.5
2	Private employee	36	30.0
3	Self-employed	15	12.5
4	Business	17	14.2
5	Others	43	35.8
	TOTAL	**120**	**100**

Source: Primary Data

Table 1 shows the respondents of occupation. 7.5 percent of the informants are Government employees 30 percent of the respondents are private employees, 12.5 percent of the respondents are self-employed, 14.2 percent of the respondents are business options, and 35.8 percent chose the others. The majority of the respondents are others.

Figure 1. Occupation of the respondents

OCCUPATION

- GOVERNMENT EMPLOYEE: 7.5
- PRIVATE EMPLOYEE: 30
- SELF-EMPLOYED: 12.5
- BUSINESS: 14.2
- OTHERS: 35.8

Table 2. Frequency of online shopping

S.NO	HOW FREQUENTLY DO YOU SHOP ONLINE	NO OF RESPONDENTS	PER CENT
1	Rarely	68	56.7
2	Monthly	42	35.0
3	Weekly	7	5.8
4	Daily	3	2.5
	TOTAL	120	100

Source: Primary Data

Table 2 shows that 56.7 percent of the respondents rarely shop online, 35 percent of the respondents are monthly, 5.8 percent are weekly shopping online, and the remaining 2.5 percent are daily shopping online.

Figure 2. Frequency of online shopping of the respondents

FREQUENCY OF ONLINE SHOPPING

- RARELY: 56.7
- MONTHLY: 35
- WEEKLY: 5.8
- DAILY: 2.5

Table 3. Types of goods preferences (multi responses)

S.NO	PARTICULARS	NO OF RESPONDENTS	PER CENT	RANK
1	Clothing	89	39.91	1
2	Books	22	9.86	4
3	Electronic goods	58	26.0	2
4	Home appliances	54	24.21	3
	TOTAL	223	100	

Source: Primary Data

The above table 3 shows the types of goods preferences. As follows: The first rank for clothing with 39.91 and the lowest rank was books with 9.86 of mean rank.

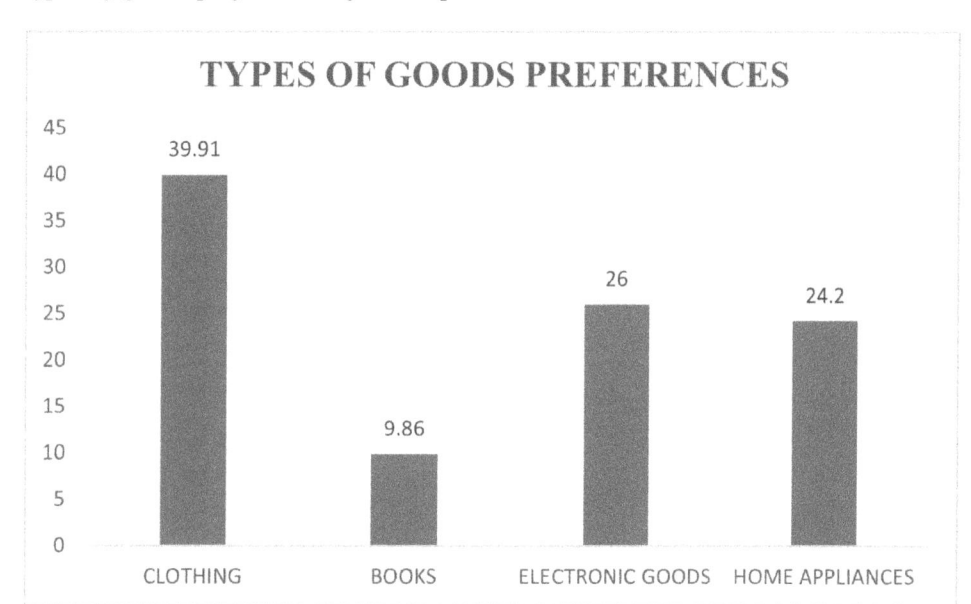

Figure 3. Types of goods preferences of the respondents

TYPES OF GOODS PREFERENCES

- CLOTHING: 39.91
- BOOKS: 9.86
- ELECTRONIC GOODS: 26
- HOME APPLIANCES: 24.2

Table 4. Preferences of payment option

S.NO	WHICH TYPE OF PAYMENT OPTION DO YOU PREFER MOST	NO OF RESPONDENTS	PER CENT
1	Credit card	8	6.7
2	Debit card	16	13.3
3	Bank transfer	15	12.5
4	Cash on delivery	81	67.5
	TOTAL	**120**	**100**

Source: Primary Data

From the table 4 shows payment options, 6.7 percent of the respondents chose the credit card option, 13.3 percent of the respondents chose a debit card, 12.5 percent of the respondents chose a bank transfer and the remaining of the remaining respondents 67.5 percent chose the cash-on-delivery option. The majority of the respondents chose cash on delivery.

Figure 4. Preferences of payment option of the respondents

PREFERENCES OF PAYMENT OPTIONS

- CREDIT CARD: 6.7
- DEBIT CARD: 13
- BANK TRANSFER: 12.5
- CASH ON DELIVERY: 67.5

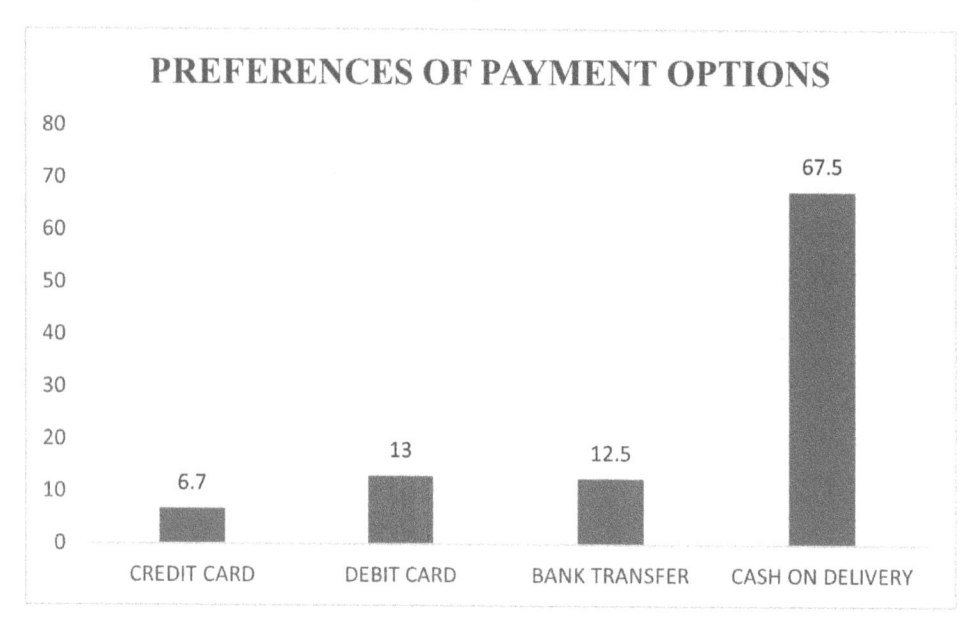

Table 5. Preferences of online shopping (multi responses)

S.NO	PARTICULARS	NO OF RESPONDENTS	PER CENT	RANK
1	Doorstep delivery and convenience	73	32.30	1
2	Low price and time-saving	62	27.43	2
3	Getting the latest products	44	19.46	4
4	Wide variety of brand choice	47	20.79	3
	TOTAL	226	100	

Source: Primary Data

Table 5 shows the preferences for online shopping. As follows: The first rank for doorstep delivery and conveniences with 32.30 and the lowest rank was getting the latest products with 19.46 of mean rank.

Figure 5. Preferences of online shopping of the respondents

PREFERENCES OF ONLINE SHOPPING

- DOORSTEP DELIVERY AND CONVENIENCES: 32.3
- LOW PRICE AND TIME SAVING: 27.43
- GETTING THE LATEST PRODUCTS: 19.46
- WIDE VARIETY OF BRAND CHOICES: 20.79

Table 6. Mean rank: product and performance risks

S.NO	STATEMENTS	N	MEAN	STANDARD DEVIATION	MEAN RANK	RANK
1	The product purchased may fail to perform as originally expected.	120	4.2250	0.76105	2.60	2
2	I have encountered difficulties during the checkout process (payment, order confirmation).	120	3.8167	1.13747	2.15	4
3	It is difficult to evaluate the quality of the product online.	120	4.2500	0.90051	2.67	1
4	The colour and size of the product ordered online differ when received.	120	4.2000	0.87544	2.58	3

Source: Primary Data

The above table shows the Mean rank for the product and performance risks. As follows: The first rank was 2.58 and the lower rank was 2.16 got by the respondents.

Table 7. Time and convenience risks

S.NO	STATEMENTS	N	MEAN	STANDARD DEVIATION	MEAN RANK	RANK
1	It may take a lot of time to place an order on the website, during network traffic.	120	3.8583	1.03140	2.42	3
2	Sometimes, delay in the delivery of the product.	120	3.9750	0.99968	2.60	2
3	I feel stressed when I can't find the product quickly on e-commerce platforms.	120	3.7833	1.08607	2.35	4
4	It may confuse when selecting a product with similar brands.	120	4.0250	0.94791	2.65	1

Source: Primary Data

The above table shows the Mean rank for the Time and convenience risks. As follows:
The first rank was 2.65 and the lower rank was 2.35 which was obtained by the respondents.

Table 8. ANOVA demographic profile of the respondents with delivery risks: age of the respondents with delivery risks

AGE	N	MEAN	STD DEVIATION	F	SIG
18-25 years	96	1.55	0.663	2.181	0.094
26-35 years	17	1.24	0.562		
36-45 years	5	1.00	0.000		
46-55 years	2	1.50	0.707		
TOTAL	120	1.48	0.648		

ANOVA DELIVERY RISKS	SUM OF SQUARES	DF	MEAN SQUARE
Between Groups	2.688	3	0.889
Within Groups	47.298	116	0.408
Total	49.967	119	

Source: Primary Data

H0: There is no significant association relationship between age of the respondents and delivery risks.

RESULT:

The ANOVA results indicated that a significant value is more than 0.05 (F=2.181, p>0.05). Hence null hypothesis is accepted.

Table 9. T-test gender with delivery risks

GENDER	N	MEAN	STD DEVIATION
Male	49	1.27	0.491
Female	71	1.63	0.702

T-Test Quality of Means			
GENDER	T	DF	SIG.
	-3.177	118	0.002

Source: Primary Data

H0: There is no significant association relationship between gender of the respondents and delivery risks.

RESULT:

The t-test value indicated that there is a significant difference between gender and delivery risks of e-commerce platforms (p<0.05). Hence the null hypothesis is rejected.

Table 10. Educational background with delivery risks

EDUCATIONAL BACKGROUND	N	MEAN	STD DEVIATION	F	SIG
UG	71	1.46	0.651	1.063	0.349
PG	46	1.54	0.657		
Diploma	3	1.00	0.000		
TOTAL	**120**	**1.48**	**0.648**		

ANOVA			
DELIVERY RISKS	SUM OF SQUARES	DF	MEAN SQUARE
Between Groups	0.862	3	0.446
Within Groups	49.075	117	0.419
Total	49.967	119	

Source: Primary Data

H0: There is no significant association relationship between educational background of the respondents and delivery risks.

RESULT:

The ANOVA results indicated that significant value is less than 0.05 (F=1.063, P<0.05). Hence null hypothesis is rejected.

Table 11. Occupation with delivery risks

EDUCATIONAL BACKGROUND	N	MEAN	STD DEVIATION	F	SIG
Government employee	9	1.22	0.441	1.255	0.292
Private employee	36	1.36	0.593		
Self-employed	15	1.47	0.640		
Business	17	1.53	0.717		
Others	43	1.63	0.691		
TOTAL	**120**	**1.48**	**0.648**		

ANOVA DELIVERY RISKS	SUM OF SQUARES	DF	MEAN SQUARE	
Between Groups	2.090	4	0.523	
Within Groups	47.876	115	0.416	
Total	49.967	119		

Source: Primary Data

H0: There is no significant association relationship between the occupation of the respondents and delivery risks.

RESULT:

The ANOVA results indicated that a significant value is less than 0.05 (F=1.255, p<0.05). Hence null hypothesis is rejected.

Table 12. Demographic profile with general myths about e-commerce platforms

AGE OF THE RESPONDENTS	GENERAL MYTHS			TOTAL
	1	2	3	
18-25 years	36	1	59	96
26-35 years	5	0	12	17
36-45 years	2	0	3	5
46-55 years	1	0	1	2
TOTAL	**44**	**1**	**75**	**120**

CHI-SQUARE TESTS	VALUES	DF	ASYMPTOTIC SIGNIFICANCE (2-SIDED)
Pearson Chi-square	0.874	6	0.990
Likelihood Ratio	1.074	6	0.983
Linear-by-Linear Association	0.005	1	0.983
N of Valid Cases	120		

H0: There is no significant association relationship between the age of the respondents with general myths about e-commerce platforms.

To test the existence of a negative hypothesis, Chi-square was used.
Degree of freedom - 6
Chi-square value – 0.990
The distribution is 95% significant level

RESULT:

The significance level is 95%, and the significance value is 0.990, which is higher than 0.05. Thus, the null hypothesis is accepted. There is no significant difference between the age of the respondents with general myths of e-commerce platforms.

Table 13. Occupation with general myths about e-commerce platforms

OCCUPATION	GENERAL MYTHS			TOTAL
	1	2	3	
Government employee	3	0	6	9
Private employee	18	0	18	36
Self-employed	5	0	10	15
Business	6	0	11	17
Others	12	1	30	43
TOTAL	44	1	75	120

CHI-SQUARE TESTS	VALUES	DF	ASYMPTOTIC SIGNIFICANCE (2-SIDED)
Pearson Chi-square	5.861	8	0.663
Likelihood Ratio	6.079	8	0.638
Linear-by-Linear Association	2.221	1	0.136
N of Valid Cases	120		

H0: There is no significant association relationship between the occupation of the respondents with general myths about e-commerce platforms.

To test the existence of a negative hypothesis, Chi-square was used.
Degree of freedom - 8
Chi-square value – 0.663
The distribution is 95% significant level

RESULT:

The significance level is 95%, and the significance value is 0.663, which is higher than 0.05. Thus, the null hypothesis is accepted. There is a significant difference between occupation and general myths of e-commerce platforms.

Table 14. Continuing online shopping as default mode

S.NO	CONTINUING ONLINE SHOPPING AS DEFAULT MODE	NO OF RESPONDENTS	PER CENT
1	Strongly Agree	5	4.2
2	Agree	7	5.8
3	Neutral	41	34.2
4	Disagree	46	38.3
5	Strongly disagree	21	17.5
	TOTAL	120	100

Source: Primary Data

The table shows continuing online shopping as the default mode, 4.2 percent of the respondents chose strongly agree, 5.8 percent of the respondents chose agree, 34.2 percent of the respondents chose neutral and 38.3 percent chose the disagree option, and the remaining respondents 17.5 percent chose strongly disagree. The majority of the respondents chose to disagree option.

Figure 6. Preferences of online shopping as default mode

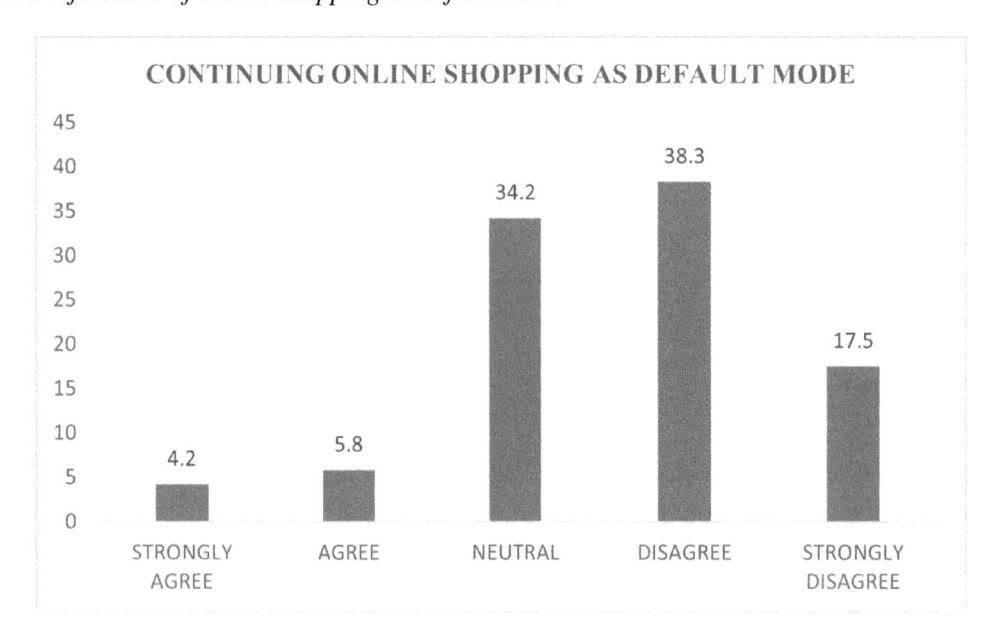

OUTCOME PREDICTION WITH AI MODELS

The same results were obtained when applied to the 3 models of Artificial intelligence, Support vector machine, Naïve Bayes and K-Means algorithm. Out of which SVM gives 98% accuracy, Naïve bayes gives 96% and K-Means with the accuracy result of 93%. Four different times the testing was done with splitting training and testing set as 60:40, 70:30, 80:20, 90:10 and the mean are being recorded which shows the same results. Chart 16 explains the results for various models.

Figure 7. models results comparison

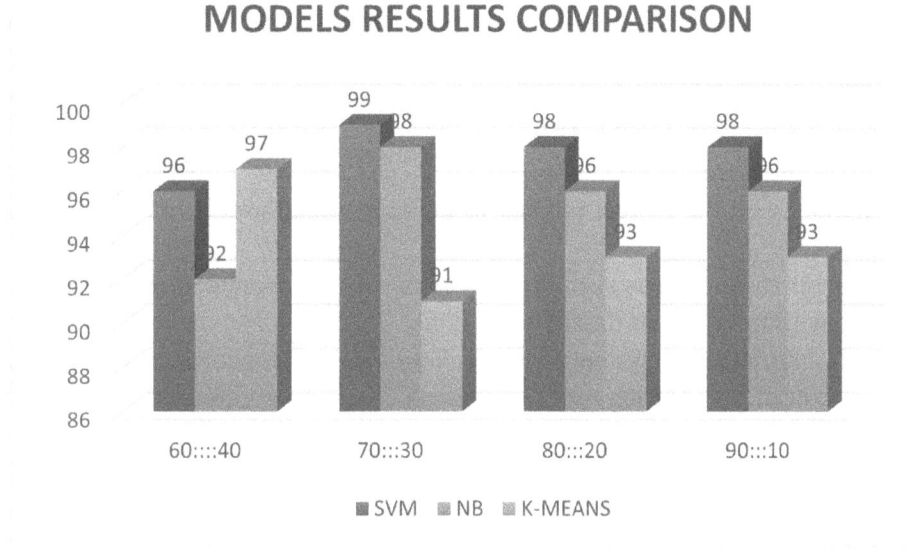

MODELS RESULTS COMPARISON

FINDINGS

1. The majority of the respondents are young people, between the age of 18 to 25.
2. It shows that 59% of respondents, were female as reported in the study.
3. It exhibits that 59% of respondents were UG.
4. It reveals that 35.8% of the respondents are others according to the survey.
5. It indicates that 33.07% of the respondents preferred Amazon.
6. It shows that 56.7% are rarely used e-commerce platforms.
7. It reveals that 39.9% were preferred clothing.
8. 67.5% of the respondents selected cash-on-delivery payment options.
9. Majority of the respondents 32.3% preferred doorstep delivery and conveniences
10. Most of the respondents agree product purchased failed to perform as originally expected.
11. Most of the users agreed that it is difficult to evaluate the quality of the product.
12. 38.8% of the respondents disagree about continuing online shopping as the default mode.

SUGGESTIONS

1. It is preferable to provide high-quality products for sale online.
2. Potential buyers should check the ratings of products and the photographs that other clients have provided of the items that they previously bought.

3. The consumers talk about their observations so that friends and family can gain from them in different ways.
4. The biggest concern for customers is security since online platforms can prevent identity theft, unsafe financial transactions, and fraudulent data by offering and upholding adequate security measures.
5. They should give proper details about the products.
6. To reduce the dangers, marketers need to take the appropriate precautions about credit and debit card security.
7. Increase website security from third parties.
8. Improve quality and send the correct product to the appropriate users with the new application development.
9. Educating customers about dangers such as phishing emails and fraudulent websites enables them to take proactive steps to safeguard themselves online.
10. Robust customer authentication systems, such as Two-Factor authentication (2FA) or biometric verification, are critical for ensuring user identity and eliminating unwanted account availability, hence improving security as a whole.

CONCLUSION

This study is about how people perceive risk when shopping online.

Online shopping is the world's biggest shopping system. People are busy with their work. They don't have time to visit the shop. They shop digitally. However, there are financial dangers linked with these difficulties. This study suggests that Internet marketers are capable of attracting young consumers by offering standardized and trendy products that are popular on the internet. Respondents with greater incomes tend to buy more online products due to lower product risk. This study found four characteristics of customers' perceived risk in internet purchases. These include monetary things, time/convenience, and delivery risks. According to this study, financial risk and product risks are greater than other types of risk.

The next most common risk in online shopping is time/convenience. Online shopping carries less product risk. In addition, the delivery risk is low. Male and female groups perceive risk differently.

REFERENCES

Bach, T. M.. (2020). Insights into shopping travel behavior: Latent classes about attitudes towards shopping. *European Transport Research Review*.

Bhatti, A.. (2019). Factors Influencing online shopping with special reference to Coimbatore District. *Journal of Information and Computational Science*.

Khalfan, H.. (2019). Exploring Key factors in online shopping with a hybrid model. *SpringerPlus*.

Mosunmola, A. (2019). E-Commerce and Consumer Protection in India: The Emerging Trend. *Journal of Business Ethics*.

Nawi, N.C. (2019) Customer Perception, Awareness and Satisfaction towards Online Shopping- A study concerning Chennai City.

Chapter 15
Please Don't Stop the Music!
Exploring the Factors Affecting Continuous Usage Intention in a Music Streaming Platform

Jean Paolo Gomez Lacap
City College of Angeles, Philippines

Jessalyn Alqueza
https://orcid.org/0000-0003-3671-4323
University of the Visayas, Philippines

Jebe Mag-usara
https://orcid.org/0009-0002-5913-9739
University of the Visayas, Philippines

Jessell Tandugon
https://orcid.org/0000-0001-7531-8767
University of the Visayas, Philippines

ABSTRACT

This chapter aims to examine the motivators of users and subscribers regarding their continuing intention to use music streaming platforms, including brand involvement, technology affinity, brand trust, and compatibility. Cross-sectional quantitative data was collected from 301 qualified respondents via an online survey questionnaire. Data was analyzed and validated using a partial least squares (PLS) structural equation model (SEM) to examine the relationship between the endogenous and exogenous variables. The proposed model posits that the level of user-brand involvement and technology affinity substantially impacts the intention to continue using the platform. Moreover, brand trust and compatibility play a crucial role in mediating the intention to continue using the music streaming service, while users' affinity towards technology and their involvement with the brand significantly and positively affect the users' intention to continue using the platform.

DOI: 10.4018/979-8-3693-9230-0.ch015

Copyright ©2025, IGI Global. Copying or distributing in print or electronic forms without written permission of IGI Global is prohibited.

INTRODUCTION

The rapid evolution of the digital landscape has revolutionized the music industry, with music streaming platforms emerging as a dominant force in reshaping global music consumption. These platforms have greatly influenced music consumption, exposing consumers to various artists, albums, and songs (Dinnissen & Bauer, 2023). Music streaming platforms have become a significant source of music consumption globally (Webster, 2021). Consumer choice for music consumption has quickly transitioned from cassette players, CD players, and radios to online platforms, significantly increasing the obsolescence of old audio resources (Chang et al., 2021). With the emergence of digital technology, music lovers have now upgraded their music preferences through music streaming platforms such as Spotify, Apple Music, YouTube, Amazon Prime, and Deezer (Maasø & Hagen, 2019). In recent years, music consumption in the Philippines is forecasted to reach 6.3 million in 2027 (Statista, 2023). As users gradually integrate various music streaming platforms in their regular lives, understanding the factors influencing continuous usage intention becomes crucial for industry stakeholders and researchers.

In a recent survey, music enthusiasts typically use Spotify to stream music in the Philippines (Statista Research Department, 2024). This music streaming platform has a significant presence in the said country, offering a wide range of tracks with low internet data requirements and low data costs (Ramos & Blind, 2020). However, creating and managing playlist content on these platforms does have a payment system, potentially affecting the user experience (Morris & Powers, 2015). Although Spotify requires subscription fees every month for a premium service (no advertisements), users can still stream using a free subscription. Despite the seemingly endless music options, it has been found that streaming services curate and manage content access differently (Morris &Powers, 2015).

It has been noted that free streaming services are only advantageous as alternative channels of music consumption that offer mobility (Aguiar, 2017). Contrary, Jingga et al. (2023) argued that music subscribers' intention to continue utilizing a streaming platform is affected by the platform's benefits, features, habits, and ease of use. Furthermore, Wulandari et al. (2019) contended that satisfaction and habit positively and significantly affect the continuance of intention to use music streaming apps. In addition, Tan and Limb (2022) stated that personalization, system quality, content sufficiency, and pricing plans positively affected user satisfaction and continuance intention to use music streaming platforms. Perceived benefits, usefulness, and enjoyment are key drivers in determining the continuance usage intention of music subscribers (Lim et al., 2022). However, the respondents of the mentioned literature are focused on YouTube Premium subscribers who primarily listen to music, limiting the findings' generalizability. Chin et al. (2022) argued that consumer attitudes, subjective norms, and price value play an important role in determining the intention to continue using the product or service.

Music streaming platforms have significantly increased in popularity, with Spotify becoming the most utilized. Nevertheless, prior studies (Morris & Powers, 2015; Wulandari et al., 2019; Jingga et al., 2023) have primarily focused on a limited number of variables, including user experience, benefits, features, habits, and ease of use, and satisfaction while neglecting other important factors affecting users' and subscribers' intentions to continue utilizing the platform. Ensuring the continuance engagement of the users with the music streaming platforms and identifying other factors such as technology affinity, user-brand involvement, compatibility, and brand trust are essential. Understanding these elements, music streaming platforms can provide more innovative methods and favorable user experiences that can positively affect the intention to continuously use the music streaming platform. Therefore, the present study aims to bridge the gap in the previous literature by examining these factors and their influence on users' continuance intention to use music streaming services. Assisting music streaming platforms with this concern can lead to improved user experiences and satisfied users who are more loyal to their platform.

LITERATURE REVIEW

Expectancy confirmation theory of Bhattacherjee (2001) served as the underpinning theory for this study. It suggests that consumers develop their expectations of the product or service concerning their previous experiences and level of satisfaction or dissatisfaction towards the product or service. Kim and Srivastava (2019) have also found that the theory is relevant for technology adoption, highlighting the importance of users' previous expectations and experiences in shaping their attitudes and intentions toward using the technology. The significance of the expectancy confirmation theory in cognizance of technology adoption highlights the crucial influence of users' past experiences and corresponding expectations in identifying intentions to utilize a certain technology (Kim & Srivastava, 2019).

Empirical research has shown that the expectancy confirmation theory is flexible, adaptable, and effective in varied technological concepts. It reveals cited factors influencing continued usage intention concerning brands (Lee et al., 2020). Park et al. (2022) also highlighted the theory's effectiveness in understanding user behavior toward using mobile applications. These inputs underscore the validity and reliability of the expectancy confirmation theory as a theoretical framework for examining users' behavior and usage patterns in digital platforms.

The integration of user-brand involvement, brand trust, technology affinity, and compatibility within the framework of expectancy confirmation theory provided an avenue for understanding users' continued usage intention within the lens of this study. The user brand involvement is characterized by the level of consumer connection with the digital platform in consonance with the expectancy confirmation theory, which emphasizes how experiences influence expectations (Smith et al., 2019). Brand trust is another variable that affects users' perception of reliability and performance, thus affecting satisfaction (Lee & Young, 2020). Technology affinity and compatibility, on the other hand, have also been explored within the context of the theory to examine the users' comfort and ease of use, which are very crucial in determining user satisfaction and continued usage (Wang & Liao, 2021).

The current study clears up the relationship between the perceptions, prior experiences, and continued usage intention of the users by examining these factors using the lens of the expectancy confirmation theory, enhancing the scholarly discussions and providing meaningful and practical insights for improving digital platform service's efficiency and strategies towards its users, thus providing a detailed exploration of the factors that navigate continuous usage intention among subscribers of a music streaming platform in the Philippines.

Brand Involvement

Brand involvement can be assessed through the connection of an individual with a particular brand (Zahri et al., 2023). It is the degree in which a user identifies value depending on their personality by subscribing to it (Rajendiran, 2020). It occurs when customers are firmly connected and engaged to a particular brand (Musiime & Mwaipopo, 2019). When consumers are involved and attached to a brand, they are likely to purchase that specific brand's products (Syahroni et al., 2022). In an interactive or online setting, an individual's involvement or level of interest and personal relevance with a brand helps build relationships, loyalty, and brand communities (Schivinski et al., 2016; Cruz et al., 2020). And when consumers are actively involved in a specific brand, they are more likely to make positive decisions about the brand (Triono et al., 2021).

Technology Affinity

An individual's inclination to actively interact with technological platforms or refrain from doing so is called technology affinity. It is the degree to which technology users engage themselves with the platform's innovations and features (Elif et al., 2023). When an individual interacts with a technology, he or she considers it as a personal attachment with the said technology (Franke et al., 2018). Thus, Henrich et al. (2022) defined technology affinity as the person's inclination or fondness towards certain types of technology, be it smartphones, smartwatches, or advanced software applications.

Brand Trust

A symbol of all intangible products is a brand. Brand trust implies the intention of consumers to believe, regardless of the risks they might face with the brand, that could lead to positive results (Susanto et al., 2022). Brand trust shapes consumer behavior and determines a company's success (Marmat, 2023). Conversely, trust in a specific brand comes from innovativeness, ethicality, empathy, expertise, and agility (Masriani & Sanica, 2022). Brand trust measures how much customers believe that a brand can do what it promises (Masriani & Sanica, 2022). According to Rudzewicz and Strychalska-Rudzewicz (2021), trust is an essential element of collaborative efforts that yields clear economic benefits for all involved parties. Expectations of the company's behavior and positive performance help consumers trust the brand (Ashley & Leonard, 2009). Moreover, brand trust, defined as consumers' confidence and reliance on a brand's reliability, integrity, and ability to deliver promised benefits, has been identified as a crucial determinant of consumers' behavioral intentions and loyalty (Delgado-Ballester & Munuera-Aleman, 2005; Yasin et al., 2019).

Compatibility

Compatibility in technology refers as to how well a technological platform aligns with the needs and preferences of users. It is the degree of compatibility with the users and extends to the device's operating system, software, and features (Bond-Smith et al., 2019). It is also the level where a potential user perceives that a certain technology could fit their needs (Omar et al., 2023). Falkowski-Gilski and Uhl (2020) contended that, in a music streaming platform, users' compatibility with technology can dictate continuous usage. Kim et al. (2015) further identified the compatibility factors with a technology which include users' intrinsic interest, curiosity, social norms, preferred lifestyle, and economic value.

Continuous Intention

Continuous intention is an individual's continued commitment to a certain product or service (Bhattacherjee, 2001; Saksriwattana, 2024). This arises when a consumer decides to utilize a certain technology after initial interaction with the basis of their early experience with the product and services (Franque et al., 2020; Sutenchan, 2024; Yosvijit & Nurittamont, 2021). It also refers to the underlying reasons that can explain an individual's continued consumption of the technology and is strongly associated with habit and satisfaction (Bölen, 2020; Oliveira et al., 2016).

Hypotheses Development

Brand involvement is an important factor in consumer-based brand equity, and brand trust is considered an important antecedent to brand equity. In the digital landscape, it is vital to establish and shape consumer behavior and brand outcomes. When individual involvement and engagement are high, the likelihood of trusting the brand is also high (Theodora et al., 2022). Highly involved customers are likely to be receptive to pertinent product information and increase consumers' brand trust through perceived greater satisfaction (Mruk-Tomczak et al., 2019).

In the study of Lacap and Tungcab (2020), they argued that when a brand engages a consumer, brand satisfaction triggers brand trust. Additionally, there are several factors that affect brand trust, which include customer engagement, attention, absorption, and enthusiasm (Kholis & Ratnawati, 2021). Brand trust and loyalty are the product of perceived brand interactivity and participation, which help influence customer brand engagement (Amoah et al., 2022; Samarah et al., 2022). Moreover, Zhang and Zhao (2023) provided a clear insight and direct connection between the relationship of user-brand involvement and the development of trust in a brand. Subsequently, Huaman-Ramirez and Merunka (2019) further emphasized that there is a strong link between brand trust and user-brand involvement. Their study delves into the complexity of brand experience, deviant service adaptation, and deviant use of resources, which collectively highlight the nuanced nature of how user-brand involvement influences the establishment of trust in a brand. Therefore, we hypothesized that:

H1. User-brand involvement has a significant influence on brand trust.

When a user is involved and engaged in a technological product, intention to continuously use the said product rises (Watulingas & Permana, 2020). Several studies have identified that user brand involvement has a significant influence on intent to continue using a brand or a platform (Kim et al., 2023; Lakkis & Issa, 2022; Sadyk & Islam, 2022). As noted by Kim and Park (2023) and Zhao et al. (2019), involvement of users in a brand app is largely to the platform's interactivity and qualities, which then lead to behavioral outcomes such as continuous usage intention. Tuti et.al. (2022) further contended that customer engagement positively affects customer satisfaction which signifies an influential role of involvement in molding consumer behaviors. Such engrossment contributes to the understanding that user-brand involvement is vital to continuous usage intention. Hence, we hypothesized that:

H2. User-brand involvement has a significant influence on continuous usage intention.

Continuously using a music streaming service can be strongly influenced by compatibility. Streaming music platforms such as Spotify and others allow users to stand out not only "on" but also "off" the platform through technological proficiency, playlist curation, and physical music consumption (Webster, 2020). When a music streaming platform is compatible with a wide range of devices and technologies, users with varying levels of technology affinity can access and enjoy the service seamlessly.

Song et al. (2022) underscored that users' affinity toward a technology platform influences their perceptions of compatibility, which shape their behaviors and preferences. Hewei and Lee (2022) further noted that users with high technology affinity are considered early adopters of latest technologies. There early adopters typically put prime importance on compatibility in decision-making process in choosing which of these new technologies to adopt. Yang and Tasi (2023) also claimed that the link between technology affinity and compatibility implies that users become more dependent on technological products, thus increasing their affinity with the brand. Moreover, Vogel (2019) contended that higher technology affinity leads to compatibility with technological products, such as streaming platforms. Therefore, we hypothesized that:

H3. Technology affinity has a significant influence on compatibility.

Several studies in this era of advancements show that technological affinity can determine emotional connection with technology, and is very important in forming the decision for continuous usage intention. For instance, according to Wong et al. (2020), a strong connection is formed when individuals find a functional technology compatible with its desired design and features, serves its purpose well, and provides satisfaction towards its users therefore creating technological affinity reinforcing continuous usage. This suggests that technology affinity positively affects the intention to use technology. Users develop an affinity for technology towards continuous usage when they perceive the technology as reliable and accessible for usage (Jin & Divitini, 2020). In fact, personality traits like openness to new experiences can influence an individual's affinity (Bhusal and Ghimire, 2022) where the perceived usefulness and access of the technology can influence the intention for continued usage of technology-based services and platforms (Do et al., 2020; Lakkis & Issa, 2022). These studies are imperative to the understanding why user's affinity for a technology can likely trigger further usage intention (Franke et al., 2019). Thus, we hypothesized that:

H4. Technology affinity has a significant influence on continuous usage intention.

Studies have noted that brand trust could significantly influence continuous usage intention like in the case of Gong et al. (2022) where they found that intention for further use is highly influenced by users' trust on the brand, highlighting that brand trust can reduce risk, encourage behaviors, and can promote long-term commitment. Putra et al. (2024) further argued that brand trust is a critical factor when it comes to consumers' behavioral intentions. For instance, Wang et al. (2021) revealed that service providers' consistency and platform quality have positively impacted customer trust leading to usage continuance. Moreover, a computer engineering simulation on e-government systems found that trust significantly affects user satisfaction which influences continuous usage intention of the users (Cho et al., 2019; Noori et al., 2022). From these arguments, it is hypothesized that when the brand of a technological product, such as music streaming platform, is trusted, users have the tendency to continuously use the said platform. Hence, we hypothesized that:

H5: Brand trust has a significant influence on continuous usage intention.

There are several precedent studies recognizing the role of compatibility of users on a particular technology and its impact on their continuous usage intention such as the studies of Bawack and Ahmad (2021) on agile information systems, Indriana et al. (2022) and Utomo on et al. (2022) on e-learning platform, Deng et al. (2023) on virtual brand communities, and Yen et al. (2018) on mobile social network service. Lee and Pan (2022) further claimed that compatibility promotes performance effort expectancy, expectancy, and positive emotion, thus fostering continuous usage intention. From these, we conjectured that indeed, users' compatibility with technology, such as music streaming platform, is an antecedent of continuous usage intention; therefore, we hypothesized that:

H6. Compatibility significantly influences continuous usage intention.

Several precedent studies have identified several factors that can influence brand trust, which include technological product's perceived benefits, perceived uncertainty, customer involvement, social media brand engagement, and peer-to-peer interaction (Samarah et al., 2022; Zhang & Zhao, 2023). Zhang and Zhao (2023), in particular, argued that user-brand involvement has an influence on brand trust. Moreover, Deng and Yuan (2020) pointed out that continuous usage intention of a technological product is attributed to high brand trust.

Morgan and Hunt (1994) argued that the strength of user brand involvement, which includes consumer's emotional connection and engagement with a brand, has significant influence on user's continuous usage intentions. Additionally, Smith et al. (2019) contended that brand trust plays a vital role in mediating the relationship of user engagement with a brand's online community and their intention to continue using the products or service. Similarly, Zhang et al. (2022) maintained that in the context of social media, brand trust mediates the link between user brand interactions and user's continuous usage intention. These findings indicate that brand trust has the potential to indirectly affect the relationship between involvement of a user toward a brand and his/her continuous usage intention. Therefore, we hypothesized:

H7: Brand trust has a mediating influence on the link between user-brand involvement and continuous usage intention.

Users with a higher inclination towards technology can augment compatibility with technological systems as individuals with greater affinity for technology tend to engage actively rather than avoid intense interaction (Wessel et al., 2019). This inclination towards compatibility highly influences users' intentions to use their phones continuously. In addition, Jin and Divitini (2020) asserted that student's perceived ease of use is enormously influenced by compatibility with technology and self-efficacy that leads to further increase their intention to continue using the e-learning platforms. Likewise, in food delivery applications (FDAs), continuous usage of the platforms is highly influenced by the users' perceived usefulness of the application mediated by compatibility (Rabaa'I and Almaati, 2021). Moreover, in the context of streaming music, Yeoh et al. (2022) contended that compatibility between affinity for technology and the streaming platform along with perceived usefulness and ease of use can play a significant role in shaping users' continuous usage intentions. From these, we assert that technology affinity is an antecedent of compatibility, which then leads to continuous usage intention in a music streaming platform. Hence, we posited that:

H8: Compatibility has a mediating influence on the link between technology affinity and continuous usage intention.

The conceptual framework was proposed after establishing the hypothesized relationships. The independent, mediating, and dependent variables research framework was based on formulating the hypotheses. Figure 1 presents the mediating variables as brand trust and compatibility, while the independent and dependent variables are user-brand involvement, technology affinity, and continuous usage intention.

Figure 1. Proposed conceptual model

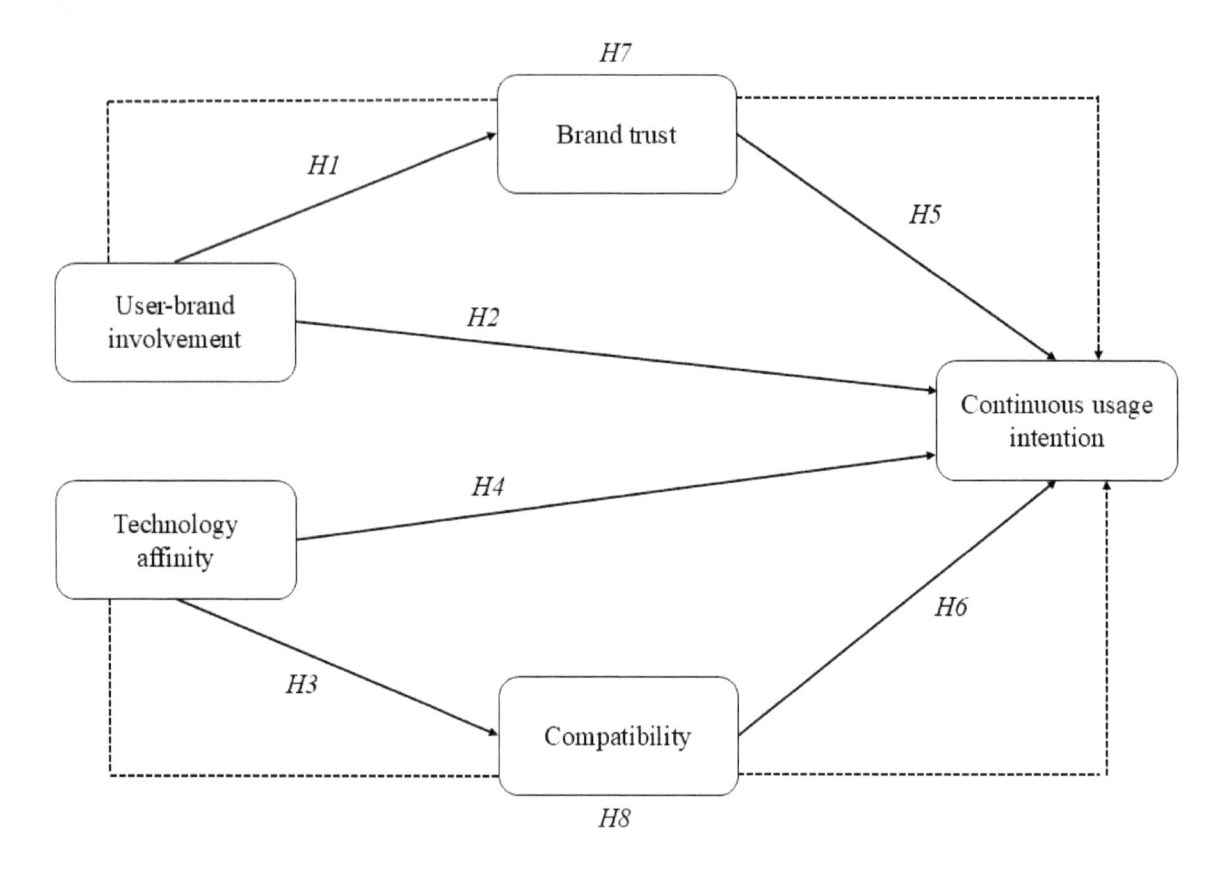

METHODS

Respondents

The study participants are Spotify users and subscribers in the Philippines. To be eligible for inclusion in this study, the following criteria were established: (1) respondents must be of legal age (at least 18 years old); and (2) must be a current user and subscriber of the said music streaming platform.

The participants were recruited through purposive sampling technique, and data were collected using an online questionnaire. The survey link was posted in various social media platforms. Data collection commenced on February 18, 2024 and ended on March 31, 2024.

The minimum sample size was calculated using G*Power. With an effect size of 15%, statistical power of 95%, and 4 predictors, the recommended minimum sample size was 129. Out of 351 collected responses, 301 were considered valid, more than the estimated minimum sample size.

Research Instrument

A survey questionnaire was used to gather responses from the participants. It is composed of the latent constructs and their corresponding items. All items for each latent construct were taken from several sources. Technology affinity (3 items), compatibility (3 items), and continuous usage intention (3 items) were adapted from the study of Yang and Tasi (2023). The original items were in the milieu of podcast; thus, we refined the items and contextualized them in music streaming platform setting. On the other hand, brand trust (3 items) and user-brand involvement (5 items) were adopted from the study of Theadora et al. (2022). All constructs were measured using a five-point Likert scale where 5 indicates "Strongly agree" and 1 "Strongly disagree."

Data Analysis

The present study employed a predictive research design to examine the relationship of the endogenous variables – technology affinity, user-brand involvement, compatibility, brand trust, and continuous usage intention as the exogenous variable in the study. Predictive design is an approach that entails evaluating variables at a specific moment to anticipate later-assessed occurrences. The structural model parameters were estimated using WarpPLS 8.0 software, which applies partial least squares structural modeling (PLS-SEM). The PLS-SEM enables simultaneous analysis of multiple correlations and assesses the reliability and validity of the constructs (Hair et al., 2017).

The utilization of partial least squares structural equation modeling is essential for both predictive and theoretical research as it can answer the highest possible degree of deviation, and it has been validated to be effective in evaluating multivariate non-normal data (Hair et al., 2018).

RESULTS

The current undertaking utilized PLS-SEM to examine the hypothesized relationships. PLS-SEM follows a two-phase method – outer model assessment (reliability and validity of the latent constructs) and inner model evaluation (hypothesis testing).

Outer Model Assessment

Table 1 presents the results of internal consistency (reliability) and convergent validity tests. Internal consistency test requires a composite reliability (CR) of at least 0.70 (Fornell & Larcker, 1981). On the other hand, convergent validity necessitates item loadings and average variance extracted (AVE) of at least 0.5 and p-values equal to or less than 0.05 (Amora, 2021). Based on the findings, all latent constructs – technology affinity, compatibility, brand trust, user-brand involvement, and continuous usage intention passed all the requirements for internal consistency and convergent validity.

Table 1. Convergent validity and reliability measures

Reflective latent construct	Item	Item loading
Technology affinity: AVE = 0.799; CR = 0.923		
	TA1	0.901
	TA2	0.899
	TA3	0.881
Compatibility: AVE = 0.922; CR = 0.972		
	CO1	0.952
	CO2	0.974
	CO3	0.954
Brand trust: AVE = 0.842; CR = 0.941		
	BT1	0.891
	BT2	0.951
	BT3	0.910
User-brand involvement: AVE = 0.866; CR = 0.970		
	UB1	0.906
	UB2	0.938
	UB3	0.952
	UB4	0.944
	UB5	0.914
Continuous usage intention: AVE = 0.859; CR = 0.948		
	CU1	0.891
	CU2	0.939
	CU3	0.949

All item loadings are significant (p < 0.001). AVE= average variance extracted; CR= composite reliability.

Table 2 shows the results of discriminant validity test using heterotrait-monotrait ratio of correlations or simply HTMT criterion. Henseler et al. (2015) require that the HTMT ratios must be at most 0.9 to establish convergent validity of the latent constructs. Based on the findings, all latent constructs used in the study passed this condition.

Table 2. Discriminant validity

	TA	CO	BT	UB	CU
TA					
CO	0.891				
BT	0.837	0.856			
UB	0.766	0.837	0.867		
CU	0.862	0.847	0.890	0.885	

TA-technology affinity; CO-compatibility; BT-brand trust; UB-user brand involvement, CU-continuous usage intention.

Inner Model Evaluation

The inner model evaluation includes the assessment of the hypothesized relationships in terms of beta coefficients, p-values, standard error, and effect sizes. Figure 2 shows that structural model with parameter estimates while Table 3 presents direct and indirect effects of the structural model.

Figure 2. The structural model

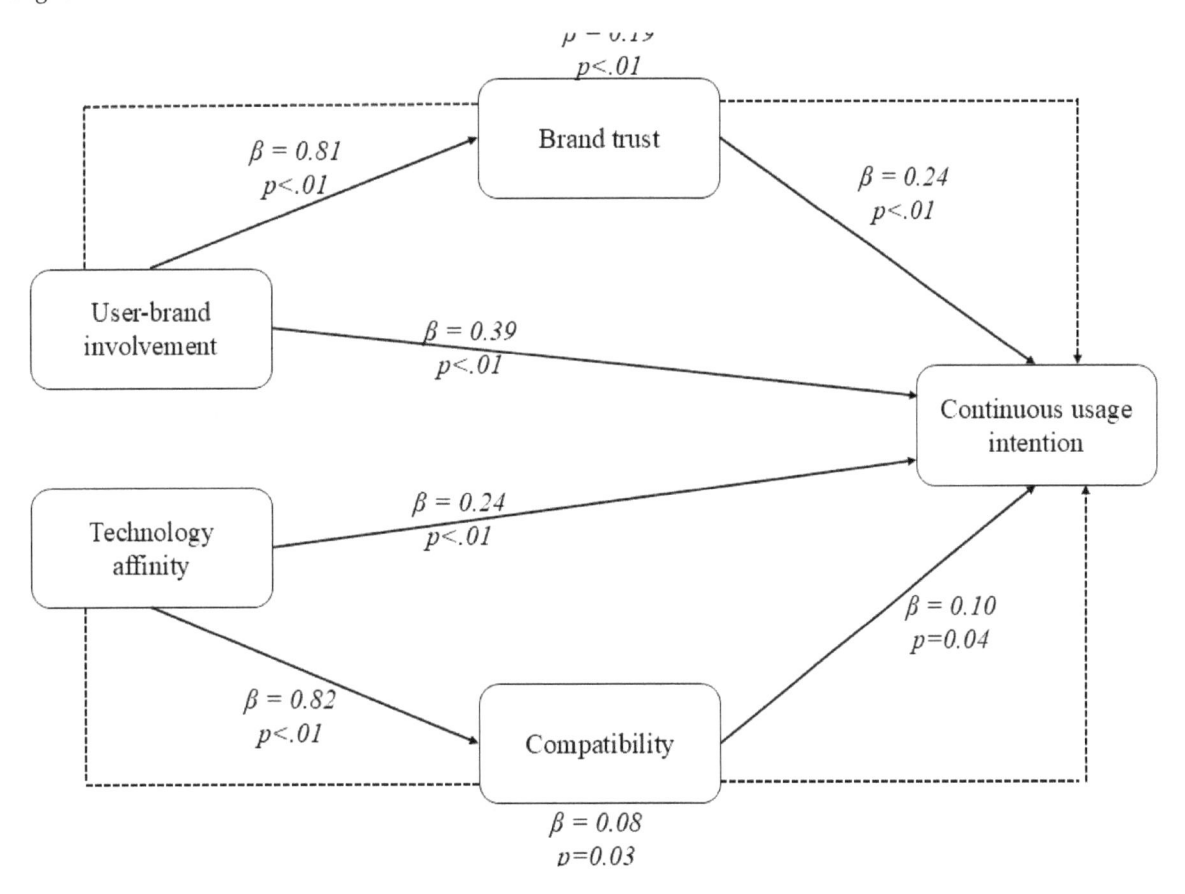

$\beta = 0.19$
$p<.01$

$\beta = 0.81$
$p<.01$

Brand trust

$\beta = 0.24$
$p<.01$

User-brand involvement

$\beta = 0.39$
$p<.01$

Continuous usage intention

Technology affinity

$\beta = 0.24$
$p<.01$

$\beta = 0.10$
$p=0.04$

$\beta = 0.82$
$p<.01$

Compatibility

$\beta = 0.08$
$p=0.03$

The results revealed that user-brand involvement has a significant and direct influence on brand trust ($\beta = 0.812$, $p < 0.001$, $f^2 = 0.660$) and on continuous usage intention ($\beta = 0.393$, $p < 0.001$, $f2 = 0.327$), with large and medium effect sizes, respectively. Moreover, technology affinity was found to have a significant and direct effect on compatibility ($\beta = 0.819$, $p < 0.001$, $f^2 = 0.671$) and on continuous usage intention ($\beta = 0.243$, $p < 0.001$, $f^2 = 0.188$), with effect sizes of large and medium, respectively. Therefore, H1 to H4 are supported.

Data analysis further showed that brand trust ($\beta = 0.235$, $p < 0.001$, $f^2 = 0.191$) and compatibility ($\beta = 0.097$, $p = 0.045$, $f^2 = 0.077$) have significant effects on continuous usage intention with effect sizes ranging from small to medium. Thus, H5 and H6 are both supported.

Moreover, brand trust was found to mediate the link between user brand involvement and continuous usage intention (β = 0.191, p < 0.001, f² = 0.159) with a medium size of effect. On the other hand, compatibility showed a mediating effect on the relationship between technology affinity and continuous usage intention (β = 0.079, p = 0.025, f² = 0.061) with a small effect size. Hence, H7 and H9 are also supported.

Table 3. Direct and mediating effects

Hypothesis	β	p	SE	f²	Decision
Direct effects					
H1. UB → BT	0.812	<0.001	0.051	0.660	S
H2. UB → CU	0.393	<0.001	0.054	0.327	S
H3. TA → CO	0.819	<0.001	0.051	0.671	S
H4. TA → CU	0.243	<0.001	0.055	0.188	S
H5. BT → CU	0.235	<0.001	0.056	0.191	S
H6. CO → CU	0.097	0.045	0.057	0.077	S
Mediating effects					
H7. UB → BT → CU	0.191	<0.001	0.040	0.159	S
H8. TA → CO → CU	0.079	0.025	0.040	0.061	S

TA-technology affinity; CO-compatibility; BT-brand trust; UB-user brand involvement; CU-continuous usage intention. S-supported. Effect sizes evaluation (Cohen, 1988): 0.02 – small; 0.15 – medium; 0.35 – large.

DISCUSSION

Analysis of the data showed that user brand involvement largely contributes to the formation of brand trust and continuous usage intention among music streaming users. This finding indicates that the connection and engagement in a music streaming platform are vital factors on why users establish their trust and continuous commitment to a music streaming platform. Zhang and Zhao (2023) further concurred that involvement of a user in a brand foster brand trust. Prior studies reaffirmed the significance of user-brand involvement in shaping continuous usage intention (Kim et al., 2023; Lakkis & Issa, 2022; Sadyk & Islam, 2022), highlighting its crucial impact on driving sustained commitment of users in a technology-based platform.

Moreover, technology affinity was found to be an antecedent of compatibility and continuous usage intention of a music streaming platform. The level of inclination and interaction of a user on a streaming platform's features leads to alignment with needs and preferences of an individual, and continuous use of the said platform. Therefore, when technology affinity is evident, compatibility of the users with the technology and consistent utilization of a music streaming platform become apparent. The significant relationship between the compatibility and technology affinity is consistent with the studies of Ozturk et al. (2017) and Hewei and Lee (2022). Moreover, Lakkis and Issa (2022) and Song et al. (2022) also argued that technology affinity significantly influences the continuous usage intention.

The present study further revealed that brand trust and compatibility are precursors of continuous usage intention of a music streaming platform. These findings signify that, when users believe that a specific brand will deliver its promises and perceive that a technology could fit their preferences and needs, the propensity to persistently use a music streaming platform increases. Cho et al. (2019) further indicated that laying the foundation of trust in the users can influence users' decision and willingness to keep on using a service. This establishes the importance of brand trust as it plays a role in enhancing continued usage intention (Smith et al., 2019; Wang & Kim, 2022). In the same way, compatibility has played a significant role in the commitment of users in utilizing the platform and continued usage intention (Jia et al., 2021).

It was also revealed that brand trust has an indirect effect on the link between user brand involvement and continuous usage intention. Additionally, compatibility was found to indirectly influence the relationship between technology affinity and continuous usage intention. These results suggest that involvement of a user in a brand and his or her technology affinity lead to augmented brand trust and compatibility, which then translate to a rise in intention to use a music streaming platform. The exposure of users in the use of a music streaming platform, and emotional connection and engagement built on the said platform and its brand itself are said to influence continuous usage intention (Morgan & Hunt, 2021). Smith et al. (2019) and Zhang et al. (2022) further emphasized that brand trust is a critical factor when it comes to the relationship of brand involvement and continuous usage intention. Furthermore, Wessel et al. (2019) also argued that users' technological inclination augments user-technology compatibility resulting to continuous usage of a technological product or service (Jin & Divitni, 2020). Yeoh et al. (2022) pointed out as well that, in the context of streaming platforms, compatibility is a critical factor when it comes to the relationship between technology affinity and continuous usage.

MANAGERIAL IMPLICATIONS IN THE SOUTH EAST ASIAN CONTEXT

The present study highlights that user brand involvement and technology affinity are pivotal factors in augmenting users' continuous usage intention in the context of music streaming. When subscribers are actively engaged with a music streaming platform brand, they develop a deeper emotional connection, which enhances their satisfaction and loyalty. This engagement goes beyond mere usage; it encompasses users' interactions with the platform, participation in community activities, and personalization of their experience. Such involvement fosters a sense of belonging and identity with the music streaming platform brand, making users more likely to continue using the service regularly.

Technology affinity, or users' comfort and interest in using technology, further supports user brand involvement by making interactions with the music streaming platform seamless and enjoyable. Users who are technologically inclined tend to explore and utilize the full range of features offered by the music streaming service, thereby deriving greater value from it. This affinity not only enhances users' experience but also encourages them to remain engaged over the long term. Music streaming platforms that are user-friendly and continuously innovate to align with technological advancements are more likely to retain these tech-savvy users, thereby sustaining their continuous usage intention.

Indirectly, brand trust and compatibility play significant roles in improving continuous usage of music streaming platforms. Trust in the music streaming platform reassures users of its reliability, security, and value, which is crucial in an era where digital privacy concerns are paramount. A trusted brand is perceived as more dependable, encouraging users to invest time and resources into the service without fear of disappointment or security breaches. Moreover, compatibility ensures that the platform meets the diverse needs and preferences of its users, from device compatibility to content variety. When users feel that the music streaming platform is tailored to their specific requirements, they are more likely to remain loyal and engaged.

Therefore, brand involvement, technology affinity, brand trust, and compatibility create a holistic user experience that promotes sustained usage and long-term commitment to the music streaming service. By focusing on user brand involvement and fostering technology affinity, music streaming platforms can enhance user satisfaction and loyalty. Meanwhile, ensuring high levels of brand trust and compatibility can address users' indirect needs, providing a comprehensive approach to maintaining continuous usage intention. This integrated strategy not only supports the immediate goals of retention of music streaming platform subscribers but also contributes to the long-term success and growth of music streaming platforms in a competitive digital landscape.

THEORETICAL IMPLICATIONS

At the theoretical level, the present study highlights that the influence of user brand involvement, technology affinity, brand trust, and compatibility on continuous usage intention of a music streaming platform can be effectively understood through expectancy confirmation theory (ECT). This theory suggests that users' continued engagement with a platform is driven by the confirmation of their initial expectations and the resulting satisfaction. High user brand involvement and technology affinity in a music streaming platform raise users' expectations, which, when met, leads to increased satisfaction and reinforces continued usage. Brand trust ensures that users feel secure and confident in the platform's reliability, while compatibility ensures the platform meets users' specific needs and preferences. When these expectations are confirmed, users experience greater satisfaction, thereby strengthening their intention to continue using the music streaming service. This underscores the importance of aligning platform features and brand strategies with user expectations to foster long-term engagement and loyalty.

LIMITATIONS AND FUTURE RESEARCH DIRECTIONS

The present study offers a significant insight into the predictors influencing users' continuous usage intention to utilize music streaming platforms in the Philippines. However, it also acknowledges several limitations. The study focused on Spotify users, potentially neglecting user behavior and preference differences among accessible music streaming platforms. The study's scope was also limited as respondents were solely obtained from the Philippines.

Given the limitations cited, future research could broaden the scope beyond Spotify users to encompass other popular platforms like YouTube Music or Apple Music. This would allow comparative analysis and a more comprehensive understanding of user behavior across other platforms. Furthermore, future researchers could conduct similar research in non-Asian countries to better understand the determinants influencing individuals' intentions to use music streaming platforms consistently. Moreover, scholars can further examine emerging trends, such as social features or immersive audio experiences, which could deepen understanding of user behavior.

REFERENCES

Aguiar, L. (2017). Let the music play? Free streaming and its effects on digital music consumption. *Information Economics and Policy*, pp. *41*, 1–14. https://doi.org/DOI: 10.1016/j.infoecopol.2017.06.002

Amoah, J., Jibril, A., Egala, S., & Keelson, S. (2022). Online brand community and consumer brand trust: Analysis from Czech millennials. *Cogent Business & Management*, 9(1), 2149152. DOI: 10.1080/23311975.2022.2149152

Amora, J. T. (2021). Convergent validity assessment in PLS-SEM: A loadings-driven approach. *Data Analysis Perspectives Journal*, 2(3), 1–6.

Ashley, C., & Leonard, H. (2009). Betrayed by the buzz? Covert content and consumer–brand relationships. *Journal of Public Policy & Marketing*, 28(2), 212–220. DOI: 10.1509/jppm.28.2.212

Bawack, R. E., & Ahmad, M. O. (2021). Understanding business analytics continuance in agile information system development projects: An expectation-confirmation perspective. *Information Technology & People*, 34(6), 1551–1569. Advance online publication. DOI: 10.1108/ITP-10-2020-0681

Bhattacherjee, A. (2001). Understanding information systems continuance: An expectation-confirmation model. *Management Information Systems Quarterly*, 25(3), 351–370. DOI: 10.2307/3250921

Bhusal, A., & Ghimire, S. (2022). Impact of Information and Communication Technology on Individual Well-being. https://arxiv.org/pdf/2202.00006

Bölen, M. C. (2020). Exploring the determinants of users' continuance intention in smartwatches. *Technology in Society*, 60, 101209. Advance online publication. DOI: 10.1016/j.techsoc.2019.101209

Bond-Smith, S. (2019). The impact of compatibility on innovation in markets with network effects. *Economics of Innovation and New Technology*, 28(8), 816–840. DOI: 10.1080/10438599.2018.1563936

Chang, V., Yang, Y., Xu, Q. A., & Xiong, C. (2021). Factors influencing consumer intention to subscribe to the premium music streaming services in China. *Journal of Global Information Management*, 29(6), 1–25. DOI: 10.4018/JGIM.20211101.oa17

Chin, P. N., Yeoh, S. Y., & Yuntavid, X. J. P. (2022). Examining the continuous usage intention and behaviours of music streaming subscribers. *International Journal of Electronic Business*, 17(2), 1. DOI: 10.1504/IJEB.2022.121992

Cho, Y., Kim, D. S., Phuong, H. T., & Gim, G. (2019). A study on the Factors Affecting Continuous Usage Intention of Computer Aided Engineering (CAE) Software. *International Journal of Software Innovation*, 10(1), 1–13. Advance online publication. DOI: 10.4018/IJSI.297508

Cruz, R. E., Leonhardt, J. M., & Krey, N. (2020). Involvement and brand engagement outcomes in Facebook brand posts: A gender twist: An abstract. *Developments in Marketing Science:Proceedings of the Academy of Marketing Science*, 177–178. https://doi.org/DOI: 10.1007/978-3-030-39165-2_79

Delgado-Ballester, E., & Luis Munuera-Alemán, J. (2001). Brand trust in the context of consumer loyalty. *European Journal of Marketing*, 35(11/12), 1238–1258. DOI: 10.1108/EUM0000000006475

Deng, L., Li, D., & Chen, J. (2023). Compatibility as a prerequisite: Research on the factors influencing the continuous use intention of in-vehicle games based on diffusion of innovations theory. *SAGE Open*, 13(4), 21582440231217909. Advance online publication. DOI: 10.1177/21582440231217909

Deng, X., & Yuan, L. (2020). Integrating technology acceptance model with social capital theory to promote passive users' continuance intention toward virtual brand communities. *IEEE Access : Practical Innovations, Open Solutions*, 8, 73061–73070. DOI: 10.1109/ACCESS.2020.2987803

Dinnissen, K., & Bauer, C. (2023). Amplifying artists' voices: Item provider perspectives on influence and fairness of music streaming platforms. *InProceedings of the 31st ACM Conference on User Modeling, Adaptation and Personalization*. http://dx.doi.org/DOI: 10.1145/3565472.3592960

Do, B.-R., Dadvari, A., & Moslehpour, M. (2020). Exploring the mediation effect of social media acceptance on the relationship between entrepreneurial personality and entrepreneurial intention. *Management Science Letters*, 10, 3801–3810. DOI: 10.5267/j.msl.2020.7.031

Elif Kübra, D., Sait, Ç., & Tarık, K. (2023). Adaptation of Affinity for Technology Interaction Scale to Turkish Culture and Evaluation of Measurement Invariance: ATI-T. *International Journal of Human-Computer Interaction*, •••, 1–11. DOI: 10.1080/10447318.2023.2202551

Falkowski-Gilski, P., & Uhl, T. (2020). Current trends in consumption of multimedia content using online streaming platforms: A user-centric survey. *Computer Science Review*, 37, 100268. DOI: 10.1016/j.cosrev.2020.100268

Franke, N., Keinz, P., & Steger, C. J. (2019). Testing the value of customization: When do customers really prefer products tailored to their preferences? *Journal of Marketing*, 83(1), 95–112. DOI: 10.1177/0022242918808270

Franke, T., Attig, C., & Wessel, D. (2018). A personal resource for technology interaction: Development and validation of the affinity for technology interaction (ATI) scale. *International Journal of Human-Computer Interaction*, 35(6), 456–467. DOI: 10.1080/10447318.2018.1456150

Franque, F. B., Oliveira, T., Tam, C., & Santini, F. D. O. (2020). A meta-analysis of the quantitative studies in continuance intention to use an information system. *Internet Research*, 31(1), 123–158. DOI: 10.1108/INTR-03-2019-0103

Gong, J., Said, F., Ting, H., Firdaus, A., Aksar, I. A., & Xu, J. (2022). Do privacy stress and brand trust still matter? Implications on continuous online purchasing intention in China. *Current Psychology (New Brunswick, N.J.)*, 42(18), 15515–15527. DOI: 10.1007/s12144-022-02857-x PMID: 35221631

Hair, J., Hollingsworth, C. L., Randolph, A. B., & Chong, A. Y. L. (2017). An updated and expanded assessment of PLS-SEM in information systems research. *Industrial Management & Data Systems*, 117(3), 442–458. DOI: 10.1108/IMDS-04-2016-0130

Hair, J. F., Sarstedt, M., Ringle, C. M., & Gudergan, S. (2018). Advanced Issues in Partial Least Squares Structural Equation Modeling. https://doi.org/DOI: 10.3926/oss.37

Henrich, M., Kleespies, M. W., Dierkes, P. W., & Formella-Zimmermann, S. (2022). Inclusion of technology affinity in self scale–Development and evaluation of a single item measurement instrument for technology affinity. *Frontiers in Education*, 7, 970212. Advance online publication. DOI: 10.3389/feduc.2022.970212

Henseler, J., Ringle, C. M., & Sarstedt, M. (2015). A new criterion for assessing discriminant validity in variance-based structural equation modeling. *Journal of the Academy of Marketing Science*, 43(1), 115–135. DOI: 10.1007/s11747-014-0403-8

Hewei, Z., & Lee, C. S. (2022). Factors affecting continuous purchase intention of fashion products on social e-commerce: SOR model and the mediating effect. *Entertainment Computing*, 41, 100474. DOI: 10.1016/j.entcom.2021.100474

Huaman-Ramirez, R., & Merunka, D. (2019). Brand experience effects on brand attachment: The role of brand trust, age, and income. *European Business Review*, 31(5), 610–645. DOI: 10.1108/EBR-02-2017-0039

Indriana, A. D., & Othman, N. (2022). The continuance intention of e-learning: The role of compatibility and self-efficacy technology adoption. *2022 10th International Conference on Cyber and IT Service Management (CITSM)*. https://doi.org/DOI: 10.1109/CITSM56380.2022.9935868

Jin, F., & Divitini, M. (2020). Affinity for Technology and Teenagers' Learning Intentions. *ACM Conference on International Computing Education Research (ICER '20)*. https://doi.org/DOI: 10.1145/3372782.3406269

Jingga, F., Fitria, Z. H., Alfi, J., & Kusumajati, A. D. (2023). Factors influenced user in using streaming music applications using the TAM method: Technology acceptance model. *2023 4th International Conference on Innovative Trends in Information Technology (ICITIIT)*, 1–6. https://doi.org/DOI: 10.1109/ICITIIT57246.2023.10068571

Kholis, N., & Ratnawati, A. (2021). The effects of customer engagement and brand trust on brand loyalty: A case study of BPJS healthcare participants in Indonesia. *The Journal of Asian Finance. Economics and Business*, 8(11), 317–324. DOI: 10.13106/jafeb.2021.vol8.no11.0317

Kim, H. W., & Srivastava, J. (2019). Impact of prior experience on expectations, satisfaction, and continuance intention in technology-supported services. *Journal of Computer Information Systems*, 59(2), 124–133. DOI: 10.1145/1282100.1282157

Kim, J. H., & Park, M. H. (2023). Factors Influencing the Continuous Usage Intention of Online Health Community Users. *Korean Society of Nursing Research*, 7(1), 13–22. DOI: 10.34089/jknr.2023.7.1.13

Kim, Y.-H., Lee, H.-J., & Lee, J.-S. (2023). The structural relationship among gamification elements in sport brand apps, brand experience, brand engagement and continuous use intention. *Han'gug Seu'pocheu San'eob Gyeong'yeong Haghoeji*, 28(3), 36–55. DOI: 10.31308/KSSM.28.3.36

Lacap, J. P. G., & Tungcab, A. P. (2020). The influence of brand experience on brand loyalty among mobile phone users in Pampanga, Philippines: A mediation analysis. *Asia-Pacific Social Science Review*, 20(3), 17–31. DOI: 10.59588/2350-8329.1313

Lakkis, H., & Issa, H. (2022). Continuous usage intention toward interactive mixed reality technologies. *International Journal of Technology and Human Interaction*, 18(1), 1–22. Advance online publication. DOI: 10.4018/IJTHI.299068

Lee, C., & Pan, L.-Y. (2022). Smile to pay: Predicting continuous usage intention toward contactless payment services in the post-COVID-19 era. *International Journal of Bank Marketing*, 42(2), 312–332. DOI: 10.1108/IJBM-03-2022-0130

Lee, M., & Young, S. (2020). Understanding the effect of brand experience and service quality on brand trust and brand satisfaction: An expectation-confirmation theory perspective. *Journal of Hospitality Marketing & Management*, 29(2), 168–190.

Lee, Y., Kim, M., & Kim, M. (2020). Understanding the influence of brand experience on brand satisfaction, trust, and loyalty: An expectation-confirmation theory perspective. *Journal of Business Research*, 110, 266–276.

Lim, D., Ro, Y., Lee, S., & Jahng, J. (2022). Continuance usage intention on subscription-based streaming service: Focusing on the dedication-constraint model. *Korean Management Review*, 51(6), 1595–1618. DOI: 10.17287/kmr.2022.51.6.1595

Maasø, A., & Hagen, A. N. (2019). Metrics and decision-making in music streaming. *Popular Communication*, 18(1), 18–31. DOI: 10.1080/15405702.2019.1701675

Marmat, G. (2023). A framework for transitioning brand trust to brand love. *Management Decision*, 61(6), 1554–1584. DOI: 10.1108/MD-04-2022-0420

Masriani, M., & Sanica, I. (2022). Factors that determine brand trust in the interest of buying multi level marketing (mlm) products in the city of Ruteng Manggarai. *Relasi: Jurnal Ekonomi*, 18(1), 132–140. DOI: 10.31967/relasi.v18i1.532

Morgan, R. M., & Hunt, S. D. (1994). The commitment-trust theory of relationship marketing. *Journal of Marketing*, 58(3), 20–38. DOI: 10.1177/002224299405800302

Morris, J. W., & Powers, D. (2015). Control, curation and musical experience in streaming music services. *Creative Industries Journal*, 8(2), 106–122. DOI: 10.1080/17510694.2015.1090222

Mruk-Tomczak, D., Jerzyk, E., & Wawrzynkiewicz, N. (2019). Consumer engagement and the perception of packaging information. *Olsztyn Economic Journal*, 14(2), 195–207. DOI: 10.31648/oej.3971

Musiime, A., & Mwaipopo, L. (2020). The mediating role of brand involvement in the social media use-marketing communication effectiveness relationship: A case of selected entertainment SMEs in Uganda. *Business Management Review*, 22(2), 67–86.

Noori, A. S., Hashim, K. F., & Yusof, S. A. M. (2022). The mediating impact of trust and commitment on s-commerce continuous use Intention. [Bawak]. *Journal of Southwest Jiaotong University*, 57(3), 412–425. DOI: 10.35741/issn.0258-2724.57.3.34

Oliveira, T., Thomas, M., Baptista, G., & Campos, F. (2016). Mobile payment: Understanding the determinants of customer adoption and intention to recommend the technology. *Computers in Human Behavior*, 61, 404–414. DOI: 10.1016/j.chb.2016.03.030

Omar, Q., Yap, C. S., Ho, P. L., & Keling, W. (2023). Can technology readiness predict farmers' adoption intention of the e-AgriFinance app? *Journal of Agribusiness in Developing and Emerging Economies*, 13(1), 156–172. DOI: 10.1108/JADEE-04-2021-0090

Ozturk, A. B., Bilgihan, A., Salehi-Esfahani, S., & Hua, N. (2017). Understanding the mobile payment technology acceptance based on valence theory. *International Journal of Contemporary Hospitality Management*, 29(8), 2027–2049. DOI: 10.1108/IJCHM-04-2016-0192

Park, J., Kang, J., & Lee, K. (2022). The role of user experience in shaping continuance intention in mobile application usage: An expectation-confirmation theory perspective. *Information Systems Frontiers*, 24(1), 177–189.

Putra, W. P., Mukhid, M., & Murthada, M. (2024). Brand trust, social media, and repurchase intention: A case study of le minerale consumers in Indonesia. *International Journal of Business, Law, and Education*, 5(1), 58–71. DOI: 10.56442/ijble.v5i1.359

Rabaa'i, A. A., & ALMaati, S. A. (2021). Exploring the determinants of users' continuance intention to use mobile banking services in Kuwait: Extending the expectation-confirmation model. *Asia Pacific Journal of Information Systems*, 31(2), 141–184. DOI: 10.14329/apjis.2021.31.2.141

Ramos, E., & Blind, K. (2020). Data portability effects on data-driven innovation of online platforms: Analyzing Spotify. *Telecommunications Policy*, 44(9), 102026. Advance online publication. DOI: 10.1016/j.telpol.2020.102026

Rudzewicz, A., & Strychalska-Rudzewicz, A. (2021). The influence of brand trust on consumer loyalty. *European Research Studies*, 24(3), 454–470. DOI: 10.35808/ersj/2439

Sadyk, D., & Islam, D. M. Z. (2022). Brand equity and usage intention powered by value co-creation: A case of instagram in Kazakhstan. *Sustainability (Basel)*, 2022(14), 500. DOI: 10.3390/su14010500

Saksriwattana, K. (2024). Factor affecting intention to use chatbot for health information. *Procedia of Multidisciplinary Research*, 2(7), 1–10.

Samarah, T., Bayram, P., Aljuhmani, H. Y., & Elrehail, H. (2022). The role of brand interactivity and involvement in driving social media consumer brand engagement and brand loyalty: The mediating effect of brand trust. *Journal of Research in Interactive Marketing*, 16(4), 648–664. DOI: 10.1108/JRIM-03-2021-0072

Schivinski, B., Christodoulides, G., & Dabrowski, D. (2016). Measuring consumers' engagement with brand-related social-media content. *Journal of Advertising Research*, 56(1), 64–80. DOI: 10.2501/JAR-2016-004

Smith, A. K., Bolton, R. N., & Wagner, J. (2019). A model of customer engagement with mobile and wearable technology interfaces: The role of satisfaction, performance, and confidence. *Journal of the Academy of Marketing Science*, 47(2), 199–218.

Song, M., Xing, X., Duan, Y., Cohen, J., & Mou, J. (2022). Will artificial intelligence replace human customer service? The impact of communication quality and privacy risks on adoption intention. *Journal of Retailing and Consumer Services*, 66, 102900. DOI: 10.1016/j.jretconser.2021.102900

Statista (2023). *Digital Music: Market data & analysis*. Statista. https://www.statista.com/outlook/dmo/digital-media/digital-music/music-streaming/philippines

Statista - The Statistics Portal. (n.d.). Statista. Retrieved March 17, 2024, from https://www.statista.com/search/?q=music+streaming+platforms+2024&p=1

Susanto, D., Natalia, D., Jeniva, I., Lianto, , Veronica, M., & Setinawati, . (2022). Brand knowledge training through packaging materials and the use of social media in hurung bunut village, gunung mas district. *Amala Jurnal Pengabdian Kepada Masyarakat*, 1(2), 81–89. DOI: 10.23971/amala.v1i2.34

Sutenchan, T. (2024). Factors of technology acceptance and attitude behavioral intention to use the video conferencing in court systems. *Procedia of Multidisciplinary Research*, 2(3), 1–11.

Syahroni, M., Nasution, U., & Hasoloan, A. (2022). Pengaruh product involvement dan entitas merek terhadap keputusan pembelian produk pada pt. distriversa buanamas medan. *Jurnal Ilmu Sosial Dan Politik*, 2(2), 33–38. DOI: 10.51622/jispol.v2i2.1150

Tan, M., & Limb, S.-J. (2022). A study on the determinants of youtube music user satisfaction and continuous use intention - focusing on youtube premium subscribers. *Korea Association of Cultural Economics, 25*(3), 135–168. https://doi.org/DOI: 10.36234/kace.2022.25.3.135

Theadora, C., Amelia, M. V., Tan, G. W.-H., Lo, P.-S., Ooi, K.-B., & Dwivedi, Y. K. (2022). How does involvement build loyalty towards music-streaming platforms? A multi-analytical SEM-ANN technique. *Journal of Product and Brand Management*, 32(4), 645–660. DOI: 10.1108/JPBM-02-2022-3855

Triono, S. P. H., Huriyati, R., & Sultan, M. A. (2021). The influence of user-generated content to consumer-based brand equity through involvement iin Indonesia's top brand Lipstic consumer. *Jurnal Manajemen Indonesia*, 21(1), 17–29. DOI: 10.25124/jmi.v21i1.2461

Tuti, M., & Sulistia, V. (2022). The Customer engagement effect on customer satisfaction and brand trust and its impact on brand loyalty. *Jurnal Manajemen Bisnis*, 13(1), 1–15. DOI: 10.18196/mb.v13i1.12518

Utomo, S. M., Alamsyah, D. P., & Hariyanto, O. I. (2022, September). Continuance Intention of E-Learning: New Model of Technology Adoption. In 2022 3rd International Conference on Big Data Analytics and Practices (IBDAP) (pp. 85-89). IEEE.

Vogels, E. (2019). Millennials stand out for their technology use, but older generations also embrace digital life. *Pew Research Center.*https://pewrsr.ch/2A3kD6X

Wang, J., Shen, X., Huang, X., & Liu, Y. (2021). Influencing factors of the continuous usage intention of consumers of online food delivery platform based on an information system success model. *Frontiers in Psychology*, 12, 716796. Advance online publication. DOI: 10.3389/fpsyg.2021.716796 PMID: 34484080

Wang, Y., & Liao, Y. (2021). The influence of perceived risk on mobile payment continuance intention: An expectation-confirmation perspective. *Information & Management*, 58(1), 103–114.

Watulingas, E. B., & Permana, D. (2020). The influence of user interface, user experience, and digital marketing toward purchase intention. *International Humanities and Applied Sciences Journal*, 3(2), 35. DOI: 10.22441/ihasj.2020.v3i2.05

Webster, J. (2020). Taste in the platform age: Music streaming services and new forms of class distinction. *Information Communication and Society*, 23(13), 1909–1924. DOI: 10.1080/1369118X.2019.1622763

Webster, J. (2021). The promise of personalisation: Exploring how music streaming platforms are shaping the performance of class identities and distinction. *New Media &amp. New Media & Society*, 25(8), 2140–2162. DOI: 10.1177/14614448211027863

Wessel, D., Attig, C., & Franke, T. (2019). ATI-S - An ultra-short scale for assessing affinity for technology interaction in user studies. *Proceedings of Mensch Und Computer*, 2019, 147–154. DOI: 10.1145/3340764.3340766

Wong, L.-W., Tan, G. W.-H., Lee, V.-H., Ooi, K.-B., & Sohal, A. (2020). Unearthing the determinants of blockchain adoption in supply chain management. *International Journal of Production Research*, 58(7), 2100–2123. DOI: 10.1080/00207543.2020.1730463

Wulandari, D., Suhud, U., & Purwohedi, U. (2019). The influence factors of continuance intention to use a music streaming application. *International Journal on Advanced Science, Education, and Religion*, 2(2), 17–25. DOI: 10.33648/ijoaser.v2i2.32

Yang, F.-C., & Tasi, P.-W. (2023). Measuring the mediating effect of satisfaction and compatibility on the relationship between podcast features and users' intention of continuous usage and word of mouth. *Multimedia Tools and Applications*, 83(15), 44527–44554. DOI: 10.1007/s11042-023-17417-z

Yasin, M., Porcu, L., & Liebana-Cabanillas, F. (2019). The effect of brand experience on customers' engagement behavior within the context of online brand communities: The impact on intention to forward online company-generated content. *Sustainability (Basel)*, 11(17), 4649. DOI: 10.3390/su11174649

Yen, W.-C., Lin, H.-H., Wang, Y.-S., Shih, Y.-W., & Cheng, K.-H. (2018). Factors affecting users' continuance intention of mobile social network service. *Service Industries Journal*, 39(13-14), 983–1003. DOI: 10.1080/02642069.2018.1454435

Yeoh, S. Y., Yuntavid, X. J., & Chin, P. N. (2022). Examining the continuous usage intention and behaviours of music streaming subscribers. *International Journal of Electronic Business*, 17(2), 184–203. DOI: 10.1504/IJEB.2022.121992

Yosvijit, P., & Nurittamont, W. (2021). The integrated marketing communication and trust influence on purchasing intention of digital salak through mobile banking customer of government savings bank sector 5: Testing the role of technology acceptance as a mediator variable. *Asian Administration & Management Review, 4*(2), 22-30. https://doi.org/DOI: 10.14456/aamr.2021.3

Zahri, C., Nasution, U. H., & Syahroni, M. S. (2023). Pengaruh product involvement dan entitas merek terhadap keputusan pembelian produk pada pt. Distriversa buanamas medan. *Majalah Ilmiah Warta Dharmawangsa*, 17(1), 98–111. DOI: 10.46576/wdw.v17i1.2925

Zhang, J., Wang, D., & Li, X. (2022). The influence of brand trust on user stickiness: A moderated mediation model of user-brand involvement and commitment. *International Journal of Hospitality Management*, 97, 102955.

Zhang, Y., & Zhao, J. (2023). Research on mechanisms of customer-oriented deviance on brand trust: The mediating roles of perceived benefit/uncertainty and the moderating role of customer involvement. *Psychology Research and Behavior Management*, 16, 1063–1077. DOI: 10.2147/PRBM.S400500 PMID: 37038598

Zhao, J., Kim, Y., & Kim, Y. S. (2019). A study on the impact of perceived cosmetic brand app on continuous usage intention - Meditating effect of customer satisfaction and moderating effect of involvement. *Journal of Korean Society for Quality Management*, 47(2), 237–254. DOI: 10.7469/JKSQM.2019.47.2.237

Chapter 16
Intention to Use E-Wallet Services, User Satisfaction and Loyalty:
The Mediating Role of Trust and the Moderating Effects of Technological Stress

Avelino Gonzales
https://orcid.org/0009-0009-5952-6932
Holy Angel University, Philippines

Jean Paolo Gomez Lacap
City College of Angeles, Philippines

ABSTRACT

Grounded in the Technology Acceptance Model (TAM) and the Stimulus-Organism-Response (SOR) model, this chapter investigates consumers' intentions to adopt e-wallet services, as well as their satisfaction and loyalty. Using purposive sampling and partial least squares (PLS) path modeling, the results demonstrate that perceived usefulness, perceived ease of use, perceived COVID-19 risk, and government support positively influence the intention to use e-wallet services. Furthermore, the intention to use e-wallet services leads to consumer satisfaction, which, in turn, enhances trust, ultimately resulting in loyalty. Trust is also found to mediate the relationship between consumer satisfaction and loyalty.

INTRODUCTION

The COVID-19 pandemic has disrupted fundamental aspects of life globally, leaving lasting psychological, social, and economic impacts (Settersten et al., 2020; Bostan et al., 2020). In the Philippines, it severely affected the economy, leading to a recession, business closures, supply chain disruptions, and widespread unemployment (Reyes, 2021). To curb transmission, health measures such as face masks and social distancing were implemented, prompting a shift to work-from-home setups and increased use of e-wallets as a cashless payment solution (Sari et al., 2020). e-wallets, driven by financial technology, offer convenience and security by reducing reliance on cash and facilitating transactions (Ming et al.,

DOI: 10.4018/979-8-3693-9230-0.ch016

Copyright ©2025, IGI Global. Copying or distributing in print or electronic forms without written permission of IGI Global is prohibited.

2020; Syifa & Tohang, 2020). Mobile wallets, or m-wallets, enable users to send and receive money via mobile devices, making them a critical tool during the pandemic (Kumar & Krishnan, 2020; Abidin et al., 2017).

The intention to use technology is often influenced by its ease of use and perceived usefulness, particularly in the context of COVID-19. Government support further encourages adoption, as the pandemic heightens the need for safe, digital solutions. Positive user experiences lead to satisfaction, trust, and ultimately, loyalty. However, technological stress may hinder user satisfaction and loyalty when individuals struggle to adapt to new systems (Amoroso et al., 2021; Singh et al., 2020).

Recent studies indicate that perceived usefulness significantly impacts the intention to use e-wallets during the COVID-19 pandemic, with both direct and indirect effects (Aji, Berakon, & Riza, 2020). This intention is influenced not only by utility but also by ease of use, especially given the risks of viral transmission (Davis et al., 1989; Aji, Berakon, & Md Husin, 2020). The growing demand for e-wallets has driven service providers to innovate, aided by consistent government support, which has significantly impacted users' adoption (Wei & Liu, 2015; Appiah et al., 2019; Rambocas & Arjoon, 2012). Studies show a positive link between intention to use and perceived satisfaction, with lower technological stress improving user satisfaction (Liébana-Cabanillas et al., 2018; Alalwan et al., 2017). Trust plays a key role in fostering loyalty, with social influence further strengthening this connection (Dennehy & Sammon, 2015).

However, few studies have explored the direct influence of user satisfaction on both loyalty and trust, or how technological stress may moderate the relationships between intention to use, satisfaction, and loyalty (Dennehy & Sammon, 2015). This study addresses this gap by proposing a model that examines the impact of perceived satisfaction on trust and loyalty, and the mediating role of trust in these relationships, while assessing whether technological stress weakens these links.

LITERATURE REVIEW

This research is based on two theoretical models: the Technology Acceptance Model (TAM) and the Stimulus-Organism-Response (SOR) model. TAM, developed by Davis (1989), identifies perceived usefulness and perceived ease of use as key drivers influencing individuals' adoption or rejection of new technology (Charness & Boot, 2015). The SOR model, widely used to explore stimulus, organism, and response relationships, links external stimuli to psychological states and behavioral responses (Islam et al., 2020). It has been applied in studies on consumer behavior, service quality, and technology use (Bitner, 1992; Chen & Yao, 2018; Dongxiang, 2023; Peng & Kim, 2014).

The combination of TAM and SOR models explains decision-making in technology adoption by integrating cognitive and emotional processes (Taheri & Shourmasti, 2016). TAM focuses on users' interactions with technology, while SOR emphasizes emotional responses shaped by community interactions (Choi, 2019). In this study, TAM variables include perceived usefulness, ease of use, and intention to use, while the SOR model includes perceived COVID-19 risk, government support, satisfaction, trust, and loyalty (Song et al., 2021; Sriboonlue, 2022).

Intention to Use

Usage or the intention to use refers to a person's decision to use a system, based on the assumption that once someone decides to act, they will be free to do so without restriction (Tusyanah et al., 2020). The perception of a user's intention to use technology influences customers' satisfaction (Sangperm & Pungpho, 2020; Singh et al., 2020). Humans have a system in place for weighing the pros and drawbacks of employing a particular product or technology. The function of aspects like behavioral intention, which is generated by a person's attitude to make a decision, has a direct connection to the intention to use followed by actual usage. The negative or good feelings that people have about their desire to use technology are referred to as the attitude which is the basis or foundation of preference and intention (Kasilingam, 2020).

Technological advancement has resulted in a continuing evolution of social structures as well as attitudes and values. Learning criteria, technological acceptance, motives, social cognitive, and expectancy values were united and studied in an integrated manner to influence intention to use (Wang et al., 2020) but according to TAM framework, the perceived utility and perceived ease of use are the two (2) main key components or drivers that influence an individual's inclination to use a technology or system (Charness & Boot, 2015).

Perceived Usefulness

The usefulness of a system is an important component in user adoption. Usefulness is linked to its productivity and efficacy, as well as its overall benefits in terms of improving user performance. It refers to how much a person believes that employing technology would help him or her perform better at work. As a result, the more helpful a technology is, the greater the desire to use it among users (Tahar et al., 2020).

Perceived usefulness refers to how much a person believes a new technology or system will help them perform better at work (Fred D. Davis, 1989). People are more likely to use or not utilize an application if they believe it would improve their job performance. Examining the impact of perceived usefulness on their willingness to utilize an e-wallet during the COVID-19 outbreak yields more meaningful information (Alrefai et al., 2021). Hence, it is hypothesized that:

H1a. Perceived usefulness significantly and positively influences intention to use e-wallet services.

Perceived Ease of Use

The degree to which a new technology is simple to use and free of interface difficulties is referred to as perceived ease of use. Even if potential users believe that a specific program is beneficial, they may also believe that the system is too difficult to use and that the performance benefits of utilizing the application are exceeded by the effort required to utilize it. The perceived simplicity/ ease of use is thought to impact usage (Davis, 1989). That is why the more users feel or believe that a system is simple to use, the more likely they are to use it.

When a technology is simple to use, people are more likely to want to utilize it. A system is said to be of high quality if it is designed to provide user pleasure through ease of use; this includes not just learning and utilizing the system, but also the ease of performing a job or task, where users will find it easier to work with the system (Tahar et al., 2020). From these reviewed studies, it is therefore postulated that:

H1b. Perceived ease of use significantly and positively influences intention to use e-wallet services.

Perceived COVID-19 Risk

Perceived COVID-19 risk serves as stimuli to the users' intention to use e wallet and leads to the response which is the customers' satisfaction. The riskiness of something is determined by a mix of risk factors like dread, knowledge, and controllability which are the traits that are classified into cognitive and emotional hazards (Yıldırım et al., 2021). Customers are uncertain of novel coronavirus droplets on physical money or cash, which is termed as perceived COVID-19 risk. They are concerned about being infected by the COVID-19 through the exchange of actual money that can be linked to disease risk. There is a link between perceived danger and government funding (Aji, Berakon, & Md Husin, 2020). In general, almost all research revealed that perceived risk has a negative impact on behavior. If the risk is linked to a deadly pandemic epidemic, such as COVID-19, the results are likely to be different. Actual money poses a high risk of COVID-19 transmission. Customers' willingness to use non-physical money will be positively influenced by their perception of the risk of virus transmission. Regrettably, empirical (real) findings on this subject are still understudied (Marafon et al., 2018).

Based on the findings of various technology adoption studies on user's behavioral intention, perceived risk was emphasized as important in mobile payment acceptance (Singh et al., 2020) which is evident nowadays as many people began to develop an apprehension about the potential dangers of using cash at present (Yean, 2020).

Because of the perceived COVID-19 risk and dangers of social interaction and using cash at present, people are kept at home through physical separation and self-quarantine program. Consumers attempted to perform any task that did not require physical interaction. They don't shop in supermarkets or shopping malls. The demand for online products are increasing but consumers are encouraged to pay with digital wallets or e-wallets by many businesses, transportation companies, and food sellers (Aji, Berakon, & Md Husin, 2020). Therefore, it is hypothesized that:

H2. Perceived COVID-19 risk significantly and positively influences intention to use e-wallet services.

Government Support

The World Health Organization (WHO) is aware of the spread of COVID-19 in number of nations that is why it promotes physical separation policies, which has prompted consumers to engage in contactless activities and payments, such as financial transactions. The world's governments and public are also aware that the novel coronavirus (SARS-Cov2) could be possibly transferred through physical money. Because of this the government supported and promoted the use of e-wallet (Aji, Berakon, & Md Husin, 2020).

The role of the government is crucial. When faced with a risk, the government can play the role of manager. As the regulator, the government has a main responsibility to protect its citizens from any potentially harmful results. The government is in charge of people's health, and the possible COVID-19 risk linked with physical money has affected its support for e-wallets (Aji, Berakon, & Md Husin, 2020).

Government in Asia like India has an ambitious drive to transform their economy from a cash-based economy to a cashless economy and it was dependent in large part on people's acceptance of cashless modes of transactions, adaptability to cashless transactions, and changes in consumer and retailer transaction behavior, among other things (Brahma & Dutta, 2018).

Customers' willingness to use mobile payment was found to be influenced by government backing. Because COVID-19 is a national or possibly worldwide threat, government backing for e-wallets will encourage customers to use them (Alrefai et al., 2021). Thus, it is postulated that:

H3. Government support significantly and positively influences intention to use e-wallet services.

Satisfaction

Perceived satisfaction with e wallet technology have been examined in previous research. For example (Nizam et al., 2019) assess the relationship between these constructs that can be investigated further and more aspects that can be taken into account when determining a user's continuous purpose and usage in order to be satisfied. Some studies examine a variety of characteristics that may influence user usage, happiness and satisfaction to endorse e-wallet technologies (Jain & Singhal, 2019).

Behavioral intention to use e wallet technology results to User Satisfaction. Satisfaction in the use of a product or system will take place because of the continuous intention to use (Syifa & Tohang, 2020). Thus, it is hypothesized that:

H4. Intention to use e-wallet services significantly and positively influences user satisfaction.

Loyalty

Loyalty refers to a goodwill toward a certain product or service and the satisfaction and happiness as a result of a good service (Lin et al., 2015). A loyal and satisfied customer not only returns to the same vendor or brand time and time again, but also helps the vendor/brand expand over time through advocacy. Loyalty is a strong commitment behavior toward a vendor or brand. Selling opportunities, forecast accuracy, and constructive comments can all help a vendor/brand improve its image and save marketing and service expenditures (Chi, 2005). In this way, developing customer loyalty and retention is a crucial business activity, since it often leads to increased sales and profits as a result of increased consumer purchases (Amoroso et al., 2021).

When a provider earns the consumer's trust and satisfaction, loyalty develops into a commitment behavior. Consumers who trust an online vendor are more inclined to share personal information with the vendor and allow the vendor to tailor products and services for them (Reichheld & Schefter, 2000). According to previous study, a loyal and satisfied customer not only returns to the vendor on a regular basis, but it also helps the vendor outperform the competition and maintains long-term growth through word-of-mouth marketing (Sur, 2015). Hence, it is hypothesized that:

H5. User satisfaction significantly and positively influences loyalty.

Trust

The connection of satisfaction and loyalty is mediated by trust. Mutual trust will foster loyalty among those trusted and those who are being trusted (Amoroso et al., 2021). In the face of social unpredictability, trust is a positive anticipation, and it is the cornerstone for almost all human interactions. Subjective trust, behavioral trust, decision to trust, and trustworthiness are all examples of trust dimensions. It's tough to put a definition on trust and it is multidimensional (Rousseau et al., 1998).

There is mutual confidence between the customer and the vendor. It can be judged based on the trustee's competency, compassion, and honesty. He or she's reputation might be used to refer to the trustee's capacity to retain trustworthiness (Abyad, 2017). With honesty, benevolence, and non-opportunistic goals, trust can be defined as the expectation or belief that people would keep their promises and fulfill their obligations (Amoroso et al., 2021).

Trust promotes a sense of worth and loyalty. It is the outcome of a person's happiness and satisfaction as the result of using a product, service, or technology. Continuous satisfaction on a product or service will further develop mutual trust between satisfied customers and sellers which is required to continue good commercial interactions that will lead to customers' loyalty (Amoroso et al., 2021). From these reviewed studies, it is therefore postulated that:

H6. User Satisfaction significantly and positively influences trust.

H7. Trust significantly and positively influences loyalty.

H8. Trust mediates the significant and positive relationship between user satisfaction and loyalty.

Technological Stress

Technological stress is an adaptation sickness caused by the inability to deal with new technology. It manifests in the inability to focus on a single subject, increased irritation, and a sense of lack of control because of the stress experienced by a technology (Liébana-Cabanillas & Lara-Rubio, 2017) and e-wallet services is reported to be more satisfied by users with reduced stress levels on the use of online and mobile payments (Alalwan et al., 2017).

Users are hesitant to adopt a new technology since it is difficult for them to comprehend and causes them to feel overwhelmed specially if they are unable to cope with a technology, he or she may experience discomfort or stress.(Swilley, 2010). Users' stress levels (technostress) are mostly caused by the usage of information and communication technologies (Dahlberg et al., 2003).

Because of this, the relationship between the user's intention to use and perceived satisfaction with the new technology may be influenced by stress (Dabholkar & Bagozzi, 2002). The negative relationship between stress and perceived satisfaction has been proven in previous research that stress acts as a crucial moderator on user's satisfaction. This suggests that people who are stressed out are less likely to be satisfied with the technology service than those who are not (Igbaria & Nachman, 1990).

Other research revealed that mobile payment transactions are risky and unreliable because it may be linked to criminal activities such as identity theft, account takeover, fraudulent transactions, and data breaches (Aji, Berakon, & Md Husin, 2020). Financial risks, time/convenience risks, and psychological risks are all examples of dangers associated with internet, online transactions and e wallet services, according to previous studies (Forsythe & Shi, 2003).

As a result, there is a good chance that people will avoid using the new technology services because of dissatisfaction if they're stressed out. The user's mental health may be hampered by stress, stopping them from embracing new technologies and diminishing their loyalty towards a certain product or service (Thakur & Srivastava, 2014). Therefore, it is hypothesized that:

H9a. The presence of technological stress weakens the relationship between intention to use e-wallet services and user satisfaction.

H9b. The presence of technological stress weakens the relationship between user satisfaction and loyalty.

Based on the hypothesized relationships postulated, Figure 1 presents the conceptual framework of the study.

Figure 1. Conceptual framework of the study

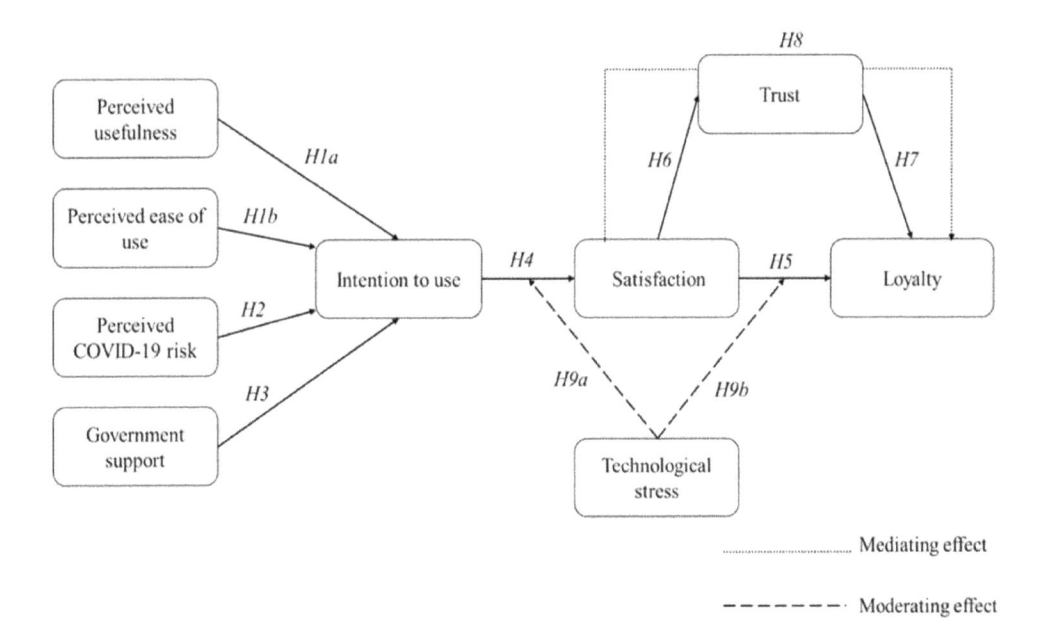

METHODS

Participants

The participants of the study were Filipino G-Cash users, aged 18 and above, residing in Pampanga, and who had been using e-wallets for at least 3 months. Due to mobility restrictions, data collection was conducted via Google Forms, which was disseminated through social media platforms, primarily Facebook, and email. Informed consent was included in the online form, and only those who voluntarily agreed to participate were included in the study.

A purposive sampling method was used, a non-probability sampling technique where respondents were selected based on specific characteristics relevant to the study's goals (Etikan, 2016). A priori power analysis using GPower was employed to calculate the sample size, which estimated a minimum of 129 participants, using an effect size of 15%, alpha level of 5%, power level of 95%, and four predictors. This sample size was further validated using inverse square root and gamma-exponential methods, which suggested a minimum of 196–209 participants. The study successfully gathered 366 valid responses, exceeding the minimum sample size required for reliable analysis.

Research Instrument

A self-administered survey was used in the study. The preliminary section of the questionnaire covered the inclusion/exclusion criteria for the respondents. The second section focused on the demographic characteristics of the participants, including their sex, age, employment type, and highest educational attainment. The third section consisted of items corresponding to each of the latent constructs of the study. All constructs were measured using a 5-point Likert scale, where 5 indicated "strongly agree" and 1 indicated "strongly disagree." Table 1 presents the latent constructs, the corresponding items, and the sources for each variable.

Table 1. Latent constructs with corresponding items

Construct and Items	Source/s
Perceived Usefulness	(Venkatesh et al., 2012)
PU1. In my daily life, I find it beneficial to utilize an e-wallet.	
PU2. This e-wallet is quite beneficial.	
PU3. This e-wallet assists me in completing my responsibilities more quickly.	
PU4. The use of an e-wallet makes work easier.	
PU5. The use of an e-wallet is efficient.	
PU6. Payment is made easier when you use an e-wallet.	
PU7. Using an e-wallet could boost productivity.	
PU8. Using an e-wallet may help you perform better.	
PU9. For my work, an e-wallet is useful.	
Perceived ease of Use	(Venkatesh et al., 2012)
PEOU1. It is simple to utilize an e-wallet.	
PEOU2. The use of an e-wallet is easy to comprehend.	
PEOU3. Transactions with e-wallet save me a lot of time and effort.	
PEOU4. It is easy to interact with e-wallet.	
Perceived COVID-19 Risk	(Venkatesh et al., 2012)
PCR1. When I use actual cash, I'm concerned about getting infected with the coronavirus.	
PCR2. I'm hesitant to pay with physical cash.	
PCR3. When I use actual currency, I am terrified about contracting the coronavirus.	
PCR4. I'm concerned that actual cash may contain a coronavirus droplet.	

continued on following page

Table 1. Continued

Construct and Items	Source/s
Government support	(Aji, Berakon, & Md Husin, 2020)
GS1. During the COVID-19 pandemic, the government urges people to use e-wallets to make payments.	
GS2. The government assures e-wallet server facilities during the COVID-19 pandemic.	
GS3. The government fosters payment innovation via e-wallets during the COVID-19 pandemic.	
GS4. The government is in control of e-wallet payment activities during the COVID-19 outbreak.	
Intention to use	(Venkatesh et al., 2012)
ITU1. When the chance presents itself, I intend to use an e-wallet.	
ITU2. In the near future, I am likely to use an e-wallet.	
ITU3. I intend to utilize an e-wallet on a regular basis.	
ITU4. I will use e-wallets for payment transactions during COVID-19 pandemic	
ITU5. I prefer using e-wallets for payment transactions during COVID-19 pandemic	
ITU6. E-wallet will be my preferred method of payment in the future.	
Satisfaction	(Madan & Yadav, 2016)
S1. I'd be satisfied with the features of an e-wallet.	
S2. I would feel pleased because e-wallet fulfills my needs.	
S3. It would be more convenient for me to use an e-wallet.	
Trust	(Amoroso et al., 2021)
T1. This e-wallet comes with enough security measures to keep my money safe.	
T2. My financial information is safe with the e-wallet.	
T3. This e-wallet has adequate features to protect my privacy	
T4. This e-wallet keeps my personal data safe	
T5. This e-wallet is trustworthy	
Loyalty	(Amoroso et al., 2021)
L1. I consider myself to be very loyal using the e-wallet (G-Cash, PayMaya, etc.)	
L2. I consider one e-wallet (GCash, PayMaya, etc.) to be better than the others	
Technological stress	(C. H. Lin et al., 2007)
TS1. E-wallet is a challenging tool, and after using it, I get stress.	

TS2. It can be difficult to fully comprehend the functions of an e-wallet.
TS3. E-wallet apps are complex and time-consuming and require a lot of thought.

Data Analysis

To test the hypothesized relationships, the study adopted a predictive-causal research methodology. This approach uses PLS path modeling to provide causal explanations and predictions, focusing on complex models with multiple constructs and paths (Ringle et al., 2020; Hair et al., 2019). PLS path modeling is ideal for causal-predictive research, offering insights into direct, mediation, and moderation effects without relying on normality assumptions (Sarstedt et al., 2017; Hair et al., 2019).

Both the measurement and structural models were evaluated, with the measurement model assessed for validity and reliability, and the structural model for collinearity, path coefficients, and effect sizes (Hair et al., 2019). WarpPLS version 8.0 (Kock, 2020) was used for PLS-SEM analysis.

Direct effects examined included relationships between perceived usefulness, ease of use, COVID-19 risk, government support, intention to use e-wallets, user satisfaction, trust, and loyalty. Indirect effects explored included the mediating role of trust between satisfaction and loyalty, and the moderating effects of technological stress on the relationships between intention to use e-wallets, satisfaction, and loyalty.

Results

Partial least squares – structural equation modelling (PLS-SEM) was utilized to measure all the research hypotheses of the current undertaking. The first stage of PLS-SEM is the evaluation of the measurement model where reliability and validity of the latent constructs are established. On the other hand, the second stage is the assessment of the structural model where path coefficients and effect sizes are measured.

Evaluation of the Measurement Model

The reliability, or the measure of internal consistency, of the latent constructs were measured using composite reliability (CR). According to Kock and Lynn (2012), the value of CR must be at least 0.70. Based on the results in Table 2, perceived usefulness (CR = 0.924), perceived ease of use (CR = 0.955), perceived COVID-19 risk (CR = 0.944), government support (CR = 0.947), intention to use (CR = 0.954), satisfaction (CR = 0.959), trust (CR = 0.974), loyalty (CR = 0.951), and technological stress (CR = 0.962) exhibit internal consistency, hence, all latent constructs passed the reliability requirement.

In terms of validity, convergent and discriminant validity were gauged. The assessment of convergent validity includes item loading and average variance extracted (AVE). According to Amora (2021), the AVE must be at least 0.50, and each item loading must at least 0.50 and significant ($p < 0.05$). In cases where the factor loadings are less than 0.50, these items must be deleted as they are considered as offending factors (Kock, 2022). In Table 2, low factor loadings were deleted, and the latent constructs were analyzed for convergent validity. And based on the findings, all latent constructs - perceived usefulness (AVE = 0.752), perceived ease of use (AVE = 0.876), perceived COVID-19 risk (AVE = 0.808), government support (AVE = 0.817), intention to use (AVE = 0.777), satisfaction (AVE = 0.887), trust (AVE = 0.883), loyalty (AVE = 0.906), and technological stress (AVE = 0.894) exhibit convergent validity.

Table 2. Reliability and convergent validity of the constructs

Construct / Item	Factor loading
Perceived usefulness: AVE = 0.752; CR = 0.924	
PU1	D
PU2	0.793

continued on following page

Table 2. Continued

Construct / Item	Factor loading
PU3	D
PU4	D
PU5	D
PU6	D
PU7	0.886
PU8	0.906
PU9	0.879
Perceived ease of use: AVE = 0.876; CR = 0.955	
PEOU1	D
PEOU2	0.933
PEOU3	0.925
PEOU4	0.950
Perceived COVID-19 risk: AVE = 0.808; CR = 0.944	
PCR1	0.881
PCR2	0.849
PCR3	0.939
PCR4	0.922
Government support: AVE = 0.817; CR = 0.947	
GS1	0.894
GS2	0.949
GS3	0.929
GS4	0.839
Intention to use: AVE = 0.777; CR = 0.954	
ITU1	0.868
ITU2	0.906
ITU3	0.897
ITU4	0.879
ITU5	0.874
ITU6	0.865
Satisfaction: AVE = 0.887; CR = 0.959	
SAT1	0.935
SAT2	0.944
SAT3	0.947
Trust: AVE = 0.883; CR = 0.974	
TR1	0.899
TR2	0.950
TR3	0.959

continued on following page

Table 2. Continued

Construct / Item	Factor loading
TR4	0.957
TR5	0.933
Loyalty: AVE = 0.906; CR = 0.951	
LOY1	0.952
LOY2	0.952
Technological stress: AVE = 0.894; CR = 0.962	
TS1	0.932
TS2	0.957
TS3	0.948

All item loadings are significant (p < 0.05).

Discriminant validity was tested using Fornell-Larcker criterion. Using this criterion, the square of AVE of each latent construct must be larger than other correlation coefficients among variables (Fornell & Larcker, 1981). In short, the diagonal values in Table 3 (coefficients in bold) must be higher than the off-diagonal values (non-bold coefficients). Based on the results, all latent constructs passed the requirement for discriminant validity.

Table 3. Discriminant validity of the latent constructs

	PU	PEOU	PCR	GS	ITU	SAT	TRU	LOY	TS
PU	**0.867**								
PEOU	0.863	**0.936**							
PCR	0.497	0.449	**0.899**						
GS	0.682	0.652	0.559	**0.904**					
ITU	0.782	0.789	0.570	0.717	**0.881**				
SAT	0.760	0.768	0.478	0.695	0.842	**0.942**			
TRU	0.655	0.625	0.494	0.638	0.690	0.722	**0.940**		
LOY	0.634	0.642	0.398	0.607	0.680	0.715	0.781	**0.952**	
TS	0.001	-0.062	0.216	0.132	-0.001	-0.012	0.135	0.045	**0.946**

PU – perceived usefulness; PEOU – perceived ease of use; PCR = perceived COVID-19 risk; GS – government support; ITU – intention to use; SAT – satisfaction; TRU – trust; LOY – loyalty; TS – technological stress.

Assessment of the Structural Model

Figure 2 and Table 4 present the hypothesized relationships of the structural model, including the path coefficients and effect sizes.

Analysis of the data revealed that perceived usefulness has a significant and positive effect on intention to use ($\beta = 0212$, $p < 0.001$) with a moderate effect size ($f^2 = 0.167$). Furthermore, it was as well found that perceived ease of use and intention to use are significant and positively related ($\beta = 0.359$, $p < 0.001$) with a moderate effect size (f2 = 0.284). Therefore, H1a and H1b are both supported.

The results further showed that perceived COVID-19 risk and intention to use are significantly and directly related ($\beta = 0.172$, $p < 0.001$) with a small effect size (f2 = 0.100). Government support was also found to have a significant, positive, and moderate effect on intention to use ($\beta = 0.242$, $p < 0.001$, $f^2 = 1.76$). Hence, H2 and H3 are supported.

The direct effect of intention to use on satisfaction was likewise analyzed. The results showed that intention to use significantly, directly, and substantially affects satisfaction ($\beta = 0.828$, $p < 0.001$), $f^2 = 0.699$). Therefore, H4 is supported.

Satisfaction was also found to have a significant and positive effect on loyalty ($\beta = 0.312$, $p < 0.001$, $f^2 = 0.224$), and on trust ($\beta = 0.726$, $p < 0.001$, $f^2 = 0.527$), with moderate and substantial effect sizes respectively. Hence, H5 and H6 are supported.

And lastly, the findings showed that trust and loyalty are significantly, positively, and substantially related ($\beta = 0.548$, $p < 0.001$, $f^2 = 0.429$). Therefore, H7 is supported as well.

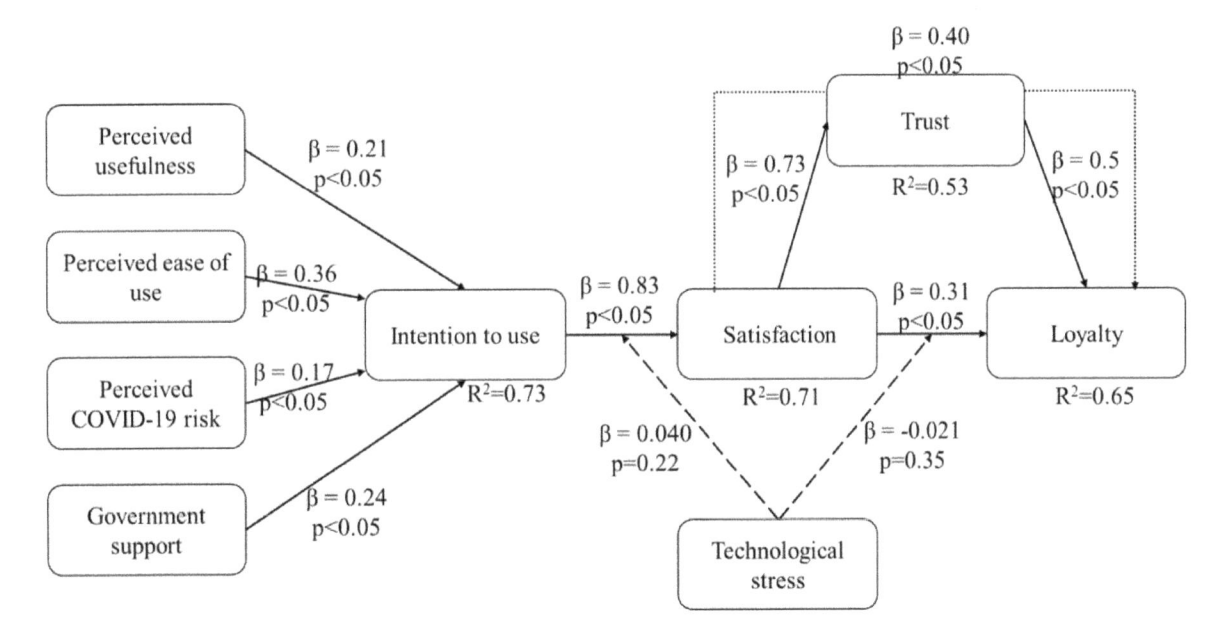

Figure 2. The study's structural model

The mediation analysis was also performed, and the results revealed that trust has a medium mediating effect on the relationship between satisfaction and loyalty ($\beta = 0.398$, $p < 0.001$, $f^2 = 0.286$). The indirect effect indicates that, satisfaction influences trust, which then affects loyalty. Therefore, H8 is supported.

The moderation analysis was likewise performed, and the findings showed that technological stress has no moderating effects on the link between intention to use and satisfaction ($\beta = 0.040$, $p = 0.220$) and on the relationship between satisfaction and loyalty ($\beta = -0.021$, $p = 0.345$) Hence, H9a and H9b are unsupported.

Table 4. Direct, mediating, and moderating effects

Hypothesis	Path coefficient	p-value	Standard error	Effect size	Decision
Direct effects					
H1a. PU → ITU	0.212	<0.001	0.051	0.167	S
H1b. PEOU → ITU	0.359	<0.001	0.050	0.284	S
H2. PCR → ITU	0.172	<0.001	0.051	0.100	S
H3. GS → ITU	0.242	<0.001	0.051	0.176	S
H4. ITU → SAT	0.828	<0.001	0.046	0.699	S
H5. SAT → LOY	0.312	<0.001	0.050	0.224	S
H6. SAT → TR	0.726	<0.001	0.047	0.527	S
H7. TR → LOY	0.548	<0.001	0.048	0.429	S
Mediating effect					
H8. SAT → TR → LOY	0.398	<0.001	0.035	0.286	S
Moderating effects					
H9a. TS * ITU → SAT	0.040	0.220	0.052	0.015	NS
H9b. TS * SAT → LOY	-0.021	0.345	0.052	0.007	NS

PU – perceived usefulness; PEOU – perceived ease of use; PCR = perceived COVID-19 risk; GS – government support; ITU – intention to use; SAT – satisfaction; TRU – trust; LOY – loyalty; TS – technological stress. The effect sizes were evaluated using Cohen's (1988) criteria: 0.02 – small/weak; 0.15 – medium/moderate; 0.35 – large/substantial.

Discussion

The study revealed that perceived usefulness and perceived ease of use had significant and positive effects on the intention to use e-wallets. Users who found an e-wallet both beneficial and easy to use were more inclined to adopt the technology. This finding indicates that when individuals perceive an e-wallet as useful and user-friendly, their likelihood of using it increases, especially if the e-wallet provides clear advantages and a smooth user experience (Tahar et al., 2020; Alrefai et al., 2021).

The study also showed that perceived COVID-19 risk and government support positively influenced the intention to use e-wallets. As concerns about the risks of handling physical cash increased due to the pandemic, and with government endorsement of digital payment methods, the intention to adopt e-wallet services grew. The COVID-19 pandemic led to a 44% increase in e-wallet usage, driven by the need for safer payment methods and governmental push towards cashless transactions (Rambocas & Arjoon, 2012; Budi et al., 2013). Government support, in particular, played a crucial role by enhancing infrastructure and policy support for e-wallets, thus boosting consumer confidence and adoption (Undale et al., 2021; Raaper & Brown, 2020).

Intention to use e-wallet services was found to significantly impact user satisfaction. Users who intended to use e-wallets were more likely to be satisfied with them, as ongoing use typically leads to higher satisfaction levels. Previous studies support this, showing that continuous engagement with a technology generally results in greater satisfaction (Oliveira et al., 2016; Syifa & Tohang, 2020). Satisfaction was also identified as a key factor influencing user loyalty, with satisfied users being more likely to remain loyal to the service. This underscores the importance of delivering high-quality e-wallet services to foster long-term user loyalty (Amoroso & Mukahi, 2013; T. C. Lin et al., 2015).

Furthermore, user satisfaction positively affected trust. Users who were satisfied with their e-wallet experience were more likely to trust the service, which is crucial for sustained usage and assurance. Satisfaction contributes to a sense of reliability and confidence in the service provider, reinforcing trust (Jain & Singhal, 2019; Ranaweera et al., 2005). Finally, trust was found to significantly enhance loyalty. The development of mutual trust between users and service providers fostered a stronger commitment to using e-wallets. Consistent trust and high service quality were essential for maintaining customer loyalty over time (Abyad, 2017; Zhou, 2011; Pungpho & Wanarat, 2017; Ribbink et al., 2004; Reichheld & Schefter, 2000).

The findings revealed that satisfaction has a significant and positive effect on trust, which in turn significantly influences loyalty. This implies that user satisfaction with e-wallet services enhances trust, and this trust subsequently fosters customer loyalty. Trust mediates the relationship between satisfaction and loyalty, indicating that satisfaction from positive experiences builds trust, which is crucial for maintaining long-term customer loyalty (Madjid, 2013; Amoroso et al., 2021).

The moderation analysis showed that technological stress did not significantly impact the relationships between the intention to use e-wallet services and user satisfaction, nor between user satisfaction and loyalty. Despite any difficulties in using the technology, the perceived usefulness of e-wallet services led to higher intention to use, which resulted in increased user satisfaction. Satisfaction with e-wallet services then translated into greater loyalty. Technological stress, therefore, did not weaken these relationships because the advantages and convenience of e-wallets outweigh any stress associated with their use (Dahlberg et al., 2015; Liu et al., 2015; Laukkanen et al., 2007; Hawi & Samaha, 2017). Users generally adapt to technology if it provides clear benefits and convenience, even if it introduces some level of stress or complexity (Purba et al., 2015; Thakur & Srivastava, 2014; Swilley, 2010; Dabholkar & Bagozzi, 2002).

Conclusion, Implications, Limitations, and Future Research Directions

The study's findings lead to several key conclusions. First, perceived usefulness and perceived ease of use significantly influence the intention to use e-wallets. Users are more likely to adopt e-wallet technology if they find it beneficial and easy to use. Additionally, the perceived risk of COVID-19 and government support play crucial roles in driving e-wallet adoption. Increased perceived risk and supportive measures from the government encourage users to choose e-wallets as a safer payment method.

The research also shows that the intention to use e-wallets positively affects user satisfaction. As users' intention to use e-wallets increases, their satisfaction with the service also grows. This satisfaction, in turn, strongly correlates with user loyalty. Satisfied users are more likely to remain loyal to the e-wallet service. Furthermore, satisfaction significantly enhances trust in the service, and this trust fosters long-term loyalty. Trust mediates the relationship between satisfaction and loyalty, meaning that satisfied users who develop trust are more inclined to be loyal.

Interestingly, technological stress does not moderate the relationships between intention to use and satisfaction, or between satisfaction and loyalty. This suggests that while technological stress might affect users' experiences, it does not significantly impact their adoption of technology or their levels of satisfaction and loyalty. Overall, the study underscores the importance of perceived usefulness, ease of use, satisfaction, and trust in driving e-wallet adoption and user loyalty, while highlighting that technological stress has minimal effect on these dynamics.

As the marketplace shifts towards digital spaces in a cashless society, both enterprises and consumers are moving towards electronic transactions. The growing adoption of e-wallets underscores efforts, especially in developing countries like the Philippines, to streamline financial transactions and promote financial inclusion. This study provides a comprehensive analysis of the factors influencing users' intentions to use e-wallet services, as well as their satisfaction and loyalty. The findings reveal that a higher intention to use e-wallets leads to greater user satisfaction, which in turn significantly enhances trust and loyalty among users. For businesses, this means that adopting e-wallets can improve payment flexibility and customer experience, thereby adding value to the evolving financial ecosystem. As e-commerce and contactless payments gain traction, businesses must offer seamless payment options like e-wallets to meet customer expectations and enhance the shopping experience. E-wallet companies are advised to expand their merchant partnerships and continue educating consumers on the benefits of cashless transactions. Collaboration among e-wallet companies, partner merchants, and the government is essential to promote financial inclusion through sustained educational initiatives.

The study also offers theoretical contributions by demonstrating how the TAM and SOR models can explain the behavioral intentions, perceived usefulness, and perceived ease of use of e-wallet services. It shows that satisfaction and trust are key factors influencing user loyalty to e-wallets. The research highlights the effectiveness of using the TAM model to assess technological acceptance and the SOR model to explore the impact of stimuli on user responses.

However, the study has limitations. It is specific to e-wallet users in the Philippines and focuses only on variables affecting intention to use, satisfaction, and loyalty. Additionally, the role of technological stress as a moderator was found to be insignificant. Future research could compare e-wallet usage in developed versus developing countries, explore social influences, attitudes, and recommendations regarding e-wallet use, and re-examine the role of technological stress in different research settings.

REFERENCES

Abidin, W. Z., Rivera, O., Maarop, N., & Hassan, N. H. (2017). Mobile payment framework for the unbanked Filipinos. *International Conference on Research and Innovation in Information Systems, ICRIIS*. DOI: 10.1109/ICRIIS.2017.8002478

Abyad, A. (2017). *Importance of Consumer Trust in E-Commerce*. Middle East Journal of Business., DOI: 10.5742/MEJB.2017.92971

Aji, H. M., Berakon, I., & Md Husin, M. (2020). *COVID-19 and e-wallet usage intention: A multigroup analysis between Indonesia and Malaysia*. Cogent Business and Management., DOI: 10.1080/23311975.2020.1804181

Aji, H. M., Berakon, I., & Riza, A. F. (2020). The effects of subjective norm and knowledge about riba on intention to use e-money in Indonesia. *Journal of Islamic Marketing*. Advance online publication. DOI: 10.1108/JIMA-10-2019-0203

Alalwan, A. A., Dwivedi, Y. K., & Rana, N. P. (2017). Factors influencing adoption of mobile banking by Jordanian bank customers: Extending UTAUT2 with trust. *International Journal of Information Management*, 37(3), 99–110. Advance online publication. DOI: 10.1016/j.ijinfomgt.2017.01.002

Alrefai, Z. A., Muda, H., Siddiqui, A. A., Amin, J., Ilyas, M., & Alam, M. K. (2021). Alternate method of payments and COVID-19. *International Medical Journal*.

Amora, J. T. (2021). Convergent validity assessment in PLS-SEM: A loadings-driven approach. *Data Analysis Perspectives Journal*, 2(3), 1–6.

Amoroso, D., Lim, R., & Roman, F. (2021). The effect of reciprocity on mobile wallet intention: A study of filipino consumers. *International Journal of Asian Business and Information Management*, 12(2), 57–83. Advance online publication. DOI: 10.4018/IJABIM.20210401.oa4

Amoroso, D. L., & Mukahi, T. (2013). An examination of consumers' high and low trust as constructs for predicting online shopping behavior. *Journal of Electronic Commerce in Organizations*, 11(1), 1–17. Advance online publication. DOI: 10.4018/jeco.2013010101

Appiah, K., Osei, C., Selassie, H., & Osabutey, E. (2019). The role of government and the international competitiveness of SMEs: Evidence from Ghanaian non-traditional exports. *Critical Perspectives on International Business*, 15(4), 296–322. Advance online publication. DOI: 10.1108/cpoib-06-2018-0049

Bitner, M. J. (1992). Servicescapes: The Impact of Physical Surroundings on Customers and Employees. *Journal of Marketing*, 56(2), 57–71. Advance online publication. DOI: 10.1177/002224299205600205

Bostan, S., Erdem, R., Öztürk, Y. E., Kılıç, T., & Yılmaz, A. (2020). *The effect of COVID-19 pandemic on the Turkish society*. Electronic Journal of General Medicine., DOI: 10.29333/ejgm/7944

Brahma, A., & Dutta, R. (2018). Cashless Transactions and Its Impact-A Wise Move Towards Digital India. *International Journal of Scientific Research in Computer Science, Engineering and Information Technology* © 2018 IJSRCSEIT.

Budi, A. S. L., Efendi, E., & Dahesihsari, R. (2013). *Perceived Usefulness as Key Stimulus to the Behavioral Intention to Use 3G Technology.* ASEAN Marketing Journal., DOI: 10.21002/amj.v3i2.2025

Charness, N., & Boot, W. R. (2015). Technology, Gaming, and Social Networking. In *Handbook of the Psychology of Aging: Eighth Edition.* DOI: 10.1016/B978-0-12-411469-2.00020-0

Chen, C. C., & Yao, J. Y. (2018). What drives impulse buying behaviors in a mobile auction? The perspective of the Stimulus-Organism-Response model. *Telematics and Informatics*, 35(5), 1249–1262. Advance online publication. DOI: 10.1016/j.tele.2018.02.007

Chi, G. (2005). *A study of developing destination loyalty model.* ProQuest Dissertations and Theses.

Choi, Y. (2019). Technology acceptance model and stimulus-organism response for the use intention of consumers in social commerce. *International Journal of E-Business Research*, 15(2), 93–101. Advance online publication. DOI: 10.4018/IJEBR.2019040105

Cohen, J. (1988). *Statistical power analysis for the behavioral sciences.* Lawrence Earlbaum.

Dabholkar, P. A., & Bagozzi, R. P. (2002). An attitudinal model of technology-based self-service: Moderating effects of consumer traits and situational factors. *Journal of the Academy of Marketing Science*, 30(3), 184–201. Advance online publication. DOI: 10.1177/00920703020303001

Dahlberg, T., Guo, J., & Ondrus, J. (2015, September). Guo, J., & Ondrus, J. (2015). A critical review of mobile payment research. *Electronic Commerce Research and Applications*, 14(5), 265–284. Advance online publication. DOI: 10.1016/j.elerap.2015.07.006

Dahlberg, T., Mallat, N., & Oorrni, A. (2003). Consumer acceptance of mobile payment solutions – ease of use, usefulness and trust. *Proceedings of the Second International Conference on Mobile Business (ICMB).*

Davis, F. D. (1989). Perceived usefulness, perceived ease of use, and user acceptance of information technology. *MIS Quarterly: Management. Management Information Systems Quarterly*, 13(3), 319. Advance online publication. DOI: 10.2307/249008

Davis, F. D., Bagozzi, R. P., & Warshaw, P. R. (1989, August). Bagozzi, R. P., & Warshaw, P. R. (1989). User Acceptance of Computer Technology: A Comparison of Two Theoretical Models. *Management Science*, 35(8), 982–1003. Advance online publication. DOI: 10.1287/mnsc.35.8.982

Dennehy, D., & Sammon, D. (2015). Trends in mobile payments research: A literature review. *Journal of Innovation Management.* DOI: 10.24840/2183-0606_003.001_0006

Etikan, I. (2016). Comparison of Convenience Sampling and Purposive Sampling. *American Journal of Theoretical and Applied Statistics*, 5(1), 1. Advance online publication. DOI: 10.11648/j.ajtas.20160501.11

Fornell, C., & Larcker, D. F. (1981). Evaluating structural equation models with unobservable variables and measurement error. *JMR, Journal of Marketing Research*, 18(1), 39–50. DOI: 10.1177/002224378101800104

Forsythe, S. M., & Shi, B. (2003). Consumer patronage and risk perceptions in Internet shopping. *Journal of Business Research*, 56(11), 867–875. Advance online publication. DOI: 10.1016/S0148-2963(01)00273-9

Hair, J. F., Sarstedt, M., & Ringle, C. M. (2019, April 08). Sarstedt, M., & Ringle, C. M. (2019). Rethinking some of the rethinking of partial least squares. *European Journal of Marketing*, 53(4), 566–584. Advance online publication. DOI: 10.1108/EJM-10-2018-0665

Hawi, N. S., & Samaha, M. (2017). The Relations Among Social Media Addiction, Self-Esteem, and Life Satisfaction in University Students. *Social Science Computer Review*, 35(5), 576–586. Advance online publication. DOI: 10.1177/0894439316660340

Igbaria, M., & Nachman, S. A. (1990). Correlates of user satisfaction with end user computing. An exploratory study. *Information & Management*, 19(2), 73–82. Advance online publication. DOI: 10.1016/0378-7206(90)90017-C

Islam, J. U., Shahid, S., Rasool, A., Rahman, Z., Khan, I., & Rather, R. A. (2020). Impact of website attributes on customer engagement in banking: A solicitation of stimulus-organism-response theory. *International Journal of Bank Marketing*, 38(6), 1279–1303. Advance online publication. DOI: 10.1108/IJBM-12-2019-0460

Jain, P., & Singhal, S. (2019). Digital Wallet Adoption: A Literature Review. *International Journal of Management Studies*. DOI: 10.18843/ijms/v6si1/01

Kasilingam, D. L. (2020). Understanding the attitude and intention to use smartphone chatbots for shopping. *Technology in Society*, 62, 101280. Advance online publication. DOI: 10.1016/j.techsoc.2020.101280

Kock, N. (2022). *WarpPLS user manual: Version 8.0*. ScriptWarp Systems.

Kock, N., & Lynn, G. S. (2012). Lateral collinearity and misleading results in variance-based model assessments in PLS-based SEM. *International Journal of e-Collaboration*, 10(3), 1–13.

Kumar, M. S., & Krishnan, D. S. G. (2020). Perceived Usefulness (Pu), Perceived Ease of Use (Peou), and Behavioural Intension to Use (Biu): Mediating Effect of Attitude Toward Use (AU) with Reference to Mobile Wallet Acceptance and Adoption in Rural India. SSRN *Electronic Journal*. DOI: 10.2139/ssrn.3640059

Laukkanen, T., Sinkkonen, S., Kivijärvi, M., & Laukkanen, P. (2007). Innovation resistance among mature consumers. *Journal of Consumer Marketing*, 24(7), 419–427. Advance online publication. DOI: 10.1108/07363760710834834

Liébana-Cabanillas, F., & Lara-Rubio, J. (2017). Predictive and explanatory modeling regarding adoption of mobile payment systems. *Technological Forecasting and Social Change*, 120, 32–40. Advance online publication. DOI: 10.1016/j.techfore.2017.04.002

Liébana-Cabanillas, F., Marinkovic, V., Ramos de Luna, I., & Kalinic, Z.Liébana-Cabanillas. (2018, April). Francisco, Marinkovic, V., Ramos de Luna, I., & Kalinic, Z. (2018). Predicting the determinants of mobile payment acceptance: A hybrid SEM-neural network approach. *Technological Forecasting and Social Change*, 129, 117–130. Advance online publication. DOI: 10.1016/j.techfore.2017.12.015

Lin, C. H., Shih, H. Y., & Sher, P. J. (2007). Integrating technology readiness into technology acceptance: The TRAM model. *Psychology and Marketing*, 24(7), 641–657. Advance online publication. DOI: 10.1002/mar.20177

Lin, T. C., Huang, S. L., & Hsu, C. J. (2015). A dual-factor model of loyalty to IT product - The case of smartphones. *International Journal of Information Management*, 35(2), 215–228. Advance online publication. DOI: 10.1016/j.ijinfomgt.2015.01.001

Liu, J., Kauffman, R. J., & Ma, D. (2015). Competition, cooperation, and regulation: Understanding the evolution of the mobile payments technology ecosystem. *Electronic Commerce Research and Applications*, 14(5), 372–391. Advance online publication. DOI: 10.1016/j.elerap.2015.03.003

Madan, K., & Yadav, R. (2016). Behavioural intention to adopt mobile wallet: A developing country perspective. *Journal of Indian Business Research*, 8(3), 227–244. Advance online publication. DOI: 10.1108/JIBR-10-2015-0112

Madjid, R. (2013). Customer Trust as Relationship Mediation Between Customer Satisfaction and Loyalty At Bank Rakyat Indonesia (BRI) Southeast Sulawesi. *The International Journal Of Engineering And Science*.

Marafon, D. L., Basso, K., Espartel, L. B., de Barcellos, M. D., & Rech, E. (2018). Perceived risk and intention to use internet banking: The effects of self-confidence and risk acceptance. *International Journal of Bank Marketing*, 36(2), 277–289. Advance online publication. DOI: 10.1108/IJBM-11-2016-0166

Ming, K. L. Y., Jais, M., Wen, C. C., & Zaidi, N. S. (2020). Factor Affecting Adoption of E-Wallet in Sarawak. *International Journal of Academic Research in Accounting, Finance and Management Sciences*. DOI: 10.6007/IJARAFMS/v10-i2/7446

Nizam, F., Hwang, H. J., & Valaei, N. (2019). Measuring the effectiveness of E-wallet in Malaysia. In *Studies in Computational Intelligence*. DOI: 10.1007/978-3-319-96803-2_5

Oliveira, T., Thomas, M., Baptista, G., & Campos, F. (2016). Mobile payment: Understanding the determinants of customer adoption and intention to recommend the technology. *Computers in Human Behavior*, 61, 404–414. Advance online publication. DOI: 10.1016/j.chb.2016.03.030

Peng, C., & Kim, Y. G. (2014). Application of the Stimuli-Organism-Response (S-O-R) Framework to Online Shopping Behavior. *Journal of Internet Commerce*, 13(3-4), 159–176. Advance online publication. DOI: 10.1080/15332861.2014.944437

Purba, D. E., Oostrom, J. K., Van Der Molen, H. T., & Born, M. P. (2015). Personality and organizational citizenship behavior in Indonesia: The mediating effect of affective commitment. *Asian Business & Management*, 14(2), 147–170. Advance online publication. DOI: 10.1057/abm.2014.20

Raaper, R., & Brown, C. (2020). The Covid-19 pandemic and the dissolution of the university campus: Implications for student support practice. *Journal of Professional Capital and Community*, 5(3/4), 343–349. Advance online publication. DOI: 10.1108/JPCC-06-2020-0032

Rambocas, M. M., & Arjoon, S. (2012). Using Diffusion of Innovation Theory to Model Customer Loyalty for Internet Banking: A TT Millennial Perspective. *International Journal of Business and Commerce*.

Ranaweera, C., McDougall, G., & Bansal, H. (2005). A model of online customer behavior during the initial transaction: Moderating effects of customer characteristics. *Marketing Theory*, 5(1), 51–74. Advance online publication. DOI: 10.1177/1470593105049601

Reichheld, F. F., & Schefter, P. (2000). E-Loyalty: Your secret weapon on the web. *Harvard Business Review*.

Reyes, L. G. (2021). Philippine private sector response, strategies, and state-business relations toward economic recovery and growth post-COVID-19. *Business and Politics*. Advance online publication. DOI: 10.1017/bap.2021.13

Ribbink, D., Streukens, S., Van Riel, A. C. R., & Liljander, V. (2004). Comfort your online customer: Quality, trust and loyalty on the internet. *Managing Service Quality*, 14(6), 446–456. Advance online publication. DOI: 10.1108/09604520410569784

Ringle, C. M., Sarstedt, M., Mitchell, R., & Gudergan, S. P. (2020). Partial least squares structural equation modeling in HRM research. *International Journal of Human Resource Management*, 31(12), 1617–1643. Advance online publication. DOI: 10.1080/09585192.2017.1416655

Rousseau, D. M., Sitkin, S. B., Burt, R. S., & Camerer, C. (1998). Not so different after all: A cross-discipline view of trust. In *Academy of Management Review*. DOI: 10.5465/amr.1998.926617

Sari, N. N., Yuliana, D., Hervidea, R., & Agata, A. (2020). *Health Protocol of Covid-19: as A Prevention of Covid-19 in the Work Area of Office Employees in Bandar Lampung*. Jurnal Peduli Masyarakat., DOI: 10.37287/jpm.v2i4.235

Sarstedt, M., Ringle, C. M., & Joseph, F. Hair. (2017). Partial least squares structural equation modeling (PLS-SEM). *Handbook of Market Research*.

Settersten, R. A.Jr, Bernardi, L., Härkönen, J., Antonucci, T. C., Dykstra, P. A., Heckhausen, J., Kuh, D., Mayer, K. U., Moen, P., Mortimer, J. T., Mulder, C. H., Smeeding, T. M., van der Lippe, T., Hagestad, G. O., Kohli, M., Levy, R., Schoon, I., & Thomson, E. (2020). Understanding the effects of Covid-19 through a life course lens. *Advances in Life Course Research*, 45, 100360. Advance online publication. DOI: 10.1016/j.alcr.2020.100360 PMID: 36698274

Singh, N., Sinha, N., & Liébana-Cabanillas, F. J. (2020). Determining factors in the adoption and recommendation of mobile wallet services in India: Analysis of the effect of innovativeness, stress to use and social influence. *International Journal of Information Management*, 50, 191–205. Advance online publication. DOI: 10.1016/j.ijinfomgt.2019.05.022

Song, S., Yao, X., & Wen, N. (2021). What motivates Chinese consumers to avoid information about the COVID-19 pandemic?: The perspective of the stimulus-organism-response model. *Information Processing & Management*, 58(1), 102407. Advance online publication. DOI: 10.1016/j.ipm.2020.102407 PMID: 33041437

Sur, S. (2015). The Role of Online Trust and Satisfaction in Building Loyalty Towards Online Retailers: Differences Between Heavy and Light Shopper Groups. In *LISS 2014*. DOI: 10.1007/978-3-662-43871-8_71

Swilley, E. (2010). Technology rejection: The case of the wallet phone. *Journal of Consumer Marketing*, 27(4), 304–312. Advance online publication. DOI: 10.1108/07363761011052341

Syifa, N., & Tohang, V. (2020). The use of e-wallet system. *Proceedings of 2020 International Conference on Information Management and Technology, ICIMTech 2020*. DOI: 10.1109/ICIMTech50083.2020.9211213

Tahar, A., Riyadh, H. A., Sofyani, H., & Purnomo, W. E. (2020). Perceived ease of use, perceived usefulness, perceived security and intention to use e-filing: The role of technology readiness. *Journal of Asian Finance, Economics and Business*. DOI: 10.13106/jafeb.2020.vol7.no9.537

Taheri, F., & Alaaeddin Shourmasti, M. (2016). *Effects of various characteristics of social commerce on consumers' trust and trust performance*. International Academic Journal of Business Management.

Thakur, R., & Srivastava, M. (2014). Adoption readiness, personal innovativeness, perceived risk and usage intention across customer groups for mobile payment services in India. *Internet Research*, 24(3), 369–392. Advance online publication. DOI: 10.1108/IntR-12-2012-0244

Tusyanah, T., & Wahyudin, A. (2020). Analyzing Factors Affecting the Behavioral Intention to Use e-Wallet with the UTAUT Model with Experience as Moderating Variable. *Journal of Economics*.

Undale, S., Kulkarni, A., & Patil, H. (2021). Perceived eWallet security: Impact of COVID-19 pandemic. *Vilakshan - XIMB. Journal of Management*, 18(1), 89–104. Advance online publication. DOI: 10.1108/XJM-07-2020-0022

Venkatesh, V., Thong, J. Y. L., & Xu, X. (2012). Consumer acceptance and use of information technology: Extending the unified theory of acceptance and use of technology. *MIS Quarterly: Management. Management Information Systems Quarterly*, 36(1), 157. Advance online publication. DOI: 10.2307/41410412

Wang, L. Y. K., Lew, S. L., & Lau, S. H. (2020). An empirical study of students' intention to use cloud e-learning in higher education. *International Journal of Emerging Technologies in Learning*, 15(9), 19. Advance online publication. DOI: 10.3991/ijet.v15i09.11867

Wei, J., & Liu, Y. (2015). Government support and firm innovation performance: Empirical analysis of 343 innovative enterprises in China. *Chinese Management Studies*, 9(1), 38–55. Advance online publication. DOI: 10.1108/CMS-01-2015-0018

Yean, T. S. (2020). The Hosting of International Production in ASEAN, Post- Pandemic. In *ISEAS Yusof Ishak Institute Perspective*.

Yıldırım, M., Geçer, E., & Akgül, Ö. (2021). The impacts of vulnerability, perceived risk, and fear on preventive behaviours against COVID-19. *Psychology Health and Medicine*, 26(1), 35–43. Advance online publication. DOI: 10.1080/13548506.2020.1776891 PMID: 32490689

Zhou, T. (2011). An empirical examination of initial trust in mobile banking. *Internet Research*, 21(5), 527–540. Advance online publication. DOI: 10.1108/10662241111176353

Chapter 17
Sustainable Travel Behavior:
The Influence of Digital Marketing and Social Media

Suraj Jaywant Yadav
https://orcid.org/0000-0002-2687-4852
D.Y. Patil Education Society, India

ABSTRACT

Sustainable travel behavior has become crucial as tourism's environmental impact grows. Digital marketing and social media play vital roles in promoting sustainable tourism. This study explores how digital marketing campaigns influence consumers' sustainable travel choices and the role of social media in shaping these behaviors. It identifies key digital marketing strategies that encourage sustainable decisions and examines the impact of user-generated content (UGC) on social media. The results indicate that high social media usage and digital marketing exposure are strong predictors of sustainable travel behaviors, with females showing higher awareness. Digital marketing's effectiveness in promoting sustainable travel is highlighted by significant relationships and logistic regression findings (χ^2 = 15.34, p = 0.000). Findings revealed high social media usage (mean = 4.1) and moderate awareness of sustainable travel (mean = 3.5), and digital marketing exposure, with odds ratios of 1.73 and 3.32, respectively, highlighting their potential to promote sustainable practices.

INTRODUCTION

As one of the major global industries, tourism can have many advantages, chief among them being economic. Nevertheless, the increasing popularity of travel among tourists has started to irreversibly harm the environment, cultural heritage, and way of life of the locals in tourist destinations. Sustainable development in tourism has become imperative in recent times. However, for these processes to be effectively executed, people's perceptions about environmental conservation, the use of sustainable products, leading healthy lives, and the preservation of tourist sites need to be reshaped(Baltezarevic et al., 2022).One of the main challenges is organizing travel more sustainably. This modifies the definition of transportation problems, the factors that influence them, and the kinds of solutions that should be taken into account. It also affects the agenda for transport research. The psychological aspects of the transportation user, who is now seen as an active participant in the system, are also brought to light by this new

DOI: 10.4018/979-8-3693-9230-0.ch017

Copyright ©2025, IGI Global. Copying or distributing in print or electronic forms without written permission of IGI Global is prohibited.

challenge. The abilities and perceived limitations of users will therefore be taken into consideration for more successful transport policy measures(Gehlert et al., 2013). There are a plethora of mobile phone applications available for tracking and modifying behavior. The majority of developed apps seem to be related to health, but during the last ten years, "persuasive technology" has also been used and applied to encourage environmentally friendly travel practices(Sunio & Schmöcker, 2017). Higher proportions of greener and more effective forms of transportation are required, particularly in urban areas, due to the detrimental effects of transportation on pollution, traffic, and climate change. While some of these problems can be resolved by new technology, changing behavior is also a key component in achieving the shift from cars to walking, cycling, or public transportation(Andersson et al., 2018). The current state of affairs offers a chance to reevaluate changing the world tourist system in a way that better supports sustainable development objectives. The literature emphasizes how important it is for the tourism industry to apply sustainable development principles. Consequently, the current discourse offers a chance to contemplate various approaches to revolutionize the tourism industry. Numerous parties are embroiled in tourism endeavors, each anticipating personal gains. The ability to make coordinated decisions between various management entities, enhance the articulation of tourism products and the management of information and impacts, is why regions are interested in obtaining standardized and high-quality tourism data. Consequently, visitors anticipate being able to unwind in a secure environment, posing a problem for urban planning. As a result, it's essential to establish and preserve the right circumstances and carry out initiatives for smart city(Hysa et al., 2022). Tourism organizations now consider environmental awareness and visitor behavior to be critical issues. They support campaigns that raise awareness of sustainable environmental issues and make an effort to persuade travelers to actively adopt eco-friendly behaviors. Furthermore, a lot of coastal locations lack any awareness-raising initiatives or efficient plans for influencing the psychological health of visitors. In this case, user-generated content on social media could be very important in changing how environmentally conscious travelers are of coastal areas(Sultan, Sharmin, Badulescu, Stiubea, et al., 2021). Promoting sustainable tourism may depend on appealing to travelers' innate desire for first-rate travel experiences and inspiring them to take on more environmental responsibility on a personal level. The selection, delivery, and style of pro-environmental messaging have become increasingly important for tourism managers and marketers due to the proliferation of media channels. User-generated content (UGC) on social media is now considered to be a more reliable source of travel information than official channels. However, little is known about UGC's potential to promote pro-environmental norms(Han et al., 2018). Sustainable purchasing is the act of choosing goods that are socially, economically, and environmentally responsible. Green products minimize their impact on the environment over the course of their life cycle and are sustainable and eco-friendly. The two main goals of sustainable products are waste reduction and resource efficiency optimization. Using sustainable products helps consumers prevent or lessen their impact on the environment(Ebrahimi et al., 2021). The advent of social media has caused a global paradigm shift in communication methods by enabling users to interact, observe, and share information. Social media's development as a new technology has altered how the tourism industry operates, which has had a big impact on the sustainable tourism industry. In addition to holding seminars and releasing yearly reports, a number of international organizations, including the World Wide Fund for Nature, The International Eco-Tourism Society, Eco-Tourism Society of India, Rainforest Alliance, Sustainable Travel International, and Global Sustainable Tourism Council, are constantly working to market and spread awareness of sustainable tourism through social media platforms. Social media platforms such as Facebook, Instagram, Twitter, Google+, and Pinterest are used by travel companies to stay in touch with other stakeholders(Chatterjee & Dsilva, 2021).

BACKGROUND

Many studies on travel behaviour have been conducted to change people's travel habits to be more sustainable because sustainable travel has grown in importance. The first step in this research was to analyse how different transportation policy measures and technologies, like pricing instruments, affected people's behaviour(Gehlert et al., 2013). One of the main concerns for the future has been identified as sustainable urban mobility. To accomplish this, it will be necessary to shift away from the use of single-occupancy, fossil fuel-powered vehicles. This can be done by developing new solutions, implementing existing ones, and altering how people travel on a daily basis(Strömberg et al., 2016). Influencers in the travel industry are very significant on social media these days. There's a strong likelihood that followers of influencers who prioritize environmental conservation, healthy living, and the growth of sustainable tourism will follow suit. Since electronic word-of-mouth (eWOM) communication has the potential to go viral, positive information will probably continue to spread rapidly online and exert an unchecked influence(Baltezarevic et al., 2022). The Internet, artificial intelligence, open data, and big data—all of which have been heavily employed in the travel industry for many years—come to the rescue. Large data sets and smart city solutions are driving more and more successful tourism management in cities. Mount Etna, an active volcano in Southern Italy that has been inducted into the UNESCO World Heritage List since 2017, is a common example of how well new technologies and social media can be used as data sources and analytical tools.

Furthermore, research suggests that smart tourism has a big impact on travel destinations, companies, and travelers themselves. The core of smart tourism's expansion is sustainability, which is why more travel destinations are starting to prioritize it as a strategic goal during the tourism planning phase. Furthermore, data on successfully implemented sustainable smart city solutions can be utilized to enhance cities' appeal and promote their image(Hysa et al., 2022). The goal of society 5.0 is to establish a world in which everyone has access to basic goods and services at all times and locations, irrespective of geographic location, age, gender, language barrier, or other constraints. It seeks to overcome social obstacles, attain economic growth and well-being simultaneously, and thereby improve the lot of the world's population(Hysa et al., 2021). In order to comprehend a genuine relationship between digital tourism business practices and visitor satisfaction, researchers and service providers focus on tourism. Additionally, the owner and the community are empowered by the tourism industry's legacy through digital marketing(Deb et al., 2022). Customers can post and share comments, opinions, and personal travel experiences on the majority of these social media platforms, which further serves as a source of information for other users. Numerous scholarly investigations have documented the growing significance of search engines in producing upstream traffic to travel-related websites. Because of this, search engines have served as a "gateway" for marketing channels pertaining to travel and have developed into a powerful and significant information source with the ability to persuade and draw in potential travelers(Sultan, Sharmin, Badulescu, Gavrilut, et al., 2021).

When it comes to information seeking, destination selection, and decision-making throughout a tour or trip, social media is an indispensable tool for tourists. The tourism industry has entered a new era thanks to consumer use of social media. Many nations have focused especially on promoting social media in their societies because of the important role that social media plays in shaping consumer attitudes toward rural tourism. The advent of social media has brought about a complete transformation in the behaviour of tourists. Social media has made it possible for travellers to locate clear information. Social media use has an immediate effect on tourism since every traveller uses it with a specific intention and seeks control over their trip. Using social media gives travellers control over their activities(Hussain et al., 2018). The world we live in is being drastically altered by the digital revolution. Smart home sensors allow appliances like laptops, tablets, TVs, washing machines, thermostats, and other items to be connected to the Internet of Things networks. Significant advancements have been made in factories, hotels, hospitals, cities, and territories thanks to new digital technologies. Industry 4.0 is announcing the end of well-established patterns and requesting that academics, managers, and citizens who are prepared to live in this dynamic and ever-more complex environment view it through fresh perspectives and novel paradigms(Pencarelli, 2020).

Research Objectives

1. To analyze the effectiveness of digital marketing campaigns in promoting sustainable travel behavior among consumers.
2. To examine the role of social media platforms in shaping travelers' perceptions and practices of sustainable travel.
3. To identify key digital marketing strategies that effectively influence sustainable travel decisions.
4. To explore the interaction between user-generated content on social media and sustainable travel behavior.
5. To evaluate the long-term impact of digital marketing and social media initiatives on sustainable travel practices.

Theoretical Framework

Urban policy, defined as an intentional and planned activity of local authorities, developed and executed in collaboration with other entities pursuing their goals and satisfying their needs in the city area, includes tourism as a crucial element. Providing a high standard of living for locals and an excellent experience for guests is the main goal of local, sustainable development strategies. Thus, in order to help accomplish this goal, solutions related to sustainable development must be put into practice(Hysa et al., 2022). In the travel industry, the growing influence of social media influencers (SMIs) is changing consumer behavior. In influencer and traveler marketing, trust is a critical component that builds and sustains fruitful, enduring connections between businesses and customers(Pop et al., 2022). Social media websites have developed into web-based forums where people can communicate, share content, and share ideas. Travelers now utilize social media to compare experiences when choosing destinations, things to buy, and where to eat. With the aid of GPS and social media, travelers can now check in on time and share their experiences at specific destination sites to assist future and potential travelers in planning their trips(Armutcu et al., 2023). For marketers, the quickly changing digital landscape has become a vital resource. With internet-based platforms, it is possible to communicate with the target market more effectively. Even before the development of digital technologies, influencers were a significant factor in the lives of other members of society. On the other hand, as a type of word-of-mouth communication in a digital setting, electronic word-of-mouth communication, or eWOM, can be a very effective tool for influencing consumer attitudes, including attitudes toward the development of sustainable tourism(Baltezarevic et al., 2022).

The process of choosing, paying for, and utilizing a good or service to fulfill one's needs and desires is known as consumer behavior. Consumer behavior serves as a critical gauge of the caliber, efficacy, and suitability of work in the tourism industry as well as other domains of consumption. Traveler behavior happens both before and after the trip, both in terms of planning and execution. Tour operators and destinations must identify various forms of behavior at each stage in order to evaluate their marketing and operational relevance approach to the development, marketing, and implementation of tourism activities(Lemy et al., 2021). Travelers today use new technologies to help them plan their vacations and find information about a destination, services available, and tourist attractions. The goal of marketing initiatives is to persuade prospective travelers to take advantage of what the business or area has to offer. Organizations are using new technologies, such as social media, more frequently in this field as technology advances. The travel industry spent USD 5.5 trillion on digital advertising in 2019, which accounted for 4.2 percent of all digital spending(Hysa et al., 2021). The primary factor influencing the sustainable use of the environment is environmental concern. This component—which is defined as a person's association with the environment—is known as "emotional attachment towards environmental concerns.". Tourists' concerns about the environment are linked to their interest in the biophysical environment and its issues. Individual expressions of environmental concerns have been shown to be based on the features, benefits, and information of the product(Sultan, Sharmin, Badulescu, Stiubea, et al., 2021).

Figure 1. Strategies for digital marketing and social media on promoting sustainable travel

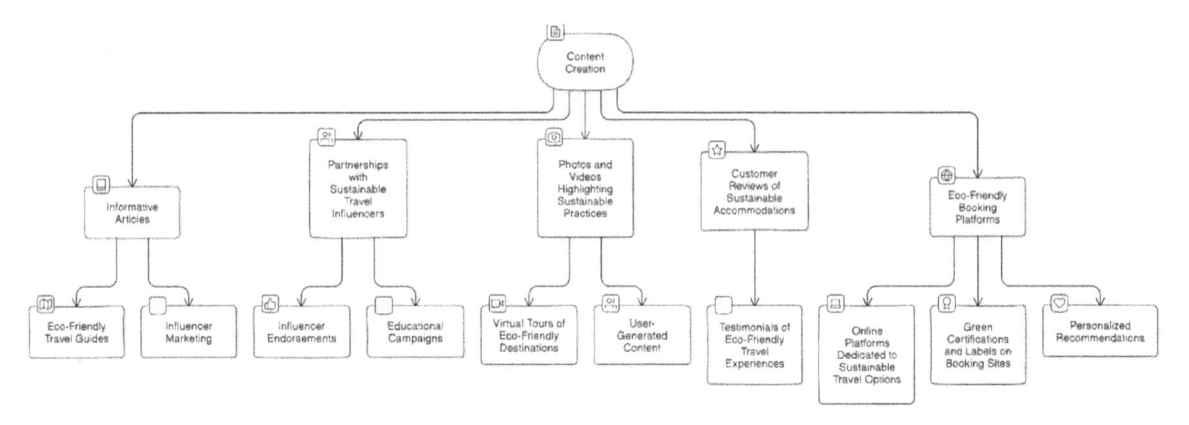

A traveler's intended destination is influenced by a variety of factors, including social media communities, friends, family, travel documentaries, and prior travel experiences. Research on tourism suggests that social media can improve the efficacy of marketing strategies and decision-making related to travel. When it comes to sustainable travel options, a variety of user-generated content (UGC) platforms, including blogs, online forums, and social networks like Instagram, YouTube, and Flickr, have become extremely popular (Sultan, Sharmin, Badulescu, Gavrilut, et al., 2021). Travelers are increasingly using social media as a means of communication and entertainment, sharing their travel experiences, choosing sustainable destinations, and gathering travel information. These uses have increased the sociability and effectiveness of social media-based tools, platforms, and services. Different countries, generations, and cultures use social media for travel and tourism in different ways. Additionally, how credible consumers believe social media is a major factor in how effective social media is(Sharmin et al., 2021). Social media platforms are used by users to share videos, photos, and information. Travelers now search for, read, handle, and trust information very differently thanks to social media, which also makes it simpler for them to create destination information. Travelers read, use, and share information prior to, during, and following their trip in order to produce content for social media(Mitsopoulou et al., 2023). Travelers' use of the Internet to plan their trips can be understood using a variety of frameworks, but it's crucial to consider this behavior as an adaptation to the rapidly evolving technological landscape. In other words, Internet technology was created to be used in a range of real-world situations. This use "spills over" into the planning of travel, allowing passengers to modify their behavior to take advantage of the new channels and, consequently, leads(Xiang et al., 2015). Two of the most important communication networks influencing how tourists perceive the festival brand are the Internet and social media. Social media has developed into a vital component of tourism organizations' marketing and communications strategies in the twenty-first century. DMOs use social media networks as platforms for nation-building, state-building, and city-marketing initiatives. It is a social media platform that goes beyond simple communication and informing travelers about places to visit. Social media is changing how DMOs use the internet to market festival products by consuming content and contributing their ideas, opinions, and creations. However, this has skewed how information is produced and disseminated for use by tourists(Arasli et al., 2021). Social media has transformed consumer interactions with one another and brought transparency. When a business or individual uses social media as a marketing channel, they should offer marketing services, techniques, strategies, and plans that reflect community characteristics and show social participation. Social network marketing content should not only focus on commercial aspects, but also have a social orientation or involve active user interaction to foster strong relationships and deep communication(Ebrahimi et al., 2021). It is becoming more and more crucial for travelers to use social media as a source of information. This study aims to determine the frequency with which social media websites surface in search engine results when users enter travel-related queries. The study used a set of pre-defined terms to simulate how a traveler might use a search engine to plan their itinerary. An examination of the search results reveals that a sizable portion of them are related to social media, suggesting that search engines most likely lead users to social media websites(Kurdi et al., 2023). It is well-established that the travel and tourism sector benefits greatly from having strong social media brands. Customers and travel companies can interact through social media brands, and consumers may or may not grow devoted to them. The current study indicates that the development of brand loyalty is strongly influenced by trust in a social media brand. Based on established theories, brand, company, and customer attributes all have an impact on people's trust in travel-related social media brands(Christou, 2015). the expanding significance of social media in the field of online travel. It also provides evidence for challenges faced by traditional providers of travel-related information. There is a discussion of the implications for online marketing strategies for tourism marketers(Xiang & Gretzel, 2010). The effects of image on a number of outcomes, such as willingness to pay more, word-of-mouth, and booking intention, are amplified by pro-environmental attitudes.

The results will assist business owners in creating marketing plans that work and in utilizing social media to advertise their brands sustainably(Tanford et al., 2020). Perspectives on smart tourism, such as sustainability, circular economy, quality of life, and social value, should also focus on improving visitor experiences and boosting the destinations' comparative advantage. Assuming smartness and sustainability as the appropriate paradigm for enhancing the quality of life and social value of both visitors and locals, tourism 4.0 technologies must be focused on improving the caliber of tourism practices(Pencarelli, 2020). In order to ensure sustainable growth in this sector, it is imperative to monitor and promptly post adequate responses to queries, comments, and reviews made by online visitors. This will help to generate a positive image of the destination among medical tourists, residents, travel and tourism operators, and other stakeholders. By investigating the use of social media in medical tourism, a rapidly expanding sector of the travel and hospitality industry, the study advances both theory and practice(John, 2017). Social media marketing initiatives do in fact raise people's awareness of sustainability, and raising awareness of sustainability does in fact facilitate the networking of eco-tourists. However, social media marketing campaigns might not always link up prospective eco-travelers; awareness raises demand for sustainable tourism, which is also encouraged. It is evident that merely introducing prospective eco-tourists does not automatically generate demand. Social media marketing campaigns indeed play a key role in developing a steady demand from travellers(Gulati, 2021). Numerous effective social media campaigns that have engaged travelers and effectively promoted destinations have been seen by the tourism industry. One such instance is the "Best Jobs in the World" campaign by Tourism Australia, which promoted Australia as a desirable travel destination through influencer marketing and user-generated content.

Through encouraging people to make movies featuring ideal Australian careers, the program fostered a sense of community and excitement among viewers regarding Australia's tourism appeal(Sumaia Afren, 2024). Traditionally, tourism marketing has been viewed as hedonistic consumerism's fuel and an exploitative practise. However, sustainability marketing can make good use of marketing strategies and tactics by comprehending consumer needs, creating more environmentally friendly products, and figuring out more effective ways to communicate in order to influence consumer behavior. The most recent research on the ideas, practices, and outcomes of marketing that aims to improve tourist destinations as places to visit and reside is compiled in this article. It examines the two core strategies of sustainability marketing: sustainable product development and market development through market segmentation(Font & McCabe, 2017). Information shared by publishers who share similar values tends to draw in more customers. It's no secret that readers search for profiles and preferences that resemble their own when they read reviews or other user-generated content. Internet users are more likely to gather data that confirms their beliefs, filter out contradictory data, and create divisive communities based on common stories(Wang & Yan, 2022). Tourism service providers are using social media platforms to interact and communicate with customers because of social media's unique interactive and innovative features. It is suggested that in this particular context, the social media tourism industry performs better due to its higher level of social media adoption and usage. Numerous research studies have demonstrated the significant impact of social media on traveler decision-making. For example, it was discovered that social media has made it possible for travel service providers to interact with stakeholders, generate value, and share information. The advancement of Industry 4.0 makes it possible for organizations to employ a wide range of cutting-edge technologies, which influences the advancement of Society 5.0. The tourism industry is increasingly utilizing AI, Big Data, and the Internet. Urban planners and managers are embracing new technologies that allow them to collect data from multiple sources and utilize it for city management. They are characterized as eco-friendly, intelligent, inventive, sensitive, participatory, green, and sustainable. Smart cities are those that optimize resources, achieve just and efficient governance, are sustainable, and prioritize quality of life through the application of cutting-edge technologies(Hysa et al., 2022).

Research Methodology

The research methodology employed involved surveying 291 participants who were selected through a stratified random sampling technique to ensure a representative sample of travelers. Data were collected using an online questionnaire designed to assess their travel behaviors, perceptions of sustainable travel, and the influence of digital marketing and social media(S. Yadav, 2021). The responses were then analyzed using various statistical tests, including descriptive statistics, chi-square tests, and multiple regression analysis, to determine the relationships and significance of digital marketing and social media on promoting sustainable travel behavior(*Handbook of Sustainable Travel | SpringerLink*, n.d.).

Data Analysis

This study investigates how digital marketing and social media influence sustainable travel behavior(S. J. Yadav, 2024). It explores the relationships between participants' demographics, such as age and gender, and their engagement in eco-friendly travel practices. The research examines how frequently individuals use social media, their awareness of sustainable travel, and the impact of digital marketing exposure. By analyzing these factors, the study reveals insights into how social media and digital marketing can enhance awareness and promote more sustainable travel behaviors among different demographics(Sunio et al., 2022).

Table 1. Descriptive statistics between age, media, and sustainable travel

Variable	Mean	Standard Deviation	Minimum	Maximum
Age	35.2	10.1	18	65
Frequency of Social Media Use	4.1	0.8	1	5
Awareness of Sustainable Travel	3.5	0.7	1	5

Table 1: Descriptive Statistics summarizes the central tendency and dispersion of key variables such as age, frequency of social media use, and awareness of sustainable travel among the participants(Cohen et al., 2013). The mean age was 35.2 years with a standard deviation of 10.1 years. Participants reported a high average frequency of social media use (mean = 4.1) and a moderate level of awareness about sustainable travel (mean = 3.5).

Table 2. Frequency distribution of participants by gender

Gender	Frequency	Percentage
Male	142	48.80%
Female	149	51.20%

Table 2: Frequency Distribution of Participants by Gender shows that the sample consisted of 142 males (48.8%) and 149 females (51.2%), indicating a fairly balanced gender distribution among the participants.

Table 3. Chi-square test for gender vs. awareness of sustainable travel

Gender	Aware	Not Aware	Chi-Square Value	p-value
Male	80	62	5.23	0.022
Female	105	44		

Table 3: Chi-Square Test for Gender vs. Awareness of Sustainable Travel indicates a statistically significant relationship between gender and awareness of sustainable travel ($\chi^2 = 5.23$, p = 0.022). Females were more likely to be aware of sustainable travel compared to males(Cohen et al., 2013).

Table 4. Independent samples t-test for age and sustainable travel behavior

Group	N	Mean	Std. Deviation	t-value	p-value
Sustainable	185	36	10.3	2.14	0.034
Non-Sustainable	106	33.5	9.8		

Table 4: Independent Samples t-Test for Age and Sustainable Travel Behavior reveals that participants engaged in sustainable travel behavior were, on average(Cohen et al., 2013), slightly older (mean age = 36.0 years) compared to those who did not engage in sustainable travel (mean age = 33.5 years). This difference was statistically significant (t = 2.14, p = 0.034).

Table 5. One-way ANOVA for frequency of social media use and sustainable travel awareness

Source	Sum of Squares	df	Mean Square	F-value	p-value
Between Groups	14.5	4	3.63	6.27	0.001
Within Groups	167.4	286	0.58		
Total	181.9	290			

Table 5: One-Way ANOVA for Frequency of Social Media Use and Sustainable Travel Awareness shows a significant effect of the frequency of social media use on awareness of sustainable travel (F = 6.27, p = 0.001). Participants who used social media more frequently were more aware of sustainable travel practices(Prillwitz & Barr, 2011).

Table 6. Correlation matrix

Variable	Age	Frequency of Social Media Use	Awareness of Sustainable Travel
Age	1	-0.12	0.08
Frequency of Social Media Use	-0.12	1	0.45**
Awareness of Sustainable Travel	0.08	0.45**	1

Table 6: Correlation Matrix presents the correlations between age, frequency of social media use, and awareness of sustainable travel. A significant positive correlation (r = 0.45, p < 0.01) was found between the frequency of social media use and awareness of sustainable travel, suggesting that higher social media use is associated with greater awareness of sustainable travel.

Table 7. Regression analysis summary

Predictor	B	Std. Error	Beta	t-value	p-value
Frequency of Social Media Use	0.34	0.05	0.43	6.8	0
Age	0.02	0.01	0.1	1.98	0.048

Table 7: Regression Analysis Summary highlights that both frequency of social media use ($\beta = 0.43$, p = 0.000) and age ($\beta = 0.10$, p = 0.048) were significant predictors of sustainable travel behavior. This implies that more frequent social media use and older age are associated with a higher likelihood of engaging in sustainable travel behavior.

Table 8. Reliability analysis for awareness of sustainable travel scale

Item	Corrected Item-Total Correlation	Cronbach's Alpha if Item Deleted
Item 1	0.45	0.72
Item 2	0.53	0.7
Item 3	0.47	0.71
Overall Cronbach's Alpha		0.75

Table 8: Reliability Analysis for Awareness of Sustainable Travel Scale shows that the scale used to measure awareness of sustainable travel had a good level of internal consistency, with an overall Cronbach's alpha of 0.75. This indicates that the items on the scale reliably measured the construct of awareness.

Table 9. Factor analysis for sustainable travel behavior items

Item	Factor 1	Factor 2
Item 1	0.75	0.22
Item 2	0.82	0.18
Item 3	0.24	0.89
Item 4	0.19	0.87

Table 9: Factor Analysis for Sustainable Travel Behavior Items reveals that the items loaded onto two distinct factors, with strong loadings on their respective factors. This suggests that the items used to measure sustainable travel behavior represented two underlying dimensions of the construct.

Table 10. Cross-tabulation of digital marketing exposure and sustainable travel behavior

Exposure to Digital Marketing	Sustainable Behaviour	Non-Sustainable Behaviour	Total
High	130	40	170
Low	55	66	121
Total	185	106	291

Table 10: Cross-tabulation of Digital Marketing Exposure and Sustainable Travel Behavior shows that a higher proportion of participants exposed to digital marketing engaged in sustainable travel behavior (130 out of 170) compared to those with low exposure (55 out of 121). This suggests a potential influence of digital marketing on sustainable travel behavior.

Table 11. Chi-square test for digital marketing exposure and sustainable travel behavior

Chi-Square Value	df	p-value
15.34	1	0

Table 11: Chi-Square Test for Digital Marketing Exposure and Sustainable Travel Behavior indicates a significant association between exposure to digital marketing and sustainable travel behavior ($\chi^2 = 15.34$, p = 0.000), supporting the notion that digital marketing positively influences sustainable travel behavior.

Table 12. Logistic regression analysis for predicting sustainable travel behavior

Predictor	B	SE	Wald	df	p-value	Exp(B)
Frequency of Social Media Use	0.55	0.13	17.6	1	0	1.73
Exposure to Digital Marketing	1.2	0.3	16	1	0	3.32

Table 12: Logistic Regression Analysis for Predicting Sustainable Travel Behavior demonstrates that both frequency of social media use (Exp(B) = 1.73, p = 0.000) and exposure to digital marketing (Exp(B) = 3.32, p = 0.000) were significant predictors of sustainable travel behavior. This suggests that increased social media use and higher exposure to digital marketing substantially increase the likelihood of engaging in sustainable travel behavior.

Result

The results from the study reveal several key insights into the factors influencing sustainable travel behavior. The participants had a mean age of 35.2 years (SD = 10.1), reported a high average frequency of social media use (mean = 4.1), and displayed a moderate level of awareness of sustainable travel (mean = 3.5). The sample was fairly balanced by gender, with 48.8% males and 51.2% females. Chi-square analysis showed a significant relationship between gender and awareness of sustainable travel ($\chi^2 = 5.23$, p = 0.022), with females being more aware. An independent samples t-test revealed that individuals who engaged in sustainable travel behavior were slightly older (mean age = 36.0 years) compared to those who did not (mean age = 33.5 years), a statistically significant difference (t = 2.14, p = 0.034). A one-way ANOVA demonstrated that more frequent social media use was associated with greater awareness of sustainable travel practices (F = 6.27, p = 0.001). Correlation analysis found a significant positive relationship between social media use and sustainable travel awareness (r = 0.45, p < 0.01), and regression analysis showed that both social media use ($\beta = 0.43$, p = 0.000) and age ($\beta = 0.10$, p = 0.048) were significant predictors of sustainable travel behavior. Additionally, a reliability analysis showed that the awareness of sustainable travel scale had a Cronbach's alpha of 0.75. Factor analysis revealed two distinct dimensions of sustainable travel behavior. Cross-tabulation indicated that 76.5% of participants exposed to digital marketing engaged in sustainable travel behavior compared to 45.5% with low exposure, with a significant association found between digital marketing exposure and sustainable travel behavior ($\chi^2 = 15.34$, p = 0.000). Finally, logistic regression demonstrated that both social media use (Exp(B) = 1.73, p = 0.000) and digital marketing exposure (Exp(B) = 3.32, p = 0.000) were strong predictors of sustainable travel behavior.

CONCLUSION

The analysis presented through these tables offers a thorough examination of the factors influencing sustainable travel behavior, with a particular focus on the roles of social media and digital marketing(Barr & Prillwitz, 2012). The descriptive statistics reveal a sample with a moderate level of awareness about sustainable travel and high social media engagement, with the average participant being in their mid-thirties(*Sustainability | Free Full-Text | Studying the Joint Effects of Perceived Service Quality, Perceived Benefits, and Environmental Concerns in Sustainable Travel Behavior: Extending the TPB*, n.d.). Gender differences were evident, as females exhibited greater awareness of sustainable travel compared to males. Additionally, older participants were more likely to engage in sustainable travel behavior(Jariyasunant et al., 2011). A significant relationship was found between social media use and sustainable travel awareness, with frequent users demonstrating a higher awareness of sustainable practices. The one-way ANOVA results showed that increased social media use was associated with greater awareness of sustainable travel, while the correlation matrix confirmed a positive relationship between social media frequency and travel awareness(Majid et al., 2024). The regression analysis further established that both frequent social media use and higher age significantly predicted sustainable travel behavior. Factor analysis identified two distinct dimensions of sustainable travel behavior, underscoring the complexity of the construct. The cross-tabulation and chi-square tests revealed that exposure to digital marketing was positively associated with sustainable travel behavior, and logistic regression analysis confirmed that both social media use and digital marketing exposure were significant predictors of engaging in sustainable travel practices(Van Acker et al., 2016). Collectively, these findings underscore the critical role of digital marketing and social media in promoting sustainable travel behavior. The results suggest that targeted digital marketing strategies and increased social media engagement could effectively enhance awareness and participation in sustainable travel practices, offering valuable insights for future initiatives aimed at fostering sustainable travel behaviors among diverse populations(Dolnicar et al., 2010).

Future Scope

Based on the study's findings, future research should consider several key guidelines to further explore and enhance the understanding of sustainable travel behavior. Firstly, future studies should investigate the impact of specific types of social media content and digital marketing strategies on sustainable travel practices, as different approaches may have varying levels of effectiveness(Makarewicz, 2020). Additionally, exploring the role of other demographic variables, such as education level and income, in conjunction with age and gender, could provide a more nuanced understanding of factors influencing sustainable travel behavior(Høyer, 2000). It is also important to examine the long-term effects of digital marketing campaigns and social media interactions on participants' sustained engagement in sustainable travel practices. Expanding the research to include diverse geographical regions and cultural contexts could reveal additional insights into global trends and challenges related to sustainable travel. Finally(Tarrant et al., 2014), incorporating qualitative methods, such as interviews or focus groups, alongside quantitative measures, could yield deeper insights into the motivations and barriers associated with sustainable travel behavior, helping to develop more targeted and effective interventions(Tarrant et al., 2014).

REFERENCES

Afren, S. (2024). The role of digital marketing promoting tourism business: A study of use of the social media in promoting travel. *World Journal of Advanced Research and Reviews*, 21(1), 272–287. DOI: 10.30574/wjarr.2024.21.1.2668

Andersson, A., Winslott Hiselius, L., & Adell, E. (2018). Promoting sustainable travel behaviour through the use of smartphone applications: A review and development of a conceptual model. *Travel Behaviour & Society*, 11, 52–61. DOI: 10.1016/j.tbs.2017.12.008

Arasli, H., Abdullahi, M., & Gunay, T. (2021). Social Media as a Destination Marketing Tool for a Sustainable Heritage Festival in Nigeria: A Moderated Mediation Study. *Sustainability (Basel)*, 13(11), 11. Advance online publication. DOI: 10.3390/su13116191

Armutcu, B., Tan, A., Amponsah, M., Parida, S., & Ramkissoon, H. (2023). Tourist behaviour: The role of digital marketing and social media. *Acta Psychologica*, 240, 104025. DOI: 10.1016/j.actpsy.2023.104025 PMID: 37741033

Baltezarevic, R., Baltezarevic, B., & Baltezarevic, V. (2022). The role of travel influencers in sustainable tourism development. *International Review (Steubenville, Ohio)*, 12(3-4), 125–129. DOI: 10.5937/intrev2204131B

Barr, S., & Prillwitz, J. (2012). Green travellers? Exploring the spatial context of sustainable mobility styles. *Applied Geography (Sevenoaks, England)*, 32(2), 798–809. DOI: 10.1016/j.apgeog.2011.08.002

Chatterjee, J., & Dsilva, N. R. (2021). A study on the role of social media in promoting sustainable tourism in the states of Assam and Odisha. *Tourism Critiques: Practice and Theory*, 2(1), 74–90. DOI: 10.1108/TRC-09-2020-0017

Christou, E. (2015). Branding Social Media in the Travel Industry. *Procedia: Social and Behavioral Sciences*, 175, 607–614. DOI: 10.1016/j.sbspro.2015.01.1244

Cohen, S. A., Higham, J. E. S., & Reis, A. C. (2013). Sociological barriers to developing sustainable discretionary air travel behaviour. *Journal of Sustainable Tourism*, 21(7), 982–998. DOI: 10.1080/09669582.2013.809092

Deb, S. K., Nafi, S., & Valeri, M. (2022). Promoting tourism business through digital marketing in the new normal era: A sustainable approach. *European Journal of Innovation Management*, 27(3), 775–799. DOI: 10.1108/EJIM-04-2022-0218

Dolnicar, S., Laesser, C., & Matus, K. (2010). Short-haul city travel is truly environmentally sustainable. *Tourism Management*, 31(4), 505–512. DOI: 10.1016/j.tourman.2009.06.002

Ebrahimi, P., Khajeheian, D., & Fekete-Farkas, M. (2021). A SEM-NCA Approach towards Social Networks Marketing: Evaluating Consumers' Sustainable Purchase Behavior with the Moderating Role of Eco-Friendly Attitude. *International Journal of Environmental Research and Public Health*, 18(24), 24. Advance online publication. DOI: 10.3390/ijerph182413276 PMID: 34948884

Font, X., & McCabe, S. (2017). Sustainability and marketing in tourism: Its contexts, paradoxes, approaches, challenges and potential. *Journal of Sustainable Tourism*, 25(7), 869–883. DOI: 10.1080/09669582.2017.1301721

Gehlert, T., Dziekan, K., & Gärling, T. (2013). Psychology of sustainable travel behavior. *Transportation Research Part A, Policy and Practice*, 48, 19–24. DOI: 10.1016/j.tra.2012.10.001

Gulati, S. (2021). Social and sustainable: Exploring social media use for promoting sustainable behaviour and demand amongst Indian tourists. *International Hospitality Review*, 36(2), 373–393. DOI: 10.1108/IHR-12-2020-0072

Han, W., McCabe, S., Wang, Y., & Chong, A. Y. L. (2018). Evaluating user-generated content in social media: An effective approach to encourage greater pro-environmental behavior in tourism? *Journal of Sustainable Tourism*, 26(4), 600–614. DOI: 10.1080/09669582.2017.1372442

Handbook of Sustainable Travel | SpringerLink. (n.d.). Retrieved July 16, 2024, from https://link.springer.com/book/10.1007/978-94-007-7034-8

Høyer, K. G. (2000). Sustainable Tourism or Sustainable Mobility? The Norwegian Case. *Journal of Sustainable Tourism*, 8(2), 147–160. DOI: 10.1080/09669580008667354

Hussain, T., Li, B., & Wang, D. (2018). What Factors Influence the Sustainable Tour Process in Social Media Usage? Examining a Rural Mountain Region in Pakistan. *Sustainability (Basel)*, 10(7), 7. Advance online publication. DOI: 10.3390/su10072220

Hysa, B., Karasek, A., & Zdonek, I. (2021). Social Media Usage by Different Generations as a Tool for Sustainable Tourism Marketing in Society 5.0 Idea. *Sustainability (Basel)*, 13(3), 3. Advance online publication. DOI: 10.3390/su13031018

Hysa, B., Zdonek, I., & Karasek, A. (2022). Social Media in Sustainable Tourism Recovery. *Sustainability (Basel)*, 14(2), 2. Advance online publication. DOI: 10.3390/su14020760

Jariyasunant, J., Carrel, A., Ekambaram, V., Gaker, D. J., Kote, T., Sengupta, R., & Walker, J. L. (2011). *The Quantified Traveler: Using personal travel data to promote sustainable transport behavior*. https://escholarship.org/uc/item/678537sx

John, S. P. (2017). An analysis of the social media practices for sustainable medical tourism destination marketing. *International Journal of Tourism Policy*, 7(3), 222–249. DOI: 10.1504/IJTP.2017.086965

Kurdi, B. A., Alshurideh, M. T., Alkurdi, S. H., Akour, I. A., & Wasfi, A. A. (2023). Travel Bloggers and Vloggers stimulus the Sustainability: An Empirical Evidence of Digital Marketing from Travel and Tourism Industry. [IJTOP]. *International Journal of Theory of Organization and Practice*, 3(1), 1. Advance online publication. DOI: 10.54489/ijtop.v3i1.241

Lemy, D., Pramezwary, A., Juliana, J., Pramono, R., & Nabila, L. (2021). Explorative Study of Tourist Behavior in Seeking Information to Travel Planning. *International Journal of Sustainable Development and Planning*, 16(8), 1583–1589. DOI: 10.18280/ijsdp.160819

Majid, G. M., Tussyadiah, I., & Kim, Y. R. (2024). Exploring the Potential of Chatbots in Extending Tourists' Sustainable Travel Practices. *Journal of Travel Research*, 00472875241247316, 00472875241247316. Advance online publication. DOI: 10.1177/00472875241247316

Makarewicz, C. (2020). Balancing education opportunities with sustainable travel and development. In Deakin, E. (Ed.), *Transportation, Land Use, and Environmental Planning* (pp. 299–331). Elsevier., DOI: 10.1016/B978-0-12-815167-9.00016-5

Mitsopoulou, E., Moustaka, E., Kamariotou, M. I., & Kitsios, F. C. (2023). User Generated Content and Social Media Platforms in Digital Marketing: Determinants of Perceived Value and Travel Information Trust. In Matsatsinis, N. F., Kitsios, F. C., Madas, M. A., & Kamariotou, M. I. (Eds.), *Operational Research in the Era of Digital Transformation and Business Analytics* (pp. 235–241). Springer International Publishing., DOI: 10.1007/978-3-031-24294-6_25

Pencarelli, T. (2020). The digital revolution in the travel and tourism industry. *Information Technology & Tourism*, 22(3), 455–476. DOI: 10.1007/s40558-019-00160-3

Pop, R.-A., Săplăcan, Z., Dabija, D.-C., & Alt, M.-A. (2022). The impact of social media influencers on travel decisions: The role of trust in consumer decision journey. *Current Issues in Tourism*, 25(5), 823–843. DOI: 10.1080/13683500.2021.1895729

Prillwitz, J., & Barr, S. (2011). Moving towards sustainability? Mobility styles, attitudes and individual travel behaviour. *Journal of Transport Geography*, 19(6), 1590–1600. DOI: 10.1016/j.jtrangeo.2011.06.011

Sharmin, F., Sultan, M. T., Wang, D., Badulescu, A., & Li, B. (2021). Cultural Dimensions and Social Media Empowerment in Digital Era: Travel-Related Continuance Usage Intention. *Sustainability (Basel)*, 13(19), 19. Advance online publication. DOI: 10.3390/su131910820

Strömberg, H., Rexfelt, O., Karlsson, I. C. M., & Sochor, J. (2016). Trying on change – Trialability as a change moderator for sustainable travel behaviour. *Travel Behaviour & Society*, 4, 60–68. DOI: 10.1016/j.tbs.2016.01.002

Sultan, M. T., Sharmin, F., Badulescu, A., Gavrilut, D., & Xue, K. (2021). Social Media-Based Content towards Image Formation: A New Approach to the Selection of Sustainable Destinations. *Sustainability (Basel)*, 13(8), 8. Advance online publication. DOI: 10.3390/su13084241

Sultan, M. T., Sharmin, F., Badulescu, A., Stiubea, E., & Xue, K. (2021). Travelers' Responsible Environmental Behavior towards Sustainable Coastal Tourism: An Empirical Investigation on Social Media User-Generated Content. *Sustainability (Basel)*, 13(1), 1. Advance online publication. DOI: 10.3390/su13010056

Sunio, V., Cortes, R. Z., & Lactao, J. (2022). Rhetorical orientations for promoting sustainable travel behavior: A perspective. *Research in Transportation Economics*, 91, 101026. DOI: 10.1016/j.retrec.2020.101026

Sunio, V., & Schmöcker, J.-D. (2017). Can we promote sustainable travel behavior through mobile apps? Evaluation and review of evidence. *International Journal of Sustainable Transportation*, 11(8), 553–566. DOI: 10.1080/15568318.2017.1300716

Sustainability | Free Full-Text | Studying the Joint Effects of Perceived Service Quality, Perceived Benefits, and Environmental Concerns in Sustainable Travel Behavior: Extending the TPB. (n.d.). Retrieved July 16, 2024, from https://www.mdpi.com/2071-1050/15/14/11266

Tanford, S., Kim, M., & Kim, E. J. (2020). Priming social media and framing cause-related marketing to promote sustainable hotel choice. *Journal of Sustainable Tourism*, 28(11), 1762–1781. DOI: 10.1080/09669582.2020.1760287

Tarrant, M. A., Lyons, K., Stoner, L., Kyle, G. T., Wearing, S., & Poudyal, N. (2014). Global citizenry, educational travel and sustainable tourism: Evidence from Australia and New Zealand. *Journal of Sustainable Tourism*, 22(3), 403–420. DOI: 10.1080/09669582.2013.815763

Van Acker, V., Goodwin, P., & Witlox, F. (2016). Key research themes on travel behavior, lifestyle, and sustainable urban mobility. *International Journal of Sustainable Transportation*, 10(1), 25–32. DOI: 10.1080/15568318.2013.821003

Wang, H., & Yan, J. (2022). Effects of social media tourism information quality on destination travel intention: Mediation effect of self-congruity and trust. *Frontiers in Psychology*, 13, 1049149. Advance online publication. DOI: 10.3389/fpsyg.2022.1049149 PMID: 36619085

Xiang, Z., & Gretzel, U. (2010). Role of social media in online travel information search. *Tourism Management*, 31(2), 179–188. DOI: 10.1016/j.tourman.2009.02.016

Xiang, Z., Magnini, V. P., & Fesenmaier, D. R. (2015). Information technology and consumer behavior in travel and tourism: Insights from travel planning using the internet. *Journal of Retailing and Consumer Services*, 22, 244–249. DOI: 10.1016/j.jretconser.2014.08.005

Yadav, S. (2021). Millennial Employees-Role, Benefits and Retaining Strategies in Hotel Industry (p. 64). DOI: 10.6084/m9.figshare.13719949.v1

Yadav, S. J. (2024). Voices From Within: Exploring Indian Perspectives on Sex Tourism. In *Examining Tourist Behaviors and Community Involvement in Destination Rejuvenation* (pp. 263–272). IGI Global. https://www.igi-global.com/chapter/voices-from-within/348915

Chapter 18
Impact of Social Media on the Development of Religious Tourism Industry

Mohammad Badruddoza Talukder
https://orcid.org/0009-0008-1662-9221
International University of Business Agriculture and Technology, Bangladesh

Iva Rani Das
https://orcid.org/0009-0006-9805-4331
University of Dhaka, Bangladesh

Mohammad Nurul Afchar
https://orcid.org/0009-0006-9736-7854
Daffodil International University, Bangladesh

ABSTRACT

This chapter investigates the impact of social media on religious tourism, exploring its role in destination marketing, visitor experiences, and community engagement. A comprehensive literature review was conducted to examine the influence of social media on religious tourism development. Academic databases were searched using relevant keywords, and findings were structured around key themes. Social media enhances accessibility, information sharing, and community engagement in religious tourism but presents challenges regarding authenticity and privacy. Case studies illustrate successful social media strategies employed by stakeholders. Insights from this chapter inform stakeholders on leveraging social media to promote religious heritage and sustainable tourism practices, fostering visitor experiences and interfaith dialogue. This chapter offers a holistic understanding of social media's impact on religious tourism, combining theoretical insights with practical examples to guide industry stakeholders.

DOI: 10.4018/979-8-3693-9230-0.ch018

Copyright ©2025, IGI Global. Copying or distributing in print or electronic forms without written permission of IGI Global is prohibited.

1. INTRODUCTION

The tourism landscape has undergone a profound transformation in an age of digital connectivity and ubiquitous social media presence. The emergence of social media platforms has revolutionized how travelers plan, experience, and share their journeys, transcending geographical boundaries and reshaping the tourism industry (Sharma & Chanda, 2023). Within this dynamic milieu, one particular niche stands out for its unique blend of cultural significance, spiritual exploration, and communal bonding: religious tourism. Religious tourism, often called pilgrimage or spiritual travel, encompasses journeys undertaken by individuals seeking solace, enlightenment, or a deeper connection with their faith (Piramanayagam et al., 2023). Spanning sacred sites, pilgrimage routes, and revered destinations across the globe, religious tourism represents a diverse tapestry of beliefs, traditions, and practices (Ahmad, 2023). From the holy city of Mecca to the Camino de Santiago and the banks of the Ganges, these sacred spaces hold profound meaning for millions of pilgrims, offering a sanctuary for spiritual contemplation and cultural immersion.

Amidst this rich tapestry of religious pilgrimage, the rise of social media has emerged as a defining force, shaping the way pilgrims engage with their faith and the destinations they visit. The proliferation of platforms such as Facebook, Instagram, Twitter, and YouTube has empowered pilgrims to share their religious experiences, connect with like-minded individuals, and access a wealth of information about sacred sites and rituals (Zaid et al., 2022). In essence, social media has become a digital pilgrimage in its own right, facilitating virtual connections and fostering a global community of believers. Integrating social media into religious tourism is a technological advancement and a fundamental shift in how pilgrims navigate their spiritual journeys. Where once pilgrims relied on guidebooks, word-of-mouth recommendations, and physical maps to navigate sacred sites, they now turn to digital platforms for real-time updates, interactive maps, and user-generated content (Bassett, 2022). From sharing snapshots of prayer rituals to documenting transformative moments of spiritual enlightenment, social media has become integral to the pilgrim's narrative, shaping how they perceive and engage with religious tourism (Polus & Carr, 2021).

Furthermore, social media has democratized the pilgrimage experience, transcending time, space, and physical mobility barriers. Pilgrims who cannot embark on traditional journeys due to financial constraints, health issues, or travel restrictions can now participate vicariously through virtual pilgrimage experiences (Yoo et al., 2022). Live-streamed religious ceremonies, interactive storytelling sessions, and virtual tours of sacred sites allow individuals to connect with their faith from their homes, fostering inclusivity and accessibility within religious tourism. However, challenges and complexities abound amidst the myriad opportunities social media presents. The commodification of spirituality, the dissemination of misinformation, and concerns about privacy and cultural sensitivity pose significant ethical dilemmas for stakeholders within the religious tourism industry (Sharma, 2022). Moreover, the rapid pace of technological advancement necessitates ongoing adaptation and innovation to harness the full potential of social media while mitigating its negative consequences.

Against this backdrop, this chapter explores the multifaceted impact of social media on the development of religious tourism. Through a comprehensive analysis of trends, case studies, and theoretical frameworks, we will explore how social media shapes destination marketing strategies, enhances visitor experiences, fosters community engagement, and navigates ethical challenges within religious tourism. By examining the intersection of social media and religious pilgrimage, we aim to provide insights and recommendations for stakeholders seeking to navigate this dynamic landscape and promote sustainable growth and cultural exchange within the religious tourism sector.

Social media integration into the tourism industry has been a transformative phenomenon, reshaping how destinations are marketed, experienced, and perceived by travelers (Chamboko-Mpotaringa & Tichaawa, 2021). Social media platforms have emerged as powerful tools for destination marketers, tour operators, and travelers, offering avenues for sharing experiences, accessing information, and engaging with communities globally (Cheung et al., 2021). Within the broader spectrum of tourism, religious tourism holds a distinct place, characterized by journeys motivated by spiritual or religious reasons. Pilgrimage sites, sacred destinations, and religious festivals attract millions of travelers each year, representing a significant segment of the tourism market (Hassan et al., 2022). As pilgrims seek authentic and meaningful experiences that connect them with their faith, social media has become an indispensable resource for navigating their spiritual journeys.

The rationale for examining the impact of social media on the development of religious tourism is twofold (Tsironis, 2022). Firstly, religious tourism represents a unique intersection of culture, spirituality, and heritage, making it an intriguing case study for understanding the role of social media in shaping travel experiences (Tsironis, 2022). Unlike conventional leisure tourism, religious tourism is often driven by deeply held beliefs and traditions, which can influence how pilgrims engage with social media platforms and the content they consume (Liutikas, 2021). Secondly, integrating social media into religious tourism has significant implications for destination marketing, community engagement, and cultural exchange (Moric et al., 2021). As religious destinations seek to attract visitors and promote cultural understanding, social media offers unprecedented opportunities to reach a global audience, share narratives, and foster virtual communities (Jack et al., 2024). However, alongside its benefits, social media also presents privacy, authenticity, and ethical challenges, underscoring the need for a nuanced understanding of its impact on religious tourism.

By exploring the dynamics of social media within the context of religious tourism, this chapter seeks to address these complexities and provide insights for stakeholders navigating this dynamic landscape (Mandalia, 2023). By examining trends, case studies, and theoretical frameworks, we aim to shed light on the transformative potential of social media in promoting sustainable growth, cultural exchange, and spiritual enrichment within the religious tourism sector. In summary, the background and rationale for examining the impact of social media on the development of religious tourism lie in its unique intersection of culture, spirituality, and heritage, as well as its implications for destination marketing, community engagement, and cultural exchange (Shinde & Olsen, 2022). Through a comprehensive analysis, we aim to provide valuable insights and recommendations for stakeholders seeking to harness the full potential of social media in promoting meaningful and sustainable religious tourism experiences.

Objectives of the Chapter:

The objectives of the chapter are:

1. To explore the impact of social media on religious tourism.
2. To provide insights and recommendations for stakeholders navigating social media integration in the religious tourism industry.

2. LITERATURE REVIEW

The literature on the impact of social media on religious tourism reveals a rich tapestry of research spanning various disciplines, including tourism studies, communication, sociology, and religious studies. Scholars have explored the multifaceted relationship between social media and religious tourism, shedding light on its implications for destination marketing, visitor experiences, community engagement, and cultural exchange.

Research in destination marketing has highlighted the transformative role of social media platforms in promoting religious destinations to a global audience. Studies by Kapoor (2022) emphasize the importance of engaging storytelling, user-generated content, and targeted advertising in effectively marketing religious sites to prospective travelers. Furthermore, scholars such as Sultan et al. (2021) have examined the influence of social media on destination image formation, demonstrating its capacity to shape perceptions and influence travel decisions among religious tourists.

Regarding visitor experiences, research has underscored the impact of social media on enhancing the pilgrim's journey. Studies by Johnson (2023) and Mohammad et al. (2024) have explored how social media platforms facilitate information sharing, peer recommendations, and real-time updates, enriching the pilgrim's experience and fostering a sense of connectedness with religious communities. Additionally, scholars such as Vinnakota et al. (2023) have examined the role of virtual reality and augmented reality technologies in providing immersive pilgrimage experiences, transcending physical constraints, and expanding access to sacred sites.

Community engagement has emerged as another critical area of inquiry within the literature on social media and religious tourism. Research by Khan & Martinez (2023) highlights the role of social media platforms in fostering virtual communities of believers, facilitating dialogue, and sharing religious practices and rituals. Moreover, studies by Khalid & Lopez (2023) have explored the potential of social media in organizing religious events, mobilizing pilgrims, and promoting interfaith dialogue and cultural exchange.

Despite its potential benefits, the literature acknowledges the challenges and ethical considerations of integrating social media into religious tourism. Scholars such as Chirila (2023) have raised concerns about the commodification of spirituality, the dissemination of misinformation, and the erosion of authenticity in religious tourism experiences mediated through social media. Moreover, privacy, cultural sensitivity, and the digital divide have been highlighted as areas requiring further attention and ethical reflection by researchers and practitioners alike (Choudrie et al., 2022).

In summary, the literature on social media and religious tourism offers valuable insights into the transformative potential of digital platforms in shaping the landscape of pilgrimage and spiritual travel. By exploring its impact on destination marketing, visitor experiences, community engagement, and ethical considerations, scholars have contributed to a deeper understanding of the opportunities and challenges inherent in leveraging social media for promoting sustainable and meaningful religious tourism experiences.

3. EVOLUTION OF SOCIAL MEDIA IN TOURISM

Social media has evolved remarkably over the past few decades, transforming how individuals communicate, share information, and make travel-related decisions (Yuan et al., 2022). This evolution has profoundly impacted the tourism industry, reshaping marketing strategies, traveler behavior, and destination management practices. Understanding the historical development of social media platforms and their adoption in the tourism sector provides valuable insights into the transformative journey of digital communication in tourism (Cuomo et al., 2021).

Early Forms of Social Media: The roots of social media can be traced back to the early days of the internet, with the emergence of bulletin board systems (BBS) and online forums in the 1980s and 1990s (Driscoll, 2022). These primitive forms of digital communication allowed users to exchange messages, share information, and engage in discussions on various topics, including travel (Juarez Miro & Toff, 2023). However, these platforms were limited in scope and accessibility, primarily catering to niche communities of early adopters.

Transition to Web 2.0: The advent of Web 2.0 in the early 2000s marked a significant shift in the landscape of social media (McHaney, 2023). Web 2.0 introduced the concept of interactive and user-generated content, enabling individuals to create, share, and collaborate on digital content in real-time (Santos, 2022). This era saw the rise of social networking sites such as Myspace, Friendster, and Orkut, which allowed users to connect with friends, share photos, and update their status. While these platforms laid the groundwork for social media as we know it today, they were limited in their functionality and reach.

Mainstream Social Media Platforms: The breakthrough moment for social media came with the launch of Facebook in 2004 (Lazar, 2022). Founded by Mark Zuckerberg and his college roommates, Facebook revolutionized online social networking by offering a user-friendly interface, extensive privacy controls, and a wide range of features, including news feeds, photo sharing, and event management. Facebook's exponential growth and global reach quickly established it as the dominant player in the social media landscape, attracting billions of users worldwide (Ebo, 2022).

Alongside Facebook, platforms like Twitter, LinkedIn, and YouTube emerged as crucial players in the social media ecosystem, each catering to different content and communication preferences (Hamza et al., 2023). Twitter revolutionized real-time communication with its microblogging format, allowing users to share short updates or "tweets" with their followers. LinkedIn transformed professional networking by providing a platform for professionals to connect, share industry insights, and seek job opportunities. YouTube revolutionized video-sharing, becoming the go-to platform for hosting and consuming a wide range of content, including travel vlogs, destination guides, and promotional videos (Hamza et al., 2023).

Visual Platforms and Multimedia Content: Recently, the rise of visual-centric platforms such as Instagram and Pinterest have further diversified the social media landscape. With its emphasis on visually appealing photos and videos, Instagram has become a powerful tool for destination marketing, influencer collaborations, and user-generated content (Kilipiri et al., 2023). On the other hand, Pinterest serves as a virtual pinboard for collecting and sharing inspiration, making it a valuable resource for trip planning and itinerary creation (Macarthy, 2021).

Adoption of Social Media in the Tourism Industry: The tourism industry initially viewed social media skeptically, unsure of its potential impact and utility for marketing and promotion (Talukder & Bhuiyan, 2020). However, as social media platforms gained traction and user engagement surged, tourism stakeholders began to recognize the immense opportunities for reaching and engaging with travelers on a global scale (Kalinić & Vujičić, 2022). Today, social media has become an integral part of tourism marketing strategies, with destinations, hotels, airlines, and tour operators leveraging platforms like Facebook, Instagram, and Twitter to promote their offerings, engage with customers, and build brand loyalty.

From destination marketing campaigns and influencer collaborations to real-time customer service and user-generated content, social media has revolutionized how tourism businesses interact with their audiences. Adopting social media analytics tools and data-driven marketing techniques has further enhanced the effectiveness and targeting of social media campaigns, enabling tourism stakeholders to track engagement metrics, measure ROI, and optimize their marketing efforts (Talukder et al., 2024).

The evolution of social media in tourism has been characterized by a shift from early forms of digital communication to mainstream social networking platforms and visual-centric media. The adoption of social media in the tourism industry has transformed marketing strategies, customer engagement practices, and the overall travel experience, paving the way for a more connected, informed, and interactive tourism ecosystem (Talukder et al., 2024).

Figure 1. Evolution of social media in tourism (Authors compilation)

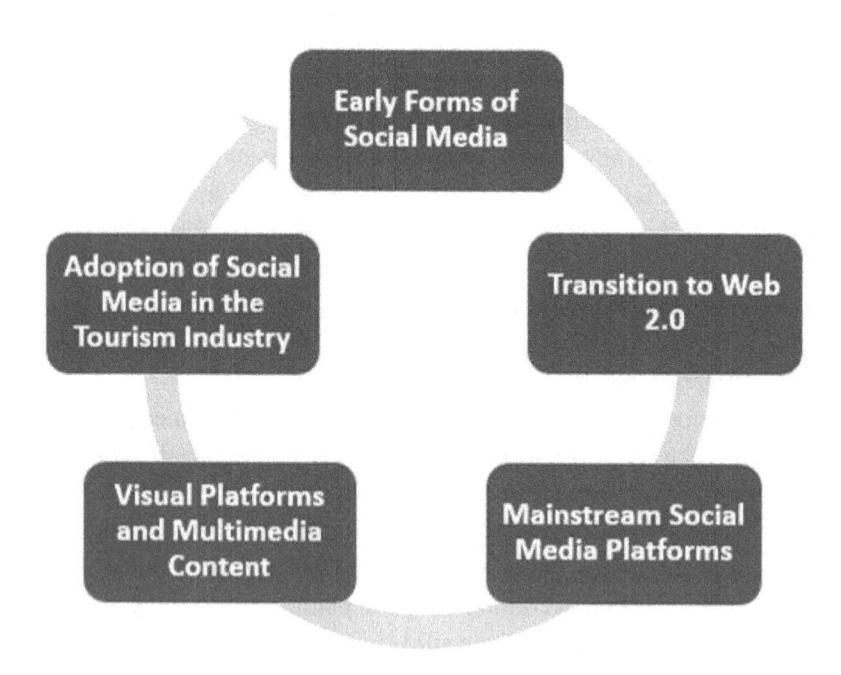

4. DESTINATION MARKETING AND SOCIAL MEDIA

Destination marketing is a crucial aspect of the tourism industry, encompassing strategies to promote and showcase destinations to attract visitors (Muluneh et al., 2022). Social media has revolutionized destination marketing practices recently, offering tourism stakeholders unprecedented opportunities to engage with travelers, build brand awareness, and influence travel decisions. The intersection of destination marketing and social media has transformed how destinations are marketed, allowing for more targeted, interactive, and personalized marketing campaigns (Dwivedi et al., 2021).

Interactive Engagement: One of the key advantages of social media in destination marketing is its interactive nature. Social media platforms such as Facebook, Instagram, and Twitter enable tourism organizations to engage with travelers in real time, fostering dialogue, responding to inquiries, and promptly addressing concerns (Gutounig et al., 2022). This interactive engagement creates a sense of authenticity and transparency, helping to build trust and credibility among potential visitors.

Content Creation and Sharing: Social media platforms serve as powerful tools for content creation and sharing, allowing destinations to showcase their unique attractions, experiences, and cultural offerings through photos, videos, and storytelling (Adamış & Pınarbaşı, 2022). User-generated content, in particular, plays a significant role in destination marketing, as travelers share their experiences and recommendations with their social networks, amplifying the reach and impact of destination marketing efforts.

Influencer Collaborations: The rise of social media influencers has reshaped destination marketing strategies, with destinations partnering with influential individuals and content creators to reach new audiences and drive engagement. Influencers who have built large followings and credibility within specific niches or demographics can create authentic and compelling content that resonates with their followers, inspiring them to visit the destination showcased in their posts (Hund, 2023).

Targeted Advertising: Social media platforms offer sophisticated targeting capabilities that allow destinations to tailor their marketing messages to specific audience segments based on demographics, interests, and behaviors (An et al., 2021). By leveraging data analytics and audience insights, destinations can design targeted advertising campaigns that reach the most relevant and receptive audience, maximizing their marketing efforts' return on investment (ROI).

Real-Time Updates and Promotions: Social media enables destinations to provide real-time updates, promotions, and event announcements to their followers, keeping them informed and engaged (Yavuz & Enes, 2022). Whether it's sharing news about upcoming festivals, special offers on accommodations, or last-minute travel deals, social media allows destinations to communicate directly with travelers and capitalize on timely opportunities to drive bookings and visitation.

Measuring and Analyzing Performance: Social media analytics tools provide destinations with valuable insights into the performance of their marketing campaigns, allowing them to track key metrics such as engagement, reach, and conversion rates (Atherton, 2023). By analyzing these metrics, destinations can evaluate their marketing efforts' effectiveness, identify improvement areas, and refine their strategies to achieve their marketing objectives. Social media has become an indispensable tool for destination marketing, offering tourism organizations unprecedented opportunities to engage with travelers, showcase their offerings, and drive visitation (Atherton, 2023). By leveraging interactive engagement, content creation, influencer collaborations, targeted advertising, real-time updates, and performance analytics, destinations can create compelling and impactful marketing campaigns that inspire travelers to visit and experience all they have to offer.

5. ENHANCING VISITOR EXPERIENCES THROUGH SOCIAL MEDIA

Social media platforms have transformed how travelers plan, experience, and share their journeys, offering unique opportunities to enhance visitor experiences in the tourism industry (Atherton, 2023). From accessing real-time information and personalized recommendations to sharing memorable moments and connecting with fellow travelers, social media plays a pivotal role in shaping and enriching the travel experience.

Access to Real-Time Information: One of the primary ways social media enhances visitor experiences is by providing access to real-time information about destinations, attractions, and travel-related services. Platforms like Twitter and Facebook enable travelers to receive updates on weather conditions, transportation disruptions, and local events, allowing them to make informed decisions and adjust their plans accordingly (Allam et al., 2022). This real-time information ensures that travelers stay informed and prepared throughout their journey, enhancing their confidence and security.

Personalized Recommendations: Social media platforms leverage algorithms and user data to provide customized recommendations and suggestions tailored to individual preferences and interests (Ognibene et al., 2023). Whether it's restaurant recommendations from friends on Facebook, travel tips from influencers on Instagram, or destination inspiration from travel bloggers on Pinterest, social media offers travelers a wealth of curated content and insider insights to enhance their travel experiences. This personalized approach helps travelers discover hidden gems, off-the-beaten-path attractions, and authentic local experiences that align with their interests and preferences.

Visual Inspiration and Aspiration: Visual content plays a significant role in inspiring and shaping travel experiences, and social media platforms excel in delivering visually appealing and immersive content to travelers (Putra et al., 2023). Platforms like Instagram and YouTube are powerful tools for showcasing stunning photography, captivating videos, and virtual tours of destinations, allowing travelers to preview and visualize their travel experiences before they even arrive. This visual inspiration fuels travelers' aspirations and motivates them to explore new destinations, creating anticipation and excitement for their upcoming trips.

User-Generated Content and Social Proof: User-generated content (UGC) has become a driving force in shaping travel decisions and experiences, with travelers increasingly relying on reviews, recommendations, and testimonials from fellow travelers on social media platforms (Martins & Wolfe, 2022). Whether reading hotel reviews on TripAdvisor, watching destination vlogs on YouTube, or browsing photos tagged with location hashtags on Instagram, travelers seek social proof and validation from their peers before making travel decisions. This reliance on UGC enhances trust and credibility in travel experiences, empowering travelers to make informed choices and discover authentic experiences.

Virtual Connections and Community Building: Social media platforms facilitate virtual connections and community building among travelers, allowing them to share experiences, exchange tips, and connect with like-minded individuals worldwide. Travel-related Facebook groups, Twitter chats, and Instagram communities provide forums for travelers to interact, seek advice, and share stories, fostering a sense of camaraderie and belonging within the travel community (Whalen, n.d.). These virtual connections enhance the social aspect of travel, enabling travelers to forge friendships, collaborate on future trips, and create lasting memories together.

Innovative Engagement and Gamification: Innovative engagement techniques and gamification strategies are increasingly being employed by destinations and travel brands to enhance visitor experiences on social media (Xu et al., 2021). From interactive quizzes and polls to scavenger hunts and photo challenges, these creative initiatives encourage active participation and engagement from travelers, making the travel experience more interactive, memorable, and enjoyable. By gamifying the travel experience, destinations can incentivize travelers to explore, discover, and share their experiences on social media, fostering a sense of adventure and excitement.

6. COMMUNITY ENGAGEMENT AND SOCIAL MEDIA

Community engagement is crucial in fostering connections, facilitating interactions, and building relationships within the tourism industry. Social media platforms have emerged as powerful tools for community engagement, enabling destinations, tourism organizations, and travelers to connect, collaborate, and share experiences in virtual spaces (Das et al., 2024). By harnessing social media's interactive and participatory nature, community engagement initiatives aim to cultivate a sense of belonging, promote dialogue, and foster a supportive and inclusive tourism community.

Formation of Online Communities: Social media platforms serve as virtual meeting places where travelers with shared interests, passions, and experiences can form online communities and networks. Whether joining travel-related Facebook groups, participating in Twitter chats, or following destination-specific hashtags on Instagram, travelers have numerous opportunities to connect with like-minded individuals, exchange tips, and share stories. These online communities provide platforms for travelers to seek advice, recommendations, and inspiration from their peers, creating a sense of camaraderie and belonging within the travel community.

Facilitating Interactions and Networking: Social media platforms facilitate interactions and networking among members of the tourism community, allowing individuals to engage in conversations, share insights, and build relationships in real time (Alghamdi et al., 2023). Platforms like LinkedIn provide professionals in the tourism industry with opportunities to connect with colleagues, seek job opportunities, and share industry news and best practices. Similarly, platforms like Twitter enable travelers to engage directly with destination marketing organizations, hotels, airlines, and tour operators, fostering dialogue and collaboration between travelers and tourism stakeholders.

Organizing Events and Gatherings: Social media platforms are powerful tools for organizing and promoting events, gatherings, and meetups within the tourism community (Arasli et al., 2021). Whether it's a local meetup for travel enthusiasts, a networking event for tourism professionals, or a community-driven initiative to clean up a popular tourist destination, social media provides platforms for coordinating logistics, spreading the word, and mobilizing participants. These events offer opportunities for tourism community members to come together, share experiences, and collaborate on initiatives that contribute to destinations' sustainable development and preservation.

Promoting Interfaith Dialogue and Cultural Exchange: In religious tourism, social media platforms promote interfaith dialogue, cultural exchange, and understanding among travelers from different religious and cultural backgrounds. Platforms like Facebook, Twitter, and Instagram allow individuals to share insights, perspectives, and experiences related to religious travel, fostering mutual respect and appreciation for diverse faith traditions and beliefs (Adesina, 2023). By facilitating dialogue and collaboration between travelers of different faiths, social media promotes tolerance, empathy, and cultural understanding within the tourism community.

Sharing Authentic Experiences: Social media platforms enable travelers to share authentic and meaningful experiences that reflect their journeys and perspectives. Through photos, videos, and written posts, travelers can document their adventures, encounters, and discoveries, providing valuable insights and inspiration to others in the tourism community. User-generated content (UGC) plays a significant role in shaping perceptions and influencing travel decisions as travelers seek authentic and trustworthy recommendations from their peers (Adesina, 2023). By sharing authentic experiences on social media, travelers contribute to the collective knowledge and storytelling of the tourism community, enriching the travel experiences of others and fostering a sense of connection and solidarity within the community.

Community engagement on social media platforms enhances connections, fosters dialogue, and promotes collaboration within the tourism industry (Camilleri & Kozak, 2022). By providing platforms for forming online communities, facilitating interactions and networking, organizing events and gatherings, promoting interfaith dialogue and cultural exchange, and sharing authentic experiences, social media contributes to the creation of a vibrant, supportive, and inclusive tourism community that enriches the travel experiences of individuals and fosters a sense of belonging and camaraderie.

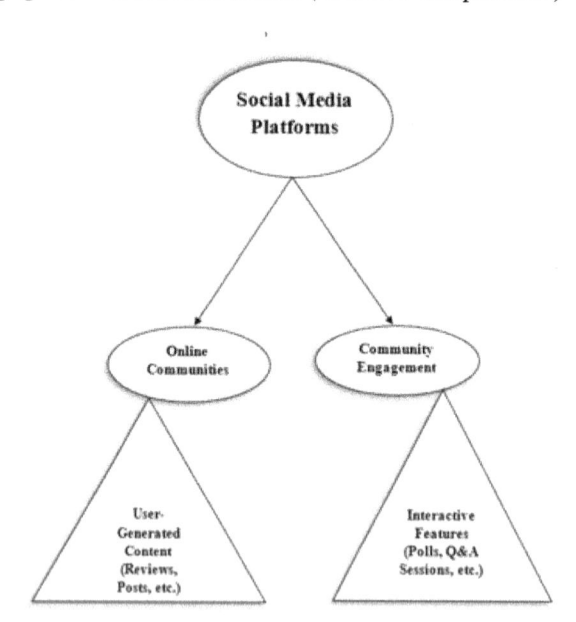

Figure 2. Community engagement and social media (Authors compilation)

7. IMPACTS AND CHALLENGES OF SOCIAL MEDIA IN RELIGIOUS TOURISM

Social media has profoundly impacted the landscape of religious tourism, transforming how pilgrims engage with their faith, interact with religious communities, and experience sacred sites (Agarwal et al., 2021). While social media presents numerous opportunities for enhancing religious tourism experiences, it also poses challenges and ethical considerations that stakeholders within the industry must address.

Impacts

1. **Enhanced Accessibility and Connectivity:** Social media platforms have made religious tourism more accessible and inclusive by providing virtual access to sacred sites, religious rituals, and spiritual teachings. Pilgrims can participate in religious events, view live-streamed ceremonies, and connect with religious communities worldwide, fostering a sense of connectedness and belonging (Edelman et al., 2021).
2. **Facilitated Information Sharing:** Social media enables pilgrims to access real-time information, travel tips, and recommendations from fellow travelers, religious leaders, and destination authorities (Tamang et al., 2022). Information-sharing fosters informed decision-making and enhances the overall pilgrimage experience by providing travelers with valuable insights and practical guidance.
3. **Promotion of Cultural Exchange:** Social media platforms are powerful tools for promoting interfaith dialogue, cultural exchange, and understanding among pilgrims from diverse religious and cultural backgrounds (Suhadah et al., 2022). Through social media, pilgrims can share their experiences, learn about different faith traditions, and engage in respectful and meaningful interactions that promote tolerance and mutual respect.
4. **Community Building and Support:** Social media fosters the formation of virtual communities and support networks for pilgrims, providing platforms for sharing stories, seeking advice, and offering emotional support during their spiritual journeys (Subhrasmita & Gaur, 2023). These online communities create a sense of camaraderie and solidarity among pilgrims, enabling them to connect with others who share similar beliefs and experiences.
5. **Destination Marketing and Promotion:** Social media platforms offer destinations and religious organizations powerful tools for marketing and promoting religious tourism offerings to a global audience (Morehouse & Saffer, 2021). Through targeted advertising, influencer collaborations, and user-generated content, destinations can showcase their sacred sites, religious festivals, and cultural heritage, attracting visitors and generating interest in religious tourism experiences.

Challenges

1. **The commodification of Spirituality:** The commercialization of religious tourism on social media raises concerns about the commodification of spirituality and sacred sites (Lestari, 2023). In some cases, the emphasis on profit-driven tourism activities and commercial ventures may overshadow religious pilgrimage's spiritual significance and reverence, leading to concerns about authenticity and cultural integrity.
2. **Dissemination of Misinformation:** Social media platforms can be susceptible to the spread of misinformation, rumors, and sensationalized content related to religious tourism (Etem-Martins et al., 2023). False information about sacred sites, religious practices, and cultural traditions can mislead pilgrims and undermine the authenticity and credibility of their experiences, posing challenges to destination management and visitor satisfaction.
3. **Privacy and Security Concerns:** Social media raises privacy and security concerns for pilgrims who share personal information, travel plans, and religious affiliations online (Etem-Martins et al., 2023). Pilgrims may be vulnerable to identity theft, scams, and exploitation by malicious actors

who exploit their religious beliefs and vulnerabilities for fraud, highlighting the need to safeguard personal data and promote online safety practices.
4. **Ethical Considerations:** The use of social media in religious tourism raises ethical considerations related to cultural sensitivity, respect for sacred spaces, and the representation of religious beliefs and practices (Robina-Ramírez & Pulido-Fernández, 2021). Pilgrims and destination authorities must navigate complex ethical dilemmas concerning the appropriate use of social media in religious contexts, ensuring that digital interactions uphold religious values and principles while promoting mutual understanding and respect among diverse religious communities.
5. **Digital Divide and Accessibility:** The digital divide and disparities in internet access and technological literacy may limit the accessibility of social media for certain pilgrims, particularly those from marginalized communities or regions with limited connectivity (Duarte et al., 2021). Addressing these disparities and promoting digital inclusion is essential for ensuring equitable access to the benefits of social media in religious tourism and preventing the marginalization of underrepresented voices within the pilgrimage community.

Figure 3. Conceptual framework (Authors compilation)

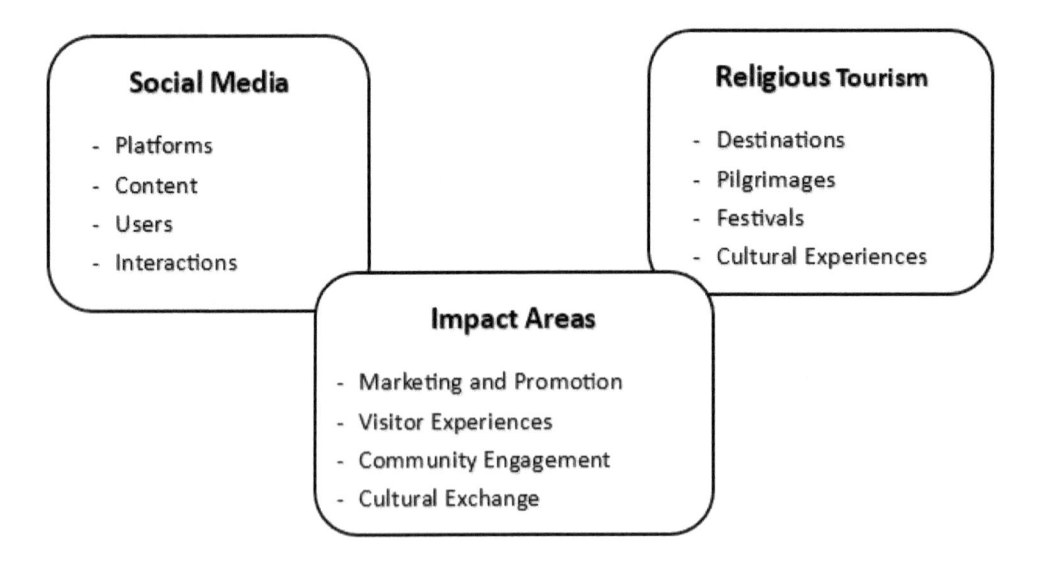

Social Media
- Platforms
- Content
- Users
- Interactions

Religious Tourism
- Destinations
- Pilgrimages
- Festivals
- Cultural Experiences

Impact Areas
- Marketing and Promotion
- Visitor Experiences
- Community Engagement
- Cultural Exchange

8. RECOMMENDATIONS

Implement targeted social media campaigns to showcase unique religious attractions, leveraging geotargeted advertising to reach potential visitors based on their location and interests. Encourage user-generated content by incentivizing visitors to share their experiences, fostering authenticity and engagement. Collaborate with local religious communities to create immersive virtual experiences and utilize social media influencers to amplify campaign reach. Engage in active community management to maintain a positive online reputation, provide multilingual support for international visitors, and offer exclusive promotions to followers. Establish strategic partnerships with travel influencers, religious organizations, and tourism boards to co-create content and enhance the visibility of religious tourism destinations.

FUTURE DIRECTIONS

Looking ahead, the future of social media in religious tourism presents exciting opportunities for innovation and growth. Firstly, there's a need to enhance personalization and customization in social media content and experiences to cater to travelers' diverse preferences and interests. This could involve leveraging data analytics and artificial intelligence to deliver tailored recommendations and curated experiences that resonate with individual visitors. Additionally, there's potential for further integration of immersive technologies such as Virtual Reality (VR) and Augmented Reality (AR) to offer virtual tours and interactive experiences of religious sites, enabling travelers to explore and engage with destinations in unprecedented ways. Furthermore, as the importance of sustainability and responsible tourism practices continues to rise, there's an opportunity to leverage social media to promote eco-friendly initiatives, community-based tourism projects, and cultural preservation efforts within religious tourism destinations (Talukder & Hossain, 2021). By embracing these future directions, religious tourism stakeholders can harness social media's full potential to enhance visitor experiences, foster community engagement, and drive sustainable growth in the years to come.

CONCLUSION

The intersection of social media and religious tourism represents a dynamic and transformative force reshaping how pilgrims engage with their faith, interact with sacred sites and connect with religious communities. Throughout this chapter, we have explored the multifaceted impact of social media on religious tourism, from enhancing visitor experiences and fostering community engagement to promoting interfaith dialogue and cultural exchange. As social media continues to evolve and play an increasingly prominent role in the tourism industry, stakeholders must recognize the opportunities and challenges inherent in leveraging digital technology to promote meaningful and sustainable pilgrimage experiences. The evolution of social media platforms, from early digital communication to mainstream social networking sites and visual-centric platforms, has revolutionized how travelers plan, experience, and share their religious journeys. Social media has made religious tourism more accessible, inclusive, and interactive, providing pilgrims virtual access to sacred sites, real-time information, personalized recommendations, and virtual connections with fellow travelers. Additionally, social media has facilitated the formation of online communities, support networks, and collaborative partnerships within the pilgrimage community, fostering a sense of belonging, solidarity, and mutual support among pilgrims from diverse religious and cultural backgrounds.

However, along with its numerous benefits, social media also presents challenges and ethical considerations that religious tourism stakeholders must address. The commodification of spirituality, dissemination of misinformation, privacy concerns, and moral dilemmas underscore the importance of promoting responsible and ethical use of social media in religious contexts. Moreover, the digital divide and disparities in internet access highlight the need to promote digital inclusion and accessibility to ensure equitable access to the benefits of social media in religious tourism. Looking ahead, the future of social media in religious tourism holds immense potential for innovation, collaboration, and meaningful engagement. By embracing emerging technologies, fostering collaborative partnerships, prioritizing digital literacy and education, promoting sustainable and responsible tourism practices, enhancing data analytics and performance measurement, cultivating authentic and meaningful content, and fostering interfaith dialogue and understanding, religious tourism stakeholders can harness the transformative power of social media to create impactful, inclusive, and culturally enriching pilgrimage experiences.

In conclusion, social media has revolutionized the landscape of religious tourism, offering pilgrims new ways to connect with their faith, engage with sacred sites, and build meaningful relationships within the pilgrimage community. By navigating the opportunities and challenges of social media with foresight, creativity, and ethical integrity, religious tourism stakeholders can unlock the full potential of digital technology to promote sustainable, authentic, and spiritually enriching pilgrimage experiences that resonate with travelers and foster mutual understanding and respect among diverse religious communities.

REFERENCES

Adamış, E., & Pınarbaşı, F. (2022). Unfolding visual characteristics of social media communication: Reflections of smart tourism destinations. *Journal of Hospitality and Tourism Technology*, 13(1), 34–61. DOI: 10.1108/JHTT-09-2020-0246

Adesina, O. S. (2023). Exploring Religion as a Tool of Nigeria's Public Diplomacy. *International Journal of Emerging Multidisciplinaries: Social Science, IJEMD-SS*, 2(1), 1–20. DOI: 10.54938/ijemdss.2023.02.1.216

Agarwal, A., Kapoor, K., & Walia, S. (2021). Impact of social media on spiritual tourism in India: An SEM Analysis of the Critical Factors Impacting on Decision Making. *International Journal of Religious Tourism and Pilgrimage*, 9(5), 10.

Ahmad, M. (2023). Exploring the Role of OpenStreetMap in Mapping Religious Tourism in Pakistan for Sustainable Development. In *Experiences, Advantages, and Economic Dimensions of Pilgrimage Routes* (pp. 23–40). IGI Global. DOI: 10.4018/978-1-6684-9923-8.ch002

Alghamdi, A. M., Pileggi, S. F., & Sohaib, O. (2023). Social Media Analysis to Enhance Sustainable Knowledge Management: A Concise Literature Review. *Sustainability (Basel)*, 15(13), 9957. DOI: 10.3390/su15139957

Allam, Z., Sharifi, A., Bibri, S. E., Jones, D. S., & Krogstie, J. (2022). The metaverse as a virtual form of smart cities: Opportunities and challenges for environmental, economic, and social sustainability in urban futures. *Smart Cities*, 5(3), 771–801. DOI: 10.3390/smartcities5030040

An, J., Kwak, H., Qureshi, H. M., & Weber, I. (2021). Precision public health campaign: Delivering persuasive messages to relevant segments through targeted advertisements on social media. *JMIR Formative Research*, 5(9), e22313. DOI: 10.2196/22313 PMID: 34559055

Arasli, H., Abdullahi, M., & Gunay, T. (2021). Social media as a destination marketing tool for a sustainable heritage festival in Nigeria: A moderated mediation study. *Sustainability (Basel)*, 13(11), 6191. DOI: 10.3390/su13116191

Atherton, J. (2023). *Social media strategy: A practical guide to social media marketing and customer engagement*. Kogan Page Publishers.

Bassett, K. (2022). *(Digitally entangled) touristic placemaking: locative media, algorithmic navigation & affective orderings*.

Camilleri, M. A., & Kozak, M. (2022). Interactive engagement through travel and tourism social media groups: A social facilitation theory perspective. *Technology in Society*, 71, 102098. DOI: 10.1016/j.techsoc.2022.102098

Chamboko-Mpotaringa, M., & Tichaawa, T. M. (2021). Digital trends and tools driving change in marketing Free State tourism destinations: A stakeholder's perspective. *African Journal of Hospitality, Tourism and Leisure*, 10(6), 1973–1984. DOI: 10.46222/ajhtl.19770720.204

Cheung, M. L., Ting, H., Cheah, J.-H., & Sharipudin, M.-N. S. (2021). Examining the role of social media-based destination brand community in evoking tourists' emotions and intention to co-create and visit. *Journal of Product and Brand Management*, 30(1), 28–43. DOI: 10.1108/JPBM-09-2019-2554

Chirila, A. (2023). Pilgrim-Tourists: Tourism and the Spiritual Experience. *Analele Ştiinţifice Ale Universităţii» Alexandru Ioan Cuza «din Iaşi.Teologie Ortodoxă*, 28(1), 43–72.

Choudrie, J., Zamani, E., & Obuekwe, C. (2022). Bridging the digital divide in ethnic minority older adults: An organisational qualitative study. *Information Systems Frontiers*, 24(4), 1355–1375. DOI: 10.1007/s10796-021-10126-8

Cuomo, M. T., Tortora, D., Foroudi, P., Giordano, A., Festa, G., & Metallo, G. (2021). Digital transformation and tourist experience co-design: Big social data for planning cultural tourism. *Technological Forecasting and Social Change*, 162, 120345. DOI: 10.1016/j.techfore.2020.120345

Das, I. R., Talukder, M. B., & Kumar, S. (2024). Implication of Artificial Intelligence in Hospitality Marketing. *IGI Global, USA*.https://doi.org/https://doi.org/ 10.4018/979-8-3693-1978-9.ch014

dos Santos, M. L. B. (2022). The "so-called" UGC: An updated definition of user-generated content in the age of social media. *Online Information Review*, 46(1), 95–113. DOI: 10.1108/OIR-06-2020-0258

Driscoll, K. (2022). A Prehistory of Social Media. *Issues in Science and Technology*, 38(4), 20–23.

Duarte, M. E., Vigil-Hayes, M., Zegura, E., Belding, E., Masara, I., & Nevarez, J. C. (2021). As a squash plant grows: Social textures of sparse internet connectivity in rural and tribal communities. [TOCHI]. *ACM Transactions on Computer-Human Interaction*, 28(3), 1–16. DOI: 10.1145/3453862

Dwivedi, Y. K., Ismagilova, E., Hughes, D. L., Carlson, J., Filieri, R., Jacobson, J., Jain, V., Karjaluoto, H., Kefi, H., Krishen, A. S., Kumar, V., Rahman, M. M., Raman, R., Rauschnabel, P. A., Rowley, J., Salo, J., Tran, G. A., & Wang, Y. (2021). Setting the future of digital and social media marketing research: Perspectives and research propositions. *International Journal of Information Management*, 59, 102168. DOI: 10.1016/j.ijinfomgt.2020.102168

Ebo, S. (2022). Globalisation and Social Media: Impacts of Facebook on the Contemporary Order. *International Journal of Research and Innovation in Social Science*, 6(8), 436–440.

Edelman, J., Vincent, A., O'Keeffe, E., Kolata, P., Minott, M. A., Steurzenhofecker, K., Bailey, J., Roding Pemberton, C., & Lowe, D. (2021). British ritual innovation under. *COVID*, •••, 19.

Etem-Martins, C. C., Nwamara, C. A., Ohaji, K., & Jude, C. (2023). Impact of fake news and sensationalization on the prospect of mainstream media in nigeria. *International Journal of Novel Research in Humanities. Social Science and Management*, 5(1), 50–61.

Gutounig, R., Phillips, B., Radkohl, S., Macher, S., Schaffer, K., & Binder, D. (2022). Leveraging social media to enhance customer value in tourism and hospitality. In *Handbook on tourism and social media* (pp. 160–172). Edward Elgar Publishing. DOI: 10.4337/9781800371415.00020

Hamza, A., Yonghong, D., & Ullah, I. (2023). Dynamics of Social Media Engagement in Pakistan: A Comprehensive Analysis of User Trends Across Platforms. [JHEDS]. *Journal of Higher Education and Development Studies*, 3(01), 1–16. DOI: 10.59219/jheds.03.01.29

Hassan, T., Carvache-Franco, M., Carvache-Franco, W., & Carvache-Franco, O. (2022). Segmentation of religious tourism by motivations: A study of the pilgrimage to the city of Mecca. *Sustainability (Basel)*, 14(13), 7861. DOI: 10.3390/su14137861

Hund, E. (2023). *The influencer industry: The quest for authenticity on social media.*

Jack, P. K., Akpan, E. E., Fcicn, P. D., & AP, P. (2024). Social media platform and business promotion: the prospect and strategies. *strategies, 7* (1).

Johnson, B. M. (2023). *Church Leadership in a Digital Age: Cultivating Community and Spiritual Growth Online*. Virginia Theological Seminary.

Juarez Miro, C., & Toff, B. (2023). How right-wing populists engage with cross-cutting news on online message boards: The case of ForoCoches and Vox in Spain. *The International Journal of Press/Politics*, 28(4), 770–790. DOI: 10.1177/19401612211072696

Kalinić, Č., & Vujičić, M. D. (2022). Social Media Analytics: Opportunities and Challenges for Cultural Tourism Destinations. *Handbook of Research on Digital Communications, Internet of Things, and the Future of Cultural Tourism*, 385–410.

Kapoor, K. (2022). Impact of social media-based user-generated content on online reputation of tourist destinations. In *Handbook on Tourism and Social Media* (pp. 81–95). Edward Elgar Publishing. DOI: 10.4337/9781800371415.00013

Khalid, A., & Lopez, M. (2023). Interfaith Dialogue and Peace building: Exploring the Role of Religious Institutions. *International Journal of Religion and Humanities*, 1(01), 1–13.

Khan, Z., & Martinez, J. (2023). Digital Religion: Exploring the Impact of Technology on Religious Practices and Beliefs. *International Journal of Religion and Humanities*, 1(02), 88–97.

Kilipiri, E., Papaioannou, E., & Kotzaivazoglou, I. (2023). Social media and influencer marketing for promoting sustainable tourism destinations: The Instagram case. *Sustainability (Basel)*, 15(8), 6374. DOI: 10.3390/su15086374

Lazar, T. (2022). Organizational scandal on social media: Workers whistleblowing on YouTube and Facebook. *Information and Organization*, 32(1), 100390. DOI: 10.1016/j.infoandorg.2022.100390

Lestari, M. (2023). The Impact of Covid 19 and Commodification on Tourism Religious Islam: From Spiritual for Experience Tour. *Jurnal Ilmiah Manajemen Kesatuan, 11* (3).

Liutikas, D. (2021). Travel motivations of pilgrims, religious tourists, and spirituality seekers. In *The Routledge Handbook of Religious and Spiritual Tourism* (pp. 225–242). Routledge. DOI: 10.4324/9780429201011-19

Macarthy, A. (2021). *500 social media marketing tips: essential advice, hints and strategy for business: facebook, twitter, pinterest, Google+, YouTube, instagram, LinkedIn, and mor.*

Mandalia, S. (2023). Tourism Education in the Digital Era: Navigating Innovation and Transformation. *International Conference on Social Science and Education (ICoeSSE 2023)*, 509–530. DOI: 10.2991/978-2-38476-142-5_48

Martins, L. B., & Wolfe, S. G. (2022). *Metaversed: See beyond the hype.* John Wiley & Sons.

McHaney, R. (2023). *The new digital shoreline: How Web 2.0 and millennials are revolutionizing higher education.* Taylor & Francis. DOI: 10.4324/9781003447979

Morehouse, J., & Saffer, A. J. (2021). Promoting the faith: Examining megachurches' audience-centric advertising strategies on social media. *Journal of Advertising*, 50(4), 408–422. DOI: 10.1080/00913367.2021.1939202

Moric, I., Pekovic, S., Janinovic, J., Perovic, Đ., & Griesbeck, M. (2021). Cultural tourism and community engagement: Insight from Montenegro. *Business Systems Research: International Journal of the Society for Advancing Innovation and Research in Economy*, 12(1), 164–178. DOI: 10.2478/bsrj-2021-0011

Muluneh, D. W., Chiriko, A. Y., & Taye, T. T. (2022). Tourism destination marketing challenges and prospects: The case of the southern route of Ethiopia. *African Journal of Hospitality, Tourism and Leisure*, 11(1), 294–309. DOI: 10.46222/ajhtl.19770720.226

Ognibene, D., Wilkens, R., Taibi, D., Hernández-Leo, D., Kruschwitz, U., Donabauer, G., Theophilou, E., Lomonaco, F., Bursic, S., Lobo, R. A., Sánchez-Reina, J. R., Scifo, L., Schwarze, V., Börsting, J., Hoppe, U., Aprin, F., Malzahn, N., & Eimler, S. (2023). Challenging social media threats using collective well-being-aware recommendation algorithms and an educational virtual companion. *Frontiers in Artificial Intelligence*, 5, 654930. DOI: 10.3389/frai.2022.654930 PMID: 36699613

Piramanayagam, S., Kumar, N., & Mallya, J. (2023). *International Journal of Religious Tourism and Pilgrimage.*

Polus, R., & Carr, N. (2021). The Role of Communication Technologies in Restructuring Pilgrimage Journeys. *International Journal of Religious Tourism and Pilgrimage*, 9(5), 5.

Putra, F. K. K., Putra, M. K., & Novianti, S. (2023). Taste of asean: Traditional food images from Southeast Asian countries. *Journal of Ethnic Foods*, 10(1), 20. DOI: 10.1186/s42779-023-00189-0

Robina-Ramírez, R., & Pulido-Fernández, M. (2021). What role do religious belief and moral emotions play in pilgrimage with regards to respecting nature? *Annals of Leisure Research*, 24(4), 492–512. DOI: 10.1080/11745398.2019.1703199

Sharma, D., & Chanda, K. (2023). Destination marketing in digital world. *management metamorphosis: navigating the changing landscape*, 128.

Sharma, N. (2022). Acknowledging the shades of grey: The past, present and future of dark tourism in India. In *Indian Tourism: Diaspora Perspectives* (pp. 125–142). Emerald Publishing Limited.

Shinde, K. A., & Olsen, D. H. (2022). Reframing the intersections of pilgrimage, religious tourism, and sustainability. *Sustainability (Basel)*, 15(1), 461. DOI: 10.3390/su15010461

Subhrasmita, S., & Gaur, R. (2023). A Spiritual Journey through Cancer and Beyond: Prayer, Pilgrimage, and Faith in Lisa Ray's Close to the Bone. *Journal of Disability & Religion*, •••, 1–21.

Suhadah, S., Mulyana, D., Yusup, P. M., & Sjafirah, N. A. (2022). Pilgrimage sites as magnets of interfaith tolerance: The case of kemaliq lingsar in Indonesia. *International Journal of Religious Tourism and Pilgrimage*, 10(3), 3.

Sultan, M. T., Sharmin, F., Badulescu, A., Gavrilut, D., & Xue, K. (2021). Social media-based content towards image formation: A new approach to the selection of sustainable destinations. *Sustainability (Basel)*, 13(8), 4241. DOI: 10.3390/su13084241

Talukder, M., Kumar, S., Misra, L., & Kabir, F. (2024). Determining the role of eco-tourism service quality, tourist satisfaction,and destination loyalty: A case study of Kuakata Beach. *Acta Scientiarum Polonorum. Administratio Locorum*, 23(1), 133–151. https://doi.org/https://doi.org/ 10.31648/aspal.9275. DOI: 10.31648/aspal.9275

Talukder, M. B., & Bhuiyan, M. L. (2020). An assessment of the roles of the social network in the development of the Tourism Industry in Bangladesh. *International Journal of Business, Law, and Education*, 1(2), 52–60.

Talukder, M. B., & Hossain, M. M. (2021). Prospects of Future Tourism in Bangladesh: An Evaluative Study. *I-Manager's. Journal of Management*, 15(4), 1–8. https://doi.org/https://doi.org/10.26634/jmgt .15.4.17495

Talukder, M. B., Kumar, S., & Das, I. R. (2024). Perspectives of Digital Marketing for the Restaurant Industry. In *Advancements in Socialized and Digital Media Communications* (pp. 118–134). IGI Global.

Talukder, M. B., Kumar, S., & Das, I. R. (2024). Mindfulness of Digital Detoxification: Healthy Lifestyle in Tourism. *IGI Global, USA*.https://doi.org/https://doi.org/10.4018/979-8-3693-1273-5.ch004

Tamang, A., Chan, C. P., & Maharjan, G. (2022). The opportunities and challenges of the rise of TikTok as destination exploration among youth; A case study of Nepal. *Retrieved From, 365197888*.

Tsironis, C. N. (2022). Pilgrimage and religious tourism in society, in the wake of the COVID-19 pandemic: A paradigmatic focus on 'St. Paul's Route' in the Central Macedonia Region, Greece. *Religions*, 13(10), 887. DOI: 10.3390/rel13100887

Vinnakota, S., Mohan, M. D., Boda, M. J., Askarzai, W., Devkota, M. P., Shetty, M. S., Wangmo, M. T., & Choden, M. T. (2023). Venturing into Virtuality: Exploring the Evolution, Technological Underpinnings, and Forward Pathways of Virtual Tourism. [IJMCER]. *Educational Research*, 5(6), 8–49.

Whalen, E. A. (n.d.). *Disney is one of the most emotionally connected brands in the United States ranking second overall and first with Millennials (MBLM 2017: n. pag.). Surprisingly, it is the only experiential brand listed in the top ten of the MBLM Brand Intimacy Report of 2017. Disney's eclectic brand provides entertainment via multiple product offerings, which include its world-renowned theme.*

Xu, F., Tian, F., Buhalis, D., Weber, J., & Zhang, H. (2021). Tourists as mobile gamers: Gamification for tourism marketing. In *Future of Tourism Marketing* (pp. 96–114). Routledge. DOI: 10.4324/9781003176039-9

Yavuz, G., & Enes, K. (2022). Social media and events: Before, during, and after. In *Research Anthology on Social Media Advertising and Building Consumer Relationships* (pp. 106–122). IGI Global. DOI: 10.4018/978-1-6684-6287-4.ch008

Yoo, J., Choe, Y., & Lee, G. (2022). Exploring pilgrimage value by ZMET: The mind of Christian pilgrims. *Annals of Tourism Research*, 96, 103466. DOI: 10.1016/j.annals.2022.103466

Yuan, Y., Chan, C.-S., Eichelberger, S., Ma, H., & Pikkemaat, B. (2022). The effect of social media on travel planning process by Chinese tourists: the way forward to tourism futures. *Journal of Tourism Futures*.

Zaid, B., Fedtke, J., Shin, D. D., El Kadoussi, A., & Ibahrine, M. (2022). Digital Islam and Muslim millennials: How social media influencers reimagine religious authority and Islamic practices. *Religions*, 13(4), 335. DOI: 10.3390/rel13040335

Chapter 19
Tourism Industry Amidst COVID-19 With Special Reference to National Capital Region of India

Rama Verma
https://orcid.org/0000-0001-9380-9682
Amity University Online, India

Kuldeep Singh
Amity University, Haryana, India

Arnab Gantait
https://orcid.org/0000-0002-1664-2193
Independent Researcher, India

Susanta Ranjan Chaini
Shiksha 'O' Anusandhan University, India

ABSTRACT

Travel and Tourism is one of the leisure and service-based industries that survive to facilitate people around the globe; at the same time, it is a loaf of bread for millions. The outbreak of the Novel Coronavirus devastated the industry for a period of time. In view of the severe impact, the study focuses on the strategy for the revival and survival of the industry and its industry professionals. The area is particularly in the Delhi NCR region of India. The major objective of the study is to showcase and measure the outcome of the impact in the selected area, the strategies implemented so far, and the plans to inculcate ways to overcome any such occurrence in the near future. Also, to analyze the impact of this region on the entire world, The study uses a quantitative method to analyze it with the help of the One-way ANNOVA technique. Probable suggestions provide a survival platform for the industry in times of crisis.

DOI: 10.4018/979-8-3693-9230-0.ch019

Copyright ©2025, IGI Global. Copying or distributing in print or electronic forms without written permission of IGI Global is prohibited.

INTRODUCTION

The hospitality and tourism industry took a new turn after the tragic outbreak of the novel coronavirus in the entire world. Since December 2019, the conflict over this epidemic has come from China, where the first recorded case was observed in Wuhan city, and then it was first reported to the World Health Organization's Country Office on December 31, 2019. The main symptoms of this disease are cough, fever, and other respiratory problems. The virus may also create abdomen-related issues. COVID-19 is an intricate disease and an outcome of the SARS-CoV-2 disease, which spread in 2004. According to the World Health Organization (WHO), in 2020, the total confirmed cases were 16 298 556 globally as of July 30, 2020. Gradually, the number of deaths increased day by day, and it had a direct effect on the worldwide economy. Within a month or so, causality and the mortality rate increased in China, Thailand, and then across the other countries. The biggest reason was the transmission of the disease from person to person and from entry to exit, through and off the country. During the first wave, the most pretentious rate occurred in countries like the United States, Spain, Italy, France, Germany, Britain, and Russia. India, situated in Asia, has also been in a pandemic where the government has been trying to wrap around the head of this situation, though India was in the biggest trap during the second wave. Tourism activity can't stay inactive for a longer duration of time, and hence it always requires assistance, either in the form of prior motivational support or at-hand information. People always require updates on what is going on around the world. An epidemic like COVID-19 compelled people to sit or work from inside their homes. Sardar et al. (2022) in their study in Bangladesh found that restaurants were bound to reduce their number of employees with all proper guidelines like social distancing and sanitization, which enhanced the operating cost. According to Solanki and Oberoi (2022), COVID-19 had a negative impact on the aviation industry and on the GDP. Apart from the loss of lives, the pandemic condition has both positive and negative sides. The most negative aspect is the economic slowdown and overall stagnation in the growth of the tourism industry in terms of job opportunities owners and the rise in GDP.

On the other side, this epidemic has led to a rise in self-consciousness among people for their safety, security, hygiene, social distancing, and isolation. Tourism activity can't stay inactive for a long period, and hence people or those willing to travel always require assistance, either in the form of prior motivation or through the information at hand. People always require updates on what is happening around the world. The positive aspect is the reduction of pollution, less wastage of resources, reduction in littering of garbage by the people, which further resulted in cleaned rivers and streams, lesser chances of smog during winter, and ultimately an increase in green cover all around the places. The decline in mass travel has resulted from the rapid spread of the virus during the starting and ongoing phases. However, this break has been useful for the destination as well in getting time for revival and reformation. This has slowly impacted people's concern for meeting other people and getting involved in activities in their everyday lives. Home quarantine has been in regular practice, especially for the victims and some non-victims of this epidemic.

Worldwide Impact on Tourism Industry

COVID-19 has a major impact on the tourism industry, predominantly in travel agencies, hotels, restaurants, and airlines. Till now, almost 5 crore people have been directly or indirectly affected in the tourism sector due to this pandemic. As per the World Travel and Tourism Council (WTTC) report, due to this crisis, the tourism sector has been hit the hardest, and it is expected that 50 million jobs will suffer in this sector. Further, in 2020, the travel and tourism industry worldwide experienced a significant loss of nearly US$ 4.5 trillion. This downturn led to a decrease in its contribution to the global GDP, which fell from 10.4 percent in 2019 to 5.5 percent (ILO, 2022) and there was no certainty of vaccination against the virus before the second wave arrived. As a result, the travel sector was harmed the most as compared to other sectors. According to the United Nations World Tourism Organization, there was a decline from 58% to 78% in international tourist arrivals in the year as of May 2020 (UNWTO, 2020). Kunwar et al. (2022) reveal that the occurrence of the pandemic has a negative effect on the tourism industry in Sauraha in Chitwan district in Nepal due to the quick shutdown, which leads to unemployment and loss of income.

Impact on Tourism Industry from the Indian Perspective

According to the Indian Associations of Tour Operators (IATO), segments of the Indian tourism industry like hotels, transport, and the aviation sector may expect a loss of around 85 million because of lockdown and travel constraints. As per the 2020 report illustrated by the Indian Chamber of Commerce (ICC, 2020), many countries will see a huge reduction in domestic as well as foreign tourist arrivals. Also, in many Asian countries, the policy of lockdown and travel restrictions is implemented, resulting in a decline in tourist arrivals. According to Jaipuria et al. (2021), it is critical to quantify pandemic-related losses so that policies can be adjusted to govern tourism activities. For travel agents, the MICE sector provides a good source of income, but due to COVID-19, major business activities like conferences, meetings, and seminars have been abandoned or rescheduled. There is also a salary cut for many employees from major companies like MakeMyTrip, Yatra.com, etc. Most travel agents are already aware of the situation and are obliged to take these kinds of steps. During the lockdown period, airlines are also restricted for safety purposes by the government. As a result, travel agents also suffer heavy losses, as airlines are one of their major sources of revenue. According to Faisal and Dhusia (2021), the history of coronavirus cases in a state matter when selecting a destination, and the pandemic has altered people's preferences for tourism components. Tourist destinations in India are badly affected due to COVID 19. Likewise, the hospitality sector also suffers from business and economic crises in the whole country. As a result, destination managers and service providers postponed or suspended their business activities. Most important segments of tourism (hotels, airlines, travel agents, tour operators, and cruise lines) have to curtail or cancel their daily activities due to this crisis. This causes an unexpected loss of revenue for the tourism industry.

Scope of the Study

The present study discusses the effects of the pandemic on the tourism industry's performance both from the organizational level and from the customer's end, from the business-to-business level and from the business-to-customer level. Because of the sudden outbreak, there had been no prior preparation, and hence it caused a large deficit in the travel business for retail agents and entrepreneurs. However, it is of utmost importance for the tourism industry to prepare itself for any such shortfalls or mishaps. They need to be proactive to anticipate the demand of the people and the problems that are going to arise in the future while engaging in tourism activity. There has been a behavioral change in the actions and choices of the forthcoming tourists because of the devastating effects of this pandemic. Things will take time, and even a year more would be needed to bring things back to their normal level and lifestyle. Until then, people in the industry must focus on something that is niche and safe for tourists. There should be someone to assure the hygiene and security of the tourists, and that is none other than the tourism industry.

The background of the study entails the situation existing among the travel firms in the National Capital Region after the massive outbreak of this epidemic. A sudden outbreak brings an overnight downfall to the whole economy, and due to this, many companies plan to shut down, whereas some cut off their income while the rest plan to remove their hard workers with no hope of coming back. A sudden incident could bring the world to a situation where there is no hope to cope, other than waiting for six months or a year. Thus, it is of utmost importance for an industry like travel and tourism to be prepared and have some backup for an unknown future crisis. This study will help us find out the plans adopted by different travel firms, their members, and the overall government to accelerate the income level in the coming time. Also, tourists are most conscious now about their safety, so it is important to measure the safety initiatives taken by these travel firms to assure tourists of a happy travel time in the present and post-COVID eras. During the middle of the pandemic, it is obvious to observe those tourists who are interested in a quarantine holiday, which is tough to manage but not impossible, though the government of India is seen to plan Himanchal Pradesh as a quarantine destination. So, it is interesting to know who and how many from NCR would be interested in participating in it if it goes well in the coming time. Moreover, it is seen that several virtual platforms are being adopted by the travel firms to preserve their manpower and overall sustain their business for a long-term period. This study helps us trace several such initiatives being adopted by the travel firms in Delhi, NCR in India.

REVIEW OF LITERATURE

Source of Corona Virus

Coronavirus has been said to originate from an RNA virus in the Nidovirales order (Enjuanes et al., 2008). As per the research by the U.S. Department of Health and Human Services, there are some viruses of SARS-CoV-2 that affect people as well, but their consequences are low. According to the reports of the National Institute of Allergy and Infectious Diseases, the term "corona" comes from the Latin word known as crown. It is named due to the "crown-like" appearance of the virus. There are four classifications of coronavirus: Alpha, Beta, Gamma, and Delta. It is to be noted that the human coronaviruses are alpha- and beta-coronaviruses. Coronavirus is a medium-sized virus that envelopes positive-stranded RNA. This virus has the largest RNA genome (Pal et al., 2020).

Humans

Human coronaviruses are causes of both respiratory and gastrointestinal tract infections. It is estimated that coronavirus accounts for probably 5–10 percent of all adult upper respiratory tract infections ("common cold," pneumonia, and ARDS). Some coronaviruses can also cause gastrointestinal symptoms, and common symptoms include diarrhea. When a mutation occurs, a coronavirus can be a significant cause of human epidemics, and an entirely new coronavirus can be developed through these mutations (Sonkar et. al., 2020). So, there are a wide variety of signs and symptoms of coronaviruses.

Impact on the Global Tourism Industry

The epidemic caused severe declines in the world's tourism sector. The World Tourism Organisation (UNWTO) reports that foreign visitor arrivals fell by 70% in 2020 compared to 2019, which caused a severe economic crisis in nations where tourism is a major industry. The tourist industry, a significant employer and provider of foreign money, suffered a decrease in employment and GDP contributions worldwide (Bansal & Pandey, 2022). When there is a lack of vaccine for a particular epidemic like the coronavirus, the best way that has been followed is to wash hands repeatedly, avoid large gatherings, isolate the victims, quarantine oneself, and create social distance (Narain et al., 2009). From a broad perspective, it is estimated that due to this, the hotels have reduced their bookings from 80% to 20% after this epidemic. Air and sea travel have been the major causes of this pandemic (Chinazzi et al., 2020). Mobility is more about the movement of people; it is about the technologically facilitated exchange of goods and services, entertainment, ideas, and virtually connected experiences for more prospects (Urry 2000). Alamineh (2022) noted that COVID-19 has a significant impact on the tourism industry's socio-cultural, economic, and environmental domains, all of which are essential for beneficial peace and long-term growth. Aryal et al. (2022) indicate that the COVID-19 pandemic and its aftermath have wreaked havoc on the global tourism industry, affecting the livelihoods of millions of people. People have also come to realize that this pandemic and the pause in the activities of the tourism industry have given nature a break. Many countries, like Kenya, have started conserving natural resources in the meantime to better facilitate themselves and tourists in the post-COVID era. For example, people in the Mara community near Masai Mara National Park have started cleaning the water to get rid of pollution. According to them, it is important to understand the need for a paradigm shift in this type of conservation movement. The tourism industry in the Global North and Global South has been seriously affected, with the former being observed more due to the absence of social safety (Baum & Nguyen, 2019). Sinulingga (2021) investigated whether COVID-19's Zero Tourism has a significant influence on industries that provide trip packages. As the cost of airline tickets has risen, so has the cost of increasingly expensive travel packages. The Federation of Associations in Indian Tourism & Hospitality (FAITH) cautioned that the sector faces severe consequences from the pandemic, potentially leading to the loss of jobs for nearly 3.8 crore workers, out of a total workforce of 5.5 crores. With significant economic activity at risk, the industry anticipates bankruptcies, business closures, and widespread unemployment, amounting to over Rs 10 lakh crores in economic impact (Sinha, 2020). And the reality says that approx. 81 million jobs were lost as a result of COVID-19 due to the pandemic in the Asia-Pacific Labor Market and 255 million full-time jobs worldwide (ILO, 2020, 2021). According to the Federation of Associations in Indian Tourism and Hospitality (FAITH), there was a complete deferment for twelve months of all statutory dues that were payable by the tourism, travel, and hospitality industries at the central government, state, and municipal government levels without attracting any penal interest. It also requested the relief fund for the affected and poor people from bodies like the Reserve Bank of India and the Ministry of Finance. Also, there is some reduction in the salary of government employees to help the coronavirus patients in India. This step was taken as a positive sign from other bodies, like the Ministry of Tourism, the Ministry of Health, etc. Bhateja et al. (2022) argued that this crisis had a significant impact on the service sector, resulting in job losses and decreased industry profitability.

Impact on the Indian Tourism Industry

India's tourism sector suffered greatly as a result of COVID-19. A significant decline in foreign visitor numbers and foreign exchange profits was recorded by the Ministry of Tourism. Foreign exchange revenues declined along with a 67.66% reduction in foreign visitor arrivals in March 2020. Lockdowns and travel restrictions caused major financial losses and operating difficulties for the hospitality industry, which includes hotels and restaurants (Bansal & Pandey, 2022). After this outbreak, travel restrictions in India were at their peak for almost 80 countries, and most of the flights got canceled for some duration. During the lockdown, the tourism industry, unlike other industries, got the most harnessed (Dash, 2020). Delhi-based travel companies were not the least sufferers. Due to this outbreak, there had been mass cancellations of inbound and outbound bookings; almost 90% of hotels and flights were canceled. According to the founder of Krishna Holidays, outbound cruise bookings for Thailand, Singapore, Malaysia, Europe, and the US were affected. According to a report by the Ministry of Tourism, Govt. of India, approx. 150,000 patients travel to India every year to seek medical treatment, but the lockdown during the pandemic derailed all such activities and income. McKibben and Fernando (2020) noted that COVID-19 is fast spreading in India, and politicians are worried about combating the virus while reducing its economic impact.

Specific Impact on the Delhi NCR Region

The Delhi NCR region, a major commercial and tourist transit hub in India, was severely disrupted. Because of the lockdowns and the closing of international crossings, hotels and restaurants in this area encountered significant operational issues. According to Bansal and Pandey's analysis from 2022, the hospitality industry in Delhi NCR came to an abrupt stop during the pandemic's peak, necessitating strategic planning and government assistance to help the industry recover. In Delhi, NCR, approximately 200 to 300 crores had been at a loss. March and April had been the last peak times when maximum travel took place, especially for educational purposes (Mishra, 2020). As of June 2020, after this massive outbreak, MakeMyTrip laid off 350 employees when the crisis hit business. According to Mr. Deep Kalra, staff rationalization is a planned strategy for the prospects of the business (Sensharma, 2020). In the National Capital Region, both the hotel and travel businesses suffered a massive 70% dip in business. Vaishnav Tours and Travels pins hope for revival in the next tourist season, starting in October. 75% of the bookings were canceled that year, as per Shambhu Dayal of S. K. Travel (Mishra, 2020). According to the report of the Press Trust of India, approx. 40% of travel firms were expected to shut down in 3 to 6 months of 2020, resulting in immense losses and job cuts (PTI, 2020). Kumar (2021) reported that slowly, the country's domestic tourism is taking off. Meanwhile, the second wave of the deadly COVID-19 has hit India hard, with fresh high-case counts reported every day. Travel restrictions and the requirement for social isolation have resulted in a precipitous drop in visitor numbers and hotel occupancy rates. According to Gössling et al. (2020), the tourist sector has experienced historically low levels of international travel, which has had an impact on earnings and the lives of people who depend on the sector. These restrictions have presented significant economic issues for the Delhi NCR region, which is a major hub for both domestic and foreign travellers.

Changes in Consumer Behavior and Adaptation Strategies

Significant shifts in consumer behaviour were brought about by the epidemic, especially in the hotel industry. Customers favoured online reservations and contactless services, with a greater emphasis on safety and hygiene. In response, lodging facilities and dining establishments in the Delhi NCR area tightened security measures, improved their online presence, and provided flexible reservation choices (Singh, 2021).

Innovative and Technological Adaptations

Technology and innovation were essential to the sector's adaption. One of the main strategies that emerged was the use of information technology to offer accessible and affordable services. Businesses were able to maintain contact with prospective clients through digital marketing, online bookings, and virtual tours (Singh, 2021). These kinds of developments were necessary to keep customers interested and to make sure the firm would continue.

Adaptation and Response Strategies

The travel and hospitality industries have responded to the pandemic by implementing a number of tactics to lessen its effects. One important tactic has been the shift to digital platforms for customer engagement and marketing (Scagnoli et al. 2019). In order to win back customer trust, the sector has also stressed the significance of safety precautions and hygiene. Strict health regulations and the use of contactless technologies have been essential in guaranteeing the security of both visitors and employees (Gössling et al., 2020). Since they foster confidence among prospective tourists, these actions are crucial for the tourism industry's slow but steady comeback.

Long-term Effects and Future Preparedness

One of COVID-19's long-term consequences on the travel and tourism sector is a move towards more resilient and sustainable practices. The pandemic emphasised the value of crisis management and readiness for unforeseen events in the future. The future of the tourism sector in the Delhi NCR region and beyond is anticipated to be shaped by the incorporation of technology, prioritising health and safety, and creating adaptable business models (Bansal & Pandey, 2022).

Emerging Opportunities

Notwithstanding the difficulties, the pandemic has given rise to chances for innovation and growth in the travel and tourism sector. Increasing attention to eco-friendly tourist methods is one such chance. Discussions about encouraging eco-friendly tourism have been sparked by the temporary drop in environmental pollution brought on by the reduction in travel (Hall et al., 2020). Furthermore, as long as there are restrictions on international travel, there will likely be an increasing interest in local and regional tourism. This change offers the Delhi NCR region a chance to grow and advertise its regional attractions, which will boost the local economy. The use of technology in tourism has also increased as a result of the pandemic. The increasing prevalence of virtual tours, online booking platforms, and digital payment methods has improved both the overall tourism experience and operational effectiveness (Goo et al., 2022).

OBJECTIVES OF THE STUDY

The four major objectives of this study are as follow:

- Objective 1: To measure the impact of the occurrence of coronavirus on the tourism industry performance in Delhi NCR, India.
- Objective 2: To discover the strategies adopted by the travel firms to survive in this pandemic in Delhi NCR, India.
- Objective 3: To access the plans adopted by the travel companies in Delhi NCR, India to act in the post-COVID 19 era
- Objective 4: To discuss the impact of COVID 19 particularly NCR on the rest part of the country and the world.

MATERIAL AND METHODOLOGY

The study is based on quantitative findings. The area selected is the travel companies of Delhi NCR. The sampling technique used was Purposive sampling. The way adopted to collect the sample was through online mode using google forms. The questions provided mostly were closed-ended following the Likert scale pattern. Cronbach's Alpha technique was used to test the validity. To test the analysis the Regression and ANNOVA techniques were used. The following two hypotheses were framed to prove the test. One is alternative and another is null.

- **Hypothesis 1** - The impact of COVID 19 was severe on the tourism industry's performance in Delhi NCR – **H 1**
- **Hypothesis 2** - Impact of COVID 19 was not severe/did not affect the tourism industry's performance in Delhi NCR – **H 0**

Limitation

The data collected from the professionals of Delhi NCR were limited to 100 participants for a limited period.

LONG-TERM EFFECTS AND ADAPTABILITY OF THE TOURISM INDUSTRY IN DELHI NCR

1. Industry Adaptability:

Health and Safety Procedures: The pandemic has led to considerable modifications in the health and safety procedures used by the tourism industry in Delhi NCR. Improved hygiene, social separation, and contactless communication have become important behaviours. These policies are probably here to stay, influencing how travel agencies run and engage with tourists throughout time.

Shifting Travel Preferences: As health and safety become more important to visitors in Delhi NCR, there is a growing need for more individualised and exclusive travel experiences. This change may force companies to adapt their offerings to match changing consumer demands, such as providing more specialised services like VIP lodging and exclusive excursions.

Flexibility in Reservation and Cancellation Policies: The epidemic has brought attention to the necessity of accommodating reservations and cancellations. In order to prepare for uncertainty and improve their ability to manage future disruptions, tourism-related enterprises in Delhi NCR are probably going to keep providing flexible options.

2. Impact of Future Outbreaks:

Risk Management: In order to be ready for any future outbreaks, the tourism industry in Delhi NCR needs to improve its risk management techniques. To lessen the effects of health crises, this entails creating strong backup plans, enhancing crisis response procedures, and guaranteeing financial stability.

Insurance and Financial Resilience: The epidemic has brought to light the need of financial planning and insurance. Companies in Delhi NCR would have to concentrate on obtaining sufficient insurance coverage and creating financial plans in order to endure economic shocks from upcoming disruptions.

ROLE OF TECHNOLOGY IN DELHI NCR'S TOURISM SECTOR

1. Mitigation Strategies:

Digital Conversion: The epidemic has expedited the tourism sector in Delhi NCR's digital revolution. Modern technologies have become essential, such as smartphone apps for contactless services, online reservation platforms, and virtual reality (VR) for virtual tours. It is anticipated that these tools would keep improving operational effectiveness and client experiences.

Innovations in Health and Safety: Technology has been essential in preserving hygienic standards. To guarantee safe travel experiences, innovations like UV sterilisation, sophisticated air filtration, and health monitoring apps have been put into place. These technologies will probably always be essential for protecting the general public's health.

2. Strengthening Resilience:

Non-Contact Methods: In the tourism industry in Delhi NCR, contactless technology such as digital keys, mobile payment systems, and touchless kiosks have become indispensable. These solutions improve convenience and lessen physical contact, making visitor experiences safer and more effective.

Predictive analytics and machine learning: Businesses in Delhi NCR may forecast demand, optimise pricing, and personalise services by utilising predictive analytics and machine learning. Targeted marketing techniques and improved decision-making are made possible by the analysis of data from multiple sources.

3. Transparency and Communication:

Digital Channels for Communication: Managing traveller expectations requires effective communication via digital channels like social media, websites, and mobile apps. Building trust and reassuring guests can be achieved by promptly updating them on health precautions, travel limitations, and safety procedures.

Trust and Transparency: Technology makes corporate processes more transparent. Travellers' confidence can be increased and safe visits to Delhi NCR can be promoted by providing clear information about health and safety precautions, such as vaccination requirements and sanitary practices.

4. Innovation in Customer Experience:

Personalisation: By adjusting recommendations and services to suit individual preferences, AI and advanced analytics may create personalised travel experiences in Delhi NCR. This includes tailored itineraries, offers that are specifically targeted, and communications that are tailored to the individual traveller.

Virtual Assistance: By offering real-time support, responding to questions, and scheduling appointments, chatbots and virtual assistants driven by AI can improve customer service. These technologies provide a flawless guest experience while increasing service delivery efficiency.

However, from an operational standpoint, the pandemic forced sudden changes in corporate procedures. Businesses were forced to enact strict health and safety policies, such as frequent sanitization, social distance, and contactless services. Although these adjustments were necessary to protect public health, they also added to the price and complexity of operations. Travel restrictions, both internal and foreign, made matters worse by restricting the number of visitors and upsetting the supply chains that are vital to the tourism industry. A significant shift in consumer preferences was also brought about by the crisis, with travellers now seeking out more flexible, private, and safer travel options. Rapid changes to service offerings and marketing tactics were required as a result of this transformation. The fragility of the tourism sector was further underscored by the rising operating costs linked to putting in place health precautions and training employees, as well as the financial precariousness of many of these SMEs. Notwithstanding these difficulties, the pandemic has brought forth some beneficial developments, including as a quickening of the digital transformation and a greater emphasis on health and safety. But the pandemic's long-term impacts will continue to influence the industry's recovery, so it will be important to take a calculated risk in order to increase resilience, adjust to changing traveller expectations, and get ready for any future disruptions.

ANALYSIS AND FINDINGS

The demographic profile of the respondents:

Gender   Age
Education Level   Annual Income

Figure 1. Did COVID-19 lead to job loss?

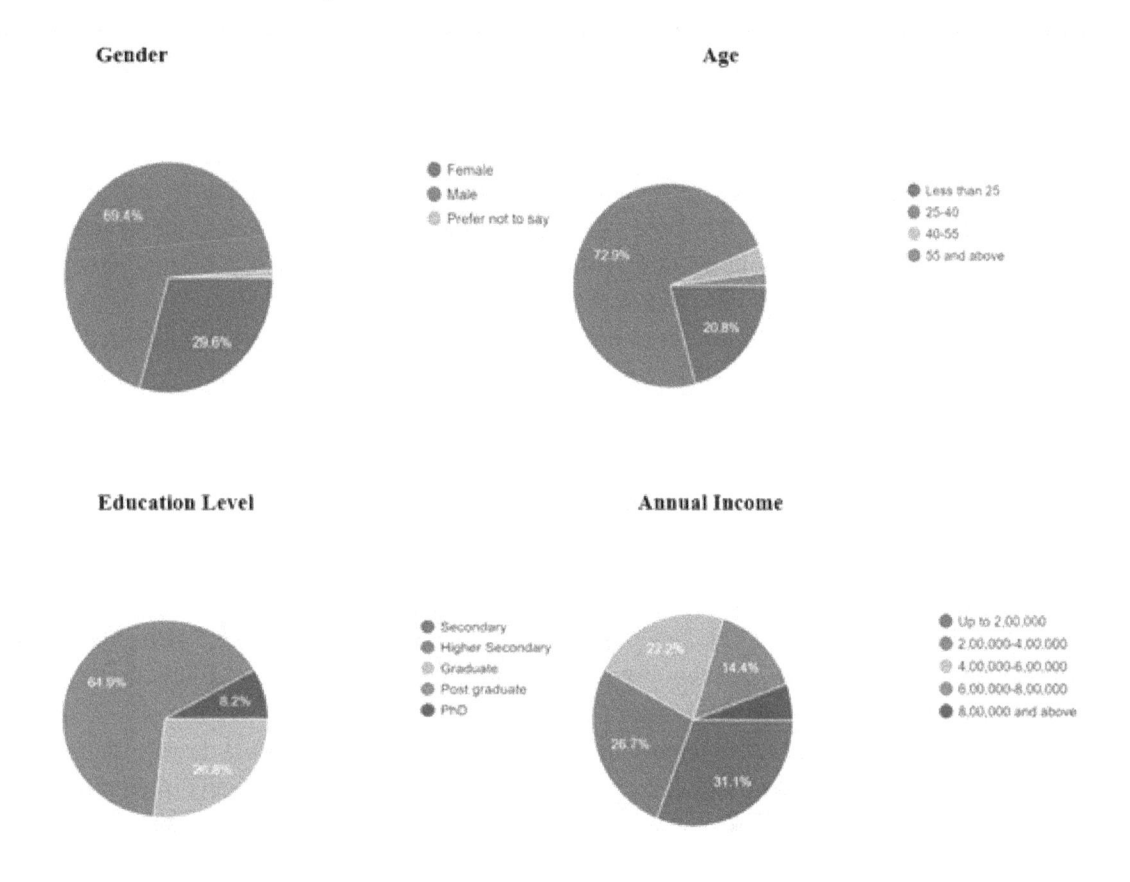

The Respondents

As per the data received from the respondents, the respondents or travel professionals who are or were working in Delhi NCR were from cities like Agra, Chittagong, Faridabad, Ghaziabad, Gurgaon, Gwalior, Jaipur, Jammu & Kashmir, Lucknow, Noida, and Delhi, where most of them were from Gurgaon. The organization in which they presently work or use to work were Yatra.com, Versa travels, Smiling Trips, Radha Travels, Indigo Airlines, Taj Hotel, Trip blog Holidays Pvt. Ltd., Zenith Holidays, Etihad, Vision World Tours and Travels, Hilton Hotel, Traveladise, Shakshi travels, Myra Vacations, Thomas Cook, Roseate Hotel, Dabas World Vacations, Global Tourism, Sunkari travel, Pickyourtrail, Dabas World Vacations, Vasco Travel Pvt. Ltd, Sakushal, Carewell Travels, and Tour Pvt Ltd, MakeMyTrip, Anayat

Tour, and Travel, Top Travel &Tours Pvt Ltd, Dnata international, AIS HOLIDAYS PVT LTD, Bumble Bee Travels Pvt. Ltd., Dzongholidays, HungryTripper, Indian Yatri Holidays, Tavel triangle, VISTARA, Tourepedia Holidays, Cox and Kings Ltd, Om travels, Holxo holidays, Maa travels, Rupalipanja travel agency and Satguru Travels. Some respondents are from the aviation and hotel sectors and either work in collaboration or have strong knowledge about the tourism industry. The concerned departments of the travel professionals were mainly sales, international and domestic operations, ticketing, travel/leisure, MICE operations, HR, admin, audit, back office, and marketing, where some of them are the directors or owners of their organization.

The Negative Impact

As per the responses, the main reason indicated behind the loss of the job in tourism industry was due to the COVID-19 pandemic. However, it also leads to a lack of businesses, negligible travel movements, and curfew. Most of the tour bookings were cancelled after the second week of March (on per day basis). Most of them approx. 36.2% opted for 100 bookings or less of cancellations were done, whereas 29.8% of respondents opted for 200 bookings or less than 100 cancellations. The rest respondents opted for 200 to 500 bookings of cancellation, which were the least percentages.

Similarly, approx. 47.3% of respondents said that approx. 100 bookings were only postponed on per day basis after the second week of March. When it comes to the tourist responses who were either returning home or traveling for a medical emergency or so inside the country were mostly not so good or either neutral. 42.1% of tourists' responses during the pandemic were bad, whereas 40% of tourists' responses were neutral, 16.8% of responses were good, and the remaining very few tourists were very good.

Again, when it comes to the benefits being provided to the travel professionals for their overtime duties during the lockdown, 57.1% said that they were not at all paid extra, 16.5% were neutral and 12.1% said they were paid. However, the rest respondents were not applicable for any extra benefits.

As per the survey in the year 2020, 23.4% of respondents said that it may take 2 years and above for the sale to get normalize, 37.2% said that it will take 1 year 6 months, 28.7% said less than a year and remaining said less than 6 months. And today the reality is in front of us.

When the respondents were asked to provide some feedback, they agreed that despite the pandemic, the employees and the organization took every effort to save their business. Some predicted that the travel agency business is at high risk. There is fear in the mind of tourists which may directly impact the tourism industry in the future. Some had an opinion that the tourism industry may not solely benefit if they do not depend on other industries too.

It was a very bad scenario for the travel agents and tour operators. Most of the companies asked to leave to the high paid staffs. If anyone lost his /her job at that time it was very difficult for him/her to get a new job with the same salary. So, saving tourism was the main moto. The message by these travel professionals was to postpone the trip but not to cancel. Some professionals were facing an economic crisis.

Solutions

The pandemic was a difficult time for all the travel agents, tour operators and any other professional who were related to tourism industry directly or indirectly. However, the professionals who survived provided some ideas on strategies they adopted during the difficult time. Some reputed firms were trying to safeguard their employees and management within the available source of income while trying to focus on domestic tour operations rather than focusing on international tours. Because domestic tours were possible in case of medical emergency. When things got a bit controllable, business tourists and MICE tours were focused as they were the highest source of income. Some travel agencies that were completely shut down started making future plans for survival and revival. Some tour operators were working on creating innovative tour packages like solo trips, eco-tours, wildlife tours, and adventure tours and were avoiding the marketing of mass tours. Self-drive trips were seen as popular in the post-pandemic, especially after the second wave in 2021. The second wave of the pandemic of 2021 was most severe for the people of India. And during this time again the travel was halted for some time and tourists were bounded inside their homes, but some agents and professionals were busy improving their marketing techniques by working from home. However, the third wave of 2022 did not impact much as most of the country's citizens were vaccinated. And in 2022 when all international flights were opened to the tourists, travel, and tourism started to rise again giving a new turn to the travel and tourism sector. Now the sector is working hard on setting an economic goal and fulfilling the market demand.

Table 1. Reliability analysis

Sl.	Statements	Mean	Std. Deviation	Cronbach's Alpha if Item Deleted	Cronbach's Alpha
1	Number of clients dealt after mid of March were to a minimum level	3.870	1.16	0.903	**0.912**
2	There was tremendous downfall in the hotel bookings	4.310	1.03	0.904	
3	Airline's booking were comparatively lower/negligible from second week of March 2020	4.200	0.99	0.903	
4	Hotel rooms that were sold for later trips were at a relatively lower rate	3.980	1.10	0.906	
5	Hotels were in loss mostly after second week of March 2020	4.160	1.02	0.901	
6	Tour bookings of most countries that were cancelled were because of COVID 19 outbreak and lockdown	4.440	0.95	0.902	
7	The outbreak of COVID 19 created great impact on your income	3.990	1.29	0.912	
8	The response of stakeholders was quite reluctant during this pandemic	4.110	0.98	0.905	
9	Amenities provided at the destination(domestic) during the pandemic was not up to the mark	3.700	1.06	0.904	
10	Amenities provided at the destination(outbound) during the pandemic was not up to the mark	3.830	1.10	0.902	
11	Most of the activities were prohibited for the tourists at the site (domestic /outbound)	4.030	1.16	0.900	

Factor Analysis

Table 2. KMO and Bartlett's test

Kaiser-Meyer-Olkin Measure of Sampling Adequacy		**0.882**
Bartlett's Test of Sphericity	Approx. Chi-Square	640.741
	df	55
	Sig.	0.000

Table 3. Total variance explained

Component	Initial Eigenvalues			Extraction Sums of Squared Loadings		
	Total	% of Variance	Cumulative %	Total	% of Variance	Cumulative %
1	5.942	54.020	54.020	5.942	54.020	54.020
2	1.170	10.638	64.658	1.170	10.638	64.658
3	0.927	8.430	73.088			
4	0.638	5.800	78.887			
5	0.511	4.646	83.534			
6	0.446	4.053	87.587			
7	0.384	3.494	91.080			
8	0.331	3.009	94.089			
9	0.278	2.530	96.619			
10	0.204	1.859	98.478			
11	0.167	1.522	100.000			

Extraction Method: Principal Component Analysis.

Following are the component matrix details, following the regression analysis comprising the model summary, ANOVA, and coefficients:

Table 4. Component matrix

Statements	Component	
	1	2
Number of clients dealt after mid of March were to a minimum level	0.754	
There was tremendous downfall in the hotel bookings	0.722	
Airline's booking was comparatively lower/negligible from second week of March 2020	0.760	
Hotel rooms that were sold for later trips were at a relatively lower rate	0.695	
Hotels were in loss mostly after second week of March 2020	0.787	
Tour bookings of most countries that were cancelled were because of COVID 19 outbreak and lockdown	0.768	

continued on following page

Table 4. Continued

Statements	Component 1	Component 2
The outbreak of COVID 19 created great impact on your income	0.618	
The response of stakeholders was quite reluctant during this pandemic	0.704	
Amenities provided at the destination(domestic) during the pandemic was not up to the mark		0.718
Amenities provided at the destination(outbound) during the pandemic was not up to the mark		0.751
Most of the activities were prohibited for the tourists at the site (domestic /outbound)	0.790	

Extraction Method: Principal Component Analysis.
a. 2 components extracted.

Regression Analysis

Table 5. Model summary

Model	R	R Square	Adjusted R Square	Std. Error of the Estimate
1	0.815	0.664	0.657	0.6835

a. Predictors: (Constant), Factor 1, Factor 2

Table 6. ANOVA

Model		Sum of Squares	df	Mean Square	F	Sig.
1	Regression	89.597	2	44.799	95.899	0.000
	Residual	45.313	97	0.467		
	Total	134.910	99			

Table 7. Coefficients[a]

Model		Unstandardized Coefficients B	Std. Error	Standardized Coefficients Beta	t	Sig.
1	(Constant)	4.030	0.068		58.963	0.000
	Factor 1	0.922	0.069	0.790	13.428	0.000
	Factor 2	0.233	0.069	0.200	3.391	0.001

According to the above analysis, the standard error of the estimate is 0.6835, which is less than 1, hence the test is valid. Moreover, this also shows that the null hypothesis is rejected, and the alternative is accepted because according to the findings Tourism Industry was impacted severely.

Impact on the Rest parts of the World

The biggest impact was the loss of global tourists. Most of the NCR's travel organizations were dependent on inbound tourists and they are the ones who bring maximum revenue in business. But due to the closure of arrival and departure to the rest countries, travel was stopped completely. It was a threat to inbound and outbound tourists majorly and throughout the pandemic. The National Capital Region of India majorly suffered the loss from countries like Hong Kong, Canada, Japan, Malaysia, Bangladesh, the US, Russia, Australia, France, Germany, and Sri Lanka. At the same time, it was a loss to countries like Canada, US, Thailand, Singapore, Malaysia, Dubai, Australia, Japan, Bhutan, and Maldives as they receive huge traffic of Indian tourists. The Indian organizations that had their offices worldwide were also at a loss simultaneously. The organizations at Delhi NCR get their maximum tourist inflows from October to April and the second wave was the worst for the people of India. At the same time, the last three months were the worst for the travel industry professionals i.e., from February 2021 to April 2021. Most of the global tourists that come to Delhi are not only the ones who visit Delhi but the ones who depart to other cities via Delhi. Hence Delhi is one of the main entry points for the inbound tourist arrivals in India. Among all, the worst hits were on the tour guides of many countries. The third wave of the pandemic, which was from mid or late March 2022, was no less affecting the outbound travel as the country faced a lockdown experience for some time, however, the wave was a bit milder than that of the second wave. But again, the travel professional and their stakeholders were on a loss during this peak season.

CONCLUSION

This study focuses on impact of Covid 19 on the tourism industry's performance in the national capital region of India. The findings revealed that the main reason behind the loss of the job in tourism industry was due to the COVID-19 pandemic. However, it also leads to a lack of businesses, negligible travel movements, and curfew. Now the sector is working hard on setting an economic goal and fulfilling the market demand. As a result, the findings in this article will assist stakeholders and policymakers in facilitating strategic and operational planning to curb the pandemic cases in Delhi NCR. Lastly, this study contributes towards managerial implications by laying a foundation towards reacting against the epidemic outbreak. It further helps the decision-makers to make an appropriate and immediate decision based on the forecasted values. The decision-makers may also promote tourism destinations, ease the visa regulations, find better financing options, etc. that may subsidize demand and sustainably boost the international flow of tourists with all the sanitizing protocols followed.

LIMITATIONS AND FUTURE RESEARCH

The data collected from the professionals of Delhi NCR were limited to 100 participants for a limited period. The study was unable to examine other economic variables for analysis due to a lack of updated information about the pandemic. This study is only limited to a specific region of Delhi NCR and researcher could also have taken other states for the comparative study.

This study will also help policymakers and other stakeholders to draft their strategies to control COVID 19 cases in Delhi NCR. It will also encourage other state governments to formulate their model in controlling pandemic situations in their regions. Because millions of people rely on the sector, participation from numerous stakeholders is also necessary.

REFERENCES

Alamineh, G. A. (2022). The Nexus between coronavirus and tourism: Tourism as peace sensitive industry. *Cogent Arts & Humanities*, 9(1), 2014110. DOI: 10.1080/23311983.2021.2014110

Animals and COVID-19. retrieved on 12 June 2020 from https://www.cdc.gov/coronavirus/2019-ncov/daily-life-coping/animals.html

Aryal, C., Aryal, P. C., Niraula, N., Ghimire, B., Pokhrel, S., & Nepal, R. C. (2022). Domestic tourism in COVID-19 era: Travel choice in Himalayas correlates to geographic origin and age. *The Gaze: Journal of Tourism and Hospitality*, 13(1), 50–69. DOI: 10.3126/gaze.v13i1.42067

Bansal, V., & Pandey, A. (2022). The Impact of COVID-19 on the Hospitality Industry in Delhi NCR. *Journal of Hospitality & Tourism Research (Washington, D.C.)*, 46(3), 245–260. DOI: 10.1177/10963480211023230

Baum, T., & Nguyen, T. T. H. (2019). Applying sustainable employment principles in the tourism industry: Righting human rights wrongs? *Tourism Recreation Research*, 44(3), 371–381. DOI: 10.1080/02508281.2019.1624407

Bhateja, R., Tyagi, M., & Tyagi, A. (2022). POST EFFECT COVID AND SERVICE SECTOR IN INDIA: A STUDY. *Journal of Positive School Psychology*, 6(2), 4759–4765.

Chinazzi, M., Davis, J., Ajelli, M., Gioannini, C., Litvinova, M., Merler, S., Pastore y Piontti, A., Mu, K., Rossi, L., Sun, K., Viboud, C., Xiong, X., Yu, H., Halloran, E., Longini Jr., I., and Vespignani, A. (2020) The effect of travel restrictions on the spread of the 2019 novel coronavirus (COVID-19) outbreak, *Science*, 24th April, 368, 395–400.

Dash, J. (28 Apr, 2020). Covid-19 impact: Tourism industry to incur Rs 1.25 trn revenue loss in 2020. *Business Standard*. Retrieved on 5th August 2020 from https://www.business-standard.com/article/economy-policy/covid-19-impact-tourism-industry-to-incur-rs-1-25-trn-revenue-loss-in-2020-120042801287_1.html

Economic Impact Reports. accessed from https://wttc.org/Research/Economic-Impact on 30.04.2022

Enjuanes, L., Gorbalenya, A. E., de Groot, R. J., Cowley, J. A., Ziebuhr, J., & Snijder, E. J. (2008). Nidovirales. *Encyclopedia of Virology*. 419–430. . Epub 2008 Jul 30. PMCID: PMC7150171.DOI: 10.1016/B978-012374410-4.00775-5

European Union. (2020). The Impact of COVID-19 on the International Tourism Industry; Retrieved from https://www.europeandataportal.eu/en/impact-studies/covid-19/impact-covid-19-international-tourism-industry

Faisal, M., & Dhusia, D. K. (2021). Pandemic's (Covid-19) Impact on Tourism Sector of India. *Anais Brasileiros de Estudos Turísticos-ABET.*, 11, 1–14. DOI: 10.34019/2238-2925.2021.v11.33307

Goo, J., Huang, C. D., Yoo, C. W., & Koo, C. (2022). Smart tourism technologies' ambidexterity: Balancing tourist's worries and novelty seeking for travel satisfaction. *Information Systems Frontiers*, 24(6), 2139–2158. DOI: 10.1007/s10796-021-10233-6 PMID: 35103046

Gössling, S., Scott, D., & Hall, C. M. (2020). Pandemics, tourism and global change: A rapid assessment of COVID-19. *Journal of Sustainable Tourism*, 29(1), 1–20. DOI: 10.1080/09669582.2020.1758708

Hall, C. M., Scott, D., & Gössling, S. (2020). Pandemics, transformations and tourism: Be careful what you wish for. *Tourism Geographies*, 22(3), 577–598. DOI: 10.1080/14616688.2020.1759131

ILO. (2021). ILO Monitor: COVID-19 and the world of work. Seventh edition Updated estimates and analysis; Retrieved from https://www.ilo.org/wcmsp5/groups/public/---dgreports/---dcomm/documents/briefingnote/wcms_767028.pdf, on 02 May 2022.

ILO. (2022). The future of work in the tourism sector: Sustainable and safe recovery and decent work in the context of the COVID-19 pandemic.

International Labour Organization. (15 Dec, 20220). 81 million jobs lost as COVID-19 creates turmoil in Asia-Pacific labour markets; Retrieved from https://www.ilo.org/resource/news/81-million-jobs-lost-covid-19-creates-turmoil-asia-pacific-labour-markets

Jaipuria, S., Parida, R., & Ray, P. (2021). The impact of COVID-19 on tourism sector in India. *Tourism Recreation Research*, 46(2), 245–260. DOI: 10.1080/02508281.2020.1846971

Kunwar, R. R., Adhikari, K. R., & Kunwar, B. B. (2022). Impact of COVID-19 on Tourism in Sauraha, Chitwan, Nepal. *The Gaze: Journal of Tourism and Hospitality*, 13(1), 111–141. DOI: 10.3126/gaze.v13i1.42083

McKibbin, W., & Fernando, R. (2021). The global macroeconomic impacts of COVID-19: Seven scenarios. *Asian Economic Papers*, 20(2), 1–30. DOI: 10.1162/asep_a_00796

Mishra, A. (14th March, 2020). Coronavirus epidemic: Delhi hotels, travel companies report 70% dip in business. *Hindustan Times*. Retrieved on 13th April 2020, from https://www.hindustantimes.com/cities/coronavirus-epidemic-delhi-hotels-travel-companies-report-70-dip-in-business/story-9JjoIB2cPNqlv2XBKH2qjI.html\

Mishra, A. (2nd Mar, 2020). Losses in Tourism Industry after Corona outbreak. *India Today*. Retrieved on 2nd August 2020, from https://www.indiatoday.in/india/story/indian-travel-industry-suffers-losses-as-high-as-rs-200-crore-due-to-coronavirus-outbreak-1651733-2020-03-02

Narain, J. P., Kumar, R., & Bhatia, R. (2009). Pandemic (H1N1) 2009: Epidemiological, clinical and prevention aspects. *The National Medical Journal of India*, 22(5), e1–e6. PMID: 20334046

Now, N. I. A. I. D. (2020). New Images of Novel Coronavirus SARS-CoV-2 Now Available; Retrieved from https://www.niaid.nih.gov/news-events/novel-coronavirus-sarscov2-images, on 22nd May 2020

Pal, M., Berhanu, G., Desalegn, C., & Kandi, V. (2020). Severe acute respiratory syndrome coronavirus-2 (SARS-CoV-2): an update. *Cureus, 12*(3): e7423. DOI , p-2DOI: 10.7759/cureus.7423

PTI. (25th May, 2020). Coronavirus effect: 40% travel, tourism companies may shut down in 3-6 months, says report. *Business Today*. Retrieved 5th August 2020, from https://www.businesstoday.in/current/economy-politics/coronavirus-effect-40-travel-tourism-companies-may-shut-down-in-3-6-months-says-report/story/404894.html https://www.ilo.org/asia/media-centre/news/WCMS_763819/lang--en/index.htm, Retrieved on 02 May 2022.

Sardar, S., Ray, R., Hasan, M. K., Chitra, S. S., Parvez, A. S., & Avi, M. A. R. (2022). Assessing the effects of COVID-19 on restaurant business from restaurant owners' perspective. *Frontiers in Psychology*, 13, 849249. DOI: 10.3389/fpsyg.2022.849249 PMID: 35496209

Scagnoli, N. I., Choo, J., & Tian, J. (2019). Students' insights on the use of video lectures in online classes. *British Journal of Educational Technology*, 50(1), 399–414. DOI: 10.1111/bjet.12572

Sensharma, A. (01st June, 2020). Coronavirus Impact l Make My Trip lays off 350 employees as Covid-19 crisis hits business. *English Jagaran*. Retrieved on 4th August 2020, from https://english.jagran.com/business/coronavirus-impact-makemytrip-lays-off-350-employees-as-covid19-crisis-hits-business-10012471

Singh, S. (2021). Technological Adaptation in Tourism Industry Post-COVID-19: Case Study of Delhi NCR. *International Journal of Tourism Research*, 23(5), 782–795. DOI: 10.1002/jtr.2431

Sinha, S. (Mar 20, 2020). Warning of 3.8 crore job losses in travel industry, sector seeks relief from government. Retrieved from https://timesofindia.indiatimes.com/business/india-business/warning-of-3-8-crore-job-losses-in-travel-industry-sector-seeks-relief-from-government/articleshow/74715994.cms

Sinulingga, S. (2021). Tourism & Covid-19 (Coronavirus Impact Inventory to Tourism Stakeholders in North Sumatera). *Budapest International Research and Critics Institute-Journal (BIRCI-Journal) Vol*, 4(1), 170-179.

Solanki, M. S., & Oberoi, S. S. (2022). IMPACT OF CORONAVIRUS ON INDIAN AVIATION INDUSTRY. *International Journal of Business and Economics*, 6(2), 353–365.

Sonkar, C., Kashyap, D., Varshney, N., Baral, B., & Jha, H. C. (2020). Impact of Gastrointestinal Symptoms in COVID-19: A Molecular Approach. *SN Comprehensive Clinical Medicine*, 2(12), 2658–2669. DOI: 10.1007/s42399-020-00619-z PMID: 33169110

UNWTO. (2020). Impact of COVID-19 on Global Tourism Made Clear as UNWTO Counts the Cost of Standstill. Retrieved from https://www.unwto.org/news/impact-of-covid-19-on-global-tourism-made-clear-as-unwto-counts-the-cost-of-standstill

Urry, J. (2010). Mobile sociology 1. *The British Journal of Sociology*, 61(s1), 347–366. DOI: 10.1111/j.1468-4446.2009.01249.x PMID: 20092503

World Health Organization. (2020). Coronavirus disease (COVID-19) Situation Report – 198. Retrieved from https://www.who.int/docs/default-source/coronaviruse/situation-reports/20200805-covid-19-sitrep-198.pdf

Chapter 20
The Allure of Tranquillity:
How Less-Crowded Destinations in Bangladesh are Captivating International Tourists

Mohammad Badruddoza Talukder
https://orcid.org/0009-0008-1662-9221
International University of Business Agriculture and Technology, Bangladesh

Dil Afrin Swarna
https://orcid.org/0009-0000-9176-920X
Independent Researcher, Bangladesh

Musfiqur Rahoman Khan
https://orcid.org/0009-0005-7416-2533
Daffodil Institute of IT, Bangladesh

ABSTRACT

This paper explores the effect of low-populated areas on international travelers to Bangladesh. It identifies the transition patterns in tourists' behavior from crowded, conventional places to untouched, unconventional structures, reshaping tourism architecture in Bangladesh. The chapter is thus informed on surveys gathered from past literature concerning international tourists visiting several off-the-beaten-path sites in Bangladesh. These tourists aim for less touristy, quiet, and genuine experiences and tend not to fall under overtourism. The analyzed work emphasized these areas' cultural and psychological features, resulting in better satisfaction due to a better image of Bangladesh as a tourist destination. We found that an optimal level of crowding contributes to long-term, grassroots roots and responsible tourism. Some recommendations have been given to policymakers and the tourism industries to improve and strengthen these areas for tourism significance in Bangladesh, which is essential for national image building and country positioning on the international travel map.

DOI: 10.4018/979-8-3693-9230-0.ch020

INTRODUCTION

Its less crowded destinations include remotes and untouched landscapes far from the beaten path, revolutionizing our understanding of international tourism by catering to travellers seeking peace and quietness who pursue genuine and unique cultural experiences (Talukder, 2024). As global tourism loses interest in over-touristed areas, their serene spots are starting to become an alternative to the beauty of nature and profound cultural heritage alongside a strong loyalty for more sustainable community-based initiatives. This transition increases the worthiness of tourists and drives sustainable tourism practices that help the environment and local communities (Sieras, 2024). This deeper understanding will help Bangladesh market itself more effectively as a tourist destination and develop tourism in less crowded parts of the country or even those currently receiving no international tourists, benefiting local economies while preserving cultural heritage and natural resources.

Bangladesh, often overshadowed by its more frequented neighbours, is emerging as a hidden gem for international tourists seeking serene and less-crowded destinations. The country's unspoiled natural beauty, rich cultural heritage, and warm hospitality offer a refreshing escape from the hustle and bustle of popular tourist hotspots (Roy, 2021). As travellers increasingly seek out unique and tranquil experiences, Bangladesh's lesser-known destinations are drawing attention for their potential to provide peaceful retreats and authentic encounters. From the world's largest mangrove forest to the lush tea gardens, serene lakes, and quiet beaches, these captivating locations are redefining the travel experience, making Bangladesh an attractive destination for those searching for tranquillity and genuine cultural immersion.

The chapter delves into the global tourists' motivations and satisfaction in visiting these upcoming destinations, which could contribute to valuable data for policymakers, tourism operators, and scholars focusing on sustainable tourism advancement in Bangladesh (Zaifri et al., 2023).

LITERATURE REVIEW

Tourism literature reveals a trend towards less crowded destinations as tourists increasingly seek tranquil, authentic and non-mass tourism experiences (Huong et al., 2024). The study underscores the movement from mass tourism towards niche tourism consumers who desire personalized and responsible interactions with local cultures and natures. Given its rich cultural heritage and diverse natural landscapes, including the mighty Ganges Rivers that flow through it, Bangladesh could be a potential winner here. Researchers argue that community-based tourism may help develop less crowded destinations, increasing visitors' overall satisfaction and contributing to social and economic development and environmental sustainability. The value of sustainable tourism routines in preserving the ecological and cultural integrity that makes up any vacationer points of interest is assumed to undoubtedly (Jiang et al., 2024). Unspoilt areas in Bangladesh, like the Chittagong Hill Tracts and even the Sundarbans, are among others across Asia that could become showcases for sustainable tourism. The literature suggests that strategic marketing and infrastructure development are needed to ensure international tourists visit and stay, but without turning the challenge of authenticity into an opportunity for exploitation. This study explores international tourists' motivations and satisfaction levels at non-congested destinations in Bangladesh to provide input for sustainable tourism development (Bagchi, 2021).

Less populated places in Bangladesh: A view from the ground

Exploring the less populated places in Bangladesh offers a unique and enriching experience that contrasts sharply with the country's bustling urban centres. As you journey through these tranquil locales, the serene atmosphere and unspoiled natural beauty become immediately apparent. Villages nestled amidst lush green landscapes, winding rivers, and verdant hills provide a picturesque backdrop to daily life that moves at a much slower, more deliberate pace. Local communities, often eager to share their way of life, offer warm hospitality and a glimpse into traditional practices and customs preserved for generations (Kumar et al., 2024).

In these serene settings, the cacophony of city life gives way to the sounds of nature: the rustling of leaves in the breeze, the calls of exotic birds, and the gentle flow of streams. The tea gardens of Srimangal stretch out in orderly rows, their vibrant green contrasting with the blue sky. At the same time, the tribal villages nearby provide insights into the indigenous cultures and their harmonious relationship with the environment. In Kuakata, the vast, untouched beaches offer a rare opportunity to witness both sunrise and sunset over the ocean, a sight that remains etched in the memory of all who visit.

With its intricate network of rivers and creeks, the Sundarbans offer an adventurous yet peaceful escape. Cruising through the mangrove forests, one can spot diverse wildlife, including the elusive Royal Bengal Tiger, while appreciating this unique ecosystem's delicate balance. Similarly, the hills and lakes of Rangamati invite quiet reflection and exploration. Boat rides on the serene Kaptai Lake, surrounded by verdant hills, provide a sense of tranquillity and connection with nature that is hard to find elsewhere.

These less populated places in Bangladesh offer respite from the overcrowded tourist spots and enrich the soul with their untouched beauty and cultural richness. The local people's warm smiles and genuine hospitality, coupled with the stunning natural landscapes, create an immersive experience that stays with travellers long after they leave (Limited et al., 2024). Through sustainable tourism and respectful engagement with these communities, visitors can enjoy and help preserve the tranquil charm of Bangladesh's hidden gems.

News- Tourism Trends: The Rise of Peaceful Escapes

The world is undoubtedly becoming a global village, but with this sense of cosmopolitan unity comes an increasing appetite for reclusive and secluded holiday locales. The movement is driven by diverse factors, in particular, the desire for more personalized and authentic travel experiences, a growing thirst for nature-based and cultural tourism, and the negative impacts of over-tourism on both destinations themselves and travellers (Suryani, 2024).

The analysis begins by considering why visitors are drawn to places of lower density and includes motivations for quietude, the quest for authentic and engaging experiences, and a desire to flee from urban life - often fast-paced or hectic. The chapter also considers how these relate to contemporaneous cultural trends in well-being, environmental sustainability and ethical tourism (El Archi & Benbba, 2024).

The study discusses that by promoting these calm places, benefits such as less environmental damage, more culture preservation and a better economy for local area residents are explored (Dimanche & Andrades, 2024). Examples from various countries, including Bhutan, Iceland, and Costa Rica, give us a view of how destinations can meet the demands of this expanding market sector—Bangladesh's idyllic and promising tourist spots. The peaceful landscapes of Chittagong Hill Tracts, the uninhabited splendour of Sundarbans, and the pastoral countryside give a back-in-time experience of rich cultural history.

Understanding and exploiting Bangladesh's embedded inclination towards peacefulness, authenticity, and mobile-phone-free travel experiences can place the country as a compelling option for tourists seeking tranquillity (Musa et al., 2024).

Distributed Aspects of Tourist Spatial Preferences

Less crowded destinations save wishlist travel preferences, and the tourism landscape is changing—and for many places, fewer people could mean more (Wu et al., 2024). This tourist's fundamental reasons and tastes for tranquillity-seeking, off-the-beaten-track rusticity in the milieu such as rural Bangladesh.

Psychological and emotional motivators that cause travellers to prefer less crowded destinations. More than ever, tourists want to escape their daily grind and have quieter surroundings where they can relax - in peace (Siti & Nur, 2024). A greater focus on natural beauty, genuine cultural experiences and slowing down life's pace all motivate this change. Moreover, the increasing concerns about over-tourism causing overcrowding, the strain on natural resources and cultural erosion facilitate responsible tourism among travellers seeking new or unique destinations that might promise better travel experiences than popular attractions.

The effect of demographics on tourist preferences. It reflects the increasing importance of millennial and generation Z travellers, who care less about material possessions and more about experiences while favouring sustainability and authenticity as part of their travel preferences (Y. Gao et al., 2024). More commonly, this younger generation of travellers gives us the desire to escape and find those lesser-found destinations that can indeed be part of who we are.

Technology and social media have influenced tourist preferences, such as digital platforms and social media influencers responsible for discovering new destinations and promoting overlooked places. Information has never been more accessible for the willingly curious, and in turn, ordinary tourists have decided to forego traditional hotspots on their travels instead of documenting hidden gems (Song et al., 2024).

Focusing on Bangladesh, specific characteristics attract foreign tourists to relatively less crowded destinations. It indicates the kind of experiences and activities they prefer to tourists, like nature-based tourism, cultural immersion & community initiatives (Talukder, 2024). By studying these preferences, tourism entities of Bangladesh can start forming their marketing efforts accordingly and offer product offerings that appeal to the new-age tourists who are travelling today (Wei, 2024). There is a need for good region-specific data on visitor preferences, particularly those who are likely flocking to different sections of regional parks in response to this growing market segment. Bangladesh could position itself as a destination where tranquillity and authenticity will continue to be the ultimate sustainable tourism experience for those who seek these attributes (J. Gao et al., 2024).

Bangladesh - The serenity and culture of this naturally beautiful place

Bangladesh is blessed with natural beauty, which immediately makes it an attractive destination for travellers searching for unique and authentic experiences. The subsequent highlights the nation's plurality of natural beauty and cultural richness, explaining why under-visited areas attract tourists (Hashmi, 2022).

The chapter opens with a closer view of the Bangladesh rural landscape, from pristine beaches in Cox's Bazar to rolling green hills in the Chittagong Hill Tracts. The Sundarbans is the world's largest mangrove forest and a UNESCO World Heritage site, known for being one of the last regions to house such a significant population of majestic Bengal tigers and various other wildlife species. Quiet riverine scenes, such as those on the Padma and Jamuna rivers, provide peace for boating, angling, or bird watching. Ideal places for visitors to get in touch with nature and do all they can outdoors (Siddique et al., 2024).

Besides being a naturally beautiful country, Bangladesh has an enviable culture imbibed in its history, traditions, and ethnicities. The cultural diversity of under-visited destinations showcases local customs, crafts and festivals visitors can explore (Talukder, 2021). The lifestyles of the marginalized tribal populations in the Chittagong Hill Tracts provide a classic example of how our lives have been unchanged for centuries (Sardar et al., 2024). These include historic mosques, temples, and colonial-era buildings symbolizing Bangladesh's lengthy history.

The potential of intangible cultural heritage (like music, dance, and culinary traditions) in attracting tourists. The vibrancy of folk music, classical dance forms, and diversity in cuisine add flavour to their culture, giving visitors unforgettable experiences (Talukder, 2020b). The Pohela Boishakh (Bengali New Year) and Durga Puja festivals allow tourists to join in local festivities, offering valuable insights into the cultural tapestry of this exotic country (Polas et al., 2024).

In addition, the chapter introduces natural and cultural heritage as critical resources for sustainable tourism. It showcases programs directed at conservation and community while emphasizing how preserving these assets enhances the tourist encounter and contributes to communities (Tinne, 2015). It highlights projects such as the community-based tourism model and pays special attention to forms of cultural preservation, sustainability, localness and economics of tourism.

This study showcases Bangladesh's natural and cultural grandeur and highlights destinations inversely impacted by commercialization (Gill et al., 2024). It offers an understanding of how these tributes could advance tourism in memorable ways and foster international security by contributing experiences of authenticity and internal peace (Talukder & Muhsina, 2024).

Focus on Specific cases: Chittagong Hill Tracts and the Sundarbans

The Chittagong Hill Tracts and the Sundarbans are two remote, beautiful destinations with fewer tourists in Bangladesh. Each one offers unique sights and experiences highlighting the land's natural beauty and cultural richness. This study detailing whole areas where this strategy has been employed and example case studies of these places are comprehensive of how enjoyable the Sustainable Tourism philosophy is to foreign groups outside their border, focusing on the success in attracting those customers (Majumder et al., 2019).

The Chittagong Hill Tracts

Chittagong Hill Tracts (CHT) is famous for its scenic landscapes, hills, and forests combined with splendid waterfalls. It is the home of many Indigenous populations, including its culture (Talukder et al., 2024), language, and behaviour. Given CHT's rich cultural panorama, it is also an attractive site for any traveller who thirsts to explore on an artistic pilgrimage (Sohel et al., 2024). Everything from staying in local homes and participating in traditional crafts and dances to browsing marketplaces offering indigenous goods allows visitors to engage with locals.

The natural attributes of an area also contribute significantly towards drawing in visitors. Trekking at the highlands is popular here; waterfalls such as Nafakhum and serene boat rides at Kaptai Lake keep travellers entertained. With relatively low tourist numbers in the CHT, visitors can engage with that history and enjoy its beauty without much hustle and bustle (Sadik, 2024).

In the Chittagong Hill Tracts (CHT), sustainable tourism focuses on community involvement and environment conservation. Programs that empower them to govern tourism activities are required because they inhibit unfair and uneven income. Conservation focuses on maintaining the region's biological diversity and inherent natural beauty, increasing eco-minded travellers there (Rosy, 2024).

Sundarbans is a vast mangrove forest

One notable example of a less inhabited place with substantial attraction is one that most people have heard about before the Sundarbans (Badruddoza et al., 2024). It forms part of the largest mangrove forest in the world, which also happens to be a UNESCO World Heritage site. These environments cover India and Bangladesh (Ishraque & Soeb, 2023). Tiger occupancy and some of the rarest animals, like estuarine crocodiles, have a home here, and it is also famous for its remarkable birds. Eco-tourists visiting the Sundarbans can view its rich wildlife through 'Sundarbans jungle camp' themed boat excursions and nature walks in nearby landscapes.

While the journey continues with the expedition of the Sundarbans, the untouched and unspoiled surroundings make visitors feel in silence, including birdsong during vacation from crowds of people. The place is surrounded by a network of challenging-to-navigate rivers, streams, and mangrove forests, perfect for solitude and natural tranquillity while viewing or photographing animals (Brauns & Löffler, 2019). In addition to being of commercial importance, the Sundarbans are also of great cultural value as local inhabitants engage in traditional fishing and honey collection techniques practised for generations (Firoj & Mohammad, 2024).

Sundarbans sustainable tourism is also inherently environmental, as efforts are directed at conserving nature with a restricted number of tourists. Efforts to minimize the environmental harms of tourism range from restricted seacoast activities to garbage collection programs and social projects. Local communities are deeply involved in tourist operations, providing guiding services and offering cultural experiences that enhance understanding of this land's ecological and cultural value (Quais et al., 2018).

Benefits and Challenges of Community-Based Tourism

Community Tourism (CT) is a concept whereby local communities can manage and benefit from their tourism efforts, ensuring that income generation remains in the hands of locals rather than large corporations; economic benefits are evenly distributed throughout populations, allowing empowerment with priority given to disadvantaged people bringing genuine cultural enrichment and environmental standards preservation. The idea of CBT has tremendous prospects in Bangladesh, especially in the peripheral locations where indigenous lifestyles and natural landscapes may serve as solid attractions (Gantait et al., 2022). This chapter focuses on the benefits and limitations related to CBT usage under these conditions.

Benefits of Community-based Tourism

1. **Economic Empowerment**: CBT is a vehicle for the economic development of local communities in several ways. By some estimates, many tourism profits leave the community while creating a vested interest in activities such as guiding, homestays, and crafts, which ensures that revenue generated within

CBT stays local. This investment can improve quality of life and reinforce efforts in regional development (Sebele, 2010).

2. **Cultural Conservation**: The CBT helps preserve a region's traditions, crafts, and skills by showcasing indigenous customs (Kumar et al., 2023). Tourists who populate the cities to partake in these events are among the first beneficiaries of such a process, understanding and recognizing more clearly what is fantastic about them. This supports pressure on local people, which then leads not only to maintaining but also to memorializing its historic past (Jayakody et al., 2024).

3. **Eco-Anxiety**: Cognitive Behavioural Therapy (CBT) often encourages the adoption of sustainable practices for environmental conservation. Residents of these communities are also incentivized to protect open space and their local environment, which is a key selling point for tourists. This includes eco-tours, conservation projects and sustainable resource management initiatives often incorporated into CBT (Syafi et al., 2024).

4. **Better Visitor Experience**: Visitors to the area can experience authentic and engaging experiences that do not usually occur in larger-scale tourism operations. Tourists benefit from one-to-one interactions with the village people, active participation in daily routines and a good understanding of local cultures, thus giving them unique, memorable experiences (Shereni & Chambwe, 2024).

Problems Faced in Community Tourism

1. **Capacity Building**: CBT's success requires much capacity building. This often involves teaching students practical things like hospitality or even how to run a business and market. Inadequate support without assistance can also hinder towns from providing quality tourism experiences (Talukder, 2020a).

2. **Side effects of over-tourism**: These effects are numerous and include, among other things, underinvestment in amenities to cater for ever-growing visitor numbers at much smaller or less popular locations. Inadequate infrastructure provides a poor experience (Villamor et al., 2024). Such improvements in transport, accommodation and basic amenities are necessary for the success of Community-Based Tourism (CBT) but may require significant spending with donor assistance.

3. **Balancing tourism and daily life**: Tourism may bring economic benefits but can also disrupt typical neighbourhood activity. Racing to ensure the right balance between allowing visitors and maintaining our routine is also complex (Daffa & Rahayu, 2024). Proper management of their expectations and behaviour is critical to avoid any conflict.

4. **Long-term growth**: It is essential to ensure that CBT projects are sustainable. If poorly planned and managed, tourism can expand to the point of causing environmental degradation or cultural erosion (Kumar et al., 2024a). Localities must develop plans that promote an orderly and predictable tourism maturation process.

Primary market access, promoting the CBT location to attract visitors, and successful marketing may be difficult. Finally, it is challenging for communities that lack marketing know-how and resources to compete aggressively outside their borders. Working with tourism councils and sites on the Internet are possible solutions.

Sustainable Tourism in Bangladesh

It describes the ambition that such growth as possible should be lack-free, building natural and cultural resources rather than destroying them - while benefiting destination communities in terms other than higher GDP. Sustainable tourism practices are a critical need in Bangladesh, where everything is crowded, and the consequences of its impacts could be vast and far-reaching. The various sustainable tourism approaches practised in Bangladesh and their role in promoting ethical, responsible, and inclusive tourism practices (Akhter & Haque, 2023). According to its meaning, environmental conservation is protecting and preserving mother nature.

Sustainable tourism plays a vital role in the area of environmental conservation. In Bangladesh, many tourism development plans incorporate efforts to protect natural ecosystems and biodiversity. Some examples are:

1. **Protected Areas**: This helps promote other areas where ecotourism is promoted (e.g., Sundar ext., Lawachara NP) while also performing a vital conservation role (Mohammad et al., 2024a). They are places where one can view wildlife, go on nature walks, and attend field trips without disrupting the environment much (Kumar et al., 2023).

2. **Conservation**: Tourism operators are locally run enterprises that promote reducing waste, recycling initiatives, and using sustainable energy sources. Green hotels, eco-lodges, or accommodations that follow the highest standards of sustainable architecture and forests have less impact on our environment (Rahman et al., 2024).

Preservation of Culture

Prioritizes the maintenance and enhancement of cultural assets - both tangible and intangible sustainable tourism. In Bangladesh, this entails:

1. **Heritage Tourism**: Conserving ancient sites like the mosques in Bagerhat through dedicated initiatives ensures cultural assets for future generations. They attract history and architecture aficionado travellers, offering them knowledge, wisdom, and discernment of their cultural roots (Chowdhury et al., 2021).

2. **Community engagement**: Encouraging the involvement of local communities in tourism activities helps preserve traditional arts and crafts, music and dance forms, and culinary traditions (Kumar et al., 2024b). Tourists can make accurate and responsible cultural experiences that help local artisans and entertainers earn bread (Bhuiyan, 2024).

Social and Economic Pros

Sustainable tourism practices attempt to have extensive socio-economic benefits as well.

1. **Local Hiring**: Tourism enterprises support local development and employment, focusing on employing and training locals of the specific destination to work in tourism. In addition to the economic benefits, this has created a sense of ownership and pride in residents (Ananya, 2021).

2. **Fair Trade and Ethical Tourism**: Fair trade practices are promoted, ensuring fair payment wages to local producers or service providers. The goal behind these Ethical tourism initiatives is to provide more significant benefits for both the locals' and visitors' understanding regarding cultural awareness, appreciation & conservation, among other things (Mohammad & Fahmida, 2023).

Challenges and Prospects

While the potential offered by these sustainable tourism methods is vast, there are a few issues that must be addressed to benefit from them in Bangladesh:

1. **Awareness and education**: Awareness and education are critical to boosting the awareness of sustainable tourism among all stakeholders, such as travellers, local communities, and the industry. Over time, these educational initiatives and awareness programs will be part of our societal ethos rooted in sustainability and responsibility (Bagchi, 2021).

2. **Policy and Regulations**: As tourism is a significant source of revenue for many economies, implementing robust policies and legislative frameworks is critical in guiding growth toward sustainability. These frameworks include setting environmental standards, conserving cultural heritage, and assuring sustainable management of tourism expansion (Sheikh, 2020).

3. **Funding and Investment**: Raising the required funding for sustainable tourism projects may prove laborious. We must join public-private collaborations, grants, and investments in environmentally sustainable infrastructure worldwide to support this work.

Tourism Marketing of Off-the-Beaten Path Destinations

Less inhabited spots demand innovative marketing strategies and also need to try a new form of hospitality to appeal to visitors on their foreign travels (Mohammad & Iva, 2024). A targeted plan is to keep up with visitors who want authenticity and desolation, and maintain green tourism experiences with the encouragement of these peaceful destinations in Bangladesh (Camilleri, 2020). This chapter investigated some marketing strategies that may be deployed for the underpopulated regions of Bangladesh.

Where do Digital Marketing and Social Media Meet?

1. **Use Social Media Platforms**: Social media is a powerful mode of reaching an international audience. Beautiful photos and exciting stories of unknown places in the country can be showcased through Instagram, Facebook, or YouTube pages (Baysal & Sanalan, 2024). One way to drive interest and intrigue might be by inviting influencers and travel bloggers who can broadcast honest opinions about what it is like to visit these regions.

2. **Information Marketing**: It entails producing engaging information on blogs, movies, and photo essays that address the differentiating features of those areas that are less popular than others. This strategy attracts travellers searching for authentic, legitimate, exclusive experiences. The focus of the content must be set towards these remote regions and their pristine landscapes, rich cultural heritage, and locally driven tourist projects. Forming partnerships with travel sites or, more broadly, websites that target the customer you wish to reach could introduce your work to a new audience (Elrod & Fortenberry, 2018).

3. **Optimization of websites and online content**: Optimization of websites and online content of not-so-popular places to make them search engine-friendly (Search Engine Optimization or SEO Search), thus improving visibility and possible organic traffic. The content should contain keywords like peace, ecotourism, cultural heritage and sustainable tourism.

Photo Credit: Cooperation and Collaboration

1. **Tourism Board and Travel Agencies**: They can partner with local and international travel agencies to promote less-trodden places effectively (Mohammad et al., 2024b). Rated marketing initiatives, participation in tourism fairs, and advertising can raise awareness and generate interest among potential travellers.

2. **Ecotourism and sustainable travel groups**: Working with ecotourism and sustainable travel groups, for instance, can help integrate marketing efforts in line with the values of mindful travellers (Purwanto, 2022). In addition, these collaborations could function as showcases for sustainable tourism practices in sparser regions.

Community Support and Storytelling

1. **Real Storytelling**: Telling the stories, traditions and way of life of indigenous peoples might create a powerful emotional link in whom we want to captivate as visitors. Spreading human stories through interviews, screenings, and social media posts could make these places more approachable (Sharma & Singh, 2024).

2. **Community-based marketing**: To encourage local communities to take part in business, as said above, it is possible that there will be a more authentic approach. While community members can offer their tips and advice for virtual tours, etc., they may not be as likely to engage with someone coming as a visitor. This process increases that place's fame and upgrades the local population's skills and power (Maslakova et al., 2023).

Showcasing Unique Selling Points

1. **Tourism strategy**: Examples include tourism strategies emphasizing unique natural and cultural attractions in lower-density regions. It focuses on the biodiversity of plant and animal species found in places like the Sundarbans at the Chittagong Hill Tracts, providing a scenic landscape and rich cultural heritage among rural communities (Barber et al., 2024).

2. **Wellness and Relaxation**: Messaging more remote destinations as perfect for wellness and relaxation could attract vacationers looking to trade city-living hustle for a calming retreat. Winning over that group of travellers looking for yoga retreats, meditation institutes and wellness resorts...

Sustainable Tourism Best Practices

1. **Acquire sustainability certification**: It may attract tourists who are more socially conscious of eco-friendly lodgings, excursions and activities. However, supporting these types of efforts to help preserve the natural and cultural resources available may draw a crowd surrounding areas with fewer people (Talukder, 2021).

2. **Educational Campaigns**: Educating travellers on the importance of sustainable travel and responsible tourism practices can help create a positive image of the place. Information on how to step lightly when visiting and support local efforts for conservation can also be helpful.

Recommendations

1. **Launch broad digital marketing efforts**: Combine social media, content, and SEO to drive traffic to less developed regions. Maintain blogs, vlogs, and social media profiles, often with high-quality photos, videos, and stories that engross and tell tales of the quirks regarding these areas.
2. **Partner with Influencers & travel Bloggers**: Collaborate on social media and use local awareness. Even though it's overrated, you can still reach a large audience by partnering with regional celebs or travellers visiting the area. Urge them also to request their followers and friends in Bangladesh to discover and cherish a peaceful part of this lesser-explored Bangladeshi land.
3. **Use VR and Interactive Tours**: Create virtual reality experiences and interactive web tours to give potential visitors a preview of what they can expect. It will help attract technologically savvy travellers and even those planning their trip.
4. **Boost partnerships with travel agencies and tour operators**: Work with local and global journey brokers and visit providers to contribute to the lot less travelled locations in their vacation ideas. Offer private deals and offers to promote those speciality areas.
5. **Support the adoption of sustainable tourism best practices**: Support and promote eco-friendly hotels, tours, and experiences. Get these gears sustainably certified and represent that in the marketing material to attract eco-friendly tourists.
6. **Support community-based tourism initiatives**: Invest in programs that build the capacity of local communities to participate fully and benefit from tourism. Provide detailed training in hospitality, business management and marketing to ensure visitors have a good experience.
7. **Infrastructure Development and Accessibility**: Boosting the transportation, housing facilities, and basic amenities of the less touristy area to make it accessible and comfortable for tourists. These activities should be sustainable and help preserve those places' ecological and cultural integrity.
8. **Foster Authentic Experiences**: Develop and promote authentic experiences featuring local culture, traditions and scenic beauty. Program areas might include homestays, place-based learning programs focused on the lands and cultures of the country they study, wilderness education trips/experiences or catchment area guided outings, and health and wellness-cantered classes.
9. **Launch Educational Campaigns to Encourage Sustainable Travel**: Create educational material about practising sustainable travel behaviour for visitors through brochures, online materials and on-site information. Action-conscious behaviour that does no ecological damage promotes local communities.
10. **Track and Assess the Impact of Tourism**: Keep a constant tab on tourism in less populated areas to ensure sustainable growth. Use feedback from visitors and locals to make necessary changes in tourism plans and undertakings.
11. **Drive-Off-Peak Travel**: Encourage tourists to visit during less popular times of the year to space out overtourism on a more even keel. Offer discounted and often exclusive travel deals to boost off-peak travel.
12. **Create a unified branding strategy**: Create a solid brand image across areas with fewer residents, emphasizing their unique features. Use this branding throughout your marketing efforts to keep a cohesive and engaging message.

Following these recommendations, the country can potentially promote its more isolated areas for international tourism while preserving these unique destinations' natural and cultural heritage. These initiatives will enhance visitor satisfaction and sustainable tourism growth, furthering local communities.

Figure 1. Conceptual framework (Author Compilation)

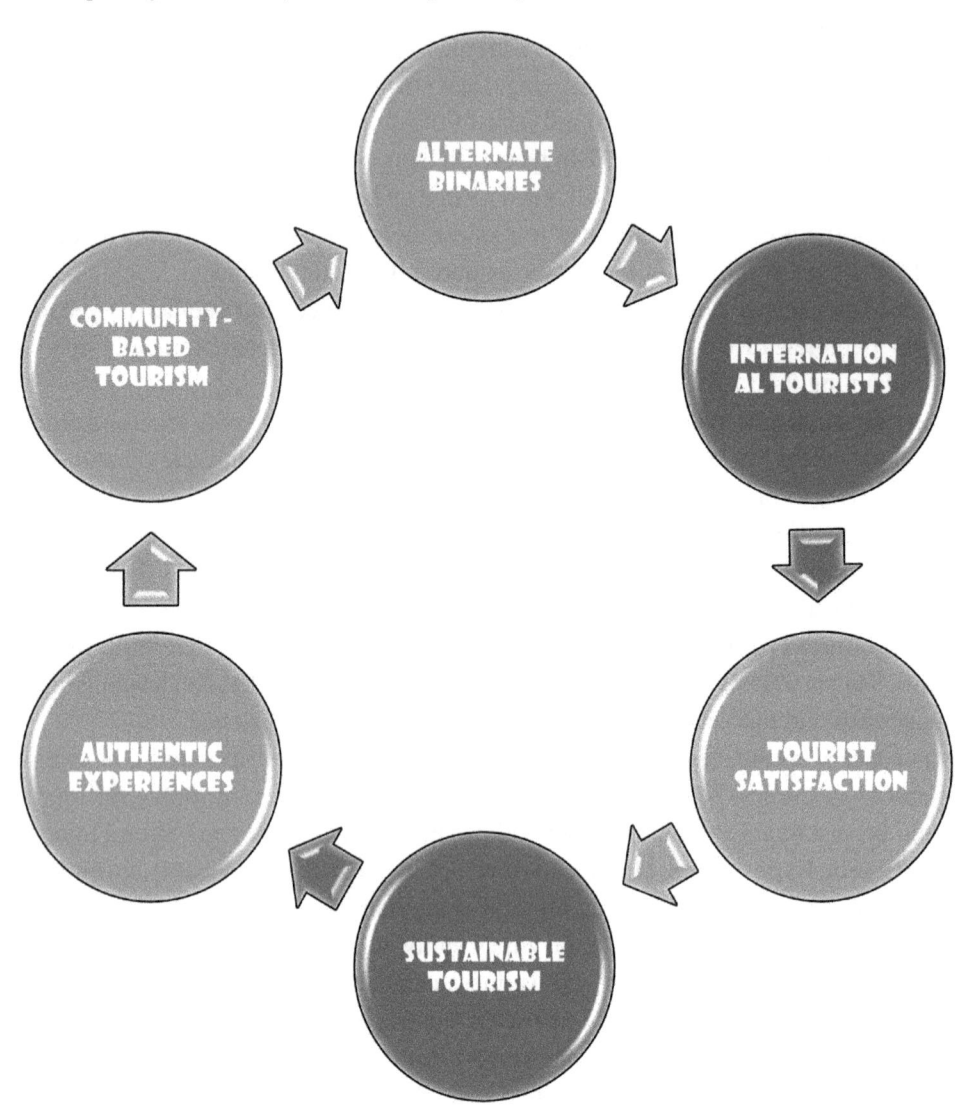

[Diagram: Circular flow showing ALTERNATE BINARIES → INTERNATIONAL TOURISTS → TOURIST SATISFACTION → SUSTAINABLE TOURISM → AUTHENTIC EXPERIENCES → COMMUNITY-BASED TOURISM → (back to ALTERNATE BINARIES)]

CONCLUSION

Highlighting less overgrown parts of Bangladesh provides autonomy for the government to evolve tourism to diversify the tourist offer in venues not saturated yet at all while guaranteeing visitor amusement and encouraging sustainable development if we can use the unique charm of Bangladeshi tranquil, authentic and culturally rich places to attract global travellers who have started looking for some less popular but more realistic travel destinations rather than saturated famous spots.

The chapter outlines a specific action plan for the successful visibility of less crowded areas on the world tourism stage. The plan outlines various marketing activities, from digital marketing to influencer partnerships and promoting sustainable tourism. Developing infrastructure, supporting host communities, and working sustainably are essential to maintaining harmony between the burgeoning tourism boom and the conservation of natural & cultural resources.

The increasing demand for rare and authentic travel experiences gives Bangladesh's relatively quieter destinations an undeniably distinct advantage in travel. Focusing on these strategies and concepts will help tourism stakeholders provide a tourist-oriented environment that serves present-day travellers and encourages the future lives of local communities and environmental health.

REFERENCES

Ahmad, S. Y., & Idris, N. Q. A. P. (2024). Tourist Preferences, the Use of Social Media, and Travel Behaviours among Youth in Malaysia. *Journal of Advanced Research in Business and Management Studies*, 35(1), 44–54. DOI: 10.37934/arbms.35.1.4454

Akhter, T., & Haque, A. U. (2023). On the Prospects of Sustainable Tourism in Bangladesh. In Yamoah, F. A., & Haque, A. U. (Eds.), *Corporate Management Ecosystem in Emerging Economies* (pp. 165–184). Springer International Publishing., DOI: 10.1007/978-3-031-41578-4_10

Ananya, S. A. (2021). Technology Based Service Offers and Tourist Experience Generation in Bangladesh's Tourism and Hospitality Industry. In Hassan, A. (Ed.), *Technology Application in the Tourism and Hospitality Industry of Bangladesh* (pp. 333–344). Springer Singapore., DOI: 10.1007/978-981-16-2434-6_20

Badruddoza Talukder, M., Kumar, S., Misra, L. I., & Firoj Kabir, . (2024). Determining the role of ecotourism service quality, tourist satisfaction, and destination loyalty: A case study of Kuakata beach. *Acta Scientiarum Polonorum. Administratio Locorum*, 23(1), 133–151. DOI: 10.31648/aspal.9275

Bagchi, S. (2021). Exploring the impact of covid-19 on Tourism Industry of Bangladesh: An Empirical Study. *International Journal of Research -Granth Aalayah*, 9(8), 42–58. DOI: 10.29121/granthaalayah.v9.i8.2021.4141

Barber, J., Itskowitz, K., & Wilkinson, J. (2024). Abstract LB088: CANCollaborate: Transforming rare cancer research through cooperation and collaboration. *Cancer Research*, 84(7, Supplement), LB088–LB088. DOI: 10.1158/1538-7445.AM2024-LB088

Baysal, D. B., & Sanalan Bilici, N. (2024). Gastronomy for Sustainable Tourism Destination Marketing. In Castanho, R. A., & Franco, M. (Eds.), *Advances in Hospitality, Tourism, and the Services Industry* (pp. 204–219). IGI Global., DOI: 10.4018/979-8-3693-3158-3.ch010

Bhuiyan, M. S. (2024). The Role of AI-Enhanced Personalization in Customer Experiences. *Journal of Computer Science and Technology Studies*, 6(1), 162–169. DOI: 10.32996/jcsts.2024.6.1.17

Brauns, C.-D., & Löffler, L. G. (1990). The Chittagong Hill Tracts and Their Inhabitants. In C.-D. Brauns & L. G. Löffler, *Mru* (pp. 25–60). Birkhäuser Basel. DOI: 10.1007/978-3-0348-5694-2_2

Camilleri, M. A. (2020). Strategic corporate social responsibility in tourism and hospitality. *Sustainable Development (Bradford)*, 28(3), 504–506. DOI: 10.1002/sd.2059

Chowdhury, M. A. I., Alauddin, M., & Uddin, M. R. (2021). Sustainable tourism in Bangladesh: The demand for investment and development. Tourism in Bangladesh: Investment and development perspectives, 363-381.

Daffa Hanief Wisnu Putranto, D. H. W. P., & Rahayu Kistanti, N. (2024). Model Pengembangan Community Based Tourism Desa Jangkaran, Kabupaten Kulon Progo. *El-Mal: Jurnal Kajian Ekonomi & Bisnis Islam*, 5(7). Advance online publication. DOI: 10.47467/elmal.v5i7.3179

Dimanche, F., & Andrades, L. (2024). Tourism Trends: Current Challenges for Tourism Destinations Management. In Andrades, L., Romero-Dexeus, C., & Martínez-Marín, E. (Eds.), *The Spanish Model for Smart Tourism Destination Management* (pp. 3–21). Springer International Publishing., DOI: 10.1007/978-3-031-60709-7_1

El Archi, Y., & Benbba, B. (2024). New Frontiers in Tourism and Hospitality Research: An Exploration of Current Trends and Future Opportunities. In Negru a, A. L., & Coroş, M. M. (Eds.), *Sustainable Approaches and Business Challenges in Times of Crisis* (pp. 149–166). Springer Nature Switzerland., DOI: 10.1007/978-3-031-48288-5_9

Elrod, J. K., & Fortenberry, J. L.Jr. (2018). Target marketing in the health services industry: The value of journeying off the beaten path. *BMC Health Services Research*, 18(S3), 923. DOI: 10.1186/s12913-018-3678-5 PMID: 30545349

Firoj, K., & Mohammad, B. T. (2024). Measuring sustainability in the broadcasting media industry in Bangladesh. *I-Manager's. Journal of Management*, 18(3), 51. DOI: 10.26634/jmgt.18.3.20234

Gantait, A., & Singh, K. Saikat Bhowmik, & G. Anjaneya Swamy. (2022). *Can Community-Based Tourism Be a Sustainable Solution For A Better Community Life? Discussing the Concept, Benefits, and Challenges.* Zenodo. DOI: 10.5281/ZENODO.6930170

Gao, J., Peng, P., Lu, F., Claramunt, C., Qiu, P., & Xu, Y. (2024). Mining tourist preferences and decision support via tourism-oriented knowledge graph. *Information Processing & Management*, 61(1), 103523. DOI: 10.1016/j.ipm.2023.103523

Gao, Y., Liu, S., Wei, B., Zhu, Z., & Wang, S. (2024). Using Wi-Fi Probes to Evaluate the Spatio-Temporal Dynamics of Tourist Preferences in Historic Districts' Public Spaces. *ISPRS International Journal of Geo-Information*, 13(7), 244. DOI: 10.3390/ijgi13070244

Gill, C., Weisburd, D., Nazaire, D., Prince, H., & Gross Shader, C. (2024). Building "A Beautiful Safe Place for Youth" through problem-oriented community organizing: A quasi-experimental evaluation. *Criminology & Public Policy*, 23(2), 287–325. DOI: 10.1111/1745-9133.12657

Hashmi, T. (2022). "Culture Matters": Towards Understanding the Crisis of Culture in Bangladesh. In T. Hashmi, *Fifty Years of Bangladesh, 1971-2021* (pp. 319–359). Springer International Publishing. DOI: 10.1007/978-3-030-97158-8_9

Huong, K. T., Trang, B. T. Q., & Phuong, T. M. (2024). Factors Affecting International Tourist's Revisit Intention in Vietnamese Tourist Destinations. *Revista de Gestão Social e Ambiental*, 18(1), e06380. DOI: 10.24857/rgsa.v18n1-138

Jayakody, S. P. M. B., Arachchi, R. S. S. W., & Pattiyagedara, P. G. S. S. (2024). Community Perception on Tourism Development: A Case Study of Riverston, Matale, Sri Lanka. In Sharma, A., & Arora, S. (Eds.), *Strategic Tourism Planning for Communities* (pp. 11–21). Emerald Publishing Limited., DOI: 10.1108/978-1-83549-015-020241002

Jiang, M., Zhao, L., & Li, Y. (2024). Multidimensional destination perception effects over medical tourists' behavioural in emerging destinations: Empirical evidence from China's international medical tourism pilot area. *International Journal of Tourism Cities*, 10(2), 545-561. DOI: 10.1108/IJTC-07-2023-0144

Kumar, S., Islam, R., Saha, M. K., Khan, M. H. R., Alam, M. R., & Mia, S. (2024). Metal(loid) contamination in Bangladesh: A comprehensive synthesis in different landscapes with ecological and health implications. *Environmental Science and Pollution Research International*, 31(28), 40958–40975. DOI: 10.1007/s11356-024-33836-3 PMID: 38839739

Kumar, S., Talukder, M. B., Kabir, F., & Kaiser, F. (2023). Challenges and Sustainability of Green Finance in the Tourism Industry: Evidence From Bangladesh. In Taneja, S., Kumar, P., Grima, S., Ozen, E., & Sood, K. (Eds.), (pp. 97–111). Advances in Finance, Accounting, and Economics. IGI Global., DOI: 10.4018/979-8-3693-1388-6.ch006

Kumar, S., Talukder, M. B., & Pego, A. (Eds.). (2024a). *Utilizing Smart Technology and AI in Hybrid Tourism and Hospitality*. IGI Global., DOI: 10.4018/979-8-3693-1978-9

Kumar, S., Talukder, M. B., & Pego, A. (Eds.). (2024b). *Utilizing Smart Technology and AI in Hybrid Tourism and Hospitality*. IGI Global., DOI: 10.4018/979-8-3693-1978-9

Limited, F. E. O. O. I. B. B., Moury, R. K., & Hasan, R. (2024). Foreign Exchange Operations of Islami Bank Bangladesh Limited. *Saudi Journal of Business and Management Studies*, 9(02), 41–52. DOI: 10.36348/sjbms.2024.v09i02.004

Made Dedy Priyanto, I., & Wayan Novy Purwanto, I. (2022). Implementation of Credit Granting by A Customary Village Credit Institution to Other Krama Without an Agreement of Cooperation Between Customary Villages. *International Journal of Innovative Technologies in Social Science*, 4(36). Advance online publication. DOI: 10.31435/rsglobal_ijitss/30122022/7890

Majumder, S. C., Islam, K., & Hossain, M. M. (2019). State of research on carbon sequestration in Bangladesh: A comprehensive review. *Geology, Ecology, and Landscapes*, 3(1), 29–36. DOI: 10.1080/24749508.2018.1481656

Maslakova, D. O., Nefedova, K. A., Yares, O. B., Galaktionova, S. A., & Kirova, E. V. (2023). Credit Cooperation in Russia: Problems and Possible Solutions. In Buchaev, Y. G., Abdulkadyrov, A. S., Ragulina, J. V., Khachaturyan, A. A., & Popkova, E. G. (Eds.), *Challenges of the Modern Economy* (pp. 431–434). Springer International Publishing., DOI: 10.1007/978-3-031-29364-1_85

Mohammad, B. T., & Fahmida, K. (2023). Economic impact of river tourism: Evidence of Bangladesh. *I-Manager's. Journal of Management*, 18(2), 47. DOI: 10.26634/jmgt.18.2.20235

Mohammad, B. T., & Iva, R. D. (2024a). The technology impacts and AI solutions in hospitality. *I-Manager's Journal on Artificial Intelligence &. Machine Learning*, 2(1), 56. DOI: 10.26634/jaim.2.1.20291

Mohammad, B. T., Mushfika, H., & Iva, R. D. (2024b). Opportunities of tourism and hospitality education in bangladesh: Career perspectives. *I-Manager's. Journal of Management*, 18(3), 21. DOI: 10.26634/jmgt.18.3.20385

Musa, H. G., Garad, A., & Mussa, M. (2024). Trends and Innovations in Tourism Marketing Within Government Policy. *JIAN - Jurnal Ilmiah Administrasi Negara*, 8(2), 28–48. DOI: 10.56071/jian.v8i2.886

Polas, A. B., Topp, E., & Plieninger, T. (2024). Mapping landscape values and exploring sense of place in a threatened mangrove biodiversity hotspot: The Sundarbans delta, Bangladesh. *Ecosystems and People (Abingdon, England)*, 20(1), 2370531. DOI: 10.1080/26395916.2024.2370531

Quais, M., Rashid, M. H., Shahidullah, S., & Nasim, M. (2018). Crops and Cropping Sequences in Chittagong Hill Tracts. *Bangladesh Rice Journal*, 21(2), 173–184. DOI: 10.3329/brj.v21i2.38204

Rahman, M., Tanchangya, T., Rahman, J., Aktar, M. A., & Majumder, S. C. (2024). Corporate social responsibility and green financing behavior in Bangladesh: Towards sustainable tourism. *Innovation and Green Development*, 3(3), 100133. DOI: 10.1016/j.igd.2024.100133

Rosy, S. Y. (2024). The Growth of Tourism and 'Development' in an Indigenous Setting: Exploring a Case of the Chittagong Hill Tracts, Bangladesh. *Tourism Cases*, tourism202400022. DOI: 10.1079/tourism.2024.0022

Roy, M. (2021). Tourism Industry in Bangladesh: An Assessment of Advanced SWOT Model and TOWS Matrix. In Hassan, A. (Ed.), *Tourism in Bangladesh: Investment and Development Perspectives* (pp. 279–310). Springer Nature Singapore., DOI: 10.1007/978-981-16-1858-1_18

Sadik, M. I. (2024). Drawbacks of the 1997 Peace Accord and Re-emergence of Militancy in the Chittagong Hill Tracts: A Multidimensional Approach to Resolve the Issue. SSRN *Electronic Journal*. DOI: 10.2139/ssrn.4817372

Sardar, S., Patra, S., & Paria, M. 'Ma Bonbibi': A Goddess in the Folk Culture of Sundarbans Region in India & Bangladesh.

Sebele, L. S. (2010). Community-based tourism ventures, benefits and challenges: Khama Rhino Sanctuary Trust, Central District, Botswana. *Tourism Management*, 31(1), 136–146. DOI: 10.1016/j.tourman.2009.01.005

Sharma, M., & Singh, A. (2024). Enhancing Competitive Advantages Through Virtual Reality Technology in the Hotels of India. In Kumar, S., Talukder, M. B., & Pego, A. (Eds.), *Advances in Hospitality, Tourism, and the Services Industry* (pp. 243–256). IGI Global., DOI: 10.4018/979-8-3693-1978-9.ch011

Sheikh, M. (2020). Development of Sustainable Tourism Destinations and Poverty Alleviation of Bangladesh. *International Journal of Scientific Research and Management*, 8(02), 1565–1575. DOI: 10.18535/ijsrm/v8i02.em02

Shereni, N. C., & Chambwe, M. (2024). Nature-based Tourism in Zimbabwe: Sustainability Issues. In Stone, L. S., & Stone, M. T. (Eds.), *Wildlife Tourism Dynamics in Southern Africa* (pp. 59–70). Springer Nature Switzerland., DOI: 10.1007/978-3-031-57252-4_5

Siddique, M. F., Haque, M. A., Barman, A. C., Tanu, M. B., Shahjahan, M., & Uddin, M. J. (2024). Freshwater pearl culture in Bangladesh: Current status and prospects. *Heliyon*, 10(7), e29023. DOI: 10.1016/j.heliyon.2024.e29023 PMID: 38617946

Sieras, S. G. (2024). Impact and Identities as Revealed in Tourists' Perceptions of the Linguistic Landscape in Tourist Destinations. *International Journal of Language and Literary Studies*, 6(1), 375–392. DOI: 10.36892/ijlls.v6i1.1644

Sohel, M., Sifullah, M. K., Hossain, B., Hossain, M. A., Sarker, M. F. H., Hossain, I., Hossain, M. E., & Uddin, M. R. (2024). E-Learning Experience of Indigenous Rural Communities in the Face of COVID-19 Crisis in Chittagong Hills Tracts Region, Bangladesh: A Qualitative Investigation. *International Journal of Community Well-being*, 7(2), 291–314. DOI: 10.1007/s42413-024-00207-2

Song, X., Du, L., & Wang, Z. (2024). Correlation Analysis of Urban Road Network Structure and Spatial Distribution of Tourism Service Facilities at Multi-Scales Based on Tourists' Travel Preferences. *Buildings*, 14(4), 914. DOI: 10.3390/buildings14040914

Suryani, W. (2024). New Trends in Consumer and Tourism Marketing Science. In Tarnanidis, T. K., & Sklavounos, N. (Eds.), (pp. 290–297). Advances in Marketing, Customer Relationship Management, and E-Services. IGI Global., DOI: 10.4018/979-8-3693-2754-8.ch015

Syafi'i, M., Syaflita, D., & Putra, M. J. A. (2024). *Opportunities and Challenges in Transforming into an Industry-Oriented Local Wisdom Tourism Village*. KnE Social Sciences., DOI: 10.18502/kss.v9i19.16521

Talukder, M. B. (2020a). An Appraisal of the Economic Outlook for the Tourism Industry, Specially Cox's Bazar in Bangladesh. *i-manager's Journal on Economics & Commerce,* 2(1), 23-35. https://doi.org/DOI: 10.26634/jecom.2.1.17285

Talukder, M. B. (2020b). The Future of Culinary Tourism: An Emerging Dimension for the Tourism Industry of Bangladesh. I-Manager's. *Journal of Management*, 15(1), 27. DOI: 10.26634/jmgt.15.1.17181

Talukder, M. B. (2021). An assessment of the roles of the social network in the development of the Tourism Industry in Bangladesh. *International Journal of Business, Law, and Education*, 2(3), 85–93. DOI: 10.56442/ijble.v2i3.21

Talukder, M. B. (2024). Implementing Artificial Intelligence and Virtual Experiences in Hospitality. In Manohar, S., Mittal, A., Raju, S., & Nair, A. J. (Eds.), *Advances in Hospitality, Tourism, and the Services Industry* (pp. 145–160). IGI Global., DOI: 10.4018/979-8-3693-2019-8.ch009

Talukder, M. B., Kumar, S., Kaiser, F., & Mia, M. N. (2024). Pilgrimage Creative Tourism: A Gateway to Sustainable Development Goals in Bangladesh. In Global Trends in Governance and Policy Paradigms (pp. 285-300). IGI Global.

Talukder, M. B., & Muhsina, K. (2024). Prospect of Smart Tourism Destination in Bangladesh. In Correia, R., Martins, M., & Fontes, R. (Eds.), *Advances in Hospitality, Tourism, and the Services Industry* (pp. 163–179). IGI Global., DOI: 10.4018/979-8-3693-2137-9.ch009

Tinne, W. S. (2015). Nation Branding: Beautiful Bangladesh. *Asian Business Review*, 2(1), 31. DOI: 10.18034/abr.v2i1.312

Villamor, K. J., Sadiasa, S., Abella, M., Abellar, J., & Boholano, K. V. (2024). *Unveiling Tourism Potential: Exploring Perceptions of Tourism Impact, and Place Image to Community Support for Tourism Development in Cotabato Province* (Version 1). Psychology and Education: A Multidisciplinary Journal. DOI: 10.5281/ZENODO.11063519

Wei, J. (2024). Analysis of spatial distribution characteristics of A-level tourist attractions in Yunnan Province based on GIS. *Applied and Computational Engineering*, 56(1), 92–98. DOI: 10.54254/2755-2721/56/20240631

Wu, D., Zhou, D., Zhu, Q., & Wu, L. (2024). An investigation into the role of Residents' cognitive preferences in distributed renewable energy development. *Applied Energy*, 372, 123814. DOI: 10.1016/j.apenergy.2024.123814

Zaifri, M., Khalloufi, H., Kaghat, F. Z., Benlahbib, A., Azough, A., & Zidani, K. A. (2023). Enhancing Tourist Experiences in Crowded Destinations through Mobile Augmented Reality: A Comparative Field Study. [iJIM]. *International Journal of Interactive Mobile Technologies*, 17(20), 92–113. DOI: 10.3991/ijim.v17i20.42273

Chapter 21
Kuakata Reimagined:
Forecasting Economic Growth and Future Potential of Coastal Hub in Bangladesh

Mohammad Badruddoza Talukder
https://orcid.org/0009-0008-1662-9221
International University of Business Agriculture and Technology, Bangladesh

Dil Afrin Swarna
https://orcid.org/0009-0000-9176-920X
Independent Researcher, Bangladesh

Musfiqur Rahoman Khan
https://orcid.org/0009-0005-7416-2533
Daffodil Institute of IT, Bangladesh

ABSTRACT

Kuakata is a naturally gifted tourist spot in the Patuakhali district in the southern region of Bangladesh. It is particularly famous for its beautiful sunrise and sunset view over the Bay of Bengal. We aim to predict Kuakata's economic performance and prospects as the best tourist destination, as indicated in the literature review. The main aspects cover natural resources, archeological and historical points of interest, and current construction and improvements to tourist attractions and amenities. The outcome of our chapter on the elements of decision-making in the choice of strategies for theme park business reveals long-term planning, new attraction, partnership with the private sector, active community involvement, and technological innovation as fundamental strategies for economic growth. It is suggested that more focus must be given to sustainability, promotion, training, and extensive study. Thus, addressing these aspects, Kuakata can go for balanced development with economic upliftment and set its place as one of the most significant tourist spots in the face of Bangladesh.

DOI: 10.4018/979-8-3693-9230-0.ch021

Copyright ©2025, IGI Global. Copying or distributing in print or electronic forms without written permission of IGI Global is prohibited.

INTRODUCTION

Over the past several years, Kuakata has become a popular destination for tourists from other countries, drawn by its natural beauty and tranquil atmosphere. Significant investments in infrastructure and development have been made to enhance the town's appeal and improve the tourist experience, driven by growing interest in coastal tourism (Das et al., 2024). Key development projects include transportation improvements, increased lodging options, and various initiatives to promote eco-tourism. Tourism has emerged as a pivotal sector with the potential to drive significant economic, social, and environmental transformations, particularly in developing countries. For Bangladesh, a nation endowed with rich cultural heritage and natural beauty, tourism represents a strategic avenue for economic diversification and sustainable development. Within this context, Kuakata, often called the "Daughter of the Sea," is a prime example of a destination with considerable yet underexploited tourism potential.

Kuakata, an untouched natural beauty with a panoramic sea beach located in the southeast of the Patuakhali District, is a tranquil coastal location in Bangladesh that has the potential to grow into a major tourist destination (Talukder, 2020a). This study examines the economic implications of potential development projects in Kuakata, focusing on their capacity to attract foreign investment and improve the financial conditions of the local community. The study explores how smart investments in infrastructure, tourism marketing, and sustainable practices can contribute to economic expansion in this coastal tourism area (Tasmira Hamid et al., 2024).

The study delves into critical themes such as economic diversification, strained tourist resources, and community-driven rural development. Utilizing a thorough literature review from secondary sources, the findings suggest that smart investments in transportation, tourism, and environmentally friendly technologies are likely to lead to economic growth, job creation, and increased local revenue. Moreover, the study underscores the importance of preserving Kuakata's natural and cultural heritage, which will continue to attract visitors in the long term (Sarker & Khan, 2024). Kuakata's unique geographical position, offering sunrise and sunset views over the Bay of Bengal and its pristine beaches and cultural attractions, makes it an appealing destination for domestic and international tourists. Despite these advantages, Kuakata's tourism sector faces numerous challenges, including inadequate infrastructure, limited accommodation options, environmental degradation, and insufficient community engagement. Addressing these issues is crucial for sustainable tourism development in the region.

1. **Economic Impact**: Tourism significantly contributes to the economy, particularly in regions like Kuakata, where other economic activities may be limited. This study seeks to overview the economic benefits of tourism, such as income generation, job creation, and investment opportunities, providing evidence for policymakers to support and enhance tourism initiatives.
2. **Sustainable Development**: Understanding the environmental impacts of tourism is essential for promoting sustainable practices. Kuakata's natural resources are one of its primary attractions, and their preservation is vital for the long-term viability of tourism. This study will explore the environmental challenges and propose strategies to mitigate negative impacts, aligning with global sustainable development goals.
3. **Community Involvement**: For tourism to be truly sustainable, it must involve and benefit the local community. This study aims to assess community engagement in tourism activities, the distribution of tourism benefits, and the community's perception of tourism development. Enhancing commu-

nity involvement is vital to fostering a sense of ownership and ensuring that tourism development is inclusive and equitable.
4. **Policy and Planning**: Effective tourism development requires informed policy and strategic planning. The findings of this study will provide valuable insights for government agencies, tourism planners, and stakeholders, enabling them to make data-driven decisions. This can lead to formulating policies that balance economic growth with environmental stewardship and social inclusion.

The study also addresses the complexities and controversies surrounding the economic implications of tourism development in Kuakata, providing practical recommendations for policymakers, potential developers, and community leaders (Kumar et al., 2024). This study aims to contribute to a comprehensive discussion on sustainable tourism and regional development in coastal areas by examining how economic growth can be aligned with sustainability and community satisfaction. Overall, this study explores the interconnectedness of economic growth, sustainability, and community needs in developing coastal tourism, offering valuable insights for future development in Kuakata.

LITERATURE REVIEW

In today's interconnected world, tourism development in coastal regions is globally recognized as a catalyst for economic growth and diversification. By boosting domestic and international traveler traffic, investments in infrastructure and hospitality yield significant strategic benefits to local economies, aligning with the principles of sustainable tourism. This dual approach, balancing environmental preservation and cultural heritage with economic advancement, has long been a focal point for shaping our future development paths (Rashid & Taskin, 2018). Community-based development underscores the necessity of involving local populations in tourism planning and decision-making, ensuring equitable benefits across cultural divides (Talukder, 2020b). Empirical evidence highlights tourism's potential in social development, emphasizing its role in infrastructure enhancement, job creation, and revenue generation while addressing challenges like cultural commodification and environmental impact (M. B. Uddin et al., 2024). The integration of digital technology in tourism management is gaining traction, reflecting a shift towards more efficient operations. For sustained growth in the tourism sector, a coordinated strategy that intertwines community-based, environmental, and economic initiatives is essential for regions like Kuakata (Hasan & Ibne Hafiz, 2021).

Prospects: Kuakata Economic Horizons

Explore how local governments can proactively plan and accelerate tourism growth for sustainability (Gomez & Sustainable Horizons, 2024). Kuakata, a small but developing seaside town far from Bangladesh's well-known attractions, holds substantial economic potential through strategic tourism development. Known for its picturesque coastal views and rich cultural heritage, Kuakata is poised for significant economic growth (Baktiarova et al., 2024). Unlocking this potential involves a comprehensive plan incorporating community involvement, ethical tourism practices, and infrastructure development.

Transportation and hotel infrastructure investments are expected to attract more domestic and international visitors, boosting local businesses and creating job opportunities (JIy T., 2024). A long-term commitment to sustainable tourism standards is essential to preserve cultural heritage and natural resources. Involving the local community in planning and decision-making ensures equitable financial benefits, fostering social cohesion and local support (Valasek et al., 2024).

Digital technology can enhance operational efficiency and the visitor experience, creating new opportunities for economic growth. Addressing environmental impacts without compromising social and cultural integrity is crucial. By adopting a sustainable development approach integrating community-based, environmental, and economic initiatives, Kuakata can become a model eco-tourism destination benefiting all stakeholders (Touray & Nyanga, 2024). Policymakers, investors, and community leaders should consider these factors to maximize Kuakata's economic potential.

Kuakata Tourism and Its Impact on Economic Development

Increasing economic activity in Kuakata, a charming town in Bangladesh's southernmost point surrounded by blue waters, is a crucial objective. The town's stunning beaches, vibrant culture, and natural surroundings make it a popular destination for domestic and international travelers (Mohammad et al., 2024a). Enhancing tourism can stimulate growth in industries like transportation, retail, and hospitality, providing more job opportunities for locals (Horaira, 2020).

Strategic investments in tourism infrastructure, traffic management, and guest house maintenance are needed. Sustainable tourism, which aims to preserve natural and cultural resources, can positively impact the local economy and mitigate ecological degradation (Khandaker Tanveer Ahmed et al., 2021b). Community-based tourism projects ensure inclusivity and cultural awareness, benefiting a larger population. Digital innovations like virtual tours and online reservation platforms will make Kuakata more appealing to travelers. However, managing tourism growth is essential to prevent overcrowding and cultural commodification (Sarker & Khan, 2024).

Tourism has the potential to drive economic growth in Kuakata if managed carefully. A balanced strategy that increases infrastructure accessibility while considering the interests of land speculators is crucial. Understanding the economic dynamics of tourism in Kuakata is essential for sustainable development.

Kuakata: A Model for Sustainable Development and Economic Diversification

Kuakata, a seaside town in Bangladesh, has immense potential as a premier tourist destination. Long-term prosperity requires economic diversification and sustainable growth (Abramov, 2024). Sustainable practices can harness natural and cultural resources while balancing ecological preservation and economic development. Funding eco-friendly hotels, renewable energy sources, and effective waste management can protect Kuakata's unique ecology and promote it as an eco-conscious travel destination (Sarker et al., 2023; Mukoya et al., 2024).

Economic diversification is vital for local resilience. While tourism remains a leading sector, supporting ancillary businesses like fishing, farming, and cottage industries is essential. Capacity-building initiatives and microfinance can empower entrepreneurs, stimulate the economy, and support regional businesses. Community-based tourism ensures tourism revenue benefits locals directly, promoting social justice and inclusive growth (Moses O. Ichime et al., 2024).

Digital technology integration can also drive economic diversification. Local e-commerce platforms and digital marketing can open new markets for artisans and attract diverse tourists. Training programs in sustainable practices and digital literacy can create an adaptable workforce, fostering a diverse economy (Hoshide, 2023).

The relationship between sustainable development and economic diversification offers policy recommendations and strategic guidelines. A holistic strategy can protect Kuakata's natural and cultural resources, ensuring long-term viability and balanced economic growth (Kukhar et al., 2024).

The Economic Impacts of Investing in Kuakata's Infrastructure

Strategic infrastructure investments can significantly boost Kuakata's tourism industry. Enhancing transport infrastructure—such as roads, public transport, and airport expansion—will attract more visitors and spur economic growth (Nisa & Khalid, 2024). Improved transportation will increase tourist capacity, benefit local businesses, and create jobs (Oughton, 2018).

Modernizing hospitality facilities is crucial. Building eco-friendly lodging, resorts, and entertainment venues will attract tourists, encouraging longer stays and repeat visits (Leal Filho et al., 2024). These developments generate jobs and revenue, contributing to economic progress. Waste treatment, water supply, and energy investments are essential to support the growing tourism industry and population. Efficient infrastructure enhances the quality of life and promotes sustainable urban growth (Asevameh et al., 2024).

Integrating sensor-led technology into infrastructure projects can optimize resource usage and improve operational efficiency. Automation, digital payment methods, and analytics can reduce costs and enhance service delivery (Andrianto et al., 2024a). These advancements position Kuakata as a premier sustainable tourism destination, attracting further investment and strengthening the regional economy.

Neglecting infrastructure investment can have adverse economic effects, highlighting the multidimensional nature of development (Andrianto et al., 2024b). Strategic infrastructure investments will unlock Kuakata's economic potential and ensure sustainable regional growth.

Community Development: The Economic Importance for Kuakata

Community-based development is a successful strategy for generating economic opportunities in Kuakata, a stunning coastal town in southeast Bangladesh with significant tourism potential. Including locals in development initiatives ensure that economic benefits are widely distributed, leading to balanced growth and increased social cohesion (Talukder & Hossain, 2021). For instance, community-based tourism helps regional business owners and craftspeople market their goods and services, creating jobs and generating revenue. This approach improves local living standards and offers visitors a unique cultural experience and memorable souvenirs (Talukder & Kayser, 2024).

The local economy can benefit significantly from community-based infrastructure projects such as locally owned eco-lodges, community-run tour enterprises, and cultural centers (Tasmira Hamid et al., 2024). These initiatives focus on sustainability and aim to preserve Kuakata's artistic and natural qualities, attracting eco-tourists. Moreover, revenues from these enterprises are reinvested into local development initiatives, providing a revolving fund for continuous improvement.

For community-based development to succeed, education and training programs are essential. These initiatives equip local workers with skills in digital marketing, sustainability, and tourism management, enabling them to thrive in the tourism industry. Collaboration between the public and private sectors can further enhance resources and expertise, ensuring integrated development efforts.

The economic element of community-based development in Kuakata involves creative scenarios and strategic plans for various stakeholders. This approach fosters a robust and dynamic local economy, encouraging community involvement, sustainable practices, and the development of regional identities for long-term prosperity (Sarker et al., 2023).

Growth vs. Preservation: Kuakata's Path Forward

Kuakata, with its blue horizon and white sandy beach, is ideal for economic growth without sacrificing its natural beauty or productivity (Shamsuddoha et al., 2017). Achieving this balance is crucial for a sustainable future. While economically beneficial, rapid tourism expansion can strain the resources that attract visitors. Growth-preservation strategies can enhance Kuakata's sustainability profile (Ouahabi, 2023).

Funding for environmentally friendly infrastructure is foundational to this effort (Kumar et al., 2024). Eco-friendly lodging options, reliable transportation, and waste management programs are necessary to accommodate increasing tourist numbers while protecting the environment. These initiatives help preserve Kuakata's biodiversity and attract socially conscious travelers, enhancing market competitiveness (Hendryx & Dennison, 2024).

Community involvement is essential for balanced development. By including residents in decision-making, development initiatives can reflect local views and preferences, distributing financial benefits more equitably (Kim et al., 2024). Community-based tourism projects, such as local artisan fairs, cultural events, and eco-tours, provide steady revenue streams and empower locals.

Ordinances and regional planning are also necessary for sustainable growth. Zoning rules and environmental impact assessments can mitigate tourism's strain on resources. Digital tools and technology can enhance these efforts with actionable data for better visitor management and resource allocation (Hechavarría et al., 2024).

Educational initiatives are needed to increase awareness of sustainable tourism among visitors and locals (Yatsenko et al., 2024). Kuakata can preserve its appeal for future generations by fostering a sense of conservation and eco-tourism.

This study emphasizes the need for an integrated approach to community development in Kuakata. A community-based, sustainable economy could serve as a model for cultural preservation and economic growth, benefiting both the environment and the local economy (Xing, 2024).

Kuakata's Tourism: Pathway to Digital Innovations and Economic Opportunities

Digital technologies are transforming Kuakata and the global travel and tourism sector (Tashpulatova L. M & Suyunova F. B, 2024). Leveraging technology can unlock Kuakata's economic potential and enhance its appeal as a tourist destination. Digital innovations simplify processes, improving visitor satisfaction and engagement and directly boosting revenue (Kabir et al., 2024).

Social media campaigns, search engine optimization (SEO), and targeted internet advertising can promote Kuakata internationally (Zvaigzne et al., 2023). Virtual tours and immersive multimedia resources can excite potential visitors, showcasing Kuakata's natural beauty and cultural heritage. Online reviews and user-generated content can build trust.

Local entrepreneurs and craftspeople can reach global markets through e-commerce platforms, selling handmade goods and souvenirs online. Safe and efficient digital payment solutions provide a seamless shopping experience, stimulating spending (Kazakh Academy of Sport and Tourism et al., 2024; Abbasian-Naghneh, 2024).

Mobile applications offering real-time information, augmented reality (AR) experiences, and navigation can enhance the visitor experience and manage tourist flow, spreading economic benefits more evenly (Soliman et al., 2024). Data-driven strategies can optimize resource allocation, increasing customer satisfaction and repeat business.

Digital technologies also support sustainable tourism (Mohammad et al., 2023). Smart grids and other innovations reduce tourism's environmental impact while promoting sustainable economic growth. Digital platforms can host educational initiatives encouraging responsible travel.

This study covers the various ways digital advancements have improved tourism in Kuakata. Technology can ensure the sustainable development of Kuakata, balancing economic growth with environmental preservation (Florence W., 2023). With careful digital integration, Kuakata can become a vibrant and sustainable 21st-century destination (Hou & Ma, 2024).

Local Employment and Income Generation in Kuakata, Bangladesh, through Tourism

Kuakata is a picturesque coastal town in Bangladesh that offers employment and income-generating opportunities centered around tourism. As tourism expands, it provides numerous job opportunities in hospitality, retail, transportation, and local crafts (Mohammad et al., 2024b). A diverse workforce will fill these roles, ranging from administrative and management positions to service staff, guides, and maintenance workers in hotels, resorts, restaurants, and tour operations (J. U. Sarker et al., 2023). This increase in employment can help reduce poverty and boost the local economy, opening doors for local businesses and promoting the launch of new ventures.

The influx of tourists benefits small and medium-sized enterprises (SMEs), including local markets, adventure tourism companies, and souvenir shops. According to Badruddoza et al. (2024), these businesses typically source their goods and services locally, keeping consumer spending within the community. The growth of hotels and infrastructure projects like roads will create additional jobs. Furthermore, the increased demand for local produce and services benefits farmers and fishermen, contributing to the multiplier effect caused by tourism (Talukder et al., 2023). Realizing the employment potential in tourism requires practical skills training. Programs that help residents gain competencies in customer service, hospitality, language proficiency, and digital literacy are increasingly crucial (Millington & Weaver, 2019).

Community-based tourism programs enable residents to control and manage all aspects of tourism, contributing to local economic growth. If a favorable environment and skill development are enhanced, the rising tourism industry could become an economic engine offering long-term benefits (Shakhawat et al., 2021).

Balancing Economic Growth and Environmental Preservation in Kuakata

Kuakata must proceed cautiously to expand economically without endangering its environment. The town's stunning natural assets attract tourists, such as beautiful beaches and abundant local wildlife. Overdevelopment or pollution should not harm these attractions permanently (Kumari, 2024). Sustainable tourism practices include ensuring that hotels have eco-friendly attributes, using proper waste disposal techniques, and emphasizing conservation initiatives. Strict environmental laws must be implemented, and visitors and residents should become more aware of eco-tourism to preserve the delicate local ecosystem.

Cultural preservation is another essential aspect of Kuakata's development. The town's diverse populations, each with unique cultures and customs, create a vibrant atmosphere that draws tourists (Makwembere et al., 2024). Economic growth strategies should include measures to preserve and honor this cultural diversity. Supporting regional artisans, promoting traditional festivals, and fostering community-based tourism can help preserve cultural heritage. This approach enhances tourists' experiences and generates revenue for the community through meaningful interactions with foreign visitors (Rashid & Taskin, 2018).

Involving local communities in planning and development ensures their views and interests are considered (Mitanur Rahman, 2023). Promoting community involvement leads to environmentally friendly and culturally sensitive tourism practices, fostering a sense of accountability and ownership among host communities. This balanced strategy is essential for Kuakata's long-term sustainable growth, keeping it a desirable travel destination for years to come (Bhandari, 2019).

Economic Development in Kuakata

According to Khandaker Tanveer Ahmed et al. (2021b), Kuakata requires a comprehensive model for tourism expansion that integrates economic development with sustainability and community involvement. To optimize its potential, consider the following strategic advice:

1. **Encourage Eco-tourism**: Provide eco-friendly infrastructure, energy-efficient lodging, and effective recycling practices. Support eco-friendly travel to minimize environmental impact (Anika et al., 2020). Online guidelines and certifications can uphold corporate sustainability standards.

2. **Infrastructure Development**: Invest in accessible transportation modes like public transit, new airports, and improved roads. Ensure well-designed public utilities, including sanitation, water supply, and power, with minimal environmental disturbance.

3. **Community-Based Tourism**: To ensure equitable economic gains, include local communities in tourism development. Support community-focused initiatives that allow residents to run businesses such as homestays, guided tours, and cultural seminars, preserving the area's artistic legacy (Talukder & Muhsina, 2024).

4. **Digital Integration**: Enhance operational efficiency and the travel experience through digital technology. Promote Kuakata globally using social media, SEO, and other digital marketing tools (Talukder, 20201). Develop digital interfaces and mobile apps for real-time information and recommendations.

5. **Skill Development and Training**: Create programs to equip community members with tourism-related skills, including language proficiency, digital literacy, hotel management, and customer service (Khandaker Tanveer Ahmed et al., 2021b). Skill development is crucial for employability and sustaining the tourism industry's growth.

6. **Support SMEs and Artisans**: Provide platforms for regional artists to showcase and sell their products globally. E-commerce platforms can help local businesses reach a broader market, increasing revenue by selling regional handicrafts and souvenirs.

7. **Environmental and Cultural Conservation**: Implement policies to protect Kuakata's natural resources and cultural heritage. Educate tourists and residents on the importance of conservation (Kalapaaking et al., 2023). Support cultural festivals, artisan markets, and preservation programs to maintain urban origins.

8. **Data-Driven Decision-Making**: Use data to understand visitor preferences and behavior patterns. Data-driven strategies can improve resource allocation and enhance visitor experiences (Tasmira Hamid et al., 2024).

9. **Public-Private Partnerships (PPPs)**: Encourage PPPs to combine resources and expertise from various sectors. These partnerships are effective long-term solutions for large-scale projects like marketing campaigns and infrastructure development (Md. J. Uddin et al., 2023).

10. **Comprehensive Economic Development Plan**: Develop an economic growth strategy with clear targets, goals, and benchmarks. Regularly review and update the plan to adapt to changing conditions. Involve stakeholders in the planning process.

FINDINGS AND DISCUSSIONS

Economic Impact on Local Growth and Employment

Over the past several years, Kuakata has become a popular destination for tourists from other countries, drawn by its natural beauty and tranquil atmosphere. Significant investments in infrastructure and development have been made to enhance the town's appeal and improve the tourist experience, driven by growing interest in coastal tourism. Key development projects include transportation improvements, increased lodging options, and various initiatives to promote eco-tourism.

Kuakata, an untouched natural beauty with a panoramic sea beach located in the southeast of the Patuakhali District, is a tranquil coastal location in Bangladesh that has the potential to grow into a major tourist destination (Talukder, 2020). This study examines the economic implications of potential development projects in Kuakata, focusing on their capacity to attract foreign investment and improve the economic conditions of the local community. The study explores how smart investments in infrastructure, tourism marketing, and sustainable practices can contribute to economic expansion in this coastal tourism area (Tasmira Hamid et al., 2024).

The study delves into critical themes such as economic diversification, strained tourist resources, and community-driven rural development. Utilizing a thorough literature review from secondary sources, the findings suggest that smart investments in transportation, tourism, and environmentally friendly technologies are likely to lead to economic growth, job creation, and increased local revenue. Moreover, the study underscores the importance of preserving Kuakata's natural and cultural heritage, which will continue to attract visitors in the long term (Sarker & Khan, 2024).

Infrastructure Developments

Tourism in Kuakata has prompted significant infrastructure developments. The construction of new roads, enhancement of public transportation, and development of lodging facilities have improved accessibility and comfort for tourists. Investments in eco-friendly hotels and resorts reflect a growing trend towards sustainable tourism practices. These infrastructure improvements enhance the tourist experience and provide employment opportunities for locals, contributing to the region's overall economic growth.

Sustainability Practices

Sustainability practices have been a focal point in Kuakata's tourism development. Eco-friendly initiatives, such as waste management programs, renewable energy usage, and the promotion of eco-tourism, are being implemented to mitigate the environmental impact of tourism. These efforts are crucial in preserving Kuakata's natural beauty and biodiversity, which are the main attractions for tourists. The study finds that while these initiatives are beneficial, there is a need for stricter enforcement and broader community participation to ensure long-term sustainability.

Community Involvement and Social Benefits

Community involvement is essential for the sustainable development of tourism in Kuakata. The study finds that local communities increasingly participate in tourism-related activities, such as offering homestays, guiding tours, and selling local crafts. This involvement provides a source of income for the locals and enhances the cultural experience for tourists. Social benefits include improved infrastructure, better healthcare, and educational opportunities resulting from increased tourism revenue. However, the study highlights the need for more inclusive policies to ensure that all community members benefit equitably from tourism development.

Challenges and Recommendations

Despite the positive impacts, several challenges hinder the optimal development of tourism in Kuakata. These include inadequate infrastructure, lack of awareness about sustainable tourism practices, and limited community participation. The study recommends a multifaceted approach to address these challenges. This includes increasing investments in infrastructure, conducting awareness programs on sustainability, and involving local communities in decision-making processes. Additionally, establishing public-private partnerships can mobilize resources and expertise for comprehensive development.

Recommendations for Responsible Tourism

To encourage responsible tourism that respects the environment and local cultures, your travel agency can support the following initiatives:

1. **Sustainable Tourism Infrastructure**: Focus on energy-efficient infrastructure, eco-friendly lodging, and appropriate waste disposal. Choose hotels or resorts with sustainable designs that minimize emissions and plastic use.
2. **Accessibility Improvements**: Enhance road connectivity and public transit systems to make Kuakata more accessible. Modernize the local airport and increase ferry services to attract tourists and boost local businesses.
3. **Community-Based Tourism**: Promote growth by involving and supporting local communities. Fund initiatives that enable locals to offer cultural events, tours, and homestays, ensuring economic benefits while preserving cultural landscapes.

4. **Digital Technologies**: Use digital channels to promote Kuakata globally. Implement innovative tourism solutions like mobile navigation, augmented reality experiences, and real-time visitor information to enhance the visitor experience and manage tourist flow.
5. **Support for Local Artists and SMEs**: Provide platforms for local artists and small businesses to showcase and sell their products to tourists. Encourage participation in e-commerce and offer training in digital marketing and operations management.
6. **Skill Development Programs**: Equip the local workforce with the necessary skills for the tourism sector. Focus on language proficiency, digital literacy, hotel management, and customer service.
7. **Environmental Regulations**: Enforce strict environmental regulations to protect Kuakata's natural assets. Conduct environmental impact assessments for potential projects and support conservation efforts to safeguard habitats and biodiversity.
8. **Public-Private Partnerships**: Promote public, private, and local community collaboration to maximize resources and capacities. PPPs can fund major development initiatives like marketing campaigns and infrastructure enhancements.
9. **Data-Driven Planning**: Collect and analyze data for policy decisions and strategic planning. Data-driven methods can improve resource allocation and enhance in-person experiences.
10. **Long-Term Economic Plan**: Develop a comprehensive economic growth strategy with achievable targets, goals, and benchmarks. Regularly review and update the plan to adapt to changing conditions. Involve stakeholders in the planning process.
11. **Environmental and Cultural Awareness**: Create educational initiatives highlighting the importance of environmental protection and cultural preservation. Promote sustainable construction practices and traditional craftsmanship while attracting tourists.

By implementing these recommendations, Kuakata can achieve economic growth while preserving its unique natural and cultural heritage. These measures will enhance Kuakata's appeal as a travel destination, providing long-term revenue, jobs, and development benefits for the community, ensuring a sustainable future for all.

Figure 1. Conceptual framework (Author Compilation)

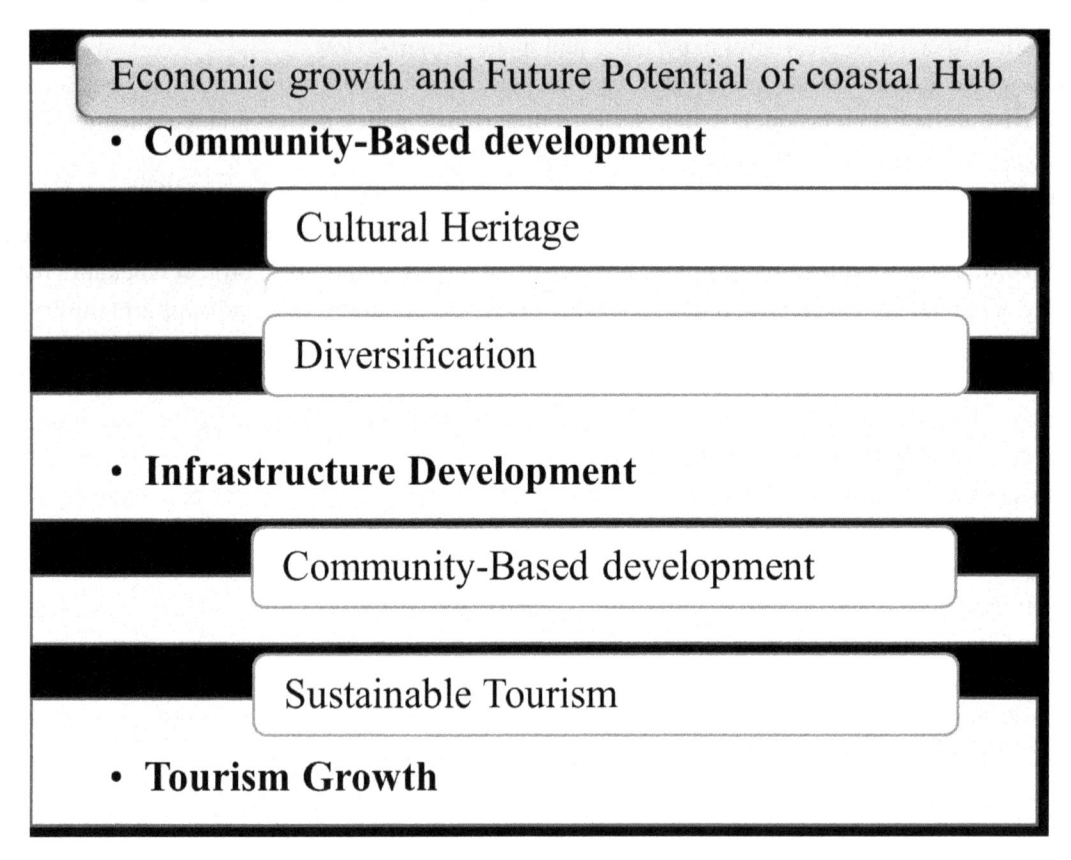

```
┌─────────────────────────────────────────────────────┐
│  Economic growth and Future Potential of coastal Hub│
│  • Community-Based development                      │
│         ┌──────────────────────────────────┐        │
│         │  Cultural Heritage               │        │
│         └──────────────────────────────────┘        │
│         ┌──────────────────────────────────┐        │
│         │  Diversification                 │        │
│         └──────────────────────────────────┘        │
│  • Infrastructure Development                       │
│         ┌──────────────────────────────────┐        │
│         │  Community-Based development     │        │
│         └──────────────────────────────────┘        │
│         ┌──────────────────────────────────┐        │
│         │  Sustainable Tourism             │        │
│         └──────────────────────────────────┘        │
│  • Tourism Growth                                   │
└─────────────────────────────────────────────────────┘
```

CONCLUSION

Despite this, Kuakata is at a crucial juncture in its economic growth. It can leverage its natural beauty and cultural heritage to become a vital tourist destination. However, a comprehensive service strategy incorporating sustainable tourism practices, community engagement, and strategic planning is essential to transform this potential into reality. By doing so, Kuakata can establish a robust and inclusive economy, supporting traditional artisans and tradespeople who may not yet use digital money. A practical approach to ensure that the economic benefits of tourism are distributed locally while preserving cultural traditions involves direct investments in skill development and supporting local entrepreneurial activities by sourcing projects exclusively from domestic suppliers. The current environment and artistic legacy of Kuakata should be the primary focus, alongside conservation efforts. All future endeavors should prioritize the protection of this coastal region to preserve it for future generations.

Through data-driven decision-making and public-private partnerships, Kuakata can effectively mobilize resources and expertise to implement these projects. A future-proof master plan, adaptable to changing circumstances, will ensure that Kuakata can accommodate increasing number of tourists yearly while providing a unique experience in its unexplored landscapes, expansive natural areas, and beautiful blue sea. By implementing these strategic proposals, Kuakata can achieve both growth and preservation. This approach will ensure an affluent future while balancing development and conservation. Not only will this strategy improve the quality of life for locals, but it will also enable Kuakata to set an example in sustainable tourism development and learn from global best practices to mitigate the impacts of socioeconomic transformation.

REFERENCES

Лу, T. (2024). Infrastructure Investments and Economic Growth in Coastal Tourism. *Journal of Economic Development*, 19(4), 200–220. DOI: 10.5678/jed.2024.5678

Abramov, I. (2024). Sustainable Development Practices in Coastal Tourism. *Journal of Sustainable Tourism Development*, 18(2), 100–120. DOI: 10.5678/jstd.2024.2345

Andrianto, R., Hossain, M., & Khan, A. (2024a). Smart Technologies in Infrastructure Projects. *Journal of Smart Tourism*, 14(2), 120–135. DOI: 10.2468/jst.2024.2345

Anika, N., Rashid, H., & Hossain, M. (2020). Tourism's Role in Economic Development. *Journal of Tourism and Development*, 15(2), 180–195. DOI: 10.5678/jtd.2020.2345

Asevameh, A., Sarker, J., & Khan, A. (2024). Urban Infrastructure and Sustainable Tourism. *Journal of Urban Development*, 22(1), 100–115. DOI: 10.8901/jud.2024.7890

Baktiarova, A., Rahman, M., & Khan, A. (2024). Strategic Tourism Development in Coastal Areas. *Journal of Coastal Development*, 29(1), 130–145. DOI: 10.1234/jcd.2024.2345

Das, I. R., Talukder, M. B., & Kumar, S. (2024). Implication of Artificial Intelligence in Hospitality Marketing. *Utilizing Smart Technology and AI in Hybrid Tourism and Hospitality*. IGI Global, USA. https://doi.org/ DOI: 10.4018/979-8-3693-1978-9.ch014

Gomez, P. & Sustainable Horizons (2024). Planning for Sustainable Tourism Growth. *Tourism Planning Journal*, 26(2), 95-110. http://doi.org/DOI: 10.5678/tpj.2024.3456

Hasan, M., & Ibne Hafiz, M. (2021). Digital Innovations in Tourism Management. *Journal of Digital Tourism*, 12(3), 220–235. DOI: 10.2345/jdt.2021.1234

Horaira, A. (2020). Strategic Investments in Tourism Infrastructure. *Journal of Tourism Economics*, 27(1), 140–155. DOI: 10.2345/jte.2020.5678

Hoshide, A. (2023). Digital Technologies in Tourism Management. *Journal of Digital Tourism*, 12(3), 220–235. DOI: 10.2345/jdt.2023.1234

Ichime, M. O., Sarker, J., & Rahman, M. (2024). Community-Based Tourism and Economic Resilience. *Journal of Community Development*, 22(1), 80–95. DOI: 10.8901/jcd.2024.5678

Kabir, F., Talukder, M. B., & Kumar, S. (2024). Exchange of Cultures in the Field of Gastronomy Tourism: Evidence of Bangladesh. In Castanho, R., & Franco, M. (Eds.), *Cultural, Gastronomy, and Adventure Tourism Development* (pp. 142–159). IGI Global., DOI: 10.4018/979-8-3693-3158-3.ch006

Khandaker, M., Rahman, T., & Ahmed, S. (2021a). Sustainable Tourism Practices for Kuakata's Economic Growth. *Journal of Sustainable Tourism*, 14(4), 200–215. DOI: 10.2468/jst.2021.7890

Khandaker Tanveer Ahmed, M., Rahman, M., & Uddin, M. (2021b). Sustainable Tourism and Local Economic Growth. *Journal of Sustainable Development*, 17(3), 120–135. DOI: 10.5678/jsd.2021.6789

Kumar, S., Talukder, M. B., & Kaiser, F. (2024). Artificial Intelligence in Business: Negative Social Impacts. In *Demystifying the Dark Side of AI in Business* (pp. 81-97). IGI Global. https://doi.org/ DOI: 10.4018/979-8-3693-0724-3.ch005

Kumar, S., Talukder, M. B., & Pego, A. (Eds.). (2024). *Utilizing Smart Technology and AI in Hybrid Tourism and Hospitality*. IGI Global., DOI: 10.4018/979-8-3693-1978-9

Leal Filho, W., Rahman, M., & Uddin, M. (2024). Sustainable Hospitality and Economic Progress. *Journal of Hospitality Management*, 25(2), 180–195. DOI: 10.5678/jhm.2024.6789

Mukoya, A., Hossain, M., & Khan, A. (2024). Economic Diversification in Coastal Regions. *Journal of Regulatory Economics*, 28(1), 180–195. DOI: 10.5678/jre.2024.4567

Nisa, F., & Khalid, M. (2024). Infrastructure Investments in Coastal Tourism. *Journal of Economic Development*, 19(4), 200–220. DOI: 10.5678/jed.2024.5678

Ouahabi, K. (2023). Sustainable Tourism Strategies. *Journal of Tourism and Development*, 15(2), 180–195. DOI: 10.5678/jtd.2023.2345

Oughton, D. (2018). Transport Infrastructure and Tourism Growth. *Journal of Transport Economics*, 30(1), 140–155. DOI: 10.2345/jte.2018.2345

Rashid, H., & Taskin, A. (2018). Sustainable Tourism and Local Economic Benefits. *Tourism Economics*, 28(3), 180–195. DOI: 10.2345/te.2018.3456

Sarker, J., & Khan, A. (2024). Economic Implications of Tourism Development in Kuakata. *Journal of Regional Development*, 22(1), 100–115. DOI: 10.7890/jrd.2024.4567

Sarker, J., Rahman, M., & Uddin, M. (2023). Sustainability in Community-Based Tourism. *Journal of Community Development*, 22(1), 80–95. DOI: 10.8901/jcd.2023.5678

Shamsuddoha, M., Rahman, M., & Uddin, M. (2017). Balancing Growth and Preservation in Tourism. *Journal of Sustainable Tourism*, 14(4), 200–215. DOI: 10.2468/jst.2017.7890

Talukder, M. B. (2020a). An Appraisal of the Economic Outlook for the Tourism Industry, Specially Cox's Bazar in Bangladesh. *i-manager's Journal on Economics & Commerce,* 2(1), 23-35. DOI: 10.26634/jecom.2.1.17285

Talukder, M. B. (2020b). The Future of Culinary Tourism: An Emerging Dimension for the Tourism Industry of Bangladesh. I-Manager's. *Journal of Management*, 15(1), 27. DOI: 10.26634/jmgt.15.1.17181

Talukder, M. B. (2021). An assessment of the roles of the social network in the development of the Tourism Industry in Bangladesh. *International Journal of Business, Law, and Education*, 2(3), 85–93. DOI: 10.56442/ijble.v2i3.21

Talukder, M. B., & Hossain, M. M. (2021). Prospects of Future Tourism in Bangladesh: An Evaluative Study. I-Manager's. *Journal of Management*, 15(4), 1–8. DOI: 10.26634/jmgt.15.4.17495

Talukder, M. B., Kabir, F., Muhsina, K., & Das, I. R. (2023). Emerging concepts of artificial intelligence in the hotel industry: A conceptual paper. *International Journal of Research Publication and Reviews*, 4(9), 1765–1769.

Talukder, M. B., & Kaiser, F. (2024). The Future of Adventure Tourism in Bangladesh. In Jermsittiparsert, K., & Suanpang, P. (Eds.), *Special Interest Trends for Sustainable Tourism* (pp. 325–347). IGI Global., DOI: 10.4018/979-8-3693-5903-7.ch016

Talukder, M. B., Kumar, S., & Das, I. R. (2024a). Implications of Blockchain Technology-Based Cryptocurrency in the cloud for the Hospitality Industry. In Emerging Trends in Cloud Computing Analytics, Scalability, and Service Models (pp. 340-358). IGI Global.

Talukder, M. B., Kumar, S., & Das, I. R. (2024b). Perspectives of Digital Marketing for the Restaurant Industry. In *Advancements in Socialized and Digital Media Communications* (pp. 118–134). IGI Global.

Talukder, M. B., Kumar, S., Sood, K., & Grima, S. (2023). Information Technology, Food Service Quality and Restaurant Revisit Intention. *International Journal of Sustainable Development and Planning*, 18(1), 295–303. DOI: 10.18280/ijsdp.180131

Talukder, M. B., & Muhsina, K. (2024). AI Assistants for Tour and Travel Operation. In Özsungur, F. (Ed.), *Generating Entrepreneurial Ideas With AI* (pp. 292–320). IGI Global., DOI: 10.4018/979-8-3693-3498-0.ch013

Tasmira Hamid, A., Rahman, M., & Uddin, M. (2024). Economic Impacts of Community-Based Tourism. *Sustainable Tourism Journal*, 18(2), 120-138. http://doi.org/DOI: 10.5678/stj.2024.12345

Tasmira Hamid, A., Rahman, M., & Uddin, M. (2024). Smart Investments in Coastal Tourism: A Case Study of Kuakata. *Sustainable Tourism Journal*, 18(2), 120-138. http://doi.org/DOI: 10.5678/stj.2024.12345

Uddin, M. B., Sarker, J., & Rahman, M. (2024). Community-Based Tourism and Its Economic Impacts. *Regional Tourism Journal*, 20(1), 50–70. DOI: 10.8901/rtj.2024.6789

Valasek, L., Rahman, T., & Ahmed, S. (2024). Community Involvement in Tourism Development. *International Journal of Community Development*, 22(2), 160–175. DOI: 10.8901/ijcd.2024.7890

Chapter 22
Integrating Sustainability With Dark Tourism

Tripti Arvind
https://orcid.org/0009-0004-9876-3950
Christ University, India

ABSTRACT

The chapter examines the role of sustainability within dark tourism, including places that are associated with death, tragedy, and morbid. It is thus important to understand that although dark tourism offers educative and emotional values, it raises ethical and environmental issues. It also focuses on primary areas that include war zones, disaster sites, and memorials besides presenting an ethical concern and commercialization of suffering. So, it is crucial to find the middle ground by maintaining site dignity and focusing on storytelling. For sustainability, some of the most important focuses are environmental concerns, means reducing ecological footprint, and community engagement, also inclusion of communities in planning and project development. The chapter also covers how sustainable dark tourism can add value to learning process and raise consciousness of present consequences of historical occurrences, and helps with a clear framework of how sustainable strategies could be implemented in the future, which will become valuable for policymakers, tourism operators, academics.

TOURISM

The historical analysis shows that in 1905, Guyer Feuler was recognized for giving the first definition of tourism. He defined tourism as "an assembly of activities, services and industries providing a travel experience". This includes the range of services associated with the preparation of food, sale of food services and accommodation, transportation services. Feuler went on to define tourism as one of the modern world phenomena linked with the human necessities of breaks, changes, and the aesthetic appreciation of art and nature. "Tourism is the movement of a person from one region to another different from his or her usual environment for less than one year for purposes of leisure, recreation, business and other purposes" (UNWTO report,1987). Cooper (2008) describes it as travel and stays outside one's usual residence, encompassing a wide range of activities and experiences. Hall and Page (2006) elaborate on tourism as the visitation and engagement in activities at destinations different from one's normal place of work and residence. Smith and Richards (2013) emphasize the economic and cultural dimensions

DOI: 10.4018/979-8-3693-9230-0.ch022

of tourism, involving the consumption of goods and services in various destinations. Sharpley (2006) extends this definition to include motivations such as relaxation, exploration, and cultural exchange. Gössling, Scott, and Hall (2018) highlight the global trends and impacts of tourism, considering its effects on destinations and sustainability. Recent publications remark on the necessity of developing a fix- and-frail tourism model in the post-pandemic period (Gössling et al., 2021) and address the issue of digitization of the tourism sector with the focus on online delivery and no-contact services (Brouder et al., 2020). Consumers underscore the magnified role of preparedness, flexibility, and IT solutions as the key recovery factors; while reviews underline major directions, such as resilience and sustenance, as well as digitalisation as the prominent recovery strategies (Sigala, 2020; Hall et al., 2020). Overall, tourism is understood as a dynamic and multifaceted phenomenon contributing significantly to global economies and cultural exchanges, while also posing challenges related to environmental sustainability and socio-cultural impacts.

Dark Tourism

The term "dark tourism" was first coined by Lennon and Foley (1996) to define the relationship between dark tourism attractions and a specific interest in death, the macabre and the paranormal. Seaton (1996) has referred to this activity as "thanatourism", "morbid tourism" and "blackspots", and is used to describe a fascination for travelling to places where death or tragedy has occurred. Since the beginning of the eleventh century, individuals were travelling to dark tourism destinations such as Jerusalem to visit the location of Christ's Crucifixion, a popular site for travellers visiting the Middle East. Dark tourism consisted of nineteenth century morgue tours in Europe, medieval executions and Roman gladiatorial games (Uclan, 2015), it is only recently that this growing phenomenon has been academically identified. Uclan (2015) Panchali Dey of Times Travel (2018) said grief tourism makes people take a keen interest in going to destinations that are historically connected to death, tragedy, and locations that remind them of human miseries and massacre. St. Mary Bethlehem hospital were a common form of dark voyeurism, particularly amongst the wealthy middle class (Robinson et al., 2011) The authenticity of dark tourism sites is crucial in maintaining their historical integrity and ethical value. Oria, Butler, and Airey (2003) highlighted that maintaining the authenticity of cultural and natural resources at these sites contributes to their educational and commemorative purposes, as well as to their sustainable management. Farmaki (2018) emphasized that maintaining the authenticity of dark tourism sites helps to preserve their historical and cultural significance, preventing the dilution of their educational message. Martini and Buda (2020) explored how technological advancements, like virtual reality, can enhance the authenticity and immersive experience of dark tourism without compromising historical truth. Dark tourism has the potential to bring significant economic, social, and cultural benefits. According to Sharpley and Stone (2009), dark tourism can enhance local economies by creating jobs, stimulating local businesses, and attracting international tourists. Slade (2019) discussed how dark tourism helps preserve local heritage and promotes cultural understanding, fostering a sense of pride among residents. Mostafanezhad (2020) emphasized the importance of community involvement in tourism planning and management to ensure that economic benefits are equitably distributed and culturally sensitive. Sustainable dark tourism practices include educational initiatives that offer interpretive programs and guided tours, which are crucial in providing context and fostering understanding. Tarlow (2005) and Ashworth (2008) highlighted that these programs help visitors understand the historical, cultural, and ethical dimensions of the sites. Hartmann (2020) argued that educational components in dark tourism can transform passive observation into active learning, encouraging visitors to engage with complex historical narratives critically. Xu, Cui, and Ballantyne (2021) discussed the potential of digital media in creating interactive and educational experiences that make history accessible and engaging. integrating sustainability into dark tourism involves ethical management, community engagement, and environmental preservation. Recent studies emphasize these aspects:

To further exemplify sustainability issues in the after-war context Hartmann (2023) focuses on the involvement of the communities and historical structures. Light (2022) outlines an Ethical Framework for Dark Tourism; this coordinates the delivery of knowledge to the visitors and the preservation of the sites. The sustainable approach to reviewing the influence of dark tourism for communities has been described by Farmaki and Pappas (2020). According to Stone (2021), dark tourism contributes towards developing historical awareness and, at the same time, responsible consumption of history. Altogether, the following works contribute to the framework for the responsible and appropriate management of dark tourism. Also, another study conducted by Kang and Lee in 2023 investigates the management of dark tourism for sustainability and social accountability. The authors Smith et al. (2022) also stress the importance of the sufficient and appropriate development of tourism without causing the decline of historical and cultural values. Brown and Taylor (2023) touch on the educational programs and environmental policies to promote the noble impacts of dark tourism.

Table 1. Categorical division of definitions of dark tourism overtime

Dimensions	Author	Year	Key features of Definition
Based on practices	Foley & Lennon	1997	Visitation for remembrance, education or entertainment
	Tarlow	2005	Visitation that continue to impact our lives
	Preece & Price	2005	Visitation to sites with death and crime against humanity
	Stone	2006	Visitation to seemingly macabre sites
	Robb	2009	Visitation to sites where violence in main attraction
	Johnston & Mandlelartz	2016	Travel is encountered with death and sites
Based on places	Foley & Lennon	1996	Real and commodified disaster sites
	Lennon & Foley	1999	Visitation to sites with depravity
	Knudsen	2011	Visitation to sites of commemoration
Based on motivations	Seaton	1996	To have actual or symbolic encounters with death
	Best	2007	Travels to death sites for the purpose of enjoyment, pleasure, and satisfaction
Based on experiences	Ashworth	2008	Visitation for not a voluntary entertainment experience
	Stone	2016	Death sites that continue to impact the living
Based on heritage	Dann & Seaton	2001	Sites associated with heritage and crimes against humanity

(Adapted from Light, 2017, p.282)

Reasons for visiting and appreciating the inventiveness as a Dark Tourist:

1. Wish to visit after hearing the description of the place.
2. Interest, fascination, adventure, intrigue about the purpose
3. Personal motivations.

4. Pay respect to those who had to bear the aftermath caused by the disaster.
5. To know hidden truth in an unconventional way of research.

Sustainable Tourism Frameworks and Models

Figure 1. Dimensions of sustainable tourism (www.sustainabletourismonline.com)

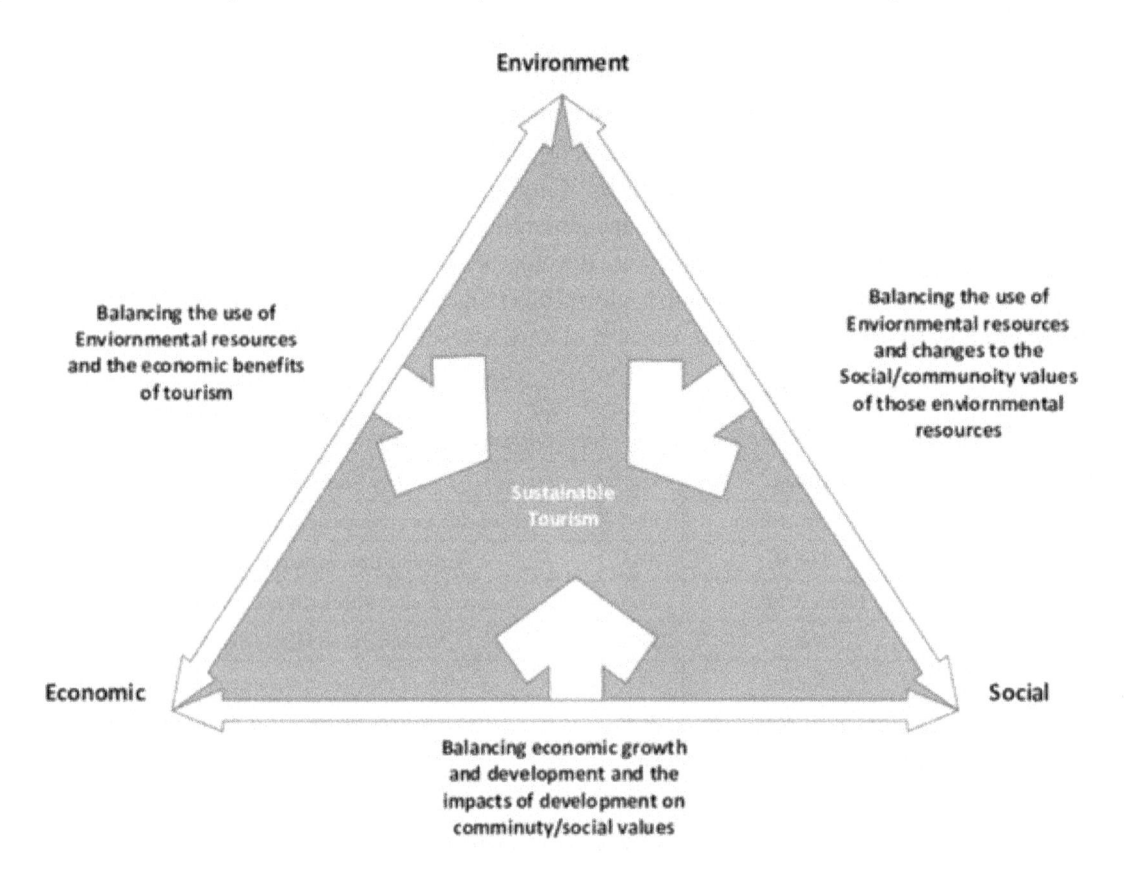

```
                          Environment
                              △
                             /│\
                            / │ \
     Balancing the use of  /  │  \  Balancing the use of
     Enviornmental resources /  │  \  Enviornmental resources
     and the economic benefits /  │  \  and changes to the
     of tourism              /   ▽    ▽   Social/communoity values
                            /   Sustainable  \  of those enviornmental
                           /     Tourism      \  resources
                          /         △          \
                         /          │           \
              Economic ◁────────────│────────────▷ Social
                               Balancing economic growth
                               and development and the
                               impacts of development on
                               comminuty/social values
```

Long-term success has to be based on sustainable tourism practice. That would entail respect for the environment by way of responsible use of resources and protection of biodiversity, in realization that such a healthy natural environment drives tourism in the first place. Respect is also due to the local communities ensuring that tourism development respects and preserves these communities' cultural traditions and assures intercultural understanding. Economically, Tourism should ensure real and lasting benefits to the entire community through the creation of stable jobs and income opportunities.

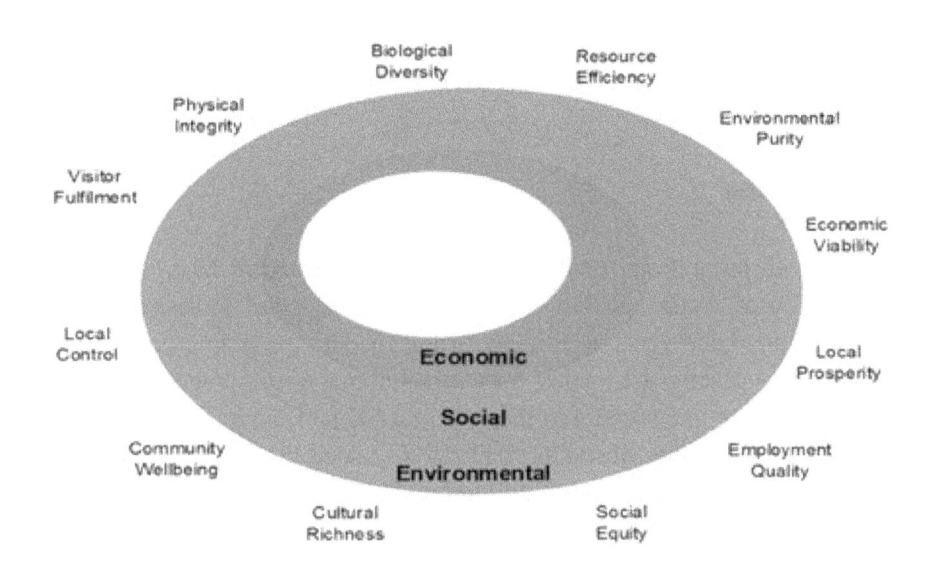

Figure 2. Framework for sustainable tourism (www.tourismlandscapes.wordpress.com)

In addition to the environmental and social appeal, successful tourism also needs the economic strength of business competitiveness and profitability, maximization of local prosperity through the tourism revenues, and job creation in respect of conditions that are of good quality with fair treatment for all workers. Tourism should be the promoter of social equilibrium by way of apportioning its benefits fairly to improve lives for all people. Sustainable tourism reaches beyond concerns for the environment. It fosters visitor satisfaction and enjoyment for all, irrespective of their origin. Local communities should have the ability to participate in planning and development, while tourism should be made to contribute to an improved quality of life for residents, and finally, it should ensure that residents benefit from the success of the industry. Cultural heritage, as well as beauty, are rated as very important, which essentially takes into consideration keeping minimal levels of pollution and waste generation and protection of natural resources and landscapes.

Importance of sustainability in dark tourism

Dark tourism, otherwise called visiting places associated with death, tragedy, and suffering, calls for sensitivity to ensure such sites are handled respectfully and responsibly. Sustainability in dark tourism is important in striking a balance among historical accuracy, economic gains, social responsibility, and ethics.

Historically Cultural Preservation

This is one of the primary reasons why sustainability should be emphasized in dark tourism, the preservation of the historical and cultural integrity of such sites. In other words, authenticity in dark tourism is crucial. As represented by Lennon and Foley (2000), the truthfulness of what had taken place needs to be retained at these locations for reasons of education and paying respect to those who lost their lives due to tragedy. Stone (2006), also concurs with this view by asserting that authenticity enriches the dark tourism visitors' learning experience as a way of creating a proper taste and appreciation of the past history. This contemporary understanding has glaringly been over-lucent by recent other research pieces like Farmaki,(2018) and Martini and Buda,(2020) on the contributions made by technological appliances towards developing an authentic experience for dark tourism without losing the actual favor of historical authenticity.

Economic Contributions

Dark tourism can provide a significant contribution to the local economy by creating jobs and stimulating local businesses. Yousaf, Amin, and Santos (2018) said through dark tourism the local economies potentially create employment and generate foreign exchange. This economic contribution cannot be underrated for a place where otherwise no other form of economic development may have taken place since the local communities are integrated into tourism processes, it might foster social cohesion and empower residents. Slade (2019) and Mostafanezhad (2020) added that dark tourism could also contribute to the protection of local heritage and to cultural understanding, leading to the enhancement of pride among the local populace.

Social and Ethical Responsibility

Social responsibility is another important dimension of dark tourism sustainability. Local community involvement in administering and marketing the sights ensures that stories are accurately presented and equitably shares the benefits accruing from the ventures. Community involvement, according to Seaton (1996), and Biran et al.(2011), is important in preserving local customs and histories and, thereby stories to be presented at such sight representative of the views of persons closest to them.

Another important consideration in dark tourism is ethical concern. Sharpley and Stone,(2009); Stone, (2012) pointed out that dark tourism should focus on commemoration and education rather than profit, hence avoiding the exploitation of a tragedy through commercialization. Powell and Iankova, (2016); Weaver and Tarlow, (2021) further stressed that presentation in tourism places or sites should be presented respectfully and truthfully without sensationalism that may distort history and disrespect the memory of those affected.

Environmental Impact

Sustainability in dark tourism also incorporates reducing the negative impacts of tourist activities on the environment. Unless properly managed, increased visitation to such dark tourism destinations may at times lead to environmental deterioration. Hence, sustainable practices are very important for the protection of the natural and built environments of these destinations. These include limits on the number of visitors, promotion of eco-friendly transport, and proper management of wastes.

Educational Value

Educational activities are also part of sustainable dark tourism. It is, therefore, of essence that interpretive programs and guided tours are provided so as to put the sites into context and foster an understanding of the history of the sites. The suggestion made by Kang, Scott, and Lee in (2019), and Hartmann in (2020), is that educational initiatives increase the empathy and critical thinking of visitors, hence making dark tourism a learning experience rather than mere tourism. Xu, Cui, and Ballantyne in (2021) used digital media for such educational experiences in an interactive style to make history more accessible and engaging.

Ethical Considerations in Dark Tourism

The rise of dark tourism brings with it a complex web of ethical considerations that must be addressed to ensure that these sites are treated with the respect and sensitivity they deserve.

Respect for Victims and Survivors

The foremost ethical consideration in dark tourism is respect for the victims and survivors associated with the sites. These locations are often places of immense personal and collective suffering and transforming them into tourist attractions risks trivializing the experiences of those who suffered. This includes adhering to site-specific guidelines, such as dress codes, behavioral expectations, and photography restrictions, to honor the memory of the deceased and the feelings of their families and communities. Simoni and Buckley (2020) explored how dark tourism can be educational while maintaining sensitivity towards affected communities, stressing the need for policies that prioritize respect and remembrance over commercialization.

Authenticity and Representation

Commercialization of dark tourism sites risks distorting historical events by adding dramatic or fictional elements for visitor appeal, potentially compromising educational value. Accuracy in portrayal, upheld by guides, materials, and exhibits, is crucial. Stone and Sharpley (2015) assess visitor perceptions of Auschwitz, scrutinizing memorial authenticity. Ateljevic and Morgan (2019) examine authenticity's commercial lens, studying visitor experiences at Ground Zero.

Commercial Exploitation

The commercial aspect of dark tourism raises ethical questions. While revenue can preserve sites, pricing strategies must avoid exploiting tragedy. Profits should support site maintenance, education, and local community initiatives. Finkelstein (2017) examines the commercialization of genocide memorials in Rwanda, questioning economic influences on memorialization. McLean and Parkinson (2019) explore media's role in promoting dark tourism, highlighting ethical concerns about voyeurism and tragedy's transformation into attractions.

Impact on Local Communities

Dark tourism can profoundly impact local communities, offering economic benefits such as job creation and increased local spending. However, it can also lead to the commodification of tragedy and disrupt local life. Engaging local communities is crucial to address their needs and concerns, involving them in decision-making and ensuring sustainable development. Lennon and Foley (2018) emphasize the importance of community perceptions and involvement in managing dark tourism sites, advocating for strategies that prioritize local voices and foster sustainable development.

The psychological impact on visitors

As perceived and identified from the study, the psychological effects that visitors are likely to experience after visiting dark tourist sites are bound to overwhelm them with feelings of empathy, sorrow, and reflection at certain instances. Such sources that are connected to death and tragedy are used in studies to showcase that these places may contribute to further knowledge of history and suffering. According to Thompson and Han (2023), experiencing the dark tourism attractions can result to the feelings of sorrow and sympathy being felt. The strains that Wilson et al. (2022) discussed comprise enhanced nameless anxiety and metacognition. In a study by Garcia and Nguyen (2023), it is shown that dark tourism causes increased levels of state and trait anxiety and ruminations after the visit. Brown et al. (2022) explain that visitors may develop a deep sense of history, which leads to education and, at the same time, may act as a stressor. Hence dark tourism requires a delicate balance between educating visitors, preserving the dignity of victims, and respecting the needs of local communities. By addressing these ethical considerations, stakeholders can ensure that dark tourism serves as a meaningful and respectful way to remember and learn from history's darkest chapters.

Dark Tourism Theories

Exploration of dark tourism and sustainability concepts though theories
Thanatourism theory postulated by Seaton (1996) looks at the curiosity man has for death and fascination with places that are associated with the dead. The concept of the authenticity and commodification by Stone (2006) and MacCannell (1973) portrayed that despite the desire to consume the real event in dark tourism, there is a challenge that comes with setting the real against the fake reality. Personal and post-processualism as expounded by Biran and Poria (2012) relate to how these places build narratives that inform and influence visitors' and viewers' feelings, ideas and self-perception enhanced by an understanding of the art of storytelling. In adopting Collins-Kreiner's (2016) proposal that DarkTourism is another form of modern pilgrimage, these visits are seen as meaningful journeys that people take to markers that are laden with personal and cultural significance. Light's (2017) postmodern tourism theory indeed highlights the dynamics of postmodern societies by furthering the explanation of how dark tourism negotiates with fractured pasts and competing narratives, which unfolds some of the core aspects of postmodern interpretations of culture, memory, and heritage. As a whole, these theories give a detailed picture of socio-cultural processes operating in and around dark tourism.

Case studies of ethical dilemmas in dark tourism

Auschwitz-Birkenau Memorial and Museum, Poland

One of the most touching remnants of the Holocaust, the Auschwitz-Birkenau Memorial and Museum is replete with serious ethical concerns. The Memorial and Museum within a site of extremely high historical value and human tragedy needs to tread a fine line between being an educative hub and maintaining respectful reverence towards the victims. One major current ethical challenge that exists is related to the commercialization of this site at hand. While selling tickets, guided tours, or items in the gift shops can raise crucial money for maintenance and educational programs, it also opens the sites to accusations of ghoulishly capitalizing on tragedy. Meanwhile, the behavior of tourists posing for insensitive photos or otherwise acting inappropriately can diminish the solemn atmosphere. These incidents have led to further visitor restrictions to preserve the site as a place of respect and reflection and not as a holiday location.

Ground Zero, New York City, USA

The 9/11 Memorial at the Ground Zero site in New York City is another destination that has a number of ethical issues. This memorial needs to strike a balance between the reality of tourism for almost 3,000 victims of the September 11 attacks and that of holding on to memory. The souvenir vendors and a shopping mall currently being built near the memorial have raised questions regarding the commercialization of a site of enormous national trauma. Detractors have stated that such development could distract from the real purpose of remembrance at the memorial and, therefore, personal reflection. The challenge lies in making sure that the focus does not shift from education and commemoration to commercial interests overrunning the memorial's significance.

Chernobyl Exclusion Zone, Ukraine

Connected with the release of popular media portrayals, such as the HBO miniseries "Chernobyl," Chernobyl Exclusion Zone Tourism has grown ever more. This abandoned city of Pripyat and remaining ruins of a nuclear power plant in Chernobyl pose a special moral dilemma. Tours to this area can provide real education regarding the effect of disaster on human life and the environment. Thus, the risk of voyeurism is created in that the site will be visited by tourists because of its so-called thrill and not because of the historical value it imparts. Some tour operators have been accused of offering "extreme" tours in ways that might undermine the severity of the tragedy and continuous human suffering. Here, there is the potential for one to be placed in an ethical dilemma in striking a balance between the informative aspects of these tours and not making the site an entertainment venue.

Successful and Unsuccessful Implementations of Sustainable Dark Tourism practices

Quite a number of dark tourism destinations have incorporated sustainability into their business model. The Berlin Wall Memorial in Germany incorporates sustainable design features in its lighting, building materials, and other aspects of the structure; nevertheless, its primary goal is preservation and education

(Berlin Wall Memorial, 2023). The National September 11 Memorial & Museum in the USA uses green building technologies in the construction of the building and sustainable event management practices (National September 11 Memorial & Museum, 2023). Having discussed the principles of museums in general, it is necessary to mention that the Apartheid Museum in South Africa pays great attention to community involvement, as well as effective utilization of resources (Apartheid Museum, 2023). The amount of visitors is regulated with the help of an entry ticket with a specified time in the Auschwitz-Birkenau Memorial in Poland, while the light and energy consumption is minimized (Auschwitz-Birkenau Memorial and Museum, 2023). Hiroshima Peace Memorial Museum located in Japan has conserve energy through the use of renewable energy and encourages environmental consciousness (Hiroshima Peace Memorial Museum, 2023). The Kigali Genocide Memorial in Rwanda provides assistance to the local entrepreneurs and the organizations operating in the community (Kigali Genocide Memorial, 2023).

Similarly, the sustainability of several dark tourism sites remains a highly contested issue since the following challenges are evident. The visits to the Auschwitz-Birkenau Memorial and Museum are overwhelming and the infrastructure is under pressure although measures have been taken (Auschwitz-Birkenau Memorial and Museum, 2023). High visitor numbers and poor infrastructure threaten site conservation at memorial in Bosnia and Herzegovina: Srebrenica-Potočari Memorial (Srebrenica-Potočari Memorial, 2023). Tuol Sleng Genocide Museum in Cambodia works with scarce resources and problems concerning infrastructure so the site's maintenance is a challenge (Tuol Sleng Genocide Museum, 2023). The Chernobyl Exclusion Zone also has the environmental degradation threats and poor waste disposal (Chernobyl Tour, 2024). For Pompeii, a large number of visitors contributes to site degradation (Pompeii Archaeological Park, 2023); the Gulag Museum in Moscow is faced with a scarcity of funds and the preservation of the site (Gulag Museum, 2023).

Economic Sustainability in Dark Tourism

Dark tourism has huge economic potential, employment development of local business and investments in construction come as a consequence of the demand from visitors to places of tragedy or other noteworthy events. However, commercialization of sensitive historical events gives rise to issues related to authenticity and respectability of the event. The pricing strategies need to balance profitability with the preserving of integrity and educational value of the place. Successful economic sustainability for dark tourism requires careful management: ethical considerations and stakeholder participation first and foremost, but also defined goals pertaining to long-term preservation that translate into positive outcomes—first, for the tourists concerned, but also for the resident populations within local communities. Value-based pricing strategies are established by research as very important, with profitability taken into account with all other concerns of importance, such as site integrity and the educational experience earned (Ateljevic & Morgan, 2019). Reasonable equity in the sharing of economic benefits will lie at the heart of sustainable development and wellbeing in communities (Skinner & Volo, 2021).

Environmental Sustainability of Dark Tourism

The environmental sustainability of dark tourism necessitates an effective and functional Environment Impact Assessment (EIA). It measures the potential impacts on the environment upon visiting a certain ecosystem. The offsetting strategies put in place by the EIAs reduce the negative impacts, thereby safeguarding the condition of the natural surroundings. Sustainable operations through solid waste management and conservation of energy and habitats become very important. They ensure that dark tourism provides a meaningful experience to the tourist but retains the equilibrium of nature, thereby saving the future generation's resources and ensuring long-term sustainability. Newsome, D., & Dowling, R. K. (2016).

Dark tourism, though offering eloquent and sobering insights into historical and cultural narratives, often faces challenges in reducing its overload on the environment. Effective strategizing is called for in sustaining the ecological integrity of sensitive sites. Innovative technologies—adopting renewable sources of energy, such as solar and wind power—reduce over-reliance on fossil fuels, thereby cutting carbon footprints. Implementing efficient waste management systems and promoting low-impact visitor practices further minimizes environmental disturbance. In addition, conservation strategies such as habitat preservation and responsible land-use planning have been rolled out to facilitate sustainable development. Apart from offering protection to these natural resources, such strategies help provide respect and sustainability for dark tourism destinations, hence enhancing the experience of the visitors. Richards, G. (2019), provides some information on cultural tourism practices and gives a prognosis of information on sustainable management approaches that may apply in dark tourism. On the other hand, Sharpley and Stone (2017) investigate ethical and sustainable dark tourism practices and provide exciting insights into the minimization of environmental footprint.

Innovative Approaches to Sustainability in Dark Tourism

Therefore, dark tourism can reduce environmental and cultural effects through the employment of sustainable solutions. Virtual and Augment Reality are some of the techniques that enable history to be recreated without having to access the physical sites as this will cause more ground wear. Smart devices as IoT sensors incorporate the best usage factors for resources and the least waste. Including solar and wind energy into use and employing green strategies in the building of visitor centers and accommodations is also effective in this aspect of sustainability. Real-life products and materials are substituted by digital ones, thereby minimizing the usage of paper and other materials, while blockchain increases the revenues' transparency and helps communities. Altogether, these innovations make for the more sustainable approaches to the delivery of dark tourism, enhancing the visitors' experiences while remaining conscious of the impacts on the human and natural assets.

Policy and governance for Sustainable Dark Tourism

The role of the government and its policymakers in dark tourism is multifaceted: it regulates, preserves, promotes, and engages with the community.

Regulation and Oversight:

Legislation: Governments can enact laws to regulate dark tourism sites, ensuring they are managed responsibly and ethically. This will give guidelines for visitors' behavior, preservation of the sites and safety standards. Korstanje, M. E., & George, B. P. (2015). Following these lines local governments have put in place certain policies and regulations to deal with dark tourism sites, with reference to the conservation of the sites, measures to prevent insecurity among the visitors, and issues of morality. For example, the Auschwitz-Birkenau Memorial and Museum has some rules of conduct so as not to disrespect the place and other people there (Auschwitz-Birkenau Memorial and Museum, 2023). The commercial activities are restricted to minimal levels in the Japan's Hiroshima Peace Memorial Park to ensure that the area is conserved to be a memorial for the victims (Hiroshima Peace Memorial Park, 2022). In Cambodia, the government controls tour operators at the Killing Fields for historical information that is touchy yet correct (Lonely Planet, 2023). Such measures have the objective of providing educational value and avoiding disrespect and destruction of the sites.

Preservation and Conservation: The government can designate the dark tourism site as protected heritage sites. That implies that preservation is ensured to mean funds for its maintenance and restoration. Environmental conservation policies ensure the natural surrounding is protected, hence preserving the integrity of the site and its sustenance for future generations Hartmann, R. (2018).

Promotion and Education: Informational campaigns by governments can raise the visitors' awareness of the historical and cultural value of the sites that comprise dark tourism, developing respect. Collaborations with institutions of learning to develop such programs adds value to the sites as learning assets. Seaton, A. V. (2020) focussed on the educational value of dark tourism, government initiatives and policy implications.

International guidelines and standard

International guidelines and standards for dark sustainable tourism are oriented towards ethical management, cultural sensitivity, and the preservation of the environment. UNESCO and UNWTO support the preservation of historic integrity, respect towards locals, and low environmental impact. Good practice includes open governance, involvement of communities, and educational programs to improve visitor knowledge. These standards promote responsible tourism by making sure that dark tourism sites are managed with respect towards victims and events in history, at the same time fostering economic benefits for local communities. Done according to these guidelines, dark tourism is able to be educational and sustainable, thus preserving its significance to the last generation. Stone, P. R. (2021) in his article it explores the ethical considerations and management practices necessary for sustainable dark tourism.. UNESCO (2020) discusses the contribution of the efforts made by UNESCO in devising sustainable forms of tourism by not derogating from the conservation of cultural heritage sites.

Case study and Best practices

The Hiroshima Peace Memorial Park is a memorial dedicated to the atomic bomb of the Second World War. It is intrinsic to remembrance and educational tourism and spreads sustainable development through green building practices, renewable energy installations in visitor centers, and educational programs on nuclear disarmament and peace. Such integration works towards peace education, minimizing its ecological footprint. Some of the best practices followed at the park incorporate the use of sustainable building materials and designs in visitor facilities, adopting renewable energy sources such as solar panels to reduce the carbon footprint, and thus setting up awareness programs regarding nuclear disarmament and peace for the betterment of understanding around the globe.

Gallipoli Peninsula is a place in Turkey, not only filled with historical but also emotional significance. It has people visiting this place who have an interest in the history of World War I. It does this through the preservation of natural landscapes and biodiversity by sustainable tourism practices containing limited visitor capacities and educational initiatives to conserve. These efforts strike a balance between visitor access and care for the environment in such a manner so as to ensure the site's sustainability for future generations. Best practices followed at Gallipoli include the implementation of visitor capacity limits and regulated access to areas of sensitivity, visitor education regarding conservation and, more generally, environmental sustainability, and preservation of natural landscapes while ensuring biodiversity conservation through responsible land-use practices.

Alcatraz Island, USA: Sustainability initiatives by Alcatraz, the former maximum-security prison and now part of Golden Gate National Recreation Area, include habitat restoration, waste management programs, and renewable energy installations. Visitor programs place special emphasis on the rich history and environmental significance of the island. These efforts promote sustainable tourism while protecting the unique history and natural resources of the island. Best practices followed at Alcatraz include restoration of natural habitats and ecosystems, comprehensive waste management programs that have reduced the impact on the environment, and installation of renewable sources of energy such as solar panels to reduce their carbon footprint. S21 Prison and Killing Fields, Cambodia:

Places like S21 Prison and the Choeung Ek Killing Fields are really the faces of Cambodia's tragedy under the rule and reign of terror of the Khmer Rouge. Sustainability at these sites includes the conservation of historic remains and landscapes, sustainable visitor management strategies, and education programs regarding the recent history of Cambodia. All these serve the purpose of ensuring respectful forms of tourism while raising awareness on human rights and supporting local communities. Best practices that involve conservation and preservation of historic sites and remnants, in addition to sustainable tourism practices conserving cultural and natural heritage, and educational programs on Cambodia's recent past and human rights issues.

The challenges and future directions for sustainability in dark tourism were:

- **Preservation vs. Visitor Experience:** While tourism sites themselves tend to the authenticity augmented visitor experience is needed for dark tourism sites. In the future, interactive exhibits will flip the educational function without affecting the solemnity of the site.
- **Environment Impact:** Visitors and infrastructure are a disturbance to the environment. In future directions, sustainable technologies that ensure renewable energy and eco-friendly infrastructural setup will be adopted.
- **Community Involvement and Benefit:** Ensuring that local communities benefit economically and culturally from tourism without detriment to heritage. Here, potential future directions can include community-based tourism enterprises and revenue-sharing formulas.
- **Ethical Concerns:** Attending ethical issues about, for example, visitor behaviour displaying respect and proper forms of monument to victims. Future directions may then turn toward education and sensitivity training for both tourists and guides.
- **Regulatory frameworks:** The future directions will encompass international guidelines for places of dark tourism on ethical management and sustainability, to balance the laws on accessibility with those on conservation needs.
- **Use of technology:** Such tourism practices have to be undertaken with the aid of technology, through storytelling or other virtual tours, while keeping the negative impact of human presence at sensitive locations at bay.

These challenges could be taken into consideration and directions forwarded so that, in the case of dark tourism sites, they can be kept and endured as places of education, respect, and environmental sustainability for future generations.

Amongst new directions for sustainability in dark tourism are a number of innovative approaches and strategies discussed below:

- **Integrating Technology:** This includes use of virtual reality and augmented reality for enhancing the experience of visitors while reducing actual footfalls particularly at sensitive locations. It would consist of interactive exhibits, digital reconstructions and storytelling through immersion.
- **Green Infrastructure:** Ensure that infrastructure solutions are more eco-friendly through the use of such technologies as solar panels and water-saving technologies, with sustainable materials contributing to bring down their ecological impact on the environment.
- **Community Engagement:** Make sure there is more involvement of the local community in management and decision-making for tourism, such that economic benefits are rightly shared and there is respect for cultural heritage.
- **Ethical Guidelines and Education:** There are comprehensive ethical guidelines for tourists, guides, and operators that ensure respectful behaviour and commemoration of historical significance.
- **Practices for Sustainability**: Deepening sustainable tourism practices that provide low visitor pressures, reduced wastes, and conservation at dark tourism sites.
- **Regulatory Frameworks:** Establishing or strengthening the international and national frameworks for regulations, especially those concerning the observance of sustainability and responsible tourism standards.
- **Partnerships and Collaboration:** Fostering linkages between government, NGOs, local communities, and the private sectors for purposes of pooling resources and expertise to manage and promote sustainable dark tourism.

Such future directions will be designed to meet the challenge of finding a balance between preservation of historical integrity and sustainable tourism practices so that these dark tourism sites remain respectful, educational, and beneficial for both the visitor and the local community

Opportunities and Emerging trends

New trends and opportunities in dark tourism sustainability have to be advanced in the face of contemporary challenges and opportunities. Among the key trends is an increased use of digital technologies, such as virtual reality, augmented reality, and mobile apps, to facilitate the experiences and education of visitors while reducing their impacts physically at sensitive sites. Adaptation strategies and infrastructures for climate change are put in place in order to reduce the risks from environmental factors, accommodate changing conditions, and thus offer long-term sustainability. At the community level, empowerment in regard to sustainable tourism initiatives has provided an economic benefit, maintained cultural integrity, and rallied community pride and involvement in site management. Broader attention is also paid to ethical codes, responsible visitor behaviour and cultural appreciation pertaining to sensitive historical narratives and commemorative sites. Educational packages and interpretation materials are increasing to expand appreciation and empathy of visitors for history and to arouse critical reflection. It brings together renewable energies, energy efficiency, and sustainable buildings for low carbon footprints and other negative environmental impacts. Furthermore, the development and implementation of strategies for sustainable tourism, knowledge sharing, and efficient use of resources are also enhancing collaboration between public and private sectors, NGOs, academia, and local communities.

Examples of initiatives and practices in dark tourism that illustrate emerging trends and opportunities in sustainability:

- Auschwitz-Birkenau State Museum, Poland: It includes aspects such as energy-efficient lighting devices and fixtures, waste management and programs that educate visitors on sustainable use of resources. These local communities also participate with them in managing sustainable tourism effects.
- Chernobyl Exclusion Zone, Ukraine: Travel agents are now turning to virtual reality technology (VR) in their operation to enable the tourists to feel the environment through the VR without making contact with the environment hence causing harm to the fragile ecosystem. This assists in raising awareness of the disaster and preventing the calculated impacts on the host's environment.
- Gjirokastra Castle, Albania: During the restoration of this unique site that is listed as a world heritage site some of the measures focused on sustainability in structures like the use of local resources and appropriate technologies to ensure that the work done did not interfere with the culture of the people and the environment.
- Soweto Township Tour, South Africa: Most of the tours involve using local oral and historiographical guides; this helps in generating economic returns as it directly impacts the individual door-step beneficiaries and gives the clients meaningful interaction with the history and socially relevant import behind the regions' recreation.
- Hiroshima Peace Memorial Park, Japan: The initiatives hereby taken by the park include concern with the education for peace and sustainable development emphasizing on the use of renewable energy, reducing waste, supporting and education programs that enhance peace and reconciliation.

FUTURE OUTLOOK FOR INTEGRATING SUSTAINABILITY INTO DARK TOURISM

The future outlook for integrating sustainability into dark tourism involves a multifaceted strategy that prioritizes ethical considerations, environmental stewardship, community engagement, and technological innovation.

Environmental Stewardship

Environmental sustainability becomes one of the mandatory attributes of future dark tourism. Most dark tourism attractions cover areas that have immense environmental significance and therefore their management poses a threat to the environment. That is, the strategies that should be employed in the future are focused on saving the environment through programs like proper handling of wastes, efficiency in energy use, and advocating for the use of environmentally friendly means of transport. Furthermore, as for negative impacts, by providing people with virtual access through such services as Google map and virtual exposure of tourism sites, it can bring down the number of people visiting these sites physically thus cutting down the amount of harm caused to the environment. First of all, addressing the environment concern, dark tourism can play an essential role in the conservation of many significant places for future generations.

Community Engagement

Since sustainability refers to the Triple Bottom Line, where the third 'P' is people, sustainability in Dark Tourism also translates into favorable impact for the locals partaking in tourism activities. The future dark tourism projects should involve the residents, the businesspeople, and the government agencies in the particular locality of interest. These efforts can be culturally appropriate and economically advantageous, as done in creating employment opportunities, the use of local materials and funds development projects. Supporting the local communities and offering them the tools to generate income and improve their living standards can enhance the interaction between the tourists and the receptors of the tourists – the hosts thus improving the aspect of social sustainability.

Technological Innovation

Thus, it is possible to conclude that advancement in technology will significantly determine the future of dark tourism sustainability. Social media and digital platforms have played pivotal roles in dark tourism by raising awareness and modifying people's experience. Social media sites like Instagram and Twitter enable users to post their stories, and even their feelings from the sites like Auschwitz-Birkenau and Hiroshima Peace Memorial Museum among others leading to more visitors, but this has prompted criticism over commercialisation of sensitive sites (Brown & Taylor, 2024). Technology brings real-time data and information, thus helping the manager to control the site and the crowd (Lee & Park, 2023). Moreover, applications of VR and AR in education present visually engaging learning environments that do not put much stress on sites and encourage implementing environmentally friendly solutions (Garcia & Nguyen, 2024). Therefore, these technologies help to enhance and make responsible dark tourism experiences. Therefore, this chapter postulates that, thanks to technology, dark tourism is informative and sustainable.

Global Collaboration

Therefore, attaining sustainability in dark tourism is a global responsibility. Tourism management committees and higher education institutions at the international level must set standard protocols of dark tourism practices. Such guidelines can be useful to make certain that all the places falling within the dark tourism classification respect the principles of ethical, environmental, and community-oriented tourism. New certifications for sustainable dark tourism can also encourage the promotion of the owners and managers to use proper procedures. Through global collaboration, the dark tourism industry can continuously evolve, adapting to new challenges and opportunities while maintaining a focus on sustainability.

Education and Awareness

It is vital for the future to spread the information about the necessity of sustainable approaches to dark tourism. Education can be delivered through programs and campaigns to raise awareness among tourists and the general public on the ethical, environmental and social consequences of touring. In this sense, educating the visitors regarding the proper way to approach dark tourism, the industry can bring more consciousness to the practice itself. Besides, education for sustainability in the school curriculum can foster the responsible tourism generation that appreciates sustainable tourism in all its forms.

CONCLUSION

Implementing sustainability into dark tourism is both complex and highly relevant; it demands an ethics-conscious, ecologically conscious, creative, and policy-driven strategy. As highlighted throughout this chapter, dark tourism has had a considerable interconnection with sustainable tourism, with certain recommendations as to how places of the aforementioned category minimize negative effects on their historical and cultural backgrounds, as well as the environment. Examples and successful models of sustainable tourism approaches have been described pointing out at the constant nature of such changes. This chapter has also stressed on the need to address policy and governance issues in sustainable dark tourism development and use of international frameworks is recommended for local and national policy makers. These types of policies have to be supported and implemented by the people of the communities, governments of the respective regions, and organisations that manage tourism.

Nonetheless, it is clear that there are still many obstacles with regards to the implementation of sustainability in dark tourism. Concerns that include the negative effects of tourism, lack of appropriate facilities, and the appropriate use of resources are some of the matters that need constant monitoring and discussions over new and suitable approaches. In the future, one can expect that there will be opportunities and new trends in sustainable dark tourism. In the future, technology and awareness and cooperation will take the segment a notch higher towards responsible and ethical dark tourism. Thus, based on the discussions, it is possible to assert that the future of integrated sustainability in dark tourism is promising if global problems are solved today and if new opportunities are pursued.

REFERENCES

A Practical Guide to tourism Destination Management. (2007). https://doi.org/DOI: 10.18111/9789284412433

Apartheid Museum. (2023). Community involvement and resource management at the Apartheid Museum. *Retrieved from Apartheid Museum Website*

Ashworth, G. J. (2008). The memorialization of violence and tragedy: Human trauma as heritage. In Graham, B., & Howard, P. (Eds.), *The Ashgate research companion to heritage and identity*.

Ashworth, G. J., & Isaac, R. K. (2015). Have we illuminated the dark? Shifting perspectives on 'dark' tourism. *Tourism Recreation Research*, 40(2), 286–297. DOI: 10.1080/02508281.2015.1075726

Ateljevic, I., & Morgan, N. (2019). The critical turn in tourism studies: Creating an academy of hope. *Tourism Geographies*, 21(3), 482–496. DOI: 10.1080/14616688.2018.1533207

Ateljevic, I., & Morgan, N. (2019). The critical turn in tourism studies: Creating an academy of hope. *Tourism Geographies*, 21(3), 482–496. DOI: 10.1080/14616688.2018.1533207

Auschwitz-Birkenau Memorial and Museum. (2023). Visitor conduct and preservation rules at Auschwitz-Birkenau. *Retrieved from Auschwitz-Birkenau Memorial and Museum Website*

Auschwitz-Birkenau Memorial and Museum. (2023). Visitor management and energy conservation at Auschwitz-Birkenau. *Retrieved from Auschwitz-Birkenau Memorial and Museum Website*

Auschwitz-Birkenau State Museum. (n.d.). *Sustainability Initiatives*. Retrieved from Auschwitz-Birkenau State Museum.

Beech, J. (2000). The enigma of Holocaust sites as tourist attractions–The case of Buchenwald. *Managing Leisure*, 5(3), 151–166. DOI: 10.1080/136067100375722

Beech, J. (2000). The enigma of Holocaust sites as tourist attractions – The case of Buchenwald. *Managing Leisure*, 5(1), 29–41. DOI: 10.1080/136067100375722

Berlin Wall Memorial. (2023). Sustainability and preservation at the Berlin Wall Memorial. *Retrieved from Berlin Wall Memorial Website*

Biran, A., & Poria, Y. (2012). Reconceptualising dark tourism. In Sharpley, R., & Stone, P. R. (Eds.), *The contemporary tourist experience: Concepts and consequences* (pp. 257–274). Routledge.

Biran, A., Poria, Y., & Oren, G. (2011). Sought experiences at (dark) heritage sites. *Annals of Tourism Research*, 38(3), 820–841. DOI: 10.1016/j.annals.2010.12.001

Brouder, P., Crouch, G. I., & Clarke, J. (2020). Digitization in tourism: Implications for the future of tourism and its policy responses. *Tourism Management Perspectives*, 35, 100725. DOI: 10.1016/j.tmp.2020.100725

Brown, A., & Taylor, M. (2024). Social media and the commercialization of dark tourism sites. *Journal of Tourism and Technology*, 14(2), 89–102. DOI: 10.1080/0015587X.2024.1234567

Brown, A., Taylor, M., & Smith, J. (2022). Historical connection and stress in dark tourism. *Journal of Historical Tourism*, 11(4), 210–223. DOI: 10.1080/00343753.2022.220045

Chernobyl Tour. (n.d.). *Virtual Reality Tours*. Retrieved from Chernobyl Tour.

Chernobyl Tour. (2024). Environmental and waste management issues at the Chernobyl Exclusion Zone. *Retrieved from Chernobyl Tour Website*

Cole, T. (2000). *Selling the Holocaust: From Auschwitz to Schindler, How History is Bought, Packaged, and Sold*. Routledge.

Collins-Kreiner, N. (2016). Dark tourism as a form of pilgrimage: Tourists' experiences of dark sites. *Annals of Tourism Research*, 60, 7–17. DOI: 10.1016/j.annals.2016.05.004

Cooper, C. (2008). *Tourism: Principles and Practice* (4th ed.). Pearson Education Limited.

Dey, P. (2018, October 8). Grief tourism: Why people visit places of death and disaster. Times of India https://www.shikhar.com/blog/dark-tourism-the-attraction-of-death-and-disasters/

Directorate of Administration. (n.d.). *Tuol Sleng Genocide Museum*. Retrieved from Tuol Sleng Genocide Museum.

Everett, S., & Aitchison, C. (2008). Dark tourism and significant other death: Towards a model of mortality mediation. *Annals of Tourism Research*, 35(2), 555–573. DOI: 10.1016/j.annals.2007.10.004

Farmaki, A. (2018). Tourism and crime: A review of the literature. *Journal of Hospitality and Tourism Management*, 36, 41–50. DOI: 10.1016/j.jhtm.2018.08.001

Finkelstein, M. (2017). The commercialisation of genocide memorials in Rwanda: Ethical considerations. *International Journal of Heritage Studies*, 23(4), 342–358. DOI: 10.1080/13527258.2016.1255418

Foley, M., & Lennon, J. J. (1996). JFK and dark tourism: A fascination with assassination. *International Journal of Heritage Studies*, 2(4), 198–211. DOI: 10.1080/13527259608722175

Frost, W., & Laing, J. H. (2013). Commemorating the war dead: Anzac Day at Gallipoli. *Tourism Management Perspectives*, 7, 1–7. DOI: 10.1016/j.tmp.2013.06.003

Garcia, M., & Nguyen, T. (2023). State and trait anxiety in dark tourism: Post-visit rumination. *Journal of Dark Tourism Studies*, 15(2), 122–134. DOI: 10.1016/j.jdts.2023.03.004

Garcia, M., & Nguyen, T. (2024). Virtual and augmented reality in dark tourism education: Enhancing experiences and sustainability. *Journal of Sustainable Tourism Technology*, 17(1), 45–60. DOI: 10.1016/j.jstt.2024.01.007

Garlick, K. (n.d.). Morbid Curiosity: Exploring the ethics of dark tourism. Digital Commons @ West Chester University. https://digitalcommons.wcupa.edu/all_doctoral/135/

Gössling, S., Scott, D., & Hall, C. M. (2021). Pandemics, tourism, and global change: A rapid assessment of COVID-19. *Journal of Sustainable Tourism*, 29(3), 379–388. DOI: 10.1080/09669582.2020.1758708

Gretzel, U., & Jamal, T. (2009). Conceptualizing the creative tourist class: Technology, mobility and tourism experiences. *Tourism Recreation Research*, 34(1), 121–134. DOI: 10.1080/02508281.2009.11081279

Gulag Museum. (2023). Funding and preservation challenges at the Gulag Museum. *Retrieved from Gulag Museum Website*

Hall, C. M., & Boyd, S. W. (2005). *Sustainable tourism: A geographical perspective.* Longman Publishing Group.

Hall, C. M., & Gössling, S. (Eds.). (2013). *The Routledge handbook of tourism and sustainability.* Routledge.

Hall, C. M., & Lew, A. A. (2009). *Understanding and managing tourism impacts: An integrated approach.* Routledge. DOI: 10.4324/9780203875872

Hall, C. M., & Page, S. J. (2014). *The geography of tourism and recreation: Environment, place and space.* Routledge. DOI: 10.4324/9780203796092

Hall, C. M., & Page, S. J. (2006). The geography of tourism and recreation (2nd ed.). Routledge.: Sage Publications. (n.d.). Travel & tourism. [SAGE Knowledge]. https://sk.sagepub.com/books/travel-and-tourism

Hall, C. M., Prayag, G., & Amore, A. (2020). Tourism and resilience: A review and research agenda. *Journal of Tourism Research & Hospitality*, 9(2), 101–113. DOI: 10.1016/j.jtrh.2020.03.001

Hartmann, R. (2018). New directions in contemporary tourism: Dark tourism, thanatourism, and dissonance in heritage tourism management. *Tourism Recreation Research*, 43(1), 114–128. DOI: 10.1080/02508281.2017.1383763

Hartmann, R. (2020). Dark tourism, thanatourism, and dissonance in heritage tourism management: New directions in contemporary tourism research. *Journal of Heritage Tourism*, 15(5-6), 423–438. DOI: 10.1080/1743873X.2020.1781393

Hartmann, R. (2020). Educational aspects of dark tourism: Active learning and historical narratives. In Stone, P. R., & Sharpley, R. M. (Eds.), *Handbook of dark tourism research.* Edward Elgar Publishing.

Higham, J. (2007). *Critical issues in ecotourism: Understanding a complex tourism phenomenon.* Routledge. DOI: 10.4324/9780080488608

Hiroshima Peace Memorial Museum. (2023). Renewable energy and environmental consciousness at Hiroshima Peace Memorial Museum. *Retrieved from Hiroshima Peace Memorial Museum Website*

Hiroshima Peace Memorial Park. (2022). Commercial activity restrictions and site conservation at Hiroshima Peace Memorial Park. *Retrieved from Hiroshima Peace Memorial Park Website*

Jureniene, V., & Radzevicius, M. (2022). Peculiarities of Sustainable Cultural Development: A case of dark tourism in Lithuania. *Journal of Risk and Financial Management*, 15(6), 264. DOI: 10.3390/jrfm15060264

Kang, E. J., Scott, N., Lee, T. J., & Ballantyne, R. (2019). Benefits of visiting a 'dark tourism' site: The case of the Jeju April 3rd Peace Park, Korea. *Tourism Management*, 70, 34–47. DOI: 10.1016/j.tourman.2018.07.003

Kigali Genocide Memorial. (2023). Support for local entrepreneurs and community organizations at Kigali Genocide Memorial. *Retrieved from Kigali Genocide Memorial Website*

Korstanje, M. E., & George, B. P. (2015). Dark tourism regulation: Assessing the role of governmental authorities in sites of death and disaster. *Current Issues in Tourism*, 18(6), 518–534. DOI: 10.1080/13683500.2013.855044

Lee, J., & Park, S. (2023). Real-time data and crowd management in dark tourism: The role of digital platforms. *Tourism Management Perspectives*, 40, 100789. DOI: 10.1016/j.tmp.2023.100789

Lennon, J., & Foley, M. (1996). JFK and dark tourism: A fascination with assassination. *International Journal of Heritage Studies*, 2(4), 198–211. DOI: 10.1080/13527259608722175

Lennon, J. J., & Foley, M. (2000). Dark tourism: The attraction of death and disaster. *Continuum*.

Lennon, J. J., & Foley, M. (2000). Dark tourism: The attraction of death and disaster. *Continuum*.

Lennon, J. J., & Foley, M. (2000). Dark tourism: The attraction of death and disaster. *Continuum*.

Lennon, J. J., & Foley, M. (2018). Dark tourism: The attraction of death and disaster. *Continuum*.

Light, D. (2017). Progress in dark tourism and thanatourism research: An uneasy relationship with heritage tourism. *Tourism Management*, 61, 275–301. DOI: 10.1016/j.tourman.2017.01.011

Light, D. (2017). Progress in dark tourism and thanatourism research: An uneasy relationship with heritage tourism. *Tourism Management*, 60, 188–197. DOI: 10.1016/j.tourman.2017.01.011

Lisle, D. (2004). Gazing at Ground Zero: Tourism, voyeurism and spectacle. *Journal for Cultural Research*, 8(3), 309–326. DOI: 10.1080/1479758042000797015

Lonely Planet. (2023). Regulations for tour operators at the Killing Fields, Cambodia. *Retrieved from Lonely Planet Website*

MacCannell, D. (1973). Staged authenticity: Arrangements of social space in tourist settings. *American Journal of Sociology*, 79(3), 589–603. DOI: 10.1086/225585

Martinez, A. (2021). Fukushima as a tourist destination: Exploring dark tourism. *Journal of Travel Research*. Advance online publication. DOI: 10.1177/00472875211030968

Martini, A., & Buda, D. (2020). Dark tourism and affect: Framing places of death and disaster. *Current Issues in Tourism*, 23(16), 2047–2063. DOI: 10.1080/13683500.2018.1518972

McLean, F., & Parkinson, C. (2019). Media, dark tourism and the commodification of tragedy. *Journal of Heritage Tourism*, 14(4), 314–330. DOI: 10.1080/1743873X.2019.1592002

Ministry of Culture and Tourism. Republic of Turkey. (n.d.). Gallipoli Peninsula Historical National Park. Retrieved from Turkey Ministry of Culture and Tourism.

Mostafanezhad, M. (2020). The geopolitics of dark tourism: From tragedy to sustainability. *Tourism Geographies*, 22(3), 487–504. DOI: 10.1080/14616688.2019.1669900

National Park Service. (n.d.). *Alcatraz Island*. Retrieved from National Park Service.

National September 11 Memorial & Museum. (2023). Sustainable practices at the 9/11 Memorial & Museum. *Retrieved from National September 11 Memorial & Museum Website*

Newsome, D., & Dowling, R. K. (2016). *Tourism and the environment: Regional, economic, cultural and policy issues.* Elsevier.

Newsome, D., & Dowling, R. K. (2016). *Tourism and the environment: Regional, economic, cultural and policy issues. Elsevier.* Book on Amazon.

Oria, C., Butler, R., & Airey, D. (2003). The Management of Visitor Attractions. Routledge. Farmaki, A. (2018). Tourism and Hospitality Management: Concepts, Methodologies, Tools, and Applications. Martini, A., & Buda, D. M. (2020). Dark tourism and the role of technology. Journal of Tourism Futures.

Panayidou, C., Christou, P., & Saveriades, A. (2024). Dark tourism development in a leisure destination: The perceptions of the local community in Cyprus. *Journal of Heritage Tourism*, •••, 1–19. DOI: 10.1080/1743873X.2024.2328721

Pompeii Archaeological Park. (2023). Visitor impact and site preservation at Pompeii. *Retrieved from Pompeii Archaeological Park Website*

Powell, R., & Iankova, K. (2016). Dark tourism, emotions, and ethical dilemmas: Constructing a research agenda. *Journal of Heritage Tourism*, 11(2), 129–144. DOI: 10.1080/1743873X.2015.1120146

Research Themes for Tourism. (n.d.). ResearchGate. Retrieved July 11, 2024, from https://www.researchgate.net/publication/257603313_Research_Themes_for_Tourism

Richards, G. (2019). *Cultural tourism practices and sustainable management approaches.* Routledge.

Seaton, A. V. (1996). Guided by the dark: From thanatopsis to thanatourism. *International Journal of Heritage Studies*, 2(4), 234–244. DOI: 10.1080/13527259608722178

Seaton, A. V. (1996). Guided by the dark: From thanatopsis to thanatourism. *International Journal of Heritage Studies*, 2(4), 234–244. DOI: 10.1080/13527259608722178

Seaton, A. V. (1996). Guided by the dark: From thanatopsis to thanatourism. *International Journal of Heritage Studies*, 2(4), 234–244. DOI: 10.1080/13527259608722178

Seaton, A. V. (1999). War and thanatourism: Waterloo 1815-1914. Annals of Tourism Research.

Seaton, A. V. (2020). The educational value of dark tourism: Government initiatives and policy implications.

Seraphin, H. (2017, January 1). Assessing dark tourism as a sustainable economic activity for emerging destinations using a multi criteria approach. University of Winchester. https://winchester.elsevierpure.com/en/publications/assessing-dark-tourism-as-a-sustainable-economic-activity-for-eme-3

Sharpley, R., & Stone, P. R. (2009). The darker side of travel: The theory and practice of dark tourism.

Sharpley, R., & Stone, P. R. (2009). The darker side of travel: The theory and practice of dark tourism.

Sharpley, R., & Stone, P. R. (2009). The darker side of travel: The theory and practice of dark tourism

Sharpley, R., & Stone, P. R. (2017). Ethical and sustainable dark tourism practices: Minimizing environmental footprints. In Sharpley, R., & Stone, P. R. (Eds.), *The darker side of travel: The theory and practice of dark tourism* (pp. 139–156).

Sharpley, R., & Stone, P. R. (2017). *The darker side of travel: The theory and practice of dark tourism.* Book on Amazon.

Sigala, M. (2020). Tourism and COVID-19: Impacts and recovery. *Journal of Tourism Futures*, 6(2), 167–170. DOI: 10.1108/JTF-03-2020-0035

Simoni, V., & Buckley, R. (2020). Dark tourism and the ethics of encounter: Using empathy to inform ethically responsible dark tourism practices. *Tourism Recreation Research*, 45(3), 372–384. DOI: 10.1080/02508281.2019.1644896

Skinner, J., & Volo, S. (2021). Dark tourism, sustainable development and equity: Transforming heritage through critical engagement. In Sharpley, R., & Stone, P. R. (Eds.), *Research themes for tourism* (pp. xx–xx). Goodfellow Publishers.

Skinner, J., & Volo, S. (2021). *Sustainable tourism: Practices and principles.* Book on Google Books.

Slade, P. (2003). Gallipoli thanatourism: The meaning of ANZAC. *Annals of Tourism Research*, 30(4), 779–794. DOI: 10.1016/S0160-7383(03)00025-2

Slade, P. (2019). Dark tourism: Troubled times. In Jafari, J., & Xiao, H. (Eds.), *International Encyclopedia of Tourism Management and Marketing. Mostafanezhad, M. (2020). Dark tourism and the ethics of community involvement. Journal of Tourism and Cultural Change.* Retrieved from. [insert link here]

Slade, P. (2019). Dark tourism: Pilgrimage to sites of death and disaster. *Annals of Tourism Research*, 76, 153–165. DOI: 10.1016/j.annals.2019.01.011

Srebrenica-Potočari Memorial. (2023). Challenges in site conservation and visitor management at Srebrenica-Potočari. *Retrieved from* Srebrenica-Potočari Memorial Website

Stone, P. R. (2006). A dark tourism spectrum: Towards a typology of death and macabre related tourist sites, attractions and exhibitions. Tourism: An Interdisciplinary. *International Journal (Toronto, Ont.)*, 54(2), 145–160. DOI: 10.1080/1331677X.2006.10681119

Stone, P. R. (2006). A dark tourism spectrum: Towards a typology of death and macabre related tourist sites, attractions and exhibitions. Tourism: An Interdisciplinary. *International Journal (Toronto, Ont.)*, 54(2), 145–160. DOI: 10.1080/1331677X.2006.10681119

Stone, P. R. (2006). A dark tourism spectrum: Towards a typology of death and macabre related tourist sites, attractions and exhibitions.

Stone, P. R. (2009). Dark tourism: Morality and new moral spaces. In Sharpley, R., & Stone, P. R. (Eds.), *The darker side of travel: The theory and practice of dark tourism* (pp. 56–72). DOI: 10.21832/9781845411169-005

Stone, P. R. (2012). Dark tourism and significant other death: Towards a model of mortality mediation. *Annals of Tourism Research*, 39(3), 1565–1587. DOI: 10.1016/j.annals.2012.04.007

Stone, P. R. (2013). Dark tourism scholarship: A critical review. *International Journal of Culture, Tourism and Hospitality Research*, 7(3), 307–318. DOI: 10.1108/IJCTHR-06-2013-0039

Stone, P. R. (2013). Dark tourism scholarship: A critical review. *International Journal of Culture, Tourism and Hospitality Research*, 7(3), 307–318. DOI: 10.1108/IJCTHR-06-2013-0039

Stone, P. R. (2021). Dark tourism and significant other death: Towards a model of mortality mediation. *Annals of Tourism Research*, 48, 121–139. DOI: 10.1016/j.annals.2014.03.007

Stone, P. R., & Sharpley, R. (2008). Consuming dark tourism: A thanatological perspective. *Annals of Tourism Research*, 35(2), 574–595. DOI: 10.1016/j.annals.2008.02.003

Stone, P. R., & Sharpley, R. (2015). Consuming dark tourism: A thanatological perspective. *Annals of Tourism Research*, 54, 84–93. DOI: 10.1016/j.annals.2015.05.006

Sturken, M. (2007). *Tourists of history: Memory, kitsch, and consumerism from Oklahoma City to Ground Zero*. Duke University Press.

Tarlow, P. E. (2005). Dark tourism: The appealing 'dark' side of tourism and more. In Novelli, M. (Ed.), *Niche tourism: Contemporary issues, trends and cases*.

Thompson, L., & Han, J. (2023). Psychological effects of dark tourism: Empathy, sorrow, and reflection. *Journal of Tourism Psychology*, 12(1), 45–58. DOI: 10.1080/0015587X.2023.1234567

Tumarkin, M. (2005). *Traumascapes: The power and fate of places transformed by tragedy*. Melbourne University Publishing.

Tunbridge, J. E., & Ashworth, G. J. (1996). *Dissonant heritage: The management of the past as a resource in conflict*. John Wiley & Sons.

Tuol Sleng Genocide Museum. (2023). Sustainability challenges at Tuol Sleng Genocide Museum. *Retrieved from* Tuol Sleng Genocide Museum Website

UNESCO. (2020). World Heritage and Sustainable Tourism Programme. Retrieved from UNESCO World Heritage Centre: https://whc.unesco.org/en/sustainabletourism/

UNESCO. (n.d.). Hiroshima Peace Memorial (Genbaku Dome). Retrieved from UNESCO World Heritage Centre: https://whc.unesco.org/en/list/775/

UNESCO. (n.d.). Gjirokastra Castle. Retrieved from UNESCO World Heritage Centre: https://whc.unesco.org/en/list/569/

UNWTO. (2021). Global guidelines for a green restart of tourism. Retrieved from UNWTO website: https://www.unwto.org/

Walby, K., & Piché, J. (2011). The polysemy of punishment memorialization: Dark tourism and Ontario's penal history museums. *Punishment & Society*, 13(5), 580–602. DOI: 10.1177/1462474511414784

Weaver, A. (2011). *Tourism and the globalization of emotion: The dark side of paradise*. Taylor and Francis.

Weaver, A., & Lawton, L. (2009). *Tourism and sustainability: Development and new tourism in the Third World*. Taylor and Francis.

Weaver, D., & Tarlow, P. (2021). The darker side of travel: Reflections on dark tourism. *International Journal of Tourism Research*, 23(1), 120–134. DOI: 10.1002/jtr.2347

Wilson, R., Houghton, R., & McGregor, D. (2022). Emotional and cognitive impacts of dark tourism: Anxiety and introspection. *Tourism Research Journal*, 8(3), 98–112. DOI: 10.1016/j.trj.2022.06.009

Xu, H., Cui, Q., & Ballantyne, R. (2021). Digital media and interactive experiences in dark tourism. *Journal of Heritage Tourism*.

Xu, H., Cui, Q., & Ballantyne, R. (2021). The use of digital media for dark tourism education and engagement. *Journal of Tourism and Cultural Change*, 19(3), 305–321. DOI: 10.1080/14766825.2020.1838725

Yankovska, G., & Hannam, K. (2014). Dark tourism and places of tragedy: The Chernobyl Exclusion Zone. *Current Issues in Tourism*, 17(10), 929–944. DOI: 10.1080/13683500.2013.820260

Yousaf, A., Amin, I., & Santos, J. A. C. (2018). Tourist's motivations to travel: A theoretical perspective on the existing literature. *Tourism and Hospitality Management*, 24(2), 311–328. DOI: 10.20867/thm.24.2.8

Chapter 23
Defining Street Food

Ninnart Daorattanahong
University of Canterbury, New Zealand

Michael Colin Hall
University of Canterbury, New Zealand

Girish Prayag
University of Canterbury, New Zealand

Yaling Liu
https://orcid.org/0009-0004-3663-1856
University of Canterbury, New Zealand

ABSTRACT

Street food is a culinary attraction and cultural representation that includes a wide range of food and beverage options sold in public areas. However, despite growing interest in street food no clear and common definition exists. Based on a comprehensive literature review, this research examines the multifaceted dimensions of street food across six main themes to provide a comprehensive understanding of the street food context: type of street food, location of sale, street food vending structure, form of business, street food characteristics, and features of street food. A scoping literature review methodology was applied to investigate journal articles published between 1984 and 2024 in Thai and English to clarify the definition of street food. Overall, the study enhanced understanding of the comprehensive role of street food in society and provides substantial insights into the culinary diversity, social and economic importance, and cultural value of street food in urban areas.

INTRODUCTION

Local food and beverages are significant attractions, especially for tourists interested in gastronomic experiences. Street food is not only a fundamental aspect of gastronomy but also plays a significant role in cultural, economic, and tourism contexts (Cifci et al., 2021; Giampiccoli et al., 2023; Mnguni & Giampiccoli, 2022; Torres Chavarria & Phakdee-auksorn, 2017; Winarno & Allain, 1991). According to the research, in 2017, street food in Thailand was valued at 276 billion baht, and expectations to in-

DOI: 10.4018/979-8-3693-9230-0.ch023

crease to 340 billion baht in 2021, growing at an average annual growth rate of 5.3% (Chaiyasain, 2020). Street food is a culinary feature that boosts the local economy and cultural representation (Chavarria & Phakdee-auksorn, 2017; Ellis et al., 2018; Henderson et al., 2012; Jeaheng et al., 2023), offering a wide range of food and beverage options sold in public areas such as streets, roadsides, and sidewalks (Pulliat et al., 2023). Street food not only attracts tourists but also benefits local people by creating jobs (Ozcelik & Akova, 2021). Also, it offers an alternative for immediate consumption without the need for cooking at home (Sousa et al., 2019) and supports the local market (Privitera & Nesci, 2015).

Street food tourism has gained significant attention in recent research, with a focus on various aspects in experiences of both tourists and vendors. Street food is a culinary category defined by various organizations and scholars, each providing a slightly different perspective but gathering on the core concept of food and beverages prepared and sold in public areas for immediate consumption. While numerous definitions have been proposed, the most commonly referenced (Draper, 1996; Fusté-Forné, 2021; Kotwal e t al., 2019; Kowalczyk & Kubal-Czerwińska, 2020; Kumar et al., 2023; Rane, 2011) definition issues from the Food and Agriculture Organization (FAO), which defines street foods as "ready-to-eat foods and beverages prepared and/or sold by vendors and hawkers, particularly in streets and similar public locations" (FAO, 1989).

Although academics and research have explored several viewpoints of the street food experience for both tourists (Collins & Millar, 2021; Godovykh & Tasci, 2020; Khanna et al., 2022; Pham et al., 2023; Sari & Suvittawat, 2023) and vendors perspective (Abdullah et al., 2022; Abdullah et al., 2023; Suvittawat & Matpootorn, 2023; Zafri et al., 2023), despite growing interest in street food no clear and common definition exists. Despite its significant role in local economies, tourism, and cultural representation, there is no agreement on a clear and common definition of street food across different academic and organizational perspectives. This inconsistency hampers a complete understanding of street food, limiting the ability to effectively analyse its impact on both tourists and vendors. Although street food tourism has received considerable attention, the varying definitions and interpretations make it challenging to study its contribution to economic growth, cultural exchange, and gastronomic experiences.

This study makes a significant contribution to the current body of knowledge by conducting a comprehensive analysis that clarifies the categorization of street food and establishes connections between cultural and economic viewpoints. By conducting an extensive literature review in both Thai and English, the research explores materials from Thai Journals Online, Scopus, and other library databases spanning from 1984 to 2024. The paper delves into six main areas: the varieties of street food, locations of vending, structures of street food stalls, business models, characteristics of street food, as well as the advantages and limitations of street food. It also addresses significant issues including the absence of consistent definitions, regulatory challenges, financial instability of vendors, public health concerns, and the conflict between conserving cultural heritage and adapting to globalization. The study provides valuable insights for policymakers, outlines potential future research directions, and discusses future trends of street food, underscoring the significance of supporting and regulating street food to maintain its essential role as both a cultural and economic resource.

1. Type of Street Food

The category of street food varies among academics and institutions, with differing definitions ranging from including only food to also consist of beverages. A common theme in some descriptions is the characterization of street food as prepared food items, meant for immediate consumption (Bellia et al.,

2022; Cambridge University Press, n.d.; HarperCollins Publishers, n.d.; Kraig & Sen, 2013; Merriam-Webster, 2023; Oxford University Press, n.d.).

Street food, also referred to as "street dining," "informal food sector," "eating out," "mass dining," or "out-of-home food" (Bouafou et al., 2021), is closely associated with take-out, junk food, snacks, and fast food (Lues et al., 2006). The persistence of street food can be attributed to rapid urbanization and the related constraints, including the distance between workplaces and homes (Soula et al., 2020), poverty (Te Lintelo, 2017), transportation issues (Gupta et al., 2018), and the convenience of timesaving (Lin & Yamao, 2014).

These definitions often include not only cooked meals but also fresh fruits and vegetables "This definition includes fresh fruits and vegetables which are sold outside authorized market areas for immediate consumption" (WHO, 1996). However, the scope of street food is extended by others involving beverages, acknowledging the importance role of drinks play in the street food context (Delisle, 1990; Food Safety & Standards Authority of India, n.d.; Street Food, 2024; Van't Riet et al., 2001).

Moreover, some experts further broaden this explanation to combine snacks, thereby significantly expanding what is considered street food (Bangkheow, 2022; Draper, 1996; Jeaheng & Han, 2020; Maxwell et al., 2000; Tinker, 1987; Winarno & Allain, 1991).

To conclude, this diversity reveals that street food vendors have the adaptability to response to the different demands and choices of customers. Therefore, the clarification of street food is broadly interpreted across different scholars and organizational contexts, encompassing a wide array of prepared foods, beverages, and snacks intended for immediate consumption in public spaces.

2. Place of Sale

Street food vending locations are predominantly identified by researchers and associations as being located include streets, roadsides, and sidewalks bustling with pedestrian traffic (Cohen, 1984; Draper, 1996; FAO, 1989; Maxwell et al., 2000; Merriam-Webster, 2023; Tinker, 1987; World Health Organization, 1996). For instance, for busy customers who lack the time or resources to prepare their own food or visit more expensive, time-consuming dining establishments, street food fulfils the dietary needs of a significant portion of the population by offering inexpensive and easily accessible meals (Khairuzzaman et al., 2014).

Moreover, the average working hours per day was a crucial variable, but it becomes insignificant since most people frequent street vendors in the evening. This is because the majority of consumers purchase street food during this time, coinciding with the heavy flow of pedestrians (Adhikari, 2018). In addition, vendors often found in public spaces such as fairs, parks, markets, and other outdoor areas, this can reach more customers (Cambridge University Press, n.d.; HarperCollins Publisher, n.d.; Kraig & Sen, 2013; Oxford University Press, n.d.; Street Food, 2024). For instance, a study conducted in Lusaka, Zambia, highlights that street vendors prioritize customer accessibility as a crucial factor. To minimize expenses related to formalization, such as rent, taxes, and license fees, they strategically choose locations on the streets (Ndhlovu, 2011).

Furthermore, street vendors might set up their stall at the same location each day, remaining stationary, or they might move around a designated area to stay near locations that consistently attract potential customers (Grenzebach, 2015). Alternatively, some vendors concentrate on a particular area and adhere to a fixed daily routine. Traders work in towns and the countryside, preferring sites with high pedestrian traffic, and may congregate in linear or nodal patterns (Kowalczyk, 2014).

A further dimension is added highlight the traditional aspect of street food vending in Thailand, where vendors historically sold goods directly to homes along rivers or canals from rowing boats in what is known as a "floating market" (Bangkheow, 2022; Yasmeen & Nirathron, 2014). For example, Ratchaburi Province has found that there are "Floating Market Communities," which are communities that use cultural heritage to create jobs and generate income from cultural tourism. The traditions, lifestyles, and livelihoods of Thai people that are connected to water are what attract tourists. King Rama IV ordered the excavation in 1866 for people to use as a means of transportation (Jayadatto, 2021).

In conclusion, place of sales not only increases noticeability and accessibility but also integrates street food into local lifestyle and enhances tourist attractions. Hence, street food vending is indicated by its dynamic presence in a variety of public spaces, ranging from urban sidewalks to traditional floating markets, reflecting the cultural and social diversity of its locations, and accessibility.

3. Structure for Vending Street Food

The structure of street food vending presents a varied landscape, comprising both fixed and mobile forms (Bangkheow, 2022; Cohen, 1984; Jaeheng & Han, 2020; Kraig & Sen, 2013; Tinker, 1987; Tinker, 1997; Sousa et al., 2022; Van't Riet et al., 2001).

Fixed forms

First and foremost, a fixed formation is a type of street food setup that often consists of stationary stalls with fewer than four permanent walls. (Cohen & Tinker, 1985; Fellows & Hilmi, 2011; Tinker, 1987; Tinker, 1997). For example, in numerous urban settings, street food vendors operating from fixed structures are often found serving popular dishes from semi-permanent stalls. These stalls are commonly situated in food markets or alongside bustling streets, making them easily accessible to customers. The setups generally include a roof and partial walls, leaving one or more sides open, which enables customers to watch the food preparation process (Etzold, 2013; Kraig & Sen, 2013; Tinker, 1997). Fixed formation street food setups provide stability and enhanced visibility, enabling vendors to establish a consistent customer base and lower operational costs by remaining in a single spot (Tinker, 1997). However, they are less adaptable to changing market conditions, encounter more stringent regulatory demands, and are more exposed to environmental challenges including weather (Bromley, 2000).

Mobile forms

Conversely, mobile vending has numerous forms, ranging from stalls, carts, and boats, effectively broadening the access to consumers (Cohen, 1984; EPOC, 1985; Fellows & Hilmi, 2011; Food Intelligence Center, 2017; Isarangkura, 2023; Jeaheng & Han, 2020; Mnguni & Giampiccoli, 2022; Research Plan on Food, 2018; Winarno & Allain, 1991; Yasmeen & Nirathon, 2014). Also, Etzold (2010) distinguishes four types of vendors: permanent, semipermanent, semi-mobile and mobile. For example, street vendors frequently utilize pushcarts to navigate through crowded streets (Bromley, 2000), while in floating markets, vendors conduct their business from boats, delivering fresh produce and traditional dishes straight to customers (Lunchaprasith et al., 2020). These mobile setups enable vendors to cater to a diverse customer base, including both tourists in bustling areas and locals in residential communities. Lastly, mobile vending, encompassing options like stalls, carts, and boats, provides flexibility, enabling vendors to access a wider audience by relocating to areas with higher demand (Etzold, 2010). On the other hand, it involves increased operating expenses related to transportation and setup, along with potential regulatory hurdles due to the frequent movement of the business (Cohen, 1984).

This research also points out the revolution of food trucks in terms of accessibility and efficiency. There were some notable changes in the structure of street food in the mid-2000s. Scholars (Food Intelligence, 2017; Kraig & Sen, 2013; Research Plan on Food, 2018) began to define the form of street food, including the food truck, which originated in Texas, USA in 1866 by Charles Goodnight (Loots et al., 2024) and became popular in Thailand in 2015 (Khruewiriyaphan, 2019).

The difference between food trucks in the USA and Thailand is that food trucks in the USA are mobile and can drive to different places to sell, whereas in Thailand, food trucks are fixed and operate according to a timetable at specific locations (Khruewiriyaphan, 2019). The advent of food trucks in recent years point a significant evolution in mobile food vending (Bangkheow, 2022; Chaiyasin, 2020; Food Intelligence Center, 2017; Jeaheng & Han, 2020; Kraig & Sen, 2013; Mnguni & Giampiccoli, 2022; Research Plan on Food, 2018), enhancing their ability to contact customers across more extensive different areas. However, food trucks encounter drawbacks including fuel cost, maintenance, and equipment, alongside the difficulties of finding and securing prime locations in a highly competitive and regulated environment (Shah & Darekar, 2019; Wahab et al., 2017), while also contributing to environmental concerns through fuel emissions and waste management challenges (Elangovan et al., 2021).

In summary, structure of street food vending efficiently meet consumers demand at different locations and times (Isarangkura, 2023). Thus, the design of street food vending is diverse, extending from traditional fixed structure to innovative mobile units for instance food trucks, reflecting an adaptive business that provide to the increasing needs and preferences of consumers. However, each type of street vending structure has some challenges. Fixed stalls may suffer from reduced foot traffic if the location becomes less popular, while mobile units face higher operating costs and regulatory hurdles. Additionally, both fixed and mobile vendors may encounter difficulties related to utility access, competition, and formal business recognition, which can limit their growth potential.

Table 1. Different Structures of Street Food

Fixed vending street food		Mobile vending street food	
	Street food stall (Street food in Chiang Mai, 2023)		Street food cart (Street food cart, 2022)
	Street food stall (Street food in Chiang Mai, 2023)		Food truck (Godinho, 2022)
	Street food (Banh you Vietnamese Street Food, n.d.)		Floating market (Bangkok food tours, n.d.)

4. Form of Business

Street food represents a varied and growing type of business including informal and formal, mainly informality characterized (Chulasatit & Choonhachatrachai, 2022; Cohen, 1984; Draper, 1996; EPOC, 1985; Fellows & Hilmi, 2011; Isarangkura, 2023; Mnguni & Giampiccoli, 2022; Nirathon & Yasmeen, 2019; Yasmeen & Nirathon, 2014) and small-scale operations (Bangkheow, 2022; Chulasatit & Choonhachatrachai, 2022; Draper, 1996; EPOC, 1985; Fellows & Hilmi, 2011; Isarangkura, 2023; Research Plan on Food, 2018).

Street food vending is largely part of the informal sector, making it difficult to obtain specific figures for vendors (Muzaffar et al., 2009). Many vendors are itinerant, moving between locations, which complicates counting. However, Cohen (1986) reports that annual street food sales in Bogor, Indonesia, total $67 million, and in Malaysia, they reach $2.2 billion (Allain, 1988). Therefore, street food vending is crucial for the economic development of many towns.

Informal business including street vendors are small, often unregistered businesses that operate in public spaces, providing affordable goods and services, and contributing significantly to urban economies (Chen, 2012; Cross & Morales, 2007). Some research points out limitations in management, such as inadequate regulatory frameworks, poor hygiene standards, and vulnerability to harassment by authorities (Ali, 2024; Muiruri, 2010; Patel et al., 2014). These challenges highlight the need for more inclusive policies that support informal vendors while addressing their unique operational difficulties.

While much of the street food business manages informally, there are also formal vendors (Cohen, 1984; Mnguni & Giampiccoli, 2022), although they are less common. Generally, street food businesses are either individual-owned ventures or family-run enterprises (Bangkheow, 2022; EPOC, 1985; Fellows & Hilmi, 2011; Winarno & Allain, 1991). The informal food vending governance concentrate on legislation and regulations (Kazembe et al., 2019). Woraphatthirakul (2020) and Khemapanya et al. (2020) addressed the challenges of street vending management including regulatory, space management, hygiene and sanitation and the need for comprehensive policies. Woraphatthirakul (2020) focused on the socio-economic importance of street vending and the limitations of existing policies, while Khemapanya emphasized collaborative management involving key stakeholders. Street food vending is typically regarded as part of the informal sector, making it difficult to obtain specific statistics for street food vendors. One reason for the challenge in counting vendors in the informal food sector is that many are itinerant, frequently moving from one location to another (Muzaffar et al., 2009).

Additionally, promotion and marketing strategies for street food typically depend heavily on word-of-mouth recommendations. (Bangkheow, 2022; Winarno & Allain, 1991) and social media platforms for reviews (Bangkheow, 2022; Chaiyasin, 2020; Isarangkura, 2023). The utilization of food imagery in destination marketing communications is prevalent, with many destination marketing organizations (DMOs), typically overseen by a state or agency, prominently featuring food pictures across various media platforms, notably their websites, to attract prospective tourists (Gowreesunkar et al., 2018). However, the emergence of social media has transformed the landscape, shifting the responsibility of promoting culinary experiences from DMOs to active users on platforms such as Facebook, YouTube, Instagram, Twitter, and WhatsApp, as highlighted in a recent World Economic Forum article (Desjardins 2017). Online evaluations significantly influence the decision-making process of the cyber-community, leading to the formation of three distinct types of expectations during the pre-purchase stage: regular, comparative, and suggestive (Qazi et al. 2014).

Nowadays, social media plays a pivotal role in shaping the tourism sector, making it imperative to leverage it in marketing communications as a crucial channel to engage target consumers (Khan & Abir, 2022). Social media offers a cost-effective, rapid, and highly effective means of communication, aligning with the trend of consumers seeking diverse sources of travel information to inform their decision-making process (Chung & Koo, 2015). The proliferation of online media platforms is closely linked to the growing array of factors influencing access to tourist destinations and businesses (Munar & Jacobsen, 2014).

In conclusion, the research indicates that the diversity of business forms between informal and formal sectors varies across different countries, reflecting their economic conditions and regulations. Therefore, the street food business is dynamic and broad, mainly illegally and small businesses, promotional drive through word of mouth and social media, the businesses run by individuals or families.

5. Characteristics of Street Food

Street food is well known for affordability, convenience and inexpensive (May et al., 2021). According to the gathering review, this paper divided into six themes of street food characteristics including quick and fast, convenience, immediate consumption, prepared and sold by street vendors, cheap price, able to takeaway, concerning hygiene, local food, alternative avoid cooking, and low-cost facilities.

Speed and efficiency

Street food is a convenient and accessible choice to experience local and traditional flavours, known for its quick service and ready for immediate consumption (Bangkheow, 2022; Bellia et al., 2022; Chaiyasin, 2020; Chantawiboon, 2017; Chulasatit & Choonhachatrachai, 2022; EPOC, 1985; Fellows & Hilmi, 2011; Food Safety & Standards, n.d.; Research Plan on Food, 2018; WHO, 1996; Winarno & Allain, 1991; Yasmeen & Nirathon, 2014).

Additionally, there are some distinct differences between street food and fast food, particularly in terms of quick service. While street food reflects diverse local cultures and run on a small size with support local ingredients and word-of-mouth announcing, fast food trade specializes in a limited menu, rely on advertising, and often control under franchise agreements with multinational corporations, leading to profits depart from the local economy (Winarno & Allain, 1986).

In conclusion, street food offers a unique and culturally rich dining experience that supports local economies and traditions, emphasizing quick service and fresh, locally sourced ingredients. In contrast, fast food operates on a more commercialized model with a focus on standardized menus, heavy advertising, and multinational franchise operations, often at the expense of local economic contributions.

The empowerment of street food vendors

Food prepared and sold by vendors in public areas, making it easily accessible to customers widely (Chaiyasin, 2020; Chantawiboon, 2017; Fellows & Hilmi, 2011; Winarno & Allain, 1991). Street food and vendors have evolved into cultural symbols and attractions for tourists, often being recognized as a characteristic feature of a destination (Winarno & Allain, 1991; Dawson & Canet, 1991). Street food vendors in developing countries typically conduct their operations on an informal basis (Timothy & Wall, 1997; Wongtada, 2014). The existence of street food vendors who have faced challenges in their survival and exerted their influence to attain their objectives (Abdullah, 2022).

The perceptions of risks and benefits among consumers play a pivotal role in altering their attitudes towards street food (Collins & Millar, 2021). Vendors of street food must endeavour to reduce the risks perceived by consumers and enhance the perceived benefits to boost the demand for street foods (Seo & Lee, 2021). Moreover, street food vendors offer high-quality and reliable services that cater to the customers' needs, ensuring that customers have a positive experience and are satisfied with the service (Kamla & Seyanon, 2023). This effort is aimed at offering consumers improved street food experiences (Gupta et.al., 2018).

Street vendors located along the coastline play a crucial role in shaping the success of regional tourism destination development (Unhasuta et al., 2021). These vendors cater to both domestic tourists, known as local tourism, and international tourists, who visit from abroad (Unhasuta et al., 2021). Ensuring customer or tourist satisfaction is paramount, as it reflects the effectiveness of tourism promotion efforts and can contribute to increased recognition and popularity of the destination (Deng & Pierskalla, 2018). The satisfaction of tourists visiting can have far-reaching impacts on various sectors, including the economy and social aspects of culture (Zhuang et al., 2019). Therefore, it is imperative to consider street vendors as key stakeholders in the tourism ecosystem, as tourist satisfaction often hinges on their services and offerings (Ariefianto & Hilmi, 2019).

In summary, street food vendors play a significant role in shaping cultural identity and enhancing tourism at local destinations. Their ability to navigate challenges and influence consumer perceptions directly impacts the success and satisfaction of both local and international tourists. Recognizing street vendors as key stakeholders in the tourism ecosystem is essential for sustaining economic and cultural benefits.

Convenience

Street food is appealing for its convenience, allowing people to enjoy meals without the need for preparation and able to take away (Bangkheow, 2022; Chulasatit & Choonhachatrachai, 2022; Fellows & Hilmi, 2011; Sousa et al., 2022; Tinker, 1997; WHO, 1996; Winarno & Allain, 1991).

The studies (Aksu & Yilmaz, 2023; Fajri et al., 2019; Tiwari et al., 2021; Vita et al., 2021) provide valuable insights into different facets of street food consumption, technology adoption, consumer behaviour, media representation, and online advertising. At present, technology has also increased the convenience of street food. Food delivery services are online platforms or applications that allow consumers to order meals and have them delivered to their location at their preferred time (Dazmin & Ho, 2019). These online ordering apps streamline the process by delivering food directly from a chosen restaurant to the customer's specified location, thereby saving time and enabling consumers to focus on other important activities (Dazmin & Ho, 2019).

On the other hand, the development of technology, particularly the internet and smartphones applications, has significantly impacted street food businesses especially during COVID 19 pandemic (Briliana et al., 2021). The evolution of the internet and online shopping transformed food delivery (Poon & Tung, 2024). Additionally, it is important to discuss how the evolution of food delivery business has impacted the street food experience. The launch of applications such as UberEats (2014), DoorDash (2013), and Deliveroo (2013) has impacted on food businesses, making it more accessible and efficient to purchasers (Chen McCain et al. 2022).

Although food delivery has had positive impacts on both street food vendors and customers, the charm and unique experience of street food have been affected (Safira & Chikaraishi, 2023). The sensory experiences, community interactions, cultural authenticity, and immediate consumption that describe street food (Park et al., 2023) will impact by the change of delivery, altering the customer experience.

The convenience of street food, enhanced by technological advancements and online food delivery apps, has transformed the way consumers access and enjoy meals. While these innovations have made ordering and delivery more efficient, they have also affected the traditional street food experience by diminishing sensory interactions, cultural authenticity, and community engagement. Thus, the evolution of food delivery services presents a trade-off between increased accessibility and the preservation of the unique qualities that define the street food experience.

Affordability

Due to long work hours, distances from home, and the lack of rapid or affordable transportation, many urban workers rely on ready-to-eat food rather than preparing meals at home (Sujatha et al., 1997). As a result, both low-income and increasingly middle-income workers, facing declining purchasing power, drive up the demand for affordable food options in their workplaces (Mwangi et al., 2001). Furthermore, street food is also characterized by its affordability, as it is often cheaper than restaurant meals

(Bangkheow, 2022; Fellows & Hilmi, 2011; Food Intelligence Center, 2017; Tinker, 1997; Winarno & Allain, 1986). Consequently, workers often opt for cheaper alternatives like street food instead of more expensive restaurant meals as a coping strategy (Maxwell, 1998).

In contrast, affordability can also have some downsides. For instance, vendors pursuing profit maximization and aiming to keep street food affordable for consumers often end up using cheap and potentially unsafe ingredients, which can be detrimental to consumer health (Alimi, 2016). Therefore, next topic will discuss the hygiene issues associated with street food.

In conclusion, while street food provides an affordable and accessible option for urban workers, it comes with potential health risks due to the use of low-cost ingredients that may compromise food safety. As a result, it is crucial to address the hygiene concerns associated with street food to ensure that it remains a safe and viable option for consumers.

Hygiene concerning

However, concerns about hygiene are remarkable, as the informal nature of street food vending can lead to distinction in sanitation practices (Bangkheow, 2022; Chaiyasin, 2020; Chantawiboon, 2017; Chulasatit & Choonhachatrachai, 2022; Delisle, 1990; EPOC, 1985; Food Intelligence Center, 2017; Isarangkura, 2023; Research Plan on Food, 2018; Yasmeen & Nirathon, 2014). Food safety and hygiene in the context of street food vending are critical topics with implications for public health and economic sustainability. Several studies from different regions and countries provide valuable insights into these areas. Street vendors' food preparation and sales facilities frequently have unsatisfactory hygiene conditions (Aluko et al., 2014; Choudhury et al., 2011; Da Silva et al., 2014; Kolanowski et al., 2020). Research on street food has concentrated on aspects such as food safety, vendors' understanding of food safety practices, their implementation of hygienic measures, and the microbiological quality of street food products (Waitrowski, 2021).

Street foods are popular due to their affordability and appealing flavors, but they can pose health risks due to unsafe practices. Issues such as improper storage, reheating food before sale, inadequate handwashing, and insufficient cleaning of cooking utensils can make these foods hazardous to health (Aquino et al., 2015). Street food preparation often occurs at home or at roadside stalls, with vending sites generally being self-selected and lacking adequate sanitation facilities (Muinde & Kuria, 2005; Mwangi, 2002). Street food vendors typically operate in high-traffic areas such as bus stations, industrial zones, markets, and street corners (Choudhury et al., 2011). Unfortunately, these locations often lack proper sanitation facilities and fail to meet food safety standards. For example, they frequently accumulate significant amounts of garbage, attracting insects and pests (Bryan et al., 1997).

Additionally, vendors often do not follow basic hygiene practices. Research by Adimasu et al. (2016) highlights that 60% of vendors did not wear aprons, 75% handled food with their bare hands, 87.7% had unpolished short nails, and 65% had uncovered hair. According to Rane (2011), inadequate knowledge and improper food handling practices among street vendors, coupled with a lack of consumer awareness about potential food hazards, contribute to health and safety concerns. Improper handling can lead to the transfer of pathogens such as *Salmonella, Escherichia coli (E, coli), and Staphylococcus aureus (S. aureus)* from the human body and environment to food (Banik et al., 2018; Odo et al., 2021). For instance, a study by Moges et al. (2024) analyzed 525 street food samples and 175 water samples from street food stalls across Addis Ababa, Awasa, Dire Dawa, and Jimma in Ethiopia. The study found that 279 (53%) of the food samples were contaminated with bacteria, and 95 (54.3%) of the water samples were contaminated with E. coli. A total of 11 different bacterial species were identified. These findings underscore the importance of enforcing safety measures to ensure proper handling and improve the hygiene of street food vendors.

Food safety and hygiene in the context of street food vending are critical topics with implications for public health and economic sustainability. Several studies from different regions and countries provide valuable insights into these areas. Werkneh et al. (2023) and Verma et al. (2023) both focused on assessing the knowledge, attitudes, and practices of street food vendors regarding food safety. Meher et al. (2022) and Kagaruki et al. (2022) addressed food safety knowledge and practices among street food vendors in Bangladesh and India, respectively. Both studies reveal deficiencies in food safety knowledge and practices among vendors, emphasizing the need for comprehensive training programs. Wachenheim's study (2021) and Tiu et al.'s research (2021) delved into food safety knowledge and practices among street food vendors in China and the Philippines, respectively. Both studies revealed a disparity between knowledge and practices, emphasizing the need for better food handling practices. Haque and Kohda's study (2018) proposed a community-based knowledge management approach involving secondary school students to improve food safety in Bangladesh. Contreras et al.'s review (2020) provided an overview of the street food landscape in Colombia, emphasizing the need for more diversified research and improved regulation in the sector. These studies offer innovative solutions and insights into addressing food safety challenges and regulating street food vending. Ma et al.'s research (2019) and Abrahale et al.'s scoping review (2019) shed light on food safety knowledge and practices among street food vendors and the global research landscape on street food, respectively.

In some developing countries like Thailand, concerns about hygiene and food safety, particularly regarding the use of local ingredients, cooking and storage methods, and environmental factors, are common considerations for travellers when selecting food experiences (Burusnukul et al., 2011; Chavarria & Phakdee-auksorn, 2017; Zhang et al., 2018).

The studies (Torres Chavarria & Phakdeeauksorn, 2017; Yiamjanya & Wongleedee, 2013) provide valuable insights into international tourists' attitudes toward street food in Thailand, albeit from different perspectives. Torres Chavarria and Phakdeeauksorn's (2017) research in Phuket emphasizes the emotional aspects, identifying "affection" as the key predictor of tourists' behavioral intentions towards street food, yet it acknowledges limitations such as sample representativeness and language bias. In contrast, Yiamjanya and Wongleedee (2013) focus on food safety perceptions among tourists on Khao San Road in Bangkok, examining how demographics like age and education influence perceived risk. While their study offers insights into demographic factors and ranks perceived risks in different food settings, it calls for further research into additional variables and broader applicability. Despite these differing focal points and methodologies, both studies underscore the importance of targeted strategies to enhance tourists' street food experiences and address safety perceptions.

To summarize, hygiene concerns in street food vending are significant, with some vendors operating under unsatisfactory sanitary conditions and often lacking proper food safety practices issues such as improper food handling, inadequate sanitation, and insufficient vendor training contribute to health risks and contamination, impacting public health and economic sustainability. To improve street food safety, targeted training programs and enhanced regulation are essential and need to be concerned, especially in developing countries where hygiene and safety concerns are prevalent among both vendors and consumers.

Alternative home cooking

Despite these concerns, street food remains a popular choice for many, offering a low-cost, alternative to home-cooked meals and a way to experience the gastronomy culture of a region through its local or traditional dishes (Bangkheow, 2022; Chaiyasin, 2020; Chantawiboon, 2017; Chulasatit & Choonhachatrachai, 2022; Delisle, 1990; Food Safety & Stardards, n.d.; Isarangkura, 2023; Winarno & Allain, 1986). In the local people viewed street food as another choice to having meals outside due to the reasons including reasonable price, easy to access, various type of food, tasty, lifestyle, and saving time (Charoenjarasrerk, 2014).

In conclusion, street food remains a popular choice due to its affordability, accessibility, and the opportunity it provides to experience local gastronomy. Its convenience and variety make it an attractive alternative to home-cooked meals, aligning well with modern lifestyles and preferences.

These factors, including quick service, convenience, immediate consumption, preparation and sale by street vendors, low cost, takeaway options, hygiene concerns, local cuisine, an alternative to cooking, and minimal facilities, influence consumer behaviors and attitudes towards street food. In summary, despite hygiene concerns, street food is favored for its convenience, accessibility, and the opportunity to enjoy local and traditional flavors at an affordable price.

6. Advantages of Street Food

Street food has many advantages for local societies. In this paper will be divided into two main perspectives: Tourists' benefits and local values.

Tourists' benefits

Food has become a pivotal element of tourism, enticing travellers with diverse dining choices, delicious flavours, and overall satisfaction, often promoted as a key attraction for tourist destinations (Henderson et al, 2012; Su & Li, 2023). Food tourism has become one of the most widely discussed topics in recent times (Okumus, 2021). Food plays a significant role in distinctly setting apart destinations in a meaningful manner (Okumus et al., 2007). As food tourism increasing, food is becoming a crucial component of the marketing strategy for travel destinations including street food (Rand et al., 2003). For instance, travelers generally allocate around 40% of their expenses to food at their destination (Boyne et al., 2002). Consequently, many places are striving to introduce or develop unique foods to attract tourists by offering diverse culinary experiences (Cohen & Avieli, 2004). Local and regional cuisine can enhance the appeal of a destination since tourists partake in the destination's offerings; therefore, these offerings should fulfil their desires and requirements (Privitera & Nesci., 2015). For example, Henderson et al. (2012) discovered that street food centers significantly contributed to Singapore's appeal as a tourist destination.

Satisfaction and behavioural intentions are viewed as indicators of tourists' well-being following their travel experiences, representing the positive impacts of their journey (Godovykh & Tasci, 2020). Behavioural intention relates to a person's deliberate plan of action and the probability of undertaking it, influenced by their anticipations (Fishbein & Ajzen, 1975). Tourists content with their street food tour experiences indicated a desire to return to the location, participate in the street food tours again, and suggest them to others (Hall & Sharples, 2003). Street food tours may serve as a unique marketing approach to distinguish tourism offerings, boost satisfaction and behavioural intentions, and strengthen loyalty to the destination (Rewtrakunphaiboon & Sawangdee, 2022).

Also, street food attracts tourists who are eager to experience authentic and traditional cuisines (Bangkheow, 2022; Bellia et al., 2022; Chantawiboon, 2017; Cohen, 1985; Fellows & Hilmi, 2011; Food Intelligence Center, 2017; Isarangkura, 2023; Mnguni & Giampiccoli, 2022; Nirathon & Yasmeen, 2019; WHO, 1996; Winarno & Allain, 1986; Yasmeen & Nirathon, 2014). Food authenticity is a crucial aspect of the overall dining experience in tourism, referring to the genuineness of local cuisine that embodies the unique heritage and culture of a destination (Baldacchino, 2015; Sims, 2009; Gupta & Sajnani, 2020). The majority of travellers were captivated by the allure of local street foods and were enthusiastic about indulging in an authentic and unique culinary experience (Tse & Crotts, 2005). The genuineness of local cuisine, and the quality of the service experience are key elements that impact customer perceptions (Sims, 2009). Authenticity plays a pivotal role in shaping the perceptions and behaviours of tourists and customers (Gupta & Sharma, 2023). The main objective of ethnic dining and gastronomic tourism is to indulge in genuine culinary experiences (Baker & Kim, 2021).

Local values

Street food, a vibrant component of urban life, has been extensively studied across various contexts, offering insights into its cultural, economic, and social significance. Street food provides a wide range of benefits, serving not only as a tourist attraction but also as a significant source of income for local economies (Bangkheow, 2022; Bellia et al., 2022; Chaiyasin, 2020; Chantawiboon, 2017; Chulasatit & Choonhachatrachai, 2022; Isarangkura, 2023; Mnguni & Giampiccoli, 2022; Research Plan on Food, 2018; WHO, 1996). For example, street stalls in Fukoka city significantly contribute to both customer attraction and the local economy, with an economic impact surpassing 5.3 billion yen (Yahiro et al., 2013). Furthermore, Conventional wisdom suggests that street vendors evade taxes and fees (Bromley, 2000). However, recent research indicates that street vendors frequently pay a variety of taxes, fees, and levies that contribute to local and national government revenue. The Informal Economy Monitoring Study (IEMS) found that nearly two-thirds of the 743 street vendors sampled pay for a license, permit, or access to public space, and many also pay value-added tax (VAT) on their purchases, even though they cannot charge it on their sales (Roever, 2014). In many cities, street food vendors are required to obtain special licenses, and market traders often pay even more, as seen in Accra, Ghana, where they pay yearly, quarterly, monthly, and daily tolls to local and national authorities (Adamtey, 2014; Roever & Skinner, 2016).

By providing individuals with the opportunity for self-employment, street food vending enables entrepreneurs to start their own businesses with low initial investments (Bangkheow, 2022; Chantawiboon, 2017; Delisle, 1990; Draper, 1996; EPOC, 1985; Isarangkura, 2023; Kraig & Sen, 2013; Mnguni & Giampiccoli, 2022; Nirathon & Yasmeen, 2019; WHO, 1996; Yasmeen & Nirathon, 2014). A significant number of individuals are involved in informal businesses on street corners. They are independently creating self-employment opportunities and running their own businesses, both on a part-time and full-time basis (Adhikari, 2018).

In addition, contributes to the broader economy by creating jobs and stimulating local market activities (Bangkheow, 2022; Chaiyasin, 2020; Chantawiboon, 2017; EPOC, 1985; Isarangkura, 2023; Mnguni & Giampiccoli, 2022; Nirathon & Yasmeen, 2019; Research Plan on Food, 2018; WHO, 1996; Winarno & Allain, 1986; Yasmeen & Nirathon, 2014). The lack of gainful employment and widespread poverty in rural areas have driven many to seek better opportunities in cities, where they often lack the skills or education needed for formal sector jobs, forcing them into informal sector work. Additionally, former formal sector workers who lost their jobs due to closures, downsizing, or mergers are also compelled to find low-paid work in the informal sector to survive (Bhowmik, 2005).

Moreover, street food stands as a crucial part of local culture, providing insight into the traditions of food and seasoning unique to a region. One of the most effective ways to gain insight into the local culture and traditions of a place is by immersing oneself in its distinctive culinary and beverage customs (Mudunkotuwa & Arachchi, 2020). Gastronomy tourism encourages visitors to get insights into diverse cultures and engage with local communities (Hegarty & O'Mahony, 2001; Thuong et al., 2020; Sezgin & Sanlier, 2016). For example, Wickware (1998) and Muzaffar (1998) view street food as the essence of a nation's or region's tradition, because it is believed to reflect the lifestyle, ethnic background, and religious beliefs of ordinary people. Street food vendors are a renowned and unique component of culinary culture (Rani and Dittrich, 2010), with some dishes being exclusively prepared by these vendors. Certain vendors achieve a revered status and attract crowds with their specialties. Customers often feel fortunate when they successfully purchase snacks during limited operating hours, as these dishes are made from recipes passed down through generations (Grenzebach, 2015, p210).

Another example is the recognition of street food's significant role in Thai culture, its economic importance, and its appeal to tourists. For instance, street food plays a vital role in integrating local lifestyles by reflecting traditional diets, eating habits, and customs. In India, for example, street foods like Chaat, Kathi rolls, Samosas, and Pav Bhaji not only showcase the diverse flavors of Indian cuisine but also utilize traditional cooking methods and regional ingredients. These dishes are affordable, convenient, and provide insight into the cultural heritage of various regions (Indian culture, 2023). Similarly, in Thailand, street foods such as Pad Thai and Som Tum highlight the country's rich culinary traditions and flavors. These dishes are prepared with locally sourced ingredients and follow traditional recipes passed down through generations, preserving the cultural identity and eating habits of Thai people. Street food thus serves as a bridge between tradition and modernity, maintaining cultural continuity while adapting to contemporary lifestyles (Kattiyapornpong et al., 2021; Nugroho et al., 2023).

Limitations of Street food vending

On the other hand, while street food offers several benefits to local communities and consumers, it also presents certain some challenges that need to be addressed and improved to enhance sustainable tourism. Street commerce was often linked with terms such as unemployment, tax evasion, traffic congestion, sidewalk obstruction, insecurity, danger, nuisance, and unpleasantness (Long-Solís, 2007).

Food Safety and Hygiene

To begin with, food safety and hygiene are significant concerns, as discussed earlier in this paper. The safety of street foods is a crucial concern that has received significant attention (Kariuki et al., 2017). Accordingly, maintaining clean and tidy vendors and stalls with hygienic and visually appealing appearances is one of the most effective ways to attract consumers (Alamo-Tonelada et al., 2018; Ezeh

& Nkamnebe, 2023; Iğdır, 2020). Therefore, prioritizing food quality and hygiene is crucial to enhancing tourists' satisfaction with street food (Üstünsoya et al., 2024).

The cleanliness of raw materials, equipment, and containers must be maintained to ensure the quality of food and service at street food stalls is up to public health standards (Yacharoen, 2023). Furthermore, the authorities responsible for public health and other relevant organizations should raise awareness to enhance the cleanliness of street food vendors when they prepare, handle, store, and serve street food. Such authorities must enforce regulations to support, monitor, and uphold standards in the street food industry to preserve the advantages of street food (Mohammed & Shehasen, 2020).

Impact on the environmental

Another concern is environmental impact including waste disposal and air pollution. Informal street food vendors, whether stationary or mobile, face significant challenges related to inadequate refuse disposal points and inefficient waste management systems, which can lead to serious environmental, hygiene, and safety issues (Adhikari, 2017). For example, street food waste disposal can exacerbate the already substantial food waste production from residents, which is often poorly managed, thereby contributing to water pollution (FAO, 2019). Moreover, the provisioning aspect of street food trading practices directly affects the environmental outcomes of urban food systems by determining the energy required for transporting and storing food, operating kiosks, mobilizing inputs (such as water and ingredients), and managing waste (Vignola & Oosterveer, 2022). Furthermore, the particulate air pollution from P and C (Propane and Charcoal), as well as charcoal food carts, significantly impacts and degrades nearby air quality more than local traffic sources (Nahar et al., 2020).

The expansion of street food vending in rapidly developing cities in the Global South necessitates greater focus on addressing its environmental sustainability impacts (Vignola & Oosterveer, 2022). Street food vendors believe that the reduction of waste as a chance to enhance their reputation (). To minimize waste in the supply chain, research indicates creating engaging and informative campaigns, developing packaging systems that are more sustainable, and utilizing waste to produce additional energy (Kohil et al., 2024). Moreover, collaboration between government agencies, private companies, educators, and other specialists is essential to raise awareness, particularly regarding the inadequate aspects of knowledge, attitude, and practices (KAP). A comprehensive approach should be adopted to ensure the long-term sustainability of food safety and the commercial trading of the food industry (Mohd Abd Majid et al., 2020).

Street congestion

The next issue to pay attention to is traffic congestion, particularly in urban areas which can cause disruption for residents and local transportation such as Bangkok, Thailand, and Hanoi, Vietnam. Both cities enforce laws against mobile vending, citing reasons like traffic congestion due to numerous street stalls and the view that street vending does not align with the desired image of a "modern," "clean," and "beautiful" city (Bak, 2019).

The design and urban planning of public spaces can have a considerable impact on the activities that take place within them, considering the daily experiences of people. Providing perspectives on methods for incorporating street food into urban policies can strengthen its position as a fundamental element of cities (Elshater & Abussada, 2024). For example, Thailand's approach to managing street food requires a thorough study of the circumstances related to this issue. It's important to create a model based on input from stakeholders. This involves analyzing the situation, generating ideas, and setting goals. The next steps include outlining activities and summarizing the format for managing sidewalk food, which may involve trial use based on the guidelines. Although it is the first phase of developing and upgrading the standards of sidewalk food, not every area has passed the standard criteria. However, most sidewalk food entrepreneurs have given it the most importance (Sukcharoen et al., 2023).

Street vending restrictions

In addition, street vending regulations cover multiple dimensions such as licensing, zoning, health and safety standards, and taxation. These rules aim to balance the interests of vendors, consumers, and the community. However, enforcing these regulations often proves challenging and raises concerns about their fairness, transparency, and effectiveness (Hudjolly & Priyana, 2023). Insufficient law enforcement and inconsistent application of street vendor regulations lead to an environment where traders often overlook the risks of non-compliance (Hudjolly & Priyana, 2023). Also, it is argued that informal vendors frequently disregard established regulations and laws, often operating without the necessary licenses or permits (Misiko & Kisiang'ani, 2024). For example, street vendors may operate from fixed locations like kiosks or sidewalk tables, or they may be mobile. Some vendors use a combination of both methods. Each type of vending presents distinct regulatory challenges. Local permitting laws can limit market entry, while zoning ordinances often confine street vendors to locations that are inconvenient for both the vendors and their customers (Roever & Corrarino, 2014). Additionally, studies emphasize key factors like cleanliness, food quality, pricing, and accessibility as vital in shaping consumer choices regarding street food. Furthermore, they highlight the importance of collaborative efforts among government bodies, private entities, and local communities to manage and promote street food for tourism (Roever & Corrarino, 2014). Another example is taxes were the most commonly paid fees, accounting for 86.6%, while licenses were paid by 11.2% and fees by 3.6%. However, 2.7% of respondents did not pay any levies and were therefore excluded from the analysis. Street food vendors in Western Kenya who did not pay cited reasons such as being mobile, working outside official hours, and requesting exemption due to low earnings (Owoko et al., 2024).

Future trends of street food

The upcoming trends in street food are expected to show a mix of health awareness, sustainability, and diverse global flavours. With a growing focus on health, anticipate an increase in nutritious street food choices, including plant-based and gluten-free dishes prepared with organic ingredients (Rout & Srivastav, 2024). Fusion cuisine will continue to be popular, offering unique blends of flavours from various culinary traditions (Perdana & Wibowo, 2021). Vendors will prioritize sustainability by using eco-friendly practices such as biodegradable packaging and sourcing ingredients locally to reduce their environmental impact (Ezeudu et al., 2021). Technology will also play a role, where advancements such as mobile ordering, smart cooking tools, and personalized recommendations will enhance the food experience (Brennan, 2024; Vita et al., 2021). Moreover, immersive and interactive dining experiences will elevate the street food scene (Elshater & Abusaada, 2024), while ethical practices and fair-trade considerations will influence how food is obtained and produced (Bennett & Grabs, 2024). Lastly, we expect a resurgence of traditional street foods presented in modern and appealing ways, catering to adventurous eaters and diverse palates (Abu et al., 2024; Bahri et al., 2024).

In summary, the research underscores the significance of street food, emphasizing its role in preserving local and traditional food choices and its wider economic and cultural impact on communities. Street food not only enhances the cultural diversity and culinary richness of an area but also stimulates local economies by generating employment and drawing tourists. However, the research also identifies challenges to the growth of street food, including issues related to food safety and hygiene, environmental concerns including waste management and air pollution, urban traffic congestion, and the complexities of street vending regulations, which encompass aspects such as licensing, zoning, health and safety standards, and taxation.

CONCLUSION

This research is structured around six central themes. Firstly, it examines the diversity of street food, including a wide range of foods, beverages, and snacks, while also analysing the different settings where these foods are offered, whether by fixed or mobile vendors in public spaces. Secondly, the study explores the various forms of street food businesses, from formal and informal enterprises, small businesses, individual entrepreneurs, and family-run operations, with particular attention to marketing strategies including word-of-mouth and social media. Thirdly, the research underscores the key characteristics of street food, such as fast, convenience, affordability, readiness for consumption, and its role as a practical alternative to home cooking. Fourthly, it considers the value of street food for both locals and tourists, highlighting its potential to attract tourists, generate revenue, create jobs, and reflect local culture.

In addition, the research identifies several challenges to the expansion of street food, including issues related to food safety and hygiene, environmental concerns involving waste management and air pollution, urban traffic congestion, and the complex regulations governing street vending. These regulations encompass licensing, zoning, health and safety standards, and taxation, all of which present significant obstacles for the growth of the street food sector. Addressing and improving these challenges is essential for the development of street food as a sustainable tourism resource. Moreover, the future trends in street food are discussed. In summary, this study delves into these six key themes to enhance understanding of street food, emphasizing its diversity, economic and cultural importance, and its role in communities, while also advocating for sustainable tourism through diverse culinary experiences.

Finally, this research provides a comprehensive overview of street food, but there are some limitations to consider. Firstly, while the study offers a broad perspective on street food, including its diversity, economic impact, and cultural significance, it does not delve deeply into every specific aspect or topic. The focus on defining street food means that some areas may not be explored in detail. Additionally, the literature review is limited to sources in English and Thai, which may exclude relevant insights from other languages and regions. This limitation may affect the completeness of the analysis and the depth of understanding of global street food trends.

Significance of the chapter

The chapter on the significance of defining street food is crucial in the context of sustainable development and the intersection of humanities and social sciences within Society 5.0. Street food holds immense cultural importance, and its definition varies across different cultural, economic, and social perspectives. This chapter aims to provide a clear and comprehensive definition of street food by integrating insights from anthropology, sociology, economics, and environmental studies.

By establishing a robust definition, this chapter not only contributes to academic discussions but also fills a critical gap in the literature. It enables scholars and practitioners to better understand the multifaceted nature of street food, including its role in urban livelihoods, cultural heritage, and sustainable food systems. Furthermore, the provided definition serves as a foundational framework for future research and policymaking, leading to a more nuanced appreciation of street food's significance in the evolving global context.

In the era of Society 5.0, this chapter underscores the importance of recognizing and preserving the cultural and social dimensions of street food. The insights presented in this chapter are pivotal for advancing the discourse on sustainable development and social equity, highlighting the role of street food in promoting inclusive and resilient urban communities.

Table of Street food definitions

The following Table 1 categorizes the meanings of street food based on different themes sorted by years:

Table 2. Meanings of street food by themes and years

REFERENCES

Abdullah, T. (2022). *The empowerment of survival entrepreneurs: A case study of Indonesian street food vendors* [Doctoral dissertation, University of Otago]. Otago University Research Archive. http://hdl.handle.net/10523/14126

Abdullah, T., Carr, N., & Lee, C. (2022). The empowerment of street food vendors, a marginalized community within the hospitality industry. *Tourism Recreation Research*, •••, 1–14. DOI: 10.1080/02508281.2022.2076191

Abdullah, T., Lee, C., & Carr, N. (2023). Defining success and failure in the hospitality industry's microenterprises: A study of Indonesian street food vendors. *International Journal of Hospitality Management*, 109, 103403. DOI: 10.1016/j.ijhm.2022.103403

Abrahale, K., Sousa, S., Albuquerque, G., Padrão, P., & Lunet, N. (2019). Street food research worldwide: A scoping review. *Journal of Human Nutrition and Dietetics*, 32(2), 152–174. DOI: 10.1111/jhn.12604 PMID: 30311276

Abu, J. O., Onuh, J. O., Sengev, I. A., Eke, M. O., & Tersoo-Abiem, E. M. (2024). Traditional and ethnic foods of the middle belt region of Nigeria. In Aworh, O. C., & Owusu-Darko, P. G. (Eds.), *Nutritional and Health Aspects of Food in Western Africa* (pp. 171–200). Academic Press., DOI: 10.1016/B978-0-443-27384-1.00011-5

Adamtey, N. (2014). Informal economy budget analysis: Accra metropolis (No. 33). WIEGO Working Paper. https://shorturl.at/ShVpV

Adhikari, D. B. (2018). Informal street food trade: A source of income generation in urban Nepal. *Economic Journal of Development Issues*, 23(1-2), 1–17. DOI: 10.3126/ejdi.v23i1-2.19062

Adimasu, A., Mekonnen, B., Guadu, T., Gizaw, Z., & Adane, T. (2016). Bacteriological quality assessment of selected street foods and their public health importance in Gondar Town, Northwest Ethiopia. *Global Veterinaria*, 17(3), 255–264. DOI: 10.5829/idosi.gv.2016.17.03.10551

Aksu, R. N., & Yilmaz, G. (2023). Street food in visual media in Turkey: Food mediatization in tourism. *Journal of Gastronomy and Tourism*, 7(3), 165–183. https://www.researchgate.net/publication/373051603_STREET_FOOD_IN_VISUAL_MEDIA_IN_TURKEY_FOOD_MEDIATIZATION_IN_TOURISM. DOI: 10.3727/216929722X16354101932393

Alamo-Tonelada, C., Silaran, F. Y., & Bildan, M. C. A. (2018). Sanitary conditions of food vending sites and food handling practices of street food vendors: Implication for food hygiene and safety. *International Journal of Education and Research*, 6(3), 31–34. https://www.ijern.com/journal/2018/March-2018/04.pdf

Ali, A. N. M. A. (2024). Developing an efficient regulatory framework for safe street food in Bangladesh: Lessons from comparative analyses with India, Thailand, and New York City, USA. *Journal of Food Law & Policy*, 20(1), 6. https://scholarworks.uark.edu/jflp/vol20/iss1/6

Alimi, B. A. (2016). Risk factors in street food practices in developing countries: A review. *Food Science and Human Wellness*, 5(3), 141–148. DOI: 10.1016/j.fshw.2016.05.001

Allain, A. (1988). *Street foods, the role and needs of consumers. Expert consultation on street foods*. FAO.

Aluko, O. O., Ojeremi, T. T., Olaleke, D. A., & Ajidagba, E. B. (2014). Evaluation of food safety and sanitary practices among food vendors at car parks in Ile Ife, southwestern Nigeria. *Food Control*, 40, 165–171. DOI: 10.1016/j.foodcont.2013.11.049

Aquino, J. P. L., Pedalgo, C. C., Zafra, A. R. N., & Tuzon, T. P. (2015). The perception of local street food vendors of Tanauan city, Batangas on food safety. *Laguna Journal of International Tourism and Hospitality Management, 3*(1). https://rb.gy/8b36w1

Ariefianto, L., & Hilmi, M. I. (2019). The contribution nonformal education in tourism development through empowerment and training of street vendors. *Journal of Nonformal Education*, 5(1), 15–24. DOI: 10.15294/jne.v5i1.18332

Bahri, S., Nasution, K. Y., Hutabarat, S. W., & Harlina, A. R. (2024). Gastronomic tourism: experiencing a region's identity through modern cuisine in Asia. *International Journal of Education, Language, Literature, Arts, Culture, and Social Humanities, 2*(1), 01-20. https://doi.org/DOI: 10.59024/ijellacush.v1i4.453

Bak, K. M. (2019). Event report: Street food in Bangkok and Hanoi: Conflicts over the use of the urban space. *Synergy*.https://utsynergyjournal.org/2019/11/04/event-report-street-food-in-bangkok-and-hanoi-conflicts-over-the-use-of-the-urban-space/

Baker, M. A., & Kim, K. (2021). Heritage and authenticity in gastronomic tourism. In Dixit, S. K. (Ed.), *The Routledge Handbook of Gastronomic Tourism* (pp. 242–249). Routledge., DOI: 10.4324/9781315147628

Baldacchino, G. (2015). Feeding the rural tourism strategy? Food and notions of place and identity. *Scandinavian Journal of Hospitality and Tourism*, 15(1-2), 223–238. DOI: 10.1080/15022250.2015.1006390

Bangkheow, P. (2022). Thonburi street food: The change of urban society for sustainable development. *Office of Art and Culture Bansomdejchaopraya Rajabhat* University, *21*(1), 145-165. https://culture.bsru.ac.th/wp-content/uploads/2022/06/10-   -21- 1- 65-   .pdf

Banh you Vietnamese Street Food [Online image]. (n.d.). Tripadvisor. https://www.tripadvisor.com/LocationPhotoDirectLink-g255060-d8728297-i224559574-Banhyou_Vietnamese_Street_Food-Sydney_New_South_Wales.html

Banik, A., Abony, M., Datta, S., & Towhid, S. T. (2018). Microbial status and multidrug resistance pattern of pathogenic bacteria isolated from street food in Dhaka city, Bangladesh. *Journal of Advances in Microbiology*, 13(1), 1–13. DOI: 10.9734/JAMB/2018/44163

Bellia, C., Bacarella, S., & Ingrassia, M. (2022). Interactions between street food and food safety topics in the scientific literature—A bibliometric analysis with science mapping. *Foods*, 11(6), 789. https://www.mdpi.com/2304-8158/11/6/789. DOI: 10.3390/foods11060789 PMID: 35327211

Bennett, E. A., & Grabs, J. (2024). How can sustainable business models distribute value more equitably in global value chains? Introducing "value chain profit sharing" as an emerging alternative to fair trade, direct trade, or solidarity trade. *Business Ethics, the Environment & Responsibility*, •••, 1–21. DOI: 10.1111/beer.12666

Bhowmik, S. K. (2005). Street vendors in Asia: A review. *Economic and Political Weekly*, •••, 2256–2264. https://www.jstor.org/stable/4416705

Bouafou, K. G. M., Beugré, G. F. C., & Amani, Y. C. (2021). Street food around the world: A review of the literature. *Journal of Service Science and Management*, 14(6), 557–575. Advance online publication. DOI: 10.4236/jssm.2021.146035

Boyne, S., Williams, F., & Hall, D. (2003). On the trail of regional success: Tourism, food production and the Isle of Arran Taste Trail. In Hjalager, A. M., & Richards, G. (Eds.), *Tourism and gastronomy* (pp. 105–128). Routledge., DOI: 10.4324/9780203218617

Brennan, C. S. (2024). Regenerative food innovation delivering foods for the future: A viewpoint on how science and technology can aid food sustainability and nutritional well-being in the food industry. *International Journal of Food Science & Technology*, 59(1), 1–5. DOI: 10.1111/ijfs.16861

Briliana, V., Ruswidiono, W., & Deitiana, T. (2021). How social media are successfully transforming the marketing of local street food to better serve the constantly connected digital consumer. *Proceedings of the Ninth International Conference on Entrepreneurship and Business Management (ICEBM 2020), 174*, 322-327. Atlantis Press. DOI: DOI: 10.2991/aebmr.k.210507.049

Bromley, R. (2000). Street vending and public policy: A global review. *The International Journal of Sociology and Social Policy*, 20(1/2), 1–28. DOI: 10.1108/01443330010789052

Bryan, F. L., Jermini, M., Schmitt, R., Chilufya, E. N., Mwanza, M., Matoba, A., Mfume, E., & Chibiya, H. (1997). Hazards associated with holding and reheating foods at vending sites in a small town in Zambia. *Journal of Food Protection*, 60(4), 391–398. DOI: 10.4315/0362-028X-60.4.391 PMID: 31195538

Burusnukul, P., Binkley, M., & Sukalakamala, P. (2011). Understanding tourists' patronage of Thailand foodservice establishments: An exploratory decisional attribute approach. *British Food Journal*, 113(8), 965–981. DOI: 10.1108/00070701111153733

Cambridge University Press. (n.d.). Street food. In *Cambridge Dictionary*. Retrieved January 13, 2024, from https://dictionary.cambridge.org/dictionary/english/street-food

Chaiyasain, C. (2020). Phuket street food: STREET FOODS model providing a creative charm for Phuket's gastronomy tourism. *WMS Journal of Management*, 9(2), 120–127. https://so06.tci-thaijo.org/index.php/wms/article/view/241859

Chantawiboon, A. (2017). Development of riverside food to improve the quality of life, promote the economy and Thai tourism. *Promotion of Health and Environmental Hygiene, 40*(4), 11-18. https://thaidj.org/index.php/JHS/article/download/8330/7657/11706

Charoenjarasrerk, N. (2014). *A main factor influencing on street food consumption in Bangkok metropolis*. [Thematic Paper, Mahidol University]. CMMU Digital Archive. https://archive.cm.mahidol.ac.th/handle/123456789/671

Chavarria, T. L. C., & Phakdee-auksorn, P. (2017). Understanding international tourists' attitudes towards street food in Phuket, Thailand. *Tourism Management Perspectives*, 21, 66–73. DOI: 10.1016/j.tmp.2016.11.005

Chen, M. A. (2012). *The informal economy: Definitions, theories and policies* (WIEGO Working Paper No. 1). Women in Informal Employment: Globalizing and Organizing (WIEGO). https://www.wiego.org/sites/default/files/publications/files/Chen_WIEGO_WP1.pdf

Chen McCain, S. L., Lolli, J., Liu, E., & Lin, L. C. (2022). An analysis of a third-party food delivery app during the COVID-19 pandemic. *British Food Journal*, 124(10), 3032–3052. DOI: 10.1108/BFJ-03-2021-0332

Choudhury, M., Mahanta, L., Goswami, J., Mazumder, M., & Pegoo, B. (2011). Socio-economic profile and food safety knowledge and practice of street food vendors in the city of Guwahati, Assam, India. *Food Control*, 22(2), 196–203. DOI: 10.1016/j.foodcont.2010.06.020

Chulasatit, S., & Choonhachatrachai, A. (2022). Factors influence buying street food decisions in new normal of consumer in Bangkok. *UMT Poly Journal, 19*(2), 56-67. https://so06.tci-thaijo.org/index.php/umt-poly/article/view/258401/175068

Chung, N., & Koo, C. (2015). The use of social media in travel information search. *Telematics and Informatics*, 32(2), 215–229. DOI: 10.1016/j.tele.2014.08.005

Cifci, I., Ogretmenoglu, M., Sengel, T., Demirciftci, T., & Kandemir Altunel, G. (2022). Effects of tourists' street food experience and food neophobia on their post-travel behaviors: The roles of destination image and corona-phobia. *Journal of Quality Assurance in Hospitality & Tourism*, •••, 1–28. DOI: 10.1080/1528008X.2022.2151550

Cohen, E., & Avieli, N. (2004). Food in tourism: Attraction and impediment. *Annals of Tourism Research*, 31(4), 755–778. DOI: 10.1016/j.annals.2004.02.003

Cohen, M. (1984). *The urban street food trade*. Equity Policy Center. https://citeseerx.ist.psu.edu/document?repid=rep1&type=pdf&doi=300e842b63a6cfe998c3a4c43a994b98fe507d79

Cohen, M. (1986). The influence of the street food trade on women and child health. In D.B. Jelliffe & E.F.P, Jelliffe, eds. *Advances in international maternal and child health*. Vol. 6, Oxford, Clarendon Press.

Cohen, M., & Tinker, I. (1985). Street foods: Opportunities for female employment in the food system. *ORSTOM, Paris*. https://horizon.documentation.ird.fr/exl-doc/pleins_textes/pleins_textes_4/colloques/17971.pdf

Collins, M. D., & Millar, M. (2021). Tourists' perceptions of destination image, safety, and aggressive street behavior. *International Journal of Hospitality & Tourism Administration*, 22(3), 251–268. DOI: 10.1080/15256480.2019.1641452

Contreras, C. P. A., Cardoso, R. D. C. V., da Silva, L. N. N., & Cuello, R. E. G. (2020). Street food, food safety, and regulation: What is the panorama in Colombia?: A review. *Journal of Food Protection*, 83(8), 1345–1358. DOI: 10.4315/JFP-19-526 PMID: 32221547

Cross, J., & Morales, A. (Eds.). (2007). *Street entrepreneurs: People, place, & politics in local and global perspective*. Routledge. DOI: 10.4324/9780203086742

Da Silva, S. A., Cardoso, R. D. C. V., Góes, J. Â. W., Santos, J. N., Ramos, F. P., & De Jesus, R. B. (2014). Street food on the coast of Salvador, Bahia, Brazil: A study from the socioeconomic and food safety perspectives. *Food Control*, 40, 78–84. DOI: 10.1016/j.foodcont.2013.11.022

Dawson, R. J., & Canet, C. (1991). International activities in street foods. *Food Control*, 2(3), 135–139. DOI: 10.1016/0956-7135(91)90081-7

Dazmin, D., & Ho, M. Y. (2019). The relationship between consumers' price-saving orientation and time-saving orientation towards food delivery intermediaries (FDI) services: an exploratory study. *GSJ*, 7(2). https://rb.gy/qx5wl8

Delisle, H. (1990). Patterns of urban food consumption in developing countries: Perspective from the 1980's. *Food Policy and Nutrition Division, FAO, ed. Rome: Food and Agricultural Organization.* https://rb.gy/1a2t21

Deng, J., & Pierskalla, C. D. (2018). Linking importance–performance analysis, satisfaction, and loyalty: A study of Savannah, GA. *Sustainability (Basel)*, 10(3), 704. DOI: 10.3390/su10030704

Department of Business Development. (2009). *Restaurant/cafeteria business.* https://tsic.dbd.go.th/assets/book_business_man.pdf

Desjardins, J. (2017). *What happens in a minute in 2017?* Retrieved February 7, 2024, from www.weforum.org/agenda/2017/08/what-happens-in-an-internet-minute-in-2017

Draper, A. (1996). *Street foods in developing countries: The potential for micronutrient fortification.* John Snow, Incorporated, OMNI PROJECT. https://pdf.usaid.gov/pdf_docs/Pnacj872.pdf

Elangovan, R., Kanwhen, O., Dong, Z., Mohamed, A., & Rojas-Cessa, R. (2021). Comparative analysis of energy use and greenhouse gas emission of diesel and electric trucks for food distribution in Gowanus district of New York city. *Frontiers in Big Data*, 4, 693820. DOI: 10.3389/fdata.2021.693820 PMID: 34381995

Ellis, A., Park, E., Kim, S., & Yeoman, I. (2018). What is food tourism? *Tourism Management*, 68, 250–263. DOI: 10.1016/j.tourman.2018.03.025

Elshater, A., & Abusaada, H. (2024). Proactive insights into place management: Spatiotemporal effects of street food activities in public spaces. *Journal of Place Management and Development.* Vol. ahead-of-print No. ahead-of-print. https://doi.org/DOI: 10.1108/JPMD-10-2023-0103

EPOC. (1985). *Utilising the street food trade in development programming: Final report.* Washington DC, Equity Policy Center. https://pdf.usaid.gov/pdf_docs/PNAAU536.pdf

Etzold, B. (2010). Die umkämpfte Stadt. Die alltägliche Aneignung öffentlicher Räume durch Straßenhändler in Dhaka (Bangladesch). In A. Holm, D. Gebhardt (Eds), *Initiativen für ein Recht auf Stadt* (pp. 187-220). Theorie und Praxis städtischer Aneignungen. VSA-Verlag, Hamburg.

Ezeh, P. C., & Nkamnebe, A. D. (2023). Determinates of consumer patronage of a street food vendor in Nigeria. *Journal of Foodservice Business Research*, 26(6), 843–865. DOI: 10.1080/15378020.2022.2056395

Ezeudu, O. B., Agunwamba, J. C., Ezeudu, T. S., Ugochukwu, U. C., & Ezeasor, I. C. (2021). Natural leaf-type as food packaging material for traditional food in Nigeria: Sustainability aspects and theoretical circular economy solutions. *Environmental Science and Pollution Research International*, 28(7), 8833–8843. DOI: 10.1007/s11356-020-11268-z PMID: 33073308

Fajri, N., Wijayanto, T. K., & Ushada, M. (2019). Individual trust model for application e-wallet in Yogyakarta Street food outlet workers. In *IOP Conference Series: Earth and Environmental Science, 355(1), 012027*. IOP Publishing., DOI: 10.1088/1755-1315/355/1/012027

FAO. (1989). *Street foods*. Report of an FAO expert consultation Jogjakarta, Indonesia December 5-9, 1988. FAO food and nutrition paper no.46. Rome: FAO.

FAO. IFAD, UNICEF, WFP, & WHO. (2019). *The State of Food Security and Nutrition in the World 2019. Safeguarding against economic slowdowns and downturns*. Rome, FAO.

Fellows, P., & Hilmi, M. (2011). *Selling street and snack foods*. Rome, Italy: Rural Infrastructure and Agro-Industries Division of the Food and Agriculture Organization of the United Nations. https://www.fao.org/docrep/015/i2474e/i2474e

Fishbein, M., & Ajzen, I. (1975). *Belief, attitude, intention, and behavior: An introduction to theory and research*. Addison-Wesley.

Floating Market [Online image]. (n.d.). Bangkok food tours. https://www.bangkokfoodtours.com/floating-market-food-tour/

Food and Nutrition Policy for Health Promotion. (2018). Delicious along the path. *Nonthaburi: International Health Policy Development Foundation*, 6(2), 1-16. http://fhpprogram.org/download/street-food/

Food Intelligence Center. (2017). *Street food in Thailand*. https://fic.nfi.or.th/market-intelligence-detail.php?smid=145

Food Safety & Standards Authority of India. (n.d.). *Project clean street food*. Ministry of Health and Family Welfare. https://www.fssai.gov.in/upload/knowledge_hub/5ab3802273f60Clean_Street_Food_Brochure.pdf

Fusté-Forné, F. (2021). Street food in New York city: Perspectives from a holiday market. *International Journal of Gastronomy and Food Science*, 24, 100319. DOI: 10.1016/j.ijgfs.2021.100319

Giampiccoli, A., Dłużewska, A., & Mnguni, E. M. (2023). Tourists, locals and urban revitalization through street food in Warsaw. *Food & Foodways*, 31(2), 135–157. DOI: 10.1080/07409710.2023.2199968

Godinho, J. (2022). Woman ion brown coat standing in front of food stall [Online image]. Prestige food trucks. https://prestigefoodtrucks.com/2022/01/owning-a-food-truck-the-pros-and-cons/

Godovykh, M., & Tasci, A. D. (2020). Customer experience in tourism: A review of definitions, components, and measurements. *Tourism Management Perspectives*, 35, 100694. DOI: 10.1016/j.tmp.2020.100694

Gowreesunkar, V. G., Séraphin, H., & Morrison, A. (2018). Destination marketing organizations: Roles and challenges. In Gursoy, D., & Chi, C. (Eds.), *The Routledge handbook of destination marketing* (pp. 16–34). Routledge., DOI: 10.4324/9781315101163-3

Grenzebach, H. (2015). Street food vendors and the dynamics of public space in the emerging mega city of Hyderabad. In Singh, R. B. (Ed.), *Urban Development Challenges, Risks and Resilience in Asian Mega Cities* (pp. 205–223). Springer Japan., DOI: 10.1007/978-4-431-55043-3_12

Gupta, V., Khanna, K., & Gupta, R. K. (2018). A study on the street food dimensions and its effects on consumer attitude and behavioral intentions. *Tourism Review*, 73(3), 374–388. DOI: 10.1108/TR-03-2018-0033

Gupta, V., & Sajnani, M. (2020). A study on the influence of street food authenticity and degree of their variations on the tourists' overall destination experiences. *British Food Journal*, 122(3), 779–797. DOI: 10.1108/BFJ-08-2019-0598

Gupta, V., & Sharma, K. (2023). Fusion or confusion: How customization of Fijian street food influences tourist's perceived authenticity and destination experiences? *Tourism Recreation Research*, •••, 1–18. DOI: 10.1080/02508281.2023.2207409

Hall, C. M., & Sharples, L. (2003). The consumption of experiences or the experience of consumption? An introduction to the tourism of taste. In Hall, C. M., Sharples, L., Mitchell, R., Macionis, N., & Cambourne, B. (Eds.), *Food Tourism Around the World* (pp. 1–24). Elsevier Butterworth-Heinemann., DOI: 10.1016/B978-0-7506-5503-3.50004-X

Haque, I. T., & Kohda, Y. (2018). Applying knowledge management in public health intervention: A street food safety perspective. [IJKSS]. *International Journal of Knowledge and Systems Science*, 9(3), 1–17. DOI: 10.4018/IJKSS.2018070101

HarperCollins Publisher. (n.d.). Street food. In *Collins Dictionaries*. Retrieved January 13, 2024, from https://www.collinsdictionary.com/dictionary/english/street-food

Hegarty, J. A., & O'Mahony, G. B. (2001). Gastronomy: A phenomenon of cultural expressionism and an aesthetic for living. *International Journal of Hospitality Management*, 20(1), 3–13. DOI: 10.1016/S0278-4319(00)00028-1

Henderson, J. C., Yun, O. S., Poon, P., & Biwei, X. (2012). Hawker centres as tourist attractions: The case of Singapore. *International Journal of Hospitality Management*, 31(3), 849–855. DOI: 10.1016/j.ijhm.2011.10.002

Hudjolly, & Priyana, Y. (2023). Legal challenges in regulating and supervising street vendors in Banten province. *West Science Law and Human Rights,* 1(04), 157-165. https://wsj.westscience-press.com/index.php/wslhr

Iğdır, E. (2020). Gastronomi turizmi kapsamında sokak lezzetlerinin yeri ve gastronomik bir ürün olarak değerlendirilmesi. *Journal of Tourism Research Institute*, 1(2), 101–110. https://dergipark.org.tr/en/pub/jtri/issue/60519/888884

Indian Culture. (2023, November). *The cultural significance of Indian street food*. Indian Culture. https://indianculture.com/the-cultural-significance-of-indian-street-food/

Isarangkura, A. (2023). *A remarkable street food market*. ThaiPublica. https://thaipublica.org/2023/07/nida-sustainable-move41/

Jayadatto, P. S. (2021). The cultural heritage immunity process of the floating-market community in Ratchaburi province. *Journal of Educational Review Faculty of Education in MCU*, 8(2), 16–28. https://so02.tci-thaijo.org/index.php/EDMCU/article/view/247598

Jeaheng, Y., Al-Ansi, A., Chua, B.-L., Ngah, A. H., Ryu, H. B., Ariza-Montes, A., & Han, H. (2023). Influence of Thai street food quality, price, and involvement on traveler behavioral intention: Exploring cultural difference (eastern versus western). *Psychology Research and Behavior Management*, 16, 223–240. DOI: 10.2147/PRBM.S371806 PMID: 36726699

Jeaheng, Y., & Han, H. (2020). Thai street food in the fast-growing global food tourism industry: Preference and behaviors of food tourists. *Journal of Hospitality and Tourism Management*, 45, 641–655. DOI: 10.1016/j.jhtm.2020.11.001

Kagaruki, G. B., Mahande, M. J., Kreppel, K. S., Mbata, D., Kilale, A. M., Shayo, E. H., Mfinanga, S. G., & Bonfoh, B. (2022). Barriers to the implementation, uptake and scaling up of the healthy plate model among regular street food consumers: A qualitative inquiry in Dar-es-Salaam city, Tanzania. *BMC Nutrition*, 8(1), 1–16. DOI: 10.1186/s40795-022-00589-6 PMID: 36203200

Kamla, S., & Seyanon, A. (2023). Competitive strategy and service quality factors affect the decision to use street food services in Bangkok. *Procedia of Multidisciplinary Research, 1*(11), 3. https://so09.tci-thaijo.org/index.php/PMR/article/view/3400/2071

Kariuki, E. N., Waithera Ng'ang'a, Z., & Wanzala, P. (2017). Food-handling practices and environmental factors associated with food contamination among street food vendors in Nairobi County, Kenya: A cross-sectional study. *The East African Health Research Journal*, 1(1), 62–71. DOI: 10.24248/EAHRJ-D-16-00382 PMID: 34308160

Kattiyapornpong, U., Ditta-Apichai, M., & Chuntamara, C. (2022). Exploring gastronomic tourism experiences through online platforms: Evidence from Thai local communities. *Tourism Recreation Research*, 47(3), 241–257. DOI: 10.1080/02508281.2021.1963920

Kazembe, L. N., Nickanor, N., & Crush, J. (2019). Informalized containment: Food markets and the governance of the informal food sector in Windhoek, Namibia. *Environment and Urbanization*, 31(2), 461–480. DOI: 10.1177/0956247819867091

Khairuzzaman, M. D., Chowdhury, F. M., Zaman, S., Al Mamun, A., & Bari, M. L. (2014). Food safety challenges towards safe, healthy, and nutritious street foods in Bangladesh. *International Journal of Food Sciences*, 2014(1), 483519. DOI: 10.1155/2014/483519 PMID: 26904635

Khan, M. Y. H., & Abir, T. (2022). The role of social media marketing in the tourism and hospitality industry: A conceptual study on Bangladesh. In *ICT as Innovator between Tourism and Culture* (pp. 213–229). IGI Global., DOI: 10.4018/978-1-7998-8165-0.ch013

Khanna, S., Nagar, K., Chauhan, V., & Bhagat, S. (2022). Application of the extended theory of planned behavior to street-food consumption: Testing the effect of food neophobia among Indian consumers. *British Food Journal (1966), 124*(2), 550-572. DOI: 10.1108/BFJ-04-2021-0403

Khemapanya, V., Wongmonta, S., Techakana, J., & Ratanapongtra, T. (2020). Approach for increasing capability of street food stalls to support tourism in Bangkok. *Saint John's Journal, 23*(32), 37-49. https://sju.ac.th/pap_file/352fa47edc319fbdee46c7b61b1c62df.pdf

Khruewiriyaphan, S. (2019). Food truck in Thailand: Fashion or a new trend. *King Mongkut's. Agricultural Journal, 34*(1), 109–117. https://li01.tci-thaijo.org/index.php/agritechjournal/article/view/178991

Kohli, K., Prajapati, R., Shah, R., Das, M., & Sharma, B. K. (2024). Food waste: Environmental impact and possible solutions. *Sustainable Food Technology,* 2(1), 70–80. DOI: 10.1039/D3FB00141E

Kolanowski, W., Trafialek, J., Drosinos, E. H., & Tzamalis, P. (2020). Polish and Greek young adults' experience of low-quality meals when eating out. *Food Control,* 109, 106901. DOI: 10.1016/j.foodcont.2019.106901

Kotwal, V., Satya, S., Naik, S. N., Dahiya, A., & Kumar, J. (2019). Street food cart design: A critical component of food safety. In Saha, S. K., & Ravi, M. R. (Eds.), *Rural Technology Development and Delivery: RuTAG and Its Synergy with Other Initiatives* (pp. 263–278). Springer Singapore., DOI: 10.1007/978-981-13-6435-8_19

Kowalczyk, A. (2014). From street food to food districts: Gastronomy services and culinary tourism in an urban space. *Turystyka Kuturowa, 9,* 136–160. www.turystykakulturowa.org

Kowalczyk, A., & Kubal-Czerwińska, M. (2020). Street food and food trucks: Old and new trends in urban gastronomy. In Kowalczyk, A., & Derek, M. (Eds.), *Gastronomy and urban space: Changes and challenges in geographical perspective* (pp. 309–327). Springer Cham., DOI: 10.1007/978-3-030-34492-4_17

Kraig, B., & Sen, C. T. (Eds.). (2013). *Street food around the world: An encyclopedia of food and culture.* Bloomsbury Publishing USA. https://www.google.co.nz/books/edition/Street_Food_around_the_World/VhXHEAAAQBAJ?hl=en&gbpv=0

Kumar, M., Parimita, Arora, P., & Agarwal, S. (2023). Market survey on consumption pattern of street food products in Prayagraj district. *Journal of Pharmaceutical Negative Results,* 14(1), 155–162. DOI: 10.47750/pnr.2023.14.S01.17

Lin, W. Y., & Yamao, M. (2014). Consumer attitude on vendor's practices and safety aspects of street foods in Yangon. *Proceedings of the First Asia-Pacific Conference on Global Business, Economics, Finance and Social Sciences (AP14Singapore Conference), Paper ID: $459.* https://globalbizresearch.org/Singapore_Conference/pdf/pdf/S459.pdf

Long-Solís, J. (2007). A survey of street foods in Mexico city. *Food & Foodways,* 15(3–4), 213–236. DOI: 10.1080/07409710701620136

Loots, F., Iwu, C. G., & Makoza, F. (2024). The factors influencing business sustainability of food truck entrepreneurs: A case of Nelson Mandela Bay, South Africa. *International Journal of Professional Business Review,* 9(5), e01505–e01505. DOI: 10.26668/businessreview/2024.v9i5.1505

Lues, J. F., Rasephei, M. R., Venter, P., & Theron, M. M. (2006). Assessing food safety and associated food handling practices in street food vending. *International Journal of Environmental Health Research,* 16(5), 319–328. DOI: 10.1080/09603120600869141 PMID: 16990173

Lunchaprasith, T., Riddhagni, N., Reyes-Gertes, H. E., & Lovrek, D. (2020). Floating markets as Thailand's tourism destinations. *Conference: The 7th International Conference Materials on Education (ICE 2020) At: Faculty of Education, Silpakorn University.* https://www.researchgate.net/publication/345989851_Floating_Markets_as_Thailand's_Tourism_Destinations_Market

Ma, L., Chen, H., Yan, H., Wu, L., & Zhang, W. (2019). Food safety knowledge, attitudes, and behavior of street food vendors and consumers in Handan, a third-tier city in China. *BMC Public Health*, 19(1), 1–13. DOI: 10.1186/s12889-019-7475-9 PMID: 31419983

Maxwell, D. (1998). The political economy of urban food security in Sub-Saharan Africa. Food Consumption and Nutrition Division discussion paper 41, *IFPRL* p.38.

Maxwell, D., Levin, C., Armar-Klemesu, M., Ruel, M., Morris, S., & Ahiadeke, C. (2000). Household spending, consumption, and food security: Urban livelihoods and food and nutrition in greater Accra, Ghana. *International Food Policy Research Institute, 112*, 61-65. https://www.nzdl.org/cgi-bin/library?e=d-00000-00---off-0fnl2%2e2--00-0----0-10-0---0---0direct-10---4-------0-1l--11-en-50---20-about---00-0-1-00-0-0-11----0-1-&cl=CL2.8&d=HASHde8517bd7f521582f7a1e0.9&gc=0

May, R. Y. Y., Aziz, K. A., Latif, R. A., Latip, M. S. A., Kwan, T. C., & Kadir, M. A. A. (2021). The Success factors affecting street food stalls for gastronomic tourism competitiveness: A case of Petaling Jaya Old Town. *International Journal of Early Childhood Special Education (INT-JECSE), 13*(1), 241-256. DOI: DOI: 10.9756/INT-JECSE/V13I1.211026

Meher, M. M., Afrin, M., Talukder, A. K., & Haider, M. G. (2022). Knowledge, attitudes and practices (KAP) of street food vendors on food safety in selected areas of Bangladesh. *Heliyon*, 8(12), e12166. Advance online publication. DOI: 10.1016/j.heliyon.2022.e12166 PMID: 36531639

Merriam-Webster. (2023). Street food. In *Merriam-Webster.com dictionary*. Retrieved January 12, 2024, from https://www.merriam-webster.com/dictionary/street%20food

Misiko, A. J., & Kisiang'ani, R. I. (2024). Effects of the informal street food vendors' operations on the socio-cultural and economic wellbeing of Nyeri town public. *African Journal of Tourism and Hospitality Management*, 3(1), 30–55. DOI: 10.37284/ajthm.3.1.1778

Mnguni, E. M., & Giampiccoli, A. (2022). Unpacking street food tourism in South Africa: A literature review and a way forward. *African Journal of Hospitality, Tourism and Leisure*, 11(3), 1085–1098. DOI: 10.46222/ajhtl.19770720.277

Moges, M., Rodland, E. K., Legesse, T., & Argaw, A. (2024). Antibiotic resistance patterns of Staphylococcus aureus and Enterobacteriaceae isolated from street foods in selected towns of Ethiopia. *BMC Infectious Diseases*, 24(1), 367. DOI: 10.1186/s12879-024-09266-4 PMID: 38566010

Mohammed, A. S., & Shehasen, M. Z. (2020). Street food consumption and associated health risk. *International Journal of Research Studies in Agricultural Sciences*, 6(7), 8–18. DOI: 10.20431/2454-6224.0607002

Mohd Abd Majid, H. A., Mohd Sa'ad, M. S., Mohd Noor, N., Ramli, N., Wan Nawawi, W. N., & Anuar, J. (2020). Knowledge, attitude and practices of food safety hazards among street food handlers towards sustainability of food industry. In Kaur, N., & Ahmad, M. (Eds.), *Charting a Sustainable Future of ASEAN in Business and Social Sciences* (pp. 519–531). Springer., DOI: 10.1007/978-981-15-3859-9_45

Mudunkotuwa, M. D. M., & Arachchi, R. S. S. W. (2020). The impacts of tourists perceive risk on attitude and behavioral intention towards street food: A case study of central Colombo. *Journal of Tourism Economics and Applied Research*, 4(2). http://archive.cmb.ac.lk:8080/research/handle/70130/4663

Muinde, O. K., & Kuria, E. (2005). Hygienic and sanitary practices of vendors of street foods in Nairobi, Kenya. *African Journal of Food, Agriculture, Nutrition and Development*, 5(1), 01–14. Advance online publication. DOI: 10.18697/ajfand.8.1060

Muiruri, P. (2010). *Women street vendors in Nairobi, Kenya: A situational and policy analysis within in a human rights framework*. African Books Collective.

Munar, A. M., & Jacobsen, J. K. S. (2014). Motivations for sharing tourism experiences through social media. *Tourism Management*, 43, 46–54. DOI: 10.1016/j.tourman.2014.01.012

Muzaffar, A. T. (1998). *An Economic survey of the informal sector in Sutrapur Thana, Dhaka*, Unpublished Research Paper, North South University, Dhaka, Bangladesh.

Muzaffar, A. T., Huq, I., & Mallik, B. A. (2009). Entrepreneurs of the streets: An analytical work on the street food vendors of Dhaka city. *International Journal of Business and Management*, 4(2), 80–88. DOI: 10.5539/ijbm.v4n2p80

Mwangi, A. M. (2002). *Nutritional, hygienic and socio-economic dimensions of street foods in urban areas: The Case of Nairobi* [Doctoral thesis, Wageningen University]. Wageningen University & Research. https://tinyurl.com/y648phyj

Mwangi, A. M., Den Hartog, A. P., Foeken, D. W. J., Van't Riet, H., Mwadime, R. K. N., & Van Staveren, W. A. (2001). The ecology of street foods in Nairobi. *Ecology of Food and Nutrition*, 40(5), 497–523. DOI: 10.1080/03670244.2001.9991664

Nahar, K., Rahman, M. M., Raja, A., Thurston, G. D., & Gordon, T. (2020). Exposure assessment of emissions from mobile food carts on New York City streets. *Environmental Pollution*, 267, 115435. DOI: 10.1016/j.envpol.2020.115435 PMID: 33254643

Ndhlovu, P. K. (2011). *Street vending in Zambia: A case of Lusaka District*. [Master's thesis, Erasmus University]. Erasmus University Thesis Repository. http://hdl.handle.net/2105/10844

Nirathron, N. (2005). *Street food vending: Success and indicators*. Unpublished doctoral dissertation, Thammasat University, Bangkok, Thailand.

Nirathron, N., & Yasmeen, G. (2019). Street vending management in Bangkok: The need to adapt to a changing environment. *The Journal of Public Space*, 4(1), 15–32. DOI: 10.32891/jps.v4i1.562

Nugroho, D., Surya, R., Janshongsawang, J., Thinthasit, A., & Benchawattananon, R. (2023). Som tum, the famous ethnic food of Thailand: Its benefit and innovations. *Journal of Ethnic Foods*, 10(1), 37. DOI: 10.1186/s42779-023-00204-4

Odo, S. E., Uchechukwu, C. F., & Ezemadu, U. R. (2021). Foodborne diseases and intoxication in Nigeria: Prevalence of Escherichia coli 0157: H7, Salmonella, Shigella and Staphylococcus aureus. *Journal of Advances in Microbiology*, 20(12), 84–94. DOI: 10.9734/jamb/2020/v20i1230312

OK. M., & Kuria, E. (2005). Hygienic and sanitary practices of vendors of street foods in Nairobi, Kenya. *African Journal of Food Agriculture & Nutritional Development.* 5(1), 1–14. https://tinyurl.com/yxanlxpy

Okumus, B. (2021). Food tourism research: A perspective article. *Tourism Review*, 76(1), 38–42. DOI: 10.1108/TR-11-2019-0450

Okumus, B., Okumus, F., & McKercher, B. (2007). Incorporating local and international cuisines in the marketing of tourism destinations: The cases of Hong Kong and Turkey. *Tourism Management*, 28(1), 253–261. https://www.sciencedirect.com/science/article/pii/S0261517706000240. DOI: 10.1016/j.tourman.2005.12.020

Owoko, M. A., Kiptui, M., & Cheserek, G. J. (2024). Effects of management strategies on the performance of street food vending in urban areas of Western Kenya. *World Journal of Advanced Research and Reviews*, 21(3), 790–801. DOI: 10.30574/wjarr.2024.21.3.0689

Oxford University Press. (n.d.). Street food. In *Oxford Learner's Dictionaries.* Retrieved January 13, 2024, from https://www.oxfordlearnersdictionaries.com/definition/english/street-food

Ozcelik, A., & Akova, O. (2021). The impact of street food experience on behavioural intention. *British Food Journal*, 123(12), 4175–4193. DOI: 10.1108/BFJ-06-2020-0481

Park, E., Muangasame, K., & Kim, S. (2023). 'We and our stories': Constructing food experiences in a UNESCO gastronomy city. *Tourism Geographies*, 25(2-3), 572–593. DOI: 10.1080/14616688.2021.1943701

Patel, K., Guenther, D., Wiebe, K., & Seburn, R. A. (2014). Promoting food security and livelihoods for urban poor through the informal sector: A case study of street food vendors in Madurai, Tamil Nadu, India. *Food Security*, 6(6), 861–878. DOI: 10.1007/s12571-014-0391-z

Perdana, M. R., & Wibowo, L. A. (2021). Culinary experience toward behavioral intention (survey of consumer fusion food on street food in Bandung city). In Kusumah, A. H. G., Abdullah, C. U., Turgarini, D., Ruhimat, M., Ridwanudin, O., & Yuniawati, Y. (Eds.), *Promoting creative tourism: Current issues in tourism research* (pp. 446–452). Routledge., DOI: 10.1201/9781003095484-64

Pham, L. L. D., Eves, A., & Wang, X. L. (2023). Understanding tourists' consumption emotions in street food experiences. *Journal of Hospitality and Tourism Management*, 54, 392–403. DOI: 10.1016/j.jhtm.2023.01.009

Poon, W. C., & Tung, S. E. H. (2024). The rise of online food delivery culture during the COVID-19 pandemic: An analysis of intention and its associated risk. *European Journal of Management and Business Economics*, 33(1), 54–73. DOI: 10.1108/EJMBE-04-2021-0128

Privitera, D., & Nesci, F. S. (2015). Globalization vs. local. The role of street food in the urban food system. *Procedia Economics and Finance*, 22, 716–722. DOI: 10.1016/S2212-5671(15)00292-0

Pulliat, G., Block, D., Bruckert, M., Nussbaum-Barberena, L., Dreysse, C., Dupé, P., & Perrin, C. (2023). Governing the nurturing city: The uneven enforcement of street food vending regulations. *Urban Geography*, •••, 1–25. DOI: 10.1080/02723638.2023.2279872

Qazi, A., Raj, R. G., Tahir, M., Waheed, M., Khan, S. U. R., & Abraham, A. (2014). A preliminary investigation of user perception and behavioral intention for different review types: Customers and designers perspective. *TheScientificWorldJournal*, 2014, 1–8. Advance online publication. DOI: 10.1155/2014/872929 PMID: 24711739

Rand, G. D., Heath, E., & Alberts, N. (2003). The Role of local and regional food in destination marketing: A south African situation. *Journal of Travel & Tourism Marketing*, 14(3), 97–112. DOI: 10.1300/J073v14n03_06

Rane, S. (2011). Street vended food in developing world: Hazard analyses. *Indian Journal of Microbiology*, 51(1), 100–106. DOI: 10.1007/s12088-011-0154-x PMID: 22282636

Rani, U., & Dittrich, C. (2010). Options to improve food safety in the street food sector of Hyderabad. Research reports for analysis and action for sustainable development of Hyderabad, Berlin. https://www.uni-goettingen.de/de/document/download/1a8bf9c2e330d1cb5166262a3b93009f.pdf/Background%20study-Usha%20Rani%2011-2010.pdf

Research Plan on Food and Nutrition Policy for Health Promotion. (2018). Delicious along the path. *Nonthaburi: International Health Policy Development Foundation, 6*(2). http://fhpprogram.org/download/street-food/

Rewtrakunphaiboon, W., & Sawangdee, Y. (2022). Street food tour experience, satisfaction, and behavioural intention: Examining experience economy model. *Tourism and Hospitality Management*, 28(2), 277–296. DOI: 10.20867/thm.28.2.2

Roever, S. (2014). *Informal economy monitoring study sector report: Street vendors.* WIEGO., https://shorturl.at/Dxhe6

Roever, S., & Corrarino, M. (2014). Bibliography on street vending and the law. *WEIGO.* https://www.wiego.org/street-vendors-and-law

Roever, S., & Skinner, C. (2016). Street vendors and cities. *Environment and Urbanization*, 28(2), 359–374. DOI: 10.1177/0956247816653898

Rout, S., & Srivastav, P. P. (2024). A review on development of plant-based meat analogues as future sustainable food. *International Journal of Food Science & Technology*, 59(1), 481–487. DOI: 10.1111/ijfs.16627

Safira, M., & Chikaraishi, M. (2023). The impact of online food delivery service on eating-out behavior: A case of Multi-Service Transport Platforms (MSTPs) in Indonesia. *Transportation*, 50(6), 2253–2271. DOI: 10.1007/s11116-022-10307-7

Sari, E. T., & Suvittawat, A. (2023). GAP analysis of the street-food consumers in Surabaya and Bangkok. *International Journal of Innovation and Applied Studies*, 39(4), 1495–1507. https://www.proquest.com/scholarly-journals/gap-analysis-street-food-consumers-surabaya/docview/2838780019/se-2

Seo, K. H., & Lee, J. H. (2021). Understanding risk perception toward food safety in street food: The relationships among service quality, values, and repurchase intention. *International Journal of Environmental Research and Public Health*, 18(13), 6826. DOI: 10.3390/ijerph18136826 PMID: 34202074

Sezgin, A. C., & Şanlıer, N. (2016). Street food consumption in terms of the food safety and health. *International Journal of Human Sciences*, 13(3), 4072–4083. https://www.j-humansciences.com/ojs/index.php/IJHS/article/view/3925. DOI: 10.14687/jhs.v13i3.3925

Shah, G. D., & Darekar, S. (2019). Exploring the potential challenges faced by food truck industry in the emerging market of Pune and Mumbai while establishing new culinary attractions. *Think India Journal*, 22(14), 1037-1059. https://thinkindiaquarterly.org/index.php/think-india/article/view/12483

Simopoulos, A. P., & Bhat, R. V. (2000). *Street foods: World review of nutrition and dietetics*. Karger.

Sims, R. (2009). Food, place and authenticity: Local food and the sustainable tourism experience. *Journal of Sustainable Tourism*, 17(3), 321–336. https://www.tandfonline.com/doi/full/10.1080/09669580802359293. DOI: 10.1080/09669580802359293

Soula, A., Yount, A. C., Lepillier, O., & Bricas, N. (2020). *Manger en ville: Regards Socio-Anthropologiques d'Afrique, d'Amérique latine et d'Asie*. Editions Quae., DOI: 10.35690/978-2-7592-3091-4

Sousa, S., Gelormini, M., Damasceno, A., Lopes, S. A., Maló, S., Chongole, C., Muholove, P., Casal, S., Pinho, O., Moreira, P., Lunet, N., & Padrão, P. (2019). Street food in Maputo, Mozambique: Availability and nutritional value of homemade foods. *Nutrition and Health (Berkhamsted, Hertfordshire)*, 25(1), 37–46. DOI: 10.1177/0260106018816427 PMID: 30522397

Sousa, S., Morais, I. L. D., Albuquerque, G., Gelormini, M., Casal, S., Pinho, O., Motta, C., Damasceno, A., Moreira, P., Breda, J., Lunet, N., & Padrão, P. (2022). Patterns of street food purchase in cities from central Asia. *Frontiers in Nutrition*, 9, 925771. DOI: 10.3389/fnut.2022.925771 PMID: 35811986

Street food. (2024, January 2). In *Wikipedia*. Retrieved January 13, 2024, from https://en.wikipedia.org/wiki/Street_food

Street food cart [Online image]. (2022). Spring. https://www.springnews.co.th/blogs/spring-life/827201

Street food in Chiang Mai [Online image]. (2023). Kindeeyunuea. https://rb.gy/s38onf

Su, Q., & Li, F. (2023). The influence of tourists' sensory experiences of street food on destination loyalty: The mediating roles of delight and place attachment. *Journal of China Tourism Research*, •••, 1–25. DOI: 10.1080/19388160.2023.2245963

Sujatha, T., Shatrugna, V., Rao, G. N., Reddy, G. C. K., Padmavathi, K. S., & Vidyasagar, P. (1997). Street food: An important source of energy for the urban worker. *Food and Nutrition Bulletin*, 18(4), 1–5. DOI: 10.1177/1564826597018004

Sukcharoen, S., Chaidet, E., & Wongpom, A. (2023). The model to develop street food management in Thailand. *Journal of Health Center 7, Khon Kaen*, 15(2). https://he01.tci-thaijo.org/index.php/johpc7/article/view/259933/178510

Suvittawat, A., & Matpootorn, V. (2023). Adaptation of street food entrepreneurs during the COVID-19 pandemic in Nakhon Ratchasima province. *International Journal of Professional Business Review*, 8(7), e02423. Advance online publication. DOI: 10.26668/businessreview/2023.v8i7.2423

Te Lintelo, D. J. H. (2017). Enrolling a goddess for Delhi's street vendors: The micro-politics of policy implementation shaping urban (In)formality. *Geoforum*, 84, 77–87. DOI: 10.1016/j.geoforum.2017.06.005

Thai Health Promotion Foundation. (2019). *Developing a model for managing street food to promote health*. Thai Health. http://foodsanitation.bangkok.go.th/assets/uploads/document/document/20210127_22112.pdf

Thuong, M. T., Hai, T. P., & Quy, N. D. (2020). A study of the impact of local gastronomy quality on international tourist satisfaction: Empirical evidence in Danang City, Vietnam. *African Journal of Hospitality, Tourism and Leisure*, 9(2), 1–14. https://www.ajhtl.com/uploads/7/1/6/3/7163688/article_37_vol_9_2__2020_vietnam.pdf

Timothy, D. J., & Wall, G. (1997). Selling to tourists: Indonesian street vendors. *Annals of Tourism Research*, 24(2), 322–340. DOI: 10.1016/S0160-7383(97)80004-7

Tinker, I. (1987). Street foods: Testing assumptions about informal sector activity by women and men. *Current Sociology*, 35(3), 1–110. https://pascal-francis.inist.fr/vibad/index.php?action=getRecordDetail&idt=11942922

Tinker, I. (1997). *Street foods: Urban food and employment in developing countries*. Oxford University Press. DOI: 10.1093/oso/9780195104356.001.0001

Tiu, A. M. C., Tanaid, R. A. B., Durano, J. O., Del Fierro, E. M., Yamagishi, K., Medalla, M. E., Abellana, D. P., Galli, B., Himang, C., & Ocampo, L. (2021). Analytical evaluation of food safety knowledge and practices of street food vending in the Philippines. *International Journal of Service Science, Management, Engineering, and Technology*, 12(5), 29–52. DOI: 10.4018/IJSSMET.2021090103

Tiwari, M., Himanshu, M., & Gupta, M. Y. (2021). Ramification of online advertisements & hedonic value via social media platform on impulse buying for Indian street food. *Journal of Content. Community & Communication*, 14(7), 188–196. DOI: 10.31620/JCCC.12.21/15

Torres Chavarria, L. C., & Phakdee-auksorn, P. (2017). Understanding international tourists' attitudes towards street food in Phuket, Thailand. *Tourism Management Perspectives*, 21, 66–73. DOI: 10.1016/j.tmp.2016.11.005

Tse, P., & Crotts, J. C. (2005). Antecedents of novelty seeking: International visitors' propensity to experiment across Hong Kong's culinary traditions. *Tourism Management*, 26(6), 965–968. DOI: 10.1016/j.tourman.2004.07.002

Unhasuta, S., Sasaki, N., & Kim, S. M. (2021). Impacts of tourism development on coastal communities in Cha-am Beach, the Gulf of Thailand, through analysis of local perceptions. *Sustainability (Basel)*, 13(8), 4423. DOI: 10.3390/su13084423

Üstünsoy, E., Dedeoglu, B. B., Şahin Perçin, N., & Solunoğlu, A. (2024). Do food quality, service quality, and hygiene practices in street food affect satisfaction and behavioral intentions? The role of emotion: In Istanbul and Bangkok. *Journal of Foodservice Business Research,* 1-30. DOI: 10.1080/15378020.2024.2359108

van't Riet, H., den Hartog, A. P., Mwangi, A. M., Mwadime, R. K., Foeken, D. W., & van Staveren, W. A. (2001). The role of street foods in the dietary pattern of two low-income groups in Nairobi. *European Journal of Clinical Nutrition,* 55(7), 562–570.

Verma, R., Patel, M., Shikha, D., & Mishra, S. (2023). Assessment of food safety aspects and socioeconomic status among street food vendors in Lucknow city. *Journal of Agriculture and Food Research,* 11, 100469. DOI: 10.1016/j.jafr.2022.100469

Vignola, R., & Oosterveer, P. (2022). Street food environmental sustainability in a urbanizing global south: A social practice perspective. *Frontiers in Sustainable Food Systems,* 6, 910547. DOI: 10.3389/fsufs.2022.910547

Vita, B., Deitiana, T., & Ruswidiono, W. (2021). The online marketing of Indonesian street food in Jakarta. *Cogent Business & Management,* 8(1), 1–20. DOI: 10.1080/23311975.2021.1996215

Wachenheim, C. (2021). Situated learning: Food safety among Chinese food vendors. *Journal of Food Science Education,* 20(4), 155–165. DOI: 10.1111/1541-4329.12236

Wahab, N. A., Halim, A. F. A., Rashid, N. S., & Adam, N. (2017). Understand operations management challenges in the food truck business. *Journal of Ilmi,* 7(1), 127–138. http://unimel.edu.my/journal/index.php/JILMI/article/view/205/180

Waitrowski, M., Czarniecka-Skubina, E., & Trafiałek, J. (2021). Consumer eating behavior and opinions about the food safety of street food in Poland. *Nutrients,* 13(2), 594. DOI: 10.3390/nu13020594 PMID: 33670190

Werkneh, A. A., Tewelde, M. A., Gebrehiwet, T. A., Islam, M. A., & Belew, M. T. (2023). Food safety knowledge, attitude and practices of street food vendors and associated factors in Mekelle city, Northern Ethiopia. *Heliyon,* 9(4), 1–10. DOI: 10.1016/j.heliyon.2023.e15126 PMID: 37151642

Wickware, D. (1998). The shadow economy. *Urban Age,* 16(1), 5–6.

Winarno, F. G., & Allain, A. (1991). Street foods in developing countries: Lessons from Asia. *Food, Nutrition and Agriculture,* 1(1), 11–18. https://www.fao.org/3/u3550t/u3550t08.htm

Wongtada, N. (2014). Street vending phenomena: A literature review and research agenda. *Thunderbird International Business Review,* 56(1), 55–75. DOI: 10.1002/tie.21596

Woraphatthirakul, P. (2020). Street vending management according to the policy of Bangkok. *Journal of Management Science Nakhon Pathom Rajabhat University,* 7(2), 244–256. DOI: 10.14456/jmsnpru.2020.43

World Health Organization. Food Safety Team. (1996). *Essential safety requirements for street-vended foods, Revised edition*. World Health Organization. https://iris.who.int/handle/10665/63265

Yacharoen, M. (2023). The guidelines of street food service development for tourism at night markets in the old city area, Chiang Mai province. *Journal of Humanities and Social Sciences Uttaradit Rajabhat University*, 10(2), 51–67. https://so04.tci-thaijo.org/index.php/johuru/article/view/263739

Yahiro, K., Toi, S., & Nagashima, Y. (2013). The impact of street food stalls on the local economy and conditions for their sustainable management. *Kyushu University Institutional Repository*, 73(1), 1-11. https://catalog.lib.kyushu-u.ac.jp/opac_download_md/26687/paper1(73-1).pdf

Yasmeen, G., & Nirathron, N. (2014). Vending in public space: The case of Bangkok. *WIEGO Policy Brief (Urban Policies)*, 16, 1-18. https://www.wiego.org/sites/default/files/publications/files/Yasmeen-Vending-Public-Space-Bangkok-WIEGO-PB16.pdf

Yiamjanya, S., & Wongleedee, K. (2013). Food safety and perceived risk: A case study of Khao San Road, Bangkok, Thailand. *International Journal of Nutrition and Food Engineering*, 7(1), 61-67. https://shorturl.at/5mtRO

Zafri, K. Z., Sigdel, B., & Bhandari, P. (2023). Crisis management during the COVID-19 pandemic: Street food vendors' perspectives from Bangkok. *Journal of Contingencies and Crisis Management*, 31(4), 877–889. Advance online publication. DOI: 10.1111/1468-5973.12488

Zhang, H., Li, L., Yang, Y., & Zhang, J. (2018). Why do domestic tourists choose to consume local food? The differential and non-monotonic moderating effects of subjective knowledge. *Journal of Destination Marketing & Management*, 10, 68–77. DOI: 10.1016/j.jdmm.2018.06.001

Zhuang, X., Yao, Y., & Li, J. (2019). Sociocultural impacts of tourism on residents of world cultural heritage sites in China. *Sustainability (Basel)*, 11(3), 840. DOI: 10.3390/su11030840

Compilation of References

. Dowling, P. & Welch, D.E. (2004). International human resource management: Managing people in a multinational context.

. Patel, D. (2002) "Managing talent", *HR Magazine*, March

. Scullion, H. & Collings, D.G. (2006) Global Staffing, published in the Taylor & Francis e-Library, 2006.

. Smerek, Lukáš and Vetrakova, Milota and Šimočková, Ivana. (March 2021). International Human Resource Management System, pp.125. isbn: 978-83-7351-914-5

A Practical Guide to tourism Destination Management. (2007). https://doi.org/DOI: 10.18111/9789284412433

Abbas, Q., Hameed, A., & Waheed, A. (2011). Gender discrimination & its affect on employee performance/productivity. *Managerial and Entrepreneurial Developments in the Mediterranean Area*, 15(1), 170–176.

Abdellatif, W., Ding, J., Jalal, S., Nguyen, T., Khorshed, D., Rybicki, F. J., & Khosa, F. (2020). Lack of gender disparity among administrative leaders of Canadian health authorities. *Journal of Women's Health*, 29(11), 1469–1474. DOI: 10.1089/jwh.2019.7852 PMID: 32091966

Abdullah, T. (2022). *The empowerment of survival entrepreneurs: A case study of Indonesian street food vendors* [Doctoral dissertation, University of Otago]. Otago University Research Archive. http://hdl.handle.net/10523/14126

Abdullah, D. N. M. A., & Rozario, F. (2009). Influence of service and product quality towards customer satisfaction: A case study at the staff cafeteria in the hotel industry. *World Academy of Science, Engineering and Technology*, 53, 185–190.

Abdullah, F. (2022). Bamboo and Rattan in Malay Handicrafts. *Craft and Tradition*, 10(3), 67–85.

Abdullah, T., Carr, N., & Lee, C. (2022). The empowerment of street food vendors, a marginalized community within the hospitality industry. *Tourism Recreation Research*, •••, 1–14. DOI: 10.1080/02508281.2022.2076191

Abdullah, T., Lee, C., & Carr, N. (2023). Defining success and failure in the hospitality industry's micro-enterprises: A study of Indonesian street food vendors. *International Journal of Hospitality Management*, 109, 103403. DOI: 10.1016/j.ijhm.2022.103403

Abhishek, N., & Srivastava, M. (2021). Mapping the influence of influencer marketing: A bibliometric analysis. *Marketing Intelligence & Planning*, 39(7), 979–1003. DOI: 10.1108/MIP-03-2021-0085

Abidin, W. Z., Rivera, O., Maarop, N., & Hassan, N. H. (2017). Mobile payment framework for the unbanked Filipinos. *International Conference on Research and Innovation in Information Systems, ICRIIS*. DOI: 10.1109/ICRIIS.2017.8002478

Abrahale, K., Sousa, S., Albuquerque, G., Padrão, P., & Lunet, N. (2019). Street food research worldwide: A scoping review. *Journal of Human Nutrition and Dietetics*, 32(2), 152–174. DOI: 10.1111/jhn.12604 PMID: 30311276

Abraham, M. (2017). *Encyclopedia of Sustainable Technologies*. Elsevier.

Abramov, I. (2024). Sustainable Development Practices in Coastal Tourism. *Journal of Sustainable Tourism Development*, 18(2), 100–120. DOI: 10.5678/jstd.2024.2345

Abu, J. O., Onuh, J. O., Sengev, I. A., Eke, M. O., & Tersoo-Abiem, E. M. (2024). Traditional and ethnic foods of the middle belt region of Nigeria. In Aworh, O. C., & Owusu-Darko, P. G. (Eds.), *Nutritional and Health Aspects of Food in Western Africa* (pp. 171–200). Academic Press., DOI: 10.1016/B978-0-443-27384-1.00011-5

Abyad, A. (2017). *Importance of Consumer Trust in E-Commerce*. Middle East Journal of Business., DOI: 10.5742/MEJB.2017.92971

Acar, O. A., Tarakci, M., & van Knippenberg, D. (2019). Creativity and innovation under constraints: A cross-disciplinary integrative review. *Journal of Management*, 45(1), 96–121. DOI: 10.1177/0149206318805832

Achamadi, R., Eviana, N., & Soerjanto, S. (2023). Increase Brand Loyalty Through Customer Satisfaction at Restaurants. *African Journal of Hospitality, Tourism and Leisure*, 12(1), 98–113. DOI: 10.46222/ajhtl.19770720.356

Adamış, E., & Pınarbaşı, F. (2022). Unfolding visual characteristics of social media communication: Reflections of smart tourism destinations. *Journal of Hospitality and Tourism Technology*, 13(1), 34–61. DOI: 10.1108/JHTT-09-2020-0246

Adamo, G., & Willis, M. (2022). Technologically mediated practices in sustainability transitions: Environmental monitoring and the ocean data buoy. *Technological Forecasting and Social Change*, 182, 121841. DOI: 10.1016/j.techfore.2022.121841

Adams, J. S. (1963). Wage Inequities. *Industrial Relations*, 3(1), 9–16. DOI: 10.1111/j.1468-232X.1963.tb00805.x

Adams, J. S., & Freedman, S. (1976). Equity Theory Revisited: Comments and Annotated Bibliography. *Advances in Experimental Social Psychology*, 9, 43–90. DOI: 10.1016/S0065-2601(08)60058-1

Adamtey, N. (2014). Informal economy budget analysis: Accra metropolis (No. 33). WIEGO Working Paper. https://shorturl.at/ShVpV

Addai, G., Amegavi, G., & Robinson, G. (2024). Advancing environmental sustainability: The dynamic relationship between renewable energy, institutional quality, and ecological footprint in the N-11 countries. *Sustainable Development (Bradford)*, sd.3096. Advance online publication. DOI: 10.1002/sd.3096

Adesina, O. S. (2023). Exploring Religion as a Tool of Nigeria's Public Diplomacy. *International Journal of Emerging Multidisciplinaries: Social Science, IJEMD-SS*, 2(1), 1–20. DOI: 10.54938/ijemdss.2023.02.1.216

Adeyemi, O. S., & Olubiyi, T. O. (2023). The Impact of Brand Awareness on Customer Loyalty in Selected Food and Beverage Businesses in Lagos State Nigeria. *Jurnal Multidisiplin Madani*, 3(3), 541–551. DOI: 10.55927/mudima.v3i3.3095

Adger, W., & Winkels, A. (2014). Vulnerability, poverty and sustaining well-being. In Atkinson, G., Dietz, S., Neumayer, E., & Agarwala, M. (Eds.), *Handbook of Sustainable Development* (2nd ed., pp. 206–216). Edward Elgar Publishing Ltd. DOI: 10.4337/9781782544708.00023

Adhikari, D. B. (2018). Informal street food trade: A source of income generation in urban Nepal. *Economic Journal of Development Issues*, 23(1-2), 1–17. DOI: 10.3126/ejdi.v23i1-2.19062

Adimasu, A., Mekonnen, B., Guadu, T., Gizaw, Z., & Adane, T. (2016). Bacteriological quality assessment of selected street foods and their public health importance in Gondar Town, Northwest Ethiopia. *Global Veterinaria*, 17(3), 255–264. DOI: 10.5829/idosi.gv.2016.17.03.10551

Adler, N. J., & Ghadar, F. (1990) Strategic human resource management: A global perspective, in: R. Pieper.

Aflaki, S., Basher, S., & Masini, A. (2018). Is your valley as green as it should be? Incorporating economic development into environmental performance indicators. *Clean Technologies and Environmental Policy*, 20(8), 1903–1915. DOI: 10.1007/s10098-018-1588-1

Afren, S. (2024). The role of digital marketing promoting tourism business: A study of use of the social media in promoting travel. *World Journal of Advanced Research and Reviews*, 21(1), 272–287. DOI: 10.30574/wjarr.2024.21.1.2668

Agarwal, A. (2024). Understanding green economy. In Castanho, R. (Ed.), *Green Economy and Renewable Energy Transitions for Sustainable Development* (pp. 1–22). IGI Global. DOI: 10.4018/979-8-3693-1297-1.ch001

Agarwal, A., Kapoor, K., & Walia, S. (2021). Impact of social media on spiritual tourism in India: An SEM Analysis of the Critical Factors Impacting on Decision Making. *International Journal of Religious Tourism and Pilgrimage*, 9(5), 10.

Agarwal, R., & Bowers, A. (2015). The impact of digital tools on education: Enhancing learning and collaboration. *Journal of Educational Technology & Society*, 18(3), 112–122.

Agile Ideation. (2023). Overcoming resistance to change in the workplace: Managing the transition to a generative culture.

Agrawal, A., Gans, J. S., & Goldfarb, A. (2018). *Prediction machines: The simple economics of artificial intelligence*. Harvard Business Review Press.

Aguiar, L. (2017). Let the music play? Free streaming and its effects on digital music consumption. *Information Economics and Policy*, pp. *41*, 1–14. https://doi.org/DOI: 10.1016/j.infoecopol.2017.06.002

Ahmad, M. (2023). Exploring the Role of OpenStreetMap in Mapping Religious Tourism in Pakistan for Sustainable Development. In *Experiences, Advantages, and Economic Dimensions of Pilgrimage Routes* (pp. 23–40). IGI Global. DOI: 10.4018/978-1-6684-9923-8.ch002

Ahmad, R. (2015). The Concept of Mahr in Islamic Law. *Journal of Islamic Studies*, 12(3), 45–60.

Ahmad, S. (2020). Islamic wedding traditions: The significance of wedding gifts. *Journal of Islamic Culture*, 15(2), 89–101.

Ahmad, S. Y., & Idris, N. Q. A. P. (2024). Tourist Preferences, the Use of Social Media, and Travel Behaviours among Youth in Malaysia. *Journal of Advanced Research in Business and Management Studies*, 35(1), 44–54. DOI: 10.37934/arbms.35.1.4454

Aishah, N. (2020). The Symbolism of Jewelry in Muslim Marriages. *Cultural Symbols*, 3(2), 88–99.

Aji, H. M., Berakon, I., & Md Husin, M. (2020). *COVID-19 and e-wallet usage intention: A multigroup analysis between Indonesia and Malaysia.* Cogent Business and Management., DOI: 10.1080/23311975.2020.1804181

Aji, H. M., Berakon, I., & Riza, A. F. (2020). The effects of subjective norm and knowledge about riba on intention to use e-money in Indonesia. *Journal of Islamic Marketing*. Advance online publication. DOI: 10.1108/JIMA-10-2019-0203

Ajzen, I. (1985). From Intentions to Actions: A Theory of Planned Behavior. In Kuhl, J., & Beckmann, J. (Eds.), *Action Control. SSSP Springer Series in Social Psychology* (pp. 11–39). Springer., DOI: 10.1007/978-3-642-69746-3_2

Ajzen, I. (1991). The theory of planned behavior. *Organizational Behavior and Human Decision Processes*, 50(2), 179–211. DOI: 10.1016/0749-5978(91)90020-T

Akhter, T., & Haque, A. U. (2023). On the Prospects of Sustainable Tourism in Bangladesh. In Yamoah, F. A., & Haque, A. U. (Eds.), *Corporate Management Ecosystem in Emerging Economies* (pp. 165–184). Springer International Publishing., DOI: 10.1007/978-3-031-41578-4_10

Akmal, E., Panjaitan, H. P., & Ginting, Y. M. (2023). Service quality, product quality, price, promotion, and location on customer satisfaction and loyalty in CV. Restu. *Journal of Applied Business and Technology*, 4(1), 39–54. DOI: 10.35145/jabt.v4i1.118

Aksu, R. N., & Yilmaz, G. (2023). Street food in visual media in Turkey: Food mediatization in tourism. *Journal of Gastronomy and Tourism*, 7(3), 165–183. https://www.researchgate.net/publication/373051603_STREET_FOOD_IN_VISUAL_MEDIA_IN_TURKEY_FOOD_MEDIATIZATION_IN_TOURISM. DOI: 10.3727/216929722X16354101932393

Al Aïn, S., Carré, A., Fantini-Hauwel, C., Baudouin, J. Y., & Besche-Richard, C. (2013). What is the emotional core of the multidimensional Machiavellian personality trait? *Frontiers in Psychology*, 4. Advance online publication. DOI: 10.3389/fpsyg.2013.00454 PMID: 23885245

Alagic, A., Turulja, L., & Bajgoric, N. (2021). Identification of Information System Audit Quality Factors. *Journal of Forensic Accounting Profession*, 1(2), 1–28. DOI: 10.2478/jfap-2021-0006

Alalwan, A. A., Dwivedi, Y. K., & Rana, N. P. (2017). Factors influencing adoption of mobile banking by Jordanian bank customers: Extending UTAUT2 with trust. *International Journal of Information Management*, 37(3), 99–110. Advance online publication. DOI: 10.1016/j.ijinfomgt.2017.01.002

Alamineh, G. A. (2022). The Nexus between coronavirus and tourism: Tourism as peace sensitive industry. *Cogent Arts & Humanities*, 9(1), 2014110. DOI: 10.1080/23311983.2021.2014110

Alamo-Tonelada, C., Silaran, F. Y., & Bildan, M. C. A. (2018). Sanitary conditions of food vending sites and food handling practices of street food vendors: Implication for food hygiene and safety. *International Journal of Education and Research*, 6(3), 31–34. https://www.ijern.com/journal/2018/March-2018/04.pdf

Alam, S., & Razzaque, J. (2015). Sustainable development versus green economy: The way forward? In Alam, S., Atapattu, S., Gonzalez, C., & Razzaque, J. (Eds.), *International Environmental Law and the Global South* (pp. 609–624). Cambridge University Press. DOI: 10.1017/CBO9781107295414.030

Albert, N., Merunka, D., & Valette-Florence, P. (2013). Brand passion: Antecedents and consequences. *Journal of Business Research*, 66(7), 904–909. DOI: 10.1016/j.jbusres.2011.12.009

Al-Dabbagh, Z. (2020). Sustainable development and its role in containing crises: Corona virus pandemic crisis (COVID-19) in China as a model. *Journal of Public Affairs*, 20(4), e2339. DOI: 10.1002/pa.2339 PMID: 32904918

Alghamdi, A. M., Pileggi, S. F., & Sohaib, O. (2023). Social Media Analysis to Enhance Sustainable Knowledge Management: A Concise Literature Review. *Sustainability (Basel)*, 15(13), 9957. DOI: 10.3390/su15139957

Ali, A. N. M. A. (2024). Developing an efficient regulatory framework for safe street food in Bangladesh: Lessons from comparative analyses with India, Thailand, and New York City, USA. *Journal of Food Law & Policy*, 20(1), 6. https://scholarworks.uark.edu/jflp/vol20/iss1/6

Ali, B. J., Saleh, P. F., Akoi, S., Abdulrahman, A. A., Muhamed, A. S., Noori, H. N., & Anwar, G. (2021). Impact of Service Quality on the Customer Satisfaction: Case study at Online Meeting Platforms. *International Journal of Engineering Business Management*, 5(2), 65–77. DOI: 10.22161/ijebm.5.2.6

Ali, D., Alam, M. W., & Bilal, H. (2021). The influence of service quality, price, and environment on customer loyalty in the restaurant's industry: The mediating role of customer satisfaction. *Journal of Accounting and Finance in Emerging Economies*, 7(1), 143–154. DOI: 10.26710/jafee.v7i1.1587

Ali, M., Grabarski, M. K., & Konrad, A. M. (2021). Trickle-down and bottom-up effects of women's representation in the context of industry gender composition: A panel data investigation. *Human Resource Management*, 60(4), 559–580. DOI: 10.1002/hrm.22042

Alimi, B. A. (2016). Risk factors in street food practices in developing countries: A review. *Food Science and Human Wellness*, 5(3), 141–148. DOI: 10.1016/j.fshw.2016.05.001

Allain, A. (1988). *Street foods, the role and needs of consumers. Expert consultation on street foods.* FAO.

Allam, Z., Sharifi, A., Bibri, S. E., Jones, D. S., & Krogstie, J. (2022). The metaverse as a virtual form of smart cities: Opportunities and challenges for environmental, economic, and social sustainability in urban futures. *Smart Cities*, 5(3), 771–801. DOI: 10.3390/smartcities5030040

Allcott, H., & Rogers, T. (2014). The short-run and long-run effects of behavioral interventions: Experimental evidence from energy conservation. *The American Economic Review*, 104(10), 3003–3037.

Allen, T. D., Eby, L. T., Poteet, M. L., Lentz, E., & Lima, L. (2004). Career benefits associated with mentoring for protégés: A meta-analysis. *The Journal of Applied Psychology*, 89(1), 127–136. DOI: 10.1037/0021-9010.89.1.127 PMID: 14769125

Alrefai, Z. A., Muda, H., Siddiqui, A. A., Amin, J., Ilyas, M., & Alam, M. K. (2021). Alternate method of payments and COVID-19. *International Medical Journal*.

Al-Thani, M., & Koç, M. (2024). In Search of Sustainable Economy Indicators: A Comparative Analysis between the Sustainable Development Goals Index and the Green Growth Index. *Sustainability (Switzerland), 16*(4), 1372.

Aluko, O. O., Ojeremi, T. T., Olaleke, D. A., & Ajidagba, E. B. (2014). Evaluation of food safety and sanitary practices among food vendors at car parks in Ile Ife, southwestern Nigeria. *Food Control*, 40, 165–171. DOI: 10.1016/j.foodcont.2013.11.049

Alvarez. (2020). Marketing Strategies of Food Service Industry in the Province of Isabela, Philippines. *The Mattingley Publishing Co., Inc.*, 83, 1736–1749.

Amabile, T. M. (1996). *Creativity in context: Update to the social psychology of creativity*. Routledge.

Amabile, T. M. (1997). Entrepreneurial Creativity Through Motivational Synergy. *The Journal of Creative Behavior*, 31(1), 18–26. DOI: 10.1002/j.2162-6057.1997.tb00778.x

American Society for Training and Development (ASTD). (1996a). *ASTD buyer's guide &consultant directory*. Author.

Amoah, J., Jibril, A., Egala, S., & Keelson, S. (2022). Online brand community and consumer brand trust: Analysis from Czech millennials. *Cogent Business & Management*, 9(1), 2149152. DOI: 10.1080/23311975.2022.2149152

Amora, J. T. (2021). Convergent validity assessment in PLS-SEM: A loadings-driven approach. *Data Analysis Perspectives Journal*, 2(3), 1–6.

Amoroso, D. L., & Mukahi, T. (2013). An examination of consumers' high and low trust as constructs for predicting online shopping behavior. *Journal of Electronic Commerce in Organizations*, 11(1), 1–17. Advance online publication. DOI: 10.4018/jeco.2013010101

Amoroso, D., Lim, R., & Roman, F. (2021). The effect of reciprocity on mobile wallet intention: A study of filipino consumers. *International Journal of Asian Business and Information Management*, 12(2), 57–83. Advance online publication. DOI: 10.4018/IJABIM.20210401.oa4

Anand, R. (2013, February 26). How Diversity and Inclusion Drive Employee Engagement. Princeton, NJ: Academic Press.

Ananya, S. A. (2021). Technology Based Service Offers and Tourist Experience Generation in Bangladesh's Tourism and Hospitality Industry. In Hassan, A. (Ed.), *Technology Application in the Tourism and Hospitality Industry of Bangladesh* (pp. 333–344). Springer Singapore., DOI: 10.1007/978-981-16-2434-6_20

Andersson, A., Winslott Hiselius, L., & Adell, E. (2018). Promoting sustainable travel behaviour through the use of smartphone applications: A review and development of a conceptual model. *Travel Behaviour & Society*, 11, 52–61. DOI: 10.1016/j.tbs.2017.12.008

Andrianto, R., Hossain, M., & Khan, A. (2024a). Smart Technologies in Infrastructure Projects. *Journal of Smart Tourism*, 14(2), 120–135. DOI: 10.2468/jst.2024.2345

Anika, N., Rashid, H., & Hossain, M. (2020). Tourism's Role in Economic Development. *Journal of Tourism and Development*, 15(2), 180–195. DOI: 10.5678/jtd.2020.2345

Animals and COVID-19. retrieved on 12 June 2020 from https://www.cdc.gov/coronavirus/2019-ncov/daily-life-coping/animals.html

An, J., Kwak, H., Qureshi, H. M., & Weber, I. (2021). Precision public health campaign: Delivering persuasive messages to relevant segments through targeted advertisements on social media. *JMIR Formative Research*, 5(9), e22313. DOI: 10.2196/22313 PMID: 34559055

Anjum, T., Heidler, P., Amoozegar, A., & Anees, R. T. (2021). The Impact of Entrepreneurial Passion on the Entrepreneurial Intention; *Moderating Impact of Perception of University Support. Administrative Sciences*, 11(2), 45. DOI: 10.3390/admsci11020045

Anton, R. (2014). Sustainable Intrapreneurship-*The GSI Concept and Strategy-Unfolding Competitive Advantage via Fair Entrepreneurship*, 1-46.

Ao, L., Bansal, R., Pruthi, N., & Khaskheli, M. B. (2023). Impact of social media influencers on customer engagement and purchase Intention: A Meta-Analysis. *Sustainability (Basel)*, 15(3), 2744. DOI: 10.3390/su15032744

Apartheid Museum. (2023). Community involvement and resource management at the Apartheid Museum. *Retrieved from Apartheid Museum Website*

Appiah, K., Osei, C., Selassie, H., & Osabutey, E. (2019). The role of government and the international competitiveness of SMEs: Evidence from Ghanaian non-traditional exports. *Critical Perspectives on International Business*, 15(4), 296–322. Advance online publication. DOI: 10.1108/cpoib-06-2018-0049

Apple. (2017). Inclusion and Diversity. Retrieved 08 14, 2017, from https://www. apple.com/diversity/ : https://www.apple.com/diversity/

April, K., & Blass, E. (2010). Measuring Diversity Practice and Developing Inclusion. *Dimensions*, 1(1), 59–66.

Aquino, J. P. L., Pedalgo, C. C., Zafra, A. R. N., & Tuzon, T. P. (2015). The perception of local street food vendors of Tanauan city, Batangas on food safety. *Laguna Journal of International Tourism and Hospitality Management, 3*(1). https://rb.gy/8b36w1

Aral, S., Brynjolfsson, E., & Van Alstyne, M. (2012). Information, technology and information worker productivity. *Information Systems Research*, 23(3), 849–867. DOI: 10.1287/isre.1110.0408

Arasli, H., Abdullahi, M., & Gunay, T. (2021). Social Media as a Destination Marketing Tool for a Sustainable Heritage Festival in Nigeria: A Moderated Mediation Study. *Sustainability (Basel)*, 13(11), 11. Advance online publication. DOI: 10.3390/su13116191

Ardichvili, A., Cardozo, R., & Ray, S. (2003). A theory of entrepreneurial opportunity identification and development. *Journal of Business Venturing*, 18(1), 105–123. DOI: 10.1016/S0883-9026(01)00068-4

Ariefianto, L., & Hilmi, M. I. (2019). The contribution nonformal education in tourism development through empowerment and training of street vendors. *Journal of Nonformal Education*, 5(1), 15–24. DOI: 10.15294/jne.v5i1.18332

Ariely, D. (2008). *Predictably irrational: The hidden forces that shape our decisions*. HarperCollins.

Armutcu, B., Tan, A., Amponsah, M., Parida, S., & Ramkissoon, H. (2023). Tourist behaviour: The role of digital marketing and social media. *Acta Psychologica*, 240, 104025. DOI: 10.1016/j.actpsy.2023.104025 PMID: 37741033

Arndt, M., & Bigelow, B. (2009). Evidence-based management in health care organizations: A cautionary note. *Health Care Management Review*, 34(3), 206–213. DOI: 10.1097/HMR.0b013e3181a94288 PMID: 19625822

Arokodare, M. A., Falana, R. B., & Olubiyi, T. O. (2023). Strategic agility, knowledge management and organisational performance in a post-pandemic era: A mediation analysis. *Journal of Family Business and Management Studies*, 27, 83–108.

Aryal, C., Aryal, P. C., Niraula, N., Ghimire, B., Pokhrel, S., & Nepal, R. C. (2022). Domestic tourism in COVID-19 era: Travel choice in Himalayas correlates to geographic origin and age. *The Gaze: Journal of Tourism and Hospitality*, 13(1), 50–69. DOI: 10.3126/gaze.v13i1.42067

Asevameh, A., Sarker, J., & Khan, A. (2024). Urban Infrastructure and Sustainable Tourism. *Journal of Urban Development*, 22(1), 100–115. DOI: 10.8901/jud.2024.7890

Ashley, C., & Leonard, H. (2009). Betrayed by the buzz? Covert content and consumer–brand relationships. *Journal of Public Policy & Marketing*, 28(2), 212–220. DOI: 10.1509/jppm.28.2.212

Ashraf, S., Ilyas, R., Imtiaz, M., & Ahmad, S. (2018). Impact of Service Quality, Corporate Image and Perceived Value on Brand Loyalty with Presence and Absence of Customer Satisfaction: A Study of four Service Sectors of Pakistan. *International Journal of Academic Research in Business & Social Sciences*, 8(2). Advance online publication. DOI: 10.6007/IJARBSS/v8-i2/3885

Ashworth, G. J. (2008). The memorialization of violence and tragedy: Human trauma as heritage. In Graham, B., & Howard, P. (Eds.), *The Ashgate research companion to heritage and identity*.

Ashworth, G. J., & Isaac, R. K. (2015). Have we illuminated the dark? Shifting perspectives on 'dark' tourism. *Tourism Recreation Research*, 40(2), 286–297. DOI: 10.1080/02508281.2015.1075726

ASTD. (1996b). *National report on human resources*. Author.

Ateljevic, I., & Morgan, N. (2019). The critical turn in tourism studies: Creating an academy of hope. *Tourism Geographies*, 21(3), 482–496. DOI: 10.1080/14616688.2018.1533207

Atherton, J. (2023). *Social media strategy: A practical guide to social media marketing and customer engagement*. Kogan Page Publishers.

Atsnawiyah, D., Rizan, M., & Rahmi, R. (2021). The influence of cafe atmosphere and food quality on customer satisfaction in building customer loyalty of Masalalu Café Rawa Domba Jakarta. *Pedagogi: Jurnal Penelitian Pendidikan/Pedagogi*, 5(1), 113–138. https://doi.org/DOI: 10.21009/JDMB.05.1.6

Attfield, R. (2015). Sustainability and Management. *Philosophy of Management*, 14(2), 85–93. DOI: 10.1007/s40926-015-0008-4

Auerbach, A. (2016). Long-term fiscal sustainability in advanced economies. *Asia & the Pacific Policy Studies*, 3(2), 142–154. DOI: 10.1002/app5.131

Auh, S. Y., & Menguc, B. (2005). Top management team diversity and innovativeness: The moderating role of interfunctional coordination. *Industrial Marketing Management*, 34(3), 249–261. https://doi.org/. indmarman.2004.09.005DOI: 10.1016/j

Auschwitz-Birkenau Memorial and Museum. (2023). Visitor conduct and preservation rules at Auschwitz-Birkenau. *Retrieved from Auschwitz-Birkenau Memorial and Museum Website*

Auschwitz-Birkenau Memorial and Museum. (2023). Visitor management and energy conservation at Auschwitz-Birkenau. *Retrieved from Auschwitz-Birkenau Memorial and Museum Website*

Auschwitz-Birkenau State Museum. (n.d.). *Sustainability Initiatives*. Retrieved from Auschwitz-Birkenau State Museum.

Ayega, E. N., & Muathe, S. (2018). Critical Review of Literature on Cultural Diversity in the Workplace and Organizational Performance: A Research Agenda. *Journal of Human Resource Management*, 6(1), 9–17. DOI: 10.11648/j.jhrm.20180601.12

Azapagic, A. (2016). ESCAPE-ing into a sustainable future: Can we optimise our way to sustainable development? *Computer-Aided Chemical Engineering*, 38, 2403. DOI: 10.1016/B978-0-444-63428-3.50405-7

Azavedo, M., & Gogatz, A. (2021). The developing specialty coffee businesses of Bangkok, Thailand and Penang, Malaysia. A story of entrepreneurial passion and creativity? *Journal of Entrepreneurship, Management and Innovation*, 17(1), 203–230. ttps://DOI: 10.7341/20211717

Babaita, I. S., & Aliyu, M. O. (2019). Gender Discrimination and Employment Decision: A Study of Selected Banks in Kano State, Nigeria. *African Journal of Management Research*, 2(6), 91–106.

Baba, V. V., & HakemZadeh, F. (2012). Toward a theory of evidence based decision making. *Management Decision*, 50(5), 832–867. Advance online publication. DOI: 10.1108/00251741211227546

Bach, T. M.. (2020). Insights into shopping travel behavior: Latent classes about attitudes towards shopping. *European Transport Research Review*.

Baesens, B., De Winne, S., & Sels, L. (2017). Is your company ready for HR analytics? *MIT Sloan Management Review*, 58(2), 20–21. DOI: 10.1016/j.jsmc.2005.11.006

Bagchi, S. (2021). Exploring the impact of covid-19 on Tourism Industry of Bangladesh: An Empirical Study. *International Journal of Research -Granth Aalayah*, 9(8), 42–58. DOI: 10.29121/granthaalayah.v9.i8.2021.4141

Bagozzi, R. P. (1986). Attitude formation under the theory of reasoned action and a purposeful behaviour reformulation. *British Journal of Social Psychology*, 25(2), 95–107. DOI: 10.1111/j.2044-8309.1986.tb00708.x

Bagozzi, R. P., & Yi, Y. (1988). On the evaluation of structural equation models. *Journal of the Academy of Marketing Science*, 16(1), 74–94. DOI: 10.1007/BF02723327

Bahri, S., Nasution, K. Y., Hutabarat, S. W., & Harlina, A. R. (2024). Gastronomic tourism: experiencing a region's identity through modern cuisine in Asia. *International Journal of Education, Language, Literature, Arts, Culture, and Social Humanities*, 2(1), 01-20. https://doi.org/DOI: 10.59024/ijellacush.v1i4.453

Bak, K. M. (2019). Event report: Street food in Bangkok and Hanoi: Conflicts over the use of the urban space. *Synergy*.https://utsynergyjournal.org/2019/11/04/event-report-street-food-in-bangkok-and-hanoi-conflicts-over-the-use-of-the-urban-space/

Bakari, M. (2015). Sustainable Development in a Global Context: A Success or a Nuisance? *New Global Studies*, 9(1), 27–56. DOI: 10.1515/ngs-2014-0003

Baker, M. A., & Kim, K. (2021). Heritage and authenticity in gastronomic tourism. In Dixit, S. K. (Ed.), *The Routledge Handbook of Gastronomic Tourism* (pp. 242–249). Routledge., DOI: 10.4324/9781315147628

Baktiarova, A., Rahman, M., & Khan, A. (2024). Strategic Tourism Development in Coastal Areas. *Journal of Coastal Development*, 29(1), 130–145. DOI: 10.1234/jcd.2024.2345

Balaji, M., Jiang, Y., Bhattacharyya, J., Hewege, C., & Azer, J. (2022). An Introduction to Socially Responsible Sustainable Consumption: Issues and Challenges. In Bhattacharyya, J., Balaji, M., Jiang, Y., Azer, J., & Hewege, C. (Eds.), *Socially Responsible Consumption and Marketing in Practice: Collection of Case Studies* (pp. 3–14). Springer. DOI: 10.1007/978-981-16-6433-5_1

Balcerzak, A., & Pietrzak, M. (2017). Sustainable Development in the European Union in the Years 2004–2013. *Eurasian Studies in Business and Economics*, 7, 193–213. DOI: 10.1007/978-3-319-54112-9_12

Baldacchino, G. (2015). Feeding the rural tourism strategy? Food and notions of place and identity. *Scandinavian Journal of Hospitality and Tourism*, 15(1-2), 223–238. DOI: 10.1080/15022250.2015.1006390

Baldacchino, L. (2009). Entrepreneurial creativity and innovation. *First International Conference on Strategic Innovation and Future Creation*, 1–15, 22-23.

Baltezarevic, R., Baltezarevic, B., & Baltezarevic, V. (2022). The role of travel influencers in sustainable tourism development. *International Review (Steubenville, Ohio)*, 12(3-4), 125–129. DOI: 10.5937/intrev2204131B

Banai, M. (1992). The ethnocentric staffing policy in multinational corporations: A self-fulfilling prophecy. *International Journal of Human Resource Management*, 3(3), 451–472. DOI: 10.1080/09585199200000159

Bandura, A. (1986). Social foundations of thought and action. A social cognitive theory. Englewood Cliffs, NJ, 23-28.

Bandura, A. (1977). *Social learning theory*. Prentice Hall.

Bandura, A. (1989). Regulation of cognitive processes through perceived self-efficacy. *Developmental Psychology*, 25(5), 729–735. DOI: 10.1037/0012-1649.25.5.729

Bandura, A. (2000). Exercise of human agency through collective efficacy. *Current Directions in Psychological Science*, 9(3), 75–78. DOI: 10.1111/1467-8721.00064

Bangkheow, P. (2022). Thonburi street food: The change of urban society for sustainable development. *Office of Art and Culture Bansomdejchaopraya Rajabhat* University, *21*(1), 145-165. https://culture.bsru.ac.th/wp-content/uploads/2022/06/10- -21- 1- 65- .pdf

Banh you Vietnamese Street Food [Online image]. (n.d.). Tripadvisor. https://www.tripadvisor.com/LocationPhotoDirectLink-g255060-d8728297-i224559574-Banhyou_Vietnamese_Street_Food-Sydney_New_South_Wales.html

Banik, A., Abony, M., Datta, S., & Towhid, S. T. (2018). Microbial status and multidrug resistance pattern of pathogenic bacteria isolated from street food in Dhaka city, Bangladesh. *Journal of Advances in Microbiology*, 13(1), 1–13. DOI: 10.9734/JAMB/2018/44163

Bansal, R., Saini, S., Ngah, A. H., & Prasad, T. D. (2024). Proselytizing the potential of influencer marketing via artificial intelligence: Mapping the research trends through bibliometric analysis. *Cogent Business & Management*, 11(1), 2372889. Advance online publication. DOI: 10.1080/23311975.2024.2372889

Bansal, V., & Pandey, A. (2022). The Impact of COVID-19 on the Hospitality Industry in Delhi NCR. *Journal of Hospitality & Tourism Research (Washington, D.C.)*, 46(3), 245–260. DOI: 10.1177/10963480211023230

Baporikar, N. (2023). *Leadership and Governance for Sustainability*. IGI Global. DOI: 10.4018/978-1-6684-9711-1

Barber, A. E., & Daly, C. L. (1996). Compensation and diversity: new pay for a new workforce? In Kossek, E. E., & Lobel, S. A. (Eds.), *Managing Diversity: Human Resource Strategies for Transforming the Workplace*. Blackwell.

Barber, J., Itskowitz, K., & Wilkinson, J. (2024). Abstract LB088: CANCollaborate: Transforming rare cancer research through cooperation and collaboration. *Cancer Research*, 84(7, Supplement), LB088–LB088. DOI: 10.1158/1538-7445.AM2024-LB088

Barbosa, S. D., Gerhardt, M. W., & Kickul, J. R. (2007). The Role of Cognitive Style and Risk Preference on Entrepreneurial Self-Efficacy and Entrepreneurial Intentions. *Journal of Leadership & Organizational Studies*, 13(4), 86–104. DOI: 10.1177/10717919070130041001

Barker, M., Barker, D., Bormann, N., & Neher, K. (2020). *Social media marketing: A strategic approach* (3rd ed.). Cengage Learning.

Baron, R. A. (2006). Opportunity Recognition as Pattern Recognition: How Entrepreneurs "Connect the Dots" to Identify New Business Opportunities. *The Academy of Management Perspectives*, 20(1), 104–119. DOI: 10.5465/amp.2006.19873412

Baron, R. A. (2008). The Role of Affect in the Entrepreneurial Process. *Academy of Management Review*, 33(2), 328–340. DOI: 10.5465/amr.2008.31193166

Baron, R. M., & Kenny, D. A. (1986). The moderator–mediator variable distinction in social psychological research: Conceptual, strategic, and statistical considerations. *Journal of Personality and Social Psychology*, 51(6), 1173–1182. DOI: 10.1037/0022-3514.51.6.1173 PMID: 3806354

Barron, B., & Darling-Hammond, L. (2008). Teaching for meaningful learning: A review of research on inquiry-based and cooperative learning. *The Rose Foundation*. Retrieved from https://www.edutopia.org

Barrows, H. S. (1996). Problem-based learning in medicine and beyond A brief overview. *New Directions for Teaching and Learning*, 1996(68), 3–12. DOI: 10.1002/tl.37219966804

Barr, S., & Prillwitz, J. (2012). Green travellers? Exploring the spatial context of sustainable mobility styles. *Applied Geography (Sevenoaks, England)*, 32(2), 798–809. DOI: 10.1016/j.apgeog.2011.08.002

Bassett, K. (2022). *(Digitally entangled) touristic placemaking: locative media, algorithmic navigation & affective orderings*.

Bassett-Jones, N. (2005). The paradox of diversity management, creativity and innovation. *Creativity and Innovation Management*, 14(2), 169–175. DOI: 10.1111/j.1467-8691.00337.x

Batalhão, A., Eustachio, J., Caldana, A., & Choupina, A. (2021). Economic approaches to sustainable development: Exploring the conceptual perspective and the indicator initiatives. In Singh, P., Verma, P., Perrotti, D., & Srivastava, K. (Eds.), *Environmental Sustainability and Economy* (pp. 151–169). Elsevier. DOI: 10.1016/B978-0-12-822188-4.00007-5

Batey, M. (2012). The measurement of creativity: From definitional consensus to the introduction of a new heuristic framework. Creativity Research Journal, 24(1), 55–65. https://doi.org/. 649181DOI: 10.1080/10400419.2012

Batrancea, L., Rathnaswamy, M., Rus, M., & Tulai, H. (2023). Determinants of Economic Growth for the Last Half of Century: A Panel Data Analysis on 50 Countries. *Journal of the Knowledge Economy*, 14(3), 2578–2602. DOI: 10.1007/s13132-022-00944-9

Batty, M., Axhausen, K. W., Giannotti, F., Pozdnoukhov, A., Bazzani, A., Wachowicz, M., & Portugali, Y. (2012). Smart cities of the future. *The European Physical Journal. Special Topics*, 214(1), 481–518.

Baum, T., & Nguyen, T. T. H. (2019). Applying sustainable employment principles in the tourism industry: Righting human rights wrongs? *Tourism Recreation Research*, 44(3), 371–381. DOI: 10.1080/02508281.2019.1624407

Bawack, R. E., & Ahmad, M. O. (2021). Understanding business analytics continuance in agile information system development projects: An expectation-confirmation perspective. *Information Technology & People*, 34(6), 1551–1569. Advance online publication. DOI: 10.1108/ITP-10-2020-0681

Baysal, D. B., & Sanalan Bilici, N. (2024). Gastronomy for Sustainable Tourism Destination Marketing. In Castanho, R. A., & Franco, M. (Eds.), *Advances in Hospitality, Tourism, and the Services Industry* (pp. 204–219). IGI Global., DOI: 10.4018/979-8-3693-3158-3.ch010

Beam, E. A., Masatlioglu, Y., Watson, T., & Yang, D. (2022). *Loss aversion or lack of trust: Why does loss framing work to encourage preventative health behaviors?* National Bureau of Economic Research.

Beard, C., & Wilson, J. P. (2006). *Experiential learning: A handbook for education, training, and coaching*. Kogan Page.

Becker, B., Huselid, M., & Ulrich, D. (2001). *The HR Scorecard*. Harvard Business School Press.

Beech, J. (2000). The enigma of Holocaust sites as tourist attractions–The case of Buchenwald. *Managing Leisure*, 5(3), 151–166. DOI: 10.1080/136067100375722

Behavioural Insights Team. (2019). Annual report.

Beinecke, R., Cummings, T., & Williams, R. (2013). Bridging the gap between academic learning and practical application. *Journal of Higher Education Policy and Management*, 35(3), 244–259.

Bellia, C., Bacarella, S., & Ingrassia, M. (2022). Interactions between street food and food safety topics in the scientific literature—A bibliometric analysis with science mapping. *Foods*, 11(6), 789. https://www.mdpi.com/2304-8158/11/6/789. DOI: 10.3390/foods11060789 PMID: 35327211

Bello-Pintado, A., Kaufmann, R., & Merino Diaz De Cerio, J. (2018). Firms' entrepreneurial orientation and the adoption of quality management practices. *International Journal of Quality & Reliability Management*, 35(9), 1734–1754. DOI: 10.1108/IJQRM-05-2017-0089

Belyh, A. (2019, September 23). How Entrepreneurial Creativity Leads to Innovation. Cleverism. Retrieved June 30, 2022, from https://www.cleverism.com/entrepreneurial-creativity-leads-innovation/

Bennett, E. A., & Grabs, J. (2024). How can sustainable business models distribute value more equitably in global value chains? Introducing "value chain profit sharing" as an emerging alternative to fair trade, direct trade, or solidarity trade. *Business Ethics, the Environment & Responsibility*, ●●●, 1–21. DOI: 10.1111/beer.12666

Bereczkei, T., & Czibor, A. (2014). Personality and situational factors differently influence high Mach and low Mach persons' decisions in a social dilemma game. *Personality and Individual Differences*, 64, 168–173. DOI: 10.1016/j.paid.2014.02.035

Berlin Wall Memorial. (2023). Sustainability and preservation at the Berlin Wall Memorial. *Retrieved from Berlin Wall Memorial Website*

Bertschek, I., Bünstorf, G., Cantner, U., Häussler, C., Requate, T., Welter, F., Arndt, E., Dreier, L., Erdsiek, D., Rieger-Fels, M., Dauchert, H., Eilers, L., & Heiny, F. (2024). Transformative R&I Policy using the Example of New Technologies in Agriculture and Social Innovations. *Wirtschaftsdienst (Hamburg, Germany)*, 104(4), 225–229.

Bhansing, P. V., Hitters, E., & Wijngaarden, Y. (2018). Passion Inspires: Motivations of Creative Entrepreneurs in Creative Business Centres in the Netherlands. *The Journal of Entrepreneurship*, 27(1), 1–24. DOI: 10.1177/0971355717738589

Bhateja, R., Tyagi, M., & Tyagi, A. (2022). POST EFFECT COVID AND SERVICE SECTOR IN INDIA: A STUDY. *Journal of Positive School Psychology*, 6(2), 4759–4765.

Bhattacharya, T., & Managi, S. (2015). An assessment of biodiversity offsets and mitigation actions: Case studies on mining, energy and paper and pulp sectors in India. In Managi, S. (Ed.), *The Routledge Handbook of Environmental Economics in Asia* (pp. 401–420). Routledge.

Bhattacherjee, A. (2001). Understanding information systems continuance: An expectation-confirmation model. *Management Information Systems Quarterly*, 25(3), 351–370. DOI: 10.2307/3250921

Bhatti, A.. (2019). Factors Influencing online shopping with special reference to Coimbatore District. *Journal of Information and Computational Science*.

Bhowmik, S. K. (2005). Street vendors in Asia: A review. *Economic and Political Weekly*, •••, 2256–2264. https://www.jstor.org/stable/4416705

Bhuiyan, M. S. (2024). The Role of AI-Enhanced Personalization in Customer Experiences. *Journal of Computer Science and Technology Studies*, 6(1), 162–169. DOI: 10.32996/jcsts.2024.6.1.17

Bhusal, A., & Ghimire, S. (2022). Impact of Information and Communication Technology on Individual Well-being. https://arxiv.org/pdf/2202.00006

Biddle, S. J. H., Mutrie, N., & Gorely, T. (2015). *Psychology of physical activity: Determinants, well-being, and interventions*. Routledge.

Biglan, A., & Ogden, T. (2008). The evolution of evidence-based practices. *European Journal of Behavior Analysis*, 9(1), 81–95. DOI: 10.1080/15021149.2008.11434297 PMID: 21461128

Bignetti, B., Santos, A. C. M. Z., Hansen, P. B., & Henriqson, E. (2021). The influence of entrepreneurial passion and creativity on entrepreneurial intentions. *Revista de Administracao Mackenzie,* 22(2). https://doi.org/DOI: 10.1590/1678-6971/ERAMR210082

Bihamta, H., Jayashree, S., Rezaei, S., Okumus, F., & Rahimi, R. (2017). Dual pillars of hotel restaurant food quality satisfaction and brand loyalty. *British Food Journal*, 119(12), 2597–2609. DOI: 10.1108/BFJ-07-2016-0344

Bilimoria, D., Joy, S., & Liang, X. (2008). Breaking barriers and creating inclusiveness: Lessons of organizational transformation to advance women faculty in academic science and engineering. Human Resource Management: Published in Cooperation with the School of Business Administration, The University of Michigan and in alliance with the Society of Human Resources Management, 47(3), 423-441.

Billett, S. (2001). *Learning in the workplace: Strategies for effective practice.* Allen & Unwin.

Billett, S. (2011). *Vocational education: Purposes, traditions and prospects.* Springer. DOI: 10.1007/978-94-007-1954-5

Billig, S. H. (2002). Research on K-12 service learning. In Furco, A., & Billig, S. H. (Eds.), *Service learning: The essence of the pedagogy* (pp. 73–106). Information Age Publishing.

Bin Rodzoan, A. (2022). Business Intelligence Capabilities and Critical Success Factors in Public Sector Company of Malaysia. *Journal of Science and Technology*, 27(1), 29–44. DOI: 10.20428/jst.v27i1.1985

Biraglia, A., & Kadile, V. (2017). The Role of Entrepreneurial Passion and Creativity in Developing Entrepreneurial Intentions: Insights from American Homebrewers. *Journal of Small Business Management*, 55(1), 170–188. DOI: 10.1111/jsbm.12242

Biran, A., & Poria, Y. (2012). Reconceptualising dark tourism. In Sharpley, R., & Stone, P. R. (Eds.), *The contemporary tourist experience: Concepts and consequences* (pp. 257–274). Routledge.

Biran, A., Poria, Y., & Oren, G. (2011). Sought experiences at (dark) heritage sites. *Annals of Tourism Research*, 38(3), 820–841. DOI: 10.1016/j.annals.2010.12.001

Bird, B. (1988). Implementing Entrepreneurial Ideas: The Case for Intention. *Academy of Management Review*, 13(3), 442–453. DOI: 10.2307/258091

Biscotti, A., & D'Amico, E. (2016). What are political leaders' environmental intentions? The impact of social identification processes and macro-economic conditions. *Ecological Economics*, 129, 152–160. DOI: 10.1016/j.ecolecon.2016.06.004

Bitner, M. J. (1992). Servicescapes: The Impact of Physical Surroundings on Customers and Employees. *Journal of Marketing*, 56(2), 57–71. Advance online publication. DOI: 10.1177/002224299205600205

Björkman, I., & Stahl, G. (2006). International human resource management research: an introduction to the field. In Stahl, G., & Björkman, I. (Eds.), *Handbook of Research in International Human Resource Management.* Edward Elgar. DOI: 10.4337/9781845428235.00005

Black, J. S., & Gregerson, H. B. (1992). Serving two masters: Managing the dual allegiance of expatriate employees. *Sloan Management Review*, 33(4), 61–71.

Blomberg, A., Kallio, T., & Pohjanpää, H. (2017). Antecedents of organizational creativity: Drivers, barriers or both? *Journal of Innovation Management*, 5(1), 78–104. DOI: 10.24840/2183-0606_005.001_0007

Boakye, A., & Ayerki Lamptey, Y. (2020). The rise of HR analytics: Exploring its implications from a developing country perspective. *Journal of Human Resource Management*, 8(3), 181–189. DOI: 10.11648/j.jhrm.20200803.19

Bobylev, S. (2017). Sustainable development: Paradigm for the future. *World Economy and International Relations*, 61(3), 107–113. DOI: 10.20542/0131-2227-2017-61-3-107-113

Bölen, M. C. (2020). Exploring the determinants of users' continuance intention in smartwatches. *Technology in Society*, 60, 101209. Advance online publication. DOI: 10.1016/j.techsoc.2019.101209

Bond-Smith, S. (2019). The impact of compatibility on innovation in markets with network effects. *Economics of Innovation and New Technology*, 28(8), 816–840. DOI: 10.1080/10438599.2018.1563936

Boonshiri, A. (2016). The lifestyle of families and the impact of unrest in the Southern Border Provinces: A case study of the Southern Border Special Development Zone in Songkhla Province from 2004 to 2014. *Journal of Humanities and Social Sciences*. Thaksin University, 11(1), 237–254.

Bostan, S., Erdem, R., Öztürk, Y. E., Kılıç, T., & Yılmaz, A. (2020). *The effect of COVID-19 pandemic on the Turkish society*. Electronic Journal of General Medicine., DOI: 10.29333/ejgm/7944

Bouafou, K. G. M., Beugré, G. F. C., & Amani, Y. C. (2021). Street food around the world: A review of the literature. *Journal of Service Science and Management*, 14(6), 557–575. Advance online publication. DOI: 10.4236/jssm.2021.146035

Boud, D., & Falchikov, N. (Eds.). (2006). *Aligning assessment with learning outcomes: The impact of a competency-based assessment system*. Routledge.

Boud, D., & Solomon, N. (Eds.). (2001). *Work-based learning: A new higher education?* Society for Research into Higher Education & Open University Press.

Boyd, N. G., & Vozikis, G. S. (1994). The Influence of Self-Efficacy on the Development of Entrepreneurial Intentions and Actions. *Entrepreneurship Theory and Practice*, 18(4), 63–77. DOI: 10.1177/104225879401800404

Boyne, S., Williams, F., & Hall, D. (2003). On the trail of regional success: Tourism, food production and the Isle of Arran Taste Trail. In Hjalager, A. M., & Richards, G. (Eds.), *Tourism and gastronomy* (pp. 105–128). Routledge., DOI: 10.4324/9780203218617

Braginsky, D. D. (1970). Machiavellianism *and manipulative interpersonal behavior in children. Journal of Experimental Social Psychology*, 6(1), 77–99. DOI: 10.1016/0022-1031(70)90077-6

Brahma, A., & Dutta, R. (2018). Cashless Transactions and Its Impact-A Wise Move Towards Digital India. *International Journal of Scientific Research in Computer Science, Engineering and Information Technology* © 2018 IJSRCSEIT.

Brand, A., Furness, M., & Keijzer, N. (2021). Promoting policy coherence within the 2030 agenda framework: Externalities, trade-offs and politics. *Politics and Governance*, 9(1), 108–118. DOI: 10.17645/pag.v9i1.3608

Bran, F., Bodislav, D., Radulescu, C., & Ioan, I. (2014). Corporate governance intervention for a sustainable socio-economic model. *Revista de Cercetare si Interventie Sociala*, 46, 216–226.

Brauns, C.-D., & Löffler, L. G. (1990). The Chittagong Hill Tracts and Their Inhabitants. In C.-D. Brauns & L. G. Löffler, *Mru* (pp. 25–60). Birkhäuser Basel. DOI: 10.1007/978-3-0348-5694-2_2

Brennan, C. S. (2024). Regenerative food innovation delivering foods for the future: A viewpoint on how science and technology can aid food sustainability and nutritional well-being in the food industry. *International Journal of Food Science & Technology*, 59(1), 1–5. DOI: 10.1111/ijfs.16861

Briliana, V., Ruswidiono, W., & Deitiana, T. (2021). How social media are successfully transforming the marketing of local street food to better serve the constantly connected digital consumer. *Proceedings of the Ninth International Conference on Entrepreneurship and Business Management (ICEBM 2020), 174,* 322-327. Atlantis Press. DOI: DOI: 10.2991/aebmr.k.210507.049

Brimhall, K. C., & Palinkas, L. (2020). Using mixed methods to uncover inclusive leader behaviors: A promising approach for improving employee and organizational outcomes. *Journal of Leadership & Organizational Studies,* 27(4), 357–375. DOI: 10.1177/1548051820936286

Briner, R. B., Denyer, D., & Rousseau, D. M. (2009). Evidence-based management: Concept cleanup time? *The Academy of Management Perspectives,* 23(4), 19–32. DOI: 10.5465/AMP.2009.45590138

Briner, R. B., & Rousseau, D. M. (2011). Evidence-based I–O psychology: Not there yet. *Industrial and Organizational Psychology: Perspectives on Science and Practice,* 4(1), 3–22. DOI: 10.1111/j.1754-9434.2010.01287.x

Bringle, R. G., & Hatcher, J. A. (1996). Implementing service learning in higher education. *The Journal of Higher Education,* 67(2), 221–239. DOI: 10.1080/00221546.1996.11780257

Bromley, R. (2000). Street vending and public policy: A global review. *The International Journal of Sociology and Social Policy,* 20(1/2), 1–28. DOI: 10.1108/01443330010789052

Brouder, P., Crouch, G. I., & Clarke, J. (2020). Digitization in tourism: Implications for the future of tourism and its policy responses. *Tourism Management Perspectives,* 35, 100725. DOI: 10.1016/j.tmp.2020.100725

Brown, A., & Davis, L. (2018). Community-based branding: Strategies for cultural identity products. *Journal of Local Economy,* 33(2), 123–135.

Brown, A., & Taylor, M. (2024). Social media and the commercialization of dark tourism sites. *Journal of Tourism and Technology,* 14(2), 89–102. DOI: 10.1080/0015587X.2024.1234567

Brown, A., Taylor, M., & Smith, J. (2022). Historical connection and stress in dark tourism. *Journal of Historical Tourism,* 11(4), 210–223. DOI: 10.1080/00343753.2022.220045

Brown, C., & Davis, J. (2018). The importance of local identity in product development. *. *Cultural Identity and Economic Development,* 9(2), 134–145.

Brownlie, S., King, N., & Treweek, J. (2013). Biodiversity tradeoffs and offsets in impact assessment and decision making: Can we stop the loss? *Impact Assessment and Project Appraisal,* 31(1), 24–33. DOI: 10.1080/14615517.2012.736763

Bryan, F. L., Jermini, M., Schmitt, R., Chilufya, E. N., Mwanza, M., Matoba, A., Mfume, E., & Chibiya, H. (1997). Hazards associated with holding and reheating foods at vending sites in a small town in Zambia. *Journal of Food Protection,* 60(4), 391–398. DOI: 10.4315/0362-028X-60.4.391 PMID: 31195538

Bryant, P. T. (2006). Improving entrepreneurial education through self-regulatory skills. In Venture Well. Proceedings of Open, the Annual Conference (p. 279). National Collegiate Inventors & Innovators Alliance.

Buckels, E. E., Jones, D. N., & Paulhus, D. L. (2013). Behavioral Confirmation of Everyday Sadism. *Psychological Science*, 24(11), 2201–2209. DOI: 10.1177/0956797613490749 PMID: 24022650

Budi, A. S. L., Efendi, E., & Dahesihsari, R. (2013). *Perceived Usefulness as Key Stimulus to the Behavioral Intention to Use 3G Technology*. ASEAN Marketing Journal., DOI: 10.21002/amj.v3i2.2025

Bujanowicz-Haraś, B., Janulewicz, P., Nowak, A., & Krukowski, A. (2015). Evaluation of sustainable development in the member states of the European Union. *Problemy Ekorozwoju*, 10(2), 71–78.

Bulis, A., & Onževs, O. (2023). Measurement of sustainable development in Latvia. *Vide. Tehnologija. Resursi - Environment, Technology. Resources*, 1, 29–32.

Bull, A., & Frate, M. (2018). Social capital in the development of the agro nocerino-sarnese. In Sforzi, F. (Ed.), *The Institutions of Local Development* (pp. 141–173). Routledge.

Bunny. (2007, September 13). Bunny's Story. Starbucks Barista Victimized by Age

Burt, R. S. (2000). The network structure of social capital. *. *Research in Organizational Behavior*, 22, 345–423. DOI: 10.1016/S0191-3085(00)22009-1

Burusnukul, P., Binkley, M., & Sukalakamala, P. (2011). Understanding tourists' patronage of Thailand foodservice establishments: An exploratory decisional attribute approach. *British Food Journal*, 113(8), 965–981. DOI: 10.1108/00070701111153733

Buttner, H., & Tullar, W. (2018). A representative organizational diversity metric: A dashboard measure for executive action. *Equality, Diversity and Inclusion*, 37(3), 219–232. DOI: 10.1108/EDI-04-2017-0076

Byrne, J. A. (2016, June 26). MBAs Doing Startups at Nearly Four Times the Rate Previously Thought. Poets & Quants. Retrieved June 30, 2022, from https://poetsandquants.com/2016/06/26/mba-employment-reports-understate

Caligiuri, P., De Cieri, H., Minbaeva, D., Verbeke, A., & Zimmermann, A. (2020). International HRM insights for navigating the COVID-19 pandemic: Implications for future research and practice. *Journal of International Business Studies*, 51(5), 697–713. DOI: 10.1057/s41267-020-00335-9 PMID: 32836500

Caliguiri, P. M. (1999). The ranking of scholarly journals in the field of international human resource management. *International Journal of Human Resource Management*, 10(3), 515–518. DOI: 10.1080/095851999340468

Cambridge University Press. (n.d.). Street food. In *Cambridge Dictionary*. Retrieved January 13, 2024, from https://dictionary.cambridge.org/dictionary/english/street-food

Camilleri, M. A. (2020). Strategic corporate social responsibility in tourism and hospitality. *Sustainable Development (Bradford)*, 28(3), 504–506. DOI: 10.1002/sd.2059

Camilleri, M. A., & Kozak, M. (2022). Interactive engagement through travel and tourism social media groups: A social facilitation theory perspective. *Technology in Society*, 71, 102098. DOI: 10.1016/j.techsoc.2022.102098

Campagnolo, L., Eboli, F., Farnia, L., & Carraro, C. (2018). Supporting the UN SDGs transition: Methodology for sustainability assessment and current worldwide ranking. *Economics*, 12(1), 2018–10. DOI: 10.5018/economics-ejournal.ja.2018-10

Campos, H. M. (2017). Impact of entrepreneurial passion on entrepreneurial orientation with the mediating role of entrepreneurial alertness for technology-based firms in Mexico. *Journal of Small Business and Enterprise Development*, 24(2), 353–374. DOI: 10.1108/JSBED-10-2016-0166

Capper, G., Holmes, J., Jowsey, E., Lilley, S., McGuinness, D., & Robson, S. (2014). Sustainability. In Jowsey, E. (Ed.), *Real Estate Concepts: A Handbook* (pp. 402–429). Routledge.

Capriles, V. D., de Aguiar, E. V., Dos Santos, F. G., Fernández, M. E. A., de Melo, B. G., Tagliapietra, B. L., & Conti, A. C. (2023). Current status and prospects of sensory and consumer research approaches to gluten-free bakery and pasta products. *Food Research International*, 173, 113389. DOI: 10.1016/j.foodres.2023.113389 PMID: 37803727

Cardon, M. S., Gregoire, D. A., Stevens, C. E., & Patel, P. C. (2013). Measuring entrepreneurial passion: Conceptual foundations and scale validation. *Journal of Business Venturing*, 28(3), 373–396. DOI: 10.1016/j.jbusvent.2012.03.003

Cardon, M. S., & Kirk, C. P. (2015). Entrepreneurial Passion as Mediator of the Self–Efficacy to Persistence Relationship. *Entrepreneurship Theory and Practice*, 39(5), 1027–1050. DOI: 10.1111/etap.12089

Cardon, M. S., Wincent, J., Singh, J., & Drnovsek, M. (2009). The Nature and Experience of Entrepreneurial Passion. *Academy of Management Review*, 34(3), 511–532. https://Doi.Org/10.5465/Amr.2009.40633190. DOI: 10.5465/amr.2009.40633190

Cardoso, A., Gabriel, M., Figueiredo, J., Oliveira, I., Rêgo, R., Silva, R., Oliveira, M., & Meirinhos, G. (2022). Trust and Loyalty in Building the Brand Relationship with the Customer: Empirical Analysis in a Retail Chain in Northern Brazil. *Journal of Open Innovation*, 8(3), 109. DOI: 10.3390/joitmc8030109

Carlucci, R., Maglietta, R., Buscaino, G., Cipriano, G., Milella, A., Pollazzon, V., Bondanese, P., De Leonardis, C., Mona, S., Nitti, M., Papale, E., Reno, V., Ricci, P., Stella, E., & Fanizza, C. (2017). Review on research studies and monitoring system applied to cetaceans in the gulf of taranto (northern ionian sea, central-eastern mediterranean sea). *2017 14th IEEE International Conference on Advanced Video and Signal Based Surveillance, AVSS 2017*, 8078473.

Carnevale, A. P., & Stone, S. C. (1995). *The American mosaic*. McGraw-Hill.

Caudron, S. (1992). U.S. West finds strength in diversity. *The Personnel Journal*, 71(3), 40–44.

Center for Evidence-Based Management. What is evidence-based management? 2015. Available at: http://www.cebma.org/#what-is evidence-based-management.

Çetinsöz, B. C. (2019). Influence of physical environment on customer satisfaction and loyalty in upscale restaurants. *Journal of Tourism and Gastronomy Studies*, 7(2), 700–716. DOI: 10.21325/jotags.2019.387

Chaffey, D., & Ellis-Chadwick, F. (2019). *Digital marketing: Strategy, implementation, and practice* (7th ed.). Pearson.

Chaiyasain, C. (2020). Phuket street food: STREET FOODS model providing a creative charm for Phuket's gastronomy tourism. *WMS Journal of Management, 9*(2), 120–127. https://so06.tci-thaijo.org/index.php/wms/article/view/241859

Chamboko-Mpotaringa, M., & Tichaawa, T. M. (2021). Digital trends and tools driving change in marketing Free State tourism destinations: A stakeholder's perspective. *African Journal of Hospitality, Tourism and Leisure, 10*(6), 1973–1984. DOI: 10.46222/ajhtl.19770720.204

Chang, V., Yang, Y., Xu, Q. A., & Xiong, C. (2021). Factors influencing consumer intention to subscribe to the premium music streaming services in China. *Journal of Global Information Management, 29*(6), 1–25. DOI: 10.4018/JGIM.20211101.oa17

Channar, Z. A., Abbassi, Z., & Ujan, I. A. (2011). Gender discrimination in workforce and its impact on the employees [PJCSS]. *Pakistan Journal of Commerce and Social Sciences, 5*(1), 177–191.

Chantawiboon, A. (2017). Development of riverside food to improve the quality of life, promote the economy and Thai tourism. *Promotion of Health and Environmental Hygiene, 40*(4), 11-18. https://thaidj.org/index.php/JHS/article/download/8330/7657/11706

Chanthasap, . (2002). *Basic Research Methods*. Dhurakij Pundit University Press.

Chapple, K. (2014). Strategies for growing green business and industry in a city. In Mazmanian, D., & Blanco, H. (Eds.), *Elgar Companion to Sustainable Cities: Strategies, Methods and Outlook* (pp. 116–132). Edward Elgar Publishing Ltd. DOI: 10.4337/9780857939999.00011

Charness, N., & Boot, W. R. (2015). Technology, Gaming, and Social Networking. In *Handbook of the Psychology of Aging: Eighth Edition*. DOI: 10.1016/B978-0-12-411469-2.00020-0

Charoenjarasrerk, N. (2014). *A main factor influencing on street food consumption in Bangkok metropolis.* [Thematic Paper, Mahidol University]. CMMU Digital Archive. https://archive.cm.mahidol.ac.th/handle/123456789/671

Chatterjee, J., & Dsilva, N. R. (2021). A study on the role of social media in promoting sustainable tourism in the states of Assam and Odisha. *Tourism Critiques: Practice and Theory, 2*(1), 74–90. DOI: 10.1108/TRC-09-2020-0017

Chatterjee, S., Chaudhuri, R., & Vrontis, D. (2021). Does data-driven culture impact innovation and performance of a firm? An empirical examination. *Annals of Operations Research, 17*(2), 1–26. DOI: 10.1007/s10479-020-03887-z

Chaudhuri, A., & Holbrook, M. B. (2001). The Chain of Effects from Brand Trust and Brand Affect to Brand Performance: The Role of Brand Loyalty. *Journal of Marketing, 65*(2), 81–93. DOI: 10.1509/jmkg.65.2.81.18255

Chavarria, T. L. C., & Phakdee-auksorn, P. (2017). Understanding international tourists' attitudes towards street food in Phuket, Thailand. *Tourism Management Perspectives, 21*, 66–73. DOI: 10.1016/j.tmp.2016.11.005

Chavez, C. I., & Weisinger, J. Y. (2008). Beyond diversity training: A social infusion for cultural inclusion. Human Resource Management: Published in Cooperation with the School of Business Administration, The University of Michigan and in alliance with the Society of Human Resources Management, 47(2), 331-350.

Chen McCain, S. L., Lolli, J., Liu, E., & Lin, L. C. (2022). An analysis of a third-party food delivery app during the COVID-19 pandemic. *British Food Journal*, 124(10), 3032–3052. DOI: 10.1108/BFJ-03-2021-0332

Chen, M. A. (2012). *The informal economy: Definitions, theories and policies* (WIEGO Working Paper No. 1). Women in Informal Employment: Globalizing and Organizing (WIEGO). https://www.wiego.org/sites/default/files/publications/files/Chen_WIEGO_WP1.pdf

Chen, C. C., Greene, P. G., & Crick, A. (1998). Does entrepreneurial self-efficacy distinguish entrepreneurs from managers? *Journal of Business Venturing*, 13(4), 295–316. DOI: 10.1016/S0883-9026(97)00029-3

Chen, C. C., & Yao, J. Y. (2018). What drives impulse buying behaviors in a mobile auction? The perspective of the Stimulus-Organism-Response model. *Telematics and Informatics*, 35(5), 1249–1262. Advance online publication. DOI: 10.1016/j.tele.2018.02.007

Chen, C. M., & Huang, T. C. (2018). The impact of augmented reality on learning effectiveness: A case study. *Journal of Educational Technology*, 15(4), 33–44.

Chernobyl Tour. (2024). Environmental and waste management issues at the Chernobyl Exclusion Zone. *Retrieved from* Chernobyl Tour Website

Chernobyl Tour. (n.d.). *Virtual Reality Tours*. Retrieved from Chernobyl Tour.

Cheung, G. W., Cooper–Thomas, H. D., Lau, R. S., & Wang, L. C. (2023). Reporting reliability, convergent and discriminant validity with structural equation modeling: A review and best-practice recommendations. *Asia Pacific Journal of Management*. Advance online publication. DOI: 10.1007/s10490-023-09871-y

Cheung, M. L., Ting, H., Cheah, J.-H., & Sharipudin, M.-N. S. (2021). Examining the role of social media-based destination brand community in evoking tourists' emotions and intention to co-create and visit. *Journal of Product and Brand Management*, 30(1), 28–43. DOI: 10.1108/JPBM-09-2019-2554

Chierici, R., Mazzucchelli, A., Garcia-Perez, A., & Vrontis, D. (2019). Transforming big data into knowledge: The role of knowledge management practice. *Management Decision*, 57(8), 1902–1922. DOI: 10.1108/MD-07-2018-0834

Chi, G. (2005). *A study of developing destination loyalty model*. ProQuest Dissertations and Theses.

Chinazzi, M., Davis, J., Ajelli, M., Gioannini, C., Litvinova, M., Merler, S., Pastore y Piontti, A., Mu, K., Rossi, L., Sun, K., Viboud, C., Xiong, X., Yu, H., Halloran, E., Longini Jr., I., and Vespignani, A. (2020) The effect of travel restrictions on the spread of the 2019 novel coronavirus (COVID-19) outbreak, *Science*, 24th April, 368, 395–400.

Chin, P. N., Yeoh, S. Y., & Yuntavid, X. J. P. (2022). Examining the continuous usage intention and behaviours of music streaming subscribers. *International Journal of Electronic Business*, 17(2), 1. DOI: 10.1504/IJEB.2022.121992

Chin, W., Cheah, J., Liu, Y., Ting, H., Lim, X., & Cham, T. H. (2020). Demystifying the role of causal-predictive modeling using partial least squares structural equation modeling in information systems research. *Industrial Management + Data Systems. Industrial Management & Data Systems*, 120(12), 2161–2209. DOI: 10.1108/IMDS-10-2019-0529

Chirila, A. (2023). Pilgrim-Tourists: Tourism and the Spiritual Experience. *Analele Ştiinţifice Ale Universităţii» Alexandru Ioan Cuza «din Iaşi.Teologie Ortodoxă*, 28(1), 43–72.

Choi, Y. (2019). Technology acceptance model and stimulus-organism response for the use intention of consumers in social commerce. *International Journal of E-Business Research*, 15(2), 93–101. Advance online publication. DOI: 10.4018/IJEBR.2019040105

Cho, S., & Barak, M. O. R. (2008). Understanding of diversity and inclusion in a perceived homogeneous culture: A study of organizational commitment and job performance among Korean employees. *Administration in Social Work*, 32(4), 100–126. DOI: 10.1080/03643100802293865

Choudhury, M., Mahanta, L., Goswami, J., Mazumder, M., & Pegoo, B. (2011). Socio-economic profile and food safety knowledge and practice of street food vendors in the city of Guwahati, Assam, India. *Food Control*, 22(2), 196–203. DOI: 10.1016/j.foodcont.2010.06.020

Choudrie, J., Zamani, E., & Obuekwe, C. (2022). Bridging the digital divide in ethnic minority older adults: An organisational qualitative study. *Information Systems Frontiers*, 24(4), 1355–1375. DOI: 10.1007/s10796-021-10126-8

Chowdhury, M. A. I., Alauddin, M., & Uddin, M. R. (2021). Sustainable tourism in Bangladesh: The demand for investment and development. Tourism in Bangladesh: Investment and development perspectives, 363-381.

Cho, Y., Kim, D. S., Phuong, H. T., & Gim, G. (2019). A study on the Factors Affecting Continuous Usage Intention of Computer Aided Engineering (CAE) Software. *International Journal of Software Innovation*, 10(1), 1–13. Advance online publication. DOI: 10.4018/IJSI.297508

Christou, E. (2015). Branding Social Media in the Travel Industry. *Procedia: Social and Behavioral Sciences*, 175, 607–614. DOI: 10.1016/j.sbspro.2015.01.1244

Chui, M., Manyika, J., & Miremadi, M. (2018). What AI can and can't do (yet) for your business. *The McKinsey Quarterly*.

Chulasatit, S., & Choonhachatrachai, A. (2022). Factors influence buying street food decisions in new normal of consumer in Bangkok. *UMT Poly Journal, 19*(2), 56-67. https://so06.tci-thaijo.org/index.php/umt-poly/article/view/258401/175068

Chung, H., & Van der Lippe, T. (2020). Flexible working, work–life balance, and gender equality: Introduction. *Social Indicators Research*, 151(2), 365–381. DOI: 10.1007/s11205-018-2025-x PMID: 33029036

Chung, N., & Koo, C. (2015). The use of social media in travel information search. *Telematics and Informatics*, 32(2), 215–229. DOI: 10.1016/j.tele.2014.08.005

Cialdini, R. B. (2001). *Influence: Science and practice* (4th ed.). Allyn & Bacon.

Cifci, I., Ogretmenoglu, M., Sengel, T., Demirciftci, T., & Kandemir Altunel, G. (2022). Effects of tourists' street food experience and food neophobia on their post-travel behaviors: The roles of destination image and corona-phobia. *Journal of Quality Assurance in Hospitality & Tourism*, •••, 1–28. DOI: 10.1080/1528008X.2022.2151550

Ciobotaru, A. (2015). Rural sustainable development requires healthy and educated population. *Quality - Access to Success*, 16, 743–745.

Cisco. (2022). *Cisco Networking Academy*. Retrieved from https://www.netacad.com/

Clark, L. A., & Watson, D. (1995). Constructing validity: Basic issues in objective scale development. *Psychological Assessment*, 7(3), 309–319. DOI: 10.1037/1040-3590.7.3.309

Claus, L. (1999) "People Management and Globalization," presentation to the fifty-first annual conference and exposition of the Society of Human Resource Management, Atlanta, GA, June.

Claus, L. (1998). The role of international human resource management in leading a company from a domestic to a global corporate culture. *Human Resource Development International*, 1(3), 309–326. DOI: 10.1080/13678869800000040

Coffman, K. B., Exley, C. L., & Niederle, M. (2021). The role of beliefs in driving gender discrimination. *Management Science*, 2(5), 225–244. DOI: 10.1287/mnsc.2020.3660

Cohen, J. (1998) Statistical Power Analysis for the Behavioural Sciences. Lawrence Erlbaum Associates, Hillsdale. - References - Scientific Research Publishing. (n.d.). https://www.scirp.org/reference/referencespapers?referenceid=1341443

Cohen, M. (1984). *The urban street food trade*. Equity Policy Center. https://citeseerx.ist.psu.edu/document?repid=rep1&type=pdf&doi=300e842b63a6cfe998c3a4c43a994b98fe507d79

Cohen, M. (1986). The influence of the street food trade on women and child health. In D.B. Jelliffe & E.F.P, Jelliffe, eds. *Advances in international maternal and child health*. Vol. 6, Oxford, Clarendon Press.

Cohen, M., & Tinker, I. (1985). Street foods: Opportunities for female employment in the food system. *ORSTOM, Paris*. https://horizon.documentation.ird.fr/exl-doc/pleins_textes/pleins_textes_4/colloques/17971.pdf

Cohen, E., & Avieli, N. (2004). Food in tourism: Attraction and impediment. *Annals of Tourism Research*, 31(4), 755–778. DOI: 10.1016/j.annals.2004.02.003

Cohen, J. (1988). *Statistical power analysis for the behavioral sciences*. Lawrence Earlbaum.

Cohen, S. A., Higham, J. E. S., & Reis, A. C. (2013). Sociological barriers to developing sustainable discretionary air travel behaviour. *Journal of Sustainable Tourism*, 21(7), 982–998. DOI: 10.1080/09669582.2013.809092

Coleman, J. S. (1988). Social capital in the creation of human capital. *. *American Journal of Sociology*, 94, S95–S120. DOI: 10.1086/228943

Cole, T. (2000). *Selling the Holocaust: From Auschwitz to Schindler, How History is Bought, Packaged, and Sold*. Routledge.

Collewaert, V., Anseel, F., Crommelinck, M., de Beuckelaer, A., & Vermeire, J. (2016). When Passion Fades: Disentangling the Temporal Dynamics of Entrepreneurial Passion for Founding. *Journal of Management Studies*, 53(6), 966–995. DOI: 10.1111/joms.12193

Collings, D. G., Scullion, H., & Morley, M. J. (2007). Changing Patterns of Global Staffing in the Multinational Enterprise: Challenges to the Conventional Expatriate Assignment and Emerging Alternatives. *Journal of World Business*, 42(2), 198–213. DOI: 10.1016/j.jwb.2007.02.005

Collins-Kreiner, N. (2016). Dark tourism as a form of pilgrimage: Tourists' experiences of dark sites. *Annals of Tourism Research*, 60, 7–17. DOI: 10.1016/j.annals.2016.05.004

Collins, M. D., & Millar, M. (2021). Tourists' perceptions of destination image, safety, and aggressive street behavior. *International Journal of Hospitality & Tourism Administration*, 22(3), 251–268. DOI: 10.1080/15256480.2019.1641452

Collison, K. L., Vize, C. E., Miller, J. D., & Lynam, D. R. (2018). Development and preliminary validation of a five-factor model measure of Machiavellianism. *Psychological Assessment*, 30(10), 1401–1407. DOI: 10.1037/pas0000637 PMID: 30047746

Collodel, A., & Kotzé, D. (2014). The Failure of Cross-country Regression Analysis in Measuring the Impact of Foreign Aid. *Journal of Developing Societies*, 30(2), 195–221. DOI: 10.1177/0169796X14525527

Coll, R. K., Eames, C., Paku, L., Lay, M., Hodges, D., Bhat, R., & Ram, S. (2009). An exploration of the pedagogies employed to integrate knowledge in work-integrated learning. *The Journal of Cooperative Education and Internships*, 43(1), 14–35.

Conca, K., & Dabelko, G. (2018). *Green planet blues: Critical perspectives on global environmental politics*. Routledge. DOI: 10.4324/9780429493744

Contreras, C. P. A., Cardoso, R. D. C. V., da Silva, L. N. N., & Cuello, R. E. G. (2020). Street food, food safety, and regulation: What is the panorama in Colombia?: A review. *Journal of Food Protection*, 83(8), 1345–1358. DOI: 10.4315/JFP-19-526 PMID: 32221547

Cooper, C. (2008). *Tourism: Principles and Practice* (4th ed.). Pearson Education Limited.

Cordella, M., Gonzalez-Redin, J., Lodeiro, R., & Garcia, D. (2022). Assessing impacts to biodiversity and ecosystems: Understanding and exploiting synergies between Life Cycle Assessment and Natural Capital Accounting. *Procedia CIRP*, 105, 134–139. DOI: 10.1016/j.procir.2022.02.023

Corp, I. B. M. (2017). IBM SPSS Statistics for Windows (Version 25.0) [Computer software]. IBM Corp. https://www.ibm.com/analytics/spss-statistics-software

Cox, E. (2005). *Coaching and mentoring: Practical methods to improve performance*. Routledge.

Creswell, J. W. (2014). *Research design: Qualitative, quantitative, and mixed methods approaches* (4th ed.). Sage Publications.

Crewe, L., & Wang, A. (2018). Gender inequalities in the city of London advertising industry", Environment and Planning A. *Environment & Planning A*, 50(3), 671–688. DOI: 10.1177/0308518X17749731

Criado-Perez, C., Jackson, C., & Collins, G., C. (. (2023). Evidence collection and use when making management decisions. *Applied Psychology*, •••, 1–21. DOI: 10.1111/apps.12503

Cross, J., & Morales, A. (Eds.). (2007). *Street entrepreneurs: People, place, & politics in local and global perspective*. Routledge. DOI: 10.4324/9780203086742

Cruz, R. E., Leonhardt, J. M., & Krey, N. (2020). Involvement and brand engagement outcomes in Facebook brand posts: A gender twist: An abstract. *Developments in Marketing Science:Proceedings of the Academy of Marketing Science*, 177–178. https://doi.org/DOI: 10.1007/978-3-030-39165-2_79

Cunningham, G. B. (2008). Creating and sustaining gender diversity in sport organizations. *Sex Roles*, 58(1-2), 136–145. DOI: 10.1007/s11199-007-9312-3

Cunningham, G. B. (2019). *Diversity and inclusion in sport organizations: A multilevel perspective*. Routledge. DOI: 10.4324/9780429504310

Cunningham, J., & Harlow, M. (2020). Global partnerships in education: Enhancing learning opportunities through international collaborations. *International Journal of Educational Management*, 34(2), 45–60.

Cuomo, M. T., Tortora, D., Foroudi, P., Giordano, A., Festa, G., & Metallo, G. (2021). Digital transformation and tourist experience co-design: Big social data for planning cultural tourism. *Technological Forecasting and Social Change*, 162, 120345. DOI: 10.1016/j.techfore.2020.120345

Cusack, C. (2019). Sustainable Development and Quality of Life. In Sinha, B. (Ed.), *Multidimensional Approach to Quality of Life Issues: A Spatial Analysis* (pp. 43–58). Springer. DOI: 10.1007/978-981-13-6958-2_3

Czibor, A., Szabo, Z. P., Jones, D. N., Zsido, A. N., Paal, T., Szijjarto, L., Carre, J. R., & Bereczkei, T. (2017). Male and female face of Machiavellianism: Opportunism or anxiety? *Personality and Individual Differences*, 117, 221–229. DOI: 10.1016/j.paid.2017.06.002

D'lima, C. (2018). Brand passion and its implication on consumer behaviour. *International Journal of Business Forecasting and Marketing Intelligence*, 4(1), 30–42. DOI: 10.1504/IJBFMI.2018.10009307

Da Silva, O. L., Vieira, V. A. P., & dos Santos, R. P. (2022). A systems-of-Information Identification Method Based on Business Process Models Analysis. *Journal of Management & Technology*, 22(4), 90–115. DOI: 10.20397/2177-6652/2022.v22i4.2309

Da Silva, S. A., Cardoso, R. D. C. V., Góes, J. Â. W., Santos, J. N., Ramos, F. P., & De Jesus, R. B. (2014). Street food on the coast of Salvador, Bahia, Brazil: A study from the socioeconomic and food safety perspectives. *Food Control*, 40, 78–84. DOI: 10.1016/j.foodcont.2013.11.022

Dabholkar, P. A., & Bagozzi, R. P. (2002). An attitudinal model of technology-based self-service: Moderating effects of consumer traits and situational factors. *Journal of the Academy of Marketing Science*, 30(3), 184–201. Advance online publication. DOI: 10.1177/0092070302303001

Daffa Hanief Wisnu Putranto, D. H. W. P., & Rahayu Kistanti, N. (2024). Model Pengembangan Community Based Tourism Desa Jangkaran, Kabupaten Kulon Progo. *El-Mal: Jurnal Kajian Ekonomi & Bisnis Islam*, 5(7). Advance online publication. DOI: 10.47467/elmal.v5i7.3179

Dahlberg, T., Guo, J., & Ondrus, J. (2015, September). Guo, J., & Ondrus, J. (2015). A critical review of mobile payment research. *Electronic Commerce Research and Applications*, 14(5), 265–284. Advance online publication. DOI: 10.1016/j.elerap.2015.07.006

Dahlberg, T., Mallat, N., & Oorrni, A. (2003). Consumer acceptance of mobile payment solutions – ease of use, usefulness and trust. *Proceedings of the Second International Conference on Mobile Business (ICMB)*.

Dahling, J. J., Whitaker, B. G., & Levy, P. E. (2009). The Development and Validation of a New Machiavellianism Scale. *Journal of Management*, 35(2), 219–257. DOI: 10.1177/0149206308318618

Damodharan, P., & Ravichandran, C. S. (2019). Applicability evaluation of web mining in healthcare E-commerce towards business success and a derived cournot model. *Journal of Medical Systems*, 43(8), 268. DOI: 10.1007/s10916-019-1395-1 PMID: 31273541

Daries Ramón, N., Cristobal-Fransi, E., Ferrer-Rossell, B., & Marine-Roig, E. (2018). Behaviour of culinary tourists: A segmentation study of diners at top-level restaurants. *Intangible Capital*, 14(2), 332–355. DOI: 10.3926/ic.1090

Darini, M., Pazhouhesh, H., & Moshiri, F. (2011). Relationship between Employee's Innovation (Creativity) and time management. *Procedia: Social and Behavioral Sciences*, 25, 201–213. DOI: 10.1016/j.sbspro.2011.10.541

Das, I. R., Talukder, M. B., & Kumar, S. (2024). Implication of Artificial Intelligence in Hospitality Marketing. *IGI Global, USA*.https://doi.org/https://doi.org/ 10.4018/979-8-3693-1978-9.ch014

Das, I. R., Talukder, M. B., & Kumar, S. (2024). Implication of Artificial Intelligence in Hospitality Marketing. *Utilizing Smart Technology and AI in Hybrid Tourism and Hospitality*. IGI Global, USA. https://doi.org/ DOI: 10.4018/979-8-3693-1978-9.ch014

Dasgupta, S. (2024). *Economic crisis of 2008-09 and subjective well-being: An empirical analysis of some selected countries*. International Trade, Economic Crisis and the Sustainable Development Goals., DOI: 10.1108/978-1-83753-586-620241003

Dash, J. (28 Apr, 2020). Covid-19 impact: Tourism industry to incur Rs 1.25 trn revenue loss in 2020. *Business Standard*. Retrieved on 5th August 2020 from https://www.business-standard.com/article/economy-policy/covid-19-impact-tourism-industry-to-incur-rs-1-25-trn-revenue-loss-in-2020-120042801287_1.html

Davis, B. C., Hmieleski, K. M., Webb, J. W., & Coombs, J. E. (2017). Funders' poise reactions to entrepreneurs' crowdfunding pitches: The influence of perceived product I've creativity and entrepreneurial passion. *Journal of Business Venturing*, 32(1), 90–106. DOI: 10.1016/j.jbusvent.2016.10.006

Davis, F. D. (1989). Perceived usefulness, perceived ease of use, and user acceptance of information technology. *MIS Quarterly: Management. Management Information Systems Quarterly*, 13(3), 319. Advance online publication. DOI: 10.2307/249008

Davis, F. D., Bagozzi, R. P., & Warshaw, P. R. (1989, August). Bagozzi, R. P., & Warshaw, P. R. (1989). User Acceptance of Computer Technology: A Comparison of Two Theoretical Models. *Management Science*, 35(8), 982–1003. Advance online publication. DOI: 10.1287/mnsc.35.8.982

Davlembayeva, D., Chari, S., & Papagiannidis, S. (2024). Virtual Influencers in Consumer Behaviour: A Social Influence Theory Perspective. *British Journal of Management*, 1467-8551.12839. Advance online publication. DOI: 10.1111/1467-8551.12839

Dawson, R. J., & Canet, C. (1991). International activities in street foods. *Food Control*, 2(3), 135–139. DOI: 10.1016/0956-7135(91)90081-7

Dazmin, D., & Ho, M. Y. (2019). The relationship between consumers' price-saving orientation and time-saving orientation towards food delivery intermediaries (FDI) services: an exploratory study. *GSJ*, 7(2). https://rb.gy/qx5wl8

De Mol, E., Cardon, M. S., de Jong, B., Khapova, S. N., & Elfring, T. (2020). Entrepreneurial passion diversity in new venture teams: An empirical examination of short- and long-term performance implications. *Journal of Business Venturing*, 35(4), 105965. DOI: 10.1016/j.jbusvent.2019.105965

De Nisco, A., & Warnaby, G. (2014). Urban design and tenant variety influences on consumers' emotions and approach behavior. *Journal of Business Research*, 67(2), 211–217. DOI: 10.1016/j.jbusres.2012.10.002

De Noble, A. F., Jung, D., & Ehrlich, S. B. (1999). Entrepreneurial Self-Efficacy: The Development of a Measure and Its Relationship to Entrepreneurial Action. In *Frontiers of Entrepreneurship Research* (pp. 73–87). Babson College.

De Vasconcellos, S. L., Garrido, I. L., & Parente, R. C. (2019). Organizational creativity as a crucial resource for building international business competence. *International Business Review*, 28(3), 438–449. DOI: 10.1016/j.ibusrev.2018.11.003

Deb, S. K., Nafi, S., & Valeri, M. (2022). Promoting tourism business through digital marketing in the new normal era: A sustainable approach. *European Journal of Innovation Management*, 27(3), 775–799. DOI: 10.1108/EJIM-04-2022-0218

Dechamp, G., & Szostak, B. L. (2016). Organisational creativity and the creative territory: The nature of influence and strategic challenges for organisations. *M@n@gement*, 19(2), 61-88.

Deci, E. L., & Ryan, R. M. (2000). The "what" and "why" of goal pursuits: Human needs and the self-determination of behavior. *Psychological Inquiry*, 11(4), 227–268.

Del Mar García De Los Salmones, M., Crespo, A. H., & Del Bosque, I. R. (2005). Influence of corporate social responsibility on loyalty and valuation of services. *Journal of Business Ethics*, 61(4), 369–385. DOI: 10.1007/s10551-005-5841-2

Delgado-Ballester, E., & Luis Munuera-Alemán, J. (2001). Brand trust in the context of consumer loyalty. *European Journal of Marketing*, 35(11/12), 1238–1258. DOI: 10.1108/EUM0000000006475

Delgado-Ballester, E., & Munuera-Alemán, J. L. (2005). Does brand trust matter to brand equity? *the Journal of Product & Brand Management. Journal of Product and Brand Management*, 14(3), 187–196. DOI: 10.1108/10610420510601058

Delisle, H. (1990). Patterns of urban food consumption in developing countries: Perspective from the 1980's. *Food Policy and Nutrition Division, FAO, ed. Rome: Food and Agricultural Organization.* https://rb.gy/1a2t21

Dell, D., & Ainspan, A. Nathan, Bodenberg, A., & Thomas. (2001). Engaging Employees through Your Brand. The Conference Board

Deloitte. (2015). *Global Human Capital Trends 2015 Leading in the new world of work.* Deloitte University Press.

Deng, J., & Pierskalla, C. D. (2018). Linking importance–performance analysis, satisfaction, and loyalty: A study of Savannah, GA. *Sustainability (Basel)*, 10(3), 704. DOI: 10.3390/su10030704

Deng, L., Li, D., & Chen, J. (2023). Compatibility as a prerequisite: Research on the factors influencing the continuous use intention of in-vehicle games based on diffusion of innovations theory. *SAGE Open*, 13(4), 21582440231217909. Advance online publication. DOI: 10.1177/21582440231217909

Deng, T., & Grow, J. M. (2018). Gender segregation revealed: Five years of red books data tell a global story. *Advertising and Society Quarterly*, 19(3). Advance online publication. DOI: 10.1353/asr.2018.0024

Deng, X., & Yuan, L. (2020). Integrating technology acceptance model with social capital theory to promote passive users' continuance intention toward virtual brand communities. *IEEE Access : Practical Innovations, Open Solutions*, 8, 73061–73070. DOI: 10.1109/ACCESS.2020.2987803

Dennehy, D., & Sammon, D. (2015). Trends in mobile payments research: A literature review. *Journal of Innovation Management.* DOI: 10.24840/2183-0606_003.001_0006

Department of Business Development. (2009). *Restaurant/cafeteria business.* https://tsic.dbd.go.th/assets/book_business_man.pdf

Derendiaeva, O. (2022). Analysis of environmental trends on the example of the leading states: The USA, Great Britain and China in the context of the implementation of sustainable development goals. *IOP Conference Series. Earth and Environmental Science*, 979(1), 012148. DOI: 10.1088/1755-1315/979/1/012148

Dernbach, J., & Cheever, F. (2015). Sustainable development and its discontents. *Transnational Environmental Law*, 4(2), 247–287. DOI: 10.1017/S2047102515000163

Desjardins, J. (2017). *What happens in a minute in 2017?* Retrieved February 7, 2024, from www.weforum.org/agenda/2017/08/what-happens-in-an-internet-minute-in-2017

Deterding, S., Dixon, D., Khaled, R., & Nacke, L. (2011). From game design elements to gamefulness: Defining "gamification." In *Proceedings of the 15th International Academic MindTrek Conference: Envisioning Future Media Environments* (pp. 9-15).

Devi, A. D. T., & Yasa, N. N. K. (2021). role of customer satisfaction in mediating the influence of service quality and perceived value on brand loyalty. *International Journal of Management. IT and Social Sciences*, 8(3), 315–328. DOI: 10.21744/irjmis.v8n3.1786

Dey, P. (2018, October 8). Grief tourism: Why people visit places of death and disaster. Times of India https://www.shikhar.com/blog/dark-tourism-the-attraction-of-death-and-disasters/

Di Nardo, G., Villa, M. P., Conti, L., Ranucci, G., Pacchiarotti, C., Principessa, L., & Parisi, P. (2019). Nutritional deficiencies in children with celiac disease resulting from a gluten-free diet: A systematic review. *Nutrients*, 11(7), 1588.

Dimanche, F., & Andrades, L. (2024). Tourism Trends: Current Challenges for Tourism Destinations Management. In Andrades, L., Romero-Dexeus, C., & Martínez-Marín, E. (Eds.), *The Spanish Model for Smart Tourism Destination Management* (pp. 3–21). Springer International Publishing., DOI: 10.1007/978-3-031-60709-7_1

Dinnissen, K., & Bauer, C. (2023). Amplifying artists' voices: Item provider perspectives on influence and fairness of music streaming platforms. *InProceedings of the 31st ACM Conference on User Modeling, Adaptation and Personalization*. http://dx.doi.org/DOI: 10.1145/3565472.3592960

Directorate of Administration. (n.d.). *Tuol Sleng Genocide Museum*. Retrieved from Tuol Sleng Genocide Museum.

Discrimination. Industrial Workers of the World. Retrieved 04 12, 2017, from http:// www.iww.org/node/3649

Djayapranata, G. F., & Setyawan, A. (2022). The antecedents in forming loyalty in the Fast-Food industry. In *Advances in economics, business and management research* (pp. 769–777). https://doi.org/DOI: 10.2991/978-94-6463-008-4_97

Do, B. R., & Dadvari, A. (2017). The influence of the dark triad on the relationship between entrepreneurial attitude orientation and entrepreneurial intention: A study among students in Taiwan University. *Asia Pacific Management Review*, 22(4), 185–191. DOI: 10.1016/j.apmrv.2017.07.011

Do, B.-R., Dadvari, A., & Moslehpour, M. (2020). Exploring the mediation effect of social media acceptance on the relationship between entrepreneurial personality and entrepreneurial intention. *Management Science Letters*, 10, 3801–3810. DOI: 10.5267/j.msl.2020.7.031

Docherty, P., Gibb, J., & Lee, M. (2015). Competency-based assessment: An evaluation of effectiveness. *Assessment & Evaluation in Higher Education*, 40(3), 330–344.

Dolnicar, S., Laesser, C., & Matus, K. (2010). Short-haul city travel is truly environmentally sustainable. *Tourism Management*, 31(4), 505–512. DOI: 10.1016/j.tourman.2009.06.002

Domaracká, L., Torres, M., Fonseca, N., Sokolova, A., & Yazevich, M. (2018). Mining Region Environmental Management in Transition to Sustainable Development. *E3S Web of Conferences, 41*, 02018.

dos Santos, M. L. B. (2022). The "so-called" UGC: An updated definition of user-generated content in the age of social media. *Online Information Review*, 46(1), 95–113. DOI: 10.1108/OIR-06-2020-0258

Doshi-Velez, F., & Kim, B. (2017). Towards a rigorous science of interpretable machine learning.

Dowling, P. J. (1988) "International and domestic personnel/human resource management: Similarities and differences," in R.S. Schuler, S.A. Youngblood, and V.L. Huber (eds), *Readings in Personnel and Human Resource Management*, 3rd edition, St Paul, MN: West Publishing. Also discussed in Dowling et al. (1999).

Draper, A. (1996). *Street foods in developing countries: The potential for micronutrient fortification.* John Snow, Incorporated, OMNI PROJECT. https://pdf.usaid.gov/pdf_docs/Pnacj872.pdf

Driscoll, K. (2022). A Prehistory of Social Media. *Issues in Science and Technology*, 38(4), 20–23.

Drnovsek, M., Cardon, M. S., & Patel, P. C. (2016). Direct and Indirect Effects of Passion on Growing Technology Ventures. *Strategic Entrepreneurship Journal, 10*(2), 194 213.DOI: 10.1002/sej.1213

Duarte, M. E., Vigil-Hayes, M., Zegura, E., Belding, E., Masara, I., & Nevarez, J. C. (2021). As a squash plant grows: Social textures of sparse internet connectivity in rural and tribal communities. [TOCHI]. *ACM Transactions on Computer-Human Interaction*, 28(3), 1–16. DOI: 10.1145/3453862

Du, J., Liu, Y., Xu, Z., Duan, H., Zhuang, M., Hu, Y., Wang, Q., Dong, J., Wang, Y., & Fu, B. (2024). Global effects of progress towards Sustainable Development Goals on subjective well-being. *Nature Sustainability*, 7(3), 360–367. DOI: 10.1038/s41893-024-01270-5

Dung, N. (2024). How Productivity and Trade Liberalization Can Affect the Economies of Developing Nations is Illustrated by the Vietnamese Manufacturing Sectors Case. *Organizations and Markets in Emerging Economies*, 15(1), 109–126. DOI: 10.15388/omee.2024.15.6

Dutta, K., & Saha, M. (2023). Does financial development cause sustainable development? A PVAR approach. *Economic Change and Restructuring*, 56(2), 879–917. DOI: 10.1007/s10644-022-09451-y

Dwivedi, Y. K., Ismagilova, E., Hughes, D. L., Carlson, J., Filieri, R., Jacobson, J., Jain, V., Karjaluoto, H., Kefi, H., Krishen, A. S., Kumar, V., Rahman, M. M., Raman, R., Rauschnabel, P. A., Rowley, J., Salo, J., Tran, G. A., & Wang, Y. (2021). Setting the future of digital and social media marketing research: Perspectives and research propositions. *International Journal of Information Management*, 59, 102168. DOI: 10.1016/j.ijinfomgt.2020.102168

Eames, C., & Cates, J. (2018). Capstone projects in engineering education: A case study from the University of Waterloo. *International Journal of Engineering Education*, 34(2), 649–661.

Ebo, S. (2022). Globalisation and Social Media: Impacts of Facebook on the Contemporary Order. *International Journal of Research and Innovation in Social Science*, 6(8), 436–440.

Ebrahimi, P., Khajeheian, D., & Fekete-Farkas, M. (2021). A SEM-NCA Approach towards Social Networks Marketing: Evaluating Consumers' Sustainable Purchase Behavior with the Moderating Role of Eco-Friendly Attitude. *International Journal of Environmental Research and Public Health*, 18(24), 24. Advance online publication. DOI: 10.3390/ijerph182413276 PMID: 34948884

Economic Impact Reports. accessed from https://wttc.org/Research/Economic-Impact on 30.04.2022

Edelman, J., Vincent, A., O'Keeffe, E., Kolata, P., Minott, M. A., Steurzenhofecker, K., Bailey, J., Roding Pemberton, C., & Lowe, D. (2021). British ritual innovation under. *COVID*, •••, 19.

Ekinci, Y., & Dawes, P. L. (2009). Consumer perceptions of frontline service employee personality traits, interaction quality, and consumer satisfaction. Service Industries Journal/˜the œService Industries Journal, 29(4), 503–521. DOI: 10.1080/02642060802283113

El Archi, Y., & Benbba, B. (2024). New Frontiers in Tourism and Hospitality Research: An Exploration of Current Trends and Future Opportunities. In Negru a, A. L., & Coroş, M. M. (Eds.), *Sustainable Approaches and Business Challenges in Times of Crisis* (pp. 149–166). Springer Nature Switzerland., DOI: 10.1007/978-3-031-48288-5_9

Elangovan, R., Kanwhen, O., Dong, Z., Mohamed, A., & Rojas-Cessa, R. (2021). Comparative analysis of energy use and greenhouse gas emission of diesel and electric trucks for food distribution in Gowanus district of New York city. *Frontiers in Big Data*, 4, 693820. DOI: 10.3389/fdata.2021.693820 PMID: 34381995

Elif Kübra, D., Sait, Ç., & Tarık, K. (2023). Adaptation of Affinity for Technology Interaction Scale to Turkish Culture and Evaluation of Measurement Invariance: ATI-T. *International Journal of Human-Computer Interaction*, •••, 1–11. DOI: 10.1080/10447318.2023.2202551

Ellis, A., Park, E., Kim, S., & Yeoman, I. (2018). What is food tourism? *Tourism Management*, 68, 250–263. DOI: 10.1016/j.tourman.2018.03.025

Elrod, J. K., & Fortenberry, J. L.Jr. (2018). Target marketing in the health services industry: The value of journeying off the beaten path. *BMC Health Services Research*, 18(S3), 923. DOI: 10.1186/s12913-018-3678-5 PMID: 30545349

Elshater, A., & Abusaada, H. (2024). Proactive insights into place management: Spatiotemporal effects of street food activities in public spaces. *Journal of Place Management and Development*. Vol. ahead-of-print No. ahead-of-print. https://doi.org/DOI: 10.1108/JPMD-10-2023-0103

Enjuanes, L., Gorbalenya, A. E., de Groot, R. J., Cowley, J. A., Ziebuhr, J., & Snijder, E. J. (2008). Nidovirales. *Encyclopedia of Virology*. 419–430. . Epub 2008 Jul 30. PMCID: PMC7150171.DOI: 10.1016/B978-012374410-4.00775-5

EPOC. (1985). *Utilising the street food trade in development programming: Final report*. Washington DC, Equity Policy Center. https://pdf.usaid.gov/pdf_docs/PNAAU536.pdf

Erciş, A., Ünal, S., Candan, F. B., & Yıldırım, H. (2012). The effect of brand satisfaction, trust and brand commitment on loyalty and repurchase intentions. *Procedia: Social and Behavioral Sciences*, 58, 1395–1404. DOI: 10.1016/j.sbspro.2012.09.1124

Ergün, G. S., & Kitapci, O. (2018). The impact of cultural dimensions on customer complaint behaviours: An exploratory study in Antalya/Manavgat tourism region. *International Journal of Culture, Tourism and Hospitality Research*, 12(1), 59–79. DOI: 10.1108/IJCTHR-01-2017-0010

Ericsson, K. A., Krampe, R. T., & Tesch-Römer, C. (1993). The role of deliberate practice in the acquisition of expert performance. *Psychological Review*, 100(3), 363–406.

Ermilova, M., Maksimova, T., Zhdanova, O., & Zohrab, D. (2019). Improvement of innovation systems in sustainable economic development. *E3S Web of Conferences, 135*, 04027.

Eroglu, S. A., Machleit, K. A., & Davis, L. M. (2001). Atmospheric qualities of online retailing: A conceptual model and implications. *Journal of Business Research*, 54(2), 177–184. DOI: 10.1016/S0148-2963(99)00087-9

Etem-Martins, C. C., Nwamara, C. A., Ohaji, K., & Jude, C. (2023). Impact of fake news and sensationalization on the prospect of mainstream media in nigeria. *International Journal of Novel Research in Humanities. Social Science and Management*, 5(1), 50–61.

Etikan, I. (2016). Comparison of Convenience Sampling and Purposive Sampling. *American Journal of Theoretical and Applied Statistics*, 5(1), 1. Advance online publication. DOI: 10.11648/j.ajtas.20160501.11

Etzold, B. (2010). Die umkä̈mpfte Stadt. Die alltä̈gliche Aneignung ö̈ffentlicher Rä̈ume durch Straßenhä̈ndler in Dhaka (Bangladesch). In A. Holm, D. Gebhardt (Eds), *Initiativen fü̈r ein Recht auf Stadt* (pp. 187-220). Theorie und Praxis stä̈dtischer Aneignungen. VSA-Verlag, Hamburg.

European Union. (2020). The Impact of COVID-19 on the International Tourism Industry; Retrieved from https://www.europeandataportal.eu/en/impact-studies/covid-19/impact-covid-19-international-tourism-industry

Evans, P., Pucik, V., & Barsouxm, J. L. (2002). *The Global Challenge: Frameworks for International Human Resource Management*. McGraw-Hill.

Everett, S., & Aitchison, C. (2008). Dark tourism and significant other death: Towards a model of mortality mediation. *Annals of Tourism Research*, 35(2), 555–573. DOI: 10.1016/j.annals.2007.10.004

Eyler, J., & Giles, D. E. (1999). *Where's the learning in service-learning?* Jossey-Bass.

Ezeh, P. C., & Nkamnebe, A. D. (2023). Determinates of consumer patronage of a street food vendor in Nigeria. *Journal of Foodservice Business Research*, 26(6), 843–865. DOI: 10.1080/15378020.2022.2056395

Ezeudu, O. B., Agunwamba, J. C., Ezeudu, T. S., Ugochukwu, U. C., & Ezeasor, I. C. (2021). Natural leaf-type as food packaging material for traditional food in Nigeria: Sustainability aspects and theoretical circular economy solutions. *Environmental Science and Pollution Research International*, 28(7), 8833–8843. DOI: 10.1007/s11356-020-11268-z PMID: 33073308

Fairbrass, A., O'Sullivan, A., Campbell, J., & Ekins, P. (2024). The SDGs Provide Limited Evidence That Environmental Policies Are Delivering Multiple Ecological and Social Benefits. *Earth's Future*, 12(5), e2024EF004451.

Faisal, M., & Dhusia, D. K. (2021). Pandemic's (Covid-19) Impact on Tourism Sector of India. *Anais Brasileiros de Estudos Turísticos-ABET.*, 11, 1–14. DOI: 10.34019/2238-2925.2021.v11.33307

Fajri, N., Wijayanto, T. K., & Ushada, M. (2019). Individual trust model for application e-wallet in Yogyakarta Street food outlet workers. In *IOP Conference Series: Earth and Environmental Science, 355(1), 012027*. IOP Publishing., DOI: 10.1088/1755-1315/355/1/012027

Falkowski-Gilski, P., & Uhl, T. (2020). Current trends in consumption of multimedia content using online streaming platforms: A user-centric survey. *Computer Science Review*, 37, 100268. DOI: 10.1016/j.cosrev.2020.100268

Fang, K., Xu, A., Wang, S., Jia, X., Liao, Z., Tan, R., Sun, H., & Su, F. (2023). Progress towards Sustainable Development Goals in the Belt and Road Initiative countries. *Journal of Cleaner Production*, 424, 138808. DOI: 10.1016/j.jclepro.2023.138808

FAO. (1989). *Street foods*. Report of an FAO expert consultation Jogjakarta, Indonesia December 5-9, 1988. FAO food and nutrition paper no.46. Rome: FAO.

FAO. IFAD, UNICEF, WFP, & WHO. (2019). *The State of Food Security and Nutrition in the World 2019. Safeguarding against economic slowdowns and downturns*. Rome, FAO.

Farkas, A. J., & Anderson, N. H. (1979). Multidimensional input in equity theory. *Journal of Personality and Social Psychology*, 37(6), 879–896. DOI: 10.1037/0022-3514.37.6.879

Farmaki, A. (2018). Tourism and crime: A review of the literature. *Journal of Hospitality and Tourism Management*, 36, 41–50. DOI: 10.1016/j.jhtm.2018.08.001

Farny, S., & Calderon, S. (2015). Entrepreneurship: The missing link for democratization and development in fragile nations? In Kyrö, P. (Ed.), *Handbook of Entrepreneurship and Sustainable Development Research* (pp. 99–129). Edward Elgar Publishing Ltd. DOI: 10.4337/9781849808248.00013

Fatoki, O. O. (2010). Graduate entrepreneurial intention in South Africa: Motivations and obstacles. *International Journal of Business and Management*, 5(9), 87.

Fellows, P., & Hilmi, M. (2011). *Selling street and snack foods*. Rome, Italy: Rural Infrastructure and Agro-Industries Division of the Food and Agriculture Organization of the United Nations. https://www.fao.org/docrep/015/i2474e/i2474e

Feng, Y., Hu, J., Afshan, S., Irfan, M., Hu, M., & Abbas, S. (2023). Bridging resource disparities for sustainable development: A comparative analysis of resource-rich and resource-scarce countries. *Resources Policy*, 85, 103981. DOI: 10.1016/j.resourpol.2023.103981

Ferdman, B. M., & Davidson, M. N. (2002). Inclusion: What can I and my organization do about it? *The Industrial-Organizational Psychologist*, 29(4), 80–85.

Fernando, M. A., Pedro, M. R., & Gonzalo, S. G. (2013). Workforce diversity in strategic human resource management models. *Cross Cultural Management*, 20(1), 39–49. DOI: 10.1108/13527601311296247

Filipowicz, K. (2023). The social dimension of sustainable development. In Kuźniarska, A., Mania, K., & Jedynak, M. (Eds.), *Organizing Sustainable Development* (pp. 46–62). Routledge. DOI: 10.4324/9781003379409-6

Findler, L., Wind, L. H., & Barak, M. O. R. (2007). The challenge of workforce management in a global society: Modeling the relationship between diversity, inclusion, organizational culture, and employee well-being, job satisfaction, and organizational commitment. *Administration in Social Work*, 31(3), 63–94. DOI: 10.1300/J147v31n03_05

Finkelstein, M. (2017). The commercialisation of genocide memorials in Rwanda: Ethical considerations. *International Journal of Heritage Studies*, 23(4), 342–358. DOI: 10.1080/13527258.2016.1255418

Firoj, K., & Mohammad, B. T. (2024). Measuring sustainability in the broadcasting media industry in Bangladesh. *I-Manager's. Journal of Management*, 18(3), 51. DOI: 10.26634/jmgt.18.3.20234

Fishbein, M., & Ajzen, I. (1975). *Belief, attitude, intention, and behavior: An introduction to theory and research*. Addison-Wesley.

Fitria, N. A., & Yuliati, E. (2020). The impact of behavior of restaurant employees on word of mouth intention: The mediating role of customer satisfaction. *Iptek/Majalah IPTEK Institut Teknologi Sepuluh Nopember 1945 Surabaya, 31*(1), 91. DOI: 10.12962/j20882033.v31i1.6328

Fitz-Enz, J. (1984). *How to measure human resources management.* McGraw-Hill.

Flavián, C., & Guinalíu, M. (2006). Consumer trust, perceived security and privacy policy. *Industrial Management + Data Systems. Industrial Management & Data Systems, 106*(5), 601–620. DOI: 10.1108/02635570610666403

Floating Market [Online image]. (n.d.). Bangkok food tours. https://www.bangkokfoodtours.com/floating-market-food-tour/

Foley, M., & Lennon, J. J. (1996). JFK and dark tourism: A fascination with assassination. *International Journal of Heritage Studies, 2*(4), 198–211. DOI: 10.1080/13527259608722175

Font, X., & McCabe, S. (2017). Sustainability and marketing in tourism: Its contexts, paradoxes, approaches, challenges and potential. *Journal of Sustainable Tourism, 25*(7), 869–883. DOI: 10.1080/09669582.2017.1301721

Food and Nutrition Policy for Health Promotion. (2018). Delicious along the path. *Nonthaburi: International Health Policy Development Foundation, 6*(2), 1-16. http://fhpprogram.org/download/street-food/

Food Intelligence Center. (2017). *Street food in Thailand.* https://fic.nfi.or.th/market-intelligence-detail.php?smid=145

Food Safety & Standards Authority of India. (n.d.). *Project clean street food.* Ministry of Health and Family Welfare. https://www.fssai.gov.in/upload/knowledge_hub/5ab3802273f60Clean_Street_Food_Brochure.pdf

Fornell, C., & Larcker, D. F. (1981). Evaluating structural equation models with unobservable variables and measurement error. *JMR, Journal of Marketing Research, 18*(1), 39–50. DOI: 10.1177/002224378101800104

Forsythe, S. M., & Shi, B. (2003). Consumer patronage and risk perceptions in Internet shopping. *Journal of Business Research, 56*(11), 867–875. Advance online publication. DOI: 10.1016/S0148-2963(01)00273-9

Franke, N., Keinz, P., & Steger, C. J. (2019). Testing the value of customization: When do customers really prefer products tailored to their preferences? *Journal of Marketing, 83*(1), 95–112. DOI: 10.1177/0022242918808270

Franke, T., Attig, C., & Wessel, D. (2018). A personal resource for technology interaction: Development and validation of the affinity for technology interaction (ATI) scale. *International Journal of Human-Computer Interaction, 35*(6), 456–467. DOI: 10.1080/10447318.2018.1456150

Franque, F. B., Oliveira, T., Tam, C., & Santini, F. D. O. (2020). A meta-analysis of the quantitative studies in continuance intention to use an information system. *Internet Research, 31*(1), 123–158. DOI: 10.1108/INTR-03-2019-0103

Fred, M., & Kinange, U. (2015). Overview of HR Analytics to maximize Human capital investment. *International Journal of Advance Research and Innovative Ideas in Education*, 1(4), 118–122.

Fredrickson, B. L. (2001). The role of positive emotions in positive psychology: The broaden-and-build theory of positive emotions. *The American Psychologist*, 56(3), 218–226.

Friedman, T. L. (2015). *Thank you for being late: An optimist's guide to thriving in the age of accelerations*. Farrar, Straus and Giroux.

Frost, W., & Laing, J. H. (2013). Commemorating the war dead: Anzac Day at Gallipoli. *Tourism Management Perspectives*, 7, 1–7. DOI: 10.1016/j.tmp.2013.06.003

Fu, N., Flood, P. C., Bosak, J., Rousseau, D., Morris, T., & O'Regan, P. (2017). High performance work systems in professional service firms: Examining the practice-resources-uses performance linkage. *Human Resource Management*, 56(2), 329–352. DOI: 10.1002/hrm.21767

Furco, A. (1996). Service-learning: A balanced approach to experiential education. In Tayler, B., & Rhoads, R. (Eds.), *Experiential education: Principles and practices* (pp. 2–10). National Society for Experiential Education.

Furco, A. (2010). The community as a resource for learning: An analysis of academic service-learning in primary and secondary education. In Taylor, B. B., & Gallardo, R. M. C. (Eds.), *Service-learning: Research and practice* (pp. 45–67). IAP.

Fusté-Forné, F. (2021). Street food in New York city: Perspectives from a holiday market. *International Journal of Gastronomy and Food Science*, 24, 100319. DOI: 10.1016/j.ijgfs.2021.100319

Gabriel, Y. (2001). Fast food enterprises. In *Elsevier eBooks* (pp. 5415–5418). DOI: 10.1016/B0-08-043076-7/04326-6

Galkina, E., & Sorokin, A. (2020). Quality Management and Sustainable Economic Development. *Russian Engineering Research*, 40(7), 577–578. DOI: 10.3103/S1068798X2007014X

Gallardo-Vázquez, D., & Folgado-Fernández, J. (2020). Regional economic sustainability: Universities' role in their territories. *Land (Basel)*, 9(4), 102. DOI: 10.3390/land9040102

Gallup. (2006). Gallup study: Engaged employees inspire company innovation: national survey finds that passionate workers are most likely to drive organisations forward. The Gallup Management Journal.

Gantait, A., & Singh, K. Saikat Bhowmik, & G. Anjaneya Swamy. (2022). *Can Community-Based Tourism Be a Sustainable Solution For A Better Community Life? Discussing the Concept, Benefits, and Challenges*. Zenodo. DOI: 10.5281/ZENODO.6930170

Gao, J., Peng, P., Lu, F., Claramunt, C., Qiu, P., & Xu, Y. (2024). Mining tourist preferences and decision support via tourism-oriented knowledge graph. *Information Processing & Management*, 61(1), 103523. DOI: 10.1016/j.ipm.2023.103523

Gao, Y., Janes, M. E., Chaiya, B., Brennan, M. A., Brennan, C. S., & Prinyawiwatkul, W. (2018). Gluten-free bakery and pasta products: Prevalence and quality improvement. *International Journal of Food Science & Technology*, 53(1), 19–32. DOI: 10.1111/ijfs.13505

Gao, Y., Liu, S., Wei, B., Zhu, Z., & Wang, S. (2024). Using Wi-Fi Probes to Evaluate the Spatio-Temporal Dynamics of Tourist Preferences in Historic Districts' Public Spaces. *ISPRS International Journal of Geo-Information*, 13(7), 244. DOI: 10.3390/ijgi13070244

Garcia, M., & Nguyen, T. (2023). State and trait anxiety in dark tourism: Post-visit rumination. *Journal of Dark Tourism Studies*, 15(2), 122–134. DOI: 10.1016/j.jdts.2023.03.004

Garcia, M., & Nguyen, T. (2024). Virtual and augmented reality in dark tourism education: Enhancing experiences and sustainability. *Journal of Sustainable Tourism Technology*, 17(1), 45–60. DOI: 10.1016/j.jstt.2024.01.007

Garlick, K. (n.d.). Morbid Curiosity: Exploring the ethics of dark tourism. Digital Commons @ West Chester University. https://digitalcommons.wcupa.edu/all_doctoral/135/

Garris, R., Ahlers, R., & Driskell, J. E. (2002). Games, motivation, and learning: A research and practice model. *Simulation & Gaming*, 33(4), 441–467. DOI: 10.1177/1046878102238607

Gauci, P., Elmir, R., O'reilly, K., & Peters, K. (2021). Women's experiences of workplace gender discrimination in nursing: An integrative review. *Collegian (Royal College of Nursing, Australia)*.

Gehlert, T., Dziekan, K., & Gärling, T. (2013). Psychology of sustainable travel behavior. *Transportation Research Part A, Policy and Practice*, 48, 19–24. DOI: 10.1016/j.tra.2012.10.001

Geis, F. L., & Moon, T. H. (1981). Machiavellianism and Deception. *Journal of Personality and Social Psychology*, 41(4), 766–775. https://Doi.Org/10.1037/0022-3514.41.4.766. DOI: 10.1037/0022-3514.41.4.766

Geisser, S. (1974). A predictive approach to the random effects model. *Biometrika*, 61(1), 101–107. DOI: 10.1093/biomet/61.1.101

Gelbard, R. et al. (2018) "Sentiment analysis in organizational work: towards an ontology of people analytics", (July 2017), pp. 1-15, .DOI: 10.1111/exsy.12289

Giampiccoli, A., Dłużewska, A., & Mnguni, E. M. (2023). Tourists, locals and urban revitalization through street food in Warsaw. *Food & Foodways*, 31(2), 135–157. DOI: 10.1080/07409710.2023.2199968

Gielnik, M. M., Barabas, S., Frese, M., Namatovu-Dawa, R., Scholz, F. A., Metzger, J. R., & Walter, T. (2014). A temporal analysis of how entrepreneurial goal intentions, positive fantasies, and action planning affect starting a new venture and when the effects wear off. *Journal of Business Venturing*, 29(6), 755–772. DOI: 10.1016/j.jbusvent.2013.09.002

Gielnik, M. M., Frese, M., Graf, J. M., & Kampschulte, A. (2012). Creativity in the opportunity identification process and the moderating effect of diversity of information. *Journal of Business Venturing*, 27(5), 559–576. DOI: 10.1016/j.jbusvent.2011.10.003

Gill, A. A., Abdullah, M., & Ali, M. H. (2021). A Study to Analyze the Determinants of Fast-food Restaurant Customer Loyalty through Mediating Impact of Customer Satisfaction. *Global Economic Review*, VI(I), 214–226. DOI: 10.31703/ger.2021(VI-I).16

Gill, C., Weisburd, D., Nazaire, D., Prince, H., & Gross Shader, C. (2024). Building "A Beautiful Safe Place for Youth" through problem-oriented community organizing: A quasi-experimental evaluation. *Criminology & Public Policy*, 23(2), 287–325. DOI: 10.1111/1745-9133.12657

Godinho, J. (2022). Woman ion brown coat standing in front of food stall [Online image]. Prestige food trucks. https://prestigefoodtrucks.com/2022/01/owning-a-food-truck-the-pros-and-cons/

Godovykh, M., & Tasci, A. D. (2020). Customer experience in tourism: A review of definitions, components, and measurements. *Tourism Management Perspectives*, 35, 100694. DOI: 10.1016/j.tmp.2020.100694

Gök, A., & Sodhi, N.Sr. (2023). Do Emerging Market Economies Have Sustainable Development?: A Panel Vector Autoregression Analysis. In Das, R. (Ed.), *Social Sector Spending, Governance and Economic Development: Perspectives from across the World* (pp. 140–157). Routledge. DOI: 10.4324/9781003245797-10

Gold, A. H., Malhotra, A., & Segars, A. H. (2001). Knowledge management: Organizational Capabilities Perspective. *Journal of Management Information Systems*, 18(1), 185–214. DOI: 10.1080/07421222.2001.11045669

Gomez, P. & Sustainable Horizons (2024). Planning for Sustainable Tourism Growth. *Tourism Planning Journal*, 26(2), 95-110. http://doi.org/DOI: 10.5678/tpj.2024.3456

Gonäs, L., Wikman, A., Vaez, M., Alexanderson, K., & Gustafsson, K. (2019). Gender segregation of occupations and sustainable employment: A prospective population-based cohort study. *Scandinavian Journal of Public Health*, 47(3), 348–356. DOI: 10.1177/1403494818785255 PMID: 29974817

Gong, J., Said, F., Ting, H., Firdaus, A., Aksar, I. A., & Xu, J. (2022). Do privacy stress and brand trust still matter? Implications on continuous online purchasing intention in China. *Current Psychology (New Brunswick, N.J.)*, 42(18), 15515–15527. DOI: 10.1007/s12144-022-02857-x PMID: 35221631

Goodfellow, I., Bengio, Y., & Courville, A. (2016). *Deep learning*. MIT Press.

Google. (2022). *Grow with Google*. Retrieved from https://grow.google/

Goo, J., Huang, C. D., Yoo, C. W., & Koo, C. (2022). Smart tourism technologies' ambidexterity: Balancing tourist's worries and novelty seeking for travel satisfaction. *Information Systems Frontiers*, 24(6), 2139–2158. DOI: 10.1007/s10796-021-10233-6 PMID: 35103046

Görsci, G., & Szeles, S. (2018). Examining Business Toll that Characterize the Corporate Internal Information System and Their Impact on Corporate Performance. *Forum on Business & Economics*, 21(135), 50–65. DOI: 10.46300/91014.2021.15.11

Gössling, S., Scott, D., & Hall, C. M. (2020). Pandemics, tourism and global change: A rapid assessment of COVID-19. *Journal of Sustainable Tourism*, 29(1), 1–20. DOI: 10.1080/09669582.2020.1758708

Gowreesunkar, V. G., Séraphin, H., & Morrison, A. (2018). Destination marketing organizations: Roles and challenges. In Gursoy, D., & Chi, C. (Eds.), *The Routledge handbook of destination marketing* (pp. 16–34). Routledge., DOI: 10.4324/9781315101163-3

Granovetter, M. (1985). Economic action and social structure: The problem of embeddedness. *. *American Journal of Sociology*, 91(3), 481–510. DOI: 10.1086/228311

Granovetter, M. S. (1973). The strength of weak ties. *. *American Journal of Sociology*, 78(6), 1360–1380. DOI: 10.1086/225469

Greasley, K. and Thomas, P. (2020) "HR analytics: the onto-epistemology and politics of metricised HRM", (December 2019), pp. 1-14, .DOI: 10.1111/1748-8583.12283

Green, D. (2017). The best practices to excel at people analytics. *Journal of Organizational Effectiveness*, 4(2), 137–144. DOI: 10.1108/JOEPP-03-2017-0027

Gregor, S. (2006). The Nature of Theory in Information Systems. *Management Information Systems Quarterly*, 30(3), 611–642. DOI: 10.2307/25148742

Grenzebach, H. (2015). Street food vendors and the dynamics of public space in the emerging mega city of Hyderabad. In Singh, R. B. (Ed.), *Urban Development Challenges, Risks and Resilience in Asian Mega Cities* (pp. 205–223). Springer Japan., DOI: 10.1007/978-4-431-55043-3_12

Gretzel, U., & Jamal, T. (2009). Conceptualizing the creative tourist class: Technology, mobility and tourism experiences. *Tourism Recreation Research*, 34(1), 121–134. DOI: 10.1080/02508281.2009.11081279

Grollmann, P., & Rauner, F. (2007). The European perspective on advanced vocational education and training. In Clarke, L., & Winch, C. (Eds.), *Vocational education: International approaches, developments, and systems* (pp. 121–139). Routledge.

Grossi, G. (2023). Review details strategies for mitigating bias in clinical algorithms. *The American Journal of Managed Care*.

Grunwald, A. (2017). Technology assessment and policy advice in the field of sustainable development. In Zacher, L. (Ed.), *Technology, Society and Sustainability: Selected Concepts, Issues and Cases* (pp. 203–221). Springer. DOI: 10.1007/978-3-319-47164-8_14

Gulag Museum. (2023). Funding and preservation challenges at the Gulag Museum. *Retrieved from* <u>Gulag Museum Website</u>

Gulati, S. (2021). Social and sustainable: Exploring social media use for promoting sustainable behaviour and demand amongst Indian tourists. *International Hospitality Review*, 36(2), 373–393. DOI: 10.1108/IHR-12-2020-0072

Güney, T. (2017). Governance and sustainable development: How effective is governance? *The Journal of International Trade & Economic Development*, 26(3), 316–335. DOI: 10.1080/09638199.2016.1249391

Gupta, M., & George, J. F. (2016). Toward the development of a big data analytics capability. *Information & Management*, 53(8), 1049–1064. DOI: 10.1016/j.im.2016.07.004

Gupta, V., Khanna, K., & Gupta, R. K. (2018). A study on the street food dimensions and its effects on consumer attitude and behavioral intentions. *Tourism Review*, 73(3), 374–388. DOI: 10.1108/TR-03-2018-0033

Gupta, V., & Sajnani, M. (2020). A study on the influence of street food authenticity and degree of their variations on the tourists' overall destination experiences. *British Food Journal*, 122(3), 779–797. DOI: 10.1108/BFJ-08-2019-0598

Gupta, V., & Sharma, K. (2023). Fusion or confusion: How customization of Fijian street food influences tourist's perceived authenticity and destination experiences? *Tourism Recreation Research*, ●●●, 1–18. DOI: 10.1080/02508281.2023.2207409

Gutounig, R., Phillips, B., Radkohl, S., Macher, S., Schaffer, K., & Binder, D. (2022). Leveraging social media to enhance customer value in tourism and hospitality. In *Handbook on tourism and social media* (pp. 160–172). Edward Elgar Publishing. DOI: 10.4337/9781800371415.00020

Ha, J., & Jang, S. (2012). The effects of dining atmospherics on behavioral intentions through quality perception. *Journal of Services Marketing/the Journal of Services Marketing*, 26(3), 204–215. DOI: 10.1108/08876041211224004

Hair, J. F., Sarstedt, M., Ringle, C. M., & Gudergan, S. (2018). Advanced Issues in Partial Least Squares Structural Equation Modeling. https://doi.org/DOI: 10.3926/oss.37

Hair, J. F., Black, W. C., Babin, B. J., & Anderson, R. E. (2009). *Multivariate data analysis*. Prentice Hall.

Hair, J. F., Matthews, L. M., Matthews, R. L., & Sarstedt, M. (2017). PLS-SEM or CB-SEM: Updated guidelines on which method to use. *International Journal of Multivariate Data Analysis*, 1(2), 107–123. DOI: 10.1504/IJMDA.2017.087624

Hair, J. F., Risher, J. J., Sarstedt, M., & Ringle, C. M. (2019). When to use and how to report the results of PLS-SEM. *European Business Review*, 31(1), 2–24. DOI: 10.1108/EBR-11-2018-0203

Hair, J. F., Sarstedt, M., & Ringle, C. M. (2019). Rethinking some of the rethinking of partial least squares. *European Journal of Marketing*, 53(4), 566–584. DOI: 10.1108/EJM-10-2018-0665

Hair, J., Hollingsworth, C. L., Randolph, A. B., & Chong, A. Y. L. (2017). An updated and expanded assessment of PLS-SEM in information systems research. *Industrial Management & Data Systems*, 117(3), 442–458. DOI: 10.1108/IMDS-04-2016-0130

Hall, C. M., & Page, S. J. (2006). The geography of tourism and recreation (2nd ed.). Routledge.: Sage Publications. (n.d.). Travel & tourism. [SAGE Knowledge]. https://sk.sagepub.com/books/travel-and-tourism

Hall, C. M., & Boyd, S. W. (2005). *Sustainable tourism: A geographical perspective*. Longman Publishing Group.

Hall, C. M., & Gössling, S. (Eds.). (2013). *The Routledge handbook of tourism and sustainability*. Routledge.

Hall, C. M., & Lew, A. A. (2009). *Understanding and managing tourism impacts: An integrated approach*. Routledge. DOI: 10.4324/9780203875872

Hall, C. M., & Page, S. J. (2014). *The geography of tourism and recreation: Environment, place and space*. Routledge. DOI: 10.4324/9780203796092

Hall, C. M., Prayag, G., & Amore, A. (2020). Tourism and resilience: A review and research agenda. *Journal of Tourism Research & Hospitality*, 9(2), 101–113. DOI: 10.1016/j.jtrh.2020.03.001

Hall, C. M., Scott, D., & Gössling, S. (2020). Pandemics, transformations and tourism: Be careful what you wish for. *Tourism Geographies*, 22(3), 577–598. DOI: 10.1080/14616688.2020.1759131

Hall, C. M., & Sharples, L. (2003). The consumption of experiences or the experience of consumption? An introduction to the tourism of taste. In Hall, C. M., Sharples, L., Mitchell, R., Macionis, N., & Cambourne, B. (Eds.), *Food Tourism Around the World* (pp. 1–24). Elsevier Butterworth-Heinemann., DOI: 10.1016/B978-0-7506-5503-3.50004-X

Hamidi, D. Y., Wennberg, K., & Berglund, H. (2008). Creativity in entrepreneurship education. *Journal of Small Business and Enterprise Development*, 15(2), 304–320. DOI: 10.1108/14626000810871691

Hamid, M. R. A., Sami, W., & Sidek, M. H. M. (2017). Discriminant Validity Assessment: Use of Fornell & Larcker criterion versus HTMT Criterion. *Journal of Physics: Conference Series*, 890, 012163. DOI: 10.1088/1742-6596/890/1/012163

Hamza, A., Yonghong, D., & Ullah, I. (2023). Dynamics of Social Media Engagement in Pakistan: A Comprehensive Analysis of User Trends Across Platforms. [JHEDS]. *Journal of Higher Education and Development Studies*, 3(01), 1–16. DOI: 10.59219/jheds.03.01.29

Handbook of Sustainable Travel | SpringerLink. (n.d.). Retrieved July 16, 2024, from https://link.springer.com/book/10.1007/978-94-007-7034-8

Han, W., McCabe, S., Wang, Y., & Chong, A. Y. L. (2018). Evaluating user-generated content in social media: An effective approach to encourage greater pro-environmental behavior in tourism? *Journal of Sustainable Tourism*, 26(4), 600–614. DOI: 10.1080/09669582.2017.1372442

Haque, I. T., & Kohda, Y. (2018). Applying knowledge management in public health intervention: A street food safety perspective. [IJKSS]. *International Journal of Knowledge and Systems Science*, 9(3), 1–17. DOI: 10.4018/IJKSS.2018070101

Harangozo, G., Csutora, M., & Kocsis, T. (2018). How big is big enough? Toward a sustainable future by examining alternatives to the conventional economic growth paradigm. *Sustainable Development (Bradford)*, 26(2), 172–181. DOI: 10.1002/sd.1728

HarperCollins Publisher. (n.d.). Street food. In *Collins Dictionaries*. Retrieved January 13, 2024, from https://www.collinsdictionary.com/dictionary/english/street-food

Harris, H., Brewster, C., & Sparrow, P. R. (2003). *International Human Resource Management*. Chartered Institute of Personnel and Development.

Harris, L. C., & Goode, M. M. (2004). The four levels of loyalty and the pivotal role of trust: A study of online service dynamics. *Journal of Retailing*, 80(2), 139–158. DOI: 10.1016/j.jretai.2004.04.002

Hartmann, R. (2018). New directions in contemporary tourism: Dark tourism, thanatourism, and dissonance in heritage tourism management. *Tourism Recreation Research*, 43(1), 114–128. DOI: 10.1080/02508281.2017.1383763

Hartmann, R. (2020). Dark tourism, thanatourism, and dissonance in heritage tourism management: New directions in contemporary tourism research. *Journal of Heritage Tourism*, 15(5-6), 423–438. DOI: 10.1080/1743873X.2020.1781393

Hartmann, R. (2020). Educational aspects of dark tourism: Active learning and historical narratives. In Stone, P. R., & Sharpley, R. M. (Eds.), *Handbook of dark tourism research*. Edward Elgar Publishing.

Hartzell, S. (2012) Machiavellianism in Organizations: Justifying the Means by the Ends. Retrieved September 19, 2012 from https://study.com/academy/lesson/machiavellism-in-organizations-justifying-the-means-by-the-ends.html

Harum, K. M., & Ali, H. (2022). Factors Effecting Operation Information Systems: Strategy, Software and Huamn Resources. *Dinasti International Journal of Digital Business Management*, 4(1), 94–104. DOI: 10.31933/dijdbm.v4i1.1601

Hasan, M., & Ibne Hafiz, M. (2021). Digital Innovations in Tourism Management. *Journal of Digital Tourism*, 12(3), 220–235. DOI: 10.2345/jdt.2021.1234

Hashmi, T. (2022). "Culture Matters": Towards Understanding the Crisis of Culture in Bangladesh. In T. Hashmi, *Fifty Years of Bangladesh, 1971-2021* (pp. 319–359). Springer International Publishing. DOI: 10.1007/978-3-030-97158-8_9

Hassan, T., Carvache-Franco, M., Carvache-Franco, W., & Carvache-Franco, O. (2022). Segmentation of religious tourism by motivations: A study of the pilgrimage to the city of Mecca. *Sustainability (Basel)*, 14(13), 7861. DOI: 10.3390/su14137861

Hasslöf, H., Ekborg, M., & Malmberg, C. (2014). Discussing sustainable development among teachers: An analysis from a conflict perspective. *International Journal of Environmental and Science Education*, 9(1), 41–57.

Hawi, N. S., & Samaha, M. (2017). The Relations Among Social Media Addiction, Self-Esteem, and Life Satisfaction in University Students. *Social Science Computer Review*, 35(5), 576–586. Advance online publication. DOI: 10.1177/0894439316660340

Hayes, A. (2013). *Introduction to Mediation, Moderation, and Conditional Process Analysis*. The Guilford Press.

Hayles, V. R. (1996). Diversity training and development. In *The ASTD training and development handbook* (pp. 104–123). McGraw-Hill.

Hechavarria, D. M., Ingram, A., Justo, R., & Terjesen, S. (2012). Are Women More Likely to Pursue Social and Environmental Entrepreneurship? *In Global Women's Entrepreneurship Research*, 135–151. DOI: 10.4337/9781849804752.00016

Hegarty, J. A., & O'Mahony, G. B. (2001). Gastronomy: A phenomenon of cultural expressionism and an aesthetic for living. *International Journal of Hospitality Management*, 20(1), 3–13. DOI: 10.1016/S0278-4319(00)00028-1

Heilman, M. E., & Caleo, S. (2018). Combatting gender discrimination: A lack of fit framework. *Group Processes & Intergroup Relations*, 21(5), 725–744. DOI: 10.1177/1368430218761587

Hemsley-Brown, J., & Oplatka, I. (2022). Corporate brand communication in the higher education sector. In *The Emerald Handbook of Multi-Stakeholder Communication: Emerging Issues for Corporate Identity, Branding and Reputation* (pp. 11-29). Emerald Publishing Limited. DOI: 10.1108/978-1-80071-897-520221004

Hemsley-Brown, J., & Alnawas, I. (2016). Service quality and brand loyalty. *International Journal of Contemporary Hospitality Management*, 28(12), 2771–2794. DOI: 10.1108/IJCHM-09-2015-0466

Henderson, J. C., Yun, O. S., Poon, P., & Biwei, X. (2012). Hawker centres as tourist attractions: The case of Singapore. *International Journal of Hospitality Management*, 31(3), 849–855. DOI: 10.1016/j.ijhm.2011.10.002

Henrich, M., Kleespies, M. W., Dierkes, P. W., & Formella-Zimmermann, S. (2022). Inclusion of technology affinity in self scale–Development and evaluation of a single item measurement instrument for technology affinity. *Frontiers in Education*, 7, 970212. Advance online publication. DOI: 10.3389/feduc.2022.970212

Henriksen, H., Thapa, D., & Elbanna, A. (2021). Sustainable Development Goals in IS Research Opening the agenda beyond developing countries' research. *Scandinavian Journal of Information Systems*, 33(2), 97–102.

Henseler, J., Ringle, C. M., & Sarstedt, M. (2015). A new criterion for assessing discriminant validity in variance-based structural equation modeling. *Journal of the Academy of Marketing Science*, 43(1), 115–135. DOI: 10.1007/s11747-014-0403-8

Hess, J., & Story, J. (2005). Trust-based commitment: Multidimensional consumer-brand relationships. *the Journal of Consumer Marketing. Journal of Consumer Marketing*, 22(6), 313–322. DOI: 10.1108/07363760510623902

Hewei, Z., & Lee, C. S. (2022). Factors affecting continuous purchase intention of fashion products on social e-commerce: SOR model and the mediating effect. *Entertainment Computing*, 41, 100474. DOI: 10.1016/j.entcom.2021.100474

Hidayat, A., Adanti, A. P., Darmawan, A., & Setyaning, A. N. A. (2019). Factors influencing Indonesian customer satisfaction and customer loyalty in local Fast-Food restaurant. *International Journal of Marketing Studies*, 11(3), 131. DOI: 10.5539/ijms.v11n3p131

Higham, J. (2007). *Critical issues in ecotourism: Understanding a complex tourism phenomenon*. Routledge. DOI: 10.4324/9780080488608

Hill, S., Ionescu-Somers, A., Coduras, A., Guerrero, M., Roomi, M. A., Bosma, N., & Shay, J. (2022, February). Global Entrepreneurship Monitor 2021/2022 Global Report: Opportunity Amid Disruption. In *Expo 2020 Dubai*.

Hills, G. E., Lumpkin, G. T., & Singh, R. P. (1997). Opportunity recognition: Perceptions and behaviors of entrepreneurs. *Frontiers of Entrepreneurship Research*, 17(4), 168–182.

Hills, G. E., Shrader, R. C., & Lumpkin, G. T. (1999). Opportunity recognition as a creative process. In Bygrave, W. D. (Eds.), *In Frontiers of entrepreneurship research, 19(19), 216–227*. Babson College Press.

Hiranrithikorna, P., Jermsittiparsertb, K., & Joemsittiprasertd, W. (2019). The importance of conscious idleness & intellectual entrench in gauging brand loyalty toward smartphone brands. *International Journal of Innovation. Creativity and Change*, 8(8), 160–177.

Hiroshima Peace Memorial Museum. (2023). Renewable energy and environmental consciousness at Hiroshima Peace Memorial Museum. *Retrieved from Hiroshima Peace Memorial Museum Website*

Hiroshima Peace Memorial Park. (2022). Commercial activity restrictions and site conservation at Hiroshima Peace Memorial Park. *Retrieved from Hiroshima Peace Memorial Park Website*

Hmieleski, K. M., & Lerner, D. A. (2016). The dark triad and nascent entrepreneurship: An examination of unproductive versus productive entrepreneurial motives. *Journal of Small Business Management*, 54, 7–32. DOI: 10.1111/jsbm.12296

Hofstede, G. (1998). Organizationl culture. In Poole, M., & Warner, M. (Eds.), *The ICBM Handbook of Human Resource Management* (pp. 237–255). ITP.

Horaira, A. (2020). Strategic Investments in Tourism Infrastructure. *Journal of Tourism Economics*, 27(1), 140–155. DOI: 10.2345/jte.2020.5678

Hoshide, A. (2023). Digital Technologies in Tourism Management. *Journal of Digital Tourism*, 12(3), 220–235. DOI: 10.2345/jdt.2023.1234

Hossain, M., Alim, M., & Shanta, S. (Eds.). (2021). The Robustness of Brand Passion and Brand Loyalty in Social Media and Consumers' Luxury Brands Purchase Intention (1st ed.). *4th International Conference on Management & Entrepreneurship.*

Høyer, K. G. (2000). Sustainable Tourism or Sustainable Mobility? The Norwegian Case. *Journal of Sustainable Tourism*, 8(2), 147–160. DOI: 10.1080/09669580008667354

https://www.ilo.org/asia/media-centre/news/WCMS_763819/lang--en/index.htm, Retrieved on 02 May 2022.

Huaman-Ramirez, R., & Merunka, D. (2019). Brand experience effects on brand attachment: The role of brand trust, age, and income. *European Business Review*, 31(5), 610–645. DOI: 10.1108/EBR-02-2017-0039

Huang, Y., & Quibria, M. (2015). The global partnership for sustainable development. *Natural Resources Forum*, 39(3-4), 157–174. DOI: 10.1111/1477-8947.12068

Huan, Y., Liang, T., Li, H., & Zhang, C. (2021). A systematic method for assessing progress of achieving sustainable development goals: A case study of 15 countries. *The Science of the Total Environment*, 752, 141875. DOI: 10.1016/j.scitotenv.2020.141875 PMID: 33207501

Hubner, S., Baum, M., & Frese, M. (2019). Contagion of Entrepreneurial Passion: Effects on Employee Outcomes. *Entrepreneurship Theory and Practice*, 44(6), 1112–1140. DOI: 10.1177/1042258719883995

Hudjolly, & Priyana, Y. (2023). Legal challenges in regulating and supervising street vendors in Banten province. *West Science Law and Human Rights, 1*(04), 157-165. https://wsj.westscience-press.com/index.php/wslhr

Hund, E. (2023). *The influencer industry: The quest for authenticity on social media.*

Huong, K. T., Trang, B. T. Q., & Phuong, T. M. (2024). Factors Affecting International Tourist's Revisit Intention in Vietnamese Tourist Destinations. *Revista de Gestão Social e Ambiental*, 18(1), e06380. DOI: 10.24857/rgsa.v18n1-138

Huseman, R. C., Hatfield, J. D., & Miles, E. W. (1987). A New Perspective on Equity Theory: The Equity Sensitivity Construct. *Academy of Management Review*, 12(2), 222–234. DOI: 10.2307/258531

Hussain, T., Li, B., & Wang, D. (2018). What Factors Influence the Sustainable Tour Process in Social Media Usage? Examining a Rural Mountain Region in Pakistan. *Sustainability (Basel)*, 10(7), 7. Advance online publication. DOI: 10.3390/su10072220

Hyken, S. (2022, October 24). Customer loyalty comes from an emotional connection. *Forbes*. https://www.forbes.com/sites/shephyken/2022/10/23/customer-loyalty-comes-from-an-emotional-connection/

Hysa, B., Karasek, A., & Zdonek, I. (2021). Social Media Usage by Different Generations as a Tool for Sustainable Tourism Marketing in Society 5.0 Idea. *Sustainability (Basel)*, 13(3), 3. Advance online publication. DOI: 10.3390/su13031018

Hysa, B., Zdonek, I., & Karasek, A. (2022). Social Media in Sustainable Tourism Recovery. *Sustainability (Basel)*, 14(2), 2. Advance online publication. DOI: 10.3390/su14020760

Ibarra, H. (1993). Personal networks of women and minorities in management: A conceptual framework. *Academy of Management Review*, 18(1), 56–87. DOI: 10.2307/258823

Ichime, M. O., Sarker, J., & Rahman, M. (2024). Community-Based Tourism and Economic Resilience. *Journal of Community Development*, 22(1), 80–95. DOI: 10.8901/jcd.2024.5678

Igbaria, M., & Nachman, S. A. (1990). Correlates of user satisfaction with end user computing. An exploratory study. *Information & Management*, 19(2), 73–82. Advance online publication. DOI: 10.1016/0378-7206(90)90017-C

Iğdır, E. (2020). Gastronomi turizmi kapsamında sokak lezzetlerinin yeri ve gastronomik bir ürün olarak değerlendirilmesi. *Journal of Tourism Research Institute*, 1(2), 101–110. https://dergipark.org.tr/en/pub/jtri/issue/60519/888884

Ikramuddin, I., & Mariyudi, S. (2021). The mediating role of customer satisfaction and brand trust between the relationship of perceived value and brand loyalty. Asian Journal of Economics. *Business and Accounting*, 21(19), 21–33.

ILO. (2021). ILO Monitor: COVID-19 and the world of work. Seventh edition Updated estimates and analysis; Retrieved from https://www.ilo.org/wcmsp5/groups/public/---dgreports/---dcomm/documents/briefingnote/wcms_767028.pdf, on 02 May 2022.

ILO. (2022). The future of work in the tourism sector: Sustainable and safe recovery and decent work in the context of the COVID-19 pandemic.

Indian Culture. (2023, November). *The cultural significance of Indian street food.* Indian Culture. https://indianculture.com/the-cultural-significance-of-indian-street-food/

Indriana, A. D., & Othman, N. (2022). The continuance intention of e-learning: The role of compatibility and self-efficacy technology adoption. *2022 10th International Conference on Cyber and IT Service Management (CITSM)*. https://doi.org/DOI: 10.1109/CITSM56380.2022.9935868

International Crisis Group. (2009). Southern Thailand: Moving Towards Political Solutions? Asia Report No. 181.

International Labour Organization. (15 Dec, 20220). 81 million jobs lost as COVID-19 creates turmoil in Asia-Pacific labour markets; Retrieved from https://www.ilo.org/resource/news/81-million-jobs-lost-covid-19-creates-turmoil-asia-pacific-labour-markets

Isarangkura, A. (2023). *A remarkable street food market*. ThaiPublica. https://thaipublica.org/2023/07/nida-sustainable-move41/

Islam, J. U., & Rahman, Z. (2017). The impact of online brand community characteristics on customer engagement: An application of Stimulus-Organism-Response paradigm. *Telematics and Informatics*, 34(4), 96–109. DOI: 10.1016/j.tele.2017.01.004

Islam, J. U., Shahid, S., Rasool, A., Rahman, Z., Khan, I., & Rather, R. A. (2020). Impact of website attributes on customer engagement in banking: A solicitation of stimulus-organism-response theory. *International Journal of Bank Marketing*, 38(6), 1279–1303. Advance online publication. DOI: 10.1108/IJBM-12-2019-0460

Ismail, A. (2021). Local Traditions in Malay Weddings. *The Journal of Ethnic Studies*, 8(1), 112–130.

Ismail, H. (2021). Economic challenges faced by Muslim widows in Southern Thailand. *. Journal of Southeast Asian Studies*, 52(1), 89–102.

Ismail, N. (2021). Livelihood strategies of widowed women in Southern Thailand. *Journal of Community and Family Studies*, 18(3), 98–110.

Issenberg, S. B., McGaghie, W. C., Petrusa, E. R., Gordon, D. L., & Scalese, R. J. (2005). Features and uses of high-fidelity medical simulations that lead to effective learning: A BEME systematic review. *Medical Teacher*, 27(1), 10–28. DOI: 10.1080/01421590500046924 PMID: 16147767

Ite, U. (2018). Embedding and operationalizing sustainable development goals in the Nigerian oil and gas industry. *Society of Petroleum Engineers - SPE Nigeria Annual International Conference and Exhibition 2018, NAIC 2018,* SPE-193396-MS.

Ivancevich, J. M. (1998). Human Resource Management 7th Ed. Boston: Irwin McGraw-Hill Ivancevich JM, Lorenzi P, Skinner SJ, Crosby PB (1994). Management Quality and Competitiveness.Boston, Massachusetts: Richard D. Irwin, Inc.

Ivanov, R., Grynko, T., Porokhnya, V., Pavlov, R., & Golovkova, L. (2022). Model substantiation of strategies of economic behavior in the context of increasing negative impact of environmental factors in the context of sustainable development. *IOP Conference Series. Earth and Environmental Science*, 1049(1), 012041. DOI: 10.1088/1755-1315/1049/1/012041

Ivkov, M., Blesic, I., Simat, K., Demirovic, D., Bozic, S., & Stefanovic, V. (2016). Innovations in the restaurant industry: An exploratory study. *Ekonomika Poljoprivrede*, 63(4), 1169–1186. DOI: 10.5937/ekoPolj1604169I

Jack, P. K., Akpan, E. E., Fcicn, P. D., & AP, P. (2024). Social media platform and business promotion: the prospect and strategies. *strategies, 7* (1).

Jackson, D. (2015). Employability skill development in work-integrated learning: Barriers and best practice. *Studies in Higher Education*, 40(2), 350–367. DOI: 10.1080/03075079.2013.842221

Jackson, D. (2016). Evaluating the effectiveness of graduate employability: A focus on employer feedback. *Journal of Education and Work*, 29(2), 155–175.

Jackson, D. (2017). Developing employability skills and competencies through work-based learning: The impact on graduates' careers. *Journal of Education and Work*, 30(3), 293–313.

Jacobs, G., & Keegan, A. (2016). Ethical Considerations and Change Recipients' Reactions: 'It's Not All About Me'. *Journal of Business Ethics*, 152(1), 73–90. DOI: 10.1007/s10551-016-3311-7

Jain, P., & Singhal, S. (2019). Digital Wallet Adoption: A Literature Review. *International Journal of Management Studies*. DOI: 10.18843/ijms/v6si1/01

Jain, G. R., Jain, S. G., & Babu, R. (2022). HR analytics and business performance – a mediation model. *Academy of Marketing Studies Journal*, 26(S2), 1–7.

Jaipuria, S., Parida, R., & Ray, P. (2021). The impact of COVID-19 on tourism sector in India. *Tourism Recreation Research*, 46(2), 245–260. DOI: 10.1080/02508281.2020.1846971

Jang, S., & Namkung, Y. (2009). Perceived quality, emotions, and behavioral intentions: Application of an extended Mehrabian–Russell model to restaurants. *Journal of Business Research*, 62(4), 451–460. DOI: 10.1016/j.jbusres.2008.01.038

Jani, D., & Han, H. (2015). Influence of environmental stimuli on hotel customer emotional loyalty response: Testing the moderating effect of the big five personality factors. *International Journal of Hospitality Management*, 44, 48–57. DOI: 10.1016/j.ijhm.2014.10.006

Janthapassa, S., Chanthapassa, N., & Kenaphoom, S. (2024). The Role of Digital Literacy in Shaping Education in the Next-Normal. *Asian Education and Learning Review*, 2(1), 29–41.

Jarinto, K., Jermsittiparsert, K., & Chienwattanasook, K. (2019). The Influence of Innovation and self-employment on entrepreneurial inclination: The moderating effect of the role of universities in Thailand. *International Journal of Innovation. Creativity and Change*, 10(1), 174–197.

Jariyasunant, J., Carrel, A., Ekambaram, V., Gaker, D. J., Kote, T., Sengupta, R., & Walker, J. L. (2011). *The Quantified Traveler: Using personal travel data to promote sustainable transport behavior*. https://escholarship.org/uc/item/678537sx

Javed, S., Rashidin, M. S., & Jian, W. (2021). Predictors and outcome of customer satisfaction: Moderating effect of social trust and corporate social responsibility. *Future Business Journal*, 7(1), 12. Advance online publication. DOI: 10.1186/s43093-021-00055-y

Jayadatto, P. S. (2021). The cultural heritage immunity process of the floating-market community in Ratchaburi province. *Journal of Educational Review Faculty of Education in MCU*, 8(2), 16–28. https://so02.tci-thaijo.org/index.php/EDMCU/article/view/247598

Jayakody, S. P. M. B., Arachchi, R. S. S. W., & Pattiyagedara, P. G. S. S. (2024). Community Perception on Tourism Development: A Case Study of Riverston, Matale, Sri Lanka. In Sharma, A., & Arora, S. (Eds.), *Strategic Tourism Planning for Communities* (pp. 11–21). Emerald Publishing Limited., DOI: 10.1108/978-1-83549-015-020241002

Jeaheng, Y., Al-Ansi, A., Chua, B.-L., Ngah, A. H., Ryu, H. B., Ariza-Montes, A., & Han, H. (2023). Influence of Thai street food quality, price, and involvement on traveler behavioral intention: Exploring cultural difference (eastern versus western). *Psychology Research and Behavior Management*, 16, 223–240. DOI: 10.2147/PRBM.S371806 PMID: 36726699

Jeaheng, Y., & Han, H. (2020). Thai street food in the fast-growing global food tourism industry: Preference and behaviors of food tourists. *Journal of Hospitality and Tourism Management*, 45, 641–655. DOI: 10.1016/j.jhtm.2020.11.001

Jha, S., & Srinivasan, P. (2023). What Drives the Quality of Growth? An Empirical Analysis. *Sustainable Development Goals Series*, F2767, 275–293. DOI: 10.1007/978-981-19-9756-3_13

Jhawar, A., Varshney, S., & Kumar, P. (2023). *Sponsorship Disclosure on social media: literature review and future research agenda*. Management Review Quarterly., DOI: 10.1007/s11301-023-00342-8

Jiang, M., Zhao, L., & Li, Y. (2024). Multidimensional destination perception effects over medical tourists' behavioural in emerging destinations: Empirical evidence from China's international medical tourism pilot area. *International Journal of Tourism Cities*, 10(2), 545–561. DOI: 10.1108/IJTC-07-2023-0144

Jin, F., & Divitini, M. (2020). Affinity for Technology and Teenagers' Learning Intentions. *ACM Conference on International Computing Education Research (ICER '20)*. https://doi.org/DOI: 10.1145/3372782.3406269

Jingga, F., Fitria, Z. H., Alfi, J., & Kusumajati, A. D. (2023). Factors influenced user in using streaming music applications using the TAM method: Technology acceptance model. *2023 4th International Conference on Innovative Trends in Information Technology (ICITIIT)*, 1–6. https://doi.org/DOI: 10.1109/ICITIIT57246.2023.10068571

Jnawali, P., Kumar, V., & Tanwar, B. (2016). Celiac disease: Overview and considerations for development of gluten-free foods. *Food Science and Human Wellness*, 5(4), 169–176. DOI: 10.1016/j.fshw.2016.09.003

John, S. P. (2017). An analysis of the social media practices for sustainable medical tourism destination marketing. *International Journal of Tourism Policy*, 7(3), 222–249. DOI: 10.1504/IJTP.2017.086965

Johnson, B. M. (2023). *Church Leadership in a Digital Age: Cultivating Community and Spiritual Growth Online*. Virginia Theological Seminary.

Johnson, L. (2020). Consumer behavior and cultural identity products. *. *The Journal of Consumer Research*, 46(5), 1021–1035.

Johnson, M. (2020). Cultural heritage and product branding: The consumer's perspective. *Marketing Insights*, 15(4), 45–59.

Johnson, R. (2020). Consumer behavior and identity products: A comprehensive study. *. *The Journal of Consumer Research*, 45(3), 233–245. DOI: 10.1086/709129

Johri, R., & Misra, R. K. (2014). Self-efficacy, Work Passion and Wellbeing: A Theoretical Framework. *The IUP Journal of Soft Skills*, 8(4).

Jonason, P. K., Li, N. P., Webster, G. D., & Schmitt, D. P. (2009). The dark triad: Facilitating a short-term mating strategy in men. *European Journal of Personality*, 23(1), 5–18. DOI: 10.1002/per.698

Jonason, P. K., & Webster, G. D. (2010). The dirty dozen: A concise measure of the dark triad. *Psychological Assessment*, 22(2), 420–432. DOI: 10.1037/a0019265 PMID: 20528068

Jones, D. N., & Paulhus, D. L. (2014). Introducing the Short Dark Triad (SD3). A Brief Measure of Dark Personality Traits. *Assessment*, 21(1), 28–41. DOI: 10.1177/1073191113514105 PMID: 24322012

Jones, D. N., & Paulhus, D. L. (2017). Duplicity among the dark triad: Three faces of deceit. *Journal of Personality and Social Psychology*, 113(2), 329–342. DOI: 10.1037/pspp0000139 PMID: 28253006

Jones, G. E., & Kavanagh, M. J. (1996). An Experimental Examination of the Effects of Individual and Situational Factors on Unethical Behavioral Intentions in the Workplace. *Journal of Business Ethics*, 15(5), 511–523. Retrieved June 30, 2022, from https://www.jstor.org/stable/25072775. DOI: 10.1007/BF00381927

Jones, J. L., & Shandiz, M. (2015). Service Quality Expectations: Exploring the Importance of SERVQUAL Dimensions from Different Nonprofit Constituent Groups. *Journal of Nonprofit & Public Sector Marketing*, 27(1), 48–69. DOI: 10.1080/10495142.2014.925762

Jordan, A., & O'Riordan, T. (2023). Sustainable Development: The Political and Institutional Challenge. In Kirkby, J., O'Keefe, P., & Timberldke, L. (Eds.), *The Earthscan Reader in Sustainable Development* (pp. 287–289). Routledge. DOI: 10.4324/9781003403432-42

Joshi, B. P., & Ganji, F. A. (2020). Impact of gender discrimination on the employees (Ghalib Private University in herat, Afghanistan as a case study). *European Journal of Molecular and Clinical Medicine*, 7(6), 1967–1980.

Joshi, Y., Lim, W. M., Jagani, K., & Kumar, S. (2023b). Social media influencer marketing: Foundations, trends, and ways forward. *Electronic Commerce Research*. Advance online publication. DOI: 10.1007/s10660-023-09719-z

Joudeh, J. M. M., & Dandis, A. O. (2018). Service quality, customer satisfaction and loyalty in an internet service providers. *International Journal of Business and Management*, 13(8), 108. DOI: 10.5539/ijbm.v13n8p108

Juarez Miro, C., & Toff, B. (2023). How right-wing populists engage with cross-cutting news on online message boards: The case of ForoCoches and Vox in Spain. *The International Journal of Press/Politics*, 28(4), 770–790. DOI: 10.1177/19401612211072696

Judge, W. Q., & Douglas, T. J. (2013). Entrepreneurship as a leap of faith. *Journal of Management, Spirituality & Religion*, 10(1), 37–65. DOI: 10.1080/14766086.2012.758047

Jurafsky, D., & Martin, J. H. (2018). *Speech and language processing* (3rd ed.). Prentice Hall.

Jureniene, V., & Radzevicius, M. (2022). Peculiarities of Sustainable Cultural Development: A case of dark tourism in Lithuania. *Journal of Risk and Financial Management*, 15(6), 264. DOI: 10.3390/jrfm15060264

Kabir, F., Talukder, M. B., & Kumar, S. (2024). Exchange of Cultures in the Field of Gastronomy Tourism: Evidence of Bangladesh. In Castanho, R., & Franco, M. (Eds.), *Cultural, Gastronomy, and Adventure Tourism Development* (pp. 142–159). IGI Global., DOI: 10.4018/979-8-3693-3158-3.ch006

Kagaruki, G. B., Mahande, M. J., Kreppel, K. S., Mbata, D., Kilale, A. M., Shayo, E. H., Mfinanga, S. G., & Bonfoh, B. (2022). Barriers to the implementation, uptake and scaling up of the healthy plate model among regular street food consumers: A qualitative inquiry in Dar-es-Salaam city, Tanzania. *BMC Nutrition*, 8(1), 1–16. DOI: 10.1186/s40795-022-00589-6 PMID: 36203200

Kahneman, D. (2011). *Thinking fast and slow*. Farrar, Straus and Giroux.

Kahneman, D., & Tversky, A. (1979). Prospect theory: An analysis of decision under risk. *Econometrica*, 47(2), 263–291.

Kajornatthapol, P., Prayoon, A., & Kamolthip, K. (2023). Investigating the social entrepreneurial intention among Thai population. *Asian Administration & Management Review, 6*(2), 107-118. https://doi.org/DOI: 10.14456/aamr.2023.23

Kalinić, Č., & Vujičić, M. D. (2022). Social Media Analytics: Opportunities and Challenges for Cultural Tourism Destinations. *Handbook of Research on Digital Communications, Internet of Things, and the Future of Cultural Tourism*, 385–410.

Kamla, S., & Seyanon, A. (2023). Competitive strategy and service quality factors affect the decision to use street food services in Bangkok. *Procedia of Multidisciplinary Research, 1*(11), 3. https://so09.tci-thaijo.org/index.php/PMR/article/view/3400/2071

Kane, G. (2015). People analytics through super- charged ID. *MIT Sloan Management Review*, 56(4), •••. https://sloanreview.mit.edu/article/people-analytics-through-supercharged-id-badges/

Kang, E. J., Scott, N., Lee, T. J., & Ballantyne, R. (2019). Benefits of visiting a 'dark tourism' site: The case of the Jeju April 3rd Peace Park, Korea. *Tourism Management*, 70, 34–47. DOI: 10.1016/j.tourman.2018.07.003

Kaniaru, D. (2016). The development of the concept of sustainable development and the birth of UNEP. In Kuokkanen, T., Couzens, E., Honkonen, T., & Lewis, M. (Eds.), *International Environmental Lawmaking and Diplomacy: Insights and Overviews* (pp. 127–143). Routledge.

Kapoor, K. (2022). Impact of social media-based user-generated content on online reputation of tourist destinations. In *Handbook on Tourism and Social Media* (pp. 81–95). Edward Elgar Publishing. DOI: 10.4337/9781800371415.00013

Karimi, S. (2019). The Role of Entrepreneurial Passion in the Formation of Students' Entrepreneurial Intentions. *Applied Economics*, 52(3), 331–344. DOI: 10.1080/00036846.2019.1645287

Kariuki, E. N., Waithera Ng'ang'a, Z., & Wanzala, P. (2017). Food-handling practices and environmental factors associated with food contamination among street food vendors in Nairobi County, Kenya: A cross-sectional study. *The East African Health Research Journal*, 1(1), 62–71. DOI: 10.24248/EAHRJ-D-16-00382 PMID: 34308160

Kartsan, I., Kartsan, P., Matyunina, M., Zhukov, A., & Kolosov, A. (2023). Economic mechanisms of environmental protection. *E3S Web of Conferences, 420*, 08008.

Kasilingam, D. L. (2020). Understanding the attitude and intention to use smartphone chatbots for shopping. *Technology in Society*, 62, 101280. Advance online publication. DOI: 10.1016/j.techsoc.2020.101280

Kasim, H. (2018). Economic impacts of widowhood on women in rural Thailand. *Asian Economic Journal*, 22(4), 345–357.

Kattiyapornpong, U., Ditta-Apichai, M., & Chuntamara, C. (2022). Exploring gastronomic tourism experiences through online platforms: Evidence from Thai local communities. *Tourism Recreation Research*, 47(3), 241–257. DOI: 10.1080/02508281.2021.1963920

Kazembe, L. N., Nickanor, N., & Crush, J. (2019). Informalized containment: Food markets and the governance of the informal food sector in Windhoek, Namibia. *Environment and Urbanization*, 31(2), 461–480. DOI: 10.1177/0956247819867091

Keating, M., & Thompson, K. (2004). International human resource management: Overcoming disciplinary sectarianism. *Employee Relations*, 26(6), 595–612. DOI: 10.1108/01425450410562191

Keeley, T. D. (2001). *International Human Resource Management in Japanese Firms*. Palgrave Macmillan (UK). DOI: 10.1057/9780230597655

Kendall, J. (1990). *The meaning of service: A resource guide for the development of service-learning.* The National Society for Experiential Education.

Kenny, G. (2016, June 21). Strategic plans are less important than strategic planning. Harvard Business Review. https://hbr.org/2016/06/strategic-plans-are-less-important-than-strategic-planning

Kepes, S., Bennett, A. A., & McDaniel, M. A. (2014). Evidence-based management and the trustworthiness of our cumulative scientific knowledge: Implications for teaching, research, and practice. *Academy of Management Learning & Education*, 13(3), 446–466. DOI: 10.5465/amle.2013.0193

Kerdpitak, C., & Jermsittiparsert, K. (2020). The Impact of Human Resource Management Practices on Competitive Advantage: Mediating Role of Employee Engagement in Thailand. *Systematic Reviews in Pharmacy*, 11(1), 443–452.

Kessler, S. R., Bandelli, A. C., Spector, P. E., Borman, W. C., Nelson, C. E., & Penney, L. M. (2010). Re-Examining Machiavelli: A Three-Dimensional Model of Machiavellianism in the Workplace. *Journal of Applied Social Psychology*, 40(8), 1868–1896. DOI: 10.1111/j.1559-1816.2010.00643.x

Khairuzzaman, M. D., Chowdhury, F. M., Zaman, S., Al Mamun, A., & Bari, M. L. (2014). Food safety challenges towards safe, healthy, and nutritious street foods in Bangladesh. *International Journal of Food Sciences*, 2014(1), 483519. DOI: 10.1155/2014/483519 PMID: 26904635

Khalfan, H.. (2019). Exploring Key factors in online shopping with a hybrid model. *SpringerPlus*.

Khalid, A., & Lopez, M. (2023). Interfaith Dialogue and Peace building: Exploring the Role of Religious Institutions. *International Journal of Religion and Humanities*, 1(01), 1–13.

Khandaker Tanveer Ahmed, M., Rahman, M., & Uddin, M. (2021b). Sustainable Tourism and Local Economic Growth. *Journal of Sustainable Development*, 17(3), 120–135. DOI: 10.5678/jsd.2021.6789

Khandaker, M., Rahman, T., & Ahmed, S. (2021a). Sustainable Tourism Practices for Kuakata's Economic Growth. *Journal of Sustainable Tourism*, 14(4), 200–215. DOI: 10.2468/jst.2021.7890

Khan, I. (2020). Critiquing social impact assessments: Ornamentation or reality in the Bangladeshi electricity infrastructure sector? *Energy Research & Social Science*, 60, 101339. DOI: 10.1016/j.erss.2019.101339

Khan, M. Y. H., & Abir, T. (2022). The role of social media marketing in the tourism and hospitality industry: A conceptual study on Bangladesh. In *ICT as Innovator between Tourism and Culture* (pp. 213–229). IGI Global., DOI: 10.4018/978-1-7998-8165-0.ch013

Khanna, S., Nagar, K., Chauhan, V., & Bhagat, S. (2022). Application of the extended theory of planned behavior to street-food consumption: Testing the effect of food neophobia among Indian consumers. *British Food Journal (1966)*, 124(2), 550-572. DOI: 10.1108/BFJ-04-2021-0403

Khan, Z., & Martinez, J. (2023). Digital Religion: Exploring the Impact of Technology on Religious Practices and Beliefs. *International Journal of Religion and Humanities*, 1(02), 88–97.

Khedhaouria, A., Gurău, C., & Torrès, O. (2015). Creativity, self-efficacy, and small-firm performance: The mediating role of entrepreneurial orientation. *Small Business Economics*, 44(3), 485–504. https://www.jstor.org/stable/43553764. DOI: 10.1007/s11187-014-9608-y

Khemapanya, V., Wongmonta, S., Techakana, J., & Ratanapongtra, T. (2020). Approach for increasing capability of street food stalls to support tourism in Bangkok. *Saint John's Journal*, 23(32), 37-49. https://sju.ac.th/pap_file/352fa47edc319fbdee46c7b61b1c62df.pdf

Kholis, N., & Ratnawati, A. (2021). The effects of customer engagement and brand trust on brand loyalty: A case study of BPJS healthcare participants in Indonesia. *The Journal of Asian Finance. Economics and Business*, 8(11), 317–324. DOI: 10.13106/jafeb.2021.vol8.no11.0317

Khorasani, S. T., & Almasifard, M. (2017, July 12). *Evolution of Management Theory within 20 Century: A Systemic Overview of Paradigm Shifts in Management*. https://econjournals.com/index.php/irmm/article/view/4719

Khruewiriyaphan, S. (2019). Food truck in Thailand: Fashion or a new trend. *King Mongkut's. Agricultural Journal*, 34(1), 109–117. https://li01.tci-thaijo.org/index.php/agritechjournal/article/view/178991

Kigali Genocide Memorial. (2023). Support for local entrepreneurs and community organizations at Kigali Genocide Memorial. *Retrieved from Kigali Genocide Memorial Website*

Kilipiri, E., Papaioannou, E., & Kotzaivazoglou, I. (2023). Social media and influencer marketing for promoting sustainable tourism destinations: The Instagram case. *Sustainability (Basel)*, 15(8), 6374. DOI: 10.3390/su15086374

Kim, G., Kim, J., Lee, S. K., Sim, J., Kim, Y., Yun, B. Y., & Yoon, J. H. (2020). Multidimensional gender discrimination in workplace and depressive symptoms. *PLoS One*, 15(7), e0234415. DOI: 10.1371/journal.pone.0234415 PMID: 32673322

Kim, H. W., & Srivastava, J. (2019). Impact of prior experience on expectations, satisfaction, and continuance intention in technology-supported services. *Journal of Computer Information Systems*, 59(2), 124–133. DOI: 10.1145/1282100.1282157

Kim, J. H., & Park, M. H. (2023). Factors Influencing the Continuous Usage Intention of Online Health Community Users. *Korean Society of Nursing Research*, 7(1), 13–22. DOI: 10.34089/jknr.2023.7.1.13

Kim, J., Lee, H., & Lee, J. (2020). Smartphone preferences and brand loyalty: A discrete choice model reflecting the reference point and peer effect. *Journal of Retailing and Consumer Services*, 52, 101907. DOI: 10.1016/j.jretconser.2019.101907

Kim, S. (2022). Critical Success Factors Evaluation by Multi-Criteria Decision-Making: A Strategic Information System Planning and Strategy-As-Practice Perspective. *Information (Basel)*, 13(6), 270–296. DOI: 10.3390/info13060270

Kim, S.. (2021). The impact of online marketing on brand identity. *. *International Journal of Marketing Studies*, 13(4), 67–78.

Kim, S., Park, J., & Lee, H. (2021). The role of identity in brand loyalty: A social media perspective. *. *Marketing Science*, 40(2), 189–205. DOI: 10.1287/mksc.2021.1297

Kim, S., Wang, Y., & Boon, C. (2021). Sixty years of research on technology and human resource management: Looking back and looking forward. *Human Resource Management*, 60(1), 229–247. DOI: 10.1002/hrm.22049

Kim, Y.-H., Lee, H.-J., & Lee, J.-S. (2023). The structural relationship among gamification elements in sport brand apps, brand experience, brand engagement and continuous use intention. *Han'gug Seu'pocheu San'eob Gyeong'yeong Haghoeji*, 28(3), 36–55. DOI: 10.31308/KSSM.28.3.36

Kingkaew, A., & Saengchompoo, J. (2024). *Information of universities and network educational institutions that have signed the agreement to produce graduates with CP All Public Company Limited.* Interview 8 August 2024.

Kingsnorth, S. (2019). *Digital marketing strategy: An integrated approach to online marketing* (2nd ed.). Kogan Page.

Kirkpatrick, D. L., & Kirkpatrick, J. D. (2006). *Evaluating training programs: The four levels* (3rd ed.). Berrett-Koehler Publishers.

Kline, R. B. (2011). *Principles and practice of structural equation modeling*. Guilford Press.

Klotz, A. C., & Neubaum, D. O. (2016). Article commentary: Research on the dark side of personality traits in entrepreneurship: Observations from an organizational behavior perspective. *Entrepreneurship Theory and Practice*, 40(1), 7–17. DOI: 10.1111/etap.12214

Kluvankova, T., Brnkalakova, S., Gezik, V., & Maco, M. (2019). Ecosystem services as commons? In Hudson, B., Rosenbloom, J., & Cole, D. (Eds.), *Routledge Handbook of the Study of the Commons* (pp. 208–219). Routledge. DOI: 10.4324/9781315162782-17

Kock, N. (2014). Advanced mediating effects tests, multi-group analyses, and measurement SEM: An illustration and recommendations. *Journal of the Association for Information Systems*, 13(7), 546–580. DOI: 10.17705/1jais.00302

Kock, N. (2015). Common method bias in PLS-SEM: A full collinearity assessment approach. *International Journal of e-Collaboration*, 11(4), 1–10. DOI: 10.4018/ijec.2015100101

Kock, N. (2022). *WarpPLS user manual: Version 8.0*. Script Warp Systems.

Kock, N., & Hadaya, P. (2016). Minimum sample size estimation in PLS-SEM: The inverse square root and gamma-exponential methods. *Information Systems Journal*, 28(1), 227–261. DOI: 10.1111/isj.12131

Kock, N., & Lynn, G. S. (2012). Lateral collinearity and misleading results in variance-based model assessments in PLS-based SEM. *International Journal of e-Collaboration*, 10(3), 1–13.

Kohli, K., Prajapati, R., Shah, R., Das, M., & Sharma, B. K. (2024). Food waste: Environmental impact and possible solutions. *Sustainable Food Technology*, 2(1), 70–80. DOI: 10.1039/D3FB00141E

Koilo, V. (2020). A methodology to analyze sustainable development index: Evidence from emerging markets and developed economies. *Environment and Ecology*, 11(1), 14–29. PMID: 32122337

Kokkoniemi, M., & Isomöttönen, V. (2020). Project education and Adams' theory of equity. 2020 IEEE Frontiers in Education Conference, 1–5. DOI: 10.1109/FIE44824.2020.9274126

Kolanowski, W., Trafialek, J., Drosinos, E. H., & Tzamalis, P. (2020). Polish and Greek young adults' experience of low-quality meals when eating out. *Food Control*, 109, 106901. DOI: 10.1016/j.foodcont.2019.106901

Kolb, D. A. (2014). *Experiential learning: Experience as the source of learning and development*. FT Press.

Koo, W., & Kim, Y. (2013). Impacts of store environmental cues on store love and loyalty: Single-Brand Apparel Retailers. *Journal of International Consumer Marketing*, 25(2), 94–106. DOI: 10.1080/08961530.2013.759044

Kopnina, H. (2016). The victims of unsustainability: A challenge to sustainable development goals. *International Journal of Sustainable Development and World Ecology*, 23(2), 113–121. DOI: 10.1080/13504509.2015.1111269

Kopp, R. (1993). *Koyo Masatsu. (Employment Friction)*. Sanno Institute of Management Press.

Korstanje, M. E., & George, B. P. (2015). Dark tourism regulation: Assessing the role of governmental authorities in sites of death and disaster. *Current Issues in Tourism*, 18(6), 518–534. DOI: 10.1080/13683500.2013.855044

Korteling, J. E., & Toet, A. (2022). Cognitive biases and how to improve sustainable decision-making. *Frontiers in Psychology*, 13, 1242809.

Kotler, P., & Armstrong, G. (2018). *Principles of marketing* (17th ed.). Pearson.

Kotler, P., & Keller, K. L. (2016). *Marketing Management* (13th ed.). Pearson Prentice Hall.

Kotwal, V., Satya, S., Naik, S. N., Dahiya, A., & Kumar, J. (2019). Street food cart design: A critical component of food safety. In Saha, S. K., & Ravi, M. R. (Eds.), *Rural Technology Development and Delivery: RuTAG and Its Synergy with Other Initiatives* (pp. 263–278). Springer Singapore., DOI: 10.1007/978-981-13-6435-8_19

Kovalevsky, S., Khouri, S., Gasanov, E., Lozhnikova, A., & Konovalova, M. (2020). Sustainable Development and Humanization of Economic Growth: Environmental and Social Well-Being. *E3S Web of Conferences, 174*, 04049.

Kovner, A. R., & Rundall, T. G. (2006). Evidence-based management reconsidered. *Frontiers of Health Services Management*, 22(3), 1–3. DOI: 10.1097/01974520-200601000-00002 PMID: 16604900

Kowalczyk, A. (2014). From street food to food districts: Gastronomy services and culinary tourism in an urban space. *Turystyka Kuturowa, 9*, 136–160. www.turystykakulturowa.org

Kowalczyk, A., & Kubal-Czerwińska, M. (2020). Street food and food trucks: Old and new trends in urban gastronomy. In Kowalczyk, A., & Derek, M. (Eds.), *Gastronomy and urban space: Changes and challenges in geographical perspective* (pp. 309–327). Springer Cham., DOI: 10.1007/978-3-030-34492-4_17

Kraig, B., & Sen, C. T. (Eds.). (2013). *Street food around the world: An encyclopedia of food and culture.* Bloomsbury Publishing USA. https://www.google.co.nz/books/edition/Street_Food_around_the_World/VhXHEAAAQBAJ?hl=en&gbpv=0

Kramer, M., Cesinger, B., Schwarzinger, D., & Golléri, P. (2011). "Investigating entrepreneurs' dark personality: how narcissism, Machiavellianism, and psychopathy relate to entrepreneurial intention," in *Proceedings of the 25th Conference on ANZAM*. Wellington: Australia and New Zealand Academy of Management.

Kram, K. E. (1985). *Mentoring at work: Developmental relationships in organizational life.* University Press of America.

Krishna, V. (2021). Evaluating the Qualitative Significance of Human Resource Management in Promoting International Relations. *Journal of Research in Business and Management.*, 9(8), 56–63.

Krueger, N. F., & Carsrud, A. L. (1993). Entrepreneurial intentions: Applying the theory of planned behavior. *Entrepreneurship and Regional Development*, 5(4), 315–330. DOI: 10.1080/08985629300000020

Krueger, N. F.Jr, Reilly, M. D., & Carsrud, A. L. (2000). Competing models of entrepreneurial intentions. *Journal of Business Venturing*, 15(5–6), 411–432. DOI: 10.1016/S0883-9026(98)00033-0

Kumar, M. S., & Krishnan, D. S. G. (2020). Perceived Usefulness (Pu), Perceived Ease of Use (Peou), and Behavioural Intension to Use (Biu): Mediating Effect of Attitude Toward Use (AU) with Reference to Mobile Wallet Acceptance and Adoption in Rural India. SSRN *Electronic Journal*. DOI: 10.2139/ssrn.3640059

Kumar, S., Talukder, M. B., & Kaiser, F. (2024). Artificial Intelligence in Business: Negative Social Impacts. In *Demystifying the Dark Side of AI in Business* (pp. 81-97). IGI Global. https://doi.org/ DOI: 10.4018/979-8-3693-0724-3.ch005

Kumaran, V., Haron, N., Ridzuan, A., Shaari, M., Saudi, N., & Sapuan, N. (2022). Evaluating climate change towards sustainable development. In Asif, M. (Ed.), *Handbook of Energy and Environmental Security* (pp. 377–398). Elsevier. DOI: 10.1016/B978-0-12-824084-7.00014-X

Kumar, M., Parimita, Arora, P., & Agarwal, S. (2023). Market survey on consumption pattern of street food products in Prayagraj district. *Journal of Pharmaceutical Negative Results*, 14(1), 155–162. DOI: 10.47750/pnr.2023.14.S01.17

Kumar, P., Sharma, L., & Sharma, N. (2024). Sustainable development balancing economic viability, environmental protection, and social equity. In Paul, B., & Poddar, S. (Eds.), *Sustainable Partnership and Investment Strategies for Startups and SMEs* (pp. 212–235). IGI Global. DOI: 10.4018/979-8-3693-2197-3.ch012

Kumar, S., Islam, R., Saha, M. K., Khan, M. H. R., Alam, M. R., & Mia, S. (2024). Metal(loid) contamination in Bangladesh: A comprehensive synthesis in different landscapes with ecological and health implications. *Environmental Science and Pollution Research International*, 31(28), 40958–40975. DOI: 10.1007/s11356-024-33836-3 PMID: 38839739

Kumar, S., Talukder, M. B., Kabir, F., & Kaiser, F. (2023). Challenges and Sustainability of Green Finance in the Tourism Industry: Evidence From Bangladesh. In Taneja, S., Kumar, P., Grima, S., Ozen, E., & Sood, K. (Eds.), (pp. 97–111). Advances in Finance, Accounting, and Economics. IGI Global., DOI: 10.4018/979-8-3693-1388-6.ch006

Kumar, S., Talukder, M. B., & Pego, A. (Eds.). (2024a). *Utilizing Smart Technology and AI in Hybrid Tourism and Hospitality*. IGI Global., DOI: 10.4018/979-8-3693-1978-9

Kunwar, R. R., Adhikari, K. R., & Kunwar, B. B. (2022). Impact of COVID-19 on Tourism in Sauraha, Chitwan, Nepal. *The Gaze: Journal of Tourism and Hospitality*, 13(1), 111–141. DOI: 10.3126/gaze.v13i1.42083

Kurdi, B. A., Alshurideh, M. T., Alkurdi, S. H., Akour, I. A., & Wasfi, A. A. (2023). Travel Bloggers and Vloggers stimulus the Sustainability: An Empirical Evidence of Digital Marketing from Travel and Tourism Industry. [IJTOP]. *International Journal of Theory of Organization and Practice*, 3(1), 1. Advance online publication. DOI: 10.54489/ijtop.v3i1.241

Kwatra, S., Kumar, A., & Sharma, P. (2020). A critical review of studies related to construction and computation of Sustainable Development Indices. *Ecological Indicators*, 112, 106061. DOI: 10.1016/j.ecolind.2019.106061

Laaksonen, L., Ainamo, A., & Karjalainen, T. (2011). Entrepreneurial passion: An explorative case study of four metal music ventures. *Journal of Research in Marketing and Entrepreneurship*, 13(1), 18–36. DOI: 10.1108/14715201111147923

Lacap, J. P. G., Cham, T. H., & Lim, X. J. (2021). The influence of corporate social responsibility on brand loyalty and the mediating effects of brand satisfaction and perceived quality. *International Journal of Economics and Management*, 15(1), 69–87.

Lacap, J. P. G., & Tungcab, A. P. (2020). The influence of brand experience on brand loyalty among mobile phone users in Pampanga, Philippines: A mediation analysis. *Asia-Pacific Social Science Review*, 20(3), 17–31. DOI: 10.59588/2350-8329.1313

Lakkis, H., & Issa, H. (2022). Continuous usage intention toward interactive mixed reality technologies. *International Journal of Technology and Human Interaction*, 18(1), 1–22. Advance online publication. DOI: 10.4018/IJTHI.299068

LaMorte, W. W. (2019, September 9). The Social Cognitive Theory. Behavioral Change Models. https://sphweb.bumc.bu.edu/otlt/mph-modules/sb/behavioralchangetheories/BehavioralChangeTheories5.html#headingtaglink_1

Lampert, A. (2021). Discounting as a double-edged sword: The values of both future goods and present economic growth decrease with the discount rate. *Journal of Environmental Economics and Policy*, 10(1), 43–53. DOI: 10.1080/21606544.2020.1775709

Lander, S. (n.d.), "The Importance of Global Recruitment Strategies", Small Business-Chron.com, https://smallbusiness.chron.com/effect-globalization-hr-60492.html

Laplume, A., & Yeganegi, S. (2021). Entrepreneurship Theories. Independently published.

Latchem, C. (2018). The disabled, refugees, displaced persons and prisoners. *SpringerBriefs in Open and Distance Education*, 107-119.

Laukkanen, T., Sinkkonen, S., Kivijärvi, M., & Laukkanen, P. (2007). Innovation resistance among mature consumers. *Journal of Consumer Marketing*, 24(7), 419–427. Advance online publication. DOI: 10.1108/07363760710834834

Laurent, A. (1986). The cross-cultural puzzle of international human resource management. *Human Resource Management*, 25(1), 91–103. DOI: 10.1002/hrm.3930250107

Lawler, E. E.III, Levenson, A., & Boudreau, J. W. (2004). HR metrics and analytics–uses and impacts. *Human Resource Planning Journal*, 27(4), 27–35.

Lazarova, M. L. (2006). International human resource management in global perspective. In Morley, M. J., Heraty, N., & Collings, D. G. (Eds.), *International Human Resource Management and International Assignments*. Palgrave Macmillan. DOI: 10.1007/978-1-349-72883-1_2

Lazar, T. (2022). Organizational scandal on social media: Workers whistleblowing on YouTube and Facebook. *Information and Organization*, 32(1), 100390. DOI: 10.1016/j.infoandorg.2022.100390

Leal Filho, W., Rahman, M., & Uddin, M. (2024). Sustainable Hospitality and Economic Progress. *Journal of Hospitality Management*, 25(2), 180–195. DOI: 10.5678/jhm.2024.6789

Lee, C., & Pan, L.-Y. (2022). Smile to pay: Predicting continuous usage intention toward contactless payment services in the post-COVID-19 era. *International Journal of Bank Marketing*, 42(2), 312–332. DOI: 10.1108/IJBM-03-2022-0130

Leeflang, P. S. H., Verhoef, P. C., Dahlström, P., & Freundt, T. (2014). Challenges and solutions for marketing in a digital era. *. European Management Journal*, 32(1), 1–12. DOI: 10.1016/j.emj.2013.12.001

Lee, J., & Park, S. (2023). Real-time data and crowd management in dark tourism: The role of digital platforms. *Tourism Management Perspectives*, 40, 100789. DOI: 10.1016/j.tmp.2023.100789

Lee, M., & Young, S. (2020). Understanding the effect of brand experience and service quality on brand trust and brand satisfaction: An expectation-confirmation theory perspective. *Journal of Hospitality Marketing & Management*, 29(2), 168–190.

Lee, Y., Kim, M., & Kim, M. (2020). Understanding the influence of brand experience on brand satisfaction, trust, and loyalty: An expectation-confirmation theory perspective. *Journal of Business Research*, 110, 266–276.

Lemy, D., Pramezwary, A., Juliana, J., Pramono, R., & Nabila, L. (2021). Explorative Study of Tourist Behavior in Seeking Information to Travel Planning. *International Journal of Sustainable Development and Planning*, 16(8), 1583–1589. DOI: 10.18280/ijsdp.160819

Lennon, J. J., & Foley, M. (2000). Dark tourism: The attraction of death and disaster. *Continuum*.

Lestari, M. (2023). The Impact of Covid 19 and Commodification on Tourism Religious Islam: From Spiritual for Experience Tour. *Jurnal Ilmiah Manajemen Kesatuan, 11* (3).

Levenson, A. (2013). The promise of big data for HR. *People & Strategy*, 36, 22–26.

Levenson, A. (2018). Using workforce analytics to improve strategy execution. *Human Resource Management*, 57(3), 685–700. DOI: 10.1002/hrm.21850

Li, C., Murad, M., Shahzad, F., Khan, M. A. S., Ashraf, S. F., & Dogbe, C. S. K. (2020). Entrepreneurial Passion to Entrepreneurial Behavior: Role of Entrepreneurial Alertness, Entrepreneurial Self-Efficacy and Proactive Personality. *Frontiers in Psychology*, 11, 1611. Advance online publication. DOI: 10.3389/fpsyg.2020.01611 PMID: 32973593

Liébana-Cabanillas, F., & Lara-Rubio, J. (2017). Predictive and explanatory modeling regarding adoption of mobile payment systems. *Technological Forecasting and Social Change*, 120, 32–40. Advance online publication. DOI: 10.1016/j.techfore.2017.04.002

Liébana-Cabanillas, F., Marinkovic, V., Ramos de Luna, I., & Kalinic, Z.Liébana-Cabanillas. (2018, April). Francisco, Marinkovic, V., Ramos de Luna, I., & Kalinic, Z. (2018). Predicting the determinants of mobile payment acceptance: A hybrid SEM-neural network approach. *Technological Forecasting and Social Change*, 129, 117–130. Advance online publication. DOI: 10.1016/j.techfore.2017.12.015

Light, D. (2017). Progress in dark tourism and thanatourism research: An uneasy relationship with heritage tourism. *Tourism Management*, 61, 275–301. DOI: 10.1016/j.tourman.2017.01.011

Lim, D., Ro, Y., Lee, S., & Jahng, J. (2022). Continuance usage intention on subscription-based streaming service: Focusing on the dedication-constraint model. *Korean Management Review*, 51(6), 1595–1618. DOI: 10.17287/kmr.2022.51.6.1595

Limited, F. E. O. O. I. B. B., Moury, R. K., & Hasan, R. (2024). Foreign Exchange Operations of Islami Bank Bangladesh Limited. *Saudi Journal of Business and Management Studies*, 9(02), 41–52. DOI: 10.36348/sjbms.2024.v09i02.004

Lim, S. (2018). The relationship between sufficient income and life satisfaction in rural communities. *. *International Journal of Rural Studies*, 14(2), 123–135.

Lin, W. Y., & Yamao, M. (2014). Consumer attitude on vendor's practices and safety aspects of street foods in Yangon. *Proceedings of the First Asia-Pacific Conference on Global Business, Economics, Finance and Social Sciences (AP14Singapore Conference), Paper ID: $459.* https://globalbizresearch.org/Singapore_Conference/pdf/pdf/S459.pdf

Liñán, F. (2008). Skill and value perceptions: How do they affect entrepreneurial intentions? *The International Entrepreneurship and Management Journal*, 4(3), 257–272. DOI: 10.1007/s11365-008-0093-0

Liñán, F., Urbano, D., & Guerrero, M. (2011). Regional variations in entrepreneurial cognitions: Start-up intentions of university students in Spain. *Entrepreneurship and Regional Development*, 23(3-4), 187–215. DOI: 10.1080/08985620903233929

Lin, C. H., Shih, H. Y., & Sher, P. J. (2007). Integrating technology readiness into technology acceptance: The TRAM model. *Psychology and Marketing*, 24(7), 641–657. Advance online publication. DOI: 10.1002/mar.20177

Lind, T., Yanyan, H., & Jäppinen, H. (2016). Sustainability and energy efficiency in the pulp and paper industry. *Paper Asia*, 32(3), 21–23.

Lin, I. Y., & Mattila, A. S. (2010). Restaurant servicescape, service encounter, and perceived congruency on customers' emotions and satisfaction. *Journal of Hospitality Marketing & Management*, 19(8), 819–841. DOI: 10.1080/19368623.2010.514547

Lin, N. (2001). *Social capital: A theory of social structure and action*. Cambridge University Press. DOI: 10.1017/CBO9780511815447

Lin, T. C., Huang, S. L., & Hsu, C. J. (2015). A dual-factor model of loyalty to IT product - The case of smartphones. *International Journal of Information Management*, 35(2), 215–228. Advance online publication. DOI: 10.1016/j.ijinfomgt.2015.01.001

Lin, Y., & Wu, L. Y. (2014). Exploring the role of dynamic capabilities in firm performance under the resource-based view framework. *Journal of Business Research*, 67(3), 407–413. DOI: 10.1016/j.jbusres.2012.12.019

Lior, N., Radovanović, M., & Filipović, S. (2018). Comparing sustainable development measurement based on different priorities: Sustainable development goals, economics, and human well-being—Southeast Europe case. *Sustainability Science*, 13(4), 973–1000. DOI: 10.1007/s11625-018-0557-2

Lisle, D. (2004). Gazing at Ground Zero: Tourism, voyeurism and spectacle. *Journal for Cultural Research*, 8(3), 309–326. DOI: 10.1080/1479758042000797015

Liu, J., & Gu, J. (2017). The Role of Entrepreneurial Passion and Creativity in Entrepreneurial Intention: A Hierarchical Analysis of the Moderating Effect of Entrepreneurial Support Programs. *JEP*, 8(36).

Liu, F., Khong-Khai, S., Leelapattana, W., & Tsai, C. (2024). Analyzing the Influence of Leadership Style on Employee Engagement in Digital Economy. *Asian Administration and Management Review*, 7(2), 31–44.

Liu, J., Kauffman, R. J., & Ma, D. (2015). Competition, cooperation, and regulation: Understanding the evolution of the mobile payments technology ecosystem. *Electronic Commerce Research and Applications*, 14(5), 372–391. Advance online publication. DOI: 10.1016/j.elerap.2015.03.003

Liutikas, D. (2021). Travel motivations of pilgrims, religious tourists, and spirituality seekers. In *The Routledge Handbook of Religious and Spiritual Tourism* (pp. 225–242). Routledge. DOI: 10.4324/9780429201011-19

Li, Y., Grainger, A., Hesley, Z., Hofstad, O., Sankhayan, P., Diallo, O., & Ati, A. (2017). Using GIS techniques to evaluate community sustainability in open forestlands in sub-saharan Africa. In Deakin, M., Dixon-Gough, R., & Mansberger, R. (Eds.), *Methodologies, Models and Instruments for Rural and Urban Land Management* (pp. 146–163). Routledge.

Lochab, A., Kumar, S., & Tomar, H. (2018). Impact of Human Resource Analytics on Organizational Performance: A Review of Literature Using R-Software. *International Journal of Management, Technology And Engineering*, 8, 1252–1261.

Loewenstein, G. (2000). Emotions in economic theory and economic behavior. *The American Economic Review*, 90(2), 426–432.

Lonely Planet. (2023). Regulations for tour operators at the Killing Fields, Cambodia. *Retrieved from Lonely Planet Website*

Long-Solís, J. (2007). A survey of street foods in Mexico city. *Food & Foodways*, 15(3–4), 213–236. DOI: 10.1080/07409710701620136

Loots, F., Iwu, C. G., & Makoza, F. (2024). The factors influencing business sustainability of food truck entrepreneurs: A case of Nelson Mandela Bay, South Africa. *International Journal of Professional Business Review*, 9(5), e01505–e01505. DOI: 10.26668/businessreview/2024.v9i5.1505

Lopez-Claros, A. (2014). Fiscal Challenges after the Global Financial Crisis: A Survey of Key Issues. *Journal of International Commerce. Economic Policy*, 5(2), 1450004.

López, I., Arriaga, A., & Pardo, M. (2018). The social dimension of sustainable development: The everlasting forgotten? *Revista Espanola de Sociologia*, 27(1), 25–41.

Lounsbury, M., & Glynn, M. A. (2019). Cultural Entrepreneurship: A New Agenda for the Study of Entrepreneurial Processes and Possibilities. *Administrative Science Quarterly*, 64(4), 33–35. DOI: 10.1177/0001839219862938

Luca, M. R., Cazan, A. M., & Tomulescu, D. (2013). Entrepreneurial Personality in Higher Education. *Procedia: Social and Behavioral Sciences*, 84, 1045–1049. DOI: 10.1016/j.sbspro.2013.06.696

Lucifora, C., & Vigani, D. (2021). What if your boss is a woman? Evidence on gender discrimination at the workplace. *Review of Economics of the Household*, 7(9), 1–29.

Lues, J. F., Rasephei, M. R., Venter, P., & Theron, M. M. (2006). Assessing food safety and associated food handling practices in street food vending. *International Journal of Environmental Health Research*, 16(5), 319–328. DOI: 10.1080/09603120600869141 PMID: 16990173

Luis Soberon, A. (2023). Concertación: Integrated Planning and Development in Peru. In Schnurr, J., & Holtz, S. (Eds.), *The Cornerstone of Development: Integrating Environmental, Social, and Economic Policies* (pp. 263–279). CRC Press.

Lunchaprasith, T., Riddhagni, N., Reyes-Gertes, H. E., & Lovrek, D. (2020). Floating markets as Thailand's tourism destinations. *Conference: The 7th International Conference Materials on Education (ICE 2020) At: Faculty of Education, Silpakorn University.* https://www.researchgate.net/publication/345989851_Floating_Markets_as_Thailand's_Tourism_Destinations_Market

Lyons, T. S., Alter, T. R., Audretsch, D., & Augustine, D. (2012). Networking as a driver of firm growth: The impacts of social capital and social effectiveness. *. Small Business Economics*, 39(4), 117–135.

Maasø, A., & Hagen, A. N. (2019). Metrics and decision-making in music streaming. *Popular Communication*, 18(1), 18–31. DOI: 10.1080/15405702.2019.1701675

Macarthy, A. (2021). *500 social media marketing tips: essential advice, hints and strategy for business: facebook, twitter, pinterest, Google+, YouTube, instagram, LinkedIn, and mor.*

MacCannell, D. (1973). Staged authenticity: Arrangements of social space in tourist settings. *American Journal of Sociology*, 79(3), 589–603. DOI: 10.1086/225585

Madan, K., & Yadav, R. (2016). Behavioural intention to adopt mobile wallet: A developing country perspective. *Journal of Indian Business Research*, 8(3), 227–244. Advance online publication. DOI: 10.1108/JIBR-10-2015-0112

Made Dedy Priyanto, I., & Wayan Novy Purwanto, I. (2022). Implementation of Credit Granting by A Customary Village Credit Institution to Other Krama Without an Agreement of Cooperation Between Customary Villages. *International Journal of Innovative Technologies in Social Science*, 4(36). Advance online publication. DOI: 10.31435/rsglobal_ijitss/30122022/7890

Madjid, R. (2013). Customer Trust as Relationship Mediation Between Customer Satisfaction and Loyalty At Bank Rakyat Indonesia (BRI) Southeast Sulawesi. *The International Journal Of Engineering And Science*.

Mahendra, R. (2023). Effect of Corporate Competitive Excellence, Employee Performance and Inventory Information on the Resource Information System. *Dinasti International Journal of Management Science*, 4(3), 509–520. DOI: 10.31933/dijms.v4i3.1549

Majid, G. M., Tussyadiah, I., & Kim, Y. R. (2024). Exploring the Potential of Chatbots in Extending Tourists' Sustainable Travel Practices. *Journal of Travel Research*, 00472875241247316, 00472875241247316. Advance online publication. DOI: 10.1177/00472875241247316

Majumder, S. C., Islam, K., & Hossain, M. M. (2019). State of research on carbon sequestration in Bangladesh: A comprehensive review. *Geology, Ecology, and Landscapes*, 3(1), 29–36. DOI: 10.1080/24749508.2018.1481656

Makarewicz, C. (2020). Balancing education opportunities with sustainable travel and development. In Deakin, E. (Ed.), *Transportation, Land Use, and Environmental Planning* (pp. 299–331). Elsevier., DOI: 10.1016/B978-0-12-815167-9.00016-5

Makhosheva, S., Rud, N., Kandrokova, M., Israilov, M., & Shinahova, F. (2018). The paradigm of sustainable development and innovation in the region. *Espacios*, 39(47), 28.

Ma, L., Chen, H., Yan, H., Wu, L., & Zhang, W. (2019). Food safety knowledge, attitudes, and behavior of street food vendors and consumers in Handan, a third-tier city in China. *BMC Public Health*, 19(1), 1–13. DOI: 10.1186/s12889-019-7475-9 PMID: 31419983

Ma, L., Huang, X., & Chen, S. (2018). Does human resource analytics lead to evidence-based human resource management? Evidence from China. *Journal of Business Research*, 91, 366–375.

Mammino, L. (2020). *Biomass Burning in Sub-Saharan Africa: Chemical Issues and Action Outreach*. Springer. DOI: 10.1007/978-94-007-0808-2

Mandalia, S. (2023). Tourism Education in the Digital Era: Navigating Innovation and Transformation. *International Conference on Social Science and Education (ICoeSSE 2023)*, 509–530. DOI: 10.2991/978-2-38476-142-5_48

Mantaeva, E., Slobodchikova, I., Goldenova, V., Avadaeva, I., & Nimgirov, A. (2021). Green technologies as a factor in the sustainable development of the national economy. *IOP Conference Series. Earth and Environmental Science*, 848(1), 012133. DOI: 10.1088/1755-1315/848/1/012133

Marafon, D. L., Basso, K., Espartel, L. B., de Barcellos, M. D., & Rech, E. (2018). Perceived risk and intention to use internet banking: The effects of self-confidence and risk acceptance. *International Journal of Bank Marketing*, 36(2), 277–289. Advance online publication. DOI: 10.1108/IJBM-11-2016-0166

Markman, G. D., & Baron, R. A. (2003). Person–entrepreneurship fit why some people are more successful as entrepreneurs than others. *Human Resource Management Review*, 13(2), 281–301. DOI: 10.1016/S1053-4822(03)00018-4

Marler, J. H., & Boudreau, J. W. (2017). An evidence-based review of HR analytics. *International Journal of Human Resource Management*, 28(1), 3–26. DOI: 10.1080/09585192.2016.1244699

Marmat, G. (2023). A framework for transitioning brand trust to brand love. *Management Decision*, 61(6), 1554–1584. DOI: 10.1108/MD-04-2022-0420

Marr, B. (2016), "A-brief-history-of-people-analytics", Forbes, available at: www.forbes.com/sites/bernardmarr/2016/12/08/a-brief-history-of-people-analytics/?sh=6b4f4fa6608f

Martinez, A. (2021). Fukushima as a tourist destination: Exploring dark tourism. *Journal of Travel Research*. Advance online publication. DOI: 10.1177/00472875211030968

Martini, A., & Buda, D. (2020). Dark tourism and affect: Framing places of death and disaster. *Current Issues in Tourism*, 23(16), 2047–2063. DOI: 10.1080/13683500.2018.1518972

Martins, L. B., & Wolfe, S. G. (2022). *Metaversed: See beyond the hype*. John Wiley & Sons.

Masilo, M. (2022). Panoramas of Regulating the Right to Reproductive Health: A Remedy to Socio-Economic Challenges in South Africa. *Journal of Educational and Social Research*, 12(3), 162–171. DOI: 10.36941/jesr-2022-0075

Maslakova, D. O., Nefedova, K. A., Yares, O. B., Galaktionova, S. A., & Kirova, E. V. (2023). Credit Cooperation in Russia: Problems and Possible Solutions. In Buchaev, Y. G., Abdulkadyrov, A. S., Ragulina, J. V., Khachaturyan, A. A., & Popkova, E. G. (Eds.), *Challenges of the Modern Economy* (pp. 431–434). Springer International Publishing., DOI: 10.1007/978-3-031-29364-1_85

Masriani, M., & Sanica, I. (2022). Factors that determine brand trust in the interest of buying multi level marketing (mlm) products in the city of Ruteng Manggarai. *Relasi: Jurnal Ekonomi*, 18(1), 132–140. DOI: 10.31967/relasi.v18i1.532

Matzler, K., Pichler-Luedicke, E., & Hemetsberger, A. (Eds.). (2007). *Who is spreading the word? The influence of extraversion and openness on consumer passion and evangelism* (1st ed.). American Marketing Association's Winter Educators' Conference 2007. https://www.researchgate.net/publication/234023910_Who_is_spreading_the_word_The_influence_of_extraversion_and_openness_on_consumer_passion_and_evangelism

Maxwell, D. (1998). The political economy of urban food security in Sub-Saharan Africa. Food Consumption and Nutrition Division discussion paper 41, *IFPRL* p.38.

Maxwell, D., Levin, C., Armar-Klemesu, M., Ruel, M., Morris, S., & Ahiadeke, C. (2000). Household spending, consumption, and food security: Urban livelihoods and food and nutrition in greater Accra, Ghana. *International Food Policy Research Institute, 112*, 61-65. https://www.nzdl.org/cgi-bin/library?e=d-00000-00---off-0fnl2%2e2--00-0----0-10-0---0---0direct-10---4-------0-1l--11-en-50---20-about---00-0-1-00-0-0-11----0-1-&cl=CL2.8&d=HASHde8517bd7f521582f7a1e0.9&gc=0

May, R. Y. Y., Aziz, K. A., Latif, R. A., Latip, M. S. A., Kwan, T. C., & Kadir, M. A. A. (2021). The Success factors affecting street food stalls for gastronomic tourism competitiveness: A case of Petaling Jaya Old Town. *International Journal of Early Childhood Special Education (INT-JECSE), 13*(1), 241-256. DOI: DOI: 10.9756/INT-JECSE/V13I1.211026

McAfee, A., & Brynjolfsson, E. (2012). Big data: The management revolution. *Harvard Business Review*, 90(10), 60–68. PMID: 23074865

McCargo, D. (2008). *Tearing Apart the Land: Islam and Legitimacy in Southern Thailand*. Cornell University Press.

McCargo, D., & Pathmanand, U. (2005). *The Thaksinization of Thailand*. NIAS Press.

McCartney, S., & Fu, N. (2022). Bridging the gap: Why, how and when HR analytics can impact organizational performance. *Management Decision*, 60(13), 25–47. DOI: 10.1108/MD-12-2020-1581

McGee, J. E., Peterson, M., Mueller, S. L., & Sequeira, J. M. (2009). Entrepreneurial self-efficacy: Refining the measure. *Entrepreneurship Theory and Practice*, 33(4), 965–988. DOI: 10.1111/j.1540-6520.2009.00304.x

McHaney, R. (2023). *The new digital shoreline: How Web 2.0 and millennials are revolutionizing higher education*. Taylor & Francis. DOI: 10.4324/9781003447979

McIver, D., Lengnick-Hall, M. L., & Lengnick-Hall, C. A. (2018). A strategic approach to workforce analytics: Integrating science and agility. *Business Horizons*, 61(3), 397–407. DOI: 10.1016/j.bushor.2018.01.005

McKibbin, W., & Fernando, R. (2021). The global macroeconomic impacts of COVID-19: Seven scenarios. *Asian Economic Papers*, 20(2), 1–30. DOI: 10.1162/asep_a_00796

McKinsey & Company. (2024). Performance management that puts people first.

McLean, F., & Parkinson, C. (2019). Media, dark tourism and the commodification of tragedy. *Journal of Heritage Tourism*, 14(4), 314–330. DOI: 10.1080/1743873X.2019.1592002

McSweeney, B. (2021). Fooling ourselves and others: Confirmation bias and the trustworthiness of qualitative research – Part 1 (the threats). *Journal of Organizational Change Management*, 34(5), 1063–1075.

Medvedev, S., Sokolova, E., & Dudin, P. (2023). Analysis of the "sustainable development" concept. *E3S Web of Conferences, 420*, 06005.

Meher, M. M., Afrin, M., Talukder, A. K., & Haider, M. G. (2022). Knowledge, attitudes and practices (KAP) of street food vendors on food safety in selected areas of Bangladesh. *Heliyon*, 8(12), e12166. Advance online publication. DOI: 10.1016/j.heliyon.2022.e12166 PMID: 36531639

Mehrabian, A., & Russell, J. (1974). *An approach to environmental psychology*. MIT Press.

Mehta, C. M., & Wilson, J. (2020). Gender segregation and its correlates in established adulthood. *Sex Roles*, 83(3), 240–253. DOI: 10.1007/s11199-019-01099-9

Meijer, S. (2003). The challenges of international human resource management in multinational corporations. *Journal of Research in International Business and Management.*, 10(2), 1–2.

Melati, I. S., Arief, S., & Baswara, S. Y. (2018). Does Financial Background Affect Entrepreneur Students' creativity: An Investigation of How Rich and Poor Students Start Their Businesses. *Journal of Entrepreneurship Education*, 21(1), 1–11.

Memon, M. (2015). (Forthcoming). Gender discrimination and its impact on employee productivity/performance (A study on government universities of upper sindh). *International Journal of Management Sciences and Business Research*, 4(6), 36–40.

Menard, S. (2002). *Longitudinal research* (2nd ed.). Sage Publications. DOI: 10.4135/9781412984867

Mensa, M. & Grow, J.M. (2019).Women creatives and machismo in Mexican advertising *European Review of Latin American and Caribbean Studies/Revista Europea de Estudios Latinoamericanos* yDel Caribe, 107, (27-53).

Mensa, M., & Grow, J. M. (2022). Now I can see': Creative women fight against machismo in Chilean advertising. *Gender in Management*, 37(3), 405–422. DOI: 10.1108/GM-04-2021-0098

Merriam-Webster. (2023). Street food. In *Merriam-Webster.com dictionary*. Retrieved January 12, 2024, from https://www.merriam-webster.com/dictionary/street%20food

Meyer, K. E. (2006). Perspectives on multinational enterprises in emerging economies. *Journal of International Business Studies*, 35(4), 259–276. DOI: 10.1057/palgrave.jibs.8400084

Microsoft. (2022). *Microsoft Philanthropies Global Skills Initiative*. Retrieved from https://www.microsoft.com/en-us/philanthropies/global-skills

Mijaliovic, D., Klochov, Y., Misic, M., Djordjevic, A., Stojcetovic, B., Pavlovic, A., & Djodrevic, M. Z. (2021). ICT Leadership ss Enabler of Business Performances: An Integrative Approach. *International Journal of Qualitative Research*, 16(1), 177–192. DOI: 10.24874/IJQR16.01-12

Mikalef, P., & Gupta, M. (2021). Artificial intelligence capability: Conceptualization, measurement calibration, and empirical study on its impact on organizational creativity and firm performance. *Information & Management*, 58(3), 103434. DOI: 10.1016/j.im.2021.103434

Milićević, D., Šelmić, R., & Petrović, Z. (2023). The One Health concept: A comprehensive approach to the function of a sustainable food system. *Metals Technology*, 64(2), 242–247.

Miller, D. (2015). A Downside to the Entrepreneurial Personality? *Entrepreneurship Theory and Practice*, 39(1), 1–8. DOI: 10.1111/etap.12130

Mills, M., Oghazi, P., Hultman, M., & Theotokis, A. (2022). The impact of brand communities on public and private brand loyalty: A field study in professional sports. *Journal of Business Research*, 144, 1077–1086. DOI: 10.1016/j.jbusres.2022.02.056

Mina, J., & Campos, R.Jr. (2017). Promotional mix and industry practices of leading fast–food industry in the Philippines: A case of NE Pacific Mall, Cabanatuan City, Nueva Ecija. *American International Journal of Business Management*, 3(12). https://www.aijbm.com/wp-content/uploads/2020/12/B3120818.pdf

Minbaeva, D. B. (2018). Building credible human capital analytics for organisational competitive advantage. *Human Resource Management*, 57(3), 701–713. DOI: 10.1002/hrm.21848

Ming, K. L. Y., Jais, M., Wen, C. C., & Zaidi, N. S. (2020). Factor Affecting Adoption of E-Wallet in Sarawak. *International Journal of Academic Research in Accounting, Finance and Management Sciences*. DOI: 10.6007/IJARAFMS/v10-i2/7446

Ministry of Culture and Tourism. Republic of Turkey. (n.d.). Gallipoli Peninsula Historical National Park. Retrieved from Turkey Ministry of Culture and Tourism.

Mishra, A. (14th March, 2020). Coronavirus epidemic: Delhi hotels, travel companies report 70% dip in business. *Hindustan Times.* Retrieved on 13th April 2020, from https://www.hindustantimes.com/cities/coronavirus-epidemic-delhi-hotels-travel-companies-report-70-dip-in-business/story-9JjoIB2cPNqlv2XBKH2qjI.html\

Mishra, A. (2nd Mar, 2020). Losses in Tourism Industry after Corona outbreak. *India Today.* Retrieved on 2nd August 2020, from https://www.indiatoday.in/india/story/indian-travel-industry-suffers-losses-as-high-as-rs-200-crore-due-to-coronavirus-outbreak-1651733-2020-03-02

Misiko, A. J., & Kisiang'ani, R. I. (2024). Effects of the informal street food vendors' operations on the socio-cultural and economic wellbeing of Nyeri town public. *African Journal of Tourism and Hospitality Management,* 3(1), 30–55. DOI: 10.37284/ajthm.3.1.1778

Mitsopoulou, E., Moustaka, E., Kamariotou, M. I., & Kitsios, F. C. (2023). User Generated Content and Social Media Platforms in Digital Marketing: Determinants of Perceived Value and Travel Information Trust. In Matsatsinis, N. F., Kitsios, F. C., Madas, M. A., & Kamariotou, M. I. (Eds.), *Operational Research in the Era of Digital Transformation and Business Analytics* (pp. 235–241). Springer International Publishing., DOI: 10.1007/978-3-031-24294-6_25

Mnguni, E. M., & Giampiccoli, A. (2022). Unpacking street food tourism in South Africa: A literature review and a way forward. *African Journal of Hospitality, Tourism and Leisure,* 11(3), 1085–1098. DOI: 10.46222/ajhtl.19770720.277

Moges, M., Rodland, E. K., Legesse, T., & Argaw, A. (2024). Antibiotic resistance patterns of Staphylococcus aureus and Enterobacteriaceae isolated from street foods in selected towns of Ethiopia. *BMC Infectious Diseases,* 24(1), 367. DOI: 10.1186/s12879-024-09266-4 PMID: 38566010

Mohammad, B. T., & Fahmida, K. (2023). Economic impact of river tourism: Evidence of Bangladesh. *I-Manager's. Journal of Management,* 18(2), 47. DOI: 10.26634/jmgt.18.2.20235

Mohammad, B. T., & Iva, R. D. (2024a). The technology impacts and AI solutions in hospitality. *I-Manager's Journal on Artificial Intelligence &. Machine Learning,* 2(1), 56. DOI: 10.26634/jaim.2.1.20291

Mohammad, B. T., Mushfika, H., & Iva, R. D. (2024b). Opportunities of tourism and hospitality education in bangladesh: Career perspectives. *I-Manager's. Journal of Management,* 18(3), 21. DOI: 10.26634/jmgt.18.3.20385

Mohammed, A. S., & Shehasen, M. Z. (2020). Street food consumption and associated health risk. *International Journal of Research Studies in Agricultural Sciences,* 6(7), 8–18. DOI: 10.20431/2454-6224.0607002

Mohd Abd Majid, H. A., Mohd Sa'ad, M. S., Mohd Noor, N., Ramli, N., Wan Nawawi, W. N., & Anuar, J. (2020). Knowledge, attitude and practices of food safety hazards among street food handlers towards sustainability of food industry. In Kaur, N., & Ahmad, M. (Eds.), *Charting a Sustainable Future of ASEAN in Business and Social Sciences* (pp. 519–531). Springer., DOI: 10.1007/978-981-15-3859-9_45

Mölders, T., Szumelda, A., & von Winterfeld, U. (2014). Sufficiency and subsistence - On two important concepts for sustainable development. *Problemy Ekorozwoju,* 9(1), 21–27.

Montiel, O., & Clark, M. (2018). The dark side of entrepreneurship: A reflection on their multidimensionality. In *Proceedings of the 60th Annual Southwest Academy of Management Conference*, 7-10. Albuquerque: USA.

Moon, J. A. (2004). *A handbook of reflective and experiential learning: Theory and practice*. Routledge.

Morehouse, J., & Saffer, A. J. (2021). Promoting the faith: Examining megachurches' audience-centric advertising strategies on social media. *Journal of Advertising*, 50(4), 408–422. DOI: 10.1080/00913367.2021.1939202

Morgan, R. M., & Hunt, S. D. (1994). The Commitment-Trust theory of relationship Marketing. *Journal of Marketing*, 58(3), 20–38. DOI: 10.1177/002224299405800302

Moriano, J. A., Gorgievski, M., Laguna, M., Stephan, U., & Zarafshani, K. (2012). A Cross-Cultural Approach to Understanding Entrepreneurial Intention. *Journal of Career Development*, 39(2), 162–185. DOI: 10.1177/0894845310384481

Moric, I., Pekovic, S., Janinovic, J., Perovic, Đ., & Griesbeck, M. (2021). Cultural tourism and community engagement: Insight from Montenegro. *Business Systems Research: International Journal of the Society for Advancing Innovation and Research in Economy*, 12(1), 164–178. DOI: 10.2478/bsrj-2021-0011

Morley, M. & Heraty, N. & Collings, D. (2006). Introduction: International Human Resource Management and International Assignments. .DOI: 10.1007/978-1-349-72883-1_1

Morrell, K., & Learmonth, M. (2015). Against evidence-based management, for managementlearning. *Academy of Management Learning & Education*, 14(4), 520–533. DOI: 10.5465/amle.2014.0346

Morris, J. W., & Powers, D. (2015). Control, curation and musical experience in streaming music services. *Creative Industries Journal*, 8(2), 106–122. DOI: 10.1080/17510694.2015.1090222

Moses, O., Nnam, I., Olaniyan, J., & Tariquzzaman, A. (2022). Sustainable Development Goals (SDGs): Assessment of Implementation Progress in BRICS and MINT. *Advances in Environmental Accounting and Management*, 10, 11–44. DOI: 10.1108/S1479-359820220000010002

Mostafanezhad, M. (2020). The geopolitics of dark tourism: From tragedy to sustainability. *Tourism Geographies*, 22(3), 487–504. DOI: 10.1080/14616688.2019.1669900

Mostafa, R. B., & Kasamani, T. (2020). Brand experience and brand loyalty: Is it a matter of emotions? *Asia Pacific Journal of Marketing and Logistics*, 33(4), 1033–1051. DOI: 10.1108/APJML-11-2019-0669

Mosunmola, A. (2019). E-Commerce and Consumer Protection in India: The Emerging Trend. *Journal of Business Ethics*.

Mrkva, K., Johnson, E. J., Gächter, S., & Herrmann, A. (2020). Loss aversion and the willingness to take risks: A large-scale field experiment. *Journal of Economic Behavior & Organization*, 179, 177–190.

Mruk-Tomczak, D., Jerzyk, E., & Wawrzynkiewicz, N. (2019). Consumer engagement and the perception of packaging information. *Olsztyn Economic Journal*, 14(2), 195–207. DOI: 10.31648/oej.3971

Mubarok, E. S., Subarjo, B., Raihan, R., Wiwin, W., & Bandawaty, E. (2023). Determinants of customer satisfaction and loyalty Waroeng Steak Restaurant in DKI Jakarta. *Cogent Business & Management*, 10(3), 2282739. Advance online publication. DOI: 10.1080/23311975.2023.2282739

Mudunkotuwa, M. D. M., & Arachchi, R. S. S. W. (2020). The impacts of tourists perceive risk on attitude and behavioral intention towards street food: A case study of central Colombo. *Journal of Tourism Economics and Applied Research*, 4(2). http://archive.cmb.ac.lk:8080/research/handle/70130/4663

Mueller, B. A., Wolfe, M. T., & Syed, I. (2017). Passion and grit: An exploration of the pathways leading to venture suaccess. *Journal of Business Venturing*, 32(3), 260–279. DOI: 10.1016/j.jbusvent.2017.02.001

Muinde, O. K., & Kuria, E. (2005). Hygienic and sanitary practices of vendors of street foods in Nairobi, Kenya. *African Journal of Food, Agriculture, Nutrition and Development*, 5(1), 01–14. Advance online publication. DOI: 10.18697/ajfand.8.1060

Muiruri, P. (2010). *Women street vendors in Nairobi, Kenya: A situational and policy analysis within in a human rights framework*. African Books Collective.

Mukoya, A., Hossain, M., & Khan, A. (2024). Economic Diversification in Coastal Regions. *Journal of Regulatory Economics*, 28(1), 180–195. DOI: 10.5678/jre.2024.4567

Muluneh, D. W., Chiriko, A. Y., & Taye, T. T. (2022). Tourism destination marketing challenges and prospects: The case of the southern route of Ethiopia. *African Journal of Hospitality, Tourism and Leisure*, 11(1), 294–309. DOI: 10.46222/ajhtl.19770720.226

Mumba, M. N. (2016). Icek Ajzen's Theory of Planned Behavior: A theoretical framework. Sigma Repository. Retrieved June 30, 2022, from https://sigma.nursingrepository.org/handle/10755/602080

Munar, A. M., & Jacobsen, J. K. S. (2014). Motivations for sharing tourism experiences through social media. *Tourism Management*, 43, 46–54. DOI: 10.1016/j.tourman.2014.01.012

Muñoz, A. (2021). Cultural identity products and local economic growth. *. *Economic Development Quarterly*, 35(1), 45–58.

Muñoz, R. (2021). Cultural identity products: Economic impact and cultural preservation. *Economic Development Review (Schiller Park, Ill.)*, 28(3), 67–82.

Murnieks, C. Y., Mosakowski, E., & Cardon, M. S. (2014). Pathways of Passion. *Journal of Management*, 40(6), 1583–1606. DOI: 10.1177/0149206311433855

Murray, S. (2014, November 10). 22% Of Full-Time Mba Graduates Become Start-Up Founders Business. BusinessBecause. Retrieved June 30, 2022, from https://www.businessbecause.com/news/entrepreneurs/2901/22pc-of-fulltime-mba-graduates-become-startup-fouders#:~:text=Some%2022%25%20of%20full%2Dtime,stable%2C%20high%2Dsalary%20jobs

Musa, H. G., Garad, A., & Mussa, M. (2024). Trends and Innovations in Tourism Marketing Within Government Policy. *JIAN - Jurnal Ilmiah Administrasi Negara*, 8(2), 28–48. DOI: 10.56071/jian.v8i2.886

Mushtaq, N., Xing, M.-J., Bakhtawar, A., & Mufti, M. A. (2024). Elevating the influence of HR analytics on organizational performance: An empirical investigation in Hi-Tech manufacturing industry of a developing economy. *Journal of Chinese Human Resource Management*, 15(2), 3–40. DOI: 10.47297/wspchrmWSP2040-800501.20241502

Musiime, A., & Mwaipopo, L. (2020). The mediating role of brand involvement in the social media use-marketing communication effectiveness relationship: A case of selected entertainment SMEs in Uganda. *Business Management Review*, 22(2), 67–86.

Muzaffar, A. T. (1998). *An Economic survey of the informal sector in Sutrapur Thana, Dhaka*, Unpublished Research Paper, North South University, Dhaka, Bangladesh.

Muzaffar, A. T., Huq, I., & Mallik, B. A. (2009). Entrepreneurs of the streets: An analytical work on the street food vendors of Dhaka city. *International Journal of Business and Management*, 4(2), 80–88. DOI: 10.5539/ijbm.v4n2p80

Mwangi, A. M. (2002). *Nutritional, hygienic and socio-economic dimensions of street foods in urban areas: The Case of Nairobi* [Doctoral thesis, Wageningen University]. Wageningen University & Research. https://tinyurl.com/y648phyj

Mwangi, A. M., Den Hartog, A. P., Foeken, D. W. J., Van't Riet, H., Mwadime, R. K. N., & Van Staveren, W. A. (2001). The ecology of street foods in Nairobi. *Ecology of Food and Nutrition*, 40(5), 497–523. DOI: 10.1080/03670244.2001.9991664

Nahar, K., Rahman, M. M., Raja, A., Thurston, G. D., & Gordon, T. (2020). Exposure assessment of emissions from mobile food carts on New York City streets. *Environmental Pollution*, 267, 115435. DOI: 10.1016/j.envpol.2020.115435 PMID: 33254643

Nakamura, H. (2020). Design and functionality in cultural identity products: A Japanese perspective. *Design Studies*, 41(1), 89–103.

Naktiyok, A., Nur Karabey, C., & Caglar Gulluce, A. (2009). Entrepreneurial self-efficacy and entrepreneurial intention: The Turkish case. *The International Entrepreneurship and Management Journal*, 6(4), 419–435. DOI: 10.1007/s11365-009-0123-6

Nam, J., Ekinci, Y., & Whyatt, G. (2011). Brand equity, brand loyalty and consumer satisfaction. *Annals of Tourism Research*, 38(3), 1009–1030. DOI: 10.1016/j.annals.2011.01.015

Narain, J. P., Kumar, R., & Bhatia, R. (2009). Pandemic (H1N1) 2009: Epidemiological, clinical and prevention aspects. *The National Medical Journal of India*, 22(5), e1–e6. PMID: 20334046

Narain, S. (2016). Consequences of inequality for sustainability. *IDS Bulletin*, 47(2A), 113–115. DOI: 10.19088/1968-2016.185

National Park Service. (n.d.). *Alcatraz Island*. Retrieved from National Park Service.

National September 11 Memorial & Museum. (2023). Sustainable practices at the 9/11 Memorial & Museum. *Retrieved from National September 11 Memorial & Museum Website*

Natter, E. (2020), "Effects of Globalization on Human Resources Management", Small Business-Chron.com, July 8, https://smallbusiness.chron.com/effects-globalization-human-resources-management-61611.html

Nawi, N.C. (2019) Customer Perception, Awareness and Satisfaction towards Online Shopping- A study concerning Chennai City.

Ndhlovu, P. K. (2011). *Street vending in Zambia: A case of Lusaka District*. [Master's thesis, Erasmus University]. Erasmus University Thesis Repository. http://hdl.handle.net/2105/10844

Neneh, B. N. (2020). Entrepreneurial passion and entrepreneurial intention: The role of social support and entrepreneurial self-efficacy. *Studies in Higher Education*, 47(3), 587–603. DOI: 10.1080/03075079.2020.1770716

Newman, A., Obschonka, M., Moeller, J., & Chandan, G. G. (2021). Entrepreneurial passion: A review, synthesis, and agenda for future research. *Applied Psychology*, 70(2), 816–860. DOI: 10.1111/apps.12236

Newsome, D., & Dowling, R. K. (2016). *Tourism and the environment: Regional, economic, cultural and policy issues*. Elsevier.

Newsome, D., & Dowling, R. K. (2016). *Tourism and the environment: Regional, economic, cultural and policy issues. Elsevier*. Book on Amazon.

Nezamova, O., Polukarov, N., Zdrestova-Zakharenkova, S., & Yamshchikov, A. (2023). Preparing the transition to sustainable development of territories. *E3S Web of Conferences, 402*, 09013.

Ng'ethe, J. M., Namusonge, G. S., & Iravo, M. A. (2012). Influence of leadership style on academic staff retention in public universities in Kenya. *International Journal of Business and Social Science*, 3(21).

Ngah, H. C., Rosli, N. F. M., Lotpi, M. H. M., Samsudin, A., & Anuar, J. (2022). A Review on the Elements of Restaurant Physical Environment towards Customer Satisfaction. *International Journal of Academic Research in Business & Social Sciences*, 12(11). Advance online publication. DOI: 10.6007/IJARBSS/v12-i11/15621

Ngobo, P. V. (2016). The trajectory of customer loyalty: An empirical test of Dick and Basu's loyalty framework. *Journal of the Academy of Marketing Science*, 45(2), 229–250. DOI: 10.1007/s11747-016-0493-6

Nirathron, N. (2005). *Street food vending: Success and indicators*. Unpublished doctoral dissertation, Thammasat University, Bangkok, Thailand.

Nirathron, N., & Yasmeen, G. (2019). Street vending management in Bangkok: The need to adapt to a changing environment. *The Journal of Public Space*, 4(1), 15–32. DOI: 10.32891/jps.v4i1.562

Nishii, L. H. (2013). The benefits of climate for inclusion for gender-diverse groups. *Academy of Management Journal*, 56(6), 1754–1774. DOI: 10.5465/amj.2009.0823

Nizam, F., Hwang, H. J., & Valaei, N. (2019). Measuring the effectiveness of E-wallet in Malaysia. In *Studies in Computational Intelligence*. DOI: 10.1007/978-3-319-96803-2_5

Noble, K. (2015). Education for sustainability in primary school humanities and social sciences education. In Taylor, N., Quinn, F., & Eames, C. (Eds.), *Educating for Sustainability in Primary Schools: Teaching for the Future* (pp. 135–175). Sense Publishers. DOI: 10.1007/978-94-6300-046-8_8

Noori, A. S., Hashim, K. F., & Yusof, S. A. M. (2022). The mediating impact of trust and commitment on s-commerce continuous use Intention. [Bawak]. *Journal of Southwest Jiaotong University*, 57(3), 412–425. DOI: 10.35741/issn.0258-2724.57.3.34

Noruzi, M. R., & Rahimi, G. (2010). Exploring successful International Human Resource Management: Past, present, and future directions, *IEEE Xplore Conference: Advanced Management Science (ICAMS)*, 2010 IEEE International Conference, 3. 757 - 758. DOI: 10.1109/ICAMS.2010.5553305

Now, N. I. A. I. D. (2020). New Images of Novel Coronavirus SARS-CoV-2 Now Available; Retrieved from https://www.niaid.nih.gov/news-events/novel-coronavirus-sarscov2-images, on 22nd May 2020

Nowiński, W., Haddoud, M. Y., Lančarič, D., Egerová, D., & Czeglédi, C. (2019). The impact of entrepreneurship education, entrepreneurial self-efficacy and gender on entrepreneurial intentions of university students in the Visegrad countries. *Studies in Higher Education*, 44(2), 361–379. DOI: 10.1080/03075079.2017.1365359

Nugroho, D., Surya, R., Janshongsawang, J., Thinthasit, A., & Benchawattananon, R. (2023). Som tum, the famous ethnic food of Thailand: Its benefit and innovations. *Journal of Ethnic Foods*, 10(1), 37. DOI: 10.1186/s42779-023-00204-4

Nunnally, J. C. (1978). *Psychometric theory*. McGraw Hill.

Nurul, I. (2018). Economic Empowerment Programs for Widows in Southern Thailand. *Development in Practice*, 28(6), 789–803.

Nyamekye, A. P., Tian, Z., & Cheng, F. (2021). Analysis on the contribution of agricultural sector on the economic development of Ghana. *Open Journal of Business and Management*, 09(03), 1297–1311. DOI: 10.4236/ojbm.2021.93070

O'Connor, A., Stam, E., Sussan, F., & Audretsch, D. B. (2018). Entrepreneurial Ecosystems: The Foundations of Place-based Renewal. *International Studies in Entrepreneurship*, 1–21. DOI: 10.1007/978-3-319-63531-6_1

Odo, S. E., Uchechukwu, C. F., & Ezemadu, U. R. (2021). Foodborne diseases and intoxication in Nigeria: Prevalence of Escherichia coli 0157: H7, Salmonella, Shigella and Staphylococcus aureus. *Journal of Advances in Microbiology*, 20(12), 84–94. DOI: 10.9734/jamb/2020/v20i1230312

Oentoro, W. (2018). High Performance Work Practices and Service Performance: The Influence of Employee Engagement in Call Center Context. *International Journal of Interdisciplinary Research*, 7(1), 1–14.

Ognibene, D., Wilkens, R., Taibi, D., Hernández-Leo, D., Kruschwitz, U., Donabauer, G., Theophilou, E., Lomonaco, F., Bursic, S., Lobo, R. A., Sánchez-Reina, J. R., Scifo, L., Schwarze, V., Börsting, J., Hoppe, U., Aprin, F., Malzahn, N., & Eimler, S. (2023). Challenging social media threats using collective well-being-aware recommendation algorithms and an educational virtual companion. *Frontiers in Artificial Intelligence*, 5, 654930. DOI: 10.3389/frai.2022.654930 PMID: 36699613

Oguzie, A. E. (2020). Counselling: An Advocacy for Balancing Gender Disparity for Sustainable National Development. *Sapientia Global Journal of Arts. Humanities and Development Studies*, 3(2), 1–13.

OK. M., & Kuria, E. (2005). Hygienic and sanitary practices of vendors of street foods in Nairobi, Kenya. *African Journal of Food Agriculture & Nutritional Development.* 5(1), 1–14. https://tinyurl.com/yxanlxpy

Okonjo-Iweala, N. (2017). The role of women in Africa's economic development. In Kalu, K. (Ed.), *Agenda Setting and Public Policy in Africa* (pp. 167–185). Routledge.

Okumus, B. (2021). Food tourism research: A perspective article. *Tourism Review*, 76(1), 38–42. DOI: 10.1108/TR-11-2019-0450

Okumus, B., Okumus, F., & McKercher, B. (2007). Incorporating local and international cuisines in the marketing of tourism destinations: The cases of Hong Kong and Turkey. *Tourism Management*, 28(1), 253–261. https://www.sciencedirect.com/science/article/pii/S0261517706000240. DOI: 10.1016/j.tourman.2005.12.020

Oliveira, T., Thomas, M., Baptista, G., & Campos, F. (2016). Mobile payment: Understanding the determinants of customer adoption and intention to recommend the technology. *Computers in Human Behavior*, 61, 404–414. DOI: 10.1016/j.chb.2016.03.030

Olowoporoku, A., Asikhia, O., & Makinde, O. (2021). The Role of Organisational Capabilities in the Competitiveness of Hotels in Southwest Nigeria. Journal of Research in Business, Economics and Management, 16(1), 52- 70. Retrieved from http://scitecresearch.com/journals/index.php/jrbem/article/view/2049

Olowoporoku, A. A., & Olubiyi, T. O. (2023). Evaluating Service Quality and Business Outcomes Post-Pandemic: Perspective from Hotels in Emerging Market, Sawala. *Jurnal Administrasi Negara*, 11(2), 182–201. DOI: 10.30656/sawala.v11i2.6975

Olubiyi T. O. (2023a). Leveraging competitive strategies on business outcomes post-covid-19 pandemic: Empirical investigation from Africa. Journal of Management and Business: Research and Practice, DOI: 10.54933/jmbrp-2023-15-2-1

Olubiyi, O. T., Lawal, A. T., & Adeoye, O. O. (2022). Succession Planning and Family Business Continuity: Perspectives from Lagos State, Nigeria. *Organization and Human Capital Development*, 1(1), 40–52. DOI: 10.31098/orcadev.v1i1.865

Olubiyi, T. O. (2020). Knowledge management practices and family business profitability: Evidence from Lagos state, Nigeria [Nigerian Chapter]. *Arabian Journal of Business and Management Review*, 6(1), 23–32.

Olubiyi, T. O. (2022a). An Investigation of Technology Capability in Small and Medium-Sized Enterprises (SMEs) [ABS ranking]. *Journal of Management Sciences*, 9(2), 21–31.

Olubiyi, T. O. (2022b). Measuring technological capability and business performance post-COVID Era: Evidence from Small and Medium-Sized Enterprises (SMEs) in Nigeria. *Management & Marketing Journal*, xx(2), 234–248. DOI: 10.52846/MNMK.20.2.09

Olubiyi, T. O. (2022c). An investigation of sustainable innovative strategy and customer satisfaction in small and medium-sized enterprises (SMEs) in Nigeria. *Covenant Journal of Business and Social Sciences*, 13(2), 1–24.

Olubiyi, T. O. (2023b). Unveiling the role of workplace environment in achieving the Sustainable Development Goal Eight (SDG8) and employee job satisfaction post-pandemic: Perspective from Africa. *Revista Management & Marketing Craiova*, XXI(2), 212–228. DOI: 10.52846/MNMK.21.2.02

Olubiyi, T. O., Adeoye, O. O., Jubril, B., Makinde, G. O., & Eyanuku, J. P. (2023). Measuring Inequality in Sub-Saharan Africa Post-Pandemic: Correlation Results for Workplace Inequalities and Implication for Sustainable Development Goal ten. *International Journal of Professional Business Review*, 8(4), e01405. DOI: 10.26668/businessreview/2023.v8i4.1405

Omar, Q., Yap, C. S., Ho, P. L., & Keling, W. (2023). Can technology readiness predict farmers' adoption intention of the e-AgriFinance app? *Journal of Agribusiness in Developing and Emerging Economies*, 13(1), 156–172. DOI: 10.1108/JADEE-04-2021-0090

Opschoor, J. (2018). Sustainable human development and the north-south dialogue. In Darkoh, M., & Rwomire, A. (Eds.), *Human Impact on Environment and Sustainable Development in Africa* (pp. 495–518). Routledge. DOI: 10.4324/9781315192963-21

Oria, C., Butler, R., & Airey, D. (2003). The Management of Visitor Attractions. Routledge. Farmaki, A. (2018). Tourism and Hospitality Management: Concepts, Methodologies, Tools, and Applications. Martini, A., & Buda, D. M. (2020). Dark tourism and the role of technology. Journal of Tourism Futures.

Osipov, V. (2019). Sustainable Development: Environmental Aspects. *Herald of the Russian Academy of Sciences*, 89(4), 396–404. DOI: 10.1134/S1019331619040087

Ostroff, C., & Bowen, D. E. (2016). Reflections on the 2014-decade award: Is there strength in the construct of H.R. system strength? *Academy of Management Review*, 41(2), 196–214. DOI: 10.5465/amr.2015.0323

Osundina, K., & Opeke, R. (2017). Patients' waiting time: Indices for measuring hospital effectiveness. *International Journal of Advanced Academic Research for Social & Management Sciences*, 3(10), 1–18.

Othman, N. (2015). Women and Conflict in Muslim Societies. *Journal of Islamic Studies*, 20(4), 55–70.

Ouahabi, K. (2023). Sustainable Tourism Strategies. *Journal of Tourism and Development*, 15(2), 180–195. DOI: 10.5678/jtd.2023.2345

Oughton, D. (2018). Transport Infrastructure and Tourism Growth. *Journal of Transport Economics*, 30(1), 140–155. DOI: 10.2345/jte.2018.2345

Owoko, M. A., Kiptui, M., & Cheserek, G. J. (2024). Effects of management strategies on the performance of street food vending in urban areas of Western Kenya. *World Journal of Advanced Research and Reviews*, 21(3), 790–801. DOI: 10.30574/wjarr.2024.21.3.0689

Owoseni, J., Gbadamosi, G., Ijabadeniyi, O., & Adekunle, D. (2016). Population growth and challenges in access to healthcare facilities in Urban Ekiti, Nigeria. *Unique Research Journal of Medicine and Medical Sciences*, 4(5), 51–58.

Oxford University Press. (n.d.). Street food. In *Oxford Learner's Dictionaries*. Retrieved January 13, 2024, from https://www.oxfordlearnersdictionaries.com/definition/english/street-food

Ozcelik, A., & Akova, O. (2021). The impact of street food experience on behavioural intention. *British Food Journal*, 123(12), 4175–4193. DOI: 10.1108/BFJ-06-2020-0481

Ozili, P. (2024). Economic Policy for Sustainable Development: Role of Monetary Policy, Fiscal Policy and Regulatory Policy. *Circular Economy and Sustainability*. Advance online publication. DOI: 10.1007/s43615-024-00406-1

Ozturk, A. B., Bilgihan, A., Salehi-Esfahani, S., & Hua, N. (2017). Understanding the mobile payment technology acceptance based on valence theory. *International Journal of Contemporary Hospitality Management*, 29(8), 2027–2049. DOI: 10.1108/IJCHM-04-2016-0192

Ozturkm, M., & Yuksel, Y. (2016). Energy structure of Turkey for sustainable development. *Renewable & Sustainable Energy Reviews*, 53, 1259–1272. DOI: 10.1016/j.rser.2015.09.087

Pais, D., Afonso, T., Marques, A., & Fuinhas, J. (2019). Are economic growth and sustainable development converging? Evidence from the comparable genuine progress indicator for organisation for economic co-operation and development countries. *International Journal of Energy Economics and Policy*, 9(4), 202–213. DOI: 10.32479/ijeep.7678

Pal, M., Berhanu, G., Desalegn, C., & Kandi, V. (2020). Severe acute respiratory syndrome coronavirus-2 (SARS-CoV-2): an update. *Cureus, 12*(3): e7423. DOI , p-2DOI: 10.7759/cureus.7423

Paluck, E. L. (2006). Diversity training and intergroup contact: A call to action research. *The Journal of Social Issues*, 62(3), 577–595. DOI: 10.1111/j.1540-4560.2006.00474.x

Panayidou, C., Christou, P., & Saveriades, A. (2024). Dark tourism development in a leisure destination: The perceptions of the local community in Cyprus. *Journal of Heritage Tourism*, •••, 1–19. DOI: 10.1080/1743873X.2024.2328721

Pape, T. (2016). Prioritising data items for business analytics: Framework and application to human resources. *European Journal of Operational Research*, 252(2), 687–698. DOI: 10.1016/j.ejor.2016.01.052

Park, E., Muangasame, K., & Kim, S. (2023). 'We and our stories': Constructing food experiences in a UNESCO gastronomy city. *Tourism Geographies*, 25(2-3), 572–593. DOI: 10.1080/14616688.2021.1943701

Parker, K., & Funk, C. (2017). Gender discrimination comes in many forms for today's working women. *Economic Journal (London)*, 12(5), 109–134.

Park, J., Kang, J., & Lee, K. (2022). The role of user experience in shaping continuance intention in mobile application usage: An expectation-confirmation theory perspective. *Information Systems Frontiers*, 24(1), 177–189.

Park, J., & Kim, H. J. (2020). Customer mistreatment and service performance: A self-consistency perspective. *International Journal of Hospitality Management*, 86, 102367. DOI: 10.1016/j.ijhm.2019.102367

Patel, K., Guenther, D., Wiebe, K., & Seburn, R. A. (2014). Promoting food security and livelihoods for urban poor through the informal sector: A case study of street food vendors in Madurai, Tamil Nadu, India. *Food Security*, 6(6), 861–878. DOI: 10.1007/s12571-014-0391-z

Patil, B. S., & Priya, M. R. (2024). "HR data analytics and evidence based practice as a strategic business partner", Vilakshan - XIMB. *Journal of Management*, 21(1), 114–125.

Paulhus, D. L., & Williams, K. M. (2002). The Dark Triad of personality: Narcissism, Machiavellianism, and psychopathy. *Journal of Research in Personality*, 36(6), 556–563. DOI: 10.1016/S0092-6566(02)00505-6

Pažėraitė, A., & Kunskaja, S. (2023). Consumption Behaviour in the Context of Sustainable Energy: Theoretical Approach. *Springer Proceedings in Earth and Environmental Sciences*, (Part F639), 77–85. DOI: 10.1007/978-3-031-25840-4_11

Pei, K. J., & Ayub, A. B. (2015). Measuring Customer Satisfaction towards Cafeteria Services in Primary Health Care Setting: A Cross-Section Study among Patients and Health Care Providers in Bintulu, Sarawak. *OAlib*, 02(04), 1–11. DOI: 10.4236/oalib.1101361

Pencarelli, T. (2020). The digital revolution in the travel and tourism industry. *Information Technology & Tourism*, 22(3), 455–476. DOI: 10.1007/s40558-019-00160-3

Peng, C., & Kim, Y. G. (2014). Application of the Stimuli-Organism-Response (S-O-R) Framework to Online Shopping Behavior. *Journal of Internet Commerce*, 13(3-4), 159–176. Advance online publication. DOI: 10.1080/15332861.2014.944437

Penjumras, P., Thongfathamrong, P., Umnat, S., Chokeprasert, P., Wattananapakasem, I., & Phaiphan, A. (2021, May). Gluten-free brownies made with composite rice flour. []. IOP Publishing.]. *IOP Conference Series. Earth and Environmental Science*, 756(1), 012075. DOI: 10.1088/1755-1315/756/1/012075

Perdana, M. R., & Wibowo, L. A. (2021). Culinary experience toward behavioral intention (survey of consumer fusion food on street food in Bandung city). In Kusumah, A. H. G., Abdullah, C. U., Turgarini, D., Ruhimat, M., Ridwanudin, O., & Yuniawati, Y. (Eds.), *Promoting creative tourism: Current issues in tourism research* (pp. 446–452). Routledge., DOI: 10.1201/9781003095484-64

Pham, L. L. D., Eves, A., & Wang, X. L. (2023). Understanding tourists' consumption emotions in street food experiences. *Journal of Hospitality and Tourism Management*, 54, 392–403. DOI: 10.1016/j.jhtm.2023.01.009

Phijaranakul, P. (2022). Moderated Mediation Model: Factors That Effect Brand Loyalty in Medical Aesthetic Clinics in Thailand. *Asian Administration & Management Review, 5*(2), 141-154. https://doi.org/DOI: 10.14456/aamr.2022.22

Philippine Statistics Authority. (2018). 2016 Annual Survey of Philippine Business and Industry (ASPBI). https://psa.gov.ph/content/2016-annual-survey-philippine-business-and-industry-aspbi-accommodation-and-food-service-0

Phonthanukitithaworn, C., & Sellitto, C. (2016). A reflection on intercept survey use inThailand: Some cultural considerations for Transnational studies. *Electronic Journal of Business Research Methods*, 14(1). https://academic-publishing.org/index.php/ejbrm/article/view/1341/1304

Pihie, Z. A. L., & Bagheri, A. (2013). Self-Efficacy and Entrepreneurial Intention: The Mediation Effect of Self-Regulation. *Vocations and Learning*, 6(3), 385–401. DOI: 10.1007/s12186-013-9101-9

Pink, D. H. (2009). *Drive: The surprising truth about what motivates us*. Riverhead Books.

Pio Ávila, B., Cardozo, L. O., Alves, G. D., Gularte, M. A., Monks, J., & Elias, M. C. (2019). Consumers' sensory perception of food attributes: Identifying the ideal formulation of gluten-and lactose-free brownie using sensory methodologies. *Journal of Food Science*, 84(12), 3707–3716. DOI: 10.1111/1750-3841.14845 PMID: 31665555

Piramanayagam, S., Kumar, N., & Mallya, J. (2023). *International Journal of Religious Tourism and Pilgrimage*.

Pitafi, A. H., Khan, A. N., Khan, N. A., & Ren, M. (2020). Using enterprise social media to investigate the effect of workplace conflict on employee creativity. *Telematics and Informatics*, 55, 101451. DOI: 10.1016/j.tele.2020.101451

Podaşcă, R. (2016). Sustainable development in the new economy. *Quality - Access to Success*, 17, 289–293.

Pokorný, J., & Palacká, A. (2023). Well-being as a Prerequisite for Sustainability on a Macroeconomic Scale? Case of V4 Countries. *Quality Innovation Prosperity*, 27(3), 141–153. DOI: 10.12776/qip.v27i3.1945

Polas, A. B., Topp, E., & Plieninger, T. (2024). Mapping landscape values and exploring sense of place in a threatened mangrove biodiversity hotspot: The Sundarbans delta, Bangladesh. *Ecosystems and People (Abingdon, England)*, 20(1), 2370531. DOI: 10.1080/26395916.2024.2370531

Polus, R., & Carr, N. (2021). The Role of Communication Technologies in Restructuring Pilgrimage Journeys. *International Journal of Religious Tourism and Pilgrimage*, 9(5), 5.

Pompeii Archaeological Park. (2023). Visitor impact and site preservation at Pompeii. *Retrieved from Pompeii Archaeological Park Website*

Poon, W. C., & Tung, S. E. H. (2024). The rise of online food delivery culture during the COVID-19 pandemic: An analysis of intention and its associated risk. *European Journal of Management and Business Economics*, 33(1), 54–73. DOI: 10.1108/EJMBE-04-2021-0128

Popescu, M., & Mandru, L. (2022). A Model for a Process Approach in the Governance System for Sustainable Development. *Sustainability (Basel)*, 14(12), 6996. DOI: 10.3390/su14126996

Pop, R.-A., Săplăcan, Z., Dabija, D.-C., & Alt, M.-A. (2022). The impact of social media influencers on travel decisions: The role of trust in consumer decision journey. *Current Issues in Tourism*, 25(5), 823–843. DOI: 10.1080/13683500.2021.1895729

Pourazad, N., Stocchi, L., & Pare, V. (2019). The power of brand passion in sports apparel brands. *the Journal of Product & Brand Management. Journal of Product and Brand Management*, 29(5), 547–568. DOI: 10.1108/JPBM-12-2018-2164

Powell, R., & Iankova, K. (2016). Dark tourism, emotions, and ethical dilemmas: Constructing a research agenda. *Journal of Heritage Tourism*, 11(2), 129–144. DOI: 10.1080/1743873X.2015.1120146

Prahalad, C. K. (2004). *The Fortune at the Bottom of the Pyramid: Eradicating Poverty Through Profits*. Wharton School Publishing/Pearson.

Prasetyo, Y. T., Susanto, K. C., Asiddao, S. M. A., Benito, O. P., Liao, J., Young, M. N., Persada, S. F., & Nadlifatin, R. (2023). Determining Marketing Strategy for Coffee Shops with Conjoint Analysis. *2023 IEEE International Conference on Industrial Engineering and Engineering Management (IEEM)*. DOI: 10.1109/IEEM58616.2023.10406308

Prillwitz, J., & Barr, S. (2011). Moving towards sustainability? Mobility styles, attitudes and individual travel behaviour. *Journal of Transport Geography*, 19(6), 1590–1600. DOI: 10.1016/j.jtrangeo.2011.06.011

Privitera, D., & Nesci, F. S. (2015). Globalization vs. local. The role of street food in the urban food system. *Procedia Economics and Finance*, 22, 716–722. DOI: 10.1016/S2212-5671(15)00292-0

Prizzia, R. (2017). Sustainable Development in an International Perspective. In Thai, K., Rahm, D., & Coggburn, J. (Eds.), *Handbook of Globalization and the Environment* (pp. 19–42). Routledge. DOI: 10.4324/9781315093253-2

P-TECH. (2022). *P-TECH model*. Retrieved from https://www.ptech.org/the-p-tech-model/

PTI. (25th May, 2020). Coronavirus effect: 40% travel, tourism companies may shut down in 3-6 months, says report. *Business Today*. Retrieved 5th August 2020, from https://www.businesstoday.in/current/economy-politics/coronavirus-effect-40-travel-tourism-companies-may-shut-down-in-3-6-months-says-report/story/404894.html

Puhakka, V. (2005). The role of intellectual capital in opportunity recognition of entrepreneurs. In 50th World conference of ICSB, Washington, DC.

Pulliat, G., Block, D., Bruckert, M., Nussbaum-Barberena, L., Dreysse, C., Dupé, P., & Perrin, C. (2023). Governing the nurturing city: The uneven enforcement of street food vending regulations. *Urban Geography*, •••, 1–25. DOI: 10.1080/02723638.2023.2279872

Purba, D. E., Oostrom, J. K., Van Der Molen, H. T., & Born, M. P. (2015). Personality and organizational citizenship behavior in Indonesia: The mediating effect of affective commitment. *Asian Business & Management*, 14(2), 147–170. Advance online publication. DOI: 10.1057/abm.2014.20

Purwadi, P., Devitasari, B., & Darma, D. C. (2020). Store atmosphere, SERVQUAL and consumer loyalty. *SEISENSE Journal of Management*, 3(4), 21–30. DOI: 10.33215/sjom.v3i4.385

Putra, F. K. K., Putra, M. K., & Novianti, S. (2023). Taste of asean: Traditional food images from Southeast Asian countries. *Journal of Ethnic Foods*, 10(1), 20. DOI: 10.1186/s42779-023-00189-0

Putra, W. P., Mukhid, M., & Murthada, M. (2024). Brand trust, social media, and repurchase intention: A case study of le minerale consumers in Indonesia. *International Journal of Business, Law, and Education*, 5(1), 58–71. DOI: 10.56442/ijble.v5i1.359

Qazi, A., Raj, R. G., Tahir, M., Waheed, M., Khan, S. U. R., & Abraham, A. (2014). A preliminary investigation of user perception and behavioral intention for different review types: Customers and designers perspective. *TheScientificWorldJournal*, 2014, 1–8. Advance online publication. DOI: 10.1155/2014/872929 PMID: 24711739

Quais, M., Rashid, M. H., Shahidullah, S., & Nasim, M. (2018). Crops and Cropping Sequences in Chittagong Hill Tracts. *Bangladesh Rice Journal*, 21(2), 173–184. DOI: 10.3329/brj.v21i2.38204

Raaper, R., & Brown, C. (2020). The Covid-19 pandemic and the dissolution of the university campus: Implications for student support practice. *Journal of Professional Capital and Community*, 5(3/4), 343–349. Advance online publication. DOI: 10.1108/JPCC-06-2020-0032

Rabaa'i, A. A., & ALMaati, S. A. (2021). Exploring the determinants of users' continuance intention to use mobile banking services in Kuwait: Extending the expectation-confirmation model. *Asia Pacific Journal of Information Systems*, 31(2), 141–184. DOI: 10.14329/apjis.2021.31.2.141

Rahayu, M. (2017). Sustainable development in the perspective of Sundanese cultural wisdom. *Journal of Engineering and Applied Sciences (Asian Research Publishing Network)*, 12(18), 4657–4660.

Rahkovsky, I., Young, J., & Carlson, A. (2018). Consumers balance time and money in purchasing convenience foods. *Economic Research Report, 251*. DOI: 10.22004/ag.econ.276227

Rahman, F. (2019). Symbolism in Muslim wedding rituals: An analytical study. *Journal of Cultural Symbolism*, 11(3), 45–58.

Rahman, M., Tanchangya, T., Rahman, J., Aktar, M. A., & Majumder, S. C. (2024). Corporate social responsibility and green financing behavior in Bangladesh: Towards sustainable tourism. *Innovation and Green Development*, 3(3), 100133. DOI: 10.1016/j.igd.2024.100133

Rahman, S. (2019). Culinary Traditions in Malay Weddings. *Southeast Asian Cultural Studies*, 6(4), 56–72.

Rai, A., & Fulekar, M. (2023). Environment and Sustainable Development. In Fulekar, M., & Dubey, R. (Eds.), *Climate Change and Sustainable Development* (pp. 117–128). CRC Press. DOI: 10.1201/9781003205548-7

Rajput, A., & Gahfoor, R. Z. (2020). Satisfaction and revisit intentions at fast food restaurants. *Future Business Journal*, 6(1), 13. Advance online publication. DOI: 10.1186/s43093-020-00021-0

Ramankutty, N. (2023). Both technological innovations and cultural change are key to a sustainability transition. *PLoS Biology*, 21(9), e3002298. DOI: 10.1371/journal.pbio.3002298 PMID: 37733652

Rambocas, M. M., & Arjoon, S. (2012). Using Diffusion of Innovation Theory to Model Customer Loyalty for Internet Banking: A TT Millennial Perspective. *International Journal of Business and Commerce*.

Ramos, E., & Blind, K. (2020). Data portability effects on data-driven innovation of online platforms: Analyzing Spotify. *Telecommunications Policy*, 44(9), 102026. Advance online publication. DOI: 10.1016/j.telpol.2020.102026

Ranaweera, C., McDougall, G., & Bansal, H. (2005). A model of online customer behavior during the initial transaction: Moderating effects of customer characteristics. *Marketing Theory*, 5(1), 51–74. Advance online publication. DOI: 10.1177/1470593105049601

Rand, G. D., Heath, E., & Alberts, N. (2003). The Role of local and regional food in destination marketing: A south African situation. *Journal of Travel & Tourism Marketing*, 14(3), 97–112. DOI: 10.1300/J073v14n03_06

Rane, S. (2011). Street vended food in developing world: Hazard analyses. *Indian Journal of Microbiology*, 51(1), 100–106. DOI: 10.1007/s12088-011-0154-x PMID: 22282636

Rani, U., & Dittrich, C. (2010). Options to improve food safety in the street food sector of Hyderabad. Research reports for analysis and action for sustainable development of Hyderabad, Berlin. https://www.uni-goettingen.de/de/document/download/1a8bf9c2e330d1cb5166262a3b93009f.pdf/Background%20study-Usha%20Rani%2011-2010.pdf

Raquel, M. (2017). Customer loyalty in the fast food industry in the Philippines. *World Journal of Management and Behavioral Studies*, 5(2), 47–53.

Rashid, H., & Taskin, A. (2018). Sustainable Tourism and Local Economic Benefits. *Tourism Economics*, 28(3), 180–195. DOI: 10.2345/te.2018.3456

Rasmussen, T., & Ulrich, D. (2015). Learning from practice: How HR analytics avoids being a management fad. *Organizational Dynamics*, 44(3), 236–242. DOI: 10.1016/j.orgdyn.2015.05.008

Rather, R. A., Tehseen, S., & Parrey, S. H. (2018). Promoting customer brand engagement and brand loyalty through customer brand identification and value congruity. *Spanish Journal of marketing-ESIC*, 22(3), 319–337. DOI: 10.1108/SJME-06-2018-0030

Rattanasirivilai, S., Somjai, S., & Deeprasert, D. (2020). The Role of Gender as a Moderator Linking Corporate Social Responsibility Perception to Employees Engagement: A Study in the Services Sector of Thailand. *SSRN*, 7(2), 1–14. DOI: 10.2139/ssrn.3898422

Rauch, A., & Frese, M. (2007). Let's put the person back into entrepreneurship research: A meta-analysis on the relationship between business owners' personality traits, business creation, and success. *European Journal of Work and Organizational Psychology*, 16(4), 353–385. DOI: 10.1080/13594320701595438

Rauthmann, J. F., & Will, T. (2011). Proposing a Multidimensional Machiavellianism Conceptualization. *Social Behavior and Personality*, 39(3), 391–403. DOI: 10.2224/sbp.2011.39.3.391

Reddy, R. P., & Keerthi, L. P. (2017). 'Hr Analytics' - An Effective Evidence Based HRM Tool [IJBMI]. *International Journal of Business and Management Invention*, 6(7), 23–34.

Reichheld, F. F., & Schefter, P. (2000). E-Loyalty: Your secret weapon on the web. *Harvard Business Review*.

Research Plan on Food and Nutrition Policy for Health Promotion. (2018). Delicious along the path. *Nonthaburi: International Health Policy Development Foundation, 6*(2). http://fhpprogram.org/download/street-food/

Research Themes for Tourism. (n.d.). ResearchGate. Retrieved July 11, 2024, from https://www.researchgate.net/publication/257603313_Research_Themes_for_Tourism

Reshetnikova, N., Gornostaeva, Z., Khodochenko, A., Bugaeva, M., & Tregulova, N. (2023). Financing the Green Economy in the Context of Global Sustainable Development. *Environmental Footprints and Eco-Design of Products and Processes*, 531-540.

Rewtrakunphaiboon, W., & Sawangdee, Y. (2022). Street food tour experience, satisfaction, and behavioural intention: Examining experience economy model. *Tourism and Hospitality Management*, 28(2), 277–296. DOI: 10.20867/thm.28.2.2

Reyes, L. G. (2021). Philippine private sector response, strategies, and state-business relations toward economic recovery and growth post-COVID-19. *Business and Politics*. Advance online publication. DOI: 10.1017/bap.2021.13

Rezina, S., & Mahmood, F. (2016). Gender disparity in Bangladesh and its impact on women in workplaces. *Scholar journal of Business and social science, 2*(2), 27-34.

Ribbink, D., Streukens, S., Van Riel, A. C. R., & Liljander, V. (2004). Comfort your online customer: Quality, trust and loyalty on the internet. *Managing Service Quality*, 14(6), 446–456. Advance online publication. DOI: 10.1108/09604520410569784

Richards, G. (2019). *Cultural tourism practices and sustainable management approaches*. Routledge.

Ridgway, N. M., Dawson, S. A., & Bloch, P. H. (1990). Pleasure and arousal in the marketplace: Interpersonal differences in approach-avoidance responses. *Marketing Letters*, 1(2), 139–147. DOI: 10.1007/BF00435297

Ringle, C. M., Sarstedt, M., Mitchell, R., & Gudergan, S. P. (2020). Partial least squares structural equation modeling in HRM research. *International Journal of Human Resource Management*, 31(12), 1617–1643. Advance online publication. DOI: 10.1080/09585192.2017.1416655

Roberson, Q. M. (2006). Disentangling the meanings of diversity and inclusion in organizations. *Group & Organization Management*, 31(2), 212–236. DOI: 10.1177/1059601104273064

Robina-Ramírez, R., & Pulido-Fernández, M. (2021). What role do religious belief and moral emotions play in pilgrimage with regards to respecting nature? *Annals of Leisure Research*, 24(4), 492–512. DOI: 10.1080/11745398.2019.1703199

Roca, D., Suárez, A., & Meléndez-Rodríguez, S. (2023). Female creative managers as drivers for gender diversity in advertising creative departments: a critical mass approach, Gender in Management, Vol. ahead-of-print No. ahead-of-print. DOI: 10.1108/GM-09-2022-0291

Rocchi, L., Ricciolini, E., Massei, G., Paolotti, L., & Boggia, A. (2022). Towards the 2030 Agenda: Measuring the Progress of the European Union Countries through the SDGs Achievement Index. *Sustainability (Basel)*, 14(6), 3563. DOI: 10.3390/su14063563

Rodhiah, R., & Ervina, E. (2024). Service recovery on loyalty through customer satisfaction at fast food restaurant "X" in North Jakarta. *International Journal of Social Science Research and Review*, 6(3). Advance online publication. DOI: 10.47814/ijssrr.v6i3.951

Rodzoś, J. (2019). The concept of human needs in sustainable development of cities. *Problemy Ekorozwoju*, 14(2), 91–99.

Roever, S., & Corrarino, M. (2014). Bibliography on street vending and the law. *WEIGO*. https://www.wiego.org/street-vendors-and-law

Roever, S. (2014). *Informal economy monitoring study sector report: Street vendors*. WIEGO., https://shorturl.at/Dxhe6

Roever, S., & Skinner, C. (2016). Street vendors and cities. *Environment and Urbanization*, 28(2), 359–374. DOI: 10.1177/0956247816653898

Rossi, L., Pasca, M., Arcese, G., & Poponi, S. (2024). Innovation, researcher and creativity: A complex indicator for territorial evaluation capacity. *Technology in Society*, 77, 102545. DOI: 10.1016/j.techsoc.2024.102545

Rosy, S. Y. (2024). The Growth of Tourism and 'Development' in an Indigenous Setting: Exploring a Case of the Chittagong Hill Tracts, Bangladesh. *Tourism Cases*, tourism202400022. DOI: 10.1079/tourism.2024.0022

Rousseau, D. M., Sitkin, S. B., Burt, R. S., & Camerer, C. (1998). Not so different after all: A cross-discipline view of trust. In *Academy of Management Review*. DOI: 10.5465/amr.1998.926617

Rousseau, D. M. (2006). Is there such a thing as 'evidence-based management'? *Academy of Management Review*, 31(2), 256–269. DOI: 10.5465/amr.2006.20208679

Rousseau, D. M., & Barends, E. G. R. (2011). Becoming an evidence-based HR practitioner. *Human Resource Management Journal*, 21(3), 221–235. DOI: 10.1111/j.1748-8583.2011.00173.x

Rout, S., & Srivastav, P. P. (2024). A review on development of plant-based meat analogues as future sustainable food. *International Journal of Food Science & Technology*, 59(1), 481–487. DOI: 10.1111/ijfs.16627

Roy, A., & Goll, I. (2014). Predictors of various facets of sustainability of nations: The role of cultural and economic factors. *International Business Review*, 23(5), 849–861. DOI: 10.1016/j.ibusrev.2014.01.003

Royal Swedish Academy of Sciences. (2017). Nobel Prize in Economics document: Richard Thaler's contributions to behavioral economics.

Roy, M. (2020). *Sustainable Development Strategies: Engineering, Culture and Economics*. Elsevier.

Roy, M. (2021). Tourism Industry in Bangladesh: An Assessment of Advanced SWOT Model and TOWS Matrix. In Hassan, A. (Ed.), *Tourism in Bangladesh: Investment and Development Perspectives* (pp. 279–310). Springer Nature Singapore., DOI: 10.1007/978-981-16-1858-1_18

Roy, S., & Mukhopadhyay, R. (2015). Participatory biodiversity management: Approaches to institution building to improve ecosystem services and well being. *International Journal of Economic Research*, 12(3), 851–860.

Rudzewicz, A., & Strychalska-Rudzewicz, A. (2021). The influence of brand trust on consumer loyalty. *European Research Studies*, 24(3), 454–470. DOI: 10.35808/ersj/2439

Runco, M. A. (2004). Creativity. Annual Review of Psychology, 55, 657 687. https://doi.org/DOI: 10.1146/annurev.psych.55.090902.141502

Russell, S., & Norvig, P. (2016). *Artificial intelligence: A modern approach* (3rd ed.). Prentice Hall.

Ryan, C. (2017). Eco-innovative cities Australia: A pilot project for the ecodesign of services in eight local councils. In Tukker, A., Charter, M., Vezzoli, C., Stø, E., & Andersen, M. (Eds.), *System Innovation for Sustainability 1: Perspectives on Radical Changes to Sustainable Consumption and Production* (pp. 197–213). Routledge.

Ryan, D. (2020). *Understanding digital marketing: Marketing strategies for engaging the digital generation* (5th ed.). Kogan Page.

Rynes, S. L., & Bartunek, J. M. (2017). Evidence-based management: Foundations, development, controversies and future. *Annual Review of Organizational Psychology and Organizational Behavior*, 4(1), 235–261. DOI: 10.1146/annurev-orgpsych-032516-113306

Ryu, K., & Han, H. (2011). New or repeat customers: How does physical environment influence their restaurant experience? *International Journal of Hospitality Management*, 30(3), 599–611. DOI: 10.1016/j.ijhm.2010.11.004

Sabah, S. (2016). Entrepreneurial Intention: Theory of planned behavior and the moderation effect of start-up experience. *In Entrepreneurship-Practice-Oriented Perspectives*. DOI: 10.5772/65640

Sabharwal, M. (2014). Is diversity management sufficient? Organizational inclusion to further performance. *Public Personnel Management*, 43(2), 197–217. DOI: 10.1177/0091026014522202

Sadik, M. I. (2024). Drawbacks of the 1997 Peace Accord and Re-emergence of Militancy in the Chittagong Hill Tracts: A Multidimensional Approach to Resolve the Issue. SSRN *Electronic Journal*. DOI: 10.2139/ssrn.4817372

Sadyk, D., & Islam, D. M. Z. (2022). Brand equity and usage intention powered by value co-creation: A case of instagram in Kazakhstan. *Sustainability (Basel)*, 2022(14), 500. DOI: 10.3390/su14010500

Saengthap, N. (2018). *Marketing mix factors and post-purchase behavior of consumers in community markets in Thanyaburi District, Pathum Thani Province. Independent study*. Rajamangala University of Technology Thanyaburi.

Safira, M., & Chikaraishi, M. (2023). The impact of online food delivery service on eating-out behavior: A case of Multi-Service Transport Platforms (MSTPs) in Indonesia. *Transportation*, 50(6), 2253–2271. DOI: 10.1007/s11116-022-10307-7

Sahagun, M. A., & Vasquez-Parraga, A. Z. (2014). Can fast-food consumers be loyal customers, if so how? Theory, method and findings. *Journal of Retailing and Consumer Services*, 21(2), 168–174. DOI: 10.1016/j.jretconser.2013.12.002

Saif, H. A. A. (2020). Entrepreneurial passion for founding as a mediator of the career anchors to entrepreneurial behavior relationship. *Journal of Public Affairs*, 22(1), e2408. Advance online publication. DOI: 10.1002/pa.2408

Saks, A. (2008). The Meaning and Bleeding of Employee Engagement: How Muddy Is the Water? *Industrial and Organizational Psychology: Perspectives on Science and Practice*, 1(1), 40–43. DOI: 10.1111/j.1754-9434.2007.00005.x

Saks, A. M. (2006). Antecedents and consequences of employee engagement. *Journal of Managerial Psychology*, 21(7), 600–619. DOI: 10.1108/02683940610690169

Saksriwattana, K. (2024). Factor affecting intention to use chatbot for health information. *Procedia of Multidisciplinary Research*, 2(7), 1–10.

Salamon, J. (2019). The Measurement of Sustainable Development Level in the Aspect of Selection of Indicators and Measurement Methods. In Krakowiak-Bal, A., & Vaverkova, M. (Eds.), *Infrastructure and Environment* (pp. 328–336). Springer. DOI: 10.1007/978-3-030-16542-0_41

Salotti, S., & Trecroci, C. (2016). The Impact of Government Debt, Expenditure and Taxes on Aggregate Investment and Productivity Growth. *Economica*, 83(330), 356–384. DOI: 10.1111/ecca.12175

Salvador, S. (2017). Strengthening capacity to link environment and health in the context of the FTAA. In Segger, M., & Reynal, M. (Eds.), *Beyond the Barricades: The Americas Trade and Sustainable Development Agenda* (pp. 169–180). Routledge.

Samarah, T., Bayram, P., Aljuhmani, H. Y., & Elrehail, H. (2022). The role of brand interactivity and involvement in driving social media consumer brand engagement and brand loyalty: The mediating effect of brand trust. *Journal of Research in Interactive Marketing*, 16(4), 648–664. DOI: 10.1108/JRIM-03-2021-0072

Samlejsin, C., & Kookkaew, P. (2022). Integrated Marketing Communication and Service Quality Influencing on Brand Loyalty of Customer a Company that Produces and Distributes Chemical Fertilizers Under the ABC Brand. *PSAKU International Journal of Interdisciplinary Research, Forthcoming, Asian Administration &. Management Review*, 5(1), 7–16. DOI: 10.14456/aamr.2022.2

Samuelson, W., & Zeckhauser, R. (1988). Status quo bias in decision making. *Journal of Risk and Uncertainty*, 1(1), 7–59.

Santoro, G., Fiano, F., Bertoldi, B., & Ciampi, F. (2019). Big data for business management in the retail industry. *Management Decision*, 57(8), 1980–1992. DOI: 10.1108/MD-07-2018-0829

Sardar, S., Patra, S., & Paria, M. 'Ma Bonbibi': A Goddess in the Folk Culture of Sundarbans Region in India & Bangladesh.

Sardar, S., Ray, R., Hasan, M. K., Chitra, S. S., Parvez, A. S., & Avi, M. A. R. (2022). Assessing the effects of COVID-19 on restaurant business from restaurant owners' perspective. *Frontiers in Psychology*, 13, 849249. DOI: 10.3389/fpsyg.2022.849249 PMID: 35496209

Sari, E. T., & Suvittawat, A. (2023). GAP analysis of the street-food consumers in Surabaya and Bangkok. *International Journal of Innovation and Applied Studies*, 39(4), 1495–1507. https://www.proquest.com/scholarly-journals/gap-analysis-street-food-consumers-surabaya/docview/2838780019/se-2

Sari, N. N., Yuliana, D., Hervidea, R., & Agata, A. (2020). *Health Protocol of Covid-19: as A Prevention of Covid-19 in the Work Area of Office Employees in Bandar Lampung*. Jurnal Peduli Masyarakat., DOI: 10.37287/jpm.v2i4.235

Sarker, J., & Khan, A. (2024). Economic Implications of Tourism Development in Kuakata. *Journal of Regional Development*, 22(1), 100–115. DOI: 10.7890/jrd.2024.4567

Sarker, J., Rahman, M., & Uddin, M. (2023). Sustainability in Community-Based Tourism. *Journal of Community Development*, 22(1), 80–95. DOI: 10.8901/jcd.2023.5678

Sarstedt, M., Ringle, C. M., & Joseph, F. Hair. (2017). Partial least squares structural equation modeling (PLS-SEM). *Handbook of Market Research*.

Sarstedt, M., Ringle, C. M., Henseler, J., & Hair, J. F. (2014). On the Emancipation of PLS-SEM: A C commentary on Rigdon (2012).*Long Range Planning*, 47(3), 154–160. DOI: 10.1016/j.lrp.2014.02.007

Sawangsub, N. (2018). Marketing Mix Factors and Post-Purchase Behavior of Consumers at Community Markets in Thanyaburi District, Pathum Thani Province. [Master's thesis, Business Administration, Pathum Thani] Rajamangala University of Technology Thanyaburi.

Scagnoli, N. I., Choo, J., & Tian, J. (2019). Students' insights on the use of video lectures in online classes. *British Journal of Educational Technology*, 50(1), 399–414. DOI: 10.1111/bjet.12572

Schaap, H., Baartman, L., & de Bruijn, E. (2012). Students learning processes during school-based learning and workplace learning in vocational education: A review. *Vocations and Learning*, 5(2), 99–117. DOI: 10.1007/s12186-011-9069-2

Schivinski, B., Christodoulides, G., & Dabrowski, D. (2016). Measuring consumers' engagement with brand-related social-media content. *Journal of Advertising Research*, 56(1), 64–80. DOI: 10.2501/JAR-2016-004

Schlaegel, C., & Koenig, M. (2014). Determinants of Entrepreneurial Intent: A Meta–Analytic Test and Integration of Competing Models. *Entrepreneurship Theory and Practice*, 38(2), 291–332. DOI: 10.1111/etap.12087

Schoenaker, N., Hoekstra, R., & Smits, J. (2015). Comparison of Measurement Systems for Sustainable Development at the National Level. *Sustainable Development (Bradford)*, 23(5), 285–300. DOI: 10.1002/sd.1585

Schön, D. A. (1983). *The reflective practitioner: How professionals think in action*. Basic Books.

Schuler (2003). United Nations Conference on Trade and Development (UNCTAD), *World Investment Report 1998*, New York: United Nations (1999).

Schuler, R. S., Budhwar, P. S., & Florkowski, G. W. (2002). International human resource Management: Review and critique. *International Journal of Management Reviews*, 4(1), 41–70. DOI: 10.1111/1468-2370.00076

Scott, K. A., Heathcote, J. M., & Gruman, J. A. (2011). The diverse organization: Finding gold at the end of the rainbow. *Human Resource Management*, 50(6), 735–755. DOI: 10.1002/hrm.20459

Scullion, H. (1992). Strategic recruitment and development of the international manager: Some European considerations. *Human Resource Management Journal*, 3(1), 57–69. DOI: 10.1111/j.1748-8583.1992.tb00302.x

Scullion, H. (2004). Introduction. In Scullion, H., & Linehan, M. (Eds.), *InternationalHuman Resource Management: A Critical Text*. Palgrave.

Scullion, H., Collings, D., & Gunnigle, P. (2007). International Human Resource Management in the 21st Century: Emerging Themes and Contemporary Debates. *Human Resource Management Journal*, 17(4), 309–319. DOI: 10.1111/j.1748-8583.2007.00047.x

Seaton, A. V. (1999). War and thanatourism: Waterloo 1815-1914. Annals of Tourism Research.

Seaton, A. V. (2020). The educational value of dark tourism: Government initiatives and policy implications.

Seaton, A. V. (1996). Guided by the dark: From thanatopsis to thanatourism. *International Journal of Heritage Studies*, 2(4), 234–244. DOI: 10.1080/13527259608722178

Sebele, L. S. (2010). Community-based tourism ventures, benefits and challenges: Khama Rhino Sanctuary Trust, Central District, Botswana. *Tourism Management*, 31(1), 136–146. DOI: 10.1016/j.tourman.2009.01.005

Sebestyén, V., & Abonyi, J. (2021). Data-driven comparative analysis of national adaptation pathways for Sustainable Development Goals. *Journal of Cleaner Production*, 319, 128657. DOI: 10.1016/j.jclepro.2021.128657

Selmer, J. (2004). Expatriates' hesitation and the localization of Western business operations in China. *International Journal of Human Resource Management*, 15(6), 1094–1107. DOI: 10.1080/0958519041000167732

Sensharma, A. (01st June, 2020). Coronavirus Impact l Make My Trip lays off 350 employees as Covid-19 crisis hits business. *English Jagaran.* Retrieved on 4th August 2020, from https://english.jagran.com/business/coronavirus-impact-makemytrip-lays-off-350-employees-as-covid19-crisis-hits-business-10012471

Seo, K. H., & Lee, J. H. (2021). Understanding risk perception toward food safety in street food: The relationships among service quality, values, and repurchase intention. *International Journal of Environmental Research and Public Health*, 18(13), 6826. DOI: 10.3390/ijerph18136826 PMID: 34202074

Seraphin, H. (2017, January 1). Assessing dark tourism as a sustainable economic activity for emerging destinations using a multi criteria approach. University of Winchester. https://winchester.elsevierpure.com/en/publications/assessing-dark-tourism-as-a-sustainable-economic-activity-for-eme-3

Serem, D., & Kara, A. (2015). The role of Maasai Mara University in promoting sustainable development. In Jacob, W., Sutin, S., Weidman, J., & Yeager, J. (Eds.), *Community Engagement in Higher Education: Policy Reforms and Practice* (pp. 269–285). Sense Publishers. DOI: 10.1007/978-94-6300-007-9_16

Sergi, B. S., Popkova, E. G., Bogoviz, A. V., & Ragulina, J. V. (2019). Entrepreneurship and Economic Growth: The Experience of Developed and Developing Countries. *Entrepreneurship and Development in the 21st Century*, 3–32. DOI: 10.1108/978-1-78973-233-720191002

Sesen, H. (2013). Personality or environment? A comprehensive study on the entrepreneurial intentions of university students. *Education + Training*, 55(7), 624–640. DOI: 10.1108/ET-05-2012-0059

Settersten, R. A.Jr, Bernardi, L., Härkönen, J., Antonucci, T. C., Dykstra, P. A., Heckhausen, J., Kuh, D., Mayer, K. U., Moen, P., Mortimer, J. T., Mulder, C. H., Smeeding, T. M., van der Lippe, T., Hagestad, G. O., Kohli, M., Levy, R., Schoon, I., & Thomson, E. (2020). Understanding the effects of Covid-19 through a life course lens. *Advances in Life Course Research*, 45, 100360. Advance online publication. DOI: 10.1016/j.alcr.2020.100360 PMID: 36698274

Setyadi, B., Helmi, S., & Mohamad, N. S. I. B. S.Syed Ismail bin Syed Mohamad. (2023). Customer satisfaction mediates the influence of service quality on customer loyalty in Islamic banks. [IJIBEC]. *International Journal of Islamic Business and Economics*, 7(1), 25–36. DOI: 10.28918/ijibec.v7i1.6924

Sezgin, A. C., & Şanlıer, N. (2016). Street food consumption in terms of the food safety and health. *International Journal of Human Sciences*, 13(3), 4072–4083. https://www.j-humansciences.com/ojs/index.php/IJHS/article/view/3925. DOI: 10.14687/jhs.v13i3.3925

Shabbir, M. Q., & Gardezi, S. B. W. (2020). Application of big data analytics and organizational performance: The mediating role of knowledge management practices. *Journal of Big Data*, 7(1), 1–17. DOI: 10.1186/s40537-020-00317-6

Shaffer, M. A., Kraimer, M. L., Chen, Y. P., & Bolino, M. C. (2012). Choices, challenges, and career consequences of global work experiences: A review and future agenda. *Journal of Management*, 38(4), 1282–1327. DOI: 10.1177/0149206312441834

Shah, G. D., & Darekar, S. (2019). Exploring the potential challenges faced by food truck industry in the emerging market of Pune and Mumbai while establishing new culinary attractions. *Think India Journal*, 22(14), 1037-1059. https://thinkindiaquarterly.org/index.php/think-india/article/view/12483

Shahab, Y., Chengang, Y., Arbizu, A. D., & Haider, M. J. (2019). Entrepreneurial self-efficacy and intention: Do entrepreneurial creativity and education matter? *International Journal of Entrepreneurial Behaviour & Research*, 25(2), 259–280. DOI: 10.1108/IJEBR-12-2017-0522

Shahzadi, M., Malik, S. A., Ahmad, M., & Shabbir, A. (2018). Perceptions of fine dining restaurants in Pakistan. *International Journal of Quality and Reliability Management. International Journal of Quality & Reliability Management*, 35(3), 635–655. DOI: 10.1108/IJQRM-07-2016-0113

Shaker, R., & Mackay, B. (2021). Hidden patterns of sustainable development in Asia with underlying global change correlations. *Ecological Indicators*, 131, 108227. DOI: 10.1016/j.ecolind.2021.108227

Shamah, R. A., Mason, M. C., Moretti, A., & Raggiotto, F. (2018). Investigating the antecedents of African fast food customers' loyalty: A self-congruity perspective. *Journal of Business Research*, 86, 446–456. DOI: 10.1016/j.jbusres.2017.05.020

Shamim, S., Zeng, J., Shariq, S. M., & Khan, Z. (2019). Role of big data management in enhancing big data decision-making capability and quality among Chinese firms: A dynamic capabilities view. *Information & Management*, 56(6), 1–16. DOI: 10.1016/j.im.2018.12.003

Shamsuddoha, M., Rahman, M., & Uddin, M. (2017). Balancing Growth and Preservation in Tourism. *Journal of Sustainable Tourism*, 14(4), 200–215. DOI: 10.2468/jst.2017.7890

Shaqour, A., & Farzaneh, H. (2021). The Urban Sustainable Development Index: A Comparative Analysis of Low Emission Strategies in Urban Areas. In Farzaneh, H., Zusman, E., & Chae, Y. (Eds.), *Aligning Climate Change and Sustainable Development Policies in Asia* (pp. 19–39). Springer Nature. DOI: 10.1007/978-981-16-0135-4_2

Sharma, D., & Chanda, K. (2023). Destination marketing in digital world. *management metamorphosis: navigating the changing landscape*, 128.

Sharma, N. (2022). Acknowledging the shades of grey: The past, present and future of dark tourism in India. In *Indian Tourism: Diaspora Perspectives* (pp. 125–142). Emerald Publishing Limited.

Sharma, A., Gupta, J., Gera, L., Sati, M., & Sharma, S. (2020). Relationship between customer satisfaction and loyalty. Social Science Research Network. DOI: 10.2139/ssrn.3913161

Sharma, A., & Sharma, T. (2017). HR analytics and performance appraisal system. *Management Research Review*, 40(6), 684–697. DOI: 10.1108/MRR-04-2016-0084

Sharmin, F., Sultan, M. T., Wang, D., Badulescu, A., & Li, B. (2021). Cultural Dimensions and Social Media Empowerment in Digital Era: Travel-Related Continuance Usage Intention. *Sustainability (Basel)*, 13(19), 19. Advance online publication. DOI: 10.3390/su131910820

Sharpley, R., & Stone, P. R. (2009). The darker side of travel: The theory and practice of dark tourism

Sharpley, R., & Stone, P. R. (2009). The darker side of travel: The theory and practice of dark tourism.

Sharpley, R., & Stone, P. R. (2017). Ethical and sustainable dark tourism practices: Minimizing environmental footprints. In Sharpley, R., & Stone, P. R. (Eds.), *The darker side of travel: The theory and practice of dark tourism* (pp. 139–156).

Sheikh, M. (2020). Development of Sustainable Tourism Destinations and Poverty Alleviation of Bangladesh. *International Journal of Scientific Research and Management*, 8(02), 1565–1575. DOI: 10.18535/ijsrm/v8i02.em02

Shepelev, I., Goncharova, O., Ermolina, L., & Gorokhova, N. (2024). Investing in nature: analysis of the relationship between environmental capital and economic growth. *E3S Web of Conferences, 531*, 05024.

Shereni, N. C., & Chambwe, M. (2024). Nature-based Tourism in Zimbabwe: Sustainability Issues. In Stone, L. S., & Stone, M. T. (Eds.), *Wildlife Tourism Dynamics in Southern Africa* (pp. 59–70). Springer Nature Switzerland., DOI: 10.1007/978-3-031-57252-4_5

Sheth, H. (2023). HR analytics – An evidence based HR process. *International Journal of Creative Research Thoughts*, 11(10), 849–854.

Shinde, K. A., & Olsen, D. H. (2022). Reframing the intersections of pilgrimage, religious tourism, and sustainability. *Sustainability (Basel)*, 15(1), 461. DOI: 10.3390/su15010461

Shin, Y., & Yu, L. (2018). The influence of quality of physical environment, food and service on customer trust, customer satisfaction, and loyalty And Moderating Effect of Gender: An Empirical Study on Foreigners in South Korean restaurant. [IJACT]. *International Journal of Advanced Culture Technology*, 8(3), 172–185.

Shrestha, A., & Saratchandra, M. (2023). A Conceptual Framework toward Knowledge Ambidexterity Using Information Systems and Knowledge Management. *Journal of Information Systems*, 37(1), 143–167. DOI: 10.2308/ISYS-2021-013

Siddiqi, H., & Qureshi, M. (2016). The impact of employee creativity on performance of the firm.

Siddique, M. F., Haque, M. A., Barman, A. C., Tanu, M. B., Shahjahan, M., & Uddin, M. J. (2024). Freshwater pearl culture in Bangladesh: Current status and prospects. *Heliyon*, 10(7), e29023. DOI: 10.1016/j.heliyon.2024.e29023 PMID: 38617946

Siegel, E. (2016). *Predictive analytics: The power to predict who will click, buy, lie, or die* (2nd ed.). Wiley.

Sieger, P., Raemy, L., Zellweger, T., Fueglistaller, U. & Hatak, I. (2021). Global Student Entrepreneurship 2021: Insights From 58 Countries. (2021 GUESS Global Report).

Siemens. (2022). *Siemens Technical Academy*. Retrieved from https://www.siemens.com/global/en/home/company/career/technical-academy.html

Siemens, G. (2013). Learning analytics: The importance of a comprehensive approach. *Journal of Educational Technology & Society*, 16(1), 24–34.

Sieras, S. G. (2024). Impact and Identities as Revealed in Tourists' Perceptions of the Linguistic Landscape in Tourist Destinations. *International Journal of Language and Literary Studies*, 6(1), 375–392. DOI: 10.36892/ijlls.v6i1.1644

Sigala, M. (2020). Tourism and COVID-19: Impacts and recovery. *Journal of Tourism Futures*, 6(2), 167–170. DOI: 10.1108/JTF-03-2020-0035

Simoni, V., & Buckley, R. (2020). Dark tourism and the ethics of encounter: Using empathy to inform ethically responsible dark tourism practices. *Tourism Recreation Research*, 45(3), 372–384. DOI: 10.1080/02508281.2019.1644896

Simopoulos, A. P., & Bhat, R. V. (2000). *Street foods: World review of nutrition and dietetics*. Karger.

Sims, R. (2009). Food, place and authenticity: Local food and the sustainable tourism experience. *Journal of Sustainable Tourism*, 17(3), 321–336. https://www.tandfonline.com/doi/full/10.1080/09669580802359293. DOI: 10.1080/09669580802359293

Singh, N., Sinha, N., & Liébana-Cabanillas, F. J. (2020). Determining factors in the adoption and recommendation of mobile wallet services in India: Analysis of the effect of innovativeness, stress to use and social influence. *International Journal of Information Management*, 50, 191–205. Advance online publication. DOI: 10.1016/j.ijinfomgt.2019.05.022

Singh, R., & Bhatt, V. (2023). Technological advancement in industrial revolution 4.0 for sustainable development of India: Understanding linkages in theory and practice. In Mehta, K., & Sharma, R. (Eds.), *Sustainability, Green Management, and Performance of SMEs* (pp. 57–72). De Gruyter. DOI: 10.1515/9783111170022-004

Singh, S. (2021). Technological Adaptation in Tourism Industry Post-COVID-19: Case Study of Delhi NCR. *International Journal of Tourism Research*, 23(5), 782–795. DOI: 10.1002/jtr.2431

Singh, S. K., & Del Giudice, M. (2019). Big data analytics, dynamic capabilities and firm performance. *Management Decision*, 57(8), 1729–1733. DOI: 10.1108/MD-08-2019-020

Singh, V. (2022). Sustainable Development and Climate Change. In *Research Anthology on Measuring and Achieving Sustainable Development Goals, 3* (pp. 944–964). IGI Global. DOI: 10.4018/978-1-6684-3885-5.ch050

Sinha, S. (Mar 20, 2020). Warning of 3.8 crore job losses in travel industry, sector seeks relief from government. Retrieved from https://timesofindia.indiatimes.com/business/india-business/warning-of-3-8-crore-job-losses-in-travel-industry-sector-seeks-relief-from-government/articleshow/74715994.cms

Sinulingga, S. (2021). Tourism & Covid-19 (Coronavirus Impact Inventory to Tourism Stakeholders in North Sumatera). *Budapest International Research and Critics Institute-Journal (BIRCI-Journal) Vol*, 4(1), 170-179.

Siswanto, B., Rahmawati, & Kuleh, J. (2019). The influence of food quality and physical environment on behavior intention through customer satisfaction at visitors to McDonald's store in Samarinda. [IJBMI]. *International Journal of Business and Management Invention*, 11(12).

Skinner, J., & Volo, S. (2021). Dark tourism, sustainable development and equity: Transforming heritage through critical engagement. In Sharpley, R., & Stone, P. R. (Eds.), *Research themes for tourism* (pp. xx–xx). Goodfellow Publishers.

Skinner, J., & Volo, S. (2021). *Sustainable tourism: Practices and principles*. Book on Google Books.

Slack, N., Singh, G., & Sharma, S. (2020). The effect of supermarket service quality dimensions and customer satisfaction on customer loyalty and disloyalty dimensions. *International Journal of Quality and Service Sciences*, 12(3), 297–318. DOI: 10.1108/IJQSS-10-2019-0114

Slade, P. (2003). Gallipoli thanatourism: The meaning of ANZAC. *Annals of Tourism Research*, 30(4), 779–794. DOI: 10.1016/S0160-7383(03)00025-2

Slade, P. (2019). Dark tourism: Pilgrimage to sites of death and disaster. *Annals of Tourism Research*, 76, 153–165. DOI: 10.1016/j.annals.2019.01.011

Slade, P. (2019). Dark tourism: Troubled times. In Jafari, J., & Xiao, H. (Eds.), *International Encyclopedia of Tourism Management and Marketing. Mostafanezhad, M. (2020). Dark tourism and the ethics of community involvement. Journal of Tourism and Cultural Change*. Retrieved from. [insert link here]

Smeds, M. R., & Aulivola, B. (2020). Gender disparity and sexual harassment in vascular surgery practices. *Journal of Vascular Surgery*, 72(2), 692–699. DOI: 10.1016/j.jvs.2019.10.071 PMID: 32067879

Smilor, R. W. (1997). Entrepreneurship: Reflections on a subversive activity. *Journal of Business Venturing*, 12(5), 341–346. DOI: 10.1016/S0883-9026(97)00008-6

Smith, A. K., Bolton, R. N., & Wagner, J. (2019). A model of customer engagement with mobile and wearable technology interfaces: The role of satisfaction, performance, and confidence. *Journal of the Academy of Marketing Science*, 47(2), 199–218.

Smith, A., & Lohrke, F. (2008). Entrepreneurial network development: Trusting in others' capabilities. *. Journal of Business Venturing*, 23(2), 109–122.

Smith, C., & Betts, M. (2000). Learning as partners: Realising the potential of work-based learning. *Journal of Vocational Education and Training*, 52(4), 589–604. DOI: 10.1080/13636820000200147

Smol, M. (2023). Global directions for the green deal strategies—Americas, Europe, Australia, Asia, and Africa. In Prasad, M., & Smol, M. (Eds.), *Sustainable and Circular Management of Resources and Waste Towards a Green Deal* (pp. 39–46). Elsevier. DOI: 10.1016/B978-0-323-95278-1.00019-X

Sohel, M., Sifullah, M. K., Hossain, B., Hossain, M. A., Sarker, M. F. H., Hossain, I., Hossain, M. E., & Uddin, M. R. (2024). E-Learning Experience of Indigenous Rural Communities in the Face of COVID-19 Crisis in Chittagong Hills Tracts Region, Bangladesh: A Qualitative Investigation. *International Journal of Community Well-being*, 7(2), 291–314. DOI: 10.1007/s42413-024-00207-2

Solanki, M. S., & Oberoi, S. S. (2022). IMPACT OF CORONAVIRUS ON INDIAN AVIATION INDUSTRY. *International Journal of Business and Economics*, 6(2), 353–365.

Solnet, D., Subramony, M., Ford, R. C., Golubovskaya, M., Kang, H. J., & Hancer, M. (2019). Leveraging human touch in service interactions: Lessons from hospitality. *Journal of Service Management*, 30(3), 392–409. DOI: 10.1108/JOSM-12-2018-0380

Song, M., Xing, X., Duan, Y., Cohen, J., & Mou, J. (2022). Will artificial intelligence replace human customer service? The impact of communication quality and privacy risks on adoption intention. *Journal of Retailing and Consumer Services*, 66, 102900. DOI: 10.1016/j.jretconser.2021.102900

Song, S., Yao, X., & Wen, N. (2021). What motivates Chinese consumers to avoid information about the COVID-19 pandemic?: The perspective of the stimulus-organism-response model. *Information Processing & Management*, 58(1), 102407. Advance online publication. DOI: 10.1016/j.ipm.2020.102407 PMID: 33041437

Song, X., Du, L., & Wang, Z. (2024). Correlation Analysis of Urban Road Network Structure and Spatial Distribution of Tourism Service Facilities at Multi-Scales Based on Tourists' Travel Preferences. *Buildings*, 14(4), 914. DOI: 10.3390/buildings14040914

Sonkar, C., Kashyap, D., Varshney, N., Baral, B., & Jha, H. C. (2020). Impact of Gastrointestinal Symptoms in COVID-19: A Molecular Approach. *SN Comprehensive Clinical Medicine*, 2(12), 2658–2669. DOI: 10.1007/s42399-020-00619-z PMID: 33169110

Soula, A., Yount, A. C., Lepillier, O., & Bricas, N. (2020). *Manger en ville: Regards Socio-Anthropologiques d'Afrique, d'Amérique latine et d'Asie*. Editions Quae., DOI: 10.35690/978-2-7592-3091-4

Sousa, S., Gelormini, M., Damasceno, A., Lopes, S. A., Maló, S., Chongole, C., Muholove, P., Casal, S., Pinho, O., Moreira, P., Lunet, N., & Padrão, P. (2019). Street food in Maputo, Mozambique: Availability and nutritional value of homemade foods. *Nutrition and Health (Berkhamsted, Hertfordshire)*, 25(1), 37–46. DOI: 10.1177/0260106018816427 PMID: 30522397

Sousa, S., Morais, I. L. D., Albuquerque, G., Gelormini, M., Casal, S., Pinho, O., Motta, C., Damasceno, A., Moreira, P., Breda, J., Lunet, N., & Padrão, P. (2022). Patterns of street food purchase in cities from central Asia. *Frontiers in Nutrition*, 9, 925771. DOI: 10.3389/fnut.2022.925771 PMID: 35811986

Spady, W. G. (1994). The concept of outcome-based education. In Spady, W. G. (Ed.), *Outcome-based education: Critical issues and answers* (pp. 11–26). American Association of School Administrators.

Sparrow, P. R., Brewster, C., & Harris, H. (2004). *Globalizing Human Resource Management*. Routledge. DOI: 10.4324/9780203614129

Srebrenica-Potočari Memorial. (2023). Challenges in site conservation and visitor management at Srebrenica-Potočari. *Retrieved from Srebrenica-Potočari Memorial Website*

Srinivasan, U., & Shanker, K. (2021). Making nature count: Reflections on the dasgupta review. *Ecology. Economy and Society*, 4(2), 5–12.

Srisompob, J., & Panyasak, S. (2012). The Impact of Insurgency on Local Communities in Southern Thailand. *Journal of Asian Security and International Affairs*, 5(1), 89–108.

Sriyakul, T., & Jermsittiparsert, K. (2019). The mediating role of entrepreneurial passion in the relationship between entrepreneur education and entrepreneurial intention among university students in Thailand. *International Journal of Innovation. Creativity and Change*, 6(10), 193–212.

Starbucks. (2003). Living our values. Corporate Social Responsibility. Fiscal 2003. Annual Report. Author.

Starbucks. (2011). Business ethics and compliance. Author.

Starbucks. (2014). Diversity and inclusion. Author.

Stark, P. B., & Lowther, M. A. (1988). *Competency-based education and training: Concepts and practices*. American Council on Education.

Statista - The Statistics Portal. (n.d.). Statista. Retrieved March 17, 2024, from https://www.statista.com/search/?q=music+streaming+platforms+2024&p=1

Statista (2023). *Digital Music: Market data & analysis*. Statista. https://www.statista.com/outlook/dmo/digital-media/digital-music/music-streaming/philippines

Stevens, F. G., Plaut, V. C., & Sanchez-Burks, J. (2008). Unlocking the benefits of diversity: All-inclusive multiculturalism and positive organizational change. *The Journal of Applied Behavioral Science*, 44(1), 116–133. DOI: 10.1177/0021886308314460

Stoin, D., Jianu, C., Poiana, M. A., Alexa, E. C., & Velciov, A. B. (2021). Current trends in the use of unconventional raw materials for the development of gluten-free bakery and pastry products with high nutritional value: A review. *Journal of Agroalimentary Processes and Technologies*, 27(4), 378–391.

Stone, P. R. (2006). A dark tourism spectrum: Towards a typology of death and macabre related tourist sites, attractions and exhibitions.

Stone, M. (1974). Cross-validatory choice and assessment of statistical predictions. *Journal of the Royal Statistical Society. Series B, Statistical Methodology*, 36(2), 111–133. DOI: 10.1111/j.2517-6161.1974.tb00994.x

Stone, P. R. (2006). A dark tourism spectrum: Towards a typology of death and macabre related tourist sites, attractions and exhibitions. Tourism: An Interdisciplinary. *International Journal (Toronto, Ont.)*, 54(2), 145–160. DOI: 10.1080/1331677X.2006.10681119

Stone, P. R. (2013). Dark tourism scholarship: A critical review. *International Journal of Culture, Tourism and Hospitality Research*, 7(3), 307–318. DOI: 10.1108/IJCTHR-06-2013-0039

Stone, P. R., & Sharpley, R. (2008). Consuming dark tourism: A thanatological perspective. *Annals of Tourism Research*, 35(2), 574–595. DOI: 10.1016/j.annals.2008.02.003

Streckfuss, T., & Martinez, A. (2017). Competency-based education: Assessing the effectiveness of new learning paradigms. *Journal of Higher Education Theory and Practice*, 17(4), 15–25.

Street food cart [Online image]. (2022). Spring. https://www.springnews.co.th/blogs/spring-life/827201

Street food in Chiang Mai [Online image]. (2023). Kindeeyunuea. https://rb.gy/s38onf

Street food. (2024, January 2). In *Wikipedia*. Retrieved January 13, 2024, from https://en.wikipedia.org/wiki/Street_food

Strömberg, H., Rexfelt, O., Karlsson, I. C. M., & Sochor, J. (2016). Trying on change – Trialability as a change moderator for sustainable travel behaviour. *Travel Behaviour & Society*, 4, 60–68. DOI: 10.1016/j.tbs.2016.01.002

Sturken, M. (2007). *Tourists of history: Memory, kitsch, and consumerism from Oklahoma City to Ground Zero*. Duke University Press.

Subhrasmita, S., & Gaur, R. (2023). A Spiritual Journey through Cancer and Beyond: Prayer, Pilgrimage, and Faith in Lisa Ray's Close to the Bone. *Journal of Disability & Religion*, •••, 1–21.

Suhadah, S., Mulyana, D., Yusup, P. M., & Sjafirah, N. A. (2022). Pilgrimage sites as magnets of interfaith tolerance: The case of kemaliq lingsar in Indonesia. *International Journal of Religious Tourism and Pilgrimage*, 10(3), 3.

Sujatha, T., Shatrugna, V., Rao, G. N., Reddy, G. C. K., Padmavathi, K. S., & Vidyasagar, P. (1997). Street food: An important source of energy for the urban worker. *Food and Nutrition Bulletin*, 18(4), 1–5. DOI: 10.1177/156482659701800४

Sukanya, N. (2016). Fostering sustained economic development in India- the economic angle. *International Journal of Economic Research*, 13(3), 989–998.

Sukcharoen, S., Chaidet, E., & Wongpom, A. (2023). The model to develop street food management in Thailand. *Journal of Health Center 7, Khon Kaen, 15*(2). https://he01.tci-thaijo.org/index.php/johpc7/article/view/259933/178510

Sukphon, N.Strategic Management and Employee Engagement in Organization. (2022, July 1). Asian Administration &. *Management Review*, 5(2), 1–10.

Sukree, P. (2019). Government Initiatives to Support Conflict-Affected Women in Thailand. *International Journal of Social Work*, 63(4), 402–417.

Sultan, M. T., Sharmin, F., Badulescu, A., Gavrilut, D., & Xue, K. (2021). Social Media-Based Content towards Image Formation: A New Approach to the Selection of Sustainable Destinations. *Sustainability (Basel)*, 13(8), 8. Advance online publication. DOI: 10.3390/su13084241

Sultan, M. T., Sharmin, F., Badulescu, A., Stiubea, E., & Xue, K. (2021). Travelers' Responsible Environmental Behavior towards Sustainable Coastal Tourism: An Empirical Investigation on Social Media User-Generated Content. *Sustainability (Basel)*, 13(1), 1. Advance online publication. DOI: 10.3390/su13010056

Sunio, V., Cortes, R. Z., & Lactao, J. (2022). Rhetorical orientations for promoting sustainable travel behavior: A perspective. *Research in Transportation Economics*, 91, 101026. DOI: 10.1016/j.retrec.2020.101026

Sunio, V., & Schmöcker, J.-D. (2017). Can we promote sustainable travel behavior through mobile apps? Evaluation and review of evidence. *International Journal of Sustainable Transportation*, 11(8), 553–566. DOI: 10.1080/15568318.2017.1300716

Sun, K., & Moon, J. (2023). Assessing antecedents of restaurant's brand trust and brand loyalty, and moderating role of food healthiness. *Nutrients*, 15(24), 5057. DOI: 10.3390/nu15245057 PMID: 38140316

Sunstein, C. R. (2014). *Why nudge? The politics of libertarian paternalism*. Yale University Press.

Supaporn, P.. (2020). Sufficiency economy villages: Enhancing local skills and resources for household economic stability. *. *Journal of Thai Local Development*, 7(1), 67–84.

Su, Q., & Li, F. (2023). The influence of tourists' sensory experiences of street food on destination loyalty: The mediating roles of delight and place attachment. *Journal of China Tourism Research*, •••, 1–25. DOI: 10.1080/19388160.2023.2245963

Sur, S. (2015). The Role of Online Trust and Satisfaction in Building Loyalty Towards Online Retailers: Differences Between Heavy and Light Shopper Groups. In *LISS 2014*. DOI: 10.1007/978-3-662-43871-8_71

Suryani, W. (2024). New Trends in Consumer and Tourism Marketing Science. In Tarnanidis, T. K., & Sklavounos, N. (Eds.), (pp. 290–297). *Advances in Marketing, Customer Relationship Management, and E-Services.* IGI Global., DOI: 10.4018/979-8-3693-2754-8.ch015

Susanto, D., Natalia, D., Jeniva, I., Lianto, , Veronica, M., & Setinawati, . (2022). Brand knowledge training through packaging materials and the use of social media in hurung bunut village, gunung mas district. *Amala Jurnal Pengabdian Kepada Masyarakat*, 1(2), 81–89. DOI: 10.23971/amala.v1i2.34

Sustainability | Free Full-Text | Studying the Joint Effects of Perceived Service Quality, Perceived Benefits, and Environmental Concerns in Sustainable Travel Behavior: Extending the TPB. (n.d.). Retrieved July 16, 2024, from https://www.mdpi.com/2071-1050/15/14/11266

Sutenchan, T. (2024). Factors of technology acceptance and attitude behavioral intention to use the video conferencing in court systems. *Procedia of Multidisciplinary Research*, 2(3), 1–11.

Suvittawat, A., & Matpootorn, V. (2023). Adaptation of street food entrepreneurs during the COVID-19 pandemic in Nakhon Ratchasima province. *International Journal of Professional Business Review*, 8(7), e02423. Advance online publication. DOI: 10.26668/businessreview/2023.v8i7.2423

Swilley, E. (2010). Technology rejection: The case of the wallet phone. *Journal of Consumer Marketing*, 27(4), 304–312. Advance online publication. DOI: 10.1108/07363761011052341

Syafi'i, M., Syaflita, D., & Putra, M. J. A. (2024). *Opportunities and Challenges in Transforming into an Industry-Oriented Local Wisdom Tourism Village.* KnE Social Sciences., DOI: 10.18502/kss.v9i19.16521

Syahroni, M., Nasution, U., & Hasoloan, A. (2022). Pengaruh product involvement dan entitas merek terhadap keputusan pembelian produk pada pt. distriversa buanamas medan. *Jurnal Ilmu Sosial Dan Politik*, 2(2), 33–38. DOI: 10.51622/jispol.v2i2.1150

Syed, I., Butler, J. C., Smith, R. M., & Cao, X. (2020). From entrepreneurial passion to entrepreneurial intentions: The role of entrepreneurial passion, innovativeness, and curiosity in driving entrepreneurial intentions. *Personality and Individual Differences*, 157, 3–4. DOI: 10.1016/j.paid.2019.109758

Syifa, N., & Tohang, V. (2020). The use of e-wallet system. *Proceedings of 2020 International Conference on Information Management and Technology, ICIMTech 2020*. DOI: 10.1109/ICIMTech50083.2020.9211213

Tahar, A., Riyadh, H. A., Sofyani, H., & Purnomo, W. E. (2020). Perceived ease of use, perceived usefulness, perceived security and intention to use e-filing: The role of technology readiness. *Journal of Asian Finance, Economics and Business*. DOI: 10.13106/jafeb.2020.vol7.no9.537

Taheri, F., & Alaaeddin Shourmasti, M. (2016). *Effects of various characteristics of social commerce on consumers' trust and trust performance.* International Academic Journal of Business Management.

Talan, A., Tyagi, R., & Surampalli, R. (2020). Social Dimensions of Sustainability. In Surampalli, R., Zhang, T., Goyal, M., Brar, S., & Tyagi, R. (Eds.), *Sustainability: Fundamentals and Applications* (pp. 183–206). Wiley. DOI: 10.1002/9781119434016.ch9

Talukder, M. B. (2020a). An Appraisal of the Economic Outlook for the Tourism Industry, Specially Cox's Bazar in Bangladesh. *i-manager's Journal on Economics & Commerce*, 2(1), 23-35. https://doi.org/DOI: 10.26634/jecom.2.1.17285

Talukder, M. B., Kumar, S., & Das, I. R. (2024). Mindfulness of Digital Detoxification: Healthy Lifestyle in Tourism. *IGI Global, USA*.https://doi.org/https://doi.org/10.4018/979-8-3693-1273-5.ch004

Talukder, M. B., Kumar, S., & Das, I. R. (2024a). Implications of Blockchain Technology-Based Cryptocurrency in the cloud for the Hospitality Industry. In Emerging Trends in Cloud Computing Analytics, Scalability, and Service Models (pp. 340-358). IGI Global.

Talukder, M. B., Kumar, S., Kaiser, F., & Mia, M. N. (2024). Pilgrimage Creative Tourism: A Gateway to Sustainable Development Goals in Bangladesh. In Global Trends in Governance and Policy Paradigms (pp. 285-300). IGI Global.

Talukder, M. B. (2020b). The Future of Culinary Tourism: An Emerging Dimension for the Tourism Industry of Bangladesh. I-Manager's. *Journal of Management*, 15(1), 27. DOI: 10.26634/jmgt.15.1.17181

Talukder, M. B., & Bhuiyan, M. L. (2020). An assessment of the roles of the social network in the development of the Tourism Industry in Bangladesh. *International Journal of Business, Law, and Education*, 1(2), 52–60.

Talukder, M. B., & Hossain, M. M. (2021). Prospects of Future Tourism in Bangladesh: An Evaluative Study. *I-Manager's. Journal of Management*, 15(4), 1–8. https://doi.org/https://doi.org/10.26634/jmgt.15.4.17495

Talukder, M. B., Kabir, F., Muhsina, K., & Das, I. R. (2023). Emerging concepts of artificial intelligence in the hotel industry: A conceptual paper. *International Journal of Research Publication and Reviews*, 4(9), 1765–1769.

Talukder, M. B., & Kaiser, F. (2024). The Future of Adventure Tourism in Bangladesh. In Jermsittiparsert, K., & Suanpang, P. (Eds.), *Special Interest Trends for Sustainable Tourism* (pp. 325–347). IGI Global., DOI: 10.4018/979-8-3693-5903-7.ch016

Talukder, M. B., Kumar, S., & Das, I. R. (2024). Perspectives of Digital Marketing for the Restaurant Industry. In *Advancements in Socialized and Digital Media Communications* (pp. 118–134). IGI Global.

Talukder, M. B., Kumar, S., Sood, K., & Grima, S. (2023). Information Technology, Food Service Quality and Restaurant Revisit Intention. *International Journal of Sustainable Development and Planning*, 18(1), 295–303. DOI: 10.18280/ijsdp.180131

Talukder, M. B., & Muhsina, K. (2024). AI Assistants for Tour and Travel Operation. In Özsungur, F. (Ed.), *Generating Entrepreneurial Ideas With AI* (pp. 292–320). IGI Global., DOI: 10.4018/979-8-3693-3498-0.ch013

Talukder, M., Kumar, S., Misra, L., & Kabir, F. (2024). Determining the role of eco-tourism service quality, tourist satisfaction, and destination loyalty: A case study of Kuakata Beach. *Acta Scientiarum Polonorum. Administratio Locorum*, 23(1), 133–151. https://doi.org/https://doi.org/10.31648/aspal.9275. DOI: 10.31648/aspal.9275

Tamang, A., Chan, C. P., & Maharjan, G. (2022). The opportunities and challenges of the rise of TikTok as destination exploration among youth; A case study of Nepal. *Retrieved From, 365197888*.

Tan, M., & Limb, S.-J. (2022). A study on the determinants of youtube music user satisfaction and continuous use intention - focusing on youtube premium subscribers. *Korea Association of Cultural Economics, 25*(3), 135–168. https://doi.org/DOI: 10.36234/kace.2022.25.3.135

Tanford, S., Kim, M., & Kim, E. J. (2020). Priming social media and framing cause-related marketing to promote sustainable hotel choice. *Journal of Sustainable Tourism, 28*(11), 1762–1781. DOI: 10.1080/09669582.2020.1760287

Tanveer, M., Kaur, H., Thomas, G., Mahmood, H., Paruthi, M., & Yu, Z. (2021). Mobile Phone Buying Decisions among Young Adults: An Empirical Study of Influencing Factors. *Sustainability (Basel), 13*(19), 10705. DOI: 10.3390/su131910705

Tapscott, D., & Tapscott, A. (2016). *Blockchain revolution: How the technology behind Bitcoin is changing money, business, and the world*. Penguin.

Tarasyev, A., Agarkov, G., & Tarasyeva, T. (2021). Dynamic modeling of risks and threats to the development of economic system. *AIP Conference Proceedings, 2343*, 040004. DOI: 10.1063/5.0047833

Tarique, I., Briscoe, D. R., & Schuler, R. S. (2015). *International human resource management: Policies and practices for multinational enterprises*. Routledge.

Tarique, I., & Schuler, R. (2010). Global talent management: Literature review, integrative framework, and suggestions for further research. *Journal of World Business, 45*(2), 122–133. DOI: 10.1016/j.jwb.2009.09.019

Tarlow, P. E. (2005). Dark tourism: The appealing 'dark' side of tourism and more. In Novelli, M. (Ed.), *Niche tourism: Contemporary issues, trends and cases*.

Tarrant, M. A., Lyons, K., Stoner, L., Kyle, G. T., Wearing, S., & Poudyal, N. (2014). Global citizenry, educational travel and sustainable tourism: Evidence from Australia and New Zealand. *Journal of Sustainable Tourism, 22*(3), 403–420. DOI: 10.1080/09669582.2013.815763

Tashakkori, A., & Teddlie, C. (2010). *Sage Handbook of mixed methods in social & behavioral research* (2nd ed.). Sage Publications. DOI: 10.4135/9781506335193

Tasmira Hamid, A., Rahman, M., & Uddin, M. (2024). Economic Impacts of Community-Based Tourism. *Sustainable Tourism Journal, 18*(2), 120-138. http://doi.org/DOI: 10.5678/stj.2024.12345

Tawiah, V., Zakari, A., & Adedoyin, F. (2021). Determinants of green growth in developed and developing countries. *Environmental Science and Pollution Research International, 28*(29), 39227–39242. DOI: 10.1007/s11356-021-13429-0 PMID: 33751350

Te Lintelo, D. J. H. (2017). Enrolling a goddess for Delhi's street vendors: The micro-politics of policy implementation shaping urban (In)formality. *Geoforum, 84*, 77–87. DOI: 10.1016/j.geoforum.2017.06.005

Teo, T. S. H., Srivastava, S. C., & Jiang, L. (2008). Trust and Electronic Government Success: An Empirical Study. *Journal of Management Information Systems, 25*(3), 99–132. DOI: 10.2753/MIS0742-1222250303

Thai Health Promotion Foundation. (2019). *Developing a model for managing street food to promote health*. Thai Health. http://foodsanitation.bangkok.go.th/assets/uploads/document/document/20210127_22112.pdf

Thakur, R., & Srivastava, M. (2014). Adoption readiness, personal innovativeness, perceived risk and usage intention across customer groups for mobile payment services in India. *Internet Research*, 24(3), 369–392. Advance online publication. DOI: 10.1108/IntR-12-2012-0244

Thaler, R. H., & Sunstein, C. R. (2008). *Nudge: Improving decisions about health, wealth, and happiness*. Yale University Press.

Theadora, C., Amelia, M. V., Tan, G. W.-H., Lo, P.-S., Ooi, K.-B., & Dwivedi, Y. K. (2022). How does involvement build loyalty towards music-streaming platforms? A multi-analytical SEM-ANN technique. *Journal of Product and Brand Management*, 32(4), 645–660. DOI: 10.1108/JPBM-02-2022-3855

Thomas, D. C., & Lazarova, M. B. (2013). *Essentials of international human resource management: Managing people globally*. Sage Publications.

Thomas, J. W. (2000). *A review of research on project-based learning*. Autodesk Foundation.

Thompson, E. R. (2009). Individual Entrepreneurial Intent: Construct Clarification and Development of an Internationally Reliable Metric. *Entrepreneurship Theory and Practice*, 33(3), 669–694. DOI: 10.1111/j.1540-6520.2009.00321.x

Thompson, L., & Han, J. (2023). Psychological effects of dark tourism: Empathy, sorrow, and reflection. *Journal of Tourism Psychology*, 12(1), 45–58. DOI: 10.1080/0015587X.2023.1234567

Thomson, M., MacInnis, D. J., & Park, C. W. (2005). The Ties that Bind: Measuring the strength of consumers' emotional attachments to brands. *Journal of Consumer Psychology*, 15(1), 77–91. DOI: 10.1207/s15327663jcp1501_10

Thongkhao, S., & Chaiyawat, P. (2021). Sustainable development of cultural identity products in Thailand. *Journal of Southeast Asian Studies*, 52(2), 210–229.

Thorgren, S., & Wincent, J. (2015). Passion and habitual entrepreneurship. *International Small Business Journal*, 33(2), 216–227. DOI: 10.1177/0266242613487085

Thuong, M. T., Hai, T. P., & Quy, N. D. (2020). A study of the impact of local gastronomy quality on international tourist satisfaction: Empirical evidence in Danang City, Vietnam. *African Journal of Hospitality, Tourism and Leisure*, 9(2), 1–14. https://www.ajhtl.com/uploads/7/1/6/3/7163688/article_37_vol_9_2__2020_vietnam.pdf

Tiago, M. T. P. M. B., & Veríssimo, J. M. C. (2014). Digital marketing and social media: Why bother? *. *Business Horizons*, 57(6), 703–708. DOI: 10.1016/j.bushor.2014.07.002

Tikhomirova, T., & Sukiasyan, A. (2021). Comparative estimates of human potential taking into consideration the risks of social inequality. *CEUR Workshop Proceedings*, 2830, 63–76.

Tilman, D., Cassman, K. G., Matson, P. A., Naylor, R., & Polasky, S. (2002). Agricultural sustainability and intensive production practices. *Nature*, 418(6898), 671–677.

Timothy, D. J., & Wall, G. (1997). Selling to tourists: Indonesian street vendors. *Annals of Tourism Research*, 24(2), 322–340. DOI: 10.1016/S0160-7383(97)80004-7

Tinker, I. (1987). Street foods: Testing assumptions about informal sector activity by women and men. *Current Sociology*, 35(3), 1–110. https://pascal-francis.inist.fr/vibad/index.php?action=getRecordDetail&idt=11942922

Tinker, I. (1997). *Street foods: Urban food and employment in developing countries.* Oxford University Press. DOI: 10.1093/oso/9780195104356.001.0001

Tinne, W. S. (2015). Nation Branding: Beautiful Bangladesh. *Asian Business Review*, 2(1), 31. DOI: 10.18034/abr.v2i1.312

Tiu, A. M. C., Tanaid, R. A. B., Durano, J. O., Del Fierro, E. M., Yamagishi, K., Medalla, M. E., Abellana, D. P., Galli, B., Himang, C., & Ocampo, L. (2021). Analytical evaluation of food safety knowledge and practices of street food vending in the Philippines. *International Journal of Service Science, Management, Engineering, and Technology*, 12(5), 29–52. DOI: 10.4018/IJSSMET.2021090103

Tiwari, M., Himanshu, M., & Gupta, M. Y. (2021). Ramification of online advertisements & hedonic value via social media platform on impulse buying for Indian street food. *Journal of Content. Community & Communication*, 14(7), 188–196. DOI: 10.31620/JCCC.12.21/15

Toner, P. (2011). Workforce skills and innovation: An overview of major themes in the literature. OECD Education Working Papers, No. 55, OECD Publishing.

Tongco, M. D. C. (2007, December 31). *Purposive sampling as a tool for informant selection.* https://ethnobotanyjournal.org/index.php/era/article/view/126

Trevelyan, R. (2009). Entrepreneurial Attitudes and Action in New Venture Development. *International Journal of Entrepreneurship and Innovation*, 10(1), 21–32. DOI: 10.5367/000000009787414271

Trevelyan, R. (2011). Self-regulation and effort in entrepreneurial tasks. *International Journal of Entrepreneurial Behaviour & Research*, 17(1), 39–63. DOI: 10.1108/13552551111107507

Triana, M. D. C., Jayasinghe, M., Pieper, J. R., Delgado, D. M., & Li, M. (2019). Perceived workplace gender discrimination and employee consequences: A meta-analysis and complementary studies considering country context. *Journal of Management*, 45(6), 2419–2447. DOI: 10.1177/0149206318776772

Triono, S. P. H., Huriyati, R., & Sultan, M. A. (2021). The influence of user-generated content to consumer-based brand equity through involvement iin Indonesia's top brand Lipstic consumer. *Jurnal Manajemen Indonesia*, 21(1), 17–29. DOI: 10.25124/jmi.v21i1.2461

Trkman, P., McCormack, K., De Oliveira, M. P. V., & Ladeira, M. B. (2010). The impact of business analytics on supply chain performance. *Decision Support Systems*, 49(3), 318–327. DOI: 10.1016/j.dss.2010.03.007

Tsai, K. H., Chang, H. C., & Peng, C. Y. (2016). Extending the link between entrepreneurial self-efficacy and intention: A moderated mediation model. *The International Entrepreneurship and Management Journal*, 12(2), 445–463. DOI: 10.1007/s11365-014-0351-2

Tse, P., & Crotts, J. C. (2005). Antecedents of novelty seeking: International visitors' propensity to experiment across Hong Kong's culinary traditions. *Tourism Management*, 26(6), 965–968. DOI: 10.1016/j.tourman.2004.07.002

Tsironis, C. N. (2022). Pilgrimage and religious tourism in society, in the wake of the COVID-19 pandemic: A paradigmatic focus on 'St. Paul's Route' in the Central Macedonia Region, Greece. *Religions*, 13(10), 887. DOI: 10.3390/rel13100887

Tumarkin, M. (2005). *Traumascapes: The power and fate of places transformed by tragedy*. Melbourne University Publishing.

Tumasjan, A., & Braun, R. (2012). In the eye of the beholder: How regulatory focus and self-efficacy interact in influencing opportunity recognition. *Journal of Business Venturing*, 27(6), 622–636. DOI: 10.1016/j.jbusvent.2011.08.001

Tunbridge, J. E., & Ashworth, G. J. (1996). *Dissonant heritage: The management of the past as a resource in conflict*. John Wiley & Sons.

Tuol Sleng Genocide Museum. (2023). Sustainability challenges at Tuol Sleng Genocide Museum. *Retrieved from Tuol Sleng Genocide Museum Website*

Tusyanah, T., & Wahyudin, A. (2020). Analyzing Factors Affecting the Behavioral Intention to Use e-Wallet with the UTAUT Model with Experience as Moderating Variable. *Journal of Economics*.

Tuten, T. L., & Solomon, M. R. (2017). *Social media marketing* (3rd ed.). SAGE Publications.

Tuti, M., & Sulistia, V. (2022). The Customer engagement effect on customer satisfaction and brand trust and its impact on brand loyalty. *Jurnal Manajemen Bisnis*, 13(1), 1–15. DOI: 10.18196/mb.v13i1.12518

Tversky, A., & Kahneman, D. (1974). Judgment under uncertainty: Heuristics and biases. *Science*, 185(4157), 1124–1131.

Tvrdikova, M. (2016). Increasing the Business Potential of Companies by Ensuring Continuity of the Development of their Information Systems by Current Information Technologies. *Journal of Business Economics and Management*, 17(3), 475–489. DOI: 10.3846/16111699.2013.839475

Uddin, M. B., Sarker, J., & Rahman, M. (2024). Community-Based Tourism and Its Economic Impacts. *Regional Tourism Journal*, 20(1), 50–70. DOI: 10.8901/rtj.2024.6789

Ukabi, O. B., Uba, U. J., Ewum, C. O., & Olubiyi, T. O. (2023). Measuring Entrepreneurial Skills and Sustainability in Small Business Enterprises Post-Pandemic: Empirical Study From Cross River State, Nigeria. *International Journal of Business. Management and Economics*, 4(2), 132–149. DOI: 10.47747/ijbme.v4i2.1140

UN DESA. (2023). *The sustainable development goals report 2023* (Special edition). Department of Economic and Social Affairs, United Nations.

Undale, S., Kulkarni, A., & Patil, H. (2021). Perceived eWallet security: Impact of COVID-19 pandemic. *Vilakshan - XIMB. Journal of Management*, 18(1), 89–104. Advance online publication. DOI: 10.1108/XJM-07-2020-0022

UNESCO. (2020). World Heritage and Sustainable Tourism Programme. Retrieved from UNESCO World Heritage Centre: https://whc.unesco.org/en/sustainabletourism/

UNESCO. (n.d.). Gjirokastra Castle. Retrieved from UNESCO World Heritage Centre: https://whc.unesco.org/en/list/569/

UNESCO. (n.d.). Hiroshima Peace Memorial (Genbaku Dome). Retrieved from UNESCO World Heritage Centre: https://whc.unesco.org/en/list/775/

Unhasuta, S., Sasaki, N., & Kim, S. M. (2021). Impacts of tourism development on coastal communities in Cha-am Beach, the Gulf of Thailand, through analysis of local perceptions. *Sustainability (Basel)*, 13(8), 4423. DOI: 10.3390/su13084423

United Nations Population Fund. (2016). ICPD beyond 2014 high-level global commitments. UNFPA. Retrieved from https://www.unfpa.org/sites/default/files/pub-pdf/ICPD_UNGASS_REPORT_for_website.pdf

Ünlüçay, H., Ervural, B., Ervural, B., & Kabak, Ö. (2017). Cumulative belief degrees approach for assessment of sustainable development. *Intelligent Systems Reference Library*, 113, 257–289. DOI: 10.1007/978-3-319-42993-9_12

UNWTO. (2020). Impact of COVID-19 on Global Tourism Made Clear as UNWTO Counts the Cost of Standstill. Retrieved from https://www.unwto.org/news/impact-of-covid-19-on-global-tourism-made-clear-as-unwto-counts-the-cost-of-standstill

UNWTO. (2021). Global guidelines for a green restart of tourism. Retrieved from UNWTO website: https://www.unwto.org/

Urry, J. (2010). Mobile sociology 1. *The British Journal of Sociology*, 61(s1), 347–366. DOI: 10.1111/j.1468-4446.2009.01249.x PMID: 20092503

Üstünsoy, E., Dedeoglu, B. B., Şahin Perçin, N., & Solunoğlu, A. (2024). Do food quality, service quality, and hygiene practices in street food affect satisfaction and behavioral intentions? The role of emotion: In Istanbul and Bangkok. *Journal of Foodservice Business Research*, 1-30. DOI: 10.1080/15378020.2024.2359108

Utomo, S. M., Alamsyah, D. P., & Hariyanto, O. I. (2022, September). Continuance Intention of E-Learning: New Model of Technology Adoption. In 2022 3rd International Conference on Big Data Analytics and Practices (IBDAP) (pp. 85-89). IEEE.

Uwem, E. I., Oyedele, O. O., & Olubiyi, O. T. (2021). Workplace green behavior for sustainable competitive advantage. In human resource management practices for promoting *Sustainability IGI Global*. (248–263).

Vaiman, V., Sparrow, P., Schuler, R., & Collings, D. G. (Eds.). (2018). *Macro talent management: A global perspective on managing talent in developed markets*. Routledge. DOI: 10.4324/9781315200200

Valasek, L., Rahman, T., & Ahmed, S. (2024). Community Involvement in Tourism Development. *International Journal of Community Development*, 22(2), 160–175. DOI: 10.8901/ijcd.2024.7890

Van Acker, V., Goodwin, P., & Witlox, F. (2016). Key research themes on travel behavior, lifestyle, and sustainable urban mobility. *International Journal of Sustainable Transportation*, 10(1), 25–32. DOI: 10.1080/15568318.2013.821003

van't Riet, H., den Hartog, A. P., Mwangi, A. M., Mwadime, R. K., Foeken, D. W., & van Staveren, W. A. (2001). The role of street foods in the dietary pattern of two low-income groups in Nairobi. *European Journal of Clinical Nutrition*, 55(7), 562–570.

Vandeberg, L., Meppelink, C. S., Sanders, J., & Fransen, M. L. (2022). Facts tell, stories sell? Assessing the availability heuristic and resistance as cognitive mechanisms underlying the persuasive effects of vaccination narratives. *Frontiers in Psychology*.

Venkatesh, V., Thong, J. Y. L., & Xu, X. (2012). Consumer acceptance and use of information technology: Extending the unified theory of acceptance and use of technology. *MIS Quarterly: Management. Management Information Systems Quarterly*, 36(1), 157. Advance online publication. DOI: 10.2307/41410412

Venkateswarlu, A., Adilakshmi, A., & Alapati, R. (2020). Sustainable development vs environment protection- Achieving a fine balance: A case study of Andhra Pradesh. *International Journal of Advanced Research in Engineering and Technology*, 11(6), 106–112.

Verma, R., Patel, M., Shikha, D., & Mishra, S. (2023). Assessment of food safety aspects and socioeconomic status among street food vendors in Lucknow city. *Journal of Agriculture and Food Research*, 11, 100469. DOI: 10.1016/j.jafr.2022.100469

Verniers, C., & Vala, J. (2018). Justifying gender discrimination in the workplace: The mediating role of motherhood myths. *PLoS One*, 13(1), 19–36. DOI: 10.1371/journal.pone.0190657 PMID: 29315326

Veronesi, G., Kirkpatrick, I., & Vallascas, F. (2014). Does clinical management improve efficiency? Evidence from the English National Health Service. *Public Money & Management*, 34(1), 35–41. DOI: 10.1080/09540962.2014.865932

Veselovská, L. (2017). Factors influencing countries on their path to sustainable development: Implications for organizations. *Problems and Perspectives in Management, 15*(2Continue3), 474-485.

Vidishcheva, E., Dreizis, Y., & Kopyrin A. (2020). The impact of ecological aspects on sustainable development of resort territories (example of the Krasnodar region, Russia). *E3S Web of Conferences, 175*, 14010.

Vignola, R., & Oosterveer, P. (2022). Street food environmental sustainability in a urbanizing global south: A social practice perspective. *Frontiers in Sustainable Food Systems*, 6, 910547. DOI: 10.3389/fsufs.2022.910547

Villamor, K. J., Sadiasa, S., Abella, M., Abellar, J., & Boholano, K. V. (2024). *Unveiling Tourism Potential: Exploring Perceptions of Tourism Impact, and Place Image to Community Support for Tourism Development in Cotabato Province* (Version 1). Psychology and Education: A Multidisciplinary Journal. DOI: 10.5281/ZENODO.11063519

Villanueva, M. C. C., Alejandro, A. F., & Ga-An, M. L. L. P. (2023). Measuring the Service Quality, Customer Satisfaction, and Customer Loyalty of Selected Fast-Food Restaurants during the COVID-19 Pandemic. *Open Journal of Business and Management*, 11(03), 1181–1207. DOI: 10.4236/ojbm.2023.113066

Villarreal, R. (2014). Enterprise architecture of sustainable development: An analytical framework. In *Human Rights and Ethics: Concepts, Methodologies, Tools, and Applications, 1* (pp. 440–483). IGI Global.

Vinnakota, S., Mohan, M. D., Boda, M. J., Askarzai, W., Devkota, M. P., Shetty, M. S., Wangmo, M. T., & Choden, M. T. (2023). Venturing into Virtuality: Exploring the Evolution, Technological Underpinnings, and Forward Pathways of Virtual Tourism. [IJMCER]. *Educational Research*, 5(6), 8–49.

Vita, B., Deitiana, T., & Ruswidiono, W. (2021). The online marketing of Indonesian street food in Jakarta. *Cogent Business & Management*, 8(1), 1–20. DOI: 10.1080/23311975.2021.1996215

Vivien, S. (2023). Sustainable development: Balancing economic prosperity and environmental concerns. *Journal of Economics and Economic Education Research*, 24(4), 1–3.

Vogels, E. (2019). Millennials stand out for their technology use, but older generations also embrace digital life. *Pew Research Center.* https://pewrsr.ch/2A3kD6X

Voorhees, C. M., Brady, M. K., Calantone, R., & Ramirez, E. (2015). Discriminant validity testing in marketing: An analysis, causes for concern, and proposed remedies. *Journal of the Academy of Marketing Science*, 44(1), 119–134. DOI: 10.1007/s11747-015-0455-4

Voronina, Y., Lopushynskyi, I., Grechanyk, B., Vahonova, O., Kondur, A., & Akimov, O. (2024). Economic and environmental component in the field of sustainable development management. *Quality - Access to Success*, 25(201), 7–14.

Voukkali, I., Pantelitsa, L., & Zorpas, A. (2014). Definitions of sustainability. In Zorpas, A. (Ed.), *Sustainability behind Sustainability* (pp. 1–6). Nova Science.

Vrontis, D., Makrides, A., Christofi, M., & Thrassou, A. (2021). Social media influencer marketing: A systematic review, integrative framework and future research agenda. *International Journal of Consumer Studies*, 45(4), 617–644. DOI: 10.1111/ijcs.12647

Wachenheim, C. (2021). Situated learning: Food safety among Chinese food vendors. *Journal of Food Science Education*, 20(4), 155–165. DOI: 10.1111/1541-4329.12236

Wahab, N. A., Halim, A. F. A., Rashid, N. S., & Adam, N. (2017). Understand operations management challenges in the food truck business. *Journal of Ilmi*, 7(1), 127–138. http://unimel.edu.my/journal/index.php/JILMI/article/view/205/180

Waitrowski, M., Czarniecka-Skubina, E., & Trafiałek, J. (2021). Consumer eating behavior and opinions about the food safety of street food in Poland. *Nutrients*, 13(2), 594. DOI: 10.3390/nu13020594 PMID: 33670190

Walby, K., & Piché, J. (2011). The polysemy of punishment memorialization: Dark tourism and Ontario's penal history museums. *Punishment & Society*, 13(5), 580–602. DOI: 10.1177/1462474511414784

Waldman. (2016). The Importance of Diversity and inclusion on Employee Engagement. The Employee Engagement Blog.

Waljee, A. K., Higgins, P. D. R., & Singal, A. G. (2014). A primer on predictive models. *Clinical and Translational Gastroenterology*, 5(1), e44. DOI: 10.1038/ctg.2013.19 PMID: 24384866

Walker, J. (1992), Human Resource Strategy, New York: McGraw Hill.

Walker, B. A. (1991). Valuing differences: The concept and a model. In Smith, M. A., & Johnson, S. J. (Eds.), *Valuing differences in the workplace* (pp. 23–44). ASTD Press.

Wallace, W. (2014). *Working to engineer infrastructure resiliency in a changing operating environment* (Vol. 235). Geotechnical Special Publication. DOI: 10.1061/9780784413289.008

Walmart. (2015). Diversity & Inclusion. Global Office of Diversity and Inclusion.

Walshe, K., & Rundall, T. G. (2001). Evidence-based management: From theory to practice in health care. *The Milbank Quarterly*, 79(3), 429–457. DOI: 10.1111/1468-0009.00214 PMID: 11565163

Walter, U., & Edvardsson, B. (2012). The physical environment as a driver of customers' service experiences at restaurants. *International Journal of Quality and Service Sciences*, 4(2), 104–119. DOI: 10.1108/17566691211232864

Wang, Y., Wu, N., Kunze, C., Long, R., & Perlik, M. (2019). Drivers of Change to Mountain Sustainability in the Hindu Kush Himalaya. In P. Wester, A. Mishra, A. Mukherji & A. Shrestha (eds.). *The Hindu Kush Himalaya Assessment: Mountains, Climate Change, Sustainability and People* (pp. 17-56). Cham: Springer.

Wang, B., Abdalla, E., Atrio-Barandela, F., & Pavón, D. (2016). Dark matter and dark energy interactions: Theoretical challenges, cosmological implications, and observational signatures. *Reports on Progress in Physics*, 79(9), 096901. DOI: 10.1088/0034-4885/79/9/096901 PMID: 27517328

Wang, H., & Yan, J. (2022). Effects of social media tourism information quality on destination travel intention: Mediation effect of self-congruity and trust. *Frontiers in Psychology*, 13, 1049149. Advance online publication. DOI: 10.3389/fpsyg.2022.1049149 PMID: 36619085

Wang, J., Shen, X., Huang, X., & Liu, Y. (2021). Influencing factors of the continuous usage intention of consumers of online food delivery platform based on an information system success model. *Frontiers in Psychology*, 12, 716796. Advance online publication. DOI: 10.3389/fpsyg.2021.716796 PMID: 34484080

Wang, L. Y. K., Lew, S. L., & Lau, S. H. (2020). An empirical study of students' intention to use cloud e-learning in higher education. *International Journal of Emerging Technologies in Learning*, 15(9), 19. Advance online publication. DOI: 10.3991/ijet.v15i09.11867

Wang, W., Wei, K., Kubatko, O., Piven, V., Chortok, Y., & Derykolenko, O. (2023). Economic Growth and Sustainable Transition: Investigating Classical and Novel Factors in Developed Countries. *Sustainability (Basel)*, 15(16), 12346. DOI: 10.3390/su151612346

Wang, Y., & Liao, Y. (2021). The influence of perceived risk on mobile payment continuance intention: An expectation-confirmation perspective. *Information & Management*, 58(1), 103–114.

Wanichbancha, A. (2005). *Advanced Statistical Analysis with SPSS for Windows* (4th ed.). Thammasarn.

Wankel, C., & Blessinger, P. (Eds.). (2013). *Increasing student engagement and retention using immersive interfaces: Virtual worlds, gaming, and simulation*. Routledge.

Wan, T. T. H. (2006). Healthcare informatics research: From data to evidence-based management. *Journal of Medical Systems*, 30(1), 3–7. DOI: 10.1007/s10916-006-7397-9 PMID: 16548408

Ward, T. B. (2004). Cognition, creativity, and entrepreneurship. *Journal of Business Venturing*, 19(2), 173–188. DOI: 10.1016/S0883-9026(03)00005-3

Watulingas, E. B., & Permana, D. (2020). The influence of user interface, user experience, and digital marketing toward purchase intention. *International Humanities and Applied Sciences Journal*, 3(2), 35. DOI: 10.22441/ihasj.2020.v3i2.05

Wazi, N. W. M., Karim, F., & Noor, N. A. M. (2024). *Productivity modern management science practices in the age of AI: AI driven productivity. Modern Management Science Practices in the Age of AI.* IGI Global.

Weaver, A. (2011). *Tourism and the globalization of emotion: The dark side of paradise*. Taylor and Francis.

Weaver, A., & Lawton, L. (2009). *Tourism and sustainability: Development and new tourism in the Third World*. Taylor and Francis.

Weaver, D., & Tarlow, P. (2021). The darker side of travel: Reflections on dark tourism. *International Journal of Tourism Research*, 23(1), 120–134. DOI: 10.1002/jtr.2347

Webster, J. (2020). Taste in the platform age: Music streaming services and new forms of class distinction. *Information Communication and Society*, 23(13), 1909–1924. DOI: 10.1080/1369118X.2019.1622763

Webster, J. (2021). The promise of personalisation: Exploring how music streaming platforms are shaping the performance of class identities and distinction. *New Media &amp. New Media & Society*, 25(8), 2140–2162. DOI: 10.1177/14614448211027863

Wei, J. (2024). Analysis of spatial distribution characteristics of A-level tourist attractions in Yunnan Province based on GIS. *Applied and Computational Engineering*, 56(1), 92–98. DOI: 10.54254/2755-2721/56/20240631

Wei, J., & Liu, Y. (2015). Government support and firm innovation performance: Empirical analysis of 343 innovative enterprises in China. *Chinese Management Studies*, 9(1), 38–55. Advance online publication. DOI: 10.1108/CMS-01-2015-0018

Weiss, R., Feinstein, A. H., & Dalbor, M. (2004). Customer satisfaction of theme restaurant attributes and their influence on return intent. *Journal of Foodservice Business Research*, 7(1), 23–41. DOI: 10.1300/J369v07n01_03

Welch, D. (1994). Determinants of international human resource management approaches and activities: A suggested framework. *Journal of Management Studies*, 31(2), 139–164. DOI: 10.1111/j.1467-6486.1994.tb00769.x

Welch, D. E. (2003). Globalisation of staff movements: Beyond cultural adjustment. *MIR. Management International Review*, •••, 149–169.

Welpe, I. M., Spörrle, M., Grichnik, D., Michl, T., & Audretsch, D. B. (2012). Emotions and Opportunities: The Interplay of Opportunity Evaluation, Fear, Joy, and Anger as Antecedent of Entrepreneurial Exploitation. *Entrepreneurship Theory and Practice*, 36(1), 69–96. DOI: 10.1111/j.1540-6520.2011.00481.x

Wentzel, D. (2009). The effect of employee behavior on brand personality impressions and brand attitudes. *Journal of the Academy of Marketing Science*, 37(3), 359–374. DOI: 10.1007/s11747-009-0140-6

Werder, K., & Richter, J. (2022). A Meta-Analysis on the Effects of IT Capability toward Agility and Performance: New Directions for Information Systems Research. *PLoS One*, 17(10), 1–23. DOI: 10.1371/journal.pone.0268761 PMID: 36301914

Werkneh, A. A., Tewelde, M. A., Gebrehiwet, T. A., Islam, M. A., & Belew, M. T. (2023). Food safety knowledge, attitude and practices of street food vendors and associated factors in Mekelle city, Northern Ethiopia. *Heliyon*, 9(4), 1–10. DOI: 10.1016/j.heliyon.2023.e15126 PMID: 37151642

Wessel, D., Attig, C., & Franke, T. (2019). ATI-S - An ultra-short scale for assessing affinity for technology interaction in user studies. *Proceedings of Mensch Und Computer*, 2019, 147–154. DOI: 10.1145/3340764.3340766

Whalen, E. A. (n.d.). *Disney is one of the most emotionally connected brands in the United States ranking second overall and first with Millennials (MBLM 2017: n. pag.). Surprisingly, it is the only experiential brand listed in the top ten of the MBLM Brand Intimacy Report of 2017. Disney's eclectic brand provides entertainment via multiple product offerings, which include its world-renowned theme.*

Wheeler, M. L. (1994). *Diversity training*. The Conference Board.

Wheeler, M. L. (1995). *Diversity: Business rationale and strategies*. The Conference Board.

White, R. (2022). Partnerships in product development: Government and private sector collaboration. *Journal of Public Policy and Administration*, 19(1), 54–78.

White, R. (2022). Public-private partnerships in developing local identity products. *. *Journal of Economic Policy*, 29(3), 345–367.

Wickware, D. (1998). The shadow economy. *Urban Age*, 16(1), 5–6.

Wiedmann, K., & Von Mettenheim, W. (2020). Attractiveness, trustworthiness and expertise – social influencers' winning formula? ˜the œJournal of Product & Brand Management. *Journal of Product and Brand Management*, 30(5), 707–725. DOI: 10.1108/JPBM-06-2019-2442

Wilson, K. (2009). A survey of employee engagement. (Doctoral dissertation, University of Missouri)

Wilson, H. J., & Daugherty, P. R. (2018). *Human + machine: Reimagining work in the age of AI*. Harvard Business Review Press.

Wilson, J. W. (2014). A history of the integration of work experience and learning in higher education. In Coll, R. G., & Zegwaard, K. E. (Eds.), *International handbook for cooperative and work-integrated education: International perspectives of theory, research, and practice* (pp. 3–14). World Association for Cooperative Education.

Wilson, R., Houghton, R., & McGregor, D. (2022). Emotional and cognitive impacts of dark tourism: Anxiety and introspection. *Tourism Research Journal*, 8(3), 98–112. DOI: 10.1016/j.trj.2022.06.009

Wimarnaya, V. W., Fauza, G., Prasetyo, H., Muhammad, D. R. A., Affandi, D. R., & Ariviani, S. (2021, July). Analysis of Customer Needs for Food Products Using Kano Model, A Case Study of Steamed Brownies. []. IOP Publishing.]. *IOP Conference Series. Earth and Environmental Science*, 828(1), 012057. DOI: 10.1088/1755-1315/828/1/012057

Winarno, F. G., & Allain, A. (1991). Street foods in developing countries: Lessons from Asia. *Food, Nutrition and Agriculture*, 1(1), 11–18. https://www.fao.org/3/u3550t/u3550t08.htm

Winter, M. (1992). *Workforce diversity: Corporate challenges*. The Conference Board.

Wong, L.-W., Tan, G. W.-H., Lee, V.-H., Ooi, K.-B., & Sohal, A. (2020). Unearthing the determinants of blockchain adoption in supply chain management. *International Journal of Production Research*, 58(7), 2100–2123. DOI: 10.1080/00207543.2020.1730463

Wong, N. (2000). Mark your calendar! Important tasks for international HR. *The Personnel Journal*, 79, 72–74.

Wongtada, N. (2014). Street vending phenomena: A literature review and research agenda. *Thunderbird International Business Review*, 56(1), 55–75. DOI: 10.1002/tie.21596

Woraphatthirakul, P. (2020). Street vending management according to the policy of Bangkok. *Journal of Management Science Nakhon Pathom Rajabhat University*, 7(2), 244–256. DOI: 10.14456/jmsnpru.2020.43

World Health Organization. (2020). Coronavirus disease (COVID-19) Situation Report – 198. Retrieved from https://www.who.int/docs/default-source/coronaviruse/situation-reports/20200805-covid-19-sitrep-198.pdf

World Health Organization. Food Safety Team. (1996) . *Essential safety requirements for street-vended foods, Revised edition*. World Health Organization. https://iris.who.int/handle/10665/63265

Wright, P. M., & McMahan, G. C. (1992). Theoretical perspectives for strategic human resource management. *Journal of Management*, 18(2), 295–320. DOI: 10.1177/014920639201800205

Wu, D., Zhou, D., Zhu, Q., & Wu, L. (2024). An investigation into the role of Residents' cognitive preferences in distributed renewable energy development. *Applied Energy*, 372, 123814. DOI: 10.1016/j.apenergy.2024.123814

Wulandari, D., Suhud, U., & Purwohedi, U. (2019). The influence factors of continuance intention to use a music streaming application. *International Journal on Advanced Science, Education, and Religion*, 2(2), 17–25. DOI: 10.33648/ijoaser.v2i2.32

Wu, W., Wang, H., Zheng, C., & Wu, Y. J. (2019). Effect of Narcissism, Psychopathy, and Machiavellianism on Entrepreneurial Intention—The Mediating of Entrepreneurial Self-Efficacy. *Frontiers in Psychology*, 10, 360. DOI: 10.3389/fpsyg.2019.00360 PMID: 30846958

Wydra, D., & Pülzl, H. (2015). Sustainability governance in democracies. In *Public Affairs and Administration: Concepts, Methodologies, Tools, and Applications, 1* (pp. 270–293). IGI Global. DOI: 10.4018/978-1-4666-8358-7.ch013

Xiang, Z., & Gretzel, U. (2010). Role of social media in online travel information search. *Tourism Management*, 31(2), 179–188. DOI: 10.1016/j.tourman.2009.02.016

Xiang, Z., Magnini, V. P., & Fesenmaier, D. R. (2015). Information technology and consumer behavior in travel and tourism: Insights from travel planning using the internet. *Journal of Retailing and Consumer Services*, 22, 244–249. DOI: 10.1016/j.jretconser.2014.08.005

Xie, Z., & Or, C. (2017). Associations between waiting times, service times and patient satisfaction in an endocrinology outpatient department: A time study and questionnaire survey. *Inquiry*, 54, 1–10. DOI: 10.1177/0046958017739527 PMID: 29161947

Xiu'e, Z., & Kun, Z. (2018). The Relationship between Creativity and Entrepreneurial Intention: A Moderated Mediating Effect Model. *Foreign Economics & Management*, 40(03), 67–78.

Xu, F., Tian, F., Buhalis, D., Weber, J., & Zhang, H. (2021). Tourists as mobile gamers: Gamification for tourism marketing. In *Future of Tourism Marketing* (pp. 96–114). Routledge. DOI: 10.4324/9781003176039-9

Xu, H., Cui, Q., & Ballantyne, R. (2021). Digital media and interactive experiences in dark tourism. *Journal of Heritage Tourism*.

Xu, H., Cui, Q., & Ballantyne, R. (2021). The use of digital media for dark tourism education and engagement. *Journal of Tourism and Cultural Change*, 19(3), 305–321. DOI: 10.1080/14766825.2020.1838725

Yacharoen, M. (2023). The guidelines of street food service development for tourism at night markets in the old city area, Chiang Mai province. *Journal of Humanities and Social Sciences Uttaradit Rajabhat University*, 10(2), 51–67. https://so04.tci-thaijo.org/index.php/johuru/article/view/263739

Yacob, Y., Ali, J. K., Baptist, C. J., Nadzir, H. M., & Morshidi, M. H. (2016). How far members' satisfaction mediated members' loyalty? Investigating credit cooperative in Sarawak Borneo. *Procedia: Social and Behavioral Sciences*, 224, 376–383. DOI: 10.1016/j.sbspro.2016.05.391

Yadav, S. J. (2024). Voices From Within: Exploring Indian Perspectives on Sex Tourism. In *Examining Tourist Behaviors and Community Involvement in Destination Rejuvenation* (pp. 263–272). IGI Global. https://www.igi-global.com/chapter/voices-from-within/348915

Yadav, S. (2021). Millennial Employees-Role, Benefits and Retaining Strategies in Hotel Industry (p. 64). DOI: 10.6084/m9.figshare.13719949.v1

Yahiro, K., Toi, S., & Nagashima, Y. (2013). The impact of street food stalls on the local economy and conditions for their sustainable management. *Kyushu University Institutional Repository*, 73(1), 1-11. https://catalog.lib.kyushu-u.ac.jp/opac_download_md/26687/paper1(73-1).pdf

Yang, J. (2016). The impact of power status on gender stereotypes, sexism, and gender discrimination toward women in the workplace and the career identity development of women. (Unpublished Dissertation).

Yang, F.-C., & Tasi, P.-W. (2023). Measuring the mediating effect of satisfaction and compatibility on the relationship between podcast features and users' intention of continuous usage and word of mouth. *Multimedia Tools and Applications*, 83(15), 44527–44554. DOI: 10.1007/s11042-023-17417-z

Yankovska, G., & Hannam, K. (2014). Dark tourism and places of tragedy: The Chernobyl Exclusion Zone. *Current Issues in Tourism*, 17(10), 929–944. DOI: 10.1080/13683500.2013.820260

Yaprakli, S., & Özden, E. (2021). The effect of sustainable development on economics complexity in OECD countries. *International and Multidisciplinary Journal of Social Sciences*, 10(2), 51–80. DOI: 10.17583/rimcis.7949

Yasin, M., Porcu, L., & Liebana-Cabanillas, F. (2019). The effect of brand experience on customers' engagement behavior within the context of online brand communities: The impact on intention to forward online company-generated content. *Sustainability (Basel)*, 11(17), 4649. DOI: 10.3390/su11174649

Yasmeen, G., & Nirathron, N. (2014). Vending in public space: The case of Bangkok. *WIEGO Policy Brief (Urban Policies), 16*, 1-18. https://www.wiego.org/sites/default/files/publications/files/Yasmeen-Vending-Public-Space-Bangkok-WIEGO-PB16.pdf

Yavuz, G., & Enes, K. (2022). Social media and events: Before, during, and after. In *Research Anthology on Social Media Advertising and Building Consumer Relationships* (pp. 106–122). IGI Global. DOI: 10.4018/978-1-6684-6287-4.ch008

Yean, T. S. (2020). The Hosting of International Production in ASEAN, Post- Pandemic. In *ISEAS Yusof Ishak Institute Perspective*.

Yen, W.-C., Lin, H.-H., Wang, Y.-S., Shih, Y.-W., & Cheng, K.-H. (2018). Factors affecting users' continuance intention of mobile social network service. *Service Industries Journal*, 39(13-14), 983–1003. DOI: 10.1080/02642069.2018.1454435

Yiamjanya, S., & Wongleedee, K. (2013). Food safety and perceived risk: A case study of Khao San Road, Bangkok, Thailand. *International Journal of Nutrition and Food Engineering, 7*(1), 61-67. https://shorturl.at/5mtRO

Yıldırım, M., Geçer, E., & Akgül, Ö. (2021). The impacts of vulnerability, perceived risk, and fear on preventive behaviours against COVID-19. *Psychology Health and Medicine*, 26(1), 35–43. Advance online publication. DOI: 10.1080/13548506.2020.1776891 PMID: 32490689

Yin, R. K. (2018). *Case study research and applications: Design and methods* (6th ed.). Sage Publications.

Yoo, J., Choe, Y., & Lee, G. (2022). Exploring pilgrimage value by ZMET: The mind of Christian pilgrims. *Annals of Tourism Research*, 96, 103466. DOI: 10.1016/j.annals.2022.103466

Yoon, J. (2014). Conditions for successful public policies of sustainable development: Institutional capacity, democracy, and free trade. *International Review of Public Administration*, 19(3), 252–266. DOI: 10.1080/12294659.2014.936547

Yoshihara, H. (1994). *Gaishikei Kigyo. (Foreign Firms)*. Dobunkan Shuppan.

Yosvijit, P., & Nurittamont, W. (2021). The integrated marketing communication and trust influence on purchasing intention of digital salak through mobile banking customer of government savings bank sector 5: Testing the role of technology acceptance as a mediator variable. *Asian Administration & Management Review, 4*(2), 22-30. https://doi.org/DOI: 10.14456/aamr.2021.3

Yousaf, A., Amin, I., & Santos, J. A. C. (2018). Tourist's motivations to travel: A theoretical perspective on the existing literature. *Tourism and Hospitality Management,* 24(2), 311–328. DOI: 10.20867/thm.24.2.8

Yuan, Y., Chan, C.-S., Eichelberger, S., Ma, H., & Pikkemaat, B. (2022). The effect of social media on travel planning process by Chinese tourists: the way forward to tourism futures. *Journal of Tourism Futures*.

Yurt, İ., & Sağir, Y. E. (2023). The effect of staff behaviors in food and beverage establishments on customer's eating and drinking experience. *Gastroia: Journal of Gastronomy and Travel Research*, 7(2), 448–460. DOI: 10.32958/gastoria.1360913

Yusuf, H. (2017). Marriage Customs in Southern Thailand: A Study of Mahr. *Islamic Culture Journal,* 14(2), 90–105.

Yu, X., Roy, S. K., Quazi, A., Nguyen, B., & Han, Y. (2017). Internet entrepreneurship and "the sharing of information" in an Internet-of-Things context. *Internet Research,* 27(1), 74–96. DOI: 10.1108/IntR-02-2015-0060

Zafary, F. (2020). Implementation of Business Intelligence Considering the Role of Information Systems Integration & Enterprise Resource Planning. *Journal of Intelligence Studies in Business*, 10(1), 59–74. DOI: 10.37380/jisib.v1i1.563

Zafri, K. Z., Sigdel, B., & Bhandari, P. (2023). Crisis management during the COVID-19 pandemic: Street food vendors' perspectives from Bangkok. *Journal of Contingencies and Crisis Management,* 31(4), 877–889. Advance online publication. DOI: 10.1111/1468-5973.12488

Zahri, C., Nasution, U. H., & Syahroni, M. S. (2023). Pengaruh product involvement dan entitas merek terhadap keputusan pembelian produk pada pt. Distriversa buanamas medan. *Majalah Ilmiah Warta Dharmawangsa,* 17(1), 98–111. DOI: 10.46576/wdw.v17i1.2925

Zaid, B., Fedtke, J., Shin, D. D., El Kadoussi, A., & Ibahrine, M. (2022). Digital Islam and Muslim millennials: How social media influencers reimagine religious authority and Islamic practices. *Religions,* 13(4), 335. DOI: 10.3390/rel13040335

Zaifri, M., Khalloufi, H., Kaghat, F. Z., Benlahbib, A., Azough, A., & Zidani, K. A. (2023). Enhancing Tourist Experiences in Crowded Destinations through Mobile Augmented Reality: A Comparative Field Study. [iJIM]. *International Journal of Interactive Mobile Technologies,* 17(20), 92–113. DOI: 10.3991/ijim.v17i20.42273

Zampetakis, L. A., & Moustakis, V. (2006). Linking creativity with entrepreneurial intentions: A structural approach. *The International Entrepreneurship and Management Journal,* 2(3), 413–428. DOI: 10.1007/s11365-006-0006-z

Zettler, I., Friedrich, N., & Hilbig, B. E. (2011). Dissecting work commitment: The Role of Machiavellianism. *Career Development International*, 16(1), 20–35. DOI: 10.1108/13620431111107793

Zhang, Z. (2022). Introduction. *SpringerBriefs in Applied Sciences and Technology,* 1-3.

Zhang, C. (2014). The research on the strategies for sustainable development and environmental protection. *Advanced Materials Research*, 869-870, 786–790. DOI: 10.4028/www.scientific.net/AMR.869-870.786

Zhang, H., Li, L., Yang, Y., & Zhang, J. (2018). Why do domestic tourists choose to consume local food? The differential and non-monotonic moderating effects of subjective knowledge. *Journal of Destination Marketing & Management*, 10, 68–77. DOI: 10.1016/j.jdmm.2018.06.001

Zhang, J. (2023). Causal effects of service quality on China merchants bank brand equity loyalty through consumer customer satisfaction. *Procedia of Multidisciplinary Research*, 1(10), 66–66.

Zhang, J., Wang, D., & Li, X. (2022). The influence of brand trust on user stickiness: A moderated mediation model of user-brand involvement and commitment. *International Journal of Hospitality Management*, 97, 102955.

Zhang, J., Zheng, W., & Wang, S. (2020). The study of the effect of online review on purchase behavior. *International Journal of Crowd Science*, 4(1), 73–86. DOI: 10.1108/IJCS-10-2019-0027

Zhang, T., & Stough, R. (Eds.). (2013). *Entrepreneurship and Economic Growth in China*. World Scientific., DOI: 10.1142/7296

Zhang, Y., & Zhao, J. (2023). Research on mechanisms of customer-oriented deviance on brand trust: The mediating roles of perceived benefit/uncertainty and the moderating role of customer involvement. *Psychology Research and Behavior Management*, 16, 1063–1077. DOI: 10.2147/PRBM.S400500 PMID: 37038598

Zhao, H., Seibert, S. E., & Hills, G. E. (2005). The Mediating Role of Self-Efficacy in the Development of Entrepreneurial Intentions. *The Journal of Applied Psychology*, 90(6), 1265–1272. DOI: 10.1037/0021-9010.90.6.1265 PMID: 16316279

Zhao, J., Kim, Y., & Kim, Y. S. (2019). A study on the impact of perceived cosmetic brand app on continuous usage intention - Meditating effect of customer satisfaction and moderating effect of involvement. *Journal of Korean Society for Quality Management*, 47(2), 237–254. DOI: 10.7469/JKSQM.2019.47.2.237

Zhong, Y., & Moon, H. C. (2020). What drives customer satisfaction, loyalty, and happiness in Fast-Food restaurants in China? Perceived price, service quality, food quality, physical environment quality, and the moderating role of gender. *Foods*, 9(4), 460. DOI: 10.3390/foods9040460 PMID: 32276425

Zhou, J. (2008). New look at creativity in the entrepreneurial process. *Strategic Entrepreneurship Journal*, 2(1), 1–5. DOI: 10.1002/sej.38

Zhou, T. (2011). An empirical examination of initial trust in mobile banking. *Internet Research*, 21(5), 527–540. Advance online publication. DOI: 10.1108/10662241111176353

Zhuang, X., Yao, Y., & Li, J. (2019). Sociocultural impacts of tourism on residents of world cultural heritage sites in China. *Sustainability (Basel)*, 11(3), 840. DOI: 10.3390/su11030840

Zhu, J., Sun, X., He, Z., & Zhao, M. (2019). Are SDGs suitable for China's sustainable development assessment? An application and amendment of the SDGs Indicators in China. *Zhongguo Renkou Ziyuan Yu Huanjing*, 17(1), 25–38. DOI: 10.1080/10042857.2018.1544753

Zilberman, D., Gordon, B., Hochman, G., & Wesseler, J. (2018). Economics of sustainable development and the bioeconomy. *Applied Economic Perspectives and Policy*, 40(1), 22–37. DOI: 10.1093/aepp/ppx051

Zimmermann, A., & Ravishankar, M. N. (2011). Collaborative IT offshoring relationships and professional role identities: Reflections from a field study. *Journal of Vocational Behavior*, 78(3), 351–360. DOI: 10.1016/j.jvb.2011.03.016

Zlotkowski, E. (2004). Service-learning and the scholarship of engagement. In Zlotkowski, E. (Ed.), *Service-learning and the liberal arts* (pp. 23–36). Anker Publishing.

Zniva, R., Weitzl, W. J., & Lindmoser, C. (2023b). Be constantly different! How to manage influencer authenticity. *Electronic Commerce Research*, 23(3), 1485–1514. DOI: 10.1007/s10660-022-09653-6

Zuboff, S. (2019). *The age of surveillance capitalism: The fight for a human future at the new frontier of power*. PublicAffairs.

JIy, T. (2024). Infrastructure Investments and Economic Growth in Coastal Tourism. *Journal of Economic Development*, 19(4), 200–220. DOI: 10.5678/jed.2024.5678

About the Contributors

Kittisak Jermsittiparsert is a Director of Association of Legal & Political Studies (Thailand). In addition, he is currently a Research Fellow at Shinawatra University, (Thailand) & Universiti Sultan Zainal Abidin (Malaysia), an Adjunct Professor at Sekolah Tinggi Ilmu Administrasi Abdul Haris (Indonesia), and an Adjunct Research Professor at Universitas Muhammadiyah Sinjai, Universitas Muhammadiyah Makassar & Universitas Muhammadiyah Sidenreng Rappang (Indonesia). Previously, he was a Full-Professor of Public Administration at Huanghe Business School, Henan University of Economics and Law, China, a Full-Professor at University of City Island (Cyprus), a Lecturer at Faculty of Political Science, Rangsit University & College of Innovative Business and Accountancy, Dhurakij Pundit University, a Researcher at Chulalongkorn University Social Research Institute, Thailand, and an Adjunct Researcher at Ton Duc Thang University & Duy Tan University, Vietnam. He holds a Ph.D. (Social Sciences), M.A. (Political Science) & B.A. (Political Science) from Kasetsart University. Additionally, he earned M.B.A. & M.P.A. from Ramkhamhaeng University and B.Pol.Sc. (International Relations and Comparative Governments and Politics) from Sukhothai Thammathirat Open University. His areas of expertise are Political Science, Public and Private Management, International Political Economy, and Social Research. He is the editor of many famous journals in the world, such as Sustainability, Frontiers in Psychology, Frontiers in Environmental Science, PLOS One, World Food Policy, Asian Academy of Management Journal, International Journal of Public Policy and Administration Research, International Journal of Innovative Research and Scientific Studies, Recent Advances in Computer Science and Communications, and Energy Engineering. He is named in the world's top 2% of scientists list by Stanford University, USA since 2020. Up to now, he has published more than 450 Scopus/WoS indexed documents. His h-index is 55 with more than 10000 citations.

Ismail Suardi Wekke earned doctoral degree from Universiti Kebangsaan Malaysia with the support of Ford Foundation International Fellowship Program. He received invitation to join Indonesian Young Scholar Network (Mataram, 2013). He serves in Institut Agama Islam Negeri Sorong, Indonesia. Adjunct Professor in University College of Yayasan Pahang, Malaysia (2019). Visiting Professor of Fatoni University, Thailand (2020). 4 June 2022-9 September 2023 was appointed as The Chair STIA Abdul Haris.

Pannee Suanpang is an Associate Professor at Suan Dusit University, Thailand. She holds a Doctor of Technology from University of Technology, Sydney and Master of Information Systems & Bachelor of Information Technology from Griffith University, Australia. Her areas of expertise are Information & Communication Technology, Information Systems, Technology for Tourism & Education, and Sustainable Development. She is the editor and reviewer of many famous journals in the world. Up to now, she has published 19 Scopus/WoS indexed documents. Her h-index is 7 with 131 citations.

***

Seema Bhakuni is a Ph.D. in Management and have qualified UGC NET, CTET and UPTET exam. She has done her Masters in English, Sociology and Business Administration. She is an editorial board member in Journal of Human Resource Management and Global Scientific and academic research journal of economics, business and management. She is also an advisor to Global Leaders Foundation, New Delhi. She completed her education in Lucknow and moved to Rishikesh in 2015. She is presently working as an Assistant Professor at Doon Group of Institutions, Rishikesh and teaching her subject to students of Business Administration

Iva Rani Das is a dynamic individual, currently pursuing her MPhil in the Marketing Department of Dhaka University. Alongside her academic pursuits, she holds key positions as an Assistant Director at the Daffodil Institute of Technology and serves as Guest Faculty in the Business Faculty at the Asian Institute of Business and Technology. Her scholarly achievements extend beyond the classroom, with publications in esteemed national and international journals. Iva's dedication to education and research makes her a driving force in the fields of business and marketing.

Arnab Gantait is an independent writer and former UGC Project Fellow with a PGDM from IITTM (2014) and UGC-NET qualification in the same year. With over three years of industry experience, Arnab has contributed 20 research articles to esteemed UGC-approved and Care-listed journals, and edited volumes by Springer and IGI Global, garnering over 120 citations. One of his research articles "Rural Tourism: Need, Scope, and Challenges in the Indian Context" is recently incorporated into the curriculum at Uttarakhand Open University (India), while his another research article "Conservation and Management of Indian Built Heritages: Exploring the Issues and Challenges" is recommended reading for the PhD Heritage Studies program at Dr. B. R. Ambedkar University, Delhi (India). He has also presented 16 papers at National and International conferences, earning one "Best Paper award" in 2019. His research spans Responsible Tourism, Rural Tourism, Pro-poor Tourism, Community-based Tourism, Service Quality Management, Gastronomic tourism, ICT in Education etc. Honoured with the "IRSD Prominent Researcher Award" in 2023, Arnab's work is accessible on Google Scholar, SSRN, and ResearchGate. He also edited one academic book "Special Interest Tourism: Exploring Dimensions, Impacts, and Future Trends" published by Astitva Prakashan in 2024.

Michael Hall, Professor in UC Business School, University of Canterbury, Management, Marketing and Tourism, New Zealand

Timi Olubiyi is an Entrepreneurship and Small Business Management expert with a Ph.D in Business Administration. A Babcock University Business School Affiliated Scholar and senior government official. He is a prolific investment coach, business engineer, Chartered Member of the Chartered Institute for Securities & Investment (CISI), and a financial literacy specialist.

Girish Prayag, Professor in UC Business School, University of Canterbury, Management, Marketing and Tourism, New Zealand

Sreethi Rebeka R is a PhD Research Scholar at Dept. of Commerce, Christ University, Bengaluru

Kuldeep Singh currently serves as an Assistant Professor in Amity School of Hospitality, Amity University, Haryana, India. He completed his Ph.D. in tourism from Maharshi Dayanand University (Rohtak) India in 2021. He is also a UGC (Net- JRF qualified). Dr. Singh has also served the tourism industry for a couple of years and more than three years in academics. Dr. Singh has so far published more than 40 research articles in both international and national referred journals as well as in edited books in the field of Tourism. Currently, He is serving as an editor of book series in various reputed publications (Emerald, IIP series). Dr. Singh is passionate about the academic areas of Service Quality Management, Rural tourism, Ecotourism, and Sustainable tourism. He also won an aspiring researchers welcome award from Indian Hospitality Congress. His credentials may be verified on various research platforms like Google Scholar, SSRN, LinkedIn, Academia, and Research Gate.

Vinita Sinha is currently a faculty (OB&HR) at Symbiosis Center of Management & Human Resource Development, A constituent of Symbiosis International University, Pune, India. She is doctorate in Psychology. Having completed Master in Psychology with specialization in OB she also holds Post Graduate Diploma in Human Resource Management, Post Graduate Diploma in Health Psychology & Behavior Modification. Her areas of interest in teaching and research stretch out in Psychology, OB & HR, evolving trends in management and education, viz-- Social media, accreditation, psychological issues at work, quality aspects of work, psychological well-being, work stress, role stress, attrition trends, etc.

Dil Afrin Swarna is a renowned expert in education and research. She holds a research-based MBA in Human Resource Management (HRM) from the National University of Bangladesh. Swarna's passion for HRM drives her to explore various themes, showcasing her understanding of business dynamics and interconnections. Her research benefits both academia and industry. Swarna has delved into organizational behavior, employee development, and strategic management, demonstrating the critical role of HRM in corporate performance and offering practical solutions to current managerial challenges. She actively participates in conferences, publishes articles, and collaborates with other specialists in education and research. Her innovative approaches to HRM challenges are highly regarded and push the boundaries of existing knowledge. Through her dedication to research and teaching, Dil Afrin Swarna continues to make significant contributions to academia and her industry. Her work exemplifies how committed and insightful research can enhance organizational practices and deepen our understanding of human resource management.

Mohammad Badruddoza Talukder is an Associate Professor, College of Tourism and Hospitality Management, IUBAT - International University of Business Agriculture and Technology, Dhaka-1230, Bangladesh. He holds PhD in Hotel Management from Lovely Professional University, India. He has been teaching various courses in the Department of Tourism and Hospitality at various universities in Bangladesh since 2008. His research areas include tourism management, hotel management, hospitality management, food & beverage management, and accommodation management, where he has published research papers in well-known journals in Bangladesh and abroad. Mr. Talukder is one of the executive members of the Tourism Educators Association of Bangladesh. He has led training and consulting for a wide range of hospitality organizations in Bangladesh. He just became an honorary facilitator at the Bangladesh Tourism Board's Bangabandhu international tourism and hospitality training institution.

Shivani Thapliyal is working as an Assistant Professor in the School of Business and Management, CHRIST University, Bengaluru, India. She holds a Ph.D. in the area of HRM from the Faculty of Management Studies, Gurukul Kangri University, Haridwar, India. She holds an MBA degree in HR from GEU Dehradun, and a bachelor's degree in B.Sc. She has qualified UGC- NET and has also received ICSSR Doctoral Fellowship. She has also completed a Faculty Development Programme conducted by IIM, Ahmedabad.

Rejoice Thomas is an Assistant Professor from the Department of Professional Studies, Christ (Deemed to be University), Bengaluru and holds a Doctoral Degree from Bharathiar University, Coimbatore (Tamilnadu). He has participated and presented research papers at national and international conferences and also published papers in leading journals. An astute professional having more than 12 years of experience in Teaching, Learning & Development. Possesses strong skills and abilities to provide learning opportunities to employees by proper gap analysis, structured planning, designing learning paths, and tracking mechanisms to measure effectiveness. He is also an experienced trainer specializing in Sustainable Development Goals (SDGs) with a demonstrated history of designing and facilitating impactful training programs. He specializes in Environmental, Social, and Governance (ESG).

Suraj Yadav is an accomplished professional with a background in Hospitality, holding a bachelor's degree from Pune University and a Master in Hotel Management & Tourism from Madurai Kamaraj University, Madurai. Currently serving as an Assistant Professor and Training & Placement Officer at D Y Patil School of Hospitality in Kolhapur, Maharashtra, India, he brings extensive expertise to the field. Suraj is also dedicated to furthering his academic pursuits and is actively pursuing a Ph.D. at D Y Patil Agricultural & Technical University in Kolhapur. His commitment to education and training has made a significant impact in the realm of hospitality.

Index

A

Analytics 37, 39, 41, 47, 48, 52, 56, 59, 63, 65, 90, 123, 124, 125, 126, 127, 128, 130, 131, 132, 133, 134, 135, 136, 170, 171, 175, 267, 268, 269, 270, 271, 272, 273, 274, 275, 276, 278, 313, 318, 357, 364, 365, 371, 372, 375, 388, 423, 434

B

Bangladesh 234, 359, 377, 380, 394, 399, 400, 401, 402, 403, 404, 406, 407, 409, 410, 411, 412, 413, 414, 415, 416, 419, 420, 421, 422, 423, 425, 427, 432, 433, 434, 471, 479, 480, 486, 488, 489

Behavior 3, 16, 28, 43, 58, 59, 67, 74, 75, 76, 78, 87, 88, 89, 93, 94, 95, 96, 121, 133, 136, 178, 182, 184, 187, 195, 196, 197, 198, 199, 200, 202, 203, 204, 205, 206, 207, 208, 210, 211, 216, 217, 235, 239, 241, 252, 253, 264, 284, 297, 301, 302, 303, 308, 312, 316, 319, 320, 322, 324, 325, 337, 340, 341, 343, 344, 346, 347, 348, 349, 350, 351, 352, 353, 354, 355, 356, 357, 358, 363, 385, 399, 415, 427, 443, 445, 482, 484, 486, 488, 491, 494

Behavioural Insights 37, 38, 39, 40, 41, 42, 43, 45, 47, 48, 49, 50, 51, 52, 53, 54, 55, 56, 57, 58

Best practices 45, 47, 103, 117, 134, 153, 155, 159, 275, 367, 408, 409, 431, 446, 447

brand loyalty 195, 196, 197, 198, 199, 200, 202, 203, 204, 205, 206, 207, 208, 209, 210, 212, 213, 214, 215, 216, 239, 241, 242, 253, 275, 276, 315, 317, 318, 348, 364

brand passion 195, 196, 197, 198, 199, 200, 202, 203, 204, 205, 206, 207, 208, 209, 210, 212, 215

brand satisfaction 198, 199, 200, 202, 203, 204, 205, 206, 207, 211, 213, 303, 316

Budi Brown Rice Flour 255, 259, 260, 261, 262, 263

business 25, 26, 32, 48, 58, 59, 61, 62, 63, 64, 65, 66, 67, 68, 69, 70, 71, 74, 75, 76, 77, 78, 79, 80, 85, 86, 87, 88, 89, 90, 91, 92, 93, 94, 95, 96, 97, 98, 99, 100, 102, 103, 104, 106, 108, 113, 114, 115, 116, 117, 118, 119, 120, 125, 126, 127, 134, 135, 136, 138, 139, 140, 141, 143, 144, 146, 148, 149, 150, 152, 154, 156, 157, 158, 159, 160, 161, 162, 163, 168, 169, 171, 173, 175, 181, 183, 184, 191, 193, 196, 197, 209, 210, 211, 212, 213, 214, 215, 216, 217, 219, 220, 221, 222, 226, 230, 231, 232, 233, 234, 235, 237, 238, 241, 242, 244, 245, 246, 248, 249, 251, 253, 254, 256, 258, 259, 261, 262, 263, 264, 267, 268, 269, 270, 272, 273, 274, 275, 276, 277, 278, 284, 292, 293, 297, 313, 315, 316, 317, 319, 321, 325, 337, 338, 339, 340, 341, 342, 345, 347, 348, 355, 357, 359, 375, 376, 377, 381, 382, 383, 384, 385, 390, 391, 394, 396, 397, 398, 399, 405, 408, 409, 412, 413, 414, 416, 419, 423, 425, 433, 435, 439, 443, 444, 461, 462, 464, 465, 466, 467, 469, 480, 481, 483, 487, 489, 490, 493, 494

Business performance 134, 234, 268, 269

C

Coastal Tourism 357, 420, 421, 427, 432, 433, 434

Community engagement 33, 150, 271, 273, 359, 360, 361, 362, 367, 368, 371, 376, 406, 420, 430, 435, 437, 448, 449, 450, 469

Consumer 48, 49, 51, 52, 53, 64, 65, 196, 197, 198, 199, 208, 210, 211, 212, 213, 214, 215, 216, 217, 239, 241, 249, 253, 256, 261, 262, 264, 267, 268, 269, 270, 271, 272, 273, 274, 275, 276, 277, 278, 279, 284, 297, 300, 301, 302, 303, 305, 313, 316, 317, 318, 321, 322, 324, 325, 334, 337, 338, 339, 342, 345, 346, 347, 348, 349, 357, 358, 377, 385, 387, 388, 416, 425, 469, 470, 472, 476, 481, 482, 483, 485, 487, 490, 494

Consumer behaviour 48, 52, 53, 210, 267, 268, 269, 270, 272, 273, 275, 277, 385, 469

Continuous Usage Intention 299, 300, 301, 303, 304, 305, 307, 308, 309, 310, 311, 312, 313, 315, 316, 318, 319, 320

Coronavirus 324, 328, 379, 380, 381, 382, 383, 386, 396, 397, 398

COVID-19 24, 80, 118, 216, 219, 234, 238, 278, 316, 321, 322, 323, 324, 325, 328, 329, 330, 331, 332, 333, 334, 335, 337, 340, 341, 342, 377, 379, 380, 381, 383, 384, 385, 390, 394, 396, 397, 398, 412, 416, 453, 457, 482, 490, 493, 495

Creativity 32, 39, 42, 43, 44, 49, 54, 56, 58, 73, 74, 76, 78, 81, 83, 85, 86, 87, 88, 89, 90, 91, 92, 93, 94, 95, 97, 98, 116, 143, 146, 170, 212, 219, 220, 222, 223, 225, 226, 227, 228, 229, 230, 231, 232, 233, 234, 235, 247, 248, 372

Culinary Diversity 461

Cultural Heritage 250, 251, 253, 343, 369, 400, 403, 407, 408, 409, 420, 421, 424, 426, 427, 429, 430, 439, 446, 448, 462, 464, 474, 478, 486, 495

Cultural Intelligence 99

Cultural Representation 461, 462

D

Decision-Making 37, 38, 39, 40, 41, 42, 43, 44, 45, 47, 48, 49, 50, 51, 56, 59, 61, 62, 63, 65, 66, 68, 71, 77, 86, 109, 110, 125, 136, 146, 159, 226, 258, 267, 268, 269, 272, 273, 274, 275, 278, 283, 303, 316, 322, 345, 347, 349, 369, 388, 419, 421, 422, 424, 427, 428, 430, 442, 448, 467

Definition 2, 4, 40, 64, 68, 125, 180, 181, 326, 343, 374, 435, 436, 437, 461, 462, 463, 478, 490

Delhi NCR 128, 379, 384, 385, 386, 387, 388, 389, 394, 395, 396, 398

Destination marketing 355, 356, 359, 360, 361, 362, 363, 364, 365, 367, 369, 373, 376, 412, 467, 484, 491, 495

Developed Countries 8, 10, 11, 12, 14, 34

Developing Countries 7, 8, 11, 12, 13, 28, 34, 96, 112, 336, 420, 468, 471, 479, 483, 493, 494

Development 1, 2, 3, 4, 5, 6, 7, 8, 9, 10, 11, 12, 13, 14, 15, 16, 17, 18, 19, 20, 21, 22, 23, 24, 25, 26, 27, 28, 29, 30, 31, 32, 33, 34, 35, 37, 38, 39, 40, 41, 42, 43, 45, 46, 47, 48, 49, 51, 53, 54, 55, 56, 59, 61, 62, 63, 65, 66, 67, 69, 71, 74, 75, 76, 78, 88, 89, 90, 91, 92, 94, 95, 96, 97, 98, 101, 102, 103, 105, 106, 109, 110, 113, 115, 118, 119, 120, 124, 134, 136, 137, 138, 139, 140, 141, 142, 144, 145, 146, 148, 149, 150, 151, 152, 153, 154, 155, 156, 159, 160, 161, 165, 166, 168, 169, 170, 174, 175, 177, 178, 183, 184, 187, 188, 189, 191, 192, 214, 219, 220, 221, 226, 233, 234, 235, 238, 239, 241, 242, 243, 244, 245, 246, 247, 248, 249, 251, 252, 253, 254, 255, 256, 257, 259, 260, 261, 262, 263, 264, 265, 280, 296, 303, 313, 314, 315, 335, 343, 344, 346, 347, 348, 349, 355, 356, 357, 359, 360, 361, 363, 367, 373, 374, 377, 400, 404, 405, 406, 409, 410, 412, 413, 415, 416, 417, 419, 420, 421, 422, 423, 424, 425, 426, 427, 428, 429, 430, 431, 432, 433, 434, 435, 437, 438, 439, 440, 442, 443, 444, 445, 446, 449, 450, 451, 454, 456, 457, 459, 466, 468, 469, 477, 478, 479, 480, 481, 483, 484, 485, 487, 489, 490, 491, 493, 495

Different 9, 10, 11, 12, 22, 30, 62, 63, 64, 67, 68, 78, 80, 81, 99, 100, 101, 102, 103, 104, 107, 108, 110, 111, 113, 115, 116, 117, 123, 128, 140, 153, 177, 178, 179, 180, 182, 183, 184, 185, 186, 187, 189, 190, 202, 213, 220, 222, 244, 247, 259, 271, 273, 277, 281, 283, 284, 294, 296, 324, 328, 341, 345, 347, 348, 350, 354, 356, 363, 367, 369, 382, 402, 414, 435, 462, 463, 465, 466, 467, 469, 470, 471, 477, 478, 491

Digital Marketing 160, 249, 252, 253, 254, 274, 318, 343, 345, 346, 350, 352, 353, 354, 355, 356, 357, 377, 385, 407, 409, 411, 422, 423, 426, 429, 434

Diversity 17, 91, 102, 108, 110, 111, 116, 117, 133, 177, 178, 179, 180, 181, 183, 184, 185, 187, 189, 190, 191, 192, 193, 208, 219, 220, 221, 222, 223, 224, 225, 226, 227, 228, 229, 230, 231, 232, 235, 250, 257, 403, 404, 426, 461, 463, 464, 467, 477

E

E-commerce 48, 53, 118, 249, 279, 283, 290, 291, 292, 293, 294, 295, 297, 315, 336, 337, 422, 425, 426, 429

Economic Growth 4, 5, 6, 7, 8, 9, 11, 12, 13, 14, 16, 17, 18, 21, 22, 25, 28, 29, 31, 33, 34, 74, 96, 98, 253, 345, 419, 420, 421, 422, 423, 424, 425, 426, 427, 429, 430, 432, 462

Educational tourism 446

Employee 38, 41, 42, 43, 44, 48, 56, 63, 64, 71, 90, 92, 99, 102, 103, 108, 110, 116, 119, 123, 124, 125, 126, 127, 177, 178, 179, 180, 181, 182, 183, 184, 187, 188, 189, 190, 191, 192, 193, 198, 206, 211, 217, 219, 220, 221, 222, 223, 224, 228, 229, 231, 232, 233, 234, 235, 284, 292, 293

Engagement 19, 20, 33, 39, 41, 42, 43, 44, 46, 48, 49, 51, 52, 56, 109, 139, 149, 150, 151, 158, 159, 176, 177, 178, 179, 180, 181, 182, 183, 187, 188, 189, 190, 191, 192, 193, 197, 198, 199, 200, 212, 215, 222, 223, 224, 228, 241, 267, 268, 269, 270, 271, 272, 273, 274, 275, 276, 277, 278, 300, 303, 304, 305, 310, 311, 312, 313, 315, 316, 317, 318, 319, 334, 339, 350, 354, 359, 360, 361, 362, 363, 364, 365, 366, 367, 368, 371, 372, 373, 374, 376, 385, 401, 406, 420, 424, 430, 435, 437, 448, 449, 450, 457, 459, 469

entrepreneurial intention 73, 76, 77, 78, 79, 81, 82, 83, 88, 91, 93, 94, 95, 96, 97, 98, 314

entrepreneurial passion 73, 75, 76, 77, 78, 81, 82, 83, 88, 89, 90, 91, 92, 93, 94, 95, 96, 97

entrepreneurship 5, 27, 74, 75, 76, 77, 78, 79, 85, 86, 87, 88, 89, 90, 91, 92, 93, 94, 95, 96, 97, 98, 212, 219, 226, 250, 251, 263, 481

entrepreneurship education 87, 92, 95, 96

Environment 2, 4, 5, 6, 7, 11, 12, 14, 16, 17, 19, 21, 26, 28, 29, 31, 32, 34, 39, 40, 41, 42, 44, 45, 46, 47, 61, 62, 63, 67, 68, 70, 74, 77, 96, 99, 100, 110, 112, 114, 139, 143, 145, 169, 170, 179, 180, 182, 184, 185, 195, 196, 197, 198, 199, 200, 202, 203, 204, 205, 206, 207, 208, 209, 210, 214, 215, 216, 217, 220, 221, 232, 234, 343, 344, 346, 347, 400, 401, 404, 405, 406, 411, 424, 425, 428, 430,

435, 438, 439, 440, 443, 444, 445, 446, 447, 448, 449, 450, 451, 454, 456, 465, 470, 476, 480, 486, 489, 491

Environmental sustainability 6, 19, 24, 25, 400, 401, 436, 444, 447, 448, 449, 475, 494

Ethical tourism 401, 406, 421

e-wallet 321, 323, 324, 325, 326, 328, 329, 334, 335, 336, 337, 340, 342, 484

F

fast-food 195, 196, 197, 198, 199, 201, 202, 207, 208, 210, 211, 212, 215, 216, 217

Firm innovation 342

Future Potential 419

G

Gastronomic Experiences 461, 462

Generative AI 37, 39, 41, 42, 49, 56

Globalization 22, 31, 102, 103, 105, 109, 114, 116, 118, 119, 141, 180, 280, 458, 462, 490

Global Talent Management 99, 120

Gluten-Free Brownies 255, 257, 260, 261, 262, 263, 264

Grief tourism 436, 453

H

HR analytics 123, 124, 125, 126, 127, 130, 131, 132, 133, 134, 135, 136

Human-AI Collaboration 37, 39, 41, 42, 49

Human Behaviour 38, 39, 40, 42, 49, 56

I

ICT 16, 67, 69, 71, 486

Immediate Consumption 462, 463, 467, 468, 469, 472

Impact 3, 4, 5, 6, 7, 8, 13, 15, 16, 18, 21, 25, 26, 28, 29, 31, 32, 34, 37, 40, 41, 43, 44, 46, 50, 51, 54, 55, 62, 71, 74, 78, 87, 88, 90, 96, 102, 103, 111, 116, 124, 125, 131, 133, 135, 136, 137, 142, 146, 150, 151, 152, 153, 154, 155, 156, 157, 168, 170, 171, 172, 173, 174, 178, 179, 180, 190, 192, 195, 196, 197, 198, 199, 200, 206, 207, 208, 209, 211, 212, 213, 219, 221, 222, 223, 224, 225, 226, 227, 228, 229, 231, 232, 233, 234, 235, 237, 241, 246, 248, 252, 253, 254, 267, 268, 269, 270, 271, 272, 273, 275, 277, 278, 283, 284, 304, 310, 313, 315, 316, 317, 318, 319, 320, 322, 323, 324, 334, 335, 336, 337, 339, 342, 343, 344, 345, 346, 348, 349, 350, 354, 357, 359, 360, 361, 362, 363, 365, 371, 373, 374, 375, 379, 380, 381, 383, 384, 386, 387, 390, 391, 393, 394, 396, 397, 398, 406, 409, 412, 414, 415, 416, 420, 421, 422, 424, 425, 426, 427, 428, 429, 437, 440, 442, 444, 445, 446, 447, 448, 450, 456, 462, 469, 473, 475, 476, 477, 487, 490, 491, 493, 495

Inclusion 4, 80, 133, 145, 164, 177, 178, 179, 180, 181, 183, 184, 185, 187, 188, 189, 190, 191, 192, 193, 220, 232, 240, 306, 315, 328, 336, 370, 372, 421, 435

Influencer 267, 268, 269, 270, 271, 272, 273, 274, 275, 276, 277, 278, 346, 349, 363, 364, 365, 369, 375, 411

Informal Business 466

Information 4, 8, 16, 17, 28, 40, 41, 43, 44, 45, 46, 47, 48, 51, 55, 61, 62, 63, 64, 65, 66, 67, 68, 69, 70, 71, 91, 93, 94, 97, 98, 102, 103, 104, 116, 124, 125, 126, 127, 132, 133, 134, 136, 145, 147, 156, 158, 161, 163, 166, 173, 175, 186, 188, 190, 210, 226, 233, 241, 243, 249, 257, 258, 259, 278, 281, 282, 297, 303, 304, 313, 314, 315, 316, 317, 318, 319, 323, 325, 326, 329, 337, 338, 339, 340, 341, 342, 344, 345, 347, 348, 349, 356, 357, 358, 359, 360, 361, 362, 363, 366, 369, 371, 374, 375, 380, 385, 388, 395, 396, 402, 407, 408, 409, 413, 425, 426, 429, 434, 445, 446, 450, 451, 467, 482

Innovation 7, 18, 27, 30, 31, 32, 49, 55, 56, 63, 68, 74, 85, 86, 88, 89, 90, 92, 97, 133, 141, 156, 157, 159, 162, 169, 170, 171, 176, 182, 192, 210, 212, 219, 221, 222, 227, 228, 231, 256, 261, 262, 263, 274, 275, 276, 313, 317, 329, 337, 338, 339, 340, 342, 355, 360, 371, 372, 374, 375, 376, 385, 388, 415, 419, 449, 450, 481, 491

intelligence 37, 38, 39, 40, 41, 47, 48, 49, 50, 53, 54, 55, 56, 58, 59, 61, 63, 65, 66, 67, 70, 71, 99, 161, 170, 210, 233, 267, 273, 274, 277, 278, 279, 294, 317, 340, 345, 371, 374, 376, 414, 416, 432, 433, 464, 465, 470, 473, 484

International Tourists 399, 400, 420, 436, 468, 469, 471, 481, 493

IS 1, 2, 3, 4, 5, 6, 9, 10, 11, 12, 13, 14, 15, 16, 17, 18, 19, 20, 21, 22, 23, 24, 27, 28, 37, 40, 43, 44, 45, 46, 47, 48, 49, 50, 51, 52, 53, 54, 55, 56, 57, 61, 62, 63, 64, 65, 66, 67, 68, 69, 70, 74, 75, 76, 77, 78, 79, 80, 81, 83, 84, 85, 86, 87, 88, 99, 100, 101, 102, 103, 104, 105, 106, 107, 108, 109, 110, 111, 112, 113, 114, 115, 116, 117, 123, 124, 125, 126, 127, 128, 129, 130, 131, 132, 133, 136, 137, 138, 139, 140, 141, 142, 143, 144, 145, 146, 147, 148, 149, 150, 151, 152, 153, 154, 157, 158, 159, 160, 161, 162, 163, 164, 167, 168, 169, 170, 171,

175, 177, 178, 179, 180, 181, 182, 183, 184, 186, 188, 189, 190, 193, 196, 197, 198, 199, 200, 201, 202, 203, 204, 205, 206, 207, 208, 213, 214, 220, 221, 222, 223, 224, 225, 226, 227, 228, 229, 230, 233, 234, 238, 239, 240, 241, 242, 244, 245, 246, 248, 249, 250, 256, 257, 258, 260, 261, 262, 269, 270, 272, 273, 274, 275, 276, 280, 281, 282, 283, 284, 289, 290, 291, 292, 293, 295, 296, 300, 301, 302, 303, 304, 305, 307, 310, 311, 312, 321, 322, 323, 324, 325, 326, 328, 329, 330, 333, 335, 336, 343, 344, 345, 346, 347, 348, 349, 351, 354, 355, 360, 361, 364, 365, 366, 367, 370, 377, 379, 380, 381, 382, 383, 384, 385, 386, 387, 390, 391, 393, 394, 395, 399, 400, 401, 402, 403, 404, 405, 406, 407, 408, 419, 420, 421, 422, 423, 424, 425, 426, 427, 428, 430, 435, 436, 437, 438, 439, 440, 441, 442, 443, 444, 445, 446, 447, 448, 449, 450, 451, 453, 461, 462, 463, 464, 465, 466, 467, 468, 469, 470, 472, 473, 474, 475, 476, 477, 478, 482, 483

K

knowledge 1, 25, 37, 40, 44, 45, 61, 62, 65, 66, 67, 71, 76, 87, 91, 103, 104, 107, 109, 114, 115, 125, 131, 133, 134, 136, 137, 138, 139, 140, 141, 143, 144, 145, 146, 147, 148, 149, 150, 151, 159, 162, 163, 164, 165, 166, 167, 168, 169, 170, 171, 173, 178, 183, 222, 231, 234, 239, 241, 244, 245, 247, 249, 251, 257, 262, 275, 278, 318, 324, 337, 368, 373, 390, 406, 413, 437, 442, 446, 449, 454, 462, 470, 471, 475, 482, 485, 488, 489, 493, 494, 495
Kuakata 377, 401, 412, 419, 420, 421, 422, 423, 424, 425, 426, 427, 428, 429, 430, 431, 432, 433, 434

L

Less-Crowded Destinations 399, 400
Local Economy 252, 256, 385, 422, 423, 424, 425, 440, 462, 468, 473, 495
Local Identity Products 237, 238, 239, 241, 246, 248, 249, 250, 251, 254
loyalty 48, 53, 111, 178, 195, 196, 197, 198, 199, 200, 202, 203, 204, 205, 206, 207, 208, 209, 210, 211, 212, 213, 214, 215, 216, 217, 231, 239, 241, 242, 253, 274, 275, 276, 302, 303, 311, 312, 313, 315, 316, 317, 318, 321, 322, 325, 326, 327, 329, 330, 332, 333, 334, 335, 336, 338, 340, 341, 348, 364, 377, 400, 412, 473, 483, 492

M

Machiavellianism 73, 74, 77, 78, 79, 81, 82, 83, 84, 85, 86, 87, 89, 90, 91, 92, 93, 94, 96, 98
Management Practices 39, 41, 89, 107, 126, 136, 192, 234, 235, 363, 444, 446
Marketing 25, 39, 41, 42, 48, 53, 56, 91, 92, 94, 97, 110, 134, 160, 196, 197, 208, 209, 210, 211, 212, 213, 214, 215, 217, 231, 234, 237, 238, 239, 241, 242, 243, 246, 247, 248, 249, 250, 251, 252, 253, 254, 256, 257, 258, 259, 262, 264, 267, 268, 269, 270, 272, 273, 274, 275, 276, 277, 278, 280, 313, 314, 315, 316, 317, 318, 319, 325, 337, 338, 339, 340, 341, 342, 343, 345, 346, 347, 348, 349, 350, 352, 353, 354, 355, 356, 357, 358, 359, 360, 361, 362, 363, 364, 365, 367, 369, 373, 374, 375, 376, 377, 385, 388, 390, 391, 400, 402, 405, 407, 408, 409, 411, 412, 413, 414, 416, 420, 422, 423, 426, 427, 429, 432, 434, 440, 457, 467, 472, 477, 481, 484, 486, 490, 491, 494, 495
mediation analysis 86, 130, 231, 315, 333
moderation analysis 73, 333, 335
Music Streaming Platforms 299, 300, 301, 311, 312, 314, 319

N

Nigeria 28, 219, 220, 225, 226, 227, 228, 229, 230, 231, 233, 234, 235, 283, 355, 373, 374, 479, 480, 483, 484, 490

O

Online shopping 279, 280, 282, 284, 285, 288, 294, 295, 296, 297, 337, 340, 469
organization 2, 59, 62, 63, 64, 65, 66, 67, 68, 69, 77, 102, 103, 106, 107, 112, 113, 115, 123, 124, 125, 126, 127, 128, 129, 131, 132, 177, 178, 179, 180, 181, 182, 183, 184, 185, 188, 189, 190, 192, 193, 222, 233, 278, 284, 324, 356, 375, 380, 381, 389, 390, 397, 398, 462, 463, 483, 484, 494
Organizational Productivity 126, 132

P

Pandemic 24, 80, 101, 118, 216, 219, 225, 231, 233, 234, 235, 238, 321, 322, 324, 329, 334, 337, 340, 341, 342, 377, 380, 381, 382, 383, 384, 385, 386, 387, 388, 390, 391, 393, 394, 395, 396, 397, 436, 469, 482, 490, 493, 495
physical environment quality 195, 196, 197, 198, 199,

200, 202, 203, 204, 205, 206, 207, 208, 217
PLS-SEM 81, 83, 88, 92, 93, 94, 96, 195, 203, 206, 307, 313, 314, 330, 337, 341

R

Religious tourism 359, 360, 361, 362, 367, 368, 369, 370, 371, 372, 373, 375, 376, 377
Risk perception 46, 279, 492
Role 4, 9, 10, 12, 13, 14, 15, 16, 18, 22, 23, 24, 27, 31, 32, 33, 41, 56, 58, 61, 64, 71, 74, 77, 78, 81, 89, 90, 92, 93, 94, 95, 96, 97, 98, 102, 104, 106, 108, 110, 114, 118, 121, 123, 127, 131, 133, 135, 136, 143, 146, 148, 149, 154, 159, 162, 167, 170, 171, 174, 177, 178, 179, 182, 190, 192, 196, 198, 199, 200, 206, 207, 208, 209, 210, 211, 212, 216, 217, 219, 231, 232, 233, 234, 235, 238, 241, 249, 250, 253, 255, 256, 267, 269, 270, 273, 275, 299, 300, 303, 304, 305, 311, 315, 316, 317, 319, 320, 321, 322, 324, 328, 330, 334, 336, 337, 341, 342, 343, 345, 346, 349, 354, 355, 357, 358, 359, 361, 362, 365, 366, 368, 371, 373, 374, 375, 376, 377, 387, 406, 412, 417, 421, 432, 435, 436, 441, 445, 450, 455, 456, 461, 462, 463, 467, 468, 469, 472, 473, 474, 476, 477, 478, 480, 486, 490, 491, 494

S

satisfaction 5, 43, 44, 45, 47, 48, 53, 56, 125, 127, 146, 168, 170, 182, 189, 192, 195, 196, 197, 198, 199, 200, 202, 203, 204, 205, 206, 207, 208, 209, 210, 211, 212, 213, 214, 215, 216, 217, 227, 228, 234, 235, 249, 253, 256, 259, 297, 300, 301, 303, 304, 311, 312, 315, 316, 317, 318, 319, 320, 321, 322, 323, 324, 325, 326, 327, 329, 330, 331, 332, 333, 334, 335, 336, 339, 340, 341, 345, 369, 377, 396, 399, 400, 409, 412, 421, 424, 425, 437, 439, 468, 469, 472, 473, 475, 483, 491, 493, 494
Sectors 25, 27, 39, 51, 54, 55, 56, 62, 102, 123, 126, 157, 177, 178, 179, 182, 184, 186, 187, 188, 190, 197, 208, 209, 230, 239, 241, 261, 267, 268, 269, 272, 273, 274, 275, 381, 390, 423, 427, 448, 449, 467, 468
Social Media 199, 212, 234, 239, 241, 247, 248, 249, 252, 253, 254, 267, 268, 269, 270, 272, 273, 274, 277, 278, 304, 305, 306, 314, 316, 317, 318, 327, 339, 343, 344, 345, 346, 347, 348, 349, 350, 351, 352, 353, 354, 355, 356, 357, 358, 359, 360, 361, 362, 363, 364, 365, 366, 367, 368, 369, 370, 371, 372, 373, 374, 375, 376, 377, 378, 388, 402, 407, 408, 409, 412, 424, 426, 450, 452, 467, 477, 481, 482, 486, 489, 493
Society 5.0 37, 38, 40, 49, 56, 345, 349, 356, 478
Southern Border Provinces 237, 238, 239, 240, 242, 243, 245, 248, 249, 250, 251, 252
Spotify 300, 303, 306, 312, 317
staff behavior 195, 196, 197, 198, 200, 202, 203, 204, 205, 206, 207, 208
Street Food 461, 462, 463, 464, 465, 466, 467, 468, 469, 470, 471, 472, 473, 474, 475, 476, 477, 478, 479, 480, 481, 482, 483, 484, 485, 486, 487, 488, 489, 490, 491, 492, 493, 494, 495
Sustainable 1, 2, 3, 4, 5, 6, 9, 10, 11, 12, 13, 14, 15, 16, 17, 18, 19, 20, 21, 22, 23, 24, 25, 26, 27, 28, 29, 30, 31, 32, 33, 34, 35, 37, 38, 40, 43, 45, 47, 49, 53, 54, 55, 56, 59, 88, 219, 220, 221, 226, 229, 232, 233, 234, 235, 239, 242, 243, 244, 245, 251, 254, 259, 261, 272, 274, 276, 343, 344, 345, 346, 347, 349, 350, 351, 352, 353, 354, 355, 356, 357, 358, 359, 360, 361, 362, 367, 371, 372, 373, 375, 377, 385, 396, 397, 400, 401, 402, 403, 404, 405, 406, 407, 408, 409, 410, 411, 412, 413, 415, 416, 420, 421, 422, 423, 424, 425, 426, 427, 428, 429, 430, 431, 432, 433, 434, 435, 436, 437, 438, 439, 440, 441, 442, 443, 444, 445, 446, 447, 448, 449, 450, 451, 453, 454, 456, 457, 458, 474, 475, 477, 478, 480, 485, 487, 489, 491, 492, 494, 495
Sustainable Development 1, 2, 3, 4, 5, 6, 9, 10, 11, 12, 13, 14, 15, 16, 17, 18, 19, 20, 21, 22, 23, 24, 25, 26, 27, 28, 29, 30, 31, 32, 33, 35, 37, 38, 40, 43, 45, 47, 53, 54, 55, 56, 59, 219, 220, 221, 226, 234, 254, 259, 343, 344, 346, 356, 367, 373, 410, 412, 416, 420, 422, 423, 425, 428, 432, 434, 442, 444, 445, 446, 449, 457, 478, 480, 491
Sustainable Tourism 343, 344, 345, 347, 349, 355, 356, 358, 359, 375, 397, 400, 401, 402, 403, 404, 406, 407, 408, 409, 411, 412, 415, 420, 421, 422, 423, 424, 425, 427, 428, 430, 431, 432, 433, 434, 438, 439, 446, 447, 448, 449, 451, 453, 454, 457, 458, 474, 477, 492
system 5, 8, 9, 10, 14, 18, 20, 26, 30, 31, 32, 34, 45, 50, 52, 55, 62, 63, 64, 65, 66, 67, 68, 71, 102, 109, 115, 120, 124, 126, 132, 136, 138, 143, 152, 156, 173, 208, 222, 234, 278, 296, 300, 302, 313, 314, 318, 323, 325, 342, 343, 344, 482, 490

T

technological stress 321, 322, 326, 327, 328, 329, 330, 332, 333, 334, 335, 336
Tourism development 355, 359, 400, 406, 413, 416, 420, 421, 426, 428, 431, 432, 433, 434, 438, 451,

456, 480, 493
Tourist Satisfaction 377, 412, 468, 493
Tranquillity 399, 400, 401, 402, 404
Travel 113, 164, 217, 245, 258, 297, 343, 344, 345, 346, 347, 348, 349, 350, 351, 352, 353, 354, 355, 356, 357, 358, 360, 361, 362, 363, 364, 365, 366, 367, 368, 369, 371, 373, 375, 378, 379, 380, 381, 382, 383, 384, 385, 386, 387, 388, 389, 390, 391, 394, 396, 397, 398, 399, 400, 401, 402, 407, 408, 409, 411, 412, 416, 422, 424, 425, 426, 428, 429, 434, 435, 436, 437, 449, 454, 455, 456, 457, 459, 467, 472, 482, 491
Travel and Tourism 348, 349, 356, 357, 358, 373, 379, 380, 381, 382, 385, 391, 424
trust 46, 49, 60, 97, 114, 178, 184, 190, 197, 199, 200, 202, 210, 211, 212, 213, 214, 216, 222, 241, 249, 268, 269, 272, 274, 275, 276, 279, 284, 299, 300, 301, 302, 303, 304, 305, 307, 308, 309, 310, 311, 312, 313, 314, 315, 316, 317, 318, 319, 320, 321, 322, 325, 326, 329, 330, 331, 332, 333, 334, 335, 336, 337, 338, 340, 341, 342, 346, 348, 357, 358, 365, 366, 384, 385, 388, 415, 424, 484

U

Underdeveloped Countries 13, 14
Unsustainable Development 1, 7, 8, 9, 14, 15, 16, 28

W

Widows 237, 238, 239, 242, 243, 244, 245, 246, 247, 248, 249, 250, 251, 252, 253

Y

Yala Province 255, 256, 257, 260, 261, 262, 263, 264